SCOTT FORESMAN

READING STREET

Program Authors

Peter Afflerbach
Camille Blachowicz
Candy Dawson Boyd
Elena Izquierdo
Connie Juel
Edward Kame'enui
Donald Leu
Jeanne R. Paratore
P. David Pearson
Sam Sebesta
Deborah Simmons
Susan Watts Taffe
Alfred Tatum
Sharon Vaughn
Karen Kring Wixson

Glenview, Illinois

Boston, Massachusetts

Chandler, Arizona

Upper Saddle River, New Jersey

We dedicate Reading Street to
Peter Jovanovich.

His wisdom, courage,
and passion for education
are an inspiration to us all.

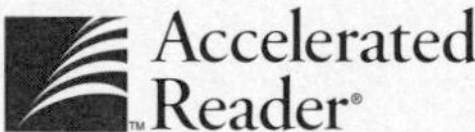

The Acknowledgments page appears in the back of the book immediately following the Oral Vocabulary section and constitutes an extension of this copyright page.

ISBN-13: 978-0-328-72516-8
ISBN-10: 0-328-72516-1
6 7 8 9 10 V064 16 15 14 13

Program Authors

Peter Afflerbach, Ph.D.
Professor; Department of Curriculum and Instruction,
University of Maryland; College Park, Maryland
Areas of Expertise: Common Core State Standards English Language Arts Work Team, Assessment, and Comprehension

Camille L. Z. Blachowicz, Ph.D.
Professor; National College of Education, National-Louis University; Skokie, Illinois
Areas of Expertise: Vocabulary and Comprehension

Candy Dawson Boyd, Ph.D.
Professor, School of Education; Saint Mary's College; Moraga, California
Areas of Expertise: Children's Literature and Professional Development

Elena Izquierdo, Ph.D.
Associate Professor, University of Texas at El Paso
Area of Expertise: English Language Learners

Connie Juel, Ph.D.
Professor of Education; Stanford University; Stanford, California
Areas of Expertise: Phonics, Oral Vocabulary, and Intervention

Edward J. Kame'enui, Ph.D.
Dean-Knight Professor of Education and Director, Institute for the Development of Educational Achievement, and the Center on Teaching and Learning; College of Education; University of Oregon
Areas of Expertise: Assessment, Intervention, and Progress Monitoring

Donald J. Leu, Ph.D.
John and Maria Neag Endowed Chair in Literacy and Technology Board of Directors, International Reading Association; University of Connecticut; Storrs, Connecticut
Areas of Expertise: Comprehension, Technology, and New Literacies

Jeanne R. Paratore, Ed.D.
Professor of Literacy, Language, and Cultural Studies; Boston University School of Education; Boston, Massachusetts
Areas of Expertise: Intervention and Small Group Instruction

P. David Pearson, Ph.D.
Professor of Language, Literacy and Culture, and Human Development; Graduate School of Education; University of California; Berkeley, California
Areas of Expertise: Common Core State Standards English Language Arts Work Team, Comprehension

Sam L. Sebesta, Ph.D.
Professor Emeritus; Curriculum and Instruction College of Education, University of Washington; Seattle, Washington
Areas of Expertise: Children's Literature, Reader Response, and Motivation

Deborah Simmons, Ph.D.
Professor in the Department of Educational Psychology, College of Education and Human Development, Texas A&M University
Areas of Expertise: Literacy Development, Phonics, and Intervention

Susan Watts Taffe, Ph.D.
Associate Professor and Program Coordinator, Literacy and Second Language Studies, School of Education; University of Cincinnati; Cincinnati, Ohio
Areas of Expertise: Vocabulary, Comprehension, and New Literacies

Alfred Tatum, Ph.D.
Associate Professor and Director, UIC Reading Clinic, University of Illinois at Chicago
Areas of Expertise: Adolescent Literacy, Reader Response, and Motivation

Sharon Vaughn, Ph.D.
H. E. Hartfelder/The Southland Corporation Regents Professor;
University of Texas; Austin, Texas
Areas of Expertise: Literacy Development, Intervention, Professional Development, English Language Learners, Vocabulary, and Small Group Instruction

Karen Kring Wixson, Ph.D.
Dean of Education, University of North Carolina, Greensboro
Areas of Expertise: Common Core State Standards English Language Arts Work Team, Assessment, Small Group Instruction

Consulting Authors

Jeff Anderson, M.Ed.
Author and National Literacy Staff Developer

Jim Cummins, Ph.D.
Professor; Department of Curriculum, Teaching and Learning; University of Toronto

Tahira A. DuPree Chase, Ed.D.
Director of Curriculum and Instruction, Mt. Vernon City School District, New York

Lily Wong Fillmore, Ph.D.
Professor Emerita; Graduate School of Education, University of California, Berkeley

Georgia Earnest Garcia, Ph.D.
Professor; Language and Literacy Division, Department of Curriculum and Instruction, University of Illinois at Urbana-Champaign

George A. Gonzalez, Ph.D.
Professor (Retired); School of Education,
University of Texas-Pan American, Edinburg

Adria Klein, Ph.D.
Professor Emeritus; School of Education, California State University, San Bernadino

Lesley Maxwell, M.S., CCC-SLP
Director of Clinical Education, Clinical Associate Professor; Department of Communication Sciences and Disorders, MGH Institute of Health Professions

Valerie Ooka Pang, Ph.D.
Professor; School of Teacher Education, San Diego State University

Sally M. Reis, Ph.D.
Board of Trustees Distinguished Professor; Department of Educational Psychology, University of Connecticut

Jon Scieszka, M.F.A.
Children's Book Author and Founder of GUYS READ, First National Ambassador for Young People's Literature 2008

Grant Wiggins, Ed.D.
President of Authentic Education, coauthor of *Understanding by Design*

Nurture the love of reading.

Help students learn to read *and* love to read. *Reading Street Common Core* supports reading, writing, and language development. Amazing literature on amazing devices inspires students in a whole new way.

Literature students love

The best literary and informational text

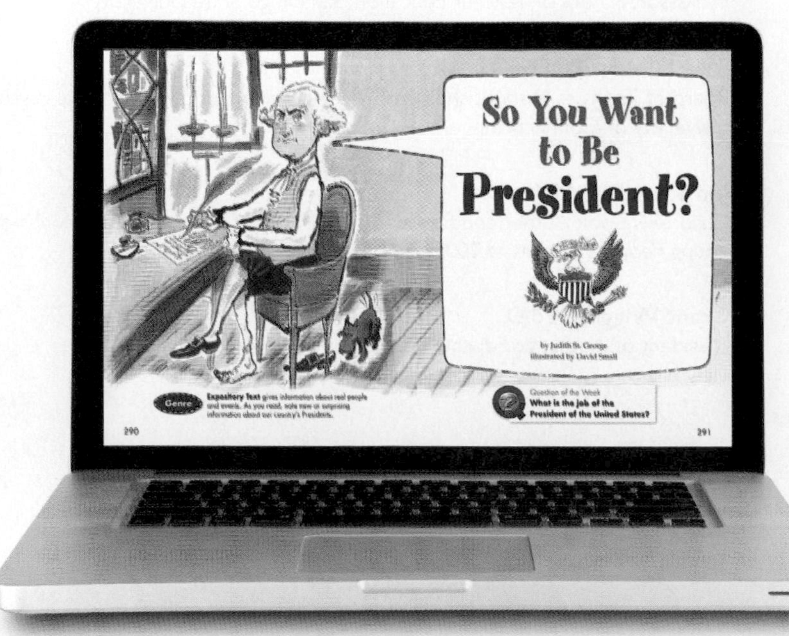

On devices they crave!

Whiteboards, tablets, computers, mobile devices

Build a foundation for reading.

Reading Street Common Core helps students develop foundational skills for reading more complex text. Common Core experts helped design the plan. Classroom results prove it works.

Early Reading Success

Reading Street students outperformed their peers by 15 percentile points, even though they started below the comparison students.

Kindergarten GRADE Total Score

50
48
46
44
42
40
38

Baseline
End of Year

Comparison
Reading Street

Greater Reading Enjoyment Later

Fourth-grade *Reading Street* students had more positive attitudes toward reading.

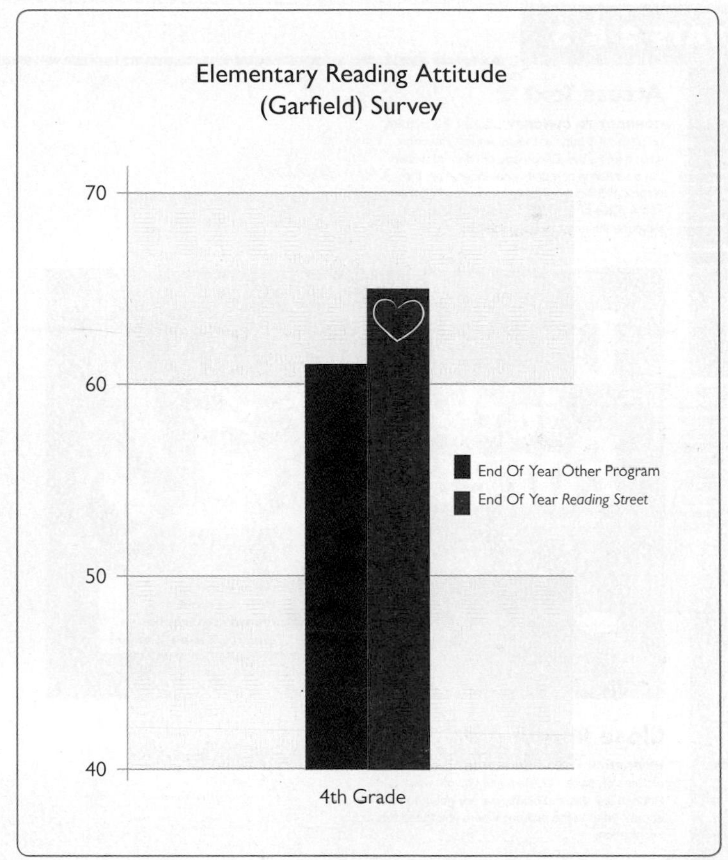

"The texts children read provide them with a foundation not just for what they're going to read, but also for what they're going to write and talk about."

Jeanne R. Paratore, Ed.D.
Program Author

Grow student capacity.

Reading Street Common Core builds students' capacity to read complex texts. Zoom in on elements critical to the Common Core State Standards.

Text-Based Comprehension

Modeling, analysis, and guided practice prepare students for more demanding text.

DAYS 2 & 3

1ST READ

Access Text — If children need help, then...

CONNECT TO CONCEPT Look at the pictures on page 147. Look at the chipmunk. Describe what it looks like. Encourage children to answer the question in complete sentences. Yes, the chipmunk is light brown with dark brown stripes. I think it is eating something. Ask children to describe the ant, raccoon, and bird.

Life in the Forest

by Claire Daniel

Genre: **Expository text** tells facts about real places. Next you will read about the plants and animals in a forest.

Question of the Week

How are plant and animal communities important to each other?

146 147

Student Edition, pp. 146–147

2ND READ

Close Reading

INFERENCE • TEXT EVIDENCE Look at the pictures on page 147. How can you tell what kinds of animals and plants you are going to read about? Point to the pictures where you found this information.

146–147 Communities • Unit 2 • Week 5

DAYS 2 & 3

AUTHOR'S PURPOSE
What is the author's purpose for writing this selection? How do you know? (The author's purpose is to give information about animals and plants in a forest. These pages tell facts about bugs and leaves.)

Common Core State Standards

Informational Text 1. Ask and answer questions about key details in a text. **Informational Text 3.** Describe the connection between two individuals, events, ideas, or pieces of information in a text. **Informational Text 8.** Identify the reasons an author gives to support points in a text. **Also Informational Text 7.**

We can find life in the forest.
It is a busy place!

Sun shines on the leaves and helps them grow. Bugs like munching on them. Yum, yum! Bugs can eat lots and lots.

Sun helped these leaves get wide and flat.

148 149

Student Edition, pp. 148–149

SYNTHESIS What if the sun never shined on leaves? How would this change the community? (If the sun never shined, the leaves would never grow. There would be no leaves for the bugs to munch on.)

CONNECT TO SCIENCE Different parts of a plant help it get what it needs to live. Roots take in water from the soil. Leaves use sunlight and a green pigment called chlorophyll to make food.

ELL

Academic Language Have pairs find other things in their environment that are *wide* and *flat*, like the leaf on page 148.

Life in the Forest **148–149**

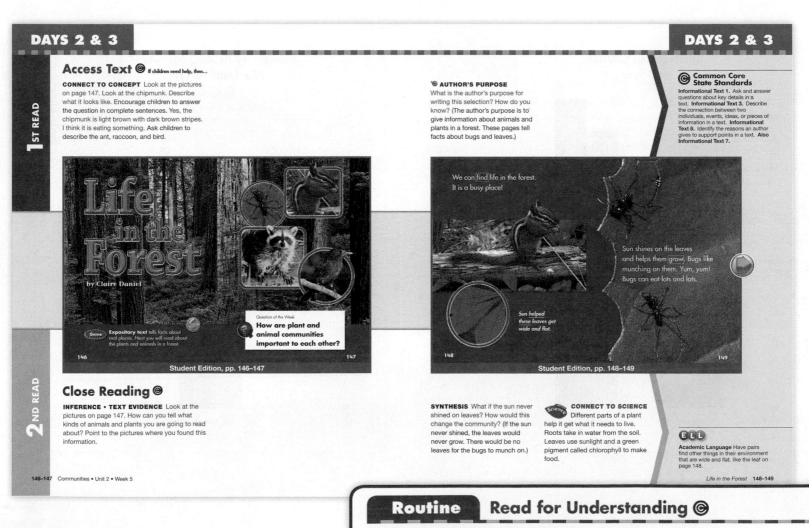

Read for Understanding Routine

Routines provide weekly opportunities to develop deep understanding and build higher-order thinking skills through Close Reading.

Routine — Read for Understanding

Deepen understanding by reading the selection multiple times.

1. **First Read**—use the **Access Text** notes to help children clarify understanding.
2. **Second Read**—use the **Close Reading** notes to help children draw knowledge from the text.

Content Knowledge

Weekly and unit instruction is built around science and social studies concepts. These concepts connect every piece of literature, vocabulary, and writing, allowing students to develop deep knowledge.

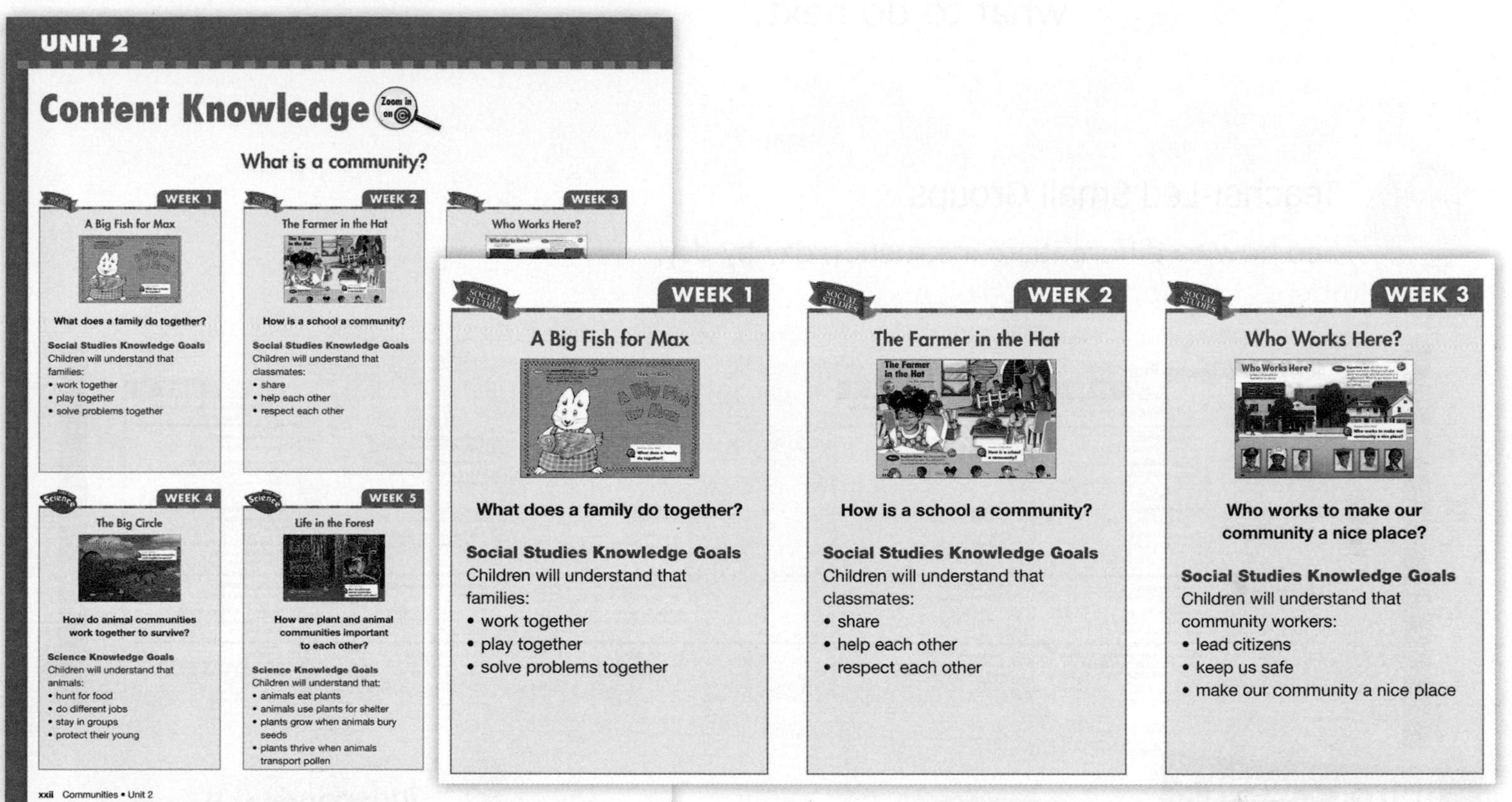

UNIT 2

Content Knowledge

What is a community?

WEEK 1	WEEK 2	WEEK 3
A Big Fish for Max	The Farmer in the Hat	Who Works Here?
What does a family do together?	How is a school a community?	Who works to make our community a nice place?
Social Studies Knowledge Goals Children will understand that families: • work together • play together • solve problems together	**Social Studies Knowledge Goals** Children will understand that classmates: • share • help each other • respect each other	**Social Studies Knowledge Goals** Children will understand that community workers: • lead citizens • keep us safe • make our community a nice place

WEEK 4	WEEK 5
The Big Circle	Life in the Forest
How do animal communities work together to survive?	How are plant and animal communities important to each other?
Science Knowledge Goals Children will understand that animals: • hunt for food • do different jobs • stay in groups • protect their young	**Science Knowledge Goals** Children will understand that: • animals eat plants • animals use plants for shelter • plants grow when animals bury seeds • plants thrive when animals transport pollen

xxii Communities • Unit 2

Writing

Varied writing tasks help students write to inform or explain.

DAILY

- 10-minute mini-lessons on writing traits and craft allow students to write in response to their reading
- Quick Write routine for writing on demand

WEEKLY

- Different writing product each week
- Writing mini-lessons and organizational models
- Mentor text to exemplify good traits

UNIT

- One- or two-week Writing Workshops
- Writing process lessons

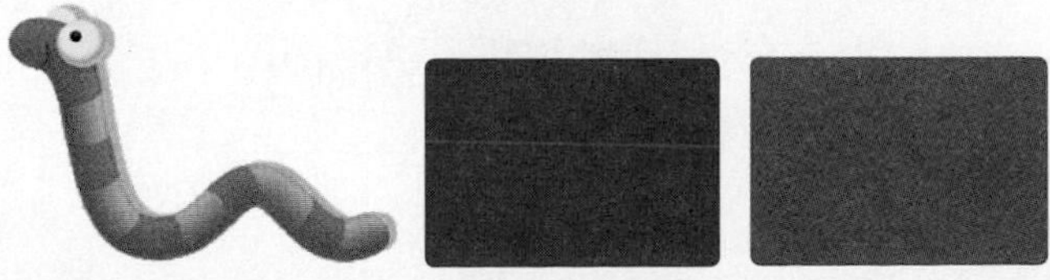

Inspire confidence.

"What do I do in group time?" Follow the simple 3-step plan. *Reading Street Common Core* provides a road map to help you teach with confidence. You'll know exactly where to go and what to do next.

1 Teacher-Led Small Groups

See how to differentiate instruction day by day.

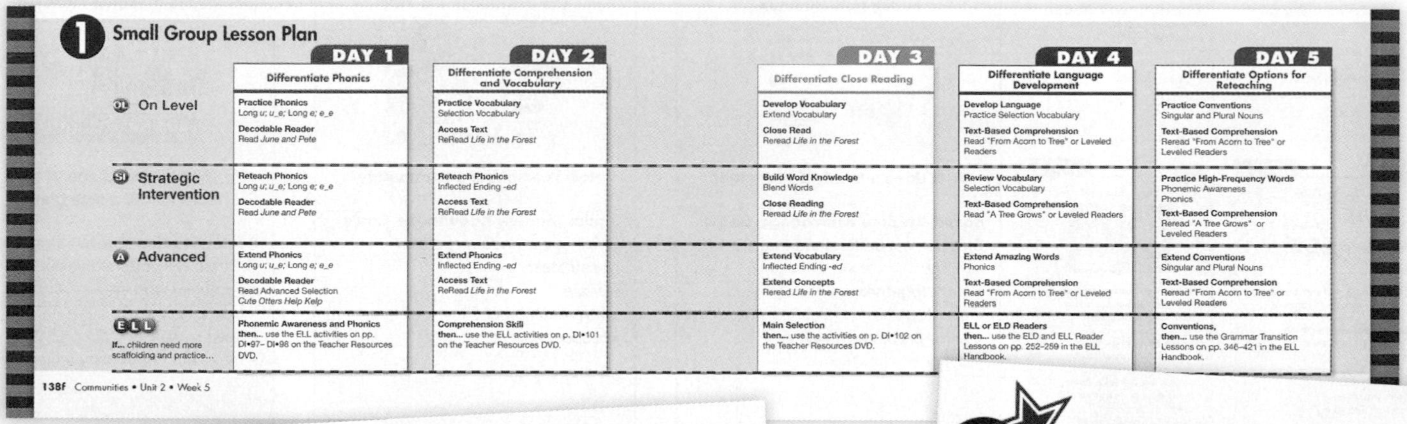

1 Small Group Lesson Plan

	DAY 1 Differentiate Phonics	DAY 2 Differentiate Comprehension and Vocabulary	DAY 3 Differentiate Close Reading	DAY 4 Differentiate Language Development	DAY 5 Differentiate Options for Reteaching
OL On Level	**Practice Phonics** Long u; u_e; Long e; e_e **Decodable Reader** Read *June and Pete*	**Practice Vocabulary** Selection Vocabulary **Access Text** ReRead *Life in the Forest*	**Develop Vocabulary** Extend Vocabulary **Close Read** Reread *Life in the Forest*	**Develop Language** Practice Selection Vocabulary **Text-Based Comprehension** Read "From Acorn to Tree" or Leveled Readers	**Practice Conventions** Singular and Plural Nouns **Text-Based Comprehension** Reread "From Acorn to Tree" or Leveled Readers
SI Strategic Intervention	**Reteach Phonics** Long u; u_e; Long e; e_e **Decodable Reader** Read *June and Pete*	**Reteach Phonics** Inflected Ending -ed **Access Text** ReRead *Life in the Forest*	**Build Word Knowledge** Blend Words **Close Reading** Reread *Life in the Forest*	**Review Vocabulary** Selection Vocabulary **Text-Based Comprehension** Read "A Tree Grows" or Leveled Readers	**Practice High-Frequency Words** Phonemic Awareness Phonics **Text-Based Comprehension** Reread "A Tree Grows" or Leveled Readers
A Advanced	**Extend Phonics** Long u; u_e; Long e; e_e **Decodable Reader** Read Advanced Selection *Cute Otters Help Kelp*	**Extend Phonics** Inflected Ending -ed **Access Text** ReRead *Life in the Forest*	**Extend Vocabulary** Inflected Ending -ed **Extend Concepts** Reread *Life in the Forest*	**Extend Amazing Words** Phonics **Text-Based Comprehension** Read "From Acorn to Tree" or Leveled Readers	**Extend Conventions** Singular and Plural Nouns **Text-Based Comprehension** Reread "From Acorn to Tree" or Leveled Readers
ELL If... children need more scaffolding and practice...	**Phonemic Awareness and Phonics** then... use the ELL activities on pp. DI•97– DI•98 on the Teacher Resources DVD.	**Comprehension Skill** then... use the ELL activities on p. DI•101 on the Teacher Resources DVD.	**Main Selection** then... use the activities on p. DI•102 on the Teacher Resources DVD.	**ELL or ELD Readers** then... use the ELD and ELL Reader Lessons on pp. 252–259 in the ELL Handbook.	**Conventions,** then... use the Grammar Transition Lessons on pp. 346–421 in the ELL Handbook.

138f Communities • Unit 2 • Week 5

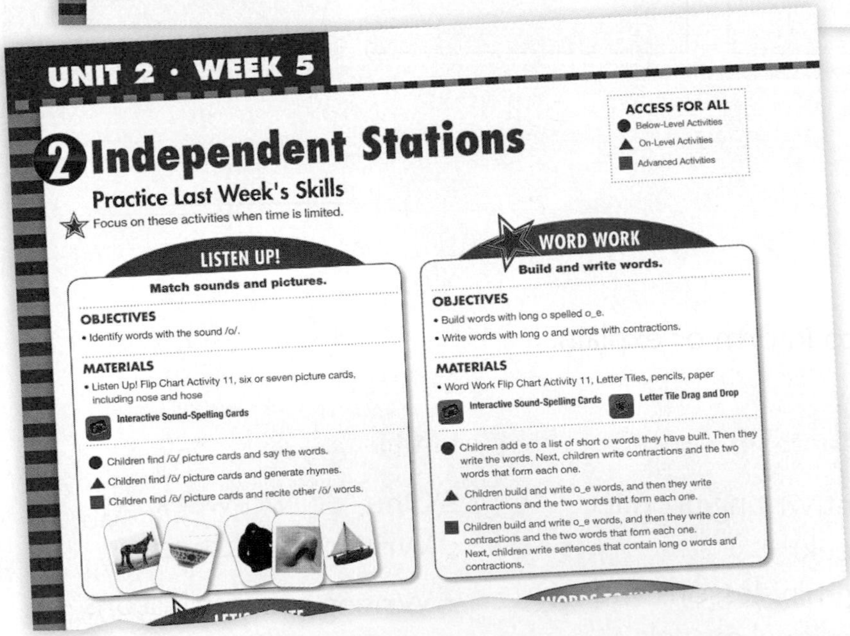

UNIT 2 • WEEK 5

2 Independent Stations

Practice Last Week's Skills

Focus on these activities when time is limited.

ACCESS FOR ALL
● Below-Level Activities
▲ On-Level Activities
■ Advanced Activities

LISTEN UP! Match sounds and pictures.

OBJECTIVES
• Identify words with the sound /o/.

MATERIALS
• Listen Up! Flip Chart Activity 11, six or seven picture cards, including nose and hose

Interactive Sound-Spelling Cards

● Children find /ō/ picture cards and say the words.
▲ Children find /ō/ picture cards and generate rhymes.
■ Children find /ō/ picture cards and recite other /ō/ words.

WORD WORK Build and write words.

OBJECTIVES
• Build words with long o spelled o_e.
• Write words with long o and words with contractions.

MATERIALS
• Word Work Flip Chart Activity 11, Letter Tiles, pencils, paper

Interactive Sound-Spelling Cards · Letter Tile Drag and Drop

● Children add e to a list of short o words they have built. Then they write the words. Next, children write contractions and the two words that form each one.
▲ Children build and write o_e words, and then they write contractions and the two words that form each one.
■ Children build and write o_e words, and then they write con contractions and the two words that form each one. Next, children write sentences that contain long o words and contractions.

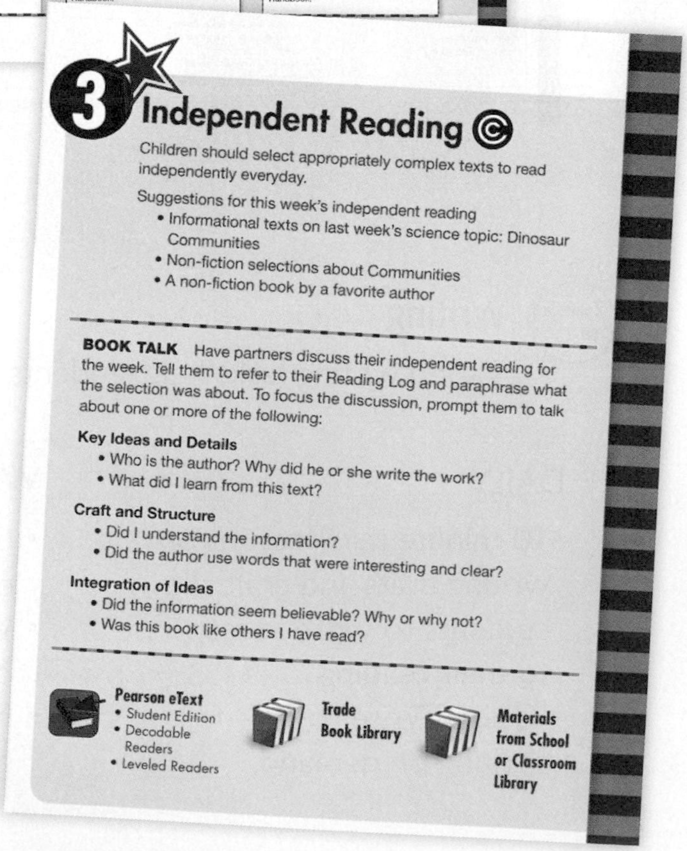

3 Independent Reading ©

Children should select appropriately complex texts to read independently everyday.

Suggestions for this week's independent reading
• Informational texts on last week's science topic: Dinosaur Communities
• Non-fiction selections about Communities
• A non-fiction book by a favorite author

BOOK TALK Have partners discuss their independent reading for the week. Tell them to refer to their Reading Log and paraphrase what the selection was about. To focus the discussion, prompt them to talk about one or more of the following:

Key Ideas and Details
• Who is the author? Why did he or she write the work?
• What did I learn from this text?

Craft and Structure
• Did I understand the information?
• Did the author use words that were interesting and clear?

Integration of Ideas
• Did the information seem believable? Why or why not?
• Was this book like others I have read?

Pearson eText • Student Edition • Decodable Readers • Leveled Readers · **Trade Book Library** · **Materials from School or Classroom Library**

2 Independent Practice Stations

Level activities and provide focus when time is limited.

3 Independent Reading

Suggest concept-related reading and partner activities.

Response to Intervention Kit

Tier 2 RTI Kit provides a targeted focus and leveled mini-lessons for individuals and small groups.

My Sidewalks Intensive Intervention

Conceptually related to *Reading Street, My Sidewalks* provides 30 weeks of instruction for struggling readers.

"What we need to do is to increase the support strategies to help students cope with complex text."

P. David Pearson
Program Author

TABLE OF CONTENTS

YOU ARE HERE

UNIT 1
Animals, Tame and Wild

UNIT 2
Communities

TABLE OF CONTENTS

UNIT 3 Changes

UNIT 4 Treasures

UNIT 5
Great Ideas

UNIT R
My World

eSTREET INTERACTIVE
www.ReadingStreet.com

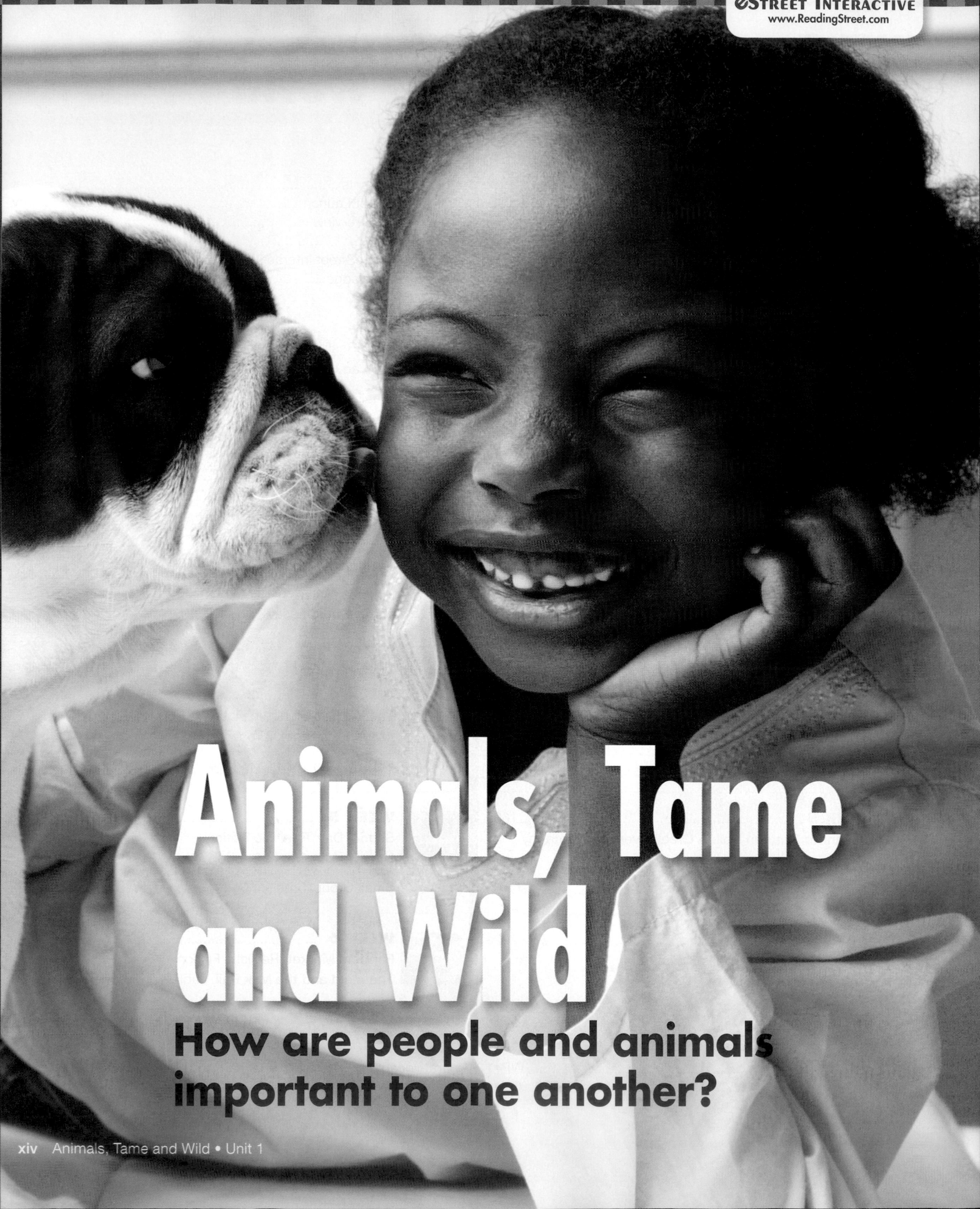

Animals, Tame and Wild

How are people and animals important to one another?

Sam, Come Back!
REALISTIC FICTION

What do pets need?

Paired Selection
Puppy Games
SING-ALONG

Pig in a Wig
ANIMAL FANTASY

Who helps animals?

Paired Selection
We Are Vets
SING-ALONG

The Big Blue Ox
ANIMAL FANTASY

How do animals help people?

Paired Selection
They Can Help
PHOTO ESSAY

A Fox and a Kit
LITERARY NONFICTION

How do wild animals take care of their babies?

Paired Selection
The Fox and the Grapes
FABLE

Get the Egg!
REALISTIC FICTION

Which wild animals live in our neighborhood?

Paired Selection
Help the Birds
HOW-TO ARTICLE

Animal Park
LITERARY NONFICTION

What can we learn about wild animals by watching them?

Paired Selection
Poetry Collection
POETRY

Skills Overview

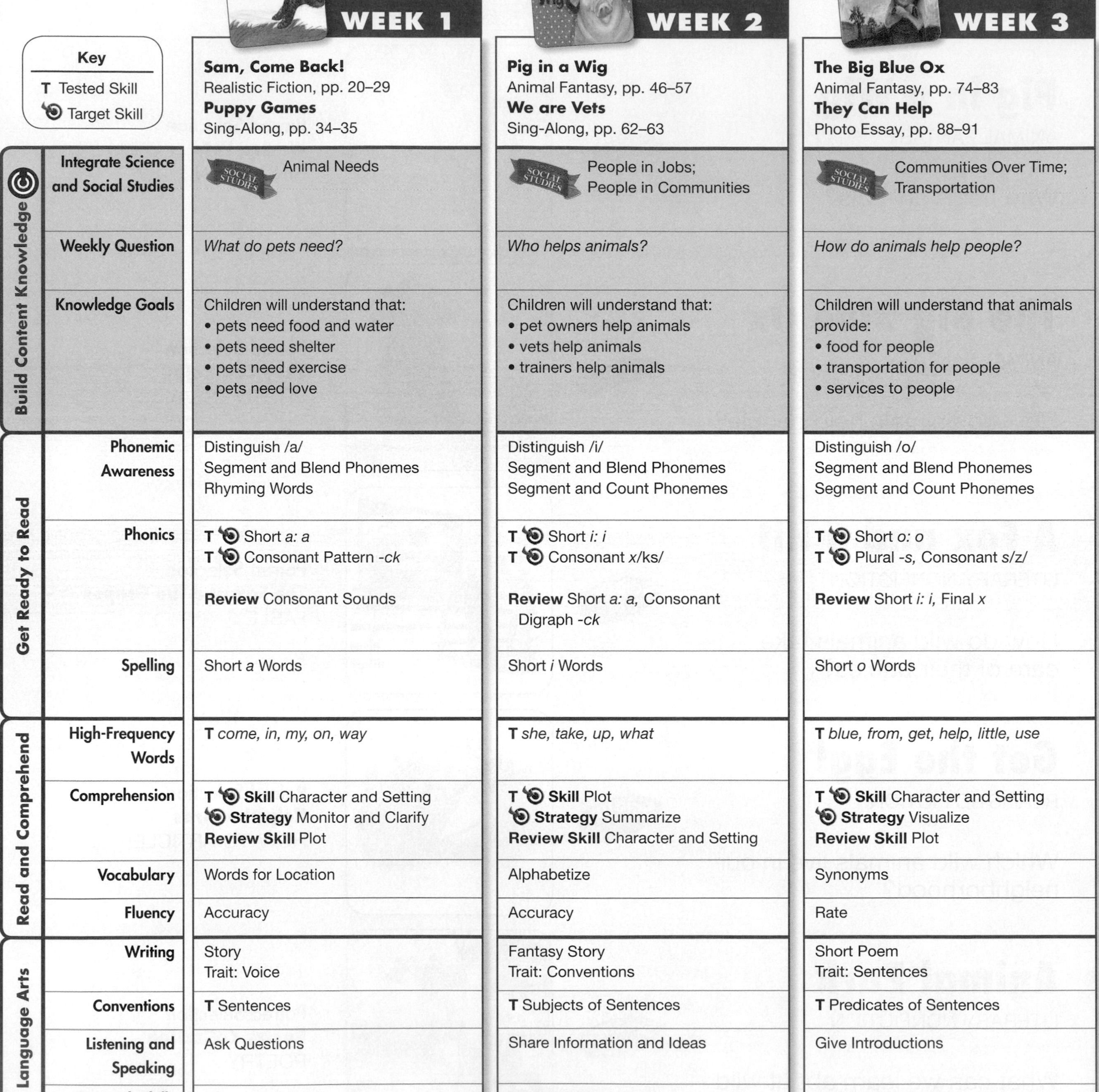

Key
T Tested Skill
◎ Target Skill

		WEEK 1	WEEK 2	WEEK 3
		Sam, Come Back! Realistic Fiction, pp. 20–29 **Puppy Games** Sing-Along, pp. 34–35	**Pig in a Wig** Animal Fantasy, pp. 46–57 **We are Vets** Sing-Along, pp. 62–63	**The Big Blue Ox** Animal Fantasy, pp. 74–83 **They Can Help** Photo Essay, pp. 88–91
Build Content Knowledge	Integrate Science and Social Studies	Animal Needs	People in Jobs; People in Communities	Communities Over Time; Transportation
	Weekly Question	*What do pets need?*	*Who helps animals?*	*How do animals help people?*
	Knowledge Goals	Children will understand that: • pets need food and water • pets need shelter • pets need exercise • pets need love	Children will understand that: • pet owners help animals • vets help animals • trainers help animals	Children will understand that animals provide: • food for people • transportation for people • services to people
Get Ready to Read	Phonemic Awareness	Distinguish /a/ Segment and Blend Phonemes Rhyming Words	Distinguish /i/ Segment and Blend Phonemes Segment and Count Phonemes	Distinguish /o/ Segment and Blend Phonemes Segment and Count Phonemes
	Phonics	**T** ◎ Short *a: a* **T** ◎ Consonant Pattern *-ck* **Review** Consonant Sounds	**T** ◎ Short *i: i* **T** ◎ Consonant *x*/ks/ **Review** Short *a: a*, Consonant Digraph *-ck*	**T** ◎ Short *o: o* **T** ◎ Plural *-s*, Consonant *s*/z/ **Review** Short *i: i*, Final *x*
	Spelling	Short *a* Words	Short *i* Words	Short *o* Words
Read and Comprehend	High-Frequency Words	**T** *come, in, my, on, way*	**T** *she, take, up, what*	**T** *blue, from, get, help, little, use*
	Comprehension	**T** ◎ **Skill** Character and Setting ◎ **Strategy** Monitor and Clarify **Review Skill** Plot	**T** ◎ **Skill** Plot ◎ **Strategy** Summarize **Review Skill** Character and Setting	**T** ◎ **Skill** Character and Setting ◎ **Strategy** Visualize **Review Skill** Plot
	Vocabulary	Words for Location	Alphabetize	Synonyms
	Fluency	Accuracy	Accuracy	Rate
Language Arts	Writing	Story Trait: Voice	Fantasy Story Trait: Conventions	Short Poem Trait: Sentences
	Conventions	**T** Sentences	**T** Subjects of Sentences	**T** Predicates of Sentences
	Listening and Speaking	Ask Questions	Share Information and Ideas	Give Introductions
	Research Skills	Selecting Books	Media Center/Library	Picture Dictionary

 WEEK 4	 WEEK 5	 WEEK 6
A Fox and a Kit Literary Nonfiction, pp. 102–111 **The Fox and the Grapes** Fable, pp. 116–117	**Get the Egg!** Realistic Fiction, pp. 128–137 **Help the Birds** How-to Article, pp. 142–143	**Animal Park** Literary Nonfiction, pp. 154–163 **Poetry Collection** Poetry, pp. 168–169
 Animal Habitats; Adult and Baby Animals; Animal Adaptation	 Animal Needs; Animal Habitats	 Habitats; Animals in Danger
How do wild animals take care of their babies?	*Which wild animals live in our neighborhood?*	*What can we learn about wild animals by watching them?*
Children will understand that wild animals: • provide food for their babies • protect their babies from harm	Children will understand that: • all kinds of animals live in our neighborhood • neighborhood animals need different kinds of food and shelter	Children will understand that: • we can learn about animals by watching them • wild animals need food, water, and shelter • we protect animals from danger
Segment and Blend Phonemes Count Syllables Segment and Blend Onset and Rime	Distinguish /e/ Segment and Blend Phonemes Segment and Blend Onset and Rime	Distinguish /u/ Segment and Blend Phonemes Segment and Blend Onset and Rime
T Inflected Endings *-s* and *-ing* **Review** Short *o: o, -s* Plurals	**T** Short *e: e* **T** Initial Consonant Blends **Review** Inflected Endings *-s* and *-ing*	**T** Short *u: u* **T** Final Consonant Blends **Review** Short *e: e*, Initial Consonant Blends
Inflected Ending *-s*	Short *e* Words	Short *u* Words with Final Consonant Blends
T *eat, five, four, her, this, too*	**T** *saw, small, tree, your*	**T** *home, into, many, them*
T **Skill** Main Idea and Details **Strategy** Important Ideas **Review Skill** Realism and Fantasy	**T** **Skill** Main Idea and Details **Strategy** Story Structure **Review Skill** Character and Setting	**T** **Skill** Cause and Effect **Strategy** Text Structure **Review Skill** Main Idea and Details
Alphabetize to the Second Letter	Sort Words	Antonyms
Accuracy and Appropriate Rate	Appropriate Phrasing	Appropriate Phrasing
Personal Narrative Trait: Voice	Realistic Story Trait: Organization	Brief Composition Trait: Focus/Ideas
T Declarative Sentences	**T** Interrogative Sentences	**T** Exclamatory Sentences
Share Information and Ideas	Give Descriptions	Give Directions
How to Read a Chart	List	Notes

Assessment

5 Steps to Success on Reading Street

RIGHT IN YOUR TEACHER'S EDITION

Step 1

Begin the Year

The Assessment Handbook provides ideas and support to begin the school year and beyond.

The Baseline Group Test helps identify where children are. Use the Baseline Test results to make initial grouping decisions and to differentiate instruction based on ability levels.

Online Assessment Save time by using digital assessments. All Reading Street assessments are available on ExamView and in SuccessTracker.

Step 2

Every Day

During the day, use these tools to monitor student progress.

- **Corrective Feedback** provides point of use support.

Corrective feedback | **If...** students are unable to answer the comprehension questions, **then...** use the Reteach lesson in *First Stop*.

- **Monitor Progress** boxes each day check phonemic awareness, phonics, retelling, and oral vocabulary.

MONITOR PROGRESS **Check Retelling**

If... students have difficulty retelling,
then... use the Retelling Cards/Story Sort to scaffold their retellings.

Step 3

Every Week

- **Weekly Assessments** found in your Teacher's Editions on Day 5 check phonics, high-frequency words, and comprehension.
- **Weekly Tests** assess target skills for the week.
- **Fresh Reads** assesses fluency and comprehension as children read a new passage.
- **Reading Street Sleuth** assesses children's ability to find clues in text through close reading.

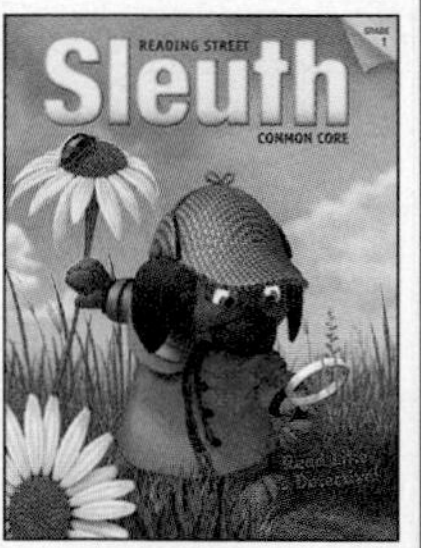

- **Writing to Sources** assesses children's ability to write an argumentative, narrative, or explanatory paragraph in response to one source and then across two sources.

Step 4

Every Unit

- **Unit Benchmark Tests** assess mastery of unit skills: comprehension, vocabulary, conventions, and writing.
- **Unit Benchmark Tests** provide professional development and support with performance-based assessment.

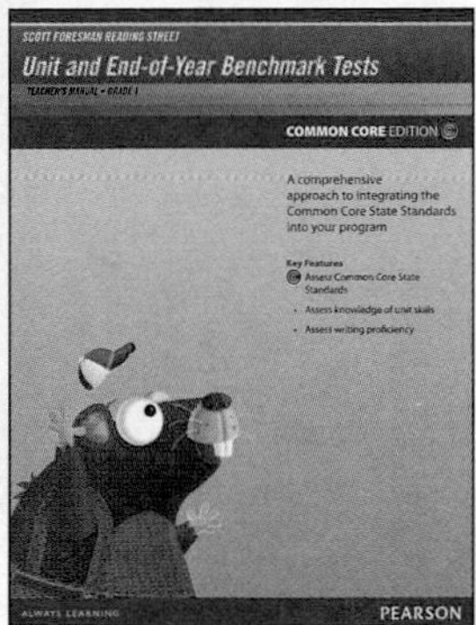

- **Performance-Based Assessments** assess children's ability to demonstrate text-based comprehension and application of higher-order thinking skills.

Step 5

End the Year

- **End-of-Year Benchmark Test** measures student mastery of skills covered in all six units with options for performance-based assessment.

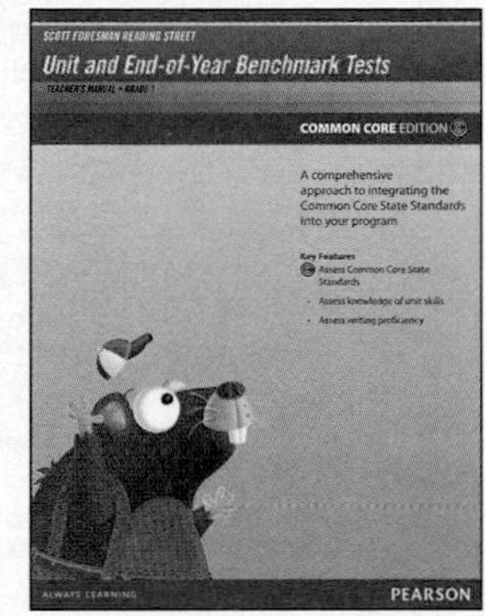

5 Steps to Success on Reading Street

1. Begin the Year
2. Every Day
3. Every Week
4. Every Unit
5. End the Year

Digital Assessment

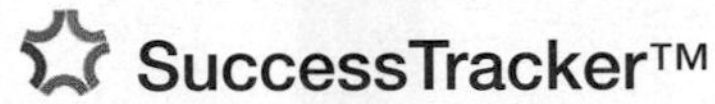

eSTREET INTERACTIVE
www.ReadingStreet.com

Implementing eStreet Interactive

Power up your classroom and put time back on your side!

eSTREET INTERACTIVE
www.ReadingStreet.com

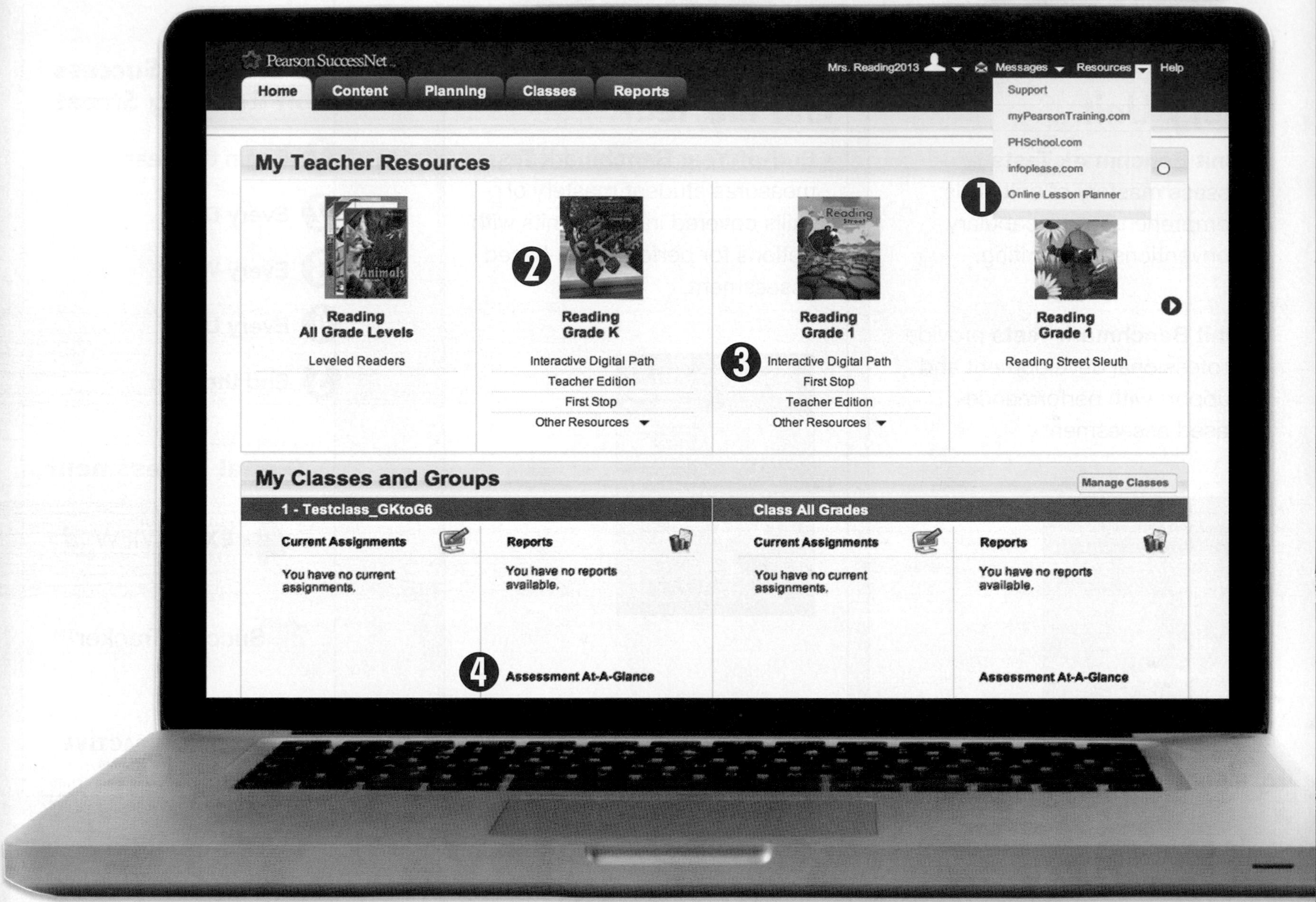

Pearson SuccessNet

Mrs. Reading2013 Messages Resources Help

Home Content Planning Classes Reports

Support
myPearsonTraining.com
PHSchool.com
infoplease.com
1 Online Lesson Planner

My Teacher Resources

Reading All Grade Levels
Leveled Readers

2 Reading Grade K
Interactive Digital Path
Teacher Edition
First Stop
Other Resources

Reading Grade 1
3 Interactive Digital Path
First Stop
Teacher Edition
Other Resources

Reading Grade 1
Reading Street Sleuth

My Classes and Groups

Manage Classes

1 - Testclass_GKtoG6

Current Assignments
You have no current assignments.

Reports
You have no reports available.

4 Assessment At-A-Glance

Class All Grades

Current Assignments
You have no current assignments.

Reports
You have no reports available.

Assessment At-A-Glance

Additional Digital Support

AudioText CD
Sing with Me CD
Background Building CD
Teacher Resources DVD

1 Plan

Customize your daily plan by clicking, dragging, and posting!

- Online Lesson Planner
- Online Teacher's Edition

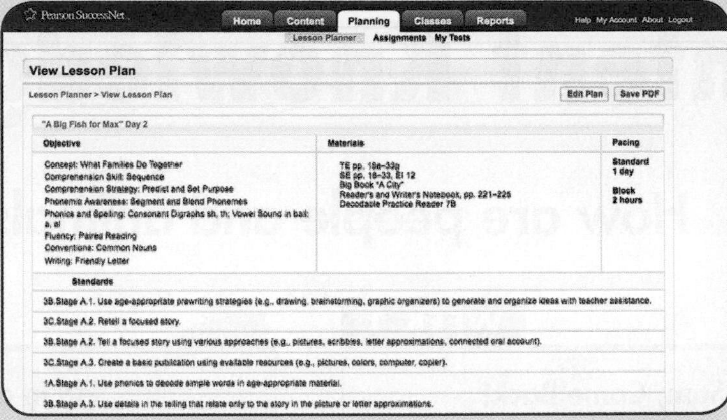

Online Lesson Planner

2 Teach

Engage through interactive media!

- Concept Talk Videos
- Interactive Sing with Me Big Book
- Interactive Sound-Spelling Cards
- Letter Tile Drag and Drop
- Envision It! Animations
- Grammar Jammer

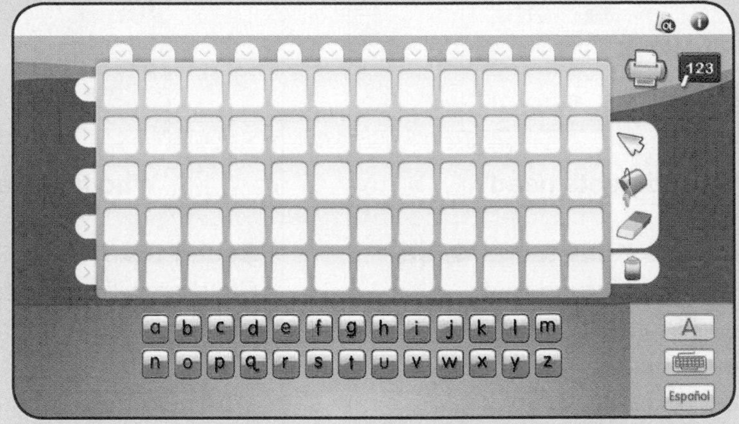

Letter Tile Drag and Drop

3 Practice

Motivate through personalized practice activities!

- Story Sort
- Pearson eText
- Journal
- Vocabulary Activities
- Leveled Reader Database

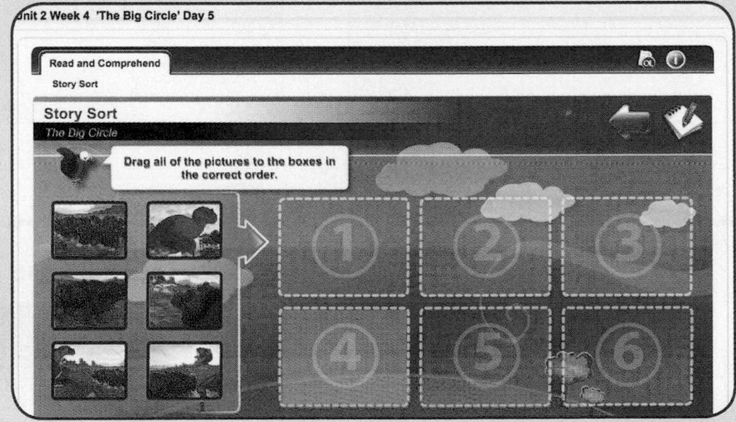

Story Sort

Manage and Assess

Respond to individual needs!

- Monitor Student Progress
- Assign
- Prescribe
- Remediate

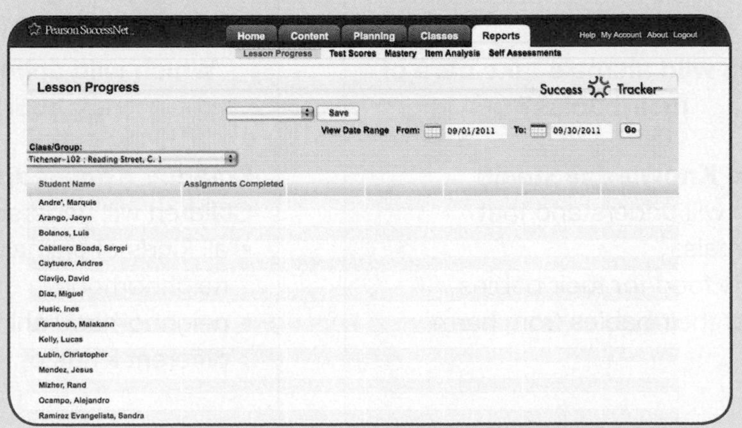

Class Management

Content Knowledge Zoom in on

How are people and animals important to one another?

WEEK 1

Sam, Come Back!

What do pets need?

Social Studies Knowledge Goals
Children will understand that:
- pets need food and water
- pets need shelter
- pets need exercise
- pets need love

WEEK 2

Pig in a Wig

Who helps animals?

Social Studies Knowledge Goals
Children will understand that:
- pet owners help animals
- vets help animals
- trainers help animals

WEEK 3

The Big Blue Ox

How do animals help people?

Social Studies Knowledge Goals
Children will understand that animals provide:
- food for people
- transportation for people
- services to people

WEEK 4

A Fox and a Kit

How do wild animals take care of their babies?

Science Knowledge Goals
Children will understand that wild animals:
- provide food for their babies
- protect their babies from harm

WEEK 5

Get the Egg!

Which wild animals live in our neighborhood?

Science Knowledge Goals
Children will understand that:
- all kinds of animals live in our neighborhood
- neighborhood animals need different kinds of food and shelter

WEEK 6

Animal Park

What can we learn about wild animals by watching them?

Science Knowledge Goals
Children will understand that:
- we can learn about animals by watching them
- wild animals need food, water, and shelter
- we protect animals from danger

This Week's Target Skills and Strategies

Target Skills and Strategies	Common Core State Standards for English Language Arts
Phonemic Awareness **Skills:** Distinguish /a/ Segment and Count Phonemes Rhyming Words	**CCSS Foundational Skills 2.c.** Isolate and pronounce initial, medial vowel, and final sounds (phonemes) in spoken single-syllable words. **(Also CCSS Foundational Skills 2.b.)**
Phonics **Skill:** Short *a*: *a* **Skill:** Consonant Pattern *-ck*	**CCSS Foundational Skills 3.** Know and apply grade-level phonics and word analysis skills in decoding words. **(Also CCSS Foundational Skills 3.a., CCSS Foundational Skills 3.b., CCSS Language 2.d., CCSS Language 2.e.)**
Text-Based Comprehension **Skill:** Character and Setting	**CCSS Literature 3.** Describe characters, settings, and major events in a story, using key details.
Strategy: Monitor and Clarify	**CCSS Literature 3.** Describe characters, settings, and major events in a story, using key details.
Fluency **Skill:** Accuracy	**CCSS Foundational Skills 4.** Read with sufficient accuracy and fluency to support comprehension.
Listening and Speaking Ask Questions	**CCSS Speaking/Listening 1.c.** Ask questions to clear up any confusion about the topics and texts under discussion.
Six-Trait Writing **Trait of the Week:** Voice	**CCSS Writing 5.** With guidance and support from adults, focus on a topic, respond to questions and suggestions from peers, and add details to strengthen writing as needed.
Writing Story	**CCSS Writing 3.** Write narratives in which they recount two or more appropriately sequenced events, include some details regarding what happened, use temporal words to signal event order, and provide some sense of closure. **(Also CCSS Writing 5.)**
Conventions **Skill:** Sentences	**CCSS Language 2.** Demonstrate command of the conventions of standard English capitalization, punctuation, and spelling when writing. **(Also CCSS Language 2.b.)**

This Week's Cross-Curricular Standards and Resources

Cross-Curricular Indiana Academic Standards for Science and Social Studies

Science
IN 1.3.4 Describe how animals' habitats, including plants, meet their needs for food, water, shelter and an environment in which they can live.

Social Studies
IN 1.3.4 Identify and describe physical features and human features of the local community including home, school and neighborhood.

Reading Street Sleuth

Are You My Kitten?
pp. 8–9

Follow the path to close reading using the Super Sleuth tips:

- Look for Clues
- Ask Questions
- Make Your Case
- Prove it!

More Reading in Science and Social Studies

Concept Literacy

Below Level

On Level

Advanced

ELL

ELD

ISBN-13: 978-0-328-73376-7 ISBN-10: 0-328-73376-8

Your 90-Minute Reading Block

	Whole Group	Formative Assessment How do I make my small groups flexible?	Small Group OL On Level SI Strategic Intervention A Advanced What are my other students reading and learning every day in Small Groups?
DAY 1	**Content Knowledge** Build Oral Language/Vocabulary **Phonemic Awareness/Phonics** **Read Decodable Reader** **Phonics/Spelling Pretest** **High-Frequency Words** **Text-Based Comprehension** Teacher Read Aloud **Research and Inquiry** Step 1–Identify and Focus Topic	**Monitor Progress** Formative Assessment: Check Word Reading	**Differentiate Phonics** OL **Practice Phonics** Blend Short *a* Words SI **Reteach Phonics** Blend Short *a* Words A **Extend Phonics** More Challenging Short *a* Words OL SI **Decodable Reader Read** *Hats* A **Advanced Selection** "Happy Dogs and Cats" A Inquiry Project ELL Access Phonemic Awareness and Phonics
DAY 2	**Content Knowledge** Build Oral Language/Vocabulary **Phonemic Awareness/Phonics** **Read Decodable Reader** **Phonics/Spelling** **High-Frequency Words/Selection Words** **Text-Based Comprehension** **Read** Main Selection, using Access Text Notes **Research and Inquiry** Step 2–Research Skill	**Monitor Progress** Formative Assessment: Check Word Reading	**Differentiate Comprehension** OL **Practice Phonics** Additional *-ck* Words SI **Reteach Phonics** Blend *-ck* Words A **Extend Phonics** Additional *-ck* Words OL SI A **Access Text Read** *Sam, Come Back!* A Inquiry Project ELL Access Comprehension Skill
DAY 3	**Content Knowledge** Build Oral Language/Vocabulary **Phonemic Awareness/Phonics** **Phonics/Spelling** **High-Frequency Words/Selection Words** **Text-Based Comprehension** **Reread** Main Selection, using Close Reading Notes **Fluency** **Research and Inquiry** Step 3–Gather and Record Information	**Monitor Progress** Formative Assessment: Check High-Frequency Words **Monitor Progress** Check Retelling	**Differentiate Close Reading** OL **Reread to Develop Vocabulary** SI **Build Word Knowledge** Blend Words with Short *a* and *-ck* A **Reread to Extend Vocabulary** OL SI **Close Reading Reread** *Sam, Come Back!* A **Extend Concepts Reread** *Sam, Come Back!* A Inquiry Project ELL Access the Main Selection
DAY 4	**Content Knowledge** Build Oral Language/Vocabulary **Phonemic Awareness/Phonics** **Read Decodable Reader** **Phonics/Spelling** **Read Content Area Paired Selection with Genre Focus** **Fluency** **Research and Inquiry** Step 4–Synthesize	**Monitor Progress** Fluency Check	**Differentiate Vocabulary** **Build Word Knowledge** OL Develop Language A Extend Amazing Words and Selection Vocabulary SI **Review Vocabulary** Review/Discuss Selection Vocabulary OL SI A **Text-Based Comprehension Read** *Reading Street Sleuth*, pp. 8–9 or Leveled Readers A Inquiry Project ELL Access Vocabulary
DAY 5	**Content Knowledge** Build Oral Language/Vocabulary **Phonemic Awareness/Phonics** **Phonics/Spelling Test** **Let's Learn It!** Vocabulary/Fluency/Listening and Speaking **Text-Based Comprehension** **High-Frequency and Selection Words** **Genre** **Assessment** Phonics, High-Frequency Words, Fluency **Research and Inquiry** Step 5–Communicate	**Monitor Progress** Formative Assessment: Check Oral Vocabulary **Monitor Progress** Word and Sentence Reading	**Differentiate Reteaching** OL **Practice Sentences** SI **Review Vocabulary** A **Extend Sentences** OL SI A **Text-Based Comprehension Reread** *Reading Street Sleuth*, pp. 8–9 or Leveled Readers A Inquiry Project ELL Access Conventions and Writing

Daily Independent Options

What do my other students do when I lead Small Groups?

★ **Independent Reading**

Suggestions for this week's independent reading:

- Informational texts on last week's social studies topic: What can we see around our neighborhood?
- Nonfiction selections about what we see around our neighborhood
- Nonfiction book by a favorite author

Book Talk

Foster critical reading and discussion skills through independent and close reading.

Students should focus on discussing one or more of the following:

- Key Ideas and Details
- Craft and Structure
- Integration of Ideas

Pearson eText
- Student Edition
- Decodable Readers
- Leveled Readers

Trade Book Library

Materials from School or Classroom Library

Independent Stations
Practice Last Week's Skills

★ Focus on these activities when time is limited.

Listen Up!
★ **Word Work**
★ **Read for Meaning**
★ **Let's Write!**
Words to Know
Get Fluent

Assessment Resources

Common Core Weekly Tests, pp. 37–42

Common Core Fresh Reads for Fluency and Comprehension, pp. 37–42

Common Core Unit 1 Benchmark Test

Common Core Success Tracker, ExamView, and Online Lesson Planner

Focus on Common Core State Standards ©

Main Selection, pp. 20–29

Paired Selection, pp. 34–35

Text-Based Comprehension

Character and Setting
CCSS Literature 3.

Monitor and Clarify
CCSS Literature 3.

Fluency

Accuracy
CCSS Foundational Skills 4.

Writing and Conventions

Trait: Voice
CCSS Writing 5.

Writing Mini-Lesson: Story
CCSS Writing 3.

Conventions: Sentences
CCSS Language 2.,
CCSS Language 2.b.

Oral Vocabulary

needs	tickle
responsibility	faithful
shelter	fetch
cuddle	heel

CCSS Language 5.c.

High-Frequency Words

come	in	my
on	way	

CCSS Foundational Skills 3.g.

Phonemic Awareness

Distinguish /a/
Segment and Count Phonemes
Rhyming Words
CCSS Foundational Skills 2.b.,
CCSS Foundational Skills 2.c.

Phonics and Spelling

Short *a*: *a*
Consonant Pattern *-ck*
CCSS Foundational Skills 3.,
CCSS Foundational Skills 3.a.,
CCSS Foundational Skills 3.b.,
CCSS Language 2.d.,
CCSS Language 2.e.

can	cat	back
dad	am	bat
mad	ran	sack
at		

Listening and Speaking

Ask Questions
CCSS Speaking/Listening 1.c.

Preview Your Week

What do pets need?

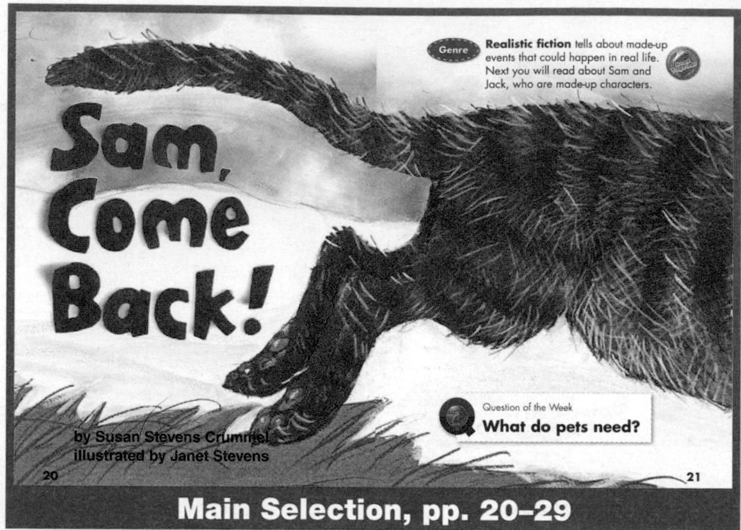

Main Selection, pp. 20–29

Genre: Realistic Fiction

Phonics: Short *a: a,* Consonant Pattern *-ck*

Text-Based Comprehension: Character and Setting

Paired Selection, pp. 34–35

Social Studies in Reading

Genre: Sing-Along

Build Content Knowledge

KNOWLEDGE GOALS
Children will understand that:

- pets need food and water
- pets need shelter
- pets need exercise
- pets need love

THIS WEEK'S CONCEPT MAP
Develop a concept-related graphic organizer like the one below over the course of this week.

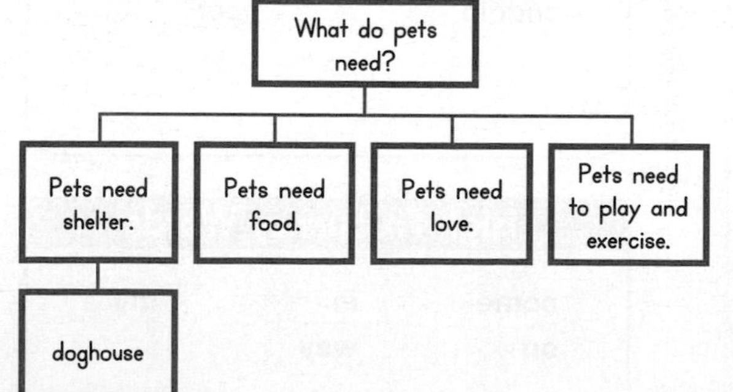

BUILD ORAL VOCABULARY
This week, children will acquire the following academic vocabulary/domain-specific words.

Amazing Words

needs	tickle	cuddle
responsibility	faithful	heel
shelter	fetch	

OPTIONAL CONCEPT-BASED READING Use the Digital Path to access readers offering different levels of text complexity.

Concept Literacy

Below Level

On Level

Advanced

ELL

ELD

This Week's Digital Resources

eStreet Interactive

www.ReadingStreet.com

Get Ready to Read

Background Building Audio CD This audio CD provides valuable background information about pets to help children read and comprehend the weekly texts.

Concept Talk Video Use this video on the Digital Path to build momentum and introduce the weekly concept of pets.

Interactive Sing with Me Big Book "Please Get Me a Pet," sung to the tune of "Camptown Races," introduces the Amazing Words with a catchy, concept-related song.

Interactive Sound-Spelling Cards With these interactive cards on the Digital Path, children see an image, hear the image name, and see the spelling for short *a* spelled *a*, and the consonant pattern *-ck*.

Pearson eText Use the eText for the Decodable Readers on the Leveled Reader Database for phonics and fluency support.

Letter Tile Drag and Drop Using this interactive tool on Pearson SuccessNet, children click and spell words to enhance their phonics skills.

Read and Comprehend

Envision It! Animations Use this colorful animation on the Digital Path to explain the target comprehension skill, Character and Setting.

Pearson eText Read the eText of the main selection, *Sam, Come Back!*, and the paired selection, "Puppy Games," with audio support on Pearson SuccessNet.

Story Sort Use the Story Sort Activity on the Digital Path after reading *Sam, Come Back!* to involve children in summarizing.

Journal: Word Bank Use the Word Bank on the Digital Path to have children write sentences using this week's high-frequency words.

Vocabulary Activities A variety of interactive vocabulary activities on the Digital Path help children practice high-frequency and concept-related words.

Language Arts

Grammar Jammer Choose a whimsical animation on the Digital Path to provide an engaging grammar lesson that will capture children's attention.

Pearson eText Find the Student Edition eText of the Let's Write It! and Let's Learn It! pages with audio support on Pearson SuccessNet.

Additional Resources

Teacher Resources DVD-ROM Use the following resources on the TR DVD or on Pearson SuccessNet throughout the week:

- Amazing Word Cards
- Reader's and Writer's Notebook
- Writing Transparencies
- Daily Fix-It Transparencies
- Scoring Rubrics
- Grammar Transparencies
- Research Transparencies
- Let's Practice It!
- Graphic Organizers
- High-Frequency Word Cards
- Vocabulary Transparencies

This Week's Skills

Phonics
Short *a: a*
Consonant Pattern *-ck*

Comprehension
Skill: Character and Setting
Strategy: Monitor and Clarify

Language
Vocabulary: Words for Location
Conventions: Sentences

Fluency
Accuracy

Writing
Story

5-Day Planner

DAY 1

Get Ready to Read

Content Knowledge 12j
Oral Vocabulary: *needs, responsibility, shelter*

Phonemic Awareness 14–15
Distinguish /a/

Phonics/Spelling 15a
Short *a: a*
READ Decodable Reader 1A
Reread for Fluency
Spelling Pretest

Monitor Progress
Check Word Reading

Read and Comprehend

High-Frequency Words 17
come, in, my, on, way

Text-Based Comprehension 17a
Character and Setting

Language Arts

Conventions 17c
Sentences

Writing 17d
Story

Research and Inquiry 17f
Identify and Focus Topic

DAY 2

Get Ready to Read

Content Knowledge 18a
Oral Vocabulary: *cuddle, tickle*

Phonemic Awareness 18c
Segment and Blend Phonemes

Phonics/Spelling 18d
Consonant Pattern *-ck*
Review Short Vowels
READ Decodable Reader 1B
Reread for Fluency
Spelling: Short *a* Words

Monitor Progress
Check Word Reading

Read and Comprehend

High-Frequency Words 19
come, in, my, on, way

Selection Vocabulary 20a
Jack, Sam
Words for Location

Text-Based Comprehension 20b
READ *Sam, Come Back!*—1st Read

Genre 29b
Realistic Fiction

Language Arts

Conventions 29c
Sentences

Writing 29d
Story

Handwriting 29f
Letter *Aa*/Letter Size

Research and Inquiry 29g
Selecting Books

DAY 3

Get Ready to Read

Content Knowledge 30a
Oral Vocabulary: *faithful*

Phonemic Awareness 30c
Rhyming Words

Phonics/Spelling 30d
Build Words
Blend and Read
Spelling: Dictation

Read and Comprehend

High-Frequency Words and Selection Words 30g
High-Frequency Words: *come, in, my, on, way*
Selection Words: *Jack, Sam*
Monitor Progress Check High-Frequency Words

Text-Based Comprehension 30h
READ *Sam, Come Back!*—2nd Read
Monitor Progress Check Retelling

Fluency 31b
Accuracy

Language Arts

Conventions 32a
Sentences

Writing 32–33
Story

Listening and Speaking 33b
Ask Questions

Research and Inquiry 33c
Gather and Record Information

DAY 4

Get Ready to Read

Content Knowledge 34a
Oral Vocabulary: *fetch, heel*

Phonemic Awareness 34c
Distinguish /a/

Phonics/Spelling 34d
Review Consonant Sounds
READ Decodable Reader 1C
Spiral Review Fluent Word Reading
Spelling: Short *a* Words

Read and Comprehend

Social Studies in Reading 34i
READ "Puppy Games" —Paired Selection

Fluency 35b
Accuracy
Monitor Progress Fluency Check

Language Arts

Conventions 35c
Sentences

Writing 35d
Story

Research and Inquiry 35f
Synthesize

DAY 5

Get Ready to Read

Content Knowledge 36a
Review Oral Vocabulary
Monitor Progress Check Oral Vocabulary

Phonemic Awareness 36c
Review Segment and Count Phonemes

Phonics/Spelling 36c
Review Short *a: a,* Consonant Pattern *-ck*
Spelling Test

Read and Comprehend

Listening and Speaking 36–37
Vocabulary 37a
Fluency 37a

Text-Based Comprehension 37b
Review Character and Setting

Vocabulary 37b
Review High-Frequency and Selection Words

Genre 37c
Review Song

Assessment 37d
Monitor Progress Word and Sentence Reading

Language Arts

Conventions 37g
Review Sentences

Writing 37h
Story

Research and Inquiry 37j
Communicate

Wrap Up Your Week! 37k

Access for All

What do I do in group time?

It's as easy as 1-2-3!

1 TEACHER-LED SMALL GROUPS → 2 INDEPENDENT PRACTICE STATIONS → 3 INDEPENDENT READING

Small Group Time

Bridge to Common Core

SKILL DEVELOPMENT

- Short *a: a*
- Consonant Pattern *-ck*
- Character and Setting
- Monitor and Clarify

DEEP UNDERSTANDING

This Week's Knowledge Goals

Children will understand that:

- pets need food and water
- pets need shelter
- pets need exercise
- pets need love

1 Small Group Lesson Plan

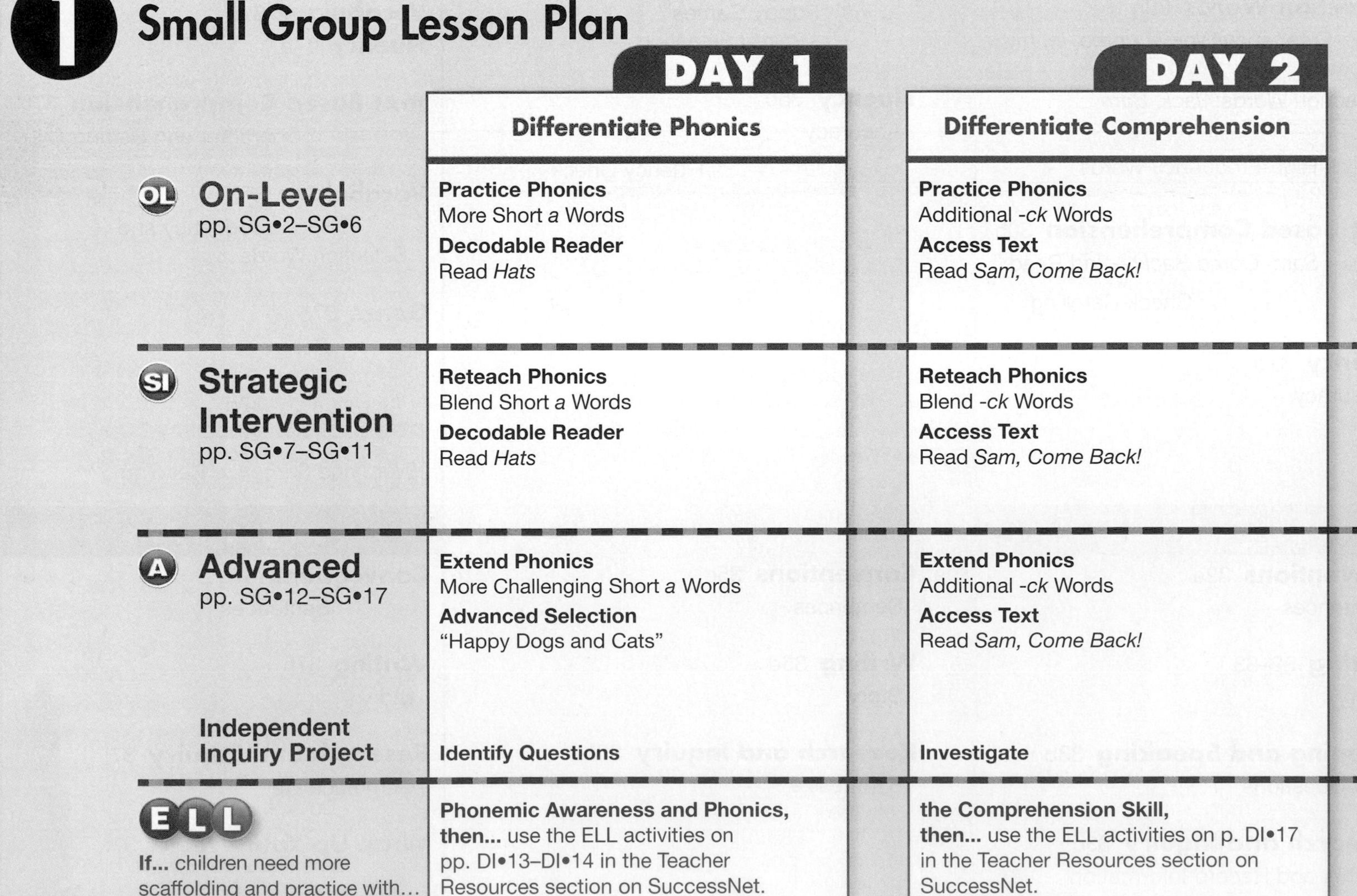

	DAY 1 Differentiate Phonics	DAY 2 Differentiate Comprehension
OL On-Level pp. SG•2–SG•6	**Practice Phonics** More Short *a* Words **Decodable Reader** Read *Hats*	**Practice Phonics** Additional *-ck* Words **Access Text** Read *Sam, Come Back!*
SI Strategic Intervention pp. SG•7–SG•11	**Reteach Phonics** Blend Short *a* Words **Decodable Reader** Read *Hats*	**Reteach Phonics** Blend *-ck* Words **Access Text** Read *Sam, Come Back!*
A Advanced pp. SG•12–SG•17	**Extend Phonics** More Challenging Short *a* Words **Advanced Selection** "Happy Dogs and Cats"	**Extend Phonics** Additional *-ck* Words **Access Text** Read *Sam, Come Back!*
Independent Inquiry Project	**Identify Questions**	**Investigate**
ELL **If...** children need more scaffolding and practice with...	**Phonemic Awareness and Phonics,** **then...** use the ELL activities on pp. DI•13–DI•14 in the Teacher Resources section on SuccessNet.	**the Comprehension Skill,** **then...** use the ELL activities on p. DI•17 in the Teacher Resources section on SuccessNet.

Reading Street Sleuth

- Provides access to grade-level text for all children
- Focuses on finding clues in text through close reading
- Builds capacity for complex text

Build Text-Based Comprehension

Zoom in on

Sam, Come Back!

Optional Leveled Readers

Concept Literacy

Below Level

On Level

Advanced

ELL

ELD

DAY 3	DAY 4	DAY 5
Differentiate Close Reading	**Differentiate Vocabulary**	**Differentiate Reteaching**
Reread to Develop Vocabulary **Close Reading** Reread *Sam, Come Back!*	**Build Word Knowledge** Develop Language **Text-Based Comprehension** Read *Reading Street Sleuth,* pp. 8–9 or Leveled Readers	**Practice Sentences** **Text-Based Comprehension** Reread *Reading Street Sleuth,* pp. 8–9 or Leveled Readers
Build Word Knowledge Blend Words with Short *a* and *-ck* **Close Reading** Reread *Sam, Come Back!*	**Review Vocabulary** Review/Discuss Selection Vocabulary **Text-Based Comprehension** Read *Reading Street Sleuth,* pp. 8–9 or Leveled Readers	**Review Vocabulary** High-Frequency Words **Text-Based Comprehension** Reread *Reading Street Sleuth,* pp. 8–9 or Leveled Readers
Reread to Extend Vocabulary **Extend Concepts** Reread *Sam, Come Back!* **Investigate**	**Build Word Knowledge** Extend Amazing Words and Selection Vocabulary **Text-Based Comprehension** Read *Reading Street Sleuth,* pp. 8–9 or Leveled Readers **Organize**	**Extend Sentences** **Text-Based Comprehension** Reread *Reading Street Sleuth,* pp. 8–9 or Leveled Readers **Communicate**
the Main Selection, **then...** use the activities on p. DI•18 in the Teacher Resources section on SuccessNet.	**Vocabulary,** **then...** use the routine on pp. xxxvi–xxxvii in the *ELL Handbook.*	**Conventions and Writing,** **then...** use the Grammar Transition Lessons on pp. 346–421 in the *ELL Handbook.*

2 Independent Stations

Practice Last Week's Skills

★ Focus on these activities when time is limited.

ACCESS FOR ALL
● Below-Level Activities
▲ On-Level Activities
■ Advanced Activities

LISTEN UP!

Match sounds and pictures.

OBJECTIVES
- Identify words with sounds /v/, /y/, /z/, or /kw/.

MATERIALS
- *Listen Up!* Flip Chart Activity 1; Picture Cards *vacuum, van, vase, vest, yak, yarn, yellow, yo-yo, zebra, zigzag, zipper, zoo, quarter, queen, quilt, five, glove, olive, puzzle*

 **Modeled Pronunciation Audio CD**

● Children find Picture Cards that begin with the same first sound as *voice, yell, zero,* and *quit.*

▲ Children find Picture Cards that begin with the same first sound as *voice, yell, zero,* and *quit.* Then find Picture cards with the same ending sound as *live.* Last, find Picture Cards with the same middle sound as *raisin.*

■ Children find Picture Cards with the same first sound as *voice, yell, zero,* and *quit* and name words that rhyme.

★ WORD WORK

Build and read words.

OBJECTIVES
- Build words that contain the consonants *v, y, z,* or *qu.*
- Read words that contain *v, y, z,* or *qu.*

MATERIALS
- *Word Work* Flip Chart Activity 1, Letter Tiles, paper, pencils

Interactive Sound-Spelling Cards  **Letter Tile Drag and Drop**

● Children use Letter Tiles to build the words *van, yam, zap,* and *quiz* and then say each word.

▲ Children use Letter Tiles to build the words *van, yam, zap,* and *quiz.* Then they write the words on their papers.

■ Children think of other words that contain consonants *v, y, z,* or *qu.* Have them build the words with Letter Tiles and write the words on their papers.

★ LET'S WRITE!

Write sentences.

OBJECTIVES
- Write sentences that include nouns, verbs, and adjectives.
- Write complete sentences.

MATERIALS
- *Let's Write!* Flip Chart Activity 1, paper, pencils

 **Grammar Jammer**

● Children write a sentence about a fruit or vegetable using nouns, verbs, and adjectives.

▲ Children write two sentences about a fruit or vegetable using nouns, verbs, and adjectives.

■ Children write sentences about a farmers market and what they might see using nouns, verbs, and adjectives.

WORDS TO KNOW

Practice high-frequency words.

OBJECTIVES
- Identify high-frequency words *where, here, for, me,* and *go.*
- Spell high-frequency words *where, here, for, me,* and *go.*

MATERIALS
- *Words to Know* Flip Chart Activity 1, Letter Tiles, paper, pencils

 **Vocabulary Activities**  **Teacher Resources**
- High-Frequency Word Cards for Unit R, Week 6

● Children use the Word Cards for *where, here, for, me,* and *go.* Match Letter Tiles to the letters on the cards.

▲ Children copy the Word Cards for *where, here, for, me,* and *go* on their papers.

■ Children write two sentences using the words *where, here, for, me,* and *go.*

READ FOR MEANING

Use text-based comprehension tools.

OBJECTIVES

- Identify realism and fantasy.

MATERIALS

- *Read for Meaning* Flip Chart Activity 1, Leveled Readers, paper, pencils, crayons

 **Pearson eText**
- Leveled eReaders

 **Envision It! Animations**

● Children read one of the Readers and identify if the selection is realistic or fantasy. Then they draw their favorite part.

▲ Children read one of the Readers. They can write a sentence explaining if the plot is realistic or fantasy.

■ Children read one of the Readers. They can draw two versions of the story, one will be realistic and the other will be fantasy. Children will label each version.

GET FLUENT

Practice fluent reading.

OBJECTIVES

- Read aloud with accuracy.

MATERIALS

- *Get Fluent* Flip Chart Activity 1, Student Edition for Unit R

 **Pearson eText**
- Leveled eReaders

Children will open their Student Editon to page 148 of *Farmers Market.* They will track the print as they listen to the AudioText CD. Notice how the reader says the words on each page. Stop the CD and have children read the book aloud themselves.

Manage the Stations

Use these management tools to set up and organize your Practice Stations:

Practice Station Flip Charts

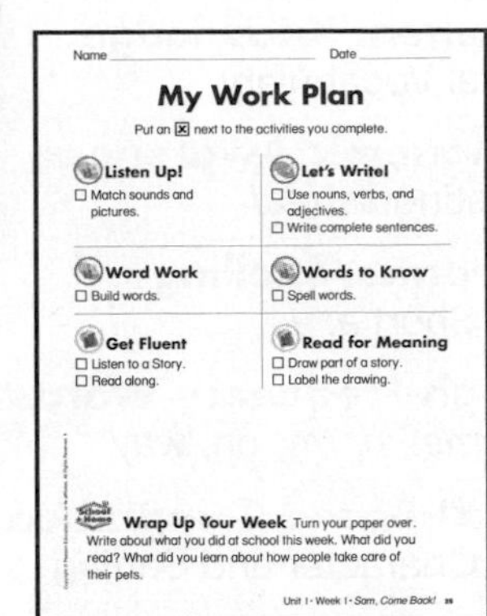
Name Date

My Work Plan

Put an ☒ next to the activities you complete.

Listen Up!
☐ Match sounds and pictures.

Let's Write!
☐ Use nouns, verbs, and adjectives.
☐ Write complete sentences.

Word Work
☐ Build words.

Words to Know
☐ Spell words.

Get Fluent
☐ Listen to a Story.
☐ Read along.

Read for Meaning
☐ Draw part of a story.
☐ Label the drawing.

Wrap Up Your Week Turn your paper over. Write about what you did at school this week. What did you read? What did you learn about how people take care of their pets.

Unit 1 • Week 1 • Sam, Come Back!

Classroom Management Handbook for Differentiated Instruction Practice Stations, p. 25

3 Independent Reading ©

Children should select appropriately complex texts to read and write about independently every day before, during, and after school.

Suggestions for this week's independent reading:
- Informational texts on last week's social studies topic: What can we see around our neighborhood?
- Nonfiction selections about what we see around our neighborhood
- Nonfiction book by a favorite author

BOOK TALK Have partners discuss their independent reading for the week. Tell them to refer to their Reading Log and paraphrase what the selection was about. To focus the discussion, prompt them to talk about one or more of the following:

Key Ideas and Details
- Who is the author? Why did he or she write the work?
- What did I learn from this text?

Craft and Structure
- Did I understand the information?
- Did the author use words that were interesting and clear?

Integration of Ideas
- Did the information seem believable? Why or why not?
- Was this book like others I have read?

 **Pearson eText**
- Student Edition
- Decodable Readers
- Leveled Readers

 **Trade Book Library**

 **Materials from School or Classroom Library**

Content Knowledge
Oral Vocabulary

Phonemic Awareness
Distinguish /a/

Phonics/Spelling
Short *a: a*

High-Frequency Words
come, in, my, on, way

Text-Based Comprehension
Character and Setting

Conventions
Sentences

Writing
Story

Research and Inquiry
Identify and Focus Topic

Materials

- Student Edition
- Sing with Me Big Book
- Sound-Spelling Cards
- Decodable Reader 1A
- Reader's and Writer's Notebook

Bridge to Common Core

INTEGRATION OF KNOWLEDGE/IDEAS
This week children read, write, and talk about pets.

Texts This Week
- "Please Get Me a Pet"
- "A Hamster for Ana"
- *A Kid's Best Friend*
- *Sam, Come Back!*
- "Puppy Games"
- "Just Fur Fun," "Hedgehog"

Social Studies Knowledge Goals
Children will understand that
- pets need food and water
- pets need shelter
- pets need exercise
- pets need love

Street Rhymes!

I will feed Puppy today,
And give him a drink in a tray.
I'll give Puppy a hug
And his leash a small tug,
And then we will go out and play.

- To introduce this week's concept, read aloud the poem several times and ask children to join you.

Content Knowledge

Pets

CONCEPT TALK To help children gain knowledge and understanding, tell them that this week they will talk, sing, read, and write about taking care of pets. Write the Question of the Week, *What do pets need?,* and track the print as you read it.

Build Oral Language

TALK ABOUT PETS Have children turn to pages 12–13 in their Student Edition. Read the title and look at the photos. Use these questions to guide discussion and create the "What do pets need?" concept map.

- The dog's owners made something to shelter, or protect, their dog. What did they build for their pet? (a doghouse) All pets need some kind of shelter. Let's add *Pets need shelter* and *doghouse* to our map.
- The boy is showing responsibility by taking care of his fish. What is he doing? (feeding the fish) All pets have to eat. Let's add *Pets need food* to our map.
- How is the girl taking care of her rabbit? (by hugging it) Yes, she's showing love and affection by hugging it. Let's add *Pets need love* to our map.

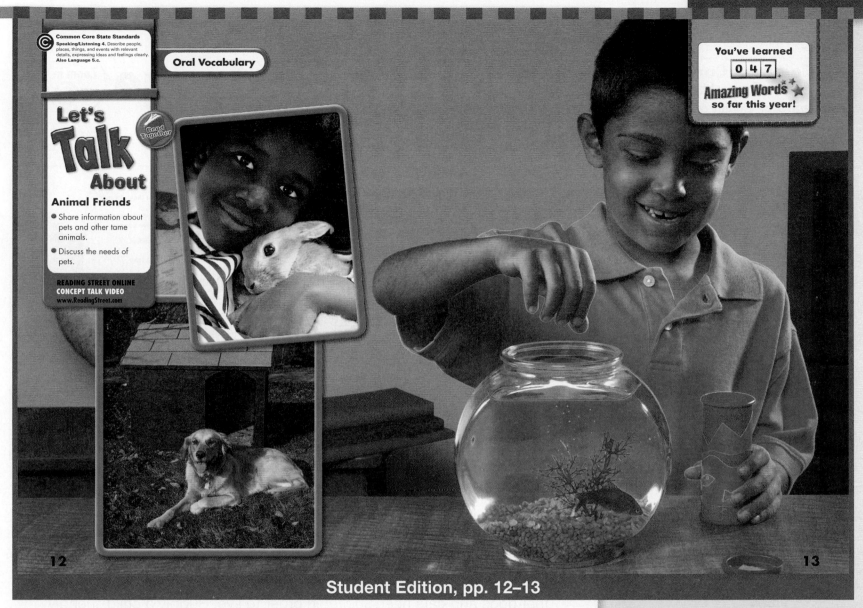

Common Core State Standards
Speaking/Listening 4. Describe people, places, things, and events with relevant details, expressing ideas and feelings clearly. **Also Language 5.c.**

Oral Vocabulary

Let's Talk About

Read Together

Animal Friends

- Share information about pets and other tame animals.
- Discuss the needs of pets.

READING STREET ONLINE
CONCEPT TALK VIDEO
www.ReadingStreet.com

You've learned 047 Amazing Words so far this year!

12 13

Student Edition, pp. 12–13

CONNECT TO READING Explain that this week children will read about a pet cat that likes to run and play. Let's add *Pets need to play and exercise* to our map.

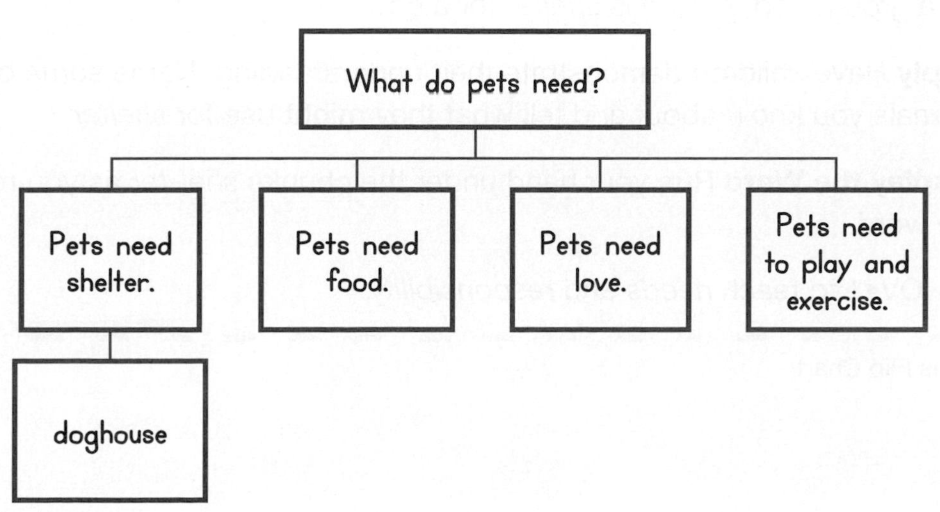

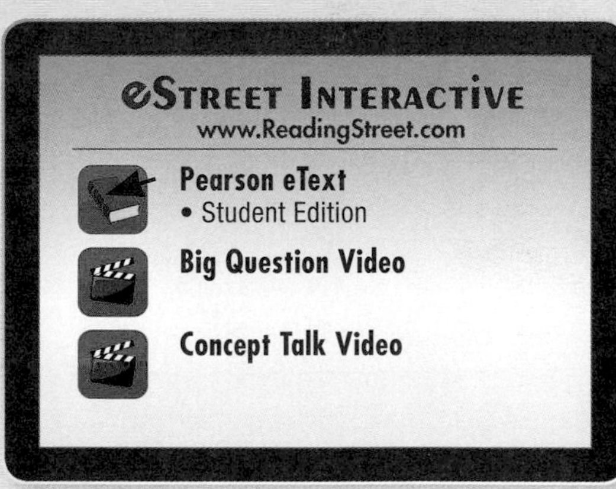

ELL

Preteach Concepts Use the Day 1 instruction on ELL Poster 1 to build knowledge and oral vocabulary.

ELL Support Additional ELL support is provided in the *ELL Handbook* on the *Teacher Resources DVD-ROM.*

Common Core State Standards

Language 5.c. Identify real-life connections between words and their use (e.g., note places at home that are *cozy*).

Content Knowledge

Build Oral Vocabulary

INTRODUCE AMAZING WORDS Display p. 1 of the *Sing with Me* Big Book. Tell children they are going to sing about a girl who wants a pet. Ask children to listen for the Amazing Words *needs*, *responsibility*, and *shelter* as you sing. Sing the song again and have children join you.

Please Get Me a Pet
Pets are great, but they all have
Needs, needs.
Dogs and cats need shelter and
Songbirds must have seeds.
Mommy, Daddy, please,
Get a pet for me.
I am old enough to take
Responsibility.

Sing with Me Big Book, p. 1

Amazing Words

You've learned **047** words so far.

You'll learn **008** words this week!

needs	tickle
responsibility	faithful
shelter	fetch
cuddle	heel

Amazing Words — Robust Vocabulary Routine

1. **Introduce the Word** Relate the word *shelter* to the song. The girl knows that dogs and cats need *shelter* in order to live. Supply a child-friendly definition. A *shelter* is a place where a person or an animal is safe and protected. Have children say the word.
2. **Demonstrate** Provide examples to show meaning. A house is *shelter* for a person. A nest in a bush is *shelter* for a bird. A hole in the ground is *shelter* for a groundhog. A barn is *shelter* for a cow.
3. **Apply** Have children demonstrate their understanding. Name some other animals you know about and tell what they might use for *shelter.*
4. **Display the Word** Run your hand under the chunks *shel-ter* as you read the word.

See p. OV•1 to teach *needs* and *responsibility.*

Routines Flip Chart

AMAZING WORDS AT WORK Have children look at the picture on page 1 of the *Sing with Me* Big Book.

- The owner of the pet shop gives each animal a safe place to live. What kind of shelter do the fish in the store have? Use the word *shelter* in your answer. (Possible response: A tank is shelter for some of the fish.)
- The workers at the shop take care of the animals' needs. What are some things that each animal must have? Use the word *needs* in your answer. (Possible response: One of an animal's needs is food.)
- If the girl in the picture gets a new puppy, she will have some responsibilities. What is one responsibility she might have? Use the word *responsibility* in your answer. (Possible response: It will be her responsibility to walk the dog.)

APPLY AMAZING WORDS Have children demonstrate their understanding of the Amazing Words by completing these sentences orally.

A ______ is a **shelter** for a ______.

Pets have a **need** for ______.

One **responsibility** I have is ______.

Corrective feedback	**If...** children have difficulty using the Amazing Words, **then...** remind them of the definitions and provide opportunities for children to use the words in sentences.

Access for All

SI Strategic Intervention

Sentence Production If children drop letters such as the *l* or *r* in *shelter,* say the word distinctly and have children repeat it. Then have them say their sentence again.

Use Cognates The word *responsibility* has a cognate in Spanish. The Spanish word *responsabilidad* may help Spanish speakers learn the English word.

Common Core State Standards
Foundational Skills 2.c. Isolate and pronounce initial, medial vowel, and final sounds (phonemes) in spoken single-syllable words. **Also Foundational Skills 2.a., 2.b.**

Phonemic Awareness

Let's Listen for Sounds

Read Together

- Find five things that contain the short *a* sound.
- Find five things that end with the sound /k/.
- Find something that rhymes with *luck*. Say each sound in the word.
- Find two things that rhyme with *pant*.

READING STREET ONLINE
SOUND-SPELLING CARDS
www.ReadingStreet.com

SHADY ACRES ANIMAL SHELTER

COME IN

14 15

Student Edition, pp. 14–15

Common Core State Standards

Foundational Skills 2.a. Distinguish long from short vowel sounds in spoken single-syllable words. **Foundational Skills 2.b.** Orally produce single-syllable words by blending sounds (phonemes), including consonant blends. **Also Foundational Skills 2.c., 3.**

Skills Trace

Short *a*: *a*
Introduce U1W1D1
Practice U1W1D3; U1W2D4
Reteach/Review U1W1D3; U1W1D4
Assess/Test Weekly Test U1W1
Benchmark Test U1
KEY: U=Unit W=Week D=Day

Phonemic Awareness

Distinguish /a/

INTRODUCE Read the first bullet point on page 14. What animal is the boy in the picture feeding? (a cat) The middle sound I hear in *cat* is /a/. The sound /a/ is called the short *a* sound. Help children name other items or actions in the picture that have the short *a* sound. (animal, ant, calf, wag, tag, crack, sack)

MODEL Listen as I say the short *a* sound: /a/, /a/, /a/. There are three sounds in *ant:* /a/ /n/ /t/. The first sound in *ant* is /a/. Read these words: *am, egg, add, ax, ape, an, odd, ate, at, in.* Guide children to raise their hands if they hear the /a/ sound at the beginning of the word.

Corrective feedback
If... children make an error,
then... model by segmenting the word, and then have them repeat the segmenting and blending of the word.

Phonics

Short *a*: *a*

CONNECT Write the letter *a*. Have children name the letter and tell if it is a consonant or a vowel. Remind them that they already know many letters and their sounds. Explain that today they will learn how to read and spell words with the /a/ sound spelled *a*.

Sound-Spelling Card 1

USE SOUND-SPELLING CARD Display Card 1. Point to *a*. The letter *a* stands for the short *a* sound, /a/, you hear at the beginning of *astronaut*. Have children say /a/ several times as you point to *a*.

MODEL Write *sat*. In this word, the letter *a* stands for the sound /a/. Segment and blend *sat;* then have children blend with you: /s/ /a/ /t/. Follow this procedure to model *mad* and *jab*.

GROUP PRACTICE Continue segmenting and blending. This time have children blend with you. Remind children that *a* often spells the short *a* sound, /a/.

bag	cat	sad	man	lap	jam
cab	tap	pat	gas	dad	ran

REVIEW What do you know about reading these words? (The letter *a* can spell the short *a* sound, /a/.)

Access for All

A Advanced

Blend Longer Words Have children who can easily blend the CVC words in Group Practice try blending these longer short *a* words: *happy, plant, sadly, thank.*

Vocabulary Support

You may wish to explain the meanings of these words.

jab to push quickly with something that is pointed; poke

cab a car with a driver that is hired to carry passengers; taxi

Produce /a/ In many languages, English short vowel sounds may not exist or may only have approximations. English learners may have a hard time hearing the differences in these sounds. Provide additional phonemic awareness activities to help children hear and pronounce words with short *a*, such as *mat, dab,* and *cap*.

Read Short *a* Spanish does not have the short *a* sound. For this reason, Spanish speakers may read a word like *sad* as *sod*. To provide more practice with short vowels, use pp. 282–283 of the *ELL Handbook*.

Common Core State Standards

Foundational Skills 3. Know and apply grade-level phonics and word analysis skills in decoding words. **Foundational Skills 3.b.** Decode regularly spelled one-syllable words.

Spelling Pattern

/a/ Spelled a The sound /a/ is usually spelled *a* at the beginning or in the middle of a word.

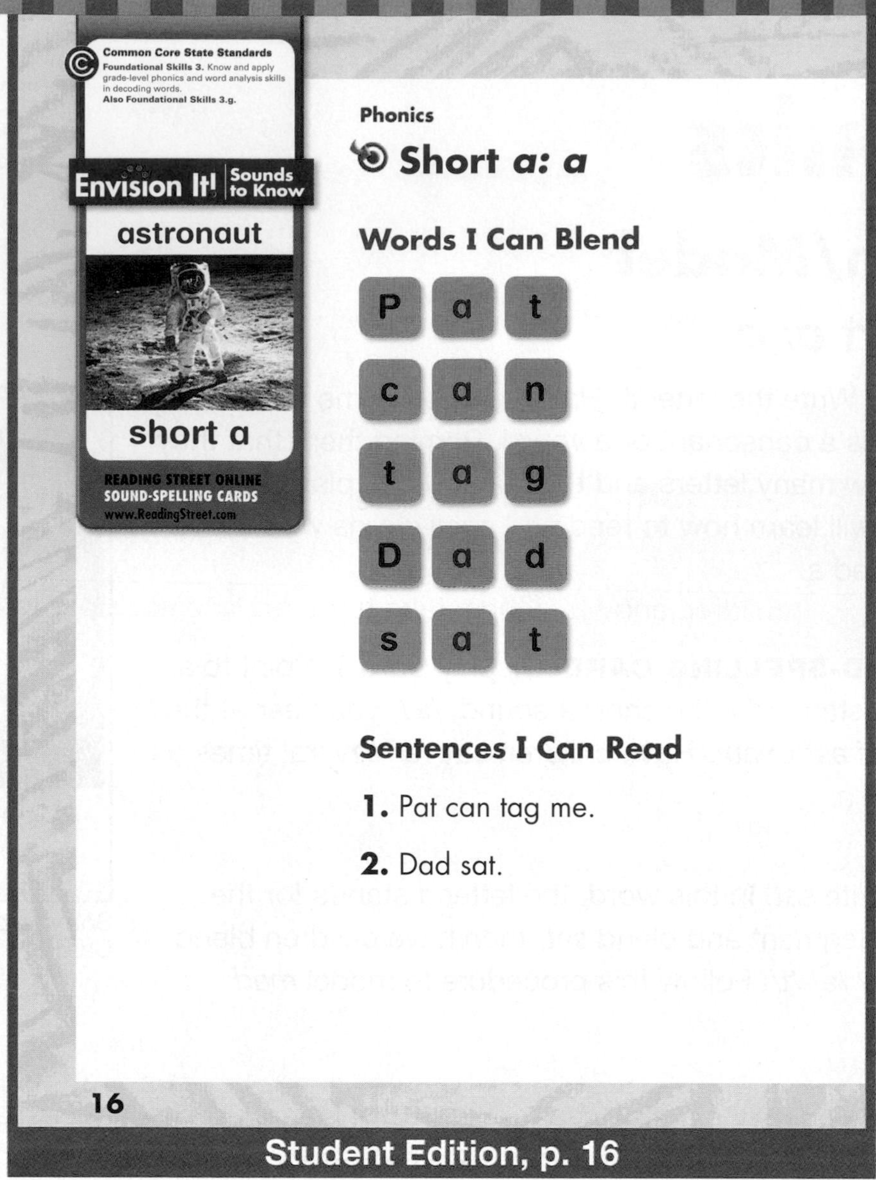

Common Core State Standards
Foundational Skills 3. Know and apply grade-level phonics and word analysis skills in decoding words.
Also Foundational Skills 3.g.

Envision It! Sounds to Know

astronaut

short a

READING STREET ONLINE
SOUND-SPELLING CARDS
www.ReadingStreet.com

Phonics

Short *a*: *a*

Words I Can Blend

P a t

c a n

t a g

D a d

s a t

Sentences I Can Read

1. Pat can tag me.

2. Dad sat.

16

Student Edition, p. 16

Phonics

Guide Practice

BLEND WORDS Have children turn to page 16 in their Student Edition. Look at the picture on this page. I see a picture of an *astronaut.* When I say *astronaut,* I hear the short *a* sound, /a/, at the beginning. The /a/ sound is spelled *a.*

GROUP PRACTICE For each word in "Words I Can Blend," ask for the sound of each letter. Make sure that children identify the correct sound for *a.* Then have children blend the whole word.

Corrective feedback	**If...** children have difficulty blending a word, **then...** model blending the word, and ask children to blend it with you.

DECODE WORDS IN ISOLATION After children can successfully segment and blend the words, point to words in random order and ask children to read them naturally.

DECODE WORDS IN CONTEXT Have children read each of the sentences. Have them identify words in the sentences that have the short *a* sound, /a/.

Team Talk Pair children and have them take turns reading each of the sentences aloud.

ON THEIR OWN Use *Reader's and Writer's Notebook,* p. 121.

MONITOR PROGRESS Short *a: a*

FORMATIVE ASSESSMENT Write the following words and have the class read them. Notice which words children miss during the group reading. Call on individuals to read some of the words.

fan	zap	had	sag	rat	**Spiral Review** Review all initial and final consonants.
pal	wag	lad	van	tap	
yak	bat	gas	jab	mat	

If... children cannot blend short *a* words at this point,

then... use the Small Group Time Strategic Intervention lesson, p. SG•7, to reteach short *a* spelled *a.* Continue to monitor children's progress using other instructional opportunities during the week. See the Skills Trace on p. 14–15.

Access for All

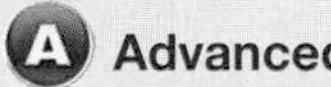

Extend Blending Provide children who can segment and blend all the words correctly with more challenging words such as *trap, plan, glad,* and *handbag.*

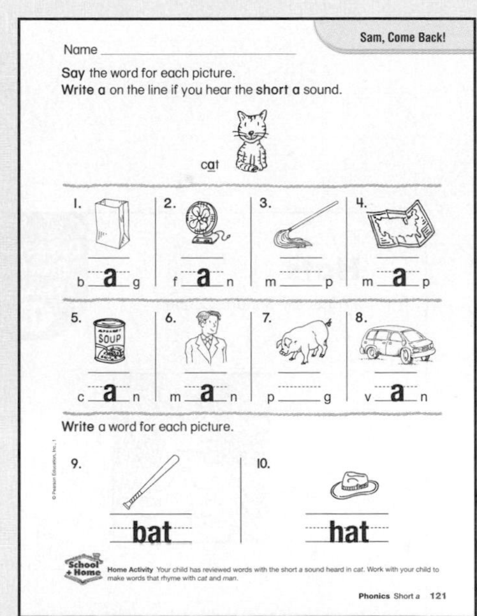
Sam, Come Back!

Name ______

Say the word for each picture.
Write *a* on the line if you hear the **short** *a* sound.

cat

1. b a g
2. f a n
3. m __ p
4. m a p
5. c a n
6. m a n
7. p __ g
8. v a n

Write a word for each picture.

9. bat
10. hat

Home Activity Your child has reviewed words with the short a sound heard in cat. Work with your child to make words that rhyme with cat and man.

Phonics Short a 121

Reader's and Writer's Notebook, p. 121

Common Core State Standards

Foundational Skills 3. Know and apply grade-level phonics and word analysis skills in decoding words. **Foundational Skills 3.b.** Decode regularly spelled one-syllable words. **Foundational Skills 3.g.** Recognize and read grade-appropriate irregularly spelled words.

Decodable Reader 1A

If children need help, then...

Read *Hats*

DECODE WORDS IN ISOLATION Have children turn to page 97. Have children decode each word.

REVIEW HIGH-FREQUENCY WORDS Review the previously taught words *a* and *with.* Have children read each word as you point to it on the Word Wall.

PREVIEW DECODABLE READER Have children read the title and preview the story. Tell them they will decode words that have the short *a* sound, /a/, spelled *a.*

DECODE WORDS IN CONTEXT Pair children for reading and listen as they decode. One child begins. Children read the entire story, switching readers after each page. Partners reread the story. This time the other child begins.

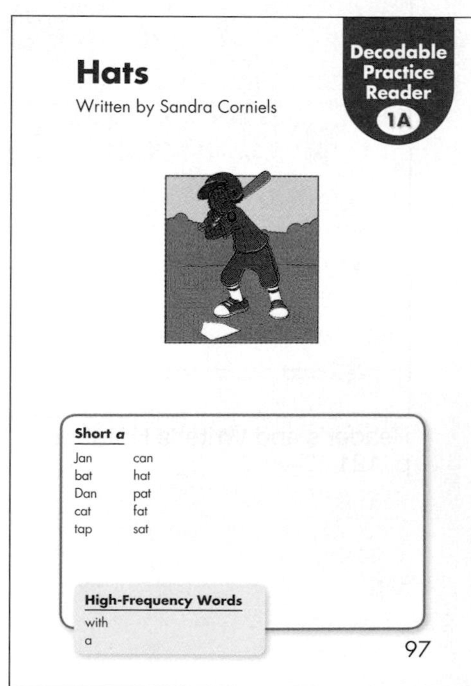

Hats

Written by Sandra Corniels

Decodable Practice Reader 1A

Short *a*

Jan	can
bat	hat
Dan	pat
cat	fat
tap	sat

High-Frequency Words

with
a

97

Decodable Practice Reader 1A

Jan can bat with a hat.

98

Dan can bat with a hat.

99

Jan can pat.
Jan can pat a cat hat.

100

Dan can pat.
Dan can pat with a fat hat.

101

Jan can tap.
Jan can tap with a hat.

102

Dan can tap.
Dan can tap with a hat.

103

Jan sat with a hat.
Dan sat with a hat.

104

Corrective feedback	**If...** children have difficulty decoding a word, **then...** refer them to the Sound-Spelling Cards to identify the sounds in the word. Then prompt them to blend the word. • What is the new word? • Is the new word a word you know? • Does it make sense in the story?

CHECK DECODING AND COMPREHENSION Have children retell the story including characters and events. Then have children find short *a* words in the story. Children should supply *Jan, can, bat, hat, Dan, pat, cat, fat, tap,* and *sat.*

Reread for Fluency

REREAD DECODABLE READER Have children reread Decodable Practice Reader 1A to develop automaticity decoding words with short *a* spelled *a.*

Routine Oral Rereading

1. **Read** Have children read the entire book orally.
2. **Reread** To achieve optimal fluency, children should reread the text three or four times.
3. **Corrective Feedback** Listen as children read. Provide corrective feedback regarding their fluency and decoding.

Routines Flip Chart

Vocabulary Development

Beginning Before children read, lead them through *Hats,* identifying Jan and Dan. Also, point out short *a* words, such as *can, bat,* and *hat,* and their corresponding pictures. Have children say those words aloud as they point to the pictures.

Intermediate After reading, have children find short *a* words, such as *can, cat, hat,* and *pat,* and use them in sentences—for example, *I can pat the cat.* Monitor children's pronunciation.

Advanced After reading, have children retell story events using complete sentences. Monitor children's pronunciation.

Common Core State Standards

Foundational Skills 3.g. Recognize and read grade-appropriate irregularly spelled words. **Language 2.d.** Use conventional spelling for words with common spelling patterns and for frequently occurring irregular words. **Language 2.e.** Spell untaught words phonetically, drawing on phonemic awareness and spelling conventions.

Access for All

A Advanced

Extend Spelling Challenge children who spell words correctly to spell more difficult words such as *jab, zap, quack, ragtag, backpack,* and *catnap.*

Phonics/Spelling Generalization

Short *a* Each spelling word is a short *a* word, which has the short *a* sound.

Name ______ Sam, Come Back!

Short *a* Words

Look at the word. **Say** it. **Listen** for the short *a* sound.

	Write each word.	Check it.
1. at	at	at
2. can	can	can
3. cat	cat	cat
4. back	back	back
5. dad	dad	dad
6. am	am	am
7. bat	bat	bat
8. mad	mad	mad
9. ran	ran	ran
10. sack	sack	sack

Words to Read

11. way way 12. come come

Home Activity Your child is learning to spell words with the short a vowel sound. To practice at home, have your child point to the short a vowel sound, pronounce the word, and write it.

DVD•30 Spelling Short a Words

Let's Practice It! TR DVD•30

ELL

If... children need more scaffolding and practice with **Phonemic Awareness and Phonics,** **then...** use the ELL activities on pp. DI•13–DI•14 in the Teacher Resources section on SuccessNet.

Spelling Pretest

Short *a* Words

DICTATE SPELLING WORDS Dictate the spelling words and read the sentences. Have children write the words. If needed, segment the words for children, clarify the pronunciations, and give meanings of words. Have children check their pretests and correct misspelled words.

1. at	I will see you **at** school.
2. can	I **can** help you build a sand castle.
3. cat*	Our **cat** likes to purr.
4. back*	Please come **back** soon.
5. dad	My mom and **dad** are home.
6. am	I **am** going to see a movie tonight.
7. bat	Swing the **bat** and hit the ball.
8. mad	He stopped being **mad** at his little brother.
9. ran*	The dog **ran** after the ball.
10. sack*	Bring your lunch in a paper **sack**.

* Words marked with asterisks come from the selection *Sam, Come Back!*

ON THEIR OWN Use Let's Practice It! p. 30 on the *Teacher Resources DVD-ROM.*

Day 1 SMALL GROUP TIME • Differentiate Phonics, p. SG•1

OL On-Level	SI Strategic Intervention	A Advanced
• **Practice Phonics** Additional Short *a* Words • **Read** Decodable Reader *Hats*	• **Reteach Phonics** Blend Short *a* Words • **Read** Decodable Reader *Hats*	• **Extend Phonics** More Short *a* Words • **Read** Advanced Selection for Short *a* Words • **Introduce** Inquiry Project

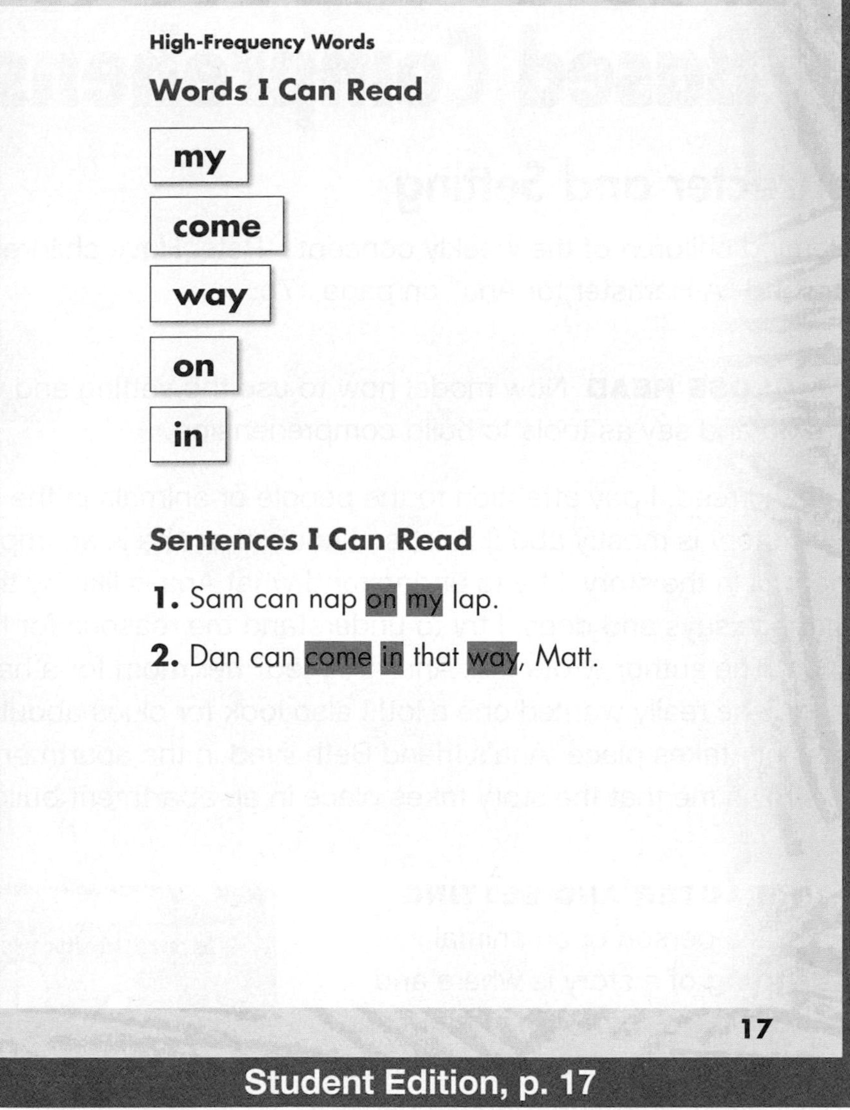

High-Frequency Words
Words I Can Read
my
come
way
on
in
Sentences I Can Read
1. Sam can nap on my lap.
2. Dan can come in that way, Matt.
17

Student Edition, p. 17

Reader's and Writer's Notebook, p. 122

High-Frequency Words

Routine Nondecodable Words

1. **Say and Spell** Some words we learn by remembering the letters. Point to *my.* Have children say and spell each word, first with you, and then without you.
2. **Identify Familiar Letter-Sounds** Point to the first letter in *my.* What is this letter and what is its sound? (*m,* /m/)
3. **Show Meaning** Tell me a sentence using the word *my.* Repeat.

Routines Flip Chart

READ Have children read the page aloud. Add the words to the Word Wall.

ON THEIR OWN Use *Reader's and Writer's Notebook,* p. 122.

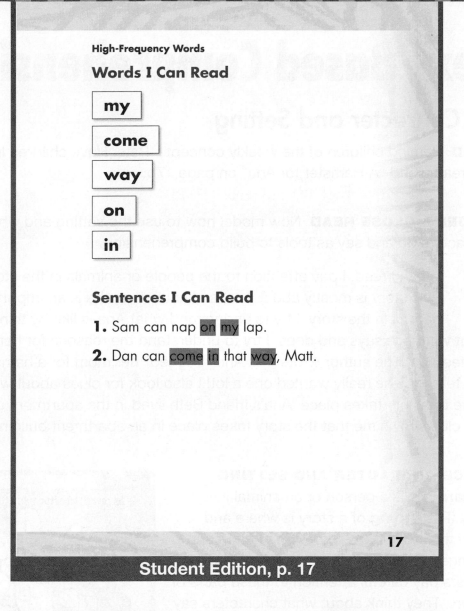

Survival Vocabulary Have children use the word *my* to talk about things that relate to them. Children might say *I like **my** school.*

Text-Based Comprehension

Character and Setting

READ Remind children of the weekly concept—Pets. Have children listen as you read aloud "A Hamster for Ana" on page 17b.

MODEL A CLOSE READ Now model how to use the setting and what the characters do and say as tools to build comprehension.

Think Aloud When I read, I pay attention to the people or animals in the story. This story is mostly about Ana, so I know that she is an important person in the story. I try to understand what Ana is like by thinking about what she says and does. I try to understand the reasons for her actions and feelings. The author wrote that Ana "begged" her mom for a hamster. That tells me she really wanted one a lot! I also look for clues about when and where the story takes place. Ana's friend Beth lived in the apartment upstairs. That clue shows me that the story takes place in an apartment building.

TEACH CHARACTER AND SETTING
A **character** is a person or an animal in a story. The **setting** of a story is where and when the story takes place. Characters and settings can be real or make-believe. Good readers pay careful attention to these parts of a story. They think about what characters say and do and how they feel.

Have children turn to p. EI•4 in their Student Edition. Discuss these questions using the pictures:

- Who are the characters? (bunnies: daddy, mommy, brother, sister)
- What is the setting? (a sunny afternoon in a field)

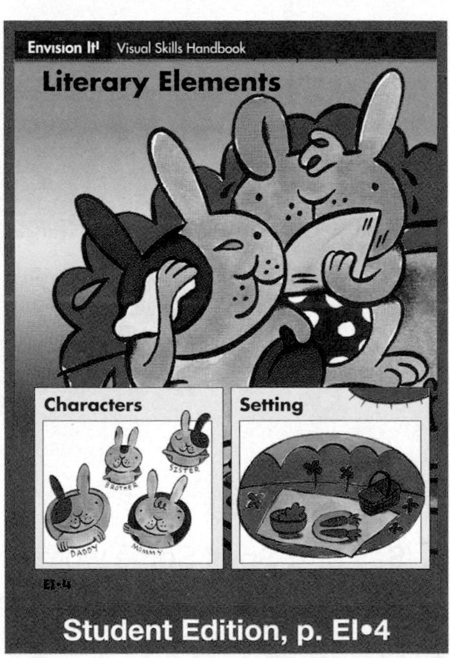

Student Edition, p. EI•4

GUIDE PRACTICE Now reread "A Hamster for Ana." After rereading, ask children to draw a picture of Ana and her mom in their apartment with Harry. Have them label each character and the setting. Ask several volunteers to share their drawings with the class. Have them read their labels and explain what each character is doing and feeling.

APPLY Use *Reader's and Writer's Notebook,* p. 123.

Common Core State Standards

Literature 3. Describe characters, settings, and major events in a story, using key details. **Literature 4.** Identify words and phrases in stories or poems that suggest feelings or appeal to the senses.

Skills Trace

Character and Setting

Introduce U1W1D1; U1W3D1; U5W1D1

Practice U1W1D2; U1W1D3; U1W1D4; U1W3D2; U1W3D3; U1W3D4; U5W1D2; U5W1D3; U5W1D4

Reteach/Review U1W1D5; U1W3D5; U2W2D2; U4W6D2; U5W1D5

Assess/Test Weekly Tests U1W1; U1W3; U5W1
Benchmark Tests U1; U5

KEY: U=Unit W=Week D=Day

Academic Vocabulary

character a person or an animal in a story

setting where and when a story takes place

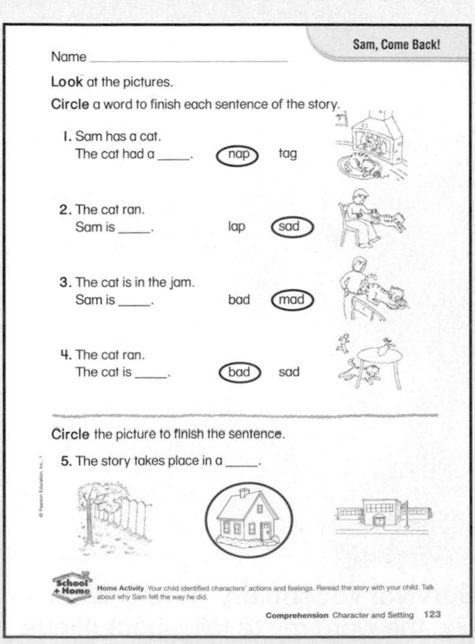
Sam, Come Back!

Name ____________

Look at the pictures.

Circle a word to finish each sentence of the story.

1. Sam has a cat.
The cat had a ____. (nap) tag
2. The cat ran.
Sam is ____. lap (sad)
3. The cat is in the jam.
Sam is ____. bad (mad)
4. The cat ran.
The cat is ____. (bad) sad

Circle the picture to finish the sentence.

5. The story takes place in a ____.

© Pearson Education, Inc. 1

School + Home **Home Activity** Your child identified characters' actions and feelings. Reread the story with your child. Talk about why Sam felt the way he did.

Comprehension Character and Setting 123

Reader's and Writer's Notebook, p. 123

Teacher Read Aloud

A Hamster for Ana

Ana wanted a hamster more than anything else in the world. Her friend Beth, who lived in the apartment upstairs, had a hamster named Harry. Harry was brown and white, and he loved to munch carrots from Beth's hand.

"Mom," Ana begged one day, "can I *please* get a hamster for my birthday next month? I don't want anything else!"

"Ana," her mother said, "having a pet is a big responsibility. Pets have lots of needs. A hamster needs shelter, and do you know what it eats and drinks?"

Ana *did* know. She had paid close attention to how Beth took care of Harry. She just needed a way to show her mom that she was ready for a pet.

The next week, Beth told Ana her family was going out of town. She asked if Ana could take care of Harry while she was away. Ana's mom said it was OK. This was just the chance Ana needed! She could show her mom that she could take care of a hamster.

Every day for a whole week, Ana fed Harry. She kept his water bottle full and his cage clean. She gave him carrots to munch from her hand. Ana's mom gave him carrots to munch too. Ana was so happy that she gave her mom an extra-tight hug.

When Beth got home and came to take Harry back, Ana felt like crying. Ana's mom was sad too. Ana could hardly believe her ears when her mom said, "Let's take the city bus to the pet store downtown to get your birthday present, honey. It's time you had a hamster of your own."

Bridge to Common Core

KEY IDEAS AND DETAILS

As children identify characters and setting in a selection, they develop an understanding of where the selection takes place and what the characters do and say and how these elements contribute to the plot of the selection. Asking questions about the characters and setting helps children better understand these elements of the selection and the key events.

Support Listening Comprehension

Use the modified Read Aloud from the *ELL Support Lesson* on the *Teacher Resources DVD-ROM* to build content knowledge.

Common Core State Standards

Foundational Skills 1.a. Recognize the distinguishing features of a sentence (e.g., first word, capitalization, ending punctuation). **Language 1.** Demonstrate command of the conventions of standard English grammar and usage when writing or speaking. **Language 2.b.** Use end punctuation for sentences. **Also Writing 3., Speaking/Listening 6.**

Academic Vocabulary

sentence a group of words that tells a complete idea

character a person or animal in a story

Daily Fix-It

1. Daad said my kat ran.
   Dad said my cat ran.
2. I im mab at that cat.
   I am mad at that cat.

Discuss the Daily Fix-It corrections with children. Review short *a* spelled *a,* /k/ spelled *c,* and the difference between *b* and *d.*

Conventions

Sentences

MAKE CONNECTIONS This week you listened to a story called "A Hamster for Ana." We can say sentences to tell about Ana. Have children use this sentence frame: *Ana* _______. Then ask children to say the sentences with you. These are *sentences.* They each tell a complete idea about Ana.

TEACH Explain that a **sentence** is a group of words that tells a complete idea. *The cat hid under the bed* is a sentence. Every sentence begins with a capital letter and ends with a punctuation mark. Remind children that a capital letter is the uppercase form of a letter and that many sentences end with a period, a punctuation mark that looks like a dot.

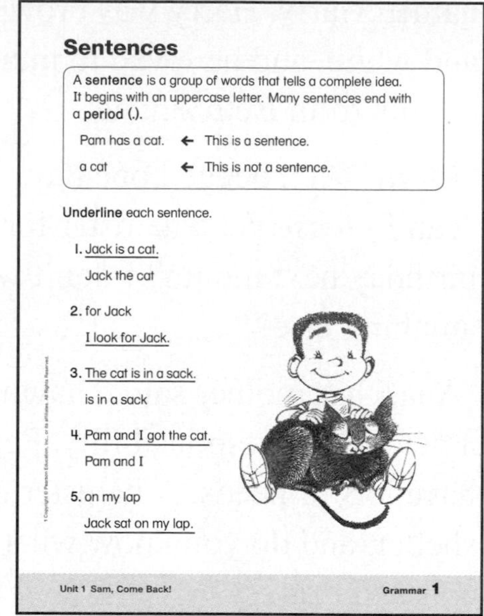

Sentences

A **sentence** is a group of words that tells a complete idea. It begins with an uppercase letter. Many sentences end with a **period** (.).

Pam has a cat. ← This is a sentence.

a cat ← This is not a sentence.

Underline each sentence.

1. Jack is a cat.
   Jack the cat
2. for Jack
   I look for Jack.
3. The cat is in a sack.
   is in a sack
4. Pam and I got the cat.
   Pam and I
5. on my lap
   Jack sat on my lap.

Unit 1 Sam, Come Back! Grammar 1

Grammar Transparency 1 TR DVD

MODEL Display Grammar Transparency 1. Read the definitions and examples aloud. Then read the directions and model number 1.

GUIDE PRACTICE Continue with items 2–5. Have children identify which group of words in each pair is a sentence and explain why.

APPLY Have the class complete these sentence frames orally, adding words to form complete sentences.

1. **A cat _______.**
2. **_______ has a pet.**

Team Talk Pair children and have them talk about their own pets or pets they know. As you circulate, check that children are speaking in complete sentences.

Story

Mini-Lesson Read Like a Writer

- **Introduce** This week you will write a story. A story tells about characters. It tells what the characters do.

  Prompt Think about a pet you know. Write a story about the pet playing.

  Trait Voice

  Mode Narrative

- **Examine Model Text** Let's listen to a story. Track the print as you read aloud "Pooky the Cat" on *Reader's and Writer's Notebook,* p. 124. Have children follow along.

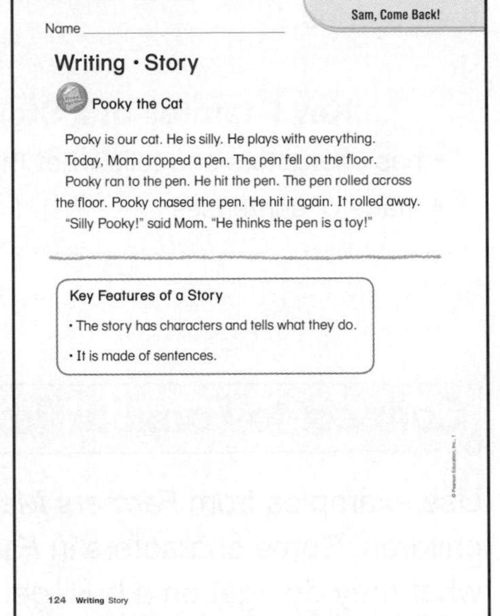

Name ______ Sam, Come Back!

Writing • Story

Pooky the Cat

Pooky is our cat. He is silly. He plays with everything. Today, Mom dropped a pen. The pen fell on the floor. Pooky ran to the pen. He hit the pen. The pen rolled across the floor. Pooky chased the pen. He hit it again. It rolled away. "Silly Pooky!" said Mom. "He thinks the pen is a toy!"

Key Features of a Story
- The story has characters and tells what they do.
- It is made of sentences.

124 Writing Story

Reader's and Writer's Notebook, p. 124

- **Key Features** Who are the two characters in this story? (Pooky and Mom) Help children find and circle the names. Ask what the characters do. Help children underline short phrases and words in the story that tell what the characters do, such as *dropped the pen* and *ran.* Then ask children to find sentences in the story. Help them circle the capital letters that begin sentences and the periods that end them.

  This story has a character who is a person and a character that is an animal. The story tells what the characters do. The writer used sentences to tell what the characters do. Each sentence tells a complete idea. Each one begins with a capital letter and ends with a period.

Writing to Sources Use More Connect the Texts on pp. 221–259 to guide children in writing text-based responses within various forms and modes.

Write Guy *by Jeff Anderson*

Powerful Words, Powerful Verbs

If children have trouble distinguishing complete sentences from fragments, have them ask this question: "Who or what did something? What did they do?" If there is no answer to the question, they know the words are a fragment. Children can have fun making a complete statement by adding together subjects (David) and powerful verbs (laughed, talked, jumped): David laughed.

Bridge to Common Core

TEXT TYPES AND PURPOSES

This week children write a story about a pet they know.

Narrative Writing

As children develop writing skills, they use narrative writing to convey real and imaginary experiences and events. This process helps them develop an understanding of the subject they are studying.

Throughout the week, children will improve the range and content of their writing through daily mini-lessons.

5-Day Plan

DAY 1	Read Like a Writer
DAY 2	Using Strong Verbs
DAY 3	Writing Trait: Voice
DAY 4	Revise: Adding Words
DAY 5	Proofread

Conventions To provide children with practice with sentences, use the modified grammar lessons in the *ELL Handbook.*

Common Core State Standards

Writing 3. Write narratives in which they recount two or more appropriately sequenced events, include some details regarding what happened, use temporal words to signal event order, and provide some sense of closure. **Writing 7.** Participate in shared research and writing projects (e.g., explore a number of "how-to" books on a given topic and use them to write a sequence of instructions). **Writing 8.** With guidance and support from adults, recall information from experiences or gather information from provided sources to answer a question.

Writing

Review Key Features

Review key features of a story with children. You may want to post these key features in the classroom to allow children to refer to them as they work on their stories.

Key Features of a Story
- has characters and tells what they do
- made of sentences

Connect to Familiar Texts

Use examples from *Farmers Market* (Unit R) or another story familiar to children. Some characters in *Farmers Market* are Pam and Dad. The story tells what they do. (get on a bus, get wet) Discuss other characters in the story and what they do. Point out that the story uses sentences to tell what the characters do.

Routine Quick Write for Fluency — Team Talk

1. **Talk** Read these questions aloud, and have children respond with sentences.
   What is a type of pet you know?
   What does the pet do when it plays?
2. **Write** Have children write short sentences to answer the questions. Make sure their sentences are complete, begin with capital letters, and end with periods.
3. **Share** Partners can read their answers to one another.

Routines Flip Chart

Research and Inquiry

Step 1 Identify and Focus Topic

TEACH Display and review the concept map about this week's question: *What do pets need?* What things that pets need would you like to know more about? Invite children to share their ideas. Point out that information in books can help them learn more about what pets need.

Think Aloud **MODEL** It is easier for me to find information in books when I know what I'm looking for. Thinking of questions can help me find what I'm looking for because I can look for answers to my questions. One question I have is about a pet's food. I know that every animal needs food, but what kind of food? My first question will be, *What kind of food does a pet need?*

GUIDE PRACTICE Give children time to think of other questions about what pets need. Record children's questions in a list. Have children think of answers and then record them in the chart.

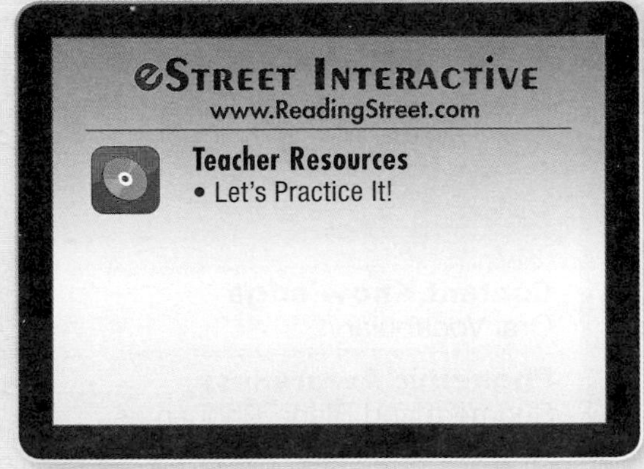

21st Century Skills

Internet Guy *Don Leu*

Weekly Inquiry Project

STEP 1	Identify and Focus Topic
STEP 2	Research Skill
STEP 3	Gather and Record Information
STEP 4	Synthesize
STEP 5	Communicate

Wrap Up Your Day!

✔ **Phonics: Short *a*: *a*** Write *bat* and *am*. Ask children what sound the *a* in *bat* has. (short *a*) Ask children what sound the *a* in *am* has. (short *a*)

✔ **Spelling: Short *a* Words** Have children name the letter that spells each sound in *ran* and write the word. Continue with *at, sad,* and *lap.*

✔ **Content Knowledge** Ask children to recall the Read Aloud "A Hamster for Ana." What does the hamster need? (water, food, shelter)

✔ **Homework** Send home this week's Family Times Newsletter from Let's Practice It! pp. 25–26 on the *Teacher Resources DVD-ROM.*

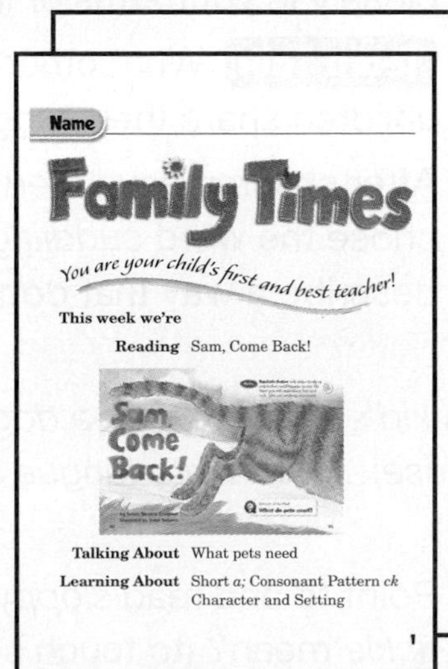

Name
Family Times
You are your child's first and best teacher!
This week we're
Reading Sam, Come Back!
Sam, Come Back!
Talking About What pets need
Learning About Short a; Consonant Pattern ck
Character and Setting
1

Let's Practice It!
TR DVD•25–26

Tell children that tomorrow they will read about a mischievous pet cat.

DAY 2 at a Glance

Content Knowledge
Oral Vocabulary

Phonemic Awareness
Segment and Blend Phonemes

Phonics/Spelling
Short *a: a*
Consonant Pattern *-ck*

High-Frequency Words
come, in, my, on, way

Selection Vocabulary
Jack, Sam
Words for Location

Text-Based Comprehension
Character and Setting
Monitor and Clarify

Conventions
Sentences

Writing
Story

Handwriting
Letter *Aa*/Letter Size

Research and Inquiry
Research Skill: Selecting Books

Materials

- Student Edition
- Sing with Me Big Book
- Big Book
- Reader's and Writer's Notebook
- Decodable Reader 1B
- Sound-Spelling Cards

Common Core State Standards

Speaking/Listening 2. Ask and answer questions about key details in a text read aloud or information presented orally or through other media. **Also Language 5.c., 6.**

Content Knowledge

Pets

EXPAND THE CONCEPT To reinforce concepts and to focus children's attention, have them sing "Please Get Me a Pet" from the *Sing with Me* Big Book. What does the girl think she is now old enough to do? (take responsibility for caring for a pet)

Build Oral Language

INTRODUCE AMAZING WORDS Display the Big Book *A Kid's Best Friend.* Read the title and identify the author. Explain that in the story, the author uses some Amazing Words. Read the story and have children listen for the words *cuddle* and *tickle.*

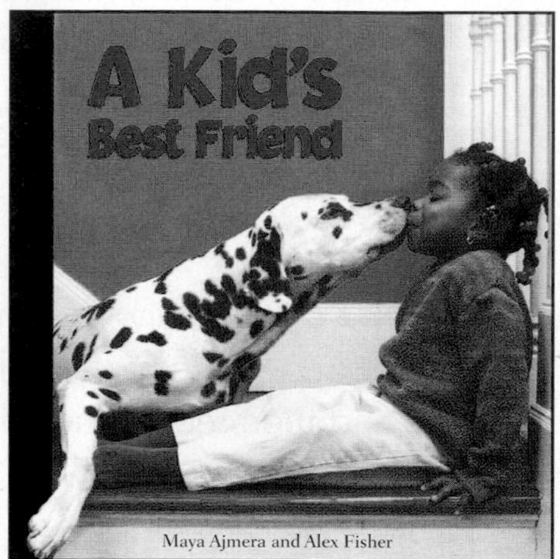

Big Book

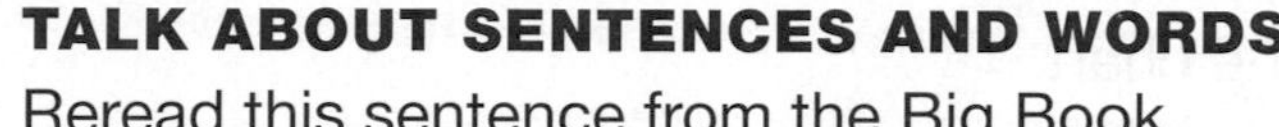

TALK ABOUT SENTENCES AND WORDS Reread this sentence from the Big Book.

A friend for cuddling and feeding and caring for each other on cold mornings and hot afternoons.

- Have children repeat the sentence with you. What does *a friend for cuddling* mean? (a friend to hold closely in your arms or lap)
- **Team Talk** What other word could we use in place of *cuddling?* Have children share their suggestions.
- After children have tried other words, ask: Why do you think the author chose the word *cuddling?* (It is an interesting word and a good way to describe a way that dogs make good friends.)

A kid's best friend is a dog with big floppy ears, a wagging tail, and a wet nose… with a big tongue and sloppy kisses to lick and tickle your face clean.

- Point to and read *sloppy kisses to lick and tickle your face clean.* What does *tickle* mean? (to touch someone lightly and make them giggle) Have children discuss what other parts of a dog the sentence tells about.
- **Team Talk** Turn to your partner and talk about the other ways to describe a dog.

Build Oral Vocabulary

Amazing Words Robust Vocabulary Routine

1. **Introduce the Word** Relate the word *cuddle* to the book. A dog is a friend you can *cuddle.* Supply a child-friendly definition. When you *cuddle* something, you hold it close and love it. Have children say the word.

2. **Demonstrate** Provide examples to show meaning. It's fun to *cuddle* a teddy bear. When you *cuddle* a puppy, you make it feel loved.

3. **Apply** Have children demonstrate their understanding. Tell us about something or someone you like to *cuddle.* Show us how you look when you *cuddle.*

4. **Display the Word** Run your hand under the chunks *cud-dle* as you read the word.

See p. OV•1 to teach *tickle.*

Routines Flip Chart

ADD TO THE CONCEPT MAP Discuss what pets eat and drink.

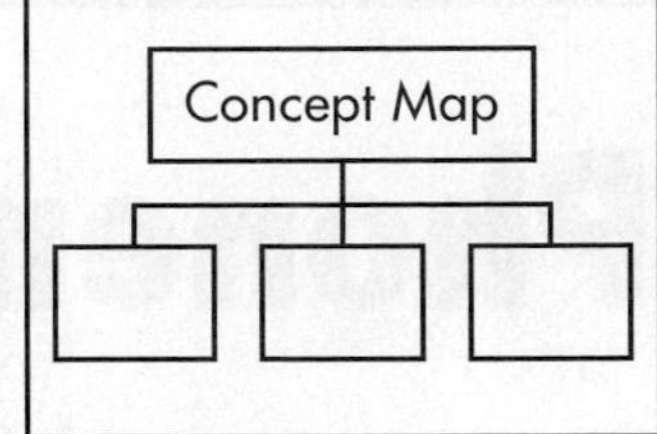

- In the song "Please Get Me a Pet," what does the girl say songbirds need? (seeds) Seeds are one kind of food that pets need. Let's add *seeds for birds* to our map.
- In yesterday's Read Aloud story "A Hamster for Ana," what did Ana give Harry the hamster to eat? (carrots) What did she give him to drink? (water) Let's add *carrots and water for hamsters* to our map.
- What are some other things that pets eat and drink?

Amazing Words

needs	tickle
responsibility	faithful
shelter	fetch
cuddle	heel

Access for All

SI Strategic Intervention

Sentence Production If children pronounce *-le* in *cuddle* or *tickle* as short *u,* pronounce each word carefully and have children repeat it after you. Then have them say their sentence again.

Reinforce Vocabulary Use the Day 2 instruction on ELL Poster 1 to reinforce the meanings of high-frequency words.

Physical Response Teach the words *cuddle* and *tickle* by demonstrating with a stuffed animal. Then have children repeat, using the animal themselves and saying each word in a sentence as they act it out.

Common Core State Standards
Foundational Skills 2.c. Isolate and pronounce initial, medial vowel, and final sounds (phonemes) in spoken single-syllable words. Also Foundational Skills 2.a., 2.b.
Phonemic Awareness
Let's Listen for Sounds
Read Together
Find five things that contain the short a sound.
Find five things that end with the sound /k/.
Find something that rhymes with luck. Say each sound in the word.
Find two things that rhyme with pant.
READING STREET ONLINE
SOUND-SPELLING CARDS
www.ReadingStreet.com
SHADY ACRES ANIMAL SHELTER
COME IN
14
15

Student Edition, pp. 14–15

Phonemic Awareness

Segment and Blend Phonemes

MODEL I see a *truck.* The last sound I hear in *truck* is /k/. I see other things that end with /k/. I see a *sack* and a *duck.* Listen to the sounds in *truck:* /t/ /r/ /u/ /k/. There are four sounds in *truck.* Let's blend those sounds to make a word: /t/ /r/ /u/ /k/. Continue with *sack.*

GROUP PRACTICE Guide children as they segment and blend these words from the picture: *black, backpack, stack, tracks, duck.*

Corrective feedback	**If...** children make an error, **then...** model by segmenting the word, and have them repeat.

ON THEIR OWN Have children segment and blend the following words.

/s/ /o/ /k/ **sock** /t/ /i/ /k/ **tick** /b/ /l/ /o/ /k/ **block**

Common Core State Standards

Foundational Skills 2.b. Orally produce single-syllable words by blending sounds (phonemes), including consonant blends. **Foundational Skills 2.c.** Isolate and pronounce initial, medial vowel, and final sounds (phonemes) in spoken single-syllable words. **Also Foundational Skills 3.**

Skills Trace

Consonant Pattern *-ck*

Introduce U1W1D2

Practice U1W1D3; U1W1D4

Reteach/Review U1W1D5; U1W2D4

Assess/Test Weekly Test U1W1
Benchmark Test U1

KEY: U=Unit W=Week D=Day

Phonics

Teach/Model

Consonant Pattern *-ck*

CONNECT Write *cat* and *kid.* Have children say the words. You studied words like these already. What letter spells the sound /k/ in *cat?* (*c*) What letter spells the sound /k/ in *kid?* (*k*) Today you will learn another way to read and spell words with the sound /k/.

Sound-Spelling Card 36

USE SOUND-SPELLING CARD Display Card 36. The sound you hear at the end of *lock* is /k/. The /k/ sound is usually spelled *-ck* when it comes at the end of a word. Have children say /k/ several times as you point to *-ck.*

MODEL Write *pack.* In this word, the letters *-ck* stand for the sound /k/. Segment and blend *pack;* then have children blend with you: /p/ /a/ /k/. Follow this procedure to model blending *back* and *sack.*

GROUP PRACTICE Continue segmenting and blending. This time have children blend with you. Remind children that *-ck* spells the sound /k/.

rack	Jack	Mack	tack	lack
sack	pack	Zack	back	quack

REVIEW What do you know about reading these words? (The letters *-ck* spell the sound /k/.)

Access for All

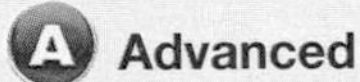

Advanced

Blend *-ck* Words If children can easily blend the words in the Guide Practice activity, have them try blending more difficult *-ck* words such as *track, black, stick,* and *clock.*

Vocabulary Support

You may wish to explain the meaning of this word.

lack not having enough

Pronounce /k/ In Spanish the letter *k* is rarely used, and the /g/ and /k/ sounds are similar. Have children practice reading and saying words that end in /g/ and /k/ and listening for the difference: *bag/back, tag/tack, sag/sack.*

Common Core State Standards

Foundational Skills 3. Know and apply grade-level phonics and word analysis skills in decoding words. **Foundational Skills 3.a.** Know the spelling-sound correspondences for common consonant digraphs.

Spelling Pattern

Consonant Pattern *-ck* The sound /k/ at the end of a word may be spelled *-ck.*

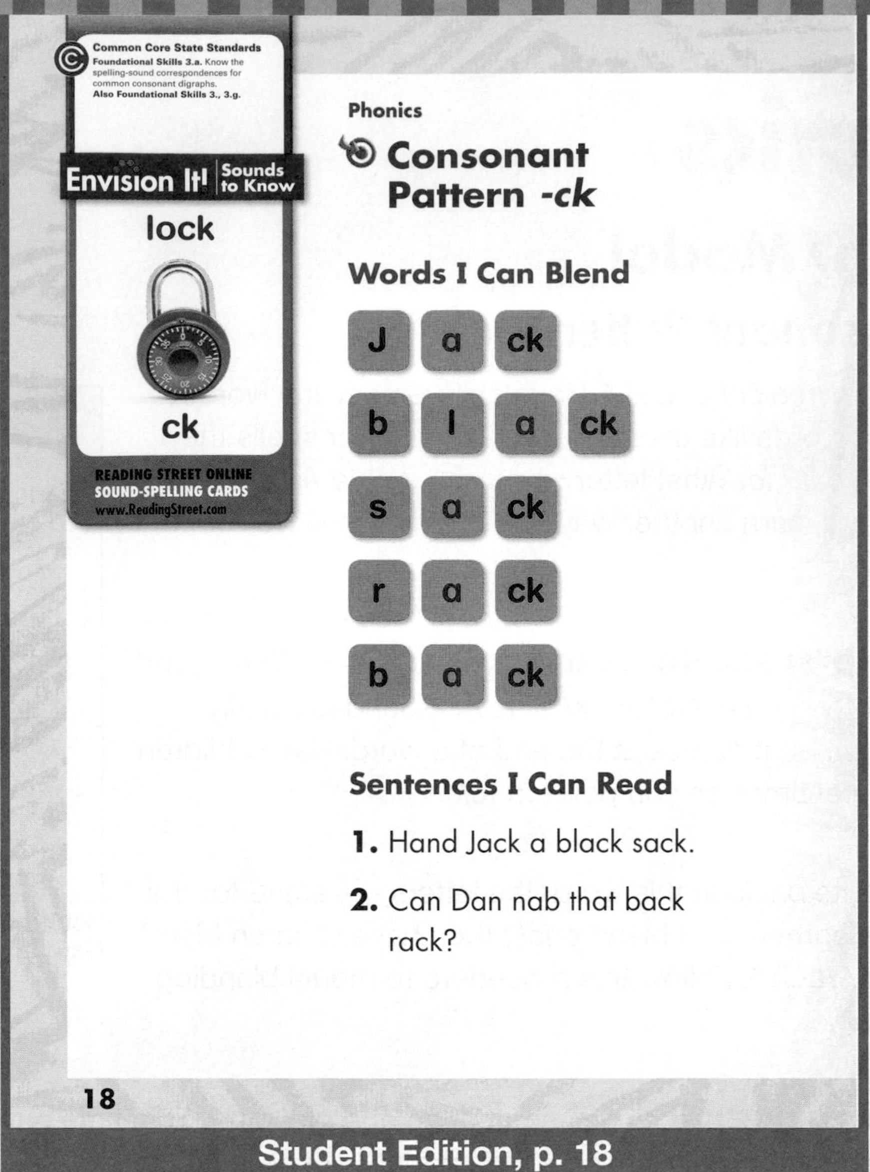

Common Core State Standards
Foundational Skills 3.a. Know the spelling-sound correspondences for common consonant digraphs.
Also Foundational Skills 3., 3.g.
Envision It! Sounds to Know
lock
ck
READING STREET ONLINE
SOUND-SPELLING CARDS
www.ReadingStreet.com
Phonics
Consonant Pattern -ck
Words I Can Blend
J a ck
b l a ck
s a ck
r a ck
b a ck
Sentences I Can Read
1. Hand Jack a black sack.
2. Can Dan nab that back rack?
18

Student Edition, p. 18

Phonics

Guide Practice

BLEND WORDS Have children turn to page 18 in their Student Edition. Look at the picture on this page. I see a picture of a lock. When I say *lock,* I hear the sound /k/ at the end. The /k/ sound is usually spelled *-ck* at the end of a word.

GROUP PRACTICE For each word in "Words I Can Blend," ask for the sound of each letter or group of letters. Make sure children identify the correct sound for *-ck.* Then have children blend the whole word.

Corrective feedback	**If...** children have difficulty blending a word, **then...** model blending the word, and ask children to blend it with you.

DECODE WORDS IN ISOLATION After children can successfully segment and blend the words, ask them to read the words naturally.

DECODE WORDS IN CONTEXT Have children read each of the sentences. Have them identify words in the sentences that have the final /k/ sound spelled *-ck.*

Team Talk Pair children and have them take turns reading each of the sentences aloud.

ON THEIR OWN Use *Reader's and Writer's Notebook,* p. 125.

MONITOR PROGRESS

Consonant Pattern *-ck*

FORMATIVE ASSESSMENT Write the following words and have the class read them. Notice which children miss words during the group reading. Call on those individuals to read some of the words.

Jack	back	sack	Zack	pack	**Spiral Review** Rows 2 and 3 review consonants.
cab	bat	ran	tack	sad	
jam	van	lack	rack	wag	

If... children cannot blend words with *-ck* at this point,

then... use the Small Group Time Strategic Intervention lesson, p. SG•8, to reteach words that end with *-ck.* Continue to monitor children's progress using other instructional opportunities during the week. See the Skills Trace on p. 18c.

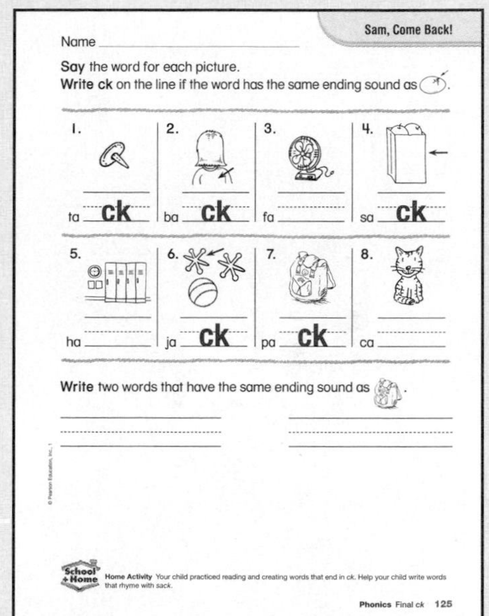
Name
Sam, Come Back!
Say the word for each picture.
Write ck on the line if the word has the same ending sound as

1. ta ck
2. ba ck
3. fa
4. sa ck
5. ha
6. ja ck
7. pa ck
8. ca

Write two words that have the same ending sound as

Home Activity Your child practiced reading and creating words that end in ck. Help your child write words that rhyme with sack.

Phonics Final ck 125

Reader's and Writer's Notebook, p. 125

Access for All

A Advanced

Blend Longer Words Provide more challenging words for children who can blend and read all the words correctly such as *quickly, chick, cracker, rocket,* and *backpack.*

ELL

Pronounce /k/ Spanish-speaking children may have difficulty reading and spelling words with *ck* because the letter *k* is rarely used in Spanish. Write examples of *-ck* words on the board: *pack, back, rack.* Point out that in English, the /k/ sound at the end of a word is usually spelled *ck.* Read the words together. Have volunteers underline the letters that spell /k/.

Common Core State Standards

Foundational Skills 3. Know and apply grade-level phonics and word analysis skills in decoding words. **Foundational Skills 3.b.** Decode regularly spelled one-syllable words. **Foundational Skills 3.g.** Recognize and read grade-appropriate irregularly spelled words. **Foundational Skills 4.** Read with sufficient accuracy and fluency to support comprehension.

Decodable Reader 1B

If children need help, then...

Read *The Pack*

DECODE WORDS IN ISOLATION Have children turn to page 105. Have children decode each word.

REVIEW HIGH-FREQUENCY WORDS Review the previously taught words *a* and *for.* Have children read each word as you point to it on the Word Wall.

PREVIEW Have children read the title and preview the story. Tell them they will read words that end with the /k/ sound spelled *-ck.*

DECODE WORDS IN CONTEXT Pair children for reading and listen as they decode. One child begins. Children read the entire story, switching readers after each page.

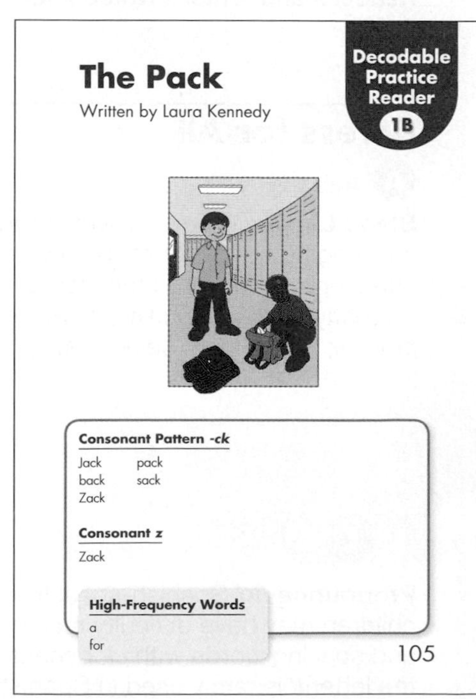
The Pack

Written by Laura Kennedy

Decodable Practice Reader 1B

Consonant Pattern -ck

Jack pack
back sack
Zack

Consonant z

Zack

High-Frequency Words

a
for

105

Decodable Practice Reader 1B

Jack can pack.
Jack can pack a back sack.

106

Pack! Pack! Pack!
Pack a sack.

107

Pack! Pack! Pack!
Pack a sack for Jack.

108

Zack can pack.
Zack can pack a sack.

109

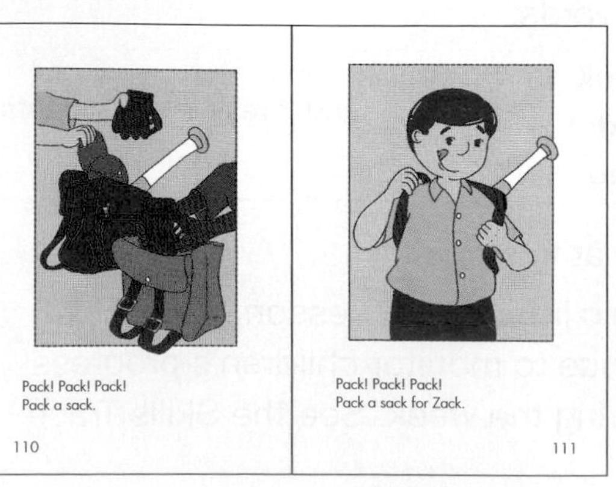
Pack! Pack! Pack!
Pack a sack.

110

Pack! Pack! Pack!
Pack a sack for Zack.

111

Jack ran.
Zack ran.

112

Corrective feedback	**If...** children have difficulty decoding a word, **then...** refer them to the Sound-Spelling Cards to identify the sounds in the word. Then prompt them to blend the word. • What is the new word? • Is the new word a word you know? • Does it make sense in the story?

CHECK DECODING AND COMPREHENSION Have children retell the story including characters, setting, and events. Then have children find words that end with the /k/ sound in the story. List words that children name. Children should supply *Jack, pack, back, sack,* and *Zack.*

Reread for Fluency

REREAD DECODABLE READER Have children reread Decodable Practice Reader 1B to develop automaticity decoding words with the /k/ sound spelled *-ck.*

Routine Paired Reading

1. **Reread** To achieve optimal fluency, have partners reread the text three or four times.
2. **Corrective Feedback** Listen as children read. Provide corrective feedback regarding their fluency and decoding.

Routines Flip Chart

Access for All

Advanced

Extend the Story Children who can read the story easily might make up another sentence to add to the story. Suggest that they use another *-ack* word, such as *black, crack, stack, tack,* or *track.*

Consonant Pattern *-ck*

Beginning Lead children on a picture walk through *The Pack,* identifying *Jack, Zack,* and the *sack.* Point to these words and other words ending with /k/ spelled *-ck,* say each word, and have children repeat it after you.

Intermediate Have children find and read words in the story that end with /k/ spelled *-ck.*

Advanced After reading, ask partners to find words in the story that end with /k/ spelled *-ck.* Have them use each word in a sentence.

Common Core State Standards

Foundational Skills 2.d. Segment spoken single-syllable words into their complete sequence of individual sounds (phonemes). **Foundational Skills 3.** Know and apply grade-level phonics and word analysis skills in decoding words. **Foundational Skills 3.b.** Decode regularly spelled one-syllable words. **Language 2.d.** Use conventional spelling for words with common spelling patterns and for frequently occurring irregular words.

Phonics

Review Short Vowels

REVIEW SOUND-SPELLINGS Review the following short vowel spelling patterns: the *a* spelling for /a/, the *e* spelling for /e/, the *i* spelling for /i/, the *o* spelling for /o/, and the *u* spelling for /u/. Use Sound-Spelling Cards 1, 6, 11, 17, and 24.

DECODE WORDS IN ISOLATION Display these words. Have the class blend the words. Then point to the words in random order and ask children to decode them quickly.

bad	**jab**	**fan**	**gas**
hid	**vat**	**set**	**fog**
tan	**jug**	**sip**	**mud**

Corrective feedback Model blending decodable words and then ask children to blend them with you.

DECODE WORDS IN CONTEXT Display these sentences. Have the class read the sentences.

Team Talk Have pairs take turns reading the sentences naturally.

I **can pet** the **cat on** the **rug.**

The **tan cup** is for you.

Jan had a **big** green **hat.**

Spelling

Short *a* Words

GUIDE PRACTICE Tell children that you will segment the sounds in each spelling word. They should repeat the sounds in each word as they write the word. Check the spelling of each word before saying the next word.

1.	/a/ /t/	**at**	**6.**	/a/ /m/	**am**
2.	/k/ /a/ /n/	**can**	**7.**	/b/ /a/ /t/	**bat**
3.	/k/ /a/ /t/	**cat**	**8.**	/m/ /a/ /d/	**mad**
4.	/b/ /a/ /k/	**back**	**9.**	/r/ /a/ /n/	**ran**
5.	/d/ /a/ /d/	**dad**	**10.**	/s/ /a/ /k/	**sack**

ON THEIR OWN Use *Reader's and Writer's Notebook,* p. 126.

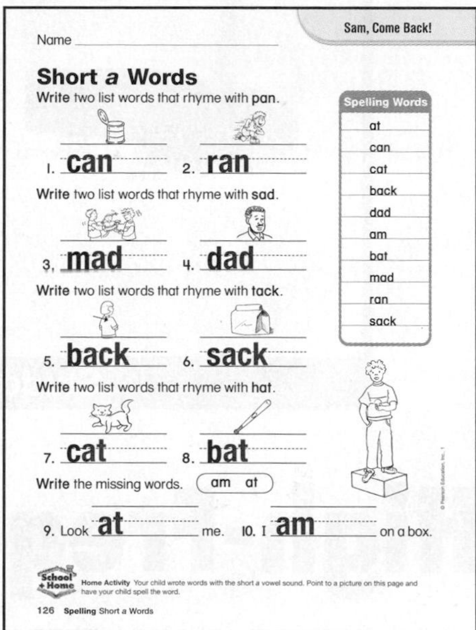
Name

Sam, Come Back!

Short *a* Words

Write two list words that rhyme with **pan**.

1. can 2. ran

Write two list words that rhyme with **sad**.

3. mad 4. dad

Write two list words that rhyme with **tack**.

5. back 6. sack

Write two list words that rhyme with **hat**.

7. cat 8. bat

Write the missing words. (am at)

9. Look at me. 10. I am on a box.

Spelling Words
at
can
cat
back
dad
am
bat
mad
ran
sack

Home Activity Your child wrote words with the short a vowel sound. Point to a picture on this page and have your child spell the word.

126 Spelling Short a Words

Reader's and Writer's Notebook, p. 126

eStreet Interactive
www.ReadingStreet.com

Interactive Sound-Spelling Cards

Teacher Resources
• Reader's and Writer's Notebook

ELL

Short Vowels The writing systems of languages such as Arabic and Hebrew focus on consonant sounds and long vowels. Short vowels are indicated with separate marks that are often optional. Write the spelling words and have speakers of these languages copy them. Emphasize the short vowel sound as you read the words with them.

Common Core State Standards

Foundational Skills 3. Know and apply grade-level phonics and word analysis skills in decoding words. **Foundational Skills 3.a.** Know the spelling-sound correspondences for common consonant digraphs. **Foundational Skills 3.g.** Recognize and read grade-appropriate irregularly spelled words. **Language 5.a.** Sort words into categories (e.g., colors, clothing) to gain a sense of the concepts the categories represent.

Name ________ Sam, Come Back!

Read the words in the box. Then **pick** one to finish each sentence. **Write** it on the line.

my way in come on

1. This is **my** cat Sam.
2. My Jack can **come** to me.
3. We go this **way** to the
4. My cat Sam is **in** the bag.
5. The book is **on** the table.

Home Activity This week your child learned to read the words my, way, on, in, and come. Write each word on a card and place the cards around the room. Name a word and have your child find that word card.

High-Frequency/Story Words DVD•29

Let's Practice It! TR DVD•29

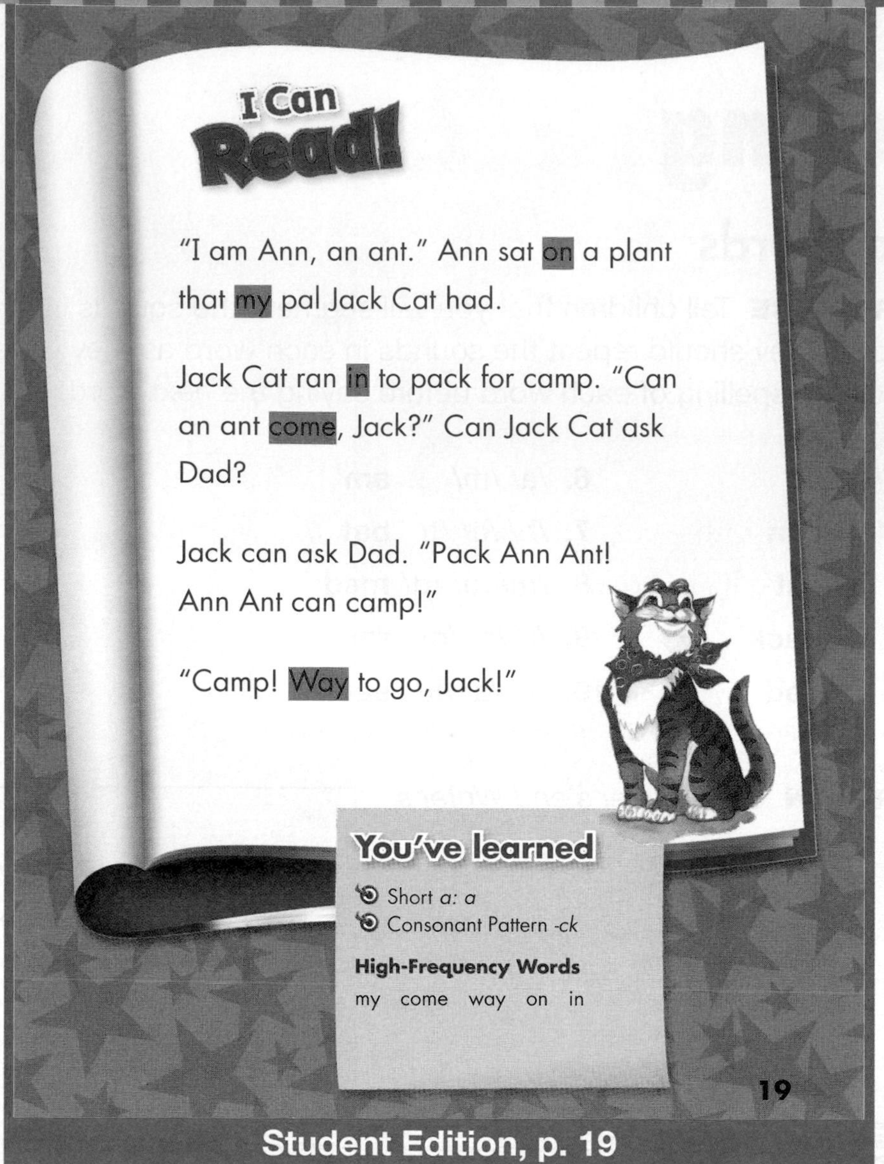

Student Edition, p. 19

High-Frequency Words

READ WORDS IN ISOLATION Remind children that there are some words we learn by remembering the letters rather than by saying the sounds. Then have them read each of the highlighted high-frequency words aloud.

READ WORDS IN CONTEXT Chorally read the "I Can Read!" passage along with children. Then have them read the passage aloud to themselves. When they are finished, ask children to reread the high-frequency words.

Team Talk Have children choose two high-frequency words and give them time to create a sentence in which both words are used properly. Then have them share their sentence with a partner.

ON THEIR OWN Use Let's Practice It! p. 29 on the *Teacher Resources DVD-ROM.*

Selection Vocabulary

INTRODUCE SELECTION WORDS Use Vocabulary Transparency 1 to introduce this week's selection words. Read each sentence as you track the print. Frame each underlined word and explain its meaning. Have children read each sentence with you.

Sam	the name of the cat in the story
Jack	the name of the boy in the story

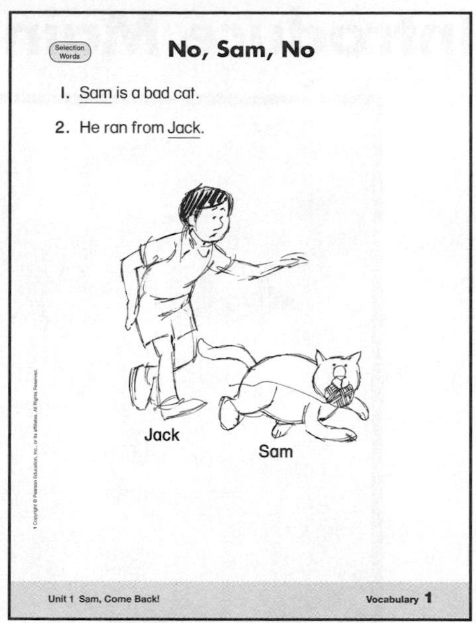

Selection Words
No, Sam, No
1. Sam is a bad cat.
2. He ran from Jack.
Jack
Sam
Unit 1 Sam, Come Back!
Vocabulary 1

Vocabulary Transparency 1 TR DVD

Vocabulary: Words for Location

TEACH Explain that words for location help tell where someone or something is. Draw a two-column chart or display Graphic Organizer 4. List these words in the left column under the heading "Where?": *in, out, up, down, over, under.*

Where?	Sentence
in	The cat is <u>in</u> my lap.
out	
up	
down	
over	
under	

Graphic Organizer 4

I see the word *in. In* is a location word that helps me know where something is. I'll write a sentence on the chart, using the word *in.* Here's my sentence: *The cat is <u>in</u> my lap.*

GUIDE PRACTICE Have children think of sentences for the remaining location words in the first column of the chart. Record their sentences in the second column. Have children suggest other location words (e.g., *left, right, beside, behind*) and sentences to add to the chart.

ON THEIR OWN Have partners choose a location word and draw and label a picture that shows its meaning. Ask children to share their drawings with the class.

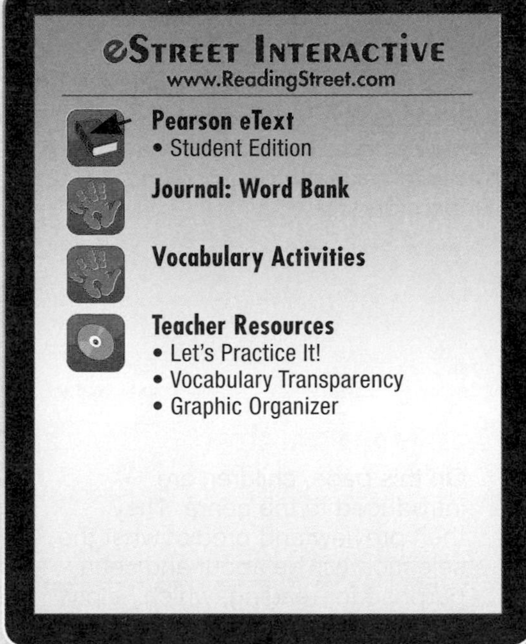

Bridge to Common Core

VOCABULARY ACQUISITION AND USE
When children interact with this week's selection vocabulary words, they are learning the names of the characters in the selection. Teaching the concept of location words helps children make real-life connections between words and their use and creates a context to build understanding of text.

Access for All

SI Strategic Intervention

Demonstrate Meaning Demonstrate physically the meanings of location words with a block and bag or other simple objects. Then have children think of additional location words and demonstrate and use the words themselves.

Multilingual Vocabulary Lists
Children can apply knowledge of their home language to acquire new English vocabulary by using the *Multilingual Vocabulary List* (*ELL Handbook*, pp. 465–476).

Common Core State Standards

Literature 1. Ask and answer questions about key details in a text. **Foundational Skills 4.a.** Read on-level text with purpose and understanding.

Bridge to Common Core

CRAFT AND STRUCTURE

On this page, children are introduced to the genre. They then preview and predict what the selection will be about and set a purpose for reading, which helps them analyze the structure of the text and the way the illustrations and text relate to each other. As they read, children can use these structures to help them understand the content and style of the selection.

Academic Vocabulary

realistic fiction a made-up story that could happen in real life

Strategy Response Log

Monitor and Clarify Before reading, have children use p. RR13 in their *Reader's and Writer's Notebook* to write what they will do if something in the story they are about to read does not make sense.

Text-Based Comprehension

Introduce Main Selection

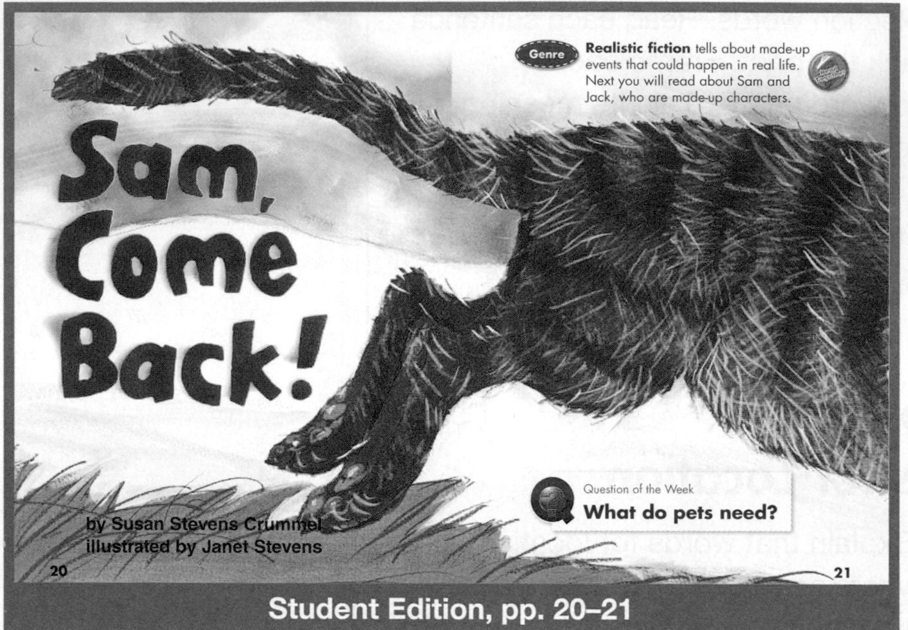
Genre
Realistic fiction tells about made-up events that could happen in real life. Next you will read about Sam and Jack, who are made-up characters.
Sam, Come Back!
by Susan Stevens Crummel
illustrated by Janet Stevens
Question of the Week
What do pets need?
20
21

Student Edition, pp. 20–21

GENRE Realistic fiction is a made-up story that could happen in real life. As they read *Sam, Come Back!,* children should identify things the made-up cat, Sam, does that a real cat might do.

PREVIEW AND PREDICT Read the names of the author and illustrator, and have children describe the role of each. Have children predict what the selection will be about.

PURPOSE Good readers read for a purpose. Setting a purpose helps us to think and understand more as we read. Model setting a purpose for reading.

MONITOR AND CLARIFY Explain that good readers ask themselves questions as they read to be sure they understand what they are reading. If part of a story is confusing, they can reread some sentences aloud and ask themselves questions to figure out what is happening. Have children turn to page EI•11 in their Student Edition.

Think Aloud

Look at these pictures. What does the girl do when something in her book is confusing? (She rereads a part.) As I read *Sam, Come Back!,* I will be sure that what I am reading makes sense. If it doesn't, I will reread aloud the part that is confusing, and I will ask myself questions.

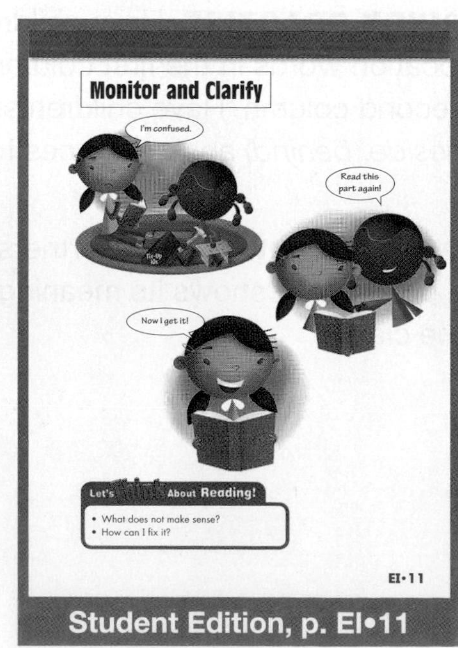
Monitor and Clarify
I'm confused.
Read this part again!
Now I get it!
Let's Think About Reading!
What does not make sense?
How can I fix it?
EI•11

Student Edition, p. EI•11

Access Main Selection

READER AND TASK SUGGESTIONS	
Preparing to Read the Text	**Leveled Tasks**
• Review consonant pattern *-ck.* • Discuss with children characteristics of realistic fiction. • Encourage children who read quickly, but with low accuracy, to slow their rate.	• **Structure** If children have a clear understanding of the text structure, ask them to draw what might happen next if the selection were to continue. • **Levels of Meaning • Analysis** To help children differentiate fiction from fantasy, ask them to tell one thing Sam did that was realistic. Then have them tell what Sam could have done instead that would have been unrealistic.

See Text Complexity Measures for *Sam, Come Back!* on the tab at the beginning of this week.

READ Tell children that today they will read *Sam, Come Back!* for the first time. Use the Read for Understanding routine.

Routine Read for Understanding ©

Deepen understanding by reading the selection multiple times.

1. **First Read**—If children need support, then use the **Access Text** notes to help them clarify understanding.
2. **Second Read**—Use the **Close Reading** notes to help children draw knowledge from the text.

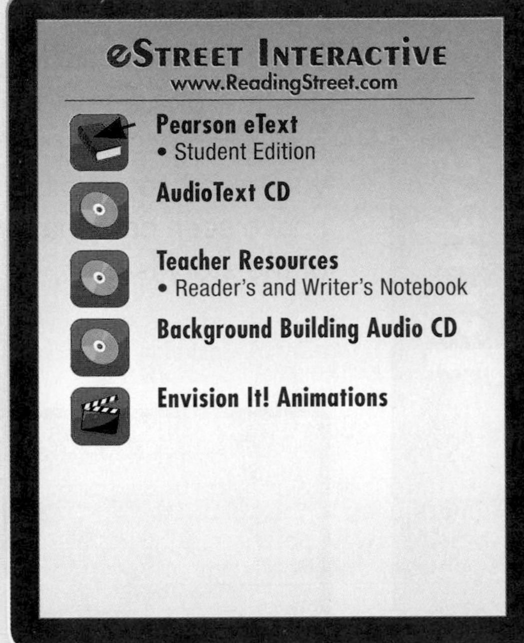

Preview Main Selection Ask children what they already know about cats using the picture on pp. 20–21. Then do a picture walk of the selection so children can talk about and see ways that cats behave.

1ST READ

Access Text © If children need help, then...

CONNECT TO CONCEPT Look at the picture and title on pages 20 and 21. What kind of animal do you think this is? (a cat) How can you tell? (I see a tail, and it's an orange color. I have seen cats that are orange.) The title of the story is *Sam, Come Back!* Who do you think might be asking Sam to come back? (Sam could be this cat. His owner could be calling him.)

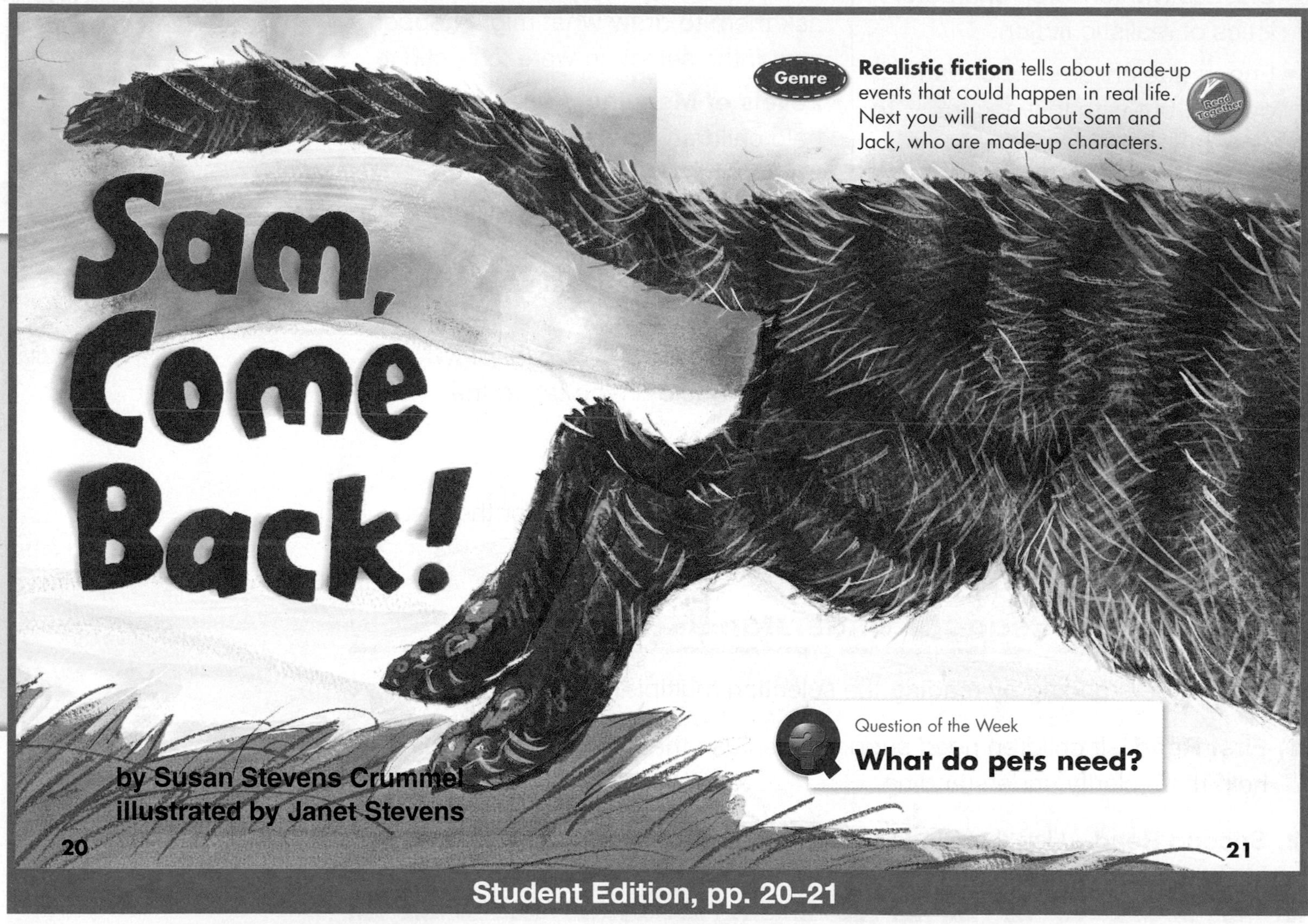

Sam, Come Back!
by Susan Stevens Crummel
illustrated by Janet Stevens
Genre
Realistic fiction tells about made-up events that could happen in real life. Next you will read about Sam and Jack, who are made-up characters.
Read Together
Question of the Week
What do pets need?
20
21

Student Edition, pp. 20–21

2ND READ

Close Reading ©

ANALYSIS • TEXT EVIDENCE On pages 20 and 21, what is the cat doing? (running) How can you tell? (Children should point to the cat's legs and tail and explain how an animal looks when it runs.)

CHARACTER AND SETTING Who are the characters in this story? (Sam the cat, a woman, a boy, and a dog) What is the setting of this story? (a home) How do you think the characters are feeling at the beginning of the story? (They feel happy and calm.) Why do you think that? Tell about the characters in the picture.

Common Core State Standards

Literature 3. Describe characters, settings, and major events in a story, using key details. **Literature 7.** Use illustrations and details in a story to describe its characters, setting, or events. **Also Literature 1., 6., 10., Foundational Skills 4.a.**

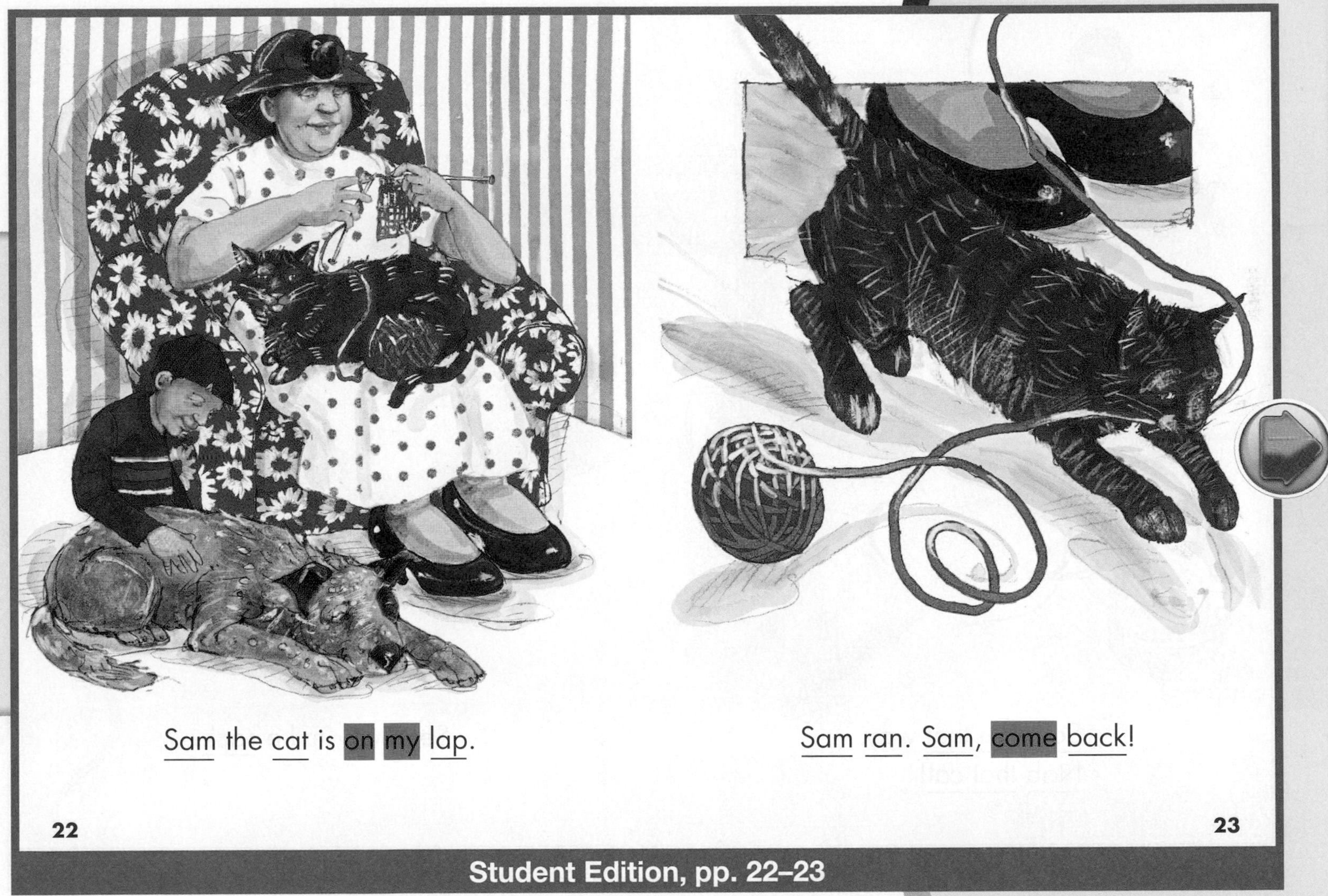

Sam the cat is on my lap.
22
Sam ran. Sam, come back!
23

Student Edition, pp. 22–23

ANALYSIS The story says that "Sam the cat is on my lap." Who does the word *my* tell about? (It is telling about the woman.) How do you know? (The picture shows the cat sitting on the woman's lap, so she must be the one who is speaking.)

1ST READ

Access Text © If children need help, then...

MONITOR AND CLARIFY Remind children that when something in a story doesn't make sense, good readers ask themselves questions and reread some sentences aloud to be sure they understand. Ask children to explain who is saying "Nab that cat!"

CHARACTER AND SETTING On page 24, the characters are now in a different setting. Where are they? (They are outside.) Why do you think Sam the cat is running away from the boy and the dog? (He is playing a game with them.)

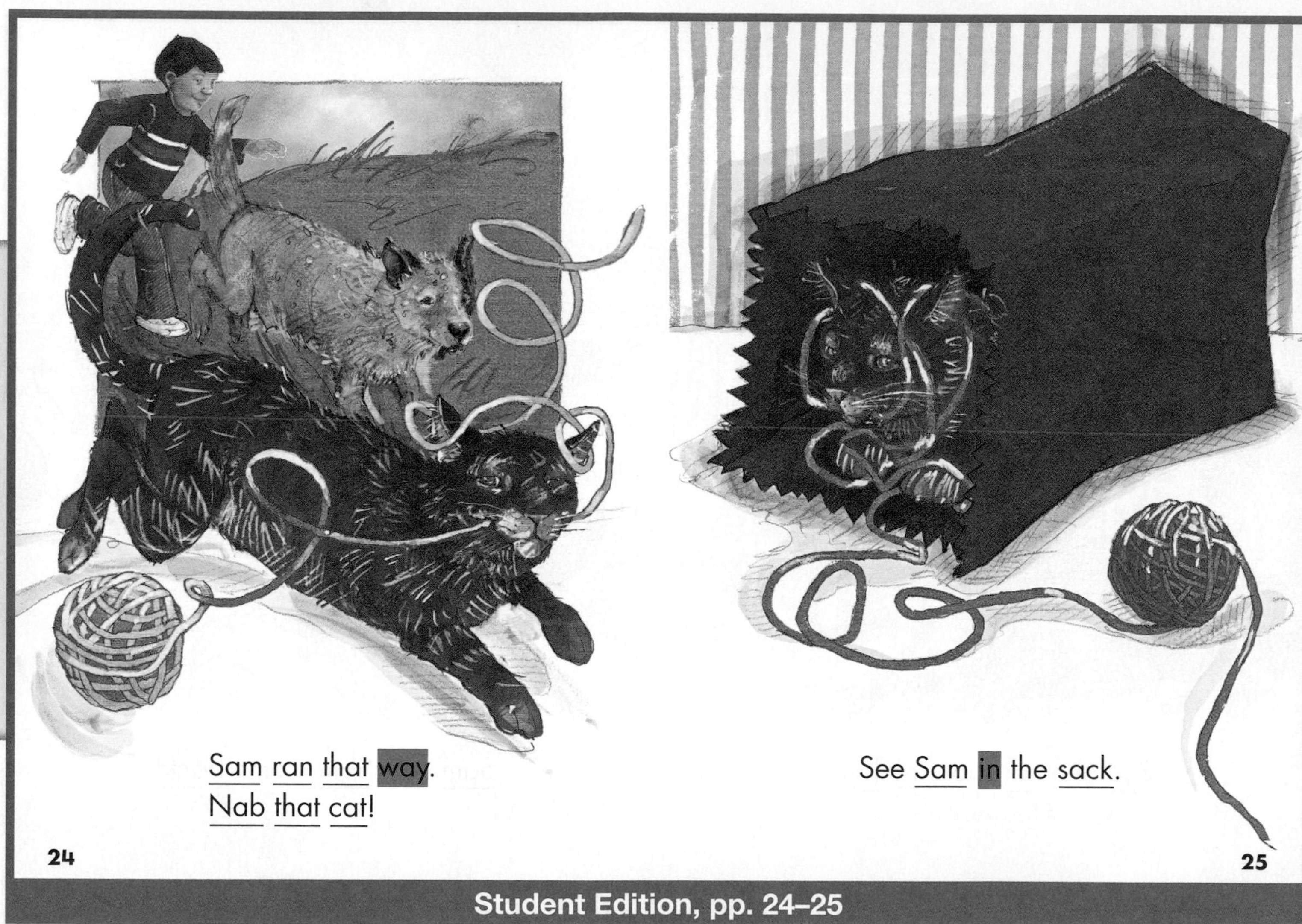

Sam ran that way.
Nab that cat!
24
See Sam in the sack.
25

Student Edition, pp. 24–25

2ND READ

Close Reading ©

EVALUATION On page 25, Sam hides in a sack. Do you think the sack is a good place for Sam to hide? Why or why not? (No, because you can still see Sam and the ball of yarn.)

Time for Science **CONNECT TO SCIENCE** Explain that there are many kinds of cats that live in different places in the world.

Team Talk Have partners discuss various cats in the cat family. Have them list both tame and wild cats, such as lions, tigers, and cheetahs.

REREAD CHALLENGING TEXT
Have children reread p. 26 and then retell what has happened in the story so far in order to better understand the phrase "Nab that cat!"

USE WORDS FOR LOCATION
Words for location, such as *under, over,* and *beside,* help explain where someone or something is. What location word on page 27 helps readers understand where Sam is? *(in)* What is Sam in? (He is in a pack.)

Common Core State Standards
Literature 7. Use illustrations and details in a story to describe its characters, setting, or events.
Literature 10. With prompting and support, read prose and poetry of appropriate complexity for grade 1.
Also Foundational Skills 4.a., 4.c., Language 4.

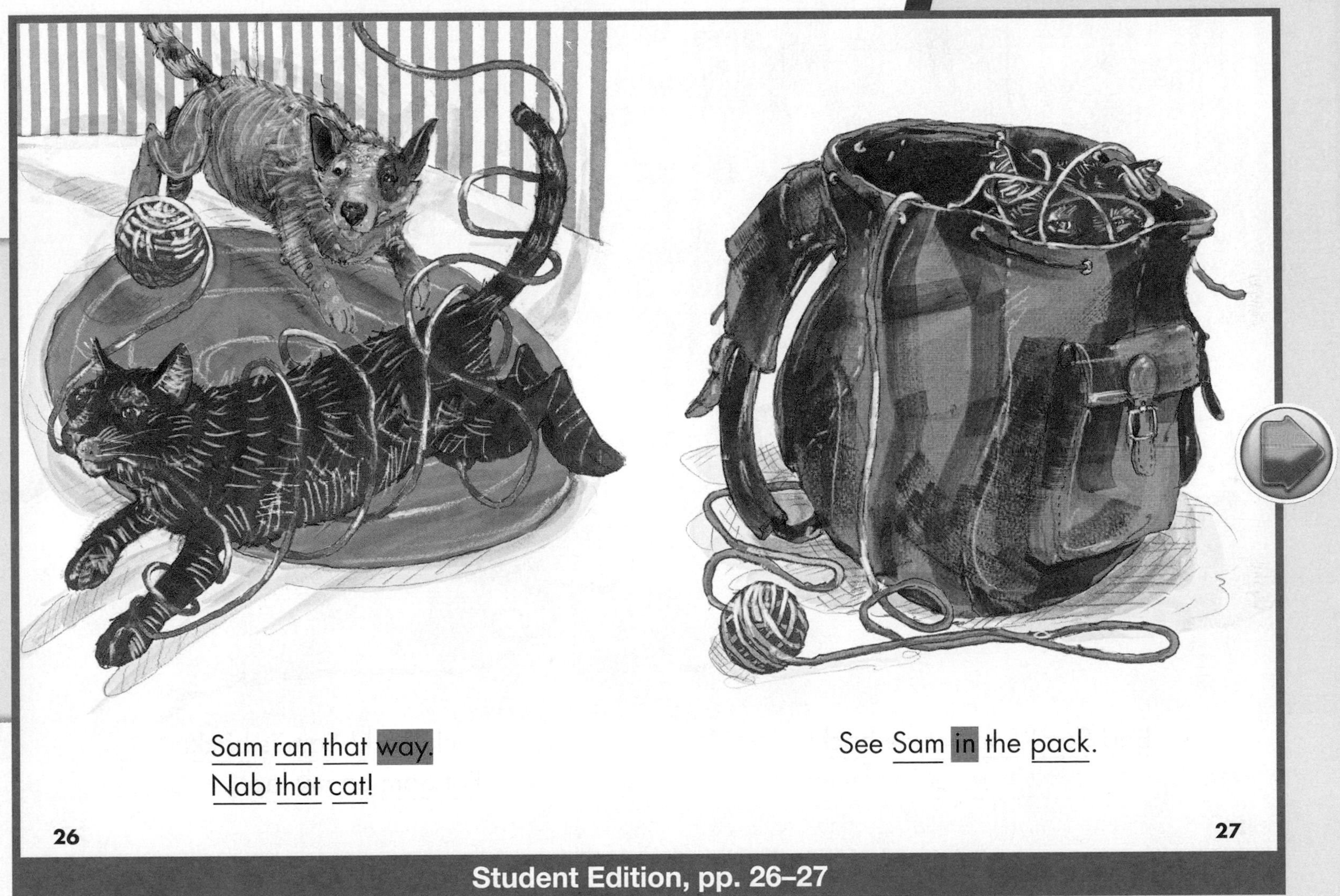

Sam ran that way.
Nab that cat!
26
See Sam in the pack.
27

Student Edition, pp. 26–27

EVALUATION • TEXT EVIDENCE
The two pets in the story are a cat and a dog. How is the behavior of the two animals alike? How do you know? (In the beginning, both animals are calm and are cuddling with their owners. The picture on page 22 shows that.) How is their behavior different? How can you tell? (The dog is well behaved and listens to the woman. The cat is naughty and teases his owners. The pictures show the dog playing and the cat running and hiding.)

1ST READ

Access Text © If children need help, then...

MONITOR AND CLARIFY When I read page 28, I asked myself why the woman says that Sam is a bad cat. What can I learn by rereading the sentences on the pages before this? (The woman says Sam is bad because he took her yarn. Then he ran away and hid.)

CROSS-TEXT EVALUATION
Use a Strategy to Self-Check How did the Read Aloud "A Hamster for Ana" help you understand this selection?

Continue to DAY 2
Text-Based Comprehension
p. 29a

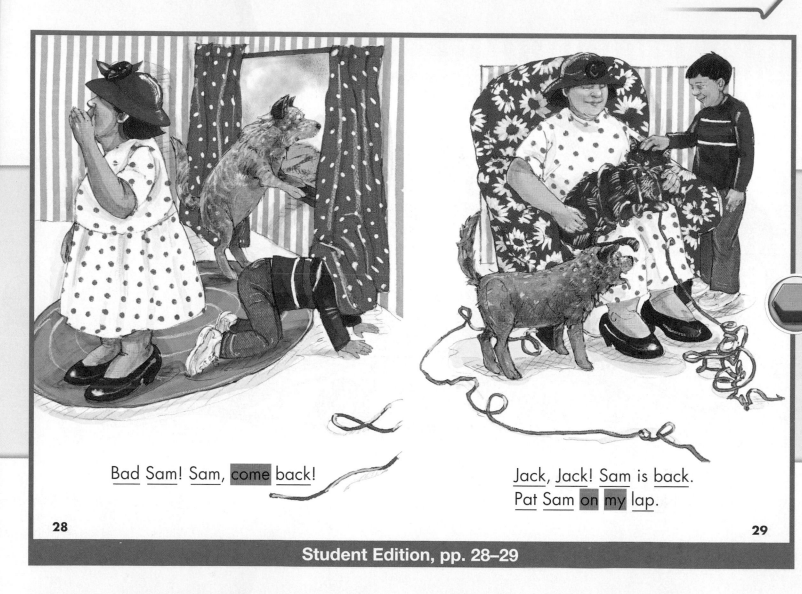

Bad Sam! Sam, come back!

28

Jack, Jack! Sam is back.
Pat Sam on my lap.

29

Student Edition, pp. 28–29

2ND READ

Close Reading ©

ANALYSIS What is the problem in the plot of this story? (Sam the cat runs away with the woman's yarn, and no one can catch him.) How does the story end? (Sam comes back on his own with the yarn.)

SYNTHESIS • TEXT EVIDENCE Using what you learned in this selection, tell what things a pet needs. Have children cite examples from the text.

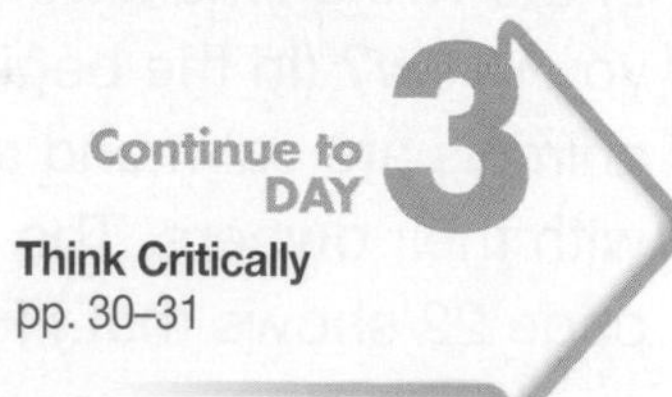
Continue to DAY 3
Think Critically
pp. 30–31

Text-Based Comprehension

Check Understanding

Have children discuss each question with a partner. Ask several pairs to share their responses.

- ✓ **Realistic fiction** Is Sam a real cat? How do you know? (Sam is a made-up cat that does things a real cat can do.)
- ✓ **Character** How do you think the woman in the story feels about her cat, Sam? Explain how you know. (The woman loves Sam. She cuddles him on her lap and smiles at him.)
- ✓ **Plot** What do the characters in the story do to try to solve their problem? (They tell Sam the cat to come back. The boy, Jack, and the dog chase after Sam and try to catch him.)
- ✓ **Confirm predictions** How did you use pictures or story clues to predict what Sam would do next? (I could tell from the pictures that Sam was running away and hiding in different places in the house.)
- ✓ **Connect text to world** In what ways is Sam like a real cat? (Sam likes to sit on people's laps, he runs, he plays with yarn, and he hides inside of things.)

Common Core State Standards

Literature 1. Ask and answer questions about key details in a text. **Literature 3.** Describe characters, settings, and major events in a story, using key details. **Literature 10.** With prompting and support, read prose and poetry of appropriate complexity for grade 1. **Foundational Skills 4.a.** Read on-level text with purpose and understanding. **Foundational Skills 4.c.** Use context to confirm or self-correct word recognition and understanding, rereading as necessary.

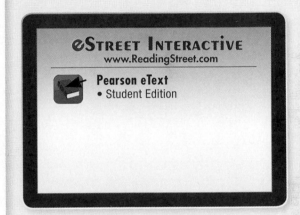

ELL

Support Discussion Ask yes or no questions to start children's responses, for example: Is Sam a real cat? (no) Then extend language opportunities by asking follow-up questions, such as: What does Sam do that real cats do?

Day 2 SMALL GROUP TIME • Differentiate Comprehension, p. SG•1

OL On-Level	SI Strategic Intervention	A Advanced
• **Practice Phonics** Additional *-ck* Words • **Read** *Sam, Come Back!*	• **Reteach Phonics** Blend *-ck* Words • **Read** *Sam, Come Back!*	• **Extend Phonics** More *-ck* Words • **Read** *Sam, Come Back!* • **Investigate** Inquiry Project

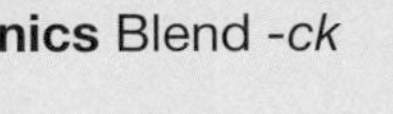

ELL

If... children need more scaffolding and practice with the **Comprehension Skill,**
then... use the ELL activities on p. DI•17 in the Teacher Resources section on SuccessNet.

Common Core State Standards

Literature 3. Describe characters, settings, and major events in a story, using key details. **Literature 9.** Compare and contrast the adventures and experiences of characters in stories. **Foundational Skills 1.a.** Recognize the distinguishing features of a sentence (e.g., first word, capitalization, ending punctuation). **Language 1.** Demonstrate command of the conventions of standard English grammar and usage when writing or speaking. **Language 2.b.** Use end punctuation for sentences.

Genre

Realistic Fiction

IDENTIFY FEATURES OF REALISTIC FICTION Use the story *Sam, Come Back!* to have children identify the features of realistic fiction.

- The story *Sam, Come Back!* is a made-up story with characters that look and act like real people and animals. Who are the characters? (a woman, Jack, Sam the cat, a dog)
- The setting of this story is also something that could be real. What is the setting? (a house in the daytime)
- The events in a story tell what happens. Are the events in this story real? (No, they are made up.) Could the events happen in real life? (Yes, the characters do things that real people and animals do.)

GUIDE PRACTICE Explain that the class will list information about two made-up stories that tell about things that could really happen. Display Graphic Organizer 25. Ask children to tell you what to write in each space. Begin by writing the title, characters, setting, and events for *Sam, Come Back!* Then repeat the process for the Read Aloud story "A Hamster for Ana." Once the chart is complete, have children compare and contrast the stories, discussing how the two selections are alike and different.

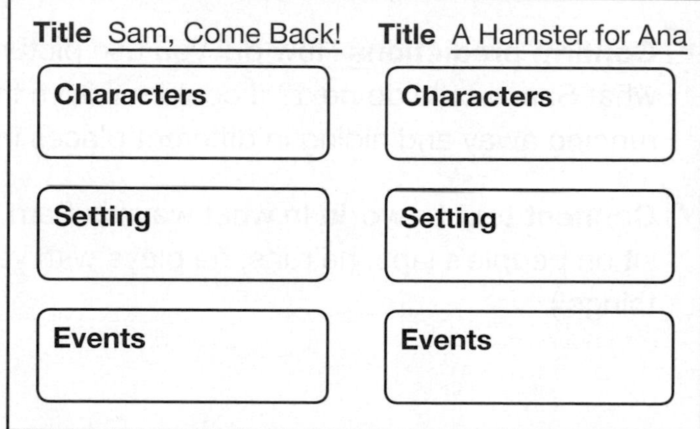

Title Sam, Come Back!
Title A Hamster for Ana
Characters
Characters
Setting
Setting
Events
Events

Graphic Organizer 25

ON THEIR OWN Organize children into small groups and assign each group a previously read realistic fiction story from the Student Edition. Have them identify the features that show that the made-up story could happen in real life. Then have them share their information with the class.

Conventions

Sentences

TEACH Write the sentence *My cat is Max* on the board and the phrase *my cat* below it. Point to each word as you read it. Have children identify which is the sentence and tell how they know it is a sentence. A sentence is a group of words that tells a complete idea. It always begins with a capital letter. Many sentences end with a period. How does a sentence begin? (with a capital letter) How do many sentences end? (with a period)

GUIDE PRACTICE Help children generate other sentences about cats. Write the sentences they suggest. Have children tell you which letter should be a capital and where to put a period.

APPLY Have the class complete these sentence frames orally, adding words to form complete sentences. Ask children to tell which word in each new sentence should begin with a capital letter.

1. **A cat has _______.**
2. **______ sometimes scare my cat.**

ON THEIR OWN Use *Reader's and Writer's Notebook,* p. 127.

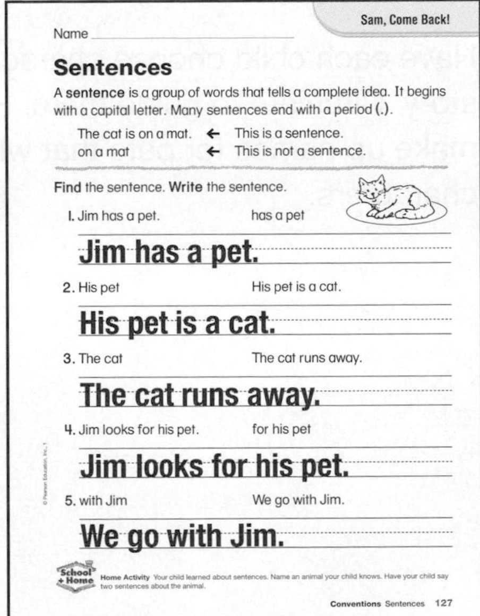

Sam, Come Back!

Name __________________

Sentences

A **sentence** is a group of words that tells a complete idea. It begins with a capital letter. Many sentences end with a period (.).

The cat is on a mat. ← This is a sentence.
on a mat ← This is not a sentence.

Find the sentence. **Write** the sentence.

1. Jim has a pet. — has a pet
   Jim has a pet.
2. His pet — His pet is a cat.
   His pet is a cat.
3. The cat — The cat runs away.
   The cat runs away.
4. Jim looks for his pet. — for his pet
   Jim looks for his pet.
5. with Jim — We go with Jim.
   We go with Jim.

School + Home **Home Activity** Your child learned about sentences. Name an animal your child knows. Have your child say two sentences about the animal.

© Pearson Education, Inc., 1

Conventions Sentences 127

Reader's and Writer's Notebook, p. 127

Daily Fix-It

3. look at the little cat
   Look at the little cat.
4. she is in that sakk.
   She is in that sack.

Discuss the Daily Fix-It corrections with children. Review sentence capitalization and punctuation, and the *ck* spelling of final /k/.

Word Order in Sentences Help children understand correct word order in English sentences. Write the following words on cards and display them: *on sat A cat hat my.* Have children read each word and explain the word's meaning. Then have children help you arrange the words in the correct sentence order: *A cat sat on my hat.* Point out that the first part of the sentence tells what the sentence is about (a cat).

Common Core State Standards

Writing 3. Write narratives in which they recount two or more appropriately sequenced events, include some details regarding what happened, use temporal words to signal event order, and provide some sense of closure. **Language 5.d.** Distinguish shades of meaning among verbs differing in manner (e.g., *look*, *peek*, *glance*, *stare*, *glare*, *scowl*) and adjectives differing in intensity (e.g., *large*, *gigantic*) by defining or choosing them or by acting out the meanings.

Writing

Story

Writer's Craft: Using Strong Verbs

INTRODUCE THE PROMPT Review with children the key features of a story. Point out that *Sam, Come Back!* is a story. Assure them that they can make up a story that tells what characters do. Explain that today children will plan their own story. It will be a story made of sentences. Read aloud the writing prompt.

Writing Prompt

Think about a pet you know. Write a story about the pet playing.

GENERATE STORY IDEAS

To plan a new story, think of different pets and how they play. Let's make a chart of pets that people have and ways the pets can play. Display a T-chart or use Graphic Organizer 4. I'll start with the word *dog.*

Guide children in identifying pets that people have and ways the pets can play. Possible ideas are shown. Record the responses, and keep the chart so that children can refer to it as they plan and draft their stories.

Have each child choose characters for a new story. Circulate to guide them. Have them make up names for pets that will be their characters.

Pets	Play
dog	play with ball
cat	jump
hamster	

Graphic Organizer 4

Mini-Lesson Using Strong Verbs

■ **Introduce** Use *Reader's and Writer's Notebook,* p. 128 to model story planning. To plan a story, I can use a chart. First, I need to choose an animal to write about. I want to write about a hamster. I'll call her Honey. I'll write her name in the Characters box. Next, I will plan what happens in the story. I will use verbs that clearly tell what Honey does.

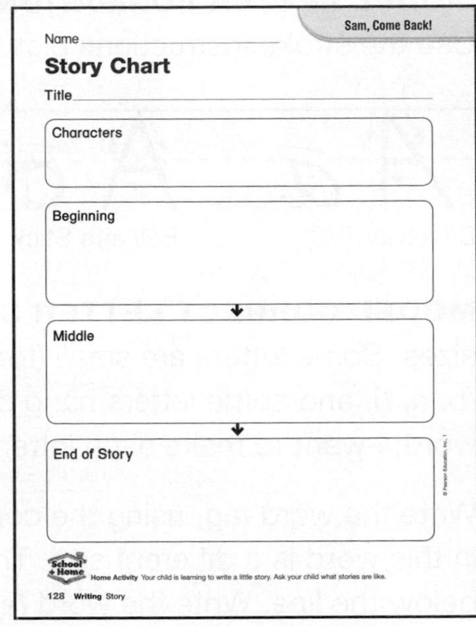

Name

Sam, Come Back!

Story Chart

Title

Characters

Beginning

Middle

End of Story

School + Home

Home Activity Your child is learning to write a little story. Ask your child what stories are like.

128 Writing Story

Reader's and Writer's Notebook, p. 128

■ **Model** At the beginning, Honey goes into my shirt. In the *Beginning* box I'll write *Honey crawls into my shirt. Crawls* is a better verb than *goes. Crawls* clearly tells what Honey does. In the middle of the story, I will tell what Honey does next. Honey crawls up my arm and gets stuck. It tickles and I laugh! I'll use the verbs *crawls, tickles,* and *laugh* when I write the middle of my story in the *Middle* box. These verbs clearly tell what Honey and I do. At the end, Honey wiggles free! *Wiggles* is a great verb! I can really picture Honey wiggling. Now I'll write that idea in the *End of Story* box. Last, I will think of a title that tells what my story is mostly about. I'll write my title on top: *Honey the Hamster Tickles.* Now plan for your story. Circulate to guide and assist children.

Routine Quick Write for Fluency

Team Talk

1. **Talk** Have children take two minutes to tell their story events to a partner.
2. **Write** Each child briefly writes about the events of the planned story, using strong verbs.
3. **Share** Partners identify the strong verbs used in each other's writing.

Routines Flip Chart

Write Guy *by Jeff Anderson*

Active Verbs

Writing snaps and sizzles when active, lively verbs are used. Using specific words gives writing voice, develops diction, and increases vocabulary.

Access for All

 Advanced

Planning with Strong Verbs Help children identify forms of the verb *to be,* such as *am, is,* and *was,* if any are used in their plans. Have them think of ways to write their ideas using different, stronger verbs.

Support Prewriting

Beginning Children can describe story events, use verbs to tell them, and share with a partner.

Intermediate Have children use verbs in short phrases to label story events. Have them describe the story plan to other children.

Advanced Have children write short sentences in their story charts. As they share the plan with partners, children can clarify it by adding strong verbs.

Common Core State Standards

Writing 7. Participate in shared research and writing projects (e.g., explore a number of "how-to" books on a given topic and use them to write a sequence of instructions). **Writing 8.** With guidance and support from adults, recall information from experiences or gather information from provided sources to answer a question. **Language 1.a.** Print all uppercase and lowercase letters.

Name ____________ **Sam, Come Back!**

A a

Copy the words. Write the letters the correct size.

Ann	Ann	nap	nap
tap	tap	ham	ham
cap	cap	ran	ran
jab	jab	yak	yak
wag	wag	sad	sad
rag	rag	pal	pal
sat	sat	Pam	Pam

Did you write all of your letters the correct size? Yes No

School + Home **Home Activity** Your child practiced writing words with A and a and the short a sound. Have your child draw a picture of two of the words he or she wrote and label the pictures with the words.

Handwriting 129

Reader's and Writer's Notebook, p. 129

Handwriting

Letter *Aa*/Letter Size

MODEL LETTER FORMATION Display uppercase and lowercase letter *Aa*. Use the stroke instructions pictured below to model proper letter formation.

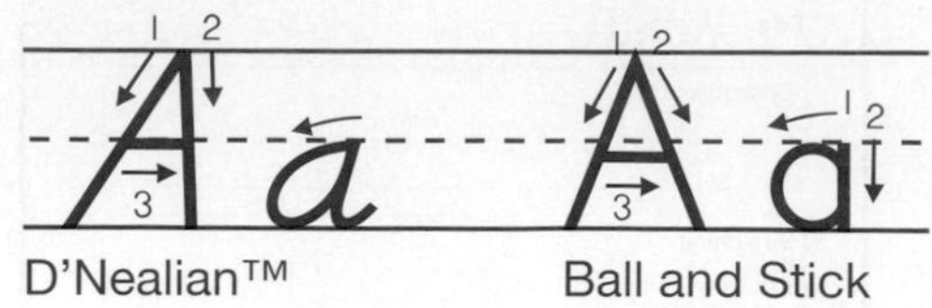

D'Nealian™ Ball and Stick

MODEL CORRECT LETTER SIZE Remind children that letters are different sizes. Some letters are small (for example, *a, c, w*), some letters are tall *(b, h, l),* and some letters hang down below the line *(g, j, p).* When I write a word, I want to make each letter the right size.

Write the word *tag,* using the correct letter size for all three letters. Each letter in this word is a different size. The letter *t* is tall, *a* is a small letter, and *g* hangs below the line. Write the word *tag* again, this time making all the letters small. Then write *tag* a third time, making all the letters tall. These two words are pretty hard to read. When I make my letters the right size, I make it easier for others to read my writing.

GUIDE PRACTICE Write the following words, making some letters too small, some too tall, and others so that they hang incorrectly below the line.

Ann sack tap Jack Pam bag

Team Talk Have children work in pairs to discuss which letters are the wrong size and how they should be fixed. Have children share with the class.

ON THEIR OWN Use *Reader's and Writer's Notebook,* p. 129.

Research and Inquiry

Step 2 Research Skill: Selecting Books

TEACH Display the front and back covers of a familiar book. Read aloud the title, the name of the author, and the name of the illustrator if it appears. Turn to the title page, modeling how to locate it. Read aloud the information given there. Point out that the title and names are the same on the cover as on the title page.

Think Aloud **MODEL** I can read the book cover and title page to find out if the book will help me answer my questions about what pets need. First, I read the title on the front cover. Then, I can look through the book for key words. Key words are important words in the book that tell what it's about. All these things give me clues about what the book is about and help me tell if the book will be useful.

GUIDE PRACTICE Give pairs of children different picture books. Have one child locate and read the cover and title page, while the partner uses key words to predict what the book is about. Take a picture walk through each book to determine if predictions were correct.

Academic Vocabulary

title the name of a book

author the person who writes a book

illustrator the person who draws the pictures in a book

key words important words in a book that tell what it's about

Bridge to Common Core

RESEARCH TO BUILD AND PRESENT KNOWLEDGE

Children will analyze how texts address similar topics in order to build knowledge about a subject through the use of books. They will also:

- learn about titles and pictures
- learn about key words to identify sources

Wrap Up Your Day!

✔ **Phonics: Consonant Pattern *-ck*** Write the words *back, sack,* and *rack.* Have children tell what sound the spelling *-ck* makes at the end of each word.

✔ **High-Frequency Words** Point to these words on the Word Wall: *my, come, way, on, in.* Have children read each word and use it in a sentence.

✔ **Content Knowledge** Monitor children's use of oral vocabulary as they respond. What needs does a pet have? (A pet needs food, water, and shelter.) Who has the responsibility of taking care of a pet? (The pet's owner has the responsibility.) What are ways to play with a pet? (cuddle and tickle him or her)

Tell children that tomorrow they will reread *Sam, Come Back!*

DAY 3
at a Glance

Content Knowledge
Oral Vocabulary

Phonemic Awareness
Rhyming Words

Phonics/Spelling
Short *a: a*
Consonant Pattern *-ck*

High-Frequency Words
come, in, my, on, way

Selection Words
Jack, Sam

Text-Based Comprehension
Review Plot

Fluency
Accuracy

Conventions
Sentences

Writing
Story
Writing Trait: Voice

Listening and Speaking
Ask Questions

Research and Inquiry
Gather and Record Information

Materials
- Student Edition
- Sing with Me Big Book
- Big Book
- Letter Tiles
- Reader's and Writer's Notebook
- Retelling Cards

Common Core State Standards

Speaking/Listening 2. Ask and answer questions about key details in a text read aloud or information presented orally or through other media. **Language 5.c.** Identify real-life connections between words and their use (e.g., note places at home that are *cozy*). **Also Language 6.**

Content Knowledge

Pets

EXPAND THE CONCEPT To reinforce concepts and to focus children's attention, have children sing "Please Get Me a Pet" from the *Sing with Me* Big Book. If you were asking for a pet, what kind would you ask for? What are some things that kind of pet would need?

Build Oral Language

LISTEN FOR AMAZING WORDS Display the Big Book *A Kid's Best Friend.* Read the story and have children listen for the word *faithful.* Have them also think about the kinds of things that kids and dogs can do together.

- What are some things kids and dogs can do together? (play, roll, run, get messy, cuddle, help each other, sleep)
- Do you think a dog can be a kid's best friend? (Yes, because a dog stays with you and plays with you.)

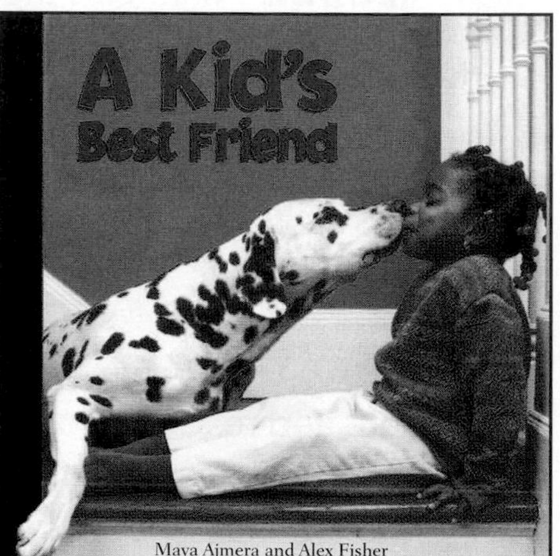

Big Book

TALK ABOUT SENTENCES AND WORDS Write the following sentence from *A Kid's Best Friend* on sentence strips on the board.

Dogs are faithful friends, but they do need care.

- Ask children to read it with you as you track the print.
- Point to and read *Dogs are faithful friends.* What does this mean? (Dogs are loyal friends.) Why did the author choose to use the word *faithful?* (It is the best word to describe a dog's friendship.) What other words could the author have used instead of *faithful?* Have children share their suggestions.
- Now point to and read *but they do need care.* What does this part of the sentence mean? (Dogs need to be taken care of.) Ask a volunteer to tell ways to take care of a dog.
- **Team Talk** Now have children work with a partner to replace key words in the sentence. Use the following sentence frame:

Dogs are _______ friends, but they do need _______.

Build Oral Vocabulary

Amazing Words Robust Vocabulary Routine

1. **Introduce the Word** Relate the word *faithful* to the book. A dog is a best friend because it is *faithful.* Supply a child-friendly definition. *Faithful* means "always there for you when you need it." Have children say the word.

2. **Demonstrate** Provide examples to show meaning. A *faithful* friend stays by you when there is trouble. A *faithful* dog loves you no matter what. When my team is losing, I am a *faithful* fan and cheer for them.

3. **Apply** Have children demonstrate their understanding. How can a dog show that it is *faithful?*

4. **Display the Word** Run your hand under the chunks *faith-ful* as you read the word.

Routines Flip Chart

ADD TO THE CONCEPT MAP Use these questions to discuss more about what pets need as you add to the concept map.

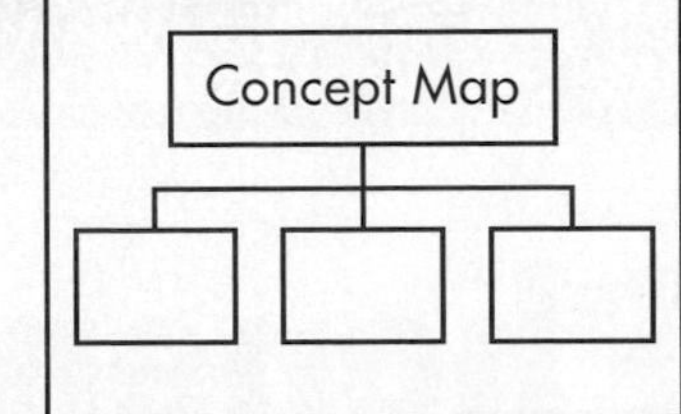

- In *Sam, Come Back!,* Sam the cat does things that many pet cats like to do. How does Sam play and get exercise? (He plays with yarn. He runs and hides.) Let's add *play with yarn* and *run and hide* to our concept map.
- We already know that pets need love. How does the woman show love for Sam the cat? (She cuddles him on her lap.) How does Jack show love for Sam? (He pets him nicely.) Let's add *cuddle on lap and pet nicely* to our map.

Amazing Words

needs	tickle
responsibility	faithful
shelter	fetch
cuddle	heel

Access for All

SI Strategic Intervention

Sentence Production Have children use the word *faithful.* Ask them to point out and explain which of the dogs in the Big Book they think are *faithful.*

ELL

Expand Vocabulary Use the Day 3 instruction on ELL Poster 1 to expand children's use of English vocabulary to communicate about lesson concepts.

Common Core State Standards
Foundational Skills 2.c. Isolate and pronounce initial, medial vowel, and final sounds (phonemes) in spoken single-syllable words. **Also Foundational Skills 2.a., 2.b.**

Phonemic Awareness

Let's Listen for Sounds

- Find five things that contain the short *a* sound.
- Find five things that end with the sound /k/.
- Find something that rhymes with *luck*. Say each sound in the word.
- Find two things that rhyme with *pant*.

Read Together

READING STREET ONLINE
SOUND-SPELLING CARDS
www.ReadingStreet.com

SHADY ACRES ANIMAL SHELTER

COME IN

14 15

Student Edition, pp. 14–15

Common Core State Standards

Foundational Skills 2. Demonstrate understanding of spoken words, syllables, and sounds (phonemes). **Foundational Skills 2.b.** Orally produce single-syllable words by blending sounds (phonemes), including consonant blends. **Foundational Skills 3.a.** Know the spelling-sound correspondences for common consonant digraphs.

Academic Vocabulary

rhyming words words that end with the same sounds

Phonemic Awareness

Rhyming Words

MODEL PRODUCING RHYMING WORDS Read together the last two bulleted points on pages 14–15. Rhyming words are words that end with the same sounds. The directions tell us to find two things that rhyme with *pant.* When I look at the picture, I see a plant near the front door of the building, and I see an ant on the lawn. The words *plant* and *ant* rhyme with *pant.*

GUIDE PRACTICE Help children use the picture to produce words that rhyme with *luck* (duck, truck) and *rag* (bag, flag, tag, wag).

ON THEIR OWN Have children produce words that rhyme with the following words.

hat back map ran sack sad

Team Talk Allow children the opportunity to create pairs of rhyming words with a partner.

Phonics

Build Words

MODEL WORD BUILDING Now we are going to build words that have the short *a* sound and that end with the /k/ sound spelled *ck.* Write *quack* and blend it. Watch me change /kw/ to /p/. Model blending the new word, *pack.*

GUIDE PRACTICE Have children spell *pack* with letter tiles. Monitor children's work as they build words.

- Change the *p* in *pack* to *b.* Say the new word together.

- Change the *b* in *back* to *r.* Say the new word together.

- Change the *r* in *rack* to *s.* Say the new word together.

- Change the *s* in *sack* to *t.* Say the new word together.

Corrective feedback | For corrective feedback, model the correct spelling and have children correct their tiles.

Fluent Word Reading

MODEL Write *sat*. I know the sounds for *s, a,* and *t.* I blend them and read the word *sat.*

GUIDE PRACTICE Write the words below. Say the sounds in your head for each spelling you see. When I point to the word, we'll read it together. Allow one second per sound previewing time for the first reading.

fan tack ham Jack pad back

ON THEIR OWN Have children read the list above three or four times, until they can read one word per second.

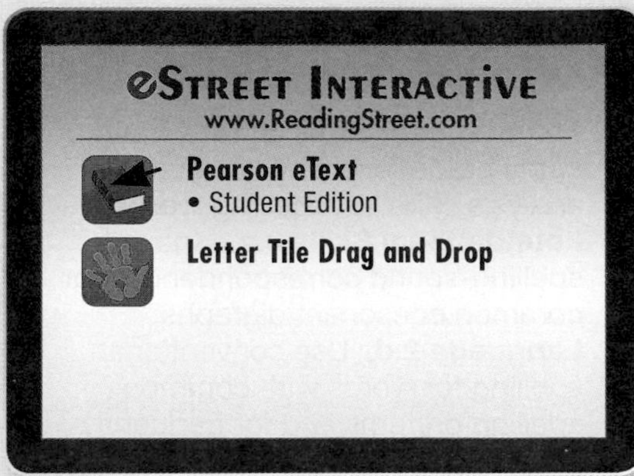

Access for All

A Advanced

Rhyming Couplets If children are able to rhyme words easily and independently, have them work with a partner to create a rhyming couplet about an animal, for example:
Sam the cat likes to run.
He plays with yarn and has lots of fun.

ELL

Visual Support As you model the rhyming words *plant* and *ant,* point to the corresponding pictures on pp. 14–15 of the Student Edition and say: An ant is a kind of insect. This plant has green leaves. To reinforce meaning, have children point to corresponding images as they produce rhyming words themselves.

Common Core State Standards

Foundational Skills 3. Know and apply grade-level phonics and word analysis skills in decoding words. **Foundational Skills 3.a.** Know the spelling-sound correspondences for common consonant digraphs. **Language 2.d.** Use conventional spelling for words with common spelling patterns and for frequently occurring irregular words.

Phonics

Blend and Read

DECODE WORDS IN ISOLATION Have children turn to pages 131–132 in the *Reader's* and *Writer's Notebook* and find the first list of words. Each word in this list has the short *a* sound. Let's blend and read these words. Be sure that children identify the correct sounds in short *a* words. Continue with the words with the consonant pattern *ck* in the second list. Next, have children read the high-frequency words.

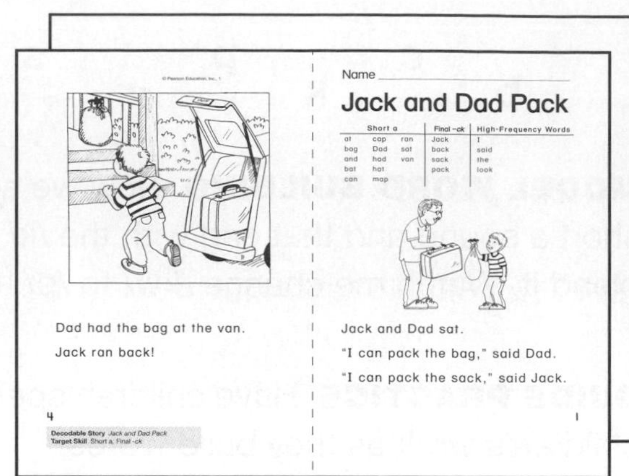

Reader's and Writer's Notebook, pp. 131–132

DECODE WORDS IN CONTEXT Chorally read the story along with children. Have children identify words in the story that have short *a* or the consonant pattern *ck.*

Team Talk Pair children and have them take turns reading the story aloud to each other. Monitor children as they read to check for proper pronunciation and appropriate pacing.

ON THEIR OWN To further develop automaticity, have children take the story home to reread.

Spelling

Short *a* Words

SPELL HIGH-FREQUENCY WORDS Write *way* and *come* and point them out on the Word Wall. Have children say and spell the words with you and then without you.

DICTATION Say each sentence. Then repeat each slowly, one word at a time. Have children write the sentences.

1. **The cat ran that way.**
2. **I can come back.**
3. **My dad is at the van.**

PROOFREAD AND CORRECT Write each sentence, spelling words one at a time. Have children circle and rewrite any misspelled words.

ON THEIR OWN Use *Reader's and Writer's Notebook,* p. 133.

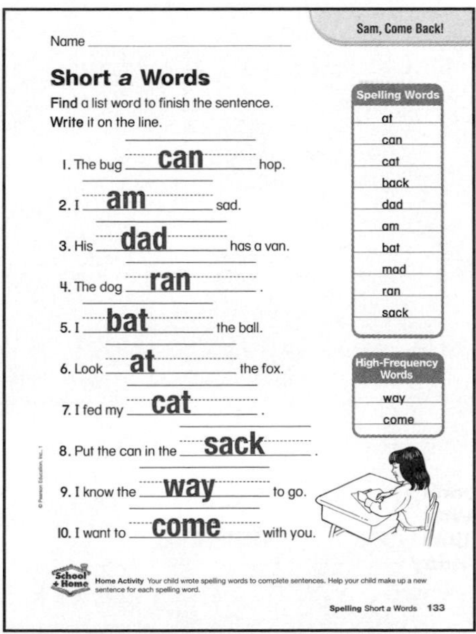
Sam, Come Back!

Name ______

Short *a* Words

Find a list word to finish the sentence.
Write it on the line.

1. The bug **can** hop.
2. I **am** sad.
3. His **dad** has a van.
4. The dog **ran**.
5. I **bat** the ball.
6. Look **at** the fox.
7. I fed my **cat**.
8. Put the can in the **sack**.
9. I know the **way** to go.
10. I want to **come** with you.

Spelling Words: at, can, cat, back, dad, am, bat, mad, ran, sack

High-Frequency Words: way, come

School + Home **Home Activity** Your child wrote spelling words to complete sentences. Help your child make up a new sentence for each spelling word.

© Pearson Education, Inc., 1

Spelling Short *a* Words 133

Reader's and Writer's Notebook, p. 133

eSTREET INTERACTIVE
www.ReadingStreet.com

Teacher Resources
- Reader's and Writer's Notebook

Spelling Words

Short *a* Words

1. at	**6. am**
2. can	**7. bat**
3. cat	**8. mad**
4. back	**9. ran**
5. dad	**10. sack**

High-Frequency Words

11. way	**12. come**

ELL

Spelling Dictation Children will benefit from hearing each dictated sentence three times. First, have children listen to understand the sentence. The second time, they should write what they hear. The third time, they can check their work.

Day 3 SMALL GROUP TIME • Differentiate Close Reading, p. SG•1

OL On-Level
- **Reread** to Develop Vocabulary
- **Reread** *Sam, Come Back!*

SI Strategic Intervention
- **Blend** Words with Short *a* and *-ck*
- **Reread** *Sam, Come Back!*

A Advanced
- **Reread** to Extend Vocabulary
- **Reread** *Sam, Come Back!*
- **Investigate** Inquiry Project

ELL

If... children need more scaffolding and practice with reading the **Main Selection,**
then... use the ELL activities on p. DI•18 in the Teacher Resources section on SuccessNet.

Common Core State Standards

Literature 3. Describe characters, settings, and major events in a story, using key details. **Foundational Skills 3.g.** Recognize and read grade-appropriate irregularly spelled words.

High-Frequency Words

come	**on**
in	**way**
my	

Selection Words

Jack the name of the boy in the story
Sam the name of the cat in the story

High-Frequency and Selection Words

READ WORDS IN ISOLATION Display and review this week's high-frequency words and selection words. Have children read the words aloud.

READ WORDS IN CONTEXT Display the following sentence frames. Have children complete the sentences using high-frequency and selection words. Have children read each completed sentence with you.

1. **______ sat on my lap. (Sam)**
2. **The man ran that ______. (way)**
3. **Jack, ______ pat the cat! (come)**
4. **The map is in ______ van. (my)**
5. **I see a hat ______ that tan bag. (in)**

Check High-Frequency Words

FORMATIVE ASSESSMENT Point to these words on the Word Wall and have the class read them. Listen for children who miss words during the reading. Call on those children to read some of the words individually.

my	**come**	**way**	**on**	**in**	**Spiral Review**
the	**is**	**that**	**see**	←	Row 2 reviews previously taught high-frequency words.

If... children cannot read these words,
then... use the Nondecodable Words Routine on p. 17 to reteach the words. Monitor children's fluency with these words during reading and provide additional practice.

Text-Based Comprehension

Read Main Selection

REVIEW PLOT Remind children that the **plot** in a story includes the problem the characters have and how they try to solve it. Thinking about the problem in a story and its solution can help us better understand story events. Have children turn to page 23 in their Student Edition. What problem do the characters in *Sam, Come Back!* have? (Sam the cat takes the woman's yarn and runs away.) Now have children turn to page 24. How do the characters try to solve their problem? (They chase Sam and try to get him to come back.)

GENRE: REALISTIC FICTION Remind children that realistic fiction is a made-up story that could happen in real life. Have children recall things that Sam in *Sam, Come Back!* does that a real cat might do. (He cuddles on his owner's lap, hides, and plays with yarn.)

READ Return to pages 20–29 and use the **2nd Read/Close Reading Notes** to reread *Sam, Come Back!*

Routine Read for Understanding

Deepen understanding by reading the selection multiple times.

1. **First Read**—If children need support, then use the **Access Text** notes to help them clarify understanding.
2. **Second Read**—Use the **Close Reading** notes to help children draw knowledge from the text.

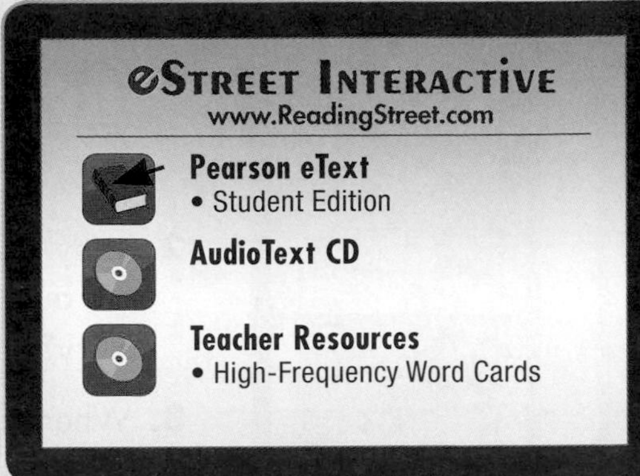

Academic Vocabulary 

plot the events that happen in the beginning, middle, and end of a story, including the problem characters have and its solution

ELL

Understanding Plot Have children use pantomime to demonstrate the problem and solution in *Sam, Come Back!* Then ask them to explain the events that they acted out.

Common Core State Standards
Literature 1. Ask and answer questions about key details in a text.
Also Literature 2., Writing 5.
Envision It! Retell
READING STREET ONLINE
STORY SORT
www.ReadingStreet.com

Think Critically

1. What part of the story do you think is funny? Why? Text to Self
2. Why do you think the author wrote this story? Author's Purpose
3. Where does Sam run? Why do you think he runs there? Character and Setting
4. Reread page 24. If you did not know what the word *nab* means, what could you do to figure it out? Monitor and Clarify
5. **Look Back and Write** Look back at page 25. Where does Sam run first? Write about it. Key Ideas and Details • Text Evidence

30

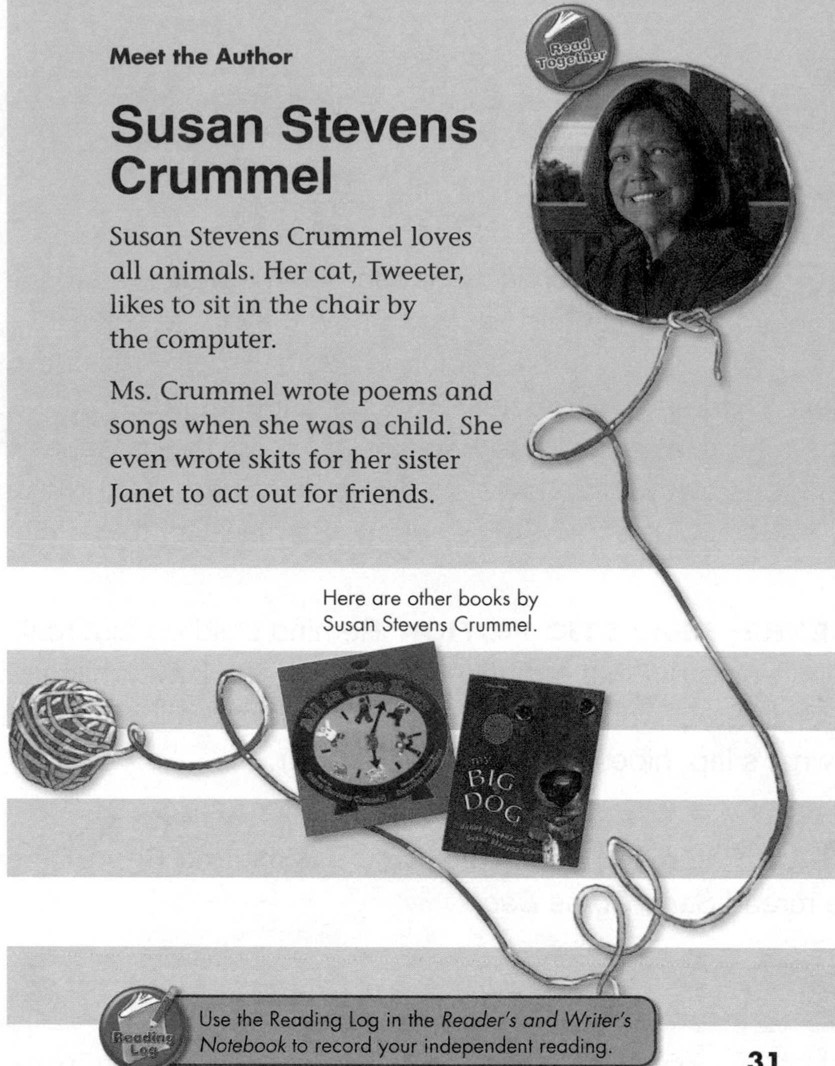

Meet the Author
Susan Stevens Crummel
Susan Stevens Crummel loves all animals. Her cat, Tweeter, likes to sit in the chair by the computer.
Ms. Crummel wrote poems and songs when she was a child. She even wrote skits for her sister Janet to act out for friends.
Here are other books by Susan Stevens Crummel.
All in One Hour
My Big Dog
Use the Reading Log in the Reader's and Writer's Notebook to record your independent reading.

31

Student Edition, pp. 30–31

Common Core State Standards

Literature 1. Ask and answer questions about key details in a text. **Literature 2.** Retell stories, including key details, and demonstrate understanding of their central message or lesson. **Also Writing 5.**

Bridge to Common Core

KEY IDEAS AND DETAILS

By reading the text multiple times, children will make logical inferences from the text and cite textual evidence when writing or discussing the knowledge they have gained. Use the Think Critically page to ensure a thorough understanding of *Sam, Come Back!*

Think Critically

1. **TEXT TO SELF** I think it's funny when Jack and the dog are chasing Sam, and they can't catch him. Even though Sam the cat is smaller than they are, he is a fast runner.
2. **AUTHOR'S PURPOSE** The author wants us to laugh about the kinds of things that all cats do.
3. **CHARACTER AND SETTING** The first place Sam runs is out the door. There are lots of places to run and hide outside.
4. **MONITOR AND CLARIFY** I could reread the sentences that come before it and look at the pictures.
5. **LOOK BACK AND WRITE • TEXT EVIDENCE** For writing fluency, assign a 5-minute time limit. As children finish, encourage them to reread their responses and proofread for errors.

Scoring Rubric Look Back and Write

TOP-SCORE RESPONSE A top-score response uses details from the text and the pictures to explain where Sam ran.

A top-score response might include:

Sam ran through the yard. Then he came back inside and hid in a bag. Next, he ran around a room. Last, he hid in a pack.

Retell

Have children use the retelling strip in the Student Edition or the Story Sort to retell the selection. Monitor children's retelling.

Scoring Rubric Narrative Retelling

	4	3	2	1
Connections	Makes connections and generalizes beyond the text	Makes connections to other events, stories, or experiences	Makes a limited connection to another event, story, or experience	Makes no connection to another event, story, or experience
Author's Purpose	Elaborates on author's purpose	Tells author's purpose with some clarity	Makes some connection to author's purpose	Makes no connection to author's purpose
Characters	Describes the main character(s) and any character development	Identifies the main character(s) and gives some information about them	Inaccurately identifies some characters or gives little information about them	Inaccurately identifies the characters or gives no information about them
Setting	Describes the time and location	Identifies the time and location	Omits details of time or location	Is unable to identify time or location
Plot	Describes the events in sequence using rich detail	Tells the plot with some errors in sequence that do not affect meaning	Tells parts of plot with gaps that affect meaning	Retelling has no sense of story

Don't Wait Until Friday

MONITOR PROGRESS Check Retelling

If... children have trouble retelling the selection,

then... use Story Sequence Graphic Organizer 23 and the Retelling Cards/ Story Sort to scaffold their retelling.

Writing to Sources

Use Write Like a Reporter on pp. 42–43 to guide children in writing text-based responses using one source.

Strategy Response Log

Monitor and Clarify Ask children to think about any parts of *Sam, Come Back!* that confused them at first. Then have children use p. RR13 in their *Reader's and Writer's Notebook* to draw and write what they did to help them understand what was happening in the story.

Plan to Assess Retelling

- ☑ **This Week** Assess Strategic Intervention children.
- ☐ **Week 2** Advanced
- ☐ **Week 3** Strategic Intervention
- ☐ **Week 4** On-Level
- ☐ **Week 5** Strategic Intervention
- ☐ **Week 6** Assess any children you have not yet checked during this unit.

Meet the Author

Read aloud page 31 as children follow along. Ask children what authors do.

Read Independently

Have children enter their independent reading into their Reading Logs.

Common Core State Standards

Foundational Skills 1.a. Recognize the distinguishing features of a sentence (e.g., first word, capitalization, ending punctuation). **Foundational Skills 4.** Read with sufficient accuracy and fluency to support comprehension. **Language 1.** Demonstrate command of the conventions of standard English grammar and usage when writing or speaking. **Language 2.b.** Use end punctuation for sentences.

Options for Oral Rereading

Use *Sam, Come Back!* or one of this week's Decodable Practice Readers.

Professional Development

Fluency To read fluently, children must be exposed to fluent reading. Auditory modeling, whether live or taped, helps children hear how text is supposed to be read.

Fluency

Accuracy

MODEL FLUENT READING Have children turn to Student Edition page 22. When I read this page, I will try to read with no mistakes. I will try not to change any words or leave any words out.

GUIDE PRACTICE Ask children to follow along as you read the page with accuracy. Have children read the page with you. Then have them reread the page as a group until they read with no mistakes. Continue in the same way with page 23.

Corrective feedback	**If...** children have difficulty reading with accuracy, **then...** prompt: • Did you change any words? • Did you leave out any words? • Try to read all the words correctly.

Reread for Fluency

Routine Choral Reading

1. **Select a Passage** For *Sam, Come Back!,* use pp. 24–25.
2. **Model** First, have children track the print as you read.
3. **Guide Practice** Then have children read along with you.
4. **Corrective Feedback** Have the class read aloud without you. Monitor progress and provide feedback. For optimal fluency, children should reread three to four times.

Routines Flip Chart

CHECK COMPREHENSION What is the problem in the plot of this story? (Sam has run away with the yarn, and Jack and the dog can't catch him.)

Conventions

Sentences

REVIEW Remind children that a sentence is a group of words that tells a complete idea. It begins with a capital letter and ends with a punctuation mark, such as a period: *The cat sleeps. Dogs run fast.*

GUIDE PRACTICE Write this sentence on the board and have children read it aloud.

Sam the cat ran back.

Guide children in describing how the sentence tells a complete idea. Who is the sentence about? (Sam the cat) What does the sentence tell us about him? (He ran back.)

Team Talk Have partners think of other sentences about pets. Have them explain why each is a complete idea by identifying who or what each sentence is about and what the sentence tells about the person, animal, or thing.

APPLY Have children complete these sentence frames orally. Ask them to explain why the sentences are complete ideas and what to put at the beginning and the end of each.

1. **My favorite pet ______.**
2. **______ likes to ______.**

ON THEIR OWN Use *Reader's and Writer's Notebook,* p. 134.

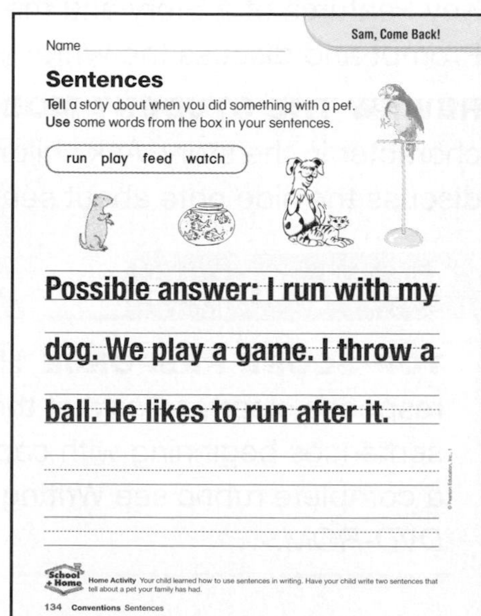
Name

Sam, Come Back!

Sentences

Tell a story about when you did something with a pet.
Use some words from the box in your sentences.

run play feed watch

Possible answer: I run with my dog. We play a game. I throw a ball. He likes to run after it.

Home Activity Your child learned how to use sentences in writing. Have your child write two sentences that tell about a pet your family has had.

134 Conventions Sentences

Reader's and Writer's Notebook, p. 134

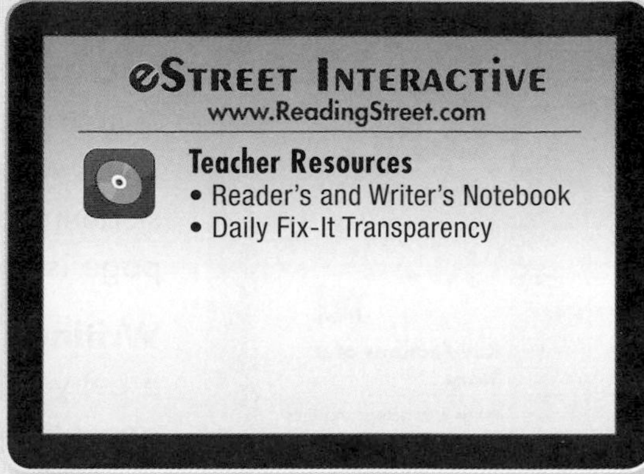

Daily Fix-It

5. My dad ren with the cat
   My dad ran with the cat.
6. the cat was in the sak.
   The cat was in the sack.

Discuss the Daily Fix-It corrections with children. Review sentence capitalization and punctuation, the *a* spelling of /a/, and the *ck* spelling of final /k/.

Support Fluency Encourage children to use the pictures as they reread for fluency. Help them associate the words with the pictures on the page.

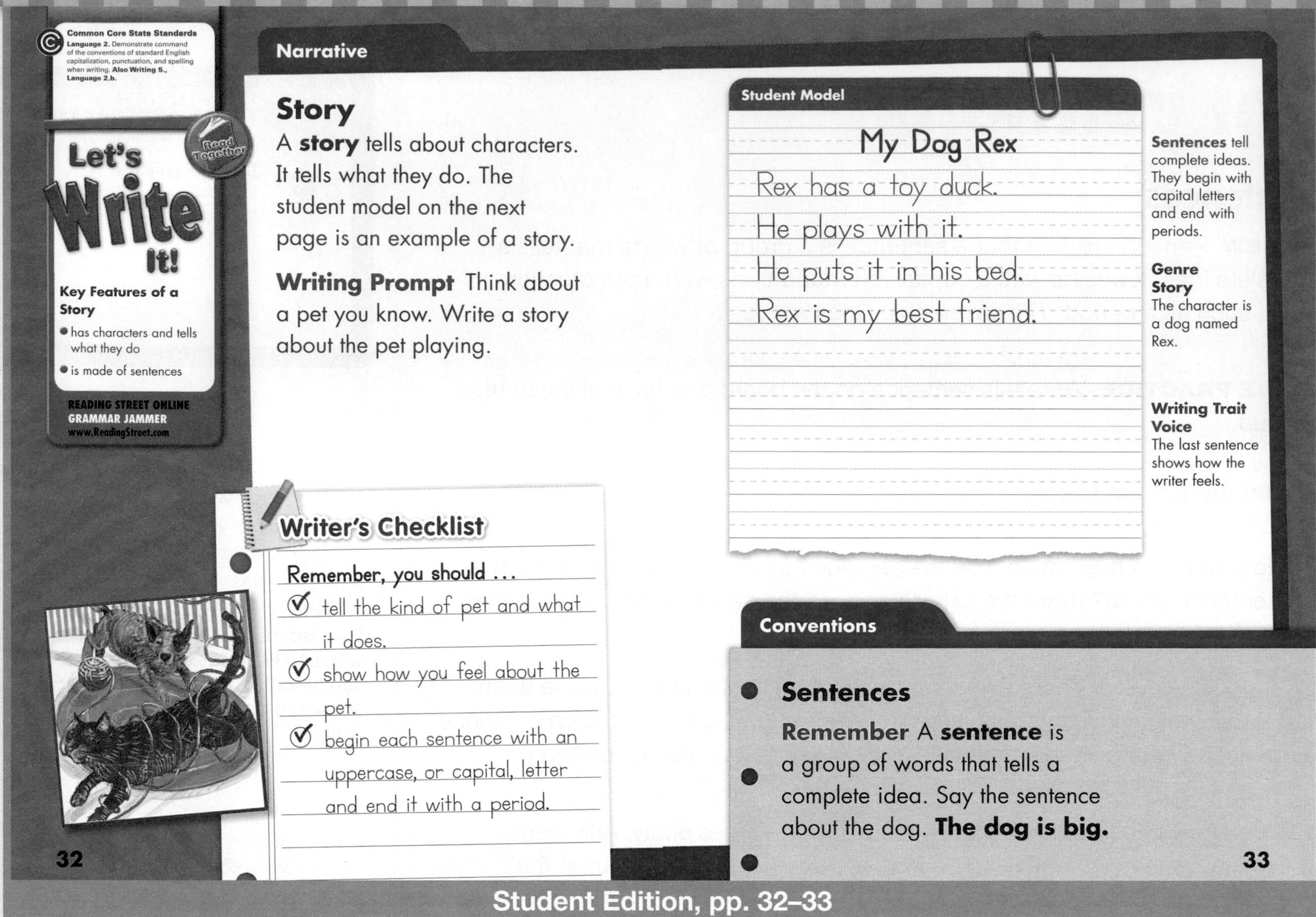

Common Core State Standards
Language 2. Demonstrate command of the conventions of standard English capitalization, punctuation, and spelling when writing. Also Writing 5., Language 2.b.
Let's Write It!
Read Together
Key Features of a Story
• has characters and tells what they do
• is made of sentences
READING STREET ONLINE
GRAMMAR JAMMER
www.ReadingStreet.com
Narrative
Story
A story tells about characters. It tells what they do. The student model on the next page is an example of a story.
Writing Prompt Think about a pet you know. Write a story about the pet playing.
Student Model
My Dog Rex
Rex has a toy duck.
He plays with it.
He puts it in his bed.
Rex is my best friend.
Sentences tell complete ideas. They begin with capital letters and end with periods.
Genre Story
The character is a dog named Rex.
Writing Trait Voice
The last sentence shows how the writer feels.
Writer's Checklist
Remember, you should ...
tell the kind of pet and what it does.
show how you feel about the pet.
begin each sentence with an uppercase, or capital, letter and end it with a period.
Conventions
Sentences
Remember A sentence is a group of words that tells a complete idea. Say the sentence about the dog. The dog is big.
32
33

Student Edition, pp. 32–33

Common Core State Standards

Writing 3. Write narratives in which they recount two or more appropriately sequenced events, include some details regarding what happened, use temporal words to signal event order, and provide some sense of closure. **Language 2.** Demonstrate command of the conventions of standard English capitalization, punctuation, and spelling when writing. **Language 2.b.** Use end punctuation for sentences.

Let's Write It!

WRITE A STORY Use pages 32–33 in the Student Edition. Read aloud the Key Features of a Story and the definition of a story. Read aloud the Writing Prompt and discuss the Writer's Checklist.

REVIEW THE STUDENT MODEL Read aloud "My Dog Rex." Point out the character in the story. Ask children to tell how the writer feels. Read aloud and discuss the side note about sentences, genre, and the writing trait.

Scoring Rubric

TOP-SCORE RESPONSE Help children understand that a top-score response clearly tells what the pet does, shows feelings, and has sentences beginning with capital letters and ending with periods. For a complete rubric see Writing Rubric 1 from the *Teacher Resources DVD-ROM.*

CONNECT TO CONVENTIONS Read to children the Conventions note about sentences. Point out the capital letters and the periods in the model story.

Story

Mini-Lesson Writing Trait: Voice

- **Introduce** Use your story chart from yesterday and Writing Transparency 1A to model expressing feelings. When I write my story, I will use my chart. First, I will introduce my character. I will use voice to introduce Honey. Good writers use voice. They show how they feel about their topic. So, I'll write *Honey is my pet hamster. It is fun to see her run and play.* These sentences tell my feelings about my topic. For example, when I write that Honey is my pet, I let readers know that I love and take care of her. I also tell that it is fun to be with her. Read aloud the draft on the transparency to show how it includes feelings about characters and story events.

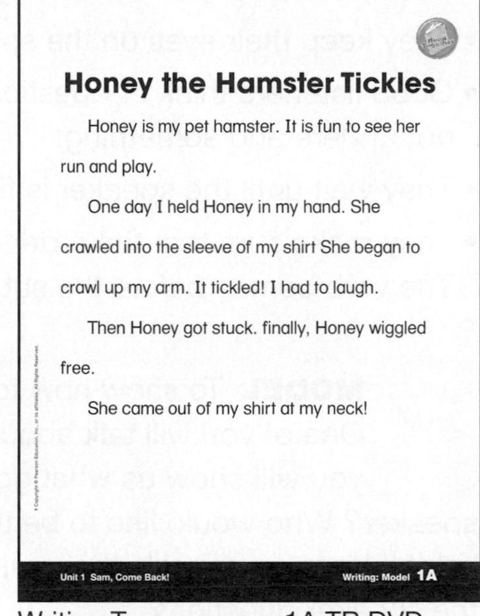
Honey the Hamster Tickles

Honey is my pet hamster. It is fun to see her run and play.

One day I held Honey in my hand. She crawled into the sleeve of my shirt She began to crawl up my arm. It tickled! I had to laugh.

Then Honey got stuck. finally, Honey wiggled free.

She came out of my shirt at my neck!

Unit 1 Sam, Come Back! Writing: Model 1A

Writing Transparency 1A TR DVD

- Explain how children can use story events they planned yesterday to draft the story. Remind them to tell about feelings in their drafts. Today's goal is to write the story but not to write each word perfectly. They can edit later to correct the words.

GUIDE WRITING Now it is time to write your story. Tell what a pet does and how you feel. Have children use their story charts. Help them finish the ideas. Then guide children as they draft the stories.

Routine Quick Write for Fluency

Team Talk

1. **Talk** Have partners take one minute to talk about what the characters in their stories do.
2. **Write** Each child writes a sentence expressing feelings about what the character does.
3. **Share** Partners point out the feelings expressed in the others' sentences.

Routines Flip Chart

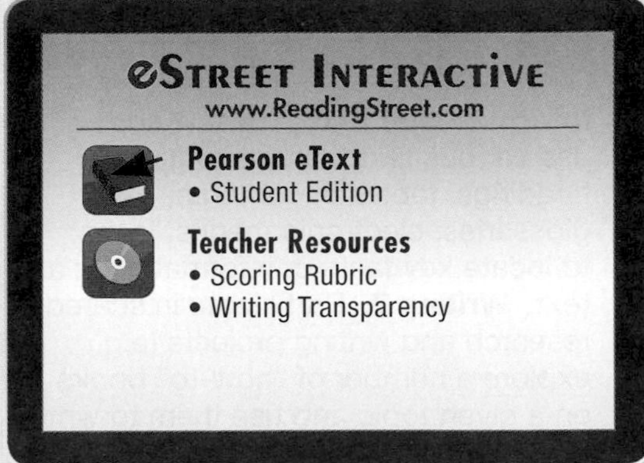
eStreet Interactive
www.ReadingStreet.com

Pearson eText
- Student Edition

Teacher Resources
- Scoring Rubric
- Writing Transparency

Access for All

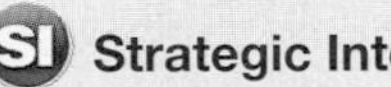
SI Strategic Intervention

Developing Voice Help children identify feelings about their topic by asking questions such as *What do you like about your character?* and *Why do you like this about your character?*

Common Core State Standards

Informational Text 5. Know and use various text features (e.g., headings, tables of contents, glossaries, electronic menus, icons) to locate key facts or information in a text. **Writing 7.** Participate in shared research and writing projects (e.g., explore a number of "how-to" books on a given topic and use them to write a sequence of instructions). **Writing 8.** With guidance and support from adults, recall information from experiences or gather information from provided sources to answer a question. **Speaking/Listening 1.c.** Ask questions to clear up any confusion about the topics and texts under discussion. **Also Speaking/Listening 2., 3.**

COMPREHENSION AND COLLABORATION

As children participate in a range of conversations and collaborations about pets, they learn to ask questions about key issues or concepts to clarify and deepen their understanding of content. This process is enhanced by developing listening and speaking habits for effective participation.

Listening and Speaking

Ask Questions

TEACH Remind children that it takes many different skills to be a good listener.

- Good listeners listen attentively and carefully.
- They keep their eyes on the speaker to show that they are paying attention.
- Good listeners think of questions to ask the speaker, especially if they do not understand something.
- They wait until the speaker is finished and then they ask their questions.
- They make sure that the order of the words in their questions is correct. The verb comes before the subject in a question.

Think Aloud **MODEL** To show how to be a good listener, let's do a little play. One of you will talk about an animal that makes a good pet. Three of you will show us what good listeners do. Who would like to be the speaker? Who would like to be the listeners? Guide the speaker and give helpful hints on animals that make good pets. Guide the listeners as they ask the speaker questions.

GUIDE PRACTICE Speak to children about a simple classroom procedure, such as turning in homework. Have children model good listening skills, including writing questions as you speak. Then put children in pairs and have them compare and contrast their questions. Have them check to make sure they didn't miss the answers to their questions. Then gather the whole class and have children ask their remaining questions. Answer their questions.

ON THEIR OWN Have children write three questions that show that they are good listeners. Have them make sure that the order of the words in their questions is correct.

Research and Inquiry

Step 3 Gather and Record Information

TEACH Tell children that today they will look through sources of information and decide which books might help them answer their questions about what pets need. They will write the title of books that will help them.

Think Aloud **MODEL** Display the list of questions the class created on Day 1. We can find answers to our questions in books, but not just any books. We need to find books about pets. Hold up a book and read the title aloud. The title tells me what the book is about. I think this book may answer some of my questions, so I'll write down the title of the book. That way I won't forget it.

GUIDE PRACTICE Give pairs of children two or three books to examine. (At least one book in each group should not be about pets' or animals' needs.) Encourage children to read the title and page through the book, looking at the table of contents, illustrations, headings, and key words. Suggest that children write the title and author of each book they feel will help them answer their questions about what pets need.

ON THEIR OWN Use *Reader's and Writer's Notebook,* p. 130.

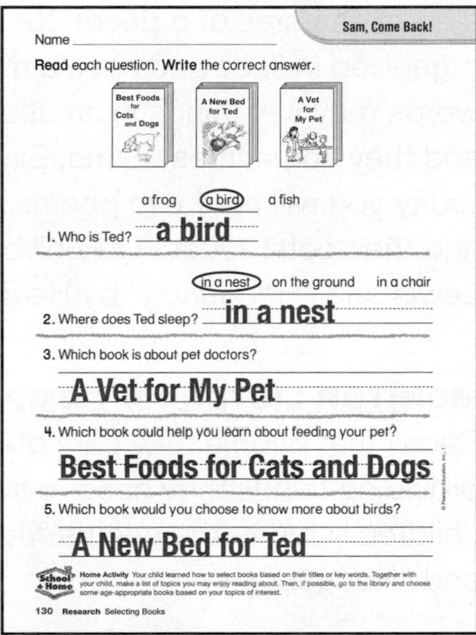
Sam, Come Back!

Name

Read each question. Write the correct answer.

Best Foods for Cats and Dogs | A New Bed for Ted | A Vet for My Pet

a frog | a bird (circled) | a fish

1. Who is Ted? **a bird**

in a nest (circled) | on the ground | in a chair

2. Where does Ted sleep? **in a nest**

3. Which book is about pet doctors?

A Vet for My Pet

4. Which book could help you learn about feeding your pet?

Best Foods for Cats and Dogs

5. Which book would you choose to know more about birds?

A New Bed for Ted

School + Home **Home Activity** Your child learned how to select books based on their titles or key words. Together with your child, make a list of topics you may enjoy reading about. Then, if possible, go to the library and choose some age-appropriate books based on your topics of interest.

© Pearson Education, Inc., 1

130 **Research** Selecting Books

Reader's and Writer's Notebook, p. 130

eStreet Interactive
www.ReadingStreet.com

Teacher Resources
- Reader's and Writer's Notebook

Access for All

SI Strategic Intervention

Reviewing Books Some children may have trouble reading the book titles. Work with children as a group. Read a book title aloud as children track the words. Allow them to page through the book and decide whether to write down its title.

Wrap Up Your Day!

- ✔ **Character and Setting** Have children think about the woman in *Sam, Come Back!* Why did the woman get upset? Where did Sam go when he ran with the yarn?
- ✔ **Monitor and Clarify** Remind children that good readers often ask themselves if they understand a story. If something is confusing or doesn't make sense, they can reread sentences and look at the pictures to clarify ideas. Ask children how they clarified confusing ideas in *Sam, Come Back!*

Tell children that tomorrow they will hear two poems about other children and their pets.

Content Knowledge
Oral Vocabulary

Phonemic Awareness
Distinguish /a/

Phonics
Review Consonant Sounds

High-Frequency Words
Review

Spelling
Short *a* Words

Social Studies in Reading
Sing-Along

Fluency
Accuracy

Conventions
Sentences

Writing
Story: Revise

Research and Inquiry
Synthesize

Materials

- Student Edition
- Sing with Me Big Book
- Read Aloud Anthology
- Decodable Reader 1C
- Reader's and Writer's Notebook

Common Core State Standards

Speaking/Listening 2. Ask and answer questions about key details in a text read aloud or information presented orally or through other media. **Language 5.c.** Identify real-life connections between words and their use (e.g., note places at home that are *cozy*). **Also Language 6.**

Content Knowledge

Pets

EXPAND THE CONCEPT To reinforce concepts and to focus children's attention, have them sing "Please Get Me a Pet" from the *Sing with Me* Big Book. The girl in the song might get a kitten at the pet shop. What are some things a little kitten needs? (milk, food, a litter box, toys)

Build Oral Language

REVIEW GENRE: POEM Have children tell the key features of a poem: the words are organized in lines and have a rhythm. The words may say things in an unusual way, and they sometimes rhyme. Explain that today you will read two poems about people and their pets: "Just Fur Fun" by J. Patrick Lewis and "Hedgehog" by Heidi Roemer.

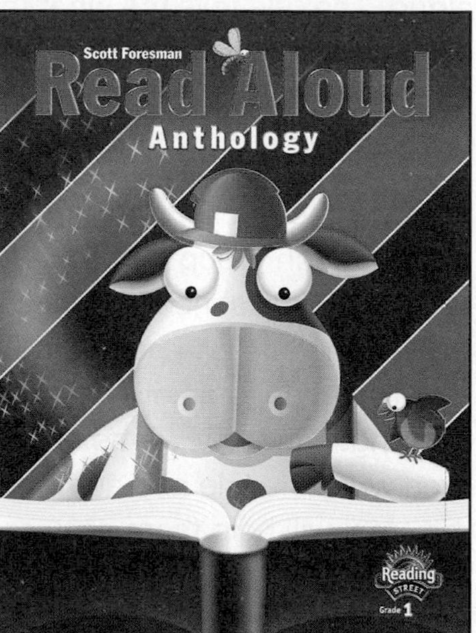

"Just Fur Fun" and "Hedgehog"

MONITOR LISTENING COMPREHENSION Recall that people take care of pets by providing things they need to live. Have children listen to the poems "Just Fur Fun" and "Hedgehog."

Team Talk **TALK ABOUT PETS** Read aloud the first stanza of "Hedgehog." Display it on the board if possible, and track the print as you read it.

- Have pairs generate questions for each other about the hedgehog they visualize when they hear this stanza. What kinds of things does a hedgehog need?
- Add words generated in the discussion to the concept map.

Build Oral Vocabulary

Amazing Words **Robust Vocabulary Routine**

1. **Introduce the Word** Relate the word *fetch* to the poem. The pet hedgehog cannot *fetch.* Supply a child-friendly definition. When you *fetch* something, you go get it. Have children say the word.
2. **Demonstrate** Provide examples to show meaning. My dog likes to *fetch* his toy bone. I will *fetch* our suitcases from the car. My mother asked me to *fetch* her glasses.
3. **Apply** Have children demonstrate their understanding. Name some things that a dog might *fetch.*
4. **Display the Word** Point out that the word begins with the sound /f/ spelled *f.* Say the word.

See p. OV•1 to teach *heel.*

Routines Flip Chart

ADD TO THE CONCEPT MAP Discuss more ideas about the things that pets need.

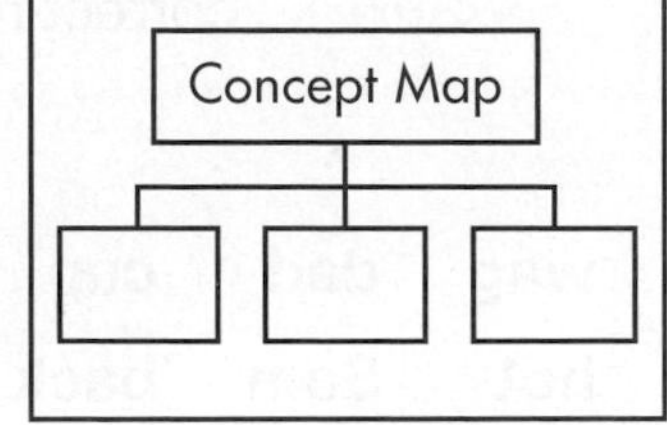

- What animal did we learn about in the poem "Just Fur Fun"? (a gerbil) What does the owner feed the gerbil? (bits of seeds) Where should we add *seeds for gerbils* to our concept map?
- Why does the hedgehog in the poem "Hedgehog" race around in his squeaky wheel? (to get exercise) Let's add *run on wheel* to our map. Where should we write that? What does the hedgehog's owner feed it? (a mealworm) We can add that to the *food* part of our map.

Amazing Words

needs	tickle
responsibility	faithful
shelter	fetch
cuddle	heel

Access for All

 **Advanced**

Extend Amazing Words Have children discuss or write answers to these questions:

- What are some things a dog can learn to *fetch?*
- Why is it important to teach a dog to *heel?*

Produce Oral Language Use the Day 4 instruction on ELL Poster 1 to extend and enrich language.

Support Listening In preparation for reading "Just Fur Fun," have children touch and name their elbows, knees, and fingers. Then have children pantomime each line of the poem as you read it and they repeat it. Before reading "Hedgehog," display a picture of a real hedgehog.

Common Core State Standards

Foundational Skills 2.c. Isolate and pronounce initial, medial vowel, and final sounds (phonemes) in spoken single-syllable words. **Foundational Skills 3.** Know and apply grade-level phonics and word analysis skills in decoding words.

Phonemic Awareness

Distinguish /a/

MODEL This week we read about a cat named Sam. Listen as I say the three sounds in *cat.* Slowly model the sounds in *cat:* /k/ /a/ /t/. The middle sound in *cat* is /a/. Now we're going to say some other words and listen for the /a/ sound.

GUIDE PRACTICE I will say a word. Repeat the word after me. Raise your hand if you hear an /a/ sound at the beginning of the word.

Corrective feedback	If children make an error, segment the word and model the correct response. Return to the word later in the practice.

and	up	elf	ask	act
it	apple	attic	ant	on

Now I will say some more words. Repeat each word after me. Raise your hand if you hear an /a/ sound in the middle of the word.

Corrective feedback	If children make an error, segment the word and model the correct response. Return to the word later in the practice.

wag	dad	cup	tack	pail
hot	Sam	back	leg	big

ON THEIR OWN Have children say each word and tell if they hear the /a/ sound at the beginning or in the middle of the word.

attic	mad	am	tag	sack
add	ash	fan	at	map

Phonics

Review Consonant Sounds

REVIEW CONSONANT SOUNDS To review consonant sounds, first write *sat.* You studied words like this one already. What do you know about the consonant sound you hear at the beginning of *sat?* (The *s* stands for the sound /s/.) What do you know about the consonant sound you hear at the end of *sat?* (The *t* stands for the sound /t/.)

Corrective feedback	If children are unable to answer your questions about the consonant sounds in *sat,* refer them to Sound-Spelling Cards 21 and 23.

GUIDE PRACTICE Continue with the words *bad, cat, fan, gas, ham, jar, lap, quack, van, wag, yak,* and *zap.* Have children identify the consonant sound at the beginning and at the end of each word.

ON THEIR OWN Use Let's Practice It! pp. 27–28 on the *Teacher Resources DVD-ROM.*

Professional Development

Model Decoding When modeling how to decode a new word, a teacher should first segment by pronouncing each sound in the word separately. Then the teacher should blend the sounds together to say the word at a normal speed. This will help teach children to consider each sound in sequence, from left to right, as well as to expect blended phonemes to sound like a word.

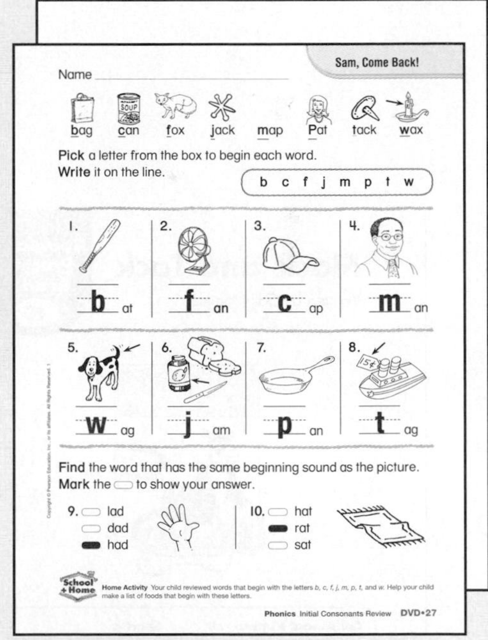

Sam, Come Back!

Name

bag can fox jack map Pat tack wax

Pick a letter from the box to begin each word.
Write it on the line.

b c f j m p t w

1. b at
2. f an
3. c ap
4. m an
5. w ag
6. j am
7. p an
8. t ag

Find the word that has the same beginning sound as the picture.
Mark the ⬭ to show your answer.

9. lad / dad / had
10. hat / rat / sat

Home Activity Your child reviewed words that begin with the letters *b, c, f, j, m, p, t,* and *w.* Help your child make a list of foods that begin with these letters.

Phonics Initial Consonants Review DVD•27

Let's Practice It!
TR DVD•27–28

Practice Final Consonants In Spanish the letters *t* and *m* cannot end a word. Spanish-speaking children may delete or substitute for these sounds. Point out these differences between Spanish and English and provide practice in saying and spelling words such as *cat* and *ham.*

Common Core State Standards

Foundational Skills 3. Know and apply grade-level phonics and word analysis skills in decoding words. **Foundational Skills 3.b.** Decode regularly spelled one-syllable words. **Foundational Skills 3.g.** Recognize and read grade-appropriate irregularly spelled words. **Foundational Skills 4.** Read with sufficient accuracy and fluency to support comprehension.

Decodable Reader 1C

If children need help, then...

Read *Mack and Tack*

DECODE WORDS IN ISOLATION Have children turn to page 113 and decode each word listed.

REVIEW HIGH-FREQUENCY WORDS Review the previously taught words *a* and *the.* Have children read each word as you point to it on the Word Wall.

PREVIEW Have children read the title and preview the story. Tell them they will read words with the short *a* sound, /a/, spelled *a* and words that end with the /k/ sound spelled *-ck.*

DECODE WORDS IN CONTEXT Pair children for reading and listen carefully as they decode. One child begins. Children read the entire story, switching readers after each page. Partners reread the story. This time the other child begins.

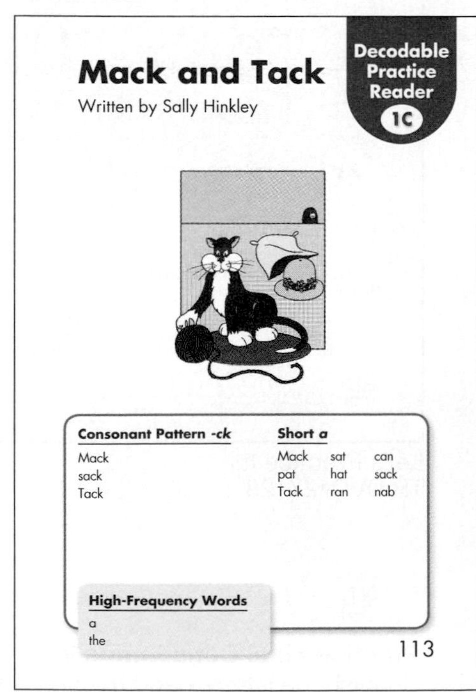

Mack and Tack

Written by Sally Hinkley

Decodable Practice Reader 1C

Consonant Pattern -ck	Short a		
Mack	Mack	sat	can
sack	pat	hat	sack
Tack	Tack	ran	nab

High-Frequency Words

a

the

113

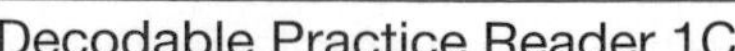

Decodable Practice Reader 1C

Mack sat.
Mack can pat.

114

Mack had a hat.
Mack had a sack.

115

Mack sat in the sack.

116

Tack sat.
Can Tack pat?

117

Tack had a hat.
Tack had a sack.

118

Tack sat on the hat.

119

Tack ran.
Mack ran.
Can Mack nab Tack?

120

Corrective feedback	**If...** children have difficulty decoding a word, **then...** refer them to the Sound-Spelling Cards to identify the sounds in the word. Then prompt them to blend the word. • What is the new word? • Is the new word a word you know? • Does it make sense in the story?

CHECK DECODING AND COMPREHENSION Have children retell the story to include characters, setting, and events. Then have children find words that end with the sound /k/ in the story. Children should supply *Mack, Tack,* and *sack.*

Reread for Fluency

REREAD DECODABLE READER Have children reread Decodable Practice Reader 1C to develop automaticity decoding words with short *a* spelled *a* and words with final /k/ spelled *-ck.*

Routine Oral Rereading

1. **Read** Have children read the entire book orally.
2. **Reread** To achieve optimal fluency, children should reread the text three or four times.
3. **Corrective Feedback** Listen as children read. Provide corrective feedback regarding their fluency and decoding.

Routines Flip Chart

Decodable Practice Reader

Beginning After reading, have children read a word in a sentence and point to the part of the illustration to which the word refers.

Intermediate After reading, refer children to the list of final *-ck* words. Have them use the words in a sentence.

Advanced Have children read a sentence and then use the illustration to elaborate. For example, they might say "Mack sat beside some yarn" or "Tack sat on the hat with flowers."

Fluent Word Reading

Spiral Review

READ WORDS IN ISOLATION Display these words. Tell children that they can blend some words on this list, and others are Word Wall words.

Have children read the list three or four times until they can read at the rate of two to three seconds per word.

cat	the	Matt	that	jam
is	a	pass	are	you
fat	have	back	I	van

Corrective feedback Word Reading	
	If... children have difficulty reading whole words, **then...** have them use sound-by-sound blending for decodable words, or have them say and spell high-frequency words. **If...** children cannot read fluently at a rate of two to three seconds per word, **then...** have pairs practice the list until they can read it fluently.

READ WORDS IN CONTEXT Display these sentences. Call on individuals to read a sentence. Then randomly point to review words and have children read them. To help you monitor word reading, high-frequency words are underlined and decodable words are italicized.

<u>I</u> <u>have</u> <u>a</u> *cat.*
<u>The</u> *cat* <u>is</u> *fat.*
Pass <u>that</u> *jam back, Matt.*
<u>Are</u> <u>you</u> *at* <u>that</u> *van?*

Corrective feedback Sentence Reading	
	If... children are unable to read an underlined high-frequency word, **then...** read the word for them and spell it, having them echo you. **If...** children have difficulty reading an italicized decodable word, **then...** guide them in using sound-by-sound blending.

Common Core State Standards

Foundational Skills 3. Know and apply grade-level phonics and word analysis skills in decoding words. **Language 2.d.** Use conventional spelling for words with common spelling patterns and for frequently occurring irregular words.

Spiral Review

These activities review

- previously taught high-frequency words *a, are, have, I, is, that, the, you.*
- initial and final consonant sounds.

Spelling

Short *a* Words

PARTNER REVIEW Supply pairs of children with index cards on which the spelling words have been written. Have one child read a word while the other writes it. Then have children switch roles. Have them use the cards to check their spelling and correct any misspelled words.

ON THEIR OWN Use *Reader's and Writer's Notebook,* p. 135.

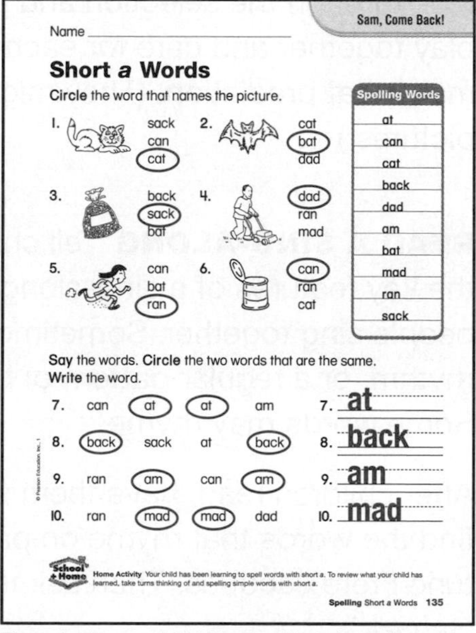

Sam, Come Back!

Name

Short *a* Words

Circle the word that names the picture.

	Spelling Words
	at
	can
	cat
	back
	dad
	am
	bat
	mad
	ran
	sack

1. sack can cat
2. cat bat dad
3. back sack bat
4. dad ran mad
5. can bat ran
6. can ran cat

Say the words. **Circle** the two words that are the same. **Write** the word.

7. can at at am — 7. at
8. back sack at back — 8. back
9. ran am can am — 9. am
10. ran mad mad dad — 10. mad

© Pearson Education, Inc. 1

School + Home — **Home Activity** Your child has been learning to spell words with short a. To review what your child has learned, take turns thinking of and spelling simple words with short a.

Spelling Short a Words 135

Reader's and Writer's Notebook, p. 135

ELL

Fluent Word Reading Have children listen to a more fluent reader say the words. Then have them repeat the words.

Day 4 SMALL GROUP TIME • Differentiate Vocabulary, p. SG•1

OL On-Level	SI Strategic Intervention	A Advanced
• **Develop** Language Using Selection Vocabulary • **Read** *Reading Street Sleuth,* pp. 8–9	• **Review/Discuss** Selection Vocabulary • **Read** *Reading Street Sleuth,* pp. 8–9	• **Extend** Amazing Words and Selection Vocabulary • **Read** *Reading Street Sleuth,* pp. 8–9 • **Organize** Inquiry Project

ELL

If... children need more scaffolding and practice with **Vocabulary,** **then...** use the routine on pp. xxxvi–xxxvii in the *ELL Handbook.*

Common Core State Standards

Literature 7. Use illustrations and details in a story to describe its characters, setting, or events. **Literature 10.** With prompting and support, read prose and poetry of appropriate complexity for grade 1.

Social Studies in Reading

Sing-Along

ACTIVATE PRIOR KNOWLEDGE Ask children what they learned from other texts this week about puppies. (Puppies like to play, bark, and chew.)

PREVIEW AND PREDICT Have children turn to page 164 in their Student Edition. Read the title and the first sentence of the selection. Have children look through the selection and predict what might happen. (A boy and dog play together and care for each other.) Ask them what clues helped them make that prediction. (They might say the title of the selection and the pictures.)

READ A SING-ALONG Tell children that they will read a sing-along. Review the key features of a sing-along: A sing-along is a poem set to music that people sing together. Sometimes new words are sung to an old tune. It has rhythm, or a regular pattern of beats. Some lines in a sing-along may repeat. Some words may rhyme.

After children read, have them pick out the lines that repeat on page 34 and find the words that rhyme on page 35. Have children sing with you using the tune Frère Jacques. Then ask them to explain why the song is called "Puppy Games."

Genre

LET'S THINK ABOUT... As you read "Puppy Games" together, use Let's Think About in the Student Edition to help children focus on the features of a sing-along.

1. The words *socks* and *blocks* and *nap* and *lap* rhyme in this sing-along. The first two lines are the same long length. The next two lines are the same short length.

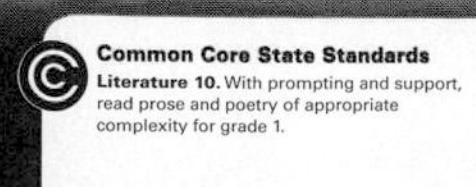

Common Core State Standards
Literature 10. With prompting and support, read prose and poetry of appropriate complexity for grade 1.

Social Studies in Reading

Genre
Sing-Along

- A sing-along is a song people sing together. Sometimes new words are sung to an old tune.
- A sing-along is a poem set to music. It has rhythm, or a regular pattern of beats.
- Some lines in a sing-along may repeat. Some words may rhyme.
- As you read "Puppy Games," think about what makes it a sing-along.

Sing to the tune of "Frère Jacques."

Puppy Games

by Linda Lott
illustrated by Maribel Suarez

Yap! Come play now!
Yap! Come play now!
Let's have fun.
Let's have fun.

I can tug on your socks.
I'll knock over your blocks.
Then I'll nap
In your lap.

Let's Think About...

What words in this sing-along rhyme? What is the sing-along's rhythm? Clap your hands to show it.
Sing-Along

Let's Think About...

Reading Across Texts How do the owners of Sam in *Sam, Come Back!* and the owner of the puppy in "Puppy Games" feel about their pets' actions?

Writing Across Texts Write sentences about what the puppy in the sing-along and Sam do. Use rhythm and rhyme.

34 35

Student Edition, pp. 34–35

Access Text

GENRE When I read these pages, I notice that there is a rhythm to the words. Some lines are long, some are short, and some words rhyme.

Think Aloud **SET PURPOSE** When readers connect what they already know with what they read, they can have a better understanding of what a story or selection is about. As I read "Puppy Games," I thought about times I've watched a puppy play. It helped me to imagine how the puppy in the sing-along tugged on socks and knocked over blocks.

Academic Vocabulary

poem writing that often has words that repeat or words that rhyme

Common Core State Standards

Literature 9. Compare and contrast the adventures and experiences of characters in stories. **Foundational Skills 4.** Read with sufficient accuracy and fluency to support comprehension.

Writing to Sources

Use Connect the Texts on pp. 44–45 to guide children in writing text-based responses using two sources.

Access Text

CONFIRM PREDICTIONS What did you learn about when you read "Puppy Games"? (I learned how a boy and his dog play together.)

SETTING What is the setting of this poem? How can you tell? (The setting is a home. The pictures give clues because the boy is sitting on a rug in a room playing with blocks.)

CHARACTER What does the puppy do in the poem? (The puppy tugs on the boy's socks, knocks over his blocks, and then naps in his lap.)

GENRE Does the puppy in the poem act like a real-life puppy? (Yes. Real puppies want to play and take naps just like the puppy in the poem.)

Reading and Writing Across Texts

Children might say that both owners love their pets, even when they are causing trouble.

Children might write about how both pets take naps. They nap in their owners' laps.

Fluency

Accuracy

- Have children turn to pp. 26–27 in *Sam, Come Back!*
- Have children follow along as you read the pages accurately.
- Have the class read the pages with you and then reread the pages as a group without you until they read with no mistakes.

Routine **Paired Reading** **Team Talk**

1. **Select a Passage** For *Sam, Come Back!,* use pp. 28–29.
2. **Model** First, have children track the print as you read.
3. **Guide Practice** Then have children read along with you.
4. **On Their Own** For optimal fluency, have partners reread three or four times.

Routines Flip Chart

Don't Wait Until Friday **MONITOR PROGRESS** **Fluency Check**

As children reread, monitor their progress toward their individual fluency goals. Mid-Year Goal: 20–30 words correct per minute. End-of-Year Goal: 60 words correct per minute. Beginning in Unit 3, children will be assessed to determine WCPM.

If... children are not on track to meet benchmark goals,

then... have children practice with text at their independent level.

Access for All

A Advanced

Rate If children already read at 60 words correct per minute, have them read more challenging text.

Options for Oral Rereading

Use *Sam, Come Back!* or one of this week's Decodable Practice Readers.

Conventions

Sentences

TEST PRACTICE Use *Reader's and Writer's Notebook,* p. 136 to help children understand complete sentences in test items. Recall that a sentence is a group of words that tells a complete idea. It begins with a capital letter and ends with a punctuation mark, such as a period: *The cat plays.* Model identifying a sentence by writing these groups of words on the board, reading them aloud, and underlining the sentence.

Jack can pat the cat.   **the cat**

ON THEIR OWN Then read the directions on *Reader's and Writer's Notebook,* p. 136. Guide children as they mark the answer for number 1.

APPLY After children mark the answers to numbers 1–6, review the correct choices aloud. Have children read each group of words that is a sentence.

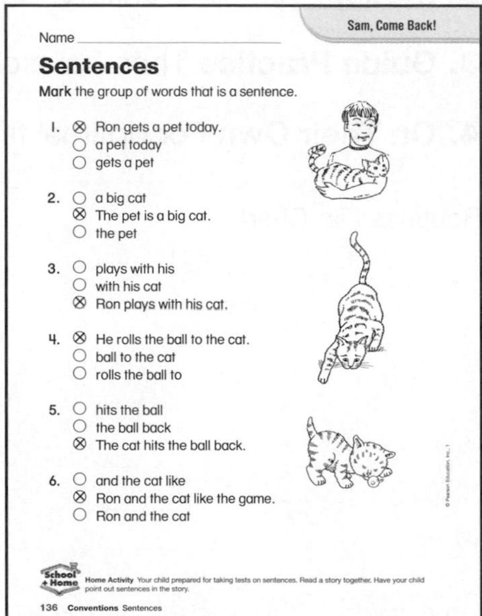
Name ____________ Sam, Come Back!

Sentences

Mark the group of words that is a sentence.

1. ⊗ Ron gets a pet today.
   ○ a pet today
   ○ gets a pet
2. ○ a big cat
   ⊗ The pet is a big cat.
   ○ the pet
3. ○ plays with his
   ○ with his cat
   ⊗ Ron plays with his cat.
4. ⊗ He rolls the ball to the cat.
   ○ ball to the cat
   ○ rolls the ball to
5. ○ hits the ball
   ○ the ball back
   ⊗ The cat hits the ball back.
6. ○ and the cat like
   ⊗ Ron and the cat like the game.
   ○ Ron and the cat

School + Home Home Activity Your child prepared for taking tests on sentences. Read a story together. Have your child point out sentences in the story.

136 Conventions Sentences

Reader's and Writer's Notebook, p. 136

Common Core State Standards

Foundational Skills 1.a. Recognize the distinguishing features of a sentence (e.g., first word, capitalization, ending punctuation). **Writing 5.** With guidance and support from adults, focus on a topic, respond to questions and suggestions from peers, and add details to strengthen writing as needed. **Language 2.** Demonstrate command of the conventions of standard English capitalization, punctuation, and spelling when writing. **Language 2.b.** Use end punctuation for sentences.

Bridge to Common Core

CONVENTIONS OF STANDARD ENGLISH

As children identify sentences, they are gaining control of the conventions of standard English grammar, usage, and mechanics. Your guidance will help them use language to convey meaning effectively as they speak and write.

Daily Fix-It

7. Sam ran bac
   Sam ran back.
8. dad is at dat.
   Dad is at bat.

Discuss the Daily Fix-It corrections with children. Review sentence capitalization and punctuation, /k/ spelled *ck,* and the difference between *b* and *d.*

Story

Mini-Lesson Revise: Adding Words

- Yesterday we wrote stories about pets playing. Today we will revise. We can help people who read the stories. We can make the stories clearer. We can add words to make our feelings clear.

- Display the Revising Tips. Explain that this is a time for making the story clear for anyone who will read it. Tomorrow children will proofread to correct any errors such as incomplete sentences, missing capital letters, or misplaced sentence periods.

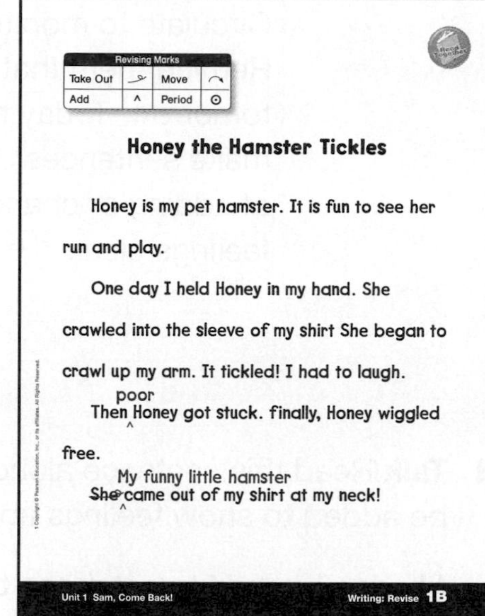

Revising Marks			
Take Out	⟋	Move	⌒
Add	^	Period	⊙

Honey the Hamster Tickles

Honey is my pet hamster. It is fun to see her run and play.

One day I held Honey in my hand. She crawled into the sleeve of my shirt She began to crawl up my arm. It tickled! I had to laugh.

Then ^poor Honey got stuck. finally, Honey wiggled free.

~~She~~ ^My funny little hamster came out of my shirt at my neck!

Unit 1 Sam, Come Back! Writing: Revise 1B

Writing Transparency 1B TR DVD

Revising Tips

✔ Make sure your story tells the kind of pet and how it plays.

✔ Add words to make your feelings clear.

- Use Writing Transparency 1B to model adding words that make feelings clear. When Honey gets stuck, I want to be clear that I feel sorry for her. I can add the word *poor* to show my feelings. Add *poor* to the sentence on the transparency. At the end, I can tell more about how I feel about Honey and how funny it was that she crawled out of my shirt. In the last sentence, cross out *She* and add *My funny little hamster.* Tell children that they can add words to their story as they revise.

PEER CONFERENCING • PEER REVISION Pair children. Tell children to spend about 30 seconds telling their partner what the story is about and one thing they need help with. Then have children silently read each other's drafts, noting suggestions and compliments. Circulate to assist children planning to revise their stories. As appropriate, suggest adding words, including words that make feelings clear.

Access for All

SI Strategic Intervention

Sentence Production If children's sentences lack subject-verb agreement, say their sentences with subject-verb agreement and have them repeat after you.

ELL

Feeling Words Review words about feelings to help children express their own voice in their stories.

Common Core State Standards

Writing 5. With guidance and support from adults, focus on a topic, respond to questions and suggestions from peers, and add details to strengthen writing as needed. **Writing 7.** Participate in shared research and writing projects (e.g., explore a number of "how-to" books on a given topic and use them to write a sequence of instructions). **Writing 8.** With guidance and support from adults, recall information from experiences or gather information from provided sources to answer a question.

Writing

Zoom in on

GUIDE PRACTICE Have children revise their stories. For those not sure how to revise, have children refer to the Revising Tips or the Key Features of a Story.

Corrective feedback	Circulate to monitor and confer with children as they write. Remind them that they will have time to proofread and edit tomorrow. Today they can make changes in story events or make sentences clearer. Help them understand the benefits of adding or changing words. Encourage them to make their feelings clear.

Routine Quick Write for Fluency

Team Talk

1. **Talk** Read this sentence aloud, and have children suggest words that could be added to show feelings about the dog.

   My dog jumped to catch the ball.

2. **Write** Have children write a short sentence expressing feelings about an animal.

3. **Share** Partners can read the sentences to one another and tell which words make the feelings expressed in their partners' sentences clear.

Routines Flip Chart

Research and Inquiry

Step 4 Synthesize

TEACH Tell children that the next step in the inquiry project is to review the books on their list to be sure they will have answers to their questions about what pets need.

Think Aloud **MODEL** We wanted to find books that would have answers to our questions about pets. First, we listed our questions. Then we learned about the parts of a book that would help us learn what was inside the book. Last, we looked at books and wrote down the names of ones that could help us answer our questions. Now I will look at the book titles I wrote down. I will be sure each title tells about a book with information about pets. If I find a book that is not about pets, I will cross that title off my list.

GUIDE PRACTICE Have children look at the information they gathered during Day 3. Instruct them to work with a partner to review the book titles they wrote down. If necessary, they can examine additional books to add titles to their list. Finally, tell children that tomorrow they will organize the book titles to share with others.

Access for All

A Advanced

Information Sources Encourage children to look for information in other sources, such as encyclopedias and nature magazines. Some children may enjoy using the computer to find more information.

Wrap Up Your Day!

✔ **Phonics Review: Short *a*** List several words with the short *a* sound spelled *a,* such as *sack, fan,* and *pad.* Have children read each word and identify the letter that stands for the /a/ sound.

✔ **Fluency** Write *Jack had that bat. That cat ran back.* Have the class reread the sentences until they can do so with accurate word recognition.

Remind children that they heard two poems about children and their pets. Tomorrow they will hear these same poems again.

DAY 5 at a Glance

Content Knowledge
Oral Vocabulary

Phonemic Awareness
Segment and Count Phonemes

Phonics/Spelling
Review Short *a: a*
Review Consonant Pattern *-ck*

Text-Based Comprehension
Review Character and Setting

Selection Words
Review

High-Frequency Words
Review

Assessment
Phonics
High-Frequency Words
Fluency

Conventions
Review Sentences

Writing
Story: Proofread

Research and Inquiry
Communicate

Materials

- Student Edition
- Read Aloud Anthology
- Weekly Test

Bridge to Common Core

INTEGRATION OF KNOWLEDGE/IDEAS
This week children have integrated content presented in diverse formats and analyzed how different texts address similar topics. They have developed knowledge about pets to expand the unit topic of Animals, Tame and Wild.

Social Studies Knowledge Goals
Children have learned that

- pets need food and water
- pets need shelter
- pets need exercise
- pets need love

Content Knowledge

Pets

REVIEW CONCEPT This week we have read and listened to stories and poems about pets and the things they need. Today you will listen to two poems about different pets and their owners. Read the poems.

- How do the owners of the gerbil and hedgehog handle their pets? (They handle the pets gently. The owner of the gerbil puts him on his elbow and knee and pets him. The owner of the hedgehog strokes his back.)

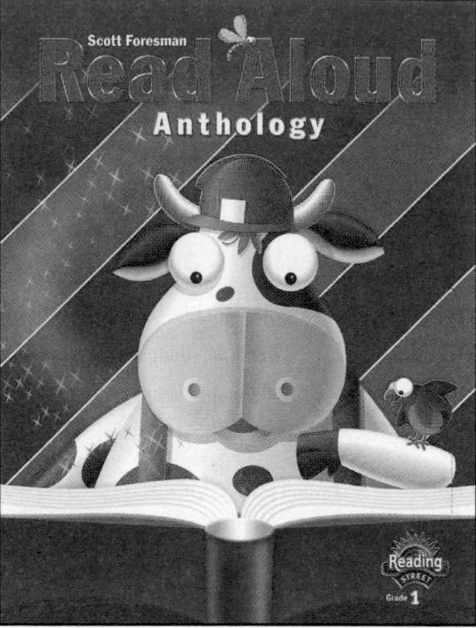

"Just Fur Fun" and "Hedgehog"

Build Oral Language

REVIEW AMAZING WORDS Orally review the meanings of this week's Amazing Words. Then display this week's concept map. Have children use Amazing Words, such as *needs, shelter,* and *cuddle,* as well as the concept map, to answer the question *What do pets need?*

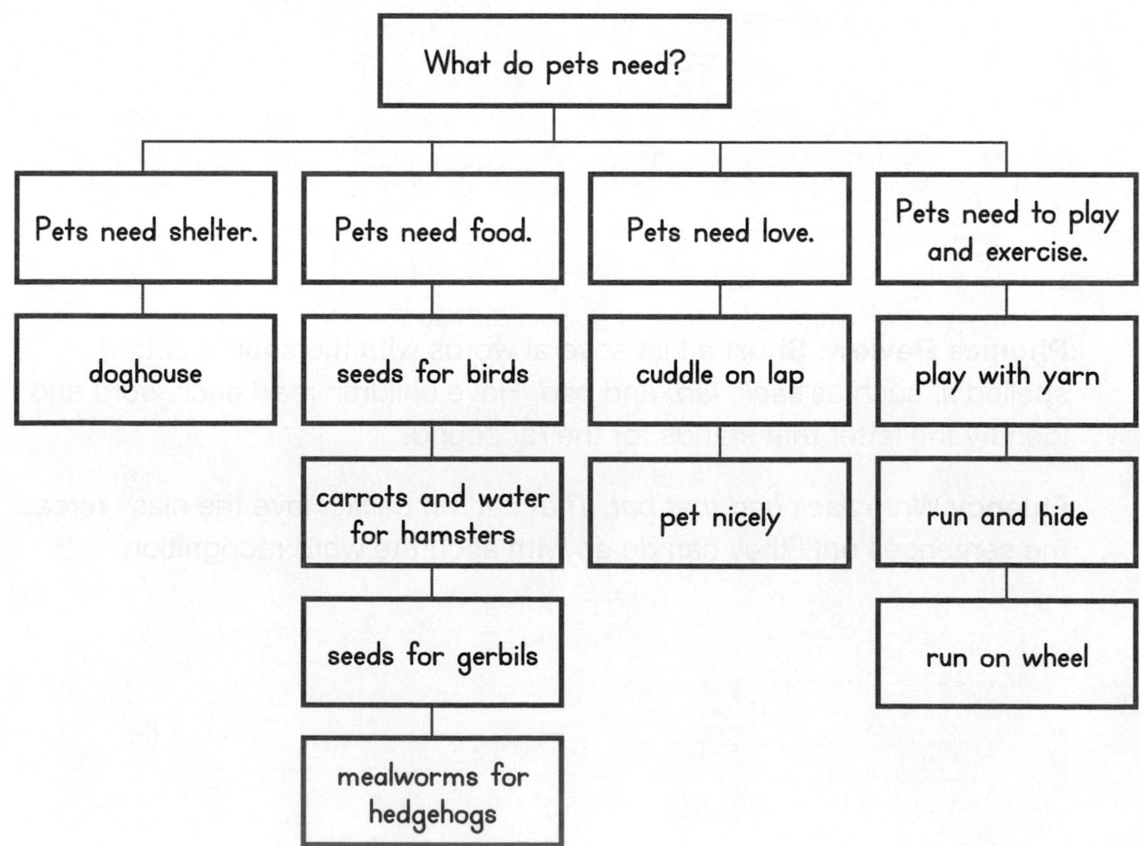

Build Oral Vocabulary

Team Talk **CONNECT TO AMAZING IDEAS** Pair children and have them discuss how the Question of the Week, *What do pets need?,* connects to the question of this unit of study: *How are people and animals important to one another?* Tell children to use the concept map and what they've learned from this week's discussions and reading selections to form an Amazing Idea—a realization or "big idea" about **animals, tame and wild.** Use the following ideas as prompts:

- What pets have we read about? (a hamster, a cat, puppies, a hedgehog)
- What types of things did each pet need?
- How do the owners feel about their pets?

Then ask each pair to share their Amazing Idea with the class. Encourage children to recall in which selection they learned their ideas.

Amazing Ideas might include:

- People and animals have very special friendships.
- People and animals love each other and help one another.

Check Oral Vocabulary

FORMATIVE ASSESSMENT Call on individuals to use this week's Amazing Words to talk about what pets need. Prompt discussion with the questions below. Monitor children's ability to use the Amazing Words and note which words children are unable to use.

- **What *needs* does a puppy have?**
- **How can a pet *tickle* you?**
- **What do dogs do when they *fetch* and *heel?***
- **What are some kinds of *shelter* for pets?**
- **How do you feel when you *cuddle* with a pet?**
- **How might you show that you could take *responsibility* for a pet?**
- **Why would you want a dog to be *faithful?***

If... children have difficulty using the Amazing Words,

then... reteach the unknown words using the Robust Vocabulary routines, pp. 13a, 18b, 30b, 34b.

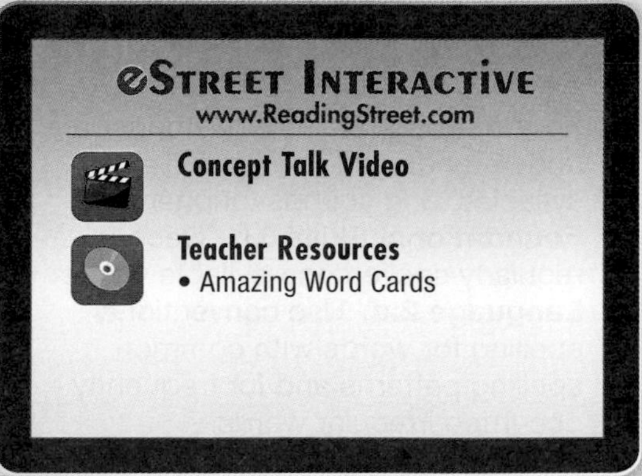

needs	tickle
responsibility	faithful
shelter	fetch
cuddle	heel

ELL

Expand Vocabulary Use the Day 5 instruction on ELL Poster 1 to monitor children's understanding of the lesson concept.

Amazing Words Use pantomime or gestures to give children clues as you review the Amazing Words.

Common Core State Standards

Foundational Skills 2. Demonstrate understanding of spoken words, syllables, and sounds (phonemes). **Foundational Skills 3.b.** Decode regularly spelled one-syllable words. **Language 2.d.** Use conventional spelling for words with common spelling patterns and for frequently occurring irregular words.

Phonemic Awareness

Review Segment and Count Phonemes

SHORT *a* AND FINAL /k/ Have children segment each word below and then count the sounds. If children make an error, model the correct response. Return to the word later in the practice.

hat	/h/ /a/ /t/	(3)	**pack**	/p/ /a/ /k/	(3)	**at**	/a/ /t/	(2)
Dan	/d/ /a/ /n/	(3)	**blast**	/b/ /l/ /a/ /s/ /t/	(5)	**racks**	/r/ /a/ /k/ /s/	(4)
ran	/r/ /a/ /n/	(3)	**sack**	/s/ /a/ /k/	(3)	**jam**	/j/ /a/ /m/	(3)

Phonics

Review Short *a: a;* Consonant Pattern *-ck*

TARGET PHONICS SKILLS Write the following sentences on the board. Have children read each one, first quietly to themselves and then aloud as you track the print.

1. **Look at the cat on the sack.**
2. **Pack a ham with the jam.**
3. **Jack ran to tag me.**
4. **I am sad to go back.**

Team Talk Have children discuss with a partner which words have short *a* and which words have the consonant pattern *-ck.* Then call on individuals to share with the class.

Spelling Test

Short *a* Words

DICTATE SPELLING WORDS Say each word, read the sentence, repeat the word, and allow time for children to write the word.

1. at	Look **at** those baby birds!
2. can	I **can** tap on a drum.
3. cat	The **cat** has a long nap.
4. back	Please come **back** soon!
5. dad	My **dad** drives a big truck.
6. am	I **am** taller than Nina.
7. bat	She swung the **bat** and hit a home run.
8. mad	Is Jack **mad** at his brother?
9. ran	Jan **ran** around the track.
10. sack	The **sack** is full of apples.

High-Frequency Words

11. way	The squirrel ran that **way.**
12. come	Dan can **come** skating with us.

Assess

- Spell words with short *a.*
- Spell high-frequency words.

Access for All

SI Strategic Intervention

Check Spelling Have children choose the correct spelling of each word from three random spellings.

A Advanced

Extend Spelling Have children who have demonstrated proficiency in spelling individual words spell each word in a self-made sentence.

Day 5 SMALL GROUP TIME • Differentiate Reteaching, p. SG•1

OL On-Level

- **Practice** Sentences
- **Reread** *Reading Street Sleuth,* pp. 8–9

SI Strategic Intervention

- **Review** High-Frequency Words
- **Reread** *Reading Street Sleuth,* pp. 8–9

A Advanced

- **Extend** Sentences
- **Reread** *Reading Street Sleuth,* pp. 8–9
- **Communicate** Inquiry Project

If... children need more scaffolding and practice with **Conventions and Writing,**
then... use the Grammar Transition Lessons on pp. 346–421 in the *ELL Handbook.*

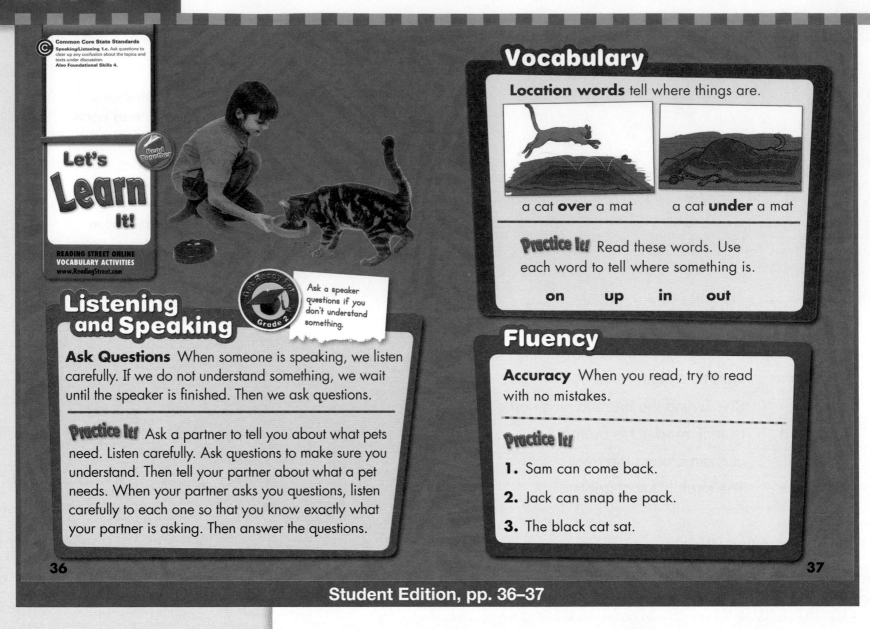

Common Core State Standards
Speaking/Listening 1.c. Ask questions to clear up any confusion about the topics and texts under discussion.
Also Foundational Skills 4.

Let's Learn It!

READING STREET ONLINE
VOCABULARY ACTIVITIES
www.ReadingStreet.com

Listening and Speaking

Ask a speaker questions if you don't understand something.

Ask Questions When someone is speaking, we listen carefully. If we do not understand something, we wait until the speaker is finished. Then we ask questions.

Practice It! Ask a partner to tell you about what pets need. Listen carefully. Ask questions to make sure you understand. Then tell your partner about what a pet needs. When your partner asks you questions, listen carefully to each one so that you know exactly what your partner is asking. Then answer the questions.

36

Vocabulary

Location words tell where things are.

a cat **over** a mat

a cat **under** a mat

Practice It! Read these words. Use each word to tell where something is.

on **up** **in** **out**

Fluency

Accuracy When you read, try to read with no mistakes.

Practice It!

1. Sam can come back.
2. Jack can snap the pack.
3. The black cat sat.

37

Student Edition, pp. 36–37

Common Core State Standards

Foundational Skills 4. Read with sufficient accuracy and fluency to support comprehension. **Speaking/Listening 1.c.** Ask questions to clear up any confusion about the topics and texts under discussion. **Language 4.** Determine or clarify the meaning of unknown and multiple-meaning words and phrases based on grade 1 reading and content, choosing flexibly from an array of strategies.

Ask Questions

Children at Grade 2 should be able to use a variety of question-building words correctly and effectively, such as *what, when, how, why, could, should,* and *would.*

Listening and Speaking

Ask Questions

TEACH Have children turn to pages 36–37 of the Student Edition. Read the Ask Questions section and discuss the photo. Remind children that good speakers use complete sentences and that good listeners ask questions about things they don't understand. Model how to ask a question about the photo. How can we ask a question about this photo? We might ask, *What does a pet cat need every day?* Have children say or write other questions about the photo.

INTRODUCE PROMPT Read the Practice It! prompt with the class. Have partners take turns telling what pets need and asking each other questions.

Team Talk Have pairs take turns asking and answering questions about things pets need. Tell children that good speakers speak clearly and slowly, and that good listeners should repeat the question before answering.

Vocabulary

Words for Location

TEACH Read and discuss the Vocabulary lesson on page 37 of the Student Edition. Use the model to explain that words for location tell where things are. Point to the first illustration. Where is the cat in this picture? The cat is *over* a mat. Point to the second illustration. Is the cat *over* the mat in this picture? No, the cat is *under* the mat. *Over* and *under* are location words that tell where things are.

GUIDE PRACTICE Read the instructions for the Vocabulary Practice It! activity. Read the first word and then have children repeat after you.

What can I see that is *on* something? I see a book *on* my desk. I will say the sentence *The book is on my desk.*

ON THEIR OWN Have children continue saying or writing sentences for the remaining location words in the list.

Corrective feedback	Circulate around the room and check that children are using each word for location correctly. Provide assistance as needed.

Fluency

Accuracy

TEACH Read and discuss the Fluency instructions.

READ WORDS IN CONTEXT Give children a moment to look at the sentences. Then have them read each sentence three or four times until they can read each sentence with accuracy.

Access for All

A Advanced

Extend the Concept Ask children who easily read and understand the location words in the Student Edition to think of additional words, such as *around, behind, beside,* and *between.* Have children draw and label a picture for each new word or demonstrate each word's meaning, using objects.

Use Sentence Frames Take two classroom objects, such as a book and a pencil. Then have children use this sentence frame to explain where you have placed the two objects in relation to one another: *The book is ________ the pencil.*

Common Core State Standards

Literature 1. Ask and answer questions about key details in a text. **Literature 3.** Describe characters, settings, and major events in a story, using key details. **Foundational Skills 3.g.** Recognize and read grade-appropriate irregularly spelled words.

Text-Based Comprehension

Review Character and Setting

Remember that in a fiction story, the author tells about people and animals that are not real. What are the people and animals in a made-up story called? (characters) The author also tells where and when the story takes place. What is that part of the story called? (the setting)

CHECK UNDERSTANDING Read aloud the following story and have children answer the questions that follow.

Angela had waited forever for this day, and now it was finally here! She could hardly sit still as her parents filled out all the papers at the animal shelter that Saturday. It wouldn't be long now. She was finally going to have a puppy of her own. Angela had already picked out the perfect name: Buttercup. Suddenly, the moment she had dreamed of came. There was Buttercup with her soft yellow fur, sitting on Angela's lap, licking her face.

1. Who are the characters in this story? (Angela, Angela's parents, Buttercup)
2. What is the setting? (Saturday at an animal shelter)
3. Why does Angela have trouble sitting still? (She is so excited because she is getting a new puppy.)

Vocabulary

Review High-Frequency and Selection Words

HIGH-FREQUENCY WORDS Review this week's high-frequency words: *come, in, my, on, way.* Provide an example of a riddle for one of the words for the class to solve, such as: I rhyme with *thin.* I have two letters. *(in)*

Team Talk Write the high-frequency words on the board. Pair children and have them make up their own word riddles for a partner to solve.

SELECTION WORDS Write the words *Sam* and *Jack.* Read them aloud together. Then have children tell what each word means.

Corrective feedback	**If...** children cannot tell what the selection words mean, **then...** review the definitions on page 20a.

Genre

Review Song

SONG Have children turn to pages 34–35 in their Student Edition. Review that a song is a poem set to music. Like a poem, the words in a song are organized in lines and have a rhythm. A song often has words that repeat and words that rhyme.

TEACH When I look at the words for the song "Puppy Games," I see that the first two lines of the song are long, and they say the same thing, "Yap! Come play now!" The next two lines of the song also repeat, but they are shorter. They both say, "Let's have fun."

MODEL I'm going to sing these first four lines of the song. As I sing, I'll clap out the rhythm of the song. Clap out the rhythm as you sing. I can hear that there are two beats in each line of the song.

GUIDE PRACTICE Ask the following questions to guide children in understanding the features of a song.

- Look at page 35 in your book. Which two lines of the song are long? (the first two lines) Which two lines of the song are short? (the last two lines)
- Which words in the first two lines rhyme? *(socks, blocks)* Which words in the last two lines rhyme? *(nap, lap)*

ON THEIR OWN Ask children to think of a song they know that has rhyming words. Have them sing a few lines of the song to the class or to a partner. Ask them to clap out the rhythm of the song as they sing and then name the words that rhyme.

Access for All

 Strategic Intervention

Words That Rhyme If children have difficulty identifying words that rhyme, say sets of three words and have children name the two that rhyme, for example: *tap, nap, tan.*

Academic Vocabulary 

rhyming words words that end with the same sound

Common Core State Standards

Foundational Skills 3. Know and apply grade-level phonics and word analysis skills in decoding words. **Foundational Skills 3.a.** Know the spelling-sound correspondences for common consonant digraphs. **Also Foundational Skills 3.b., 3.g.**

Assess

- Words with Short *a*
- Consonant Pattern *-ck*
- High-Frequency Words

Assessment

Monitor Progress

For a written assessment of words with short *a,* consonant pattern *-ck,* high-frequency words, and identifying character and setting, use Weekly Test 1, pages 37–42.

WORD READING Use the following reproducible page to assess children's ability to read words in isolation. Call on children to read the words aloud. Start over if necessary.

SENTENCE READING Use the reproducible page on page 37f to assess children's ability to read words in context. Call on children to read two sentences aloud. Start over with sentence one if necessary.

MONITOR ACCURACY Record scores using the Word/Sentence Reading Chart for this unit in *First Stop.*

MONITOR PROGRESS Word and Sentence Reading

If... children have trouble reading words with short *a* and consonant pattern *-ck,*
then... use the Reteach Lessons in *First Stop.*

If... a child cannot read all the high-frequency words,
then... mark the missed words on a high-frequency word list and have the child practice reading the words with a fluent reader.

Name ______________________________

Read the Words

1. cat
2. my
3. tap
4. back
5. way
6. man
7. in
8. sack
9. come
10. pack
11. jam
12. on

MONITOR PROGRESS

- Short *a: a*
- Consonant Pattern *-ck*
- High-Frequency Words

Name ______________________________

Read the Sentences

1. Mack sat on the mat.

2. Zack had my cap.

3. Come pat the cat, Jack.

4. Pam ran back that way.

5. Pack one hat in the bag.

MONITOR PROGRESS

- **Fluency**
- **Short *a: a***
- **Consonant Pattern *-ck***
- **High-Frequency Words**

Conventions

Review Sentences

REVIEW Remind children that a sentence is a group of words that tells a complete idea. It begins with a capital letter and ends with a punctuation mark, such as a period. Have children give several examples of sentences.

GUIDE PRACTICE Write the following groups of words. Have children tell which word groups are sentences and explain why.

1. **Tad ran back.**
2. **the bad cat**
3. **had a tan bag**
4. **Mack can pack the van.**

APPLY Write the phrase *Mack the cat* and read it aloud. Have children work in pairs to think of as many complete sentences as they can that include this phrase. Then have children share their sentences with the class, telling how each sentence should begin and end.

ON THEIR OWN Use Let's Practice It! p. 31 from the *Teacher Resources DVD-ROM.*

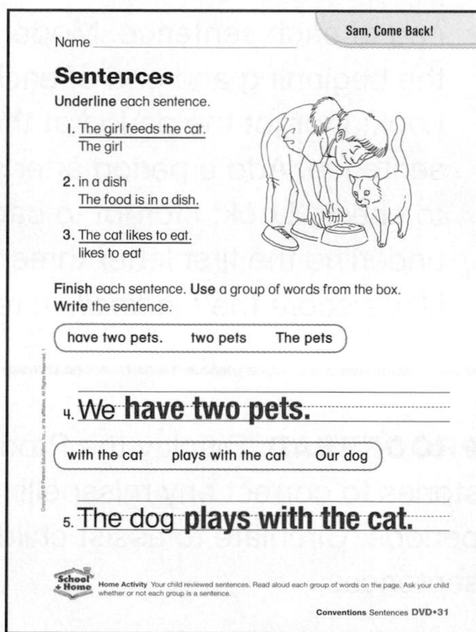

Sam, Come Back!

Name

Sentences

Underline each sentence.

1. The girl feeds the cat.
   The girl
2. in a dish
   The food is in a dish.
3. The cat likes to eat.
   likes to eat

Finish each sentence. **Use** a group of words from the box. **Write** the sentence.

have two pets.	two pets	The pets

4. We **have two pets.**

with the cat	plays with the cat	Our dog

5. The dog **plays with the cat.**

Home Activity Your child reviewed sentences. Read aloud each group of words on the page. Ask your child whether or not each group is a sentence.

Conventions Sentences DVD•31

Let's Practice It! TR DVD•31

Common Core State Standards

Foundational Skills 1.a. Recognize the distinguishing features of a sentence (e.g., first word, capitalization, ending punctuation). **Foundational Skills 3.** Know and apply grade-level phonics and word analysis skills in decoding words. **Language 2.** Demonstrate command of the conventions of standard English capitalization, punctuation, and spelling when writing. **Language 2.b.** Use end punctuation for sentences.

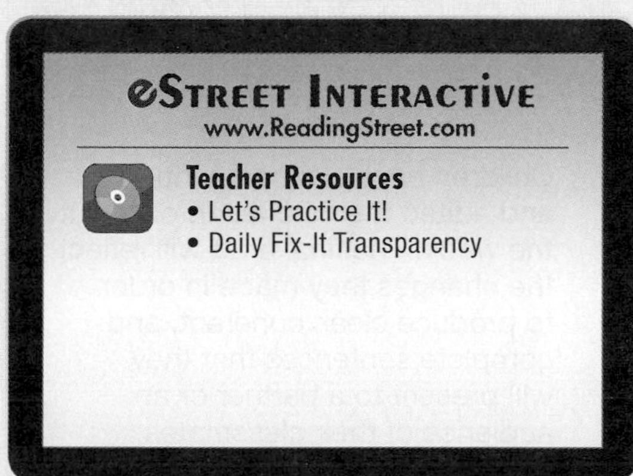

Daily Fix-It

9. dad is made at Sam.
   Dad is mad at Sam.
10. sam ran bak to Dad.
    Sam ran back to Dad.

Discuss the Daily Fix-It corrections with children. Review sentence capitalization, /a/ spelled *a,* and final /k/ spelled *-ck.*

Common Core State Standards

Writing 5. With guidance and support from adults, focus on a topic, respond to questions and suggestions from peers, and add details to strengthen writing as needed. **Language 2.** Demonstrate command of the conventions of standard English capitalization, punctuation, and spelling when writing. **Language 2.b.** Use end punctuation for sentences. **Also Writing 6.**

Bridge to Common Core

PRODUCTION AND DISTRIBUTION OF WRITING

Children have planned, written, and edited their stories throughout the week. The final draft will reflect the changes they made in order to produce clear, coherent, and complete sentences that they will present to a partner or an audience of their classmates.

Writing

Story

REVIEW REVISING Remind children that yesterday they revised their stories. They may have added words to make their feelings clearer. Today they will proofread their stories.

Mini-Lesson Proofread

Proofread for Sentences

- **Teach** In our stories, if we capitalize and punctuate the sentences correctly, readers will know where the sentences begin and end. When we proofread, we check to make sure the sentences are correct.
- **Model** Let's look at my story about Honey. Display Writing Transparency 1C. I'm going to make sure that each sentence begins with a capital letter and ends with punctuation. I'll check the beginning and end of each sentence. Model checking the beginning and end of each sentence. Look; I forgot the period at the end of this sentence. Add a period after *shirt* on the transparency and then continue to check. Look; I forgot to capitalize the beginning of this sentence. I will underline the first letter three times to show that it should be capitalized. Underscore the *f* in *finally* three times and then continue to check.

Proofreading Marks			
Take Out	⌇	Uppercase letter	≡
Add	^	Lowercase letter	/
Period	⊙	New paragraph	¶
Check spelling	⬭	Insert apostrophe	∨

Honey the Hamster Tickles

Honey is my pet hamster. It is fun to see her run and play.

One day I held Honey in my hand. She crawled into the sleeve of my shirt⊙She began to crawl up my arm. It tickled! I had to laugh.

Then poor Honey got stuck. finally, Honey wiggled free. My funny little hamster came out of my shirt at my neck!

Unit 1 Sam, Come Back! Writing: Proofread 1C

Writing Transparency 1C TR DVD

PROOFREAD Display the Proofreading Tips. Have children proofread their stories to correct any misspellings, missing capital letters, or errors with periods. Circulate to assist children with the beginnings and ends of sentences.

Proofreading Tips

- ✔ Do my sentences begin with a capital letter?
- ✔ Did I use periods correctly?
- ✔ Are my verbs spelled correctly? Check a dictionary.
- ✔ Are the words that show feelings spelled correctly?

PRESENT Have children use a computer to make a final draft of their stories, with their revisions and proofreading corrections. Help as appropriate. Choose an option for children to present their stories.

Take turns reading their stories aloud to a partner.	Read their stories aloud to the class.

When children have finished writing their stories, give them a copy of About My Writing, p. RR45 of the *Reader's and Writer's Notebook.* Then have children evaluate their writing by answering the questions on the page.

Routine **Quick Write for Fluency** Team Talk

1. **Talk** Have partners take one minute to find a word that shows feeling (such as *glad, happy,* or *laughed*) in each of their stories.
2. **Write** Each child writes a new short sentence using one of the words.
3. **Share** Partners trade sentences and read them aloud.

Routines Flip Chart

Write Guy *by Jeff Anderson*

Adding Without Hanging

A child might add worthwhile information but write a sentence fragment. I like to encourage the writer by welcoming the idea and yet helping children form solid sentences or add dependent parts in order to communicate. Children can recognize "sentences" that "leave the reader hanging" (that is, fragments). *Pacing back and forth.* That's not a complete sentence, but it may add a vivid image to a child's narrative. If it follows a sentence such as *I peeked out the window and saw Lee,* then a reader may wonder who is pacing back and forth. Let's help our young writers put images together. *I peeked out the window and saw Lee pacing back and forth.* That doesn't leave readers hanging. Kids can understand that.

Support Proofreading For children to whom the sounds and spelling of English still are not very familiar, look for spelling improvement little by little from week to week rather than rapid development. Help children make progress a word at a time and learn word meanings.

Common Core State Standards

Writing 7. Participate in shared research and writing projects (e.g., explore a number of "how-to" books on a given topic and use them to write a sequence of instructions). **Speaking/Listening 1.** Participate in collaborative conversations about grade 1 topics and texts with peers and adults in small and larger groups.

Research and Inquiry

Step 5 Communicate

TEACH Tell children that today they will create a chart of book titles. They will only use books with information about what pets need. Children will share the chart with others.

Think Aloud **MODEL** Display the list of book titles. I have a long list of book titles. It will be easier for others to read it if I sort the titles into groups and then make a chart. Adapt the discussion to the titles in your list. I see I have three books about dogs. I will put those books in my chart under the heading *Books About Dogs.* I have two books about cats. I'll list those books under the heading *Books About Cats.* I also have two books about how to make a home for a pet hamster. Those books belong together in a group too. I'll call this group *Homes for Hamsters.*

GUIDE PRACTICE Review children's charts. Work with them to sort their book titles into groups and write a heading that describes each group.

ON THEIR OWN Have children choose the group of book titles they would like to share with the class. Have those with similar groups work together to create a combined list of titles. Instruct them to read the titles aloud to one another. Remind them how to be good speakers and listeners:

- Good speakers pay close attention to the words so they read accurately.
- Good listeners pay attention to the speaker and do not talk while someone else is speaking.

Wrap Up Your Week!

Pets

What do pets need?

Think Aloud This week we explored the topic of pets and their needs. In the story *Sam, Come Back!,* we read about a cat that likes to play. In the song "Puppy Games," we sang about a puppy that likes to play. The owners of both of these animals loved their pets very much.

Team Talk Have children work with partners to talk about their Amazing Ideas about pets and their needs. Then have children use these ideas to help them demonstrate their understanding of the Question of the Week, *What do pets need?*

You've learned 008 words this week!

You've learned 055 words this year!

Next Week's Concept

Helping Animals

Who helps animals?

ELL

Poster Preview Prepare children for next week by using Unit 1, Week 2, ELL Poster 2. Read the Poster Talk-Through to introduce the concept and vocabulary. Ask children to identify and describe objects and actions in the art.

Selection Summary Send home the summary from the *ELL Handbook* of *Pig in a Wig* in English and the child's home language if available. Children can read the summary with family members.

Tell children that next week they will read more about animals and the special ways people help them.

Preview Next Week

Assessment Checkpoints for the Week

Weekly Assessment

Use pp. 37–42 of *Weekly Tests* to check:

✔ **Phonics** Short *a: a*

✔ **Phonics** Consonant Pattern *-ck*

✔ **Comprehension** Character and Setting

✔ **High-Frequency Words**

come	**on**
in	**way**
my	

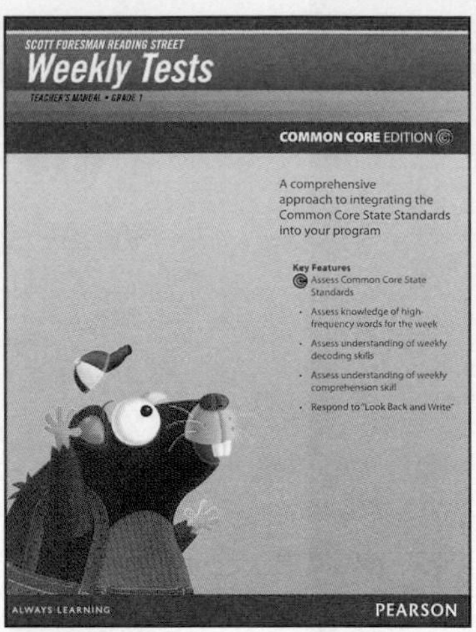

Weekly Tests

Differentiated Assessment

Advanced

On-Level

Strategic Intervention

Use pp. 37–42 of *Fresh Reads for Fluency and Comprehension* to check:

✔ **Comprehension** Character and Setting

✔ **Review Comprehension** Plot

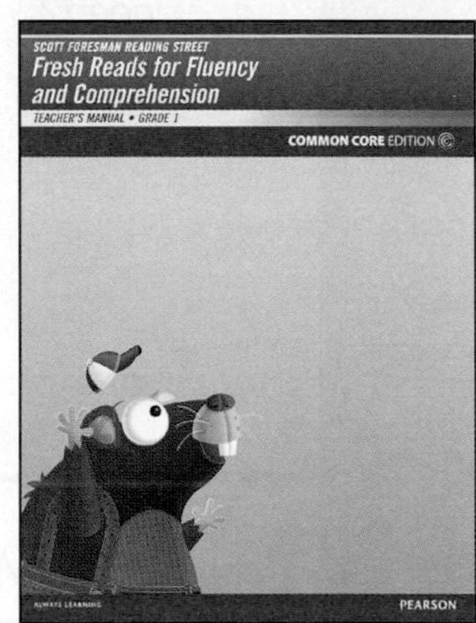

Fresh Reads for Fluency and Comprehension

Managing Assessment

Use *Assessment Handbook* for:

✔ **Weekly Assessment Blackline Masters for Monitoring Progress**

✔ **Observation Checklists**

✔ **Record-Keeping Forms**

✔ **Portfolio Assessment**

Assessment Handbook

DAY 1 Differentiate Phonics

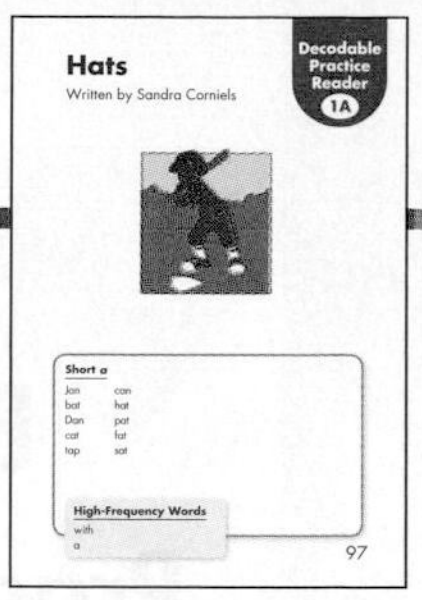

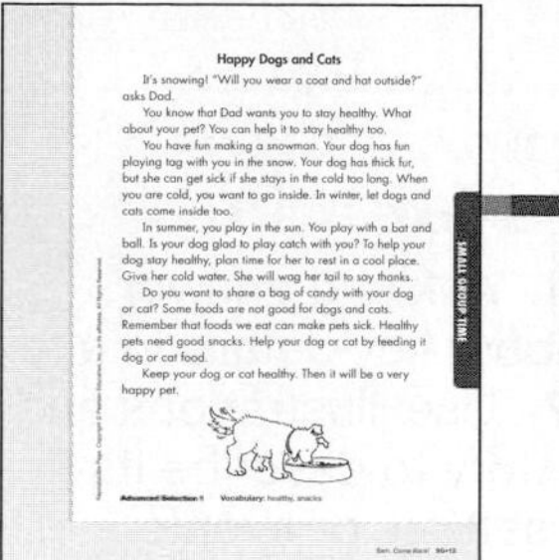

- Short *a: a*
  - Decodable Practice Reader
  - Advanced Selection "Happy Dogs and Cats"
  - **Inquiry** Identify Questions

DAY 2 Differentiate Comprehension

- Consonant Pattern *-ck*
  - **Access Text** Read *Sam, Come Back!*
  - **Inquiry** Investigate

DAY 3 Differentiate Close Reading

- Develop Vocabulary
- **Close Reading** Read *Sam, Come Back!*
- **Inquiry** Investigate

DAY 4 Differentiate Vocabulary

- Develop Language
- "Are You My Kitten?" or Leveled Readers
- **Inquiry** Organize

"Are You My Kitten?" pp. 8–9

DAY 5 Differentiate Reteaching

- Phonics and High-Frequency Words
- Conventions
- "Are You My Kitten?" or Leveled Readers
- **Inquiry** Communicate

Teacher Guides and Student pages can be found in the Leveled Reader Database.

Place English Language Learners in the groups that correspond to their reading abilities.
If... children need scaffolding and practice,
then... use the ELL notes on the page.

Independent Practice

Independent Practice Stations

See pp. 12h and 12i for Independent Stations.

Pearson Trade Book Library

See the Leveled Reader Database for Lesson Plans and student pages.

Reading Street Digital Path

Independent Practice Activities available in the Digital Path.

Independent Reading

See p. 12i for independent reading suggestions.

On-Level

Common Core State Standards

Literature 1. Ask and answer questions about key details in a text.
Literature 7. Use illustrations and details in a story to describe its characters, setting, or events.
Foundational Skills 3. Know and apply grade-level phonics and word analysis skills in decoding words.
Foundational Skills 3.b. Decode regularly spelled one-syllable words.
Foundational Skills 4.a. Read on-level text with purpose and understanding.

1 Build Word Knowledge

Practice Phonics

SHORT *a*: *a* Write the following words and have children practice reading words with short *a*.

pal **tag** **bat** **man**

Spelling

SHORT *a* WORDS Remind children that each spelling word has the letter *a*, which spells the /a/ sound. Clarify the pronunciation and meaning of each word. For example, say: A *sack* is a kind of bag. Have children identify whether the letter *a* is at the beginning or in the middle of these words: *cat, am, back, mad, at, ran.*

2 Read

Decodable Reader 1A *Hats*

HIGH-FREQUENCY WORDS Have children read the decodable reader. Then have them reread the text to develop automaticity. Have children return to the text and find the previously taught high-frequency words. Help children demonstrate their understanding of the words. Provide sentence frames such as: I go to the park _______ my friends. (with)

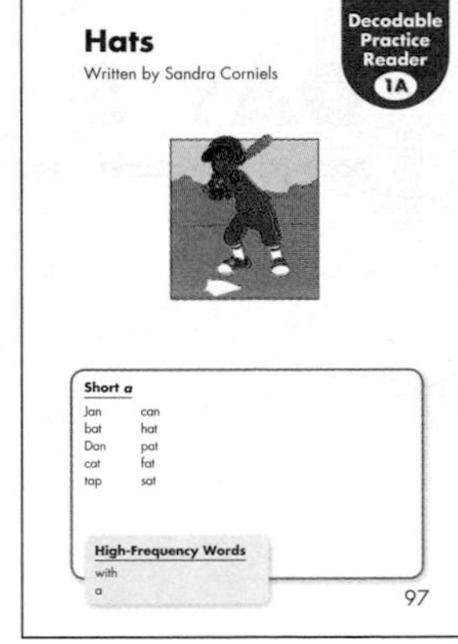

ELL

If... children need more scaffolding and practice with phonics,
then... use the ELL activities on pp. DI•13–DI•14 in the Teacher Resources section on SuccessNet.

OL

On-Level

1 Build Word Knowledge

Practice Phonics

CONSONANT PATTERN *-ck* Write the following words and have children practice reading words with the consonant pattern *-ck.*

pack **tack** **lack** **Jack**

2 Read

Sam, Come Back!

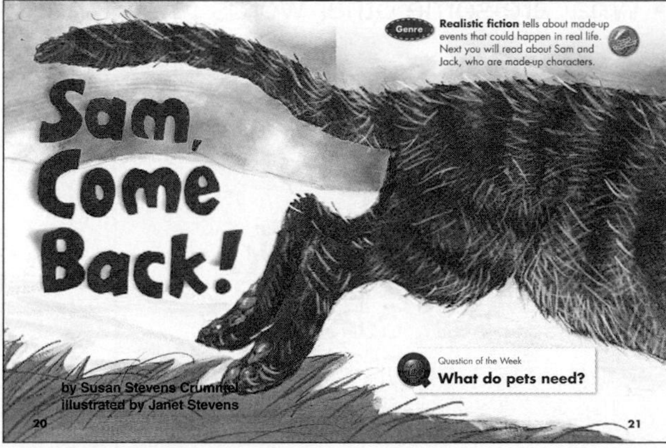
Sam, Come Back!
Genre
Realistic fiction tells about made-up events that could happen in real life. Next you will read about Sam and Jack, who are made-up characters.
by Susan Stevens Crummel
illustrated by Janet Stevens
Question of the Week
What do pets need?
20
21

If you read *Sam, Come Back!* during whole group time, then use the following instruction.

ACCESS TEXT Have children look at the pictures on pp. 22–23. Reread the sentence on p. 22.

- Who says "Sam the cat is on my lap." (the woman)
- What word in the sentence tells you that? (*my*)
- Who else do you see in the picture? (Sam the cat, a boy, and a dog)
- Look at the picture on page 23. What does the cat have in his mouth? (green yarn)
- Where does Sam get the green yarn? (The woman was using green yarn.)

If you are reading *Sam, Come Back!* during small group time, then return to pp. 20b–29a to guide the reading.

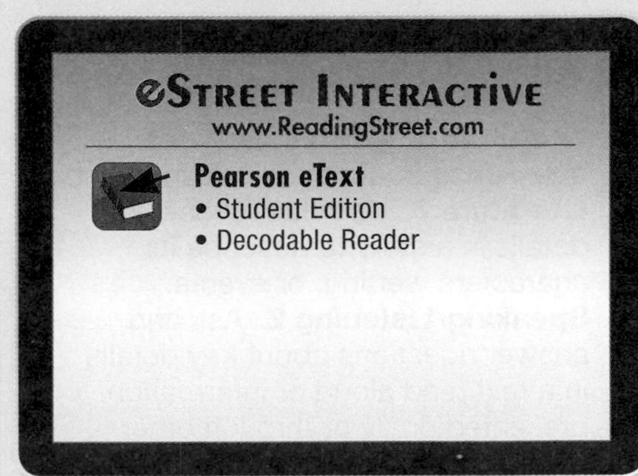
eStreet Interactive
www.ReadingStreet.com
Pearson eText
• Student Edition
• Decodable Reader

SMALL GROUP TIME

Independent Reading Options

Trade Book Library

eStreet Interactive
www.ReadingStreet.com

Teacher's Guides available on the Leveled Reader Database.

On-Level

Common Core State Standards

Literature 1. Ask and answer questions about key details in a text. **Literature 7.** Use illustrations and details in a story to describe its characters, setting, or events. **Speaking/Listening 2.** Ask and answer questions about key details in a text read aloud or information presented orally or through other media. **Language 5.c.** Identify real-life connections between words and their use (e.g., note places at home that are *cozy*). **Also Speaking/ Listening 1.**

1 Build Word Knowledge

Develop Vocabulary

REREAD FOR VOCABULARY Have children reread *Sam, Come Back!*, p. 26.

Read the following sentence and discuss the way to catch the cat. (nab)

Nab that cat!

- What does the word *nab* mean? (to catch)
- What are some other words to describe ways to catch Sam? (grab, capture)

2 Read

Sam, Come Back!

Genre
Realistic fiction tells about made-up events that could happen in real life. Next you will read about Sam and Jack, who are made-up characters.
Sam, Come Back!
by Susan Stevens Crummel
illustrated by Janet Stevens
Question of the Week
What do pets need?
20
21

If you read *Sam, Come Back!* during whole group time, then use the following instruction.

CLOSE READING Reread pp. 24–25. Have children summarize the ideas presented on these pages. Ask questions to guide deeper understanding.

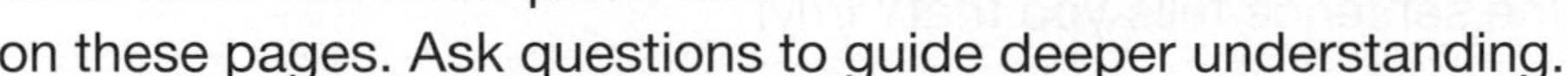

- Which way does Sam run? (that way)
- Who is trying to nab Sam? (Jack and the dog)
- Where does Sam hide? (in a sack)

Have children look at the pictures on pages 24–25 and think of one sentence to tell more information about what is happening. (Sam runs with green yarn. See Sam in the brown paper sack.)

If you are reading *Sam, Come Back!* during small group time, then return to pp. 20–29 to guide the reading.

If... children need more scaffolding and practice with the main selection, **then...** use the activities on p. DI•18 in the Teacher Resources section on SuccessNet.

On-Level

1 Build Word Knowledge

Practice Selection Vocabulary

Sam Jack

Team Talk **LANGUAGE DEVELOPMENT** Have children practice using the selection vocabulary. Ask questions such as: What is the name of the cat in the story? What is the name of the boy in the story? Turn and talk to your partner about these characters. Be prepared to explain your answer.

Allow children time to discuss each word. Ask for examples or rephrase for usage when necessary or to correct for understanding. Use the Student Edition to provide visual support.

2 Text-Based Comprehension

READ ALOUD "Are You My Kitten?" Lead children in a choral reading of "Are You My Kitten?" from *Reading Street Sleuth,* pp. 8–9. Then have partners take turns reading the paragraphs of the selection.

ACCESS TEXT Guide children as they work on the Be a Sleuth section.

Look for Clues Have children look for clues in the text. Ask children to think about what the third kitten does in the story.

Ask Questions Ask children to think of questions they might ask if they were going to take care of a baby kitten. What things would you need to know about a kitten? Remind children to ask about what a kitten eats and drinks, how and where it sleeps, and what it likes to play with when they create their questions.

Make Your Case Have children explain why Kelly chose the third kitten using the clues in the selection for evidence. Then ask them to evaluate Kelly's decision to see if it tells what they would do or if they would have made a different choice. Remind them that they can use information they know from their own experiences to support their reasons.

SMALL GROUP TIME

More Reading for Group Time

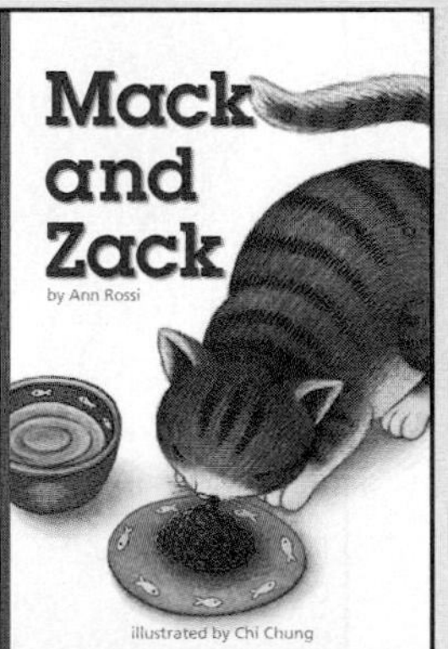

Mack and Zack
by Ann Rossi
illustrated by Chi Chung

ON-LEVEL

Reviews
- Concept Vocabulary
- Character and Setting

Use this suggested Leveled Reader or other text at children's instructional level.

eStreet Interactive
www.ReadingStreet.com

Use the Leveled Reader Database for lesson plans and student pages for *Mack and Zack.*

On-Level

Common Core State Standards

Literature 3. Describe characters, settings, and major events in a story, using key details. **Foundational Skills 1.a.** Recognize the distinguishing features of a sentence (e.g., first word, capitalization, ending punctuation). **Foundational Skills 3.** Know and apply grade-level phonics and word analysis skills in decoding words. **Foundational Skills 4.a.** Read on-level text with purpose and understanding. **Also Foundational Skills 2.c, Speaking/Listening 3., 5., Language 1.**

1 Build Word Knowledge

Practice Sentences

REVIEW If needed, revisit the conventions lesson on p. 29c.

IDENTIFY SENTENCES Have children return to "Are You My Kitten?" to identify sentences in the selection. Have children work in groups to identify the features that make each a complete sentence. (begins with a capital letter, ends with a punctuation mark, tells a complete idea)

2 Text-Based Comprehension

REREAD "Are You My Kitten?" Have partners reread "Are You My Kitten?"

EXTEND UNDERSTANDING Talk together about what Kelly will do to take care of her new kitten. Have children discuss if these are the things that all pets need.

PERFORMANCE TASK • Prove It! What must you do to take care of a pet? Have children choose a pet, such as a dog or cat, and then draw a poster showing what they would do to take care of that pet. Encourage children to use what they read in "Are You My Kitten?" but to also think of an additional task necessary for taking care of the pet that is not mentioned in the story.

COMMUNICATE Have children present their posters to the group and explain why the things they put on their poster are important for taking care of a pet.

More Reading for Group Time

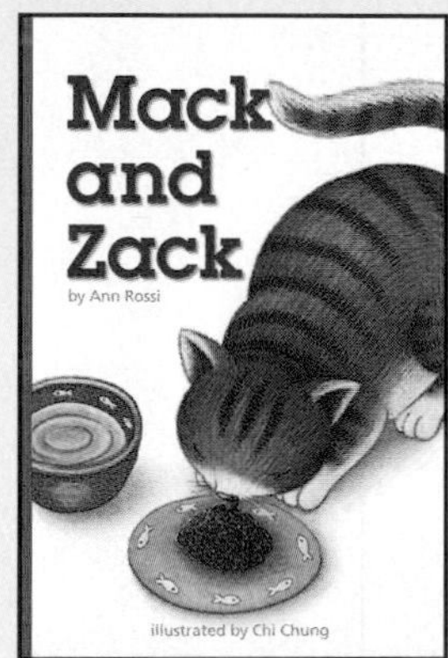

ON-LEVEL

Reviews
- Concept Vocabulary
- Character and Setting

Use this suggested Leveled Reader or other text at children's instructional level.

eSTREET INTERACTIVE
www.ReadingStreet.com

Use the Leveled Reader Database for lesson plans and student pages for *Mack and Zack.*

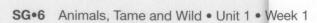

Strategic Intervention

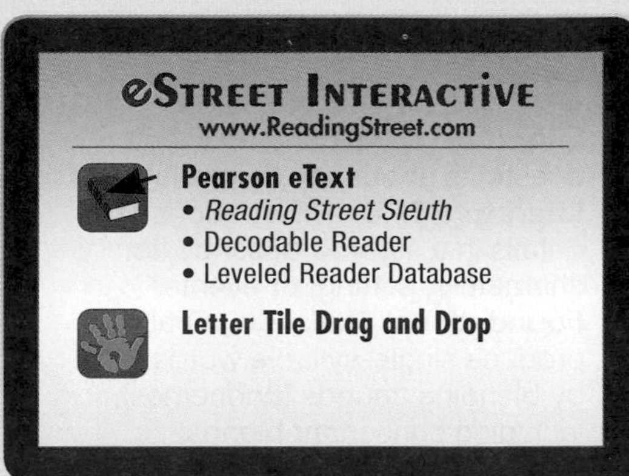

1 Build Word Knowledge

Reteach Phonemic Awareness

Reteach the lesson on p. 14–15 to model /a/. Use these additional practice items to segment and blend words.

hat **mat** **nap** **sat** **pal**

Reteach Phonics

SHORT *a: a* Reteach the lesson on p. 15a, short *a: a.* Use these additional practice words.

wag **has** **gap** **fat** **rag**

Have children spell *fan* using letter tiles. What word did you spell? Let's change a letter to make a new word and then read our new word.

- Change the *f* in *fan* to *p.* What is the new word? p a n
- Change the *n* in *pan* to *d.* What is the new word? p a d
- Change the *p* in *pad* to *b.* What is the new word? b a d

2 Read

Decodable Reader 1A *Hats*

DECODE WORDS Have children practice reading the words listed on p. 97.

Corrective feedback	**If...** children have difficulty reading the words independently, **then...** reteach the words prior to reading Decodable Reader 1A.

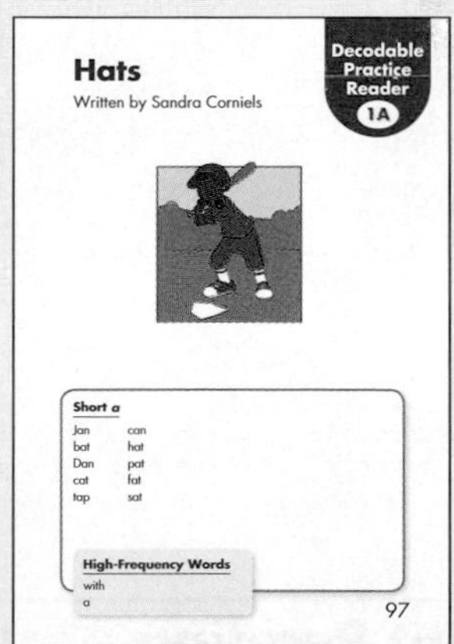

Hats
Written by Sandra Corniels
Decodable Practice Reader 1A
Short a
Jan can
bat hat
Dan pat
cat fat
tap sat
High-Frequency Words
with
a
97

READ IN CONTEXT Have children take turns reading a page in *Hats.* Have them reread the text several times to ensure accuracy.

Corrective feedback	**If...** children have difficulty reading the story independently, **then...** model reading a page and have children echo you.

3 Reread for Fluency

Have children reread the text to develop automaticity in their reading.

ELL

If... children need more scaffolding and practice with phonemic awareness and phonics, **then...** use the ELL activities on pp. DI•13–DI•14 in the Teacher Resources section on SuccessNet.

SI

Strategic Intervention

Common Core State Standards

Literature 1. Ask and answer questions about key details in a text. **Literature 7.** Use illustrations and details in a story to describe its characters, setting, or events. **Foundational Skills 2.b.** Orally produce single-syllable words by blending sounds (phonemes), including consonant blends. **Foundational Skills 3.** Know and apply grade-level phonics and word analysis skills in decoding words.

1 Build Word Knowledge

Reteach Phonemic Awareness

Reteach the lesson on p. 18c to model consonant pattern *-ck.* Use these additional practice items: *Mack, luck, tick, sock, quack, peck.*

Reteach Phonics

CONSONANT PATTERN *-ck* Reteach the lesson on p. 18d to model consonant pattern *-ck.* Use these additional words to blend: *Mack, pack, snack, tack, Zack.*

Have children spell *lack* using letter tiles. What word did you spell? Let's change a letter to make a new word and then read our new word.

- Change the *l* in *lack* to *b.* What is the new word? **b a c k**
- Change the *b* in *back* to *s.* What is the new word? **s a c k**

2 Read

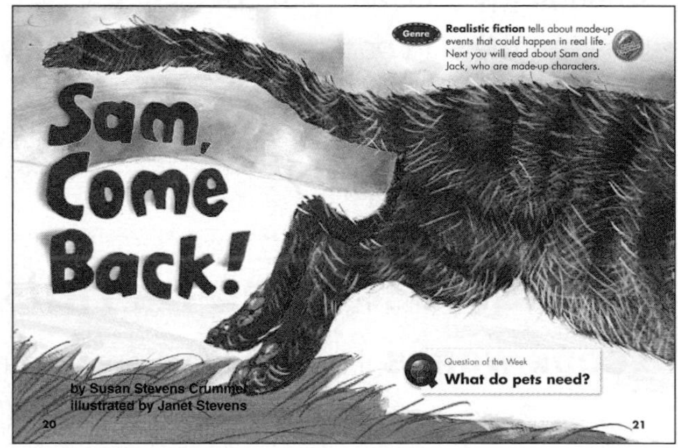
Genre
Realistic fiction tells about made-up events that could happen in real life. Next you will read about Sam and Jack, who are made-up characters.
Sam, Come Back!
by Susan Stevens Crummel
illustrated by Janet Stevens
Question of the Week
What do pets need?
20
21

Sam, Come Back!

If you read *Sam, Come Back!* during whole group time, then use the instruction below.

ACCESS TEXT Have children look at the picture on p. 29. Point to the woman in the picture. Who else do you see in the picture? (Sam the cat, Jack, and a dog) Reread the sentences on p. 29.

- Who says "Pat Sam on my lap"? (the woman)
- What word helps you understand who says that? (The word *my.* In the picture, Sam is on the woman's lap.)
- Who is being told to pat Sam? (the boy, Jack)

If you are reading *Sam, Come Back!* during small group time, then return to pp. 20b–29a to guide the reading.

Corrective feedback	**If...** children have difficulty understanding the section, **then...** read the section aloud using the Access Text Notes.

Independent Reading Options

Trade Book Library

eSTREET INTERACTIVE
www.ReadingStreet.com

Teacher's Guides available on the Leveled Reader Database.

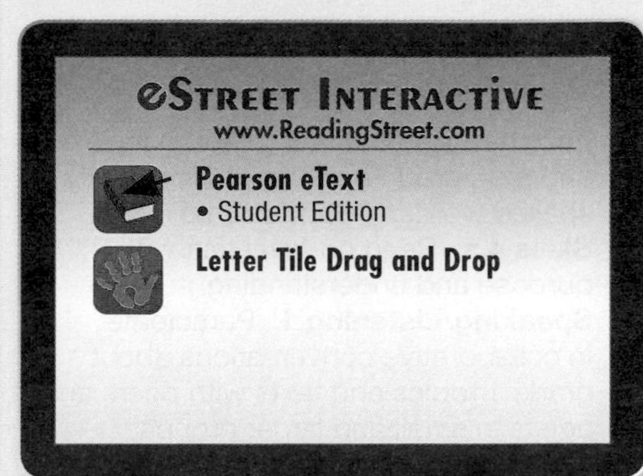

1 Build Word Knowledge

Reteach Phonemic Awareness

Reteach the activity on p. 30c to model words that rhyme. Use these additional practice items: *dog/log; sack/back; cow/now; deer/here.*

Reteach Phonics

Write these short *a* words and final *ck* words and have children blend them with you: *quack, Jack, rack, pack, lack, back, tack, Zack.*

2 Read

Sam, Come Back!

If you read *Sam, Come Back!* during whole group time, then use the instruction below.

CLOSE READING Reread page 23. Let's read this page to find out what Sam does. To help children understand what Sam does, ask questions related to the text and picture.

- What word tells what Sam does? (*ran*)
- How does the picture show what Sam does? (Sam is running in the picture.)
- What does Sam take with him when he runs? (green yarn)
- What do the other characters want Sam to do? Read the sentence on the page to find out. (They want him to come back.)

Corrective feedback	**If...** children have trouble answering questions about the text and picture on p. 23, **then...** reread the page and have them tell about the picture in their own words. Then compare their summary with the words on the page.

If you are reading *Sam, Come Back!* during small group time, then return to pp. 20–29 to guide the reading.

ELL

If... children need scaffolding and practice with the main selection, **then...** use the activities on p. DI•18 in the Teacher Resources section on SuccessNet.

Strategic Intervention

Common Core State Standards

Foundational Skills 3.g. Recognize and read grade-appropriate irregularly spelled words. **Foundational Skills 4.a.** Read on-level text with purpose and understanding. **Speaking/Listening 1.** Participate in collaborative conversations about grade 1 topics and texts with peers and adults in small and larger groups. **Also Speaking/Listening 2., 4., 5., Language 4.**

More Reading for Group Time

CONCEPT LITERACY

Practice
- Concept Words
- High-Frequency Words

BELOW LEVEL

Review
- Character and Setting
- High-Frequency Words

Use these suggested Leveled Readers or other text at children's instructional level.

eStreet Interactive
www.ReadingStreet.com

Use the Leveled Reader Database for lesson plans and student pages for *The Dog* and *Sam.*

1 Build Word Knowledge

Review Selection Vocabulary

Sam Jack

SEE IT/SAY IT/HEAR IT Write *Sam.* Scan across the word with your finger as you say it: Sam. Use the word in a sentence. **Sam** the cat ran away.

DEFINE IT How would you tell a friend who *Sam* is? Give an explanation if necessary. Yes, *Sam* is the name of the cat in the story. Restate the explanation. The name of the cat that ran away is Sam.

Team Talk Do all cats look like Sam? Turn to your partner and talk about this. Allow time for children to discuss. Ask for examples. Rephrase their examples for usage when necessary or to correct misunderstandings. Continue with *Jack.*

2 Text-Based Comprehension

READ ALOUD "Are You My Kitten?" Read aloud "Are You My Kitten?" from *Reading Street Sleuth,* pp. 8–9 and have children follow along.

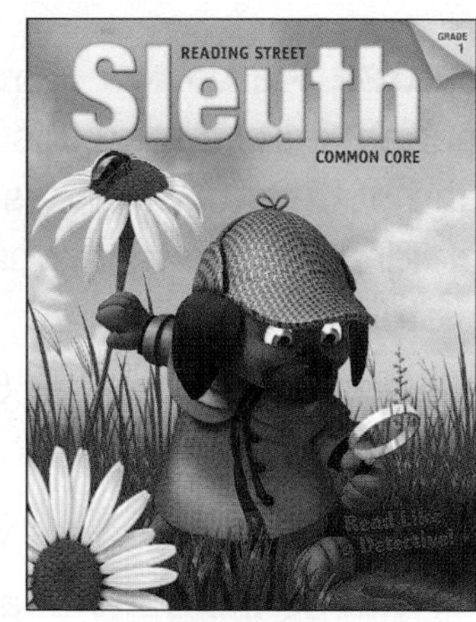

ACCESS TEXT Guide children as they work on the Be a Sleuth section.

Look for Clues Look through the selection for clues with the class. Read the descriptions and the actions of each kitten. Ask children to think about what each kitten did.

Ask Questions Have children think about a kitten as a pet. What would you need to know in order to take care of the kitten? My first question would be "What does it eat?" What would you ask?

Make Your Case Ask children to tell why they think Kelly chose the third kitten. Reread the last paragraph to help children provide evidence for their answers from the text. Then ask them to pretend that they are Kelly and decide which kitten they would have chosen and explain why.

Strategic Intervention

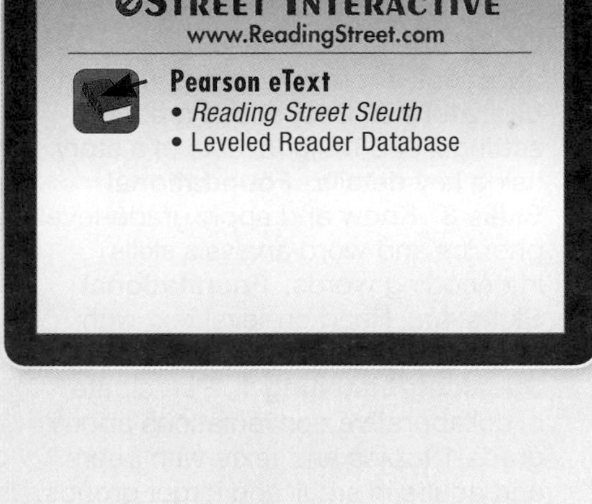

1 Build Word Knowledge

Review High-Frequency Words

Use the routine on p. 17 to review *come, in, my, on,* and *way.*

Corrective feedback	**If...** children have difficulty with any of these words, **then...** tell them the word and have them repeat it. Have children spell the word and tell what word they spelled. Have them practice in pairs with word cards.

2 Text-Based Comprehension

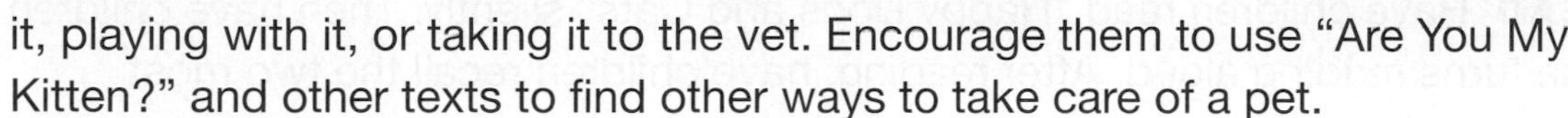

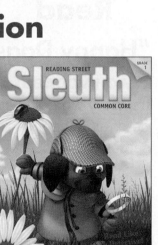

REREAD "Are You My Kitten?" Lead children in a choral reading of "Are You My Kitten?"

EXTEND UNDERSTANDING Talk together about what Kelly says to her new kitten. Have children discuss why the things she says are necessary for taking care of a pet.

PERFORMANCE TASK • Prove It! What must you do to take care of a pet? Have partners create a poster that shows what they would do to take care of a pet. Help children brainstorm ideas such as feeding it, playing with it, or taking it to the vet. Encourage them to use "Are You My Kitten?" and other texts to find other ways to take care of a pet.

COMMUNICATE Have partners show their posters to the group. Encourage the group to ask questions about the posters.

SMALL GROUP TIME

More Reading for Group Time

CONCEPT LITERACY

Practice
- Concept Words
- High-Frequency Words

BELOW LEVEL

Review
- Character and Setting
- High-Frequency Words

Use these suggested Leveled Readers or other text at children's instructional level.

eStreet Interactive
www.ReadingStreet.com

Use the Leveled Reader Database for lesson plans and student pages for *The Dog* and *Sam*.

Advanced

Common Core State Standards

Literature 1. Ask and answer questions about key details in a text. **Literature 3.** Describe characters, settings, and major events in a story, using key details. **Foundational Skills 3.** Know and apply grade-level phonics and word analysis skills in decoding words. **Foundational Skills 4.a.** Read on-level text with purpose and understanding. **Speaking/Listening 1.** Participate in collaborative conversations about grade 1 topics and texts with peers and adults in small and larger groups.

If... children need practice with phonics,
then... use the ELL activities on pp. DI•13–DI•14 in the Teacher Resources section on SuccessNet.

1 Build Word Knowledge

Extend Phonics

SHORT *a*: *a* Have children practice with more complex words. Have them spell the words using letter tiles. Then have children use the words in sentences.

plant	thank	stand	snatch	sadly
happy	hammer	advance	happen	began

2 Read

"Happy Dogs and Cats"

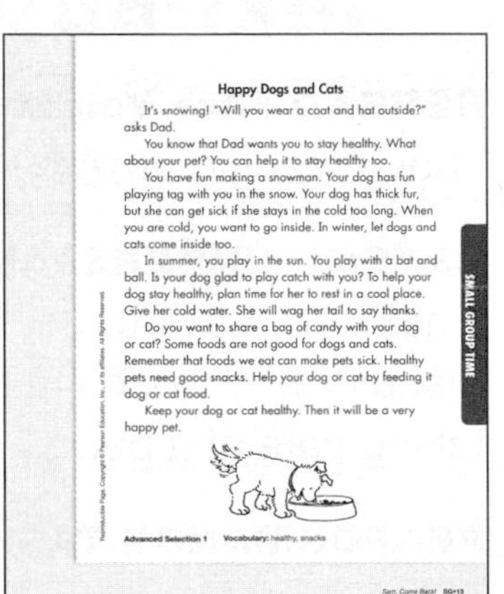

Happy Dogs and Cats

It's snowing! "Will you wear a coat and hat outside?" asks Dad.

You know that Dad wants you to stay healthy. What about your pet? You can help it to stay healthy too.

You have fun making a snowman. Your dog has fun playing tag with you in the snow. Your dog has thick fur, but she can get sick if she stays in the cold too long. When you are cold, you want to go inside. In winter, let dogs and cats come inside too.

In summer, you play in the sun. You play with a bat and ball. Is your dog glad to play catch with you? To help your dog stay healthy, plan time for her to rest in a cool place. Give her cold water. She will wag her tail to say thanks.

Do you want to share a bag of candy with your dog or cat? Some foods are not good for dogs and cats. Remember that foods we eat can make pets sick. Healthy pets need good snacks. Help your dog or cat by feeding it dog or cat food.

Keep your dog or cat healthy. Then it will be a very happy pet.

SMALL GROUP TIME

Advanced Selection 1 **Vocabulary:** healthy, snacks

TEACH VOCABULARY Before reading, introduce the story words: *healthy, snacks.* Help children determine the meaning of each word using these sentences:

1. Eating fruits and vegetables and getting enough sleep will help keep you **healthy.**
2. If you are hungry, popcorn or apples make good **snacks.**

READ Have children read "Happy Dogs and Cats" silently. Then have children take turns reading aloud. After reading, have children recall the two most important ideas of the story using details from the text.

3 Inquiry: Extend Concepts

IDENTIFY QUESTIONS Have children choose two types of pets to compare and contrast. During the week, they should learn more about each animal from reading, studying pictures, and interviewing pet owners. On Day 5, children will present what they have learned. Guide children in brainstorming possible choices.

- What are some pets that you have had?
- Think about where you live. What animal would be a good pet for where you live?

Happy Dogs and Cats

It's snowing! "Will you wear a coat and hat outside?" asks Dad.

You know that Dad wants you to stay healthy. What about your pet? You can help it to stay healthy too.

You have fun making a snowman. Your dog has fun playing tag with you in the snow. Your dog has thick fur, but she can get sick if she stays in the cold too long. When you are cold, you want to go inside. In winter, let dogs and cats come inside too.

In summer, you play in the sun. You play with a bat and ball. Is your dog glad to play catch with you? To help your dog stay healthy, plan time for her to rest in a cool place. Give her cold water. She will wag her tail to say thanks.

Do you want to share a bag of candy with your dog or cat? Some foods are not good for dogs and cats. Remember that foods we eat can make pets sick. Healthy pets need good snacks. Help your dog or cat by feeding it dog or cat food.

Keep your dog or cat healthy. Then it will be a very happy pet.

Advanced Selection 1 **Vocabulary:** healthy, snacks

A

Advanced

Common Core State Standards

Literature 1. Ask and answer questions about key details in a text. **Literature 3.** Describe characters, settings, and major events in a story, using key details. **Literature 7.** Use illustrations and details in a story to describe its characters, setting, or events. **Foundational Skills 3.** Know and apply grade-level phonics and word analysis skills in decoding words. **Language 5.a.** Sort words into categories (e.g., colors, clothing) to gain a sense of the concepts the categories represent. **Also Writing 7.**

1 Build Word Knowledge

Extend Phonics

CONSONANT PATTERN *-ck* Have children practice with additional words with *-ck.* Discuss the meanings of unfamiliar words with children. Then have them write the words on cards and sort by the number of syllables—one or two. Show children how breaking a word into syllables can help them read it.

black	check	chick	truck	bucket
locket	ticket	rocket	cracker	locker

2 Read

Sam, Come Back!

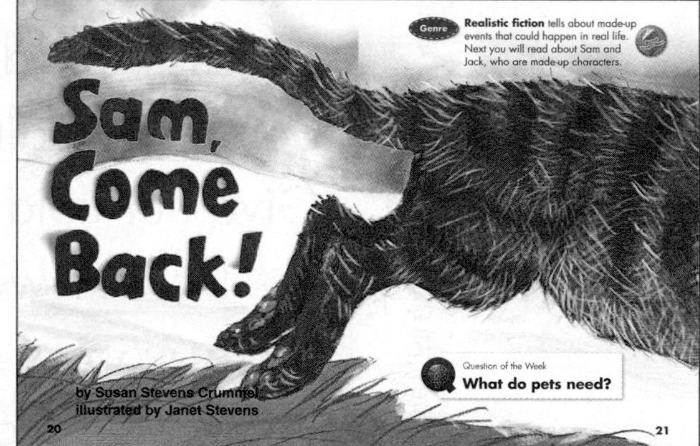
Genre
Realistic fiction tells about made-up events that could happen in real life. Next you will read about Sam and Jack, who are made-up characters.
Sam, Come Back!
by Susan Stevens Crummel
illustrated by Janet Stevens
Question of the Week
What do pets need?
20
21

If you read *Sam, Come Back!* during whole group time, then use the instruction below.

ACCESS TEXT Have children silently reread *Sam, Come Back!*, retell the selection, and identify the plot. (Beginning: Sam runs away. Middle: Jack and the dog chase him. End: Sam comes back.)

DISCUSS GENRE Discuss what makes *Sam, Come Back!* realistic fiction. Point out that the story is made up, but the events could happen in real life.

If you are reading *Sam, Come Back!* during small group time, then return to pp. 20b–29a to guide the reading.

3 Inquiry: Extend Concepts

INVESTIGATE Guide children in choosing materials at their independent reading levels.

LOOK AHEAD Help children choose formats to present their information, such as Venn diagrams, illustrated posters, or three-dimensional displays.

Independent Reading Options

Trade Book Library

eStreet Interactive
www.ReadingStreet.com

Teacher's Guides available on the Leveled Reader Database.

A

Advanced

1 Build Word Knowledge

Develop Vocabulary

REREAD FOR VOCABULARY Have children reread *Sam, Come Back!* and make a three-column chart listing the words that name animals, words that name things, and words that name actions.

Animals	Things	Actions
cat	lap	ran
	sack	pat
	pack	nab
		see

2 Read

Sam, Come Back!

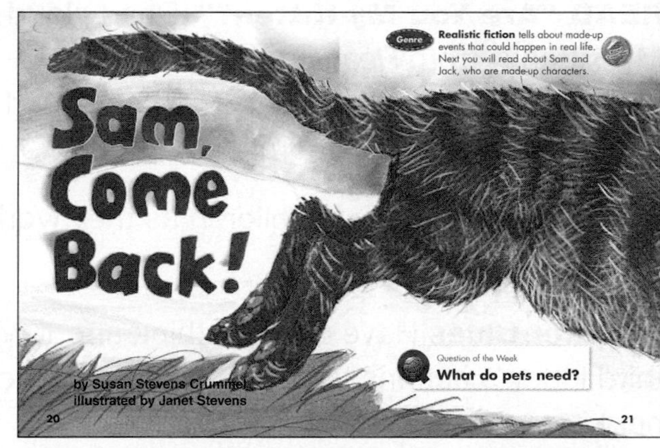
Genre
Realistic fiction tells about made-up events that could happen in real life. Next you will read about Sam and Jack, who are made-up characters.
Sam, Come Back!
by Susan Stevens Crummel
illustrated by Janet Stevens
Question of the Week
What do pets need?
20
21

If you read *Sam, Come Back!* during whole group time, then use the instruction below.

CLOSE READING Reread pp. 22–26. Have children look at the pictures on the pages. What does Sam have on each of these pages? (green yarn) Where does he get the yarn? (from the woman's lap) Look at pages 24–26. What is Sam doing with the yarn on these pages? (He is running around with it. It is unraveling and getting twisted around him.) Have children look through the rest of the selection and tell about the green yarn at the end. Ask children to explain how to clean up the yarn.

If you are reading *Sam, Come Back!* during small group time, then return to pp. 20–29 to guide the reading.

3 Inquiry: Extend Concepts

INVESTIGATE Give children time to investigate their topics by reading and studying pictures. If necessary, help children make connections between different types of pets and where each one can live.

eSTREET INTERACTIVE
www.ReadingStreet.com
Pearson eText
• Student Edition

SMALL GROUP TIME

ELL

If... children need more scaffolding and practice with the main selection,
then... use the activities on p. DI•18 in the Teacher Resources section on SuccessNet.

Common Core State Standards

Foundational Skills 1.a. Recognize the distinguishing features of a sentence (e.g., first word, capitalization, ending punctuation). **Speaking/Listening 1.** Participate in collaborative conversations about grade 1 topics and texts with peers and adults in small and larger groups. **Language 1.** Demonstrate command of the conventions of standard English grammar and usage when writing or speaking. **Language 5.c.** Identify real-life connections between words and their use (e.g., note places at home that are *cozy*). **Also Speaking/Listening 4.**

More Reading for Group Time

ADVANCED

- Extend Concept Vocabulary
- Review Target Skill

Use this suggested Leveled Reader or other text at children's instructional level.

eStreet Interactive
www.ReadingStreet.com

Use the Leveled Reader Database for lesson plans and student pages for *Carlos Picks a Pet.*

1 Build Word Knowledge

Extend Amazing Words and Selection Vocabulary

needs	tickle	shelter	Sam	Jack
responsibility	faithful	fetch		
cuddle	heel			

Team Talk Have children ask each other questions using the Amazing Words and the Selection Vocabulary, such as: Can you cuddle a fish?

2 Text-Based Comprehension

READ "Are You My Kitten?" Read aloud "Are You My Kitten?" from *Reading Street Sleuth,* pp. 8–9 and have children track the print. Then have partners take turns reading each paragraph.

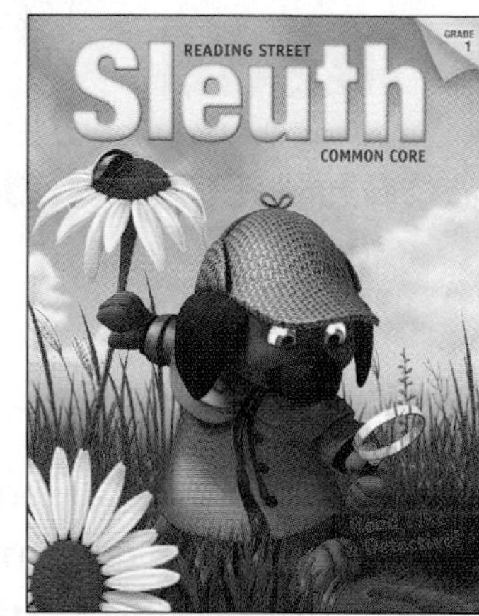

ACCESS TEXT Guide children as they work on the Be a Sleuth section.

Look for Clues Have children think about what the third kitten's actions tell about why Kelly chose it as her kitten.

Ask Questions Ask children to create questions about what they would need to know if they were going to take care of a baby kitten. What things would you need to find out about? After children create several questions, have them look for answers in sources if time permits.

Make Your Case As children answer the question about Kelly's choice, have them provide information from the text or from their background knowledge to support their reasoning for Kelly's choice. Have children with the same opinions work together to present a case for their point of view.

3 Inquiry: Extend Concepts

ORGANIZE INFORMATION Give children time to continue reading and preparing information. Provide any necessary materials, such as poster board, materials to create three-dimensional displays or models, and art supplies.

Advanced

1 Build Word Knowledge

Sentences

IDENTIFY SENTENCES Have children return to the text "Are You My Kitten?" to find sentences. Have children identify the features that make each a complete sentence. (begins with a capital letter, ends with a punctuation mark, tells a complete idea)

2 Text-Based Comprehension

REREAD "Are You My Kitten?" Have partners reread "Are You My Kitten?"

EXTEND UNDERSTANDING Talk together about what they learned about how to take care of a pet.

PERFORMANCE TASK • Prove It! What must you do to take care of a pet? Have children choose a more unique pet, such as a fish or a hamster, and then write a short paragraph telling what they would do to take care of that pet. Have children use what they learned in "Are You My Kitten?" and in other texts about taking care of pets.

COMMUNICATE Have children present their paragraphs to the group. After each child presents his or her paragraph, have the group discuss how the paragraphs are alike and different.

3 Inquiry: Extend Concepts

COMMUNICATE Have children share their inquiry projects that compare and contrast two types of pets.

SMALL GROUP TIME

More Reading for Group Time

ADVANCED

- Extend Concept Vocabulary
- Review Target Skill

Use this suggested Leveled Reader or other text at children's instructional level.

eStreet Interactive
www.ReadingStreet.com

Use the Leveled Reader Database for lesson plans and student pages for *Carlos Picks a Pet.*

TEACHER NOTES

This Week's Target Skills and Strategies

Target Skills and Strategies	Common Core State Standards for English Language Arts
Phonemic Awareness **Skills:** Distinguish /i/ Segment and Blend Phonemes Segment and Count Phonemes	**CCSS Foundational Skills 2.b.** Orally produce single-syllable words by blending sounds (phonemes), including consonant blends. **(Also CCSS Foundational Skills 2.c., CCSS Foundational Skills 2.d.)**
Phonics **Skill:** Short *i*: *i* **Skill:** Consonant *x*/ks/	**CCSS Foundational Skills 3.** Know and apply grade-level phonics and word analysis skills in decoding words. **(Also CCSS Foundational Skills 3.b., CCSS Language 2.d.)**
Text-Based Comprehension **Skill:** Plot	**CCSS Literature 3.** Describe characters, settings, and major events in a story, using key details.
Strategy: Summarize	**CCSS Literature 3.** Describe characters, settings, and major events in a story, using key details.
Fluency **Skill:** Accuracy	**CCSS Foundational Skills 4.b.** Read on-level text orally with accuracy, appropriate rate, and expression on successive readings.
Listening and Speaking Share Information and Ideas	**CCSS Speaking/Listening 1.** Participate in collaborative conversations about *grade 1 topics and texts* with peers and adults in small and larger groups. **(Also CCSS Speaking/Listening 1.a.)**
Six-Trait Writing **Trait of the Week:** Conventions	**CCSS Language 2.** Demonstrate command of the conventions of standard English capitalization, punctuation, and spelling when writing. **(Also CCSS Language 1.)**
Writing Fantasy Story	**CCSS Writing 3.** Write narratives in which they recount two or more appropriately sequenced events, include some details regarding what happened, use temporal words to signal event order, and provide some sense of closure. **(Also CCSS Writing 5.)**
Conventions **Skill:** Subjects of Sentences	**CCSS Language 1.j.** Produce and expand complete simple and compound declarative, interrogative, imperative, and exclamatory sentences in response to prompts. **(Also CCSS Language 2.)**

This Week's Cross-Curricular Standards and Resources

Cross-Curricular Indiana Academic Standards for Science and Social Studies

Science
IN 1.3.1 Classify living organisms according to variations in specific physical features (e.g., body coverings, appendages) and describe how those features may provide an advantage for survival in different environments.

Social Studies
IN 1.1.7 Explain that clocks and calendars are used to measure time.

Reading Street Sleuth

What Do You Do?
pp. 10–11

Follow the path to close reading using the Super Sleuth tips:

- Look for Clues
- Ask Questions
- Make Your Case
- Prove it!

More Reading in Science and Social Studies

Concept Literacy

Below Level

On Level

Advanced

ELL

ELD

ISBN-13: 978-0-328-73376-7 ISBN-10: 0-328-73376-8

Your 90-Minute Reading Block

	Whole Group	Formative Assessment How do I make my small groups flexible?	Small Group OL On Level SI Strategic Intervention A Advanced What are my other students reading and learning every day in Small Groups?
DAY 1	**Content Knowledge** Build Oral Language/Vocabulary **Phonemic Awareness/Phonics** **Read Decodable Reader** **Phonics/Spelling Pretest** **High-Frequency Words** **Text-Based Comprehension** Teacher Read Aloud **Research and Inquiry** Step 1–Identify and Focus Topic	**Monitor Progress** Formative Assessment: Check Word Reading	**Differentiate Phonics** OL **Practice Phonics** More Short *i* Words SI **Reteach Phonics** Blend Short *i* Words A **Extend Phonics** More Challenging Short *i* Words OL SI **Decodable Reader Read** *Did They Win?* A **Advanced Selection** "Bill and the Big Job" A Inquiry Project ELL Access Phonemic Awareness and Phonics
DAY 2	**Content Knowledge** Build Oral Language/Vocabulary **Phonemic Awareness/Phonics** **Read Decodable Reader** **Phonics/Spelling** **High-Frequency Words/Selection Words** **Text-Based Comprehension** **Read** Main Selection, using Access Text Notes **Research and Inquiry** Step 2–Research Skill	**Monitor Progress** Formative Assessment: Check Word Reading	**Differentiate Comprehension** OL **Practice Phonics** Additional *x*/ks/ Words SI **Reteach Phonics** Blend *x*/ks/ Words A **Extend Phonics** Additional *x*/ks/ Words OL SI A **Access Text Read** *Pig in a Wig* A Inquiry Project ELL Access the Comprehension Skill
DAY 3	**Content Knowledge** Build Oral Language/Vocabulary **Phonemic Awareness/Phonics** **Phonics/Spelling** **High-Frequency Words/Selection Words** **Text-Based Comprehension** **Reread** Main Selection, using Close Reading Notes **Fluency** **Research and Inquiry** Step 3–Gather and Record Information	**Monitor Progress** Formative Assessment: Check High-Frequency Words **Monitor Progress** Check Retelling	**Differentiate Close Reading** OL **Reread to Develop Vocabulary** SI **Build Word Knowledge** Blend Words with Short *i* and *x*/ks/ A **Reread to Extend Vocabulary** OL SI **Close Reading Reread** *Pig in a Wig* A **Extend Concepts Reread** *Pig in a Wig* A Inquiry Project ELL Access the Main Selection
DAY 4	**Content Knowledge** Build Oral Language/Vocabulary **Phonemic Awareness/Phonics** **Read Decodable Reader** **Phonics/Spelling** **Read Content Area Paired Selection with Genre Focus** **Fluency** **Research and Inquiry** Step 4–Synthesize	**Monitor Progress** Fluency Check	**Differentiate Vocabulary** **Build Word Knowledge** OL Develop Language A Extend Amazing Words and Selection Vocabulary SI **Review Vocabulary** Review/Discuss Selection Vocabulary OL SI A **Text-Based Comprehension Read** *Reading Street Sleuth*, pp. 10–11 or Leveled Readers A Inquiry Project ELL Access Vocabulary
DAY 5	**Content Knowledge** Build Oral Language/Vocabulary **Phonemic Awareness/Phonics** **Phonics/Spelling Test** **Let's Learn It!** Vocabulary/Fluency/Listening and Speaking **Text-Based Comprehension** **High-Frequency and Selection Words** **Genre** **Assessment** Phonics, High-Frequency Words, Fluency **Research and Inquiry** Step 5–Communicate	**Monitor Progress** Formative Assessment: Check Oral Vocabulary **Monitor Progress** Word and Sentence Reading	**Differentiate Reteaching** OL **Practice Subjects of Sentences** SI **Review Vocabulary** High-Frequency Words A **Extend Subjects of Sentences** OL SI A **Text-Based Comprehension** **Reread** *Reading Street Sleuth*, pp. 10–11 or Leveled Readers A Inquiry Project ELL Access Conventions and Writing

Daily Independent Options

What do my other students do when I lead Small Groups?

★ **Independent Reading**

Suggestions for this week's independent reading:

- Informational texts on last week's social studies topic: What do pets need?
- Nonfiction selections about what pets need
- Other books by Susan Stevens Crummel

Book Talk

Foster critical reading and discussion skills through independent and close reading.

Students should focus on discussing one or more of the following:

- Key Ideas and Details
- Craft and Structure
- Integration of Ideas

Pearson eText

- Student Edition
- Decodable Readers
- Leveled Readers

Trade Book Library

Materials from School or Classroom Library

Independent Stations
Practice Last Week's Skills

★ Focus on these activities when time is limited.

★ **Listen Up!**
Word Work
★ **Read for Meaning**
Let's Write!
Words to Know
Get Fluent

Assessment Resources

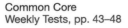

Common Core Weekly Tests, pp. 43–48

Common Core Fresh Reads for Fluency and Comprehension, pp. 43–48

Common Core Unit 1 Benchmark Test

Common Core Success Tracker, ExamView, and Online Lesson Planner

Focus on Common Core State Standards ©

Main Selection, pp. 46–57

Paired Selection, pp. 62–63

Text-Based Comprehension

 **Plot**

CCSS Literature 3.

 **Summarize**

CCSS Literature 3.

Fluency

Accuracy

CCSS Foundational Skills 4.b.

Writing and Conventions

Trait: Conventions

CCSS Language 2.

Writing Mini-Lesson: Fantasy Story

CCSS Writing 3.,
CCSS Writing 5.

Conventions: Subjects of Sentences

CCSS Language 1.j.,
CCSS Language 2.

Oral Vocabulary

career	service
tool	scrub
sloppy	exercise
comfort	search

CCSS Language 5.c.

High-Frequency Words

she	take
up	what

CCSS Foundational Skills 3.g.

Phonemic Awareness

Distinguish /i/

Segment and Blend Phonemes

Segment and Count Phonemes

CCSS Foundational Skills 2.b.,
CCSS Foundational Skills 2.d.

Phonics and Spelling

 **Consonant *x*/ks/**

Short *i*: *i*

CCSS Foundational Skills 3.,
CCSS Foundational Skills 3.b.,
CCSS Language 2.d.

six	lip	in
wig	it	did
mix	sit	pin
fix		

Listening and Speaking

Share Information and Ideas

CCSS Speaking/Listening 1.

Preview Your Week

Who helps animals?

Pig in a Wig
by Susan Stevens Crummel
illustrated by Janet Stevens
Genre
An animal fantasy is a story about animals that could not really happen. In the next story, you will read about a pig that does things a real pig cannot do.
Question of the Week
Who helps animals?
46
47

Main Selection, pp. 46–57

Genre: Animal Fantasy

Phonics: Short *i*: *i*, Consonant *x*/ks/

Text-Based Comprehension: Plot

We Are Vets
Social Studies in Reading
Genre
Sing-Along
We are vets.
We are vets.
We help pets.
We help pets.
If you have a dog who is feeling sick,
Bring him to me, and I'll fix him quick.
His tail will wag, and he'll chase a stick.
He'll feel fine. He'll feel fine.
62
63

Paired Selection, pp. 62–63

Social Studies in Reading

Genre: Sing-Along

Build Content Knowledge

Zoom in on

SOCIAL STUDIES

KNOWLEDGE GOALS
Children will understand that:

- pet owners help animals
- vets help animals
- trainers help animals

THIS WEEK'S CONCEPT MAP
Develop a concept-related graphic organizer like the one below over the course of this week.

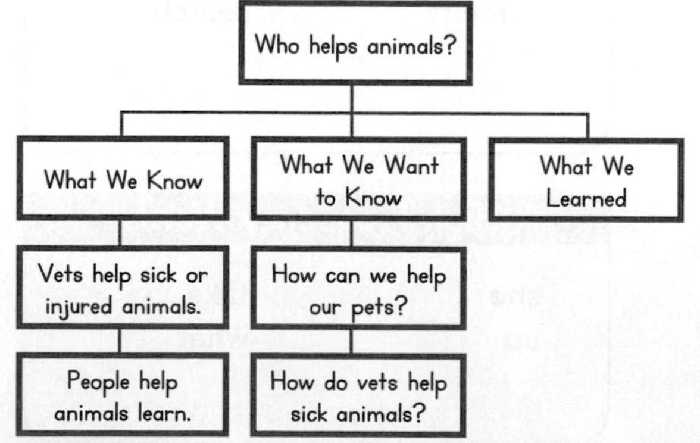
Who helps animals?
What We Know
What We Want to Know
What We Learned
Vets help sick or injured animals.
How can we help our pets?
People help animals learn.
How do vets help sick animals?

BUILD ORAL VOCABULARY
This week, children will acquire the following academic vocabulary/domain-specific words.

Amazing Words

career	service	comfort
tool	scrub	search
sloppy	exercise	

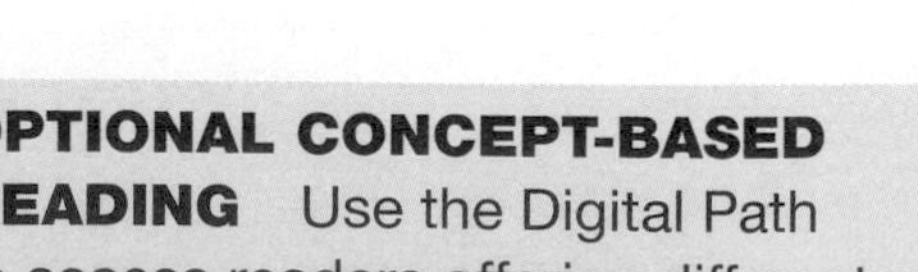

OPTIONAL CONCEPT-BASED READING Use the Digital Path to access readers offering different levels of text complexity.

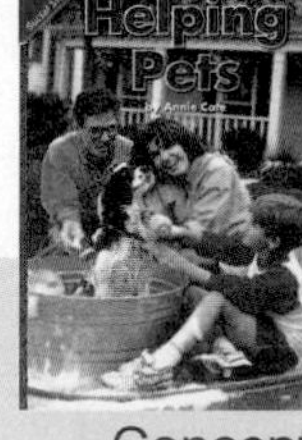
Helping Pets
Concept Literacy

Fix the Dog
Below Level

The Sick Pets
On Level

That Cat Needs Help!
Advanced

Pet Helpers
ELL

Pet Helpers
ELD

This Week's Digital Resources

eSTREET INTERACTIVE
www.ReadingStreet.com

Get Ready to Read

Background Building Audio CD This audio CD provides valuable background information about pigs to help children read and comprehend the weekly texts.

Concept Talk Video Use this video on the Digital Path to build momentum and introduce the weekly concept of helping animals.

Interactive Sing with Me Big Book "Pet Service," sung to the tune of "Yankee Doodle," introduces the Amazing Words with a catchy, concept-related song.

Interactive Sound-Spelling Cards With these interactive cards on the Digital Path, children see an image, hear the image name, and see the spelling for short *i* spelled *i*, and the consonant *x*/ks/.

Pearson eText Use the eText for the Decodable Readers on the Leveled Reader Database for phonics and fluency support.

Letter Tile Drag and Drop Using this interactive tool on Pearson SuccessNet, children click and spell words to enhance their phonics skills.

Read and Comprehend

Envision It! Animations Use this colorful animation on the Digital Path to explain the target comprehension skill, Plot.

Pearson eText Read the eText of the main selection, *Pig in a Wig,* and the paired selection, "We Are Vets," with audio support on Pearson SuccessNet.

Story Sort Use the Story Sort Activity on the Digital Path after reading *Pig in a Wig* to involve children in summarizing.

Journal: Word Bank Use the Word Bank on the Digital Path to have children write sentences using this week's high-frequency words.

Vocabulary Activities A variety of interactive vocabulary activities on the Digital Path help children practice high-frequency and concept-related words.

Language Arts

Grammar Jammer Choose a whimsical animation on the Digital Path to provide an engaging grammar lesson that will capture children's attention.

Pearson eText Find the Student Edition eText of the Let's Write It! and Let's Learn It! pages with audio support on Pearson SuccessNet.

Additional Resources

Teacher Resources DVD-ROM Use the following resources on the TR DVD or on Pearson SuccessNet throughout the week:

- Amazing Word Cards
- Reader's and Writer's Notebook
- Writing Transparencies
- Daily Fix-It Transparencies
- Scoring Rubrics
- Grammar Transparencies
- Research Transparencies
- Let's Practice It!
- Graphic Organizers
- High-Frequency Word Cards
- Vocabulary Transparencies

This Week's Skills

Phonics
- Short *i: i*
- Consonant *x*/ks/

Comprehension
- **Skill:** Plot
- **Strategy:** Summarize

Language
Vocabulary: Alphabetize
Conventions: Subjects of Sentences

Fluency
Accuracy

Writing
Fantasy Story

5-Day Planner

DAY 1

Get Ready to Read

Content Knowledge 38j
Oral Vocabulary: *career, service, tool*

Phonemic Awareness 40–41
Distinguish /i/

Phonics/Spelling 41a
Short *i: i*
READ Decodable Reader 2A
Reread for Fluency
Spelling Pretest

Monitor Progress
Check Word Reading

Read and Comprehend

High-Frequency Words 43
she, take, up, what

Text-Based Comprehension 43a
Plot

Language Arts

Conventions 43c
Subjects of Sentences

Writing 43d
Fantasy Story

Research and Inquiry 43f
Identify and Focus Topic

DAY 2

Get Ready to Read

Content Knowledge 44a
Oral Vocabulary: *scrub, sloppy*

Phonemic Awareness 44c
Segment and Blend

Phonics/Spelling 44d
Consonant *x*/ks/
Review Short *a: a*
READ Decodable Reader 2B
Reread for Fluency
Spelling: Short *i* Words

Monitor Progress
Check Word Reading

Read and Comprehend

High-Frequency Words 45
she, take, up, what

Selection Vocabulary 46a
play
Strategy: Alphabetize

Text-Based Comprehension 46b
READ *Pig in a Wig*—1st Read

Genre 57a
Animal Fantasy

Language Arts

Conventions 57b
Subjects of Sentences

Writing 57c
Fantasy Story

Handwriting 57e
Letters *Ii* and *Xx*/Letter Spacing

Research and Inquiry 57f
Media Center/Library

DAY 3

Get Ready to Read

Content Knowledge 58a
Oral Vocabulary: *exercise*

Phonemic Awareness 58c
Rhyming Words

Phonics/Spelling 58d
Build Words
Blend and Read
Spelling: Dictation

Read and Comprehend

High-Frequency Words and Selection Words 58g
High-Frequency Words: *she, take, up, what*
Selection Words: *play*
Monitor Progress Check High-Frequency Words

Text-Based Comprehension 58h
READ *Pig in a Wig*—2nd Read
Monitor Progress Check Retelling

Fluency 59b
Accuracy

Language Arts

Conventions 60a
Subjects of Sentences

Writing 60–61
Fantasy Story

Listening and Speaking 61b
Share Information About Caring

Research and Inquiry 61c
Gather and Record Information

DAY 4

Get Ready to Read

Content Knowledge 62a
Oral Vocabulary: *comfort, search*

Phonemic Awareness 62c
Distinguish /i/

Phonics/Spelling 62d
Review Short *a* Spelled *a*
Review Consonant Digraph *-ck*
READ Decodable Reader 2C
Spiral Review Fluent Word Reading
Spelling: Short *i* Words

Read and Comprehend

Social Studies in Reading 62i
READ "We Are Vets"—Paired Selection

Fluency 63b
Accuracy
Monitor Progress Fluency Check

Language Arts

Conventions 63c
Subjects of Sentences

Writing 63d
Fantasy Story

Research and Inquiry 63f
Synthesize

DAY 5

Get Ready to Read

Content Knowledge 64a
Review Oral Vocabulary
Monitor Progress Check Oral Vocabulary

Phonemic Awareness 64c
Review Segment and Count Phonemes

Phonics/Spelling 64c
Review Short *i: i,* Consonant *x*/ks/
Spelling Test

Read and Comprehend

Listening and Speaking 64–65
Vocabulary 65a
Fluency 65a

Text-Based Comprehension 65b
Review Plot

Vocabulary 65b
Review High-Frequency and Selection Words

Genre 65c
Realism and Fantasy

Assessment 65d
Monitor Progress Word and Sentence Reading

Language Arts

Conventions 65g
Review Subjects of Sentences

Writing 65h
Fantasy Story

Research and Inquiry 65j
Communicate

Wrap Up Your Week! 65k

Access for All

What do I do in group time?

It's as easy as 1-2-3!

1 TEACHER-LED SMALL GROUPS → 2 INDEPENDENT PRACTICE STATIONS → 3 INDEPENDENT READING

Small Group Time

Bridge to Common Core

SKILL DEVELOPMENT

- Consonant *x*/ks/
- Short *i: i*
- Plot
- Summarize

DEEP UNDERSTANDING

This Week's Knowledge Goals

Children will understand that:

- pet owners help animals
- vets help animals
- trainers help animals

1 Small Group Lesson Plan

	DAY 1 Differentiate Phonics	DAY 2 Differentiate Comprehension
OL On-Level pp. SG•19–SG•23	**Practice Phonics** More Short *i* Words **Decodable Reader** Read *Did They Win?*	**Practice Phonics** Additional *x*/ks/ Words **Access Text** Read *Pig in a Wig*
SI Strategic Intervention pp. SG•24–SG•28	**Reteach Phonics** Blend Short *i* Words **Decodable Reader** Read *Did They Win?*	**Reteach Phonics** Blend *x*/ks/ Words **Access Text** Read *Pig in a Wig*
A Advanced pp. SG•29–SG•34	**Extend Phonics** More Challenging Short *i* Words **Advanced Selection** "Bill and the Big Job"	**Extend Phonics** Additional *x*/ks/ Words **Access Text** Read *Pig in a Wig*
Independent Inquiry Project	**Identify Questions**	**Investigate**
ELL **If...** children need more scaffolding and practice with...	**Phonemic Awareness and Phonics,** **then...** use the ELL activities on pp. DI•34–DI•35 in the Teacher Resources section on SuccessNet.	**the Comprehension Skill,** **then...** use the ELL activities on p. DI•38 in the Teacher Resources section on SuccessNet.

Reading Street Sleuth

- Provides access to grade-level text for all children
- Focuses on finding clues in text through close reading
- Builds capacity for complex text

Build Text-Based Comprehension

Pig in a Wig

Optional Leveled Readers

Concept Literacy

Below Level

On Level

Advanced

ELL

ELD

DAY 3	DAY 4	DAY 5
Differentiate Close Reading	**Differentiate Vocabulary**	**Differentiate Reteaching**
Reread to Develop Vocabulary **Close Reading** Reread *Pig in a Wig*	**Build Word Knowledge** Develop Language **Text-Based Comprehension** Read *Reading Street Sleuth,* pp. 10–11 or Leveled Readers	**Practice Subjects of Sentences** **Text-Based Comprehension** Reread *Reading Street Sleuth,* pp. 10–11 or Leveled Readers
Build Word Knowledge Blend Words with Short *i* and *x*/ks/ **Close Reading** Reread *Pig in a Wig*	**Review Vocabulary** Review/Discuss Selection Vocabulary **Text-Based Comprehension** Read *Reading Street Sleuth,* pp. 10–11 or Leveled Readers	**Review Vocabulary** High-Frequency Words **Text-Based Comprehension** Reread *Reading Street Sleuth,* pp. 10–11 or Leveled Readers
Reread to Extend Vocabulary **Extend Concepts** Reread *Pig in a Wig* **Investigate**	**Build Word Knowledge** Extend Amazing Words and Selection Vocabulary **Text-Based Comprehension** Read *Reading Street Sleuth,* pp. 10–11 or Leveled Readers **Organize**	**Extend Subjects of Sentences** **Text-Based Comprehension** Reread *Reading Street Sleuth,* pp. 10–11 or Leveled Readers **Communicate**
the Main Selection, **then...** use the activities on p. DI•39 in the Teacher Resources section on SuccessNet.	**Vocabulary,** **then...** use the routine on pp. xxxvi–xxxvii in the *ELL Handbook.*	**Conventions and Writing,** **then...** use the activities on pp. DI•41–DI•42 in the Teacher Resources section on SuccessNet.

2 Independent Stations

Practice Last Week's Skills

★ Focus on these activities when time is limited.

ACCESS FOR ALL
- ● Below-Level Activities
- ▲ On-Level Activities
- ■ Advanced Activities

★ LISTEN UP!

Match sounds and pictures.

OBJECTIVES

- Identify words with initial and medial sound /a/.
- Identify words with final sound /k/.

MATERIALS

- *Listen Up!* Flip Chart Activity 2, Picture Cards *alligator, ant, apple, astronaut, bag, bat, black, block, brick, duck, man, truck, van*

 **Modeled Pronunciation Audio CD**

● Children find Picture Cards that have the same beginning or middle sound as *answer, had,* or ending sound as *pick.*

▲ Children find Picture Cards that have these sounds: beginning—answer, middle—had, ending—pick. Then have children think of words that rhyme with the Picture Cards.

■ Children sort the Picture Cards that have these sounds: beginning—answer, middle—had, ending—pick. Have them choose one and draw a picture.

WORD WORK

Build and read words.

OBJECTIVES

- Build words that contain the letters *a* or *ck.*
- Read words that contain the letters *a* or *ck.*

MATERIALS

- *Word Work* Flip Chart Activity 2, Letter Tiles, paper, pencils

 **Interactive Sound-Spelling Cards**  **Letter Tile Drag and Drop**

● Children use Letter Tiles to build the words *ant, bad,* and *back.* Then they say each word.

▲ Children use Letter Tiles to build the words *ant, bad,* and *back.* Then they write the words on their papers.

■ Children think of other words that contain the vowel *a* or the consonant pattern *ck.* They build the words with Letter Tiles and write them on paper.

LET'S WRITE!

Write sentences.

OBJECTIVES

- Write complete sentences.

MATERIALS

- *Let's Write!* Flip Chart Activity 2, paper, pencils

 **Grammar Jammer**

● Children write a sentence about a pet they know. Remind them to use a capital letter at the start of the sentence and a period at the end.

▲ Children write two sentences about a pet they know.

■ Children write about a pet they know or a pet they would like to own. They write several sentences with capital letters at the start and periods at the end of the sentences.

WORDS TO KNOW

Practice high-frequency words.

OBJECTIVES

- Identify high-frequency words *way, my, come, on, in.*
- Spell high-frequency words *way, my, come, on, in.*

MATERIALS

- *Words to Know* Flip Chart Activity 2; High-Frequency Word Cards for Unit 1, Week 1; Letter Tiles; paper; pencils

 **Vocabulary Activities**

 **Teacher Resources**
- High-Frequency Word Cards for Unit 1, Week 1

● Children use the Word Cards for *way, my, come, on,* and *in.* Have them match Letter Tiles to the letters on the cards.

▲ Children copy the Word Cards for *way, my, come, on,* and *in* on their papers.

■ Children write two sentences using the words *way, my, come, on,* and *in.*

Manage the Stations

Use these management tools to set up and organize your Practice Stations:

Practice Station Flip Charts

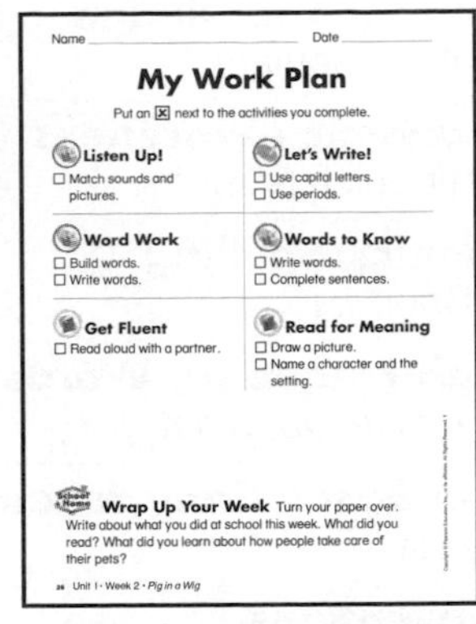

Classroom Management Handbook for Differentiated Instruction Practice Stations, p. 26

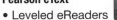

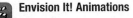

READ FOR MEANING

Use text-based comprehension tools.

OBJECTIVES

- Identify the characters in a story.
- Identify the setting in a story.

MATERIALS

- *Read for Meaning* Flip Chart Activity 2, Leveled Readers, paper, pencils, crayons

 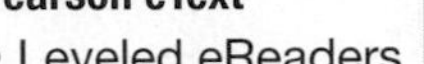 **Pearson eText**
- Leveled eReaders

 **Envision It! Animations**

● Children read *Sam* and name a character in the story. Then they draw a picture of the character and the setting.

▲ Children read *Mack and Zack* and name the characters and the setting. Then they write a sentence telling what one of the characters does.

■ Children read *Carlos Picks a Pet.* They can write two sentences, one to describe the setting and the other to describe the character. Then they draw pictures to go with the sentences.

GET FLUENT

Practice fluent reading.

OBJECTIVES

- Read aloud with accuracy.

MATERIALS

- *Get Fluent* Flip Chart Activity 2

 **Pearson eText**
- Leveled eReaders

● Children work with a partner to take turns reading from *Sam.*

▲ Children work with a partner to take turns reading from *Mack and Zack.*

■ Children work with a partner to take turns reading from *Carlos Picks a Pet.*

3 Independent Reading ©

Children should select appropriately complex texts to read and write about independently every day before, during, and after school.

Suggestions for this week's independent reading:
- Informational texts on last week's social studies topic: What do pets need?
- Nonfiction selections about what pets need
- Other books by Susan Stevens Crummel

BOOK TALK Have partners discuss their independent reading for the week. Tell them to refer to their Reading Log and paraphrase what the selection was about. To focus the discussion, prompt them to talk about one or more of the following:

Key Ideas and Details
- Who is the author? Why did he or she write the work?
- What did I learn from this text?

Craft and Structure
- Did I understand the information?
- Did the author use words that were interesting and clear?

Integration of Ideas
- Did the information seem believable? Why or why not?
- Was this book like others I have read?

 **Pearson eText**
- Student Edition
- Decodable Readers
- Leveled Readers

 **Trade Book Library**

 **Materials from School or Classroom Library**

Content Knowledge
Oral Vocabulary

Phonemic Awareness
Distinguish /i/

Phonics/Spelling
Short *i: i*

High-Frequency Words
she, take, up, what

Text-Based Comprehension
Plot

Conventions
Subjects of Sentences

Writing
Fantasy Story

Research and Inquiry
Identify and Focus Topic

Materials

- Student Edition
- Sing with Me Big Book
- Sound-Spelling Cards
- Decodable Reader 2A
- Reader's and Writer's Notebook

Bridge to Common Core

INTEGRATION OF KNOWLEDGE/IDEAS
This week children read, write, and talk about helping animals.

Texts This Week
- "Pet Service"
- "Paws and Jake"
- *A Kid's Best Friend*
- *Pig in a Wig*
- "We Are Vets"
- "The Storm Seal"

Social Studies Knowledge Goals
Children will understand that
- pet owners help animals
- vets help animals
- trainers help animals

Street Rhymes!

Kitty Kat has never met
A person kinder than the vet.
He checks her paws,
And trims her claws.
He takes such good care of my pet.

- To introduce this week's concept, read aloud the poem several times and ask children to join you.

Content Knowledge

Helping Animals

CONCEPT TALK To help children gain knowledge and understanding, tell them that this week they will talk, sing, read, and write about people who help animals. Write the Question of the Week, *Who helps animals?,* and track the print as you read it.

Build Oral Language

TALK ABOUT HELPING ANIMALS Have children turn to pp. 38–39 in their Student Edition. Read the title and look at the photos. Use these questions to guide discussion and create the "Who helps animals?" K-W-L concept map.

- Look at the picture on page 39. How is the woman helping the dog? (She is helping its leg to heal.) What is the woman's *career,* or job? (She is a vet.) Vets provide an important *service.* Let's add *Vets help sick or injured animals* to our map.
- Who is helping the dog in the picture on page 38? (a boy) He is teaching the dog to follow directions. Sometimes people use *tools,* such as whistles, to help teach dogs. Let's add *People help animals learn* under *What We Know* on our map.
- What would you like to know about who helps animals? (Possible response: How can we help our pets? How do vets help sick animals?) Let's add these questions to our map.

Common Core State Standards
Speaking/Listening 4. Describe people, places, things, and events with relevant details, expressing ideas and feelings clearly. **Also Speaking/Listening 1.**

Oral Vocabulary

Let's Talk About

Animal Friends

- Share ideas about how people help animals.
- Discuss the kinds of jobs there are in which people help animals.

READING STREET ONLINE
CONCEPT TALK VIDEO
www.ReadingStreet.com

You've learned 0 5 5 Amazing Words so far this year!

38 39

Student Edition, pp. 38–39

CONNECT TO READING Explain that this week children will read about a pig that feels sick. We will learn how a person might help a sick animal feel better. This will help us answer the questions on our map.

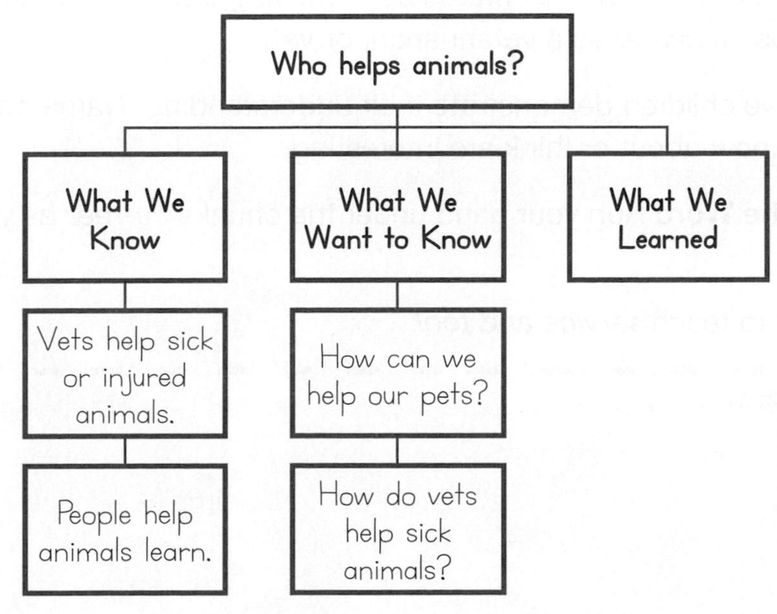

Who helps animals?
What We Know
What We Want to Know
What We Learned
Vets help sick or injured animals.
People help animals learn.
How can we help our pets?
How do vets help sick animals?

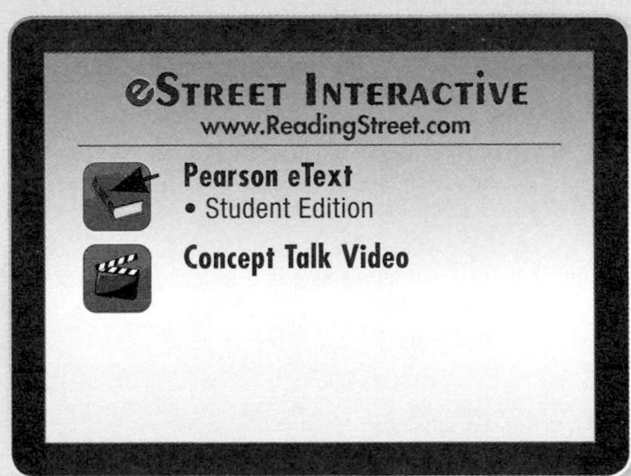

ELL

Preteach Concepts Use the Day 1 instruction on ELL Poster 2 to build knowledge and oral vocabulary.

ELL Support Additional ELL support is provided in the *ELL Handbook* and in the *ELL Support Lessons* on the *Teacher Resources DVD-ROM.*

Common Core State Standards

Language 5.c. Identify real-life connections between words and their use (e.g., note places at home that are *cozy*).

Content Knowledge

Build Oral Vocabulary

INTRODUCE AMAZING WORDS Display p. 2 of the *Sing with Me* Big Book. Tell children they are going to sing about a girl who wants a pet. Ask children to listen for the Amazing Words *career, service,* and *tool* as you sing. Sing the song again and have children join you.

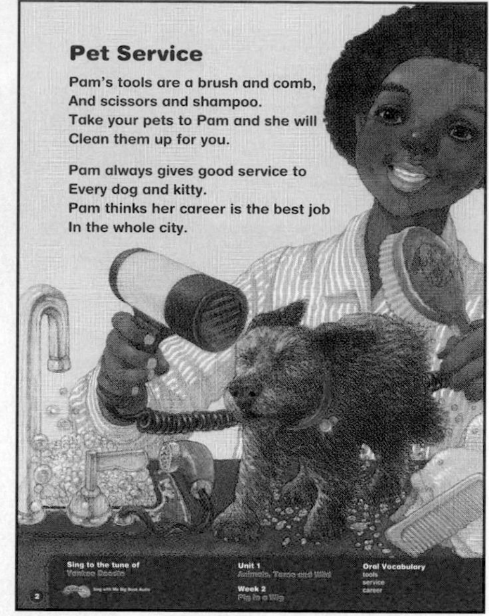

Pet Service
Pam's tools are a brush and comb,
And scissors and shampoo.
Take your pets to Pam and she will
Clean them up for you.
Pam always gives good service to
Every dog and kitty.
Pam thinks her career is the best job
In the whole city.

Sing with Me Big Book, p. 2

Amazing Words

You've learned 055 words so far.

You'll learn 008 words this week!

career	sloppy
service	exercise
tool	comfort
scrub	search

Amazing Words Robust Vocabulary Routine

1. **Introduce the Word** Relate the word *career* to the song. Pam thinks her *career* as a groomer is the best job in the whole city. Supply a child-friendly definition. A *career* is a job someone chooses to do for a long time. Have children say the word.
2. **Demonstrate** Provide examples to show meaning. Someone who is interested in helping sick or injured people may choose a *career* as a nurse or doctor. Someone who is interested in helping sick or injured animals may choose a *career* as a veterinarian, or vet.
3. **Apply** Have children demonstrate their understanding. Name some *careers* that you know about or think are interesting.
4. **Display the Word** Run your hand under the chunks *ca-reer* as you read the word.

See p. OV•2 to teach *service* and *tool.*

Routines Flip Chart

AMAZING WORDS AT WORK Have children look at the picture on p. 2 of the *Sing with Me* Big Book.

- Pam has a *career* as a groomer. What other *careers* can you have with animals? Use the word *career* in your answer. (Possible response: You can have a career as a vet if you want to work with animals.)
- Pam is providing a *service* to help the dog in the picture. What is she doing? (She is grooming the dog.) How is this a *service?* Use the word *service* in your answer. (Possible response: This is a service because Pam is helping the dog look and feel better.)
- Describe which tools Pam is using in the picture and how the tools help her. (Pam is using a hair dryer and a brush. These tools help to make the dog dry and clean.)

APPLY AMAZING WORDS Have children demonstrate their understanding of the Amazing Words by completing these sentences orally.

My ______ has a **career** as a ______.

A ______ provides **service** to ______.

A ______ is a **tool** I use to ______.

Corrective feedback | **If...** children have difficulty using the Amazing Words, **then...** remind them of the definitions and provide opportunities for children to use the words in sentences.

Access for All

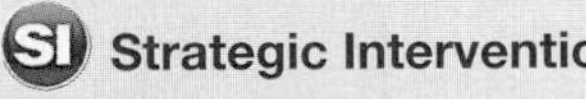

Strategic Intervention

Sentence Production If children drop *is* from the third sentence, say the sentence, stressing the verb, and have children repeat it.

Visual Aids Revisit pages 38–39 in the Student Edition to help children understand the Amazing Words. Use the photographs to provide visual examples of each word while providing definitions. Ask children to point out details in each photo that are related to each Amazing Word. For example: The man has a *career* as a fireman. He provides a *service* by saving the cat. His *tools* include an axe and a hose.

Support Sentence Production Use gestures and pantomime to help children complete the sentences.

Common Core State Standards
Foundational Skills 2.c. Isolate and pronounce initial, medial vowel, and final sounds (phonemes) in spoken single-syllable words.
Also Foundational Skills 2.b., 2.d.
Phonemic Awareness
Let's Listen for
Sounds
• Find five things that contain the short *i* sound in the middle of the word.
• Find something that has the short *i* sound at the beginning of the word. Say the word.
• Find four things that rhyme with *sick*. Say each word.
• Find something that rhymes with *six*. Say the sound at the end of that word.
• Find something that rhymes with *wish*. Say each sound in the word.
Read Together
READING STREET ONLINE
SOUND-SPELLING CARDS
www.ReadingStreet.com
Ms. Ann
40
41
Student Edition, pp. 40–41

Common Core State Standards

Foundational Skills 2.b. Orally produce single-syllable words by blending sounds (phonemes), including consonant blends. **Foundational Skills 2.c.** Isolate and pronounce initial, medial vowel, and final sounds (phonemes) in spoken single-syllable words. **Also Foundational Skills 2.d., 3.**

Skills Trace

Short *i*: *i*

Introduce U1W2D1

Practice U1W2D3; U1W2D4

Reteach/Review U1W2D5; U1W3D4

Assess/Test Weekly Test U1W2
Benchmark Test U1

KEY: U=Unit W=Week D=Day

Phonemic Awareness

Distinguish /i/

INTRODUCE Read the first two bullet points on page 40. What animal is going to the vet? (a pig) The middle sound in *pig* is /i/. Have children identify other items whose names contain the short *i* sound. (dish, fish, list, twins, stick) What are the fish doing? (jumping in the water) The first sound in the word *in* is /i/. Have children identify something whose name begins with the short *i* sound. (itch)

MODEL Listen to the sounds in the word *in:* /i/ /n/. There are two sounds. Let's blend those sounds to make a word: /i/ /n/, *in.* Continue with *pig.* Guide children as they distinguish /i/ in these words: *dish, twins, stick, itch.*

Corrective feedback	**If...** children make an error, **then...** model by sounding out the word slowly, and have them repeat the word to distinguish the sound /i/.

Phonics

Short *i*: *i*

CONNECT Write the word *sad.* Ask children what they know about the vowel sound in this word. (The vowel sound is short. *Sad* has the short vowel sound /a/.) Explain that today they will learn how to spell and read words with the short vowel sound /i/.

USE SOUND-SPELLING CARD Display Card 11. Point to *i.* The short *i* sound, /i/, is spelled *i.* Have children say /i/ several times as you point to *i.*

Ii

i

Sound-Spelling Card 11

MODEL Display pages 48 and 49 of the story *Pig in a Wig.* Read page 48 and write the word *pig* on the board. In this word, the letter *i* stands for the sound /i/. Segment and blend the sounds: /p/ /i/ /g/. Have children blend the sounds with you. Ask children to find other words in the sentence that end with the same sounds. Write each of the words on the board and have children say the sounds and read the words: *wig, big.*

GROUP PRACTICE Continue segmenting and blending with the word *tick* on page 49 and then the words below. Have children segment and blend with you. Remind children that the letter *i* can stand for the sound /i/.

sip	lit	tin	fit	sick	tick
rib	hit	will	pick	quiz	quit

REVIEW What do you know about reading these words? (The letter *i* at the beginning or in the middle of a word can spell the sound /i/.)

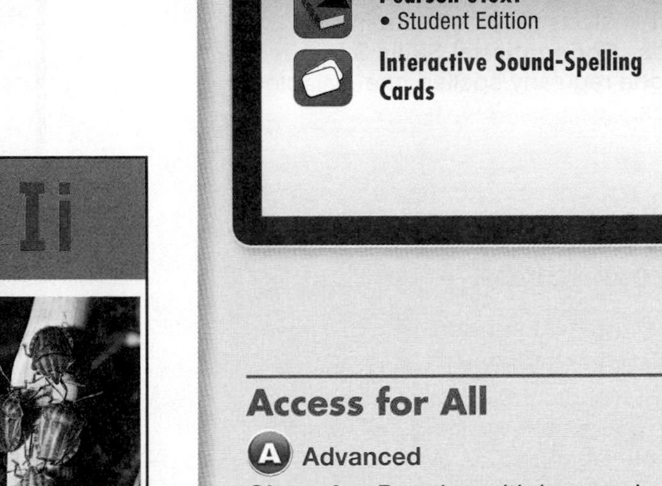

eStreet Interactive
www.ReadingStreet.com

- Pearson eText
  - Student Edition
- Interactive Sound-Spelling Cards

Access for All

A Advanced

Charades Practice with longer short *i* words such as *pinch, giggle, lifting, blink,* and *picnic.* Have children write the words on word cards and then turn them over. Then have children choose a card, read it silently, and act it out for classmates to guess.

Vocabulary Support

You may wish to explain the meaning of this word.

quiz a short test

Professional Development

Visual Learning Many children are visual in their learning. Displaying written words on the board or on a Word Wall helps children not only become more familiar with words and letters but also reminds them of the importance of language and reading.

Pronounce /i/ Sound In many languages, short vowel sounds may not exist or may only have approximations. English language learners may have a difficult time hearing the differences in these sounds. For practice, tell children to listen for the /i/ sound in the word *pig.* Emphasize the sound as you say it. Continue with these words: *hit, bin, sit.*

Common Core State Standards

Foundational Skills 3. Know and apply grade-level phonics and word analysis skills in decoding words. **Foundational Skills 3.b.** Decode regularly spelled one-syllable words.

Access for All

 Strategic Intervention

Blend Short *i* Words Use sound-by-sound blending to model blending *pig.* Write *p* and say its sound, /p/. Write *i* and say its sound, /i/. Write *g* and say its sound, /g/. Then blend the whole word, pointing to each letter as you say its sound. Continue using sound-by-sound blending with the following words: *did, fill, him, win, tip.*

Spelling Pattern

/i/ Spelled *i* The sound /i/ is usually spelled *i* at the beginning or in the middle of a word.

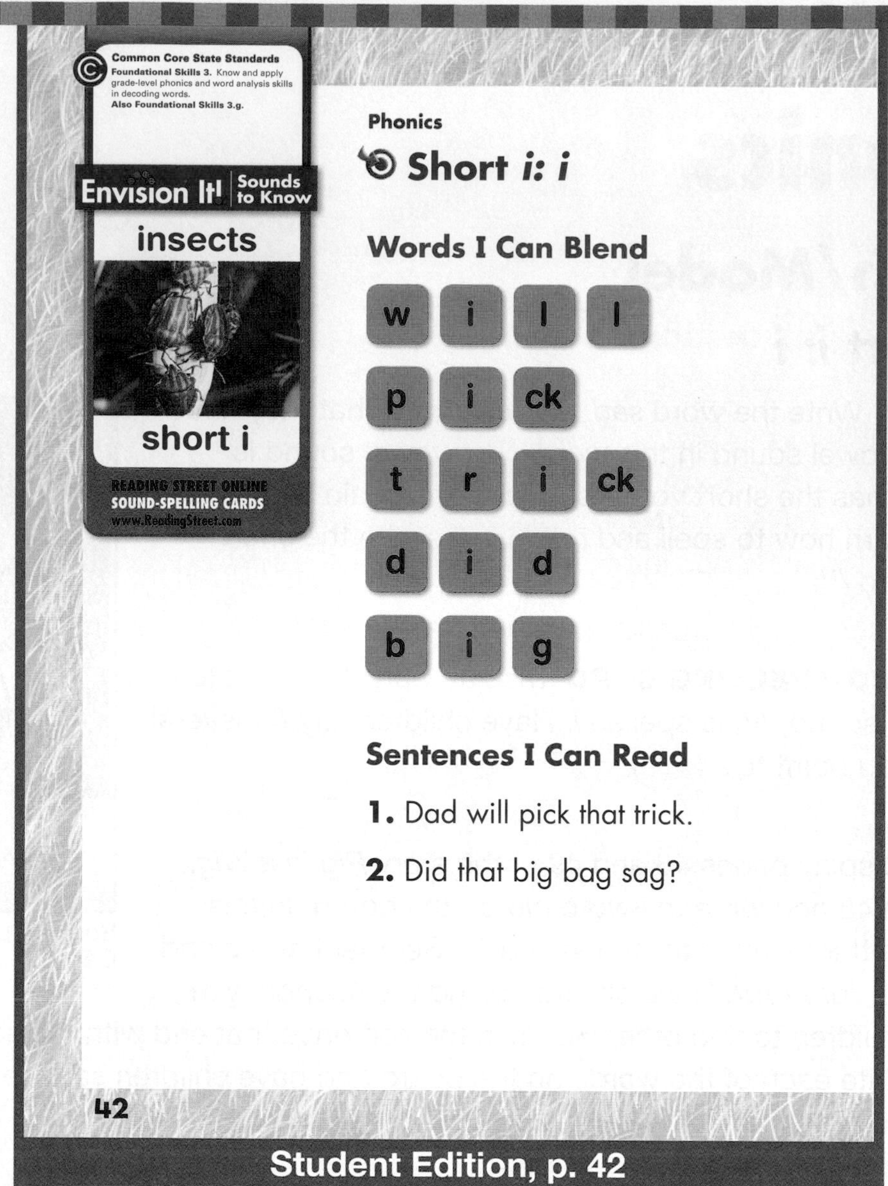

Common Core State Standards
Foundational Skills 3. Know and apply grade-level phonics and word analysis skills in decoding words.
Also Foundational Skills 3.g.
Envision It! Sounds to Know
insects
short i
READING STREET ONLINE
SOUND-SPELLING CARDS
www.ReadingStreet.com
Phonics
Short i: i
Words I Can Blend
w i l l
p i ck
t r i ck
d i d
b i g
Sentences I Can Read
1. Dad will pick that trick.
2. Did that big bag sag?
42

Student Edition, p. 42

Phonics

Guide Practice

BLEND WORDS Have children turn to page 42 in their Student Edition. Look at the picture on this page. I see a picture of *insects.* The word *insects* begins with the letter *i.* When I say *insects,* I hear /i/ at the beginning. The /i/ sound is spelled *i.*

GROUP PRACTICE For each word in "Words I Can Blend," ask for the sound of each letter or group of letters. Make sure that children identify the /i/ sound in each word. Then have children blend the whole word.

Corrective feedback	**If...** children have difficulty blending a word, **then...** model blending the word, and ask children to blend it with you.

DECODE WORDS IN ISOLATION After children can successfully segment and blend the words, point to words in random order and ask children to read them naturally.

DECODE WORDS IN CONTEXT Have children read each of the sentences. Have them identify words in the sentences that have the vowel sound /i/.

Team Talk Pair children and have them take turns reading each of the sentences aloud.

ON THEIR OWN Use *Reader's and Writer's Notebook,* p. 137.

MONITOR PROGRESS Short *i: i*

FORMATIVE ASSESSMENT Write the following words and have the class read them. Notice which words children miss during the group reading. Call on individuals to read some of the words.

bit	rip	in	hit	will	**Spiral Review** Review all initial and final consonants.
sick	bat	kiss	map	back	
sack	nip	pick	lap	dig	

If... children cannot blend short *i* words at this point,

then... use the Small Group Time Strategic Intervention lesson, p. SG•24, to reteach /i/ spelled *i.* Continue to monitor children's progress using other instructional opportunities during the week. See the Skills Trace on p. 40–41.

Pig in a Wig

Name ______

Say the word for each picture.
Write i on the line if you hear the **short i** sound.

pig

1. k i ck
2. h i ll
3. t ___ ck
4. f i n
5. p i n
6. d ___ g
7. w i g
8. z i p

Circle the word to finish each sentence. **Write** it on the line.

9. I will go. (will) wall
10. Sam hid the mat. hip (hid)

School + Home **Home Activity** Your child practiced creating words with the short i sound heard in *pig.* Help your child make up fun rhymes using short i words, such as *The big pig in the wig can dig and do a jig.*

Phonics Short i 137

Reader's and Writer's Notebook, p. 137

Support Phonics English learners from various language backgrounds may pronounce short *i* like the long *e* sound *see.* Help children practice saying and writing word pairs such as *bit/beet; fit/feet; grin/green.*

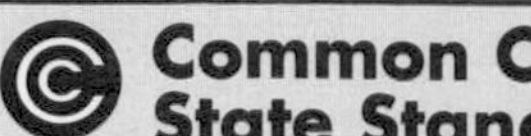

Common Core State Standards

Foundational Skills 3. Know and apply grade-level phonics and word analysis skills in decoding words. **Foundational Skills 3.b.** Decode regularly spelled one-syllable words. **Foundational Skills 3.g.** Recognize and read grade-appropriate irregularly spelled words.

Decodable Reader 2A

If children need help, then...

Read *Did They Win?*

DECODE WORDS IN ISOLATION Have children turn to page 121. Have children decode each word.

REVIEW HIGH-FREQUENCY WORDS Review the previously taught words *they, the, look,* and *to.* Have children read each word as you point to it on the Word Wall.

PREVIEW DECODABLE READER Have children read the title and preview the story. Tell them they will read words with the short vowel sound *i.*

DECODE WORDS IN CONTEXT Pair children for reading and listen as they decode. One child begins. Children read the entire story, switching readers after each page. Partners reread the story. This time the other child begins.

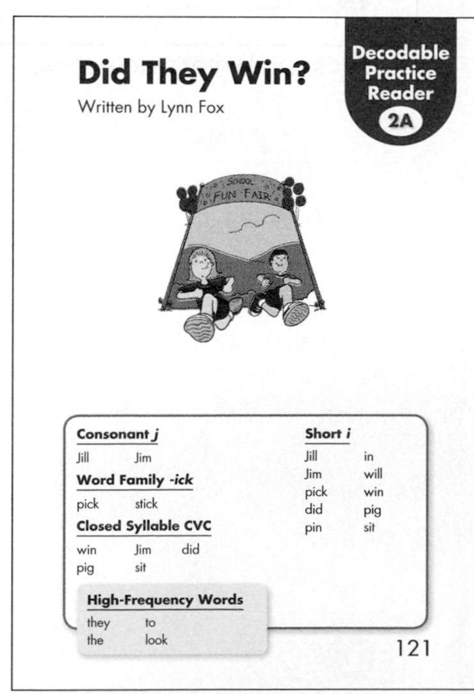

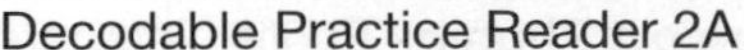
Decodable Practice Reader 2A

Corrective feedback	**If...** children have difficulty decoding a word, **then...** refer them to the Sound-Spelling Cards to identify the sounds in the word. Then prompt them to blend the word. • What is the new word? • Is the new word a word you know? • Does it make sense in the story?

CHECK DECODING AND COMPREHENSION Have children retell the story to include characters, setting, and events. Then have children find words with the short /i/ sound in the story. Explain that some words with these letters will have an *-ll* ending. Children should supply *Jill, Jim, pick, did, pin, in, will, win, pig,* and *sit.* Ask how they know these words have the short *i* sound. (The sound /i/ is usually spelled *i* at the beginning or in the middle of the word.)

Reread for Fluency

REREAD DECODABLE READER Have children reread Decodable Practice Reader 2A to develop automaticity decoding words with the short *i* sound.

Routine Oral Rereading

1. **Read** Have children read the entire book orally.
2. **Reread** To achieve optimal fluency, children should reread the text three or four times.
3. **Corrective Feedback** Listen as children read. Provide corrective feedback regarding their fluency and decoding.

Routines Flip Chart

Access for All

SI Strategic Intervention

Pronunciation Tell children that when they say the short *i* sound, their mouths are open and their tongues are slightly lowered. Have them practice with the following words: *did, lid, wig, pig, bib, zip.*

Short *i*: *i*

Beginning Before children read, lead them on a picture walk through the story. Point out and pronounce the words that have the short *i* sound. Then write a pictured word and have children pronounce it and find its picture.

Intermediate Before reading, help children pronounce the words with the short *i* sound in the story title, *Did They Win?* Then have them use the words *did* and *win* to make a prediction about what the story will be about.

Advanced After reading, have children find the words with the short *i* sound and use them to tell what might happen next, now that Jill and Jim won.

Common Core State Standards

Foundational Skills 3.g. Recognize and read grade-appropriate irregularly spelled words. **Language 2.d.** Use conventional spelling for words with common spelling patterns and for frequently occurring irregular words. **Language 2.e.** Spell untaught words phonetically, drawing on phonemic awareness and spelling conventions.

Access for All

A Advanced

Extend Spelling Challenge children who spell words correctly to spell more difficult words such as *into, limit, picnic, quick, rapid,* and *within.*

Phonics/Spelling Generalization

Short *i* Each spelling word is a short *i* word, which has the short *i* sound.

Name ______________ Pig in a Wig

Short *i* Words

Look at the word. Say it. Listen for the short *i* sound.

	Write each word.	Check it.
1. in	in	in
2. it	it	it
3. did	did	did
4. sit	sit	sit
5. six	six	six
6. fix	fix	fix
7. lip	lip	lip
8. mix	mix	mix
9. pin	pin	pin
10. wig	wig	wig

Words to Read

11. she	she	12. take	take

School + Home **Home Activity** Your child is learning to spell words with the short *i* vowel sound. To practice at home, have your child pronounce each word and spell it out loud.

DVD•38 Spelling Short *i* Words

Let's Practice It! TR DVD•38

Spelling Pretest

Short *i* Words

DICTATE SPELLING WORDS Dictate the spelling words and read the sentences. Have children write the words. If needed, segment the words for children, clarify the pronunciations, and give meanings of words. Have children check their pretests and correct misspelled words.

1. six*	I turned **six** years old yesterday.
2. lip	I have an upper **lip** and a lower **lip.**
3. in*	I live **in** a house.
4. wig	The clown had a pink **wig** on his head.
5. it*	I picked the flower and put **it** in water.
6. did*	What **did** you do today?
7. mix*	I can **mix** the batter with a spoon.
8. sit	I like to **sit** and watch the game.
9. pin	She wore a pretty **pin** on her shirt.
10. fix*	Could you **fix** my broken bike?

* Words marked with asterisks come from the selection *Pig in a Wig.*

ON THEIR OWN Use Let's Practice It! p. 38 on the *Teacher Resources DVD-ROM.*

ELL

If... children need more scaffolding and practice with **Phonemic Awareness and Phonics,** **then...** use the ELL activities on pp. DI•34–DI•35 in the Teacher Resources section on SuccessNet.

Day 1 SMALL GROUP TIME • Differentiate Phonics, p. SG•18

OL On-Level

- **Practice Phonics** Additional Short *i* Words
- **Read** Decodable Reader *Did They Win?*

SI Strategic Intervention

- **Reteach Phonics** Blend Short *i* Words
- **Read** Decodable Reader *Did They Win?*

A Advanced

- **Extend Phonics** More Short *i* Words
- **Read** Advanced Selection for Short *i* Words
- **Introduce** Inquiry Project

High-Frequency Words

Words I Can Read

she

take

what

up

Sentences I Can Read

1. She will take it back.

2. What did Bill pick up?

43

Student Edition, p. 43

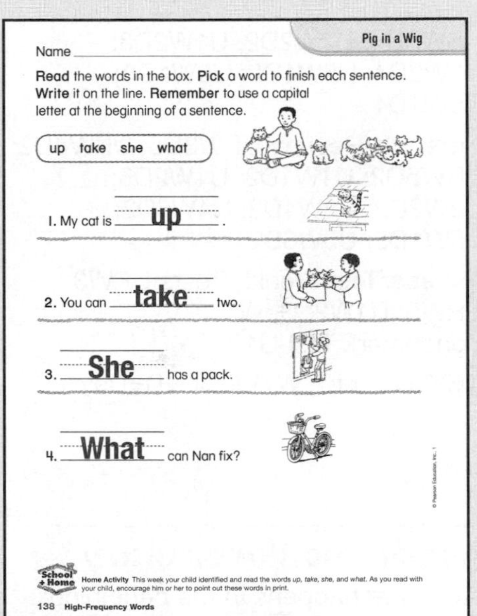
Name

Pig in a Wig

Read the words in the box. Pick a word to finish each sentence. Write it on the line. Remember to use a capital letter at the beginning of a sentence.

up take she what

1. My cat is up.

2. You can take two.

3. She has a pack.

4. What can Nan fix?

Home Activity This week your child identified and read the words up, take, she, and what. As you read with your child, encourage him or her to point out these words in print.

138 High-Frequency Words

Reader's and Writer's Notebook, p. 138

High-Frequency Words

Routine Nondecodable Words

1. **Say and Spell** Some words we learn by remembering the letters. Point to *she.* Have children say and spell each word letter by letter.

2. **Identify Familiar Letter-Sounds** Point to the first two letters in *she.* What are these letters? *(sh)* Say the sound for *sh* and have children repeat.

3. **Show Meaning** Tell me a sentence using the word *she.* Repeat.

Routines Flip Chart

READ Have children read the page aloud. Add the words to the Word Wall.

ON THEIR OWN Use *Reader's and Writer's Notebook,* p. 138.

Survival Vocabulary Have children practice using the word *she* to talk about a person. Children might say, ***She*** *likes the cat.*

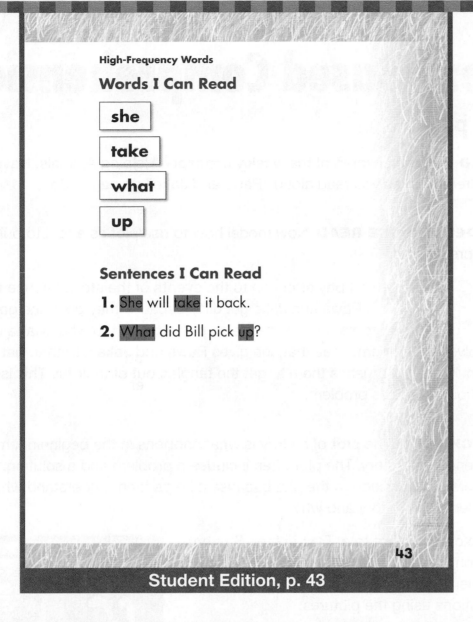

Zoom in on

Common Core State Standards

Literature 3. Describe characters, settings, and major events in a story, using key details.

Skills Trace

Plot

Introduce URW3D1; URW5D1; U1W2D1; U5W1D1

Practice URW3D2; URW3D3; URW3D4; URW5D2; URW5D3; URW5D4; U1W2D2; U1W2D3; U1W2D4; U5W1D2; U5W1D3; U5W1D4

Reteach/Review URW3D5; URW4D2; URW5D2; U1W1D2; U1W2D5; U2W2D2; U3W4D2; U4W6D2; U5W1D5; U5W6D2

Assess/Test Weekly Tests URW3; URW5; U1W2; U5W1
Benchmark Test U1

KEY: U=Unit W=Week D=Day

Academic Vocabulary

plot what happens in the beginning, middle, and end of a story

Pig in a Wig

Name ____________

Read the story.
Circle the answer to each question about the story.

Jill and Meg play with a [ball].
They hit the [ball].
They pop the [ball]!
Jill and Meg are sad.
But Dad has a [balloon] for them.
Jill and Meg play with the [balloon].

1. What happens first?
   Jill and Meg play with a [ball]. (circled)
   Jill and Meg are sad.
2. What happens that is sad?
   Jill and Meg kick the [ball].
   Jill and Meg pop the [ball]. (circled)
3. What happens so Jill and Meg are not sad?
   Dad has a [balloon] for Jill and Meg. (circled)
   Dad has a doll for Jill and Meg.
4. What happens last?
   Jill and Meg hit the [ball].
   Jill and Meg play with the [balloon]. (circled)

School + Home **Home Activity** Your child identified the plot, or what happens in a story, and the problem and solution in a story. Read a short fairy tale and have your child identify a problem and solution.

Comprehension Plot 139

Reader's and Writer's Notebook, p. 139

Text-Based Comprehension

Plot

READ Remind children of the weekly concept—Helping Animals. Have children listen as you read aloud "Paws and Jake" on page 43b.

MODEL A CLOSE READ Now model how to use plot as a tool to build comprehension.

When I read, I pay attention to the events of the story. I notice that in the story, Paws and Jake get dirty because they go in the garden. This is a problem for Marta. I also pay attention to what Marta does to solve her problem. I see that she gives Paws and Jake a bath to get them clean. Then she brushes them to get the tangles out of their fur. This is the solution to Marta's problem.

TEACH PLOT The **plot** of a story is what happens in the beginning, middle, and end of the story. The plot often includes a problem and a solution. Good readers pay attention to the plot because it helps them understand what happens in the story and why.

Have children turn to p. EI•5 in their Student Edition. These pictures show an example of problem and solution in plot. Discuss these questions using the pictures:

- What is happening in the pictures? (The bunnies are on a picnic.)
- What problem do the bunnies have in the middle picture? (The sun is making them very hot.)
- How do the bunnies solve their problem? (They put up an umbrella to block the sun.)

Student Edition, p. EI•5

GUIDE PRACTICE Now reread "Paws and Jake." After rereading, have children name other events that make up the story's plot. (Marta takes the puppies for a walk. Marta has an idea for a pet sitting service.) What other problem is there in the story? (The puppies have a lot of energy and need exercise.) What does Marta do to solve this problem? (She takes them around the block for a walk.)

APPLY Use *Reader's and Writer's Notebook,* p. 139.

Teacher Read Aloud

Paws and Jake

"Paws! Jake! Where are you?" Marta called from the back door. She didn't see her puppies anywhere in the backyard. Suddenly, two furry pups ran out of her mother's garden. They were covered in dirt!

"Oh, no," said Marta. "You two are a mess! You know you shouldn't be in Mama's tomato plants," she scolded. Paws and Jake just looked up at her and wagged their tails.

Marta brought her puppies inside and turned on the bathwater. She made sure the water wasn't too hot. In went Paws. In went Jake. Marta washed both of them while they splashed and played.

Once Marta dried the pups, she saw how tangled their hair was. "My goodness," said Marta. "This won't do at all." She found the dog brush and used it as a tool to get all the tangles out. "I could have a career as a groomer!" giggled Marta.

After Marta finished brushing them, Paws and Jake looked like their old selves again. Paws jumped up and down and Jake began running in circles.

"You both certainly have a lot of energy!" said Marta. "Would you like to go for a walk?"

Paws and Jake bounced up and down as if to say, "Yes! Yes!"

Marta put their leashes on and took them out for a long walk around the block. As she walked, Marta thought about starting her own dog sitting service. She could take care of other people's dogs for a small fee. That would give her extra money to buy treats and toys for Paws and Jake.

Marta liked her idea so much that she wanted to run home to tell her mother. "Paws! Jake! I'll race you home!" she shouted playfully.

Bridge to Common Core

KEY IDEAS AND DETAILS

As children identify the plot or sequence of events in a selection, they recognize details that tell when things happen and sequence words that indicate the order in which things happen. Retelling the selection helps children focus on the important events. Asking questions about the plot helps children better understand what happens in the beginning, middle, and end of a selection.

Support Comprehension Use the modified Read Aloud from the *ELL Support Lessons* on the *Teacher Resources DVD-ROM* to build content knowledge. Preview the compound words *backyard* and *bathwater* using visuals, and display a handful of string to visually support the meaning of the word *tangle*.

Common Core State Standards

Writing 3. Write narratives in which they recount two or more appropriately sequenced events, include some details regarding what happened, use temporal words to signal event order, and provide some sense of closure. **Language 2.** Demonstrate command of the conventions of standard English capitalization, punctuation, and spelling when writing. **Also Language 1.j.**

Academic Vocabulary

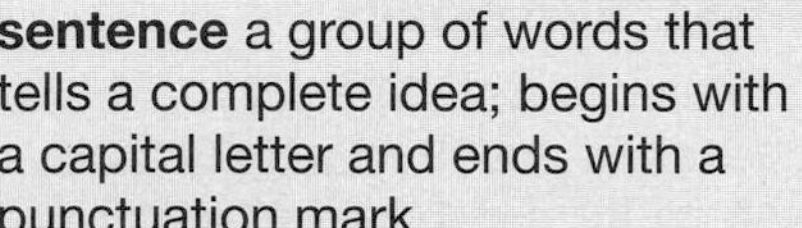

sentence a group of words that tells a complete idea; begins with a capital letter and ends with a punctuation mark

subject word or words that tell what the sentence is about

characters the people or animals in a story

fantasy a made-up story that could not really happen

Daily Fix-It

1. Ficks the wigg.
   Fix the wig.
2. the pig did id.
   The pig did it.

Discuss the Daily Fix-It corrections with children. Review sentence capitalization and punctuation, /ks/ spelled *x,* /t/ spelled *t,* and the spelling of *wig.*

Conventions

Subjects of Sentences

MAKE CONNECTIONS Today we listened to a story about Marta and her two dogs. Let's tell sentences about Marta. List children's responses. Marta is the *subject* of these sentences.

TEACH Briefly discuss word order with children. Write these sentences: *Bark to the likes dog. The dog likes to bark.* Track the words as you read each sentence and identify the sentence with the correct word order. Explain that a sentence makes sense when the words are in the correct order and you understand what it means. Explain that a **subject** tells who or what the sentence is about. It names a person, place, animal, or thing. Write the sentence *The teacher went home.* Explain that *the teacher* is the subject of the sentence because it names who the sentence is about.

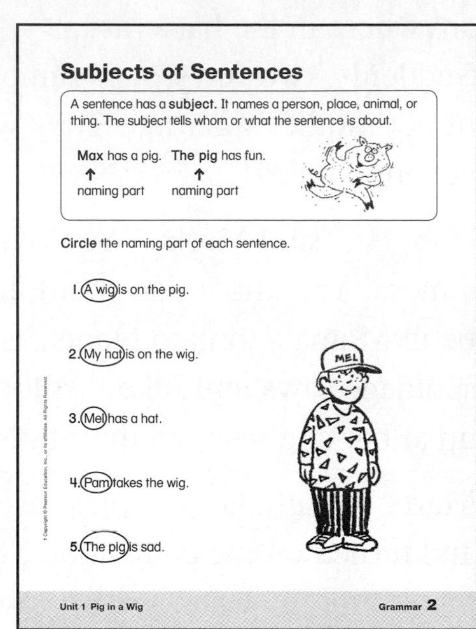

Subjects of Sentences

A sentence has a **subject.** It names a person, place, animal, or thing. The subject tells whom or what the sentence is about.

Max has a pig. **The pig** has fun.
naming part — naming part

Circle the naming part of each sentence.

1. A wig is on the pig.
2. My hat is on the wig.
3. Mel has a hat.
4. Pam takes the wig.
5. The pig is sad.

Unit 1 Pig in a Wig — Grammar 2

Grammar Transparency 2 TR DVD

MODEL Display Grammar Transparency 2. Read the top information aloud. Model identifying the subject, or naming part, in each example. Then read the directions and model number 1.

GUIDE PRACTICE Continue with items 2–5, having children identify the subject, or naming part, of each sentence.

APPLY Have the class complete these sentence frames orally using subjects.

1. **My ______ needs a bath.**
2. **______ ran up the tree.**
3. **______ caught the ball.**

Team Talk Pair children and have them take turns replacing the subject in the sentence frame: *The cat is in the box.* Remind them that a subject names a person, place, animal, or thing. Encourage them to be creative with their subjects.

Writing

Fantasy Story

Mini-Lesson Read Like a Writer

- **Introduce** This week you will write a **fantasy** story. A fantasy is a made-up story that could never really happen. In a fantasy story, **characters** do things that real people and animals cannot do.

Prompt	Write a fantasy story about a person who helps an animal. Draw a picture for your story.
Trait	Conventions
Mode	Narrative

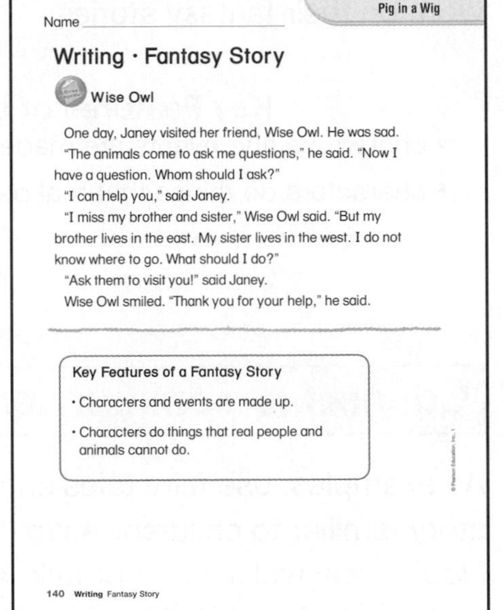

Name

Pig in a Wig

Writing • Fantasy Story

Wise Owl

One day, Janey visited her friend, Wise Owl. He was sad. "The animals come to ask me questions," he said. "Now I have a question. Whom should I ask?"

"I can help you," said Janey.

"I miss my brother and sister," Wise Owl said. "But my brother lives in the east. My sister lives in the west. I do not know where to go. What should I do?"

"Ask them to visit you!" said Janey.

Wise Owl smiled. "Thank you for your help," he said.

Key Features of a Fantasy Story
- Characters and events are made up.
- Characters do things that real people and animals cannot do.

140 Writing Fantasy Story

Reader's and Writer's Notebook, p. 140

- **Examine Model Text** Let's listen to a fantasy story. Track the print as you read aloud "Wise Owl" on *Reader's and Writer's Notebook,* p. 140. Have children follow along.

- **Key Features** Who are the two characters in this story? (Janey and Wise Owl) Help children find and circle the names. Ask if Janey and Wise Owl act like a real girl and bird. (no) Ask what they do that real people and animals cannot do. (talk to each other) Help children underline short phrases in the story that tell about the characters doing things that real people and animals do not do, such as *Wise Owl said.*

This is a made-up story that could never happen. The characters do things that real people and animals cannot do. Real girls do not have owls for friends. Real owls do not talk.

Writing to Sources Use More Connect the Texts on pp. 221–259 to guide children in writing text-based responses within various forms and modes.

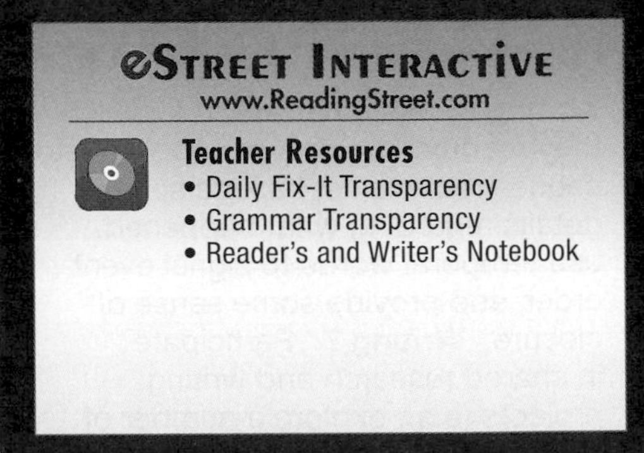

Write Guy *by Jeff Anderson*

Let's Use Books

Let's use books to solve problems! If a child wants to write dialogue, he or she can look at how the author of a recently read story wrote dialogue. Have the child ask himself or herself, "What do I like about how these characters speak?" Young writers can use models.

Bridge to Common Core

TEXT TYPES AND PURPOSES

This week children write a fantasy story about a person who helps an animal.

Narrative Writing

As children develop writing skills for creating a fantasy story, they use narrative writing to explore helping animals. The activities help children develop effective writing techniques and well-chosen details as they write their fantasy story. Throughout the week, children will improve the range and content of their writing through daily mini-lessons.

5-Day Plan

DAY 1	Read Like a Writer
DAY 2	Use Imagination
DAY 3	Writing Trait: Conventions
DAY 4	Revise: Adding a Sentence
DAY 5	Proofread

Conventions To provide children with practice on sentences, use the modified grammar lessons in the *ELL Handbook.*

Common Core State Standards

Writing 3. Write narratives in which they recount two or more appropriately sequenced events, include some details regarding what happened, use temporal words to signal event order, and provide some sense of closure. **Writing 7.** Participate in shared research and writing projects (e.g., explore a number of "how-to" books on a given topic and use them to write a sequence of instructions). **Writing 8.** With guidance and support from adults, recall information from experiences or gather information from provided sources to answer a question.

Writing

Review Key Features

Review key features of a fantasy story with children. You may want to post these key features in the classroom to allow children to refer to them as they work on their fantasy stories.

Key Features of a Fantasy Story

- characters and events are made up
- characters do things that real people and animals cannot do

Connect to Familiar Texts

As examples, use fairy tales such as *Little Red Riding Hood* or another fantasy story familiar to children. A wolf that can talk is a character in *Little Red Riding Hood.* Real wolves do not talk. Ask children to think of other examples of fantasy stories. Ask them to tell what the characters in their examples do that real people and animals do not do.

Routine Quick Write for Fluency

Team Talk

1. **Talk** Read these questions aloud, and have children respond with sentences.
   Who are people who help animals?
   How do they help animals?

2. **Write** Have children write short sentences to answer the questions. Make sure their sentences are complete, begin with capital letters, and end with periods.

3. **Share** Partners can read their answers to one another.

Routines Flip Chart

Research and Inquiry

Step 1 Identify and Focus Topic

TEACH Display and review the K-W-L chart that explores this week's question: *Who helps animals?* What do you want to know about people who help animals? Ask children to share their interests. Help them understand that many types of people help animals.

Think Aloud **MODEL** I have always wondered about what a vet does every day. I know that vets help animals feel better, but I'm not sure how. What do vets do for animals? I would like to learn more about that. I am also curious about dog trainers. I know that they can help dogs be obedient, but I have always wondered how.

GUIDE PRACTICE Give children time to think of questions they could ask about people who help animals. Record the questions in a list.

21st Century Skills

Internet Guy *Don Leu*

Weekly Inquiry Project

STEP 1	Identify and Focus Topic
STEP 2	Research Skill
STEP 3	Gather and Record Information
STEP 4	Synthesize
STEP 5	Communicate

Wrap Up Your Day!

- ✔ **Phonics: Short *i*** Write the word *pigs* and ask children how the sound /i/ is spelled in *pigs.* (/i/ is spelled *i.*) Have children name other words that have the sound /i/.
- ✔ **Spelling: Short *i* Words** Have children name the spelling for each sound in *wig.* Write the spelling as children write the letters in the air. Continue with *six, lip,* and *did.*
- ✔ **Content Knowledge** Ask children to recall what happened in the Read Aloud "Paws and Jake." How did Marta clean her pets? (She gave them a bath and brushed them.)
- ✔ **Homework** Send home this week's Family Times Newsletter from Let's Practice It! pp. 33–34 on the *Teacher Resources DVD-ROM.*

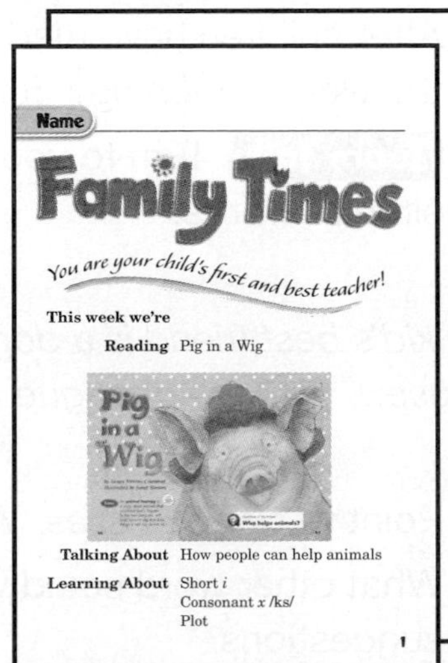

Name
Family Times
You are your child's first and best teacher!
This week we're
Reading Pig in a Wig
Pig in a Wig
Talking About How people can help animals
Learning About Short i
Consonant x /ks/
Plot
1

Let's Practice It!
TR DVD•33–34

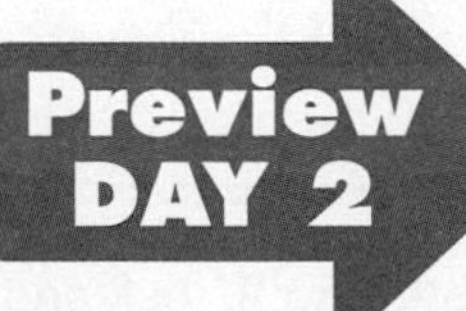

Tell children that tomorrow they will read about a sick pig that gets help.

DAY 2 at a Glance

Content Knowledge
Oral Vocabulary

Phonemic Awareness
Segment and Blend Phonemes

Phonics/Spelling
Short *i: i*
Consonant *x*/ks/

High-Frequency Words
she, take, up, what

Selection Vocabulary
play
Alphabetize

Text-Based Comprehension
Plot
Summarize

Conventions
Subjects of Sentences

Writing
Fantasy Story

Handwriting
Letters *Ii* and *Xx*/Letter Spacing

Research and Inquiry
Research Skill: Media Center/ Library

Materials

- Student Edition
- Sing with Me Big Book
- Big Book
- Sound-Spelling Cards
- Reader's and Writer's Notebook
- Decodable Reader 2B

Common Core State Standards

Speaking/Listening 2. Ask and answer questions about key details in a text read aloud or information presented orally or through other media. **Language 5.c.** Identify real-life connections between words and their use (e.g., note places at home that are *cozy*). **Also Language 6.**

Content Knowledge

Helping Animals

EXPAND THE CONCEPT To reinforce concepts and to focus children's attention, have children sing "Pet Service" from the *Sing with Me* Big Book. How does Pam help the dog feel better? (She helps him feel better by cleaning and cutting his hair.)

Build Oral Language

INTRODUCE AMAZING WORDS Display the Big Book *A Kid's Best Friend.* Read the title and identify the author. Explain that in the story, the author uses some Amazing Words. Read the story and have children listen for the words *scrub* and *sloppy.*

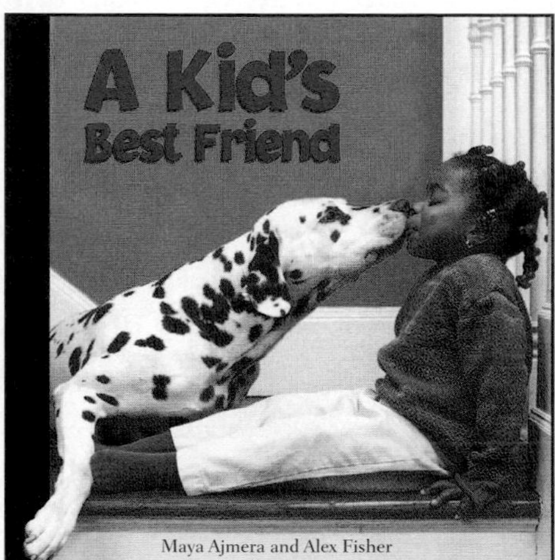

Big Book

TALK ABOUT SENTENCES AND WORDS Reread this sentence from the Big Book.

Washing and scrubbing your dog is vital to its health.

- Have children repeat the sentence with you. What does *washing and scrubbing your dog* mean? (cleaning your dog)
- What other word could we use in place of *scrubbing?* Have children share their suggestions.
- After children have tried other words, ask: Why do you think the author chose the word *scrubbing?* (It is the best way to describe how to clean a dog.)
- **Team Talk** Turn to your partner and say the sentence again using your simpler words.

A kid's best friend is a dog with big floppy ears, a wagging tail, and a wet nose… with a big tongue and sloppy kisses to lick and tickle your face clean.

- Point to *sloppy kisses.* What does *sloppy* mean? (messy)
- What other word could we use in place of *sloppy?* Have children share their suggestions.
- **Team Talk** Turn to your partner and try some other words in place of *sloppy.*

Build Oral Vocabulary

Amazing Words Robust Vocabulary Routine

1. **Introduce the Word** Relate the word *scrub* to the book. The children *scrub* the dog to get it clean. Supply a child-friendly definition. When you *scrub* something, you rub it hard to make it clean. Have children say the word.
2. **Demonstrate** Provide examples to show meaning. I had to *scrub* the rug to get the spot out. My dad *scrubs* the bathtub with a sponge.
3. **Apply** Have children demonstrate their understanding. Show me how you would *scrub* your hands to get them clean.
4. **Display the Word** Point out the sound-spelling *scr* /s/ /k/ /r/ at the beginning of *scrub.*

See p. OV•2 to teach *sloppy.*

Routines Flip Chart

ADD TO THE CONCEPT MAP Discuss the different ways that people can help animals.

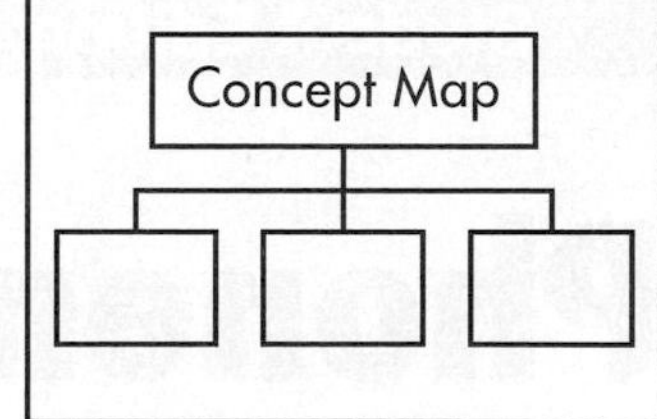

- How does the groomer in "Pet Service" help pets? (She scrubs pets to make them clean and uses tools to keep them neat, not sloppy.) Let's add this information to our K-W-L map.
- What kinds of tools does a groomer use? (A groomer uses brushes, combs, scissors, and shampoo.) Let's include this on our map also.
- In yesterday's Read Aloud "Paws and Jake," Marta took care of her pets. What did she do? (She cleaned, brushed, and exercised them.) Let's add *People take care of pets by exercising, cleaning, and brushing them* to our map. What else do we want to know about who helps animals? (Possible answer: Who helps dogs eat right?) Let's add that question to our map.

Amazing Words

career	sloppy
service	exercise
tool	comfort
scrub	search

Access for All

SI Strategic Intervention

Extend the Concept Guide children to choose materials at their reading level and gather information to extend their understanding of the weekly concept. Encourage children to present what they learned to the class.

Reinforce Vocabulary Use the Day 2 instruction on ELL Poster 2 to reinforce meanings of the high-frequency words.

Academic Language Help English learners understand the expression "running like the wind" in *A Kid's Best Friend.* Explain that dogs don't really run like the wind blows. This is just a way of saying that they run very fast. Ask children to use "running like the wind" to describe another animal that runs very fast.

Common Core State Standards
Foundational Skills 2.c. Isolate and pronounce initial, medial vowel, and final sounds (phonemes) in spoken single-syllable words.
Also Foundational Skills 2.b., 2.d.
Phonemic Awareness
Let's Listen for
Sounds
Read Together
• Find five things that contain the short *i* sound in the middle of the word.
• Find something that has the short *i* sound at the beginning of the word. Say the word.
• Find four things that rhyme with *sick*. Say each word.
• Find something that rhymes with *six*. Say the sound at the end of that word.
• Find something that rhymes with *wish*. Say each sound in the word.
READING STREET ONLINE
SOUND-SPELLING CARDS
www.ReadingStreet.com
Ms. Ann
40
41

Student Edition, pp. 40–41

Common Core State Standards

Foundational Skills 2.b. Orally produce single-syllable words by blending sounds (phonemes), including consonant blends. **Foundational Skills 2.d.** Segment spoken single-syllable words into their complete sequence of individual sounds (phonemes). **Foundational Skills 3.** Know and apply grade-level phonics and word analysis skills in decoding words.

Skills Trace

Consonant *x*/ks/

Introduce U1W2D2

Practice U1W2D3; U1W2D4

Reteach/Review U1W2D5

Assess/Test Weekly Test U1W2
Benchmark Test U1

KEY: U=Unit W=Week D=Day

Phonemic Awareness

Segment and Blend Phonemes

MODEL Look at the picture on pages 40–41. I see *six* kittens in the picture. The last sound I hear in *six* is /ks/. I also see a *fox.* The last sound in *fox* is /ks/. Now listen to the sounds in the word *six:* /s/ /i/ /ks/. Let's blend those sounds to make a word: /s/ /i/ /ks/, *six.* Continue with *fox.*

GROUP PRACTICE Guide children as they segment and blend these words from the picture: *box, fix, mix.*

Corrective feedback	**If...** children make an error, **then...** model by segmenting the word, and have them repeat.

ON THEIR OWN Have children segment and blend the following words:

/o/ /ks/ **ox** /t/ /a/ /ks/ **tax** /w/ /a/ /ks/ **wax** /f/ /a/ /ks/ **fax**

Phonics

Teach/Model

Consonant x/ks/

CONNECT Write the words *fox* and *six*. You have already heard these words. What do you know about the final sound in these words? (The final sound is /ks/.) Today you will learn how to spell words that end with the sound /ks/.

Sound-Spelling Card 27

USE SOUND-SPELLING CARD Display Card 27. The sound you hear at the end of *fox* is /ks/. This sound is spelled *x*. Have children say /ks/ several times as you point to *x*. Now I will show you how to write capital *X* and lowercase *x*. Write *X*. Watch as I trace capital *X* with my finger. Now you write capital *X*. Repeat for lowercase *x*.

MODEL Write *six*. In this word, the letter *x* stands for the sound /ks/. Segment and blend *six;* then have children blend with you: /s/ /i/ /ks/. Follow this procedure to model blending *fix*.

GROUP PRACTICE Continue the process. Write the words below and have children blend and read the words with you.

six	fax	ox
tax	mix	box

REVIEW What do you know about reading these words? (The letter *x* at the end of a word spells the sound /ks/.)

Access for All

SI Strategic Intervention

Blend Words with *x*/ks/ If children have difficulty identifying the final /ks/ sound, use sound-by-sound blending to model blending *six*. Write *s* and say its sound, /s/. Write *i* and says its sound, /i/. Write *x* and say its sound, /ks/. Then blend the whole word, pointing to each letter as you say its sound.

Vocabulary Support

You may wish to explain the meaning of this word.

fax a way of sending a picture or document over a telephone line

Visual Support Model isolating sounds while using the pictures on pages 40–41 of the Student Edition as visual support. For example: /b/ /o/ /ks/, *box*. Who can point to the box in the picture? Now let's say the sounds of *box* together: /b/ /o/ /ks/.

Common Core State Standards

Foundational Skills 3. Know and apply grade-level phonics and word analysis skills in decoding words. **Foundational Skills 3.b.** Decode regularly spelled one-syllable words. **Also Foundational Skills 3.g.**

Spelling Pattern

/ks/ spelled *x* The sound /ks/ at the end of a word is usually spelled *x*.

Access for All

Advanced

Use Word Cards Children can practice with longer words with /ks/ spelled *x*. Have children write the following words on word cards, and use each word in a sentence: *sixty, exam, fixing, relax, boxes.*

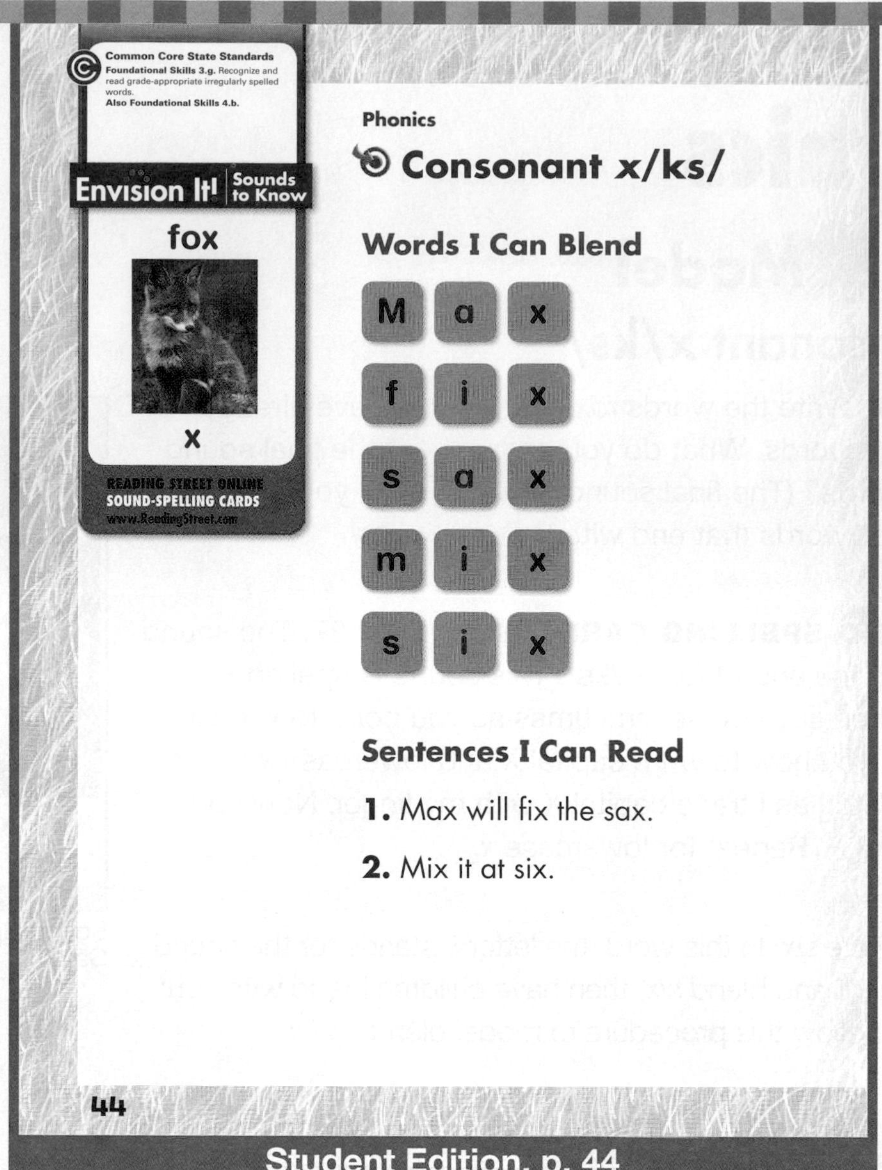

Common Core State Standards
Foundational Skills 3.g. Recognize and read grade-appropriate irregularly spelled words.
Also Foundational Skills 4.b.
Envision It! Sounds to Know
fox
x
READING STREET ONLINE
SOUND-SPELLING CARDS
www.ReadingStreet.com
Phonics
Consonant x/ks/
Words I Can Blend
M a x
f i x
s a x
m i x
s i x
Sentences I Can Read
1. Max will fix the sax.
2. Mix it at six.
44

Student Edition, p. 44

Phonics

BLEND WORDS Have children turn to page 44 in their Student Edition. Look at the picture on this page. I see a picture of a fox. When I say *fox,* I hear /ks/ at the end. In *fox,* /ks/ is spelled *x*.

GROUP PRACTICE For each word in "Words I Can Blend," ask for the sound of each letter. Make sure that children identify the correct sound for the final consonant. Then have children blend the whole word.

Corrective feedback	**If...** children have difficulty blending a word, **then...** model blending the word, and ask children to blend it with you.

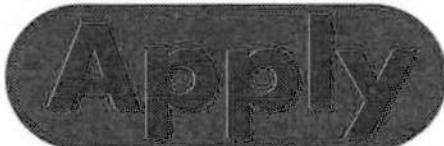

DECODE WORDS IN ISOLATION After children can successfully segment and blend the words, ask them to read the words naturally.

DECODE WORDS IN CONTEXT Have children read each of the sentences. Have them identify words in the sentences that end with the sound /ks/.

Team Talk Pair children and have them take turns reading each of the sentences aloud.

ON THEIR OWN Use *Reader's and Writer's Notebook,* p. 141.

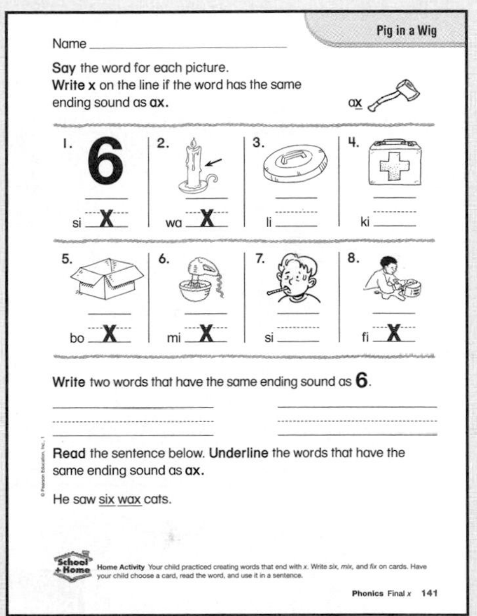

Pig in a Wig

Name ____________

Say the word for each picture.
Write x on the line if the word has the same ending sound as **ax**.

ax

1. si X
2. wa X
3. li ___
4. ki ___
5. bo X
6. mi X
7. si ___
8. fi X

Write two words that have the same ending sound as **6**.

Read the sentence below. **Underline** the words that have the same ending sound as **ax.**

He saw six wax cats.

School + Home **Home Activity** Your child practiced creating words that end with *x*. Write *six, mix,* and *fix* on cards. Have your child choose a card, read the word, and use it in a sentence.

Phonics Final *x* 141

Reader's and Writer's Notebook, p. 141

Consonant x/ks/

FORMATIVE ASSESSMENT Write the following words and have the class read them. Notice which children miss words during the group reading. Call on those individuals to read some of the words.

fix	sax	wax	mix	six	**Spiral Review**
kick	Max	back	fax	pick ←	Row 2 contrasts final *ck* and final *x* in words.

If... children cannot blend final *x* words,

then... use the Small Group Time Strategic Intervention lesson, p. SG•25, to reteach consonant *x*/ks/. Continue to monitor children's progress using other instructional opportunities during the week. See the Skills Trace on p. 44c.

Support Phonics Spanish speakers may delete or substitute consonant sounds at the end of English words because Spanish words often end in vowels. Provide practice pronouncing the final /ks/ in words such as *fix* and *mix.*

DAY 2

Common Core State Standards

Foundational Skills 3. Know and apply grade-level phonics and word analysis skills in decoding words. **Foundational Skills 3.b.** Decode regularly spelled one-syllable words. **Foundational Skills 3.g.** Recognize and read grade-appropriate irregularly spelled words. **Foundational Skills 4.a.** Read on-level text with purpose and understanding.

Decodable Reader 2B

If children need help, then...

Read *Fix It!*

DECODE WORDS IN ISOLATION Have children turn to page 129. Have children decode each word.

REVIEW HIGH-FREQUENCY WORDS Review the previously taught words *do* and *we*. Have children read each word as you point to it on the Word Wall.

PREVIEW Have children read the title and preview the story. Tell them they will read words with the consonant *x*/ks/.

DECODE WORDS IN CONTEXT Pair children for reading and listen as they decode. One child begins. Children read the entire story, switching readers after each page.

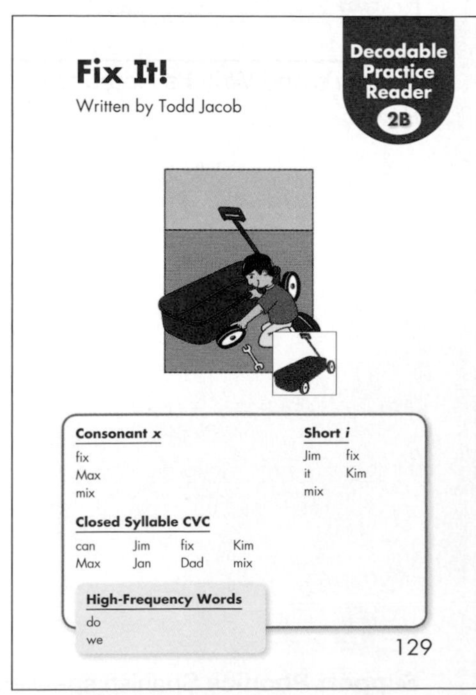
Fix It!
Written by Todd Jacob
Decodable Practice Reader 2B

Consonant x
fix
Max
mix

Short i
Jim fix
it Kim
mix

Closed Syllable CVC
can Jim fix Kim
Max Jan Dad mix

High-Frequency Words
do
we

129

Decodable Practice Reader 2B

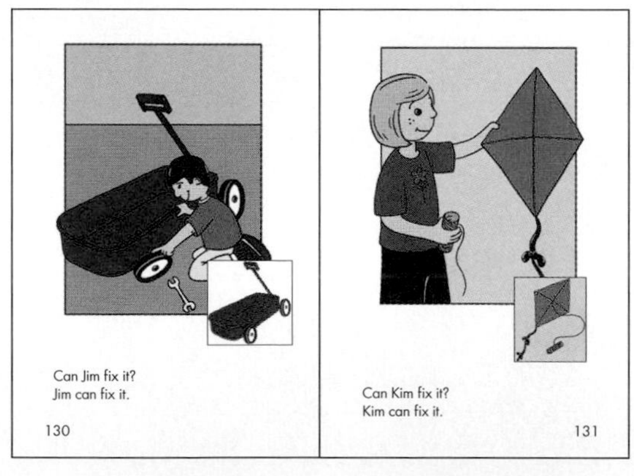

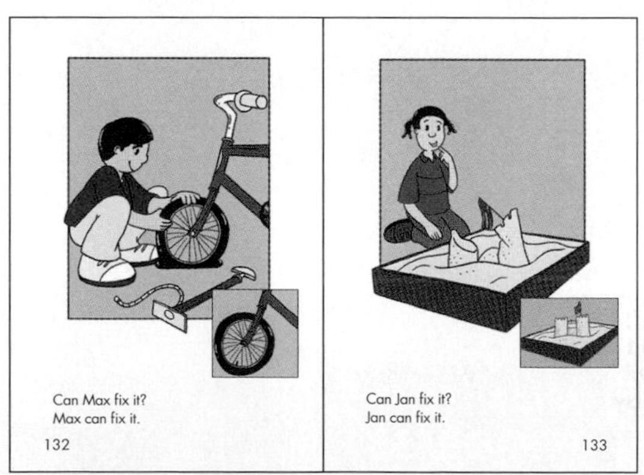

Corrective feedback	**If...** children have difficulty decoding a word, **then...** refer them to the Sound-Spelling Cards to identify the sounds in the word. Then prompt them to blend the word. • What is the new word? • Is the new word a word you know? • Does it make sense in the story?

CHECK DECODING AND COMPREHENSION Have children retell the story to include characters, setting, and events. Then have children find words with the /ks/ sound in the story. Explain that these story words will have an *-x* ending. Children should supply the words *fix, Max,* and *mix.* Ask children how they know these words have the consonant *x*/ks/ sound. (They all end with the letter *x.*)

Reread for Fluency

REREAD DECODABLE READER Have children reread Decodable Practice Reader 2B to develop automaticity decoding the consonant *x*/ks/.

Routine Paired Reading

1. **Reread** To achieve optimal fluency, have partners reread the text three or four times.
2. **Corrective Feedback** Listen as children read. Provide corrective feedback regarding their fluency and decoding.

Routines Flip Chart

Access for All

SI Strategic Intervention

Retelling If children have difficulty retelling the story, ask them direct questions regarding the events in the story.

Consonant *x*/ks/

Beginning Before children read, lead them on a picture walk through the story. Point out and pronounce the words that have the consonant *x*/ks/ sound. Then write a pictured word and have children pronounce it and find its picture.

Intermediate Before reading, help children pronounce the word with the consonant *x*/ks/ sound in the story title, *Fix It!* Then have them use the words *fix* and *it* to make a prediction about what the story will be about.

Advanced After reading, have children find words that are spelled with final *-x.* Then have children tell about something they can fix or mix. Monitor children's pronunciation.

Common Core State Standards

Foundational Skills 2.d. Segment spoken single-syllable words into their complete sequence of individual sounds (phonemes). **Foundational Skills 3.** Know and apply grade-level phonics and word analysis skills in decoding words. **Foundational Skills 3.b.** Decode regularly spelled one-syllable words. **Language 2.d.** Use conventional spelling for words with common spelling patterns and for frequently occurring irregular words.

Phonics

Review Short *a: a*

Short *i: i*

REVIEW SOUND-SPELLINGS Review the short-vowel spelling patterns *a* and *i* using Sound-Spelling Cards 1 and 11.

DECODE WORDS IN ISOLATION Display these words. Have the class blend the words. Then point to the words in random order and ask children to read them quickly.

pit	**pat**	**wig**	**ham**
pan	**pin**	**pill**	**will**
miss	**sad**	**can**	**sit**

Corrective feedback | Model blending decodable words and then ask children to blend them with you.

DECODE WORDS IN CONTEXT Display these sentences. Have the class read the sentences.

Team Talk Have pairs take turns reading the sentences naturally.

A **big pig can sit.**
Fit ham in the **pan.**
Dad ran in back.

Spelling

Short *i* Words

GUIDE PRACTICE Tell children that you will segment the sounds in each spelling word. They should repeat the sounds in each word as they write the word. Check the spelling of each word before saying the next word.

1. /s/ /i/ /ks/	**six**	**6.** /d/ /i/ /d/	**did**
2. /l/ /i/ /p/	**lip**	**7.** /m/ /i/ /ks/	**mix**
3. /i/ /n/	**in**	**8.** /s/ /i/ /t/	**sit**
4. /w/ /i/ /g/	**wig**	**9.** /p/ /i/ /n/	**pin**
5. /i/ /t/	**it**	**10.** /f/ /i/ /ks/	**fix**

ON THEIR OWN Use *Reader's and Writer's Notebook*, p. 142.

Name

Pig in a Wig

Short *i* Words

Write letters to finish the word.

1. pin 2. six
3. wig 4. lip
5. sit 6. mix
7. fix 8. in

Write the missing words. (it did)

9. I hit it.
10. Yes, I did.

Spelling Words: in, it, did, sit, six, fix, lip, mix, pin, wig

Home Activity Your child spelled words with the short *i* vowel sound. Point to a picture on this page and have your child spell the word.

142 Spelling Short *i* Words

Reader's and Writer's Notebook, p. 142

eStreet Interactive

www.ReadingStreet.com

Interactive Sound-Spelling Cards

Teacher Resources

- Reader's and Writer's Notebook

Spell Short *i* Words Clarify the pronunciation and meaning of each spelling word, such as illustrating the word *lip* by touching your lip, or the word *six* by grouping six objects.

Common Core State Standards

Foundational Skills 3.b. Decode regularly spelled one-syllable words. **Foundational Skills 3.g.** Recognize and read grade-appropriate irregularly spelled words. **Foundational Skills 4.b.** Read on-level text orally with accuracy, appropriate rate, and expression on successive readings. **Language 1.** Demonstrate command of the conventions of standard English grammar and usage when writing or speaking.

Access for All

SI Strategic Intervention

Identify High-Frequency and Selection Words If children have trouble with high-frequency and selection words, have them break into pairs and practice reading the words using word cards.

A Advanced

Extend High-Frequency and Selection Words Have children break into pairs and practice asking and answering questions that include at least one high-frequency or selection word.

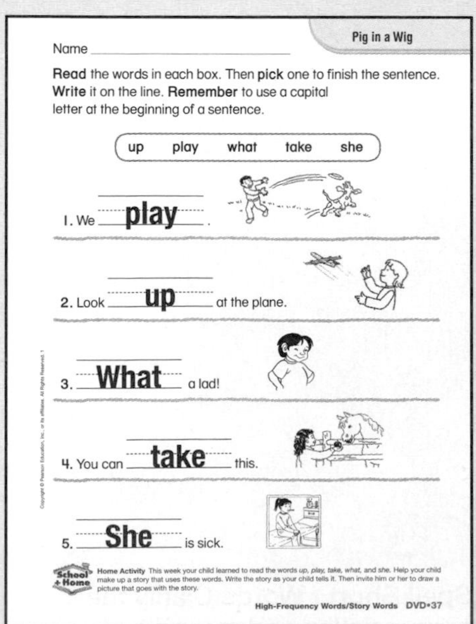

Pig in a Wig

Name ________________

Read the words in each box. Then **pick** one to finish the sentence. **Write** it on the line. **Remember** to use a capital letter at the beginning of a sentence.

up play what take she

1. We **play**.
2. Look **up** at the plane.
3. **What** a lad!
4. You can **take** this.
5. **She** is sick.

Home Activity This week your child learned to read the words up, play, take, what, and she. Help your child make up a story that uses these words. Write the story as your child tells it. Then invite him or her to draw a picture that goes with the story.

High-Frequency Words/Story Words DVD•37

Let's Practice It! TR DVD•37

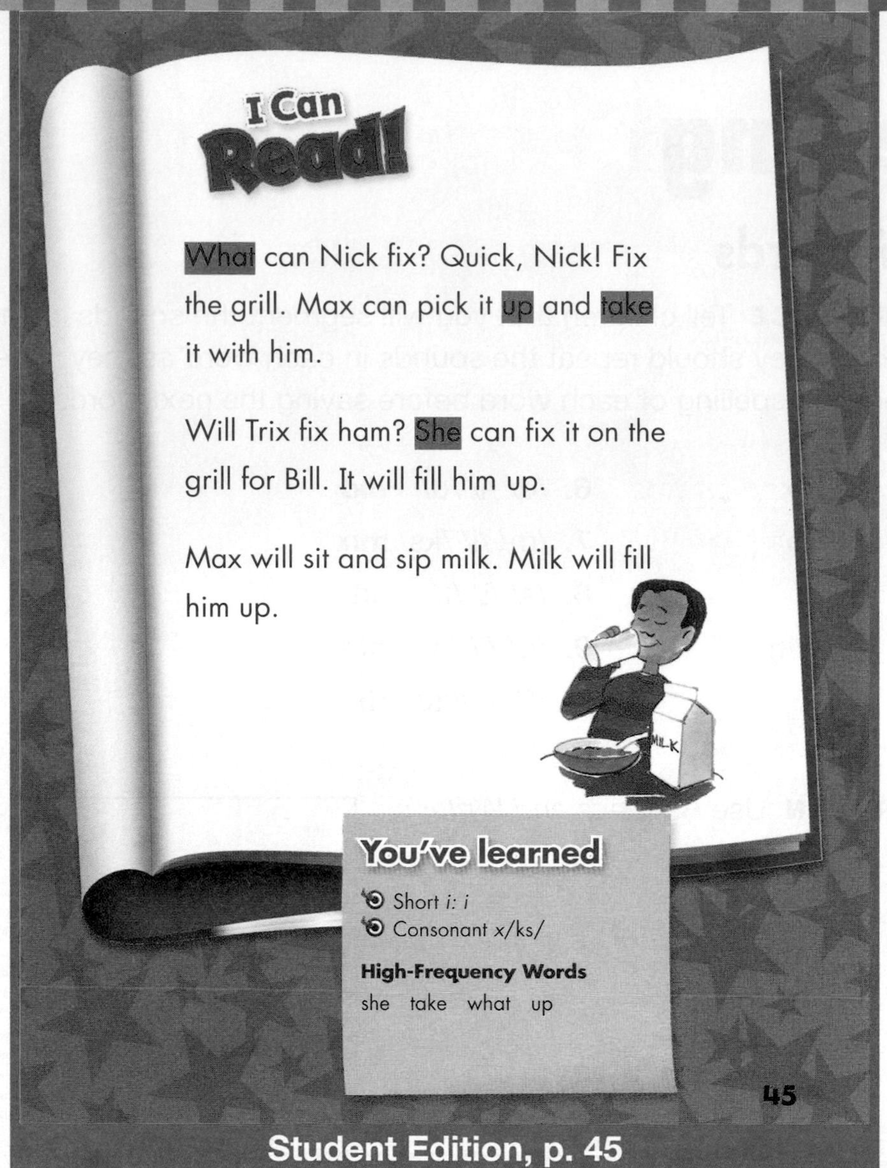

I Can Read!

What can Nick fix? Quick, Nick! Fix the grill. Max can pick it up and take it with him.

Will Trix fix ham? She can fix it on the grill for Bill. It will fill him up.

Max will sit and sip milk. Milk will fill him up.

You've learned

Short *i*: *i*
Consonant *x*/ks/

High-Frequency Words

she take what up

45

Student Edition, p. 45

High-Frequency Words

READ WORDS IN ISOLATION Remind children that there are some words we learn by remembering the letters rather than by saying the sounds. Then have them read each of the highlighted high-frequency words aloud.

READ WORDS IN CONTEXT Chorally read the "I Can Read!" passage along with children. Then have them read the passage aloud to themselves. When they are finished, ask children to reread the high-frequency words.

Team Talk Have children choose two high-frequency words and give them time to create a sentence in which both words are used properly. Then have them share their sentence with a partner.

ON THEIR OWN Use Let's Practice It! p. 37 on the *Teacher Resources DVD-ROM.*

Selection Vocabulary

INTRODUCE SELECTION WORD Use Vocabulary Transparency 2 to introduce this week's selection word. Read each sentence as you track the print. Frame the underlined word and explain its meaning. Have children read each sentence with you.

play to perform on a musical instrument

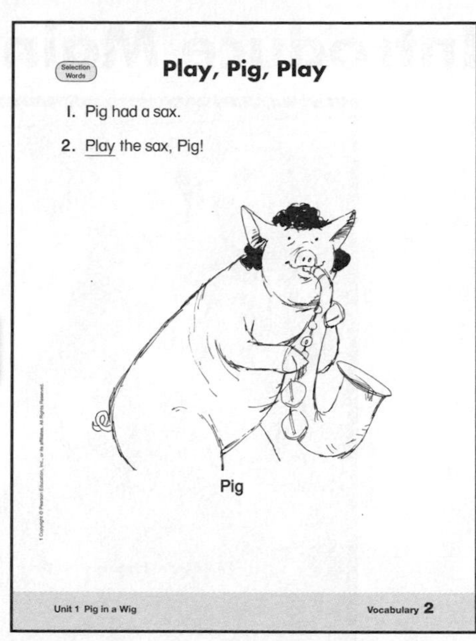

Selection Words
Play, Pig, Play
1. Pig had a sax.
2. Play the sax, Pig!
Pig
Unit 1 Pig in a Wig
Vocabulary 2

Vocabulary Transparency 2 TR DVD

Vocabulary Strategy: Alphabetize

TEACH Explain that words are **alphabetized** when they are listed in the order the letters appear in the alphabet. You can alphabetize a list of words by looking at the first letter of each word. Draw a two-column chart or display Graphic Organizer 4. List these words in the left column: *look, yellow, come, green.* Explain how to alphabetize the list of words.

I know that the letter *c* is the third letter in the alphabet: *a, b, c. C* is the first letter of the word *come.* Since there are no words that begin with *a* or *b,* I know that *come* should be listed first. I will write *come* at the top of the right column and cross it out in the left column.

look	come
yellow	green
come	look
green	yellow

Graphic Organizer 4

GUIDE PRACTICE Have a volunteer say the next word that belongs under *come* and write it in the right column *(green).* Repeat the procedure for the remaining words.

ON THEIR OWN Have children choose a new word and show where it belongs in the alphabetized list.

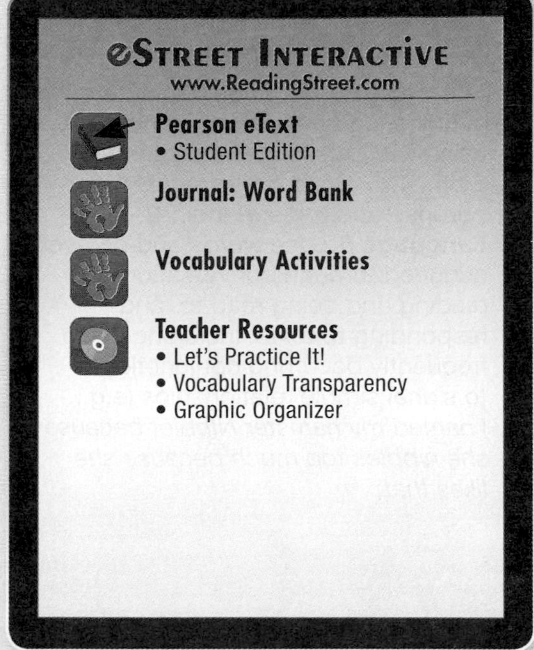

Bridge to Common Core

VOCABULARY ACQUISITION AND USE
When children interact with this week's selection vocabulary, they are learning to recognize that words can mean different things in specific contexts. Teaching the strategy of alphabetizing helps children reinforce their knowledge of the alphabet as well as increases their confidence in using a glossary or dictionary to locate the meanings of unknown words.

Academic Vocabulary 

alphabetize to place in order according to the letters of the alphabet

Multilingual Vocabulary Lists
Children can apply knowledge of their home languages to acquire new English vocabulary by using the *Multilingual Vocabulary Lists* (*ELL Handbook,* pp. 465–476).

Zoom in on ©

Common Core State Standards

Literature 3. Describe characters, settings, and major events in a story, using key details. **Foundational Skills 4.a.** Read on-level text with purpose and understanding. **Language 6.** Use words and phrases acquired through conversations, reading and being read to, and responding to texts, including using frequently occurring conjunctions to signal simple relationships (e.g., *I named my hamster Nibblet because she nibbles too much because she likes that*).

Bridge to Common Core

CRAFT AND STRUCTURE

When children are introduced to the animal fantasy genre, they learn that it is a made-up story about things that animals could not do in real life. Using the illustrations, children preview and predict what the selection will be about and set a purpose for reading. As they read, children can use their knowledge of the genre to help them understand the content, style, and structure of the selection.

Academic Vocabulary

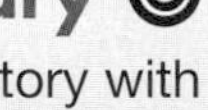

animal fantasy a made-up story with animals that could not happen in real life

summarize to recall the important ideas in a text

Strategy Response Log

Genre Have children use p. RR14 in their *Reader's and Writer's Notebook* to identify the characteristics of animal fantasy.

Text-Based Comprehension

Introduce Main Selection

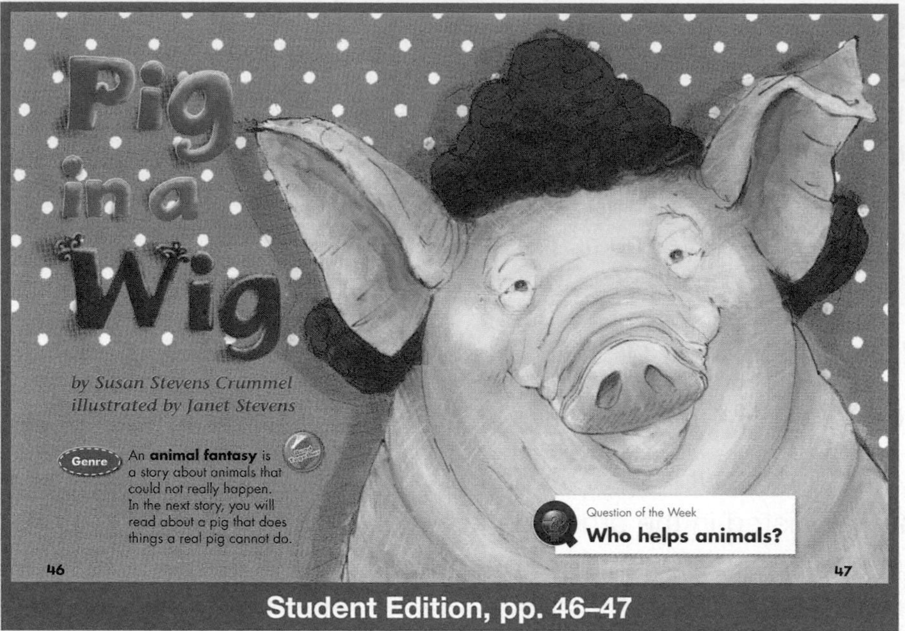
Pig in a Wig
by Susan Stevens Crummel
illustrated by Janet Stevens
Genre
An animal fantasy is a story about animals that could not really happen. In the next story, you will read about a pig that does things a real pig cannot do.
Question of the Week
Who helps animals?
46
47
Student Edition, pp. 46–47

GENRE An **animal fantasy** is a made-up story with animals that do things real animals can't do. As they read *Pig in a Wig,* children should look for things the pig does that real pigs cannot do.

PREVIEW AND PREDICT Have children identify the title of the story, the author, and the illustrator. Have children describe the role of each. Help children look through the selection and predict what might happen in the story.

PURPOSE Good readers read for a purpose. Setting a purpose helps us to think and understand more as we read. Guide children to set a purpose for reading the story.

SUMMARIZE Explain that when readers want to understand or remember what they read, they think about the most important parts. They think about how to tell what happens in a short way. Have children turn to page EI•15 in their Student Edition.

Think Aloud

Look at what is happening in this picture. What do you think this picture is mainly about? (a falling table) What do you think happened? (The dog knocked it over as it ran past.) As I read *Pig in a Wig,* I will pay attention to the most important things that happen.

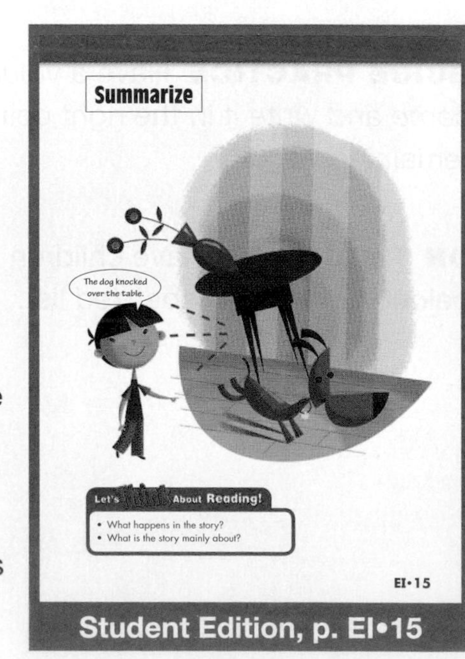
Summarize
The dog knocked over the table.
Let's Think About Reading!
• What happens in the story?
• What is the story mainly about?
EI•15
Student Edition, p. EI•15

Access Main Selection

READER AND TASK SUGGESTIONS	
Preparing to Read the Text	**Leveled Tasks**
• Review the sound of consonant *x*. • Discuss with children how they can determine a text's genre. • Remind children that to avoid misreading words, they may need to read more slowly.	• **Levels of Meaning • Evaluation** If children understand the genre, extend their understanding of genre elements by asking them to suggest something else Pig might do to add to the fantasy. • **Language Conventionality and Clarity** Children may not know the meaning of the sentence "What a ham!" Have them to use the picture on p. 57 to tell how pig is acting.

See Text Complexity Measures for *Pig in a Wig* on the tab at the beginning of this week.

READ Tell children that today they will read *Pig in a Wig* for the first time. Use the Read for Understanding routine.

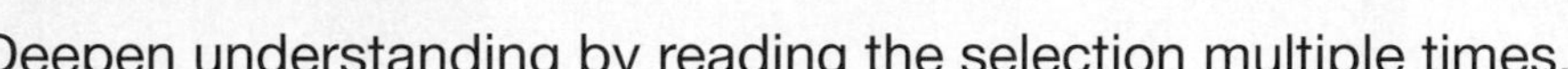

Routine Read for Understanding ©

Deepen understanding by reading the selection multiple times.

1. **First Read**—If children need support, then use the **Access Text** notes to help them clarify understanding.
2. **Second Read**—Use the **Close Reading** notes to help children draw knowledge from the text.

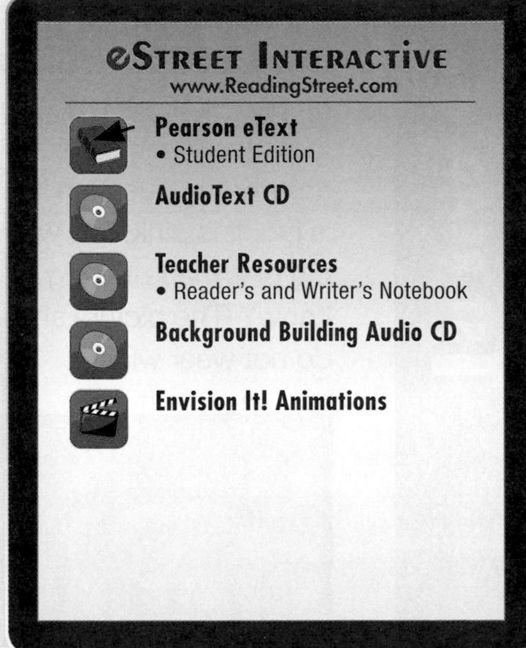

Preview Main Selection Ask children what they know about pigs. Then do a picture walk of the selection so children can talk about and see what the pig in the story does.

1ST READ

Access Text © If children need help, then...

CONNECT TO CONCEPT Look at the picture on pages 46 and 47. What is this animal? (a pig) Describe what it looks like. Encourage children to answer the question in complete sentences. (The pig is big. It is pink. It is wearing a wig.) Is this pig a real pig or a made-up pig? (a made-up pig) How do you know? (The picture shows a wig on the pig. Real pigs do not wear wigs.)

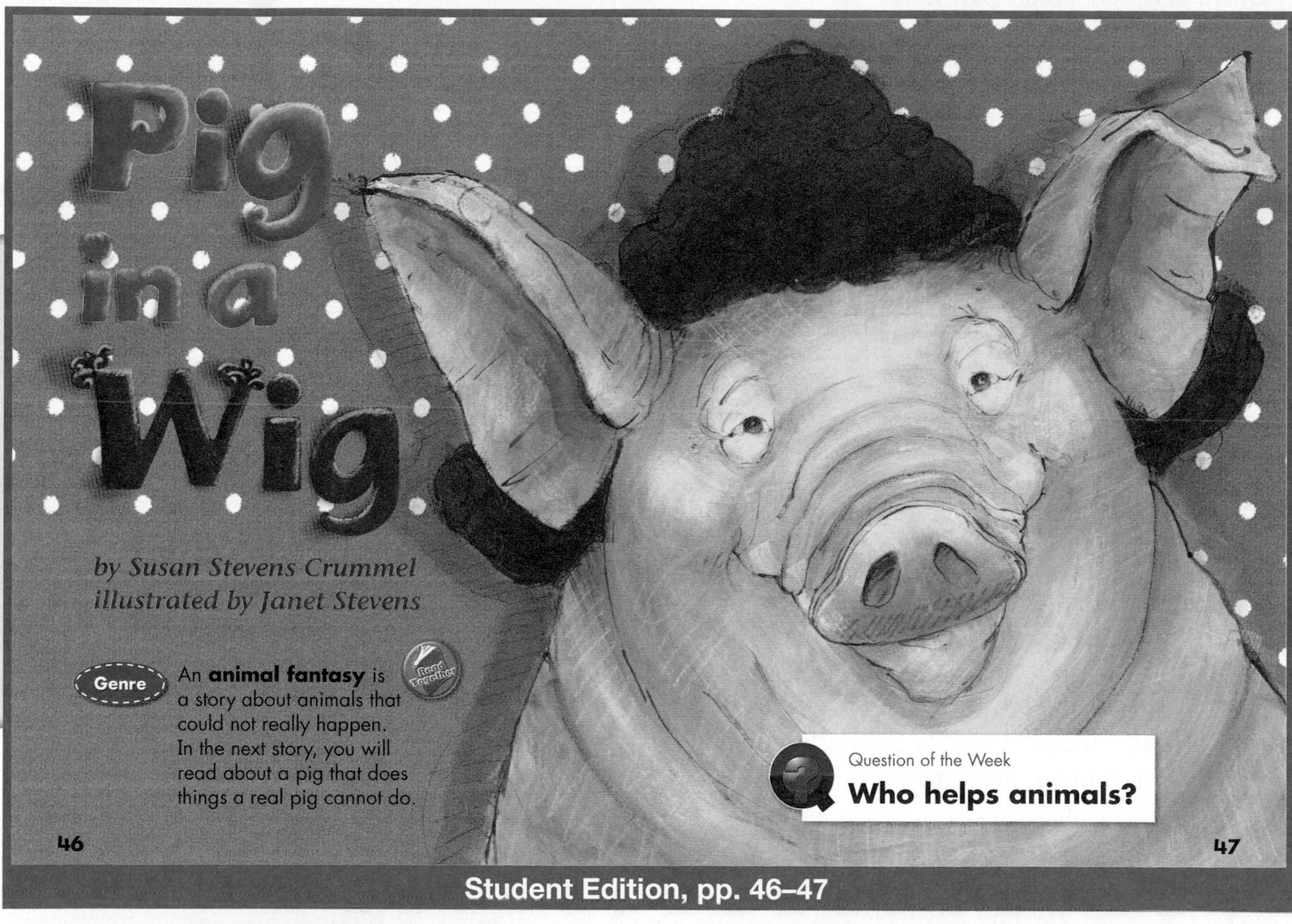

Pig in a Wig
by Susan Stevens Crummel
illustrated by Janet Stevens
Genre
An animal fantasy is a story about animals that could not really happen. In the next story, you will read about a pig that does things a real pig cannot do.
Read Together
Question of the Week
Who helps animals?
46
47

Student Edition, pp. 46–47

2ND READ

Close Reading ©

ANALYSIS • TEXT EVIDENCE How would you describe the pig in the picture on pages 46 and 47? Why? (It is funny-looking because pigs don't wear wigs.)

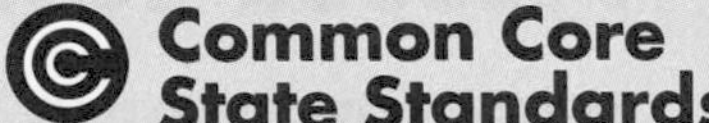

SUMMARIZE Remind children that good readers look for important ideas in a story as they read. Have them summarize the beginning of the story.

Review **CHARACTER AND SETTING** Who are the characters in this story? Point to the picture as you identify them. (a boy, a girl, a big pig) Where are the characters? (in a house) How do you know? (There is a front door.)

Common Core State Standards

Literature 3. Describe characters, settings, and major events in a story, using key details. **Literature 7.** Use illustrations and details in a story to describe its characters, setting, or events. **Literature 10.** With prompting and support, read prose and poetry of appropriate complexity for grade 1. **Foundational Skills 4.a.** Read on-level text with purpose and understanding.

Pig in a wig is big, you see.

Tick, tick, tick.
It is three.

48 49

Student Edition, pp. 48–49

SYNTHESIS • TEXT EVIDENCE What clues tell you that this part of the story takes place in the afternoon? (The story says, "Tick, tick, tick. It is three." The picture shows a clock that says three o'clock.)

ELL

Expand Vocabulary Explain to children that the words "Tick, tick, tick" are used to imitate the sound that the clock makes. Have children think of what the words *buzz* and *zip* can be used to imitate. (*Buzz* can be used to describe a bee. *Zip* can be used to describe the sound a zipper makes.)

1ST READ

Access Text If children need help, then...

CHECK DECODING Have children check their reading of new words using these questions:

- Did I blend the sounds to read the word?
- Does the word make sense in the sentence?

USE ALPHABETIZING To alphabetize is to place in order according to the letters of the alphabet. Alphabetize these words from pages 50 and 51: *pig, can, mix, dip. (can, dip, mix, pig)* Reread the sentences that have these words.

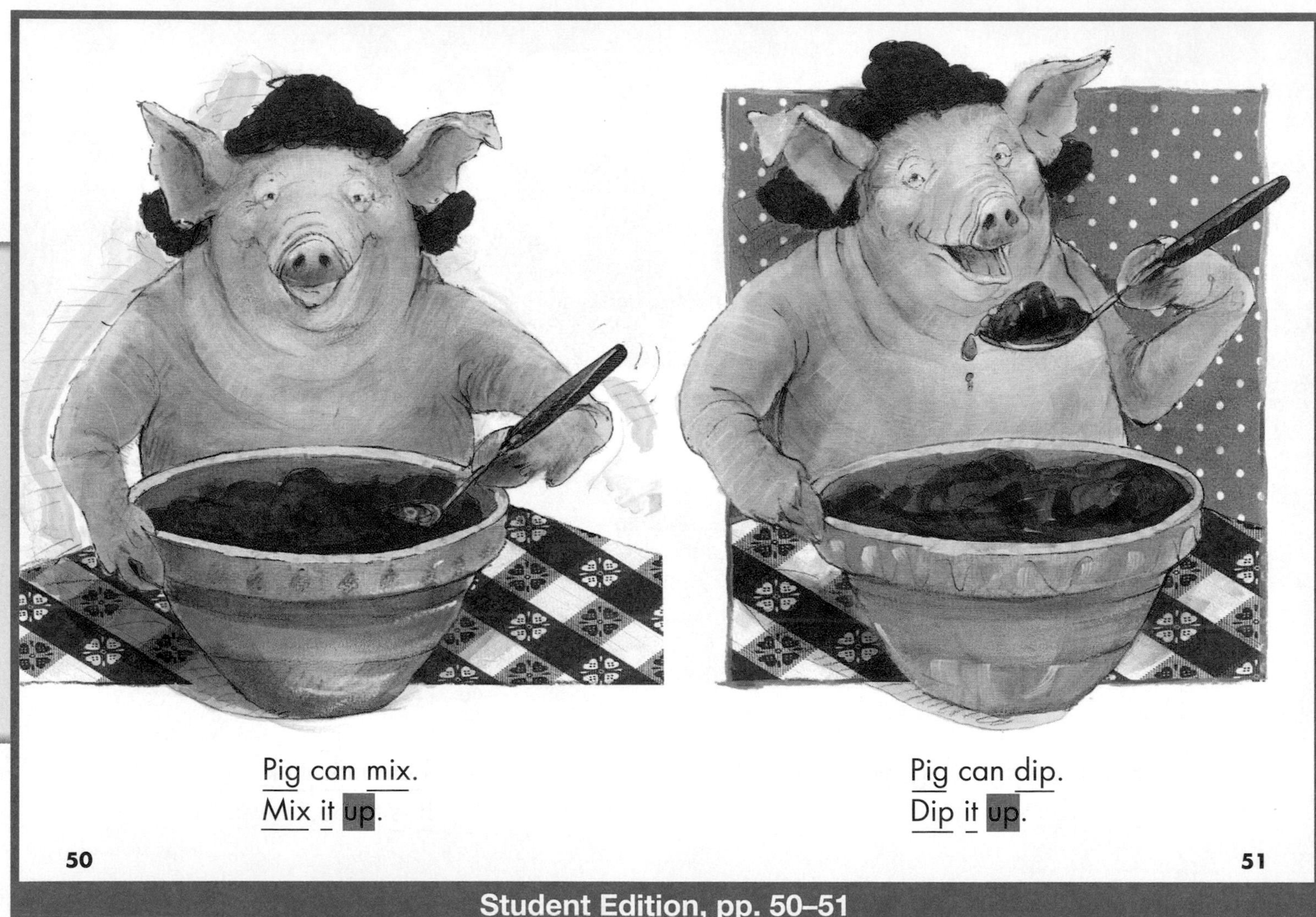
Pig can mix.
Mix it up.
50
Pig can dip.
Dip it up.
51

Student Edition, pp. 50–51

2ND READ

Close Reading

ANALYSIS • TEXT EVIDENCE Look at the pictures on pages 50 and 51. What does Pig do that shows this story is a fantasy and could not really happen? (Pig mixes food in a bowl and eats it with a spoon.)

Time for Science **CONNECT TO SCIENCE** Discuss how real pigs eat. Tell children that they usually eat from a trough or off the ground.

Team Talk Have partners name some things that real pigs eat, based on what they have learned.

SUMMARIZE Have children summarize what has happened in *Pig in a Wig* in their own words. (Pig mixes food in a bowl and eats it. She gets sick.)

PLOT What is the problem in the story? (Pig ate too much, and now she is sick.)

Common Core State Standards

Literature 2. Retell stories, including key details, and demonstrate understanding of their central message or lesson. **Literature 7.** Use illustrations and details in a story to describe its characters, setting, or events. **Also Literature 10., Foundational Skills 4.a, 4.c.**

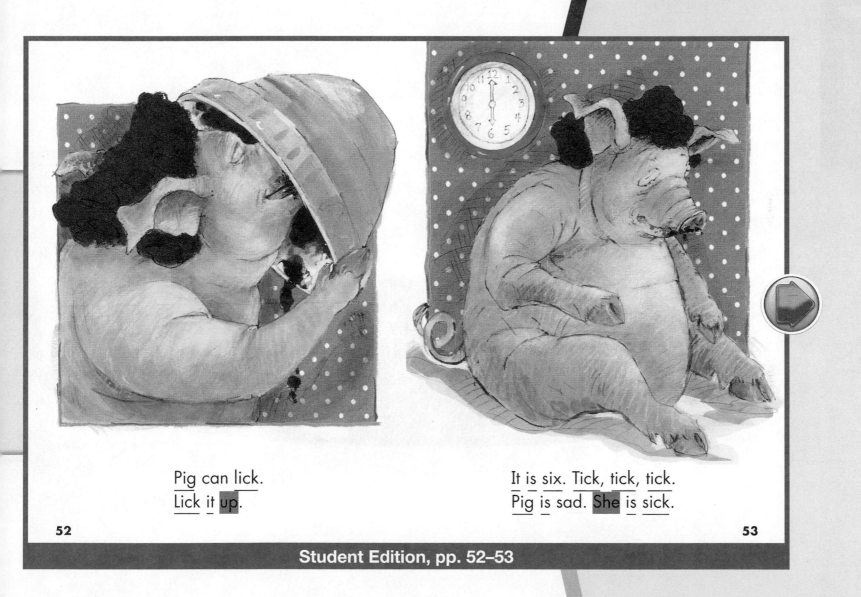

Pig can lick.
Lick it up.

52

It is six. Tick, tick, tick.
Pig is sad. She is sick.

53

Student Edition, pp. 52–53

SYNTHESIS How much time has passed at this point in the story? (Three hours.) What clues tell you that? (The clock shows it is six o'clock. At the beginning of the story, it was three o'clock.)

1ST READ

Access Text If children need help, then...

REREAD CHALLENGING TEXT Have children reread the sentence *Take a sip.* What does this sentence mean? (drink) How does someone *take a sip?* Encourage children to demonstrate how a person would take a sip of water.

Fix that pig.
Take a sip.
54
Fix that pig.
Quick, quick, quick!
55

Student Edition, pp. 54–55

2ND READ

Close Reading

EVALUATION Does the woman care about Pig? (yes) Read the words or tell about the picture that tells you that. (She gives Pig medicine because she wants Pig to feel better.)

ANALYSIS • TEXT EVIDENCE What do the words "Quick, quick, quick!" tell about Pig on page 55? (Pig is very sick and needs help right away.)

CROSS-TEXT EVALUATION
Use a Strategy to Self-Check
How did the Read Aloud "Paws and Jake" help you understand this selection?

PLOT How is Pig's problem solved? (She sips some medicine and feels better.)

Continue to DAY 2
Text-Based Comprehension
p. 57a

Common Core State Standards

Literature 2. Retell stories, including key details, and demonstrate understanding of their central message or lesson. **Literature 3.** Describe characters, settings, and major events in a story, using key details. **Literature 10.** With prompting and support, read prose and poetry of appropriate complexity for grade 1. **Foundational Skills 4.a.** Read on-level text with purpose and understanding.

Max, Max! Take the sax!
Play it, Max, and play it, Pam!
Pig in a wig did a jig.
What a ham!
56
57

Student Edition, pp. 56–57

SYNTHESIS • TEXT EVIDENCE
Using what you learned in this selection, tell who helps animals. Have children cite examples from the text.

Continue to DAY 3
Think Critically
pp. 58–59

Common Core State Standards

Literature 1. Ask and answer questions about key details in a text. **Language 1.j.** Produce and expand complete simple and compound declarative, interrogative, imperative, and exclamatory sentences in response to prompts. **Language 1.** Demonstrate command of the conventions of standard English grammar and usage when writing or speaking.

Text-Based Comprehension

Check Understanding

Have children discuss each question with a partner. Ask several pairs to share their responses.

☑ **Animal fantasy** What does Pig do that shows this story is a fantasy? (Pig wears a wig. She mixes food in a bowl and eats with a spoon.)

☑ **Confirm predictions** How did you use story clues to predict what would happen next? (I saw that "Fix that pig" was used twice. That made me guess that Pig would feel better after taking the medicine.)

☑ **Draw conclusions** What do you think Pig will think about the next time she eats? (She will try not to eat too much so she won't get sick.)

If... children need more scaffolding and practice with the **Comprehension Skill,**
then... use the ELL activities on p. DI•38 in the Teacher Resources section on SuccessNet.

Day 2 SMALL GROUP TIME • Differentiate Comprehension, p. SG•18

OL On-Level	SI Strategic Intervention	A Advanced
• **Practice Phonics** Additional /ks/ Words • **Read** *Pig in a Wig*	• **Reteach Phonics** Blend /ks/ Words • **Read** *Pig in a Wig*	• **Extend Phonics** More /ks/ Words • **Read** *Pig in a Wig* • **Investigate** Inquiry Project

Genre

Animal Fantasy

IDENTIFY FEATURES OF ANIMAL FANTASY Use *Pig in a Wig* to discuss the features of an animal fantasy. *Pig in a Wig* is an animal fantasy because it is a made-up story about a pig that does things real pigs cannot do. Discuss the components of an animal fantasy:

- includes animals
- is a made-up story
- animals do things that real animals cannot do

What is something Pig does in the story that real pigs cannot do? (Pig makes herself a meal.)

GUIDE PRACTICE Explain that the class will now list things that Pig does that show the story is an animal fantasy. Show Graphic Organizer 17 or create a web and write *Pig in a Wig* in the center. Ask children to tell what examples to include in the web.

ON THEIR OWN Arrange children into small groups. Have them revisit the story *Sam, Come Back!* and think of ideas that would make that story an animal fantasy. Have them share their ideas with the class.

Conventions

Subjects of Sentences

TEACH Write *The cat takes a nap* on the board. Point to each word as you read it. Ask children to identify the subject, or naming part, of the sentence. (the cat) Continue with *The pig sits in back.* (the pig) A subject tells who or what the sentence is about. What can the subject of a sentence name? (a person, place, animal, or thing)

GUIDE PRACTICE Write the following sentence frame:

______ can run.

Read the sentence aloud. Display the Big Book *A Kid's Best Friend,* p. 16, and point to the picture. What could be the subject that completes this sentence? (The dog) Write *The dog* on the line and read the sentence aloud. Then rewrite the sentence frame under the sentence. What is another subject that could complete this sentence? (The kid) Add *The kid* and read the sentence aloud.

APPLY Have the class complete these sentence frames orally using subjects.

1. **My ______ went to the store with me.**
2. **The ______ played catch.**
3. **______ learned some tricks.**

ON THEIR OWN Use *Reader's and Writer's Notebook,* p. 143.

Daily Fix-It

3. Pig said sitt here
   Pig said sit here.
4. he can Mix it.
   He can mix it.

Discuss the Daily Fix-It corrections with children. Review sentence capitalization, end punctuation, and spelling.

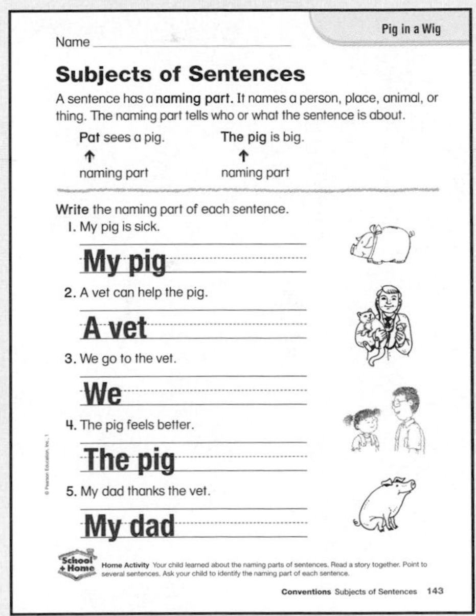

Name ______ Pig in a Wig

Subjects of Sentences

A sentence has a **naming part.** It names a person, place, animal, or thing. The naming part tells who or what the sentence is about.

Pat sees a pig. ↑ naming part — **The pig** is big. ↑ naming part

Write the naming part of each sentence.

1. My pig is sick. — **My pig**
2. A vet can help the pig. — **A vet**
3. We go to the vet. — **We**
4. The pig feels better. — **The pig**
5. My dad thanks the vet. — **My dad**

School + Home — Home Activity Your child learned about the naming parts of sentences. Read a story together. Point to several sentences. Ask your child to identify the naming part of each sentence.

Conventions Subjects of Sentences 143

Reader's and Writer's Notebook, p. 143

Practice Subjects of Sentences
Help English learners better understand subjects of sentences by using items to create sentences. For example, use a stuffed dog and make it jump in the air for the sentence *The dog is jumping.* Show them that the sentence is about the dog so the subject of the sentence is *The dog.*

Common Core State Standards

Writing 3. Write narratives in which they recount two or more appropriately sequenced events, include some details regarding what happened, use temporal words to signal event order, and provide some sense of closure. **Writing 5.** With guidance and support from adults, focus on a topic, respond to questions and suggestions from peers, and add details to strengthen writing as needed. **Language 2.** Demonstrate command of the conventions of standard English capitalization, punctuation, and spelling when writing.

Writing

Fantasy Story

Writer's Craft: Use Imagination

INTRODUCE THE PROMPT Review with children the key features of a fantasy story. Point out that *Pig in a Wig* is a fantasy story. Assure them that they can make up a brief story with characters that do things that real people and animals cannot do. Explain that today children will plan their own story with events that could not really happen. Read aloud the writing prompt.

Writing Prompt

Write a fantasy story about a person who helps an animal. Draw a picture for your story.

GENERATE STORY IDEAS

To plan a new story, think of people who help animals. Let's make a chart of people who help animals and how they help them. Display a T-chart or use Graphic Organizer 4. I'll start with the words *pet owner.*

Guide children in identifying people who help animals and how they help them. Possible ideas are shown. Record the responses and keep the chart so that children can refer to it as they plan and draft their stories.

People	How They Help Animals
pet owner	takes care of pets
groomer	keeps pets neat
vet	keeps animals healthy
pet shelter	helps animals find homes

Graphic Organizer 4

Have each child choose a topic for a new story. Circulate to guide them. Have them make up names for their characters.

Mini-Lesson Use Imagination

- **Introduce** Use *Reader's and Writer's Notebook,* p. 144 to model story planning. To plan a story, I can use a chart. I will use my imagination to think of an idea for my fantasy story. In real life, workers at animal shelters rescue animals and help people adopt them. Imagine that instead of people choosing animals to be their pets, animals got to choose whose pet they will be. In my story, I'll write about a little dog in a shelter that asks a worker at the shelter to help him pick the right girl to take him home. In real life, animals don't pick people or talk, so that makes my story a fantasy.

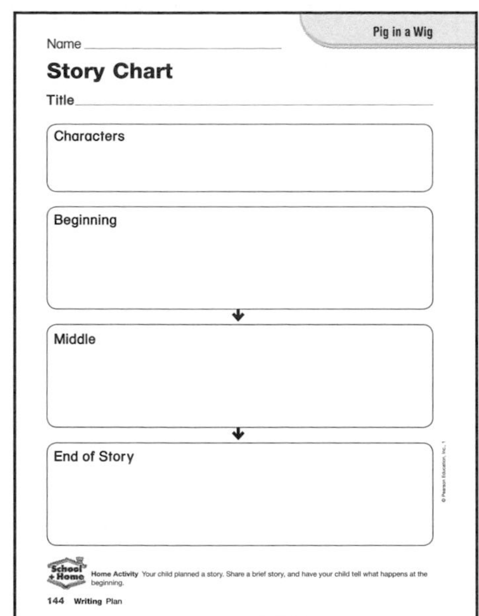
Name
Story Chart
Title
Characters
Beginning
Middle
End of Story
Home Activity Your child planned a story. Share a brief story, and have your child tell what happens at the beginning.
144 Writing Plan

Reader's and Writer's Notebook, p. 144

- **Model** Now I will write my plan. I'll call the little dog Pal. Pal will adopt a little girl who has a big smile. I'll write the characters in the *Characters* box. Now I will plan what happens in the beginning, middle, and end of my story. At the beginning, Pal will go to the shelter. I'll write that in the *Beginning* box. In the middle of the story, Pal will see a little girl named Alice. He will ask Jeff if she can take him home. I'll write that in the *Middle* box. At the end, Pal will leave the shelter with Alice. I'll write that in the *End of Story* box. Last, I will think of a title that tells what my story is mostly about. I'll write my title on top: *A New Pet.* Now plan for your story. Circulate to guide and assist children.

Routine Quick Write for Fluency

Team Talk

1. **Talk** Have children take two minutes to tell their story events to a partner.
2. **Write** Each child briefly writes about the events that could not happen in real life.
3. **Share** Each child reads the fantasy ideas to the partner.

Routines Flip Chart

Access for All

SI Strategic Intervention

Planning Fantasy If children find it difficult to include an element of fantasy in their plan, talk about things that people do but animals cannot. Help them create animal characters that do things that in real life only people do.

Support Prewriting

Beginning Children can use words and drawings to plan story events. Have them label their images and share with a partner, possibly one who speaks the same home language.

Intermediate Have children write phrases to express story event ideas. Have them describe the story plan to a partner.

Advanced Have children write short sentences in their story charts. As they share the plan with partners, children can clarify and add ideas.

Handwriting

Letters *Ii* and *Xx*/Letter Spacing

MODEL LETTER FORMATION Display uppercase and lowercase letter *Ii.* Use the stroke instructions pictured below to model proper letter formation. Review uppercase and lowercase letter *Xx.*

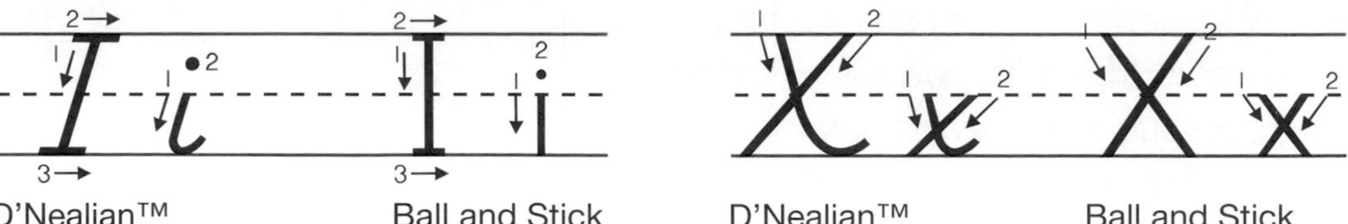

MODEL LETTER SPACING Explain that when we write a word, all the letters in that word should be evenly spaced. Write the word *six* using correct spacing. When I write the letters in a word, I need to pay attention to the spaces between each letter. The letters should not be too close together or too far apart. Write the word *six* again, with the letters too close to each other. The letters should not be so close together that they touch each other. Write *six* a third time, with the letters too far from each other. They should not be so far apart that it's hard to tell they spell out a word. If I space the letters in words correctly, I make it easier for others to understand what I write. Ask children which of the three writing examples is easiest to read and have them explain why.

GUIDE PRACTICE Write the following sentence, using letter spacing that is too far apart: *Pig can mix.*

Team Talk Have children work in pairs to discuss what is wrong with the sentence and how it should be fixed. Have them write the sentence correctly and share with the class.

ON THEIR OWN Use *Reader's and Writer's Notebook,* p. 145.

Common Core State Standards

Writing 7. Participate in shared research and writing projects (e.g., explore a number of "how-to" books on a given topic and use them to write a sequence of instructions). **Writing 8.** With guidance and support from adults, recall information from experiences or gather information from provided sources to answer a question. **Language 1.a.** Print all upper- and lowercase letters.

Name ______ Pig in a Wig

Trace and **write** the letters. Make sure you write your letters the correct size.

X X X

x x x

Check children's work.

Copy the words. Leave the correct space between letters.

X-ray X-ray six six

pig pig Ina Ina

mix mix rip rip

Did you leave the correct space between your letters? Yes No

School + Home Home Activity Your child practiced writing words with *Ii* and *Xx*. Have your child practice writing each of these letters five more times.

Handwriting 145

Reader's and Writer's Notebook, p. 145

Research and Inquiry

Step 2 Research Skill: Media Center/Library

TEACH Tell children that a **media center** or a **library** has resources to help you find answers to your questions. Discuss the types of resources found there. Explain the purposes of resources such as an encyclopedia, an atlas, and the Internet.

Think Aloud **MODEL** A **media center** or **library** has books and other materials I can use to learn about things. Suppose I want to learn more about vets. If I know where to look, I can find information about vets in a media center or library. I can look for books, CDs, and DVDs. I can also use the Internet to find information about vets.

GUIDE PRACTICE On the board, write a list of resources that would be found in a media center or library. With children, discuss each resource. Then have children determine if the resource would be helpful to find information about people who help animals.

Academic Vocabulary

media center an area that has printed resources as well as other types of media

library a place that has a collection of books and other resources

Bridge to Common Core

RESEARCH TO BUILD AND PRESENT KNOWLEDGE

Children will analyze how media centers and libraries can be used to find information to learn more about a topic. They will also:

- learn to use resources in encyclopedias, atlases, and the Internet
- learn to find information

Wrap Up Your Day!

✔ **Consonant x/ks/** Write the words *fix, Max,* and *mix.* Have children identify the final sound in each word. Ask them how they know these words end with /ks/.

✔ **High-Frequency Words** Point to these words on the Word Wall: *she, take, what, up.* Have children read each word and use it in a sentence.

✔ **Content Knowledge** Monitor children's use of oral vocabulary as they respond. Recall the Big Book *A Kid's Best Friend.* Ask: How do the children help their dog get really clean? (They scrub their dog with soap.)

Tell children that tomorrow they will reread *Pig in a Wig.*

DAY 3 at a Glance

Content Knowledge
Oral Vocabulary

Phonemic Awareness
Rhyming Words

Phonics/Spelling
Short *i: i*
Consonant *x*/ks/

High-Frequency Words
she, take, up, what

Selection Words
play

Text-Based Comprehension
Review Character and Setting

Fluency
Accuracy

Conventions
Subjects of Sentences

Writing
Fantasy Story
Writing Trait: Conventions

Listening and Speaking
Share Information About Caring

Research and Inquiry
Gather and Record Information

Materials

- Student Edition
- Sing with Me Big Book
- Big Book
- Letter Tiles
- Reader's and Writer's Notebook
- Retelling Cards

Common Core State Standards

Speaking/Listening 2. Ask and answer questions about key details in a text read aloud or information presented orally or through other media. **Language 5.c.** Identify real-life connections between words and their use (e.g., note places at home that are *cozy*). **Also Language 6.**

Content Knowledge

Helping Animals

EXPAND THE CONCEPT To reinforce concepts and to focus children's attention, have children sing "Pet Service" from the *Sing with Me* Big Book. How does Pam give good service to every dog and kitty? (She cleans them up and makes them look nice.)

Build Oral Language

LISTEN FOR AMAZING WORDS Display the Big Book *A Kid's Best Friend.* Read the story and have children listen for the word *exercise.* Have them also think about ways to help dogs get exercise.

- What are the people and their dogs doing on pages 14 and 15? (playing ball, rolling on the ground, exercising)
- What are other ways you can help animals get exercise? (run with them, take walks)

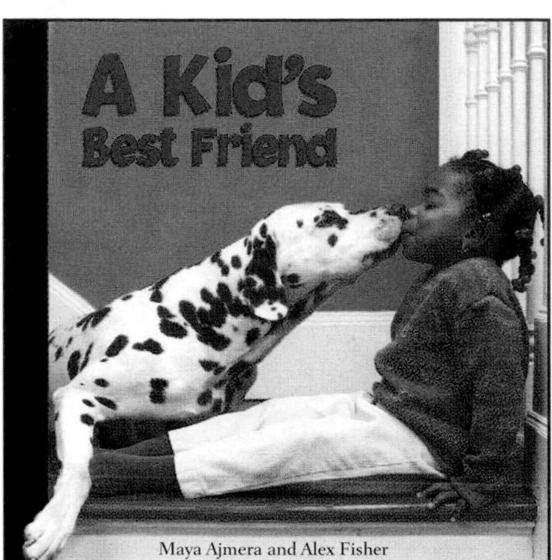

Big Book

TALK ABOUT SENTENCES AND WORDS Write the following sentence from *A Kid's Best Friend* on sentence strips or on the board.

Dogs can't go all day without exercise.

- Ask children to read it with you as you track the print.
- Point to *Dogs can't go all day without exercise.* What does this mean? (Dogs need to exercise every day.)
- What does *exercise* mean? (doing an activity) Ask volunteers to show what they might look like exercising. Why do you think the author chose to use the word *exercise?* (It's one word that tells about all forms of exercise.)
- **Team Talk** Now have children work with a partner to replace the word *exercise* in the sentence with a more specific form of exercise a dog can do. Use the following sentence frame:

  Dogs can't go all day without ______.

Build Oral Vocabulary

Amazing Words Robust Vocabulary Routine

1. **Introduce the Word** Relate the word *exercise* to the book. Dogs need *exercise* to feel good and to stay healthy. Supply a child-friendly definition. When you *exercise,* you move your body and work your muscles. Have children say the word.

2. **Demonstrate** Provide examples to show meaning. Running and swimming are forms of *exercise.* After you *exercise,* you may feel tired or sore.

3. **Apply** Have children demonstrate their understanding. What are some of your favorite ways to *exercise?*

4. **Display the Word** Run your hand under the chunks *ex-er-cise* as you read the word.

Routines Flip Chart

ADD TO THE CONCEPT MAP Use these questions to discuss how people can help animals as you add to the K-W-L concept map.

Concept Map

- In *Pig in a Wig,* Pig eats too much and gets a stomachache. Who helps Pig feel better? (a woman wearing a hat) What does the woman give Pig to make her feel better? (She gives Pig medicine.) Let's add *People can help animals feel better* to our map.
- Point out the question in the *What We Want to Know* column: Who helps dogs eat right? In *A Kid's Best Friend,* what did we learn about who helps dogs eat right? (Dog owners give their dogs good food and water.) Let's add this information to the *What We Learned* column of our map.

Amazing Words

career	sloppy
service	exercise
tool	comfort
scrub	search

Access for All

 **Strategic Intervention**

Review the Concept Review the week's concept and the Amazing Words children have learned. Have children answer the following questions: *Would you rather have a career as a groomer or a vet? Why? How would you scrub a sloppy pet? What types of exercise can you do with your pet? What is one way a person can be of service to animals?*

Expand Vocabulary Use the Day 3 instruction on ELL Poster 2 to expand children's use of vocabulary to communicate about lesson concepts.

Sentence Production Talk about different kinds of exercise children can do with their pets. Prompt children to use words such as *running, jumping, swimming,* and *playing.* Have children pantomime to show the action verbs.

Common Core State Standards
Foundational Skills 2.c. Isolate and pronounce initial, medial vowel, and final sounds (phonemes) in spoken single-syllable words.
Also Foundational Skills 2.b., 2.d.
Phonemic Awareness
Let's Listen for
Read Together
Sounds
Find five things that contain the short *i* sound in the middle of the word.
Find something that has the short *i* sound at the beginning of the word. Say the word.
Find four things that rhyme with *sick*. Say each word.
Find something that rhymes with *six*. Say the sound at the end of that word.
Find something that rhymes with *wish*. Say each sound in the word.
READING STREET ONLINE
SOUND-SPELLING CARDS
www.ReadingStreet.com
Ms. Ann
40
41
Student Edition, pp. 40–41

Common Core State Standards

Foundational Skills 2.b. Orally produce single-syllable words by blending sounds (phonemes), including consonant blends. **Foundational Skills 3.** Know and apply grade-level phonics and word analysis skills in decoding words. **Language 2.d.** Use conventional spelling for words with common spelling patterns and for frequently occurring irregular words. **Also Foundational Skills 2., 2.d.**

Academic Vocabulary

rhyming words words that end with the same sounds

Phonemic Awareness

Rhyming Words

MODEL PRODUCING RHYMING WORDS Read together the last three bullets. Today we are going to use this picture to help us produce rhyming words. Remember that **rhyming words** always end with the same sounds. When I look at the picture, I see a *brick* building, a *chick,* a puppy doing a *trick,* and a girl throwing a *stick. Brick, chick, trick,* and *stick* rhyme with *sick.*

GUIDE PRACTICE Guide children to use the picture to generate a word that rhymes with *six (fix, mix)* and a word that rhymes with *wish (dish, fish).*

ON THEIR OWN Have children generate words that rhyme with the following words.

lick	pig	fit	lip	fin	mix

Team Talk Have partners think of other short *i* words that rhyme. Ask children to share their words.

Phonics

Build Words

MODEL WORD BUILDING Now we are going to build words with the short *i* sound. Write *bin* and blend it. Watch me change *n* to *t*. Model blending the new word, *bit*.

GUIDE PRACTICE Have children spell *bit* with letter tiles. Monitor children's work as they build words.

- Change the *b* in *bit* to *s*. Say the new word together. — s i t
- Change the *s* in *sit* to *f*. Say the new word together. — f i t
- Change the *t* in *fit* to *n*. Say the new word together. — f i n
- Change the *f* in *fin* to *w*. Say the new word together. — w i n

Corrective feedback	For corrective feedback, model the correct spelling and have children correct their tiles.

Fluent Word Reading

MODEL Write *six*. I know the sounds for *s, i,* and *x*. I blend them and read the word *six*.

GUIDE PRACTICE Write the words below. Say the sounds in your head for each spelling you see. When I point to the word, we'll read it together. Allow one second per sound-previewing time for the first reading.

mix	fix	it	pig	jig	pit	six

ON THEIR OWN Have children read the list above three or four times, until they can read one word per second.

Access for All

Build Short *i* Words If children are able to build the words in the class activity easily and independently, have them use letter tiles to build these more difficult words with short *i: into, limit, picnic, quick, rapid, within.*

Short *i* Words Clarify the pronunciation and spelling of each word. Illustrate the words *sit, fit, fin,* and *win* by sitting, fitting a pencil in a box, etc.

Common Core State Standards

Foundational Skills 3. Know and apply grade-level phonics and word analysis skills in decoding words. **Foundational Skills 3.b.** Decode regularly spelled one-syllable words. **Language 2.d.** Use conventional spelling for words with common spelling patterns and for frequently occurring irregular words.

Phonics

Blend and Read

DECODE WORDS IN ISOLATION
Have children turn to pages 147–148 in the *Reader's and Writer's Notebook* and find the first list of words. Each word in this list has the short *i* sound. Let's blend and read these words. Be sure that children identify the correct sound in short *i* words. Continue with the next list of words with the consonant sound /ks/ spelled *x*. Check that children identify the correct sound for *x*. Then have children read the high-frequency words.

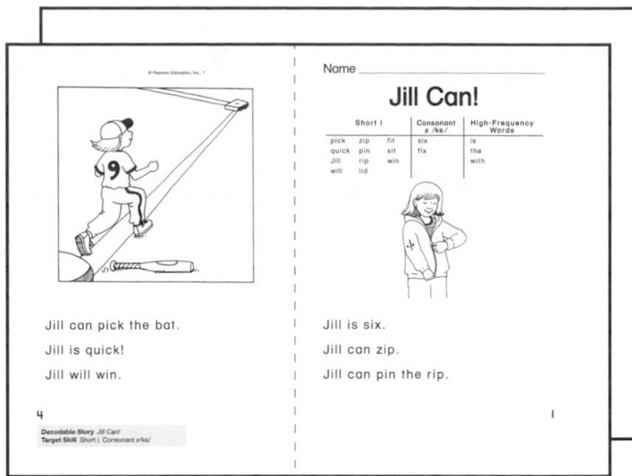
Name

Jill Can!

Short i			Consonant x /ks/	High-Frequency Words
pick	zip	fit	six	is
quick	pin	sit	fix	the
Jill	rip	win		with
will	lid			

Jill can pick the bat.
Jill is quick!
Jill will win.

Jill is six.
Jill can zip.
Jill can pin the rip.

Reader's and Writer's Notebook, pp. 147–148

DECODE WORDS IN CONTEXT Chorally read the story along with children. Have children identify words in the story that have short *i* or consonant *x*/ks/.

Team Talk Pair children and have them take turns reading the story aloud to each other. Monitor children as they read to check for proper pronunciation and appropriate pacing.

ON THEIR OWN To further develop automaticity, have children take the story home to reread.

Spelling

Short *i* Words

SPELL HIGH-FREQUENCY WORDS Write *she* and *take* and point them out on the Word Wall. Have children say and spell the words with you and then without you.

DICTATION Have children write these sentences. Say each sentence. Then repeat it slowly, one word at a time.

1. **Tim can sit and mix.**
2. **Pam did fix it.**
3. **Dad ran in to get the pin.**

PROOFREAD AND CORRECT Write each sentence, spelling words one at a time. Have children circle and rewrite any misspelled words.

ON THEIR OWN Use *Reader's and Writer's Notebook,* p. 149.

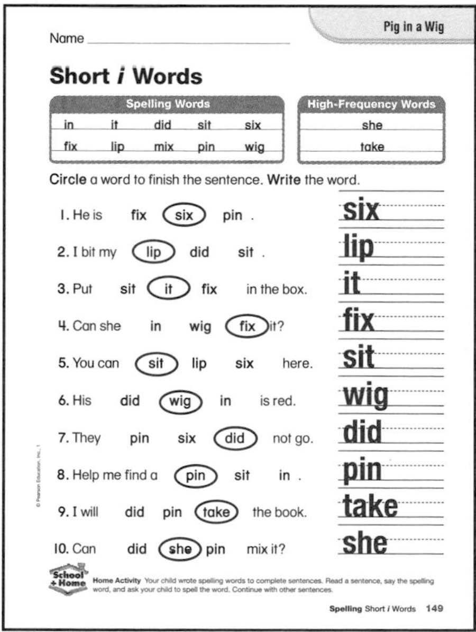

Name ____________ Pig in a Wig

Short *i* Words

Spelling Words				
in	it	did	sit	six
fix	lip	mix	pin	wig

High-Frequency Words
she
take

Circle a word to finish the sentence. Write the word.

1. He is fix (six) pin . — six
2. I bit my (lip) did sit . — lip
3. Put sit (it) fix in the box. — it
4. Can she in wig (fix) it? — fix
5. You can (sit) lip six here. — sit
6. His did (wig) in is red. — wig
7. They pin six (did) not go. — did
8. Help me find a (pin) sit in . — pin
9. I will did pin (take) the book. — take
10. Can did (she) pin mix it? — she

Home Activity Your child wrote spelling words to complete sentences. Read a sentence, say the spelling word, and ask your child to spell the word. Continue with other sentences.

Spelling Short *i* Words 149

Reader's and Writer's Notebook, p. 149

eStreet Interactive
www.ReadingStreet.com

Teacher Resources
- Reader's and Writer's Notebook

Spelling Words

Short *i* Words

1. six	6. did
2. lip	7. mix
3. in	8. sit
4. wig	9. pin
5. it	10. fix

High-Frequency Words

11. she	12. take

Spelling Dictation Write the spelling words on the board. Say the word *six,* have children repeat it, and then erase it from the board. Have partners spell the word with letter tiles. If children misspell the word, model writing it as you spell it again aloud. Continue the exercise with the remaining words.

Day 3 SMALL GROUP TIME • Differentiate Close Reading, p. SG•18

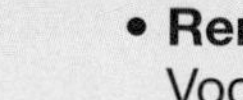

OL On-Level
- **Reread** to Develop Vocabulary
- **Reread** *Pig in a Wig*

SI Strategic Intervention
- **Blend** Words with Short *i* and *x*/ks/
- **Reread** *Pig in a Wig*

A Advanced
- **Reread** to Extend Vocabulary
- **Reread** *Pig in a Wig*
- **Investigate** Inquiry Project

ELL

If... children need more scaffolding and practice with reading the **Main Selection,**
then... use the ELL activities on p. DI•39 in the Teacher Resources section on SuccessNet.

Common Core State Standards

Literature 3. Describe characters, settings, and major events in a story, using key details. **Foundational Skills 3.b.** Decode regularly spelled one-syllable words. **Foundational Skills 3.g.** Recognize and read grade-appropriate irregularly spelled words.

High-Frequency Words

she	**up**
take	**what**

Selection Words

play to perform on a musical instrument

High-Frequency and Selection Words

READ WORDS IN ISOLATION Display and review this week's high-frequency words and selection words. Have children read the words aloud.

READ WORDS IN CONTEXT Display the following sentence frames. Have children complete the sentences using high-frequency and selection words. Have children read each completed sentence with you.

1. **Mat sat _______. (up)**
2. **Pam can _______ a cup. (take)**
3. **Dad will _______ a sax. (play)**
4. **_______ had a nap. (She)**
5. **_______ did Tom pack? (What)**

Check High-Frequency Words

FORMATIVE ASSESSMENT Point to these words on the Word Wall and have the class read them. Listen for children who miss words during the reading. Call on those children to read some of the words individually.

up	**she**	**what**	**take**	**Spiral Review**
that	**three**	**you**	←	Row 2 reviews previously taught high-frequency words.

If... children cannot read these words,

then... use the Nondecodable Words Routine on p. 43 to reteach the words. Monitor children's fluency with these words during reading and provide additional practice.

Text-Based Comprehension

Read Main Selection

REVIEW CHARACTER AND SETTING Remind children that **characters** are the people and animals in a story and the **setting** is where and when the story takes place. Paying attention to the characters and setting helps us understand what happens in a story. Who are the characters in *Pig in a Wig?* (Pig, a woman, Max, and Pam) What is the setting? (a kitchen in a home)

GENRE: ANIMAL FANTASY Remind children that an animal fantasy is a made-up story with animals that do things real animals can't do. Have children recall things Pig does in *Pig in a Wig* that real pigs can't do. (Pig wears a wig and mixes food in a bowl. She does a jig and stands on two feet.)

READ Return to pages 46–57 and use the **2nd Read/Close Reading Notes** to reread *Pig in a Wig.*

Routine Read for Understanding

Deepen understanding by reading the selection multiple times.

1. **First Read**—If children need support, then use the **Access Text** notes to help them clarify understanding.
2. **Second Read**—Use the **Close Reading** notes to help children draw knowledge from the text.

Academic Vocabulary 

characters the people and animals in a story

setting where and when the story takes place

Identify Setting Have children talk about the setting of *Pig in a Wig* in preparation for their second reading. Ask children to look at the pictures and think about what Pig is doing in order to help them identify where the story takes place. Help them use the illustrations to identify that Pig is in a kitchen.

Common Core State Standards
Literature 1. Ask and answer questions about key details in a text.
Also Literature 2., 9., Writing 5.
Envision It! Retell
READING STREET ONLINE
STORY SORT
www.ReadingStreet.com

Think Critically

1. How is Pig like Sam in *Sam, Come Back!*? Text to Text
2. How does the author make Pig seem silly? Think Like an Author
3. What problem does Pig have? How does Pig solve the problem? Plot
4. Tell about the important events in the story. Summarize
5. **Look Back and Write** Look back at page 57. How does Pig feel? Write about it. Use evidence from the story.

Key Ideas and Details • Text Evidence

58

Meet the Illustrator

Janet Stevens

Janet Stevens always wanted to draw pictures. She enjoys drawing pictures for children's books.

Ms. Stevens practices drawing all the time. "Practice helps a lot in whatever you try to do," she says. She likes to draw pigs, cats, and bears.

Here are other books illustrated by Janet Stevens.

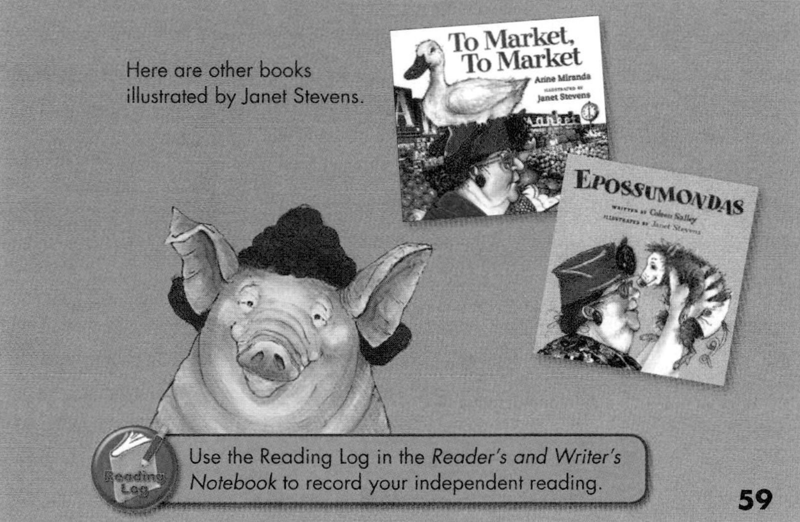

Use the Reading Log in the *Reader's and Writer's Notebook* to record your independent reading.

59

Student Edition, pp. 58–59

Common Core State Standards

Literature 1. Ask and answer questions about key details in a text. **Literature 2.** Retell stories, including key details, and demonstrate understanding of their central message or lesson. **Also Literature 9., Writing 5.**

Bridge to Common Core

KEY IDEAS AND DETAILS

By reading the text multiple times, children will make logical inferences from the text and cite textual evidence when writing or discussing the knowledge they have gained. Use the Think Critically page to ensure a thorough understanding of *Pig in a Wig*.

Think Critically

1. **TEXT TO TEXT** Both Pig and Sam are animals. They both are pets.
2. **THINK LIKE AN AUTHOR** The author shows Pig wearing a wig. Pig also does a silly jig at the end of the story.
3. **PLOT** Pig eats too much and gets a stomachache. A woman gives Pig medicine.
4. **SUMMARIZE** Pig mixes a lot of food and eats it. She does not feel well. A woman gives Pig medicine. Pig feels better.
5. **LOOK BACK AND WRITE • TEXT EVIDENCE** For writing fluency, assign a 5-minute time limit. As children finish, encourage them to reread their responses and proofread for errors.

Scoring Rubric Look Back and Write

TOP-SCORE RESPONSE A top-score response uses details from the text and the pictures to tell how Pig feels at the end of the story.

A top-score response might include:
Pig feels happy. She does a jig. She felt better after she took medicine.

Retell

Have children use the retelling strip in the Student Edition or the Story Sort to retell the selection. Monitor children's retellings.

Scoring Rubric Narrative Retelling

	4	3	2	1
Connections	Makes connections and generalizes beyond the text	Makes connections to other events, stories, or experiences	Makes a limited connection to another event, story, or experience	Makes no connection to another event, story, or experience
Author's Purpose	Elaborates on author's purpose	Tells author's purpose with some clarity	Makes some connection to author's purpose	Makes no connection to author's purpose
Characters	Describes the main character(s) and any character development	Identifies the main character(s) and gives some information about them	Inaccurately identifies some characters or gives little information about them	Inaccurately identifies the characters or gives no information about them
Setting	Describes the time and location	Identifies the time and location	Omits details of time or location	Is unable to identify time or location
Plot	Describes the events in sequence using rich detail	Tells the plot with some errors in sequence that do not affect meaning	Tells parts of plot with gaps that affect meaning	Retelling has no sense of story

Don't Wait Until Friday

MONITOR PROGRESS Check Retelling

If… children have trouble retelling the selection,

then… use Story Sequence Graphic Organizer 23 and the Retelling Cards/ Story Sort, and work with the group to scaffold their retelling.

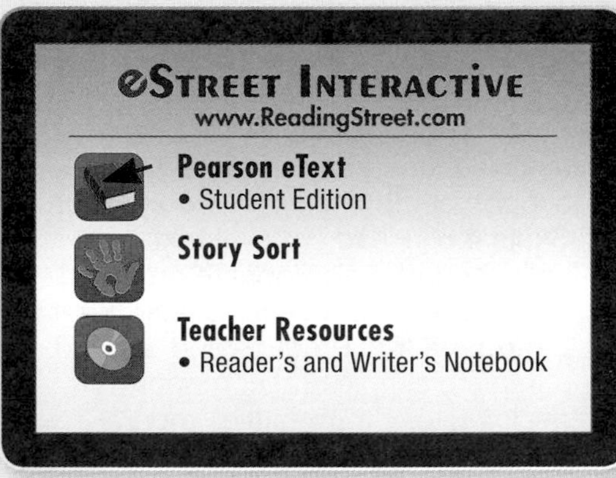

Writing to Sources

Use Write Like a Reporter on pp. 46–47 to guide children in writing text-based responses using one source.

Strategy Response Log

Summarize Have children use p. RR14 in their *Reader's and Writer's Notebook* to draw a picture that tells an important event in the story.

Plan to Assess Retelling

- ☐ **Week 1** Strategic Intervention
- ☑ **This Week** Assess Advanced children.
- ☐ **Week 3** Strategic Intervention
- ☐ **Week 4** On-Level
- ☐ **Week 5** Strategic Intervention
- ☐ **Week 6** Assess any children you have not yet checked during this unit.

Meet the Illustrator

Read aloud page 59 as children follow along. Ask children why illustrators practice drawing.

Read Independently

Have children enter their independent reading into their Reading Logs.

Fluency

Accuracy

MODEL FLUENT READING Have children turn to Student Edition page 48. Review that it is very important to read each word in a sentence correctly. When I read a sentence, I try to read each word correctly. I try not to change words or leave words out.

GUIDE PRACTICE Have children read the page with you. Then have them reread the page as a group until they read with no mistakes. Continue in the same way with pages 49–50.

Corrective feedback	**If...** children have difficulty reading with accuracy, **then...** prompt: • Did you read every word correctly? • Did you change any words? • Did you leave out any words? • Try to read all the words correctly.

Reread for Fluency

Routine Choral Reading

1. **Select a Passage** For *Pig in a Wig,* use pp. 51–53.
2. **Model** First, have children track the print as you read.
3. **Guide Practice** Then have children read along with you.
4. **Corrective Feedback** Have the class read aloud without you. Monitor progress and provide feedback. For optimal fluency, children should reread three to four times.

Routines Flip Chart

CHECK COMPREHENSION What do you think will happen next to Pig? How can you check to see if your prediction is right? (I think that Pig will take medicine to feel better. I can keep reading and looking at the pictures to confirm my prediction.)

Common Core State Standards

Foundational Skills 4. Read with sufficient accuracy and fluency to support comprehension. **Foundational Skills 4.b.** Read on-level text orally with accuracy, appropriate rate, and expression on successive readings. **Language 1.j.** Produce and expand complete simple and compound declarative, interrogative, imperative, and exclamatory sentences in response to prompts.

Options for Oral Rereading

Use *Pig in a Wig* or one of this week's Decodable Practice Readers.

Professional Development

Fluency Many children are visual learners. Displaying written words on the board or on a Word Wall helps children become more familiar with words and letters and reminds them of the importance of language and reading.

Conventions

Subjects of Sentences

REVIEW Remind children that the subject of a sentence tells who or what a sentence is about: *The boy ran. Mom ate an apple.*

GUIDE PRACTICE Write this sentence on the board and have children read it aloud.

The cat can sit in the hat.

What is the subject of this sentence? (the cat) Circle *the cat.* How do you know? (The subject tells who or what a sentence is about.)

Team Talk While in pairs, have one child perform an action. Then have the other child say a sentence that tells what the partner is doing. Ask that child to name the subject of the sentence. Then have the partners switch roles.

APPLY Have children use subjects to complete these sentence frames orally.

1. A _______ can run fast.
2. A _______ likes to play ball.
3. My _______ plays in the sink.

ON THEIR OWN Use *Reader's and Writer's Notebook,* p. 150.

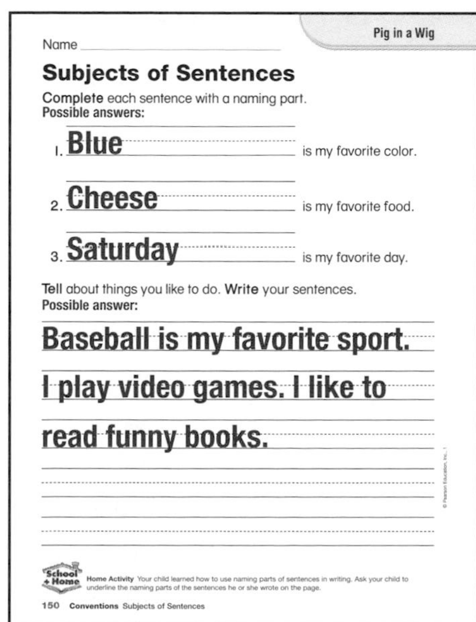
Pig in a Wig

Name

Subjects of Sentences

Complete each sentence with a naming part.
Possible answers:

1. Blue is my favorite color.
2. Cheese is my favorite food.
3. Saturday is my favorite day.

Tell about things you like to do. **Write** your sentences.
Possible answer:

Baseball is my favorite sport. I play video games. I like to read funny books.

Home Activity Your child learned how to use naming parts of sentences in writing. Ask your child to underline the naming parts of the sentences he or she wrote on the page.

150 Conventions Subjects of Sentences

Reader's and Writer's Notebook, p. 150

eSTREET INTERACTIVE
www.ReadingStreet.com

Teacher Resources
- Reader's and Writer's Notebook
- Daily Fix-It Transparency

Daily Fix-It

5. Jak can fiks it.
Jack can fix it.

6. dad can mix et
Dad can mix it.

Discuss the Daily Fix-It corrections with children. Review sentence capitalization and punctuation, /k/ spelled *ck,* /ks/ spelled *x,* and /i/ spelled *i.*

ELL

Subjects of Sentences In Spanish, subjects do not precede predicates as often as in English. Spanish verb endings allow subjects to follow verbs or to be understood. Provide many examples of English sentences with the subjects of each clearly stated to help children learn what the subjects are.

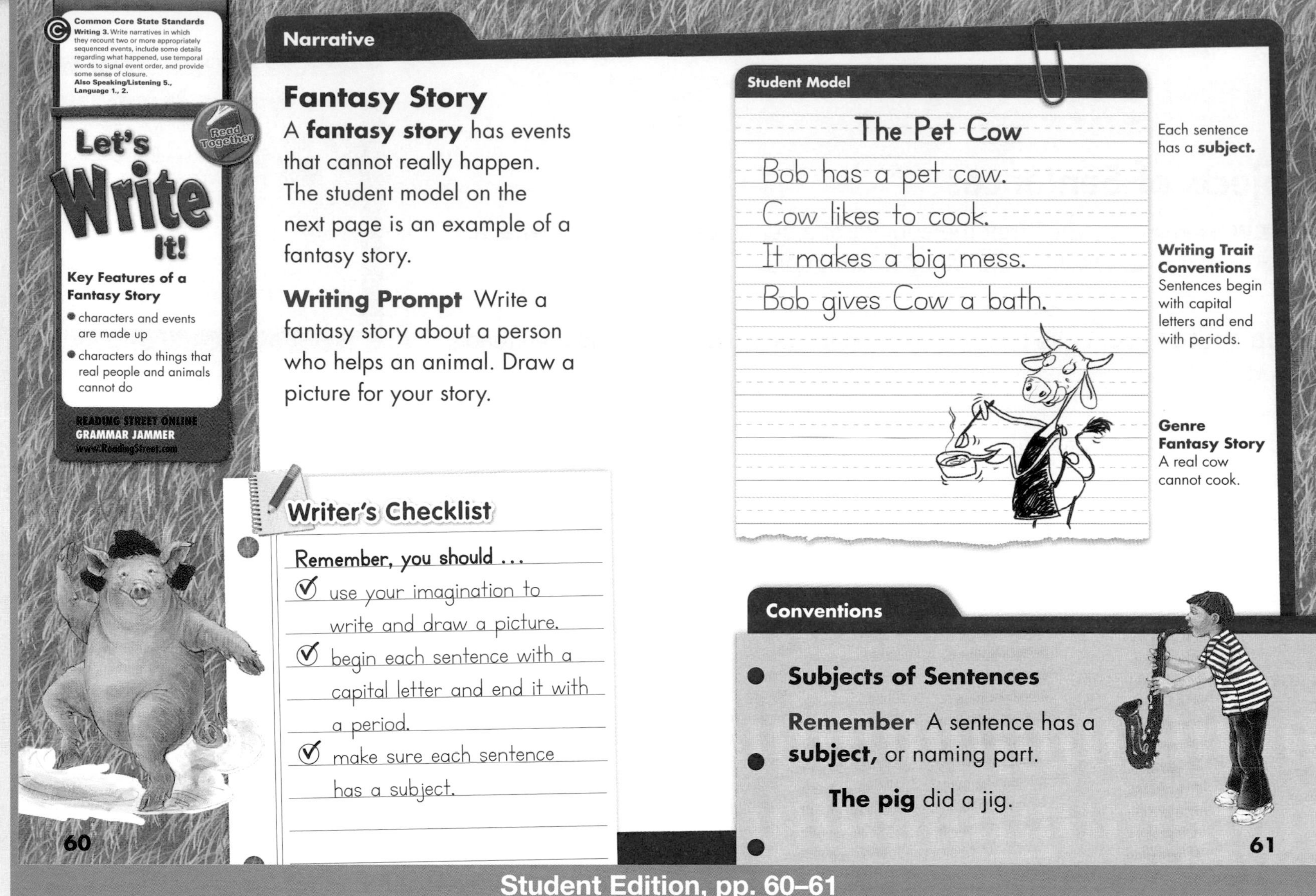

Common Core State Standards
Writing 3. Write narratives in which they recount two or more appropriately sequenced events, include some details regarding what happened, use temporal words to signal event order, and provide some sense of closure.
Also Speaking/Listening 5., Language 1., 2.

Read Together

Let's Write It!

Key Features of a Fantasy Story
- characters and events are made up
- characters do things that real people and animals cannot do

READING STREET ONLINE
GRAMMAR JAMMER
www.ReadingStreet.com

Narrative

Fantasy Story

A **fantasy story** has events that cannot really happen. The student model on the next page is an example of a fantasy story.

Writing Prompt Write a fantasy story about a person who helps an animal. Draw a picture for your story.

Writer's Checklist

Remember, you should ...
- ✓ use your imagination to write and draw a picture.
- ✓ begin each sentence with a capital letter and end it with a period.
- ✓ make sure each sentence has a subject.

60

Student Model

The Pet Cow

Bob has a pet cow.
Cow likes to cook.
It makes a big mess.
Bob gives Cow a bath.

Each sentence has a **subject.**

Writing Trait Conventions
Sentences begin with capital letters and end with periods.

Genre Fantasy Story
A real cow cannot cook.

Conventions

Subjects of Sentences

Remember A sentence has a **subject,** or naming part.

The pig did a jig.

61

Student Edition, pp. 60–61

Common Core State Standards

Writing 3. Write narratives in which they recount two or more appropriately sequenced events, include some details regarding what happened, use temporal words to signal event order, and provide some sense of closure. **Writing 5.** With guidance and support from adults, focus on a topic, respond to questions and suggestions from peers, and add details to strengthen writing as needed. **Also Speaking/Listening 5., Language 1., 2.**

Let's Write It!

WRITE A FANTASY STORY Use pages 60–61 in the Student Edition. Read aloud the Key Features of a Fantasy Story and the definition of a fantasy story. Read aloud the Writing Prompt and discuss the Writer's Checklist.

REVIEW THE STUDENT MODEL Then read "The Pet Cow" on page 61 to children. Point out the events in the story that could not happen in real life. Ask children to identify the characters. (Bob, his pet cow) Read aloud and briefly discuss the side notes about subjects, genre, and the writing trait.

Scoring Rubric

TOP-SCORE RESPONSE Help children understand that a top-score response is imaginative and has sentences that begin with capital letters, end with punctuation, and have subjects. For a complete rubric see Writing Rubric 2 from the *Teacher Resources DVD-ROM.*

CONNECT TO CONVENTIONS Read to children the Conventions note about subjects of sentences. Point out subjects in the model. *(Bob, the cow, it)*

Fantasy Story

Mini-Lesson Writing Trait: Conventions

- **Introduce** Use your story chart from yesterday and Writing Transparency 2A to model writing sentences beginning with capital letters and ending with correct punctuation. When I write my story, I will use my chart. Yesterday I wrote that the dog, Pal, will ask a worker at a shelter to help him find a new owner. I will begin my story by introducing Pal with the sentence, "One day a dog named Pal came to an animal shelter." I can help readers understand my story by beginning the sentence with a capital letter and ending it with a period. Read aloud the draft on the transparency and show the capital letters and end punctuation. Point out that the exclamation point at the end shows strong feeling.

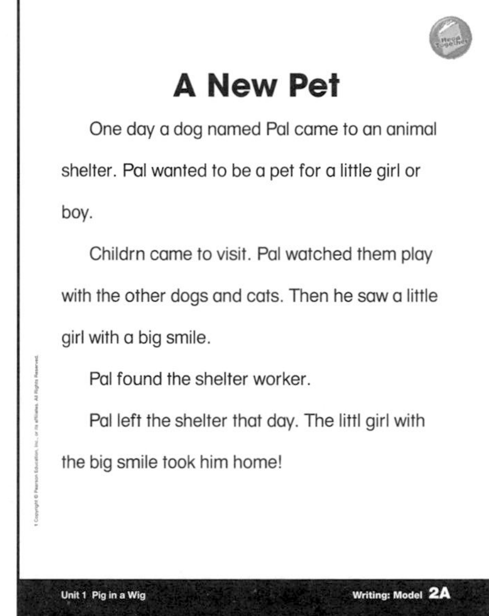

A New Pet

One day a dog named Pal came to an animal shelter. Pal wanted to be a pet for a little girl or boy.

Childrn came to visit. Pal watched them play with the other dogs and cats. Then he saw a little girl with a big smile.

Pal found the shelter worker.

Pal left the shelter that day. The littl girl with the big smile took him home!

Unit 1 Pig in a Wig — Writing: Model 2A

Writing Transparency 2A TR DVD

- Explain how children can use story events they planned yesterday to draft their story: beginning, middle, and end. Today's goal is to write the story but not to rewrite each word perfectly. They can edit later to correct the words.

GUIDE WRITING Now it is time to write your story. Tell how one of your characters helps an animal. Then draw a picture showing an important part of your story. Have children use their story charts. Help them finish the ideas. Then guide children as they draft the stories.

Routine Quick Write for Fluency — Team Talk

1. **Talk** Have partners take one minute to tell the most important event in their stories.
2. **Write** Each child writes a sentence about the important event.
3. **Share** Partners check the capitalization and punctuation of each other's sentences.

Routines Flip Chart

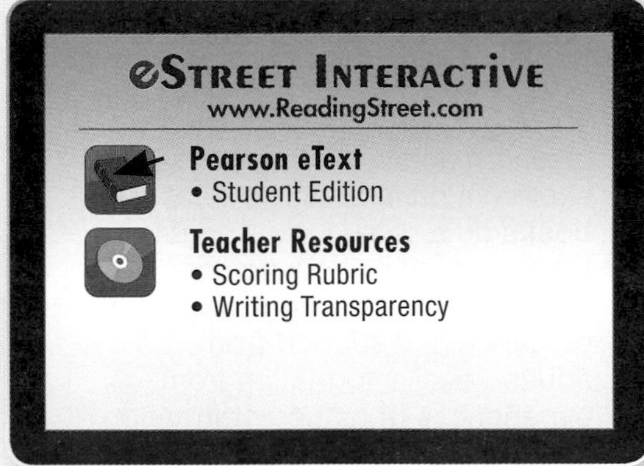

Access for All

A Advanced

Developing Sentences Children may include questions and exclamations as well as statements. Help them with the end punctuation, if necessary.

Common Core State Standards

Writing 7. Participate in shared research and writing projects (e.g., explore a number of "how-to" books on a given topic and use them to write a sequence of instructions). **Writing 8.** With guidance and support from adults, recall information from experiences or gather information from provided sources to answer a question. **Speaking/ Listening 1.** Participate in collaborative conversations about grade 1 topics and texts with peers and adults in small and larger groups. **Also Speaking/Listening 4., 6.**

Bridge to Common Core

COMPREHENSION AND COLLABORATION

Children develop listening and speaking skills as they participate in a range of conversations and collaborations to share information about caring. The instruction includes describing a caring person to develop an understanding of good citizens. They learn to ask questions about key issues or concepts to clarify and deepen their understanding of content.

Listening and Speaking

Share Information About Caring

TEACH Explain to children that caring is about being kind and helpful to others. When we care about others, we show that we are good citizens.

- A caring person helps others who are in need.
- A caring person is kind to others.
- A caring person thinks about the feelings of others.
- A caring person cares about people, animals, places, and things that are special to them.
- A caring person doesn't expect to be rewarded for their kindness.

Think Aloud **MODEL** I will share information about caring for a pet. I have a pet named Spot. He is a brown-and-white hamster. Spot is a funny hamster. He likes to run around in circles when I let him out of his cage. He also likes to exercise on his exercise wheel. I try to play with Spot as often as I can. This gives him the exercise he needs. He has a lot of fun too! I try to take very good care of Spot.

GUIDE PRACTICE Briefly discuss the model. Have children share other ideas or information about caring. Explain how to speak clearly so that everyone can hear, and the importance of speaking at an appropriate pace. Explain that speaking in sentences with subjects and verbs helps listeners understand our ideas. Ask children to explain the problems with mumbling or speaking too quickly or slowly.

ON THEIR OWN Have pairs of children take turns talking about something or someone they care about. Encourage them to explain how caring for this something or someone makes them happy. Remind children to speak clearly and to listen attentively. Remind them to speak in complete sentences.

Research and Inquiry

Step 3 Gather and Record Information

TEACH Tell children that today they will look through sources of information to learn about a topic. They will draw a picture about people who help animals, based on the information they find about the topic.

Think Aloud **MODEL** Display the list of questions the class created on Day 1. Before we can draw a picture, we have to pick a topic and learn more about it. We should choose the question that we think is the most interesting. The person the question is about will be our topic. We can gather information about our topic from sources found in a media center or library. We can use sources such as a dictionary, an encyclopedia, and the Internet.

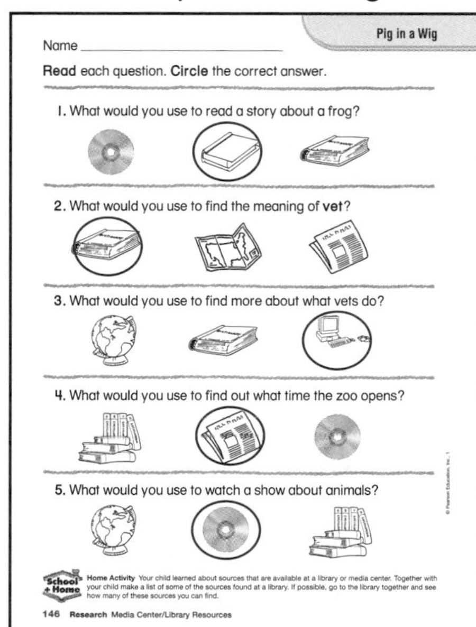

Name ___________ Pig in a Wig

Read each question. **Circle** the correct answer.

1. What would you use to read a story about a frog?
2. What would you use to find the meaning of **vet**?
3. What would you use to find more about what vets do?
4. What would you use to find out what time the zoo opens?
5. What would you use to watch a show about animals?

School + Home **Home Activity** Your child learned about sources that are available at a library or media center. Together with your child make a list of some of the sources found at a library. If possible, go to the library together and see how many of these sources you can find.

© Pearson Education, Inc., 1

146 **Research** Media Center/Library Resources

Reader's and Writer's Notebook, p. 146

GUIDE PRACTICE Have children choose a question from the list. Then have them identify their topic. Tell them to use reference works to locate information about the topic. Encourage children to find two or three facts about their topic and to record the information they have found. Explain that they will use this information to draw a picture about the topic.

ON THEIR OWN Use *Reader's and Writer's Notebook,* p. 146.

Access for All

SI Strategic Intervention

Choosing Sources Some children may have trouble knowing which source would be helpful in relation to their topic. Review each source with children and explain its use. Remind children that the same or similar information is often found in more than one source.

Wrap Up Your Day!

✔ **Plot** Have children think about what happens in *Pig in a Wig.* How would the plot be different if Pig did not eat so much? (She would not get sick and need medicine.)

✔ **Summarize** Remind children that, when they summarize, they should include only the important events in the story. What were some important events in *Pig in a Wig?*

Tell children that tomorrow they will read more about people who help animals.

Content Knowledge
Oral Vocabulary

Phonemic Awareness
Distinguish /i/

Phonics
Review Short *a* Spelled *a*
Review Consonant Digraph *-ck*

High-Frequency Words
Review

Spelling
Short *i* Words

Social Studies in Reading
Sing-Along

Fluency
Accuracy

Conventions
Subjects of Sentences

Writing
Fantasy Story: Revise

Research and Inquiry
Synthesize

Materials

- Student Edition
- Sing with Me Big Book
- Read Aloud Anthology
- Decodable Reader 2C
- Reader's and Writer's Notebook

Common Core State Standards

Speaking/Listening 2. Ask and answer questions about key details in a text read aloud or information presented orally or through other media. **Language 5.c.** Identify real-life connections between words and their use (e.g., note places at home that are *cozy*). **Also Language 6.**

Content Knowledge

Helping Animals

EXPAND THE CONCEPT To reinforce concepts and to focus children's attention, have children sing "Pet Service" from the *Sing with Me* Big Book. How is a groomer like a vet? (A groomer works with animals and helps animals feel better.) How is a groomer different from a vet? (A groomer cleans animals and cuts their hair.)

Build Oral Language

GENRE: REALISTIC FICTION Have children tell the key features of realistic fiction: It tells about made-up people and events, but the characters, events and setting seem real. The story seems like it could really happen. Explain that today you will read about an animal that needs help in "The Storm Seal" by Judy Waite.

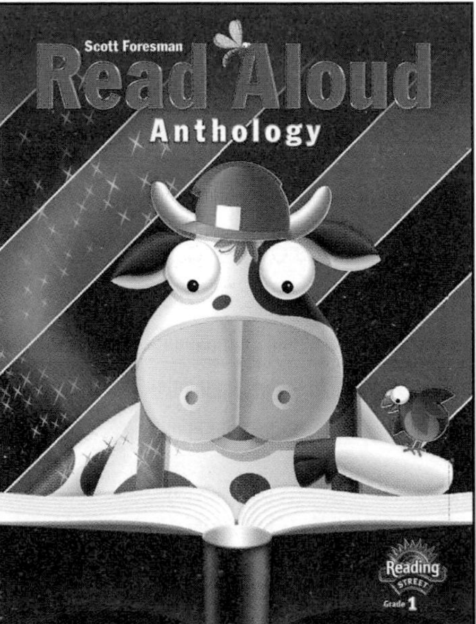

"The Storm Seal"

MONITOR LISTENING COMPREHENSION Recall that Pig needed help because she ate too much and felt sick. Have children listen to "The Storm Seal."

Team Talk **TALK ABOUT HELPING ANIMALS** Read aloud the seventh paragraph of "The Storm Seal." Display it on a whiteboard if possible, and track the print as you read.

- Have pairs of children generate questions for each other about how Peter comforts the seal.
- Add words generated in the discussion to the concept map.

Build Oral Vocabulary

Amazing Words Robust Vocabulary Routine

1. **Introduce the Word** Relate the word *search* to the story. The old man had to *search* through seaweed to find trash after the storm. Supply a child-friendly definition. When you *search,* you look carefully to try to find something. Have children say the word.

2. **Demonstrate** Provide examples to show meaning. They had to *search* for the missing coat. I have to *search* for an overdue library book.

3. **Apply** Have children demonstrate their understanding. Where would you *search* for shells on a beach?

4. **Display the Word** Point out the sound-spelling *s*/s/ at the beginning of *search.*

See p. OV•2 to teach *comfort.*

Routines Flip Chart

ADD TO THE CONCEPT MAP Discuss the kinds of animals people can help.

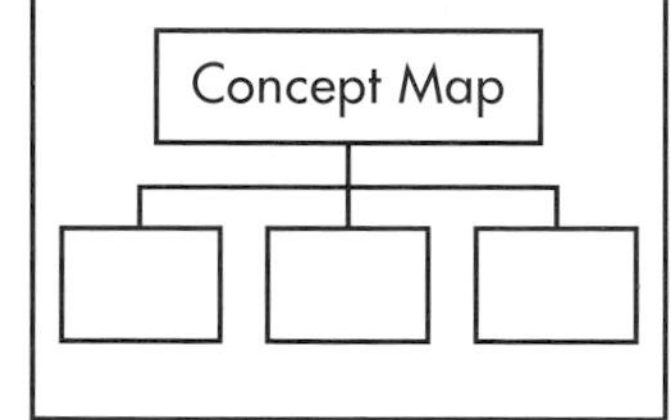

- We read about a seal today in "The Storm Seal." Was the seal a tame animal or a wild animal? (a wild animal) How do you know? (It lived with other seals and not with people.)
- How did Peter take care of the seal pup? (He comforted it, fed it, and helped it get back to the other seals.) Let's add *People help tame and wild animals* to the map.

Amazing Words

career	sloppy
service	exercise
tool	comfort
scrub	search

Access for All

Strategic Intervention

Sentence Production If children omit the sound /r/ from words such as *storm* and *Peter,* then say the word again, stressing the sound /r/, and have children repeat it.

Produce Oral Language Use the Day 4 instruction on ELL Poster 2 to extend and enrich language.

Support Listening Use ELL Poster 2 to review how people take care of animals. Discuss how the horse is taken care of. Before reading, ask children: How do you treat an animal when you take care of it?

Descriptive Language Read the first paragraph of "The Storm Seal" aloud. Explain that the writer uses strong words, such as *wild* and *angry,* to describe the storm. Talk about what these words mean and how they help describe the storm. For more advanced work, talk about the words *scratched, grumbling, heaved,* and *hurled.*

Common Core State Standards

Foundational Skills 2.c. Isolate and pronounce initial, medial vowel, and final sounds (phonemes) in spoken single-syllable words. **Foundational Skills 2.d.** Segment spoken single-syllable words into their complete sequence of individual sounds (phonemes). **Foundational Skills 3.** Know and apply grade-level phonics and word analysis skills in decoding words. **Foundational Skills 3.a.** Know the spelling-sound correspondences for common consonant digraphs.

Phonemic Awareness

Distinguish /i/

MODEL This week we read about a man who feeds a baby seal fish soup. Listen as I say the sounds in *fish.* Slowly segment the sounds in *fish,* /f/ /i/ /sh/. The middle sound I hear in *fish* is /i/. We're going to listen to other words with the beginning and middle sound /i/.

GUIDE PRACTICE I will say some words, and you can tell me if they have the /i/ sound in the middle or at the beginning. Say each word below and then guide children to decide whether the /i/ sound is in the middle or at the beginning of each one.

Corrective feedback | **If...** children make an error, **then...** segment the word and model the correct response. Return to the word later in the practice.

wish	**win**	**pick**
it	**into**	**fill**

ON THEIR OWN Have children tell you which of the following words contain the /i/ sound.

jig	**flip**	**ten**
drum	**fist**	**itch**

Phonics

Review Short *a* Spelled *a*; Consonant Digraph *-ck*

REVIEW SHORT *a* SPELLED *a* To review last week's first phonics skill, write *tag* and *cat.* You studied words like these last week. What do you know about the vowel sound in these words? (The vowel sound is /a/, the short *a* sound.) How do you spell the sound /a/? (The sound /a/ is spelled *a.*)

REVIEW CONSONANT DIGRAPH *-ck* To review last week's second phonics skill, write *pack* and *tack.* You also studied words like these. What do you know about the final sound in these words? (The final sound is /k/.) How do you spell the sound /k/ in these words? (The sound /k/ is spelled *ck* in these words.)

Corrective feedback | **If...** children are unable to answer your questions about the vowel and consonant sounds in the words you wrote, **then...** refer them to Sound-Spelling Cards 1 and 36.

GUIDE PRACTICE Use Graphic Organizer 4. When I say a word, hold up one hand if the word has the short *a* sound or two hands if it does not have the short *a* sound: *cap, wag, lick, sack, bit, sick, fan, six, quack, jig.* Write each word in the appropriate column. Have children identify words with the final /k/ sound spelled *ck (lick, sack, sick, quack).*

Short *a*	Not Short *a*
cap	lick
wag	bit
sack	sick
fan	six
quack	jig

Graphic Organizer 4

ON THEIR OWN Use Let's Practice It! pp. 35–36 on the *Teacher Resources DVD-ROM.*

Access for All

SI Strategic Intervention

Blending Words For children having difficulty blending short *a* and *ck* words, use sound-by-sound blending to model blending *pack.* Continue using sound-by-sound blending with other words such as *hack, tack, back,* and *lack.*

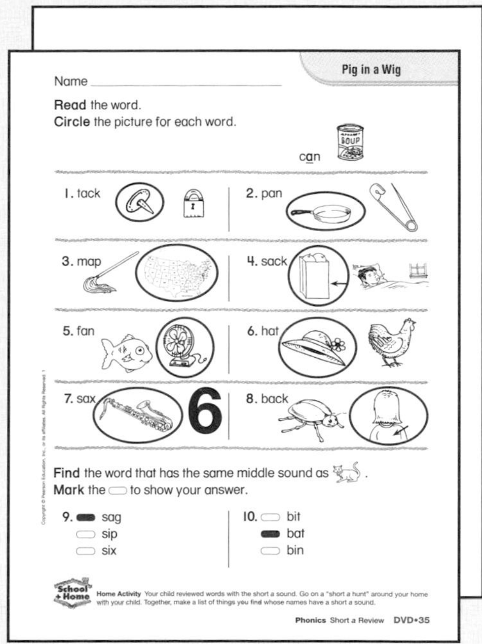
Pig in a Wig

Name ______

Read the word.
Circle the picture for each word.

can

1. tack
2. pan
3. map
4. sack
5. fan
6. hat
7. sax
8. back

Find the word that has the same middle sound as [cat]. **Mark** the ⬭ to show your answer.

9. sag / sip / six
10. bit / bat / bin

School + Home **Home Activity** Your child reviewed words with the short a sound. Go on a "short a hunt" around your home with your child. Together, make a list of things you find whose names have a short *a* sound.

Phonics Short *a* Review DVD•35

Let's Practice It! TR DVD•35–36

Pronouncing Short *a* Short vowel sounds may be challenging for English language learners because they are unfamiliar sounds. Languages such as Spanish and Chinese do not have exact equivalents. Remind children that when pronouncing short *a,* your jaw and tongue are down. Have children practice saying the /a/ sound with you.

Common Core State Standards

Foundational Skills 3. Know and apply grade-level phonics and word analysis skills in decoding words. **Foundational Skills 3.g.** Recognize and read grade-appropriate irregularly spelled words. **Foundational Skills 4.** Read with sufficient accuracy and fluency to support comprehension.

Decodable Reader 2C

If children need help, then...

Read *Mix and Fix*

DECODE WORDS IN ISOLATION Have children turn to page 137 and decode each word listed.

REVIEW HIGH-FREQUENCY WORDS Review the previously taught words *see* and *take.* Have children read each word as you point to it on the Word Wall.

PREVIEW Have children read the title and preview the story. Tell them they will read words with the short *i* sound and words with the consonant *x*/ks/.

DECODE WORDS IN CONTEXT Pair children for reading and listen as they decode. One child begins. Children read the entire story, switching readers after each page. Partners reread the story. This time the other child begins.

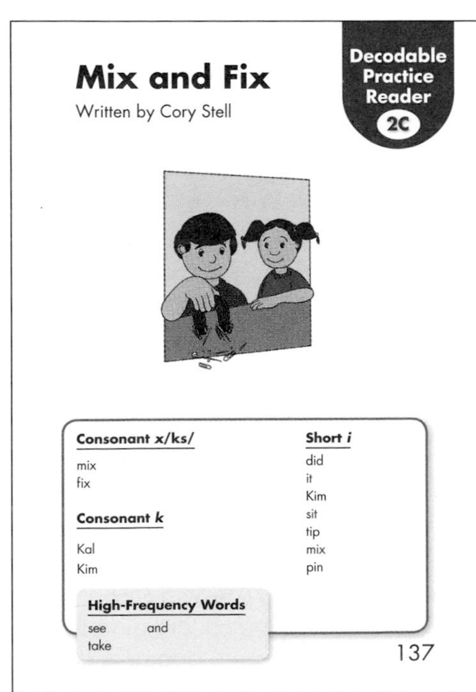
Mix and Fix

Written by Cory Stell

Decodable Practice Reader 2C

Consonant *x*/ks/: mix, fix

Consonant *k*: Kal, Kim

Short *i*: did, it, Kim, sit, tip, mix, pin

High-Frequency Words: see, and, take

137

Decodable Practice Reader 2C

Did Kal see it?
Kim did!
138
Did Kim take it?
Kim did!
139

Did Kim sit on it?
Kim did!
140
Did Kim tip it?
Kim did!
141

Did Kim mix it?
Kim did!
142
Did Kim pin it?
Kim did!
143

Did Kim fix it?
Kim and Kal did!
144

Corrective feedback	**If...** children have difficulty decoding a word, **then...** refer them to the Sound-Spelling Cards to identify the sounds in the word. Then prompt them to blend the word. • What is the new word? • Is the new word a word you know? • Does it make sense in the story?

CHECK DECODING AND COMPREHENSION Have children retell the story to include characters, setting, and events. Then have children find words with the short *i* and /ks/ sounds. Children should supply *did, it, Kim, sit, tip, pin, mix,* and *fix.* Ask children how they know these words have the short *i* and /ks/ sounds. (They have the letter *x* at the end and the *i* in the middle of the word.)

Reread for Fluency

REREAD DECODABLE READER Have children reread Decodable Practice Reader 2C to develop automaticity decoding words with the short *i* and /ks/ sounds.

Routine Oral Rereading

1. **Read** Have children read the entire book orally.
2. **Reread** To achieve optimal fluency, children should reread the text three or four times.
3. **Corrective Feedback** Listen as children read. Provide corrective feedback regarding their fluency and decoding.

Routines Flip Chart

Decodable Practice Reader

Beginning Before children read, lead them on a picture walk through *Mix and Fix.* Point out and pronounce the words that have the short *i* and /ks/ sounds. Then write a pictured word and have children pronounce it and find its picture.

Intermediate Before reading, help children pronounce the words with the short *i* and /ks/ sounds in the story title, *Mix and Fix.* Then have them use the words *mix* and *fix* to make a prediction about what the story will be about.

Advanced After reading, have children find the words with the short *i* and /ks/ sounds. Then have them make up two sentences about what the story characters, Kim and Kal, are doing, using the words *fix, mix, tip, sit,* and *did.*

Common Core State Standards

Foundational Skills 3. Know and apply grade-level phonics and word analysis skills in decoding words. **Foundational Skills 3.a.** Know the spelling-sound correspondences for common consonant digraphs. **Language 2.d.** Use conventional spelling for words with common spelling patterns and for frequently occurring irregular words.

Spiral Review

These activities review

- previously taught high-frequency words *my, the, do, that, come, to, with.*
- short *a* spelled *a;* consonant digraph *-ck;* initial and final consonants.

Fluent Word Reading

Spiral Review

READ WORDS IN ISOLATION Display these words. Tell children that they can blend some words on this list, and others are Word Wall words.

Have children read the list three or four times until they can read at the rate of two to three seconds per word.

bag	**the**	**do**	**nap**	**mad**
can	**Matt**	**Dan**	**that**	**Nan**
tack	**ran**	**sat**	**back**	**to**
my	**Dad**	**pack**	**come**	**with**

Corrective feedback

Word Reading

If... children have difficulty reading whole words,
then... have them use sound-by-sound blending for decodable words, or have them say and spell high-frequency words.

If... children cannot read fluently at a rate of two to three seconds per word,
then... have pairs practice the list until they can read it fluently.

READ WORDS IN CONTEXT Display these sentences. Call on individuals to read a sentence. Then randomly point to review words and have children read them. To help you monitor word reading, high-frequency words are underlined and decodable words are italicized.

Dan will pack* <u>**the**</u> *big bag.

Kim can nap* <u>**with**</u> *Dad.

Nan can* <u>**come**</u> *sit in back.

Matt ran back* <u>**to**</u> *Dad.

Corrective feedback

Sentence Reading

If... children are unable to read an underlined high-frequency word,
then... read the word for them and spell it, having them echo you.

If... children have difficulty reading an italicized decodable word,
then... guide them in using sound-by-sound blending.

Spelling

Short *i* Words

PARTNER REVIEW Supply pairs of children with index cards on which the spelling words have been written. Have one child read a word while the other writes it. Then have children switch roles. Have them use the cards to check their spelling and correct any misspelled words.

ON THEIR OWN Use *Reader's and Writer's Notebook,* p. 151.

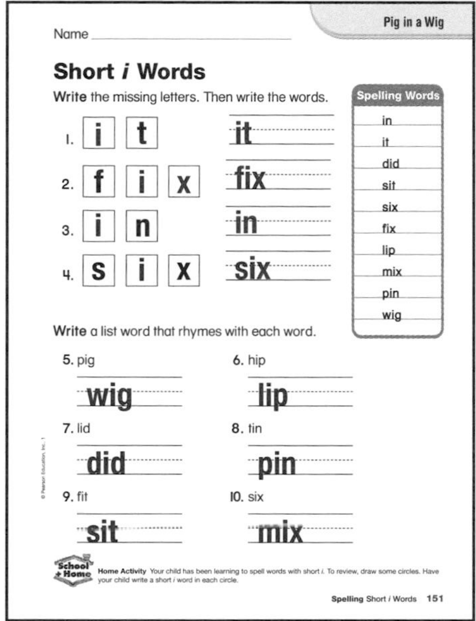
Name

Pig in a Wig

Short *i* Words

Write the missing letters. Then write the words.

1. i t — it
2. f i x — fix
3. i n — in
4. s i x — six

Spelling Words: in, it, did, sit, six, fix, lip, mix, pin, wig

Write a list word that rhymes with each word.

5. pig — wig
6. hip — lip
7. lid — did
8. tin — pin
9. fit — sit
10. six — mix

© Pearson Education, Inc., 1

School + Home **Home Activity** Your child has been learning to spell words with short *i*. To review, draw some circles. Have your child write a short *i* word in each circle.

Spelling Short *i* Words 151

Reader's and Writer's Notebook, p. 151

ELL

Fluent Word Reading Have children listen to a more fluent reader say the words. Then have them repeat the words.

Day 4 SMALL GROUP TIME • Differentiate Vocabulary, p. SG•18

OL On-Level
- **Develop** Language Using Selection Vocabulary
- **Read** *Reading Street Sleuth,* pp. 10–11

SI Strategic Intervention
- **Review/Discuss** Selection Vocabulary
- **Read** *Reading Street Sleuth,* pp. 10–11

A Advanced
- **Extend** Amazing Words and Selection Vocabulary
- **Read** *Reading Street Sleuth,* pp. 10–11
- **Organize** Inquiry Project

ELL

If... children need more scaffolding and practice with **Vocabulary, then...** use the routine on pp. xxxvi–xxxvii in the *ELL Handbook.*

Literature 1. Ask and answer questions about key details in a text. **Literature 7.** Use illustrations and details in a story to describe its characters, setting, or events. **Literature 10.** With prompting and support, read prose and poetry of appropriate complexity for grade 1.

Academic Vocabulary 

sing-along a poem set to music that people sing together

rhyme end in the same sound

Social Studies in Reading

Sing-Along

ACTIVATE PRIOR KNOWLEDGE Ask children what they learned from other texts they have read or listened to this week about how people help animals. Have children recall what the woman in *Pig in a Wig* did to help Pig feel better. (She gave Pig a spoonful of medicine.)

PREVIEW AND PREDICT Have children turn to page 62 in their Student Edition. Read the title and the author's name. Have children preview the song and predict how the characters might help animals. (Possible response: The characters will give animals medicine or treatment to help them get well.) Ask them what clues helped them make that prediction. (Possible response: They might say the title of the selection or the clothing the characters are wearing in the pictures.)

READ A SING-ALONG Tell children that this is a **sing-along.** Review the key features of a sing-along: it is a poem set to music. It has a rhythm and some words might rhyme. People sing the poem together, usually to a well-known tune. Explain that this selection is a sing-along because it is a poem with rhythm that is set to the tune "Three Blind Mice."

Genre

LET'S THINK ABOUT... As you read "We Are Vets" together, use Let's Think About in the Student Edition to help children focus on the features of a sing-along.

1. The words *vets* and *pets* rhyme, and the words *sick, quick,* and *stick* rhyme. Have children clap the rhythm of the song following the structure of "Three Blind Mice."

Common Core State Standards
Literature 10. With prompting and support, read prose and poetry of appropriate complexity for grade 1.

Social Studies in Reading

Genre
Sing-Along

- A song people sing together is sometimes called a sing-along. New words may be sung to a well-known tune.
- A sing-along is a poem set to music. It has clear rhythm, and some of the words may rhyme.
- Kids might sing a sing-along during a long car ride with their families or at summer camp with other kids.
- Read "We Are Vets." As you read, look for elements that make it a sing-along.

Read Together

We Are Vets

by Linda Lott
illustrated by Lindsey Gardiner

Sing to the tune of "Three Blind Mice."

We are vets.
We are vets.
We help pets.
We help pets.

62

If you have a dog who
is feeling sick,
Bring him to me, and I'll
fix him quick.
His tail will wag, and
he'll chase a stick.
He'll feel fine. He'll feel fine.

Let's Think About...

Which words rhyme in this sing-along? What is its rhythm? **Sing-Along**

1

Let's Think About...

Reading Across Texts The pig in *Pig in a Wig* and the dog in "We Are Vets" both feel sick. Who helps them get better? How?

Writing Across Texts Write a poem about what the two animals do after they get better. Use rhythm and rhyme in your poem.

63

Student Edition, pp. 62–63

Access Text

Think Aloud **PREDICT AND SET PURPOSE** Good readers use text and pictures to predict what will happen in a story. When I first saw this song, I wondered what it would be about. I looked at the pictures and read the first few lines. I predict that the song will be about vets and what they do to help pets. I will sing the song to find out if my prediction is correct.

GENRE As I read "We Are Vets," I notice that some words rhyme. Let's sing "We Are Vets" and use the tune from the song "Three Blind Mice" to understand the pattern of the rhythm.

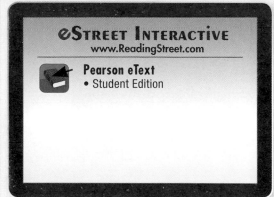

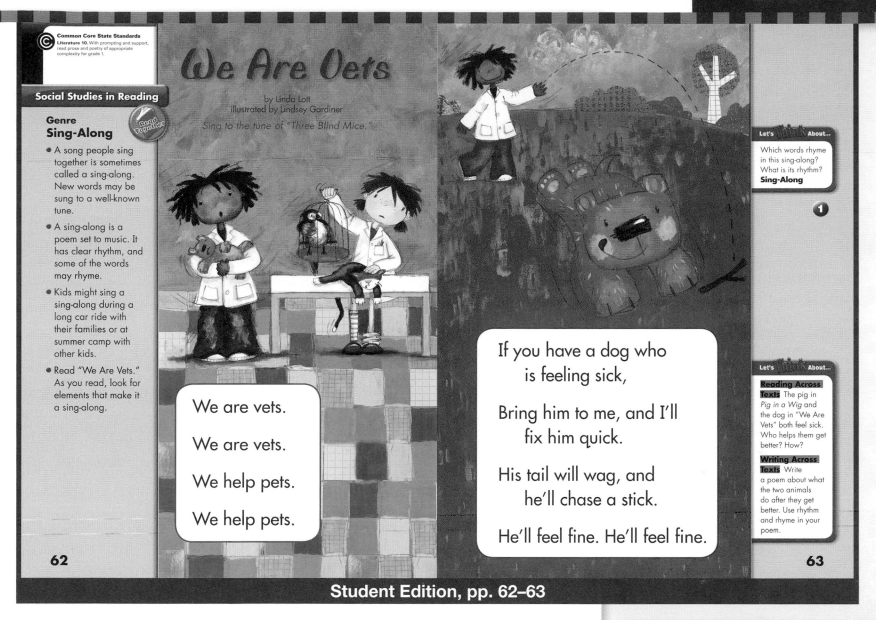

Social Studies Vocabulary

vet a doctor who takes care of animals

Common Core State Standards

Literature 1. Ask and answer questions about key details in a text. **Literature 10.** With prompting and support, read prose and poetry of appropriate complexity for grade 1. **Foundational Skills 4.** Read with sufficient accuracy and fluency to support comprehension. **Foundational Skills 4.b.** Read on-level text orally with accuracy, appropriate rate, and expression on successive readings.

Writing to Sources

Use Connect the Texts on pp. 48–49 to guide children in writing text-based responses using two sources.

Access Text

SETTING What is the setting at the beginning of the sing-along? What is the setting at the end? Explain how you know. (At the beginning of the sing-along, the setting is an animal hospital. There are vets in a room and they have pets on a table. At the end of the sing-along, the setting is a park. A dog is chasing after a stick in a place with a lot of grass.)

CONFIRM PREDICTIONS How did you use clues in the sing-along to predict what would happen next? (In the beginning, I saw that the lines "We are vets" and "We help pets" are repeated. That made me guess that a vet would help a pet in the song. I also used the pictures to see that the pets were sick in the beginning of the song and the dog felt better at the end of the song.)

PLOT What do the vets in the song do? (They help pets that aren't feeling well.)

MAIN IDEA AND DETAILS What clues in the song let us know that the sick dog is feeling better? (The song says "He'll wag his tail, and he'll chase a stick." I know that happy dogs wag their tails and chase after things. Sick dogs don't do that.)

Reading and Writing Across Texts

Have children find words and sentences in the texts of *Pig in a Wig* and "We Are Vets" to tell who helps the animals and what those people do to make the animals feel better.

Children might note that Pig in *Pig in a Wig* does a jig, while the dog in "We Are Vets" chases after a stick.

Fluency

Accuracy

- Have children turn to pp. 52–53 in *Pig in a Wig.*
- Have children follow along as you read the pages accurately.
- Have the class read the pages with you and then reread the pages as a group without you until they read with no mistakes.

Routine Paired Reading

1. **Select a Passage** For *Pig in a Wig,* use pp. 54–55.
2. **Model** First, have children track the print as you read.
3. **Guide Practice** Then have children read along with you.
4. **On Their Own** For optimal fluency, have partners reread three or four times.

Routines Flip Chart

MONITOR PROGRESS Fluency Check

As children reread, monitor their progress toward their individual fluency goals. Mid-Year Goal: 20–30 words correct per minute. End-of-Year Goal: 60 words correct per minute. Beginning in Unit 3, children will be assessed to determine WCPM.

If... children are not on track to meet benchmark goals,
then... have children practice with text at their independent level.

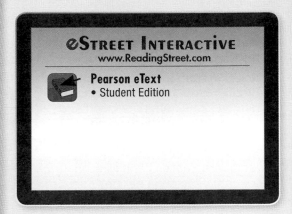

Access for All

Advanced

Rate If children already read at 60 words correct per minute, have them read more challenging text.

Options for Oral Rereading

Use *Pig in a Wig* or one of this week's Decodable Practice Readers.

Conventions

Subjects of Sentences

TEST PRACTICE Use *Reader's and Writer's Notebook,* p. 152 to help children understand subjects in sentences in test items. Recall that subjects are the naming part of a sentence. They tell who or what the sentence is about: *the cat, Pam, a dog.* Model identifying a subject in a sentence by writing this sentence on the board, reading it aloud, and underlining the subject.

The turtle was very slow.

ON THEIR OWN Then read the directions on *Reader's and Writer's Notebook,* p. 152. Guide children as they mark the answer for number 1.

APPLY After children mark the answers to numbers 1–6, review the correct choices aloud, and have children read each sentence, emphasizing the subject.

Pig in a Wig

Name ______

Subjects of Sentences

Mark the sentence that has a line under the naming part.

1. ○ My mom is a vet.
   ⊗ My mom is a vet.
   ○ My mom is a vet.
2. ⊗ She helps sick animals.
   ○ She helps sick animals.
   ○ She helps sick animals.
3. ○ That dog cut its leg.
   ○ That dog cut its leg.
   ⊗ That dog cut its leg.
4. ⊗ This cat hurt its paw.
   ○ This cat hurt its paw.
   ○ This cat hurt its paw.
5. ○ A vet will fix them.
   ⊗ A vet will fix them.
   ○ A vet will fix them.
6. ○ The animals like my mom.
   ○ The animals like my mom.
   ⊗ The animals like my mom.

School + Home **Home Activity** Your child prepared for taking tests on the naming parts of sentences. Write simple sentences about your family, such as these: *Anne is your sister. Your mother works at a bank.* Ask your child to circle each naming part.

152 **Conventions** Subjects of Sentences

Reader's and Writer's Notebook, p. 152

Common Core State Standards

Writing 5. With guidance and support from adults, focus on a topic, respond to questions and suggestions from peers, and add details to strengthen writing as needed. **Language 2.** Demonstrate command of the conventions of standard English capitalization, punctuation, and spelling when writing. **Also Language 1., 1.j.**

Bridge to Common Core

CONVENTIONS OF STANDARD ENGLISH

As children develop understanding of the subject of a sentence, they learn to produce complete sentences to gain control of the conventions of standard English grammar, usage, and mechanics. The lessons help children use language to convey meaning effectively as they speak and write.

Daily Fix-It

1. pig is en back.
   Pig is in back.
2. Take that weg
   Take that wig.

Discuss the Daily Fix-It corrections with children. Review sentence capitalization and punctuation, and short *i* spelled *i.*

Fantasy Story

Mini-Lesson Revise: Adding a Sentence

- Yesterday we wrote fantasy stories about people helping an animal. Today we will revise to help people who read the stories. One way to make the stories clearer is to add a sentence.

- Display the Revising Tips. Explain that this is a time for making the story clear for anyone who will read it. Tomorrow children will proofread to correct any errors such as misspellings, missing capital letters, or misplaced sentence periods.

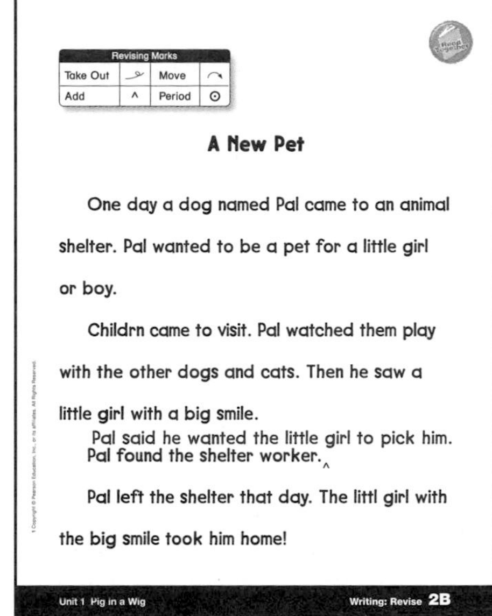

Revising Marks			
Take Out	⌒	Move	⌒
Add	^	Period	⊙

A New Pet

One day a dog named Pal came to an animal shelter. Pal wanted to be a pet for a little girl or boy.

Childrn came to visit. Pal watched them play with the other dogs and cats. Then he saw a little girl with a big smile. Pal said he wanted the little girl to pick him. Pal found the shelter worker.^

Pal left the shelter that day. The littl girl with the big smile took him home!

Unit 1 Pig in a Wig — Writing: Revise 2B

Writing Transparency 2B TR DVD

Revising Tips

✔ Make sure your characters do something real people or animals cannot do.

✔ Add a sentence if it can make your story clearer.

- Use Writing Transparency 2B to model adding sentences. In my fantasy story "A New Pet," Pal wants a little girl to take him home. I can make this part of the story clearer by adding the sentence: "Pal said he wanted the little girl to pick him." Add the sentence to the third paragraph on the transparency. Tell children that as they revise they can add sentences to their story to make them clearer or more imaginative.

PEER CONFERENCING • PEER REVISION Pair children and tell one partner to read the other's story. Allow one to two minutes. Then have the readers tell which part of the story they like most. Repeat with second partner reading and telling about the other story. Have each writer listen for any part of the story that the reader has not understood. Circulate to assist children planning to revise their stories. As appropriate, suggest adding sentences to make stories clearer.

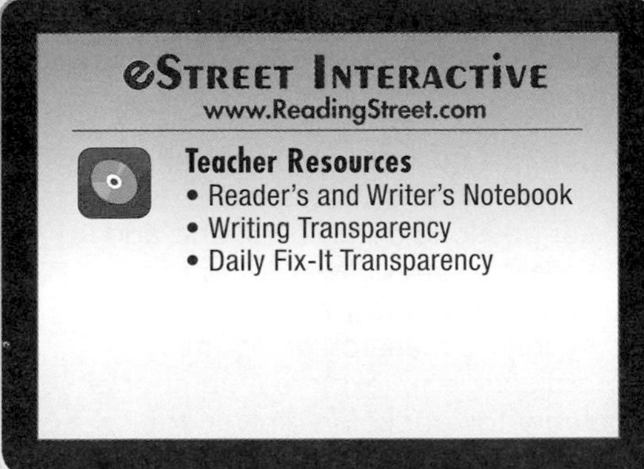

Access for All

SI Strategic Intervention

Subjects of Sentences Remind children that the subject of a sentence is who or what the sentence is about. As they read a sentence, guide them to ask a question to gain understanding of who or what it is about. For example write: *The yellow ball rolled under the car.* Ask children What rolled under the car? (the yellow ball) The *yellow ball* is the subject of the sentence.

Pronoun Agreement Be sure children understand that the words *he* and *him* can be substituted for the names of male characters and the words *she* and *her* can be substituted for the names of female characters.

Common Core State Standards

Writing 5. With guidance and support from adults, focus on a topic, respond to questions and suggestions from peers, and add details to strengthen writing as needed. **Writing 7.** Participate in shared research and writing projects (e.g., explore a number of "how-to" books on a given topic and use them to write a sequence of instructions). **Writing 8.** With guidance and support from adults, recall information from experiences or gather information from provided sources to answer a question. **Language 2.** Demonstrate command of the conventions of standard English capitalization, punctuation, and spelling when writing.

Writing

Zoom in on

GUIDE PRACTICE Have children revise their stories and begin drawing pictures for their stories. For those not sure how to revise, have children refer to the Revising Tips or the Key Features of a Fantasy Story.

Corrective feedback Circulate to monitor and confer with children as they write. Remind them that they will have time to proofread and edit tomorrow. Today they can make changes in story events or make sentences clearer. Help them understand the benefits of adding or changing sentences. Encourage them to make the beginning, middle, and end imaginative, and help them to choose an event to show in a picture.

Routine Quick Write for Fluency

Team Talk

1. **Talk** These sentences tell part of a story. Read them aloud, and have children tell what event could be missing from the story.
   We were making a salad.
   The lettuce was all over the floor!
2. **Write** Have children write a sentence that could be added to the story to make it clearer.
3. **Share** Partners can read the sentences to one another.

Routines Flip Chart

Research and Inquiry

Step 4 Synthesize

TEACH The next step in the inquiry project is to review our topic to see if we have the information we set out to find, or if our answers led to a different topic.

Think Aloud **MODEL** We wanted to learn more about a topic so that we could draw a picture about it. First, we made a list of questions. Then we learned about different resources available to us and chose a topic to focus on. We used resources to find out more about the topic we chose. Now I will see if we found any information I could use to help me draw a picture about people who help animals. If we did not, we can gather more information using the resources we learned about.

GUIDE PRACTICE Have children look at the information they gathered during Day 3. Instruct them to work with a partner to choose information for which they could draw a picture. If necessary, they can conduct research to gather more information. Finally, tell children that tomorrow they will organize all the information in order to share it with others.

Access for All

SI Strategic Intervention

Visualizing If children have difficulty visualizing pictures they could draw using the information they gathered, ask them to close their eyes and tell a partner what they see when they think of that information. Have them determine if it is something they could draw.

A Advanced

Using Judgment For children who have similar ideas for drawings, ask them to work together and create a small mural that combines their efforts.

Wrap Up Your Day!

- ✔ **Phonics** List words that end in *x*. Have children read each word and identify the final /ks/ sound.
- ✔ **Fluency** Write on the board: *Max can fit in the big box.* Have children read the sentence three or four times until they can do so fluently.

Remind children that they heard about a seal that needed some help. Tomorrow they will hear about the seal again.

DAY 5 at a Glance

Content Knowledge
Oral Vocabulary

Phonemic Awareness
Review Segment and Count Phonemes

Phonics/Spelling
Review Short *i: i*
Review Consonant *x*/ks/

Text-Based Comprehension
Review Plot

Selection Words
Review

High-Frequency Words
Review

Assessment
Phonics
High-Frequency Words
Fluency

Conventions
Review Subjects of Sentences

Writing
Fantasy Story: Proofread

Research and Inquiry
Communicate

Materials
- Student Edition
- Read Aloud Anthology
- Weekly Test

Bridge to Common Core

INTEGRATION OF KNOWLEDGE/IDEAS
This week children have integrated content presented in diverse formats and analyzed how different texts address similar topics. They have developed knowledge about people who help animals to expand the unit topic of animals, tame and wild.

Social Studies Knowledge Goals
Children have learned that
- pet owners help animals
- vets help animals
- trainers help animals

Content Knowledge

Zoom in on ©

Helping Animals

REVIEW THE CONCEPT This week we have read and listened to stories about how people help animals. Today you will listen to a story about a baby seal. Read the story.

- What gave the baby seal comfort, or made it feel better? (The baby seal sucked on Peter's hand for comfort.)

"The Storm Seal"

Build Oral Language

REVIEW AMAZING WORDS Have children use this week's Amazing Words and K-W-L concept map to answer the question, *Who helps animals?*

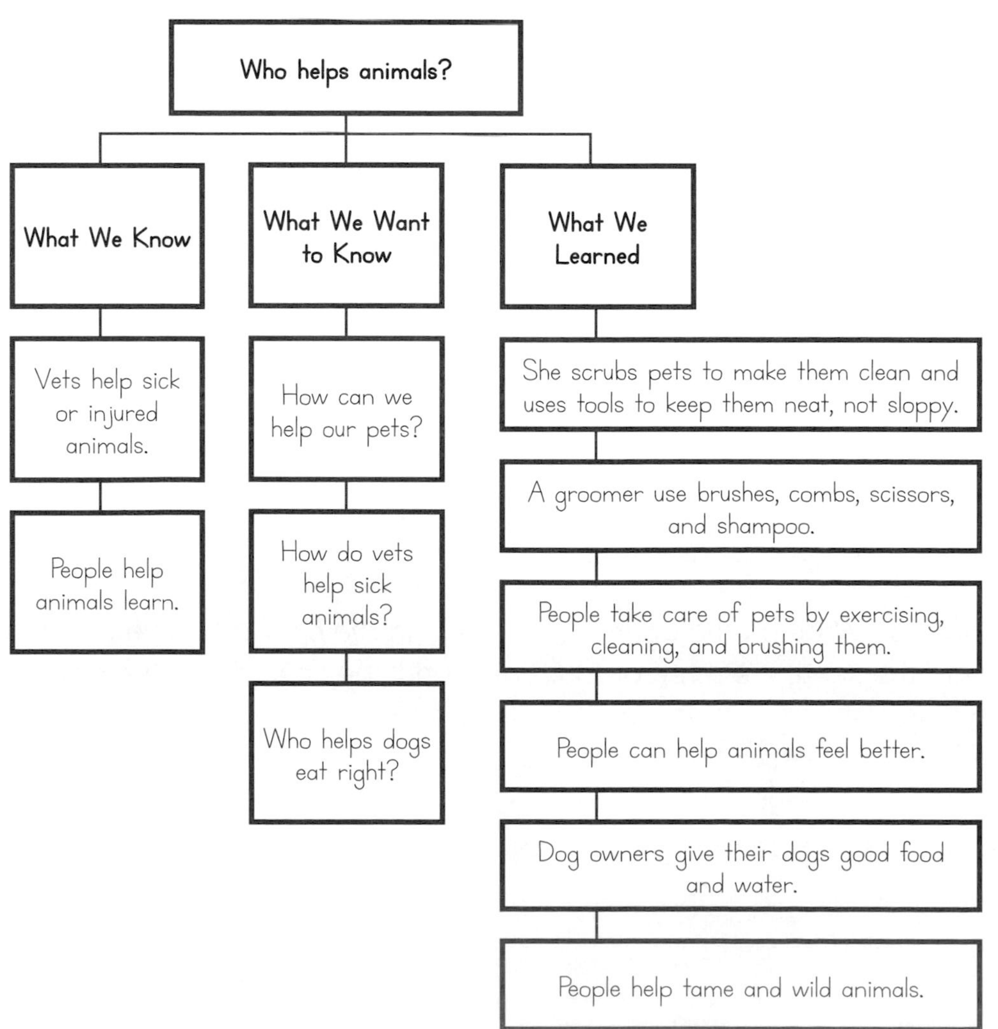

Who helps animals?
What We Know
What We Want to Know
What We Learned
Vets help sick or injured animals.
People help animals learn.
How can we help our pets?
How do vets help sick animals?
Who helps dogs eat right?
She scrubs pets to make them clean and uses tools to keep them neat, not sloppy.
A groomer use brushes, combs, scissors, and shampoo.
People take care of pets by exercising, cleaning, and brushing them.
People can help animals feel better.
Dog owners give their dogs good food and water.
People help tame and wild animals.

Build Oral Vocabulary

Team Talk **CONNECT TO AMAZING IDEAS** Pair children and have them discuss how the Question of the Week, *Who helps animals?,* connects to the question of this unit of study: *How are people and animals important to one another?* Tell children to use the K-W-L concept map and what they've learned from this week's discussions and reading selections to form an Amazing Idea—a realization or "big idea" about **animals, tame and wild.** Use the following ideas as prompts:

- Who are some people that help animals? (pet owners, vets, groomers)
- What are some ways that people help animals?

Then ask each pair to share their Amazing Idea with the class. Encourage children to recall in which selection they learned their ideas.

Amazing Ideas might include:

- People can help animals by taking care of them and comforting them.
- Pet owners clean and feed their pets and help them get exercise.
- Groomers use special tools to keep animals neat and clean.

MONITOR PROGRESS Check Oral Vocabulary

FORMATIVE ASSESSMENT Call on individuals to use this week's Amazing Words to talk about who helps animals. Prompt discussion with the questions below. Monitor children's ability to use the Amazing Words and note which words children are unable to use.

- **Which *tool* do you think pet groomers use the most when taking care of animals? Why?**
- **Why might you need to *scrub* a *sloppy* pet?**
- **What type of *career* would you choose to be of *service* to animals?**
- **How would you *search* for a lost pet? Why might your pet need *comfort* after you find it?**
- **Why is it important that your pet gets *exercise?***

If... children have difficulty using the Amazing Words,

then... reteach the unknown words using the Robust Vocabulary routines, pp. 39a, 44b, 58b, 62b.

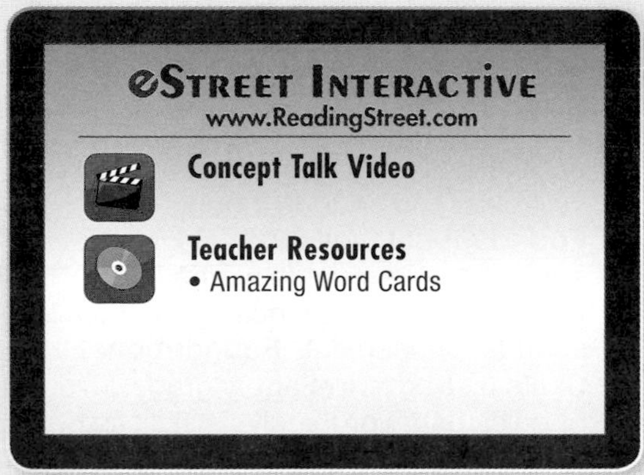

Amazing Words

career	sloppy
service	exercise
tool	comfort
scrub	search

Access for All

A Advanced

Extend the Concept Ask children who show good understanding of the concept to review the stories they read this week and add to at least one column of the existing K-W-L concept chart.

Check Concepts and Language Use the Day 5 instruction on ELL Poster 2 to monitor children's understanding of the lesson concept.

Amazing Words Create short sentence starters for children to help them use the words in sentences. For example: *Two kinds of tools are a brush and a ______.*

Common Core State Standards

Foundational Skills 2. Demonstrate understanding of spoken words, syllables, and sounds (phonemes). **Foundational Skills 2.d.** Segment spoken single-syllable words into their complete sequence of individual sounds (phonemes). **Foundational Skills 3.** Know and apply grade-level phonics and word analysis skills in decoding words. **Language 2.d.** Use conventional spelling for words with common spelling patterns and for frequently occurring irregular words.

Phonemic Awareness

Review Segment and Count Phonemes

SEGMENTING Have children segment each word below and count how many sounds are in the word. If children make an error, model the correct response. Return to the word later in the practice.

will	/w/ /i/ /l/	**rob**	/r/ /o/ /b/	**trick**	/t/ /r/ /i/ /k/
sick	/s/ /i/ /k/	**back**	/b/ /a/ /k/	**mess**	/m/ /e/ /s/
ten	/t/ /e/ /n/	**flit**	/f/ /l/ /i/ /t/	**stiff**	/s/ /t/ /i/ /f/

Phonics

Review Short *i: i;* Consonant *x*/ks/

TARGET PHONICS SKILLS Write the following sentences on the board. Have children read each one, first quietly to themselves and then aloud as you track the print.

1. **Max can fix the rip.**
2. **Mix it in the bin.**
3. **Tim hid the big ax.**
4. **Pam can hit the rim.**

Team Talk Have children discuss with a partner which words have short *i* and which words end with the consonant *x.* Then call on individuals to share with the class.

Spelling Test

Short *i* Words

DICTATE SPELLING WORDS Say each word, read the sentence, repeat the word, and allow time for children to write the word.

1. six	Jan is **six.**
2. lip	I bit my **lip.**
3. in	The jam is **in** the can.
4. wig	The **wig** will fit me.
5. it	Where is **it?**
6. did	**Did** Zack see the cat?
7. mix	**Mix** the jam.
8. sit	Max can **sit** on the sack.
9. pin	**Pin** the cap on.
10. fix	I can **fix** the rack.

High-Frequency Words

11. she	**She** is sick.
12. take	I can **take** him.

Assess

- Spell words with short *i*.
- Spell high-frequency words.

Access for All

SI Strategic Intervention

Segment Words Help children spell each word on the test by saying the individual sounds in each word, for example: /l/ /i/ /p/.

A Advanced

Extend Spelling Have children who have demonstrated proficiency in spelling individual words spell each word in a self-made sentence.

Day 5 SMALL GROUP TIME • Differentiate Reteaching, p. SG•18

OL On-Level

- **Practice** Subjects of Sentences
- **Reread** *Reading Street Sleuth,* pp. 10–11

SI Strategic Intervention

- **Review** High-Frequency Words
- **Reread** *Reading Street Sleuth,* pp. 10–11

A Advanced

- **Extend** Subjects of Sentences
- **Reread** *Reading Street Sleuth,* pp. 10–11
- **Communicate** Inquiry Project

If... children need more scaffolding and practice with **Conventions and Writing,**
then... use the activities on pp. DI•41–DI•42 in the Teacher Resources section on SuccessNet.

Common Core State Standards
Speaking/Listening 1. Participate in collaborative conversations about grade 1 topics and texts with peers and adults in small and larger groups. **Also Foundational Skills 4.b., Speaking/Listening 1.a.**

Let's Learn It!

Read Together

READING STREET ONLINE
VOCABULARY ACTIVITIES
www.ReadingStreet.com

I have a cat named Button. I feed him and give him fresh water every day. I brush him so his fur is shiny and clean. He likes that.

Listening and Speaking

Get Ready For Grade 2

Listen carefully when others are speaking.

Share Information and Ideas When we tell others our ideas, we speak clearly so that they understand us. When others tell us their ideas, we listen so that we understand them.

Practice It! When asked, tell others how you care for an animal. Then let them tell you how they care for an animal. Follow the rules. Listen carefully. Take notes to help you understand.

64

Vocabulary

These words are in **alphabetical order.** Look at the first letter in each word. Think about the alphabet.

ant bat cat

Practice It! Read these words. Write them in alphabetical order.

big dip am can

Fluency

Accuracy When you read, try to read with no mistakes.

Practice It!

1. Max can mix it.
2. The black cat licks Bill.
3. She will take the sack.

65

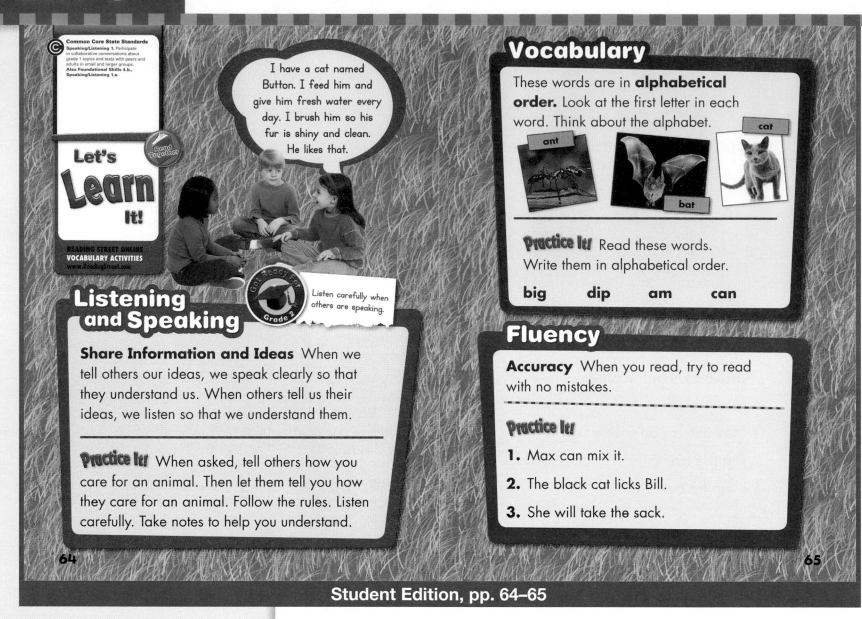

Student Edition, pp. 64–65

Common Core State Standards

Foundational Skills 4.b. Read on-level text orally with accuracy, appropriate rate, and expression on successive readings. **Speaking/Listening 1.** Participate in collaborative conversations about grade 1 topics and texts with peers and adults in small and larger groups. **Speaking/Listening 1.a.** Follow agreed-upon rules for discussions (e.g., listening to others with care, speaking one at a time about the topics and texts under discussion). **Also Speaking/Listening 6., Language 1.**

Share Information and Ideas

To prepare for Grade 2, children should be able to speak clearly and provide facts and details when sharing information and ideas.

Listening and Speaking

Share Information and Ideas

TEACH Have children turn to page 64 of the Student Edition. Read and discuss what the child in the photo is telling the other children. Remind children that good speakers speak clearly and use subjects in their sentences to name who or what the sentence is about. Explain to children that it is also important to listen carefully when others speak. Ask how the child in the photo shares information.

INTRODUCE PROMPT Read the Practice It! prompt with the class. Remind children to provide details and to always use a subject in each sentence when sharing information or ideas.

Team Talk Have pairs take turns asking and telling how they care for an animal. Remind children that good speakers speak clearly and slowly and that good listeners listen carefully.

Vocabulary

Alphabetize

TEACH Read and discuss the Vocabulary lesson on page 65 of the Student Edition. Use the model to explain how to alphabetize a series of words to the first letter.

MODEL Point to each illustration and name it. I see an *ant,* a *bat,* and a *cat.* What letter does each of these words begin with? (*a, b,* and *c*) I know that *a* is the first letter of the alphabet. *Ant* begins with *a,* so I'll write *ant* first. Continue to model alphabetizing *bat* and *cat.*

GUIDE PRACTICE Read the instructions for the Vocabulary Practice It! activity. Read the first word and then have children repeat after you.

What is the first letter of the alphabet? *(a)* Do you see a word that begins with *a? (am)* Let's write this word first.

ON THEIR OWN Have children continue alphabetizing the remaining words by stating the next letter of the alphabet.

Corrective feedback | Circulate around the room and listen as children alphabetize the words. Provide assistance as needed.

Fluency

Accuracy

TEACH Read and discuss the Fluency instructions.

READ WORDS IN CONTEXT Give children a moment to look at the sentences. Then have them read each sentence three or four times until they can read each sentence with accuracy.

Access for All

SI Strategic Intervention

Picture Cards Some children might find it helpful to use picture cards and put the cards in alphabetical order first before writing the words in order.

A Advanced

Advanced Alphabetizing For children who show ease in alphabetizing to the first letter, have them alphabetize a short list of words to the second letter: *ant, art, act.*

Use Sentence Frames Provide these sentence frames to help children structure their understanding of alphabetizing: *The letter ________ is the ________ letter of the alphabet. Does a word in this list begin with ________?*

Common Core State Standards

Literature 3. Describe characters, settings, and major events in a story, using key details. **Literature 5.** Explain major differences between books that tell stories and books that give information, drawing on a wide reading of a range of text types. **Literature 9.** Compare and contrast the adventures and experiences of characters in stories. **Foundational Skills 3.g.** Recognize and read grade-appropriate irregularly spelled words.

Text-Based Comprehension

Review Plot

Remember that plot is what happens in the beginning, middle, and end of the story. It often includes a problem and a solution. Why do good readers pay attention to the plot? (It helps them understand what is happening in the story.)

CHECK UNDERSTANDING Read aloud the following story and have children answer the questions that follow.

Amy came home from school and called her cat, Whiskers. But Whiskers did not come. Amy looked for Whiskers under her bed. She checked his spot on the sofa. She searched in her closet. Where could he be? Amy checked one last place. She looked in the laundry basket downstairs. "There you are!" Amy said. Whiskers purred to say hello.

1. What was Amy's problem in the story? (Amy could not find Whiskers.)
2. How did Amy solve her problem? (She searched for Whiskers and found him in the laundry basket.)

Vocabulary

Review High-Frequency and Selection Words

HIGH-FREQUENCY WORDS Review this week's high-frequency words: *she, take, up, what.* Model creating a rhyme that tells something about this week's selection and includes a high-frequency word in each line.

Team Talk Have children make up their own rhymes using as many of the week's high-frequency words as they can. Have them share their rhymes with the class.

SELECTION WORDS Write the word *play.* Read it aloud together. Then have children tell what the word means.

Corrective feedback	**If...** children cannot tell what the selection word means, **then...** review the definition on page 46a.

Genre

Realism and Fantasy

GENRE Review with children that *Pig in a Wig* is an animal fantasy because it is a made-up story about a pig that does things real pigs cannot do. This story could not happen in real life. Recall *Sam, Come Back!* from Week 1. Explain that this story is realistic fiction because it is a made-up story that could happen in real life.

TEACH I'm going to list some of the events in *Sam, Come Back!* that could really happen. Then I'll list events in *Pig in a Wig* that could never happen in real life. Use Graphic Organizer 4 or draw a T-chart.

Think Aloud **MODEL** In *Sam, Come Back!,* Sam sits on a lap. Then he jumps down and runs away with yarn. These are both events that could really happen, so I'll write them in my chart. In *Pig in a Wig,* Pig mixes food in a bowl. She also eats from a spoon she holds. These are events that could not really happen, so I'll add them to the chart.

Sam, Come Back!	Pig in a Wig
Sam the cat sits on a lap.	Pig mixes food in a bowl.

Graphic Organizer 4

GUIDE PRACTICE Have children continue to add events to the chart. Ask the following questions to guide children in comparing and contrasting realistic fiction and animal fantasy.

- What is true about events in realistic fiction such as *Sam, Come Back!?* (Possible response: The events could really happen.)
- What is true about the events in animal fantasy such as *Pig in a Wig?* (Possible response: The events could not really happen.)

ON THEIR OWN What are some ways that Sam and Pig are the same? (They are animals. They do things they are not supposed to do.) What are some ways they are different? (Sam does things a cat would do. Pig does things a pig would not do.)

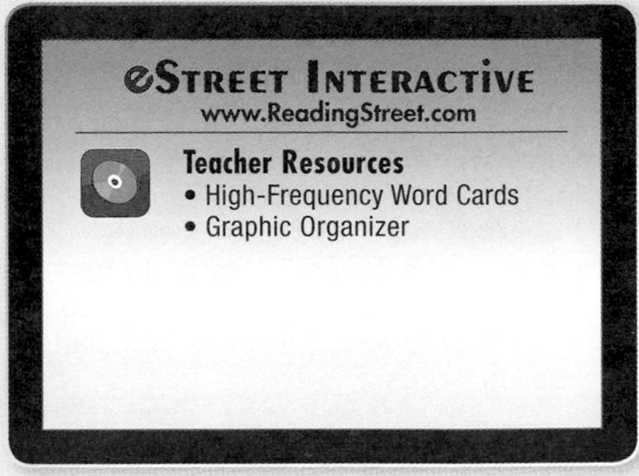

eSTREET INTERACTIVE
www.ReadingStreet.com
Teacher Resources
• High-Frequency Word Cards
• Graphic Organizer

Access for All

SI Strategic Intervention

Compare Real and Made Up If children have difficulty understanding the difference between realism and fantasy, ask them to compare the actions of the characters to real animals. Is this something a real ________ would do?

Academic Vocabulary 

events the things that happen in a story

fantasy a made-up story that could never really happen

realistic fiction a made-up story that could happen in real life

Use Illustrations Have children use the illustrations in *Pig in a Wig* and *Sam, Come Back!* to help identify what events could or could not happen in real life.

Common Core State Standards

Foundational Skills 3. Know and apply grade-level phonics and word analysis skills in decoding words. **Foundational Skills 3.b.** Decode regularly spelled one-syllable words. **Foundational Skills 3.g.** Recognize and read grade-appropriate irregularly spelled words.

Assess

- ⦿ Words with Short *i*
- ⦿ Words with Consonant *x*/ks/
- High-Frequency Words

Assessment

Monitor Progress

For a written assessment of short *i,* consonant *x*/ks/, high-frequency words, and plot, use Weekly Test 2, pages 43–48.

WORD READING Use the following reproducible page to assess children's ability to read words in isolation. Call on children to read the words aloud. Start over if necessary.

SENTENCE READING Use the reproducible page on page 65f to assess children's ability to read words in context. Call on children to read two sentences aloud. Start over with sentence one if necessary.

MONITOR ACCURACY Record scores using the Word/Sentence Reading Chart for this unit in *First Stop.*

MONITOR PROGRESS Word and Sentence Reading

If... children have trouble reading words with short *i* and consonant *x*/ks/,
then... use the Reteach Lessons in *First Stop.*

If... a child cannot read all the high-frequency words,
then... mark the missed words on a high-frequency word list and have the child practice reading the words with a fluent reader.

Name ______________________________

Read the Words

1. she
2. mix
3. fix
4. up
5. in
6. take
7. six
8. what
9. Max
10. sit
11. did
12. wig

MONITOR PROGRESS

- Short *i: i*
- Consonant *x*/ks/
- High-Frequency Words

Name ___________________________________

Read the Sentences

1. Tim can take the mix.

2. What did Sam mix?

3. Take the mix, Jim.

4. She can mix it.

5. What can Kim fix?

6. You can fix it up.

MONITOR PROGRESS

- Fluency
- Short *i: i*
- Consonant *x*/ks/
- High-Frequency Words

Conventions

Review Subjects of Sentences

REVIEW Remind children that subjects are the naming parts of sentences that tell who or what the sentence is about. Have them give examples of subjects.

GUIDE PRACTICE Write the following sentences. Have children write a subject that makes sense in each blank.

1. ________ **ran back.**
2. ________ **can fit in the sack.**
3. ________ **will fix the sick cat.**

APPLY Display and read the following sentence frame. Have children work in pairs to name as many subjects as they can that could be used to complete the sentence. Then have children share their responses with the class.

________ **can sit in a lap.**

ON THEIR OWN Use Let's Practice It! p. 39 from the *Teacher Resources DVD-ROM.*

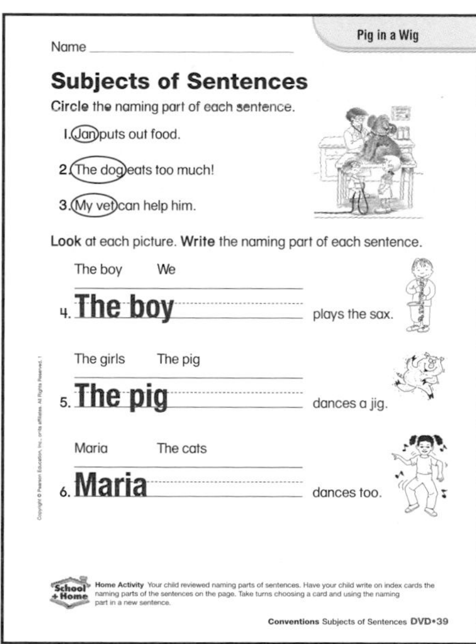
Name ________ Pig in a Wig

Subjects of Sentences

Circle the naming part of each sentence.

1. Jan puts out food.
2. The dog eats too much!
3. My vet can help him.

Look at each picture. **Write** the naming part of each sentence.

The boy We

4. The boy plays the sax.

The girls The pig

5. The pig dances a jig.

Maria The cats

6. Maria dances too.

School + Home **Home Activity** Your child reviewed naming parts of sentences. Have your child write on index cards the naming parts of the sentences on the page. Take turns choosing a card and using the naming part in a new sentence.

Conventions Subjects of Sentences **DVD•39**

Let's Practice It! TR DVD•39

Common Core State Standards

Language 1. Demonstrate command of the conventions of standard English grammar and usage when writing or speaking. **Language 1.j.** Produce and expand complete simple and compound declarative, interrogative, imperative, and exclamatory sentences in response to prompts.

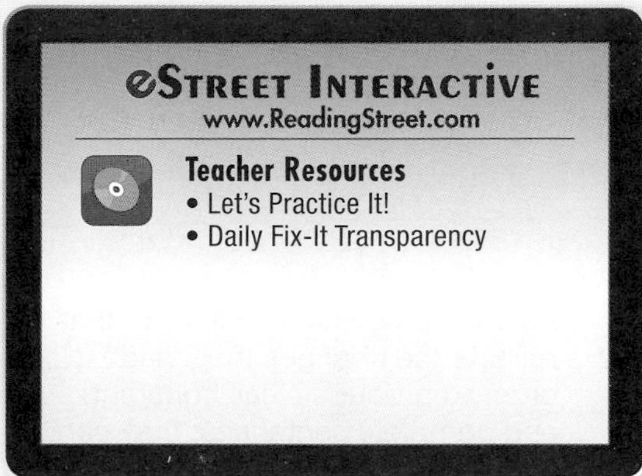

Daily Fix-It

9. sit end mix it.
   Sit and mix it.
10. Pig ded et.
    Pig did it.

Discuss the Daily Fix-It corrections with children. Review sentence capitalization and punctuation, short *a* spelled *a,* and short *i* spelled *i.*

Common Core State Standards

Writing 3. Write narratives in which they recount two or more appropriately sequenced events, include some details regarding what happened, use temporal words to signal event order, and provide some sense of closure. **Writing 5.** With guidance and support from adults, focus on a topic, respond to questions and suggestions from peers, and add details to strengthen writing as needed. **Also Writing 6.**

Bridge to Common Core

PRODUCTION AND DISTRIBUTION OF WRITING

As children create a final draft that reflects the changes they made in order to produce clear, coherent, and complete sentences, they can choose to present to a partner or create a wall display of the stories.

Writing

Zoom in on

Fantasy Story

REVIEW REVISING Remind children that yesterday they revised their stories and began drawing pictures for their stories. They may have added sentences to their stories to make the events clearer or more imaginative. Today they will proofread their stories and complete their pictures.

Mini-Lesson Proofread

Proofread for Subjects

- **Teach** In our stories, if we spell the words correctly, readers will know what words we mean. When we proofread, we check to make sure the words are correct. We can check to make sure the subject of each sentence is correct. We can use our word lists or a dictionary to check them.

- **Model** Let's look at my story about Pal. Display Writing Transparency 2C. I'm going to look at the subject of each sentence. The subjects *dog* and *Pal* are correct. But look, I don't think I spelled *children* correctly. I can look up the spelling and find out. Show how to check the spelling of *children* in a classroom dictionary or word list and write the correct spelling on the transparency. Then do the same for *little* in the subject *little girl.*

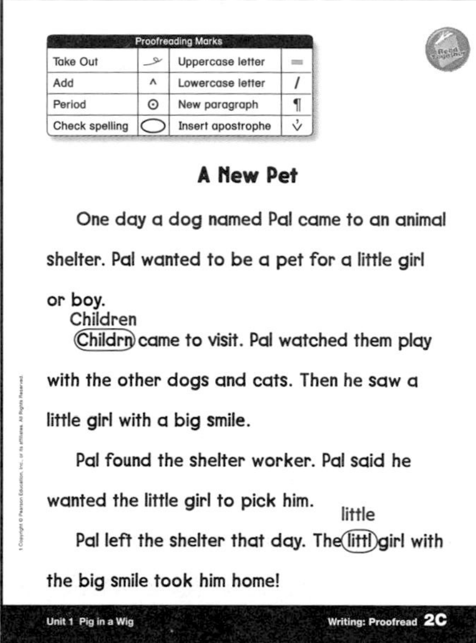

Proofreading Marks

Take Out		Uppercase letter	≡
Add	^	Lowercase letter	/
Period	⊙	New paragraph	¶
Check spelling	◯	Insert apostrophe	✓

A New Pet

One day a dog named Pal came to an animal shelter. Pal wanted to be a pet for a little girl or boy.

Children
Childrn came to visit. Pal watched them play with the other dogs and cats. Then he saw a little girl with a big smile.

Pal found the shelter worker. Pal said he wanted the little girl to pick him.

little
Pal left the shelter that day. The littl girl with the big smile took him home!

Unit 1 Pig in a Wig — Writing: Proofread 2C

Writing Transparency 2C TR DVD

PROOFREAD Display the Proofreading Tips. Have children proofread their stories to correct any misspellings, missing capital letters, or errors with periods. Then have them complete their pictures. Circulate to assist children.

Proofreading Tips

- ✔ Are my subjects spelled correctly? Check a dictionary.
- ✔ Do my sentences begin with a capital letter?
- ✔ Does each sentence end with the correct punctuation?
- ✔ Do names of characters begin with a capital letter?

PRESENT Have children use a computer to make a final draft of their stories, with their revisions and proofreading corrections. Help as appropriate. Choose an option for children to present their stories.

Create a wall display for their stories and pictures.	Read their stories to a partner.

When children have finished writing their stories, give them a copy of About My Writing, p. RR45 of the *Reader's and Writer's Notebook.* Then have children evaluate their writing by answering the questions on the page.

Routine Quick Write for Fluency

Team Talk

1. **Talk** Have partners take one minute to find the subject of a sentence in each of their stories.
2. **Write** Each child writes a new short sentence using the same subject.
3. **Share** Partners trade sentences and read them aloud.

Routines Flip Chart

Write Guy *by Jeff Anderson*

The Sunny Side

I like to look for what's *right* in children's writing rather than looking for things I can edit or fix. Most children don't write flawlessly, but they will learn what they are doing well if we point it out.

Support Editing For children to whom the sounds and spelling of English still are not very familiar, look for spelling improvement little by little from week to week rather than rapid development. Help children make progress a word at a time and learn word meanings.

Common Core State Standards

Writing 7. Participate in shared research and writing projects (e.g., explore a number of "how-to" books on a given topic and use them to write a sequence of instructions). **Writing 8.** With guidance and support from adults, recall information from experiences or gather information from provided sources to answer a question. **Speaking/Listening 1.** Participate in collaborative conversations about grade 1 topics and texts with peers and adults in small and larger groups. **Also Speaking/Listening 3., 5.**

Research and Inquiry

Step 5 Communicate

TEACH Tell children that today they will draw a picture that tells about their topic and share the information with others.

Think Aloud **MODEL** Display a list of information about the topic that could be represented in drawings. I will review the information and circle the one I think is interesting and easy to show in a drawing. I will draw a picture of that information. My topic was vets. I learned that vets can put casts on pets when they break their legs. I also learned that a cast is a hard material that keeps an arm or leg still while it heals. I can draw a picture of this information. I will draw a vet putting a cast on a dog's leg. My drawing will show how the vet is helping the dog feel better.

GUIDE PRACTICE Review children's topics and the information they gathered. Work with them to represent their information as pictures.

ON THEIR OWN Have children choose the information they would like to share with the class and draw a picture of it. Have children share their pictures in small groups. Remind them how to be good speakers and listeners:

- Good speakers speak clearly and slowly when sharing information.
- Good listeners pay attention and listen carefully to the speaker.

Wrap Up Your Week!

Helping Animals

Who helps animals?

Think Aloud This week we explored the topic of people helping animals. In the story *Pig in a Wig,* we read about a pig who gets sick and a woman who helps her feel better. In the selection "A Kid's Best Friend," we read about how kids take good care of their dogs. And in the story "The Storm Seal," we learned about a man who protects and cares for a wild baby seal.

Team Talk Have children work with partners to talk about their Amazing Ideas about how people help animals. Then have children use these ideas to help them demonstrate their understanding of the Question of the Week, *Who helps animals?*

Amazing Words

You've learned 008 words this week!

You've learned 063 words this year!

Next Week's Concept

Animals That Help

How do animals help people?

ELL

Poster Preview Prepare children for next week by using Unit 1, Week 3, ELL Poster 3. Read the Poster Talk-Through to introduce the concept and vocabulary. Ask children to identify and describe objects and actions in the art.

Selection Summary Send home the summary from the *ELL Handbook* of *The Big Blue Ox* in English and the child's home language if available. Children can read the summary with family members.

Tell children that next week they will read about how a big blue ox helps two people.

Preview Next Week

Assessment Checkpoints for the Week

Weekly Assessment

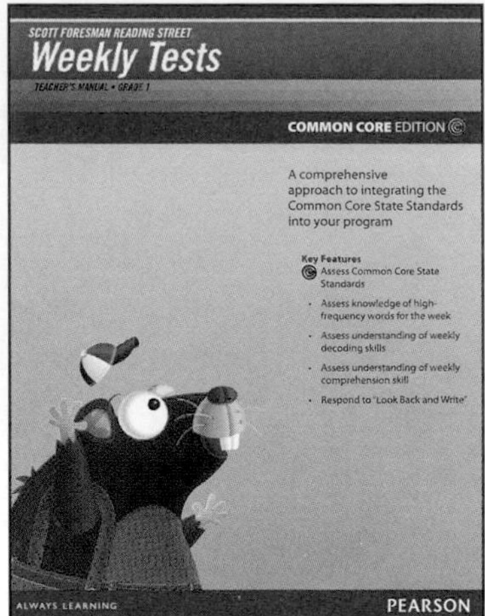

Weekly Tests

Use pp. 43–48 of *Weekly Tests* to check:

✔ **Phonics** Short *i: i*

✔ **Phonics** Consonant *x*/ks/

✔ **Comprehension** Plot

✔ **High-Frequency Words**

she	up
take	what

Differentiated Assessment

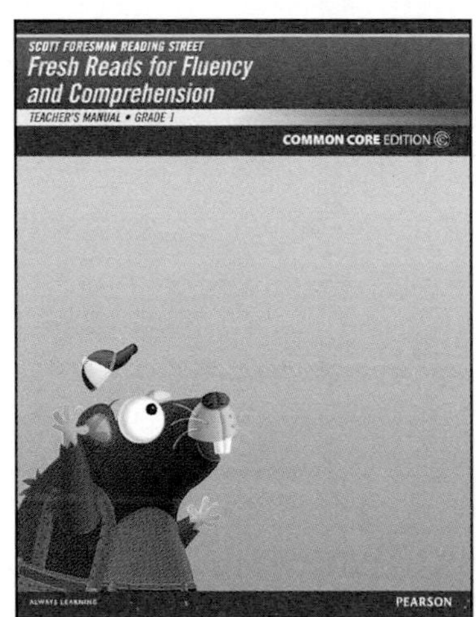

Fresh Reads for Fluency and Comprehension

Advanced

On-Level

Strategic Intervention

Use pp. 43–48 of *Fresh Reads for Fluency and Comprehension* to check:

✔ **Comprehension** Plot

✔ Review **Comprehension** Character and Setting

Managing Assessment

Assessment Handbook

Use *Assessment Handbook* for:

✔ **Weekly Assessment Blackline Masters for Monitoring Progress**

✔ **Observation Checklists**

✔ **Record-Keeping Forms**

✔ **Portfolio Assessment**

DAY 1 Differentiate Phonics

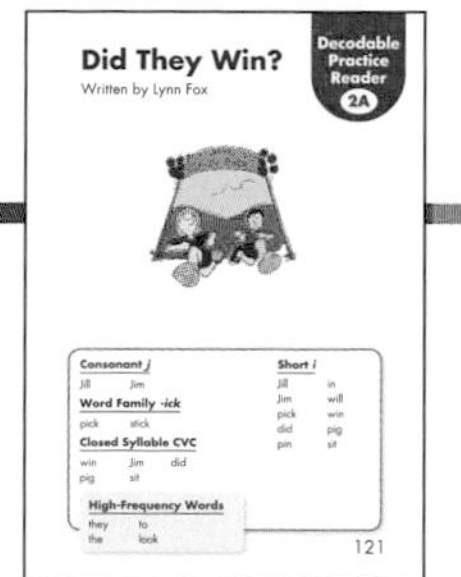

- Short *i: i*
- Decodable Practice Reader
- Advanced Selection "Bill and the Big Job"
- **Inquiry** Identify Questions

DAY 2 Differentiate Comprehension

- Consonant *x*/ks/
- **Access Text** Read *Pig in a Wig*
- **Inquiry** Investigate

DAY 3 Differentiate Close Reading

- Develop Vocabulary
- **Close Reading** Read *Pig in a Wig*
- **Inquiry** Investigate

DAY 4 Differentiate Vocabulary

"What Do You Do?" pp. 10–11

- Develop Language
- "What Do You Do?" or Leveled Readers
- **Inquiry** Organize

DAY 5 Differentiate Reteaching

- Phonics and High-Frequency Words
- Conventions
- "What Do You Do?" or Leveled Readers
- **Inquiry** Communicate

Teacher Guides and Student pages can be found in the Leveled Reader Database.

Place English Language Learners in the groups that correspond to their reading abilities.
If... children need scaffolding and practice,
then... use the ELL notes on the page.

Independent Practice

Independent Practice Stations

See pp. 38h and 38i for Independent Stations.

Pearson Trade Book Library

See the Leveled Reader Database for Lesson Plans and student pages.

Reading Street Digital Path

Independent Practice Activities available in the Digital Path.

Independent Reading

See p. 38i for independent reading suggestions.

On-Level

Common Core State Standards

Literature 1. Ask and answer questions about key details in a text. **Literature 7.** Use illustrations and details in a story to describe its characters, setting, or events. **Foundational Skills 3.** Know and apply grade-level phonics and word analysis skills in decoding words. **Foundational Skills 3.b.** Decode regularly spelled one-syllable words. **Foundational Skills 4.a.** Read on-level text with purpose and understanding.

1 Build Word Knowledge

Practice Phonics

SHORT *i*: *i* Write the following words and have children practice reading words with short *i*.

sit **dig** **kick** **mitt**

Spelling

SHORT *i* WORDS Remind children that each spelling word has the letter *i,* which spells the /i/ sound. Clarify the pronunciation and meaning of each word. For example, say: The *lip* is part of the mouth. Have children identify whether the letter *i* is at the beginning or in the middle of these words: *six, pin, in, it, did, wig.*

2 Read

Decodable Reader 2A *Did They Win?*

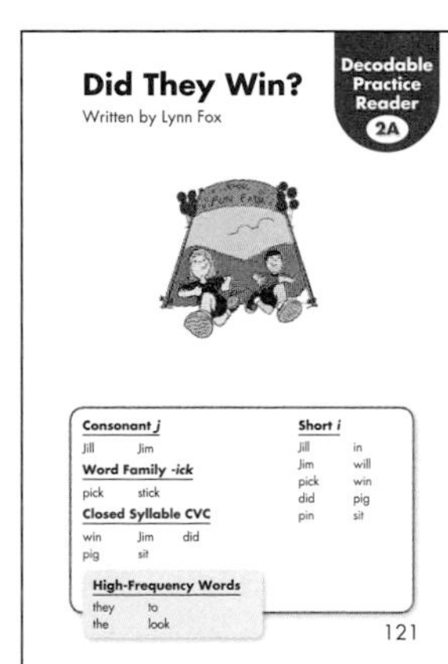

HIGH-FREQUENCY WORDS Have children read the decodable reader. Then have them reread the text to develop automaticity. Have children return to the text and find the previously taught high-frequency words. Help children demonstrate their understanding of the words. Provide sentence frames such as: The boy walks _______ the fair. (to)

ELL

If... children need more scaffolding and practice with phonics, **then...** use the ELL activities on pp. DI•34–DI•35 in the Teacher Resources section on SuccessNet.

On-Level

❶ Build Word Knowledge

Practice Phonics

CONSONANT *x*/ks/ Write the following words and have children practice reading words with *x*.

fix **tax** **mix** **six**

❷ Read

Pig in a Wig

If you read *Pig in a Wig* during whole group time, then use the following instruction.

ACCESS TEXT Have children look at the picture on p. 56 and reread the sentences on p. 56.

- What is Max doing? (playing the sax)
- Look at the picture. How does Max play the sax? (He blows in the one end and presses buttons with his fingers.)
- What is Pam doing? (playing an instrument)
- How do you know Pam is playing an instrument? (The text says "play it, Pam.")
- How does Pam play her instrument? (She holds it in one hand and hits it with her other hand.)

If you are reading *Pig in a Wig* during small group time, then return to pp. 46b–57a to guide the reading.

SMALL GROUP TIME

Independent Reading Options

Trade Book Library

eSTREET INTERACTIVE
www.ReadingStreet.com
Teacher's Guides available on the Leveled Reader Database.

On-Level

Common Core State Standards

Literature 1. Ask and answer questions about key details in a text. **Literature 7.** Use illustrations and details in a story to describe its characters, setting, or events. **Speaking/Listening 1.** Participate in collaborative conversations about grade 1 topics and texts with peers and adults in small and larger groups. **Also Language 5.c.**

1 Build Word Knowledge

Develop Vocabulary

REREAD FOR VOCABULARY Have children reread *Pig in a Wig,* p. 57.

Read the following sentence and discuss what pig is doing. (a jig)

Pig in a wig did a jig.

- What does the word *jig* mean? (a kind of dance)
- What clues tell you that the word *jig* means a kind of dance? (The pig is dancing in the picture.)
- What are some other ways you can dance? (hop, skip, wiggle)

2 Read

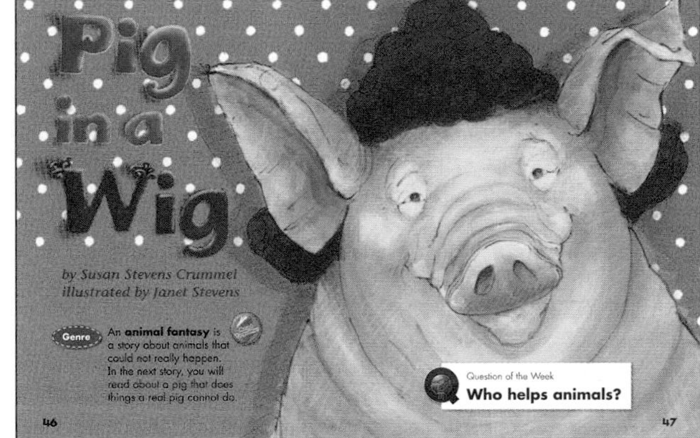
Pig in a Wig
by Susan Stevens Crummel
illustrated by Janet Stevens
Genre
An animal fantasy is a story about animals that could not really happen. In the next story, you will read about a pig that does things a real pig cannot do.
Question of the Week
Who helps animals?
46
47

Pig in a Wig

If you read *Pig in a Wig* during whole group time, then use the following instruction.

CLOSE READING Reread pp. 54–55. Have children summarize the ideas presented on these pages. Ask questions to guide deeper understanding.

- Why does the pig need to be fixed? (The pig is sick.)
- How does the woman help the pig? (She gives the pig a sip of medicine.)
- How do you know this is medicine? (When you are sick, you take medicine to feel better.)

Have children look at the pictures on pages 54–55 and think of one sentence to tell more information about what is happening. (The woman helps pig. Max and Pam watch. The woman wears a hat.)

If you are reading *Pig in a Wig* during small group time, then return to pp. 46–57 to guide the reading.

If... children need more scaffolding and practice with the main selection, **then...** use the activities on p. DI•39 in the Teacher Resources section on SuccessNet.

On-Level

1 Build Word Knowledge

Practice Selection Vocabulary

Team Talk **LANGUAGE DEVELOPMENT** Have children practice using the selection vocabulary. Ask questions such as: What do Max and Pam do at the end of the story? How do you know? Turn and talk to your partner about what Max and Pam do.

play

Allow children time to discuss the word *play.* Ask for examples or rephrase for usage when necessary or to correct for understanding. Use the Student Edition to provide visual support.

2 Text-Based Comprehension

READ ALOUD "What Do You Do?" Lead children in a choral reading of "What Do You Do?" from *Reading Street Sleuth,* pp. 10–11. Then have partners take turns reading the paragraphs of the selection.

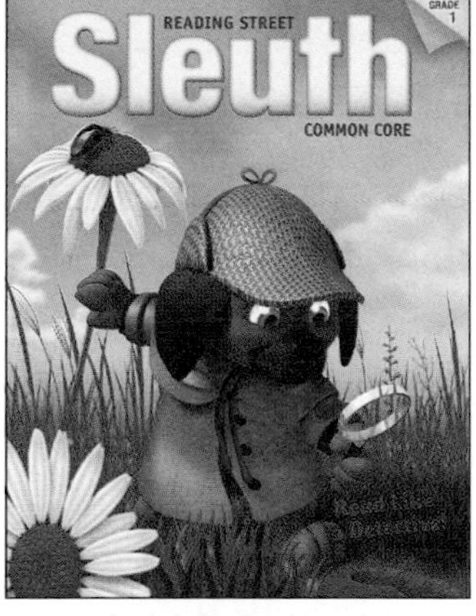

ACCESS TEXT Guide children as they work on the Be a Sleuth section.

Look for Clues Have children look for clues in the text. Ask children to think about the differences between a farm vet and a regular vet.

Ask Questions Have children think about the many kinds of animals on a farm. Then ask them to think of questions they would ask the vet to learn more about the job of a farm vet. Remind them that they can ask about specific animals or tasks related to all animals.

Make Your Case Ask children to name the kinds of animals that might be pets on a farm. Remind children to think of the needs of the different kinds of pets that people who live on a farm might have. Would a farm vet know how to take care of those pets? Ask children to provide their answer and to explain why they think it is a good choice.

SMALL GROUP TIME

More Reading for Group Time

ON-LEVEL

Reviews
- Concept Vocabulary
- Plot

Use this suggested Leveled Reader or other text at children's instructional level.

eStreet Interactive
www.ReadingStreet.com

Use the Leveled Reader Database for lesson plans and student pages for *The Sick Pets.*

On-Level

Common Core State Standards

Literature 1. Ask and answer questions about key details in a text. **Foundational Skills 3.** Know and apply grade-level phonics and word analysis skills in decoding words. **Foundational Skills 4.a.** Read on-level text with purpose and understanding. **Language 1.** Demonstrate command of the conventions of standard English grammar and usage when writing or speaking. **Also Foundational Skills 2.b., 2.c., Speaking/Listening 4.**

More Reading for Group Time

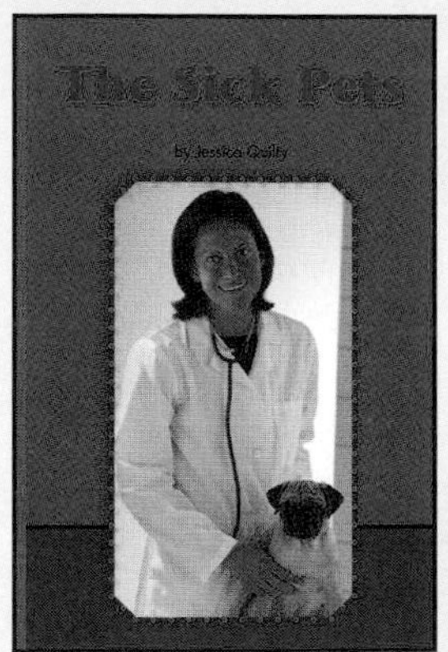

ON-LEVEL

Reviews
- Concept Vocabulary
- Plot

Use this suggested Leveled Reader or other text at children's instructional level.

eStreet Interactive
www.ReadingStreet.com

Use the Leveled Reader Database for lesson plans and student pages for *The Sick Pets.*

1 Build Word Knowledge

Practice Subjects of Sentences

REVIEW If needed, revisit the conventions lesson on p. 57b.

IDENTIFY SUBJECTS OF SENTENCES Have children return to "What Do You Do?" to identify the subjects of sentences in the selection. Have children work with a partner to identify as many subjects as they can.

2 Text-Based Comprehension

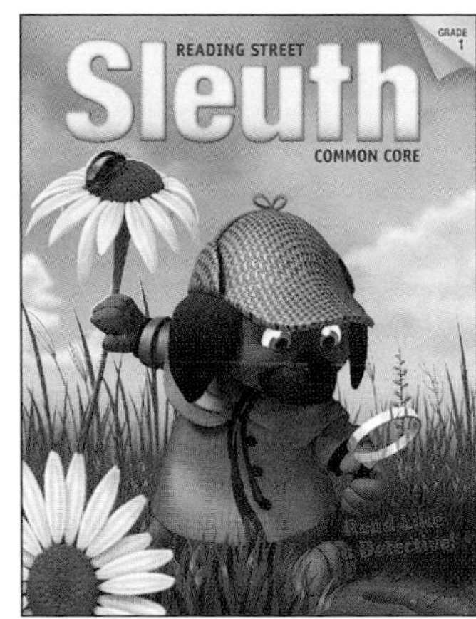

REREAD "What Do You Do?" Have partners reread "What Do You Do?"

EXTEND UNDERSTANDING Ask children if they or someone they know has ever visited a vet. What did the vet do for the pet?

PERFORMANCE TASK • Prove It! What do you think a farm vet would do for a sick pig? Have partners write two or three sentences that tell what a farm vet would do for a sick pig. Then have partners present their sentences to the class.

COMMUNICATE Have partners read their sentences to the class. Encourage the class to ask questions.

1 Build Word Knowledge

Reteach Phonemic Awareness

Reteach the lesson on p. 40–41 to distinguish /i/. Use these additional practice items.

big **tip** **did** **lid** **pig**

Reteach Phonics

SHORT *i: i* Reteach the lesson on p. 41a, short *i: i.* Use these additional practice words to blend.

dip **win** **fix** **dill** **him**

Have children spell *hill* using letter tiles. What word did you spell? Let's change a letter to make a new word and then read our new word.

- Change the *h* in *hill* to *w.* What is the new word? w i l l
- Change the *ll* in *will* to *n.* What is the new word? w i n

2 Read

Decodable Reader 2A *Did They Win?*

DECODE WORDS Have children practice reading the words listed on p. 121.

Corrective feedback	**If...** children have difficulty reading the words independently, **then...** reteach the words prior to reading Decodable Reader 2A.

READ IN CONTEXT Have children take turns reading a page in *Did They Win?* Have them reread the text several times to ensure accuracy.

Corrective feedback	**If...** children have difficulty reading the story independently, **then...** model reading a page and have children echo you.

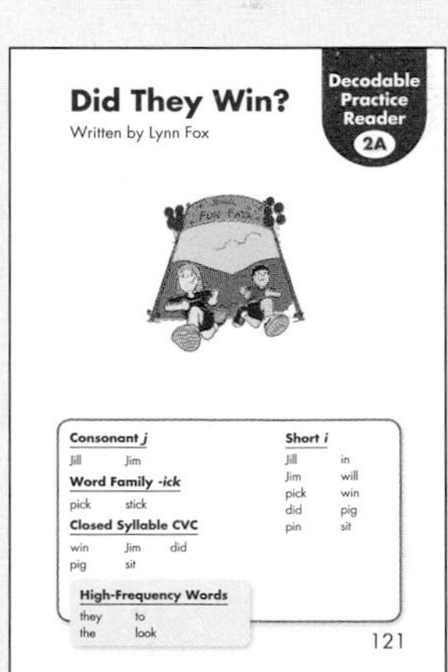

3 Reread for Fluency

Have children reread the text to develop automaticity in their reading.

SMALL GROUP TIME

ELL

If... children need more scaffolding and practice with phonemic awareness and phonics,
then... use the ELL activities on pp. DI•34–DI•35 in the Teacher Resources section on SuccessNet.

SI

Strategic Intervention

Common Core State Standards

Literature 1. Ask and answer questions about key details in a text. **Literature 7.** Use illustrations and details in a story to describe its characters, setting, or events. **Foundational Skills 2.b.** Orally produce single-syllable words by blending sounds (phonemes), including consonant blends. **Foundational Skills 3.** Know and apply grade-level phonics and word analysis skills in decoding words.

1 Build Word Knowledge

Reteach Phonemic Awareness

Reteach the lesson on p. 44c to segment and blend phonemes. Use these additional practice items: *mix, fan, big.*

Reteach Phonics

CONSONANT *x*/ks/ Reteach the lesson on p. 44d to model consonant *x*/ks/. Use these additional words to blend: *ax, Max, tax, wax, fax.*

Have children spell *fix* using letter tiles. Monitor their work.

- Change the *f* in *fix* to *m.* What is the new word? **m i x**
- Change the *m* in *mix* to *s.* What is the new word? **s i x**
- Change the *i* in *six* to *a.* What is the new word? **s a x**

2 Read

Pig in a Wig

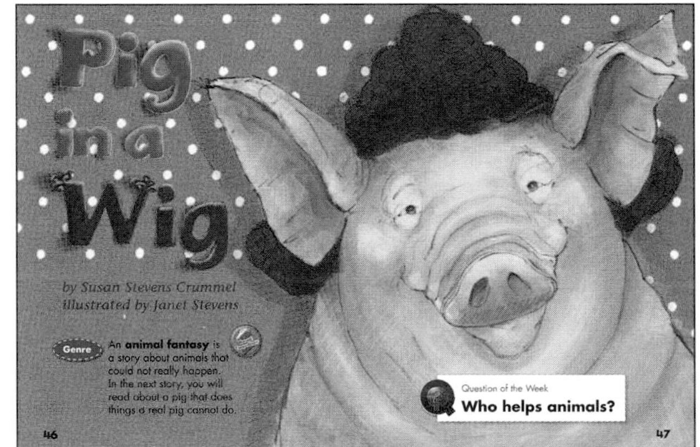
Pig in a Wig
by Susan Stevens Crummel
illustrated by Janet Stevens
Genre
An animal fantasy is a story about animals that could not really happen. In the next story, you will read about a pig that does things a real pig cannot do.
Question of the Week
Who helps animals?
46
47

If you read *Pig in a Wig* during whole group time, then use the instruction below.

ACCESS TEXT Have children look at the picture on p. 50. Point to the pig in the picture. What else do you see in the picture? (a bowl, food, a spoon, top of a table, a wig) Reread the sentences on p. 50.

- Who can mix? (the pig)
- What is the pig mixing? (food)
- What is the pig using to mix the food? (a spoon)
- How do you know the pig is using a spoon? (The picture shows she is holding a spoon.)

If you are reading *Pig in a Wig* during small group time, then return to pp. 46b–57a to guide the reading.

Corrective feedback	**If...** children have difficulty understanding the section, **then...** read the section aloud using the Access Text Notes.

Independent Reading Options

Trade Book Library

eSTREET INTERACTIVE
www.ReadingStreet.com

Teacher's Guides available on the Leveled Reader Database.

Strategic Intervention

1 Build Word Knowledge

Reteach Phonemic Awareness

Reteach the activity on p. 58c to model words that rhyme. Use these additional practice items: *fox/box; pin/in/win/twin; dish/fish.*

Reteach Phonics

Write these short *i* words and final *x* words and have children blend them with you: *fin, fix, mitt, mix, tip, tax, wig, wax.*

2 Read

Pig in a Wig

If you read *Pig in a Wig* during whole group time, then use the instruction below.

CLOSE READING Reread page 54. Let's read this page to find out what the woman is doing. To help children understand what the woman is doing, ask questions related to the text and picture.

- Why does the text say "Fix that pig"? (The pig is sick.)
- Look at the picture. Who is fixing the pig? (the woman)
- How is the woman fixing the pig? (She is feeding the pig medicine with a spoon.)
- Why is the woman giving the pig medicine? (The pig is sick, so she needs medicine.)

Corrective feedback

If... children have trouble answering questions about the text and picture on p. 54,
then... reread the page and have them tell about the picture in their own words. Then compare their summary with the words on the page.

If you are reading *Pig in a Wig* during small group time, then return to pp. 46–57 to guide the reading.

SMALL GROUP TIME

If... children need scaffolding and practice with the main selection, **then...** use the activities on p. DI•39 in the Teacher Resources section on SuccessNet.

Common Core State Standards

Foundational Skills 3.g. Recognize and read grade-appropriate irregularly spelled words. **Speaking/Listening 1.** Participate in collaborative conversations about grade 1 topics and texts with peers and adults in small and larger groups. **Language 5.c.** Identify real-life connections between words and their use (e.g., note places at home that are *cozy*). **Also Speaking/Listening 4., 5.**

1 Build Word Knowledge

Review Selection Vocabulary

play

SEE IT/SAY IT/HEAR IT Write *play.* Scan across the word with your finger as you say it: play. Use the word in a sentence. I **play** the drums.

DEFINE IT What does *play* mean in my sentence? Does it mean the same as *play outside?* Give an explanation if necessary. *Play* can mean many different things. You use it to say *play outside.* You use it to say *play a game.* You can also use it to say *play an instrument.* You make noise with an instrument if you *play* it. Restate the explanation. I *play* the drums. I make noise with them.

Team Talk What are some instruments that people play? How do they play them? Turn to your partner and talk about this. Allow time for children to discuss. Ask for examples. Rephrase their examples for usage when necessary or to correct misunderstandings.

2 Text-Based Comprehension

READ ALOUD "What Do You Do?" Read "What Do You Do?" from *Reading Street Sleuth,* pp. 10–11 as children follow along.

ACCESS TEXT Guide children as they work on the Be a Sleuth section.

Look for Clues Look through the selection for clues with the class. Ask children to think about what the farm vet does and what a regular vet does.

Ask Questions Have children name animals that they know live on a farm as you list them on the board. Then ask children to think about how a farm vet could help the animals in the list and decide what kinds of questions they would ask the farm vet to learn more.

Make Your Case Have children name animals that they think might be a pet for someone who lives on a farm. Then ask them to think of the animals on the farm that a farm vet takes care of. Next, have them answer the question by telling what the farm vet should do and providing a reason for their decision.

More Reading for Group Time

CONCEPT LITERACY

Practice
- Concept Words
- High-Frequency Words

BELOW LEVEL

Review
- Plot
- High-Frequency Words

Use these suggested Leveled Readers or other text at children's instructional level.

eSTREET INTERACTIVE
www.ReadingStreet.com

Use the Leveled Reader Database for lesson plans and student pages for *Helping Pets* and *Bix the Dog.*

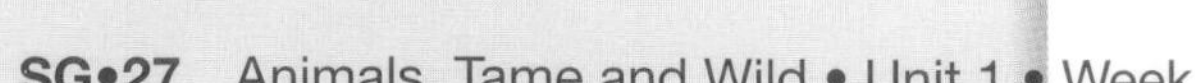

Strategic Intervention

1 Build Word Knowledge

Review High-Frequency Words

Use the routine on p. 43 to review *she, take, up,* and *what.*

Corrective feedback	**If...** children have difficulty with any of these words, **then...** tell them the word and have them repeat it. Have children spell the word and tell what word they spelled. Have them practice in pairs with word cards.

2 Text-Based Comprehension

REREAD "What Do You Do?" Lead children in a choral reread of "What Do You Do?"

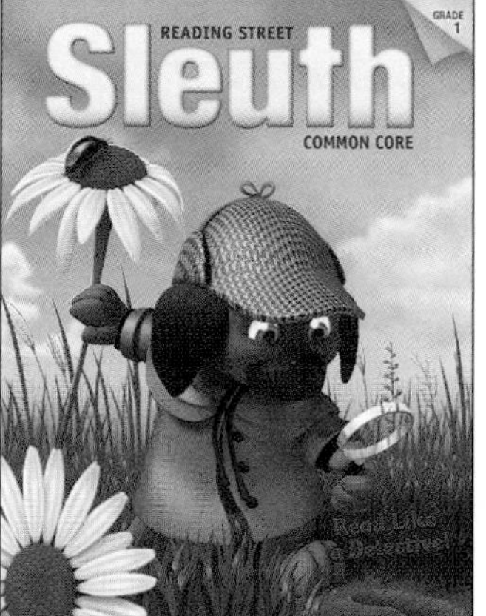

EXTEND UNDERSTANDING Ask children to name some farm animals and some pets. Ask if they think a farm animal could also be a pet.

PERFORMANCE TASK • Prove It! What do you think a farm vet would do for a sick pig? Have partners draw a picture that shows something that a farm vet might do for a sick pig. Also have them write a sentence or label for their pictures.

COMMUNICATE Have partners present their drawings and sentences to the class.

SMALL GROUP TIME

More Reading for Group Time

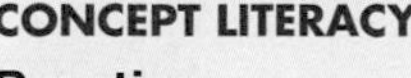

CONCEPT LITERACY

Practice
- Concept Words
- High-Frequency Words

BELOW LEVEL

Review
- Plot
- High-Frequency Words

Use these suggested Leveled Readers or other text at children's instructional level.

eSTREET INTERACTIVE
www.ReadingStreet.com

Use the Leveled Reader Database for lesson plans and student pages for *Helping Pets* and *Bix the Dog.*

Advanced

Common Core State Standards

Literature 1. Ask and answer questions about key details in a text. **Literature 3.** Describe characters, settings, and major events in a story, using key details. **Foundational Skills 3.** Know and apply grade-level phonics and word analysis skills in decoding words. **Foundational Skills 4.a.** Read on-level text with purpose and understanding. **Speaking/Listening 1.** Participate in collaborative conversations about grade 1 topics and texts with peers and adults in small and larger groups. **Also Language 4.**

1 Build Word Knowledge

Extend Phonics

SHORT *i: i* Have children practice with more complex words. Discuss the meanings of unfamiliar words and have children spell each word with letter tiles. Then have children use the words in sentences.

pinch	**skimp**	**squint**	**think**	**giggle**
wiggle	**plastic**	**picnic**	**lifting**	**grilling**

2 Read

"Bill and the Big Job"

TEACH VOCABULARY Before reading, introduce the story words: *cubs, quit.* Help children determine the meaning of each word using these sentences:

1. The young bear **cubs** followed their mother. They played in the grass.
2. Jason **quit** his job and started looking for another one.

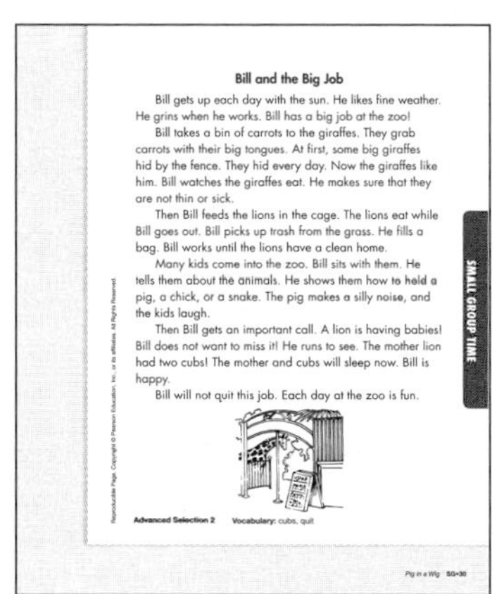

Bill and the Big Job

Bill gets up each day with the sun. He likes fine weather. He grins when he works. Bill has a big job at the zoo!

Bill takes a bin of carrots to the giraffes. They grab carrots with their big tongues. At first, some big giraffes hid by the fence. They hid every day. Now the giraffes like him. Bill watches the giraffes eat. He makes sure that they are not thin or sick.

Then Bill feeds the lions in the cage. The lions eat while Bill goes out. Bill picks up trash from the grass. He fills a bag. Bill works until the lions have a clean home.

Many kids come into the zoo. Bill sits with them. He tells them about the animals. He shows them how to hold a pig, a chick, or a snake. The pig makes a silly noise, and the kids laugh.

Then Bill gets an important call. A lion is having babies! Bill does not want to miss it! He runs to see. The mother lion had two cubs! The mother and cubs will sleep now. Bill is happy.

Bill will not quit this job. Each day at the zoo is fun.

Advanced Selection 2 Vocabulary: cubs, quit

SMALL GROUP TIME

READ Have children read "Bill and the Big Job" silently. Then have children take turns reading aloud. After reading, have children recall the two most important ideas of the story using details from the text.

3 Inquiry: Extend Concepts

IDENTIFY QUESTIONS Have children choose a career that helps animals, such as a veterinarian, zookeeper, or groomer. During the week, they will learn more about the career they pick. On Day 5, children will present what they have learned. Guide children in brainstorming possible choices.

- In "Bill and the Big Job," Bill is a zookeeper who helps animals. What are some other careers where people help animals?
- Which career do you find most interesting? Why?

ELL

If... children need practice with phonics,
then... use the ELL activities on pp. DI•34–DI•35 in the Teacher Resources section on SuccessNet.

Bill and the Big Job

Bill gets up each day with the sun. He likes fine weather. He grins when he works. Bill has a big job at the zoo!

Bill takes a bin of carrots to the giraffes. They grab carrots with their big tongues. At first, some big giraffes hid by the fence. They hid every day. Now the giraffes like him. Bill watches the giraffes eat. He makes sure that they are not thin or sick.

Then Bill feeds the lions in the cage. The lions eat while Bill goes out. Bill picks up trash from the grass. He fills a bag. Bill works until the lions have a clean home.

Many kids come into the zoo. Bill sits with them. He tells them about the animals. He shows them how to hold a pig, a chick, or a snake. The pig makes a silly noise, and the kids laugh.

Then Bill gets an important call. A lion is having babies! Bill does not want to miss it! He runs to see. The mother lion had two cubs! The mother and cubs will sleep now. Bill is happy.

Bill will not quit this job. Each day at the zoo is fun.

Advanced Selection 2 **Vocabulary:** cubs, quit

SMALL GROUP TIME

A

Advanced

Common Core State Standards

Literature 1. Ask and answer questions about key details in a text. **Literature 3.** Describe characters, settings, and major events in a story, using key details. **Literature 7.** Use illustrations and details in a story to describe its characters, setting, or events. **Foundational Skills 3.** Know and apply grade-level phonics and word analysis skills in decoding words. **Foundational Skills 3.b.** Decode regularly spelled one-syllable words. **Speaking/Listening 1.** Participate in collaborative conversations about grade 1 topics and texts with peers and adults in small and larger groups. **Also Writing 7.**

Independent Reading Options

Trade Book Library

eStreet Interactive
www.ReadingStreet.com

Teacher's Guides available on the Leveled Reader Database.

1 Build Word Knowledge

Extend Phonics

CONSONANT *x/ks/* Have children practice with additional words with *x*. Discuss the meanings of unfamiliar words with children. Then have them write the words on cards and sort by the position of the *x*/ks/—medial or final.

fax	**sixty**	**oxen**	**exam**	**extra**
boxes	**index**	**mixing**	**relax**	**tuxedo**

2 Read

Pig in a Wig

Pig in a Wig
by Susan Stevens Crummel
illustrated by Janet Stevens
Genre
An animal fantasy is a story about animals that could not really happen. In the next story, you will read about a pig that does things a real pig cannot do.
Question of the Week
Who helps animals?
46
47

If you read *Pig in a Wig* during whole group time, then use the instruction below.

ACCESS TEXT Have children silently reread *Pig in a Wig,* retell the selection, and identify the plot. (Beginning: The pig eats. Middle: The pig is sick from eating too much. End: The pig takes medicine and gets better.)

DISCUSS GENRE Discuss what makes *Pig in a Wig* an animal fantasy. Point out that this story about an animal could not really happen.

If you are reading *Pig in a Wig* during small group time, then return to pp. 46b–57a to guide the reading.

3 Inquiry: Extend Concepts

INVESTIGATE Guide children in choosing materials at their independent reading levels.

LOOK AHEAD Help children choose formats to present their information, such as in illustrated career poster or a short handbook.

Advanced

eStreet Interactive
www.ReadingStreet.com
Pearson eText
• Student Edition

1 Build Word Knowledge

Develop Vocabulary

REREAD FOR VOCABULARY Have children reread *Pig in a Wig* and make a three-column chart listing the words that name living things, words that name nonliving things, and words that name actions.

Living	Nonliving	Actions
Pig	wig	mix
Max	sax	dip
Pam		lick
Woman		fix
		take
		play

2 Read

Pig in a Wig

Pig in a Wig
by Susan Stevens Crummel
illustrated by Janet Stevens
Genre
An animal fantasy is a story about animals that could not really happen. In the next story, you will read about a pig that does things a real pig cannot do.
Question of the Week
Who helps animals?
46
47

If you read *Pig in a Wig* during whole group time, then use the instruction below.

CLOSE READING Reread pp. 50–52. Have children first look at the picture on page 50. What does the pig do first? (mix) What is the pig mixing? (food) Continue with the pig's actions on pages 51 and 52. What does the pig do with the food on these pages? (She mixes the food. Then she dips the food. Then she licks the food.) Have children look through the rest of the selection and tell about what happens to the pig because she eats all the food. Ask children to explain how the pig could have avoided getting sick.

If you are reading *Pig in a Wig* during small group time, then return to pp. 46–57 to guide the reading.

3 Inquiry: Extend Concepts

INVESTIGATE Give children time to investigate their topics by reading and studying pictures. Tell them to start thinking about how they will present what they have learned.

SMALL GROUP TIME

ELL

If... children need more scaffolding and practice with the main selection, **then...** use the activities on p. DI•39 in the Teacher Resources section on SuccessNet.

Advanced

Common Core State Standards

Literature 1. Ask and answer questions about key details in a text. **Literature 7.** Use illustrations and details in a story to describe its characters, setting, or events. **Speaking/Listening 1.** Participate in collaborative conversations about grade 1 topics and texts with peers and adults in small and larger groups. **Language 1.** Demonstrate command of the conventions of standard English grammar and usage when writing or speaking. **Also Writing 7., Speaking/Listening 4., 5.**

More Reading for Group Time

ADVANCED

- Extend Concept Vocabulary
- Review Target Skill

Use this suggested Leveled Reader or other text at children's instructional level.

eStreet Interactive
www.ReadingStreet.com

Use the Leveled Reader Database for lesson plans and student pages for *That Cat Needs Help!*

1 Build Word Knowledge

Extend Amazing Words and Selection Vocabulary

career	sloppy	service
exercise	tool	comfort
scrub	search	

play

Team Talk Have children ask each other questions using the Amazing Words and the Selection Vocabulary, such as: Where would you search for tools?

2 Text-Based Comprehension

READ "What Do You Do?" Have partners take turns reading "What Do You Do?" from *Reading Street Sleuth,* pp. 10–11 and then switch to reread the selection.

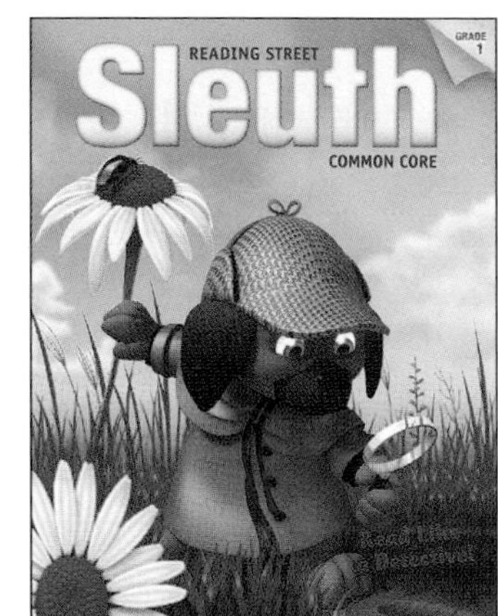

ACCESS TEXT Guide children as they work on the Be a Sleuth section.

Look for Clues Have children look for clues in the text. Ask children to think about a farm vet and a regular vet and how they are alike and different.

Ask Questions What questions would you ask to learn more about a farm vet? Would you want to know if the job is easy or hard? Remind them that they can ask about specific animals or tasks related to all animals.

Make Your Case Have children compare and contrast farm pets with farm animals. Encourage them to provide information that supports their reasoning. Remind children that they may want to look up information in other sources to make a case for their answer choice.

3 Inquiry: Extend Concepts

ORGANIZE INFORMATION Give children time to continue reading and preparing information. Provide any necessary art supplies for children to use in creating their career posters, handbooks, or other formats.

Advanced

1 Build Word Knowledge

Subjects of Sentences

IDENTIFY SUBJECTS OF SENTENCES Have children return to the text "What Do You Do?" to find subjects of sentences. Have children work independently to identify as many subjects as they can from the selection. Then have children choose one subject and create a new sentence using that subject. Have them share with a partner.

2 Text-Based Comprehension

REREAD "What Do You Do?" Have partners reread "What Do You Do?"

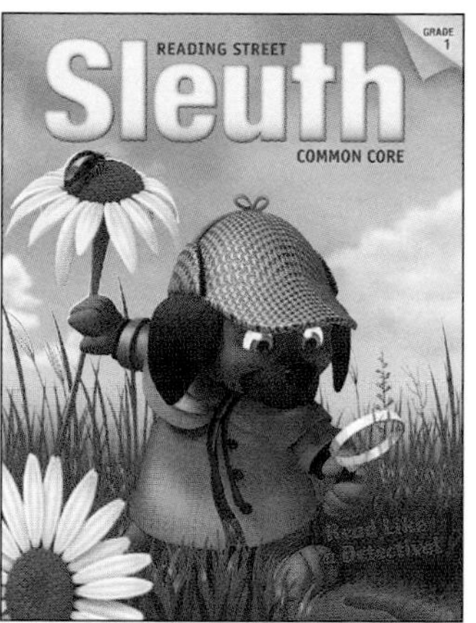

EXTEND UNDERSTANDING Ask children if they or someone they know has ever visited a vet. Ask them to think about what vets do for sick pets.

PERFORMANCE TASK • Prove It! What do you think a farm vet would do for a sick pig? Have children write a short paragraph that tells what a farm vet would do for a sick pig. Encourage them to include as many details as they can.

COMMUNICATE Have children present their paragraphs to the class. Encourage the class to ask questions.

3 Inquiry: Extend Concepts

COMMUNICATE Have children share their inquiry projects and present what they have learned about a career that helps animals.

SMALL GROUP TIME

More Reading for Group Time

ADVANCED

- Extend Concept Vocabulary
- Review Target Skill

Use this suggested Leveled Reader or other text at children's instructional level.

eSTREET INTERACTIVE
www.ReadingStreet.com

Use the Leveled Reader Database for lesson plans and student pages for *That Cat Needs Help!*

TEACHER NOTES

Indiana Common Core Edition

This Week's Target Skills and Strategies

Target Skills and Strategies	Common Core State Standards for English Language Arts
Phonemic Awareness **Skills:** Distinguish /o/ Segment and Blend Phonemes Segment and Count Phonemes	**CCSS Foundational Skills 2.c.** Isolate and pronounce initial, medial vowel, and final sounds (phonemes) in spoken single-syllable words. **(Also CCSS Foundational Skills 2., CCSS Foundational Skills 2.b.)**
Phonics **Skill:** Short *o: o* **Skill:** Plural *-s;* Consonant *s/z/*	**CCSS Foundational Skills 3.** Know and apply grade-level phonics and word analysis skills in decoding words. **(Also CCSS Foundational Skills 3.b., CCSS Language 2.d.)**
Text-Based Comprehension **Skill:** Character and Setting	**CCSS Literature 3.** Describe characters, settings, and major events in a story, using key details. **(Also CCSS Literature 7.)**
Strategy: Visualize	**CCSS Literature 3.** Describe characters, settings, and major events in a story, using key details. **(Also CCSS Literature 7.)**
Fluency **Skill:** Rate	**CCSS Foundational Skills 4.b.** Read on-level text orally with accuracy, appropriate rate, and expression on successive readings. **(Also CCSS Foundational Skills 4.)**
Listening and Speaking Give Introductions	**CCSS Speaking/Listening 4.** Describe people, places, things, and events with relevant details, expressing ideas and feelings clearly.
Six-Trait Writing **Trait of the Week:** Sentences	**CCSS Language 1.j.** Produce and expand complete simple and compound declarative, interrogative, imperative, and exclamatory sentences in response to prompts.
Writing Short Poem	**CCSS Writing 5.** With guidance and support from adults, focus on a topic, respond to questions and suggestions from peers, and add details to strengthen writing as needed.
Conventions **Skill:** Predicates of Sentences	**CCSS Language 1.j.** Produce and expand complete simple and compound declarative, interrogative, imperative, and exclamatory sentences in response to prompts.

This Week's Cross-Curricular Standards and Resources

Cross-Curricular Indiana Academic Standards for Science and Social Studies

Science
IN 1.3.5 Observe and describe ways in which animals and plants depend on one another for survival.

Social Studies
IN 1.3.4 Identify and describe physical features and human features of the local community including home, school and neighborhood.

Reading Street Sleuth

A Horse Named Chester
pp. 12–13

Follow the path to close reading using the Super Sleuth tips:

- Look for Clues
- Ask Questions
- Make Your Case
- Prove it!

More Reading in Science and Social Studies

Concept Literacy

Below Level

On Level

Advanced

ELL

ELD

ISBN-13: 978-0-328-73376-7 ISBN-10: 0-328-73376-8

Your 90-Minute Reading Block

	Whole Group	Formative Assessment How do I make my small groups flexible?	Small Group OL On Level SI Strategic Intervention A Advanced What are my other students reading and learning every day in Small Groups?
DAY 1	**Content Knowledge** Build Oral Language/Vocabulary **Phonemic Awareness/Phonics** **Read Decodable Reader** **Phonics/Spelling Pretest** **High-Frequency Words** **Text-Based Comprehension** Teacher Read Aloud **Research and Inquiry** Step 1–Identify and Focus Topic	**Monitor Progress** Formative Assessment: Check Word Reading	**Differentiate Phonics** OL **Practice Phonics** More Short *o* Words SI **Reteach Phonics** Blend Short *o* Words A **Extend Phonics** More Challenging Short *o* Words OL SI **Decodable Reader Read** *The Box* A **Advanced Selection** "How Dogs Help" A Inquiry Project ELL Access Phonemic Awareness and Phonics
DAY 2	**Content Knowledge** Build Oral Language/Vocabulary **Phonemic Awareness/Phonics** **Read Decodable Reader** **Phonics/Spelling** **High-Frequency Words/Selection Words** **Text-Based Comprehension** **Read** Main Selection, using Access Text Notes **Research and Inquiry** Step 2–Research Skill	**Monitor Progress** Formative Assessment: Check Word Reading	**Differentiate Comprehension** OL **Practice Phonics** Additional Words with Plural *-s* and Consonant *s/z/* SI **Reteach Phonics** Additional Words with Plural *-s* and Consonant *s/z/* A **Extend Phonics** Additional Words with Plural *-s* OL SI A **Access Text Read** *The Big Blue Ox* A Inquiry Project ELL Access the Comprehension Skill
DAY 3	**Content Knowledge** Build Oral Language/Vocabulary **Phonemic Awareness/Phonics** **Phonics/Spelling** **High-Frequency Words/Selection Words** **Text-Based Comprehension** **Reread** Main Selection, using Close Reading Notes **Fluency** **Research and Inquiry** Step 3–Gather and Record Information	**Monitor Progress** Formative Assessment: Check High-Frequency Words **Monitor Progress** Check Retelling	**Differentiate Close Reading** OL **Reread to Develop Vocabulary** SI **Build Word Knowledge** Blend Words with Short *o* and Plural *-s* A **Reread to Extend Vocabulary** OL SI **Close Reading Reread** *The Big Blue Ox* A **Extend Concepts Reread** *The Big Blue Ox* A Inquiry Project ELL Access the Main Selection
DAY 4	**Content Knowledge** Build Oral Language/Vocabulary **Phonemic Awareness/Phonics** **Read Decodable Reader** **Phonics/Spelling** **Read Content Area Paired Selection with Genre Focus** **Fluency** **Research and Inquiry** Step 4–Synthesize	**Monitor Progress** Fluency Check	**Differentiate Vocabulary** **Build Word Knowledge** OL Develop Language A Extend Amazing Words and Selection Vocabulary SI **Review Vocabulary** Review/Discuss Selection Vocabulary OL SI A **Text-Based Comprehension** **Read** *Reading Street Sleuth,* pp. 12–13 or Leveled Readers A Inquiry Project ELL Access Vocabulary
DAY 5	**Content Knowledge** Build Oral Language/Vocabulary **Phonemic Awareness/Phonics** **Phonics/Spelling Test** **Let's Learn It!** Vocabulary/Fluency/Listening and Speaking **Text-Based Comprehension** **High-Frequency and Selection Words** **Genre** **Assessment** Phonics, High-Frequency Words, Fluency **Research and Inquiry** Step 5–Communicate	**Monitor Progress** Formative Assessment: Check Oral Vocabulary **Monitor Progress** Word and Sentence Reading	**Differentiate Reteaching** OL **Practice Predicates of Sentences** SI **Review Vocabulary** High-Frequency Words A **Extend Predicates of Sentences** OL SI A **Text-Based Comprehension** **Reread** *Reading Street Sleuth,* pp. 12–13 or Leveled Readers A Inquiry Project ELL Access Conventions and Writing

Daily Independent Options

What do my other students do when I lead Small Groups?

★ **Independent Reading**

Suggestions for this week's independent reading:

- Informational texts on last week's social studies topic: Who helps animals?
- Nonfiction selections about who helps pets
- Other books by Janet Stevens

Book Talk

Foster critical reading and discussion skills through independent and close reading.

Students should focus on discussing one or more of the following:

- Key Ideas and Details
- Craft and Structure
- Integration of Ideas

Pearson eText

- Student Edition
- Decodable Readers
- Leveled Readers

Trade Book Library

Materials from School or Classroom Library

Independent Stations
Practice Last Week's Skills

★ Focus on these activities when time is limited.

Listen Up!
★ **Word Work**
Read for Meaning
Let's Write!
★ **Words to Know**
Get Fluent

Assessment Resources

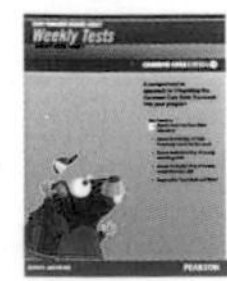

Common Core Weekly Tests, pp. 49–54

Common Core Fresh Reads for Fluency and Comprehension, pp. 49–54

Common Core Unit 1 Benchmark Test

Common Core Success Tracker, ExamView, and Online Lesson Planner

Focus on Common Core State Standards ©

The Big Blue Ox
by Susan Stevens Crummel
illustrated by Janet Stevens
Genre
An animal fantasy is a make-believe story with animals that act like people. Next you will read about an ox that acts like a person. What do you want to find out? Set a purpose for reading.
Question of the Week
How do animals help people?
Main Selection, pp. 74–83

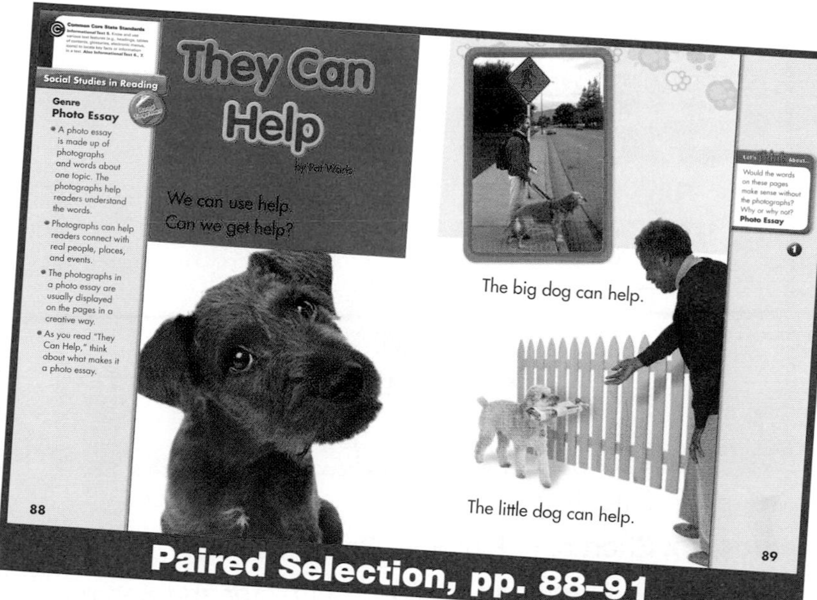
They Can Help
We can use help.
Can we get help?
The big dog can help.
The little dog can help.
Paired Selection, pp. 88–91

Text-Based Comprehension

Character and Setting
CCSS Literature 3., CCSS Literature 7.

Visualize
CCSS Literature 3., CCSS Literature 7.

Fluency

Rate
CCSS Foundational Skills 4.b.

Writing and Conventions

Trait: Sentences
CCSS Language 1.j.

Writing Mini-Lesson: Short Poem
CCSS Writing 5.

Conventions: Predicates of Sentences
CCSS Language 1.j.

Oral Vocabulary

Amazing Words

past	present
produce	transportation
danger	serve
snuggle	enormous
powerful	

CCSS Language 5.c.

High-Frequency Words

blue	from	get
help	little	use

CCSS Foundational Skills 3.g.

Phonemic Awareness

Distinguish /o/
Segment and Blend Phonemes
Segment and Count Phonemes
CCSS Foundational Skills 2.b., CCSS Foundational Skills 2.c.

Phonics and Spelling

Plural *-s;* Consonant *s/z/*
Short *o: o*
CCSS Foundational Skills 3., CCSS Foundational Skills 3.b., CCSS Language 2.d.

hot	hop	pot
pop	ox	lock
mop	got	rock
mom		

Listening and Speaking

Give Introductions
CCSS Speaking/Listening 4.

Preview Your Week

How do animals help people?

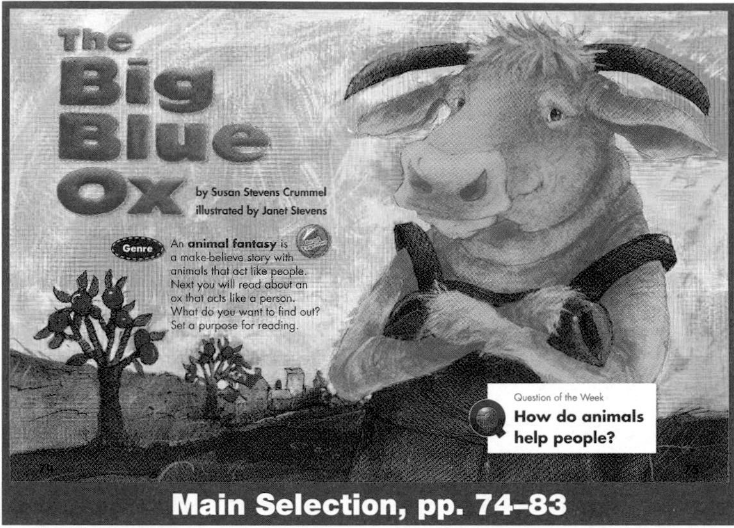
The Big Blue Ox
by Susan Stevens Crummel
illustrated by Janet Stevens
Genre
An animal fantasy is a make-believe story with animals that act like people. Next you will read about an ox that acts like a person. What do you want to find out? Set a purpose for reading.
Question of the Week
How do animals help people?

Main Selection, pp. 74–83

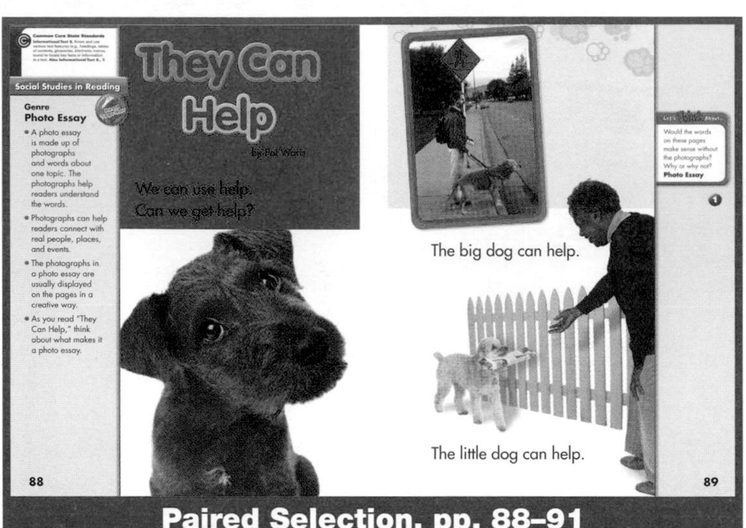
They Can Help
We can use help.
Can we get help?
The big dog can help.
The little dog can help.

Paired Selection, pp. 88–91

Genre: Animal Fantasy

Phonics: Short *o*: *o*, Plural *-s*, Consonant *s*/z/

Text-Based Comprehension: Character and Setting

Social Studies in Reading

Genre: Photo Essay

Build Content Knowledge

Zoom in on

SOCIAL STUDIES

KNOWLEDGE GOALS
Children will understand that animals provide:

- food for people
- transportation for people
- services to people

THIS WEEK'S CONCEPT MAP
Develop a concept-related graphic organizer like the one below over the course of this week.

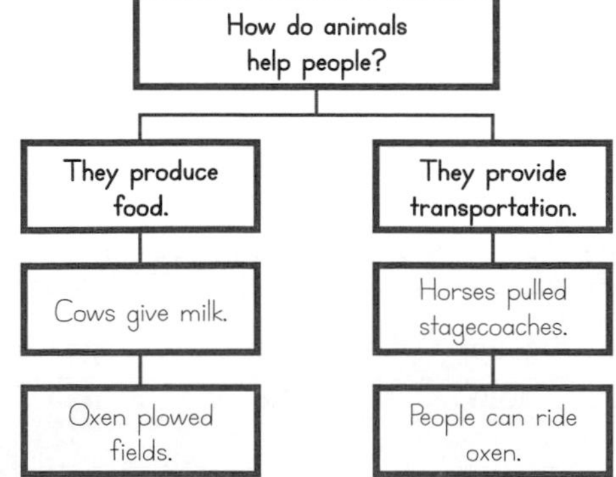
How do animals help people?
They produce food.
Cows give milk.
Oxen plowed fields.
They provide transportation.
Horses pulled stagecoaches.
People can ride oxen.

BUILD ORAL VOCABULARY
This week, children will acquire the following academic vocabulary/domain-specific words.

Amazing Words

past	serve	transportation
present	snuggle	powerful
produce	enormous	danger

OPTIONAL CONCEPT-BASED READING Use the Digital Path to access readers offering different levels of text complexity.

On the Farm

Below Level

Where They Live

On Level

Loni's Town

Advanced

We Can Help!

ELL

We Can Help!

ELD

Concept Literacy

This Week's Digital Resources

eStreet Interactive
www.ReadingStreet.com

Get Ready to Read

Background Building Audio CD This audio CD provides valuable background information about the kind of work that oxen do on a farm to help children read and comprehend the weekly texts.

Concept Talk Video Use this video on the Digital Path to build momentum and introduce the weekly concept of animals that help.

Interactive Sing with Me Big Book "The Oxen Song," sung to the tune of "My Bonnie Lies Over the Ocean," introduces the Amazing Words with a catchy, concept-related song.

Interactive Sound-Spelling Cards With these interactive cards on the Digital Path, children see an image, hear the image name, and see the spelling for short *o* spelled *o,* plural *-s,* and consonant /z/.

Pearson eText Use the eText for the Decodable Readers on the Leveled Reader Database for phonics and fluency support.

Letter Tile Drag and Drop Using this interactive tool on Pearson SuccessNet, children click and spell words to enhance their phonics skills.

Read and Comprehend

Envision It! Animations Use this colorful animation on the Digital Path to explain the target comprehension skill, Character and Setting.

Pearson eText Read the eText of the main selection, *The Big Blue Ox,* and the paired selection, "They Can Help," with audio support on Pearson SuccessNet.

Story Sort Use the Story Sort Activity on the Digital Path after reading *The Big Blue Ox* to involve children in summarizing.

Journal: Word Bank Use the Word Bank on the Digital Path to have children write sentences using this week's high-frequency words.

Vocabulary Activities A variety of interactive vocabulary activities on the Digital Path help children practice high-frequency and concept-related words.

Language Arts

Grammar Jammer Choose a whimsical animation on the Digital Path to provide an engaging grammar lesson that will capture children's attention.

Pearson eText Find the Student Edition eText of the Let's Write It! and Let's Learn It! pages with audio support on Pearson SuccessNet.

Additional Resources

Teacher Resources DVD-ROM Use the following resources on the TR DVD or on Pearson SuccessNet throughout the week:

- Amazing Word Cards
- Reader's and Writer's Notebook
- Writing Transparencies
- Daily Fix-It Transparencies
- Scoring Rubrics
- Grammar Transparencies
- Research Transparencies
- Let's Practice It!
- Graphic Organizers
- High-Frequency Word Cards
- Vocabulary Transparencies

This Week's Skills

Phonics
- Short *o: o*
- Plural *-s;* Consonant *s/z/*

Comprehension
- **Skill:** Character and Setting
- **Strategy:** Visualize

Language
- **Vocabulary:** Synonyms
- **Conventions:** Predicates of Sentences

Fluency
Rate

Writing
Short Poem

5-Day Planner

DAY 1

Get Ready to Read

Content Knowledge 67a
Oral Vocabulary: *past, present, produce, transportation*

Phonemic Awareness 68–69
Distinguish /o/

Phonics/Spelling 69a
Short *o: o*
READ Decodable Reader 3A
Reread for Fluency
Spelling Pretest

Monitor Progress
Check Word Reading

Read and Comprehend

High-Frequency Words 71
blue, from, get, help, little, use

Text-Based Comprehension 71a
Character and Setting

Language Arts

Conventions 71c
Predicates of Sentences

Writing 71d
Short Poem

Research and Inquiry 71f
Identify and Focus Topic

DAY 2

Get Ready to Read

Content Knowledge 72a
Oral Vocabulary: *danger, serve*

Phonemic Awareness 72c
Segment and Blend Phonemes

Phonics/Spelling 72d
Plural *-s;* Consonant *s/z/*
Review Short Vowels *a, i*
READ Decodable Reader 3B
Reread for Fluency
Spelling: Short *o* Words

Monitor Progress
Check Word Reading

Read and Comprehend

High-Frequency Words 73
blue, from, get, help, little, use

Selection Vocabulary 74a
town
Synonyms

Text-Based Comprehension 74b
READ *The Big Blue Ox*—1st Read

Genre 83b
Animal Fantasy

Language Arts

Conventions 83c
Predicates of Sentences

Writing 83d
Short Poem

Handwriting 83f
Letter *Oo*/Left-to-Right Progression

Research and Inquiry 83g
Picture Dictionary

DAY 3

Get Ready to Read

Content Knowledge 84a
Oral Vocabulary: *snuggle*

Phonemic Awareness 84c
Rhyming Words

Phonics/Spelling 84d
Build Words
Blend and Read
Spelling: Dictation

Read and Comprehend

High-Frequency Words and Selection Words 84g
High-Frequency Words: *blue, from, get, help, little, use*
Selection Words: *town*
Monitor Progress Check High-Frequency Words

Text-Based Comprehension 84h
READ *The Big Blue Ox*—2nd Read
Monitor Progress Check Retelling

Fluency 85b
Rate

Language Arts

Conventions 86a
Predicates of Sentences

Writing 86–87
Short Poem

Listening and Speaking 87b
Give Introductions

Research and Inquiry 87c
Gather and Record Information

DAY 4

Get Ready to Read

Content Knowledge 88a
Oral Vocabulary: *enormous, powerful*

Phonemic Awareness 88c
Distinguish /o/

Phonics/Spelling 88d
Review Short *i* Spelled *i;* Final *x*
READ Decodable Reader 3C
Spiral Review Fluent Word Reading
Spelling: Short *o* Words

Read and Comprehend

Social Studies in Reading 88i
READ "They Can Help"—Paired Selection

Fluency 91a
Rate
Monitor Progress Fluency Check

Language Arts

Conventions 91b
Predicates of Sentences

Writing 91c
Short Poem

Research and Inquiry 91e
Synthesize

DAY 5

Get Ready to Read

Content Knowledge 92a
Review Oral Vocabulary
Monitor Progress Check Oral Vocabulary

Phonemic Awareness 92c
Review Segment and Count Phonemes

Phonics/Spelling 92c
Review Short *o: o,* Plural *-s* Consonant *s/z/*
Spelling Test

Read and Comprehend

Listening and Speaking 92–93
Vocabulary 93a
Fluency 93a

Text-Based Comprehension 93b
Review Character and Setting

Vocabulary 93b
Review High-Frequency and Selection Words

Genre 93c
Review Photo Essay

Assessment 93d
Monitor Progress Word and Sentence Reading

Language Arts

Conventions 93g
Review Predicates of Sentences

Writing 93h
Short Poem

Research and Inquiry 93j
Communicate

Wrap Up Your Week! 93k

Access for All

What do I do in group time?

It's as easy as 1-2-3!

1. TEACHER-LED SMALL GROUPS
2. INDEPENDENT PRACTICE STATIONS
3. INDEPENDENT READING

Small Group Time

Bridge to Common Core

SKILL DEVELOPMENT

- Short *o: o*
- Plural *-s;* Consonant *s/z/*
- Character and Setting
- Visualize

DEEP UNDERSTANDING

This Week's Knowledge Goals

Children will understand that animals provide:

- food for people
- transportation for people
- services to people

1 Small Group Lesson Plan

	DAY 1 Differentiate Phonics	DAY 2 Differentiate Comprehension
On-Level pp. SG•36–SG•40	**Practice Phonics** More Short *o* Words **Decodable Reader** Read *The Box*	**Practice Phonics** Additional Words with Plural *-s* and Consonant *s/z/* **Access Text** Read *The Big Blue Ox*
Strategic Intervention pp. SG•41–SG•45	**Reteach Phonics** Blend Short *o* Words **Decodable Reader** Read *The Box*	**Reteach Phonics** Blend Words with Plural *-s* and Consonant *s/z/* **Access Text** Read *The Big Blue Ox*
Advanced pp. SG•46–SG•51	**Extend Phonics** More Challenging Short *o* Words **Advanced Selection** "How Dogs Help"	**Extend Phonics** Additional Words with Plural *-s* **Access Text** Read *The Big Blue Ox*
Independent Inquiry Project	**Identify Questions**	**Investigate**
ELL **If...** children need more scaffolding and practice with...	**Phonemic Awareness and Phonics,** **then...** use the Phonics Transition Lessons on pp. 249–345 in the *ELL Handbook.*	**the Comprehension Skill,** **then...** use the ELL activities on p. DI•59 in the Teacher Resources section on SuccessNet.

Reading Street Sleuth

- Provides access to grade-level text for all children
- Focuses on finding clues in text through close reading
- Builds capacity for complex text

Build Text-Based Comprehension

The Big Blue Ox

Optional Leveled Readers

Concept Literacy

Below Level

On Level

Advanced

ELL

ELD

DAY 3	DAY 4	DAY 5
Differentiate Close Reading	**Differentiate Vocabulary**	**Differentiate Reteaching**
Reread to Develop Vocabulary **Close Reading** Reread *The Big Blue Ox*	**Build Word Knowledge** Develop Language **Text-Based Comprehension** Read *Reading Street Sleuth,* pp. 12–13 or Leveled Readers	**Practice Predicates of Sentences** **Text-Based Comprehension** Reread *Reading Street Sleuth,* pp. 12–13 or Leveled Readers
Build Word Knowledge Blend Words with Short *o* and Plural *-s* **Close Reading** Reread *The Big Blue Ox*	**Review Vocabulary** Review/Discuss Selection Vocabulary **Text-Based Comprehension** Read *Reading Street Sleuth,* pp. 12–13 or Leveled Readers	**Review Vocabulary** High-Frequency Words **Text-Based Comprehension** Reread *Reading Street Sleuth,* pp. 12–13 or Leveled Readers
Reread to Extend Vocabulary **Extend Concepts** Reread *The Big Blue Ox* **Investigate**	**Build Word Knowledge** Extend Amazing Words and Selection Vocabulary **Text-Based Comprehension** Read *Reading Street Sleuth,* pp. 12–13 or Leveled Readers **Organize**	**Extend Predicates of Sentences** **Text-Based Comprehension** Reread *Reading Street Sleuth,* pp. 12–13 or Leveled Readers **Communicate**
the Main Selection, **then...** use the activities on p. DI•60 in the Teacher Resources section on SuccessNet.	**Vocabulary,** **then...** use the routine on pp. xxxvi–xxxvii in the *ELL Handbook.*	**Conventions and Writing,** **then...** use the activities on pp. DI•62–DI•63 in the Teacher Resources section on SuccessNet.

2 Independent Stations

Practice Last Week's Skills

Focus on these activities when time is limited.

ACCESS FOR ALL
- Below-Level Activities
- On-Level Activities
- Advanced Activities

LISTEN UP!

Match sounds and pictures.

OBJECTIVES
- Identify words with initial and medial sound /i/.
- Identify words with final sound /ks/.

MATERIALS
- *Listen Up!* Flip Chart Activity 3, Picture Cards *igloo, inch, insect, brick, pig, six, wig, box, fox*

Modeled Pronunciation Audio CD

● Children find Picture Cards that have the same beginning sound as *itch,* the same middle sound as *kid,* and the same final sound as *wax.*

▲ Children sort the Picture Cards into these sounds: beginning—*itch,* middle—*kid,* ending—*wax.*

■ Children look around the room. They tell a partner they see an object that begins like *itch,* middle—*kid,* ending—*wax.* The partner will guess the object. Partners take turns.

WORD WORK

Read and sort words.

OBJECTIVES
- Identify, read, and sort words with short *i.*
- Identify, read, and sort words with *x.*

MATERIALS
- *Word Work* Flip Chart Activity 3, teacher-made word cards, three sorting baskets, labeled "short *i,*" "*x,*" and "other sounds"

Interactive Sound-Spelling Cards

● Children read the words on the word cards. They sort them into the "short *i*" basket or the "*x*" basket.

▲ Children read all the words on the word cards. Then they sort the words into one of the three baskets.

■ Children read the words on the word cards. After they sort them into the correct basket, they will use one word from each basket in a sentence.

LET'S WRITE!

Write sentences.

OBJECTIVES
- Write complete sentences.
- Identify subjects of sentences.

MATERIALS
- *Let's Write!* Flip Chart Activity 3, paper, pencils

Grammar Jammer

● Children write a sentence about how to help an animal. Remind them to use a capital letter at the start of the sentence and a period at the end. Have them circle the subject.

▲ Children write two sentences about how to help an animal.

■ Children write four sentences about how to help animals. They use *vet, firefighter, pet store owner,* and *neighbor* as the subject of each sentence.

WORDS TO KNOW

Alphabetize words.

OBJECTIVES
- Identify high-frequency words *take, she, what, up.*
- Alphabetize words by first letter.

MATERIALS
- *Words to Know* Flip Chart Activity 3; paper; blank cards; pencils

Vocabulary Activities

Teacher Resources
- High-Frequency Word Cards for Unit 1, Week 2

● Children use the Word Cards and alphabetize the words to the first letter.

▲ Children place the Word Cards in alphabetical order. Then they copy them into a list, circling the first letter of each word.

■ Children place the Word Cards in alphabetical order. Then they think of other words they know, write them on the blank cards, and put them into alphabetical order along with the Word Cards.

READ FOR MEANING

Use text-based comprehension tools.

OBJECTIVES

- Identify the plot of a story.
- Identify the problem and solution in a plot.

MATERIALS

- *Read for Meaning* Flip Chart Activity 3, Leveled Readers, paper, pencils, crayons

 **Pearson eText**
- Leveled eReaders

 **Envision It! Animations**

● Children read *Bix the Dog.* Then they draw a picture showing the plot.

▲ Children read *The Sick Pets.* They write a sentence about the problem and the solution of the plot. They draw a picture to go with their sentence.

■ Children read *That Cat Needs Help!* They divide a paper in half and draw the problem on one side and the solution on the other side. Label the two drawings.

GET FLUENT

Practice fluent reading.

OBJECTIVES

- Read aloud with accuracy.

MATERIALS

- *Get Fluent* Flip Chart Activity 3, Leveled Readers

 **Pearson eText**
- Leveled eReaders

● Children work with a partner to take turns reading *Bix the Dog.*

▲ Children work with a partner to take turns reading *The Sick Pets.*

■ Children work with a partner to take turns reading *That Cat Needs Help!*

Manage the Stations

Use these management tools to set up and organize your Practice Stations:

Practice Station Flip Charts

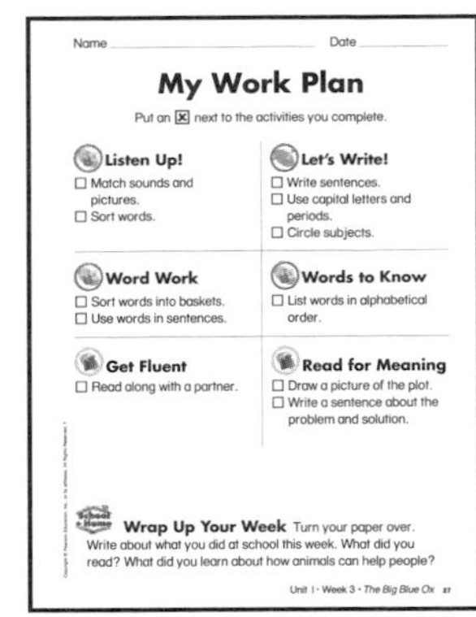
Name ______ Date ______

My Work Plan

Put an ☒ next to the activities you complete.

Listen Up!
- ☐ Match sounds and pictures.
- ☐ Sort words.

Let's Write!
- ☐ Write sentences.
- ☐ Use capital letters and periods.
- ☐ Circle subjects.

Word Work
- ☐ Sort words into baskets.
- ☐ Use words in sentences.

Words to Know
- ☐ List words in alphabetical order.

Get Fluent
- ☐ Read along with a partner.

Read for Meaning
- ☐ Draw a picture of the plot.
- ☐ Write a sentence about the problem and solution.

Wrap Up Your Week Turn your paper over. Write about what you did at school this week. What did you read? What did you learn about how animals can help people?

Unit 1 • Week 3 • *The Big Blue Ox* 27

Classroom Management Handbook for Differentiated Instruction Practice Stations, p. 27

3 Independent Reading ©

Children should select appropriately complex texts to read and write about independently every day before, during, and after school.

Suggestions for this week's independent reading:
- Informational texts on last week's social studies topic: Who helps animals?
- Nonfiction selections about who helps pets
- Other books by Janet Stevens

BOOK TALK Have partners discuss their independent reading for the week. Tell them to refer to their Reading Log and paraphrase what the selection was about. To focus the discussion, prompt them to talk about one or more of the following:

Key Ideas and Details
- Who is the author? Why did he or she write the work?
- What did I learn from this text?

Craft and Structure
- Did I understand the information?
- Did the author use words that were interesting and clear?

Integration of Ideas
- Did the information seem believable? Why or why not?
- Was this book like others I have read?

 **Pearson eText**
- Student Edition
- Decodable Readers
- Leveled Readers

 **Trade Book Library**

 **Materials from School or Classroom Library**

Content Knowledge
Oral Vocabulary

Phonemic Awareness
Distinguish /o/

Phonics/Spelling
Short *o: o*

High-Frequency Words
blue, from, get, help, little, use

Text-Based Comprehension
Character and Setting

Conventions
Predicates of Sentences

Writing
Short Poem

Research and Inquiry
Identify and Focus Topic

Materials

- Student Edition
- Sing with Me Big Book
- Sound-Spelling Cards
- Decodable Reader 3A
- Reader's and Writer's Notebook

Bridge to Common Core

INTEGRATION OF KNOWLEDGE/IDEAS

This week children read, write, and talk about animals that help.

Texts This Week

- "The Oxen Song"
- "A Perfect Visit"
- *A Kid's Best Friend*
- *The Big Blue Ox*
- "They Can Help"
- "Paul Bunyan and Babe"

Social Studies Knowledge Goals

Children will understand that animals provide
- food for people
- transportation for people
- services to people

Street Rhymes!

We get sweet milk from the cow.
The cat keeps the mice away.
The horse can pull a plow,
Or give you a ride on a sleigh.
These helpers behind the barn door
Don't have two legs but four.

- To introduce this week's concept, read aloud the poem several times and ask children to join you.

Content Knowledge

Animals That Help

CONCEPT TALK To help children gain knowledge and understanding, tell them that this week they will talk, sing, read, and write about how animals help people. Write the Question of the Week, *How do animals help people?,* on the board and track the print as you read it.

Build Oral Language

TALK ABOUT ANIMALS THAT HELP Have children turn to pages 66–67 in their Student Edition. Read the title and look at the photos. Use these questions to guide discussion and create the "How do animals help people?" concept map.

- Look at the cow in the picture. Cows *produce,* or *make,* milk. How does a cow's milk help people? (Possible response: It helps people grow big and strong.) Let's add *They produce food* and *Cows give milk* to our map.
- *Transportation* is a way to move from place to place. What does the picture of the horses have to do with transportation? (Possible response: The horses are pulling a stagecoach with people in it.) Let's add *They provide transportation* and *Horses pulled stagecoaches* to our map.
- In the past, oxen like the ones in the picture helped farmers plow fields so crops could be grown. Why didn't the farmer do this by himself? (Possible response: The plow was too heavy for the farmer to pull.) Let's add *Oxen plowed fields* to our map.

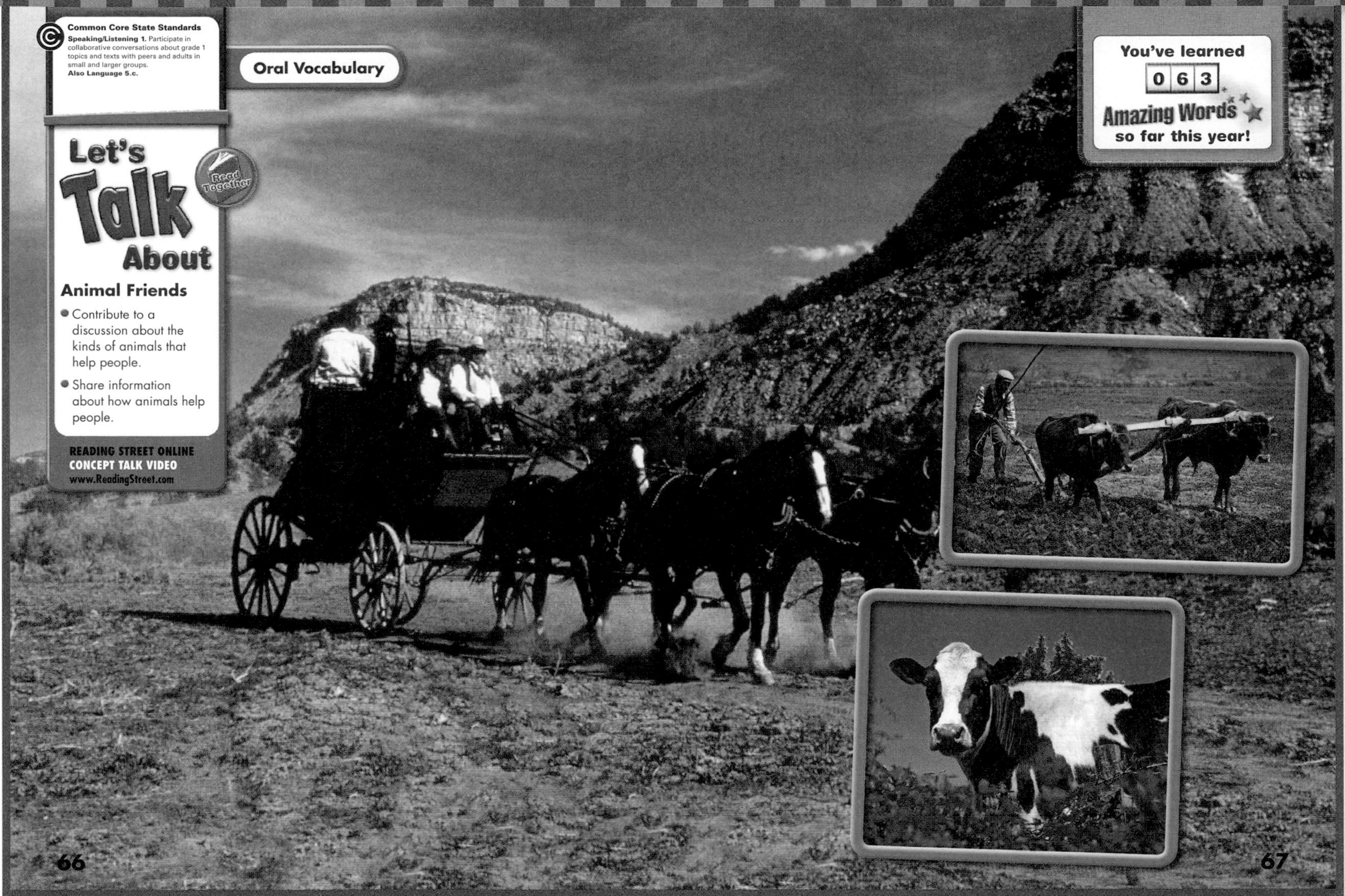

Common Core State Standards
Speaking/Listening 1. Participate in collaborative conversations about grade 1 topics and texts with peers and adults in small and larger groups.
Also Language 5.c.
Oral Vocabulary
Let's Talk About
Read Together
Animal Friends
Contribute to a discussion about the kinds of animals that help people.
Share information about how animals help people.
READING STREET ONLINE
CONCEPT TALK VIDEO
www.ReadingStreet.com
You've learned
0 6 3
Amazing Words
so far this year!
66
67

Student Edition, pp. 66–67

CONNECT TO READING Explain that this week children will read about how a make-believe blue ox helps people. Let's add *People can ride oxen* to our map.

How do animals help people?
They produce food.
They provide transportation.
Cows give milk.
Horses pulled stagecoaches.
Oxen plowed fields.
People can ride oxen.

eSTREET INTERACTIVE
www.ReadingStreet.com

- **Pearson eText**
  - Student Edition
- **Concept Talk Video**

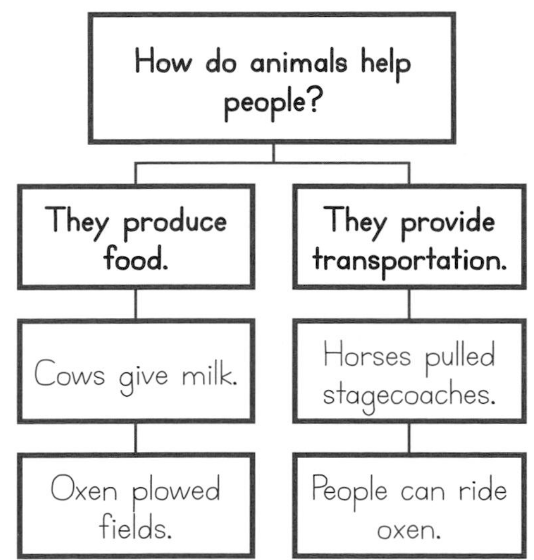

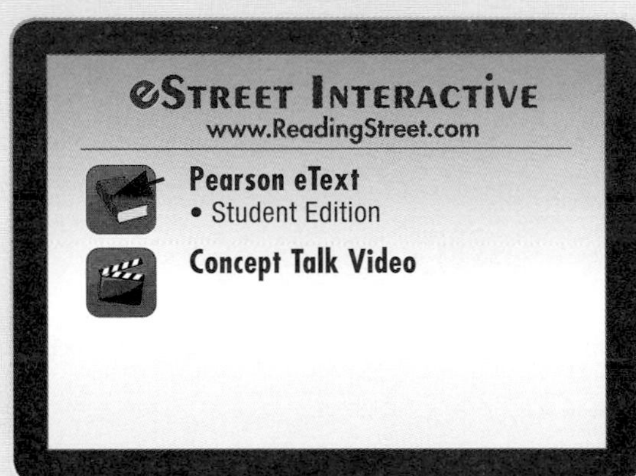

ELL

Preteach Concepts Use the Day 1 instruction on ELL Poster 3 to build knowledge and oral vocabulary.

ELL Support Additional ELL support is provided in the *ELL Handbook* and in the *ELL Support Lessons* on the *Teacher Resources DVD-ROM.*

Content Knowledge

Build Oral Vocabulary

INTRODUCE AMAZING WORDS Display p. 3 of the *Sing with Me* Big Book. Tell children they are going to sing "The Oxen Song," which is about how oxen helped farmers in the past. Ask children to listen for the Amazing Words *past, present, produce,* and *transportation* as you sing. Sing the song again and have children join you.

The Oxen Song
In olden days most farms had oxen.
They helped to produce farmers' crops.
They pulled wagons for transportation.
As helpers the oxen were tops.
Oxen, oxen,
In past times big oxen were
Everywhere.
Oxen, oxen,
In present times oxen are
Rare.

Sing with Me Big Book, p. 3

Amazing Words — Robust Vocabulary Routine

1. **Introduce the Word** Relate the word *transportation* to the song. Oxen used to pull wagons that were used for *transportation.* Supply a child-friendly definition. *Transportation* is a way to move people or things from one place to another. Have children say the word.
2. **Demonstrate** Provide examples to show meaning. Long ago, people rode horses or sailed on ships for *transportation.* Today many people use a car as their main type of *transportation.* Some children ride a school bus for *transportation* every day.
3. **Apply** Have children demonstrate their understanding. Name some forms of *transportation* you have used.
4. **Display the Word** Run your hand under the chunks *trans-por-ta-tion* as you read the word.

See p. OV•3 to teach *past, present,* and *produce.*

Routines Flip Chart

Common Core State Standards

Language 4. Determine or clarify the meaning of unknown and multiple-meaning words and phrases based on grade 1 reading and content, choosing flexibly from an array of strategies. **Language 5.c.** Identify real-life connections between words and their use (e.g., note places at home that are *cozy*).

Amazing Words

You've learned 063 words so far.

You'll learn 009 words this week!

past	serve
present	snuggle
produce	enormous
transportation	powerful
danger	

AMAZING WORDS AT WORK Have children look at the picture on p. 3. Point to the oxen.

- How did these oxen help people? Use the word *transportation* in your answer. (Possible response: They pulled wagons for transportation.)
- Why were oxen used on farms in the *past?* Use the word *past* in your answer. (Possible response: In the past, oxen made the farmer's job easier.)
- Think about *present* farms. What is used instead of oxen? Use the word *present* in your answer. (Possible response: Present farms use tractors instead of oxen.)
- Name three things that a farm may *produce.* Use the word *produce* in your answer. (Possible response: A farm may produce corn, wheat, or potatoes.)

APPLY AMAZING WORDS Have children demonstrate their understanding of the Amazing Words by completing these sentences orally.

Many people in the **past** used to get around using _______.

Many people still ride _______ in the **present.**

Factories **produce** _______.

A _______ is my favorite kind of **transportation.**

After children complete the sentences, have them write a word or a sentence with the word and draw a picture about the word. Ask them to show their page and read and tell about the word and the picture they made.

Corrective feedback	**If...** children have difficulty using the Amazing Words, **then...** remind them of the definitions and provide opportunities for children to use the words in sentences.

Access for All

SI Strategic Intervention

Amazing Words If children's oral sentences use nonstandard verb tenses, then say each sentence several times and have children repeat it.

Multiple-Meaning Words Explain that the word *present* has more than one meaning. Give an example of *present* meaning "now." Draw a simple sketch of a gift, or present, and use the word with this meaning in a sentence. Have children produce their own sentences with each meaning.

Common Core State Standards
Foundational Skills 2.c. Isolate and pronounce initial, medial vowel, and final sounds (phonemes) in spoken single-syllable words. Also Foundational Skills 2., 2.b.
Phonemic Awareness
Let's Listen for
Sounds
Read Together
• Find five things that have the short o sound in the middle.
• Find something that has the short o sound at the beginning of the word. Say the word.
• Find two things that rhyme with stop. Say each word.
• Find something that rhymes with pot. Say the sound at the end of that word.
• Find something that rhymes with rows. Say each sound in the word.
READING STREET ONLINE
SOUND-SPELLING CARDS
www.ReadingStreet.com
Bakery
$10.00
$5.00
27
68
69

Student Edition, pp. 68–69

Common Core State Standards

Foundational Skills 2.b. Orally produce single-syllable words by blending sounds (phonemes), including consonant blends. **Foundational Skills 2.c.** Isolate and pronounce initial, medial vowel, and final sounds (phonemes) in spoken single-syllable words. **Also Foundational Skills 2.d., 3., 3.b.**

Skills Trace

Short *o*: *o*

Introduce U1W3D1

Practice U1W3D3; U1W3D4

Reteach/Review U1W3D5; U1W4D4

Assess/Test Weekly Test U1W3
Benchmark Test U1

KEY: U=Unit W=Week D=Day

Phonemic Awareness

Distinguish /o/

INTRODUCE Read the first two bulleted points in the Student Edition. What is the shopkeeper using to clean up? (a mop) The middle sound in *mop* is /o/. Have children identify other items or descriptive words in the picture that contain the short *o* sound. *(shop, clock, dotted, rock, sock)* I also see things whose names begin with /o/. On the girl's shirt, I see a sea animal. Ask children to identify the sea animal whose name begins with the short *o* sound. (octopus)

MODEL Listen to the sound at the beginning of the word *octopus: /o/, octopus.* Model blending the sounds of the word *shop.*

Corrective feedback	**If...** children make an error, **then...** model by sounding out the word slowly, and have them repeat the word to distinguish the sound /o/.

Phonics

Short *o*: *o*

CONNECT Write the words *cat* and *pin.* Ask children what they know about the vowel sounds in these words. (The vowel sounds are short. *Cat* has the short vowel sound /a/ and *pin* has the short vowel sound /i/.) Explain that today they will learn how to spell and read words with the short vowel sound /o/.

Sound-Spelling Card 17

USE SOUND-SPELLING CARD Display Card 17. Point to *o.* The short *o* sound, /o/, is spelled *o.* Have children say /o/ several times as you point to *o.*

MODEL Write *top.* In this word, the letter *o* stands for the sound /o/. Segment and blend *top;* then have children blend with you: /t/ /o/ /p/. Follow this procedure to model *ox.*

GROUP PRACTICE Continue segmenting and blending. This time have children blend with you. Remind children that the letter *o* can stand for the sound /o/.

job	**hot**	**rock**	**mop**	**rod**	**jot**
lock	**hop**	**got**	**sock**	**dot**	**mom**

REVIEW What do you know about reading these words? (The letter *o* at the beginning or in the middle of a word spells the sound /o/.)

Access for All

 Advanced

Blend Short *o* Words Practice with longer short *o* words, such as *rocket, copy, jogging, body, oxen,* and *soccer.* Have children write the words on word cards and think of categories into which the words could be sorted (Things, Actions, etc.). Have children tell the class their categories and read the words.

Vocabulary Support

You may wish to explain the meanings of these words.

jot to write quickly or briefly

rod a stick or wand made of wood, metal, or another material

Say and Spell Short *o* The short *o* in English is similar to the sound of the letter *a* in Spanish. Spanish-speaking children may associate the letter *a* with the sound /o/ and spell short *o* words with *a* (e.g., *pat* for *pot*). Give these children additional practice with the pronunciation and spelling of short *o* words.

DAY 1

Common Core State Standards

Foundational Skills 3. Know and apply grade-level phonics and word analysis skills in decoding words. **Foundational Skills 3.b.** Decode regularly spelled one-syllable words.

Access for All

Advanced

Extend Blending Provide children who can segment and blend all the words correctly with more challenging words such as *trap, plan, glad,* and *handbag.*

Spelling Pattern

/o/ Spelled o The sound /o/ is usually spelled *o* at the beginning or in the middle of a word.

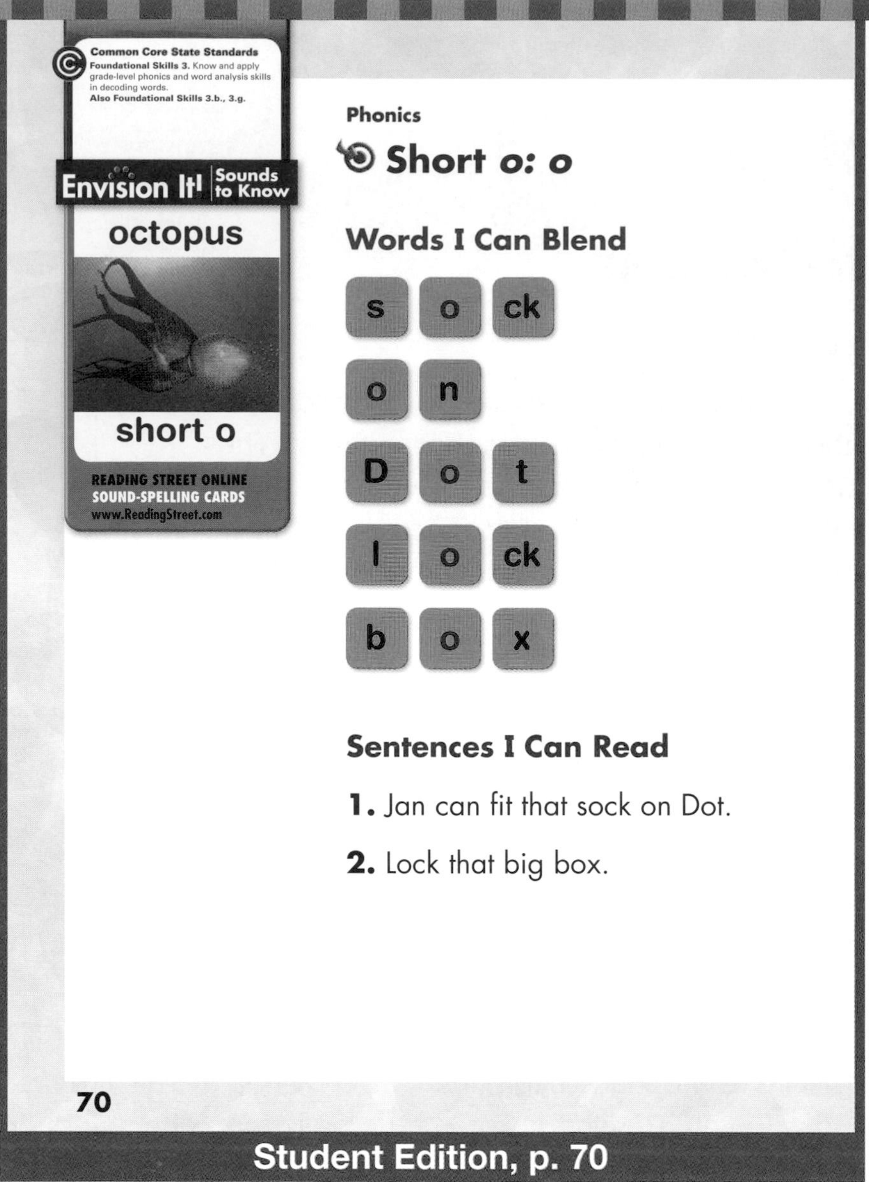
Common Core State Standards
Foundational Skills 3. Know and apply grade-level phonics and word analysis skills in decoding words.
Also Foundational Skills 3.b., 3.g.
Envision It! Sounds to Know
octopus
short o
READING STREET ONLINE
SOUND-SPELLING CARDS
www.ReadingStreet.com
Phonics
Short o: o
Words I Can Blend
s o ck
o n
D o t
l o ck
b o x
Sentences I Can Read
1. Jan can fit that sock on Dot.
2. Lock that big box.
70
Student Edition, p. 70

Phonics

Guide Practice

BLEND WORDS Have children turn to page 70 in their Student Edition. Look at the picture on this page. I see a picture of an *octopus.* When I say *octopus,* I hear /o/ at the beginning. The /o/ sound is spelled *o.*

GROUP PRACTICE For each word in "Words I Can Blend," ask for the sound of each letter or group of letters. Make sure that children identify the /o/ sound in each word. Then have children blend the whole word.

Corrective feedback	**If...** children have difficulty blending a word, **then...** model blending the word, and then ask children to blend it with you.

DECODE WORDS IN ISOLATION After children can successfully segment and blend the words, point to words in random order and ask children to read them naturally.

DECODE WORDS IN CONTEXT Have children read each of the sentences. Have them identify words in the sentences that have the vowel sound /o/.

Team Talk Pair children and have them take turns reading each of the sentences aloud.

ON THEIR OWN Use *Reader's and Writer's Notebook,* p. 153.

MONITOR PROGRESS Short *o: o*

FORMATIVE ASSESSMENT Write the following words and have the class read them. Notice which words children miss during the group reading. Call on individuals to read some of the words.

					Spiral Review
fox	mop	rock	top	not	
ran	sat	am	back	wax ←	Row 2 reviews short *a* words.
bag	lid	hop	six	van ←	Row 3 reviews short *a, i, o* words.

If... children cannot blend short *o* words at this point,

then... use the Small Group Time Strategic Intervention lesson, p. SG•41, to reteach /o/ spelled *o.* Continue to monitor children's progress using other instructional opportunities during the week. See the Skills Trace on p. 68–69.

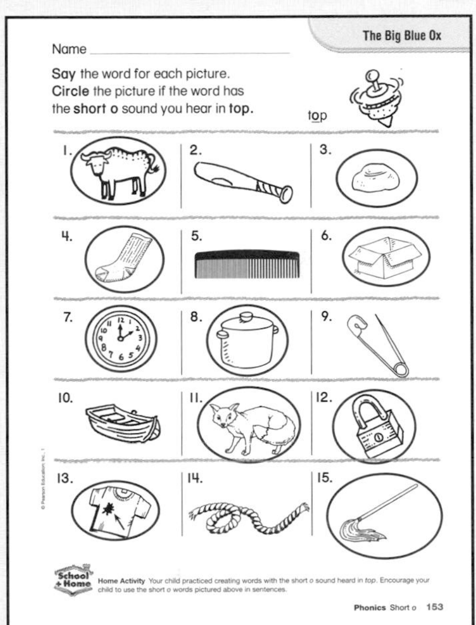
The Big Blue Ox

Name

Say the word for each picture. Circle the picture if the word has the short o sound you hear in top.

top

1. 2. 3. 4. 5. 6. 7. 8. 9. 10. 11. 12. 13. 14. 15.

Phonics Short o 153

Reader's and Writer's Notebook, p. 153

ELL

Pronunciation Children may need support pronouncing initial /, such as in *lock* and *lid.* Remind children to place their tongue behind their upper front teeth and keep it there while pronouncing the / sound.

Common Core State Standards

Foundational Skills 3. Know and apply grade-level phonics and word analysis skills in decoding words. **Foundational Skills 3.b.** Decode regularly spelled one-syllable words. **Foundational Skills 3.g.** Recognize and read grade-appropriate irregularly spelled words. **Foundational Skills 4.** Read with sufficient accuracy and fluency to support comprehension.

Decodable Reader 3A

If children need help, then...

Read *The Box*

DECODE WORDS IN ISOLATION Have children turn to page 145. Have children decode each word.

REVIEW HIGH-FREQUENCY WORDS Review the previously taught words *a, the, two, three, is,* and *they.* Have children read each word as you point to it on the Word Wall.

PREVIEW DECODABLE READER Have children read the title and preview the story. Tell them they will read words with the short vowel sound *o.*

DECODE WORDS IN CONTEXT Pair children for reading and listen as they decode. One child begins. Children read the entire story, switching readers after each page. Partners reread the story. This time the other child begins.

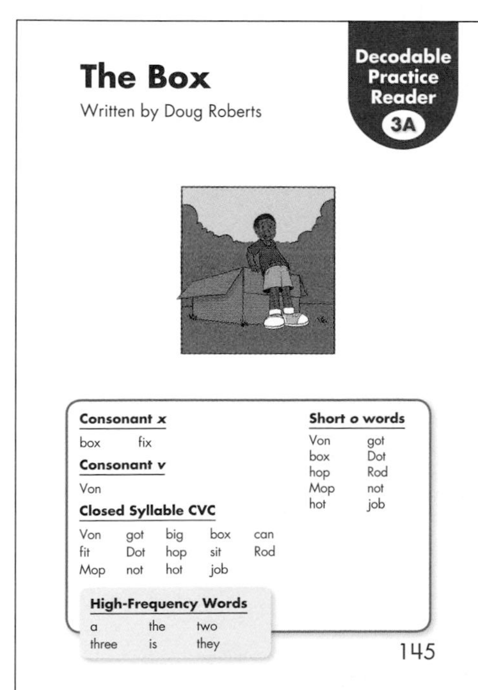
The Box

Written by Doug Roberts

Decodable Practice Reader 3A

Consonant x
box fix

Consonant v
Von

Closed Syllable CVC
Von got big box can
fit Dot hop sit Rod
Mop not hot job

Short o words
Von got
box Dot
hop Rod
Mop not
hot job

High-Frequency Words
a the two
three is they

145

Decodable Practice Reader 3A

Von got a big box.

146

Von got in the box.
Von can fit.

147

Dot will hop in.
Dot will sit in the box.
Two can fit.

148

Rod got in the box.
Rod sat in it.
Three can fit.

149

Mop will hop in.
Mop will NOT fit!

150

Von will fix the box.
It is a hot job.

151

They got back in.
Mop can fit!

152

Corrective feedback	**If...** children have difficulty decoding a word, **then...** refer them to the Sound-Spelling Cards to identify the sounds in the word. Then prompt them to blend the word. • What is the new word? • Is the new word a word you know? • Does it make sense in the story?

CHECK DECODING AND COMPREHENSION Have children retell the story to include characters, setting, and events. Then have children find words with the short *o* sound in the story. Children should supply *Von, got, box, Dot, hop, Rod, Mop, not, hot,* and *job.* Ask them how they know these words have the short *o* sound. (When the only vowel in a word is *o,* it usually spells the short *o* sound.)

Reread for Fluency

REREAD DECODABLE READER Have children reread Decodable Practice Reader 3A to develop automaticity decoding words with the short *o* sound.

Routine Oral Rereading

1. **Read** Have children read the entire book orally.
2. **Reread** To achieve optimal fluency, children should reread the text three or four times.
3. **Corrective Feedback** Listen as children read. Provide corrective feedback regarding their fluency and decoding.

Routines Flip Chart

Access for All

SI Strategic Intervention

Pronunciation After reading, have pairs ask and answer questions about the story. Monitor children's pronunciation of short *o* words.

Short *o*: *o*

Beginning Before children read, lead them on a picture walk through the story. Point out and pronounce the words that have the short *o* sound. Then write a pictured word and have children pronounce it and find its picture.

Intermediate Before reading, help children pronounce the word with the short *o* sound in the story title, *The Box.* Then have them use the word to make a prediction about what the story will be about.

Advanced After reading, have children find the words with the short *o* sound and use them to make up their own sentences about what they think will happen with the box.

Common Core State Standards

Foundational Skills 3.g. Recognize and read grade-appropriate irregularly spelled words. **Language 2.d.** Use conventional spelling for words with common spelling patterns and for frequently occurring irregular words. **Language 2.e.** Spell untaught words phonetically, drawing on phonemic awareness and spelling conventions.

Access for All

A Advanced

Extend Spelling Challenge children who spell words correctly to spell more difficult words such as *cannot, laptop, onto, potluck, solid,* and *tomcat.*

Phonics/Spelling Generalization

Short *o* Each spelling word has the short *o* sound spelled *o.*

Name ______ The Big Blue Ox

Short *o* Words

Look at the word. **Say** it. **Listen** for the short *o* sound.

	Write each word.	Check it.
1. mom	mom	mom
2. hot	hot	hot
3. hop	hop	hop
4. pot	pot	pot
5. pop	pop	pop
6. ox	ox	ox
7. lock	lock	lock
8. mop	mop	mop
9. got	got	got
10. rock	rock	rock

Words to Read

11. help help 12. use use

School + Home **Home Activity** Your child is learning to spell words with a short o vowel sound. Have your child write each word and point to the short o vowel sound.

DVD•46 **Spelling** Short o Words

Let's Practice It! TR DVD•46

Spelling Pretest

Short *o* Words

DICTATE SPELLING WORDS Dictate the spelling words and read the sentences. Have children write the words. If needed, segment the words for children, clarify the pronunciations, and give meanings of words. Have children check their pretests and correct misspelled words.

1. hot*	The sun is **hot.**
2. hop	Jon can **hop** on one foot.
3. pot	Put the lid on the **pot.**
4. pop*	It's fun to **pop** a balloon.
5. ox*	An **ox** is a big animal.
6. lock	Open the **lock** on the gate.
7. mop*	I will **mop** the floor.
8. got	Todd **got** a new pet.
9. rock	That big **rock** is heavy.
10. mom*	My **mom** will help me.

* Words marked with asterisks come from the selection *The Big Blue Ox.*

ON THEIR OWN Use Let's Practice It! p. 46 on the *Teacher Resources DVD-ROM.*

ELL

If... children need more scaffolding and practice with **Phonemic Awareness and Phonics, then...** use the Phonics Transition Lessons on pp. 249–345 in the *ELL Handbook.*

Day 1 SMALL GROUP TIME • Differentiate Phonics, p. SG•35

OL On-Level

- **Practice Phonics** Additional Short *o* Words
- **Read** Decodable Reader *The Box*

SI Strategic Intervention

- **Reteach Phonics** Blend Short *o* Words
- **Read** Decodable Reader *The Box*

A Advanced

- **Extend Phonics** More Short *o* Words
- **Read** Advanced Selection for Short *o* Words
- **Introduce** Inquiry Project

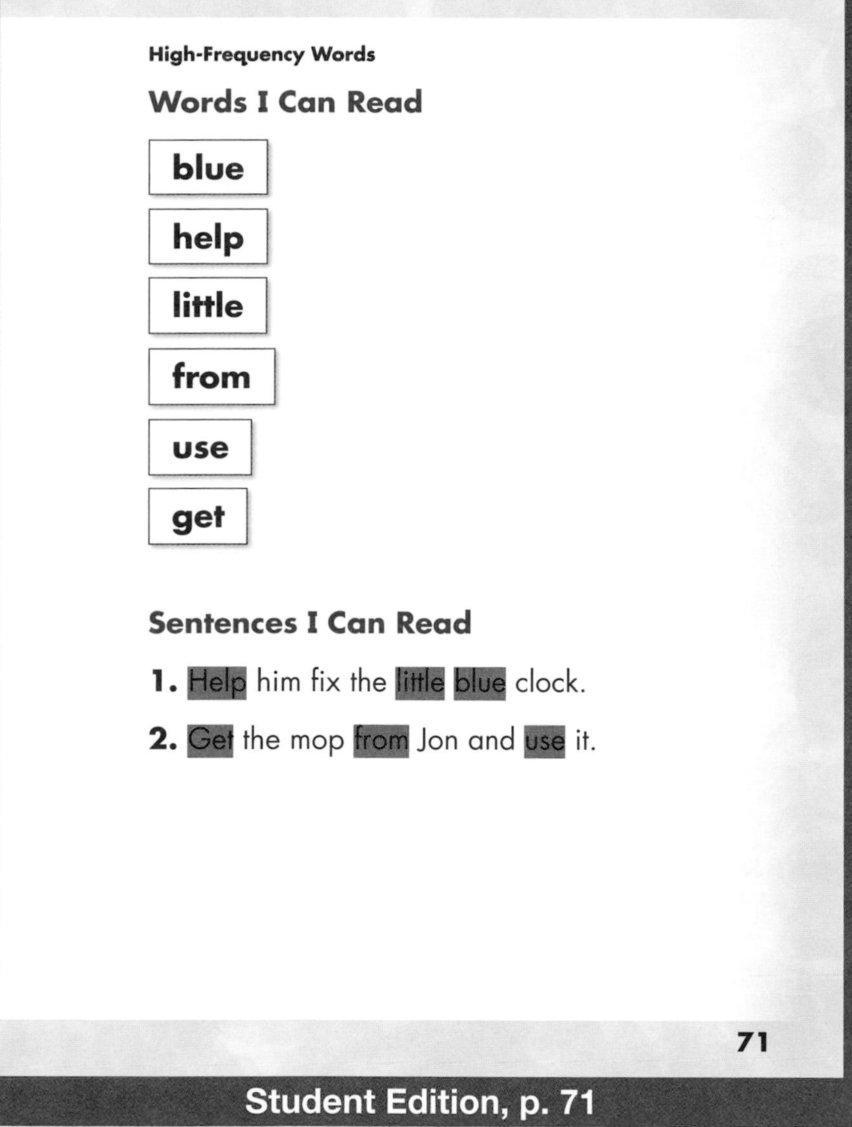
High-Frequency Words

Words I Can Read

blue

help

little

from

use

get

Sentences I Can Read

1. Help him fix the little blue clock.

2. Get the mop from Jon and use it.

71

Student Edition, p. 71

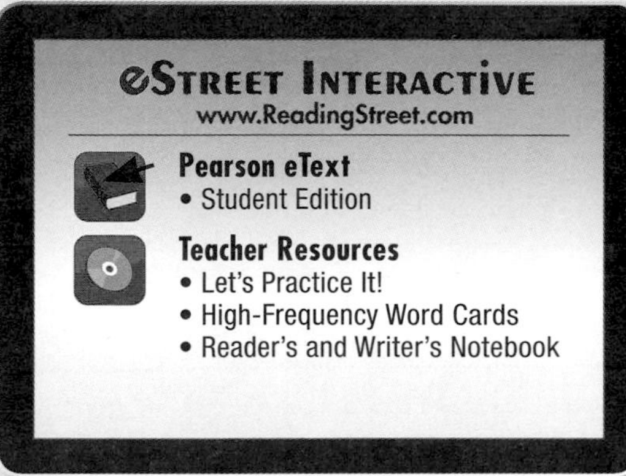

High-Frequency Words

Routine Nondecodable Words

1. **Say and Spell** Some words we learn by remembering the letters. Point to *blue.* Have children say and spell each word letter by letter.
2. **Identify Familiar Letter-Sounds** Point to the first letter in *blue.* What is this letter and what is its sound? (*b,* /b/)
3. **Show Meaning** Tell me a sentence using the word *blue.* Repeat.

Routines Flip Chart

READ Have children read the page aloud. Add the words to the Word Wall.

ON THEIR OWN Use *Reader's and Writer's Notebook,* p. 154.

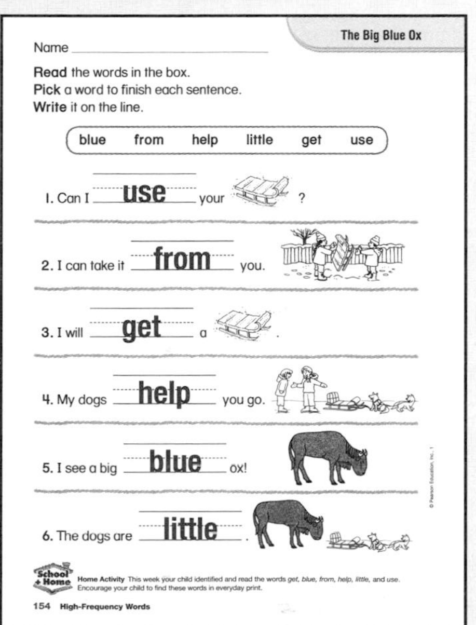
The Big Blue Ox

Name

Read the words in the box.
Pick a word to finish each sentence.
Write it on the line.

blue from help little get use

1. Can I use your ?
2. I can take it from you.
3. I will get a .
4. My dogs help you go.
5. I see a big blue ox!
6. The dogs are little .

Home Activity This week your child identified and read the words get, blue, from, help, little, and use. Encourage your child to find these words in everyday print.

154 High-Frequency Words

Reader's and Writer's Notebook, p. 154

Survival Vocabulary Have children use the word *blue* to talk about an article of clothing or other object they see in the classroom. Children might say *Max has a **blue** shirt.*

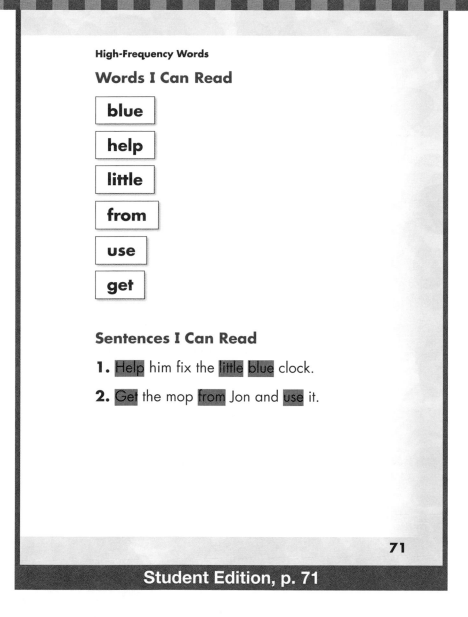

Common Core State Standards

Literature 3. Describe characters, settings, and major events in a story, using key details.

Skills Trace

Character and Setting

Introduce U1W1D1; U1W3D1; U5W1D1

Practice U1W1D2; U1W1D3; U1W1D4; U1W3D2; U1W3D3; U1W3D4; U5W1D2; U5W1D3; U5W1D4

Reteach/Review U1W1D5; U1W3D5; U2W2D2; U4W6D2; U5W1D5

Assess/Test Weekly Tests U1W1; U1W3; U5W1
Benchmark Tests U1; U5

KEY: U=Unit W=Week D=Day

Academic Vocabulary

characters the people or animals in a story

setting where and when a story takes place

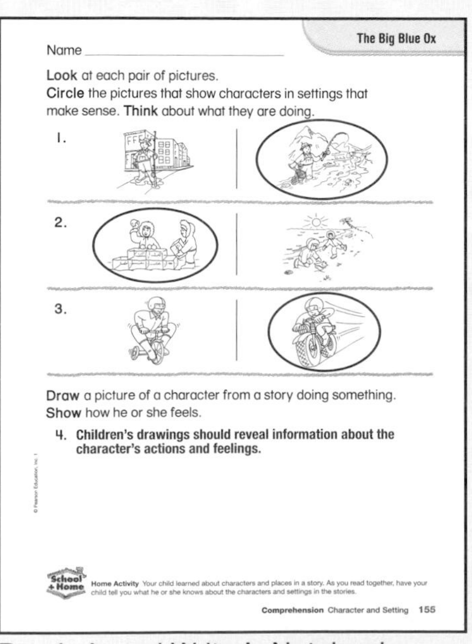

The Big Blue Ox

Name ________________

Look at each pair of pictures.
Circle the pictures that show characters in settings that make sense. **Think** about what they are doing.

1.

2.

3.

Draw a picture of a character from a story doing something.
Show how he or she feels.

4. **Children's drawings should reveal information about the character's actions and feelings.**

© Pearson Education, Inc. 1

School + Home **Home Activity** Your child learned about characters and places in a story. As you read together, have your child tell you what he or she knows about the characters and settings in the stories.

Comprehension Character and Setting 155

Reader's and Writer's Notebook, p. 155

Text-Based Comprehension

Character and Setting

READ Remind children of the weekly concept—Animals That Help. Have children listen as you read aloud "A Perfect Visit" on page 71b.

MODEL A CLOSE READ Now model how to use the setting and what the characters do and say as tools to build comprehension.

When I read, I try to figure out who the people and animals in the story are. I know the story is mostly about Farmer Bob. The animals in the story are Ox, Hen, Horse, Pig, and Cat. I also look for clues about where and when the story takes place. I know there is a farmer and farm animals in the story. Farmer Bob does work during the day, and the animals do work at night. That is a clue that the story probably takes place during one day on a farm.

TEACH CHARACTER AND SETTING **Characters** are the people and animals in a story. They can be real or make-believe. The **setting** is where and when the story takes place. It can also be a real or make-believe place. Good readers look for clues that tell them about characters and setting. Display the words *characters* and *setting.* Readers better understand a story when they can describe the reasons for a character's actions or feelings, as well as the setting of the story.

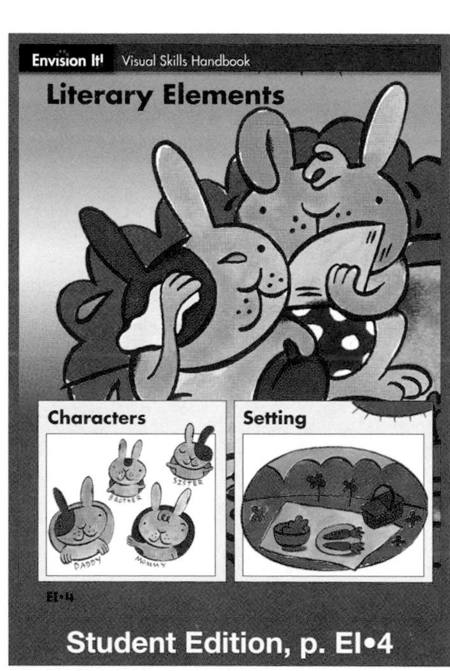

Student Edition, p. EI•4

Have children turn to p. EI•4 in their Student Edition. Discuss these questions using the pictures:

- Who are the characters? (They are bunnies: Mommy, Daddy, Sister, Brother.)
- What is the setting? (It is a field where a blanket is set up for a picnic.)

GUIDE PRACTICE Now reread "A Perfect Visit." Ask children if the characters in the story are real or make-believe and why they think so. (They are make-believe. The farmer and the animals talk to each other and the animals do things real animals can't do.) What other clues tell you that the setting is a farm? (There is a barnyard, a barn, and a farmhouse.)

APPLY Use *Reader's and Writer's Notebook,* p. 155.

Teacher Read Aloud

A Perfect Visit

Farmer Bob was very excited. His oldest, most favorite friend was coming to visit. Farmer Bob wanted everything to be just perfect. He pulled the weeds from the vegetable garden and painted the farmhouse bright white. "I want this place in tip-top shape," said Farmer Bob.

The animals in the barnyard watched as Farmer Bob worked and worked all day. That night, Farmer Bob went to the barn to feed the animals. He looked exhausted.

"Why are you working so hard, Farmer Bob?" asked Ox.

"My friend Bill is coming to visit. I want everything to be perfect." A tired Farmer Bob shuffled back to the farmhouse.

"There must be something we can do to help Farmer Bob," said Ox.

After a moment, Hen said, "I can collect eggs from the other hens and bake a cake. The hens will be happy to produce them."

"I can sweep out the barn with my tail," called Horse.

"I can pick flowers from the meadow and decorate the barnyard!" exclaimed Pig.

"Can I help too?" asked Cat.

"Yes," said Ox. "Farmer Bob and his friend will need transportation. You can help me fix up my cart."

The animals worked and worked through the night. "Oh, my!" Farmer Bob exclaimed in the morning. "The farm looks better than it ever has in the past. Who could have done all this work?"

The animals smiled as Farmer Bob filled their food bowls. "This will be the perfect visit," they all said.

Bridge to Common Core

KEY IDEAS AND DETAILS

As children identify the setting and characters in a selection, they recognize details that tell when and where the selection takes place and information about the people or animals in the selection. Retelling the selection helps children focus on the events. Asking questions about the setting and characters helps children better understand these elements of the selection.

Support Comprehension To increase children's understanding of vocabulary heard in the Read Aloud, create picture cards for words they may not know such as *barnyard, hen, horse, pig,* and *farmhouse.*

Common Core State Standards

Writing 5. With guidance and support from adults, focus on a topic, respond to questions and suggestions from peers, and add details to strengthen writing as needed. **Language 1.j.** Produce and expand complete simple and compound declarative, interrogative, imperative, and exclamatory sentences in response to prompts.

Academic Vocabulary 

predicate the action part of a sentence

sentence a group of words that tells a complete idea

poem words written in lines that may rhyme

Daily Fix-It

1. ox got Mom that pott.
   Ox got Mom that pot.
2. He can hep Pop Mop.
   He can help Pop mop.

Discuss the Daily Fix-It corrections with children. Review sentence capitalization and punctuation and the spelling of *pot* and *help.*

Conventions

Predicates of Sentences

MAKE CONNECTIONS This week you listened to a story called "A Perfect Visit." We can say sentences to tell about Farmer Bob. Have children use this sentence frame: *Farmer Bob* ______. Then ask children to say the sentences with you. The thing that Farmer Bob does is the *predicate* of the sentence.

TEACH Explain that a **sentence** is a group of words that tells a complete idea and that a **predicate** is the action part of a sentence. It tells what a person, animal, or thing does. *Skips with me, laughs aloud,* and *draws a circle* are predicates. Remind children that the word order in a sentence must make sense to know the predicate of the sentence. Tell children that word order makes sense when you can tell what the sentence means.

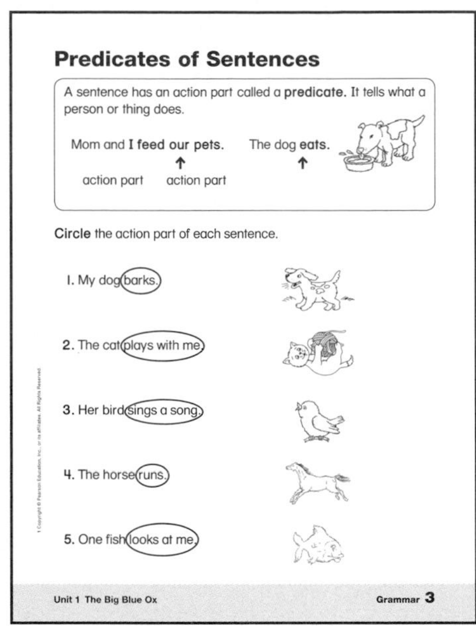

Predicates of Sentences

A sentence has an action part called a **predicate.** It tells what a person or thing does.

Mom and I **feed our pets.** (action part) The dog **eats.** (action part)

Circle the action part of each sentence.

1. My dog barks.
2. The cat plays with me.
3. Her bird sings a song.
4. The horse runs.
5. One fish looks at me.

Unit 1 The Big Blue Ox — Grammar 3

Grammar Transparency 3
TR DVD

MODEL Display Grammar Transparency 3. Read the definition aloud. Model identifying the predicate, or action part, in each example. Then read the directions and model number 1.

GUIDE PRACTICE Continue with items 2–5, having children identify the predicate, or action part, in each sentence.

APPLY Have the class complete these sentence frames orally using predicates.

1. **Our pet bird ______.**
2. **Cats ______.**
3. **My hamster and I ______.**

Team Talk Pair children and have them take turns saying a sentence about something they did today. Then have them identify the predicate in each sentence.

Writing  

Short Poem

Mini-Lesson Read Like a Writer

■ **Introduce** This week you will write a short poem. A short poem is written in lines. The lines may rhyme. The poem might describe something, or it might express feelings.

Prompt Think about a kind of animal you know. Write a two-line poem about that animal.

Trait Sentences

Mode Expository/Informative/ Explanatory

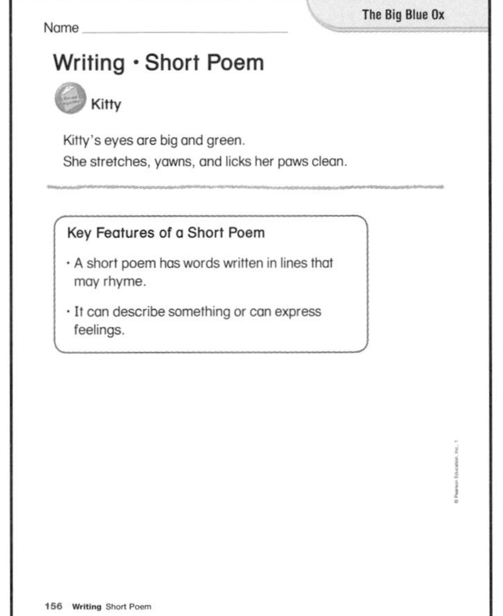
The Big Blue Ox

Name

Writing • Short Poem

Kitty

Kitty's eyes are big and green.
She stretches, yawns, and licks her paws clean.

Key Features of a Short Poem

- A short poem has words written in lines that may rhyme.
- It can describe something or can express feelings.

156 Writing Short Poem

Reader's and Writer's Notebook, p. 156

■ **Examine Model Text** Let's listen to a short poem. Track the print as you read aloud "Kitty" on *Reader's and Writer's Notebook,* p. 156. Have children follow along.

■ **Key Features** What does this poem describe? (a cat) Ask what words or phrases help children picture the cat, such as *eyes are big and green* or *stretches,* and help children underline them. Then ask which words rhyme. (*green* and *clean*) Help children circle the words that rhyme.

This short poem is written in lines. The lines in a poem sometimes rhyme and sometimes do not rhyme. The lines in this poem do rhyme.

This short poem describes a cat. The details in the poem help readers picture the cat. A short poem can also express feelings.

Writing to Sources Use More Connect the Texts on pp. 221–259 to guide children in writing text-based responses within various forms and modes.

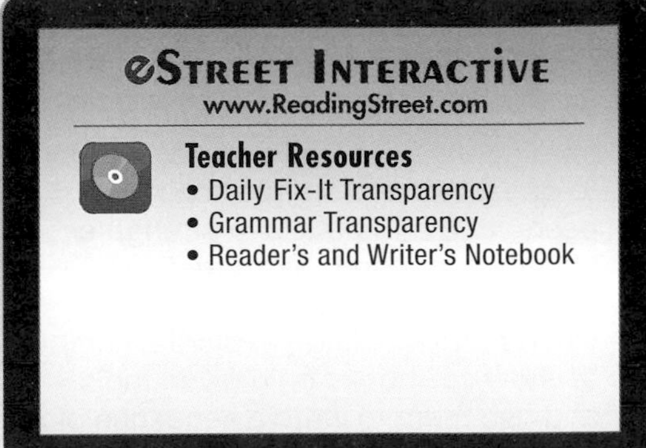

Write Guy *by Jeff Anderson*

Life in a Fishbowl

When a teacher can't confer with every child, a "fishbowl conference" with one willing child can allow other children to observe, listen, and learn. It's important to reflect what the child is doing well and how a draft might be revised and improved.

Bridge to Common Core

TEXT TYPES AND PURPOSES

This week children write a descriptive poem about a kind of animal they know.

Informative/Explanatory Writing

As children develop writing skills for creating a poem, they use descriptive writing to better understand the literary skills to learn about the structure of a poem. The activities help children develop effective writing techniques as they write their descriptive poem.

Throughout the week, children will improve their range and content of writing through daily mini-lessons.

5-Day Plan

DAY 1	Read Like a Writer
DAY 2	Sensory Details
DAY 3	Writing Trait: Sentences
DAY 4	Revise: Changing Words
DAY 5	Proofread

Conventions To provide children with practice on predicates of sentences, use the modified grammar lessons in the *ELL Handbook.*

Common Core State Standards

Writing 5. With guidance and support from adults, focus on a topic, respond to questions and suggestions from peers, and add details to strengthen writing as needed. **Writing 7.** Participate in shared research and writing projects (e.g., explore a number of "how-to" books on a given topic and use them to write a sequence of instructions).

Review Key Features

Review key features of a short poem with children. You may want to post these key features in the classroom to allow children to refer to them as they work on their poems.

Key Features of a Short Poem

- has words written in lines that may rhyme
- can describe something or can express feelings

Connect to Familiar Texts

Use examples such as "My Family" (Unit R, p. 55), "Home" (Unit R, p. 81), or other poems familiar to children. In "My Family," the lines rhyme. In "Home," the lines do not rhyme. Both poems express feelings.

Routine Quick Write for Fluency

Team Talk

1. **Talk** Read these questions aloud. If possible, challenge children to respond with words that rhyme.
   What words can help make a picture of an animal?
   What words can tell how we feel about an animal?
2. **Write** Have children use some of the words that answer the questions to write short sentences. Make sure their sentences include a subject and a verb.
3. **Share** Partners can read their answers to one another.

Routines Flip Chart

Research and Inquiry

Step 1 Identify and Focus Topic

TEACH Display and review the concept map that explores this week's question: *How do animals help people?* What would you like to learn about animals that help people? Ask children to share their interests. Help them identify what different animals do for us.

Think Aloud **MODEL** I still have some questions about how animals help people. For example: What are some ways that dogs help people who are sick or disabled? I see people with Seeing Eye dogs who help them get around when they cannot see, but I heard that dogs can help people who cannot walk or hear, also. And there are dogs that help people with different medical problems. I think that's amazing! I want to know more about the ways dogs can help people.

GUIDE PRACTICE Give children time to think about other animals that help people. Have them share questions they have about these animals.

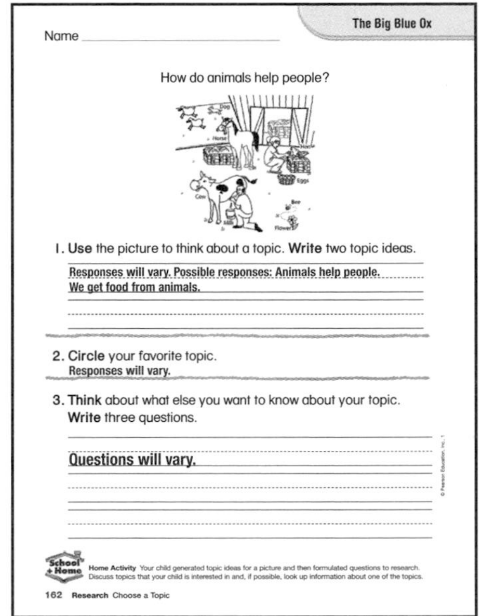

Name ______________ The Big Blue Ox

How do animals help people?

1. Use the picture to think about a topic. Write two topic ideas.
Responses will vary. Possible responses: Animals help people.
We get food from animals.

2. Circle your favorite topic.
Responses will vary.

3. Think about what else you want to know about your topic. Write three questions.
Questions will vary.

School + Home Home Activity Your child generated topic ideas for a picture and then formulated questions to research. Discuss topics that your child is interested in and, if possible, look up information about one of the topics.

162 Research Choose a Topic

Reader's and Writer's Notebook, p. 162

APPLY Use *Reader's and Writer's Notebook,* p. 162.

eStreet Interactive
www.ReadingStreet.com

Teacher Resources
- Let's Practice It!
- Reader's and Writer's Notebook

21st Century Skills

Internet Guy *Don Leu*

Weekly Inquiry Project

STEP 1	Identify and Focus Topic
STEP 2	Research Skill
STEP 3	Gather and Record Information
STEP 4	Synthesize
STEP 5	Communicate

Wrap Up Your Day!

- ✔ **Phonics: Short *o*** Write *hot* and ask children how the sound /o/ is spelled in the word.
- ✔ **Spelling: Short *o*** Say the word *pop.* Have children name the letter for each sound and write them in the air. Continue with *ox, lock,* and *got.*
- ✔ **Content Knowledge** Ask children to recall the Read Aloud "A Perfect Visit." How did the animals help Farmer Bob? (They cleaned up the farm.)
- ✔ **Homework** Send home this week's Family Times Newsletter from Let's Practice It! pp. 41–42 on the *Teacher Resources DVD-ROM.*

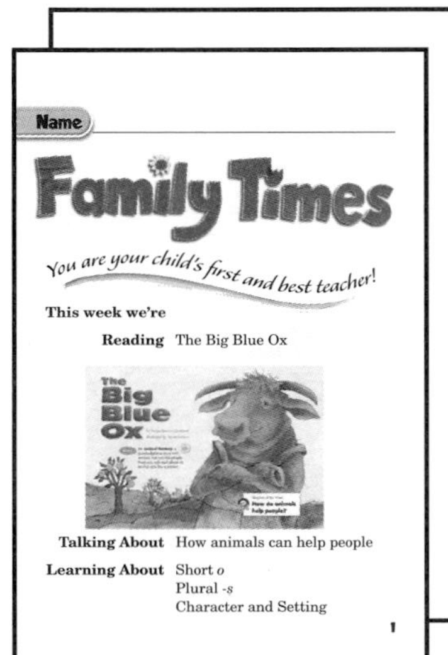

Name

Family Times

You are your child's first and best teacher!

This week we're

Reading The Big Blue Ox

Talking About How animals can help people

Learning About Short *o*
Plural *-s*
Character and Setting

1

Let's Practice It!
TR DVD•41–42

Tell children that tomorrow they will read about a big blue ox that helps a farming family.

DAY 2 at a Glance

Content Knowledge
Oral Vocabulary

Phonemic Awareness
Segment and Blend Phonemes

Phonics/Spelling
Short *o: o*
Plural *-s;* Consonant *s*/z/

High-Frequency Words
blue, from, get, help, little, use

Selection Vocabulary
town
Synonyms

Text-Based Comprehension
Character and Setting
Visualize

Conventions
Predicates of Sentences

Writing
Short Poem

Handwriting
Letter *Oo*/Left-to-Right Progression

Research and Inquiry
Research Skill: Picture Dictionary

Materials

- Student Edition
- Sing with Me Big Book
- Big Book
- Sound-Spelling Cards
- Decodable Reader 3B
- Reader's and Writer's Notebook

Common Core State Standards

Speaking/Listening 2. Ask and answer questions about key details in a text read aloud or information presented orally or through other media. **Language 4.** Determine or clarify the meaning of unknown and multiple-meaning words and phrases based on grade 1 reading and content, choosing flexibly from an array of strategies. **Language 5.c.** Identify real-life connections between words and their use (e.g., note places at home that are *cozy*). **Also Language 6.**

Content Knowledge

Animals That Help

EXPAND THE CONCEPT To reinforce concepts and to focus children's attention, have children sing "The Oxen Song" from the *Sing with Me* Big Book. Why were oxen used on farms in past times? (Oxen were able to help the farmer in different ways.)

Build Oral Language

INTRODUCE AMAZING WORDS Display the Big Book *A Kid's Best Friend.* Read the title and identify the author. Explain that in the story, the author uses some Amazing Words. Read the story and have children listen for the Words *danger* and *serve.*

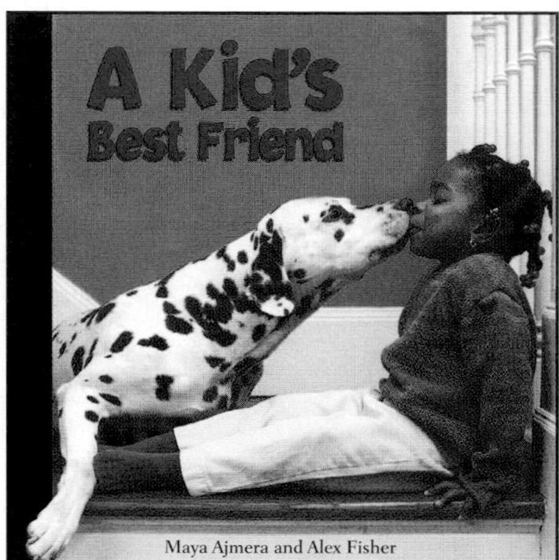

Big Book

TALK ABOUT SENTENCES AND WORDS Reread this sentence from the Big Book.

They can serve as police dogs that help the police sniff out danger.

- Have children repeat the sentence with you. What does *They can serve as police dogs* mean? (They can work as police dogs.)
- What other word could we use in place of *serve?* Have children share their suggestions.
- After children have tried other words, ask: Why do you think the author chose the word *serve?* (It sounds important.)
- **Team Talk** Turn to your partner and say the sentence again using one of your simpler words.
- Point to the phrase *sniff out danger.* What does *danger* mean? (something that can hurt you)
- **Team Talk** Turn to your partner and try some other words or phrases in place of *danger.*

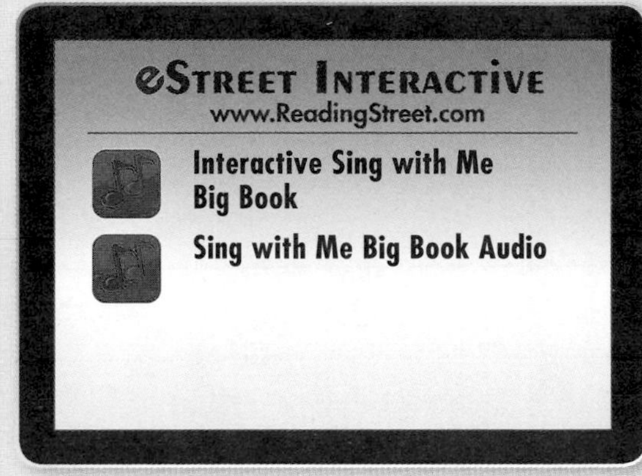

Build Oral Vocabulary

Amazing Words Robust Vocabulary Routine

1. **Introduce the Word** Relate the word *danger* to the book. A dog can help people by keeping them safe from *danger.* Supply a child-friendly definition. *Danger* is something that can hurt you. Have children say the word.

2. **Demonstrate** Provide examples to show meaning. Flooding can be a *danger* in some areas after it has rained. A fire alarm warns you of *danger* from smoke or fire.

3. **Apply** Have children demonstrate their understanding. What are some things that are a *danger* to animals?

4. **Display the Word** Run your hand under the chunks *dan-ger* as you read the word.

See p. OV•3 to teach *serve.*

Routines Flip Chart

After children are introduced to the Amazing Words, have them write the words or sentences with the words and draw a picture about the words. Ask them to show their page and read and tell about the words and the pictures they made.

ADD TO THE CONCEPT MAP Discuss how animals help people in different ways.

Concept Map

- How did the oxen in the song help farmers? (They helped to produce crops and pulled wagons.) Let's add *Oxen pulled wagons* to our map. Remember that oxen were used on farms in the *past.* They are not used as often in the *present. Past* and *present* were two of our Amazing Words from yesterday.
- In yesterday's Read Aloud "A Perfect Visit," the hens helped the farmer. What did they do? (They laid eggs.) Let's add *Hens lay eggs* to our map.

Amazing Words

past, present, produce, transportation, danger, serve, snuggle, enormous, powerful

Access for All

SI Strategic Intervention

Fiction vs. Nonfiction Reinforce the distinction between fiction and nonfiction. Have children give examples of why *A Kid's Best Friend* is nonfiction.

A Advanced

Amazing Words For children who understand the terms *danger* and *serve,* ask them to discuss with a partner how both little and big animals can serve people and protect them from danger.

Reinforce Vocabulary Use the Day 2 instruction on ELL Poster 3 to reinforce meanings of the high-frequency words.

Using Definitions Teach the words *danger* and *serve* by using definitions that children can relate to. The word *danger* means you can get *hurt.* Show the emotion of fear to reinforce the meaning. To *serve* means to *help.* Show that you are happy as reinforcement.

Common Core State Standards
Foundational Skills 2.c. Isolate and pronounce initial, medial vowel, and final sounds (phonemes) in spoken single-syllable words. Also Foundational Skills 2., 2.b.
Phonemic Awareness
Let's Listen for
Sounds
Read Together
• Find five things that have the short o sound in the middle.
• Find something that has the short o sound at the beginning of the word. Say the word.
• Find two things that rhyme with stop. Say each word.
• Find something that rhymes with pot. Say the sound at the end of that word.
• Find something that rhymes with rows. Say each sound in the word.
READING STREET ONLINE
SOUND-SPELLING CARDS
www.ReadingStreet.com
$10.00
$5.00
Bakery
27
68
69
Student Edition, pp. 68–69

Common Core State Standards

Foundational Skills 2.b. Orally produce single-syllable words by blending sounds (phonemes), including consonant blends. **Foundational Skills 2.c.** Isolate and pronounce initial, medial vowel, and final sounds (phonemes) in spoken single-syllable words. **Also Foundational Skills 3., 3.b.**

Skills Trace

Plural *-s;* Consonant *s*/z/

Introduce U1W3D2

Practice U1W3D3; U1W3D4

Reteach/Review U1W3D5; U1W4D4

Assess/Test Weekly Test U1W3
Benchmark Test U1

KEY: U=Unit W=Week D=Day

Phonemic Awareness

Segment and Blend Phonemes

MODEL Read the last bullet point on page 68. What in the picture rhymes with *rows?* (bows) The last sound in *bows* is /z/. Have children identify other items whose names end with /z/. (pies, clothes, shoes, cookies)

Listen to the sounds in the word *bows:* /b/ /ō/ /z/. There are three sounds in *bows.* Let's blends those sounds to make a word: /b/ /ō/ /z/.

GROUP PRACTICE Guide children as they segment and blend these words from the picture: *pies, kids, sales.*

Corrective feedback	**If...** children make an error, **then...** model by segmenting the word, and have them repeat.

ON THEIR OWN Have children segment and blend the following words.

/m/ /o/ /p/ /s/ **mops** /s/ /ī/ /n/ /z/ **signs** /f/ /l/ /a/ /g/ /z/ **flags**

Phonics

Teach/Model

Plural -*s;* Consonant *s/z/*

Sound-Spelling Card 141

CONNECT Write the words *job* and *top.* Have children say the words. Remind them that they already studied words with the short *o* vowel sound. Explain that today they will learn how to make and read plurals of these and other words. Tell them that a plural is a word that means "more than one."

USE SOUND-SPELLING CARD Display Card 141. The sound you hear at the end of *dogs* is /z/. Sometimes a plural ends with the sound /z/ instead of /s/. Both sounds are spelled with *s.* Have children say /z/ several times as you point to *s.*

MODEL Write *tops.* The base word is *top.* It names one thing. The ending is *-s.* It changes the word to mean "more than one top." This is how I blend this word. Segment and blend *tops.* Follow the same procedure to model blending *jobs.* Have children listen to how the *-s* at the end of *tops* sounds different than the *-s* at the end of *jobs.*

GROUP PRACTICE Continue segmenting and blending. This time have children blend with you. Remind children that a plural can end with the sound /s/ or /z/. Both sounds are spelled with *s.*

mops	**hams**	**lots**	**kids**	**cabs**	**caps**
fins	**socks**	**tabs**	**pigs**	**rods**	**bags**

REVIEW What do you know about reading these words? (When a word has an *-s* ending, it may be a plural, which means *more than one.* You may hear the sound /s/ or /z/ at the end.)

Access for All

SI Strategic Intervention

Read -*s* Plurals If children do not read the -*s* plural correctly, write the following words on the board: *cots, wigs, laps, pins.* Have children circle the root word and underline the -*s* ending in each word. Have children tell what sound ends the word and how each word is spelled.

Vocabulary Support

You may wish to explain the meanings of these words.

lots sections, or parts, of land

tabs small flaps attached to something for pulling or labeling it

Visual Support Model isolating sounds while using the pictures on pages 68–69 of the Student Edition as visual support. For example: /k/ /i/ /d/ /z/, *kids.* Who can point to the kids? Now let's say the sounds of *kids* together: /k/ /i/ /d/ /z/.

Common Core State Standards

Foundational Skills 3. Know and apply grade-level phonics and word analysis skills in decoding words. **Foundational Skills 3.b.** Decode regularly spelled one-syllable words.

Spelling Pattern

s/z/ The sound /z/ may be spelled *s*.

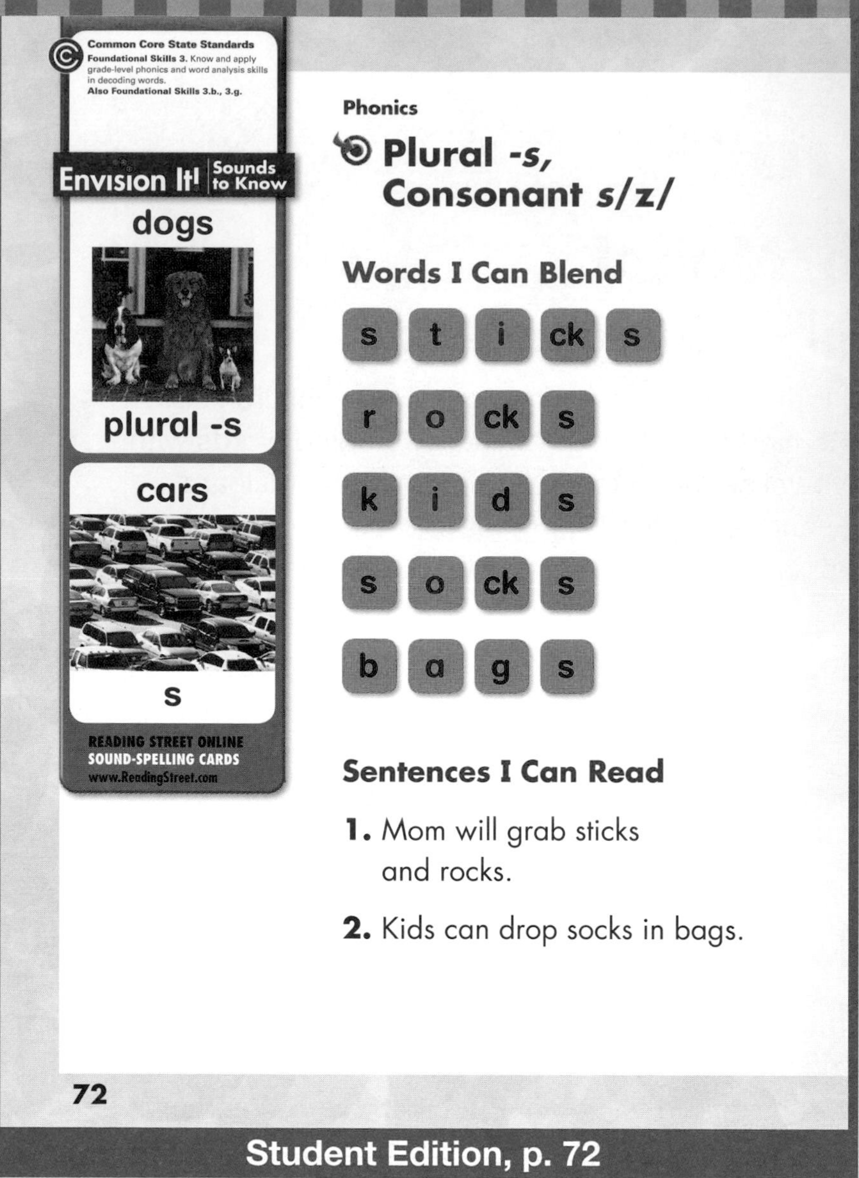

Common Core State Standards
Foundational Skills 3. Know and apply grade-level phonics and word analysis skills in decoding words.
Also Foundational Skills 3.b., 3.g.

Envision It! Sounds to Know

dogs

plural -s

cars

s

READING STREET ONLINE
SOUND-SPELLING CARDS
www.ReadingStreet.com

Phonics

Plural *-s*, Consonant *s/z/*

Words I Can Blend

s t i ck s

r o ck s

k i d s

s o ck s

b a g s

Sentences I Can Read

1. Mom will grab sticks and rocks.
2. Kids can drop socks in bags.

72

Student Edition, p. 72

Phonics

Guide Practice

BLEND WORDS Have children turn to page 72 in their Student Edition. Look at the picture on this page. I see a picture of *cars.* The word *cars* is a plural word because it means *more than one.* There is more than one car in the picture. When I say the plural word *car,* I hear the /z/ sound at the end. The /z/ sound is spelled *s.*

GROUP PRACTICE For each word in "Words I Can Blend," ask for the sound of each letter or group of letters. Make sure that children identify the /s/ or /z/ sound at the end of each word. Then have children blend the whole word.

Corrective feedback	**If...** children have difficulty blending a word, **then...** model blending the word, and ask children to blend it with you.

DECODE WORDS IN ISOLATION After children can successfully segment and blend the words, ask them to read the words naturally.

DECODE WORDS IN CONTEXT Have children read each of the sentences. Have them identify words in the sentences that have the plural -*s* sound /z/.

Team Talk Pair children and have them take turns reading each of the sentences aloud.

ON THEIR OWN Use *Reader's and Writer's Notebook,* p. 157.

MONITOR PROGRESS Plural -*s*; Consonant *s*/z/

FORMATIVE ASSESSMENT Write the following words and have the class read them. Notice which children miss words during the group reading. Call on those individuals to read some of the words.

wigs	cabs	hogs	jams	bibs	**Spiral Review** Row 3 contrasts singular and plural words.
fans	lips	bats	lids	tots	
ribs	dock	bins	van	racks ←	

If... children cannot blend -*s* plurals,

then... use the Small Group Time Strategic Intervention lesson, p. SG•42, to reteach -*s* plurals. Continue to monitor children's progress using other instructional opportunities during the week. See the Skills Trace on p. 72c.

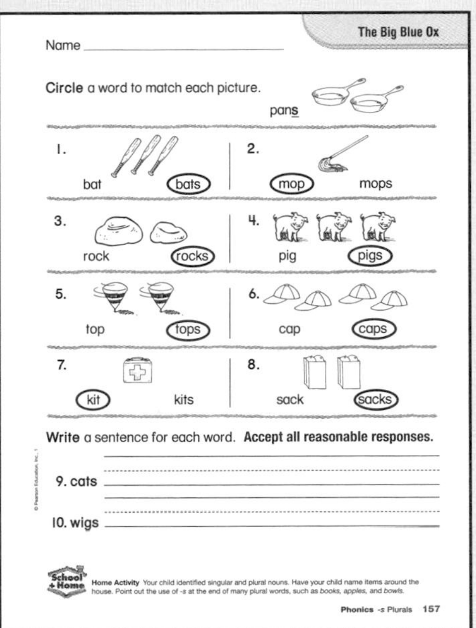
Name ____

The Big Blue Ox

Circle a word to match each picture.

pans

1. bat **(bats)**
2. **(mop)** mops
3. rock **(rocks)**
4. pig **(pigs)**
5. top **(tops)**
6. cap **(caps)**
7. **(kit)** kits
8. sack **(sacks)**

Write a sentence for each word. **Accept all reasonable responses.**

9. cats ____

10. wigs ____

Home Activity Your child identified singular and plural nouns. Have your child name items around the house. Point out the use of -*s* at the end of many plural words, such as *books, apples,* and *bowls.*

Phonics -*s* Plurals 157

Reader's and Writer's Notebook, p. 157

Access for All

A Advanced

Practice with Additional Plurals
Have children write the following words on cards: *students, umbrellas, pencils, letters, hammers, animals, tadpoles, otters.* Then have children turn the cards face down. Ask partners to take turns selecting a card and using that card in a sentence.

Practice Plural Words In Chinese, Hmong, and Vietnamese, nouns do not have a plural form. Instead, adjectives show whether a noun is singular or plural. Children who speak these languages may need additional practice with English plural word endings. Try grouping and labeling objects for visual support.

Common Core State Standards

Foundational Skills 3. Know and apply grade-level phonics and word analysis skills in decoding words. **Foundational Skills 3.b.** Decode regularly spelled one-syllable words. **Foundational Skills 3.g.** Recognize and read grade-appropriate irregularly spelled words. **Foundational Skills 4.** Read with sufficient accuracy and fluency to support comprehension.

Decodable Reader 3B

If children need help, then...

Read *Pigs, Wigs, Cats, and Bats*

DECODE WORDS IN ISOLATION Have children turn to page 153. Have children decode each word.

REVIEW HIGH-FREQUENCY WORDS Review the previously taught words *one, two, have, three, the,* and *we.* Have children read each word as you point to it on the Word Wall.

PREVIEW Have children read the title and preview the story. Tell them they will read words with the plural *-s* and the consonant *s/z/*.

DECODE WORDS IN CONTEXT Pair children for reading and listen as they decode. One child begins. Children read the entire story, switching readers after each page.

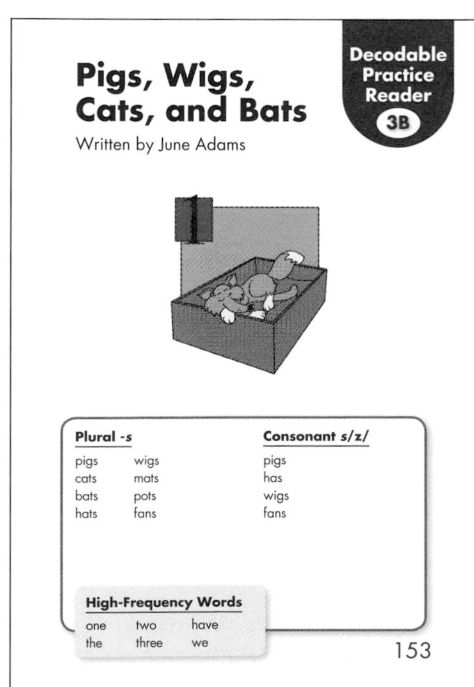
Pigs, Wigs, Cats, and Bats

Written by June Adams

Decodable Practice Reader 3B

Plural -s		Consonant s/z/
pigs	wigs	pigs
cats	mats	has
bats	pots	wigs
hats	fans	fans

High-Frequency Words

one two have

the three we

153

Decodable Practice Reader 3B

One fox can nap.
Fox is in the box.

154

Two pigs sit.
Fat pigs pin on wigs.

155

Three cats tap.
Tan cats tap on mats.

156

The bats hit.
The bats hit pots.

157

Cats can tap.
Bats can hit.

158

Pigs have hats.
Fox has fans.

159

Tap! Tap! Tap!
We can nap.

160

Corrective feedback	**If...** children have difficulty decoding a word, **then...** refer them to the Sound-Spelling Cards to identify the sounds in the word. Then prompt them to blend the word. • What is the new word? • Is the new word a word you know? • Does it make sense in the story?

CHECK DECODING AND COMPREHENSION Have children retell the story to include characters, setting, and events. Then have children find words with the plural -*s* in the story. Explain that some story words with the plural -*s* ending will have the consonant sound *s*/z/. Children should supply *pigs, wigs, cats, mats, bats, pots, hats,* and *fans.*

Reread for Fluency

REREAD DECODABLE READER Have children reread Decodable Practice Reader 3B to develop automaticity decoding the plural -*s* and the consonant *s*/z/.

Routine Paired Reading

1. **Reread** To achieve optimal fluency, have partners reread the text three or four times.
2. **Corrective Feedback** Listen as children read. Provide corrective feedback regarding their fluency and decoding.

Routines Flip Chart

Access for All

SI Strategic Intervention

Setting If children have difficulty identifying the setting, ask them to look at the illustrations and ask if the animals are inside or outside.

Plural -*s*; Consonant *s*/z/

Beginning Show children several plural nouns from the story. Break each word into its base word and its -*s* ending. Have children first say each part of the word and then blend the parts to say the whole word.

Intermediate Have children point to one animal and say its singular name. Then ask them to say the same name in its plural form.

Advanced Have children read the sentences with -*s* plurals. Then have them write sentences using the singular forms of the words.

Common Core State Standards

Foundational Skills 2.d. Segment spoken single-syllable words into their complete sequence of individual sounds (phonemes). **Foundational Skills 3.** Know and apply grade-level phonics and word analysis skills in decoding words. **Language 2.e.** Spell untaught words phonetically, drawing on phonemic awareness and spelling conventions.

Phonics

Review Short Vowels *a, i*

Short *o: o*

REVIEW SOUND-SPELLINGS Review the short-vowel spelling patterns *a, i,* and *o* using Sound-Spelling Cards 1, 11, and 17.

DECODE WORDS IN ISOLATION Display these words. Have the class blend the words. Then point to the words in random order and ask children to read them quickly.

fix	**job**	**fin**	**ran**
mop	**nap**	**ham**	**lot**
bat	**lock**	**sip**	**kit**

Corrective feedback	Model blending decodable words and then ask children to blend them with you.

DECODE WORDS IN CONTEXT Display these sentences. Have the class read the sentences.

Team Talk Have pairs take turns reading the sentences naturally.

Sam can sit on the **rock.**
Mom has a **big van.**
Liz got six tops.

Spelling

Short *o* Words

GUIDE PRACTICE Tell children that you will segment the sounds in each spelling word. They should repeat the sounds in each word as they write the word. Check the spelling of each word before saying the next word.

1. /h/ /o/ /t/ **hot**
2. /h/ /o/ /p/ **hop**
3. /p/ /o/ /t/ **pot**
4. /p/ /o/ /p/ **pop**
5. /o/ /ks/ **ox**
6. /l/ /o/ /k/ **lock**
7. /m/ /o/ /p/ **mop**
8. /g/ /o/ /t/ **got**
9. /r/ /o/ /k/ **rock**
10. /m/ /o/ /m/ **mom**

ON THEIR OWN Use *Reader's and Writer's Notebook,* p. 158.

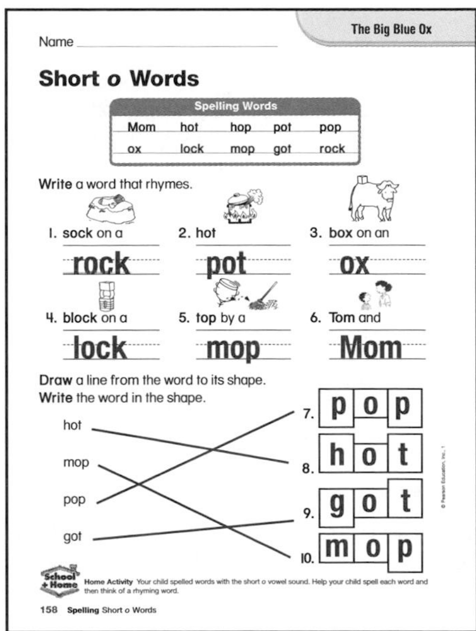
Name

The Big Blue Ox

Short *o* Words

Spelling Words				
Mom	hot	hop	pot	pop
ox	lock	mop	got	rock

Write a word that rhymes.

1. sock on a rock
2. hot pot
3. box on an ox
4. block on a lock
5. top by a mop
6. Tom and Mom

Draw a line from the word to its shape. Write the word in the shape.

hot, mop, pop, got

7. pop
8. hot
9. got
10. mop

Home Activity Your child spelled words with the short o vowel sound. Help your child spell each word and then think of a rhyming word.

158 Spelling Short o Words

Reader's and Writer's Notebook, p. 158

Physical Response Use physical gestures such as patting your head to show *top* or hopping on one foot to show *hop.* Repeat the words and gestures as needed to help children learn the words.

Common Core State Standards

Foundational Skills 3. Know and apply grade-level phonics and word analysis skills in decoding words. **Foundational Skills 3.b.** Decode regularly spelled one-syllable words. **Foundational Skills 3.g.** Recognize and read grade-appropriate irregularly spelled words. **Language 5.d.** Distinguish shades of meaning among verbs differing in manner (e.g., *look, peek, glance, stare, glare, scowl*) and adjectives differing in intensity (e.g., *large, gigantic*) by defining or choosing them or by acting out the meanings.

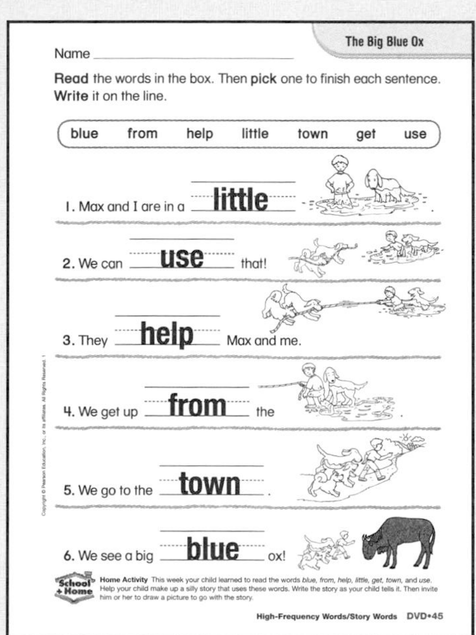
Name ______ The Big Blue Ox

Read the words in the box. Then **pick** one to finish each sentence. **Write** it on the line.

blue from help little town get use

1. Max and I are in a little.
2. We can use that!
3. They help Max and me.
4. We get up from the .
5. We go to the town.
6. We see a big blue ox!

Home Activity This week your child learned to read the words *blue, from, help, little, get, town,* and *use.* Help your child make up a silly story that uses these words. Write the story as your child tells it. Then invite him or her to draw a picture to go with the story.

High-Frequency Words/Story Words DVD•45

Let's Practice It! TR DVD•45

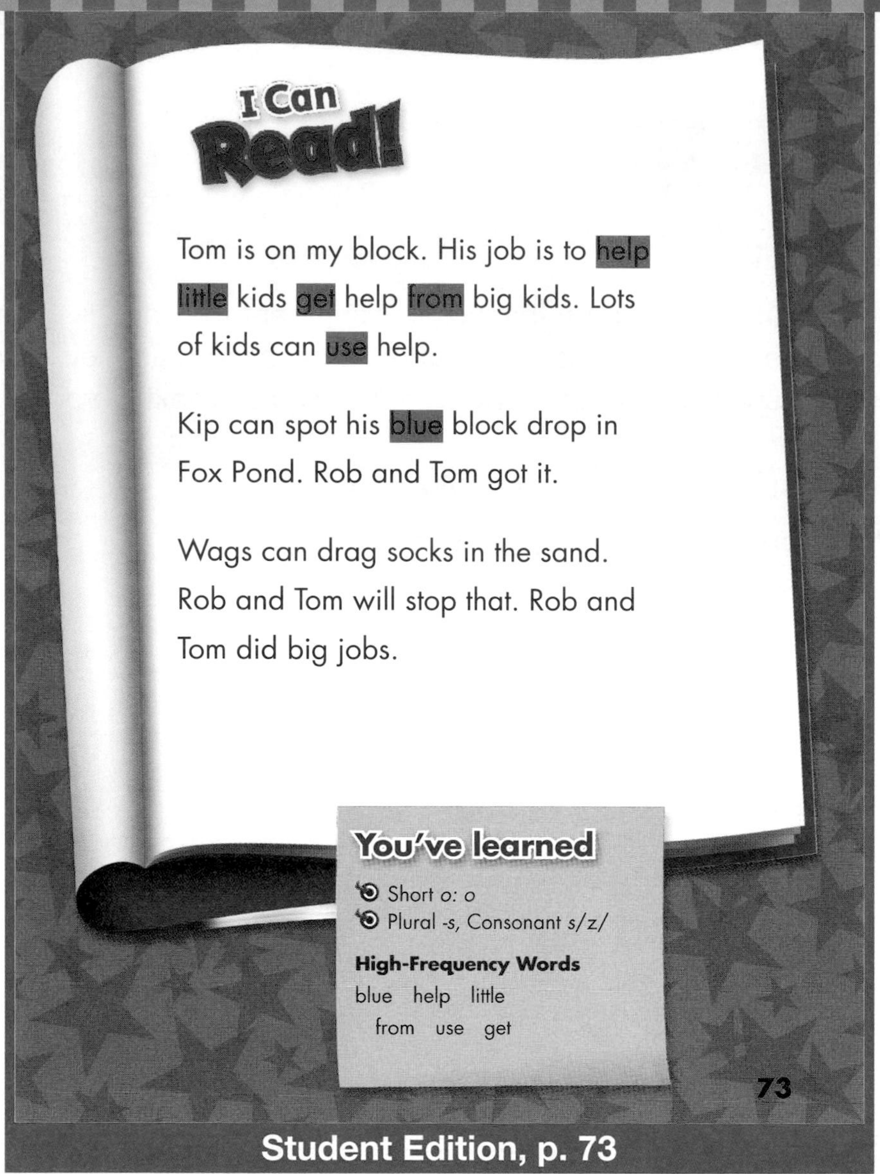

Student Edition, p. 73

High-Frequency Words

READ WORDS IN ISOLATION Remind children that there are some words we learn by remembering the letters rather than by saying the sounds. Then have them read each of the highlighted high-frequency words aloud.

READ WORDS IN CONTEXT Chorally read the "I Can Read!" passage along with children. Then have them read the passage aloud to themselves. When they are finished, ask children to reread the high-frequency words.

Team Talk Have children choose two high-frequency words and give them time to create a sentence in which both words are used properly. Then have them share their sentence with a partner.

ON THEIR OWN Use Let's Practice It! p. 45 on the *Teacher Resources DVD-ROM.*

Selection Vocabulary

INTRODUCE SELECTION WORDS Use Vocabulary Transparency 3 to introduce this week's selection word. Read each sentence as you track the print. Frame the underlined word and explain its meaning. Have children read each sentence with you.

town a large group of houses and buildings, smaller than a city

Selection Words

Ox Is Here

1. Ox naps in the mud.
2. He is back from town.

Ox

Unit 1 The Big Blue Ox Vocabulary 3

Vocabulary Transparency 3 TR DVD

Vocabulary: Synonyms

TEACH Explain that **synonyms** are words that have nearly the same meanings. Draw a web or display Graphic Organizer 18. Write *big* in the center and *huge* in one of the surrounding circles. Tell children they will add other synonyms for *big* to the web.

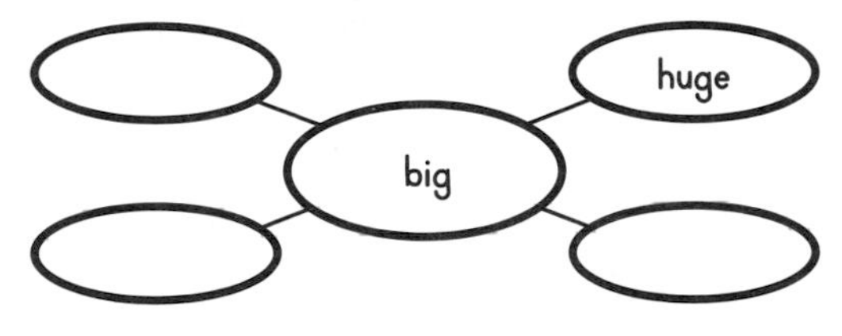

Graphic Organizer 18

Think Aloud I see the word *big* in the center of the web. I see the word *huge* in one of the smaller circles. *Huge* is a synonym for *big* because they both have nearly the same meaning. What is another synonym for *big?* One word I know is a word we will read in a story tomorrow about an *enormous* ox. *Enormous* means "very, very big." I'll write *enormous* in another circle.

GUIDE PRACTICE Have children name other synonyms for *big,* such as *large* and *massive.* Write the new words in the web, adding more circles if necessary.

ON THEIR OWN Have pairs of children use the word *big* in their own sentence. Then have them take turns replacing *big* in the sentence with each of the synonyms in the web.

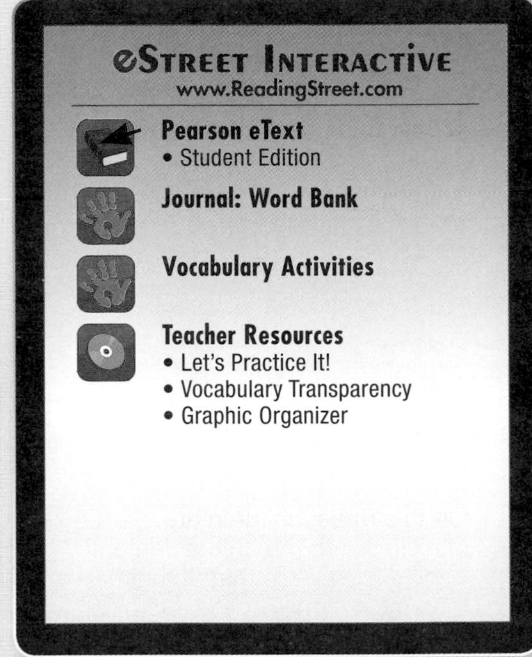

Bridge to Common Core

VOCABULARY ACQUISITION AND USE
When children interact with this week's selection vocabulary, they are learning to recognize the concepts related to the vocabulary word *town.* Teaching about synonyms or words that have the same or nearly the same meaning as another word helps children make real-life connections between words and their use.

Academic Vocabulary

synonyms words that have the same or nearly the same meaning as another word

Access for All

SI Strategic Intervention

Synonyms Provide extra support for synonyms by repeating the lesson with the word *small.*

A Advanced

Synonyms Have partners work together and discuss additional synonyms for other size words *(small, short, tall).*

Zoom in on ©

Text-Based Comprehension

Introduce Main Selection

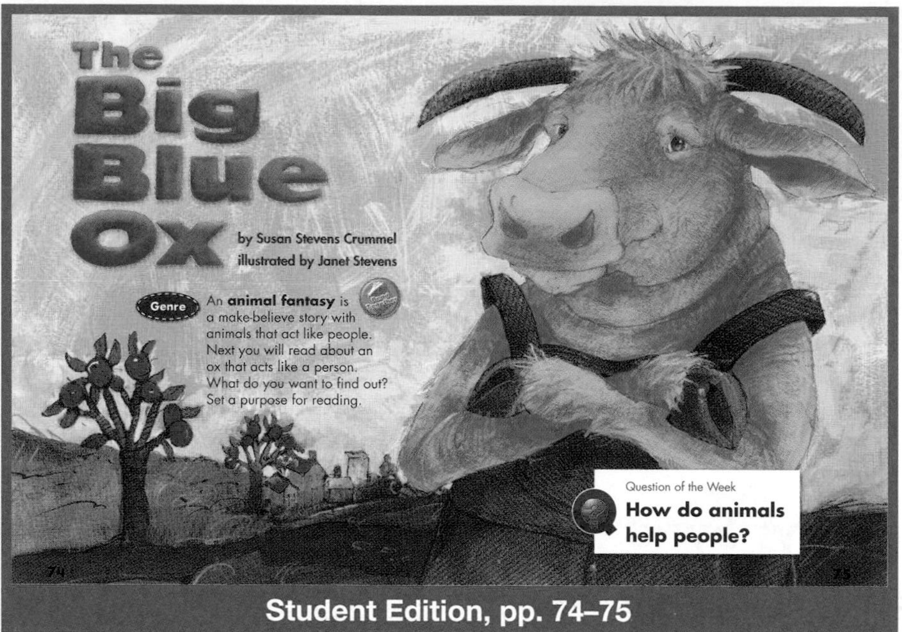

Student Edition, pp. 74–75

GENRE An **animal fantasy** is a made-up story with animals that do things real animals can't do. As they read *The Big Blue Ox,* ask children to look for things the ox does that real oxen cannot do.

PREVIEW AND PREDICT Have children identify the title of the selection, the author, and the illustrator. Read aloud the names of the author and illustrator and have children describe the role of each. Have children predict what might happen in the story.

PURPOSE Setting a purpose helps us to think and understand more as we read. Guide children to set a purpose for reading the selection.

VISUALIZE Explain that good readers make pictures in their minds to help them imagine the things they read about. Picturing a story's characters, setting, and events makes it easier to understand the story. Have children turn to page EI•17 in their Student Edition.

Look at this picture. What is the girl picturing in her mind as her mother reads to her? (dolphins jumping) When I read *Pig in a Wig,* I pictured in my mind how Pig looked wearing a wig doing a jig. I also visualized the rooms that Pig, Max, and Pam were in. As I read *The Big Blue Ox,* I will try to imagine what a big blue ox would look like and how it would act.

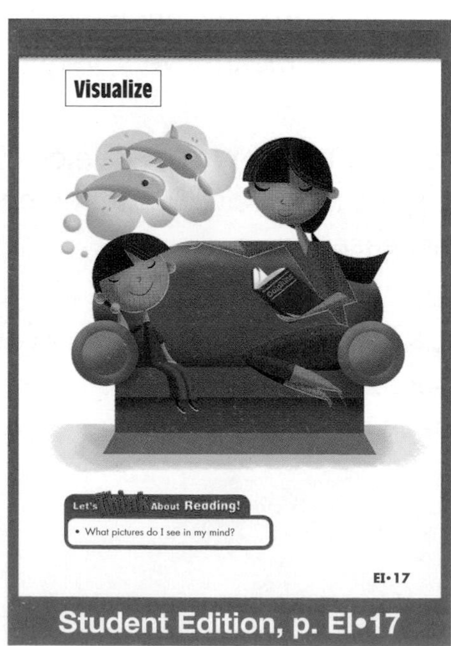

Student Edition, p. EI•17

© Common Core State Standards

Literature 3. Describe characters, settings, and major events in a story, using key details. **Literature 7.** Use illustrations and details in a story to describe its characters, setting, or events.

© Bridge to Common Core

CRAFT AND STRUCTURE

On this page, children are introduced to the animal fantasy genre. They learn that an animal fantasy is a make-believe story with animals that act like people. Using the illustrations, children preview and predict what the selection will be about and set a purpose for reading, which helps them analyze the structure of the text and the way the illustrations and text relate to each other. As they read, children can use these structures to help them understand the content and style of the selection.

Academic Vocabulary ©

animal fantasy a make-believe story with animals that act like people

visualize picture in your mind what is happening in the text

Strategy Response Log

Background Knowledge Before reading, have children use p. RR15 of their *Reader's and Writer's Notebook* to draw a picture of something an ox does on a farm. Have them write a sentence explaining how the ox is helping.

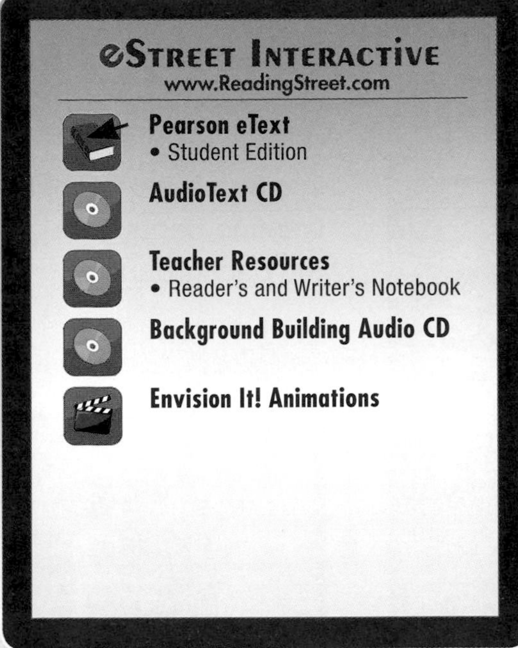

Access Main Selection

READER AND TASK SUGGESTIONS	
Preparing to Read the Text	**Leveled Tasks**
• Review short *o*. • Discuss the features of an animal fantasy. • Remind children that as they encounter unfamiliar words, they may need to slow their reading rate.	• **Structure** If children have a basic understanding of text structure, have them find the sentence that is repeated throughout the selection and tell why this sentence is repeated. • **Theme and Knowledge Demands** If children do not understand fanciful animal behavior, have them tell whether they have seen a real animal doing one of the things Ox does.

See Text Complexity Measures for *The Big Blue Ox* on the tab at the beginning of this week.

READ Tell children that today they will read *The Big Blue Ox* for the first time. Use the Read for Understanding routine.

Routine Read for Understanding

Deepen understanding by reading the selection multiple times.

1. **First Read**—If children need support, then use the **Access Text** notes to help them clarify understanding.
2. **Second Read**—Use the **Close Reading** notes to help children draw knowledge from the text.

Preview Main Selection Ask children what they already know about what kind of work oxen do on a farm. Then do a picture walk of the selection so children can talk about and see how Ox helps out on a farm.

1ST READ

Access Text © If children need help, then...

CONNECT TO CONCEPT Look at the pictures on pages 74 and 75. Look at the ox. Describe what it looks like. Encourage children to respond in complete sentences. Yes, this ox is blue and wearing pants. Ask children to describe the farm in the background.

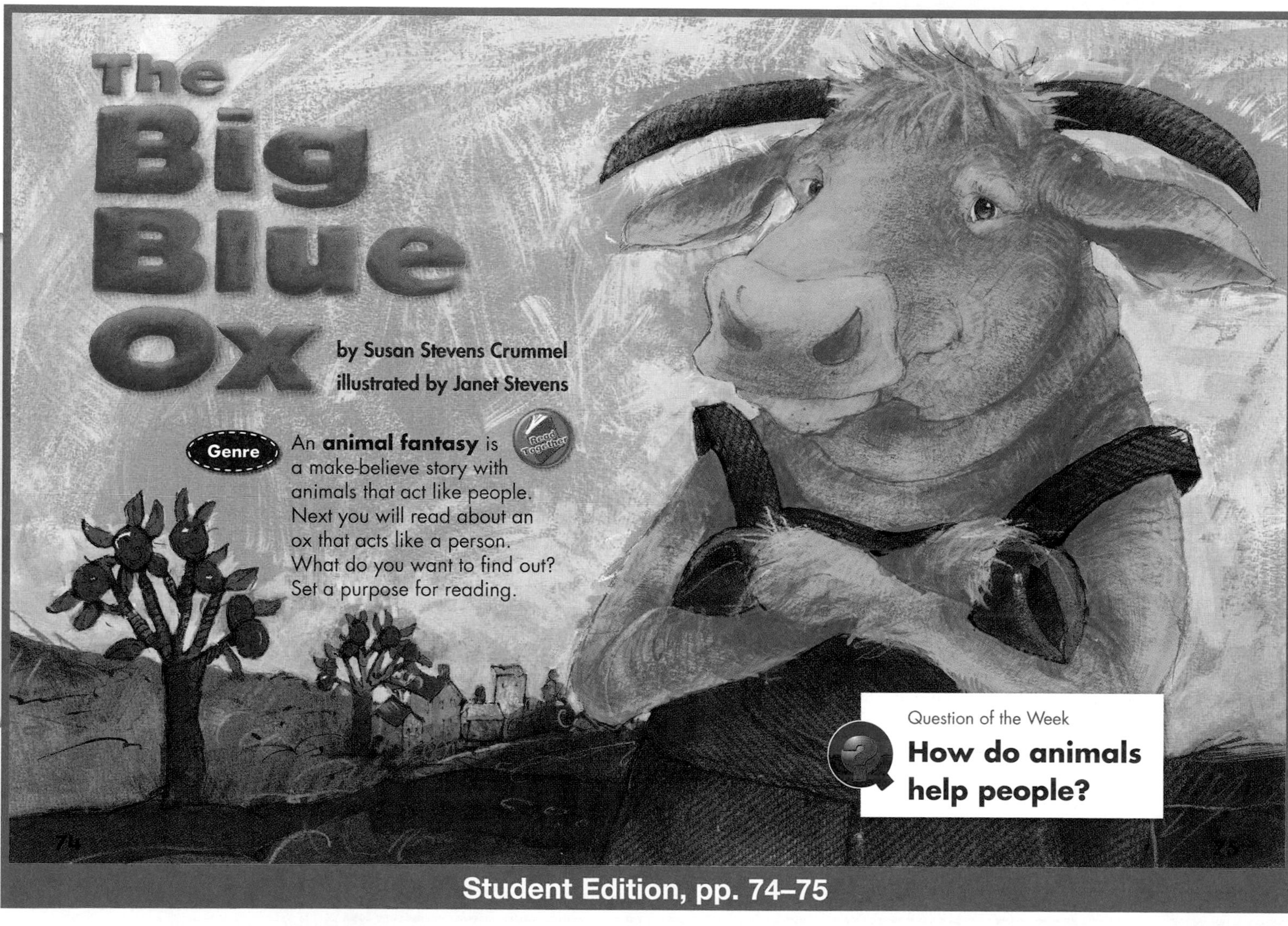

The Big Blue Ox
by Susan Stevens Crummel
illustrated by Janet Stevens
Genre
An **animal fantasy** is a make-believe story with animals that act like people. Next you will read about an ox that acts like a person. What do you want to find out? Set a purpose for reading.
Read Together
Question of the Week
How do animals help people?
74
75

Student Edition, pp. 74–75

2ND READ

Close Reading ©

EVALUATION • TEXT EVIDENCE Look at the ox in the picture on pages 74 and 75. Explain how the ox in the picture looks different from a real ox. Explain how it looks the same as a real ox. (The ox is big like a real ox, but it is blue and is wearing pants unlike a real ox.)

CHARACTER AND SETTING Who are the characters in this story? What is the setting of the story? (The characters are Ox, Mom, and Pop. The setting looks like a farm in the country. I can see the farmhouse behind the apple tree.)

VISUALIZE Remind children that good readers visualize as they read a story. They picture the story's characters, setting, and events. Have children visualize how Ox might look as he digs on the farm. Reread the part that tells about how Ox digs.

Common Core State Standards

Literature 1. Ask and answer questions about key details in a text. **Literature 3.** Describe characters, settings, and major events in a story, using key details. **Also Literature 7., Foundational Skills 4.a.**

Mom and Pop have a big blue ox.

76

Ox can help. He is big.
He can pick, and he can dig.

77

Student Edition, pp. 76–77

ANALYSIS • TEXT EVIDENCE The story says that Ox can pick. What does Ox probably pick? How do you know? (Ox picks apples from the trees. I know this because there is an apple tree behind Ox, and there are apples on Ox's horns.)

SYNTHESIS Ox is digging in the picture. What do you think he is digging? (a hole to plant an apple tree) How do you know? (You need to dig holes to put plants or seeds in the soil, and I see an apple tree in the picture.)

1ST READ

Access Text If children need help, then...

USE SYNONYMS Have children reread page 78. Words that have nearly the same meaning are called synonyms. Do the words *a little* mean a big amount or a small amount? (The words mean a small amount.)

CHARACTER AND SETTING Why does Ox want to mop the pigs? (Ox wants to mop the pigs because he thinks they are dirty. He wants to help Mom and Pop clean them.) What is the setting here? (The setting is a mud pile on the farm.)

Pigs in wigs sit in mud.
Ox can help a little!
78
Get the mop from Mom and Pop.
Mop the pigs. Fix the wigs.
79

Student Edition, pp. 78–79

2ND READ

Close Reading

SYNTHESIS • TEXT EVIDENCE Look at the pigs on pages 78 and 79. Are the pigs in the story real or make-believe? (make-believe) How do you know this? (They wear wigs. Real pigs would not wear wigs.)

CHECK SELECTION WORDS Have children locate the selection word *town.* What does "off to town" mean? (go to town)

VISUALIZE What do you picture in your mind when you read that Mom and Pop hopped on top of Ox to go to town? (Ox is very big, so I picture Mom and Pop sitting up high and holding on tight.) Let's reread the part that tells about this again.

Common Core State Standards

Literature 3. Describe characters, settings, and major events in a story, using key details. **Literature 7.** Use illustrations and details in a story to describe its characters, setting, or events. **Foundational Skills 4.a.** Read on-level text with purpose and understanding. **Also Language 4.**

Off to town go Mom and Pop.
Ox can help! Hop on top.

80

Get the cans. Pack the sack.
Ox can help! Take it back.

81

Student Edition, pp. 80–81

CONNECT TO SOCIAL STUDIES Explain that in the past, people on farms used oxen for transportation. Today machines usually do this work.

Team Talk Have partners name different ways that animals could be used for transportation.

EVALUATION Ox goes into town with Mom and Pop. Does he do a good job of helping Mom and Pop in town? (yes) How do you know? (He packs cans and helps to bring them back home. These are things that Mom and Pop would have had to do.)

1ST READ

Access Text © If children need help, then...

REVIEW HIGH-FREQUENCY WORDS Have children reread the first sentence on page 82. How does Ox help? (He uses big pans.) Read the sentence that tells you this. What clues in the picture tell you about how Ox helps? (It shows him cooking apples.)

CROSS-TEXT EVALUATION
Use a Strategy to Self-Check How did "The Oxen Song" from the *Sing with Me* Big Book help you visualize the ox in this story?

Continue to DAY 2
Text-Based Comprehension
p. 83a

Ox can help! Use big pans.
He is hot. Use big fans!

82

Mom and Pop nap on Ox.
Ox is a big, big help.

83

Student Edition, pp. 82–83

2ND READ

Close Reading ©

SYNTHESIS • TEXT EVIDENCE Using what you learned in this selection, tell how animals can help people. Have children cite examples from the text.

Continue to DAY 3
Think Critically
pp. 84–85

Text-Based Comprehension

Check Understanding

Have children discuss each question with a partner. Ask several pairs to share their responses.

- ☑ **Animal fantasy** What are some things Ox does that a real ox would not do? (Ox picks fruit, digs holes, mops the dirty pigs, packs the sack at the store, and cooks.)
- ☑ **Setting** What are some of the different settings in the story? (The story takes place on a farm, in a mud pile, in a store in town, and in a kitchen.)
- ☑ **Plot** Why is Ox tired at the end of the story? (Ox is tired because he worked hard all day. He cleaned, carried Mom and Pop, and did the cooking.)
- ☑ **Confirm predictions** How did you use pictures or story clues to predict what would happen next in the story? (I used the words "Ox can help" to predict that Ox will do a lot for Mom and Pop.)
- ☑ **Compare and contrast** Which is more helpful, a real ox or the ox in this story? The ox in this story is more helpful because he does some things that a real ox does, and he also does other things such as cook and clean.

Day 2 SMALL GROUP TIME • Differentiate Comprehension, p. SG•35

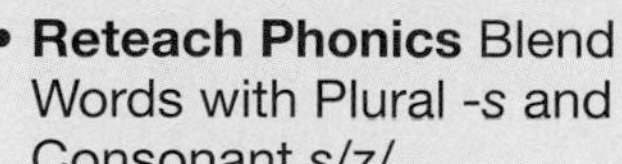

OL On-Level	SI Strategic Intervention	A Advanced
• **Practice Phonics** Additional Words with Plural *-s* and Consonant *s/z/* • **Read** *The Big Blue Ox*	• **Reteach Phonics** Blend Words with Plural *-s* and Consonant *s/z/* • **Read** *The Big Blue Ox*	• **Extend Phonics** More Words with Plural *-s* and Consonant *s/z/* • **Read** *The Big Blue Ox* • **Investigate** Inquiry Project

Common Core State Standards

Literature 1. Ask and answer questions about key details in a text. **Literature 7.** Use illustrations and details in a story to describe its characters, setting, or events. **Foundational Skills 4.a.** Read on-level text with purpose and understanding.

Access for All

SI Strategic Intervention

Discussing Setting If children have trouble identifying settings in the story, have them look through the story again and describe what they see. Keep a running list of their observations on the board and then review them afterward to identify settings.

ELL

Use Pictures Have children point to the pictures in the story as they name each thing Ox does. Assist them by providing words as needed. Ask children if a real ox would do these things. For example: Would a real ox pick fruit? (no) Extend language opportunities for children by asking follow-up questions, such as: Why? How do you know?

If... children need more scaffolding and practice with the **Comprehension Skill,**
then... use the ELL activities on p. DI•59 in the Teacher Resources section on SuccessNet.

Common Core State Standards

Literature 5. Explain major differences between books that tell stories and books that give information, drawing on a wide reading of a range of text types. **Language 1.** Demonstrate command of the conventions of standard English grammar and usage when writing or speaking. **Also Language 1.j.**

Genre

Animal Fantasy

IDENTIFY FEATURES OF ANIMAL FANTASY Use the stories *The Big Blue Ox* and *Pig in a Wig* to have children compare and contrast the features of animal fantasy.

- *The Big Blue Ox* tells about an unusual animal. Why is Ox unusual? (Ox can do things such as pick fruit and get cans at the store.)
- *Pig in a Wig* also tells about an unusual animal. Why is Pig unusual? (Pig wears a wig and can mix food in a bowl. She can also do a jig.)
- Why are both these stories animal fantasies? (Both tell made-up stories about animals that do things real animals cannot do.)

GUIDE PRACTICE Explain that the class will now compare and contrast these two stories. Use Graphic Organizer 28. Write *The Big Blue Ox* above one circle and *Pig in a Wig* above the other. Let's begin by thinking of things that are true about both stories. What do we know about Ox and Pig? (They do things that real animals can't do.) Since that is true about both stories, I will write that in the middle section where the circles overlap. Continue comparing and contrasting the stories and filling in the Venn diagram. Have children study the finished diagram. Discuss how it shows the ways the stories are the same and different.

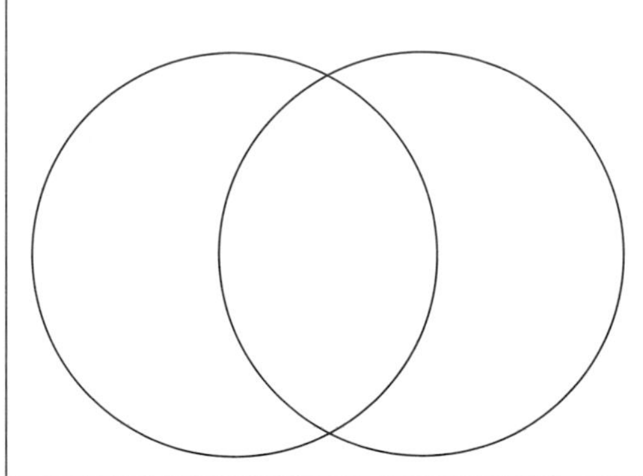

Graphic Organizer 28

ON THEIR OWN Organize children into small groups and have each group think of other animal fantasies they have read. Have them compare and contrast the features of those stories and share their information with the class.

Conventions

Predicates of Sentences

TEACH Write *The dog got the pack* on the board. Point to each word as you read it. Ask children to identify the action part of the sentence. *(got the pack)* The predicate of a sentence tells what happens. What can the predicate of a sentence tell? (what a person, animal, or thing does)

GUIDE PRACTICE Write the following sentences on the board and read them aloud. Have children read the sentences and identify the predicate in each sentence.

1. The fox sat in the box. (sat in the box)
2. Dan got the hot pot. (got the hot pot)
3. I pat the cat. (pat the cat)

APPLY Have the class complete these sentence frames orally using predicates.

1. A dog _______.
2. Horses _______.
3. Many animals _______.
4. My favorite animal _______.

ON THEIR OWN Use *Reader's and Writer's Notebook,* p. 159.

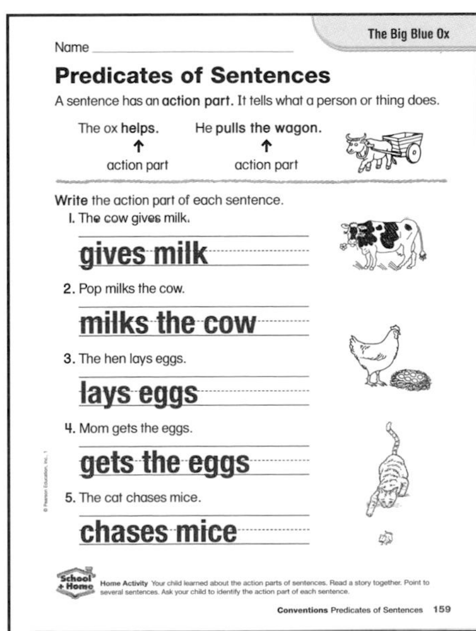

Name

The Big Blue Ox

Predicates of Sentences

A sentence has an **action part.** It tells what a person or thing does.

The ox **helps.** ↑ action part — He **pulls the wagon.** ↑ action part

Write the action part of each sentence.

1. The cow gives milk. — gives milk
2. Pop milks the cow. — milks the cow
3. The hen lays eggs. — lays eggs
4. Mom gets the eggs. — gets the eggs
5. The cat chases mice. — chases mice

School + Home **Home Activity** Your child learned about the action parts of sentences. Read a story together. Point to several sentences. Ask your child to identify the action part of each sentence.

Conventions Predicates of Sentences 159

Reader's and Writer's Notebook, p. 159

Daily Fix-It

3. mom and Pop can moop.
Mom and Pop can mop.

4. pop sat on the rok.
Pop sat on the rock.

Discuss the Daily Fix-It corrections with children. Review sentence capitalization, /o/ spelled *o,* and /k/ spelled *ck.*

Access for All

SI Strategic Intervention

Sentence Production If children's sentences lack subject-verb agreement, say the sentences with subject-verb agreement and have children repeat after you.

Support Conventions Help children recall that the action part of a sentence tells what a person or thing does. Use examples, such as *I sharpen my pencil* or *We line up for lunch,* to model the action parts of the sentences.

Act Out Predicates Remind children that a predicate tells something that happens. Say the following sentences and perform the action: I clap, I walk away, I sit down. Have children repeat the words and perform the actions themselves. Then ask them to identify the predicates.

Common Core State Standards

Writing 5. With guidance and support from adults, focus on a topic, respond to questions and suggestions from peers, and add details to strengthen writing as needed. **Language 1.j.** Produce and expand complete simple and compound declarative, interrogative, imperative, and exclamatory sentences in response to prompts.

Short Poem

Writer's Craft: Sensory Details

INTRODUCE THE PROMPT Review with children the key features of a short poem. Explain that today children will plan their own two-line poem about an animal. The poem can rhyme, if they wish, but it does not have to rhyme. Read aloud the writing prompt.

Writing Prompt

Think about a kind of animal you know. Write a two-line poem about that animal.

GENERATE POEM IDEAS

To plan a new poem, think of animals you know. Let's make a chart of animals and words that tell what they do. Display a T-chart or use Graphic Organizer 4. I'll start with the word *dog.*

Guide children in identifying animals and words that describe them. Possible ideas are shown. Record the responses, and keep the chart so that children can refer to it as they plan and draft their poems.

Animals	Words That Tell What They Do
dog	jump up; bark; fetch
cat	purr; stretch; hide
horse	run; gallop
cow	eat grass; give milk

Graphic Organizer 4

Have each child choose an animal for a poem. Circulate to guide them.

Mini-Lesson Sensory Details

- **Introduce** Use *Reader's and Writer's Notebook,* p. 160 to model planning a poem. To plan a poem, I can use a web. I want to write about a puppy named Freddie. I'll write *Freddie the puppy* in the center of my web. In the poem, I want to describe the puppy. For a description, I need words that tell how the puppy looks, sounds, feels, or smells. As I think of words, I will add them to the web.

The Big Blue Ox

Name

Web

Home Activity Your child is learning about writing a short poem. Talk with him or her about words that rhyme.

160 Writing Plan a Poem

Reader's and Writer's Notebook, p. 160

- **Model** What words tell how the puppy looks, sounds, feels, or smells? A puppy is cute. I'll add the word *cute* to the web. A puppy wags its tail. I'll add the words *wags its tail* to the web. Now use your web to plan for your poem. Write the topic of your poem in the center of the web. Then think of words that tell how your animal looks, sounds, feels, and smells, and write those words on your web. Circulate to guide and assist children.

Routine Quick Write for Fluency

Team Talk

1. **Talk** Have children take one minute to describe their animal to a partner.
2. **Write** Each child briefly writes details that describe how their animal looks, sounds, feels, and smells.
3. **Share** Each child reads the poem ideas to the partner.

Routines Flip Chart

Access for All

Strategic Intervention

Planning Sensory Details If children find it difficult to think of words that tell about sensory details, suggest words for them to choose from for each sense, such as *soft, prickly, fluffy,* and *wet* for the sense of touch.

Support Prewriting

Beginning Children can draw an animal, label it with descriptive words, and share with a partner, possibly one who speaks the same home language.

Intermediate Have children draw an animal and label it with phrases. Have them tell other children their feelings about the animal.

Advanced Have children draw pictures or write short sentences in their webs. As they share the plan with partners, children can clarify and add ideas.

Common Core State Standards

Informational Text 5. Know and use various text features (e.g., headings, tables of contents, glossaries, electronic menus, icons) to locate key facts or information in a text. **Writing 7.** Participate in shared research and writing projects (e.g., explore a number of "how-to" books on a given topic and use them to write a sequence of instructions). **Writing 8.** With guidance and support from adults, recall information from experiences or gather information from provided sources to answer a question. **Language 1.a.** Print all upper- and lowercase letters.

Name ____________ The Big Blue Ox

O o

Copy the words. Write the letters from left to right.

Oz	Oz	job	job
pot	pot	hot	hot
box	box	not	not
mom	mom	got	got
cob	cob	sob	sob
doll	doll	rod	rod
log	log	fox	fox

Did you write the letters from left to right? Yes No

School + Home **Home Activity** Your child practiced writing words with *O* and *o* and the short *o* sound. Have your child choose two words from above and write the words three more times.

Handwriting 161

Reader's and Writer's Notebook, p. 161

Handwriting

Letter *Oo*/Left-to-Right Progression

MODEL LETTER FORMATION Display uppercase and lowercase letter *Oo*. Use the stroke instructions pictured below to model proper letter formation.

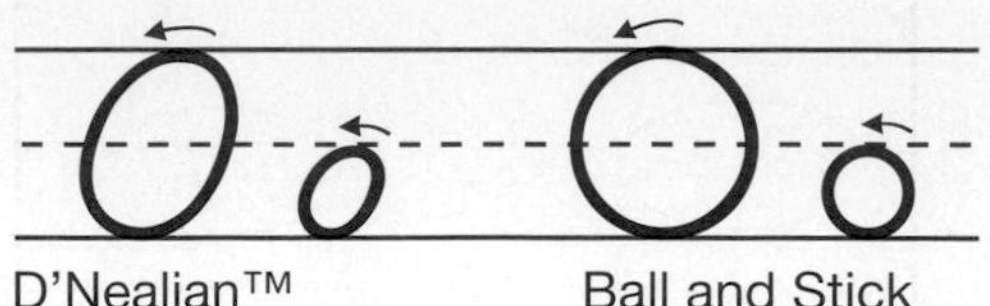

D'Nealian™ Ball and Stick

MODEL LEFT-TO-RIGHT PROGRESSION Explain that when we write a word, all the letters in that word should be written from the left side of the page to the right. This is also true when we write the words in a sentence. Turn to face the front of the room and raise your left hand. This is my left hand. Raise your left hand. Make sure children raise their left hands. Then raise your right hand and ask children to do the same.

Now look at your paper. Point to the left side of your paper. Make sure children are pointing to the correct part of the paper. Write the sentence *I got a pot.* When I write the letters in a word, I move from left to right. As I add more words, I continue to write from left to right. Write the sentence again and show children how the letters and words move from left to right.

GUIDE PRACTICE Write the following sentence.

.toh si top ehT

Team Talk Have children work in pairs to discuss what is wrong with the sentence and how it needs to be fixed. Have them rewrite the sentence correctly and share it with the class.

ON THEIR OWN Use *Reader's and Writer's Notebook,* p. 161.

Research and Inquiry

Step 2 Research Skill: Picture Dictionary

TEACH Tell children that a **picture dictionary** helps readers get information about words by showing pictures with labels. Hold up an open picture dictionary. A picture dictionary is helpful when you are not sure what a word means because it will show you an example of the word. Explain how you can use a picture dictionary to find information about animals that help people.

Think Aloud **MODEL** I know that horses help people get around. People can use horses for transportation. Horses can also pull plows in the field. I would like to know what the different parts of a horse are called. I might learn more about horses by looking in a **picture dictionary.** I might find a picture with labels that tells about the parts of a horse.

GUIDE PRACTICE With children, identify other animals that help people. Then have children look up the animals in a picture dictionary and explain how the pictures helped them locate information.

Academic Vocabulary

picture dictionary a dictionary that uses photos or drawings to show what words mean

Bridge to Common Core

RESEARCH TO BUILD AND PRESENT KNOWLEDGE

Children will analyze how to use picture dictionaries and to find information in texts in order to build knowledge about a subject. They will also:

- learn about picture dictionaries
- learn the meaning of a word
- learn to find information

Wrap Up Your Day!

✔ **Phonics: Plural *-s*** Write the words *dogs, kids, hens,* and *pigs.* Have children blend and read the words. Ask how children can tell the words name more than one.

✔ **High-Frequency Words** Point to these words on the Word Wall: *blue, little, from, use, get, help.* Have children read each word and use it in a sentence.

✔ **Content Knowledge** Monitor children's use of oral vocabulary as they respond. Recall the Read Aloud "A Perfect Visit." Ask: How did the animals in this story serve the farmer? (They cleaned up the farm and made it look pretty.) What did the hen make with the eggs she collected? (a cake)

Tell children that tomorrow they will reread *The Big Blue Ox.*

DAY 3 at a Glance

Content Knowledge
Oral Vocabulary

Phonemic Awareness
Rhyming Words

Phonics/Spelling
Short *o: o*
Plural *-s;* Consonant *s/z/*

High-Frequency Words
blue, from, get, help, little, use

Selection Words
town

Text-Based Comprehension
Review Plot

Fluency
Rate

Conventions
Predicates of Sentences

Writing
Short Poem
Writing Trait: Sentences

Listening and Speaking
Give Introductions

Research and Inquiry
Gather and Record Information

Materials

- Student Edition
- Sing with Me Big Book
- Big Book
- Letter Tiles
- Reader's and Writer's Notebook
- Retelling Cards

Common Core State Standards

Speaking/Listening 2. Ask and answer questions about key details in a text read aloud or information presented orally or through other media. **Language 4.** Determine or clarify the meaning of unknown and multiple-meaning words and phrases based on grade 1 reading and content, choosing flexibly from an array of strategies. **Also Language 5.c., 6.**

Content Knowledge

Animals That Help

EXPAND THE CONCEPT To reinforce concepts and to focus children's attention, have them sing "The Oxen Song" from the *Sing with Me* Big Book. What is another animal that can help like the oxen in the song? (Horses can help because they are big and strong. They can pull a plow or a wagon.)

Build Oral Language

LISTEN FOR AMAZING WORDS Display the Big Book *A Kid's Best Friend.* Read the story and have children listen for the word *snuggle.* Have them also think about how dogs help people through friendship.

- How do dogs show people love? (Dogs wag their tails and lick.)
- Why do you think dogs like to snuggle with kids? (Possible response: A dog likes to be close to its best friend.)

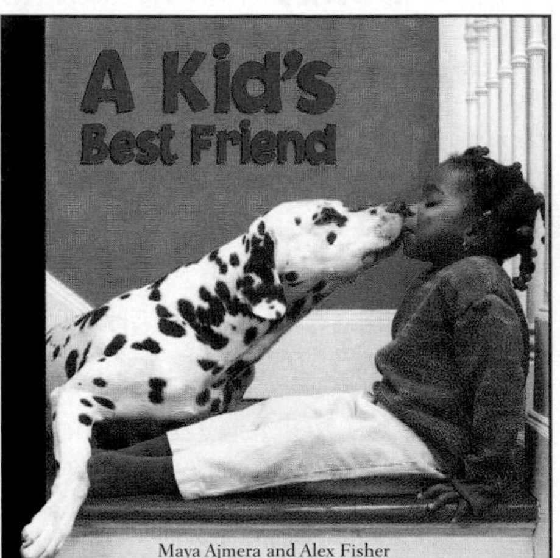

Big Book

TALK ABOUT SENTENCES AND WORDS
Write the following sentence from *A Kid's Best Friend* on sentence strips or on the board.

And when the day is over, shut your eyes with your best friend, be a pillow, and snuggle into deep sleep.

- Ask children to read it with you as you track the print.
- Point to and read *And when the day is over, shut your eyes with your best friend.* What does this mean? (At night, go to sleep with your dog, your best friend.) Why do you think the author uses the words *shut your eyes* instead of *go to sleep?* (It's a more interesting way to say *go to sleep.*)
- Now point to and read *snuggle into deep sleep.* What does *snuggle* mean? (to lay closely and comfortably together) Ask a volunteer to use a stuffed toy and show what it might look like to snuggle. Why do you think the author uses this word? (It's the best way to describe how you would sleep with a dog next to you.)
- Have children write their own sentences using the same sentence structure. Provide this sentence frame:

  And when the day is over, ______ with your best friend.

Build Oral Vocabulary

Amazing Words Robust Vocabulary Routine

1. **Introduce the Word** Relate the word *snuggle* to the book. The picture on pages 26–27 shows how a boy and his dog *snuggle.* Supply a child-friendly definition. When you *snuggle,* you get into a warm, comfortable position. Have children say the word.
2. **Demonstrate** Provide examples to show meaning. I like to *snuggle* under the covers when it's cold outside. Puppies *snuggle* together to stay warm.
3. **Apply** Have children demonstrate their understanding. Name something you like to *snuggle* with.
4. **Display the Word** Run your hand under the chunks *snug-gle* as you read the word.

Routines Flip Chart

After children are introduced to the Amazing Word, have them write the word or a sentence with the word and draw a picture about the word. Ask them to show their page and read and tell about the word and the picture they made.

ADD TO THE CONCEPT MAP Use these questions to discuss different ways that animals help people as you add to the concept map.

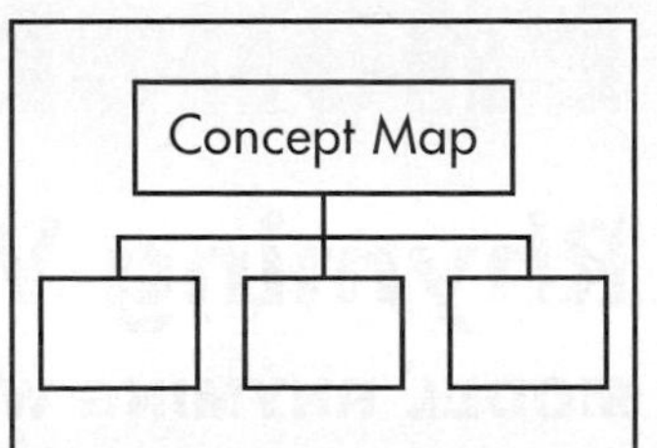

- In *The Big Blue Ox,* Ox does many different things to help Mom and Pop. Let's add *They provide services* to our concept map.
- Some things that Ox does are real and some are not real. What are some things Ox does that a real ox would do? (He carries Mom and Pop to town. He lets Mom and Pop nap on him.) We already have *People can ride oxen* on our map. Let's add *They help people feel good* to the map.

Amazing Words

past	serve
present	snuggle
produce	enormous
transportation	powerful
danger	

Access for All

SI Strategic Intervention

Sentence Production If children pronounce *-le* in *snuggle* as short *u,* pronounce the word carefully and have them repeat it after you. Then have them use the word in a sentence.

Expand Vocabulary Use the Day 3 instruction on ELL Poster 3 to expand children's use of vocabulary to communicate about lesson concepts.

Comparing Words Ask children if *snuggle* is more like *cuddle* or *tickle.* Have them explain why and then provide their own descriptions of the word.

Common Core State Standards
Foundational Skills 2.c. Isolate and pronounce initial, medial vowel, and final sounds (phonemes) in spoken single-syllable words. **Also Foundational Skills 2., 2.b.**

Phonemic Awareness

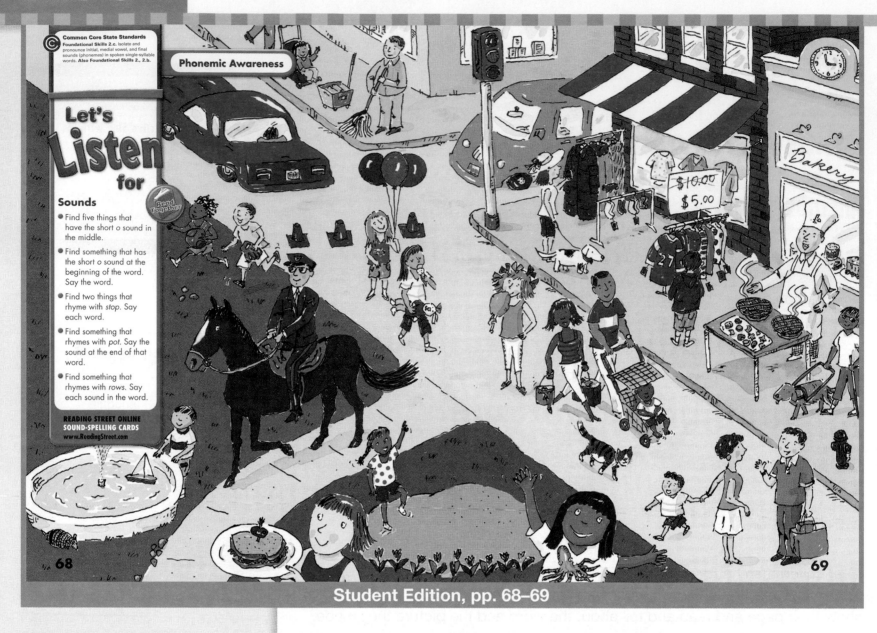

Let's Listen for Sounds

Read Together

- Find five things that have the short *o* sound in the middle.
- Find something that has the short *o* sound at the beginning of the word. Say the word.
- Find two things that rhyme with *stop*. Say each word.
- Find something that rhymes with *pot*. Say the sound at the end of that word.
- Find something that rhymes with *rows*. Say each sound in the word.

READING STREET ONLINE
SOUND-SPELLING CARDS
www.ReadingStreet.com

Bakery

$10.00
$5.00

68

69

Student Edition, pp. 68–69

Common Core State Standards

Foundational Skills 2. Demonstrate understanding of spoken words, syllables, and sounds (phonemes). **Foundational Skills 2.c.** Isolate and pronounce initial, medial vowel, and final sounds (phonemes) in spoken single-syllable words. **Foundational Skills 3.** Know and apply grade-level phonics and word analysis skills in decoding words. **Foundational Skills 3.b.** Decode regularly spelled one-syllable words.

Academic Vocabulary 

rhyming words words that end with the same sounds

Phonemic Awareness

Rhyming Words

MODEL RHYMING WORDS Read the third bulleted point on p. 68. Remember that **rhyming words** are words that end with the same sounds. Let's find three words that rhyme with *stop.* When I look at the picture, I see a *shop,* I see a shopkeeper holding a *mop,* and I see a policeman on *top* of a horse. *Shop, mop,* and *top* rhyme with *stop.* Look at the picture. Can you find a word that rhymes with *pot? (hot, dot)*

GUIDE PRACTICE Guide children to use the picture to produce words that rhyme with *clock*. *(rock, sock)*

ON THEIR OWN Have children produce words that rhyme with these words:

dot	rob	hop	ox	fog	odd

Team Talk Children create pairs of rhyming words with a partner.

Phonics

Build Words

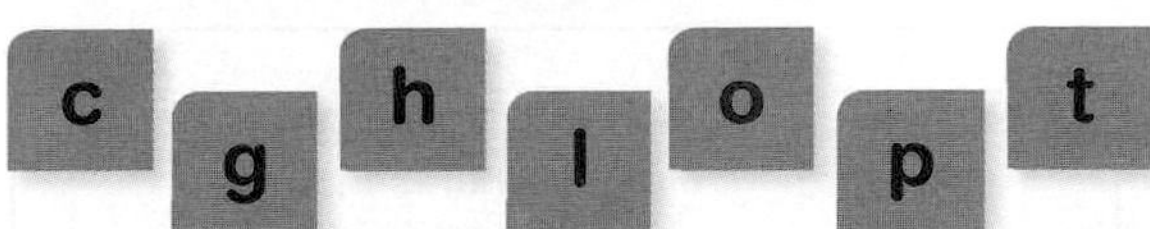

MODEL WORD BUILDING Now we are going to build words with short *o* spelled *o.* Write *pot* and blend it. Watch me change *p* to *c.* Model blending the new word, *cot.*

GUIDE PRACTICE Have children spell *cot* with letter tiles. Monitor children's work as they build words.

- Change the *c* in *cot* to *l.* Say the new word together. — l o t
- Change the *t* in *lot* to *g.* Say the new word together. — l o g
- Change the *l* in *log* to *h.* Say the new word together. — h o g
- Change the *g* in *hog* to *p.* Say the new word together. — h o p

Corrective feedback	For corrective feedback, model the correct spelling and have children correct their tiles.

Fluent Word Reading

MODEL Write *logs*. I know the sounds for *l, o, g,* and *s.* I blend them and read the word *logs.*

GUIDE PRACTICE Write the words below. Say the sounds in your head for each spelling you see. When I point to the word, we'll read it together. Allow one second per sound previewing time for the first reading.

mat **rods** **cap** **pigs** **socks** **kid**

ON THEIR OWN Have children read the list above three or four times, until they can read one word per second.

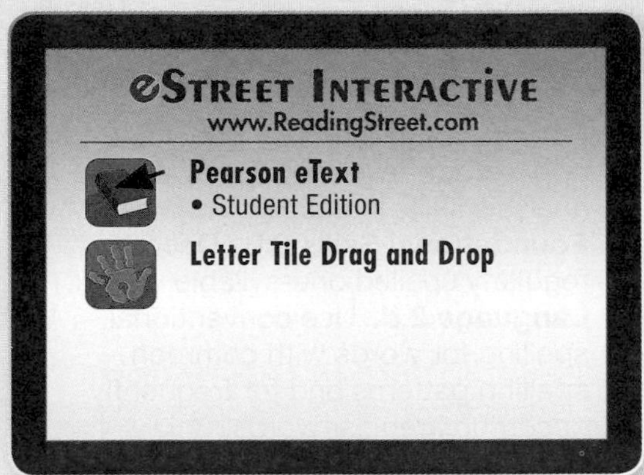

Access for All

SI Strategic Intervention

Build Short *o* Words If children have difficulty building words in the class activity, have them always switch out only the first letter to make new words: *lot, pot, hot, got.*

A Advanced

Build Short *o* Words If children are able to build the words in the class activity easily and independently, have them use letter tiles to build these more difficult words with *o: clock, stop, solid, laptop, onto.*

Pronouncing Short *o* Tell children to put their hand under their chin when making the /o/ sound. Their mouths should open and their jaws should drop. Walk around the room to ensure that children are using correct pronunciation.

Common Core State Standards

Foundational Skills 3. Know and apply grade-level phonics and word analysis skills in decoding words. **Foundational Skills 3.b.** Decode regularly spelled one-syllable words. **Language 2.d.** Use conventional spelling for words with common spelling patterns and for frequently occurring irregular words.

Phonics

Blend and Read

DECODE WORDS IN ISOLATION Have children turn to pages 163–164 in the *Reader's and Writer's Notebook* and find the first list of words. Each word in this list has short *o.* Let's blend and read these words. Continue with the second list or words with the consonant sound /z/ spelled *s.* Be sure that children identify the correct sounds in short *o* words and words that have *s*/z/. Next, have children read the high-frequency words.

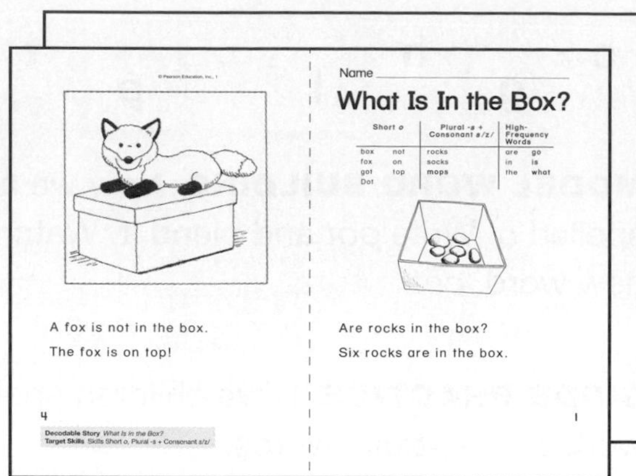

Reader's and Writer's Notebook, pp. 163–164

DECODE WORDS IN CONTEXT Chorally read the story along with children. Have children identify words in the story that have short *o* or the consonant *s*/z/.

Team Talk Pair children and have them take turns reading the story aloud to each other. Monitor children as they read to check for proper pronunciation and appropriate pacing.

ON THEIR OWN To further develop automaticity, have children take the story home to reread.

Spelling

Short *o* Words

SPELL HIGH-FREQUENCY WORDS Write *help* and *use* and point them out on the Word Wall. Have children say and spell the words with you and then without you.

DICTATION Write each sentence, spelling words one at a time. Have children circle and rewrite any misspelled words.

1. **Ox can help Mom and Pop.**
2. **Tom got the Ox to hop.**
3. **Ox can use a mop.**

PROOFREAD AND CORRECT Write each sentence, spelling words one at a time. Have children circle and rewrite any misspelled words.

ON THEIR OWN Use *Reader's and Writer's Notebook,* p. 165.

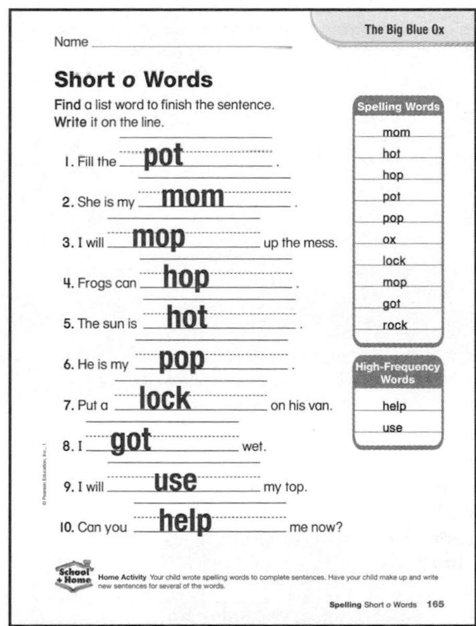
Name ______ The Big Blue Ox

Short *o* Words

Find a list word to finish the sentence. Write it on the line.

1. Fill the pot.
2. She is my mom.
3. I will mop up the mess.
4. Frogs can hop.
5. The sun is hot.
6. He is my pop.
7. Put a lock on his van.
8. I got wet.
9. I will use my top.
10. Can you help me now?

Spelling Words: mom, hot, hop, pot, pop, ox, lock, mop, got, rock

High-Frequency Words: help, use

Home Activity Your child wrote spelling words to complete sentences. Have your child make up and write new sentences for several of the words.

Spelling Short o Words 165

Reader's and Writer's Notebook, p. 165

eSTREET INTERACTIVE
www.ReadingStreet.com

Teacher Resources
- Reader's and Writer's Notebook

Spelling Words

Short *o* Words

1. hot	**6. lock**
2. hop	**7. mop**
3. pot	**8. got**
4. pop	**9. rock**
5. ox	**10. mom**

High-Frequency Words

11. help	**12. use**

Spelling Dictation Children will benefit from hearing each dictated sentence three times. First, have children listen to understand the sentence. The second time, they should write what they hear. The third time, they can check their work.

Day 3 SMALL GROUP TIME • Differentiate Close Reading, p. SG•35

OL On-Level
- **Reread** to Develop Vocabulary
- **Reread** *The Big Blue Ox*

SI Strategic Intervention
- **Blend** Words with Short *o*, Plural *-s*, and Consonant *s/z/*
- **Reread** *The Big Blue Ox*

A Advanced
- **Reread** to Extend Vocabulary
- **Reread** *The Big Blue Ox*
- **Investigate** Inquiry Project

ELL

If... children need more scaffolding and practice with reading the **Main Selection,**
then... use the ELL activities on p. DI•60 in the Teacher Resources section on SuccessNet.

Common Core State Standards

Literature 3. Describe characters, settings, and major events in a story, using key details. **Foundational Skills 3.g.** Recognize and read grade-appropriate irregularly spelled words.

High-Frequency Words

blue	help
from	little
get	use

Selection Words

town a large group of houses and buildings, smaller than a city

High-Frequency and Selection Words

READ WORDS IN ISOLATION Display and review this week's high-frequency words and selection words. Have children read the words aloud.

READ WORDS IN CONTEXT Display the following sentence frames. Have children complete the sentences using high-frequency and selection words. Have children read each completed sentence with you.

1. **Kim hugs the ______ cat. (little)**
2. **Sam can sit on the mat and ______ it. (use)**
3. **Bob can ______ the box ______ Sam. (get, from)**
4. **Dad got pans in ______. (town)**
5. **The ______ hat is big. (blue)**
6. **I got a map and I can ______. (help)**

Don't Wait Until Friday

MONITOR PROGRESS

Check High-Frequency Words

FORMATIVE ASSESSMENT Point to these words on the Word Wall and have the class read them. Listen for children who miss words during the reading. Call on those children to read some of the words individually.

blue	from	help	little	use	get	**Spiral Review**
go	he	take	have	the	←	Row 2 reviews previously taught high-frequency words.

If... children cannot read these words,

then... use the Nondecodable Words Routine on p. 71 to reteach the words. Monitor children's fluency with these words during reading and provide additional practice.

Text-Based Comprehension

Read Main Selection

REVIEW PLOT Remind children that the **plot** of a story includes the events that happen, and sometimes it includes a problem that needs to be solved. Have children turn to pages 76–83. What happens in this story? Let's see, Ox digs, he mops the pigs, he takes Mom and Pop to town, and he shops and cooks. All these things are part of the plot of the story.

GENRE: ANIMAL FANTASY Remind children that animal fantasy is a made-up story with animals that do things real animals can't do. Have children recall things the ox in *The Big Blue Ox* does that real oxen can't do. (He goes shopping and cooks.)

READ Return to pages 74–83 and use the **2nd Read/Close Reading Notes** to reread *The Big Blue Ox.*

Routine Read for Understanding

Deepen understanding by reading the selection multiple times.

1. **First Read**—If children need support, then use the **Access Text** notes to help them clarify understanding.
2. **Second Read**—Use the **Close Reading** notes to help children draw knowledge from the text.

Academic Vocabulary 

animal fantasy a made-up story with animals that do things real animals can't do

ELL

Words in Context Create a word bank on the board for children during the sentence frames review activity on page 84g. Help children find the correct words by using trial and error. Indicate with a nod of your head (yes or no) whether a sentence makes sense when you try different words. Cross out words from the word bank as you correctly complete each sentence.

Think Critically

1. Ox is a helpful friend. How do you help your friends and family? Text to Self
2. Why do you think the author decided Ox would be big? Author's Purpose
3. Who are the characters in this story? Where does this story take place? Character and Setting
4. What pictures did you see in your mind of Ox helping? Visualize
5. **Look Back and Write** Look back at pages 79–82. Write some things Ox can do to help. Be sure to use evidence from the story. Key Ideas and Details • Text Evidence

84

Meet the Author and the Illustrator

Susan Stevens Crummel and Janet Stevens

Susan Stevens Crummel and Janet Stevens are sisters! They have fun working together. Ms. Crummel writes down ideas and turns them into a story. She sends the story to her sister Janet, who draws pictures to fit the story.

Here are other books written and illustrated by Susan Stevens Crummel and Janet Stevens.

COOK-A-DOODLE-DOO!

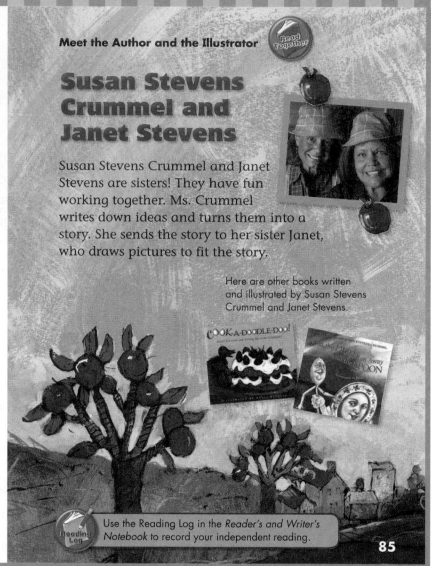

Use the Reading Log in the *Reader's and Writer's Notebook* to record your independent reading.

85

Student Edition, pp. 84–85

Common Core State Standards

Literature 1. Ask and answer questions about key details in a text. **Literature 2.** Retell stories, including key details, and demonstrate understanding of their central message or lesson. **Also Writing 5.**

Bridge to Common Core

KEY IDEAS AND DETAILS

By reading the text multiple times, children will make logical inferences from the text and cite textual evidence when writing or discussing the knowledge they have gained. Use the Think Critically page to ensure a thorough understanding of *The Big Blue Ox.*

Think Critically

1. **TEXT TO SELF** I help my mom set the table for dinner.
2. **AUTHOR'S PURPOSE** I think the author made Ox big so that he could do more things, such as carry Mom and Pop.
3. **CHARACTER AND SETTING** The characters in the story are Ox, Mom, Pop, and the pigs. The setting is Mom and Pop's farm.
4. **VISUALIZE** I pictured Ox digging a big hole and carrying Mom and Pop on his back.
5. **LOOK BACK AND WRITE • TEXT EVIDENCE** For writing fluency, assign a 5-minute time limit. As children finish, encourage them to reread their response and proofread for errors.

Scoring Rubric Look Back and Write

TOP-SCORE RESPONSE A top-score response uses details from the text and the pictures to tell how Ox can help.

A top-score response might include:
Ox can pack a sack and take it back. Ox can use big pans and big fans.

Retell

Have children use the retelling strip in the Student Edition or the Story Sort to retell the selection. Monitor children's retelling.

Scoring Rubric Narrative Retelling

	4	3	2	1
Connections	Makes connections and generalizes beyond the text	Makes connections to other events, stories, or experiences	Makes a limited connection to another event, story, or experience	Makes no connection to another event, story, or experience
Author's Purpose	Elaborates on author's purpose	Tells author's purpose with some clarity	Makes some connection to author's purpose	Makes no connection to author's purpose
Characters	Describes the main character(s) and any character development	Identifies the main character(s) and gives some information about them	Inaccurately identifies some characters or gives little information about them	Inaccurately identifies the characters or gives no information about them
Setting	Describes the time and location	Identifies the time and location	Omits details of time or location	Is unable to identify time or location
Plot	Describes the events in sequence using rich detail	Tells the plot with some errors in sequence that do not affect meaning	Tells parts of plot with gaps that affect meaning	Retelling has no sense of story

Don't Wait Until Friday

MONITOR PROGRESS Check Retelling

If... children have trouble retelling the selection,

then... use Story Sequence Graphic Organizer Flip Chart 23 and the Retelling Cards/Story Sort, and work with the group to scaffold their retelling.

Writing to Sources

Use Write Like a Reporter on pp. 50–51 to guide children in writing text-based responses using one source.

Strategy Response Log

Visualize Have children use p. RR15 in their *Reader's and Writer's Notebook* to draw a picture of the image from the story they can see the most clearly in their heads.

Plan to Assess Retelling

- ☐ **Week 1** Strategic Intervention
- ☐ **Week 2** Advanced
- ☑ **This Week** Assess Strategic Intervention children.
- ☐ **Week 4** On-Level
- ☐ **Week 5** Strategic Intervention
- ☐ **Week 6** Assess any children you have not yet checked during this unit.

Meet the Author and Illustrator

Read aloud page 85 as children follow along. Ask children how authors and illustrators work together.

Read Independently

Have children enter their independent reading into their Reading Logs.

Common Core State Standards

Literature 10. With prompting and support, read prose and poetry of appropriate complexity for grade 1. **Foundational Skills 4.** Read with sufficient accuracy and fluency to support comprehension. **Foundational Skills 4.b.** Read on-level text orally with accuracy, appropriate rate, and expression on successive readings. **Language 1.j.** Produce and expand complete simple and compound declarative, interrogative, imperative, and exclamatory sentences in response to prompts.

Options for Oral Rereading

Use *The Big Blue Ox* or one of this week's Decodable Practice Readers.

Fluency

Rate

MODEL FLUENT READING Have children turn to Student Edition page 76. Explain that the speed at which you read is very important. When I read, I try to read at a speed that sounds like I am speaking.

GUIDE PRACTICE Have children read the page with you. Then have them reread the page as a group until they read the sentence at a speed that sounds as if they are speaking. Continue in the same way with page 77.

Corrective feedback

If... children have difficulty reading at an appropriate pace/rate, **then...** prompt:

- Did you read as though you were speaking?
- Try to use an appropriate pace when you read.

Reread for Fluency

Routine Choral Reading

1. **Select a Passage** For *The Big Blue Ox,* use pp. 78–79.
2. **Model** First, have children track the print as you read.
3. **Guide Practice** Then have children read along with you.
4. **Corrective Feedback** Have the class read aloud without you. Monitor progress and provide feedback. For optimal fluency, children should reread three to four times.

Routines Flip Chart

CHECK COMPREHENSION Are the pigs in the story real or make-believe? Why do you think so? (The pigs are make-believe because pigs do not wear wigs.)

Conventions

Predicates of Sentences

REVIEW Remind children that the predicate of a sentence tells what a person, animal, or thing does. The order of the words in a sentence must be correct to be able to determine the predicate.

GUIDE PRACTICE Write this sentence on the board and have children read it aloud.

Jim sat on the cot.

What is the predicate of this sentence? *(sat on the cot)* What other predicate could we use in place of *sat on the cot* to change what the sentence means?

Team Talk Have children draw a picture of their new sentence and tell it to a partner.

APPLY Have children answer these questions orally in complete sentences.

1. **How can an ox help a boy?**
2. **How can a mom help a pop?**

ON THEIR OWN Use *Reader's and Writer's Notebook,* p. 166.

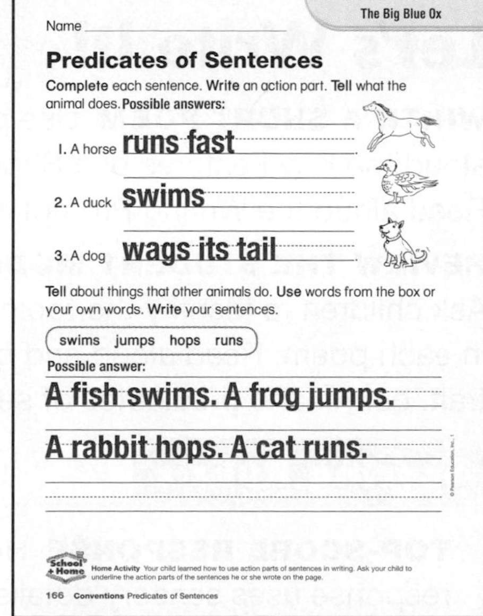
Name

The Big Blue Ox

Predicates of Sentences

Complete each sentence. **Write** an action part. **Tell** what the animal does. **Possible answers:**

1. A horse **runs fast**
2. A duck **swims**
3. A dog **wags its tail**

Tell about things that other animals do. **Use** words from the box or your own words. **Write** your sentences.

swims jumps hops runs

Possible answer:

A fish swims. A frog jumps.

A rabbit hops. A cat runs.

166 Conventions Predicates of Sentences

Reader's and Writer's Notebook, p. 166

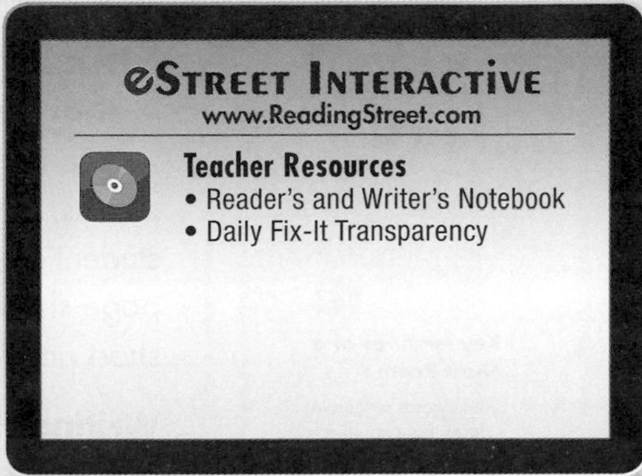
*e*Street Interactive
www.ReadingStreet.com

Teacher Resources
- Reader's and Writer's Notebook
- Daily Fix-It Transparency

Daily Fix-It

5. ox got the hot potz.
   Ox got the hot pots.
6. Pop got five lokks
   Pop got five locks.

Discuss the Daily Fix-It corrections with children. Review sentence capitalization, plural *-s,* and /k/ spelled *ck.*

ELL

Charades Have children mime actions for others to guess. Give this model: *Lu rides a bike; Lu eats an apple.* Explain that each action part is a new predicate.

Practice Building Sentences In English predicates, verbs are often followed by objects: *drank the water.* In Korean and Hindi, the verb often appears at the end of a sentence. Help children practice building English sentences with cards containing subjects, verbs, and objects.

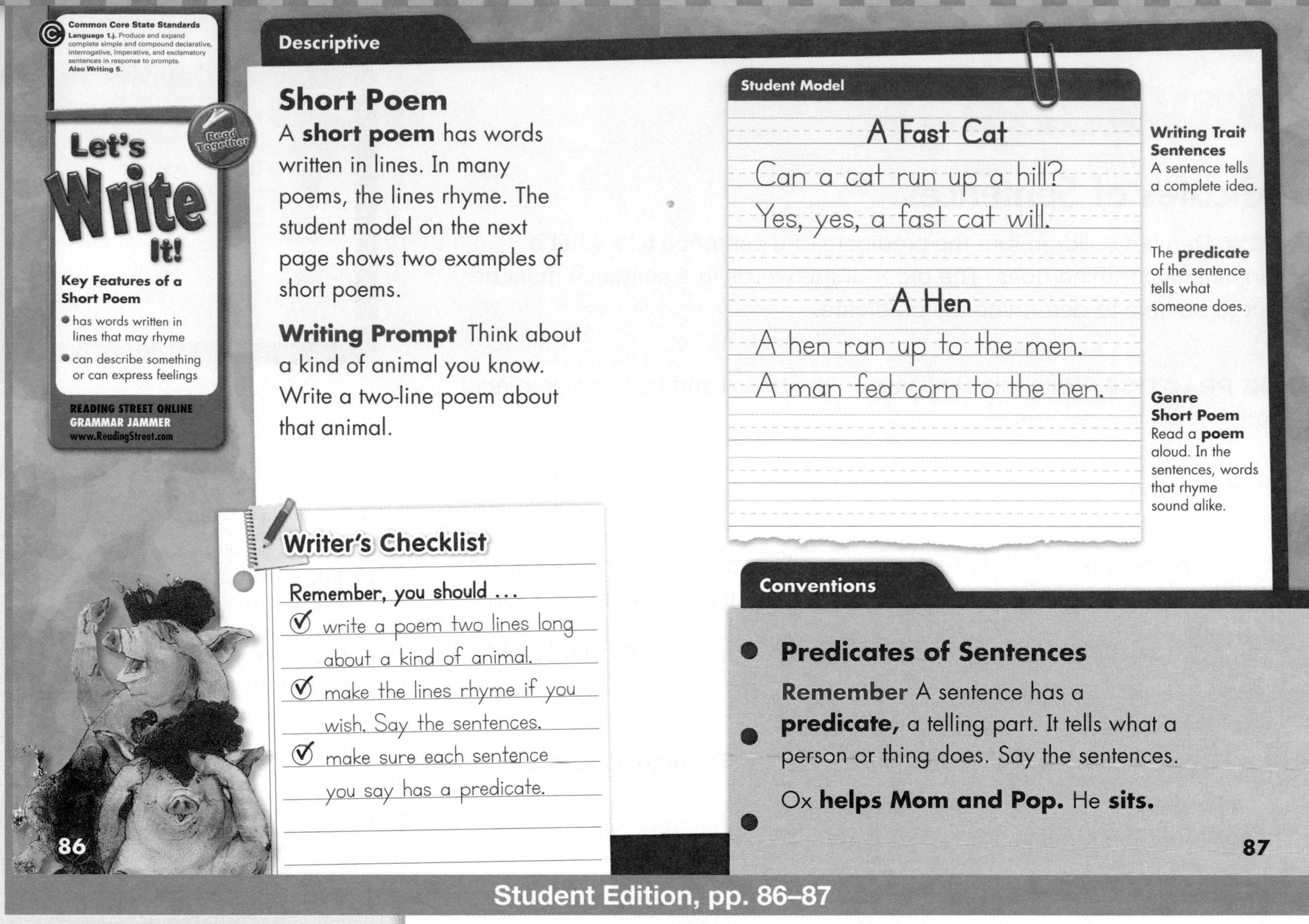

Common Core State Standards
Language 1.j. Produce and expand complete simple and compound declarative, interrogative, imperative, and exclamatory sentences in response to prompts. Also Writing 5.
Read Together
Let's Write It!
Key Features of a Short Poem
• has words written in lines that may rhyme
• can describe something or can express feelings
READING STREET ONLINE
GRAMMAR JAMMER
www.ReadingStreet.com
Descriptive
Short Poem
A short poem has words written in lines. In many poems, the lines rhyme. The student model on the next page shows two examples of short poems.
Writing Prompt Think about a kind of animal you know. Write a two-line poem about that animal.
Writer's Checklist
Remember, you should ...
write a poem two lines long about a kind of animal.
make the lines rhyme if you wish. Say the sentences.
make sure each sentence you say has a predicate.
86
Student Model
A Fast Cat
Can a cat run up a hill?
Yes, yes, a fast cat will.
A Hen
A hen ran up to the men.
A man fed corn to the hen.
Writing Trait Sentences
A sentence tells a complete idea.
The predicate of the sentence tells what someone does.
Genre Short Poem
Read a poem aloud. In the sentences, words that rhyme sound alike.
Conventions
Predicates of Sentences
Remember A sentence has a predicate, a telling part. It tells what a person or thing does. Say the sentences.
Ox helps Mom and Pop. He sits.
87

Student Edition, pp. 86–87

Common Core State Standards

Writing 5. With guidance and support from adults, focus on a topic, respond to questions and suggestions from peers, and add details to strengthen writing as needed. **Language 1.j.** Produce and expand complete simple and compound declarative, interrogative, imperative, and exclamatory sentences in response to prompts.

Let's Write It!

WRITE A SHORT POEM Use pages 86–87 in the Student Edition. Read aloud the Key Features of a Short Poem and the definition of a short poem. Read aloud the Writing Prompt and discuss the Writer's Checklist.

REVIEW THE STUDENT MODEL Read aloud "A Fast Cat" and "A Hen." Ask children to identify the topic of each poem. Point out the rhyming words in each poem. Read aloud and briefly discuss the side notes about the writing trait, genre, and predicates of sentences.

Scoring Rubric

TOP-SCORE RESPONSE Help children understand that a top-score response uses sensory details to describe or express feelings about an animal and has complete sentences with both subjects and predicates. For a complete rubric see Writing Rubric 3 from the *Teacher Resources DVD-ROM.*

CONNECT TO CONVENTIONS Read aloud the Conventions note about predicates of sentences. Point out predicates in the model poems.

Writing

Short Poem

Mini-Lesson Writing Trait: Sentences

- **Introduce** Use your web from yesterday and Writing Transparency 3A to model sentences in a poem. I will use the words in my web from yesterday to help me write my poem. I will use the words in sentences. Yesterday I wrote the word *cute* in my web. This word describes my topic, Freddie the puppy. I can use this word in a sentence about Freddie. I can write *Freddie is a cute pup.* For the second line of my poem, I can write another sentence that tells more about my topic, Freddie the puppy. I can write *He wags his tail and cheers me up.* Read aloud the draft on the transparency to show how each line of the poem is a sentence that tells about the topic.

Puppy Love
Freddie is a cute pup
He wags his tail and chers me up.
Unit 1 The Big Blue Ox
Writing: Model 3A

Writing Transparency 3A TR DVD

- Explain how children can use words from their webs to write sentences for their poems. Today's goal is to draft the poem but not to rewrite each word perfectly. They can edit later to correct the words.

GUIDE WRITING Now it is time to write your poem. Describe an animal or tell how you feel about the animal. Have children use their webs. Then guide children as they draft the poems.

Routine Quick Write for Fluency

Team Talk

1. **Talk** Have partners take one minute to tell each other the topics of their poems.
2. **Write** Each child writes a sentence about the topic of his or her partner's poem.
3. **Share** Partners identify the predicates of each other's sentences.

Routines Flip Chart

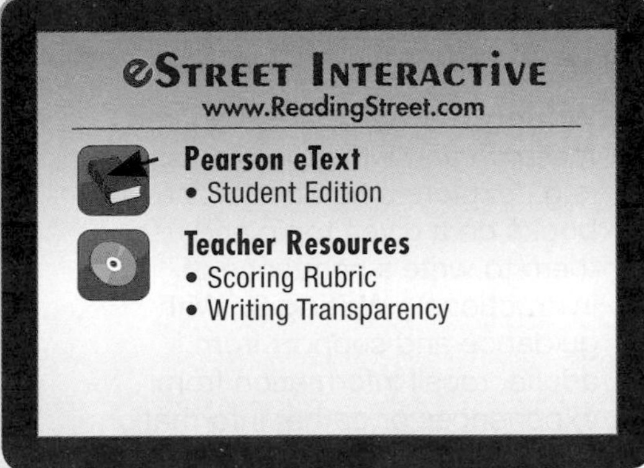

Access for All

A Advanced

Developing Rhyme Challenge children to write rhymed couplets by helping them list words that rhyme.

Write Guy *by Jeff Anderson*

Two Words: Subject, Verb!

Let's help children gain confidence in composing sentences. Guide partners as they make up fun two-word sentences: *Rex howled! Kathy giggled. Lions growl.* Then let the children continue creating sentences, checking to make sure each includes a subject and a verb. Another activity is to challenge children to find favorite sentences in books and then to whittle them to the simple subject and the verb. This paves the way for grammar to support children's writing.

Common Core State Standards

Writing 7. Participate in shared research and writing projects (e.g., explore a number of "how-to" books on a given topic and use them to write a sequence of instructions). **Writing 8.** With guidance and support from adults, recall information from experiences or gather information from provided sources to answer a question. **Speaking/Listening 4.** Describe people, places, things, and events with relevant details, expressing ideas and feelings clearly. **Also Informational Text 5., 7.**

Bridge to Common Core

PRESENTATION OF KNOWLEDGE AND IDEAS

The listening and speaking skills in this lesson focus on how to give an introduction. As children participate in a range of conversations to gather information to use in their introduction, they develop related skills. The instruction includes how to use information in an introduction to learn more about the person and to present information in order to get to know each other better.

Listening and Speaking

Give Introductions

TEACH Tell children to give introductions when two people they know meet for the first time.

- Good speakers introduce others by saying both names.
- They use predicates to tell something about each person.
- They speak clearly and slowly.
- Good listeners should be able to repeat the information they hear.

MODEL Model giving introductions: Tara, this is my friend Carl. Carl rides his bike with me after school. Carl, this is Tara. Tara goes to dance class with me on Fridays.

GUIDE PRACTICE Remind children that they must say the names of both people when giving introductions. Explain how using predicates to tell something about each person can help the people get to know each other better. Introduce two children in class and tell each child something about the other. Discuss with the class what to say before each step of the introductions.

ON THEIR OWN Place children into small groups and have each group stand in a circle. Ask children to take turns introducing the child on their left to the child on their right. Remind them to tell each child something about the other. Then have the next child in the circle give introductions.

Research and Inquiry

Step 3 Gather and Record Information

TEACH Tell children that today they will use a picture dictionary and other resources to find information about how animals help people. They will use what they learn to create a class mural, or class picture, to show the ways that animals can help.

Think Aloud **MODEL** Before we can draw a class mural, we each have to choose a topic to learn more about. On Day 1, I asked about dogs and how they are able to help people. I'll use a picture dictionary to see if I can learn more about dogs and what they look like. You can do this with your questions too.

GUIDE PRACTICE Have children choose a topic. Then tell them to use a picture dictionary and other resources to learn more about their topic. Encourage children to use the pictures and labels in the picture dictionary. Ask them to use their resources to find two or three facts about their topic and to record the information they have found. Explain that they will use this information to create a class mural later in the week.

Access for All

SI Strategic Intervention

Gathering Information Some children may have trouble utilizing the picture dictionary. Review the purpose of this resource and provide an example of its use. Show children how to search for a particular animal, such as a dog.

A Advanced

Working Together Pair up children who show advanced skills with those who still need some help. Have them work together to locate information and record facts.

Wrap Up Your Day!

- ✓ **Character and Setting** Have children think about Ox from *The Big Blue Ox.* How do you think Mom and Pop feel about Ox? Why do you think that?
- ✓ **Visualize** Write the following sentence from *The Big Blue Ox* on the board: *Mom and Pop nap on Ox.* Have children describe what they picture in their minds when they read the sentence.

Tell children that tomorrow they will hear about another ox that is a big help to people.

Content Knowledge
Oral Vocabulary

Phonemic Awareness
Distinguish /o/

Phonics
Review Short *i* Spelled *i*
Review Final *x*

High-Frequency Words
Review

Spelling
Short *o* Words

Social Studies in Reading
Photo Essay

Fluency
Rate

Conventions
Predicates of Sentences

Writing
Short Poem: Revise

Research and Inquiry
Synthesize

Materials

- Student Edition
- Sing with Me Big Book
- Read Aloud Anthology
- Decodable Reader 3C
- Reader's and Writer's Notebook

Common Core State Standards

Speaking/Listening 2. Ask and answer questions about key details in a text read aloud or information presented orally or through other media. **Language 4.** Determine or clarify the meaning of unknown and multiple-meaning words and phrases based on grade 1 reading and content, choosing flexibly from an array of strategies. **Language 5.c.** Identify real-life connections between words and their use (e.g., note places at home that are *cozy*). **Also Language 6.**

Content Knowledge

Animals That Help

EXPAND THE CONCEPT To reinforce concepts and to focus children's attention, have them sing "The Oxen Song" from the *Sing with Me* Big Book. How do animals make our lives better? (Possible response: They do things that are hard for us to do. They also spend time with us and help us with everyday jobs.)

Build Oral Language

REVIEW GENRE: ANIMAL FANTASY Have children tell the key features of an animal fantasy: it tells a made-up story. The animal characters do things that real animals don't do, but an animal fantasy may also have people as characters. The setting can be real or not real. Explain that today you will read about another ox in "Paul Bunyan and Babe."

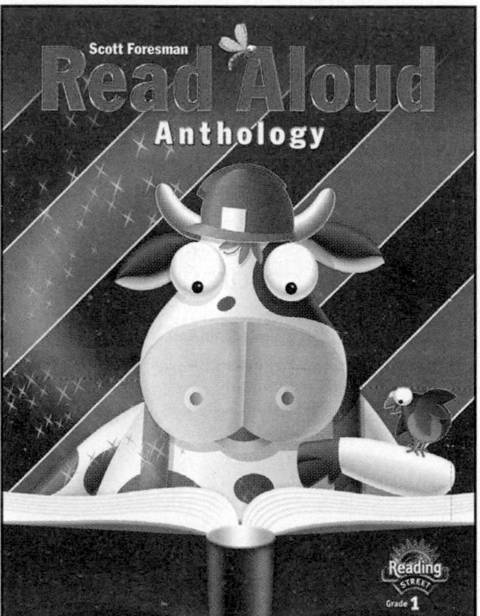

"Paul Bunyan and Babe"

MONITOR LISTENING COMPREHENSION Recall that the ox from *The Big Blue Ox* helped Mom and Pop in different ways. Have children listen to "Paul Bunyan and Babe."

Team Talk **TALK ABOUT ANIMALS THAT HELP** Read aloud the fourth paragraph of "Paul Bunyan and Babe." Display it on a whiteboard if possible, and track the print as you read.

- Have pairs of children generate ideas and examples from the story that show ways Paul Bunyan and Babe are powerful and enormous.
- Add words generated in discussion to the concept map.

Build Oral Vocabulary

Amazing Words Robust Vocabulary Routine

1. **Introduce the Word** Relate the word *enormous* to the story. Paul Bunyan was an *enormous* man. Supply a child-friendly definition. *Enormous* means "very, very, very big." Have children say the word.
2. **Demonstrate** Provide examples to show meaning. The children wondered how they would ever climb to the top of the *enormous* hill. A skyscraper is an *enormous* building.
3. **Apply** Have children demonstrate their understanding. Name and describe some things in your neighborhood that are *enormous.*
4. **Display the Word** Run your hand under the chunks *e-nor-mous* as you read the word.

See p. OV•3 to teach *powerful.*

Routines Flip Chart

After children are introduced to the Amazing Words, have them write the words or sentences with the words and draw a picture about the words. Ask them to show their page and read and tell about the words and the pictures they made.

ADD TO THE CONCEPT MAP Discuss what animals do to make people's lives easier.

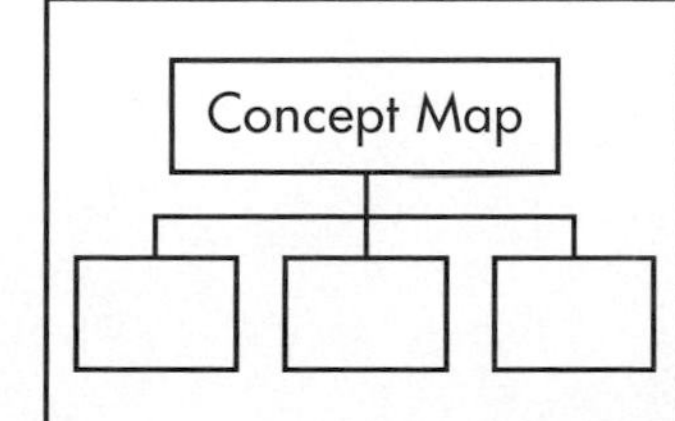

- We read about another ox today in "Paul Bunyan and Babe." How do we know the setting of this story is in the past and not the present? (The story says Paul and Babe created things that have been around for a long time, such as the Grand Canyon.)
- How did Babe help Paul Bunyan in the story? (He helped Paul Bunyan clear trees, plant crops, and build roads.) Let's add these things to our concept map. Where do they belong?

Amazing Words

past	serve
present	snuggle
produce	enormous
transportation	powerful
danger	

Access for All

Sentence Production If children do not pronounce the *r* in *enormous* and *powerful,* say the words distinctly and have children repeat after you. Then have them say each of the words in a sentence.

Produce Oral Language Use the Day 4 instruction on ELL Poster 3 to extend and enrich language.

Support Listening Use ELL Poster 3 to review ways that large and small animals can help people. Before reading, ask children: What are some things that you wish animals could do to help you? Record their answers on the board.

Use Cognates The word *enormous* has a cognate in Spanish. The Spanish word *enorme* may help Spanish speakers learn the English word.

Common Core State Standards

Foundational Skills 2. Demonstrate understanding of spoken words, syllables, and sounds (phonemes). **Foundational Skills 2.c.** Isolate and pronounce initial, medial vowel, and final sounds (phonemes) in spoken single-syllable words. **Foundational Skills 3.** Know and apply grade-level phonics and word analysis skills in decoding words.

Access for All

Strategic Intervention

Distinguishing /o/ If children still have some problems distinguishing /o/, say each word slowly. Then separate each word into its individual letters/sounds and blend:

on *o:* /o/ *n:* /n/ /o/ /n/ *on*

Advanced

Practice with Longer Words If children can easily distinguish the sound /o/ in the list of words provided, read them a list of longer words. Have them raise their hands when they hear /o/ in a word: *chomp, copy, basket, closet, follow, toothpaste, problem, bottom, stoplight.*

Phonemic Awareness

Distinguish /o/

MODEL This week we read about an ox that helps. Listen as I say the sounds in *ox.* Slowly model the sounds in *ox;* /o/ /ks/. This word begins with the sound /o/: *ox.* We're going to listen to other words with the beginning and middle sound /o/.

GUIDE PRACTICE I will say some words, and you can tell me if they have the /o/ sound in the middle or at the beginning. Say each word below and then guide children to decide whether the /o/ sound is in the middle or at the beginning of each one.

pond (middle)	**onto** (beginning)	**knock** (middle)
otter (beginning)	**box** (middle)	**frog** (middle)

Corrective feedback If children make an error, segment the word and model the correct response. Return to the word later in the practice.

ON THEIR OWN Have children tell you which of the following words contain the /o/ sound.

block	**doll**	**ox**
rest	**sob**	**track**

Phonics

Review Short *i* Spelled *i;* Final *x*

REVIEW SHORT *i* SPELLED *i* To review last week's first phonics skill, write *sip.* You studied words like this last week. What do you know about the vowel sound you hear in *sip?* (The vowel sound is /i/ spelled *i.*)

REVIEW FINAL *x* To review last week's second phonics skill, change the *p* in *sip* to *six.* You also studied words like this. What do you know about the consonant sound you hear at the end of *six?* (The consonant sound is /ks/ spelled *x.*)

Corrective feedback	**If...** children are unable to answer your questions about the vowel and consonant sounds in the words you wrote, **then...** refer them to Sound-Spelling Cards 11 and 27.

GUIDE PRACTICE Have children take out letter tiles *c, f, i, k, n, s,* and *x.* Write *sick* and have children blend it. Then have them spell it with their letter tiles.

- Change the /k/ in *sick* to /ks/.
  Which letters change? (*ck* changes to *x*)
  What is the new word? *(six)*

- Change the /s/ in *six* to /f/.
  Which letter changes? (*s* changes to *f*)
  What is the new word? *(fix)*

- Change the /ks/ in fix to /n/.
  Which letter changes? (*x* changes to *n*)
  What is the new word? *(fin)*

ON THEIR OWN Use Let's Practice It! pp. 43–44 on the *Teacher Resources DVD-ROM.*

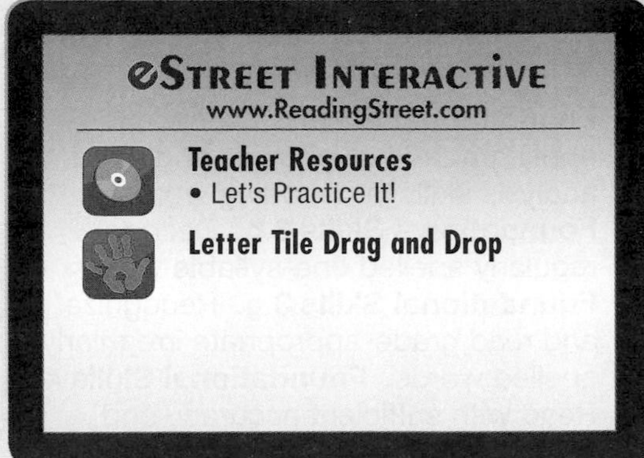

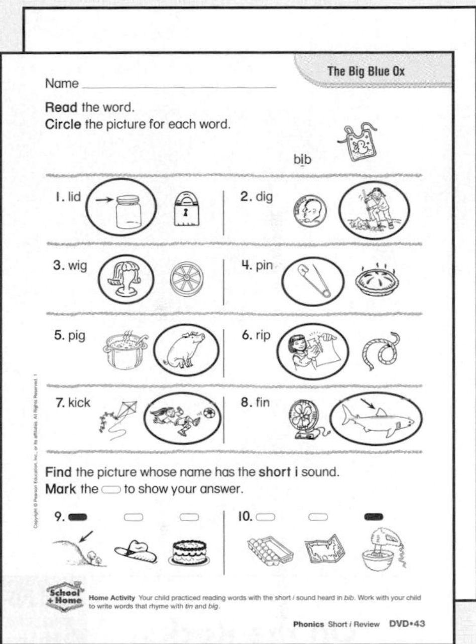
The Big Blue Ox

Name

Read the word.
Circle the picture for each word.

bib

1. lid
2. dig
3. wig
4. pin
5. pig
6. rip
7. kick
8. fin

Find the picture whose name has the **short i** sound.
Mark the ⊂⊃ to show your answer.

9.
10.

Home Activity Your child practiced reading words with the short i sound heard in bib. Work with your child to write words that rhyme with fin and big.

Phonics Short i Review DVD•43

Let's Practice It! TR DVD•43–44

ELL

Reviewing the Letter *i* For Spanish speakers, *i* is pronounced like a long *e,* as in *machine.* Remind children of the /i/ sound and demonstrate its pronunciation. Have children practice saying the following words: *tip, lip, kit, pin, hit.*

Common Core State Standards

Foundational Skills 3. Know and apply grade-level phonics and word analysis skills in decoding words. **Foundational Skills 3.b.** Decode regularly spelled one-syllable words. **Foundational Skills 3.g.** Recognize and read grade-appropriate irregularly spelled words. **Foundational Skills 4.** Read with sufficient accuracy and fluency to support comprehension.

Decodable Reader 3C

If children need help, then...

Read *On the Rocks*

DECODE WORDS IN ISOLATION Have children turn to page 161 and children decode each word listed.

REVIEW HIGH-FREQUENCY WORDS Review the previously taught words *and, the,* and *use.* Have children read each word as you point to it on the Word Wall.

PREVIEW Have children read the title and preview the story. Tell them they will read words with the short vowel *o,* the plural *-s,* and the consonant *s/z/.*

DECODE WORDS IN CONTEXT Pair children for reading and listen as they decode. One child begins. Children read the entire story, switching readers after each page. Partners reread the story. This time the other child begins.

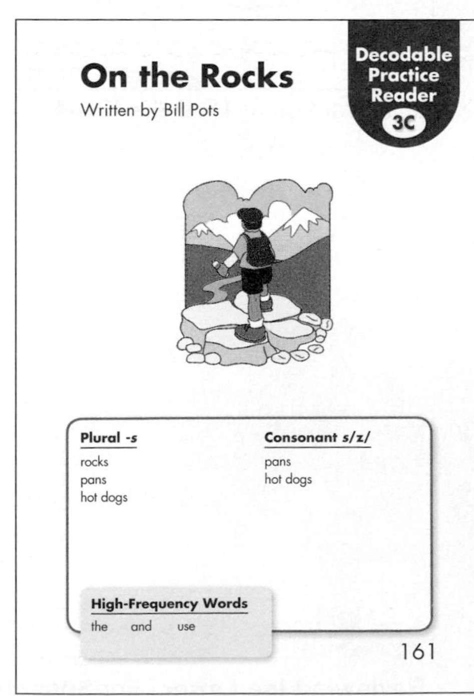
On the Rocks
Written by Bill Pots
Decodable Practice Reader 3C

Plural -s: rocks, pans, hot dogs
Consonant s/z/: pans, hot dogs
High-Frequency Words: the, and, use

161

Decodable Practice Reader 3C

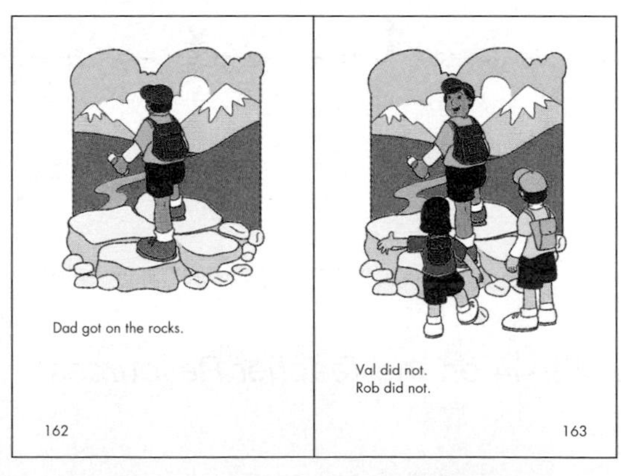
Dad got on the rocks.
162

Val did not.
Rob did not.
163

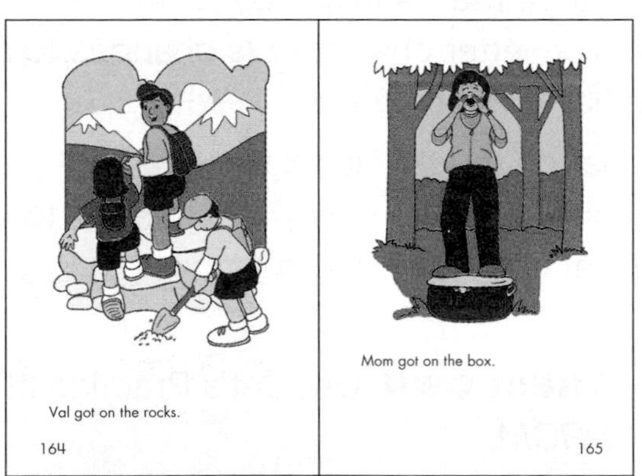
Val got on the rocks.
164

Mom got on the box.
165

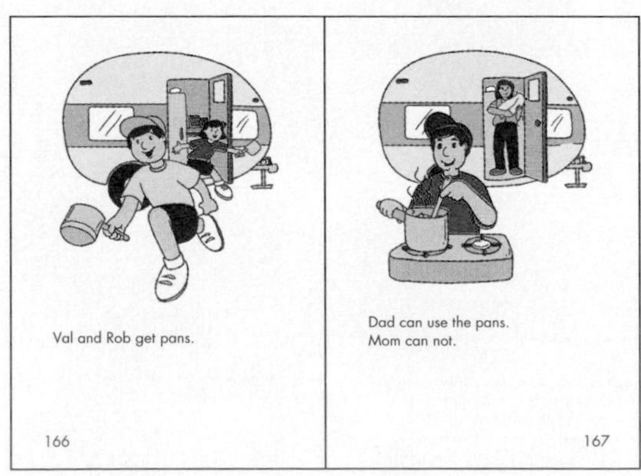
Val and Rob get pans.
166

Dad can use the pans.
Mom can not.
167

Rob, Val, and Dad
had hot dogs.
Mom did not.
168

Corrective feedback	**If...** children have difficulty decoding a word, **then...** refer them to the Sound-Spelling Cards to identify the sounds in the word. Then prompt them to blend the word. • What is the new word? • Is the new word a word you know? • Does it make sense in the story?

CHECK DECODING AND COMPREHENSION Have children retell the story to include characters, setting, and events. Then have children find words with the plural *-s* in the story. Explain that some story words with the plural *-s* ending will have the consonant sound *s/z/*. Children should supply *rocks, pans,* and *hot dogs.*

Reread for Fluency

REREAD DECODABLE READER Have children reread Decodable Practice Reader 3C to develop automaticity decoding words with the plural *-s* and consonant sound *s/z/.*

Routine Oral Rereading

1. **Read** Have children read the entire book orally.
2. **Reread** To achieve optimal fluency, children should reread the text three or four times.
3. **Corrective Feedback** Listen as children read. Provide corrective feedback regarding their fluency and decoding.

Routines Flip Chart

Decodable Practice Reader

Beginning Before children read, lead them on a picture walk through the story. Point out and pronounce the words that have the plural *-s* and consonant sound */z/*. Then write a pictured word and have children pronounce it and find its picture.

Intermediate Have children read the sentences with *-s* plurals. Then have them say the singular form of each word.

Advanced After reading, have children find the words with the short *o* and the plural *-s*. Have them write their own sentences using these words.

Common Core State Standards

Foundational Skills 3. Know and apply grade-level phonics and word analysis skills in decoding words. **Language 2.d.** Use conventional spelling for words with common spelling patterns and for frequently occurring irregular words.

Spiral Review

These activities review

- previously taught high-frequency words *she, take, what, up, a, with, way, that, for.*
- short *a* spelled *a,* short *i* spelled *i,* final *x,* and final *-ck.*

Fluent Word Reading

Spiral Review

READ WORDS IN ISOLATION Display these words. Tell children that they can blend some words on this list, and others are Word Wall words.

Have children read the list three or four times until they can read at the rate of two to three seconds per word.

up	**she**	**with**	**bag**	**that**
take	**sacks**	**six**	**rocks**	**box**
fix	**pack**	**what**	**fills**	**van**
pigs	**Rex**	**way**	**will**	**for**

Corrective feedback

Word Reading

If... children have difficulty reading whole words,
then... have them use sound-by-sound blending for decodable words, or have them say and spell high-frequency words.

If... children cannot read fluently at a rate of two to three seconds per word,
then... have pairs practice the list until they can read it fluently.

READ WORDS IN CONTEXT Display these sentences. Call on individuals to read a sentence. Then randomly point to review words and have children read them. To help you monitor word reading, high-frequency words are underlined and decodable words are italicized.

Nick can fix **<u>that</u>** ***van.***
Pam will pack **<u>a</u>** ***bag.***
Six pigs ran **<u>for</u>** ***cobs.***
Rex fills sacks **<u>with</u>** ***rocks.***

Corrective feedback

Sentence Reading

If... children are unable to read an underlined high-frequency word,
then... read the word for them and spell it, having them echo you.

If... children have difficulty reading an italicized decodable word,
then... guide them in using sound-by-sound blending.

Spelling

Short *o* Words

PARTNER REVIEW Supply pairs of children with index cards on which the spelling words have been written. Have one child read a word while the other writes it. Then have children switch roles. Have them use the cards to check their spelling and correct any misspelled words.

ON THEIR OWN Use *Reader's and Writer's Notebook,* p. 167.

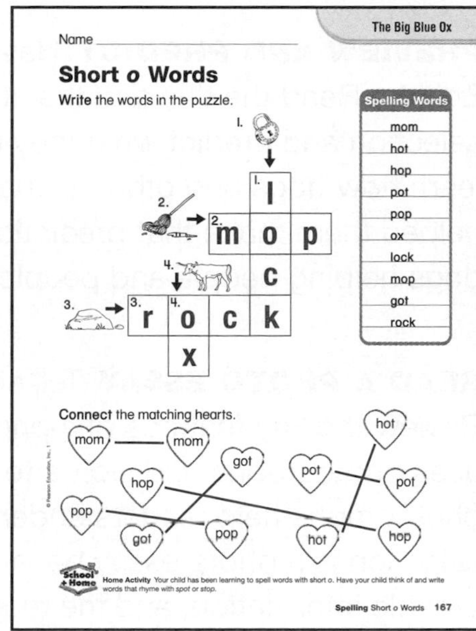

The Big Blue Ox

Name ____________

Short o Words

Write the words in the puzzle.

Spelling Words
mom
hot
hop
pot
pop
ox
lock
mop
got
rock

1. l o c k
2. m o p
3. r o c k
4. o x

Connect the matching hearts.

mom — mom, hop — hop, pop — pop, got — got, pot — pot, hot — hot

Home Activity Your child has been learning to spell words with short o. Have your child think of and write words that rhyme with spot or stop.

Spelling Short o Words 167

Reader's and Writer's Notebook, p. 167

ELL

Fluent Word Reading Have children listen to a more fluent reader say the words. Then have them repeat the words.

Day 4 SMALL GROUP TIME • Differentiate Vocabulary, p. SG•35

OL On-Level
- **Develop** Language Using Selection Vocabulary
- **Read** *Reading Street Sleuth,* pp. 12–13

SI Strategic Intervention
- **Review/Discuss** Selection Vocabulary
- **Read** *Reading Street Sleuth,* pp. 12–13

A Advanced
- **Extend** Amazing Words and Selection Vocabulary
- **Read** *Reading Street Sleuth,* pp. 12–13
- **Organize** Inquiry Project

ELL

If... children need more scaffolding and practice with **Vocabulary, then...** use the routine on pp. xxxvi–xxxvii in the *ELL Handbook.*

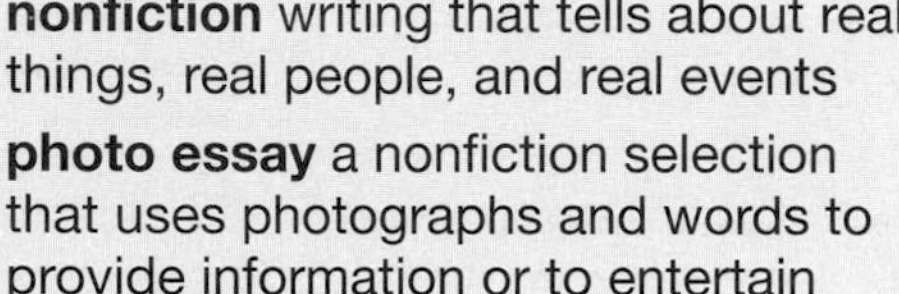

Informational Text 5. Know and use various text features (e.g., headings, tables of contents, glossaries, electronic menus, icons) to locate key facts or information in a text. **Informational Text 6.** Distinguish between information provided by pictures or other illustrations and information provided by the words in a text. **Informational Text 7.** Use the illustrations and details in a text to describe its key ideas.

Academic Vocabulary

nonfiction writing that tells about real things, real people, and real events

photo essay a nonfiction selection that uses photographs and words to provide information or to entertain

Photo Essay

ACTIVATE PRIOR KNOWLEDGE Ask children to recall what they have already learned about how animals help people. (The farm animals in "A Perfect Visit" helped make the farm neat for a friend's visit. The big blue ox helped Mom and Pop on their farm.) Remind children that these animal characters acted in ways that real animals would not.

PREVIEW AND PREDICT Have children turn to page 88 in their Student Edition. Read the title and the author's name. Have children look through the selection and predict what they might learn. (Possible response: They might learn how dogs and other animals can help people.) Ask them what clues helped them make that prediction. (Possible response: The pictures show dogs helping people and people using animals to help them get places.)

READ A PHOTO ESSAY Tell children that they will read a **photo essay.** Review the key features of a photo essay: It is a nonfiction selection that uses photographs and words to provide information or to entertain. The photographs help readers understand the words. Explain that this nonfiction selection is a photo essay because it has both photographs and words to provide information, and the reader uses the photographs to help understand the words.

Genre

LET'S THINK ABOUT... As you read "They Can Help" together, use Let's Think About in the Student Edition to help children focus on the features of a photo essay.

1. The words on these pages wouldn't make sense without the photographs. The photographs show the details of how the animals help. They explain what the words mean by giving more information.

Common Core State Standards
Informational Text 5. Know and use various text features (e.g., headings, tables of contents, glossaries, electronic menus, icons) to locate key facts or information in a text. **Also Informational Text 6., 7.**

Social Studies in Reading

Read Together

Genre
Photo Essay

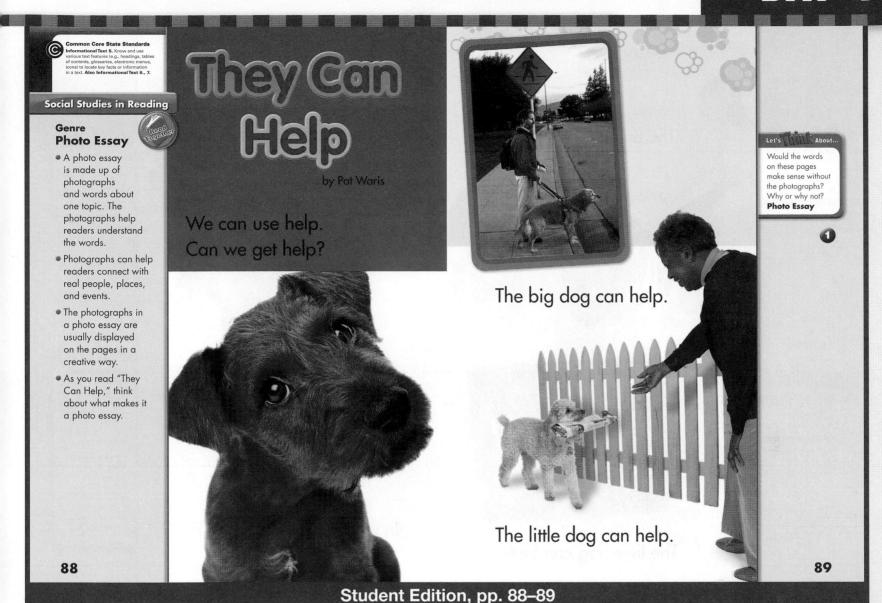

- A photo essay is made up of photographs and words about one topic. The photographs help readers understand the words.
- Photographs can help readers connect with real people, places, and events.
- The photographs in a photo essay are usually displayed on the pages in a creative way.
- As you read "They Can Help," think about what makes it a photo essay.

They Can Help

by Pat Waris

We can use help.
Can we get help?

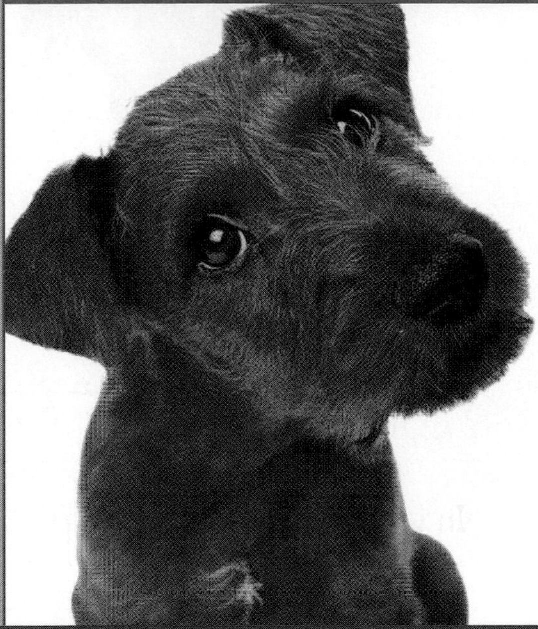

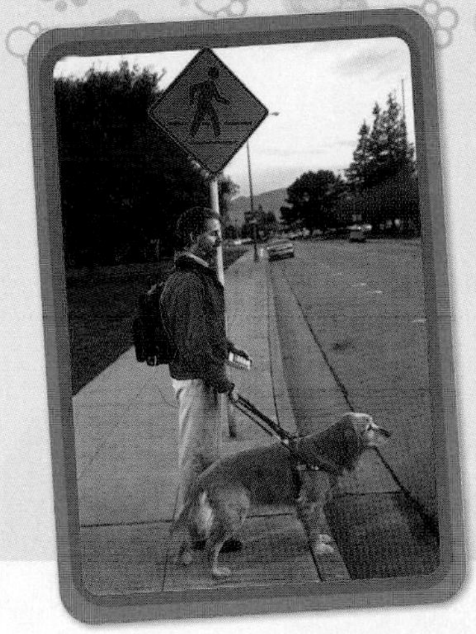

The big dog can help.

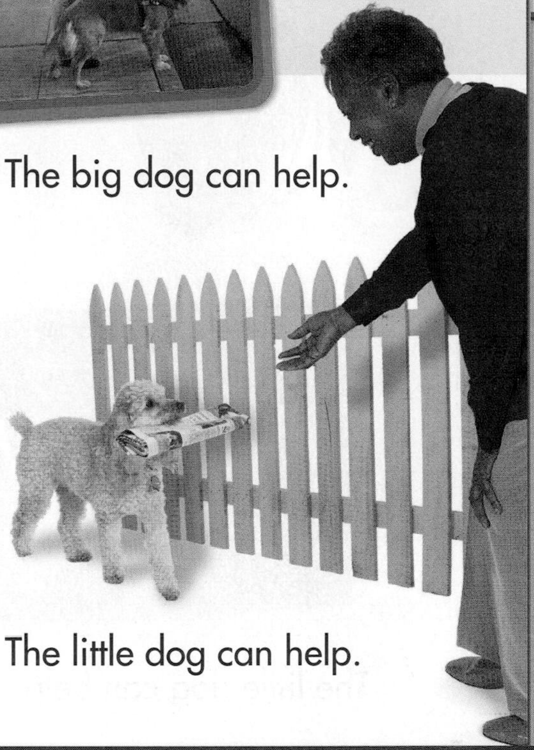

The little dog can help.

Let's Think About...
Would the words on these pages make sense without the photographs? Why or why not?
Photo Essay

1

88 89

Student Edition, pp. 88–89

Access Text

Think Aloud

SUMMARIZE Good readers look for important ideas as they read so that they can summarize a story or selection. When I finished reading *The Big Blue Ox,* I recalled that Ox did many things to help Mom and Pop. I will pay attention to the important ideas as I read "They Can Help."

eSTREET INTERACTIVE
www.ReadingStreet.com

Pearson eText
- Student Edition

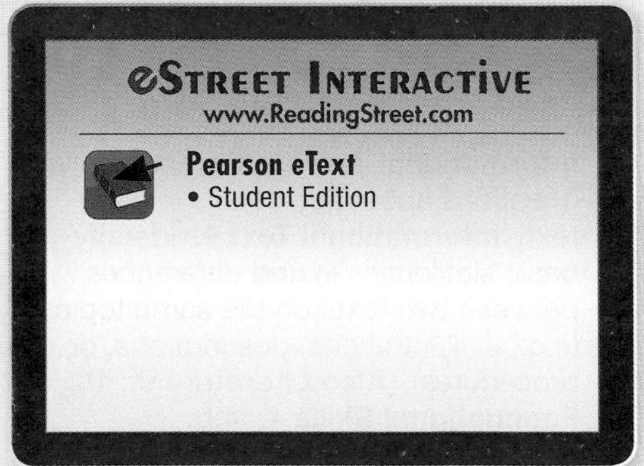

ELL

Animal Names Help children name the animals in the photographs in the selection. They may know the English names *dog, reindeer, horse, sheep,* and *camel,* or home-language words. They may not understand irregular plurals such as *reindeer* and *sheep.* Spanish speakers always add -*s* or -*es* to form plurals.

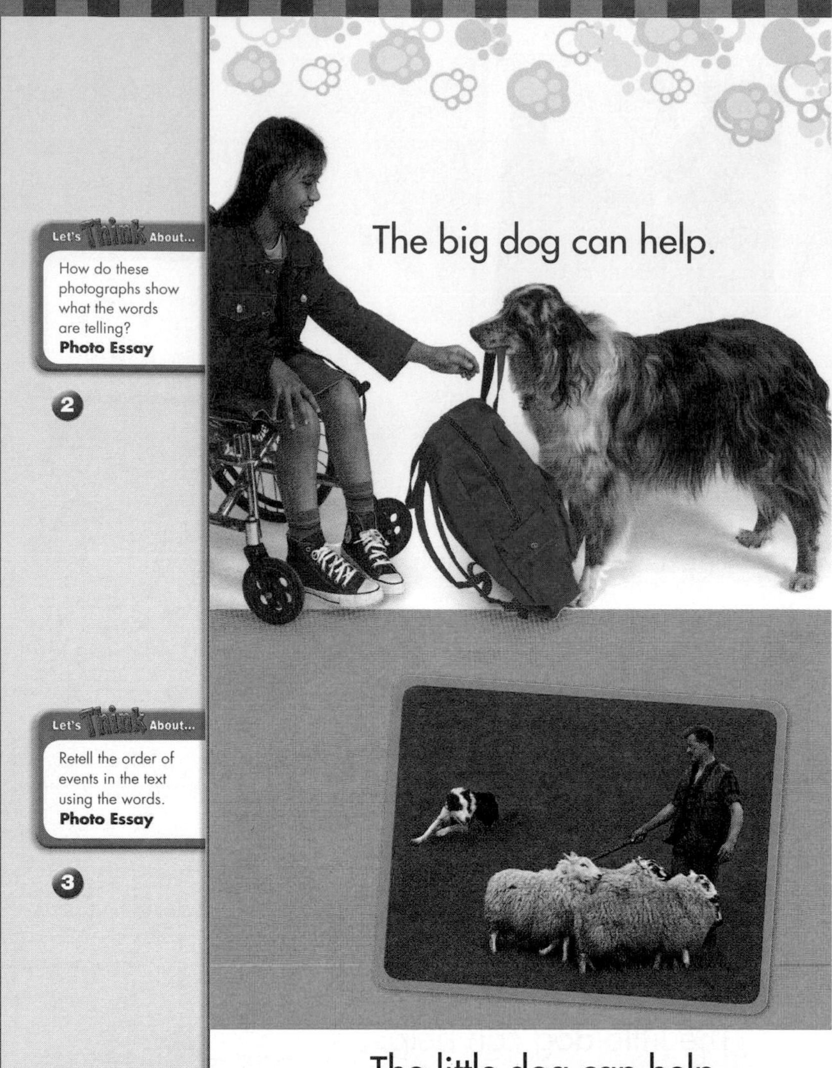

Let's Think About...
How do these photographs show what the words are telling? **Photo Essay**
2
The big dog can help.
Let's Think About...
Retell the order of events in the text using the words. **Photo Essay**
3

The little dog can help.

90

In what ways do they help?

Let's Think About...
How do these photographs answer the question on the page? **Photo Essay**
4

Let's Think About...
Reading Across Texts How are Ox in *The Big Blue Ox* and the animals in "They Can Help" different? How are the ways they help people different?
Writing Across Texts Draw pictures of Ox helping and an animal in the photo essay helping. Write sentences that tell what they are doing.

91

Student Edition, pp. 90–91

Common Core State Standards

Informational Text 1. Ask and answer questions about key details in a text. **Informational Text 9.** Identify basic similarities in and differences between two texts on the same topic (e.g., in illustrations, descriptions, or procedures). **Also Literature 9., 10., Foundational Skills 4., 4.b.**

Writing to Sources

Use Connect the Texts on pp. 52–53 to guide children in writing text-based responses using two sources.

Access Text

SUMMARIZE Summarize in one sentence what you read and saw in the photo essay "They Can Help." Remember to give only the most important information from the selection. (Animals can help in many ways.)

LET'S THINK ABOUT... features of a photo essay.

2 The photographs show the details of how the animal helps.

3 The big dog helps. The little dog helps. Many kinds of animals help.

4 The animals provide transportation for people.

Reading and Writing Across Texts

Children might note that Ox is not real and does things a real ox could not do. The animals in the photo essay are real-life animals and do only things real animals can do.

Children might draw a picture of Ox cooking in a kitchen and write the sentence: *Ox can use pans.* They might draw a picture of a dog with a newspaper in its mouth and write the sentence: *A dog can get things.*

Fluency

Rate

- Have children turn to pp. 80–81 in *The Big Blue Ox.*
- Have children follow along as you read the pages at a rate that sounds like speaking.
- Have the class read the pages with you and then reread the pages as a group without you until they read using an appropriate rate. To provide additional fluency practice, pair nonfluent readers with fluent readers.

Routine Paired Reading

1. **Select a Passage** For *The Big Blue Ox,* use pp. 82–83.
2. **Model** First, have children track the print as you read.
3. **Guide Practice** Then have children read along with you.
4. **On Their Own** For optimal fluency, have partners reread three or four times.

Routines Flip Chart

MONITOR PROGRESS Fluency Check

As children reread, monitor their progress toward their individual fluency goals. Mid-Year Goal: 20–30 words correct per minute. End-of-Year Goal: 60 words correct per minute. Beginning in Unit 3, children will be assessed to determine WCPM.

If... children are not on track to meet benchmark goals,
then... have children practice with text at their independent level.

Access for All

 Advanced

Rate If children already read at 60 words correct per minute, have them read more challenging text.

Options for Oral Rereading

Use *The Big Blue Ox* or one of this week's Decodable Practice Readers.

Conventions

Predicates of Sentences

TEST PRACTICE Use *Reader's and Writer's Notebook,* p. 168 to help children understand predicates in test items. Recall that a predicate is the action part of a sentence that tells what a person, animal, or thing does: *jumps high, goes to bed, drinks a glass of milk.* Model identifying a predicate in a sentence by writing this sentence on the board, reading it aloud, and underlining the predicate *go to the park.*

Sam and I go to the park.

ON THEIR OWN Read the directions on *Reader's and Writer's Notebook,* p. 168. Guide children as they mark the answer for number 1.

APPLY After children mark the answers to numbers 1–6, review the correct choices aloud, and have children read each sentence aloud, emphasizing the predicate.

The Big Blue Ox

Name ______________________

Predicates of Sentences

Mark the sentence that has a line under the action part.

1. ○ Ox gets a mop.
   ⊗ Ox gets a mop.
   ○ Ox gets a mop.
2. ⊗ He mops the pigs.
   ○ He mops the pigs.
   ○ He mops the pigs.
3. ○ Mom and Pop ride on Ox.
   ○ Mom and Pop ride on Ox.
   ⊗ Mom and Pop ride on Ox.
4. ⊗ Ox gets the cans.
   ○ Ox gets the cans.
   ○ Ox gets the cans.
5. ○ He packs the sack.
   ○ He packs the sack.
   ⊗ He packs the sack.
6. ○ They take a nap.
   ⊗ They take a nap.
   ○ They take a nap.

School + Home **Home Activity** Your child prepared for taking tests on the action parts of sentences. Write simple sentences about your family, such as these: *Bill plays football. Your sister feeds the baby.* Ask your child to circle each action part.

168 **Conventions** Predicates of Sentences

Reader's and Writer's Notebook, p. 168

Common Core State Standards

Writing 5. With guidance and support from adults, focus on a topic, respond to questions and suggestions from peers, and add details to strengthen writing as needed. **Language 1.j.** Produce and expand complete simple and compound declarative, interrogative, imperative, and exclamatory sentences in response to prompts.

Bridge to Common Core

CONVENTIONS OF STANDARD ENGLISH

As children develop understanding of the concept of a sentence, they learn that a predicate is the action part of a sentence that tells what a person, animal, or thing does. Children learn to produce complete sentences to gain control of the conventions of standard English grammar, usage, and mechanics. The lessons help children use language to convey meaning effectively as they speak and write.

Daily Fix-It

7. Hopp up for Mom
   Hop up for Mom.
8. ox gott a rock.
   Ox got a rock.

Discuss the Daily Fix-It corrections with children. Review sentence capitalization and punctuation and the spelling of *hop* and *got.*

Writing

Short Poem

Mini-Lesson Revise: Changing Words

- Yesterday we wrote short poems about animals we know. Today we will revise. We can help people who read the poems. We can make it easier to picture the animals the poems describe. We can do this by changing words.

Revising Marks

Take Out	⟋	Move	⌒
Add	^	Period	⊙

Puppy Love

Freddie is a ~~cute~~ floppy pup

He wags his tail and chers me up.

Unit 1 The Big Blue Ox Writing: Revise 3B

Writing Transparency 3B TR DVD

- Display the Revising Tips. Explain that this is a time for making the poem clear for anyone who will read it. Tomorrow children will proofread to correct any errors such as misspellings, missing capital letters, or misplaced sentence periods.

Revising Tips

✔ Make sure your poem tells the kind of animal it is about.

✔ Change words to make it easier to picture the animal.

- Use Writing Transparency 3B to model changing words to make it easier to picture the topic. In my poem, "Puppy Love," I wrote that Freddie is cute. One thing that makes Freddie cute is that he is so floppy. The word *floppy* really tells what Freddie looks like. I will change the word *cute* to *floppy: Freddie is a floppy pup.* Delete *cute* and replace it with *floppy* on the transparency. Tell children that they can change words in their poem as they revise.

PEER CONFERENCING • PEER REVISION Pair children and tell half to read the partner's poem. Allow one minute. Then have the readers use one or two minutes to tell which words in the poem help them to picture the animal described. Have readers ask questions about the animal to help their partners think of additional descriptive words. Repeat with second partners. Circulate to assist children planning to revise their poems.

Access for All

SI Strategic Intervention

Test Formats A child may prepare to write predicates of sentences. Make sure children understand that on *Reader's and Writer's Notebook,* p. 168, they should mark the answer choice with the predicate underlined.

Color Words Words for colors help readers picture things. Review color words to help children describe their animals.

Common Core State Standards

Writing 5. With guidance and support from adults, focus on a topic, respond to questions and suggestions from peers, and add details to strengthen writing as needed. **Writing 7.** Participate in shared research and writing projects (e.g., explore a number of "how-to" books on a given topic and use them to write a sequence of instructions). **Writing 8.** With guidance and support from adults, recall information from experiences or gather information from provided sources to answer a question.

Writing

Zoom in on

GUIDE PRACTICE Have children revise their poems. For those not sure how to revise, have children refer to the Revising Tips or the Key Features of Short Poems.

Corrective feedback	Circulate to monitor and confer with children as they write. Remind them that they will have time to proofread and edit tomorrow. Today they can change words or make sentences clearer. Help them understand the benefits of adding or changing words. Encourage them to use words that will help readers picture the animal described.

Routine Quick Write for Fluency

Team Talk

1. **Talk** Read this sentence aloud, and have children suggest words that could give a better picture of Jackson than *great* does.
   Jackson is a great horse.
2. **Write** Have children write a short sentence about an animal.
3. **Share** Partners can read the sentences to one another and tell which words help them picture the animals described in their partners' sentences.

Routines Flip Chart

Research and Inquiry

Step 4 Synthesize

TEACH The next step in the inquiry project is to review our topic to see if we have the information we set out to find. Or, did our answers lead to a different topic?

Think Aloud **MODEL** We wanted to learn more about a topic so that we could create a class mural. First, we thought of animals that help people and we asked some questions about these animals. Then we learned about picture dictionaries and used a picture dictionary to learn more about the topic we chose. We used the picture dictionary and other resources to gather two or three facts about the topic. Now I will look at the information I gathered. I will see if I found any facts that I can draw pictures about. If I did not, I can use the picture dictionary and other resources to gather more information.

GUIDE PRACTICE Have children look at the information they gathered during Day 3. Instruct them to work with a partner to choose facts about the topic that could be illustrated. If necessary, they can conduct more research to collect more facts. Finally, tell children that tomorrow they will organize all the information in order to share it with others.

Access for All

SI Strategic Intervention

Act It Out If children have difficulty knowing what information to illustrate, ask them to act out the information with a partner. This will help them visualize the information and determine if it can be drawn.

A Advanced

Mini Murals For children who have multiple ideas for the class mural, ask them to work together and create their own small mural, in addition to the class project.

Wrap Up Your Day!

✔ **Phonics Review** List CVC words with short *o.* Have children read each word and identify the letter that spells the /o/ sound.

✔ **Fluency** Write *Did the big dog nap?* Have the class reread the question until they can do so at an appropriate rate.

Remind children that they heard about Paul Bunyan and his great helper, Babe the Blue Ox. Tomorrow they will hear about Paul and Babe again.

DAY 5 at a Glance

Content Knowledge
Oral Vocabulary

Phonemic Awareness
Review Segment and Count Phonemes

Phonics/Spelling
Review Short *o: o*
Review Plural *-s;* Consonant *s/z/*

Text-Based Comprehension
Review Character and Setting

Selection Words
Review

High-Frequency Words
Review

Assessment
Phonics
High-Frequency Words
Fluency

Conventions
Review Predicates of Sentences

Writing
Short Poem: Proofread

Research and Inquiry
Communicate

Materials
- Student Edition
- Read Aloud Anthology
- Weekly Test

Bridge to Common Core

INTEGRATION OF KNOWLEDGE/IDEAS
Children have acquired an expanding body of knowledge from the diverse print and technology resources about animals that help people. They have developed a wide base of knowledge to expand the unit topic of Animals, Tame and Wild.

Social Studies Knowledge Goals
Children have learned that animals provide
- food for people
- transportation for people
- services to people

Content Knowledge

Zoom in on

Animals That Help

REVIEW CONCEPT This week we have read and listened to stories about animals that help people in different ways. Today you will listen to a story about a powerful ox. Read the story.

- Would it have been harder for Paul Bunyan to do his work without Babe? Why or why not? (It would have been harder because Babe was so powerful that he could even push and pull mountains.)

"Paul Bunyan and Babe"

Build Oral Language

REVIEW AMAZING WORDS Orally review the meanings of this week's Amazing Words. Then display this week's concept map. Have children use Amazing Words such as *produce, transportation, serve,* and *powerful,* as well as the concept map, to answer the question *How do animals help people?*

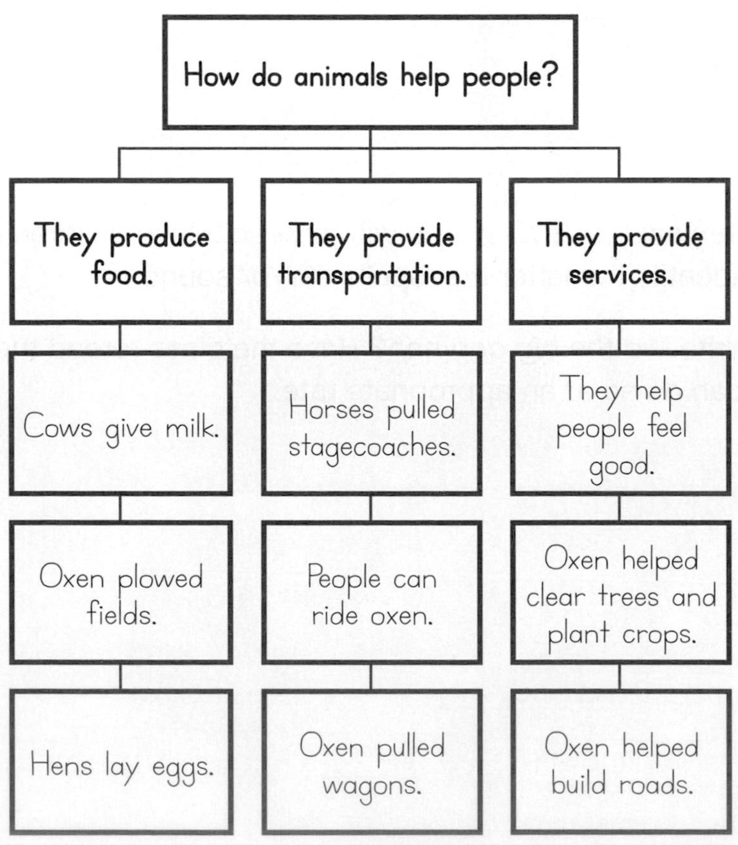
How do animals help people?
They produce food.
They provide transportation.
They provide services.
Cows give milk.
Horses pulled stagecoaches.
They help people feel good.
Oxen plowed fields.
People can ride oxen.
Oxen helped clear trees and plant crops.
Hens lay eggs.
Oxen pulled wagons.
Oxen helped build roads.

Build Oral Vocabulary

Team Talk **CONNECT TO AMAZING IDEAS** Pair children and have them discuss how the Question of the Week, *How do animals help people?*, connects to the question of this unit of study: *How are people and animals important to one another?* Tell children to use the concept map and what they've learned from this week's discussions and reading selections to form an Amazing Idea—a realization or "big idea" about **animals, tame and wild.** Use the following ideas as prompts:

- How can animals be used for transportation?
- How can animals help people do work?

Then ask each pair to share their Amazing Idea with the class. Encourage children to recall in which selection they learned their ideas.

Amazing Ideas might include:

- Animals help people produce food.
- People have used animals for transportation in the past and still do in the present.
- Animals help people do work.

MONITOR PROGRESS Check Oral Vocabulary

FORMATIVE ASSESSMENT Call on individuals to use this week's Amazing Words to talk about how animals help people. Prompt discussion with the questions below. Monitor children's ability to use the Amazing Words and note which words children are unable to use.

- **What are some ways animals were used for *transportation* in the *past* and in the *present?***
- **What are some animals that *produce* food for people?**
- **How do some animals *serve* people?**
- **How can dogs keep people safe from *danger?***
- **Would you want to *snuggle* with an *enormous* animal?**
- **Why does an ox need to be *powerful?***

If... children have difficulty using the Amazing Words,

then... reteach the unknown words using the Robust Vocabulary routines, pp. 67a, 72b, 84b, 88b.

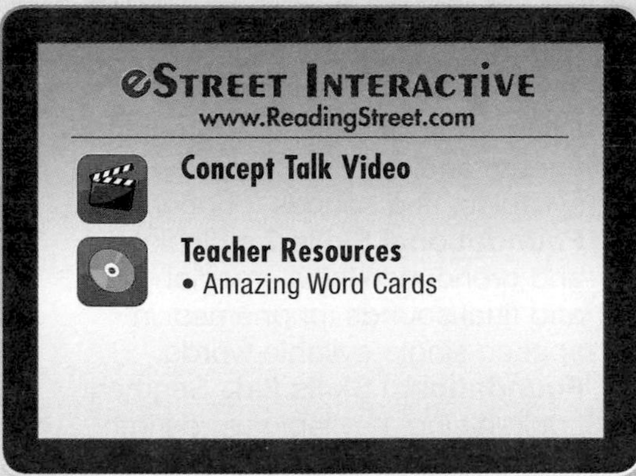

past
present
produce
transportation
danger
serve
snuggle
enormous
powerful

ELL

Check Concepts and Language Use the Day 5 instruction on ELL Poster 3 to monitor children's understanding of the lesson concept.

Amazing Words Provide sentence frames to help children answer the questions in the Check Oral Vocabulary Monitor Progress box. For example: *In the past, animals were ________ as transportation.*

Common Core State Standards

Foundational Skills 2. Demonstrate understanding of spoken words, syllables, and sounds (phonemes). **Foundational Skills 2.c.** Isolate and pronounce initial, medial vowel, and final sounds (phonemes) in spoken single-syllable words. **Foundational Skills 2.d.** Segment spoken single-syllable words into their complete sequence of individual sounds (phonemes). **Foundational Skills 3.b.** Decode regularly spelled one-syllable words. **Language 2.d.** Use conventional spelling for words with common spelling patterns and for frequently occurring irregular words.

Phonemic Awareness

Review Segment and Count Phonemes

SEGMENTING Have children segment each word below and count how many sounds are in the word. If children make an error, model the correct response. Return to the word later in the practice.

rot	/r/ /o/ /t/	(3)	**tell**	/t/ /e/ /l/	(3)	**pond**	/p/ /o/ /n/ /d/	(4)
fib	/f/ /i/ /b/	(3)	**rags**	/r/ /a/ /g/ /z/	(4)	**sock**	/s/ /o/ /k/	(3)
Tim	/t/ /i/ /m/	(3)	**kicks**	/k/ /i/ /k/ /s/	(3)	**dogs**	/d/ /o/ /g/ /z/	(4)

Phonics

Review Short *o: o;* Plural *-s;* Consonant *s/z/*

TARGET PHONICS SKILLS Write the following sentences on the board. Have children read each one, first quietly to themselves and then aloud as you track the print.

1. **Bob got a big box.**
2. **Hogs nap on the cobs.**
3. **Jog on rocks at the top.**
4. **Mom had hot pots.**

Team Talk Have children discuss with a partner which words have short *o* and which words are plurals ending with *-s.* Then call on individuals to share with the class.

Spelling Test

Short *o* Words

DICTATE SPELLING WORDS Say each word, read the sentence, repeat the word, and allow time for children to write the word.

1. hot	The wax is **hot.**
2. hop	**Hop** on the mats.
3. pot	Take the **pot** with you.
4. pop	The jam lid will **pop** up.
5. ox	Is an **ox** big?
6. lock	I see a **lock** on the box.
7. mop	**Mop** it up!
8. got	Rick **got** a tan coat.
9. rock	Sit on top of the **rock.**
10. mom	My **mom** ran up the hill.

High-Frequency Words

11. help	My dad can **help** me.
12. use	Dot can **use** a map.

Assess

- Spell words with short *o.*
- Spell high-frequency words.

Access for All

SI Strategic Intervention

Spelling Words with /l/ If children pronounce /l/ with a vowel-like quality at or near the ends of words, they may not spell *help* with an *l.* Say the word and stress the /l/ sound during dictation.

A Advanced

Extend Spelling Have children learn to spell these more difficult words with short *o* and write them in original sentences: *cannot, laptop, onto, potluck, solid, tomcat.*

Pronunciation Remind children that when we say short *o,* our mouths are open, and our jaws drop. Have children put a hand under their chins as they say the short *o* sound to experience this for themselves.

Day 5 SMALL GROUP TIME • Differentiate Reteaching, p. SG•35

OL On-Level

- **Practice** Predicates of Sentences
- **Reread** *Reading Street Sleuth,* pp. 12–13

SI Strategic Intervention

- **Review** High-Frequency Words
- **Reread** *Reading Street Sleuth,* pp. 12–13

A Advanced

- **Extend** Predicates of Sentences
- **Reread** *Reading Street Sleuth,* pp. 12–13
- **Communicate** Inquiry Project

ELL

If... children need more scaffolding and practice with **Conventions and Writing,**
then... use the activities on pp. DI•62–DI•63 in the Teacher Resources section on SuccessNet.

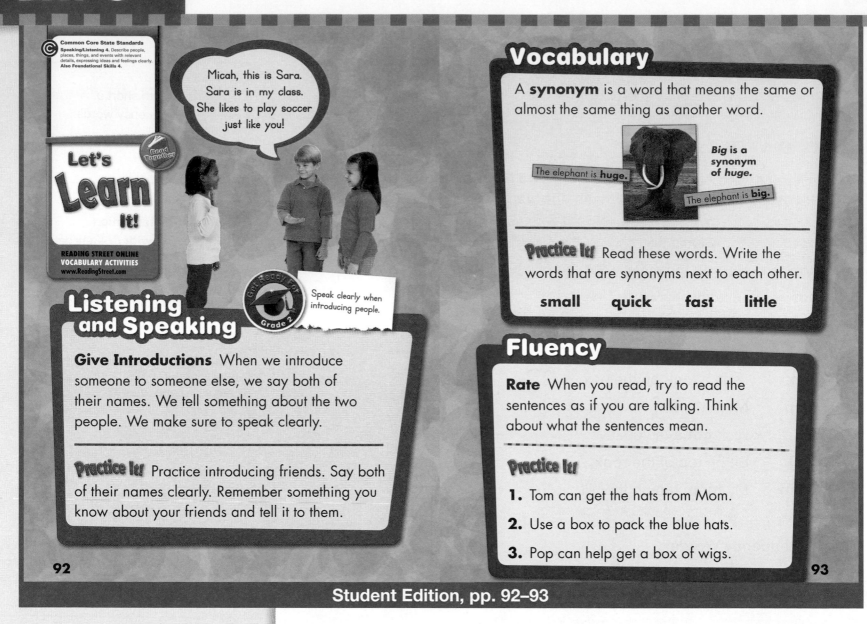

Common Core State Standards
Speaking/Listening 4. Describe people, places, things, and events with relevant details, expressing ideas and feelings clearly. **Also Foundational Skills 4.**

Let's Learn It! Read Together

READING STREET ONLINE
VOCABULARY ACTIVITIES
www.ReadingStreet.com

Micah, this is Sara. Sara is in my class. She likes to play soccer just like you!

Listening and Speaking

Get Ready For Grade 2: Speak clearly when introducing people.

Give Introductions When we introduce someone to someone else, we say both of their names. We tell something about the two people. We make sure to speak clearly.

Practice It! Practice introducing friends. Say both of their names clearly. Remember something you know about your friends and tell it to them.

92

Vocabulary

A **synonym** is a word that means the same or almost the same thing as another word.

***Big* is a synonym of *huge*.**

Practice It! Read these words. Write the words that are synonyms next to each other.

small **quick** **fast** **little**

Fluency

Rate When you read, try to read the sentences as if you are talking. Think about what the sentences mean.

Practice It!

1. Tom can get the hats from Mom.
2. Use a box to pack the blue hats.
3. Pop can help get a box of wigs.

93

Student Edition, pp. 92–93

Common Core State Standards

Foundational Skills 4. Read with sufficient accuracy and fluency to support comprehension. **Speaking/ Listening 4.** Describe people, places, things, and events with relevant details, expressing ideas and feelings clearly. **Also Language 5.d.**

Give Introductions

To prepare themselves for skills needed at 2nd grade, children should be able to speak clearly and slowly when giving introductions. Using complete sentences and an appropriate voice level, they should be able to introduce themselves as well as other people.

Listening and Speaking

Give Introductions

TEACH Have children turn to page 92 of the Student Edition. Read and discuss the introduction in the photo. Point out that the child introduces the two other children by name: Micah and Sara. Ask children why the child tells Micah that Sara likes to play soccer. (Micah likes to play soccer too. This is something they have in common.) Point out the predicates in the sentences. Have children discuss how the predicates help the child give introductions.

INTRODUCE PROMPT Read the Practice It! prompt with the class. Remind children to include the names of their friends in their introductions and to use predicates that tell something about their friends.

Team Talk Have small groups of children take turns introducing friends in the group. Tell children that good speakers speak clearly and slowly, and that good listeners should be able to repeat the information given to them.

Vocabulary

Synonyms

TEACH Read and discuss the Vocabulary lesson on page 93 of the Student Edition. Use the model to explain how synonyms are words that mean the same or almost the same thing as another word. Point to the photo and read the captions underneath. The words *big* and *huge* both describe the elephant. These words mean the same thing. So, *big* is a synonym of *huge.*

GUIDE PRACTICE Read the instructions for the Vocabulary Practice It! activity. Read the first word and then have children repeat after you.

I need to find a synonym for the word *small.* Listen as I read these words: *quick, fast, little.* Which word means the same or almost the same as *small?* *(little)* So, I will say and write the word *little* next to *small.*

ON THEIR OWN Have pairs find and write the synonym for the word *quick.* *(fast)*

Corrective feedback Circulate around the room and listen as children say the synonyms. Provide assistance as needed.

Fluency

Rate

TEACH Read and discuss the Fluency instructions.

READ WORDS IN CONTEXT Give children a moment to look at the sentences. Then have them read each sentence three or four times until they can read each sentence at an appropriate rate.

Access for All

SI Strategic Intervention

Practice Introductions To help children feel more comfortable while giving introductions, have them stand in a circle. Practice introducing yourself to one child. Then have that child practice with the next child in the circle, and so on.

Use a Web For children who are having trouble developing synonyms for the word *small,* create a web on the board and lead a discussion similar to the one in the Day 2 lesson (page 74a).

ELL

Use Sentence Frames Provide this sentence frame to help children structure their understanding of synonyms: ________ *means the same as* ________.

Common Core State Standards

Literature 1. Ask and answer questions about key details in a text. **Informational Text 6.** Distinguish between information provided by pictures or other illustrations and information provided by the words in a text. **Informational Text 7.** Use the illustrations and details in a text to describe its key ideas. **Foundational Skills 3.g.** Recognize and read grade-appropriate irregularly spelled words.

Text-Based Comprehension

Review Character and Setting

Remember that good readers pay attention to the characters and setting because it helps them know what happens in the story. What are characters? (the people and animals in a story) Readers better understand a story when they can describe why a character acts or feels a certain way. What is the setting? (where and when the story takes place)

CHECK UNDERSTANDING Read aloud the following story and have children answer the questions that follow.

Tim shouts, "You're it!" He runs in the green grass in his backyard. Chan runs after him. He wants to tag Tim. Chan and Tim like to play games in Tim's yard. It is fun to run and jump in the grass. They also like to climb Tim's big tree. They want to build a tree house there this year. "Got you!" shouts Chan as he tags Tim.

1. What is the setting of the story? (The setting is Tim's backyard, where there is green grass and a tree.)
2. Why do Tim and Chan like to play in the yard? (Tim and Chan think it is fun to run in the grass and climb the tree.)

Vocabulary

Review High-Frequency and Selection Words

HIGH-FREQUENCY WORDS Review this week's high-frequency words: *blue, help, little, from, use, get.* Create a sentence with the class that includes as many of these words as possible, such as: I will *get* the *little blue* mop to *help* you.

Team Talk Have children orally give their own sentences to a partner that include high-frequency words from the week.

SELECTION WORDS Write the word *town.* Read it aloud together. Then have children tell what the word means.

Corrective feedback	**If...** children cannot tell what the selection word means, **then...** review the definition on page 74a.

Genre

Review Photo Essay

PHOTO ESSAY Review with children that a **photo essay** is a nonfiction selection that uses photographs and words to give information or to entertain. The photographs help readers understand the words.

TEACH In "They Can Help," photographs and words are used to give information. There is a photograph next to each sentence in this photo essay. Let's see how these photographs help readers understand the words.

Think Aloud **MODEL** The first sentence in the selection says "The big dog can help." I'm not sure what that means exactly. How can the big dog help? There are many things that the big dog could do to help. I see a photograph next to this sentence. In the photograph, a big dog is helping a blind man cross the street. This photograph shows me how the big dog can help the man.

GUIDE PRACTICE Ask the following questions to guide children in describing a photo essay and determining how its photographs help readers.

- What do you see on p. 91? (I see a question and three different photographs.) What does the question ask? (In what ways do they help?)
- How do the photographs help you understand the question? (The photographs show animals doing different things to help people. You cannot answer the question without looking at the photographs.)

ON THEIR OWN Have children work with a partner. Discuss the question on p. 91. In what ways does each animal help? (The camel provides transportation for the man. The reindeer pulls a sled. The policemen ride the horses so that they don't have to walk.)

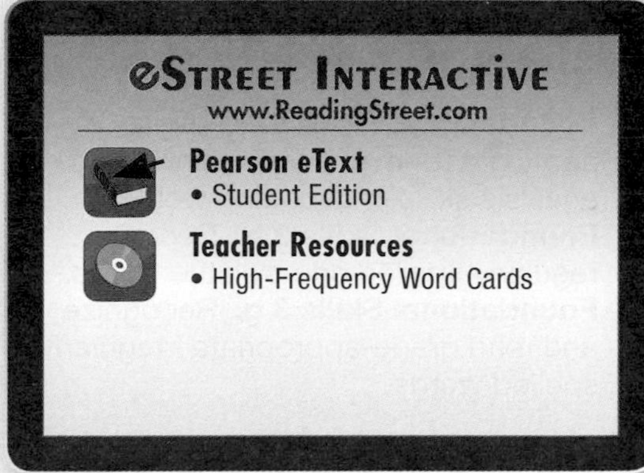

Access for All

SI Strategic Intervention

Understanding Photos If children have difficulty comprehending how the photographs help them understand the words, write the questions from the selection on the board. Ask children to answer the questions without looking at the photographs in the selection. Help them understand that the photographs are necessary.

Academic Vocabulary 

photo essay nonfiction selection that uses photographs and words to provide information or to entertain

Common Core State Standards

Foundational Skills 3. Know and apply grade-level phonics and word analysis skills in decoding words. **Foundational Skills 3.b.** Decode regularly spelled one-syllable words. **Foundational Skills 3.g.** Recognize and read grade-appropriate irregularly spelled words.

Assess

- ⦿ Words with Short *o*
- ⦿ Plural *-s,* Consonant *s*/z/
- • High-Frequency Words

Assessment

Monitor Progress

For a written assessment of short *o, -s* plurals, high-frequency words, and identifying character and setting, use Weekly Test 3, pages 49–54.

WORD READING Use the following reproducible page to assess children's ability to read words in isolation. Call on children to read the words aloud. Start over if necessary.

SENTENCE READING Use the reproducible page on page 93f to assess children's ability to read words in context. Call on children to read two sentences aloud. Start over with sentence one if necessary.

MONITOR ACCURACY Record scores using the Word/Sentence Reading Chart for this unit in *First Stop.*

MONITOR PROGRESS Word and Sentence Reading

If... children have trouble reading words with short *o* and *-s* plurals,
then... use the Reteach Lessons in *First Stop.*

If... a child cannot read all the high-frequency words,
then... mark the missed words on a high-frequency word list and have the child practice reading the words with a fluent reader.

Name ______________________________

Read the Words

1. from
2. pop
3. hot
4. mom
5. logs
6. jobs
7. little
8. get
9. fox
10. help
11. use
12. blue

MONITOR PROGRESS

- Short *o: o*
- Plural *-s;* Consonant *s*/z/
- High-Frequency Words

Name ____________________

Read the Sentences

1. Pop can get the pots.
2. The blue pots are hot.
3. Are the rocks from the box?
4. I have little pots for Mom.
5. Use a box for the rocks.
6. Mom can help fix the rocks.

MONITOR PROGRESS

- Fluency
- Short *o: o*
- Plural *-s;* Consonant *s/z/*
- High-Frequency Words

Conventions

Review Predicates of Sentences

REVIEW Remind children that a predicate is the action part of a sentence. It describes what a person, animal, or thing does. Have children give examples of predicates.

GUIDE PRACTICE Write the following sentences. Have children complete each sentence with a predicate.

1. Dad _______.
2. The pig _______.
3. Bob and Kim _______.

APPLY Display and read the following sentence frame. Have children work in pairs to make up as many predicates as they can that could be used to complete the sentence. Then have children share their responses with the class.

Mom and I _______.

ON THEIR OWN Use Let's Practice It! p. 47 from the *Teacher Resources DVD-ROM.*

The Big Blue Ox

Name ____________

Predicates of Sentences

Circle the action part of each sentence.

1. Nat rides the horse.
2. Mom feeds the ducks.
3. The girl walks her dog.

Look at each picture. **Write** the action part of each sentence.

runs sleeps

4. The cat sleeps

sings flies

5. The bird sings

swims eats

6. The dog eats

Home Activity Your child reviewed action parts of sentences. Have your child write on index cards the action parts of the sentences on the page. Take turns choosing a card and using the action part in a new sentence.

Conventions Predicates of Sentences DVD•47

Let's Practice It! TR DVD•47

Common Core State Standards

Language 1.j. Produce and expand complete simple and compound declarative, interrogative, imperative, and exclamatory sentences in response to prompts. **Language 2.** Demonstrate command of the conventions of standard English capitalization, punctuation, and spelling when writing.

Daily Fix-It

9. ox can use Pots.
   Ox can use pots.
10. Pop got the lox
    Pop got the locks.

Discuss the Daily Fix-It corrections with children. Review sentence capitalization and punctuation, and /ks/ spelled *cks.*

Common Core State Standards

Writing 5. With guidance and support from adults, focus on a topic, respond to questions and suggestions from peers, and add details to strengthen writing as needed. **Language 1.j.** Produce and expand complete simple and compound declarative, interrogative, imperative, and exclamatory sentences in response to prompts. **Also Writing 6.**

Bridge to Common Core

PRODUCTION AND DISTRIBUTION OF WRITING

As children create a final draft of their poem, the revision reflects the changes they made in order to produce a poem with the correct punctuation and capitalization. They then can choose to draw a picture for their poem to share or assemble the poems in a classroom anthology.

Writing

Zoom in on ©

Short Poem

REVIEW REVISING Remind children that yesterday they revised their poems. They may have changed words to make it easier to picture the animal described in their poems. Today they will proofread their poems.

Mini-Lesson Proofread

Proofread for Sentences

- **Teach** In our poems, if we capitalize and punctuate the sentences correctly, readers will know where the sentences begin and end. When we proofread, we check to make sure the sentences are correct. We also check to make sure the words are spelled correctly.

Proofreading Marks			
Take Out	~	Uppercase letter	≡
Add	^	Lowercase letter	/
Period	⊙	New paragraph	¶
Check spelling	◯	Insert apostrophe	∨

Puppy Love

Freddie is a floppy pup⊙

He wags his tail and (chers) me up.

cheers

Unit 1 The Big Blue Ox — Writing: Proofread 3C

Writing Transparency 3C TR DVD

- **Model** Let's look at my poem about Freddie. Display Writing Transparency 3C. I'm going to make sure that each sentence begins with a capital letter and ends with punctuation. Look: I did not end the first sentence with a period. Even though the second sentence begins a new line, I still need to end the first sentence with a period. Add the period on the transparency. I will also check that the words are spelled correctly. I don't think I spelled *cheers* correctly. I can look up the spelling and find out. Show how to check the spelling of *cheers* in a classroom dictionary or word list and write the correct spelling on the transparency.

PROOFREAD Display the Proofreading Tips. Have children proofread their poems to correct any misspellings, missing capital letters, or errors with periods. Circulate to assist children.

Proofreading Tips

- ✔ Do my sentences begin with a capital letter?
- ✔ Did I use periods correctly?
- ✔ Did I capitalize any names?
- ✔ Are descriptive words spelled correctly?

PRESENT Have children use a computer to make a final draft of their poems, with their revisions and proofreading corrections. Help as appropriate.

Choose an option for children to present their poems.

Draw a picture of their animal.	Assemble their poems in a classroom anthology.

When children have finished writing their short poems, give them a copy of About My Writing, p. RR45 of the *Reader's and Writer's Notebook*. Then have children evaluate their writing by answering the questions on the page.

Routine Quick Write for Fluency

Team Talk

1. **Talk** Have partners take one minute to choose and discuss an animal.
2. **Write** Each child writes a short sentence using the animal as the subject.
3. **Share** Partners identify the predicates of each other's sentences.

Routines Flip Chart

ELL

Support Editing For children to whom the sounds and spelling of English still are not very familiar, look for spelling improvement little by little from week to week rather than rapid development. Help children make progress a word at a time and learn word meanings.

Common Core State Standards

Writing 7. Participate in shared research and writing projects (e.g., explore a number of "how-to" books on a given topic and use them to write a sequence of instructions). **Writing 8.** With guidance and support from adults, recall information from experiences or gather information from provided sources to answer a question. **Speaking/Listening 4.** Describe people, places, things, and events with relevant details, expressing ideas and feelings clearly. **Speaking/Listening 5.** Add drawings or other visual displays to descriptions when appropriate to clarify ideas, thoughts, and feelings.

Research and Inquiry

Step 5 Communicate

TEACH Tell children that today they will create a class mural that tells about their topic.

Think Aloud **MODEL** Display a list of facts about the topic that could be illustrated. I will review the facts I gathered and circle the one I would like to illustrate. My topic was how dogs help people. I learned that dogs can be trained to press a button on the telephone to help sick people who need an ambulance. I would like to draw a picture of a dog pressing this button on a telephone. That will be part of my mural.

GUIDE PRACTICE Review children's topics and facts. Work with them to combine their information and represent it as a class mural.

ON THEIR OWN Have children share with the class the part of the mural that they illustrated. Instruct them to explain their illustration and describe how it represents animals helping people. Remind them how to be good speakers and listeners:

- Good speakers use subjects and predicates in their sentences, and speak slowly and clearly.
- Good listeners should be able to repeat the information they hear.

Wrap Up Your Week!

Animals That Help

How do animals help people?

Think Aloud This week we explored how animals helped people in the past and how they help people today. In the story *The Big Blue Ox,* we read about an ox that does many different things for a family on a farm. In the Big Book *A Kid's Best Friend,* we read about how dogs are helpful, and we saw pictures of dogs caring for kids. The animals in both selections help people in different ways.

Team Talk Have children recall their Amazing Ideas about how animals help people. Then have children use these ideas to help them demonstrate their understanding of the Question of the Week, *How do animals help people?*

You've learned 009 words this week!

You've learned 072 words this year!

Next Week's Concept

Wild Animals and Their Babies

How do wild animals take care of their babies?

ELL

Poster Preview Prepare children for next week by using Unit 1, Week 4, ELL Poster 4. Read the Poster Talk-Through to introduce the concept and vocabulary. Ask children to identify and describe objects and actions in the art.

Selection Summary Send home the summary from the *ELL Handbook* of *A Fox and a Kit* in English and the child's home language if available. Children can read the summary with family members.

Tell children that next week they will read more about animals and how we can learn from watching them.

Preview Next Week

Assessment Checkpoints for the Week

Weekly Assessment

Use pp. 49–54 of *Weekly Tests* to check:

✔ **Phonics** Short *o: o*

✔ **Phonics** Plural *-s;* Consonant Pattern *s/z/*

✔ **Comprehension** Character and Setting

✔ **High-Frequency Words**

blue	help
from	little
get	use

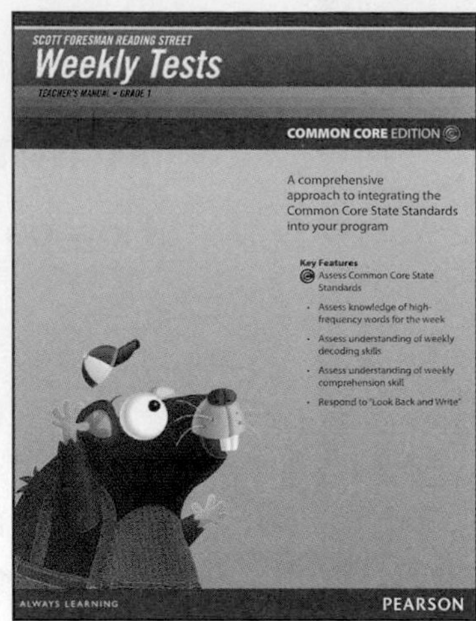

Weekly Tests

Differentiated Assessment

Advanced

On-Level

Strategic Intervention

Use pp. 49–54 of *Fresh Reads for Fluency and Comprehension* to check:

✔ **Comprehension** Character and Setting

✔ Review **Comprehension** Plot

Fresh Reads for Fluency and Comprehension

Managing Assessment

Use *Assessment Handbook* for:

✔ **Weekly Assessment Blackline Masters for Monitoring Progress**

✔ **Observation Checklists**

✔ **Record-Keeping Forms**

✔ **Portfolio Assessment**

Assessment Handbook

DAY 1 Differentiate Phonics

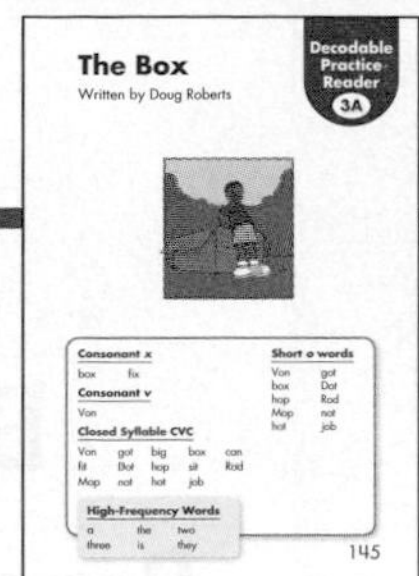
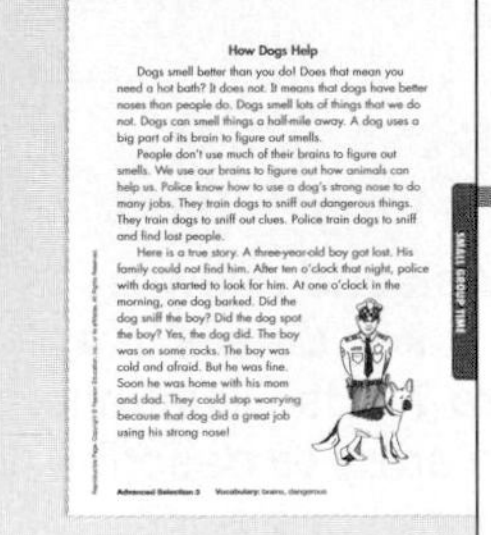

- Short *o: o*
- Decodable Practice Reader
- Advanced Selection "How Dogs Help"
- **Inquiry** Identify Questions

DAY 2 Differentiate Comprehension

- Plural *-s;* Consonant *s/z/*
- **Access Text** Read *The Big Blue Ox*
- **Inquiry** Investigate

DAY 3 Differentiate Close Reading

- Develop Vocabulary
- **Close Reading** Read *The Big Blue Ox*
- **Inquiry** Investigate

"A Horse Named Chester" pp. 12–13

DAY 4 Differentiate Vocabulary

- Develop Language
- "A Horse Named Chester" or Leveled Readers
- **Inquiry** Organize

DAY 5 Differentiate Reteaching

- Phonics and High-Frequency Words
- Conventions
- "A Horse Named Chester" or Leveled Readers
- **Inquiry** Communicate

Teacher Guides and Student pages can be found in the Leveled Reader Database.

ELL Place English Language Learners in the groups that correspond to their reading abilities.
If... children need scaffolding and practice,
then... use the ELL notes on the page.

Independent Practice

Independent Practice Stations

See pp. 66h and 66i for Independent Stations.

Pearson Trade Book Library

See the Leveled Reader Database for Lesson Plans and student pages.

Reading Street Digital Path

Independent Practice Activities available in the Digital Path.

Independent Reading

See p. 66i for independent reading suggestions.

On-Level

Common Core State Standards

Literature 1. Ask and answer questions about key details in a text. **Literature 7.** Use illustrations and details in a story to describe its characters, setting, or events. **Foundational Skills 3.** Know and apply grade-level phonics and word analysis skills in decoding words. **Also Foundational Skills 3.b., 3.g, 4.a.**

1 Build Word Knowledge

Practice Phonics

SHORT *o*: *o* Write the following words and have children practice reading words with short *o.*

not **mop** **log** **sock**

Spelling

SHORT *o* WORDS Remind children that each spelling word has the letter *o,* which spells the /o/ sound. Clarify the pronunciation and meaning of each word. For example, say: *Pop* is a sudden loud sound. Have children identify whether the letter *o* is at the beginning or in the middle of these words: *hot, ox, got, rock, mom, lock.*

2 Read

Decodable Reader 3A *The Box*

HIGH-FREQUENCY WORDS Have children read the decodable reader. Then have them reread the text to develop automaticity. Have children return to the text and find the previously taught high-frequency words. Help children demonstrate their understanding of the words. Provide sentence frames such as:
I have _______ eyes. (two)

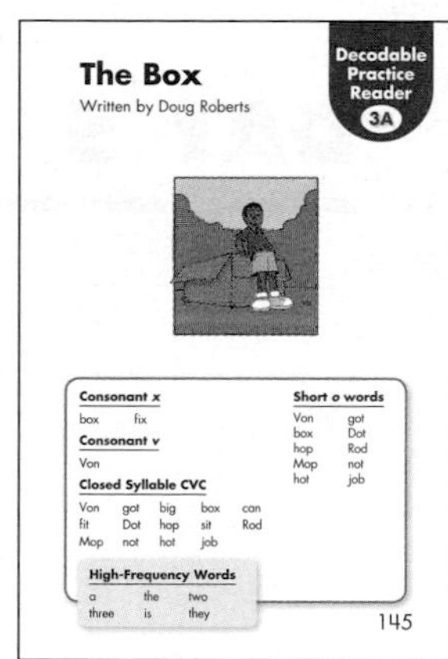

ELL

If... children need more scaffolding and practice with phonics,
then... use the Phonics Transition Lessons on pp. 249–345 in the *ELL Handbook.*

OL

On-Level

1 Build Word Knowledge

Practice Phonics

PLURAL *-s*; CONSONANT *s/z/* Write the following words and have children practice reading words with the /s/ and /z/ sounds.

locks **fins** **caps** **wigs**

2 Read

The Big Blue Ox

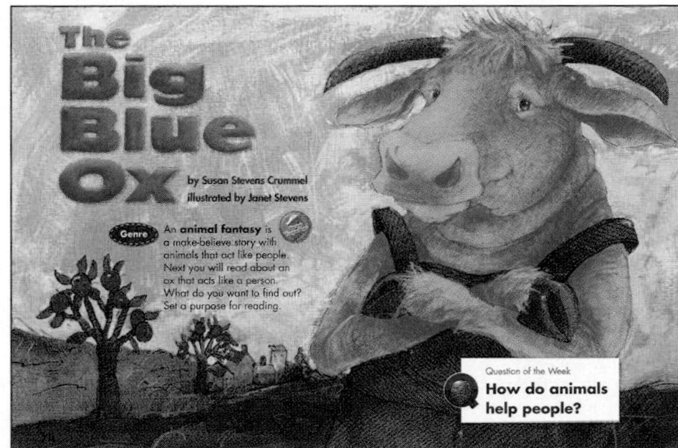
The Big Blue Ox
by Susan Stevens Crummel
illustrated by Janet Stevens
Genre
An animal fantasy is a make-believe story with animals that act like people. Next you will read about an ox that acts like a person. What do you want to find out? Set a purpose for reading.
Question of the Week
How do animals help people?

If you read *The Big Blue Ox* during whole group time, then use the following instruction.

ACCESS TEXT Have children look at the picture on p. 82. Reread the sentences.

- Look at page 82. What do you see in the picture? (Ox, fans, stove, pan, apples, apron, mitt)
- Why is Ox hot? (He is cooking over a hot stove.)
- What does Ox do to cool down? (He turns on some fans.)
- Reread the sentence that tells you this.
- Why is Ox wearing a mitt? (The pan is hot.)

If you are reading *The Big Blue Ox* during small group time, then return to pp. 74b–83a to guide the reading.

eSTREET INTERACTIVE
www.ReadingStreet.com
Pearson eText
• Student Edition
• Decodable Reader

SMALL GROUP TIME

Independent Reading Options

Trade Book Library

eSTREET INTERACTIVE
www.ReadingStreet.com

Teacher's Guides available on the Leveled Reader Database.

OL

On-Level

Common Core State Standards

Literature 1. Ask and answer questions about key details in a text. **Literature 7.** Use illustrations and details in a story to describe its characters, setting, or events. **Speaking/Listening 1.** Participate in collaborative conversations about grade 1 topics and texts with peers and adults in small and larger groups. **Also Language 6.**

1 Build Word Knowledge

Develop Vocabulary

REREAD FOR VOCABULARY Have children reread *The Big Blue Ox,* p. 79.

Read the following sentence and discuss words related to cleaning. (mop)

Mop the pigs.

- What word on this page means the same as cleaning the pigs? *(mop)*
- What are some other words that mean the same as cleaning? (clean, wipe, wash, scrub, sweep)

2 Read

The Big Blue Ox

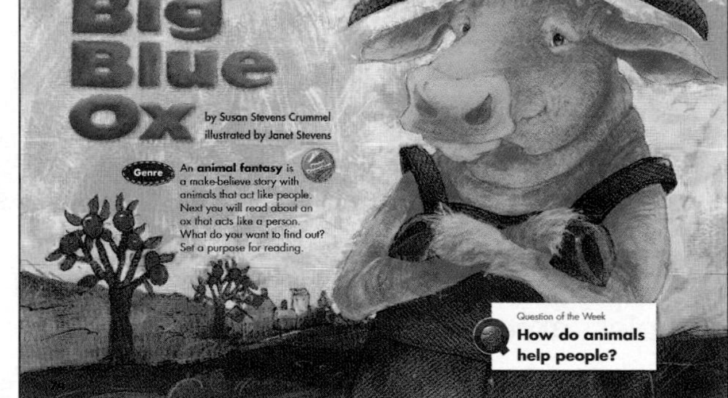
The Big Blue Ox
by Susan Stevens Crummel
illustrated by Janet Stevens
Genre
An animal fantasy is a make-believe story with animals that act like people. Next you will read about an ox that acts like a person. What do you want to find out? Set a purpose for reading.
Question of the Week
How do animals help people?

If you read *The Big Blue Ox* during whole group time, then use the following instruction.

CLOSE READING Reread pp. 80–82. Have children summarize the ideas presented on these pages. Ask questions to guide deeper understanding.

- How does Ox help Mom and Pop? (gives them rides, packs cans, cooks)
- Do you think Ox helps only a little or a lot? Why? (Ox helps a lot because he does many things for Mom and Pop.)
- How do the things Ox does help Mom and Pop? (They don't have to do them. Mom and Pop can do other things.)

Have children think of one more thing that Ox can do to help Mom and Pop. (Ox can clean. Ox can wash. Ox can sweep. Ox can cut the grass.)

If you are reading *The Big Blue Ox* during small group time, then return to pp. 74–83 to guide the reading.

ELL

If... children need more scaffolding and practice with the main selection, **then...** use the activities on p. DI•60 in the Teacher Resources section on SuccessNet.

On-Level

1 Build Word Knowledge

Practice Selection Vocabulary

Team Talk **LANGUAGE DEVELOPMENT** Have children practice using the selection vocabulary. Ask questions such as: Mom and Pop ride on Ox's back. Where do they go? What kinds of things can you do in town? Turn and talk to your partner about why Mom and Pop go to town. Be prepared to explain your answers.

town

Allow children time to discuss the word *town.* Ask for examples or rephrase for usage when necessary or to correct for understanding. Use the Student Edition to provide visual support.

2 Text-Based Comprehension

READ ALOUD "A Horse Named Chester" Lead children in a choral reading of "A Horse Named Chester" from *Reading Street Sleuth,* pp. 12–13. Then have partners take turns reading the paragraphs of the selection.

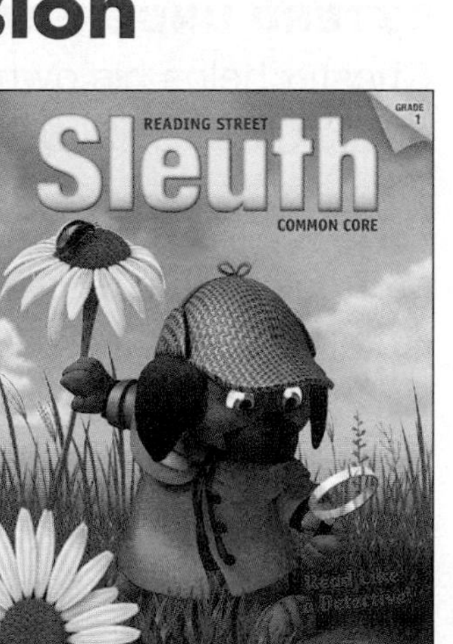

ACCESS TEXT Guide children as they work on the Be a Sleuth section.

Look for Clues Ask children to think about what Chester does for his owner. Ask them if they can think of any other ways Chester may be helpful. How does this help explain why the author wrote about service horses?

Ask Questions Create a list of children's interests about service horses. Have children choose one interest and create a question. Then discuss where they could find information to answer the question.

Make Your Case Have children make a list of things a service dog can do and things a service horse can do. Help them explore books or other sources to gather more information to make a choice. Then have them tell what they decided and present their case with reasons to the group.

eSTREET INTERACTIVE
www.ReadingStreet.com

Pearson eText
- Student Edition
- *Reading Street Sleuth*
- Leveled Reader Database

SMALL GROUP TIME

More Reading for Group Time

Where They Live
by Kristin Cashore
illustrated by Bob Brugger

ON-LEVEL

Reviews
- Concept Vocabulary
- Character and Setting

Use this suggested Leveled Reader or other text at children's instructional level.

eSTREET INTERACTIVE
www.ReadingStreet.com

Use the Leveled Reader Database for lesson plans and student pages for *Where They Live.*

On-Level

Common Core State Standards

Informational Text 1. Ask and answer questions about key details in a text. **Foundational Skills 2.b.** Orally produce single-syllable words by blending sounds (phonemes), including consonant blends. **Foundational Skills 3.** Know and apply grade-level phonics and word analysis skills in decoding words. **Language 1.** Demonstrate command of the conventions of standard English grammar and usage when writing or speaking. **Also Foundational Skills 2.c., 4.a., Speaking/ Listening 1.a., 3., 4.**

More Reading for Group Time

ON-LEVEL

Reviews
- Concept Vocabulary
- Character and Setting

Use this suggested Leveled Reader or other text at children's instructional level.

eStreet Interactive
www.ReadingStreet.com

Use the Leveled Reader Database for lesson plans and student pages for *Where They Live.*

1 Build Word Knowledge

Practice Predicates of Sentences

REVIEW If needed, revisit the conventions lesson on p. 83c.

IDENTIFY PREDICATES OF SENTENCES Have children turn to "A Horse Named Chester" to identify the predicates of sentences in the selection. Have children work in groups to identify as many predicates as they can.

2 Text-Based Comprehension

REREAD "A Horse Named Chester" Have partners reread "A Horse Named Chester."

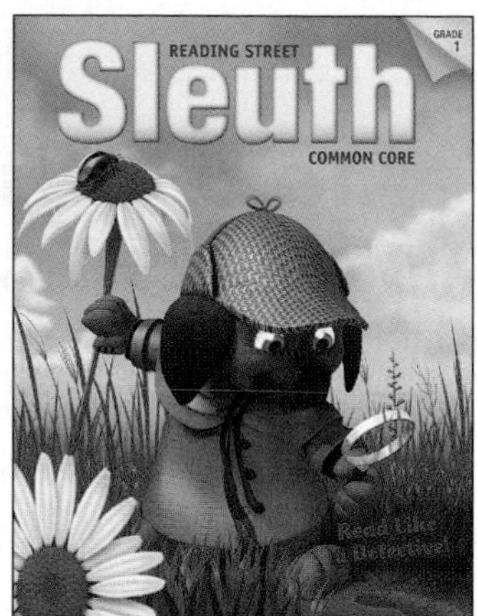

EXTEND UNDERSTANDING Talk about the ways Chester helps his owner, Mike. Ask children how difficult Mike's life would be without Chester.

PERFORMANCE TASK • Prove It! Have small groups prepare a short play that shows a day in the life of a service horse. Help children brainstorm ideas for the play, such as crossing a busy street or going to a store. Have children use the text and other references to prepare their play.

COMMUNICATE Have the groups present their plays to the class. Encourage children to ask questions after each performance.

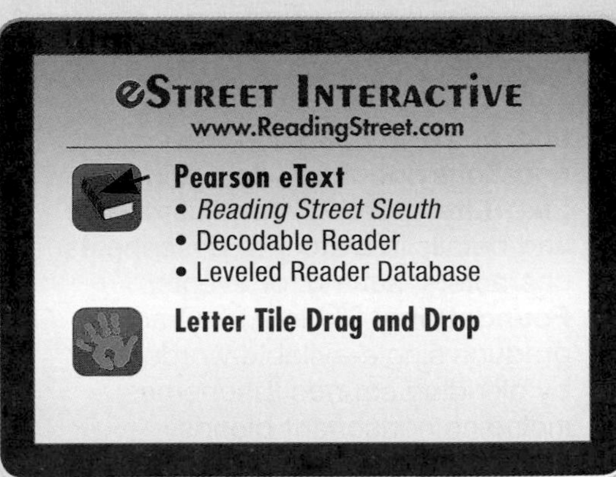

1 Build Word Knowledge

Reteach Phonemic Awareness

Reteach the lesson on p. 68–69 to distinguish /o/. Use these additional practice items.

box fox hot sob

Reteach Phonics

SHORT *o: o* Reteach the lesson on p. 69a, short *o: o.* Use these additional practice words to blend.

dot jot pop got rod

Have children spell *hop* using letter tiles. What word did you spell? Let's change a letter to make a new word and then read our new word.

- Change the *h* in *hop* to *m.* What is the new word? m o p
- Change the *m* in *mop* to *p.* What is the new word? p o p

2 Read

Decodable Reader 3A *The Box*

DECODE WORDS Have children practice reading the words listed on p. 145.

Corrective feedback	**If...** children have difficulty reading the words independently, **then...** reteach the words prior to reading Decodable Reader 3A.

READ IN CONTEXT Have children take turns reading a page in *The Box.* Have them reread the text several times to ensure accuracy.

Corrective feedback	**If...** children have difficulty reading the story independently, **then...** model reading a page and have children echo you.

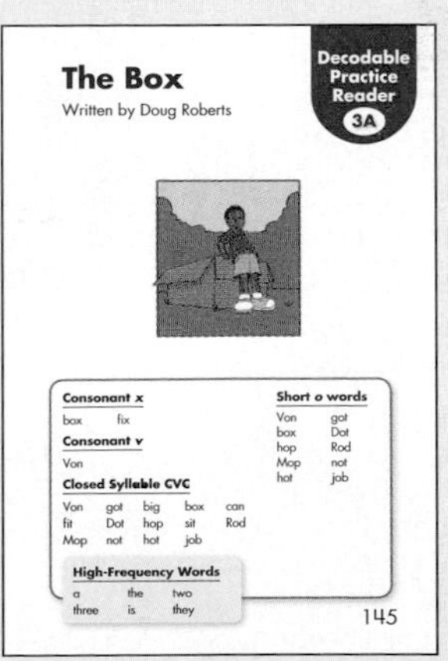

3 Reread for Fluency

Have children reread the text to develop automaticity in their reading.

SMALL GROUP TIME

ELL

If... children need more scaffolding and practice with phonemic awareness and phonics, **then...** use the Phonics Transition Lessons on pp. 249–345 in the *ELL Handbook.*

SI
Strategic Intervention

Common Core State Standards

Literature 1. Ask and answer questions about key details in a text. **Literature 7.** Use illustrations and details in a story to describe its characters, setting, or events. **Foundational Skills 2.b.** Orally produce single-syllable words by blending sounds (phonemes), including consonant blends. **Foundational Skills 3.** Know and apply grade-level phonics and word analysis skills in decoding words.

1 Build Word Knowledge

Reteach Phonemic Awareness

Reteach the lesson on p. 72c to segment and blend phonemes. Use these additional practice items: *sock–socks, hat–hats, sip–sips.*

Reteach Phonics

PLURAL *-s;* CONSONANT *s/z/* Reteach the lesson on p. 72d to model consonant *s*/z/. Use these additional words to blend: *bits, mops, cots, caps, tins.*

Have children spell *docks* using letter tiles. Monitor their work.

- Change the *d* in *docks* to *r.* What is the new word? r o c k s
- Change the *ck* in *rocks* to *d.* What is the new word? r o d s
- Change the *r* in *rods* to *p.* What is the new word? p o d s

2 Read

The Big Blue Ox

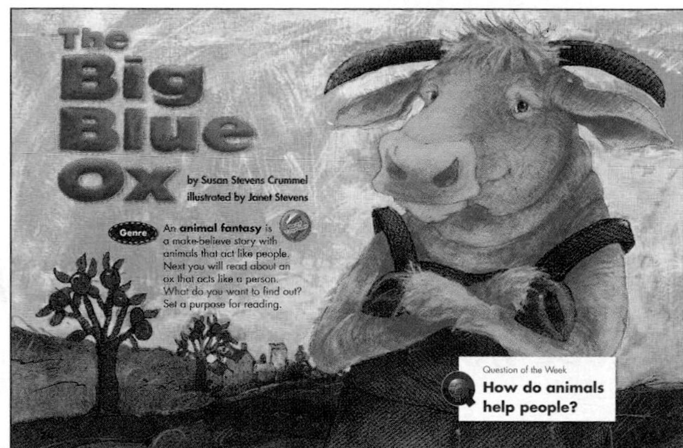
The Big Blue Ox
by Susan Stevens Crummel
illustrated by Janet Stevens
Genre
An animal fantasy is a make-believe story with animals that act like people. Next you will read about an ox that acts like a person. What do you want to find out? Set a purpose for reading.
Question of the Week
How do animals help people?

If you read *The Big Blue Ox* during whole group time, then use the instruction below.

ACCESS TEXT Have children look at the picture on p. 79. Reread the sentences.

- Look at page 79. What do you see in the picture? (Ox, mop, pigs, wigs, mud)
- What is Ox holding? (a mop)
- What is he doing with the mop? (cleaning the pigs)
- Do you think the pigs like being mopped? What clues in the picture tell you that? (Yes. The pigs are smiling.)
- Why do the pigs need to fix their wigs? (The mop messes them up.)

If you are reading *The Big Blue Ox* during small group time, then return to pp. 74b–83a to guide the reading.

Corrective feedback | **If...** children have difficulty understanding the section, **then...** read the section aloud using the Access Text Notes.

Independent Reading Options

Trade Book Library

eSTREET INTERACTIVE
www.ReadingStreet.com

Teacher's Guides available on the Leveled Reader Database.

SI

Strategic Intervention

eStreet Interactive
www.ReadingStreet.com
Pearson eText
• Student Edition
Letter Tile Drag and Drop

1 Build Word Knowledge

Reteach Phonemic Awareness

Reteach the activity on p. 84c to model words that rhyme. Use these additional practice items: *hot/tot; pop/shop/hop; clock/sock.*

Reteach Phonics

Write these short *o* words and -*s* plural words and have children blend them with you: *dot/dots, pod/pods, mop/mops, lot/lots, rod/rods, pot/pots.*

2 Read

The Big Blue Ox

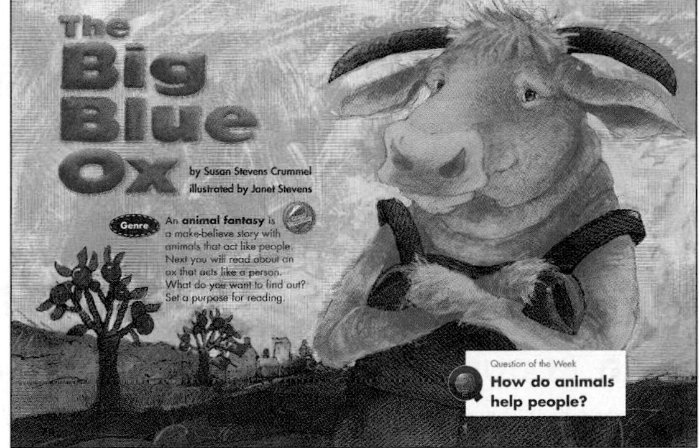
The Big Blue Ox
by Susan Stevens Crummel
illustrated by Janet Stevens
Genre
An animal fantasy is a make-believe story with animals that act like people. Next you will read about an ox that acts like a person. What do you want to find out? Set a purpose for reading.
Question of the Week
How do animals help people?

If you read *The Big Blue Ox* during whole group time, then use the instruction below.

CLOSE READING Reread p. 81. Let's read this page to find out what Ox is doing. To help children understand what Ox is doing, ask questions related to the text and picture.

- Why does *Pack the sack* mean? (Put the cans in the sack.)
- Why does Ox put cans in the sack? (to help Mom and Pop; to make the cans easier to carry)
- Where does Ox take the sack after he packs it? (takes it back; takes it home)
- Which sentence tells you that Ox takes the sack home? (Take it back.)

Corrective feedback	**If...** children have trouble answering questions about the text and picture on p. 81, **then...** reread the page and have them fill in sentence frames to summarize the ideas. **Ox gets the ______ and puts them in the ______. Then he takes the sack ______.**

If you are reading *The Big Blue Ox* during small group time, then return to pp. 74–83 to guide the reading.

SMALL GROUP TIME

ELL

If... children need scaffolding and practice with the main selection, **then...** use the activities on p. DI•60 in the Teacher Resources section on SuccessNet.

Strategic Intervention

Common Core State Standards

Informational Text 1. Ask and answer questions about key details in a text. **Foundational Skills 3.g.** Recognize and read grade-appropriate irregularly spelled words. **Speaking/Listening 1.** Participate in collaborative conversations about grade 1 topics and texts with peers and adults in small and larger groups. **Language 5.c.** Identify real-life connections between words and their use (e.g., note places at home that are *cozy*). **Also Speaking/Listening 1.a., 4.**

More Reading for Group Time

CONCEPT LITERACY

Practice
- Concept Words
- High-Frequency Words

BELOW LEVEL

Review
- Character and Setting
- High-Frequency Words

Use these suggested Leveled Readers or other text at children's instructional level.

eSTREET INTERACTIVE
www.ReadingStreet.com

Use the Leveled Reader Database for lesson plans and student pages for *Animals Help* and *On the Farm.*

1 Build Word Knowledge

Review Selection Vocabulary

SEE IT/SAY IT/HEAR IT Write *town.* Scan across the word with your finger as you say it: town. Use the word in a sentence. I live in a big **town.**

town

DEFINE IT How would you tell a friend what the word *town* means? Give an explanation if necessary. A *town* is a place with a lot of houses and buildings. Restate the explanation in child-friendly terms. A *town* is a place with a lot of houses, buildings, and people. Many people work and live in *towns.*

Team Talk Who do you know who lives in a town? What do you like about that town? Turn to your partner and talk about this. Allow time for children to discuss. Ask for examples. Rephrase their examples for usage when necessary or to correct misunderstandings.

2 Text-Based Comprehension

READ ALOUD "A Horse Named Chester" Read "A Horse Named Chester" aloud from *Reading Street Sleuth,* pp. 12–13 as children follow along.

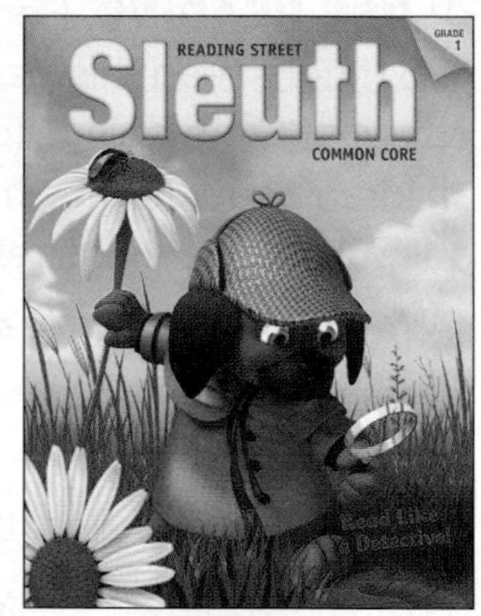

ACCESS TEXT Guide children as they work on the Be a Sleuth section.

Look for Clues Remind children that authors write for different reasons. Look through the text with children and ask them to identify any details they find about service horses that indicate the author's purpose.

Ask Questions Create a list of questions with children of things about service horses that interest them. Then have them discuss where they can find more information to answer the questions.

Make Your Case Ask children to compare several things a service dog and a service horse can do, such as leading the person, finding the way, or crossing the street. Tell children to think about what each animal does and decide which ones would be better helpers. Ask them to tell which animal they chose and why it was their choice.

1 Build Word Knowledge

Review High-Frequency Words

Use the routine on p. 71 to review *blue, help, little, from, use,* and *get.*

Corrective feedback	**If...** children have difficulty with any of these words, **then...** tell them the word and have them repeat it. Have children spell the word and tell what word they spelled. Have them practice in pairs with word cards.

2 Text-Based Comprehension

REREAD "A Horse Named Chester" Reread "A Horse Named Chester" aloud as children follow along.

EXTEND UNDERSTANDING Talk together about the selection. Ask children to think of all the ways Chester helps his owner, Mike. Ask children how difficult Mike's life would be without Chester. Remind children that Mike cannot see.

PERFORMANCE TASK • Prove It! Have small groups prepare a short play that shows one way a service horse helps, such as crossing a busy street or going to a store. Have children use the text to help them prepare the play.

COMMUNICATE Have groups present their plays to the class.

SMALL GROUP TIME

More Reading for Group Time

CONCEPT LITERACY

Practice
- Concept Words
- High-Frequency Words

BELOW LEVEL

Review
- Character and Setting
- High-Frequency Words

Use these suggested Leveled Readers or other text at children's instructional level.

eSTREET INTERACTIVE
www.ReadingStreet.com

Use the Leveled Reader Database for lesson plans and student pages for *Animals Help* and *On the Farm.*

Advanced

Common Core State Standards

Informational Text 1. Ask and answer questions about key details in a text. **Informational Text 2.** Identify the main topic and retell key details of a text. **Foundational Skills 3.** Know and apply grade-level phonics and word analysis skills in decoding words. **Speaking/Listening 1.** Participate in collaborative conversations about grade 1 topics and texts with peers and adults in small and larger groups. **Also Language 4.**

1 Build Word Knowledge

Extend Phonics

SHORT *o: o* Have children practice with more complex words. Discuss the meanings of unfamiliar words and have children spell each word with letter tiles. Then have children use the words in sentences.

drop	**clock**	**chomp**	**knob**	**blond**
copy	**body**	**oxen**	**closet**	**robot**

2 Read

"How Dogs Help"

TEACH VOCABULARY Before reading, introduce the story words: *brains, dangerous.* Help children determine the meaning of each word using these sentences:

1. We use **brains** to think. Our **brains** are in our heads.
2. A policeman's job can be very **dangerous.**

READ Have children read "How Dogs Help" silently. Then have children take turns reading aloud. After reading, have children recall the two most important ideas of the selection using details from the text.

3 Inquiry: Extend Concepts

IDENTIFY QUESTIONS Have children read and compare two other selections about real or fictional animals that help people. On Day 5, children will share their comparisons. Guide children in making their choices.

- Look through the stories before you begin to read. How do you predict the animal in each story will help people?

If... children need practice with phonics,
then... use the Phonics Transition Lessons on pp. 249–345 in the *ELL Handbook.*

How Dogs Help

Dogs smell better than you do! Does that mean you need a hot bath? It does not. It means that dogs have better noses than people do. Dogs smell lots of things that we do not. Dogs can smell things a half-mile away. A dog uses a big part of its brain to figure out smells.

People don't use much of their brains to figure out smells. We use our brains to figure out how animals can help us. Police know how to use a dog's strong nose to do many jobs. They train dogs to sniff out dangerous things. They train dogs to sniff out clues. Police train dogs to sniff and find lost people.

Here is a true story. A three-year-old boy got lost. His family could not find him. After ten o'clock that night, police with dogs started to look for him. At one o'clock in the morning, one dog barked. Did the dog sniff the boy? Did the dog spot the boy? Yes, the dog did. The boy was on some rocks. The boy was cold and afraid. But he was fine. Soon he was home with his mom and dad. They could stop worrying because that dog did a great job using his strong nose!

Advanced Selection 3 **Vocabulary:** brains, dangerous

A

Advanced

Common Core State Standards

Literature 1. Ask and answer questions about key details in a text. **Literature 3.** Describe characters, settings, and major events in a story, using key details. **Literature 7.** Use illustrations and details in a story to describe its characters, setting, or events. **Foundational Skills 3.** Know and apply grade-level phonics and word analysis skills in decoding words. **Also Foundational Skills 3.b., Writing 7., Speaking/Listening 1., Language 5.a.**

1 Build Word Knowledge

Extend Phonics

***-s* PLURALS** Have children practice with additional plural words. Discuss the meanings of unfamiliar words with children. Then have them write the words on cards and turn each card facedown. Next, have partners take turns selecting a card and using that word in a sentence. Point out that some plurals are formed by adding *-es.*

letters	pencils	students	umbrellas	animals
horses	wishes	branches	watches	tadpoles

2 Read

The Big Blue Ox

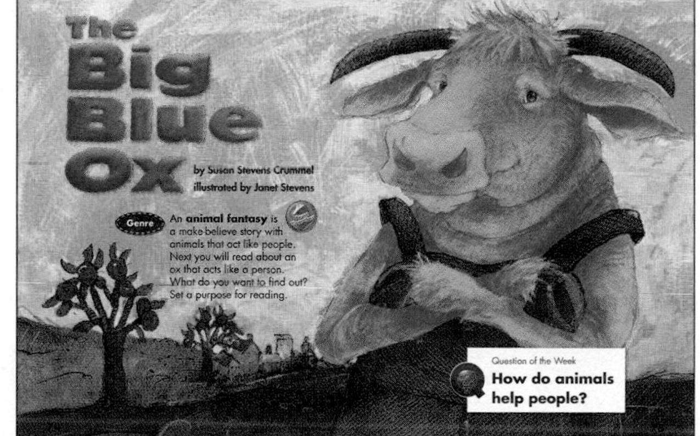
The Big Blue Ox
by Susan Stevens Crummel
illustrated by Janet Stevens
Genre
An animal fantasy is a make-believe story with animals that act like people. Next you will read about an ox that acts like a person. What do you want to find out? Set a purpose for reading.
Question of the Week
How do animals help people?

If you read *The Big Blue Ox* during whole group time, then use the instruction below.

ACCESS TEXT Have children silently reread *The Big Blue Ox,* retell the selection, and identify the plot. (Beginning: The Ox helps Mom and Pop. Middle: Mom, Pop, and Ox go to town. End: The Ox cooks, and they all nap.)

DISCUSS GENRE Discuss what makes *The Big Blue Ox* an animal fantasy. Point out that this story is about an animal that acts like a person.

If you are reading *The Big Blue Ox* during small group time, then return to pp. 74b–83a to guide the reading.

3 Inquiry: Extend Concepts

INVESTIGATE Guide children in choosing materials at their independent reading levels.

LOOK AHEAD Encourage children to make notes or drawings that help them remember each selection's setting, characters, and main ideas or events.

Independent Reading Options

Trade Book Library

eStreet Interactive
www.ReadingStreet.com

Teacher's Guides available on the Leveled Reader Database.

Advanced

eSTREET INTERACTIVE
www.ReadingStreet.com
Pearson eText
• Student Edition

1 Build Word Knowledge

Develop Vocabulary

REREAD FOR VOCABULARY Have children reread *The Big Blue Ox* and make a three-column chart listing the words that name living things, words that name nonliving things, and describing words.

Living		Nonliving		Describing
Ox	Pop	wigs	sack	big
Mom	Pigs	mop	pans	blue
		cans	fans	hot

2 Read

The Big Blue Ox

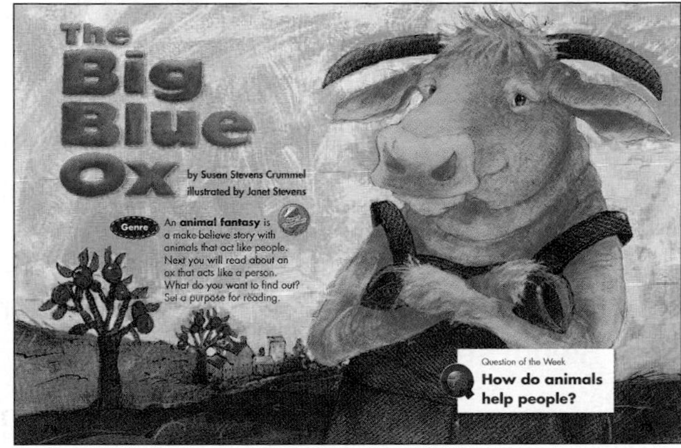
The Big Blue Ox
by Susan Stevens Crummel
illustrated by Janet Stevens
Genre
An animal fantasy is a make-believe story with animals that act like people. Next you will read about an ox that acts like a person. What do you want to find out? Set a purpose for reading.
Question of the Week
How do animals help people?

If you read *The Big Blue Ox* during whole group time, then use the instruction below.

CLOSE READING Reread pp. 77–79. Have children look at the pictures on the pages. Look at page 77. What is Ox doing? (He is digging.) What is he using to dig with? (shovel) Look at pages 78–79. What problem does the Ox help solve? (The pigs get dirty from sitting in the mud. Ox mops the pigs to clean them.) Have children look through the rest of the selection and tell about other ways Ox helps Mom and Pop. Ask children to tell about other ways Ox could help Mom and Pop.

If you are reading *The Big Blue Ox* during small group time, then return to pp. 74–83 to guide the reading.

3 Inquiry: Extend Concepts

INVESTIGATE Guide children in choosing materials at their independent reading levels.

LOOK AHEAD Help children choose formats for their selection comparisons, such as a book report, graphic organizer, or an oral presentation.

SMALL GROUP TIME

ELL

If... children need more scaffolding and practice with the main selection, **then...** use the activities on p. DI•60 in the Teacher Resources section on SuccessNet.

Advanced

Common Core State Standards

Informational Text 1. Ask and answer questions about key details in a text. **Speaking/Listening 1.** Participate in collaborative conversations about grade 1 topics and texts with peers and adults in small and larger groups. **Language 1.** Demonstrate command of the conventions of standard English grammar and usage when writing or speaking. **Also Writing 7., Speaking/Listening 1.a., 2., 3., 5.**

1 Build Word Knowledge

Extend Amazing Words and Selection Vocabulary

past	serve	present	town
snuggle	produce	enormous	
transportation	powerful	danger	

Team Talk Have children ask each other questions using the Amazing Words and the Selection Vocabulary, such as: What types of transportation can you use in a town?

2 Text-Based Comprehension

READ "A Horse Named Chester" Have children track the print as you read "A Horse Named Chester" from *Reading Street Sleuth,* pp. 12–13. Then have children read the selection independently.

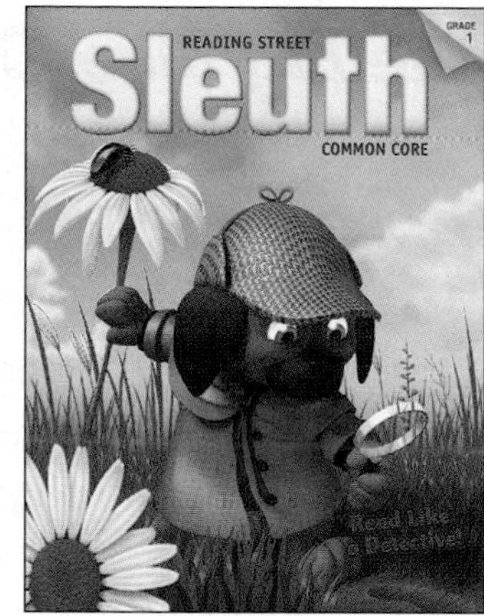

ACCESS TEXT Guide children as they work on the Be a Sleuth section.

Look for Clues Have children review the reasons an author writes. Then have them look for clues in the selection to support those reasons.

Ask Questions Have children make a list of things that interest them about service horses. Then have children make a list of questions about characteristics of service horses that interest them and that they want to learn more about.

Make Your Case Have children use a chart to compare the things a service dog can do and things a service horse can do. Then have them tell what they decided and present their case to the group using their chart to show the reasons for their decision.

3 Inquiry: Extend Concepts

ORGANIZE INFORMATION Give children time to investigate their topics by reading and studying pictures. Provide any necessary materials, such as graphic organizers or note cards.

More Reading for Group Time

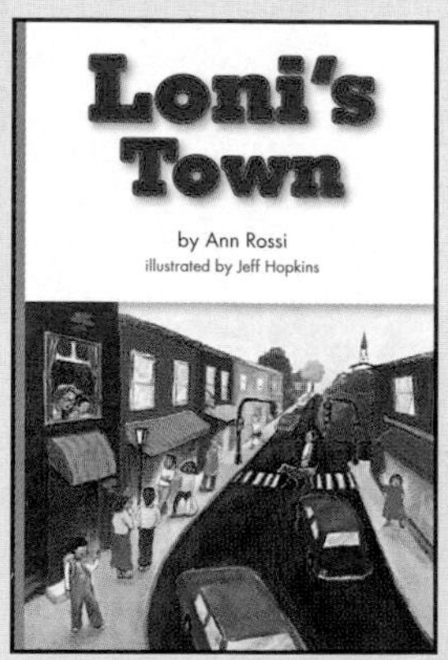

ADVANCED

- Extend Concept Vocabulary
- Review Target Skill

Use this suggested Leveled Reader or other text at children's instructional level.

eStreet Interactive
www.ReadingStreet.com

Use the Leveled Reader Database for lesson plans and student pages for *Loni's Town.*

Advanced

1 Build Word Knowledge

Predicates of Sentences

IDENTIFY PREDICATES OF SENTENCES Have children return to the text "A Horse Named Chester" to find predicates of sentences. Have children work independently to identify as many predicates of sentences as they can from the selection.

2 Text-Based Comprehension

REREAD "A Horse Named Chester" Have partners reread "A Horse Named Chester."

EXTEND UNDERSTANDING Discuss the selection together. Ask children to think of all the ways Chester helps his owner, Mike. Ask children how difficult Mike's life would be without Chester. Have children make a list of the ways Chester helps Mike.

PERFORMANCE TASK • Prove It! Have partners prepare a short play that shows a moment in the life of a service horse. Help children brainstorm ideas for the play, such as crossing a busy street or going to a store. Encourage them to use as many details as possible. Have children use the text and other references to help them prepare the play.

COMMUNICATE Have partners present their plays to the class. Encourage children to ask questions after each performance.

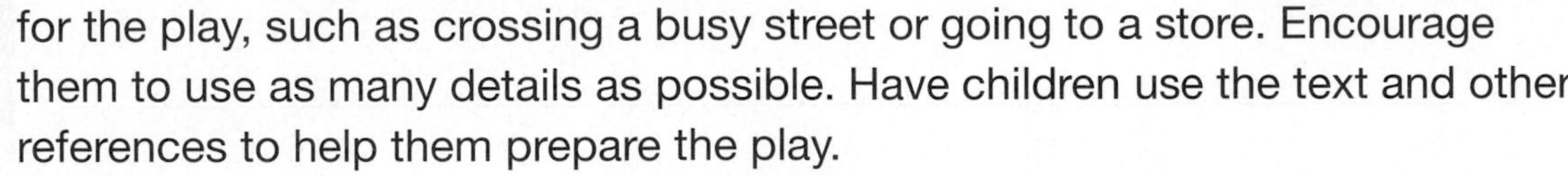

3 Inquiry: Extend Concepts

COMMUNICATE Have children share their inquiry projects and present their comparison of two other selections about real or fictional animals that help people.

SMALL GROUP TIME

More Reading for Group Time

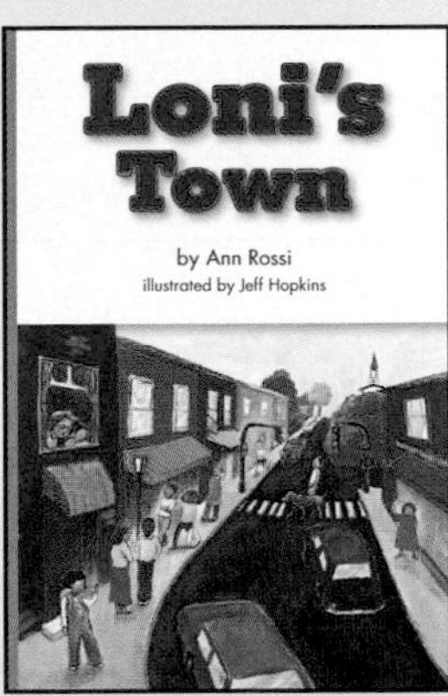

ADVANCED

- Extend Concept Vocabulary
- Review Target Skill

Use this suggested Leveled Reader or other text at children's instructional level.

eStreet Interactive
www.ReadingStreet.com

Use the Leveled Reader Database for lesson plans and student pages for *Loni's Town.*

TEACHER NOTES

Indiana Common Core Edition ©

This Week's Target Skills and Strategies

Target Skills and Strategies	© Common Core State Standards for English Language Arts
Phonemic Awareness **Skills:** Segment and Blend Phonemes Count Syllables Segment and Blend Onset and Rime	**CCSS Foundational Skills 2.b.** Orally produce single-syllable words by blending sounds (phonemes), including consonant blends. **(Also CCSS Foundational Skills 2., CCSS Foundational Skills 2.c., CCSS Speaking/Listening 6.)**
Phonics **Skill:** Inflected Endings *-s* and *-ing*	**CCSS Foundational Skills 3.f.** Read words with inflectional endings. **(Also CCSS Foundational Skills 3., CCSS Language 2.d.)**
Text-Based Comprehension **Skill:** Main Idea and Details	**CCSS Informational Text 2.** Identify the main topic and retell key details of a text.
Strategy: Important Ideas	**CCSS Informational Text 2.** Identify the main topic and retell key details of a text.
Fluency **Skill:** Accuracy and Rate	**CCSS Foundational Skills 4.b.** Read on-level text orally with accuracy, appropriate rate, and expression on successive readings.
Listening and Speaking Share Information and Ideas	**CCSS Speaking/Listening 1.b.** Build on others' talk in conversations by responding to the comments of others through multiple exchanges. **(Also CCSS Speaking/Listening 1.a., CCSS Speaking/Listening 3.)**
Six-Trait Writing **Trait of the Week:** Voice	**CCSS Writing 3.** Write narratives in which they recount two or more appropriately sequenced events, include some details regarding what happened, use temporal words to signal event order, and provide some sense of closure.
Writing Personal Narrative	**CCSS Writing 3.** Write narratives in which they recount two or more appropriately sequenced events, include some details regarding what happened, use temporal words to signal event order, and provide some sense of closure.
Conventions **Skill:** Declarative Sentences	**CCSS Language 1.j.** Produce and expand complete simple and compound declarative, interrogative, imperative, and exclamatory sentences in response to prompts. **(Also CCSS Language 2.b.)**

This Week's Cross-Curricular Standards and Resources

Cross-Curricular Indiana Academic Standards for Science and Social Studies

Science
IN 1.3.5 Observe and describe ways in which animals and plants depend on one another for survival.

Social Studies
IN 1.1.7 Explain that clocks and calendars are used to measure time.

Reading Street Sleuth

A Caring Father
pp. 14–15

Follow the path to close reading using the Super Sleuth tips:

- Look for Clues
- Ask Questions
- Make Your Case
- Prove it!

More Reading in Science and Social Studies

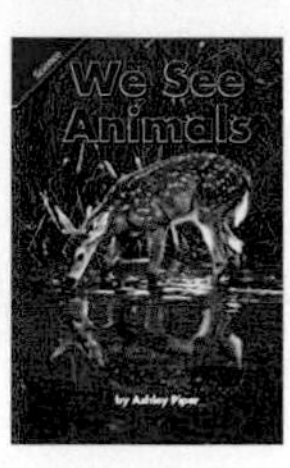

Concept Literacy

Below Level

On Level

Advanced

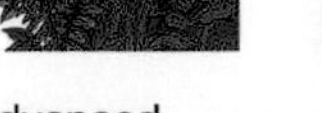

ELL

ELD

ISBN-13: 978-0-328-73376-7 ISBN-10: 0-328-73376-8

Your 90-Minute Reading Block

	Whole Group	Formative Assessment How do I make my small groups flexible?	Small Group OL On Level SI Strategic Intervention A Advanced What are my other students reading and learning every day in Small Groups?
DAY 1	**Content Knowledge** Build Oral Language/Vocabulary **Phonemic Awareness/Phonics** **Read Decodable Reader** **Phonics/Spelling Pretest** **High-Frequency Words** **Text-Based Comprehension** Teacher Read Aloud **Research and Inquiry** Step 1–Identify and Focus Topic	**Monitor Progress** Formative Assessment: Check Word Reading	**Differentiate Phonics** OL **Practice Phonics** More *-s* Words SI **Reteach Phonics** Blend *-s* Words A **Extend Phonics** More Challenging *-s* Words OL SI **Decodable Reader Read** *Big Jobs* A **Advanced Selection** "Panda Peeks at the World" A Inquiry Project ELL Access Phonemic Awareness and Phonics
DAY 2	**Content Knowledge** Build Oral Language/Vocabulary **Phonemic Awareness/Phonics** **Read Decodable Reader** **Phonics/Spelling** **High-Frequency Words/Selection Words** **Text-Based Comprehension** **Read** Main Selection, using Access Text Notes **Research and Inquiry** Step 2–Research Skill	**Monitor Progress** Formative Assessment: Check Word Reading	**Differentiate Comprehension** OL **Practice Phonics** Additional *-ing* Words SI **Reteach Phonics** Blend *-ing* Words A **Extend Phonics** Additional *-ing* Words OL SI A **Access Text Read** *A Fox and a Kit* A Inquiry Project ELL Access the Comprehension Skill
DAY 3	**Content Knowledge** Build Oral Language/Vocabulary **Phonemic Awareness/Phonics** **Phonics/Spelling** **High-Frequency Words/Selection Words** **Text-Based Comprehension** **Reread** Main Selection, using Close Reading Notes **Fluency** **Research and Inquiry** Step 3–Gather and Record Information	**Monitor Progress** Formative Assessment: Check High-Frequency Words **Monitor Progress** Check Retelling	**Differentiate Close Reading** OL **Reread to Develop Vocabulary** SI **Build Word Knowledge** Blend Words with *-s* and *-ing* A **Reread to Extend Vocabulary** OL SI **Close Reading Reread** *A Fox and a Kit* A **Extend Concepts Reread** *A Fox and a Kit* A Inquiry Project ELL Access the Main Selection
DAY 4	**Content Knowledge** Build Oral Language/Vocabulary **Phonemic Awareness/Phonics** **Read Decodable Reader** **Phonics/Spelling** **Read Content Area Paired Selection with Genre Focus** **Fluency** **Research and Inquiry** Step 4–Synthesize	**Monitor Progress** Fluency Check	**Differentiate Vocabulary** **Build Word Knowledge** OL Develop Language A Extend Amazing Words and Selection Vocabulary SI **Review Vocabulary** Review/Discuss Selection Vocabulary OL SI A **Text-Based Comprehension Read** *Reading Street Sleuth,* pp. 14–15 or Leveled Readers A Inquiry Project ELL Access Vocabulary
DAY 5	**Content Knowledge** Build Oral Language/Vocabulary **Phonemic Awareness/Phonics** **Phonics/Spelling Test** **Let's Learn It!** Vocabulary/Fluency/Listening and Speaking **Text-Based Comprehension** **High-Frequency and Selection Words** **Genre** **Assessment** Phonics, High-Frequency Words, Fluency **Research and Inquiry** Step 5–Communicate	**Monitor Progress** Formative Assessment: Check Oral Vocabulary **Monitor Progress** Word and Sentence Reading	**Differentiate Reteaching** OL **Practice Declarative Sentences** SI **Review Vocabulary** High-Frequency Words A **Extend Declarative Sentences** OL SI A **Text-Based Comprehension** **Reread** *Reading Street Sleuth,* pp. 14–15 or Leveled Readers A Inquiry Project ELL Access Conventions and Writing

Daily Independent Options

What do my other students do when I lead Small Groups?

★ **Independent Reading**

Suggestions for this week's independent reading:

- Fictional texts on last week's social studies topic: How do animals help people?
- Fiction selections about how animals help people
- Fiction book by a favorite author

Book Talk

Foster critical reading and discussion skills through independent and close reading.

Students should focus on discussing one or more of the following:

- Key Ideas and Details
- Craft and Structure
- Integration of Ideas

Pearson eText

- Student Edition
- Decodable Readers
- Leveled Readers

Trade Book Library

Materials from School or Classroom Library

Independent Stations
Practice Last Week's Skills

★ Focus on these activities when time is limited.

Listen Up!
Word Work
★ **Read for Meaning**
★ **Let's Write!**
Words to Know
Get Fluent

Assessment Resources

Common Core Weekly Tests, pp. 55–60

Common Core Fresh Reads for Fluency and Comprehension, pp. 55–60

Common Core Unit 1 Benchmark Test

Common Core Success Tracker, ExamView, and Online Lesson Planner

Focus on Common Core State Standards ©

Main Selection, pp. 102–111

Paired Selection, pp. 116–117

Text-Based Comprehension

Main Idea and Details
CCSS Informational Text 2.

Important Ideas
CCSS Informational Text 2.

Fluency

Accuracy and Rate
CCSS Foundational Skills 4.b.

Writing and Conventions

Trait: Voice
CCSS Writing 3.

Writing Mini-Lesson: Personal Narrative
CCSS Writing 3.

Conventions: Declarative Sentences
CCSS Language 1.j.,
CCSS Language 2.b.

Oral Vocabulary

Amazing Words

observe	parent
wild	canopy
screech	million
reserve	native

CCSS Language 5.c.

High-Frequency Words

eat	five	four
her	this	too

CCSS Foundational Skills 3.g.

Phonemic Awareness

Segment and Blend Phonemes

Count Syllables

Segment and Blend Onset and Rime
CCSS Foundational Skills 2.b.,
CCSS Foundational Skills 2.c.

Phonics and Spelling

Inflected Endings *-s* and *-ing*
CCSS Foundational Skills 3.f.,
CCSS Language 2.d.

sit	sits	win
wins	fit	fits
hit	hits	nap
naps		

Listening and Speaking

Share Information and Ideas
CCSS Speaking/Listening 1.b.

Preview Your Week

How do wild animals take care of their babies?

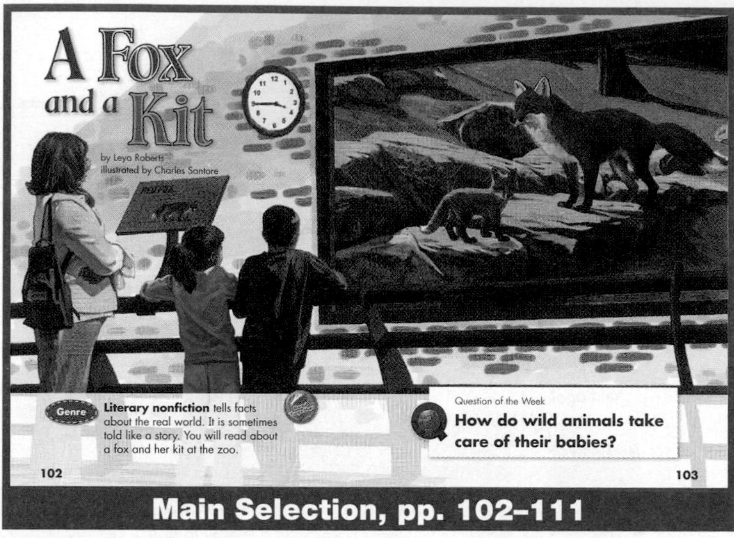

Main Selection, pp. 102–111

Paired Selection, pp. 116–117

Genre: Literary Nonfiction

Phonics: Inflected Ending *-ing,* Inflected Ending *-s*

Text-Based Comprehension: Main Idea and Details

Science in Reading

Genre: Fable

Build Content Knowledge

KNOWLEDGE GOALS
Children will understand that wild animals:

- provide food for their babies
- protect their babies from harm

THIS WEEK'S CONCEPT MAP
Develop a concept-related graphic organizer like the one below over the course of this week.

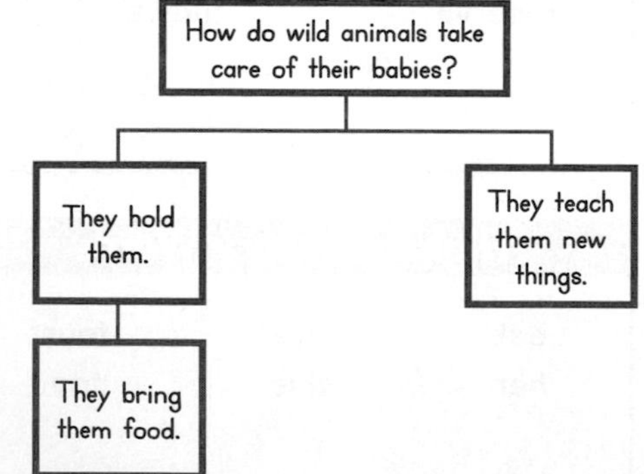

How do wild animals take care of their babies?
They hold them.
They bring them food.
They teach them new things.

BUILD ORAL VOCABULARY
This week, children will acquire the following academic vocabulary/domain-specific words.

Amazing Words

observe	screech	canopy
wild	million	reserve
parent	native	

OPTIONAL CONCEPT-BASED READING Use the Digital Path to access readers offering different levels of text complexity.

Concept Literacy

Below Level

On Level

Advanced

ELL

ELD

This Week's Digital Resources

eStreet Interactive

www.ReadingStreet.com

Get Ready to Read

Background Building Audio CD This audio CD provides valuable background information about what zookeepers do to help children read and comprehend the weekly texts.

Concept Talk Video Use this video on the Digital Path to build momentum and introduce the weekly concept of wild animals and their babies.

Interactive Sing with Me Big Book "Squirrel Song," sung to the tune of "Yellow Rose of Texas," introduces the Amazing Words with a catchy, concept-related song.

Interactive Sound-Spelling Cards With these interactive cards on the Digital Path, children see an image, hear the image name, and see the spelling for the inflected endings *-s* and *-ing*.

Pearson eText Use the eText for the Decodable Readers on the Leveled Reader Database for phonics and fluency support.

Letter Tile Drag and Drop Using this interactive tool on Pearson SuccessNet, children click and spell words to enhance their phonics skills.

Read and Comprehend

Envision It! Animations Use this colorful animation on the Digital Path to explain the target comprehension skill, Main Idea and Details.

Pearson eText Read the eText of the main selection, *A Fox and a Kit,* and the paired selection, "The Fox and the Grapes," with audio support on Pearson SuccessNet.

Story Sort Use the Story Sort Activity on the Digital Path after reading *A Fox and a Kit* to involve children in summarizing.

Journal: Word Bank Use the Word Bank on the Digital Path to have children write sentences using this week's high-frequency words.

Vocabulary Activities A variety of interactive vocabulary activities on the Digital Path help children practice high-frequency and concept-related words.

Language Arts

Grammar Jammer Choose a whimsical animation on the Digital Path to provide an engaging grammar lesson that will capture children's attention.

Pearson eText Find the Student Edition eText of the Let's Write It! and Let's Learn It! pages with audio support on Pearson SuccessNet.

Additional Resources

Teacher Resources DVD-ROM Use the following resources on the TR DVD or on Pearson SuccessNet throughout the week:

- Amazing Word Cards
- Reader's and Writer's Notebook
- Writing Transparencies
- Daily Fix-It Transparencies
- Scoring Rubrics
- Grammar Transparencies
- Research Transparencies
- Let's Practice It!
- Graphic Organizers
- High-Frequency Word Cards
- Vocabulary Transparencies

This Week's Skills

Phonics
- Inflected Ending *-s*
- Inflected Ending *-ing*

Comprehension
- **Skill:** Main Idea and Details
- **Strategy:** Important Ideas

Language
- **Vocabulary:** Alphabetize to the Second Letter
- **Conventions:** Declarative Sentences

Fluency
Accuracy and Appropriate Rate

Writing
Personal Narrative

5-Day Planner

DAY 1

Get Ready to Read

Content Knowledge 94j
Oral Vocabulary: *observe, wild, parent*

Phonemic Awareness 96–97
Segment and Blend Phonemes

Phonics/Spelling 97a
- Inflected Ending *-s*
- **READ** Decodable Reader 4A
- Reread for Fluency
- Spelling Pretest

Monitor Progress
Check Word Reading

Read and Comprehend

High-Frequency Words 99
eat, five, four, her, this, too

Text-Based Comprehension 99a
- Main Idea and Details

Language Arts

Conventions 99c
Declarative Sentences

Writing 99d
Personal Narrative

Research and Inquiry 99f
Identify and Focus Topic

DAY 2

Get Ready to Read

Content Knowledge 100a
Oral Vocabulary: *canopy, screech*

Phonemic Awareness 100c
Segment and Blend Phonemes

Phonics/Spelling 100d
- Inflected Ending *-ing*
- **Review** Inflected Ending *-s*
- **READ** Decodable Reader 4B
- Reread for Fluency
- **Spelling:** Inflected Ending *-s*

Monitor Progress
Check Word Reading

Read and Comprehend

High-Frequency Words 101
eat, five, four, her, this, too

Selection Vocabulary 102a
animals, dinner, watch
Strategy: Alphabetize to the Second Letter

Text-Based Comprehension 102b
READ *A Fox and a Kit*—1st Read

Genre 111b
Literary Nonfiction

Language Arts

Conventions 111c
Declarative Sentences

Writing 111d
Personal Narrative

Handwriting 111f
Letters *Nn* and *Gg*/Letter Slant

Research and Inquiry 111g
How to Read a Chart

DAY 3

Get Ready to Read

Content Knowledge 112a
Oral Vocabulary: *million*

Phonemic Awareness 112c
Count Syllables

Phonics/Spelling 112d
Build Words
Blend and Read
Spelling: Dictation

Read and Comprehend

High-Frequency Words and Selection Words 112g
High-Frequency Words: *eat, five, four, her, this, too*
Selection Words: *animals, dinner, watch*
Monitor Progress
Check High-Frequency Words

Text-Based Comprehension 112h
READ *A Fox and a Kit*—2nd Read
Monitor Progress Check Retelling

Fluency 113b
Accuracy and Appropriate Rate

Language Arts

Conventions 114a
Declarative Sentences

Writing 114–115
Personal Narrative

Listening and Speaking 115b
Share Information and Ideas

Research and Inquiry 115c
Gather and Record Information

DAY 4

Get Ready to Read

Content Knowledge 116a
Oral Vocabulary: *native, reserve*

Phonemic Awareness 116c
Segment and Blend Onset and Rime

Phonics/Spelling 116d
Review Short *o* Spelled *o; -s* Plurals
READ Decodable Reader 4C
Spiral Review Fluent Word Reading
Spelling: Inflected Ending *-s*

Read and Comprehend

Science in Reading 116i
READ "The Fox and the Grapes" —Paired Selection

Fluency 117b
Accuracy and Appropriate Rate
Monitor Progress Fluency Check

Language Arts

Conventions 117c
Declarative Sentences

Writing 117d
Personal Narrative

Research and Inquiry 117f
Synthesize

DAY 5

Get Ready to Read

Content Knowledge 118a
Review Oral Vocabulary
Monitor Progress
Check Oral Vocabulary

Phonemic Awareness 118c
Review Segment and Blend Onset and Rime

Phonics/Spelling 118c
Review Inflected Endings *-s* and *-ing*
Spelling Test

Read and Comprehend

Listening and Speaking 118–119
Vocabulary 119a
Fluency 119a

Text-Based Comprehension 119b
Review Main Idea and Details

Vocabulary 119b
Review High-Frequency and Selection Words

Genre 119c
Review Fable

Assessment 119d
Monitor Progress
Word and Sentence Reading

Language Arts

Conventions 119g
Review Declarative Sentences

Writing 119h
Personal Narrative

Research and Inquiry 119j
Communicate

Wrap Up Your Week! 119k

Access for All

What do I do in group time?

It's as easy as 1-2-3!

1 TEACHER-LED SMALL GROUPS → 2 INDEPENDENT PRACTICE STATIONS → 3 INDEPENDENT READING

Small Group Time

Bridge to Common Core

SKILL DEVELOPMENT
- Inflected Endings *-s* and *-ing*
- Main Idea and Details
- Important Ideas

DEEP UNDERSTANDING

This Week's Knowledge Goals

Children will understand that wild animals:
- provide food for their babies
- protect their babies from harm

1 Small Group Lesson Plan

	DAY 1 Differentiate Phonics	DAY 2 Differentiate Comprehension
On-Level pp. SG•53–SG•57	**Practice Phonics** More *-s* Words **Decodable Reader** Read *Big Jobs*	**Practice Phonics** Additional *-ing* Words **Access Text** Read *A Fox and a Kit*
Strategic Intervention pp. SG•58–SG•62	**Reteach Phonics** Blend *-s* Words **Decodable Reader** Read *Big Jobs*	**Reteach Phonics** Blend *-ing* Words **Access Text** Read *A Fox and a Kit*
Advanced pp. SG•63–SG•68	**Extend Phonics** More Challenging *-s* Words **Advanced Selection** "Panda Peeks at the World"	**Extend Phonics** Additional *-ing* Words **Access Text** Read *A Fox and a Kit*
Independent Inquiry Project	**Identify Questions**	**Investigate**
ELL **If...** children need more scaffolding and practice with...	**Phonemic Awareness and Phonics,** **then...** use the ELL activities on pp. DI•76–DI•77 in the Teacher Resources section on SuccessNet.	**the Comprehension Skill,** **then...** use the ELL activities on p. DI•80 in the Teacher Resources section on SuccessNet.

Reading Street Sleuth

- Provides access to grade-level text for all children
- Focuses on finding clues in text through close reading
- Builds capacity for complex text

Build Text-Based Comprehension

A Fox and a Kit

Optional Leveled Readers

Concept Literacy

Below Level

On Level

Advanced

ELL

ELD

DAY 3 Differentiate Close Reading	DAY 4 Differentiate Vocabulary	DAY 5 Differentiate Reteaching
Reread to Develop Vocabulary **Close Reading** Reread *A Fox and a Kit*	**Build Word Knowledge** Develop Language **Text-Based Comprehension** Read *Reading Street Sleuth,* pp. 14–15 or Leveled Readers	**Practice Declarative Sentences** **Text-Based Comprehension** Reread *Reading Street Sleuth,* pp. 14–15 or Leveled Readers
Build Word Knowledge Blend Words with *-s* and *-ing* **Close Reading** Reread *A Fox and a Kit*	**Review Vocabulary** Review/Discuss Selection Vocabulary **Text-Based Comprehension** Read *Reading Street Sleuth,* pp. 14–15 or Leveled Readers	**Review Vocabulary** High-Frequency Words **Text-Based Comprehension** Reread *Reading Street Sleuth,* pp. 14–15 or Leveled Readers
Reread to Extend Vocabulary **Extend Concepts** Reread *A Fox and a Kit* **Investigate**	**Build Word Knowledge** Extend Amazing Words and Selection Vocabulary **Text-Based Comprehension** Read *Reading Street Sleuth,* pp. 14–15 or Leveled Readers **Organize**	**Extend Declarative Sentences** **Text-Based Comprehension** Reread *Reading Street Sleuth,* pp. 14–15 or Leveled Readers **Communicate**
the Main Selection, **then...** use the activities on p. DI•81 in the Teacher Resources section on SuccessNet.	**Vocabulary,** **then...** use the routine on pp. xxxvi–xxxvii in the *ELL Handbook.*	**Conventions and Writing,** **then...** use the Grammar Transition Lessons on pp. 346–421 in the *ELL Handbook.*

2 Independent Stations

Practice Last Week's Skills

★ Focus on these activities when time is limited.

ACCESS FOR ALL
- ● Below-Level Activities
- ▲ On-Level Activities
- ■ Advanced Activities

LISTEN UP!

Match sounds and pictures.

OBJECTIVES
- Identify words with initial and medial sound /o/.
- Add final /z/ to spoken words.

MATERIALS
- *Listen Up!* Flip Chart Activity 4, Picture Cards *block, box, fox, octopus, ox, sock, fan, mug, web*

 **Modeled Pronunciation Audio CD**

● Children find Picture Cards with /o/ beginning sound and then /o/ middle sound. They add /z/ to the remaining three Picture Cards.

▲ Children find Picture Cards with /o/ beginning sound and then /o/ middle sound. They say each word on the remaining three Picture Cards in plural form. What sound did they add to the word?

■ Children sort the Picture Cards into three piles: beginning sound in *odd,* middle sound in *chop,* ending sound in *drums.*

WORD WORK

Read words.

OBJECTIVES
- Identify and read words with short *o* and *-s* plurals.

MATERIALS
- *Word Work* Flip Chart Activity 4, Teacher-made word cards, T-charts, pencils

 **Interactive Sound-Spelling Cards**

● Children sort the words into words with short *o* and other words. Repeat with words that are *-s* plurals and words that are not.

▲ Children sort the words into words with short *o* and other words. Children then add their own words to the columns. Repeat with words that are *-s* plurals and words that are not.

■ Children sort the words into words with short *o* and other words. Repeat with words that are *-s* plurals and words that are not. Then children write sentences using the words in the charts.

★ LET'S WRITE!

Write sentences.

OBJECTIVES
- Write complete sentences.
- Identify predicates of sentences.

MATERIALS
- *Let's Write!* Flip Chart Activity 4, paper, pencils

 **Grammar Jammer**

● Children write a sentence about how an animal might help someone. Have them circle the predicate of the sentence.

▲ Children write two sentences about how an animal might help someone. Have them circle the predicates of each sentence.

■ Children write a short story about how an animal might help someone.

WORDS TO KNOW

Identify high-frequency words.

OBJECTIVES
- Identify high-frequency words *help, use, from, little, blue, get.*
- Write high-frequency words.

MATERIALS
- *Words to Know* Flip Chart Activity 4; paper, pencils, crayons paper; pencils; crayons

 **Vocabulary Activities**

 **Teacher Resources**
- High-Frequency Word Cards for Unit 1, Week 3

● Children write the words from the Word Cards on their papers. Then they draw pictures of some of the words.

▲ Children write the words from the Word Cards on their papers. They draw pictures and write sentences to go with two words.

■ Children write the words from the Word Cards on their papers. Then they write sentences for each of the words.

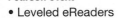

READ FOR MEANING

Use text-based comprehension tools.

OBJECTIVES

- Identify the characters in a story.
- Identify the actions of a character in a story.

MATERIALS

- *Read for Meaning* Flip Chart Activity 4, Leveled Readers, paper, pencils, crayons

Pearson eText
- Leveled eReaders

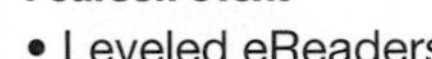

Envision It! Animations

● Children read *On the Farm.* First, they tell who the characters are, and then they draw a picture of one of them. They write the character's name on the picture.

▲ Children read *Where They Live.* First, they tell who the characters are, and then they write a sentence that describes one of the characters.

■ Children read *Loni's Town.* They draw a picture of each character, and write what the character does.

GET FLUENT

Practice fluent reading.

OBJECTIVES

- Read aloud at an appropriate rate.

MATERIALS

- *Get Fluent* Flip Chart Activity 4, Leveled Readers

Pearson eText
- Leveled eReaders

● Children work with a partner to take turns reading *On the Farm.*

▲ Children work with a partner to take turns reading *Where They Live.*

■ Children work with a partner to take turns reading *Loni's Town.*

Manage the Stations

Use these management tools to set up and organize your Practice Stations:

Practice Station Flip Charts

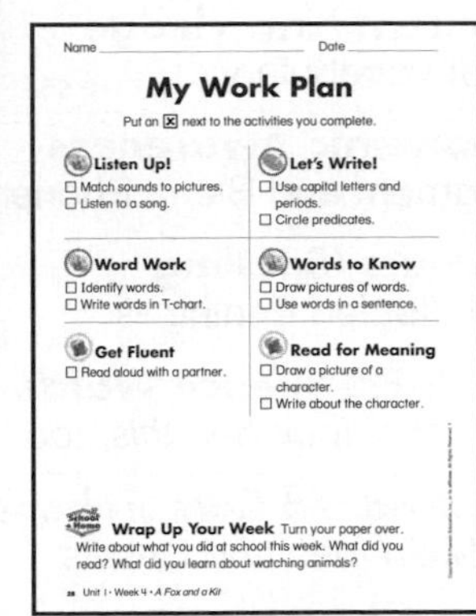
Name ______ Date ______

My Work Plan

Put an ☒ next to the activities you complete.

Listen Up!
- ☐ Match sounds to pictures.
- ☐ Listen to a song.

Let's Write!
- ☐ Use capital letters and periods.
- ☐ Circle predicates.

Word Work
- ☐ Identify words.
- ☐ Write words in T-chart.

Words to Know
- ☐ Draw pictures of words.
- ☐ Use words in a sentence.

Get Fluent
- ☐ Read aloud with a partner.

Read for Meaning
- ☐ Draw a picture of a character.
- ☐ Write about the character.

Wrap Up Your Week Turn your paper over. Write about what you did at school this week. What did you read? What did you learn about watching animals?

28 Unit 1 • Week 4 • *A Fox and a Kit*

Classroom Management Handbook for Differentiated Instruction Practice Stations, p. 28

3 Independent Reading ©

Children should select appropriately complex texts to read and write about independently every day before, during, and after school.

Suggestions for this week's independent reading:
- Fictional texts on last week's social studies topic: How do animals help people?
- Fiction selections about how animals help people
- Fiction book by a favorite author

BOOK TALK Have partners discuss their independent reading for the week. Tell them to refer to their Reading Log and paraphrase what the selection was about. To focus the discussion, prompt them to talk about one or more of the following:

Key Ideas and Details
- Who is the author? Why did he or she write the work?
- What ideas did I learn from this text?
- How do the characters interact with each other?

Craft and Structure
- Did I understand why the events happened?
- Did the author use words that were interesting and clear?

Integration of Ideas
- Did the story seem believable? Why or why not?
- Was this book like others I have read?

Pearson eText
- Student Edition
- Decodable Readers
- Leveled Readers

Trade Book Library

Materials from School or Classroom Library

Content Knowledge
Oral Vocabulary

Phonemic Awareness
Segment and Blend Phonemes

Phonics/Spelling
Inflected Ending *-s*

High-Frequency Words
eat, five, four, her, this, too

Text-Based Comprehension
Main Idea and Details

Conventions
Declarative Sentences

Writing
Personal Narrative

Research and Inquiry
Identify and Focus Topic

Materials

- Student Edition
- Sing with Me Big Book
- Sound-Spelling Cards
- Decodable Reader 4A
- Reader's and Writer's Notebook

Bridge to Common Core

INTEGRATION OF KNOWLEDGE/IDEAS
This week children read, write, and talk about wild animals and their babies.

Texts This Week
- "Squirrel Song"
- "A Rain Forest in the Zoo"
- *Jungle Drum*
- *A Fox and a Kit*
- "The Fox and the Grapes"
- "Takhi"

Science Knowledge Goals
Children will understand that wild animals
- provide food for their babies
- protect their babies from harm

Street Rhymes!

Mama Bird built her nest high;
She kept her eggs warm and dry.
When the baby birds squirm,
She brings them a worm.
Soon she will teach them to fly.

- To introduce this week's concept, read aloud the poem several times and ask children to join you.

Content Knowledge

Wild Animals and Their Babies

CONCEPT TALK To help children gain knowledge and understanding, tell them that this week they will talk, sing, read, and write about wild animals and their babies. Write the Question of the Week, *How do wild animals take care of their babies?,* and track the print as you read it.

Build Oral Language

TALK ABOUT WILD ANIMALS AND THEIR BABIES Have children turn to pages 94–95 in their Student Edition. Read the title and look at the photos. Use these questions to guide discussion and create the "How do wild animals take care of their babies?" concept map.

- What is the mother chimpanzee doing? (She is holding her baby.) Let's add *They hold them* to our map.
- How is the mother hippo helping her baby? (She is helping her baby to swim.) Let's add *They teach them new things* to our map.

Common Core State Standards
Language 5.c. Identify real-life connections between words and their use (e.g., note places at home that are cozy).
Also Speaking/Listening 1.

Oral Vocabulary

Let's Talk About

Read Together

Wild Animals

- Share information about wild animals.
- Discuss how wild animals take care of their babies.

READING STREET ONLINE
CONCEPT TALK VIDEO
www.ReadingStreet.com

You've learned 072 Amazing Words so far this year!

94 95

Student Edition, pp. 94–95

CONNECT TO READING Explain that this week children will read about a mother fox and its baby. Animal babies need to eat, so let's add *They bring them food* to our map.

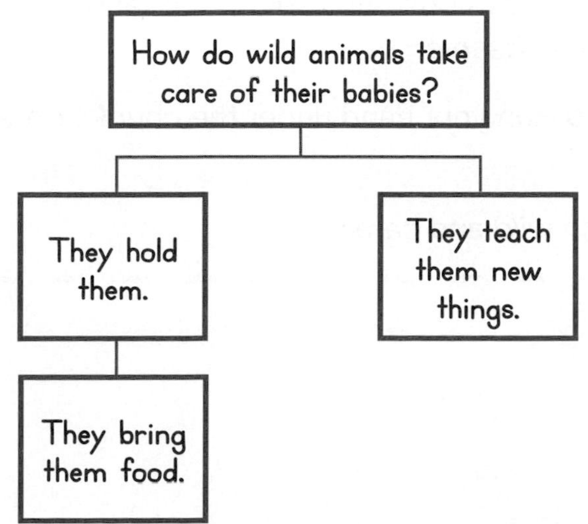
How do wild animals take care of their babies?
They hold them.
They teach them new things.
They bring them food.

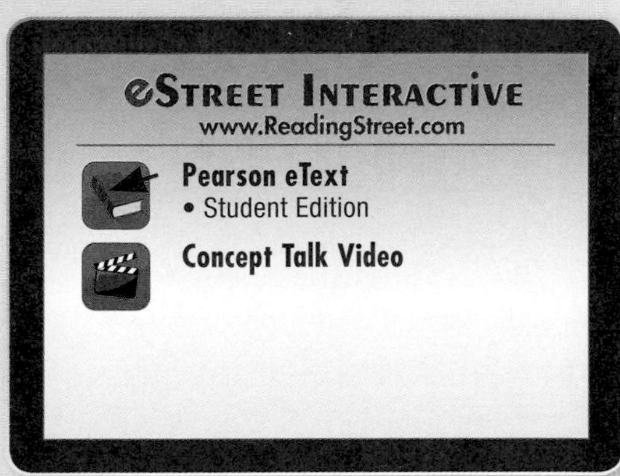
eStreet Interactive
www.ReadingStreet.com
Pearson eText
• Student Edition
Concept Talk Video

ELL

Preteach Concepts Use the Day 1 instruction on ELL Poster 4 to build knowledge and oral vocabulary.

Support Additional ELL support is provided in the *ELL Handbook* and in the *ELL Support Lessons* on the *Teacher Resources DVD-ROM.*

Common Core State Standards

Language 5.c. Identify real-life connections between words and their use (e.g., note places at home that are *cozy*). **Language 6.** Use words and phrases acquired through conversations, reading and being read to, and responding to texts, including using frequently occurring conjunctions to signal simple relationships (e.g., *I named my hamster Nibblet because she nibbles too much because she likes that*).

Amazing Words

You've learned 072 words so far.

You'll learn 008 words this week!

observe	screech
wild	million
parent	native
canopy	reserve

Content Knowledge

Build Oral Vocabulary

INTRODUCE AMAZING WORDS Display page 4 of the *Sing with Me* Big Book. Tell children they are going to sing about a mother and baby squirrel. Ask children to listen for the Amazing Words observe, wild, and parent as you sing. Sing the song again and have children join you.

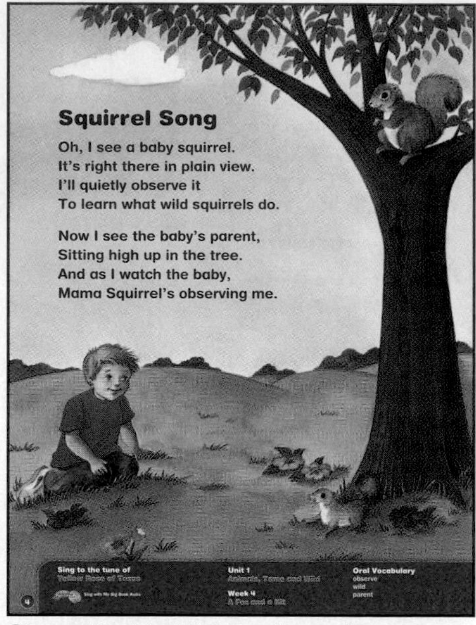

Squirrel Song
Oh, I see a baby squirrel.
It's right there in plain view.
I'll quietly observe it
To learn what wild squirrels do.
Now I see the baby's parent,
Sitting high up in the tree.
And as I watch the baby,
Mama Squirrel's observing me.

Sing with Me Big Book, p. 4

Amazing Words Robust Vocabulary Routine

1. **Introduce the Word** Relate the word *observe* to the song. The song says that the boy can observe the baby squirrel. Supply a child-friendly definition. *Observe* means to see or look at. Have children say the word.
2. **Demonstrate** Provide examples to show meaning. The boy can *observe* the baby squirrel on the ground. You can *observe* your classmates playing a game. Another teacher can *observe* this class.
3. **Apply** Have children demonstrate their understanding. Tell about something you can *observe.*
4. **Display the Word** Run your hand under the chunks *ob-serve* as you read the word.

See p. OV•4 to teach *wild* and *parent.*

Routines Flip Chart

AMAZING WORDS AT WORK Have children look at the picture on page 4.

- It is exciting to *observe* something you haven't seen before. What is something you would like to *observe?* Use the word *observe* in your answer. (Possible response: I would like to observe a soccer match.)
- In the song, the boy says he observes the squirrel to learn what *wild* squirrels do. What are some things *wild* squirrels do? Use the word *wild* in your answer. (Possible response: Wild squirrels climb trees.)
- What is something a *parent* might help a child learn? Use the word *parent* in your answer. (Possible response: A parent can help me learn to ride a bike.)

APPLY AMAZING WORDS Have children demonstrate their understanding of the Amazing Words by completing these sentences orally.

I would like to **observe a** _______.
An example of a **wild** animal is _______.
A **parent** can help me learn _______.

Corrective feedback | **If...** children have difficulty using the Amazing Words, **then...** remind them of the definitions and provide opportunities for children to use the words in sentences.

Pronunciation English learners may have trouble pronouncing the initial /r/ sound as in the word *reserve.* Have children practice the sound alone. Then have children practice words that begin with the initial /r/ sound.

Use Cognates The words *observe, million, native,* and *reserve* may have cognates in children's home languages. Invite Spanish speakers to identify cognates *observar* and *millón.* Point out how this prior knowledge can help children with learning new words.

Common Core State Standards
Foundational Skills 2. Demonstrate understanding of spoken words, syllables, and sounds (phonemes).
Also Foundational Skills 2.c., Speaking/Listening 6.

Phonemic Awareness

Let's Listen for

Sounds

- Find five people who are doing something. Tell what they are doing.
- Find two actions that rhyme with *ends*. Say the sounds in each word.
- Find two actions that rhyme with *pumping*. Say the sounds in each word.

Read Together

READING STREET ONLINE
SOUND-SPELLING CARDS
www.ReadingStreet.com

96 97

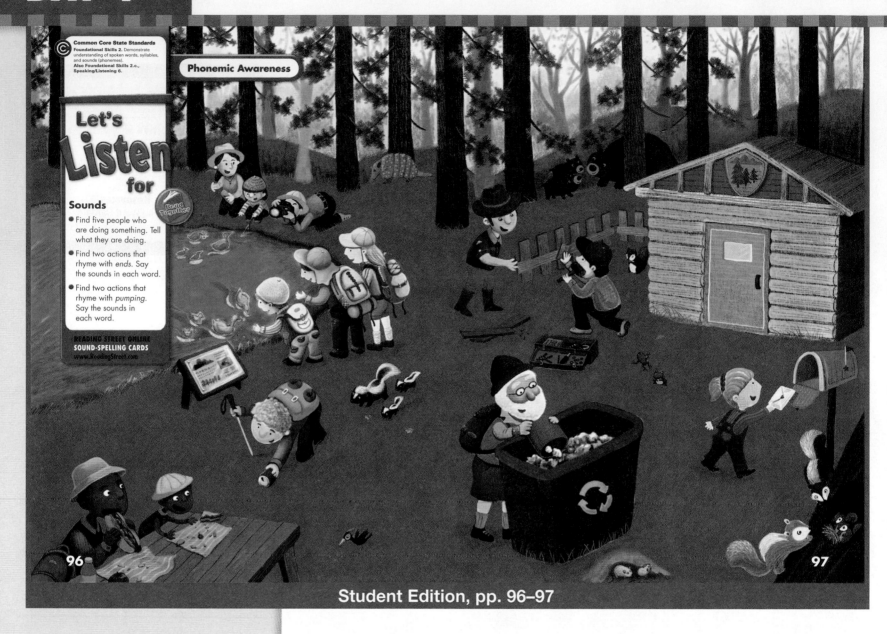

Student Edition, pp. 96–97

Common Core State Standards

Foundational Skills 2. Demonstrate understanding of spoken words, syllables, and sounds (phonemes). **Foundational Skills 2.c.** Isolate and pronounce initial, medial vowel, and final sounds (phonemes) in spoken single-syllable words. **Also Foundational Skills 3., 3.f.**

Skills Trace

Inflected Ending -*s*
Introduce U1W4D1
Practice U1W4D2; U1W4D3; U1W4D4
Reteach/Review U1W4D5; U1W5D4
Assess/Test Weekly Test U1W4
Benchmark Test U1
KEY: U=Unit W=Week D=Day

Phonemic Awareness

Segment and Blend Phonemes

INTRODUCE Have children look at the picture on pages 96–97. Point to the jumping frog. A frog jumps. The last sound in *jumps* is /s/. Have children identify other actions that end with the /s/ sound. (dumps, eats, walks, looks) A man *mends* a fence. The last sound in *mends* is /z/. Have children identify actions that contain the /z/ sound. (sends, bends, stands, feeds)

MODEL Listen to the sounds in *jumps:* /j/ /u/ /m/ /p/ /s/. There are five sounds. Let's blend those sounds: /j/ /u/ /m/ /p/ /s/. Continue with *mends.* Guide children as they segment and blend these words from the picture: *dumps, eats, stands, feeds, looks, sends, bends.*

Corrective feedback	**If...** children make an error, **then...** model by segmenting the word, and then have them repeat the segmenting and blending of the word.

Phonics

Teach/Model

Inflected Ending *-s*

CONNECT Write the words *cats* and *birds.* What do you know about the last sound of these words? (The sound /s/ is spelled *s* at the end of *cats.* The sound /z/ is spelled *s* at the end of *birds.* The *s* makes the words mean "more than one.") Explain that today they will learn more about words with the ending *-s* that don't mean "more than one."

Sound-Spelling Card 129

USE SOUND-SPELLING CARD Display Card 129. Point to the word *pulls.* We add *s* to *pull* to show that one person is doing something. The *s* has the sound /z/ for this word. Have children say *pulls* with you several times.

MODEL Write *hops.* In this word, the letter *s* stands for the sound /s/. Segment and blend *hops* and then have children blend with you: /h/ /o/ /p/ /s/. Follow this procedure to model *digs.*

GROUP PRACTICE Continue the process. This time have children blend with you. Remind children that *s* can stand for the sound /s/ or the sound /z/.

wags	**sips**	**sees**	**packs**	**gets**	**nods**
fits	**yaps**	**picks**	**digs**	**licks**	**fills**

REVIEW What do you know about reading these words? (When you see a word that ends with *-s,* you know it might be a base word with an *-s* ending. Look for the base word. The letter *s* can stand for either /s/ or /z/.)

Access for All

SI Strategic Intervention

Blend Words with *-s* If children have trouble pronouncing the final *-s* correctly, pronounce final /s/ and /z/ sounds slowly. Then have children practice with words such as *stands, eats,* and *feeds.*

Vocabulary Support

You may wish to explain the meanings of these words.

wags moves from side to side

yaps barks like a dog

nods moves head up and down

Pronunciation /s/ Speakers of other languages may need support pronouncing words with the final *-s.* Provide additional practice with words such as *dips, mops, dogs,* and *pigs.*

Language Transfer Children who speak Cantonese may have trouble telling the difference between the /s/ and /z/ sounds. Give additional practice with these sounds as needed.

Common Core State Standards

Foundational Skills 3. Know and apply grade-level phonics and word analysis skills in decoding words. **Foundational Skills 3.b.** Decode regularly spelled one-syllable words. **Foundational Skills 3.f.** Read words with inflectional endings. **Language 4.c.** Identify frequently occurring root words (e.g., *look*) and their inflectional forms (e.g., *looks, looked, looking*).

Spelling Pattern

s/z/ The sound /z/ may be spelled *s.*

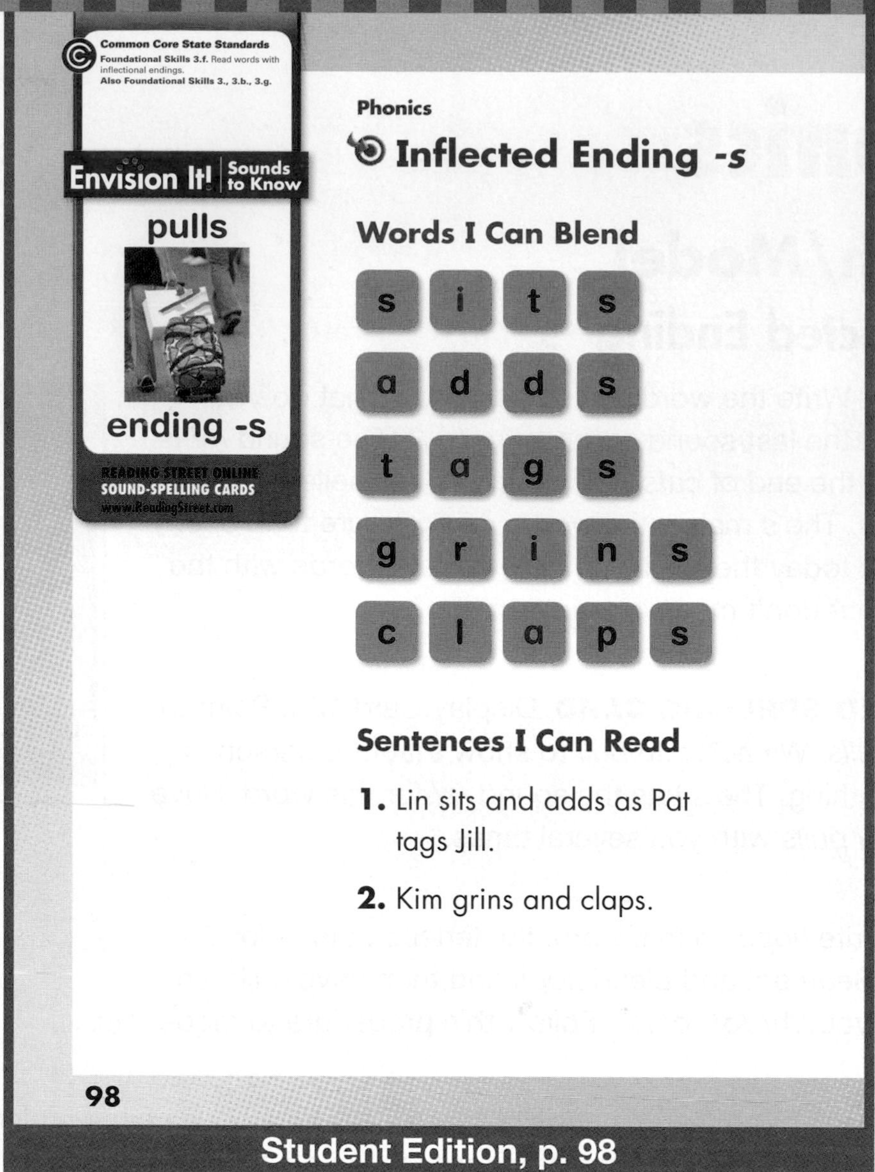

Student Edition, p. 98

Phonics

Guide Practice

BLEND WORDS Have children turn to page 98 in their Student Edition. I can see someone *pulls* a suitcase. When I say *pulls,* I hear /z/ at the end of the word. The sound /z/ can be spelled with the letter *s.* We learned that the letter *s* can spell the sound /s/ like in *sits.* The letter *s* can spell both the sound /z/ and the sound /s/.

GROUP PRACTICE For each word in "Words I Can Blend," ask for the sound of each letter or group of letters. Make sure that children identify the correct sound for /s/ or /z/. Then have children blend the whole word.

Corrective feedback	**If...** children have difficulty blending a word, **then...** model blending the word, and ask children to blend it with you.

DECODE WORDS IN ISOLATION After children can successfully segment and blend the words, point to words in random order and ask children to read them naturally.

DECODE WORDS IN CONTEXT Have children read each of the sentences. Have them identify words in the sentences that have the consonant sound /s/ or /z/.

Team Talk Pair children and have them take turns reading each of the sentences aloud.

ON THEIR OWN Use *Reader's and Writer's Notebook,* p. 169.

Inflected Ending *-s*

FORMATIVE ASSESSMENT Write the following words and have the class read them. Notice which words children miss during the group reading. Call on individuals to read some of the words.

hits	gabs	sits	hops	wins	**Spiral Review**
pops	packs	rock	jabs	bat ←	Row 2 contrasts decodable words with and without ending *-s.*
comes	takes	sees	looks	helps ←	Row 3 reviews high-frequency words with inflected ending *-s.*

If... children cannot blend words with the inflected ending *-s* at this point,

then... use the Small Group Time Strategic Intervention lesson, p. SG•58, to reteach words with inflected ending *-s.* Continue to monitor children's progress using other instructional opportunities during the week. See the Skills Trace on p. 96–97.

Access for All

A Advanced

Extend Blending Provide children who can segment and blend all the words correctly with more challenging words such as *cuddles, serves, studies,* and *scrubs.*

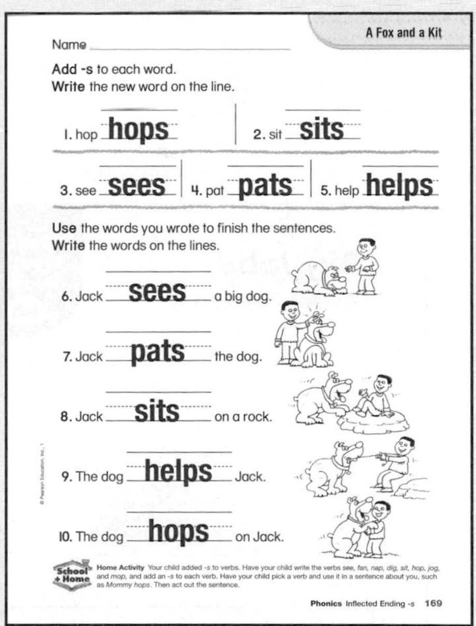

A Fox and a Kit

Name

Add -s to each word.
Write the new word on the line.

1. hop **hops**
2. sit **sits**
3. see **sees**
4. pat **pats**
5. help **helps**

Use the words you wrote to finish the sentences.
Write the words on the lines.

6. Jack **sees** a big dog.
7. Jack **pats** the dog.
8. Jack **sits** on a rock.
9. The dog **helps** Jack.
10. The dog **hops** on Jack.

Home Activity Your child added -s to verbs. Have your child write the verbs see, *fan, nap, dig, sit, hop, jog,* and *mop,* and add an -s to each verb. Have your child pick a verb and use it in a sentence about you, such as *Mommy hops.* Then act out the sentence.

Phonics Inflected Ending -s 169

Reader's and Writer's Notebook, p. 169

Common Core State Standards

Foundational Skills 3. Know and apply grade-level phonics and word analysis skills in decoding words. **Foundational Skills 3.b.** Decode regularly spelled one-syllable words. **Foundational Skills 3.f.** Read words with inflectional endings. **Foundational Skills 4.** Read with sufficient accuracy and fluency to support comprehension.

Decodable Reader 4A

If children need help, then...

Read *Big Jobs*

DECODE WORDS IN ISOLATION Have children turn to page 169. Have children decode each word.

REVIEW HIGH-FREQUENCY WORDS Review the previously taught words *a, do, have, the, we,* and *you.* Have children read each word as you point to it on the Word Wall.

PREVIEW DECODABLE READER Have children read the title and preview the story. Tell them they will decode words with inflected ending *-s.*

DECODE WORDS IN CONTEXT Pair children for reading, and listen as they decode. One child begins. Children read the entire story, switching readers after each page. Partners reread the story. This time the other child begins.

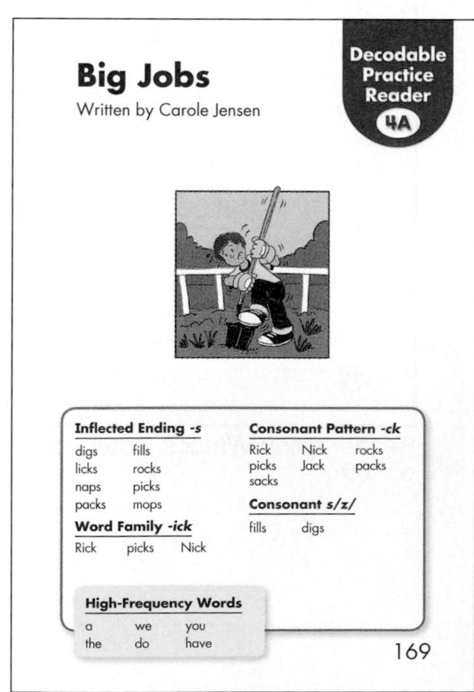

Big Jobs

Written by Carole Jensen

Decodable Practice Reader 4A

Inflected Ending -s
digs, fills, licks, rocks, naps, picks, packs, mops

Word Family -ick
Rick, picks, Nick

Consonant Pattern -ck
Rick, Nick, rocks, picks, Jack, packs, sacks

Consonant s/z/
fills, digs

High-Frequency Words
a, we, you, the, do, have

169

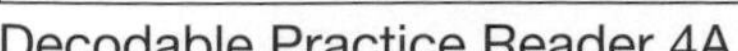

Decodable Practice Reader 4A

Corrective feedback	**If...** children have difficulty decoding a word, **then...** refer them to the Sound-Spelling Cards to identify the sounds in the word. Then prompt them to blend the word. • What is the new word? • Is the new word a word you know? • Does it make sense in the story?

CHECK DECODING AND COMPREHENSION Have children retell the story to include characters, setting, and events. Then have children find words with the inflected ending *-s* in the story. For each word, have children tell whether the *s* stands for the /s/ sound or the /z/ sound. Children should supply *digs, fills, licks, rocks, naps, picks, packs,* and *mops.*

Reread for Fluency

REREAD DECODABLE READER Have children reread Decodable Practice Reader 4A to develop automaticity decoding words with inflected ending *-s.*

Routine Oral Rereading

1. **Read** Have children read the entire book orally.
2. **Reread** To achieve optimal fluency, children should reread the text three or four times.
3. **Corrective Feedback** Listen as children read. Provide corrective feedback regarding their fluency and decoding.

Routines Flip Chart

Vocabulary Development

Beginning Write inflected ending *-s* words from *Big Jobs* on the board. Call on individuals to select a word, read it silently, and then act it out for the group to guess. Have the group pronounce the word and identify the base word and ending.

Intermediate Have children read each sentence with an *-s* word. Have them use pantomime or the picture to help identify each word as a plural noun or verb. Provide assistance with *jobs.*

Advanced Have children sort words from *Big Jobs* that mean "more than one" and words that are verbs with ending *-s* into two lists. Have them pronounce each word and explain how they sorted.

Common Core State Standards

Foundational Skills 3.g. Recognize and read grade-appropriate irregularly spelled words. **Language 2.d.** Use conventional spelling for words with common spelling patterns and for frequently occurring irregular words. **Also Foundational Skills 3.f., Language 2.e.**

Access for All

Advanced

Extend Spelling Challenge children who spell words correctly to spell more difficult words such as *eats, heats, cats, dogs,* and *tigers.*

Phonics/Spelling Generalization

Inflected *-s* Each spelling word ends in inflected *-s,* which forms the present tense.

Name ____________ A Fox and a Kit

Inflected Ending *-s*

Look at the word. **Say** it. **Think:** Does the word end in *s?*

	Write each word.	Check it.
1. nap	nap	nap
2. naps	naps	naps
3. sit	sit	sit
4. sits	sits	sits
5. win	win	win
6. wins	wins	wins
7. fit	fit	fit
8. fits	fits	fits
9. hit	hit	hit
10. hits	hits	hits

Words to Read

11. her	her	12. too	too

School + Home **Home Activity** Your child is learning to spell words that end in s. To practice at home, have your child say each word aloud. Next, help your child create a sentence using each word.

DVD•54 Spelling Inflected Ending -s

Let's Practice It! TR DVD•54

Spelling Pretest

Inflected Ending *-s*

DICTATE SPELLING WORDS Dictate the spelling words and read the sentences. Have children write the words. If needed, segment the words for children, clarify the pronunciations, and give meanings of words. Have children check their pretests and correct misspelled words.

1. sit	**Sit** in the front of the classroom.
2. sits*	Tom **sits** next to Mike on the bus.
3. win	The team will **win** the game.
4. wins	Mom **wins** the race.
5. fit	I **fit** into my new pants.
6. fits	The cat **fits** through the little door.
7. hit	I like to **hit** the drum.
8. hits	She **hits** the ball with a bat.
9. nap	I **nap** in the afternoon.
10. naps*	My brother **naps** on the couch.

* Words marked with asterisks come from the selection *A Fox and a Kit.*

ON THEIR OWN Use Let's Practice It! p. 54 on the *Teacher Resources DVD-ROM.*

ELL

If... children need more scaffolding and practice with **Phonemic Awareness and Phonics,** **then...** use the ELL activities on pp. DI•76–DI•77 in the Teacher Resources section on SuccessNet.

Day 1 SMALL GROUP TIME • Differentiate Phonics, p. SG•52

OL On-Level
- **Practice Phonics** Additional *-s* Words
- **Read** Decodable Reader *Big Jobs*

SI Strategic Intervention
- **Reteach Phonics** Blend *-s* Words
- **Read** Decodable Reader *Big Jobs*

A Advanced
- **Extend Phonics** More *-s* Words
- **Read** Advanced Selection for *-s* Words
- **Introduce** Inquiry Project

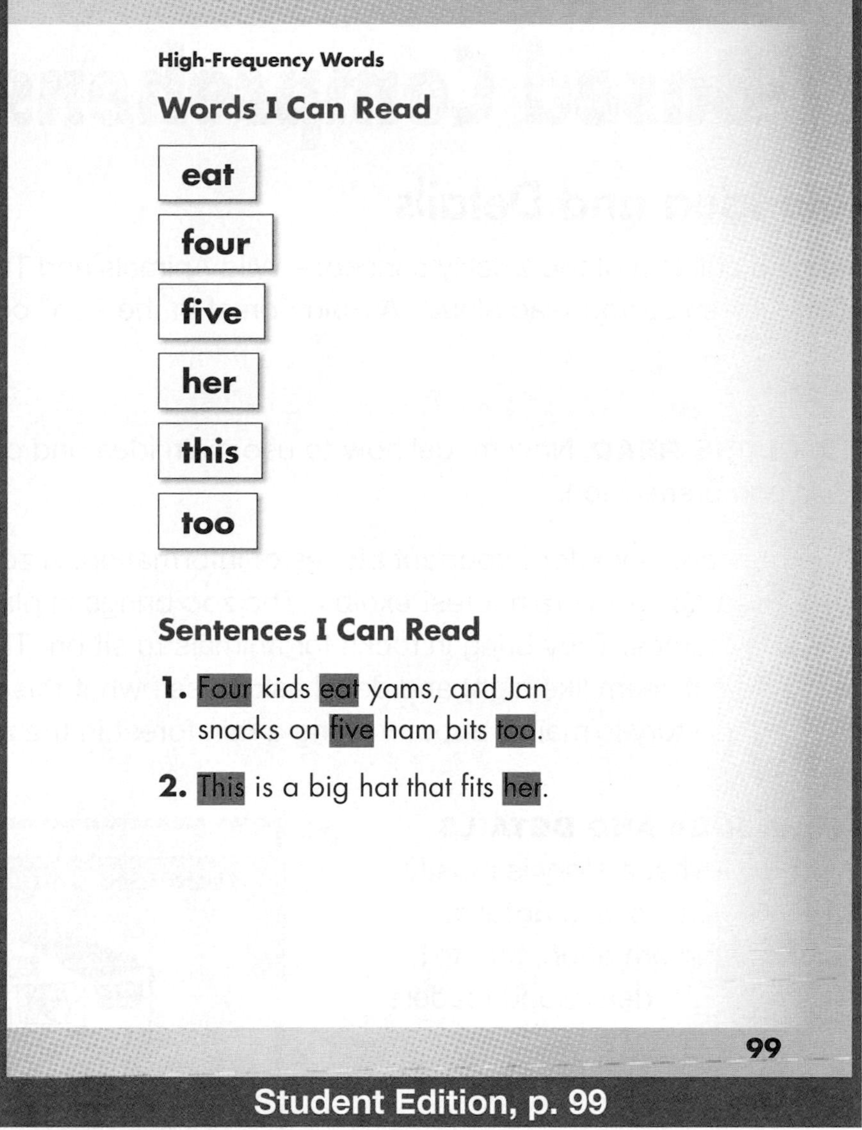

High-Frequency Words
Words I Can Read
eat
four
five
her
this
too
Sentences I Can Read
1. Four kids eat yams, and Jan snacks on five ham bits too.
2. This is a big hat that fits her.
99

Student Edition, p. 99

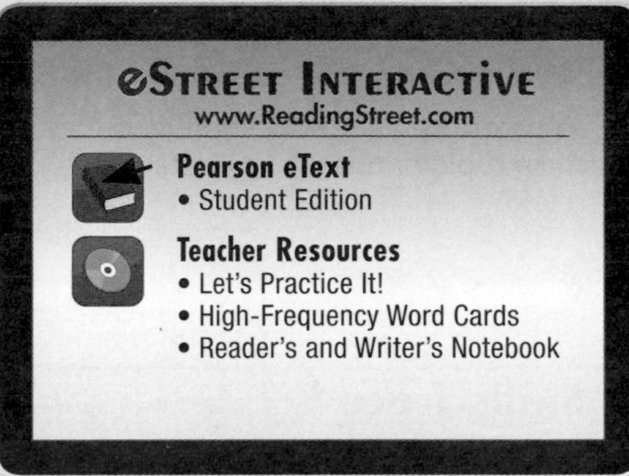

High-Frequency Words

Routine Nondecodable Words

1. **Say and Spell** Some words we have to learn by remembering the letters. Point to *eat.* Have children say and spell each word letter by letter.
2. **Identify Familiar Letter-Sounds** Point to the last letter in *eat.* What is this letter, and what is its sound? (*t,* /t/)
3. **Show Meaning** Tell me a sentence using the word *eat.* Repeat.

Routines Flip Chart

READ Have children read the page aloud. Add the words to the Word Wall.

ON THEIR OWN Use *Reader's and Writer's Notebook,* p. 170.

Name
A Fox and a Kit
Read the words in the box.
Pick a word to finish each sentence.
Write it on the line. Remember to begin a sentence with a capital letter.

eat four five her this too

1. We see four
2. The eat
3. This is a big cat.
4. This is a big cat too.
5. Can we help her?
6. We see five

Home Activity This week your child identified and read the words eat, four, five, her, too, and this. Look through books to find these words in print and have your child read them aloud.

170 High-Frequency Words

Reader's and Writer's Notebook, p. 170

Survival Vocabulary Have children use the high-frequency word *eat* in relation to their own lives. Children might say, *I **eat** breakfast every day.*

Zoom in on

Common Core State Standards

Informational Text 2. Identify the main topic and retell key details of a text.

Skills Trace

Main Idea and Details

Introduce U1W4D1; U1W5D1; U5W4D1

Practice U1W4D2; U1W4D3; U1W4D4; U1W5D2; U1W5D3; U1W5D4; U5W4D2; U5W4D3; U5W4D4

Reteach/Review U1W4D5; U1W5D5; U1W6D3; U2W3D2; U5W2D2; U5W4D5

Assess/Test Weekly Tests U1W4; U1W5; U5W4
Benchmark Tests U1; U5

KEY: U=Unit W=Week D=Day

Academic Vocabulary

main idea the big idea that tells what the selection is mainly about

details small pieces of information

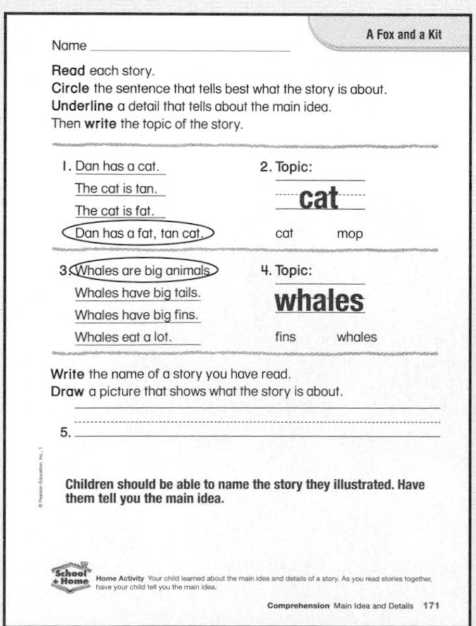

A Fox and a Kit

Name ____________

Read each story.
Circle the sentence that tells best what the story is about.
Underline a detail that tells about the main idea.
Then **write** the topic of the story.

1. Dan has a cat.
The cat is tan.
The cat is fat.
Dan has a fat, tan cat.

2. Topic: cat
cat mop

3. Whales are big animals.
Whales have big tails.
Whales have big fins.
Whales eat a lot.

4. Topic: whales
fins whales

Write the name of a story you have read.
Draw a picture that shows what the story is about.

5. ____________

Children should be able to name the story they illustrated. Have them tell you the main idea.

© Pearson Education, Inc., 1

School + Home **Home Activity** Your child learned about the main idea and details of a story. As you read stories together, have your child tell you the main idea.

Comprehension Main Idea and Details 171

Reader's and Writer's Notebook, p. 171

Text-Based Comprehension

Main Idea and Details

READ Remind children of the weekly concept—Wild Animals and Their Babies. Have children listen as you read aloud "A Rain Forest in the Zoo" on page 99b.

MODEL A CLOSE READ Now model how to use main idea and details as a tool to build comprehension.

When I read, I look for important pieces of information. A zookeeper tells Erica about the rain forest exhibit. The zoo brings in plants from animals' homes. They bring in rocks for animals to sit on. They change the lights to make it seem like night and day. I ask myself what this story is mainly about. The story is mainly about making a rain forest in the zoo.

TEACH MAIN IDEA AND DETAILS

The **main idea** is what a story is mostly about. Other sentences give **details,** or small pieces of information, that tell more about the main idea. Good readers pay attention to the details to help them understand the main idea in a story.

Main Idea and Details

Main Idea

Details

EI•3

Student Edition, p. EI•3

Have children turn to page EI•3 in their Student Edition. These pictures show an example of main idea and details. Discuss these questions using the pictures:

- When we look through the window, what details do we see? (a family at a table, a mom holding a sleeping baby, a cat on a couch)
- What do these details show? What is the main idea? (All the details show a home. The main idea is "home.")

GUIDE PRACTICE Ask children if they think the title of the selection tells the main idea. Have children explain. (Possible response: Yes, because the selection tells how people brought in things to make a rain forest in the zoo.) What is another title that you could use for this selection? (Possible response: "Erica Goes to the Rain Forest")

APPLY Use *Reader's and Writer's Notebook,* p. 171.

Teacher Read Aloud

A Rain Forest in the Zoo

Erica was very excited. Today was the day she and her dad were going to the zoo. They had been waiting all month to see the new rain forest exhibit. It finally opened today.

"Tell me about the rain forest again," Erica said to her dad as they walked into the zoo.

"A rain forest is a forest where many trees and plants grow very closely together. It rains a lot. That's why it's called a rain forest. The trees are very tall, and some birds, bugs, and other animals live in the tops of the trees. The largest animals live on the ground under the trees."

"Wow!" Erica said as they entered the exhibit. "This looks like a real forest!"

"It does!" Erica's dad said.

"That's because we try to make everything as real as we can," a zookeeper said. "Today, zoos want to build homes for the animals that look like their homes in the wild. We bring in many plants from the animals' homes. We make rocks for them to sit on. We change the lights to make it seem like night and day."

"That sounds like a lot of work!" exclaimed Erica.

"It is a lot of work," the zookeeper replied. "We do it so the animals feel right at home. We want them to feel safe and happy. Then when you observe them you can learn all about how they really live."

"Let's go look at those monkeys over there first," Erica said. "Look at that little black one. It's riding on the back of another monkey!"

The zookeeper said, "That's called a black spider monkey. Baby black spider monkeys ride on their mothers' tummies until they are about four months old. Then they ride on their mothers' backs. Monkey mothers take very good care of their babies."

"That's cool. I want to learn all about the rain forest!" Erica said.

"Me too," said Erica's dad.

Bridge to Common Core

KEY IDEAS AND DETAILS
As children read the nonfiction selection, they determine the main idea and identify the details that support that main idea. Recognizing the main idea and supporting details helps children develop knowledge in the content area. Asking questions about the content of the selection helps children better understand the selection and the key concepts.

Check Understanding Stop after reading the fifth paragraph and discuss with children. Clarify understanding by asking questions such as *What does Erica know about rain forests before she gets to the zoo?* At the end of the Read Aloud, ask children what Erica learns about the rain forest in the zoo.

DAY 1

Common Core State Standards

Foundational Skills 1.a. Recognize the distinguishing features of a sentence (e.g., first word, capitalization, ending punctuation). **Writing 1.** Write opinion pieces in which they introduce the topic or name the book they are writing about, state an opinion, supply a reason for the opinion, and provide some sense of closure. **Writing 3.** Write narratives in which they recount two or more appropriately sequenced events, include some details regarding what happened, use temporal words to signal event order, and provide some sense of closure. **Language 1.j.** Produce and expand complete simple and compound declarative, interrogative, imperative, and exclamatory sentences in response to prompts. **Also Language 1., 2.b.**

Academic Vocabulary

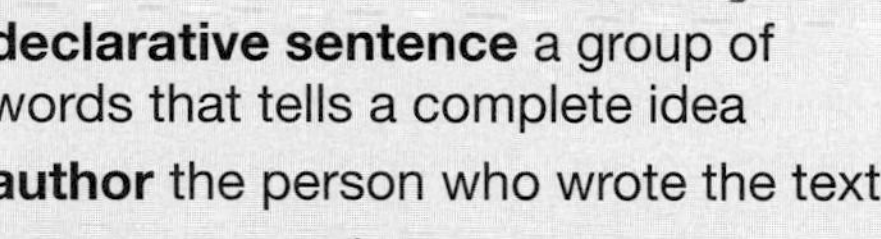

declarative sentence a group of words that tells a complete idea

author the person who wrote the text

event an experience

personal narrative a story about an event or events in the author's life

Daily Fix-It

1. Fox napz on her lap
   Fox naps on her lap.
2. frog sitts there too.
   Frog sits there too.

Discuss the Daily Fix-It corrections with children. Review sentence capitalization and punctuation, the inflected ending *-s,* and the spelling of *sits.*

Conventions

Declarative Sentences

MAKE CONNECTIONS Today we read a story about a girl who learned about a rain forest at the zoo. We learn things every day. Let's share sentences about things that you have learned. Write the sentences on the board. These sentences are called declarative sentences.

TEACH Explain that a **declarative sentence** is one that tells about something. It tells a fact or someone's point of view. A declarative sentence begins with a capital letter and ends with a period.

MODEL Display Grammar Transparency 4. Read the definition aloud. Model why each example is a declarative sentence. Then read the directions and model number 1.

GUIDE PRACTICE Continue with items 2–4, having children put a check mark by the sentence that is written correctly.

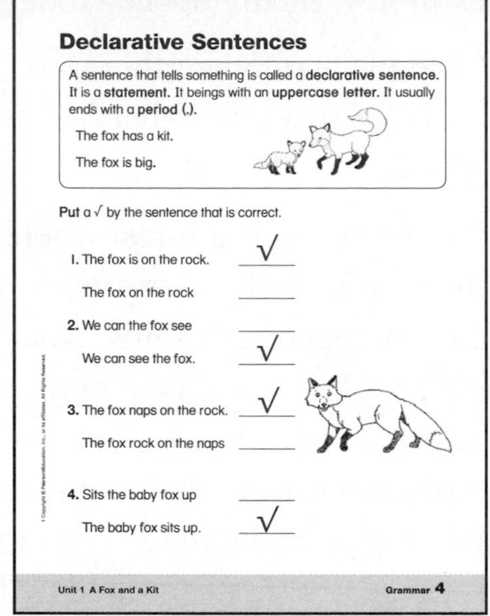

Declarative Sentences

A sentence that tells something is called a **declarative sentence.** It is a **statement.** It beings with an **uppercase letter.** It usually ends with a **period** (.).

The fox has a kit.

The fox is big.

Put a √ by the sentence that is correct.

1. The fox is on the rock. √
   The fox on the rock
2. We can the fox see
   We can see the fox. √
3. The fox naps on the rock. √
   The fox rock on the naps
4. Sits the baby fox up
   The baby fox sits up. √

Unit 1 A Fox and a Kit — Grammar 4

Grammar Transparency 4 TR DVD

APPLY Have the class complete these sentence frames orally.

1. **I can ______ animals to learn about them.**
2. **A fox is a ______ animal.**
3. **A ______ is a person with children.**

Team Talk Pair children and have them decide whether each example is a declarative sentence.

Personal Narrative

Mini-Lesson Read Like a Writer

- **Introduce** This week you will write a **personal narrative.** A personal narrative is a kind of story. It tells about an event in your life.

  Prompt Think about a time you watched some animals. Write a narrative about it.

  Trait Voice

  Mode Narrative/Opinion

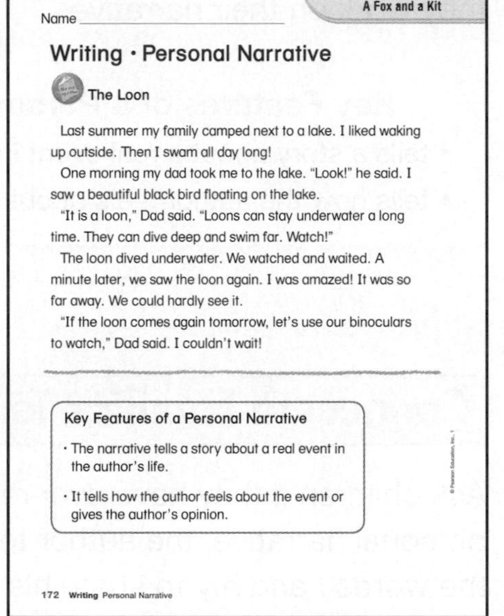

Name ____________ A Fox and a Kit

Writing • Personal Narrative

The Loon

Last summer my family camped next to a lake. I liked waking up outside. Then I swam all day long!

One morning my dad took me to the lake. "Look!" he said. I saw a beautiful black bird floating on the lake.

"It is a loon," Dad said. "Loons can stay underwater a long time. They can dive deep and swim far. Watch!"

The loon dived underwater. We watched and waited. A minute later, we saw the loon again. I was amazed! It was so far away. We could hardly see it.

"If the loon comes again tomorrow, let's use our binoculars to watch," Dad said. I couldn't wait!

Key Features of a Personal Narrative

- The narrative tells a story about a real event in the author's life.
- It tells how the author feels about the event or gives the author's opinion.

172 Writing Personal Narrative

Reader's and Writer's Notebook, p. 172

- **Examine Model Text** Let's listen to a personal narrative. Track the print as you read aloud "The Loon" on *Reader's and Writer's Notebook,* p. 172. Have children follow along.

- **Key Features** What event is this narrative mostly about? (The author and Dad watch a loon.) Help children underline words or short phrases in the story that tell the author's opinion or how the author feels about events, such as *liked, amazed,* and *I couldn't wait.*

  Like a story, this personal narrative has a beginning, middle, and end. At the beginning, Dad shows the author a loon. In the middle, they watch the loon. At the end, they decide to use binoculars the next time they see the loon.

  In the personal narrative, the author shares feelings or opinions about the events. Does the author feel excited about watching the loon? (yes)

Writing to Sources Use More Connect the Texts on pp. 221–259 to guide children in writing text-based responses within various forms and modes.

Write Guy *by Jeff Anderson*

Adjective Strings

As children learn to write, many love to "improve" sentences with adjectives—big adjectives, little adjectives, many adjectives. We don't want to encourage strings of adjectives. On the other hand, this is a problem that can correct itself. Show a sample of a sentence with too many adjectives. Ask which one adjective might be unnecessary.

Bridge to Common Core

TEXT TYPES AND PURPOSES

This week children write a personal narrative about a time when they watched animals.

Narrative Writing

As children create their personal narrative, they record events in a sequence and include details. They learn about writing a story about a real event in the author's life and how the author feels about the event. They develop effective techniques to write a well-structured personal narrative.

Throughout the week, children will improve the range and content of their writing through daily mini-lessons.

5-Day Plan

DAY 1	Read Like a Writer
DAY 2	Interesting Details
DAY 3	Writing Trait: Voice
DAY 4	Revise: Rearranging Sentences
DAY 5	Proofread

Common Core State Standards

Writing 3. Write narratives in which they recount two or more appropriately sequenced events, include some details regarding what happened, use temporal words to signal event order, and provide some sense of closure. **Writing 7.** Participate in shared research and writing projects (e.g., explore a number of "how-to" books on a given topic and use them to write a sequence of instructions). **Writing 8.** With guidance and support from adults, recall information from experiences or gather information from provided sources to answer a question.

Writing

Review Key Features

Review key features of a personal narrative with children. You may want to post these key features in the classroom to allow children to refer to them as they work on their narratives.

Key Features of a Personal Narrative

- tells a story about a real event in the author's life
- tells how the author feels about it

Connect to Familiar Texts

Ask children if they have ever read a personal narrative. Remind them that in a personal narrative, the author tells a story about a real event. The author uses the words *I* and *my* to share his or her thoughts and feelings about the event.

Routine Quick Write for Fluency

Team Talk

1. **Talk** Read these questions aloud, and give children two minutes to discuss with partners.
   What animals can we see around our school?
   What animals can we see around our community?
2. **Write** Have children write short sentences about their favorite animal among those mentioned.
3. **Share** Partners can read their answers to one another.

Routines Flip Chart

Research and Inquiry

Step 1 Identify and Focus Topic

TEACH Display and review the concept map about this week's question: *How do wild animals take care of their babies?* What are some different wild animals that take care of their babies? Ask children to share their ideas. Help children identify animals they would like to learn about.

Think Aloud **MODEL** I love animals, and I would like to learn about all the animals in the world. For now, I will focus on just a few. Bears are one of my favorite animals. I'd like to know more about how they take care of their babies, so I will put bears on my list of animals to learn about. I like foxes because they look like dogs. I wonder how foxes take care of their babies. Foxes go on my list too.

GUIDE PRACTICE Give children time to think of animals they would like to learn about. Record children's suggestions in a list.

21st Century Skills

Internet Guy *Don Leu*

Weekly Inquiry Project

STEP 1	Identify and Focus Topic
STEP 2	Research Skill
STEP 3	Gather and Record Information
STEP 4	Synthesize
STEP 5	Communicate

Wrap Up Your Day!

- ✔ **Phonics: Inflected Ending *-s*** Write *naps.* Have children identify the base word and ending. Continue with *wins, looks,* and *gets.*
- ✔ **Spelling: Inflected Ending *-s*** Have children name the letter for each sound in *hits.* Write the spelling as children write the letters in the air. Continue with *sits, kicks,* and *locks.*
- ✔ **Content Knowledge** Ask children to recall the Read Aloud "A Rain Forest in the Zoo." What did Erica and her dad see at the zoo? (a monkey and her baby)
- ✔ **Homework** Send home this week's Family Times Newsletter from Let's Practice It! pp. 49–50 on the *Teacher Resources DVD-ROM.*

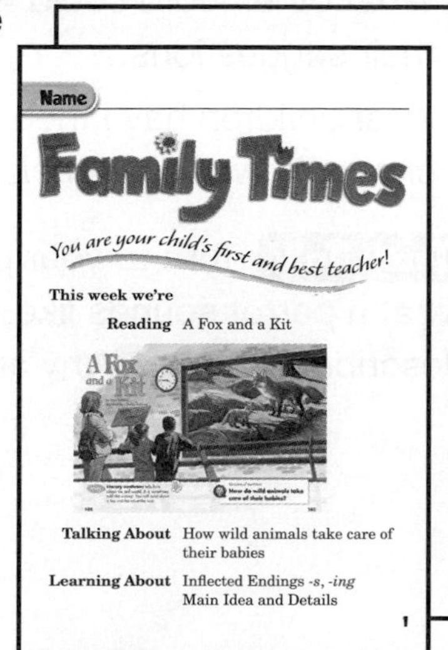

Name
Family Times
You are your child's first and best teacher!
This week we're
Reading A Fox and a Kit
Talking About How wild animals take care of their babies
Learning About Inflected Endings -s, -ing
Main Idea and Details

Let's Practice It!
TR DVD•49–50

Tell children that tomorrow they will read about how a fox takes care of its baby.

Content Knowledge
Oral Vocabulary

Phonemic Awareness
Segment and Blend Phonemes

Phonics/Spelling
Inflected Ending *-ing*
Inflected Ending *-s*

High-Frequency Words
eat, five, four, her, this, too

Selection Vocabulary
animals, dinner, watch
Alphabetize to the Second Letter

Text-Based Comprehension
Main Idea and Details
Important Ideas

Conventions
Declarative Sentences

Writing
Personal Narrative

Handwriting
Letters *Nn* and *Gg*/Letter Slant

Research and Inquiry
Research Skill: How to Read a Chart

Materials

- Student Edition
- Sing with Me Big Book
- Big Book
- Sound-Spelling Cards
- Decodable Reader 4B
- Reader's and Writer's Notebook

Common Core State Standards

Speaking/Listening 2. Ask and answer questions about key details in a text read aloud or information presented orally or through other media. **Language 6.** Use words and phrases acquired through conversations, reading and being read to, and responding to texts, including using frequently occurring conjunctions to signal simple relationships (e.g., *I named my hamster Nibblet because she nibbles too much because she likes that*).

Content Knowledge

Wild Animals and Their Babies

EXPAND THE CONCEPT To reinforce concepts and to focus children's attention, have them sing "Squirrel Song" from the *Sing with Me* Big Book. What does the boy learn about the mother squirrel? (The mother squirrel is watching her baby.)

Build Oral Language

INTRODUCE AMAZING WORDS Display the Big Book *Jungle Drum.* Read the title and identify the author. Explain that in the story, the author uses some Amazing Words. Read the story and have children listen for the words *canopy* and *screech.*

Big Book

TALK ABOUT SENTENCES AND WORDS Reread this sentence from the Big Book.

Up in the canopy, parrots are screeching. "Kahrooo! Kahrooo chooo!"

- Have children repeat the sentence with you. What does *parrots are screeching* mean? (The parrots are making loud, high-pitched sounds.)
- What other word could we use in place of *screeching?* Have children share their suggestions.
- After children have tried other words, ask: Why do you think the author chose the word *screeching?* (It is the way the author thinks parrots sound.)

Team Talk Turn to your partner and say the sentence using your word for what a parrot sounds like. Then have teams use the picture on page 14 to describe a *canopy.* Why are the parrots up in the *canopy* and not down?

Build Oral Vocabulary

Amazing Words — Robust Vocabulary Routine

1. **Introduce the Word** Relate the word *screech* to the book. We heard the parrot screech "Kahrooo chooo!" Supply a child-friendly definition. To *screech* means to make a high scream or sound. Have children say the word.

2. **Demonstrate** Provide examples to show meaning. When something frightens you, you may *screech* "Help, Help!" A cat might *screech* if it sees a big dog. The tires will *screech* if a bike stops suddenly.

3. **Apply** Have children demonstrate their understanding. If any of the things I name can screech, say *screech;* if not, say nothing: a bird, a baby, a pumpkin, a horn, a car.

4. **Display the Word** Point out the sound-spelling *scr* /s/ /k/ /r/ at the beginning of *screech.*

See p. OV•4 to teach *canopy.*

Routines Flip Chart

ADD TO THE CONCEPT MAP Discuss different ways wild animals take care of their babies.

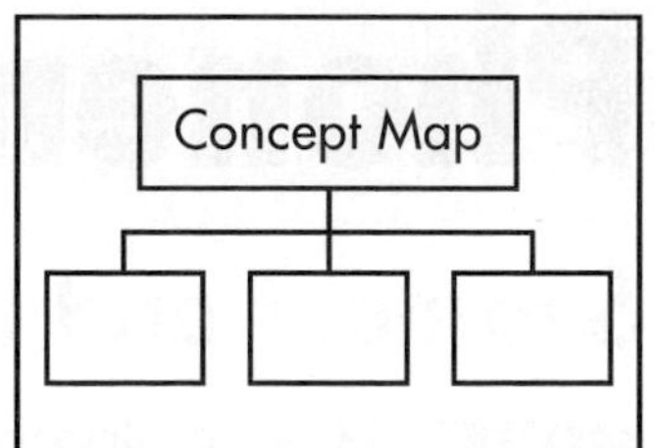

- In "Squirrel Song," what is Mama Squirrel doing? (She is watching her baby.) Let's add *They watch over them* to our map.
- In yesterday's Read Aloud "A Rain Forest in the Zoo," what did Erica see the mother monkey do? (She saw the mother monkey carrying her baby on her back.) Let's add *They carry them* to our map.

Amazing Words

observe	screech
wild	million
parent	native
canopy	reserve

Access for All

 **Advanced**

Vocabulary Tell children that **onomatopoeia** is the use of words that imitate the sounds they describe. Have children practice saying the words *blip, blop, mmm,* and *screech.*

Vocabulary Support

You may wish to explain the meanings of these words.

jungle a kind of thick forest where many bushes, vines, and trees grow

drum a musical instrument that makes a sound when you hit it

Reinforce Vocabulary Use the Day 2 instruction on ELL Poster 4 to reinforce meanings of the high-frequency words.

Onomatopoeia To help children understand sound words, point to some animals pictured in *Jungle Drum* and say the words that describe the sound they make. Have children repeat each sound word after you and then have them say it on their own.

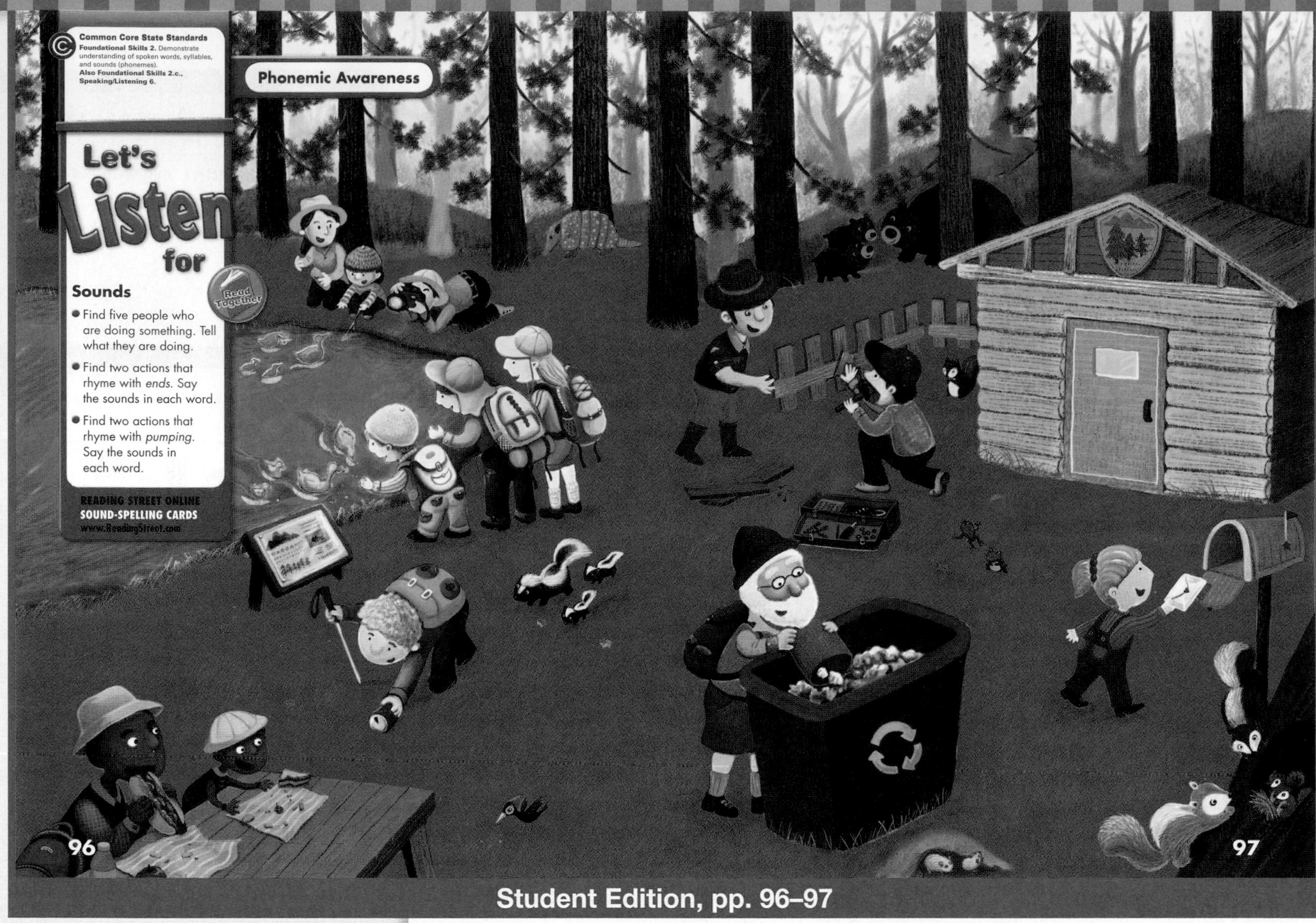

Student Edition, pp. 96–97

Common Core State Standards

Foundational Skills 2.c. Isolate and pronounce initial, medial vowel, and final sounds (phonemes) in spoken single-syllable words. **Foundational Skills 3.** Know and apply grade-level phonics and word analysis skills in decoding words. **Foundational Skills 3.f.** Read words with inflectional endings.

Skills Trace

Inflected Ending *-ing*

Introduce U1W4D2

Practice U1W4D3; U1W4D4

Reteach/Review U1W4D5, U1W5D4

Assess/Test Weekly Test U1W4
Benchmark Test U1

KEY: U=Unit W=Week D=Day

Phonemic Awareness

Segment and Blend Phonemes

MODEL Have children look at the picture on pages 96–97. I see children *bending* and *feeding* the ducks. The ducks are *eating.* The sound I hear at the end of the words *bending, feeding,* and *eating* is *-ing.*

Listen to the sounds in *bending:* /b/ /e/ /n/ /d/ *-ing.* Let's blend the sounds: /b/ /e/ /n/ /d/ *-ing, bending.* Continue with *feeding* and *eating.*

GROUP PRACTICE Guide children as they segment and blend these words from the picture: *jumping, dumping, mending, sending, standing, handing, looking.*

Corrective feedback	**If...** children make an error, **then...** model by segmenting the word and have them repeat.

ON THEIR OWN Have children segment and blend the following words.

/d/ /i/ /g/ *-ing* **digging** /l/ /o/ /k/ *-ing* **locking** /t/ /a/ /p/ *-ing* **tapping**

Phonics

Teach/Model

Inflected Ending *-ing*

CONNECT Write the words *digs* and *hops.* You studied words like these already. What do you know about reading these words? (The words have *-s* endings.) Today you will learn about words with the ending *-ing.*

Sound-Spelling Card 126

USE SOUND-SPELLING CARD Display Card 126. The sound you hear at the end of *drinking* is *-ing.* The sound *-ing* can be spelled *ing.* Have children say /ng/ several times as you point to *-ing.*

MODEL Write *fixing.* This word is *fixing.* In this word, the letters *ing* stand for *-ing.* Segment and blend *fixing;* then have children blend with you: /f/ /i/ /ks/ *-ing.* Follow this procedure to model blending *rocking.*

GROUP PRACTICE Continue the process. This time have children blend with you.

picking	locking	seeing	packing
waxing	looking	going	doing

REVIEW What do you know about reading these words? (When a word ends with *-ing,* you know it might be a base word with an *-ing* ending.)

Access for All

Strategic Intervention

Pronounce Inflected Ending *-ing* Some speakers may say *rockin* or *fixin* instead of *rocking* or *fixing,* as they might not hear the difference between *-in* and *-ing.* Have children practice pronouncing words with ending *-ing.*

Pronounce Inflected Ending *-ing* In some languages /ng/ does not exist, so there may be children who need support pronouncing words with the inflected ending *-ing.* Tell children that this sound is made by raising the back part of the tongue toward the roof of the mouth. Then demonstrate and have children follow. Provide practice with words such as *locking, mixing,* and *passing.*

Common Core State Standards

Foundational Skills 3. Know and apply grade-level phonics and word analysis skills in decoding words. **Foundational Skills 3.f.** Read words with inflectional endings.

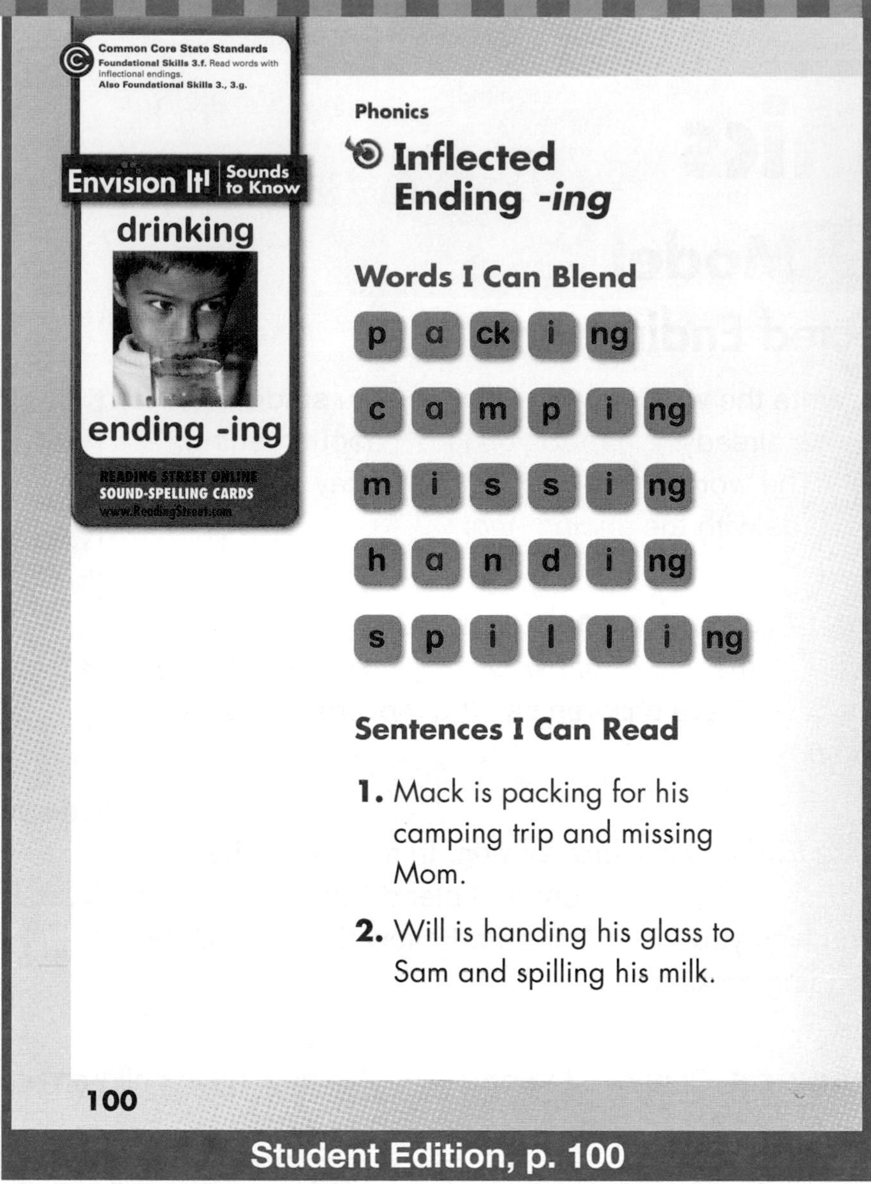

Common Core State Standards
Foundational Skills 3.f. Read words with inflectional endings.
Also Foundational Skills 3., 3.g.

Phonics

Inflected Ending *-ing*

Words I Can Blend

p a ck i ng
c a m p i ng
m i s s i ng
h a n d i ng
s p i l l i ng

Sentences I Can Read

1. Mack is packing for his camping trip and missing Mom.
2. Will is handing his glass to Sam and spilling his milk.

100

Student Edition, p. 100

Phonics

Guide Practice

BLEND WORDS Have children turn to page 100 in their Student Edition. Look at the picture on this page. The word in the picture is *drinking.* When I say *drinking,* I hear the ending *-ing.* In *drinking,* /i/ /ng/ is spelled *ing.*

GROUP PRACTICE For each word in "Words I Can Blend," ask for the sound of each letter or group of letters. Make sure that children identify the correct sound for the ending *-ing.* Then have children blend the whole word.

Corrective feedback	**If...** children have difficulty blending a word, **then...** model blending the word, and ask children to blend it with you.

DECODE WORDS IN ISOLATION After children can successfully segment and blend the words, ask them to read the words naturally.

DECODE WORDS IN CONTEXT Have children read each of the sentences. Have them identify words in the sentences that have the ending *-ing.*

Team Talk Pair children and have them take turns reading each of the sentences aloud.

ON THEIR OWN Use *Reader's and Writer's Notebook,* p. 173.

Inflected Ending *-ing*

FORMATIVE ASSESSMENT Write the following words and have the class read them. Notice which children miss words during the group reading. Call on those individuals to read some of the words.

packing	**ticking**	**locking**	**picking**	**fixing**	**Spiral Review**
wax	**waxing**	**quacking**	**fill**	**filling** ←	Row 2 contrasts decodable words with and without inflected ending *-ing.*
doing	**seeing**	**looking**	**going**	**helping** ←	Row 3 reviews high-frequency words with inflected ending *-ing.*

If... children cannot blend words with the *-ing* ending,

then... use the Small Group Time Strategic Intervention lesson, p. SG•59, to reteach *-ing* endings. Continue to monitor children's progress using other instructional opportunities during the week. See the Skills Trace on p. 100c.

Access for All

Advanced

Write Inflected Ending *-ing* Have children find and then write each word with the inflected ending *-ing* in the sentences from the "Sentences I Can Read" section. *(packing, camping, missing, handing, spilling)*

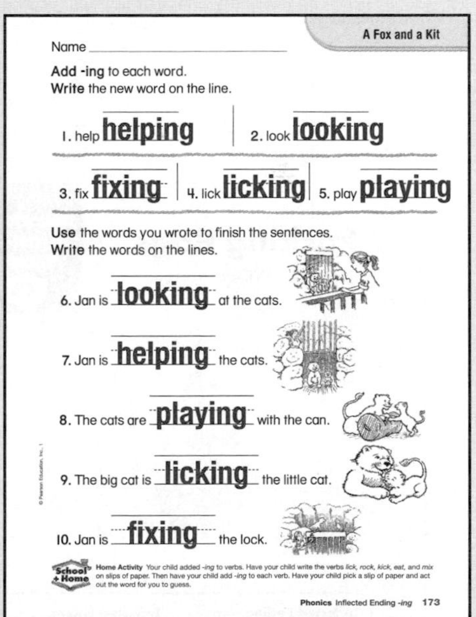

A Fox and a Kit

Name ____________

Add -ing to each word.
Write the new word on the line.

1. help **helping** 2. look **looking**
3. fix **fixing** 4. lick **licking** 5. play **playing**

Use the words you wrote to finish the sentences.
Write the words on the lines.

6. Jan is **looking** at the cats.
7. Jan is **helping** the cats.
8. The cats are **playing** with the can.
9. The big cat is **licking** the little cat.
10. Jan is **fixing** the lock.

School + Home **Home Activity** Your child added *-ing* to verbs. Have your child write the verbs *lick, rock, kick, eat,* and *mix* on slips of paper. Then have your child add *-ing* to each verb. Have your child pick a slip of paper and act out the word for you to guess.

© Pearson Education, Inc., 1

Phonics Inflected Ending *-ing* 173

Reader's and Writer's Notebook, p. 173

Support Vocabulary Help children understand the meanings of the words ending in *-ing* by pantomiming the words as you say them.

Common Core State Standards

Foundational Skills 3. Know and apply grade-level phonics and word analysis skills in decoding words. **Foundational Skills 3.f.** Read words with inflectional endings. **Foundational Skills 4.** Read with sufficient accuracy and fluency to support comprehension. **Language 4.c.** Identify frequently occurring root words (e.g., *look*) and their inflectional forms (e.g., *looks, looked, looking*).

Decodable Reader 4B

If children need help, then...

Read *Packing Bags*

DECODE WORDS IN ISOLATION Have children turn to page 177. Have children decode each word.

REVIEW HIGH-FREQUENCY WORDS Review the previously taught word *we.* Have children read the word as you point to it on the Word Wall.

PREVIEW Have children read the title and preview the story. Tell them they will read words that end in *-ing* and *-s.*

DECODE WORDS IN CONTEXT Pair children for reading, and listen as they decode. One child begins. Children read the entire story, switching readers after each page.

Packing Bags
Written by William Spree
Decodable Practice Reader 4B

Inflected Ending *-ing*		Inflected Ending *-s*	
packing	backing	helps	sits
picking		packs	

High-Frequency Words
we

177

Decodable Practice Reader 4B

Mom is packing bags.
Dad is packing bags.
Pam helps.

178

Dad is backing up.
We can get in.

179

Dad is picking up Jan.
Jan can get in.

180

Jan and Pam ran.
Mom sits.
Dad sits.

181

Jan sits. Pam sits.

182

Mom packs.
Dad packs.

183

Mom and Dad sit.
Jan and Pam sit.

184

Corrective feedback	**If…** children have difficulty decoding a word, **then…** refer them to the Sound-Spelling Cards to identify the sounds in the word. Then prompt them to blend the word. • What is the new word? • Is the new word a word you know? • Does it make sense in the story?

CHECK DECODING AND COMPREHENSION Have children retell the story to include characters, setting, and events. Then have children find words with inflected ending *-ing* in the story. Children should supply *packing, backing,* and *picking.*

Reread for Fluency

REREAD DECODABLE READER Have children reread Decodable Practice Reader 4B to develop automaticity decoding words with inflected ending *-ing.*

Routine Paired Reading

1. **Reread** To achieve optimal fluency, have partners reread the text three or four times.
2. **Corrective Feedback** Listen as children read. Provide corrective feedback regarding their fluency and decoding.

Routines Flip Chart

Access for All

SI Strategic Intervention

Retelling If children have difficulty retelling the story, ask them questions regarding the events in the story. Tell them to use the pictures to help understand what happens.

Inflected Ending *-ing*

Beginning After reading, point out the words with inflected ending *-ing.* Have children read them aloud. Then have children identify the story characters.

Intermediate After reading, have children find words with the inflected ending *-ing* and say them aloud. Have children tell you what each word means.

Advanced After reading, have children find words that have inflected ending *-ing.* Have them make up questions using the words. For example, *Who is packing?* Allow children to answer the questions.

Common Core State Standards

Foundational Skills 2.d. Segment spoken single-syllable words into their complete sequence of individual sounds (phonemes). **Foundational Skills 3.f.** Read words with inflectional endings. **Language 2.d.** Use conventional spelling for words with common spelling patterns and for frequently occurring irregular words. **Language 4.c.** Identify frequently occurring root words (e.g., *look*) and their inflectional forms (e.g., *looks, looked, looking*).

Phonics

Review Inflected Ending *-s*

REVIEW SOUND-SPELLINGS Review the inflected ending *-s* using Sound-Spelling Card 129.

DECODE WORDS IN ISOLATION Display these words. Have the class blend the words. Then point to the words in random order and ask children to decode them quickly.

digs	**locks**	**bobs**	**tips**
sits	**naps**	**sips**	**rocks**
taps	**wins**	**nods**	**pods**

Corrective feedback | Model blending decodable words and then ask children to blend them with you.

DECODE WORDS IN CONTEXT Display these sentences. Have the class read the sentences.

Team Talk Have pairs take turns reading the sentences naturally.

Jan **packs** and then **naps.**
Dad **sits** and **pats** the cat.
The little dog **yips** and **yaps.**

Spelling

Inflected Ending *-s*

GUIDE PRACTICE Tell children that you will segment the sounds in each spelling word. They should repeat the sounds in each word as they write the word. Check the spelling of each word before saying the next word.

1.	/s/ /i/ /t/	**sit**	**6.**	/f/ /i/ /t/ /s/	**fits**
2.	/s/ /i/ /t/ /s/	**sits**	**7.**	/h/ /i/ /t/	**hit**
3.	/w/ /i/ /n/	**win**	**8.**	/h/ /i/ /t/ /s/	**hits**
4.	/w/ /i/ /n/ /z/	**wins**	**9.**	/n/ /a/ /p/	**nap**
5.	/f/ /i/ /t/	**fit**	**10.**	/n/ /a/ /p/ /s/	**naps**

ON THEIR OWN Use *Reader's and Writer's Notebook,* p. 174.

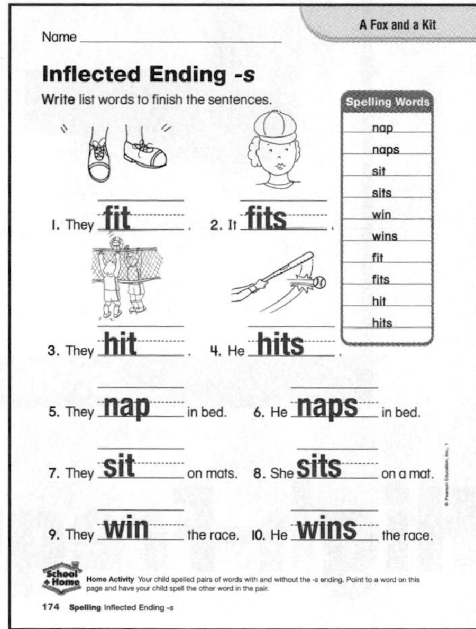
Name ______________ A Fox and a Kit

Inflected Ending -s

Write list words to finish the sentences.

Spelling Words: nap, naps, sit, sits, win, wins, fit, fits, hit, hits

1. They fit.
2. It fits.
3. They hit.
4. He hits.
5. They nap in bed.
6. He naps in bed.
7. They sit on mats.
8. She sits on a mat.
9. They win the race.
10. He wins the race.

School + Home: Home Activity Your child spelled pairs of words with and without the -s ending. Point to a word on this page and have your child spell the other word in the pair.

174 Spelling Inflected Ending -s

Reader's and Writer's Notebook, p. 174

Access for All

SI Strategic Intervention

Guide Practice To guide practice, have children write the spelling words on their own. Have children sound out the sounds in the words as they write the words. When they have finished, have them confirm their spellings by comparing them to what you have written on the board.

Physical Response Use physical gestures to demonstrate spelling words such as *sit, win,* and *nap.* Repeat the words and gestures as needed to help children learn the words.

Common Core State Standards

Foundational Skills 3. Know and apply grade-level phonics and word analysis skills in decoding words. **Foundational Skills 3.f.** Read words with inflectional endings. **Foundational Skills 3.g.** Recognize and read grade-appropriate irregularly spelled words. **Language 4.** Determine or clarify the meaning of unknown and multiple-meaning words and phrases based on grade 1 reading and content, choosing flexibly from an array of strategies.

Access for All

SI Strategic Intervention

Identify High-Frequency and Selection Words Have children practice reading *eat, five, four, her, this, too,* and *dinner.* For corrective feedback, reteach the words using Routine Cards.

A Fox and a Kit

Name ______

Read the words in each box. Then **pick** one to finish each sentence. **Write** it on the line.

five four
1. We see **five** animals.

Her This
2. **This** is a big whale.

eat too
3. We watch the [elephant] **eat** dinner.

we her
4. The big one is **her** dad.

four dinner
5. We see **four** animals.

this too
6. We see a big ox **too**.

School + Home **Home Activity** This week your child learned to read the words *animals, whale, dinner, watch, eat, four, five, her, this,* and *too.* Help your child make up a story about a day spent with friendly animals. Write the story as your child tells it. Then invite him or her to draw a picture to go with the story.

High-Frequency Words/Story Words DVD•53

Let's Practice It! TR DVD•53

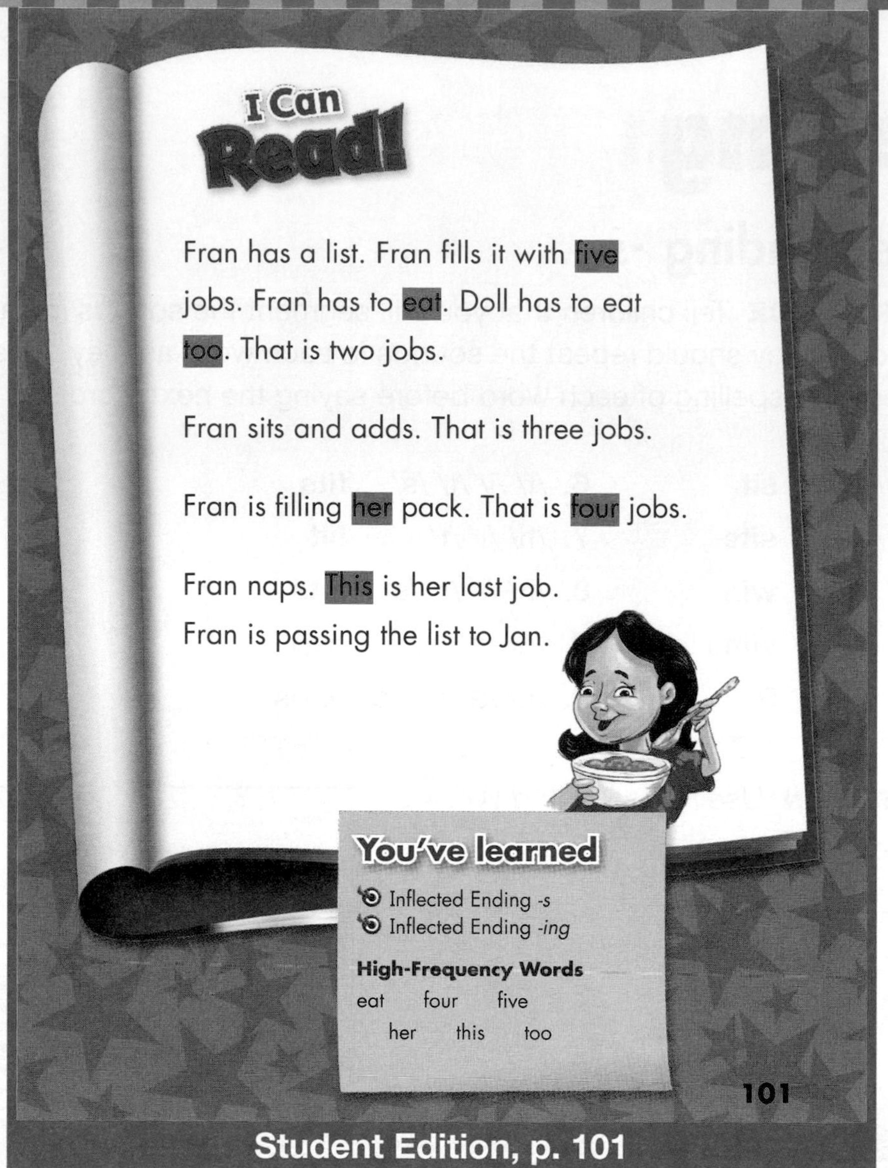

I Can Read!

Fran has a list. Fran fills it with five jobs. Fran has to eat. Doll has to eat too. That is two jobs.

Fran sits and adds. That is three jobs.

Fran is filling her pack. That is four jobs.

Fran naps. This is her last job.
Fran is passing the list to Jan.

You've learned

Inflected Ending -s
Inflected Ending -ing

High-Frequency Words
eat four five
her this too

101

Student Edition, p. 101

High-Frequency Words

READ WORDS IN ISOLATION Remind children that there are some words we learn by remembering the letters. Then have them read each of the high-lighted high-frequency words aloud.

READ WORDS IN CONTEXT Chorally read the "I Can Read!" passage along with children. Then have them read the passage aloud to themselves. When they are finished, ask children to reread the high-frequency words.

Team Talk Have children choose two high-frequency words and give them time to create a sentence in which both words are used properly. Then have them share their sentence with a partner.

ON THEIR OWN Use Let's Practice It! p. 53 on the *Teacher Resources DVD-ROM.*

Selection Vocabulary

INTRODUCE SELECTION WORDS Use Vocabulary Transparency 4 to introduce this week's selection words. Read the sentences as you track the print. Frame the underlined word and explain its meaning. Have children read each sentence with you.

animals	living things that can move around
dinner	the main meal of the day
watch	to look at something

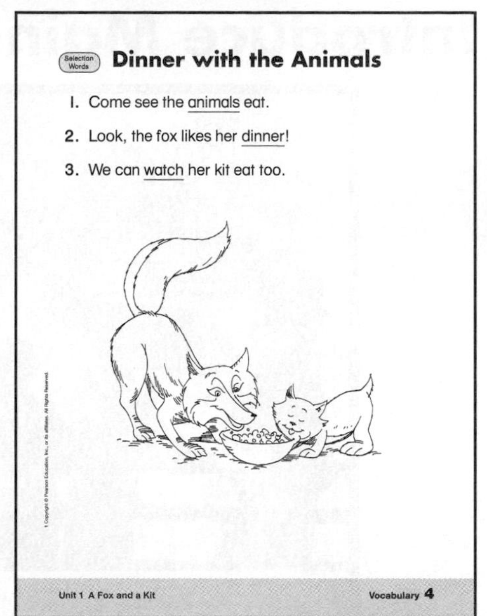
Selection Words **Dinner with the Animals**

1. Come see the animals eat.
2. Look, the fox likes her dinner!
3. We can watch her kit eat too.

Unit 1 A Fox and a Kit — Vocabulary 4

Vocabulary Transparency 4 TR DVD

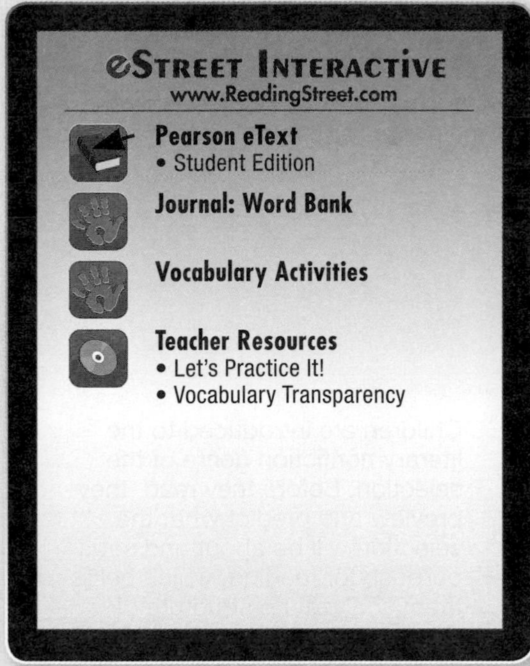

eStreet Interactive
www.ReadingStreet.com
Pearson eText
• Student Edition
Journal: Word Bank
Vocabulary Activities
Teacher Resources
• Let's Practice It!
• Vocabulary Transparency

Vocabulary Strategy: Alphabetize to the Second Letter

TEACH Explain that words are arranged in a dictionary or glossary according to the letters of the alphabet. Explain that when two or more words begin with the same letter, we need to use the second letter to put them in alphabetical order. Write the following words on the board: *dot, dim, dab.*

Think Aloud The first letter of all these words is *d,* so I need to use the second letter to put them in alphabetical order. I can see that the second letters of these words are *o, i,* and *a.* Of these letters, I know that *a* comes first in the alphabet, *i* comes second, and *o* comes third. So the correct alphabetical order is *dab, dim, dot.*

GUIDE PRACTICE Write three words on the board that begin with the same letter and have a different second letter, in nonalphabetical order. What is the second letter of each of these words? Write the letters on the board. Which letter comes first in the alphabet? Which comes second? Which comes third? What is the alphabetical order of these words? Write the words on the board in alphabetical order.

ON THEIR OWN Write three words on the board that begin with the same letter and have a different second letter, in nonalphabetical order. Have children put them in alphabetical order.

Bridge to Common Core

VOCABULARY ACQUISITION AND USE
In this week's selection, children interact with the selection vocabulary to extend understanding of the selection content. Teaching alphabetical order helps children make real-life connections to the use of references to locate definitions and understand word use to comprehend what they read.

Multilingual Vocabulary Lists
Children can apply knowledge of their home language to acquire new English vocabulary by using the *Multilingual Vocabulary List* (*ELL Handbook,* pp. 465–476).

Text-Based Comprehension

Introduce Main Selection

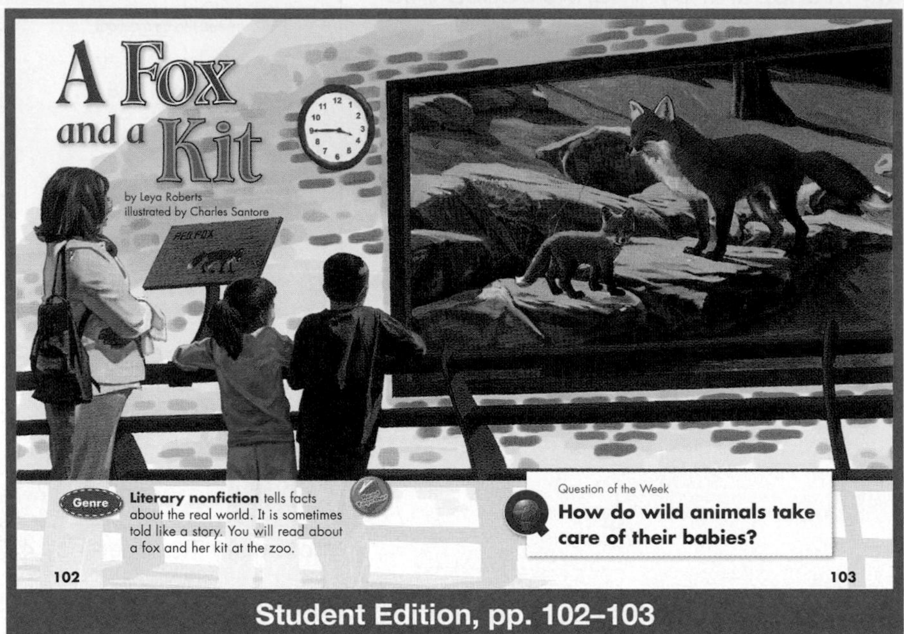

Student Edition, pp. 102–103

GENRE **Literary nonfiction** tells about real-life people, animals, or events. The setting is real. As they read *A Fox and a Kit,* ask children to look for clues that tell them that this story is about a real fox and her kit.

PREVIEW AND PREDICT Have children identify the title of the story, the author, and the illustrator. Help children look through the selection and use the illustrations to predict what it will be about.

PURPOSE Good readers read for a purpose. Setting a purpose helps us to think and understand more as we read. We will read this story to find out about the foxes in a zoo.

IMPORTANT IDEAS Explain that good readers think about the ideas that the author wants us to think about. These are the **important ideas** of a story or selection. Have children turn to page EI•9 in their Student Edition.

In this picture, I can tell that this boy wants to see a panda. The woman is pointing to a sign that says "Giant Panda." I think about what these things mean. They mean that the boy wants to see a panda and that the zoo has one, so the people will probably visit it.

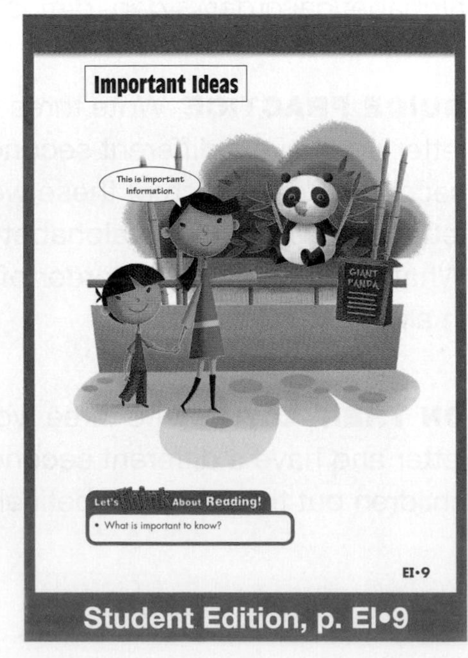

Student Edition, p. EI•9

Common Core State Standards

Informational Text 2. Identify the main topic and retell key details of a text.

Bridge to Common Core

CRAFT AND STRUCTURE

Children are introduced to the literary nonfiction genre of the selection. Before they read, they preview and predict what the selection will be about and set a purpose for reading, which helps them analyze the structure of the text. As they read, children can use the text structure to help them understand the content and style of the selection and gain knowledge to successfully read independently and closely.

Academic Vocabulary

author the person who wrote the text

Strategy Response Log

Background Knowledge Before reading, have children use p. RR16 of their *Reader's and Writer's Notebook* to draw a picture of a fox and a kit.

Access Main Selection

READER AND TASK SUGGESTIONS	
Preparing to Read the Text	**Leveled Tasks**
• Review inflected endings. • Discuss with children the kind of information found in a nonfiction text. • Remind children that to understand nonfiction text, they may need to read more slowly.	• **Theme and Knowledge Demands** If children do not understand the references to time, have them point to the pictures of the clocks and read the sentences about time. • **Levels of Meaning • Synthesis** To help with basic understanding, have children share what they have learned about foxes and kits, pointing out the part of the selection where each fact was learned.

See Text Complexity Measure for *A Fox and a Kit* on the tab at the beginning of this week.

READ Tell children that today they will read *A Fox and a Kit* for the first time. Use the Read for Understanding routine.

Routine Read for Understanding

Deepen understanding by reading the selection multiple times.

1. **First Read**—If children need support, then use the **Access Text** notes to help them clarify understanding.
2. **Second Read**—Use the **Close Reading** notes to help children draw knowledge from the text.

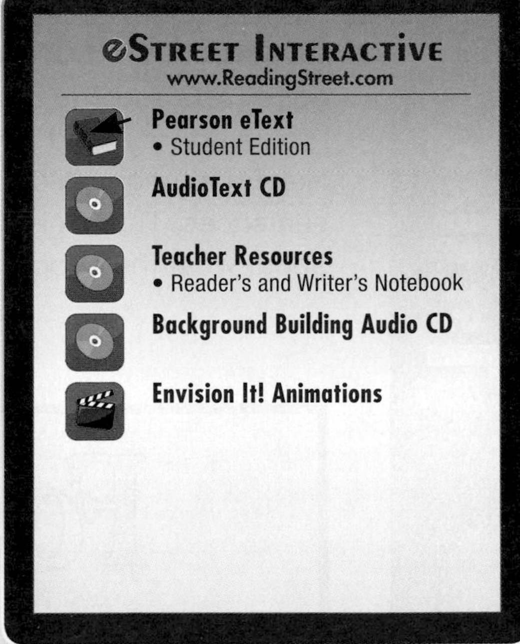

Preview Main Selection Ask children what they already know about foxes using the picture on pages 106–107. Then do a picture walk of the selection so children can talk about what they see.

1ST READ

Access Text © If children need help, then...

CONNECT TO CONCEPT Look at the picture on pages 102 and 103. Look at the fox and its baby. A baby fox is called a kit. Describe what they look like. Encourage children to answer in complete sentences. The fox is darker than the kit. Now tell about what the people are doing.

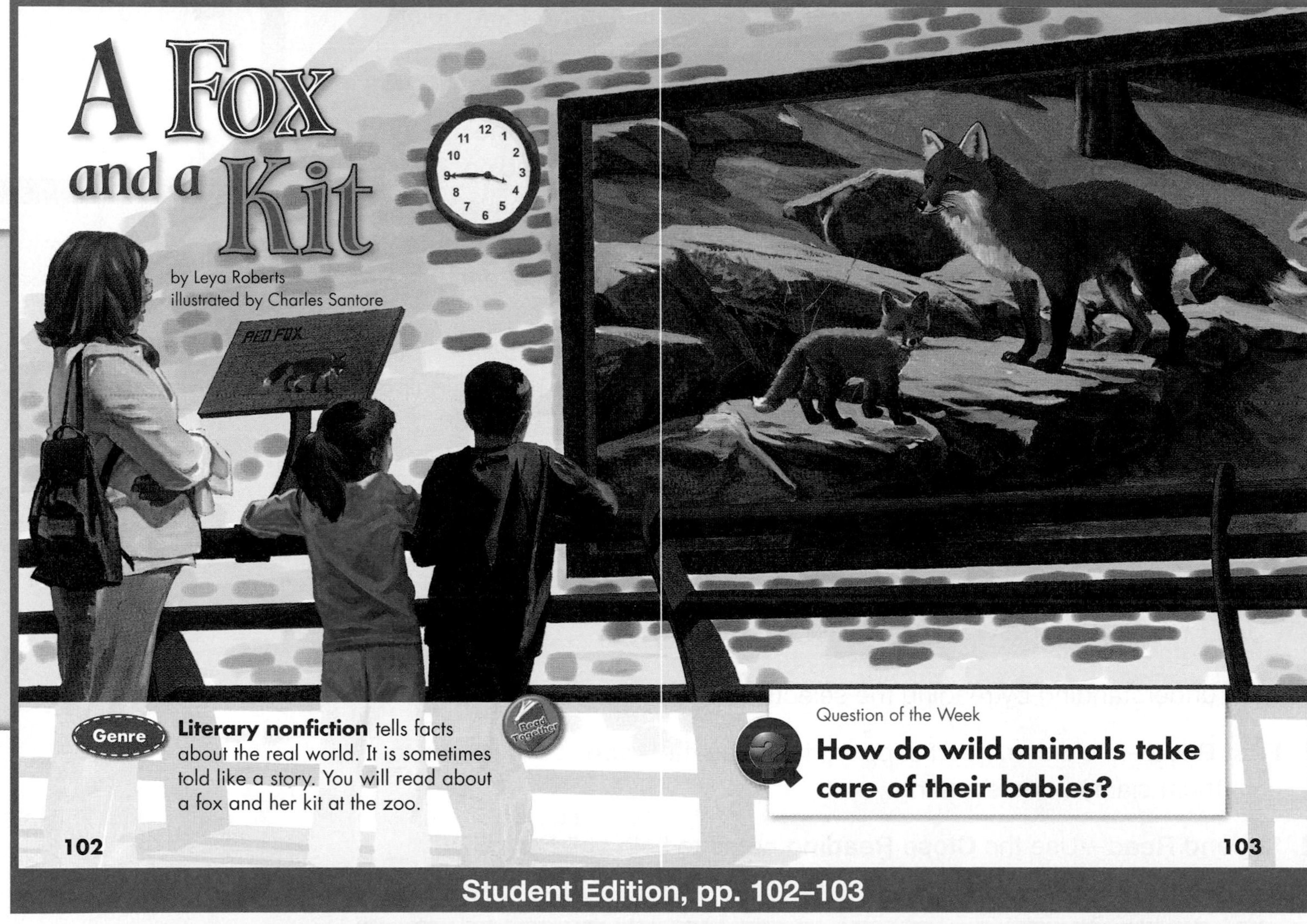

A Fox and a Kit
by Leya Roberts
illustrated by Charles Santore
RED FOX
Read Together
Genre
Literary nonfiction tells facts about the real world. It is sometimes told like a story. You will read about a fox and her kit at the zoo.
Question of the Week
How do wild animals take care of their babies?
102
103

Student Edition, pp. 102–103

2ND READ

Close Reading ©

ANALYSIS • TEXT EVIDENCE On pages 102 and 103, I see in the picture that the mother fox is watching over her kit. How can you tell? (The kit is close by. The mother fox is facing the kit.)

IMPORTANT IDEAS Remind children that good readers look for important ideas as they read. Have them suggest an important idea from what they have seen and read so far. (The fox and her kit do things together. The mother fox stays close to her kit.)

REVIEW HIGH-FREQUENCY WORDS Have children find the word *her* and reread the sentence. Who is the word *her* referring to? (the fox) How do you know? (The sentence says *her kit,* so it is talking about the mother.)

Common Core State Standards

Informational Text 1. Ask and answer questions about key details in a text. **Informational Text 2.** Identify the main topic and retell key details of a text. **Informational Text 7.** Use the illustrations and details in a text to describe its key ideas.

It is four.
This fox naps on the rocks.
Her kit naps on the rocks too.

The kit sits up.
His mom sits up.

104 105

Student Edition, pp. 104–105

ANALYSIS Are the foxes in the story real or make-believe? (They are real.) What clues tell you this? Tell about the pictures or reread the sentences. (They live in a zoo. They act like animals, not like people. They nap and sit up.)

1ST READ

Access Text If children need help, then...

MAIN IDEAS AND DETAILS • REREAD CHALLENGING TEXT What happens on these two pages? What details tell us this? (The fox and her kit have dinner. We know this because a man gives them a plate full of food, and then the plate is empty.) Have children reread the pages to find words that tell about the main idea and details.

IDENTIFY SELECTION WORDS Have children locate the word *dinner* on page 106. What time of the day do the fox and her kit eat dinner? (They eat dinner at five o'clock.)

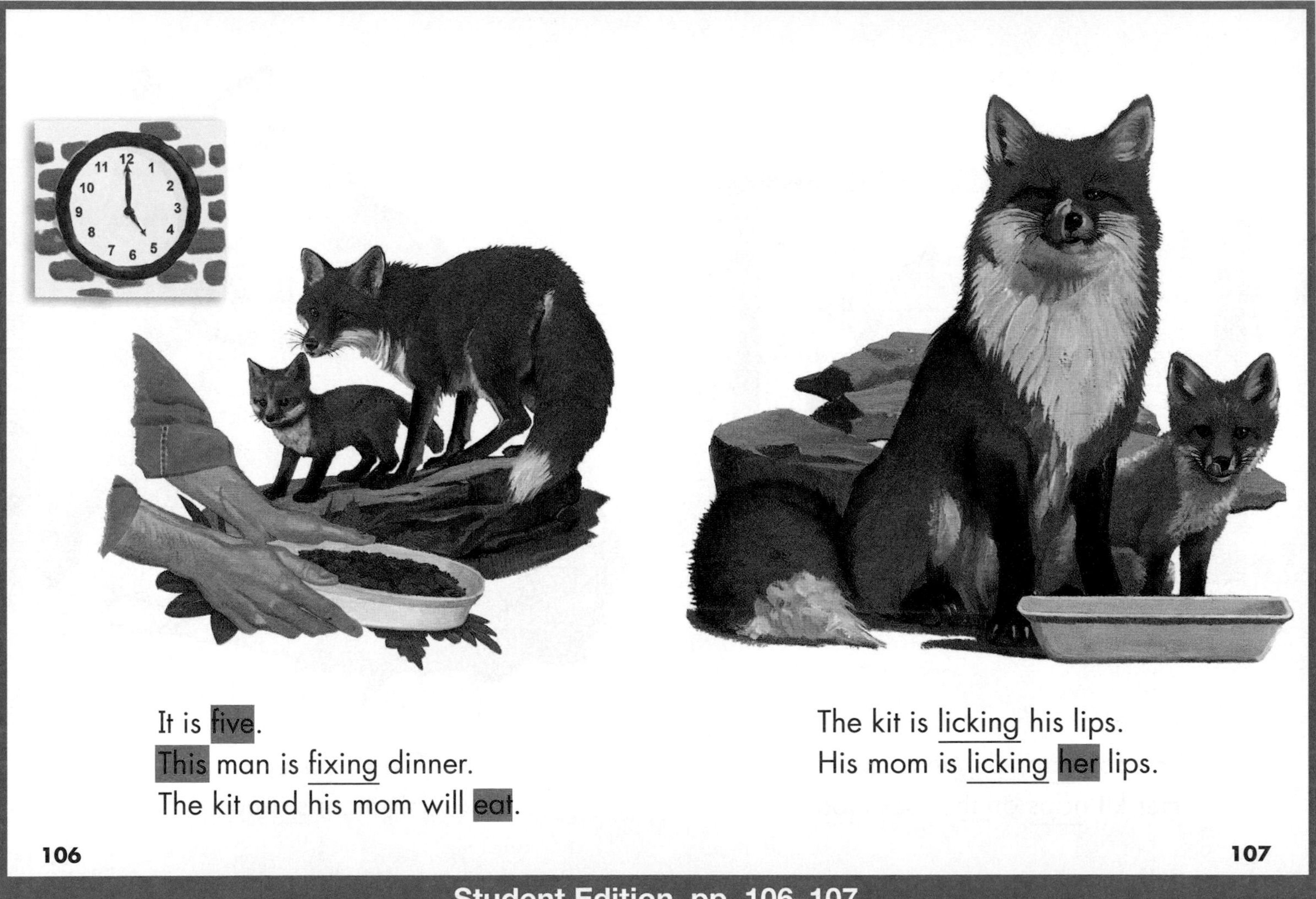

It is five.
This man is fixing dinner.
The kit and his mom will eat.
106
The kit is licking his lips.
His mom is licking her lips.
107

Student Edition, pp. 106–107

2ND READ

Close Reading

ANALYSIS Even though the foxes are wild animals, what clues tells you that they do not have to find their own food? (The words say that the man is fixing dinner, and the picture shows him giving the foxes dinner.)

SYNTHESIS • TEXT EVIDENCE Do you think the foxes liked their food? How can you tell? (They seem to look forward to eating and then they finish all their food. They lick their lips.)

MAIN IDEA AND DETAILS What is happening on these two pages? What details tell us this? (The mother fox makes sure her kit is happy and safe. We know this because the mother fox plays with her kit, and then she picks him up and takes him away from the rocks.)

Common Core State Standards

Informational Text 1. Ask and answer questions about key details in a text. **Informational Text 2.** Identify the main topic and retell key details of a text. **Informational Text 7.** Use the illustrations and details in a text to describe its key ideas.

The kit is playing.
His mom is playing.
The kit nips and tags his mom.

108

The kit is on the rocks.
His mom will get him.
She picks him up and takes him back.

109

Student Edition, pp. 108–109

EVALUATION • TEXT EVIDENCE How are the foxes behaving in these pictures? (They are playing together. The fox is protecting her kit from the rocks.) Point to the pictures that show this.

CONNECT TO SCIENCE To stay healthy, animals in a zoo need a habitat similar to their natural one.

Team Talk Have children discuss with a partner things they have observed in zoos that allow animals to behave as they would in the wild.

1ST READ

Access Text If children need help, then…

IMPORTANT IDEAS Have children discuss what they see and read on these pages. Have them suggest important ideas. (We can observe wild animals, and they can observe us.)

CROSS-TEXT EVALUATION
Use a Strategy to Self-Check How did the Read Aloud "A Rain Forest in the Zoo" help you understand this selection?

Continue to DAY 2
Text-Based Comprehension
p. 111a

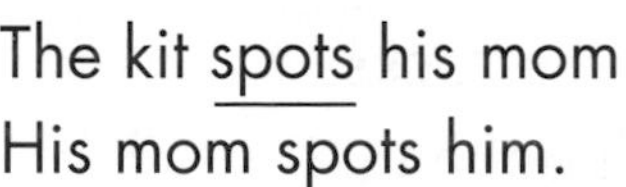

The kit spots his mom.
His mom spots him.

We like to watch this kit and his mom!
We can watch lots of animals.

110 111

Student Edition, pp. 110–111

2ND READ

Close Reading

SYNTHESIS • TEXT EVIDENCE Using what you learned in this selection, tell how wild animals take care of their babies. Have children cite examples from the text.

Continue to DAY 3
Think Critically
pp. 112–113

Text-Based Comprehension

Check Understanding

Have children discuss each question with a partner. Ask several pairs to share their responses.

- ☑ **Literary nonfiction** Do you think this selection could happen in real life? (Yes, there are zoos in real life, and they might have foxes and their kits.)
- ☑ **Main ideas and details** What is this selection mostly about? What are some of the details it tells? (The story is about a fox and a kit that live in a zoo. The details tell what they do together, such as napping, eating dinner, and playing.)
- ☑ **Setting** What is the setting of this selection? (a zoo)
- ☑ **Confirm predictions** What did you think this selection would be about from the picture at the beginning? (I thought it would be about a fox and her kit who live in a zoo.) Were your predictions correct?
- ☑ **Draw conclusions** How is the zoo a good place for the fox and her kit to live? (They get food and a place to sleep. They are safe.)

Common Core State Standards
Informational Text 1. Ask and answer questions about key details in a text. **Informational Text 2.** Identify the main topic and retell key details of a text. **Informational Text 6.** Distinguish between information provided by pictures or other illustrations and information provided by the words in a text. **Informational Text 7.** Use the illustrations and details in a text to describe its key ideas.

ELL

Support Discussion Ask yes-or-no questions to start children's responses. For example: Have you been to a zoo? (yes) Extend language opportunities for children by asking follow-up questions, such as: What animals did you see? What was their habitat like?

Day 2 SMALL GROUP TIME • Differentiate Comprehension, p. SG•52

OL On-Level	SI Strategic Intervention	A Advanced
• **Practice Phonics** Additional *-ing* Words • **Read** *A Fox and a Kit*	• **Reteach Phonics** Blend *-ing* Words • **Read** *A Fox and a Kit*	• **Extend Phonics** More *-ing* Words • **Read** *A Fox and a Kit* • **Investigate** Inquiry Project

ELL

If... children need more scaffolding and practice with the **Comprehension Skill**, **then...** use the ELL activities on p. DI•80 in the Teacher Resources section on SuccessNet.

Common Core State Standards

Informational Text 1. Ask and answer questions about key details in a text. **Informational Text 7.** Use the illustrations and details in a text to describe its key ideas. **Foundational Skills 1.a.** Recognize the distinguishing features of a sentence (e.g., first word, capitalization, ending punctuation). **Language 1.** Demonstrate command of the conventions of standard English grammar and usage when writing or speaking. **Language 1.j.** Produce and expand complete simple and compound declarative, interrogative, imperative, and exclamatory sentences in response to prompts. **Language 2.b.** Use end punctuation for sentences.

Genre

Literary Nonfiction

IDENTIFY FEATURES OF LITERARY NONFICTION Use *A Fox and a Kit* to have children identify the features of literary nonfiction. Have them use text from the selection to support their answers.

- *A Fox and a Kit* tells about a wild fox and her kit. Where do they live? (They live in a zoo.)
- What is the selection about? (It is about what the fox and her kit do.)
- Do you think this selection is real? How can you tell? (Yes, the selection is real. The foxes live in a zoo. They act like real foxes; they don't talk or act like humans.)

GUIDE PRACTICE Explain that the class will now think of all the things that tell the selection is real. Use Graphic Organizer 17, and write *What makes the selection real?* in the circle. Let's begin by thinking about the setting of the selection. Where does it take place? That's right, it takes place in a zoo. Do zoos exist in real life? Yes, zoos exist in real life, so I'll put *zoo* at the end of this spoke. Repeat this process with the characters and events in the selection. Have children study the finished web. Discuss how all the things are real.

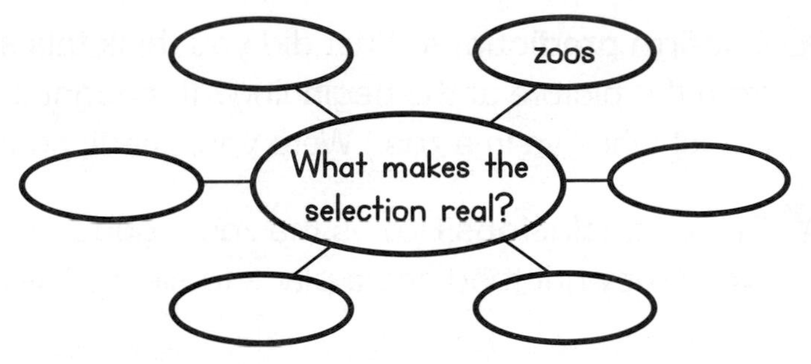

Graphic Organizer 17

ON THEIR OWN Arrange children into small groups. Have each group think about a topic they would like to learn more about. As they share their ideas with the class, reinforce that their topics are main ideas and not details.

Conventions

Declarative Sentences

TEACH Write *The green frog flips and flops* on the board. Point to each word as you read it. This is a declarative sentence that tells me that the green frog flips and flops. Ask children to identify the capital letter. Ask them to identify the period.

GUIDE PRACTICE Write the following sentences on the board. Have children tell you which words should begin with a capital letter and where to put the period in each.

a fox can do a lot
the cat napped on the mat
a tan dog sits on a box

APPLY Have the class complete these sentence frames orally.

1. **I saw a bird ______ from an egg.**
2. **A green lily pad is a ______ 's habitat.**
3. **I hope the hurt ______ survives.**

ON THEIR OWN Use *Reader's and Writer's Notebook,* p. 175.

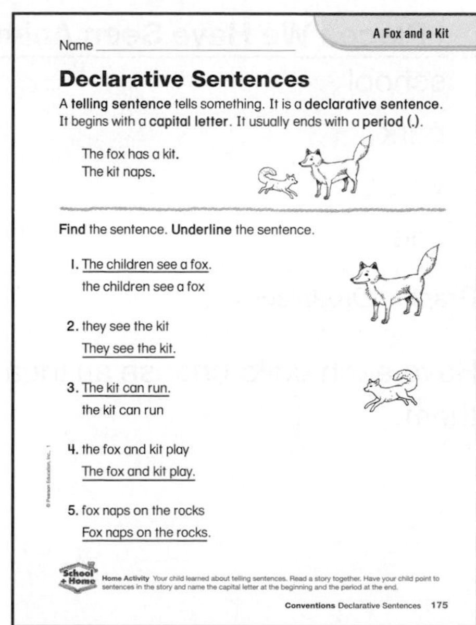
A Fox and a Kit

Name ______________

Declarative Sentences

A **telling sentence** tells something. It is a **declarative sentence**. It begins with a **capital letter**. It usually ends with a **period** (.).

The fox has a kit.
The kit naps.

Find the sentence. **Underline** the sentence.

1. The children see a fox.
   the children see a fox
2. they see the kit
   They see the kit.
3. The kit can run.
   the kit can run
4. the fox and kit play
   The fox and kit play.
5. fox naps on the rocks
   Fox naps on the rocks.

Home Activity Your child learned about telling sentences. Read a story together. Have your child point to sentences in the story and name the capital letter at the beginning and the period at the end.

Conventions Declarative Sentences 175

Reader's and Writer's Notebook, p. 175

Daily Fix-It

3. The cat her sitz with mom.
   The cat sits with her mom.
4. she fitts in a small bed.
   She fits in a small bed.

Discuss the Daily Fix-It corrections with children. Review sentence capitalization, word order, and inflected ending *-s.*

ELL

Support Grammar Reinforce to children that the word order in sentences varies in different languages. In Spanish, for example, the verb can appear before the subject. Provide extra practice with word order in sentences.

Common Core State Standards

Writing 1. Write opinion pieces in which they introduce the topic or name the book they are writing about, state an opinion, supply a reason for the opinion, and provide some sense of closure. **Writing 3.** Write narratives in which they recount two or more appropriately sequenced events, include some details regarding what happened, use temporal words to signal event order, and provide some sense of closure.

Personal Narrative

Writer's Craft: Interesting Details

INTRODUCE THE PROMPT Review with children the key features of a personal narrative. Assure them that they can write a story based on something they have seen or done themselves. Explain that today children will plan their own personal narrative. Like a made-up story, it will have a beginning, middle, and end. Read aloud the writing prompt.

Writing Prompt

Think about a time you watched some animals. Write a narrative about it.

GENERATE STORY IDEAS

Think Aloud To plan a new personal narrative, think of places where you have seen animals and what animals you have seen there. Let's make a chart of places where you have seen animals and the animals you saw. Display a T-chart. I'll start with the word *school.*

Guide children in identifying animals that they have seen. Possible ideas are shown. Record the responses, and keep the chart so that children can refer to it as they plan and draft their narratives.

Places We Have Seen Animals	Animals We Have Seen
school	robins, squirrels
park	ducks, turtles
woods	foxes, hawks, snakes
zoo	polar bears, monkeys

Graphic Organizer 4

Have each child choose an idea for a personal narrative. Circulate to guide them.

Mini-Lesson Interesting Details

- **Introduce** Use *Reader's and Writer's Notebook,* p. 176 to model planning a personal narrative. Like a made-up story, a personal narrative has a beginning, middle, and end. I can use a chart to plan my personal narrative. I've decided to write about a time I saw a bunny in a garden, so I'll write *The Bunny in the Garden* as my title. Now I will plan what happens in the beginning, middle, and end of my narrative. I want to include interesting details in my plan. Interesting details will bring my narrative to life and keep people reading it.

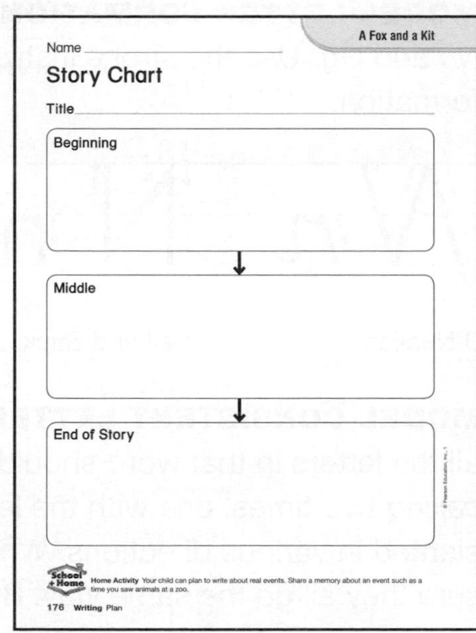
A Fox and a Kit

Name

Story Chart

Title

Beginning

Middle

End of Story

© Pearson Education, Inc., 1

School + Home **Home Activity** Your child can plan to write about real events. Share a memory about an event such as a time you saw animals at a zoo.

176 **Writing** Plan

Reader's and Writer's Notebook, p. 176

- **Model** At the beginning, I'll tell about how I like to go to the park. I'll include details about what I do there: sit under an elm tree and walk in the rose garden. Then I will tell about the bunny I saw, and I'll include details about where I saw the bunny: on a grassy path in the rose garden. I'll write that in the *Beginning* box. In the middle I'll tell what I saw the bunny do. The bunny just watched me while it filled its mouth with grass. I'll write that in the *Middle* box. I'll also include a detail that gives my opinion about how funny it looked with grass sticking out of its mouth! At the end, I'll tell that the bunny hopped away. I'll write that idea in the *End of Story* box. Now plan for your personal narrative. Circulate to guide and assist children.

Routine Quick Write for Fluency

Team Talk

1. **Talk** Have children take two minutes to tell the events in their narrative to a partner.
2. **Write** Each child briefly writes about the events at the beginning, middle, and end of the planned narrative.
3. **Share** Each child reads the story ideas to the partner.

Routines Flip Chart

Access for All

SI Strategic Intervention

Planning a Topic If children find it difficult to think of a topic for their narrative, discuss any animals that can be seen outside the classroom window. Help them write words such as *bird* or *squirrel,* and then have them write what they see the animal doing.

Support Prewriting

Beginning Children can draw a scene, label the details, and share with a partner, possibly one who speaks the same home language.

Intermediate Have children describe a scene and then write phrases to label details in the scene. Have them describe the scene to other children.

Advanced Have children draw pictures or write short sentences in their story charts. As they share the plan with partners, children can clarify by adding details.

Common Core State Standards

Writing 7. Participate in shared research and writing projects (e.g., explore a number of "how-to" books on a given topic and use them to write a sequence of instructions). **Writing 8.** With guidance and support from adults, recall information from experiences or gather information from provided sources to answer a question. **Language 1.a.** Print all upper- and lowercase letters.

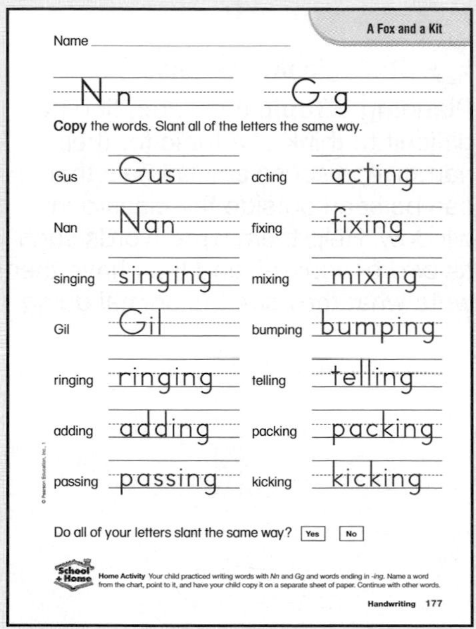
Name

A Fox and a Kit

Nn Gg

Copy the words. Slant all of the letters the same way.

Gus	Gus	acting	acting
Nan	Nan	fixing	fixing
singing	singing	mixing	mixing
Gil	Gil	bumping	bumping
ringing	ringing	telling	telling
adding	adding	packing	packing
passing	passing	kicking	kicking

Do all of your letters slant the same way? Yes No

Home Activity Your child practiced writing words with Nn and Gg and words ending in -ing. Name a word from the chart, point to it, and have your child copy it on a separate sheet of paper. Continue with other words.

Handwriting 177

Reader's and Writer's Notebook, p. 177

Handwriting

Letters *Nn* and *Gg*/Letter Slant

MODEL LETTER FORMATION Display uppercase and lowercase letters *Nn* and *Gg.* Use the stroke instructions pictured below to model proper letter formation.

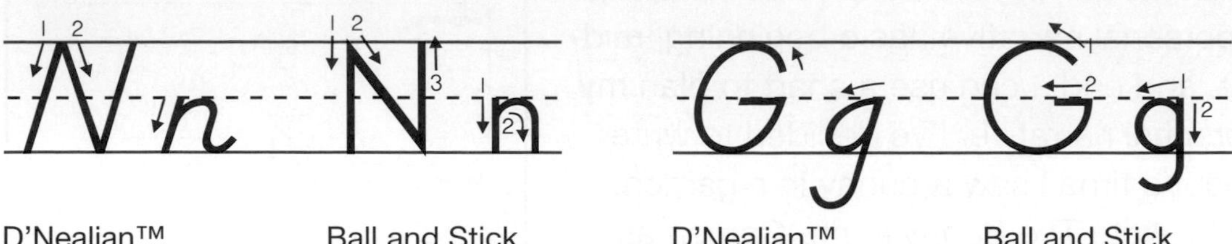

D'Nealian™ Ball and Stick D'Nealian™ Ball and Stick

MODEL CONSISTENT LETTER SLANT Explain that when we write a word, all the letters in that word should be slanted the same way. Write the word *calling* two times, one with the letters slanted correctly and one with the letters slanted in various directions. When I write the letters in a word, I need to make sure they all go the same way. By correctly slanting the letters in a word, I make it easier for others to understand what I write.

GUIDE PRACTICE Write the following words, one slanted correctly and the remaining words with letters slanting in various ways.

rolling packing camping stacking

Team Talk Have children work in pairs to discuss which letters are the wrong size and how they should be fixed. Have children share with the class.

ON THEIR OWN Use *Reader's and Writer's Notebook,* p. 177.

Research and Inquiry

Step 2 Research Skill: How to Read a Chart

TEACH Tell children that a **chart** is a diagram that organizes information and shows how facts are connected. A chart often uses a title, headings, and columns to show how the information is organized.

Think Aloud **MODEL** Display Research Transparency 4. This is an example of a chart. Let's see how this chart organizes information. Read aloud the title and the headings. Looking at the title, I can tell that the chart is about wild animals and their babies. On one side are the names of the animals. On the other side are the names of the babies. I see that the animal and the name of its babies are on the same line. Let's read the first animal and baby animal together.

Chart

Animal Name	Baby Name
fox	kit
bear	cub
hippo	calf
seal	pup
goat	kid

Unit 1 A Fox and a Kit Research 4

Research Transparency 4 TR DVD

GUIDE PRACTICE Continue reading the names of the animals and their babies. Have children tell how the chart helps them know which baby name goes with which animal name.

eStreet Interactive
www.ReadingStreet.com

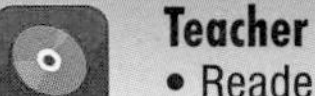

Teacher Resources
- Reader's and Writer's Notebook
- Research Transparency

Academic Vocabulary

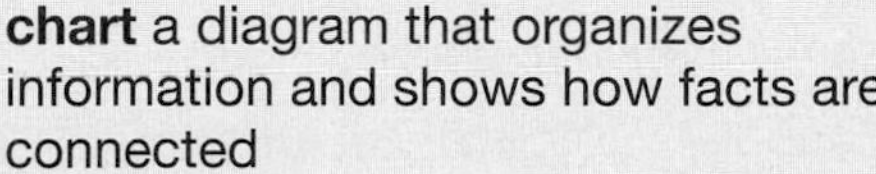

chart a diagram that organizes information and shows how facts are connected

Bridge to Common Core

RESEARCH TO BUILD AND PRESENT KNOWLEDGE

Children will explore the use and function of charts to help build knowledge about a topic. They will also:
- learn how to read a chart
- learn to organize information

Wrap Up Your Day!

✔ **Phonics: Inflected Ending *-ing*** Write the words *packing, looking,* and *picking.* Have children identify the base word and the ending.

✔ **High-Frequency Words** Write the following sentence: *This kit eats four or five times a day.* Read the sentence. Then point to the high-frequency words *this, eats, four,* and *five,* and have children read them.

✔ **Content Knowledge** Monitor children's use of oral vocabulary as they respond. Recall the wild animals children have read about. Ask: What animal lives in the canopy of a jungle? (parrots) What sound do parrots make? (Parrots screech.) What can you learn when you observe wild animals? (how a parent takes care of its babies)

Preview DAY 3

Tell children that tomorrow they will reread *A Fox and a Kit.*

DAY 3 at a Glance

Content Knowledge
Oral Vocabulary

Phonemic Awareness
Count Syllables

Phonics/Spelling
Inflected Ending *-s*
Inflected Ending *-ing*

High-Frequency Words
eat, five, four, her, this, too

Selection Words
animals, dinner, watch

Text-Based Comprehension
Review Realism and Fantasy

Fluency
Accuracy and Appropriate Rate

Conventions
Declarative Sentences

Writing
Personal Narrative
Writing Trait: Voice

Listening and Speaking
Share Information and Ideas

Research and Inquiry
Gather and Record Information

Materials

- Student Edition
- Sing with Me Big Book
- Big Book
- Letter Tiles
- Reader's and Writer's Notebook
- Retelling Cards

Common Core State Standards

Speaking/Listening 2. Ask and answer questions about key details in a text read aloud or information presented orally or through other media. **Language 6.** Use words and phrases acquired through conversations, reading and being read to, and responding to texts, including using frequently occurring conjunctions to signal simple relationships (e.g., *I named my hamster Nibblet because she nibbles too much because she likes that*).

Content Knowledge

Wild Animals and Their Babies

EXPAND THE CONCEPT To reinforce concepts and to focus children's attention, have them sing "Squirrel Song" from the *Sing with Me* Big Book. What are some things that wild squirrels do? (Possible response: They climb trees and gather nuts.)

Build Oral Language

LISTEN FOR AMAZING WORDS Display the Big Book *Jungle Drum.* Read the story and have children listen for the word *million.* Have them also think about the different sounds you might hear in the jungle.

- What sounds can you hear in the jungle? (Drops of water say blip, blop.)
- Why does the jungle sound like a drum? (It has sounds that are repeated over and over.)

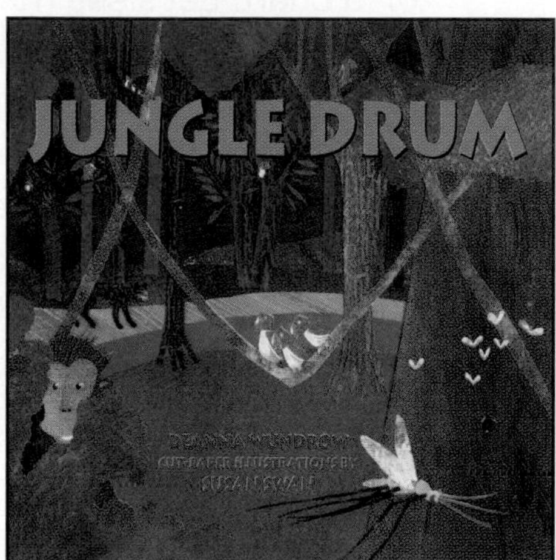

Big Book

TALK ABOUT SENTENCES AND WORDS
Write the following sentence from *Jungle Drum* on sentence strips or on the board.

And then a million insects all at once begin to sing chirp buzz whine scream.

- Ask children to read it with you as you track the print.
- What does this sentence mean? (A lot of insects start to make noise at the same time.)
- Why did the author list five different sounds? (A lot of insects probably make different sounds.) What other words could the author have used to describe sounds that insects make?
- Arrange children in five groups. Give each group a word for a sound that insects make (sing, chirp, buzz, whine, scream). Tell children that at the same time, each group will say the word for their sound to mimic what a million insects might sound like.
- **Team Talk** Write each word of the sentence on word cards and mix them up. Have partners work together to put the sentence back together.

Build Oral Vocabulary

Amazing Words Robust Vocabulary Routine

1. **Introduce the Word** Relate the word *million* to the book. A *million* different plants grow in the jungle. Supply a child-friendly definition. A *million* is a very large number. Have children say the word.
2. **Demonstrate** Provide examples to show meaning. We saw a *million* stars shining in the night sky. Mom told me a *million* times not to do that. It would take a long time to count to a *million.*
3. **Apply** Have children demonstrate their understanding. Would you prefer a *million* new toys or a *million* new friends? Why?
4. **Display the Word** Run your hand under the chunks *mil-lion* as you read the word.

Routines Flip Chart

ADD TO THE CONCEPT MAP Use these questions to discuss ideas about how wild animals take care of their babies.

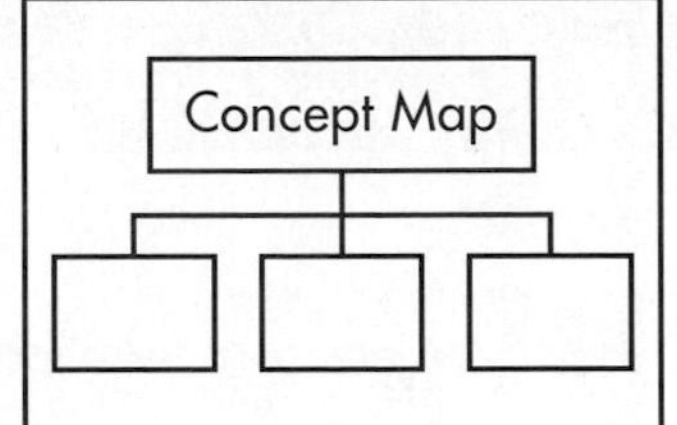

- In *A Fox and a Kit,* we watch the fox nap with her kit. Let's add *They nap with them* to our map.
- How does the mother fox move the kit? She picks him up. Let's add that to the map.

Amazing Words

observe	screech
wild	million
parent	native
canopy	reserve

ELL

Expand Vocabulary Use the Day 3 instruction on ELL Poster 4 to expand children's use of English vocabulary to communicate about lesson concepts.

Cognates Using the Spanish word *millón* will give Spanish speakers support in learning the English word *million.*

Common Core State Standards
Foundational Skills 2. Demonstrate understanding of spoken words, syllables, and sounds (phonemes). Also Foundational Skills 2.c., Speaking/Listening 6.

Phonemic Awareness

Let's Listen for Sounds

Read Together

- Find five people who are doing something. Tell what they are doing.
- Find two actions that rhyme with *ends*. Say the sounds in each word.
- Find two actions that rhyme with *pumping*. Say the sounds in each word.

READING STREET ONLINE
SOUND-SPELLING CARDS
www.ReadingStreet.com

96 97

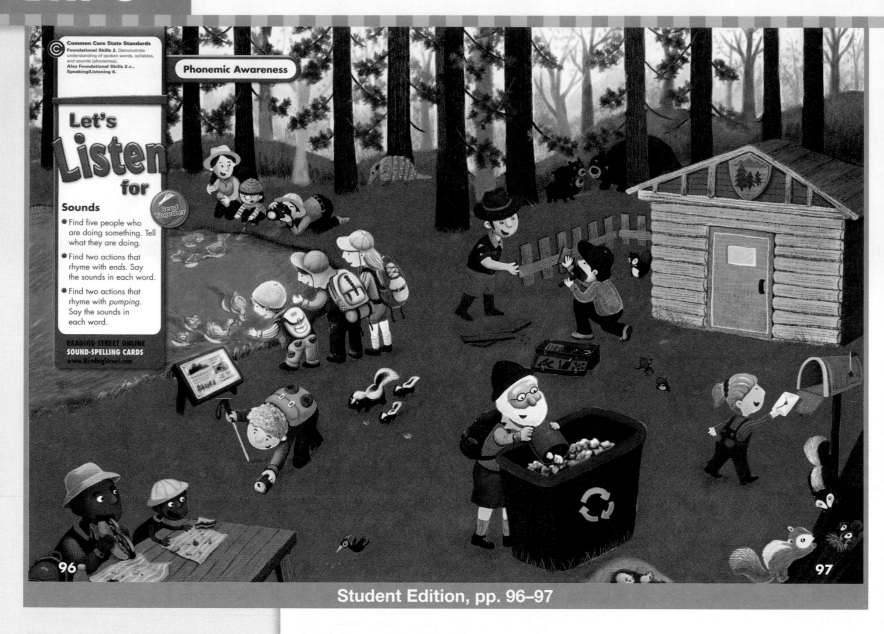

Student Edition, pp. 96–97

Common Core State Standards

Foundational Skills 2. Demonstrate understanding of spoken words, syllables, and sounds (phonemes). **Foundational Skills 3.d.** Use knowledge that every syllable must have a vowel sound to determine the number of syllables in a printed word. **Foundational Skills 3.f.** Read words with inflectional endings. **Also Language 4.c.**

Academic Vocabulary

syllable a word part that has a single vowel sound

Phonemic Awareness

Count Syllables

MODEL COUNTING SYLLABLES Look at the picture. Today we are going to count syllables. Remember that a **syllable** is a word part that has a single vowel sound. I see children bending and feeding the ducks. *Bending* has two syllables: *bend, ing. Feeding* also has two syllables: *feed, ing.*

GUIDE PRACTICE Guide children to use the picture to say words that have two syllables. *(dumping, picking)*

ON THEIR OWN Have children change each of these single-syllable words into two-syllable words by adding *-ing.*

eat	look	jump	stand	mend	hand

Team Talk Have children say other two-syllable words with a partner.

Phonics

Build Words

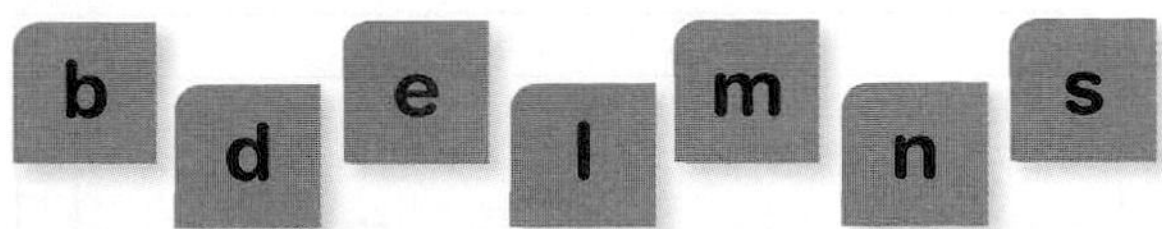

MODEL WORD BUILDING Now we are going to build words that end in *-s.* Write *mend* and blend it. Watch me add *s* to *mend.* Model blending the new word, *mends.*

GUIDE PRACTICE Have children spell *mends* with letter tiles. Monitor children's work as they build words.

- Make the word *bend.*
  Say the new word together.

- Add *s* to *bend.*
  Say the new word together.

- Make the word *lend.*
  Say the new word together.

- Add *s* to *lend.*
  Say the new word together.

Corrective feedback | For corrective feedback, model the correct spelling and have children correct their tiles.

Fluent Word Reading

MODEL Write *jumps.* I know the sounds for the letters *j, u, m, p,* and *s.* I blend them and read the word *jumps.*

GUIDE PRACTICE Write the words below. Say the sounds in your head for each spelling you see. When I point to the word, we'll read it together. Allow one second per sound-previewing time for the first reading.

sends **dumps** **looks** **eats** **stands** **naps**

ON THEIR OWN Have children read the list above three or four times, until they can read one word per second.

Access for All

SI Strategic Intervention

Pronunciation If children have trouble pronouncing words with the inflected ending *-s,* provide additional words and practice opportunities.

Academic Vocabulary 

phonics instruction in the relationship between sounds and letters

ELL

Extend Language Help children distinguish between saying singular and plural names for animals in English and in their home languages.

Common Core State Standards

Foundational Skills 3. Know and apply grade-level phonics and word analysis skills in decoding words. **Foundational Skills 3.f.** Read words with inflectional endings. **Language 2.d.** Use conventional spelling for words with common spelling patterns and for frequently occurring irregular words. **Language 4.c.** Identify frequently occurring root words (e.g., *look*) and their inflectional forms (e.g., *looks, looked, looking*).

Phonics

Blend and Read

DECODE WORDS IN ISOLATION Have children turn to pages 179–180 in the *Reader's and Writer's Notebook* and find the first list of words. Each word in this list has the ending *-s.* Let's blend and read these words. Continue with the second list that has words with the ending *-ing.* Be sure that children identify the correct sounds in words that end in *-s* and *-ing.* Next, have children read the high-frequency words.

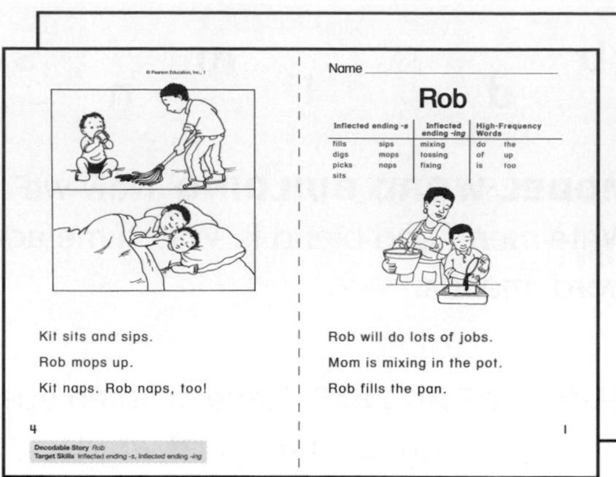

© Pearson Education, Inc., 1

Name ______________

Rob

Inflected ending -s		Inflected ending -ing	High-Frequency Words	
fills	sips	mixing	do	the
digs	mops	tossing	of	up
picks	naps	fixing	is	too
sits				

Rob will do lots of jobs.

Mom is mixing in the pot.

Rob fills the pan.

1

Kit sits and sips.

Rob mops up.

Kit naps. Rob naps, too!

4

Decodable Story *Rob*
Target Skills Inflected ending -s, Inflected ending -ing

Reader's and Writer's Notebook, pp. 179–180

DECODE WORDS IN CONTEXT Chorally read the story along with children. Have children identify words in the story that have the inflected ending *-s* or *-ing.*

Team Talk Pair children and have them take turns reading the story aloud to each other. Monitor children as they read to check for proper pronunciation and appropriate pacing.

ON THEIR OWN To further develop automaticity, have children take the story home to reread.

Spelling

Inflected Ending *-s*

SPELL HIGH-FREQUENCY WORDS Write *her* and *too* and point them out on the Word Wall. Have children say and spell the words with you and then without you.

DICTATION Have children write these sentences. Say each sentence. Then repeat it slowly, one word at a time.

1. **Emily sits with her.**
2. **I want to hit the ball too.**
3. **The dress fits her.**

PROOFREAD AND CORRECT Write each sentence, spelling words one at a time. Have children circle and rewrite any misspelled words.

ON THEIR OWN Use *Reader's and Writer's Notebook,* p. 181.

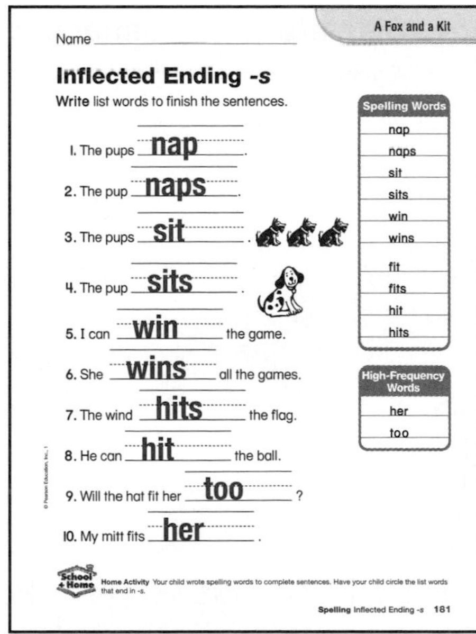
Name ______ A Fox and a Kit

Inflected Ending -s

Write list words to finish the sentences.

1. The pups nap.
2. The pup naps.
3. The pups sit.
4. The pup sits.
5. I can win the game.
6. She wins all the games.
7. The wind hits the flag.
8. He can hit the ball.
9. Will the hat fit her too?
10. My mitt fits her.

Spelling Words
nap
naps
sit
sits
win
wins
fit
fits
hit
hits

High-Frequency Words
her
too

Home Activity Your child wrote spelling words to complete sentences. Have your child circle the list words that end in -s.

Spelling Inflected Ending -s 181

Reader's and Writer's Notebook, p. 181

Day 3 SMALL GROUP TIME • Differentiate Close Reading, p. SG•52

OL On-Level
- **Reread** to Develop Vocabulary
- **Reread** *A Fox and a Kit*

SI Strategic Intervention
- **Blend** Words with -s and *-ing*
- **Reread** *A Fox and a Kit*

A Advanced
- **Reread** to Extend Vocabulary
- **Reread** *A Fox and a Kit*
- **Investigate** Inquiry Project

eSTREET INTERACTIVE
www.ReadingStreet.com

Teacher Resources
- Reader's and Writer's Notebook

Spelling Words

Inflected Ending *-s*

1. sit	**6. fits**
2. sits	**7. hit**
3. win	**8. hits**
4. wins	**9. nap**
5. fit	**10. naps**

High-Frequency Words

11. her	**12. too**

ELL

Spelling Dictation Children will benefit from hearing each dictated sentence three times. First, have children listen to understand the sentence. The second time, they should write what they hear. The third time, they can check their work.

ELL

If... children need more scaffolding and practice with reading the **Main Selection,**
then... use the ELL activities on p. DI•81 in the Teacher Resources section on SuccessNet.

 **Common Core State Standards**

Foundational Skills 3.g. Recognize and read grade-appropriate irregularly spelled words.

High-Frequency Words

eat	her
five	this
four	too

Selection Words

animals living things that can move around

dinner the main meal of the day

watch to look at something

High-Frequency and Selection Words

READ WORDS IN ISOLATION Display and review this week's high-frequency words and selection words. Have children read the words aloud.

READ WORDS IN CONTEXT Display the following sentence frames. Have children complete the sentences using high-frequency and selection words. Have children read each completed sentence with you.

1. **The fox and the kit *eat* _____ at *five.* (dinner)**
2. **We _____ the fox and the kit nap *too.* (watch)**
3. **The _____ nap on the rocks. (animals)**
4. **That man has a cap, and _____ one has a hat. (this)**
5. **My dad has a hat _____. (too)**
6. **I *eat* a snack at _____. (four)**
7. **Sis eats _____ snack *too.* (her)**

MONITOR PROGRESS **Check High-Frequency Words**

FORMATIVE ASSESSMENT Point to these words on the Word Wall and have the class read them. Listen for children who miss words during the reading. Call on those children to read some of those words individually.

eat	four	five	her	**Spiral Review** Rows 3 and 4 review previously taught high-frequency words.
this	too			
blue	from	get	help ←	
use ←				

If... children cannot read these words,

then... use the Nondecodable Words Routine on p. 99 to reteach the words. Monitor children's fluency with these words during reading and provide additional practice.

Text-Based Comprehension

Read Main Selection

REVIEW **REALISM AND FANTASY** Remind children that a realistic story could really happen and that a fantasy is a made-up story. Have children turn to pages 102–103 of their Student Edition. Is this story real or a fantasy? (real) How do you know? (The characters are animals that act like real animals. The setting is a real zoo.)

GENRE: LITERARY NONFICTION Remind children that literary nonfiction shares information about real people or animals, real places, and real events. Have children recall things in *A Fox and a Kit* that are real. (The people and animals are real, zoos are real, and the events that happen in the zoo are real.)

READ Return to pages 102–111 and use the **2nd Read/Close Reading Notes** to reread *A Fox and a Kit.*

Routine — Read for Understanding

Deepen understanding by reading the selection multiple times.

1. **First Read**—If children need support, then use the **Access Text** notes to help them clarify understanding.
2. **Second Read**—Use the **Close Reading** notes to help children draw knowledge from the text.

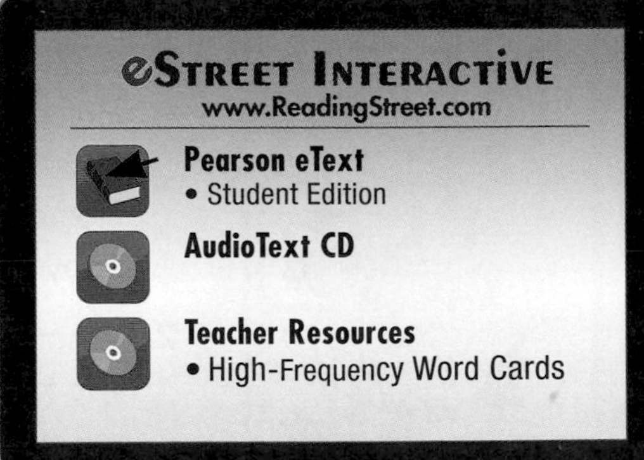

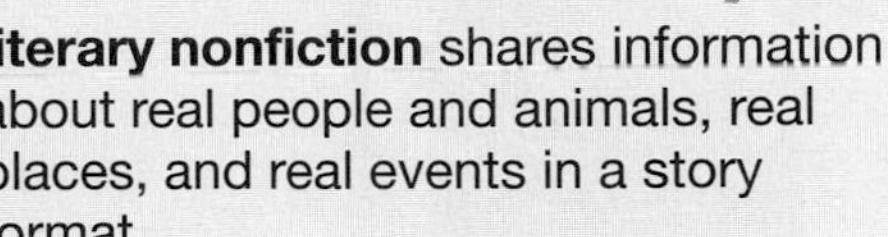

literary nonfiction shares information about real people and animals, real places, and real events in a story format

ELL

Activate Prior Knowledge Invite children to share the words for *zoo, zookeeper, fox,* and *kit* in their home languages and to describe experiences they have had with any of them.

Think Critically 

1. *A Fox and a Kit* is about a mother fox and her kit. Tell about how another animal mother takes care of her baby. Text to World
2. What does the author want you to learn by reading this selection? Author's Purpose
3. What is the selection mostly about? Main Idea and Details
4. What did you learn about foxes by reading this selection? Important Ideas
5. **Look Back and Write** Look back at page 109. Write about how the fox takes care of her kit. Use evidence from the selection.

Key Ideas and Details • Text Evidence

112

Meet the Illustrator

Charles Santore

Charles Santore went to a zoo to learn about foxes. Mr. Santore also put pictures of foxes all around his studio to help him paint the pictures he needed for this story. Animals are a big part of his work.

Here are other books illustrated by Charles Santore.

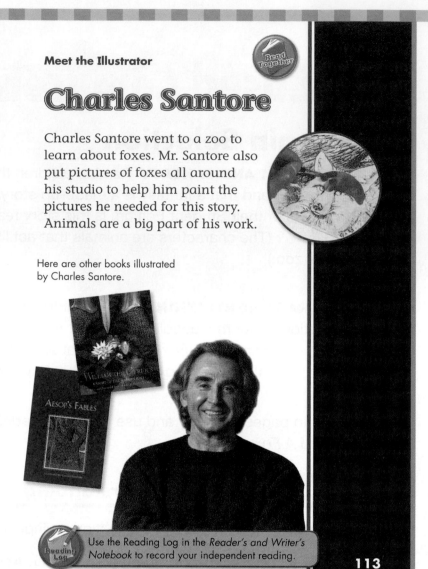

Use the Reading Log in the *Reader's and Writer's Notebook* to record your independent reading.

113

Student Edition, pp. 112–113

 Common Core State Standards

Informational Text 1. Ask and answer questions about key details in a text. **Informational Text 2.** Identify the main topic and retell key details of a text. **Also Writing 5.**

Bridge to Common Core

KEY IDEAS AND DETAILS

By reading the text multiple times, children will make logical inferences from the text and cite textual evidence when writing or discussing the knowledge they have gained. Use the Think Critically page to ensure a thorough understanding of *A Fox and a Kit.*

Think Critically

1. **TEXT TO WORLD** Mother cats take care of their babies by feeding them and moving them if they feel they are in danger. Mother cats like to keep their kittens close to them, where they are warm and safe.
2. **AUTHOR'S PURPOSE** The author wants us to learn about how mother foxes take care of their young.
3. **MAIN IDEA AND DETAILS** It is mostly about what a wild fox and her kit do. We learn that they nap, eat, and play together.
4. **IMPORTANT IDEAS** Mother foxes take care of their kits by keeping them close.
5. **LOOK BACK AND WRITE • TEXT EVIDENCE** For writing fluency, assign a five-minute time limit. As children finish, encourage them to reread their responses and proofread for errors.

Scoring Rubric **Look Back and Write**

TOP-SCORE RESPONSE A top-score response uses details from the text and the picture to tell how the fox takes care of her kit.

A top-score response might include:
The fox takes care of her kit by picking him up and moving him if he is on the rocks.

Retell

Have children use the retelling strips in the Student Edition or the Story Sort to retell the selection. Monitor children's retelling.

Scoring Rubric **Expository Retelling**

	4	3	2	1
Connections	Makes connections and generalizes beyond the text	Makes connections to other events, texts, or experiences	Makes a limited connection to another event, text, or experience	Makes no connection to another event, text, or experience
Author's Purpose	Elaborates on author's purpose	Tells author's purpose with some clarity	Makes some connection to author's purpose	Makes no connection to author's purpose
Topic	Describes the main topic	Identifies the main topic with some details early in retelling	Identifies the main topic	Retelling has no sense of topic
Important Ideas	Gives accurate information about ideas using key vocabulary	Gives accurate information about ideas with some key vocabulary	Gives limited or inaccurate information about ideas	Gives no information about ideas
Conclusions	Draws conclusions and makes inferences to generalize beyond the text	Draws conclusions about the text	Is able to tell some learnings about the text	Is unable to draw conclusions or make inferences about the text

Don't Wait Until Friday **MONITOR PROGRESS** **Check Retelling**

If... children have trouble retelling the selection,
then... use Main Idea Graphic Organizer 27, and the Retelling Cards/Story Sort, and work with the group to scaffold their retelling.

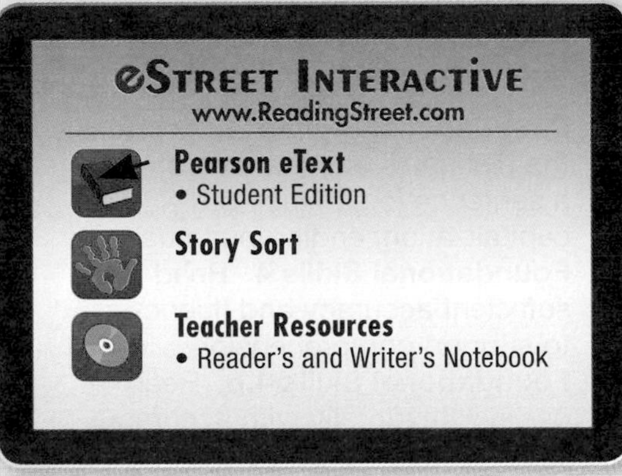

Writing to Sources

Use Write Like a Reporter on pp. 54–55 to guide children in writing text-based responses using one source.

Strategy Response Log

Important Ideas Have children revisit p. RR16 in their *Reader's and Writer's Notebook.* Have them draw a picture of what they think was the most important thing that happened in the selection.

Plan to Assess Retelling

- ☐ **Week 1** Strategic Intervention
- ☐ **Week 2** Advanced
- ☐ **Week 3** Strategic Intervention
- ☑ **This Week** Assess On-Level children.
- ☐ **Week 5** Strategic Intervention
- ☐ **Week 6** Assess any children you have not yet checked during this unit.

Meet the Illustrator

Read aloud page 113 as children follow along and track the print. Ask children what an illustrator does.

Read Independently

Have children enter their independent reading into their Reading Logs.

Common Core State Standards

Foundational Skills 1.a. Recognize the distinguishing features of a sentence (e.g., first word, capitalization, ending punctuation). **Foundational Skills 4.** Read with sufficient accuracy and fluency to support comprehension. **Foundational Skills 4.b.** Read on-level text orally with accuracy, appropriate rate, and expression on successive readings. **Language 1.j.** Produce and expand complete simple and compound declarative, interrogative, imperative, and exclamatory sentences in response to prompts. **Also Language 1., 2.b.**

Options for Oral Rereading

Use *A Fox and a Kit* or one of this week's Decodable Practice Readers.

Fluency

Accuracy and Appropriate Rate

MODEL FLUENT READING Have children turn to Student Edition pages 106–107. Follow along as I read these pages. I will try to read with no mistakes. I want to read just the way I speak.

GUIDE PRACTICE Have children read the pages with you. Then have them reread the pages chorally without you until they read with no hesitation and no mistakes. Continue in the same way with pages 108–109.

Corrective feedback	**If...** children have difficulty reading with accuracy and appropriate rate, **then...** prompt: • Which word is a problem? Let's read it together. • Read the sentence again to be sure you understand it. • Tell me the sentence. Now read it as if you are speaking it to me.

Reread for Fluency

Routine Choral Reading

1. **Select a Passage** For *A Fox and a Kit,* use pp. 110–111.
2. **Model** First, have children track the print as you read.
3. **Guide Practice** Then have children read along with you.
4. **Corrective Feedback** Have the class read aloud without you. Monitor progress and provide feedback. For optimal fluency, children should reread three to four times.

Routines Flip Chart

CHECK COMPREHENSION Who observes whom on these pages? (The fox and her kit observe each other, and then they observe the children; the children observe the foxes.)

Conventions

Declarative Sentences

REVIEW Remind children that declarative sentences tell a fact or someone's point of view. They begin with a capital letter and usually end with a period.

GUIDE PRACTICE Write *bird, pig, cat,* and *fox* on the board. Have children supply some declarative sentences about each animal. Write them on the board, asking children how each one should begin and end as you do so.

Team Talk Have children talk in pairs about what each sentence tells.

APPLY Have children complete these sentence frames orally.

1. Sam _______.
2. Pig _______ the mix.
3. Fox _______ her kit.

ON THEIR OWN Use *Reader's and Writer's Notebook,* p. 182.

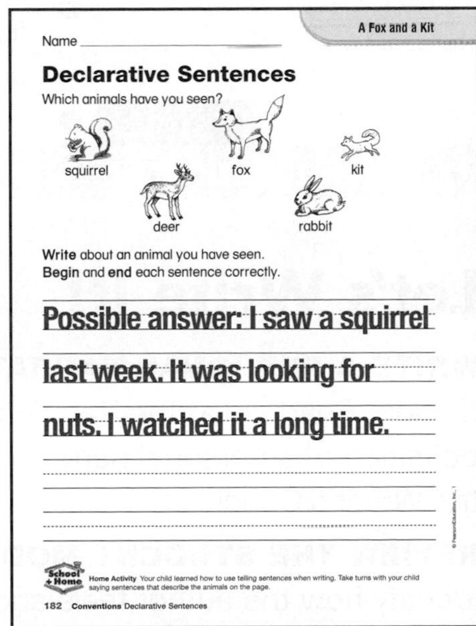
Name _______________ A Fox and a Kit

Declarative Sentences

Which animals have you seen?

squirrel fox kit deer rabbit

Write about an animal you have seen.
Begin and **end** each sentence correctly.

Possible answer: I saw a squirrel last week. It was looking for nuts. I watched it a long time.

Home Activity Your child learned how to use telling sentences when writing. Take turns with your child saying sentences that describe the animals on the page.

182 Conventions Declarative Sentences

Reader's and Writer's Notebook, p. 182

Daily Fix-It

5. The kit fitts on that rock
   The kit fits on that rock.
6. pam got a lick from her Dog.
   Pam got a lick from her dog.

Discuss the Daily Fix-It corrections with children. Review sentence capitalization and punctuation and the spelling of *fits.*

Professional Development

Fluency Having children read sentences they have produced builds both their confidence and fluency.

Support Fluency Encourage children to use the pictures as they reread for fluency. Help them associate the words with the pictures on the page.

Common Core State Standards
Writing 3. Write narratives in which they recount two or more appropriately sequenced events, include some details regarding what happened, use temporal words to signal event order, and provide some sense of closure. Also Language 1.j., 2.b.

Read Together

Let's Write It!

Key Features of a Personal Narrative

- tells a story about a real event in the author's life
- tells how the author feels about it

READING STREET ONLINE
GRAMMAR JAMMER
www.ReadingStreet.com

Narrative

Personal Narrative

A **personal narrative** tells of an event in the author's life. The student model on the next page is an example of a personal narrative.

Writing Prompt Think about a time you watched some animals. Write a narrative about it.

Writer's Checklist

Remember, you should ...

- ✓ write about a time when you saw an animal or animals.
- ✓ use words that tell how you felt about what happened.
- ✓ write sentences that tell about the event from the beginning to the end.

114

Student Model

The Ducks

Once I saw two ducks.
They swam in the pond.
They ate plants.
I wanted to swim!
I like to see ducks.

Writing Trait Voice Your writing tells how you feel. This writer shows feelings.

Genre This **personal narrative** tells about an event that happened in the writer's own life.

A **declarative sentence** begins with a capital letter and ends with a period.

Conventions

Declarative Sentences

Remember A **declarative sentence** is a telling sentence. It begins with a capital letter and ends with a period.

115

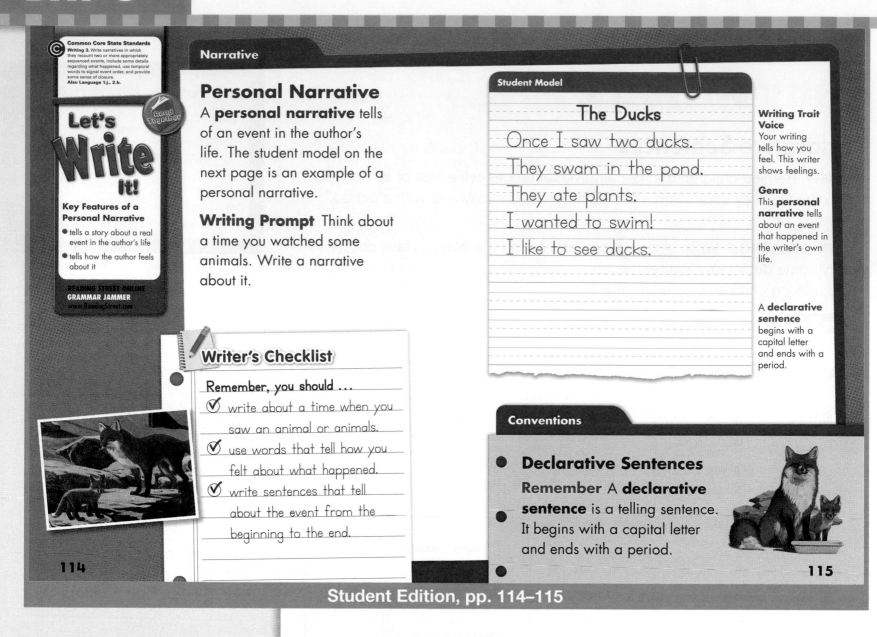

Student Edition, pp. 114–115

Writing 1. Write opinion pieces in which they introduce the topic or name the book they are writing about, state an opinion, supply a reason for the opinion, and provide some sense of closure. **Writing 3.** Write narratives in which they recount two or more appropriately sequenced events, include some details regarding what happened, use temporal words to signal event order, and provide some sense of closure. **Language 1.j.** Produce and expand complete simple and compound declarative, interrogative, imperative, and exclamatory sentences in response to prompts. **Also Language 1., 2.b.**

Let's Write It!

WRITE A PERSONAL NARRATIVE Use pages 114–115 in the Student Edition. Read aloud the Key Features of a Personal Narrative and the definition of a personal narrative. Read aloud the Writing Prompt and discuss the Writer's Checklist.

REVIEW THE STUDENT MODEL Read aloud "The Ducks." Ask children to identify how the author feels about the event. Read aloud and briefly discuss the side notes about genre, the writing trait, and declarative sentences.

Scoring Rubric

TOP-SCORE RESPONSE Help children understand that a top-score response clearly tells how they feel about what they saw and has words in an order that makes sense. For a complete rubric, see Writing Rubric 4 from the *Teacher Resources DVD-ROM.*

CONNECT TO CONVENTIONS Read aloud the Conventions note about declarative sentences. Identify the declarative sentences in the model.

Personal Narrative

Mini-Lesson Writing Trait: Voice

- **Introduce** Use your story chart from yesterday and Writing Transparency 4A to model including feelings. When I write my narrative, I will use my chart. First, I will tell about going to the park and seeing the bunny in the garden there. I will use voice and show my opinion or how I feel about my topic. So I'll write *I like to go to the park.* This sentence tells my feelings. Read aloud the draft on the transparency and point out other sentences that tell feelings or opinions, such as *It looked so funny! I was sorry to see it go.*

The Bunny in the Garden

I like to go to the park. I sit under a big elm tree I walk in the rose garden.

One Saturday I saw a bunny in the rose garden. I looked at the bunny The bunny looked at me. I saw the bunny on the grassy path.

The bunny filled its mouth with grass. It watched me while it stuffed its mouth. The grass stuck out of its mouth. It looked so funny!

Then the bunny hopped away into the rose bushes. I was sorry to see it go.

Unit 1 A Fox and a Kit Writing: Model 4A

Writing Transparency 4A TR DVD

- Explain how children can use story events they planned yesterday to draft the narrative. Remind them to include feelings about the events. Today's goal is to write the story but not to write each word perfectly. They can edit later to correct the words.

GUIDE WRITING Now it is time to write your narrative. Tell what you saw and how you felt when you watched animals. Have children use their story charts. Help them finish the ideas. Then guide children as they draft the narrative.

Routine Quick Write for Fluency

Team Talk

1. **Talk** Have partners take one minute to talk about an animal that they often see in the schoolyard or near their homes.
2. **Write** Each child writes a sentence telling a feeling or opinion about the animal.
3. **Share** Partners point out the words that tell feelings or opinions in the others' sentences.

Routines Flip Chart

Write Guy *by Jeff Anderson*

Teaching Trait: Focus

In a writing conference, choose one aspect of a child's draft, not many things. This will help the child more than trying to think about multiple writing traits at once. Maybe there is one skill at this child's growing edge of knowledge that I can help him or her improve. I'd hate to see that lost in a swarm of other comments.

Access for All

A Advanced

Developing Voice Ask children to include not just their feelings, but a sentence telling why they feel as they do about the animals and events in their narrative.

Common Core State Standards

Writing 8. With guidance and support from adults, recall information from experiences or gather information from provided sources to answer a question. **Speaking/Listening 1.a.** Follow agreed-upon rules for discussions (e.g., listening to others with care, speaking one at a time about the topics and texts under discussion). **Speaking/Listening 1.b.** Build on others' talk in conversations by responding to the comments of others through multiple exchanges.

Bridge to Common Core

COMPREHENSION AND COLLABORATION

As children share information and ideas in a range of conversations and collaborations, they explore key issues and concepts to clarify and deepen their understanding of content. This process is enhanced by developing listening and speaking habits for effective participation.

Listening and Speaking

Share Information and Ideas

TEACH Remind children that people share information and ideas in order to help each other learn more about a topic. When people share what they know and think, it helps if they speak and listen well.

- Good speakers speak clearly at an appropriate pace. They do not speak too quickly or too slowly. They also use complete sentences that listeners can understand.
- Good listeners pay attention to what the speaker is saying, wait their turn to speak, and make appropriate contributions.

Think Aloud **MODEL** Use the passage below to model sharing information. Bald eagles build nests for their eggs. After the eggs hatch, the babies depend on their parents for food and protection. At first the father collects food for the babies. The mother stays at the nest to protect them. The parents tear the food into small pieces so the babies can eat it.

GUIDE PRACTICE Briefly discuss how other animals care for their babies with the children. Have them share what they know about the birds in their neighborhood or other animals they are familiar with.

ON THEIR OWN Have pairs of children take turns listening to and speaking about how animals take care of their babies. Remind children to listen politely and to speak clearly at an appropriate pace.

Research and Inquiry

Step 3 Gather and Record Information

TEACH Tell children that today they will look through sources of information to find facts about wild animals and their babies. They will use the information to create a chart.

Think Aloud **MODEL** Display the list of animals the class created on Day 1. Before we can write a chart, we have to pick animals to include in it. It's best to choose animals you are interested in. So, I'll ask: What are your favorite animals? You can gather information about your animals from sources such as books or magazines.

GUIDE PRACTICE Have children use reference books to locate information about different animals that take care of their babies. Encourage children to find information about three or four animals. Suggest they write the name of the animal and the name of its babies. Explain that they will use this information to write a chart.

ON THEIR OWN Use *Reader's and Writer's Notebook,* p. 178.

A Fox and a Kit

Name ____________

Look at the chart. **Answer** the questions.

Adult Animals	Baby Animals
bear	cub
deer	fawn
elephant	calf
goat	kid

1. The topic of Lee's report is "Animals and Their Babies." Will this chart help?
   Yes, the chart gives information about what baby animals are called.
2. Is there enough information in the chart for Lee to write about "Animals and Their Babies"?
   No, the only information in the chart is the names of the animal babies. That is not enough.
3. **Write** a topic idea for Lee that uses only the information in the chart.

School + Home **Home Activity** Your child learned how review and revise a topic. Ask your child to choose a topic that is of interest to him or her. Have him or her list some facts about the topic. Then using a reference source, read about the topic and ask your child to revise the facts based on your research.

178 **Research** Review and Revise a Topic

Reader's and Writer's Notebook, p. 178

Access for All

SI Strategic Intervention

Reviewing Charts Some children may have trouble reading a chart. Work with children as a group. Read a chart aloud as children track the words in each section. Allow them to reread each section after you, pointing out the direction to read the columns.

Wrap Up Your Day!

✔ **Main Idea and Details** Have children think about *A Fox and a Kit.* What details did you learn about the fox and the kit? What is the main idea these details tell about?

✔ **Important Ideas** Remind children that important ideas are the bigger ideas the author wants us to think about. Have children recall why it is helpful to be able to locate bigger ideas.

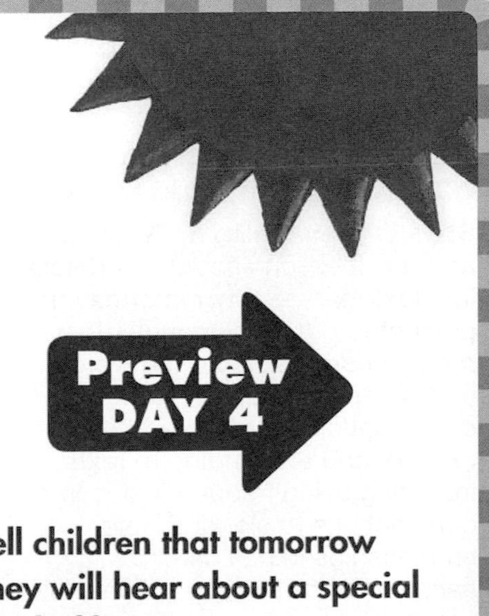

Tell children that tomorrow they will hear about a special kind of horse.

DAY 4 at a Glance

Content Knowledge
Oral Vocabulary

Phonemic Awareness
Segment and Blend Onset and Rime

Phonics
Review Short *o* Spelled *o*
Review -*s* Plurals

High-Frequency Words
Review

Spelling
Inflected Ending -*s*

Science in Reading
Fable

Fluency
Accuracy and Appropriate Rate

Conventions
Declarative Sentences

Writing
Personal Narrative: Revise

Research and Inquiry
Synthesize

Materials

- Student Edition
- Sing with Me Big Book
- Read Aloud Anthology
- Decodable Reader 4C
- Reader's and Writer's Notebook

Common Core State Standards

Speaking/Listening 2. Ask and answer questions about key details in a text read aloud or information presented orally or through other media. **Language 6.** Use words and phrases acquired through conversations, reading and being read to, and responding to texts, including using frequently occurring conjunctions to signal simple relationships (e.g., *I named my hamster Nibblet because she nibbles too much because she likes that*).

Content Knowledge

Wild Animals and Their Babies

EXPAND THE CONCEPT To reinforce concepts and to focus children's attention, have them sing "Squirrel Song" from the *Sing with Me* Big Book. How can we learn about wild squirrels? (Possible response: We can observe what they do.)

Build Oral Language

REVIEW GENRE: LITERARY NONFICTION Have children tell the key features of literary nonfiction: it tells about real people, animals, and events. The setting is real. Explain that today you will read about another animal that lives in zoos and in the wild in "Takhi" by Karen Magnuson Beil.

"Takhi"

MONITOR LISTENING COMPREHENSION Recall how people looked after the mother fox and her kit in the zoo. Have children listen to "Takhi."

Team Talk **TALK ABOUT WILD ANIMALS AND THEIR BABIES** Read aloud the first two paragraphs of "Takhi." Display them on the board if possible and track the print as you read.

- Have pairs generate questions for each other about ways these horses are wild.
- Add words generated in the discussion to the concept map.

Build Oral Vocabulary

Amazing Words Robust Vocabulary Routine

1. **Introduce the Word** Relate the word *native* to the story. People wanted to return the takhi to their *native* land. Supply a child-friendly definition. *Native* means "from a certain place." Have children say the word.

2. **Demonstrate** Provide examples to show meaning. That man is *native* to New York City. My grandparents decided to return to their *native* land. Spanish is some people's *native* language.

3. **Apply** Have children demonstrate their understanding. Tell something about your *native* country and your *native* language. Use the word *native* when you tell about it.

4. **Display the Word** Run your hand under the two syllables *na-tive* as you read the word. Point out the first sound /n/ is spelled with the letter *n.*

See p. OV•4 to teach *reserve.*

Routines Flip Chart

ADD TO THE CONCEPT MAP Discuss how wild animals take care of their babies.

Concept Map

- We read and sang about how wild animals take care of their babies. In *A Fox and a Kit,* what is the mother fox doing? (She is playing with her baby.) Let's add *They play with them* to our map.
- Referring to our concept map, what are some of the ways the takhi horses might take care of their young in the wild? (teach them new things, play with them, nap with them, watch over them)

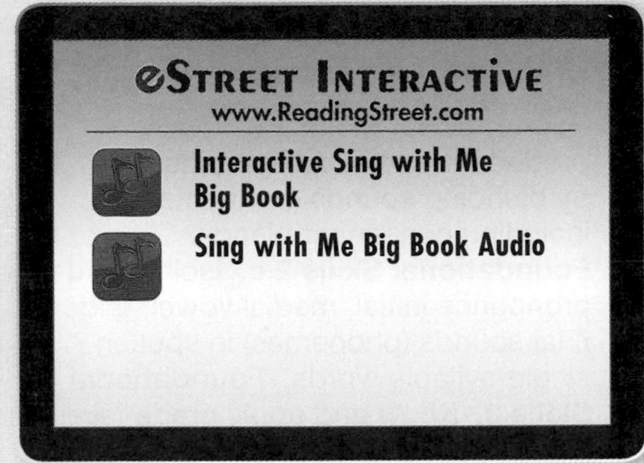

Amazing Words

observe	screech
wild	million
parent	native
canopy	reserve

Access for All

A Advanced

Extend Amazing Words Apply knowledge of oral vocabulary by asking questions that include the Amazing Words, such as: If you hear a wild animal *screech,* what might have happened? Name some *native* jungle animals. If you had a *million* dollars, how might you use it to help wild animals? Encourage children to use the words in discussion and writing.

Produce Oral Language Use the Day 4 instruction on ELL Poster 4 to extend and enrich language.

Develop Vocabulary Explain that in this selection the word *reserve* means a safe place set aside for animals. For children who need visual support, draw a simple picture to illustrate the meaning.

DAY 4

Common Core State Standards

Foundational Skills 2.b. Orally produce single-syllable words by blending sounds (phonemes), including consonant blends. **Foundational Skills 2.c.** Isolate and pronounce initial, medial vowel, and final sounds (phonemes) in spoken single-syllable words. **Foundational Skills 3.** Know and apply grade-level phonics and word analysis skills in decoding words.

Access for All

 Advanced

Extend Blending For children who master blending onset and rime, have children practice blending each individual sound in the words listed. For example, segment *sit* into /s/ /i/ /t/ and then have children blend the three sounds.

Phonemic Awareness

Segment and Blend Onset and Rime

MODEL This week we read about a fox and her kit. Listen as I say the first sound in *kit:* /k/. *Kit* ends with *-it.* Now I will blend /k/ and *-it* together to say the word: /k/ -it, *kit.*

GUIDE PRACTICE I will say the sounds in a word, and you repeat them after me. Then we will say the word together. Say the sounds in each word below, and then guide children to say the sounds. Then say the word with children.

Corrective feedback | If children make an error, model the correct response. Return to the word later in the practice.

/s/ -it	(sit)	**/d/ -ot**	(dot)	**/n/ -ap**	(nap)
/h/ -at	(hat)	**/s/ /t/ -age**	(stage)	**/l/ -og**	(log)

ON THEIR OWN Have children segment and blend the following words.

/m/ -an	(man)	**/p/ -ick**	(pick)	**/p/ -at**	(pat)
/k/ -age	(cage)	**/p/ -an**	(pan)	**/j/ -ot**	(jot)

Phonics

Review Short *o* Spelled *o*; -*s* Plurals

REVIEW SHORT *o* To review last week's first phonics skill, write *hop* and *rock.* You studied words like these last week. What do you know about the sound of *o* in a one-syllable word? (The letter *o* usually stands for the sound /o/.)

Corrective feedback	If children are unable to answer your questions about short *o*, refer them to Sound-Spelling Card 17.

REVIEW -*s* PLURALS To review last week's second phonics skill, write *kids, caps,* and *socks.* You also studied words like these. What does the letter *s* mean at the end of these words? (It makes the words plural.)

GUIDE PRACTICE Use Graphic Organizer 4. When I say a word, put up your hand if it is plural: *pins, dog, cats, mops, rat, pan, maps, sock.* Write each word in the appropriate column. Then have children read the words. Have them identify words with short *o. (dog, mops, sock)*

Singular	Plural
dog	pins
rat	cats
pan	mops
sock	maps

Graphic Organizer 4

ON THEIR OWN Use Let's Practice It! pp. 51–52 on the *Teacher Resources DVD-ROM.*

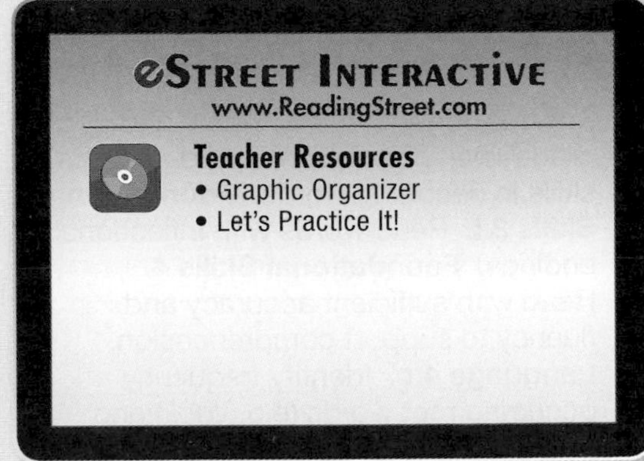

eStreet Interactive
www.ReadingStreet.com
Teacher Resources
• Graphic Organizer
• Let's Practice It!

Access for All

Strategic Intervention

Adding -*s* Remind children that plurals are words that mean "more than one." Write *The dogs sit* and *The boy sits* on the board. Explain that *dogs* means more than one dog and *sits* refers to an action, not more than one *sit.*

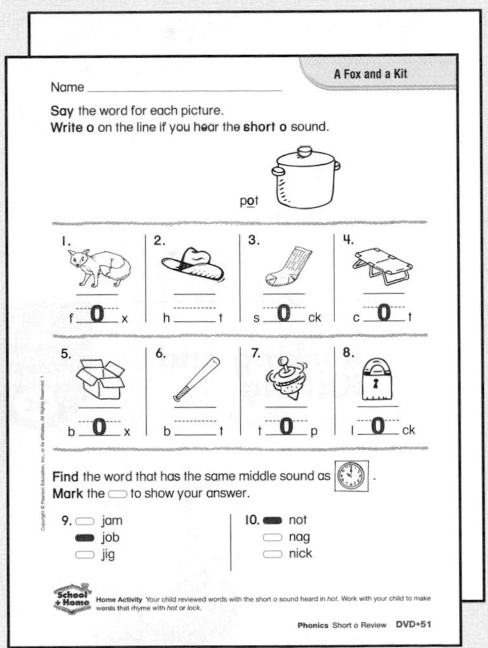

Name ____________ A Fox and a Kit

Say the word for each picture.
Write o on the line if you hear the short o sound.

pot

1. f o x
2. h _ t
3. s o ck
4. c o t
5. b o x
6. b _ t
7. t o p
8. l o ck

Find the word that has the same middle sound as [clock]. Mark the ⊂⊃ to show your answer.

9. jam / job / jig
10. not / nag / nick

Phonics Short o Review DVD•51

Let's Practice It! TR DVD•51–52

Professional Development

Model Decoding When modeling how to decode a new word, a teacher should first segment by pronouncing each sound in the word separately. Then the teacher should blend the sounds together to say the word at a normal speed. This will help teach children to consider each sound in sequence, from left to right, as well as to expect blended phonemes to sound like a word.

Common Core State Standards

Foundational Skills 3. Know and apply grade-level phonics and word analysis skills in decoding words. **Foundational Skills 3.f.** Read words with inflectional endings. **Foundational Skills 4.** Read with sufficient accuracy and fluency to support comprehension. **Language 4.c.** Identify frequently occurring root words (e.g., *look*) and their inflectional forms (e.g., *looks, looked, looking*).

Decodable Reader 4C

If children need help, then...

Read *Rocking and Kicking*

DECODE WORDS IN ISOLATION Have children turn to page 185 decode each word listed.

REVIEW HIGH-FREQUENCY WORDS Review the previously taught words *a, eats, take,* and *her.* Have children read each word as you point to it on the Word Wall.

PREVIEW Have children read the title and preview the story. Tell them they will read words that end in -*s* and words that end in *-ing.*

DECODE WORDS IN CONTEXT Pair children for reading and listen carefully as they decode. One child begins. Children read the entire story, switching readers after each page. Partners reread the story. This time the other child begins.

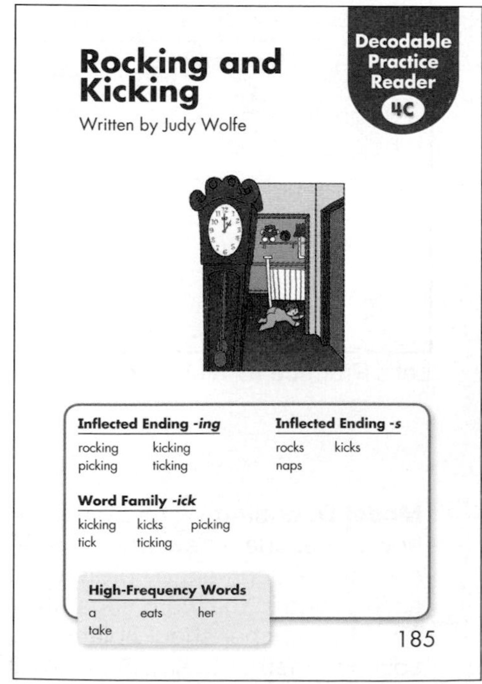

Decodable Practice Reader 4C

Corrective feedback	**If...** children have difficulty decoding a word, **then...** refer them to the Sound-Spelling Cards to identify the sounds in the word. Then prompt them to blend the word. • What is the new word? • Is the new word a word you know? • Does it make sense in the story?

CHECK DECODING AND COMPREHENSION Have children retell the story to include characters, setting, and events. Then have children find words that end in *-s* and words that end in *-ing* in the story. Children should supply *rocking, rocks, kicking, kicks, eats, picking, naps,* and *ticking.*

Reread for Fluency

REREAD DECODABLE READER Have children reread Decodable Practice Reader 4C to develop automaticity decoding words that end in *-s* and words that end in *-ing.*

Routine Oral Rereading

1. **Read** Have children read the entire book orally.
2. **Reread** To achieve optimal fluency, children should reread the text three or four times.
3. **Corrective Feedback** Listen as children read. Provide corrective feedback regarding their fluency and decoding.

Routines Flip Chart

Decodable Practice Reader

Beginning Show children the words with inflected ending *-s* in the story. Break each word into its base word and its *-s* ending. Have children first say each part of a word, and then blend the parts to say the whole word.

Intermediate Have children read each sentence in the story that has a verb with an *-s* ending. Have them pantomime the action as they pronounce the word with the *-s* ending. Monitor children's pronunciation of the words.

Advanced Have children read the sentences in the story with verbs that have the *-s* ending. Then have them produce new sentences using *helps, hits, sits,* and *wins.*

Common Core State Standards

Foundational Skills 3. Know and apply grade-level phonics and word analysis skills in decoding words. **Foundational Skills 3.f.** Read words with inflectional endings. **Language 2.d.** Use conventional spelling for words with common spelling patterns and for frequently occurring irregular words.

Spiral Review

These activities review

- previously taught high-frequency words *little, blue, from, me, what, use, help, do, for, here, is, from, a, the.*
- short *o* spelled *o,* inflected endings *-s* and *-ing,* final /k/ spelled *-ck,* and final /ks/.

Fluent Word Reading

Spiral Review

READ WORDS IN ISOLATION Display these words. Tell children that they can blend some words on this list, and others are Word Wall words.

Have children read the list three or four times until they can read at the rate of two to three seconds per word.

little	**can**	**help**	**Max**	**locks**
sack	**from**	**will**	**for**	**here**
Mick	**me**	**box**	**use**	**is**
blue	**what**	**do**	**lids**	**Dot**

Corrective feedback — Word Reading

If... children have difficulty reading whole words,
then... have them use sound-by-sound blending for decodable words, or have them say and spell high-frequency words.

If... children cannot read fluently at a rate of two to three seconds per word,
then... have pairs practice the list until they can read it fluently.

READ WORDS IN CONTEXT Display these sentences. Call on individuals to read a sentence. Then randomly point to review words and have children read them. To help you monitor word reading, high-frequency words are underlined and decodable words are italicized.

<u>What</u> *can Max* <u>do</u> <u>for</u> <u>me</u>?

***Nick will* <u>help</u> <u>from</u> <u>here</u>.**

<u>Use</u> <u>little</u> *locks on* <u>the</u> *box lids.*

Dot is packing* <u>a</u> <u>blue</u> *sack.

Corrective feedback — Sentence Reading

If... children are unable to read an underlined high-frequency word,
then... read the word for them and spell it, having them echo you.

If... children have difficulty reading an italicized decodable word,
then... guide them in using sound-by-sound blending.

Spelling

Inflected Ending *-s*

PARTNER REVIEW Supply pairs of children with index cards on which the spelling words have been written. Have one child read a word while the other writes it. Then have children switch roles. Have them use the cards to check their spelling and correct any misspelled words.

ON THEIR OWN Use *Reader's and Writer's Notebook,* p. 183.

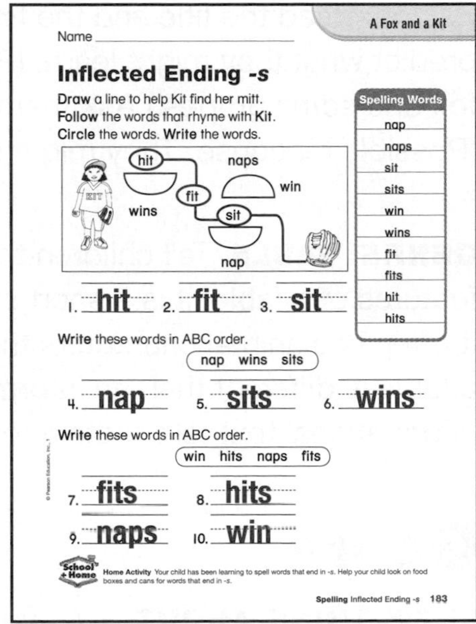
A Fox and a Kit

Name

Inflected Ending -s

Draw a line to help Kit find her mitt. **Follow** the words that rhyme with **Kit.** **Circle** the words. **Write** the words.

Spelling Words
nap
naps
sit
sits
win
wins
fit
fits
hit
hits

1. hit 2. fit 3. sit

Write these words in ABC order.

nap wins sits

4. nap 5. sits 6. wins

Write these words in ABC order.

win hits naps fits

7. fits 8. hits
9. naps 10. win

School + Home **Home Activity** Your child has been learning to spell words that end in -s. Help your child look on food boxes and cans for words that end in -s.

Spelling Inflected Ending -s 183

Reader's and Writer's Notebook, p. 183

*e*STREET INTERACTIVE
www.ReadingStreet.com

Teacher Resources
- Reader's and Writer's Notebook

ELL

Fluent Word Reading Children may benefit from first reading words in pairs to aid their decoding and pronunciation.

Day 4 **SMALL GROUP TIME • Differentiate Vocabulary, p. SG•52**

OL On-Level	SI Strategic Intervention	A Advanced
• **Develop** Language Using Selection Vocabulary • **Read** *Reading Street Sleuth,* pp. 14–15	• **Review/Discuss** Selection Vocabulary • **Read** *Reading Street Sleuth,* pp. 14–15	• **Extend** Amazing Words and Selection Vocabulary • **Read** *Reading Street Sleuth,* pp. 14–15 • **Organize** Inquiry Project

ELL

If... children need more scaffolding and practice with **Vocabulary,** **then...** use the routine on pp. xxxvi–xxxvii in the *ELL Handbook.*

Common Core State Standards

Literature 3. Describe characters, settings, and major events in a story, using key details. **Literature 5.** Explain major differences between books that tell stories and books that give information, drawing on a wide reading of a range of text types. **Literature 9.** Compare and contrast the adventures and experiences of characters in stories. **Literature 10.** With prompting and support, read prose and poetry of appropriate complexity for grade 1.

Academic Vocabulary

moral the lesson or teaching of a fable or story

Science in Reading

Fable

ACTIVATE PRIOR KNOWLEDGE Ask children what they have already learned from other texts this week about foxes. (Some foxes live in zoos and some live in the wild; mother foxes take care of their young.)

PREVIEW AND PREDICT Have children turn to page 116 of their Student Edition. Read the title and the first sentence of the story. Have children predict what they might learn. (Possible response: They might learn about a fox and some grapes.) Ask them what clue helped them make that prediction. (Possible response: They might say the title of the story or the pictures.)

GENRE: FABLE Tell children that they will read a **fable.** Review the key features of a fable: it is a short story that teaches a lesson, or moral, and it often has animal characters that speak and act like people. Explain how a fable is different than an information text. (A fable tells a story and an informational text tells facts about a topic.)

Genre

LET'S THINK ABOUT... As you read "The Fox and the Grapes" together, use Let's Think About in the Student Edition to help children focus on the features of a fable.

1. This is a fable because it is a short story that teaches a lesson, or moral, and it has an animal character who speaks and who acts like a human.
2. I can say I do not want something because I know I can never have it. If I don't have enough money for a new toy, it's easy for me to just say I never wanted it anyway.

Common Core State Standards
Literature 3. Describe characters, settings, and major events in a story, using key details. **Also Literature 9.**

Science in Reading

Genre
Fable

- A fable is a short story that teaches a lesson, or moral.
- The characters in a fable are often animals that speak and act like people.
- The author wants readers to connect a fable's moral to their personal experiences.
- Read "The Fox and the Grapes." Look for elements that make this story a fable.

Read Together

The Fox and the Grapes

adapted from Aesop

One day, a fox wanted grapes.

But he could not reach them.

The fox tried again and again.

116

At last, the fox gave up.

"I did not want those sour grapes anyway," he said.

Moral: It is easy to dislike what you cannot get.

Let's Think About...

How do you know this story is a fable? **Fable**

1

Let's Think About...

What does the moral of the fable mean? How can you connect the meaning to things that have happened to you? **Fable**

2

Let's Think About...

Reading Across Texts How are the foxes in *A Fox and a Kit* and "The Fox and the Grapes" alike? How are they different?

Writing Across Texts Imagine the foxes in *A Fox and a Kit* could talk to the fox in "The Fox and the Grapes." Write what they would say to him. Write what he would say to them.

117

Student Edition, pp. 116–117

Access Text

Think Aloud

IMPORTANT IDEAS Good readers look for the big or important ideas as they read so that they can have a better understanding of what a story or selection is about. When I finished reading *A Fox and a Kit,* I thought about all the things the mother fox and her kit did together. I will pay attention to what the fox does as I read "The Fox and the Grapes."

MAIN IDEA AND DETAILS I think about the title of this fable—"The Fox and the Grapes." I wonder if the fox will eat the grapes.

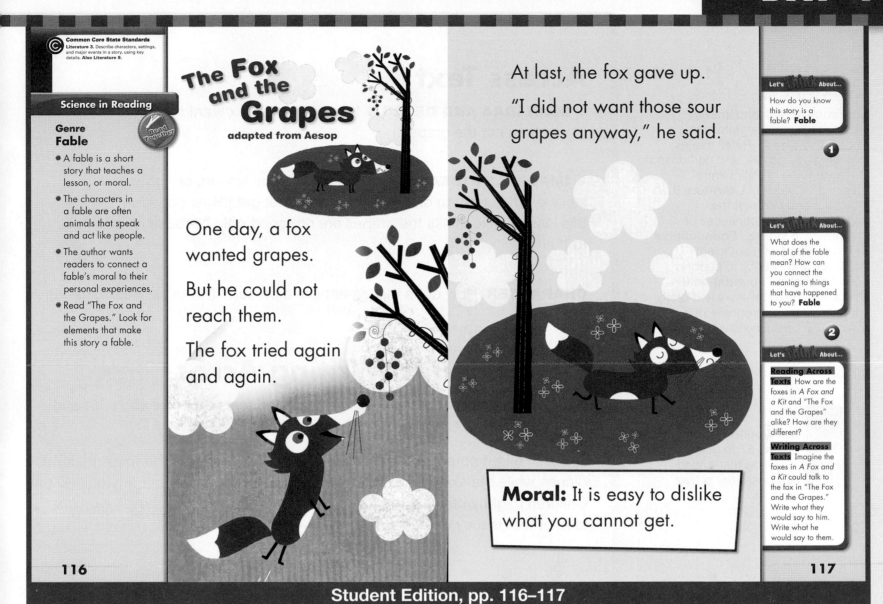

Science Vocabulary

vine a grape plant, or a long stem that trails along the ground or winds around a support such as the branch of a tree

Common Core State Standards

Literature 1. Ask and answer questions about key details in a text. **Literature 2.** Retell stories, including key details, and demonstrate understanding of their central message or lesson. **Literature 9.** Compare and contrast the adventures and experiences of characters in stories. **Foundational Skills 4.** Read with sufficient accuracy and fluency to support comprehension. **Foundational Skills 4.b.** Read on-level text orally with accuracy, appropriate rate, and expression on successive readings.

Writing to Sources

Use Connect the Texts on pp. 56–57 to guide children in writing text-based responses using two sources.

Access Text

MAIN IDEA AND DETAILS What does the fox want to do in this story? (It wants to eat the grapes.)

IMPORTANT IDEAS What do you think the lesson, or moral, of this story is? (It is easy to dislike what you cannot get.) How does the fox learn this lesson? (He thinks the grapes are not good only because he can't get to them.)

CHARACTER How does the fox act like a person? (He talks. Real foxes do not talk.)

Reading and Writing Across Texts

Have children find words and sentences in the texts of *A Fox and a Kit* and "The Fox and the Grapes" to tell what the foxes do.

Children might note that the man in *A Fox and a Kit* brings the foxes their dinner, while the fox in "The Fox and the Grapes" does not get anything to eat. Children might write how the foxes would talk about where they live or what kind of things they do every day.

Fluency

Accuracy and Appropriate Rate

- Have children turn to pages 108–109 in *A Fox and a Kit.*
- Have children follow along as you read the pages accurately and at an appropriate rate.
- Have the class read the pages with you and then reread the pages as a group until they read with no hesitation and no mistakes. To provide additional fluency practice, pair nonfluent readers with fluent readers.

Routine Paired Reading

1. **Select a Passage** For *A Fox and a Kit,* use pp. 110–111.
2. **Model** First, have children track the print as you read.
3. **Guide Practice** Then have children read along with you.
4. **On Their Own** For optimal fluency, have partners reread three or four times.

Routines Flip Chart

Access for All

A Advanced

Rate If children already read at 60 words correct per minute, have them read more challenging text.

Options for Oral Rereading

Use *A Fox and a Kit* or one of this week's Decodable Practice Readers.

MONITOR PROGRESS Fluency Check

As children reread, monitor their progress toward their individual fluency goals. Mid-Year Goal: 20–30 words correct per minute. End-of-Year Goal: 60 words correct per minute. Beginning in Unit 3, children will be assessed to determine WCPM.

If... children are not on track to meet benchmark goals,

then... have children practice with text at their independent level.

DAY 4

Common Core State Standards

Foundational Skills 1.a. Recognize the distinguishing features of a sentence (e.g., first word, capitalization, ending punctuation). **Writing 1.** Write opinion pieces in which they introduce the topic or name the book they are writing about, state an opinion, supply a reason for the opinion, and provide some sense of closure. **Writing 3.** Write narratives in which they recount two or more appropriately sequenced events, include some details regarding what happened, use temporal words to signal event order, and provide some sense of closure. **Language 1.j.** Produce and expand complete simple and compound declarative, interrogative, imperative, and exclamatory sentences in response to prompts.

Bridge to Common Core

CONVENTIONS OF STANDARD ENGLISH

As children identify declarative sentences, they learn how a sentence must make a statement and be written in a complete sentence format. As they do this, they are gaining control of the conventions of standard English grammar, usage, and mechanics.

Daily Fix-It

7. the mix is a hitt.
The mix is a hit.

8. This mix winz too
This mix wins too.

Discuss the Daily Fix-It corrections with children. Review sentence capitalization and punctuation, /z/ spelled *s*, the inflected ending *-s*, and the spelling of *hit*.

Conventions

Declarative Sentences

TEST PRACTICE Use *Reader's and Writer's Notebook,* p. 184 to help children understand identifying declarative sentences in test items. Recall that declarative sentences are statements. Model identifying a declarative sentence by writing this sentence on the board, reading it aloud, and underlining the capital letter and period.

A frog flops in the pond.

ON THEIR OWN Read the directions on *Reader's and Writer's Notebook,* p. 184. Guide children as they mark the answer for number 1.

APPLY After children mark the answers to numbers 1–6, review the correct choices aloud, and have children read each sentence aloud.

A Fox and a Kit

Name ____________

Declarative Sentences

Find the sentence. **Mark** the sentence.

1. ○ the fox is red.
   ⊗ The fox is red.
   ○ the fox is red
2. ⊗ It has a kit.
   ○ it has a kit.
   ○ It has a kit
3. ○ the kit is brown.
   ○ the kit is brown
   ⊗ The kit is brown.
4. ⊗ The man has a pan.
   ○ the man has a pan.
   ○ The man has a pan
5. ○ the pan is tan
   ○ the pan is tan.
   ⊗ The pan is tan.
6. ○ the kit sits on the rocks.
   ⊗ The kit sits on the rocks.
   ○ the kit sits on the rocks

School + Home **Home Activity** Your child prepared for taking tests on telling sentences. Name a familiar animal. Have your child say a sentence that tells about the animal.

184 **Conventions** Declarative Sentences

Reader's and Writer's Notebook, p. 184

Personal Narrative

Mini-Lesson Revise: Rearranging Sentences

- Yesterday we wrote personal narratives about watching animals. Today we will revise. We can help people who read the narratives. We can make the writing clearer or more interesting. We can make sure the sentences are in an order that makes sense.

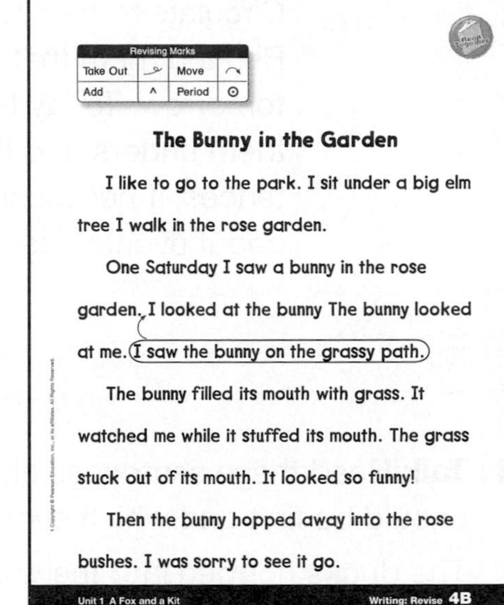

Revising Marks			
Take Out		Move	
Add	^	Period	⊙

The Bunny in the Garden

I like to go to the park. I sit under a big elm tree I walk in the rose garden.

One Saturday I saw a bunny in the rose garden. I looked at the bunny The bunny looked at me. I saw the bunny on the grassy path.

The bunny filled its mouth with grass. It watched me while it stuffed its mouth. The grass stuck out of its mouth. It looked so funny!

Then the bunny hopped away into the rose bushes. I was sorry to see it go.

Unit 1 A Fox and a Kit — Writing: Revise 4B

Writing Transparency 4B TR DVD

- Display the Revising Tips. Explain that this is a time for making the narrative clear for anyone who will read it. Tomorrow children will proofread to correct any errors such as misspellings, missing capital letters, or misplaced sentence periods.

Revising Tips

✔ Make sure you tell your feelings or opinions about events.

✔ Put sentences in an order that makes sense.

- Use Writing Transparency 4B to model rearranging sentences. I'll tell about seeing the bunny on the grassy path before I tell about the bunny and me looking at each other. I should tell events in the same order as they happened. On the transparency, show how to use revising marks to rearrange sentences. Tell children that they can rearrange sentences as they revise.

PEER CONFERENCING • PEER REVISION Pair children and tell half to read the partner's narrative. Allow two minutes. Then have the readers use one or two minutes to tell the events in the narrative in order. Repeat with second partners reading and telling about the other narrative. Have each writer listen for any part of the narrative that seems out of order or that the reader has not understood. Circulate to assist children planning to revise their narratives.

Access for All

SI Strategic Intervention

Statements If children are struggling with declarative sentences, have them tell something. Use these sentence frames to have children tell something about themselves:

I am ________.

I like ________.

I live ________.

Past Tense Help children use the inflected ending *-ed* to write their narratives in past tense. Explain that adding *-ed* to some verbs shows that the events already happened.

Common Core State Standards

Writing 3. Write narratives in which they recount two or more appropriately sequenced events, include some details regarding what happened, use temporal words to signal event order, and provide some sense of closure. **Writing 5.** With guidance and support from adults, focus on a topic, respond to questions and suggestions from peers, and add details to strengthen writing as needed. **Also Writing 7., 8.**

Writing

Zoom in on ©

GUIDE PRACTICE Have children revise their personal narratives. For those not sure how to revise, have children refer to the Revising Tips or the Key Features of a Personal Narrative.

Corrective feedback Circulate to monitor and confer with children as they write. Remind them that they will have time to proofread and edit tomorrow. Today they can make their narratives clearer. Help them understand the benefits of rearranging or adding sentences, if necessary. Encourage them to include their feelings about events described in their narratives.

Routine Quick Write for Fluency

Team Talk

1. **Talk** Read these sentences aloud, and have children tell which action should be first and which second.

   The ducks hopped into the water.
   The ducks waddled to the pond.

2. **Write** Have children write two short sentences about two things that happen one after another. Children may write the sentences in order or out of order.

3. **Share** Have children read the sentences to partners and have partners tell which sentence should be first and which should be second.

Routines Flip Chart

Research and Inquiry

Step 4 Synthesize

TEACH Tell children that the next step in the inquiry project is to review the chart to see if they have the information they set out to find, or if they need to do more research.

Think Aloud **MODEL** We planned to find out about wild animals and their babies. First, we listed wild animals. Then we picked the ones we were interested in. Last, we gathered information about the animals and their babies. Now I will look at the information I gathered. I will see if I found out enough about the wild animals and their babies. If I did not, I can always look for more information.

GUIDE PRACTICE Have children look at the information they gathered during Day 3. They will decide what kinds of information they want to include in their chart. Guide children to choose the information they want to include and to decide how they want to use a title, columns, and headings to organize this information.

Access for All

SI Strategic Intervention

Organize Information If children have difficulty organizing information, suggest they ask themselves questions to help figure out what the different pieces of information have in common.

Wrap Up Your Day!

✔ **Phonics Review** List several words with the inflected ending *-s.* Have children read each word and identify the base word and the ending.

✔ **Fluency** Write *Will the fox nap? Yes, the fox will nap.* Have the class reread the sentences until they can do so accurately and at an appropriate rate.

Remind children that they heard about wild horses. Tomorrow they will hear about the horses again.

DAY 5 at a Glance

Content Knowledge
Oral Vocabulary

Phonemic Awareness
Review Segment and Blend Onset and Rime

Phonics/Spelling
Review Inflected Ending *-s*
Review Inflected Ending *-ing*

Text-Based Comprehension
Review Main Idea and Details

Selection Words
Review

High-Frequency Words
Review

Assessment
Phonics
High-Frequency Words
Fluency

Conventions
Review Declarative Sentences

Writing
Personal Narrative: Proofread

Research and Inquiry
Communicate

Materials

- Student Edition
- Read Aloud Anthology
- Weekly Test

Bridge to Common Core

INTEGRATION OF KNOWLEDGE/IDEAS
This week children have integrated content presented in diverse formats and analyzed how different texts address similar topics. They have developed knowledge about wild animals and their babies for the unit topic of Animals, Tame and Wild.

Science Knowledge Goals
Children have learned that wild animals

- provide food for their babies
- protect their babies from harm

Content Knowledge

Zoom in on

Wild Animals and Their Babies

REVIEW CONCEPT This week we have read and listened to stories about how wild animals take care of their babies. Today you will listen to a selection about wild horses. Read the selection.

- What is something the takhi needed to learn before returning to the wild? (They had to learn how to find food.)

Scott Foresman
Read Aloud
Anthology
Reading Street
Grade 1
"Takhi"

Build Oral Language

REVIEW AMAZING WORDS Orally review the meanings of this week's Amazing Words. Then display this week's concept map. Have children use Amazing Words such as *parent, wild,* and *reserve,* as well as the concept map, to answer the question *How do wild animals take care of their babies?*

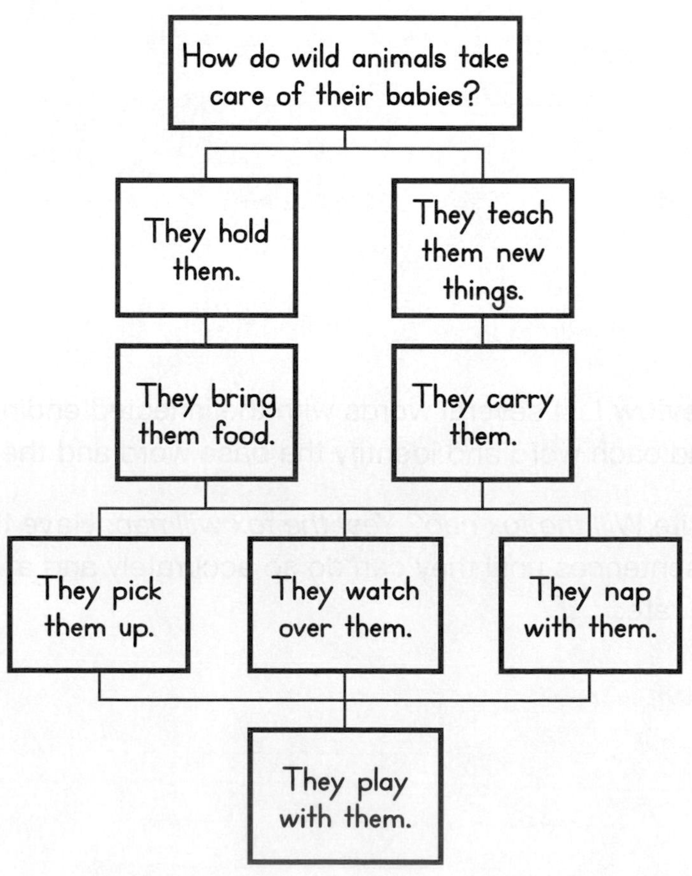
How do wild animals take care of their babies?
They hold them.
They teach them new things.
They bring them food.
They carry them.
They pick them up.
They watch over them.
They nap with them.
They play with them.

Build Oral Vocabulary

Team Talk **CONNECT TO AMAZING IDEAS** Pair children and have them discuss how the Question of the Week, *How do wild animals take care of their babies?,* connects to the question of this unit of study: *How are people and animals important to one another?* Tell children to use the concept map and what they've learned from this week's discussions and reading selections to form an Amazing Idea—a realization or "big idea" about **animals, tame and wild.** Use the following ideas as prompts:

- What kinds of wild animals have we read about? (fox, squirrel, horses)
- What is one way wild animals get food for their babies?

Then ask each pair to share their Amazing Idea with the class. Encourage children to recall in which selection they learned their ideas.

Amazing Ideas might include:

- Animal parents watch over their babies.
- People can help wild animals get food for their babies.

MONITOR PROGRESS Check Oral Vocabulary

FORMATIVE ASSESSMENT Call on individuals to use this week's Amazing Words to talk about how wild animals take care of their babies. Prompt discussion with the questions below. Monitor children's ability to use the Amazing Words and note which words children are unable to use.

- **What is something you can *observe?***
- **How is a *wild* animal different from a pet?**
- **What are some things an animal *parent* can do?**
- **Where is the *canopy* in a rain forest?**
- **Why might your little brother or sister *screech?***
- **How long do you think it would take to count to a *million?***
- **What area is *native* to the takhi?**
- **Why do some wild animals live on a *reserve?***

If... children have difficulty using the Amazing Words,

then... reteach the unknown words using the Robust Vocabulary routines, pp. 95a, 100b, 112b, 116b.

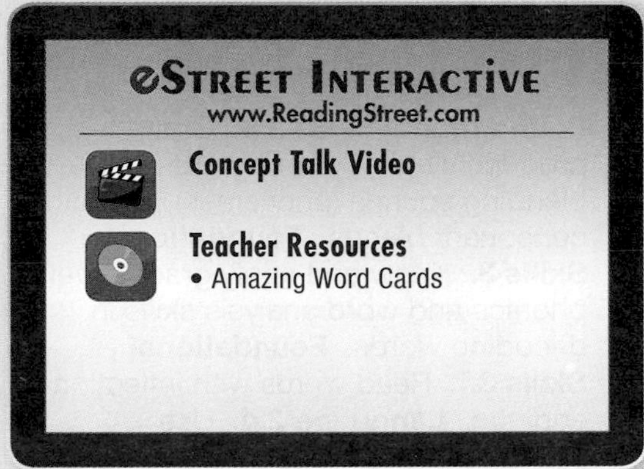

observe	screech
wild	million
parent	native
canopy	reserve

Check Concepts and Language Use the Day 5 instruction on ELL Poster 4 to monitor children's understanding of the lesson concept.

Amazing Words Rephrase the questions to make true or false statements that use the Amazing Words. Have children repeat the statements before answering: People can count to one *million* very quickly. *Wild* animals are just like pets. Your little brother or sister might *screech* when hiding from you.

Common Core State Standards

Foundational Skills 2.b. Orally produce single-syllable words by blending sounds (phonemes), including consonant blends. **Foundational Skills 3.** Know and apply grade-level phonics and word analysis skills in decoding words. **Foundational Skills 3.f.** Read words with inflectional endings. **Language 2.d.** Use conventional spelling for words with common spelling patterns and for frequently occurring irregular words.

Phonemic Awareness

Review Segment and Blend Onset and Rime

SEGMENT AND BLEND ONSET AND RIME Have children segment and blend the onset and rime in each word below. If children make an error, model the correct response. Return to the word later in the practice.

/k/ -ap	(cap)	**/p/ -age**	(page)	**/p/ -ot**	(pot)
/b/ -at	(bat)	**/s/ -ip**	(sip)	**/t/ /r/ -ick**	(trick)

Phonics

Review Inflected Endings *-s* and *-ing*

TARGET PHONICS SKILLS Write the following sentences on the board. Have children read each one, first quietly to themselves and then aloud as you track the print.

1. **Mom pins and tacks the tag on the map.**
2. **Dad is fixing and waxing the van.**
3. **Pam sits and rips the rag.**
4. **Nick is kicking and passing it.**

Team Talk Have children discuss with a partner which words have the ending *-s* and which words have the ending *-ing.* Then call on individuals to share with the class.

Spelling Test

Inflected Ending -*s*

DICTATE SPELLING WORDS Say each word, read the sentence, repeat the word, and allow time for children to write the word.

1. sit	**Sit** with me.
2. sits	Max **sits** in the van.
3. win	Will they **win?**
4. wins	Dad **wins** the top job.
5. fit	Will this cap **fit?**
6. fits	The wig **fits** Dot.
7. hit	**Hit** the two lids.
8. hits	Tim **hits** the box.
9. nap	I do not like to **nap.**
10. naps	The cat **naps** on the mat.

High-Frequency Words

11. her	Mom got **her** tan socks wet.
12. too	Did you go **too?**

Assess

- Spell words with the inflected ending -*s*.
- Spell high-frequency words.

Access for All

SI Strategic Intervention

Check Spelling Have children choose the correct spelling of each word from three random spellings.

A Advanced

Extend Spelling Have children who have demonstrated proficiency in spelling individual words spell each word in a self-made sentence.

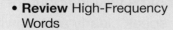

Day 5 SMALL GROUP TIME • Differentiate Reteaching, p. SG•52

OL On-Level

- **Practice** Declarative Sentences
- **Reread** *Reading Street Sleuth,* pp. 14–15

SI Strategic Intervention

- **Review** High-Frequency Words
- **Reread** *Reading Street Sleuth,* pp. 14–15

A Advanced

- **Extend** Declarative Sentences
- **Reread** *Reading Street Sleuth,* pp. 14–15
- **Communicate** Inquiry Project

If... children need more scaffolding and practice with **Conventions and Writing,**
then... use the Grammar Transition Lessons on pp. 346–421 in the *ELL Handbook.*

Common Core State Standards
Speaking/Listening 1.b. Build on others' talk in conversations by responding to the comments of others through multiple exchanges. Also Foundational Skills 4.b., Speaking/Listening 1.a., 3.

Let's Learn It! Read Together

READING STREET ONLINE
VOCABULARY ACTIVITIES
www.ReadingStreet.com

Listening and Speaking

Get Ready for Grade 2: Stay on topic when you speak.

Share Information and Ideas When we share ideas with others, we speak clearly. We listen carefully to other ideas. We ask questions if we need more information.

Practice It! Discuss your favorite animal. Speak clearly in sentences. Stay on topic during the discussion. Listen carefully, take notes, and ask questions if you do not understand something.

118

Vocabulary

When we put words in **alphabetical order,** we look at the first letter in each word. Then we think about the alphabet and remember which letter comes first. If two words start with the same letter, we look at the second letter.

Practice It! Read these words. Write them in alphabetical order.

dog **sit** **tan** **step**

Fluency

Rate When you read, try to read the sentences as if you were talking. Don't read too quickly or too slowly.

Practice It!

1. Tim can help by packing this bag.
2. The cat eats and naps.
3. The fox naps too.

119

Student Edition, pp. 118–119

Common Core State Standards

Foundational Skills 4.b. Read on-level text orally with accuracy, appropriate rate, and expression on successive readings. **Speaking/Listening 1.b.** Build on others' talk in conversations by responding to the comments of others through multiple exchanges. **Also Speaking/Listening 1.a., 3., 6., Language 1.**

Share Information and Ideas

To prepare for Grade 2, children should be able to share information and ideas and alphabetize words to the second letter.

Listening and Speaking

Share Information and Ideas

TEACH Have children turn to pages 118–119 of the Student Edition. Remind children that good speakers speak clearly and good listeners listen carefully. Remind them that we can ask questions if we want more information. Have children use declarative sentences to name their favorite zoo animals.

INTRODUCE PROMPT Read the Practice It! prompt with the class. Remind children that they should start by telling their favorite zoo animals. They can then add details about these animals.

Team Talk Have pairs take turns talking about their favorite zoo animals. Tell children that good speakers speak clearly and slowly, and that good listeners ask questions if they want more information.

Vocabulary

Alphabetize to Second Letter

TEACH Read and discuss the Vocabulary lesson on page 119 of the Student Edition. Alphabetize a series of words to the second letter. Write these words in order: *band, bed, brick.* Read and point to each word. These words are in alphabetical order. The first letter of all these words is *b,* so we need to use the second letter to put them in alphabetical order. Point to the second letter of each word in order. The second letter of *band* is *a.* The second letter of *bed* is *e.* And the second letter of *brick* is *r. A* comes before *e* in the alphabet, so *band* goes before *bed. E* comes before *r* in the alphabet, so *bed* goes before *brick.* Point to the second letter of each word. The correct order is: *band, bed, brick.*

GUIDE PRACTICE Read the instructions for the Vocabulary Practice It! activity. Read the first word and then have children repeat after you.

ON THEIR OWN Have pairs continue reading the words and writing them in alphabetical order. Have them explain how they put the word *sit* and *step* in alphabetical order.

Corrective feedback	Circulate around the room and monitor children as they say and write the words. Provide assistance as needed.

Fluency

Accuracy and Appropriate Rate

TEACH Read and discuss the Fluency instructions.

READ WORDS IN CONTEXT Give children a moment to look at the sentences. Then have them read each sentence three or four times until they can read each sentence with accuracy and at an appropriate rate.

Access for All

SI Strategic Intervention

Check Alphabetizing Reteach alphabetizing to the first letter and then alphabetizing to the second letter. Ask children to point to the first or second letter of each word as you do so.

A Advanced

Extend Alphabetizing Provide children who can alphabetize to the second letter with ease with some words to alphabetize to the third letter.

Pronounce Inflected Ending *-ing*
Some speakers may say *rockin* and *fixin,* as they may not hear the difference between *-in* and *-ing.* Have these children practice pronouncing words with ending *-ing.*

Common Core State Standards

Literature 3. Describe characters, settings, and major events in a story, using key details. **Foundational Skills 3.g.** Recognize and read grade-appropriate irregularly spelled words.

Text-Based Comprehension

Review Main Idea and Details

Remember that good readers can tell what a story or selection is mostly about. They can tell us its main idea, or what the story is mostly about. What do good readers think about to find the main idea in a story? (the details)

CHECK UNDERSTANDING Read aloud the following story and have children answer the questions that follow.

Jasper loves basketball. He watches basketball on TV and sometimes goes to big games with his parents. He goes to basketball practice after school. When he made the school team, he started playing in games on Saturday mornings.

1. What is this passage mostly about? (It is about how Jasper loves basketball.)
2. What tells you this? (He watches basketball on TV and sometimes goes to big games with his parents. He goes to practice after school and plays in games on Saturday mornings.)

Vocabulary

Review High-Frequency and Selection Words

HIGH-FREQUENCY WORDS Review this week's high-frequency words: *eat, five, four, her, this, too.* Model making up a sentence that tells something about this week's selection and includes a high-frequency word, for example: The man feeds the fox and the kit at *five.*

Team Talk Have partners retell *A Fox and a Kit* using declarative sentences. Encourage them to use at least one of the remaining five words in each sentence.

SELECTION WORDS Write the words *dinner, watch,* and *animals.* Read them aloud together. Then have children tell what the words mean.

Corrective feedback	**If...** children cannot tell what the selection words mean, **then...** review the definitions on page 102a.

Genre

Review Fable

FABLE Review with children that a fable is a short story that teaches a lesson, or moral. The characters in a fable are often animals that speak or act like people. The author wants readers to connect the moral of a fable to their own experience.

TEACH In "The Fox and the Grapes," a fox comes across some grapes hanging from a vine. He wants to eat them, but try as he might, he cannot reach them. Finally, he gives up and walks away with his nose in the air. He says, "I did not want those sour grapes anyway."

Think Aloud **MODEL** I know that in the story the fox wants something he cannot have, and I know that in real life, we sometimes want things we cannot have. When that happens, we might get annoyed and say we didn't really want the thing anyway because there was something wrong with it.

GUIDE PRACTICE Ask the following questions to guide children in describing the fable.

- Who is the character in this story, and what can he do that is different from real life? (The character is a fox, and he can talk.)
- What happens in the story? (The fox sees some grapes. He wants to eat them, but he can't reach them. He says he doesn't want them anyway because they are sour.)

ON THEIR OWN The fox doesn't really know if the grapes are sour. He just decides that they are. Why does he do this? (He does this because he is annoyed that he can't eat them. It makes him feel better.)

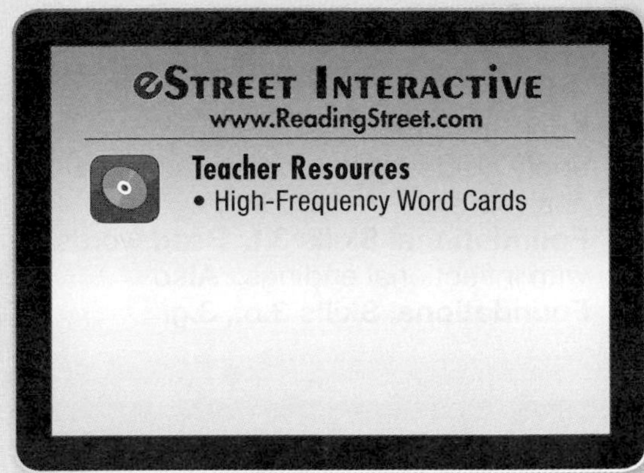

eStreet Interactive
www.ReadingStreet.com
Teacher Resources
• High-Frequency Word Cards

Access for All

SI Strategic Intervention

Support Comprehension If children have difficulty understanding why the fox got annoyed, ask them questions that put them in a similar position. For example: If you saw an ice cream vendor and wanted to buy some ice cream, but then discovered you didn't have any money with you, how might you feel? What might you say?

Academic Vocabulary

character one of the people or animals in a story

Support Vocabulary Explain to children that *sour* is a describing word. In the fable, it is meant to tell about the grapes in an unappealing way.

Common Core State Standards

Foundational Skills 3. Know and apply grade-level phonics and word analysis skills in decoding words. **Foundational Skills 3.f.** Read words with inflectional endings. **Also Foundational Skills 3.b., 3.g.**

Assess

- Verbs with the Inflected Ending *-s*
- Words with the Inflected Ending *-ing*
- High-Frequency Words

Assessment

Monitor Progress

For a written assessment of inflectional endings *-s* and *-ing,* high-frequency words, and main idea and details, use Weekly Test 4, pp. 55–60.

WORD READING Use the following reproducible page to assess children's ability to read words in isolation. Call on children to read the words aloud. Start over if necessary.

SENTENCE READING Use reproducible page 119f to assess children's ability to read words in context. Call on children to read two sentences aloud. Start over with sentence one if necessary.

MONITOR ACCURACY Record scores using the Word/Sentence Reading Chart for this unit in *First Stop.*

MONITOR PROGRESS Word and Sentence Reading

If... children have trouble reading words with inflected endings *-s* and *-ing,*
then... use the Reteach Lessons in *First Stop.*

If... a child cannot read all the high-frequency words,
then... mark the missed words on a high-frequency word list and have the child practice reading the words with a fluent reader.

Name ______________________________

Read the Words

1. hops
2. four
3. taps
4. eat
5. her
6. kicking
7. naps
8. five
9. packing
10. picking
11. rocking
12. sits
13. this
14. too

MONITOR PROGRESS

- **Inflected Ending *-s***
- **Inflected Ending *-ing***
- **High-Frequency Words**

Name ____

Read the Sentences

1. Tim hops and Mom is packing this bag.

2. Jack sits packing mix to eat.

3. The cat sits licking mix too.

4. Dad stops the four men he is passing.

5. The fox is rocking her kit that naps.

MONITOR PROGRESS

- **Fluency**
- **Inflected Ending *-s***
- **Inflected Ending *-ing***
- **High-Frequency Words**

Conventions

Review Declarative Sentences

REVIEW Remind children that declarative sentences tell a fact or someone's point of view. They begin with a capital letter and end with a period. Have children give some examples of declarative sentences.

GUIDE PRACTICE Write the following sentences on the board. In each case, have children tell you which letter should be a capital and where the period should go.

1. chickens hatch from eggs
2. toads need to be kept moist
3. worms survive in the earth

APPLY Have children form pairs to discuss what each of the sentences tell. Then have them share their responses with the class.

ON THEIR OWN Use Let's Practice It! p. 55 from the *Teacher Resources DVD-ROM.*

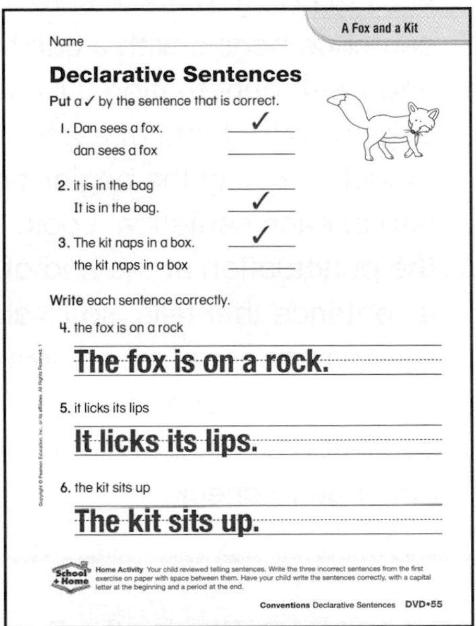

A Fox and a Kit

Name ______

Declarative Sentences

Put a ✓ by the sentence that is correct.

1. Dan sees a fox. ✓
   dan sees a fox
2. it is in the bag
   It is in the bag. ✓
3. The kit naps in a box. ✓
   the kit naps in a box

Write each sentence correctly.

4. the fox is on a rock
   The fox is on a rock.
5. it licks its lips
   It licks its lips.
6. the kit sits up
   The kit sits up.

Conventions Declarative Sentences DVD•55

Let's Practice It! TR DVD•55

Common Core State Standards

Foundational Skills 1.a. Recognize the distinguishing features of a sentence (e.g., first word, capitalization, ending punctuation). **Language 1.** Demonstrate command of the conventions of standard English grammar and usage when writing or speaking. **Language 1.j.** Produce and expand complete simple and compound declarative, interrogative, imperative, and exclamatory sentences in response to prompts.

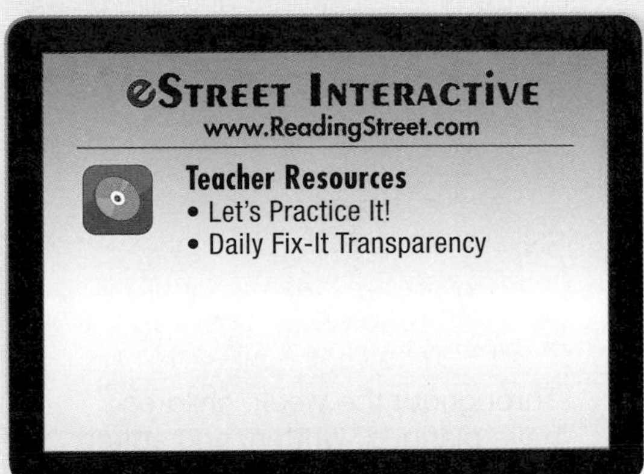

Daily Fix-It

9. The Fox sitts on a rock.
   The fox sits on a rock.
10. my dog napps with Pop.
    My dog naps with Pop.

Discuss the Daily Fix-It corrections with children. Review declarative sentences and the use of capital letters and periods.

Common Core State Standards

Writing 1. Write opinion pieces in which they introduce the topic or name the book they are writing about, state an opinion, supply a reason for the opinion, and provide some sense of closure. **Writing 3.** Write narratives in which they recount two or more appropriately sequenced events, include some details regarding what happened, use temporal words to signal event order, and provide some sense of closure. **Language 2.** Demonstrate command of the conventions of standard English capitalization, punctuation, and spelling when writing. **Language 2.b.** Use end punctuation for sentences. **Also Writing 6.**

Bridge to Common Core

PRODUCTION AND DISTRIBUTION OF WRITING

Throughout the week, children have planned, written, and edited their personal narratives. As they edit for a final draft, they will make changes as needed in order to produce clear, coherent, and complete sentences that they will present to a small group of their classmates or draw a picture and display in the classroom.

Writing

Personal Narrative

REVIEW REVISING Remind children that yesterday they revised their narratives. They may have rearranged sentences to make the events clearer. Today they will proofread their narratives.

Mini-Lesson Proofread

Proofread for Declarative Sentences

- **Teach** In our narratives, if we capitalize and punctuate the sentences correctly, readers will know where the sentences begin and end. When we proofread, we check to make sure the sentences are correct.

- **Model** Let's look at my story about the bunny I saw. Display Writing Transparency 4C. I'm going to make sure that each sentence begins with a capital letter and ends with punctuation. I'll check the beginning and end of each sentence. Model checking the beginning and end of each sentence. Look: I forgot the punctuation at the end of the sentence *I sit under a big elm tree.* It's a sentence that tells, so I'll add a period. Add a period after *tree* on the transparency, and then continue to check. Look: I forgot the punctuation at the end of the sentence *I looked at the bunny.* It's also a sentence that tells, so I'll add a period. Add a period after *bunny* on the transparency, and then continue to check.

Proofreading Marks			
Take Out		Uppercase letter	≡
Add	^	Lowercase letter	/
Period	⊙	New paragraph	¶
Check spelling	◯	Insert apostrophe	∨

The Bunny in the Garden

I like to go to the park. I sit under a big elm tree⊙I walk in the rose garden.

One Saturday I saw a bunny in the rose garden. The bunny sat on the grassy path. I looked at the bunny⊙The bunny looked at me.

The bunny filled its mouth with grass. It watched me while it stuffed its mouth. The grass stuck out of its mouth. It looked so funny!

Then the bunny hopped away into the rose bushes. I was sorry to see it go.

Unit 1 A Fox and a Kit — Writing: Proofread 4C

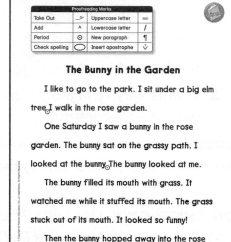

Writing Transparency 4C TR DVD

PROOFREAD Display the Proofreading Tips. Have children proofread their narratives to correct any misspellings, missing capital letters, or errors with periods. Circulate to assist children with the punctuation of sentences.

Proofreading Tips

- ✔ Are words that tell feelings or opinions spelled correctly?
- ✔ Do sentences that tell end with a period?
- ✔ Do all sentences end with punctuation?
- ✔ Do sentences begin with a capital letter?

PRESENT Have children use a computer to make a final draft of their narratives, with their revisions and proofreading corrections. Help as appropriate. Choose an option for children to present their narratives.

Draw a picture of the animal they saw to accompany the story in a wall display.	Tell the narrative aloud in a small group.

When children have finished writing their narratives, give them a copy of About My Writing, p. RR45 of the *Reader's and Writers' Notebook.* Then have children evaluate their writing by answering the questions on the page.

Routine **Quick Write for Fluency** Team Talk

1. **Talk** Have partners take one minute to find a word that tells feelings in each of their stories.
2. **Write** Each child writes a new short sentence using one of the words.
3. **Share** Partners trade sentences, read them aloud, and determine if the sentences are declarative or not.

Routines Flip Chart

Write Guy *by Jeff Anderson*

Topic Sentence? Really?

Topic sentences are excellent, but many good paragraphs actually don't have topic sentences. We want children to learn how to craft a topic sentence and a paragraph. We also want children to know that not all paragraphs consist of five sentences, beginning with a topic sentence.

Support Editing For children to whom the sounds and spelling of English still are not very familiar, look for spelling improvement little by little from week to week rather than rapid development. Help children make progress a word at a time and learn word meanings.

Common Core State Standards

Writing 7. Participate in shared research and writing projects (e.g., explore a number of "how-to" books on a given topic and use them to write a sequence of instructions). **Writing 8.** With guidance and support from adults, recall information from experiences or gather information from provided sources to answer a question. **Speaking/Listening 1.** Participate in collaborative conversations about grade 1 topics and texts with peers and adults in small and larger groups. **Speaking/ Listening 5.** Add drawings or other visual displays to descriptions when appropriate to clarify ideas, thoughts, and feelings.

Research and Inquiry

Step 5 Communicate

TEACH Tell children that today they will create a chart that tells about animals and their babies. Then they will share the information with others.

Think Aloud **MODEL** Display the chart about the topic. I will review my chart and circle the animals and animal babies I would like to tell others about. I liked the idea that a baby cow, a baby whale, and a baby elephant are all called calves. So I will include those facts in my chart. I will write the words *cow, whale,* and *elephant* on the left side of my chart. On the right side, I will write the word *calf* next to each animal name. That means I will write the word *calf* three times. How interesting!

GUIDE PRACTICE Review the animal and animal babies children learned about. Work with them to understand how to organize the information so their charts are easy to read.

ON THEIR OWN Have children choose the information about animals and baby animals they would like to share and to create a chart. Have children share their charts in small groups. Remind them how to be good speakers and listeners:

- Good speakers pay close attention to end marks such as question marks.
- Good listeners think of questions to ask the speaker when he or she is done talking.

Wild Animals and Their Babies

How do wild animals take care of their babies?

Think Aloud This week we explored the topic of how wild animals take care of their babies. In the story *A Fox and a Kit,* we read about how a mother fox takes care of her kit. In the story "The Fox and the Grapes," we read about a fox who couldn't get what he wanted.

Team Talk Have children recall their Amazing Ideas about wild animals and their babies. Then have children use these ideas to help them demonstrate their understanding of the Question of the Week, *How do wild animals take care of their babies?*

You've learned 008 words this week!

You've learned 080 words this year!

Next Week's Concept

Neighborhood Animals

Which wild animals live in our neighborhood?

Poster Preview Prepare children for next week by using Unit 1, Week 5, ELL Poster 5. Read the Poster Talk-Through to introduce the concept and vocabulary. Ask children to identify and describe objects and actions in the art.

Selection Summary Send home the summary from the *ELL Handbook* of *Get the Egg!* in English and the child's home language if available. Children can read the summary with family members.

Tell children that next week they will read about a bird and its eggs.

Preview Next Week

Assessment Checkpoints for the Week

Weekly Assessment

Use pp. 55–60 of *Weekly Tests* to check:

✔ **Phonics** Inflected Ending *-s*

✔ **Phonics** Inflected Ending *-ing*

✔ **Comprehension** Main Idea and Details

✔ **High-Frequency Words**

eat	her
five	this
four	too

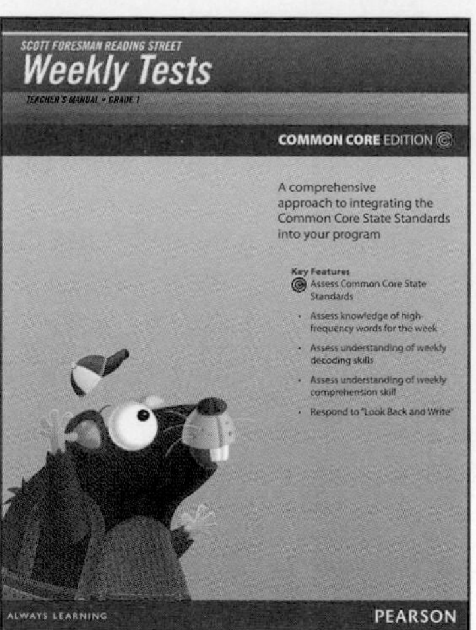

Weekly Tests

Differentiated Assessment

Advanced

On-Level

Strategic Intervention

Use pp. 55–60 of *Fresh Reads for Fluency and Comprehension* to check:

✔ **Comprehension** Main Idea and Details

✔  **Review Comprehension** Realism and Fantasy

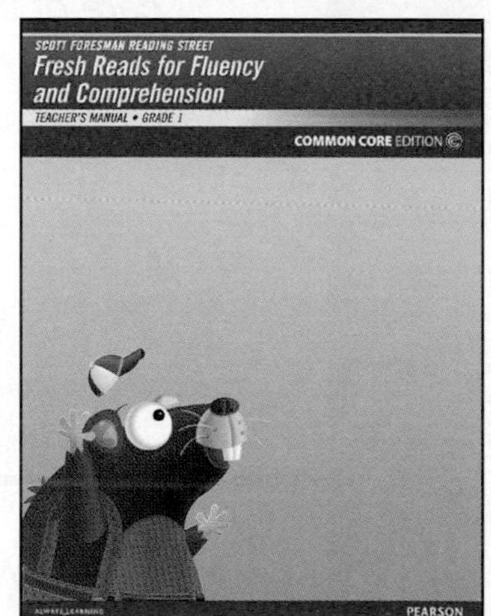

Fresh Reads for Fluency and Comprehension

Managing Assessment

Use *Assessment Handbook* for:

✔ **Weekly Assessment Blackline Masters for Monitoring Progress**

✔ **Observation Checklists**

✔ **Record-Keeping Forms**

✔ **Portfolio Assessment**

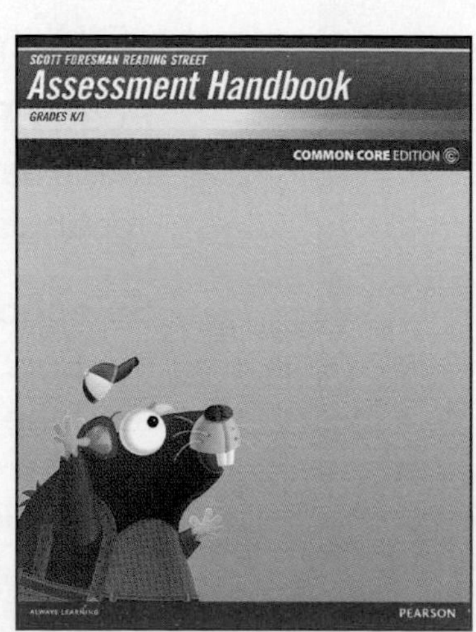

Assessment Handbook

DAY 1 Differentiate Phonics

- Inflected Ending *-s*
- Decodable Practice Reader
- Advanced Selection "Panda Peeks at the World"
- **Inquiry** Identify Questions

DAY 2 Differentiate Comprehension

- Inflected Ending *-ing*
- **Access Text** Read *A Fox and a Kit*
- **Inquiry** Investigate

DAY 3 Differentiate Close Reading

- Develop Vocabulary
- **Close Reading** Read *A Fox and a Kit*
- **Inquiry** Investigate

DAY 4 Differentiate Vocabulary

- Develop Language
- "A Caring Father" or Leveled Readers
- **Inquiry** Organize

"A Caring Father"
pp. 14–15

DAY 5 Differentiate Reteaching

- Phonics and High-Frequency Words
- Conventions
- "A Caring Father" or Leveled Readers
- **Inquiry** Communicate

Teacher Guides and Student pages can be found in the Leveled Reader Database.

Place English Language Learners in the groups that correspond to their reading abilities.
If... children need scaffolding and practice,
then... use the ELL notes on the page.

Independent Practice

Independent Practice Stations

See pp. 94h and 94i for Independent Stations.

Pearson Trade Book Library

See the Leveled Reader Database for Lesson Plans and student pages.

Reading Street Digital Path

Independent Practice Activities available in the Digital Path.

Independent Reading

See p. 94i for independent reading suggestions.

On-Level

Common Core State Standards

Informational Text 1. Ask and answer questions about key details in a text. **Foundational Skills 3.** Know and apply grade-level phonics and word analysis skills in decoding words. **Foundational Skills 3.b.** Decode regularly spelled one-syllable words. **Foundational Skills 3.f.** Read words with inflectional endings. **Foundational Skills 4.a.** Read on-level text with purpose and understanding.

1 Build Word Knowledge

Practice Phonics

INFLECTED ENDING *-s* Write the following words and have children practice reading words with inflected ending *-s*.

jogs **hits** **wins** **pats**

Spelling

INFLECTED ENDING *-s* Remind children that some of the spelling words have the ending *-s,* which can spell the sound /s/ or /z/. Clarify the pronunciation and meaning of each word. For example, say: If clothing *fits,* it is the right size. Have children identify which of the following words has the ending sound /s/ and which has the ending sound /z/: *sits, wins, fits, hits, naps.*

2 Read

Decodable Reader 4A *Big Jobs*

HIGH-FREQUENCY WORDS Have children read the decodable reader. Then have them reread the text to develop automaticity. Have children return to the text and find the previously taught high-frequency words. Help children demonstrate their understanding of the words. Provide sentence frames such as: I want to go with _______ to the store. (you)

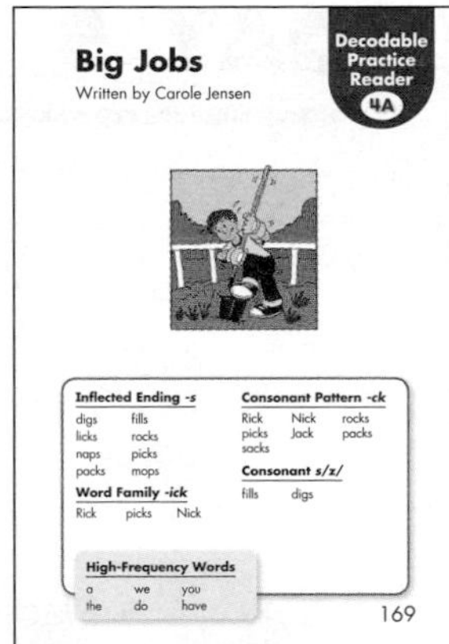

ELL

If... children need more scaffolding and practice with phonics, **then...** use the ELL activities on pp. DI•76–DI•77 in the Teacher Resources section on SuccessNet.

On-Level

1 Build Word Knowledge

Practice Phonics

INFLECTED ENDING *-ing* Write the following words and have children practice reading words with inflected ending *-ing.*

fixing **rocking** **tacking** **passing**

2 Read

A Fox and a Kit

If you read *A Fox and a Kit* during whole group time, then use the following instruction.

ACCESS TEXT Have children look at the picture and reread the sentences on pp. 106–107.

- Look at page 106. What do you see in the picture? (fox, kit, rock, plant, man's hands, dish, food, clock)
- Why do the fox and kit lick their lips? (They ate the food.)
- Do the fox and the kit live in a forest or in a zoo? (a zoo) How do you know? (A man fixed their dinner. There is a clock on the wall.)
- What time do the fox and the kit eat dinner? (five o'clock) How do you know? (The text says five. The clock on the wall says five.)

If you are reading *A Fox and a Kit* during small group time, then return to pp. 102b–111a to guide the reading.

Independent Reading Options

Trade Book Library

eStreet Interactive
www.ReadingStreet.com

Teacher's Guides available on the Leveled Reader Database.

OL

On-Level

Common Core State Standards

Informational Text 1. Ask and answer questions about key details in a text. **Informational Text 4.** Ask and answer questions to help determine or clarify the meaning of words and phrases in a text. **Speaking/Listening 1.** Participate in collaborative conversations about grade 1 topics and texts with peers and adults in small and larger groups. **Also Speaking/Listening 4., Language 6.**

1 Build Word Knowledge

Develop Vocabulary

REREAD FOR VOCABULARY Have children reread *A Fox and a Kit,* p. 110.

Read the following sentence and discuss what the fox and kit are doing.

The kit spots his mom. His mom spots him.

- What does *spot* mean? (sees, watches)
- How do you know that *spot* means to see or to watch? (The fox and the kit are looking at each other in the picture.)
- Look at page 111. How do you know the fox and the kit spot the children? (The children and the fox and kit are looking at each other.)
- What can you *spot* from your chair? (door, desk, wall, window)

2 Read

A Fox and a Kit

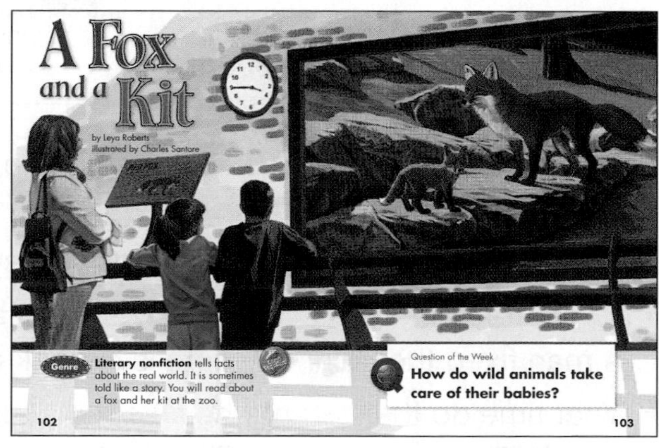
A Fox and a Kit
by Leya Roberts
illustrated by Charles Santore
Genre
Literary nonfiction tells facts about the real world. It is sometimes told like a story. You will read about a fox and her kit at the zoo.
Question of the Week
How do wild animals take care of their babies?
102
103

If you read *A Fox and a Kit* during whole group time, then use the following instruction.

CLOSE READING Reread page 108. Have children summarize the ideas presented on this page. Ask questions to guide deeper understanding.

- Look at page 108. What are the fox and the kit doing? (playing)
- What does the kit do when playing? (It nips and tags.)
- What do you do when playing? (run, play tag, laugh)

Have children combine the first two sentences on page 109 using an appropriate connecting word. (The kit is on the rocks, and his mom will get him.)

If you are reading *A Fox and a Kit* during small group time, then return to pp. 102–111 to guide the reading.

ELL

If... children need more scaffolding and practice with the main selection, **then...** use the activities on p. DI•81 in the Teacher Resources section on SuccessNet.

On-Level

1 Build Word Knowledge

Practice Selection Vocabulary

animals	dinner	watch

Team Talk **LANGUAGE DEVELOPMENT** Have children practice using the selection vocabulary. Ask questions such as: Which *animals* are fun to *watch?* Turn and talk to your partner about animals that are fun to watch. Be prepared to explain your answers.

Allow children time to discuss each word. Ask for examples or rephrase for usage when necessary or to correct for understanding. Use the Student Edition to provide visual support.

2 Text-Based Comprehension

READ ALOUD "A Caring Father" Lead children in a choral reading of "A Caring Father" from *Reading Street Sleuth,* pp. 14–15. Then have partners take turns reading the paragraphs of the selection.

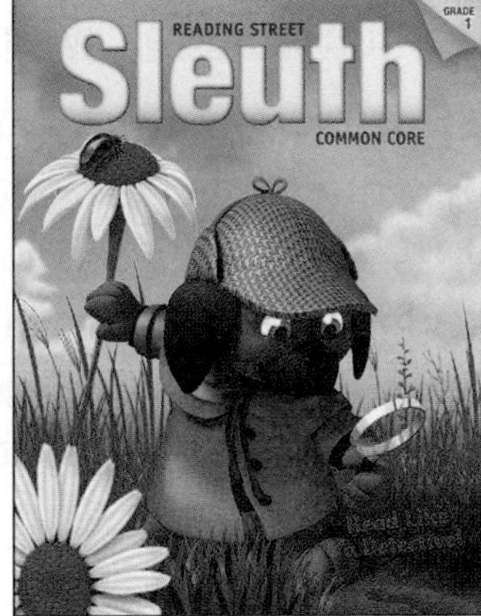

ACCESS TEXT Guide children as they work on the Be a Sleuth section.

Look for Clues Ask children to think about what the father penguin and mother penguin do to care for their egg. Ask them if they can think of any other ways penguins care for their eggs.

Ask Questions Have children tell what they know about penguins and where they live. Have them decide what they want to find out about penguins and create questions to get answers. Help them find books and other sources to use to find the answers to their questions.

Make Your Case Have children reread the selection and evaluate the information given about mother and father penguins. Ask them to make notes about their findings and then decide which penguin is more important to the penguin egg. Remind them to provide reasons for their choice when they present their ideas.

SMALL GROUP TIME

More Reading for Group Time

Life Science
WHICH FOX?
BY LINDA LOTT
ILLUSTRATED BY WENDY RASMUSSEN

ON-LEVEL

Reviews
- Concept Vocabulary
- Main Idea and Details

Use this suggested Leveled Reader or other text at children's instructional level.

eStreet Interactive
www.ReadingStreet.com

Use the Leveled Reader Database for lesson plans and student pages for *Which Fox?*

On-Level

Common Core State Standards

Foundational Skills 1.a. Recognize the distinguishing features of a sentence (e.g., first word, capitalization, ending punctuation). **Foundational Skills 2.b.** Orally produce single-syllable words by blending sounds (phonemes), including consonant blends. **Foundational Skills 3.f.** Read words with inflectional endings. **Foundational Skills 4.a.** Read on-level text with purpose and understanding. **Also Foundational Skills 2.c., 3., Speaking/Listening 3., 4., Language 1., 4.c.**

1 Build Word Knowledge

Practice Declarative Sentences

REVIEW If needed, revisit the conventions lesson on p. 111c.

IDENTIFY DECLARATIVE SENTENCES Have children return to "A Caring Father" and identify declarative sentences in the selection. Have children work in pairs to identify as many declarative sentences as they can.

2 Text-Based Comprehension

REREAD "A Caring Father" Have partners reread "A Caring Father."

EXTEND UNDERSTANDING Talk about the ways the father penguin and mother penguin care for the egg. Ask children to think about all the difficulties the penguins face while caring for the egg. Remind them that the penguins live in Antarctica.

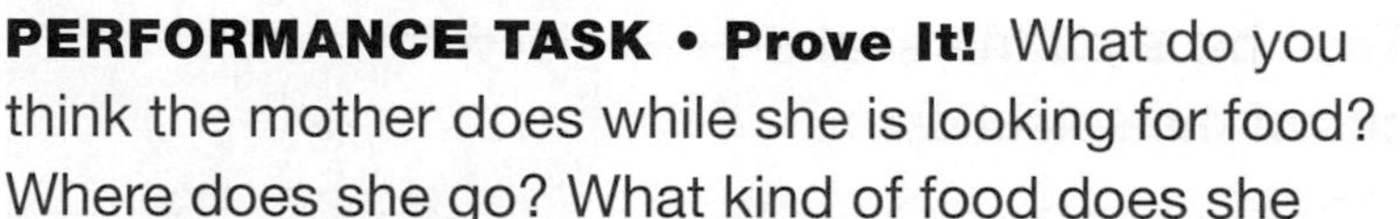

PERFORMANCE TASK • Prove It! What do you think the mother does while she is looking for food? Where does she go? What kind of food does she bring back? Have small groups work together to write short paragraphs that tell where the mother goes and what kind of food penguins eat. Have children use the text and other references to prepare their paragraphs.

COMMUNICATE Have groups present their paragraphs to the class. Encourage children to ask questions after each presentation.

More Reading for Group Time

ON-LEVEL

Reviews
- Concept Vocabulary
- Main Idea and Details

Use this suggested Leveled Reader or other text at children's instructional level.

eSTREET INTERACTIVE
www.ReadingStreet.com

Use the Leveled Reader Database for lesson plans and student pages for *Which Fox?*

SI Strategic Intervention

1 Build Word Knowledge

Reteach Phonemic Awareness

Reteach the lesson on p. 96–97 to segment and blend phonemes. Use these additional practice items: *nap-naps, tip-tips, top-tops, tack-tacks.*

Reteach Phonics

INFLECTED ENDING *-s* Reteach the lesson on p. 97a, inflected ending *-s.* Use these additional practice words to blend: *sip-sips, lock-locks, dab-dabs, jab-jabs, bid-bids.*

Write the following words under the heading *Ending -s: begs, pins, zips, tells, jogs, backs.* Have children read the words. Then have them write the base word under the heading *Base Word.*

Ending *-s*	Base Word
begs	beg
pins	pin
zips	zip
tells	tell
jogs	jog

2 Read

Decodable Reader 4A *Big Jobs*

DECODE WORDS Have children practice reading the words listed on p. 169.

> **Corrective feedback** | **If...** children have difficulty reading the words independently,
> **then...** reteach the words prior to reading Decodable Reader 4A.

READ IN CONTEXT Have children take turns reading a page in *Big Jobs.* Have them reread the text several times to ensure accuracy.

> **Corrective feedback** | **If...** children have difficulty reading the story independently,
> **then...** model reading a page and have children echo you.

3 Reread for Fluency

Have children reread the text to develop automaticity in their reading.

eStreet Interactive
www.ReadingStreet.com

Pearson eText
- *Reading Street Sleuth*
- Decodable Reader
- Leveled Reader Database

SMALL GROUP TIME

Big Jobs
Written by Carole Jensen
Decodable Practice Reader 4A

Inflected Ending -s: digs, fills, licks, rocks, naps, picks, packs, mops
Word Family -ick: Rick, picks, Nick
Consonant Pattern -ck: Rick, Nick, rocks, picks, Jack, packs, sacks
Consonant s/z/: fills, digs
High-Frequency Words: a, we, you, the, do, have

169

ELL

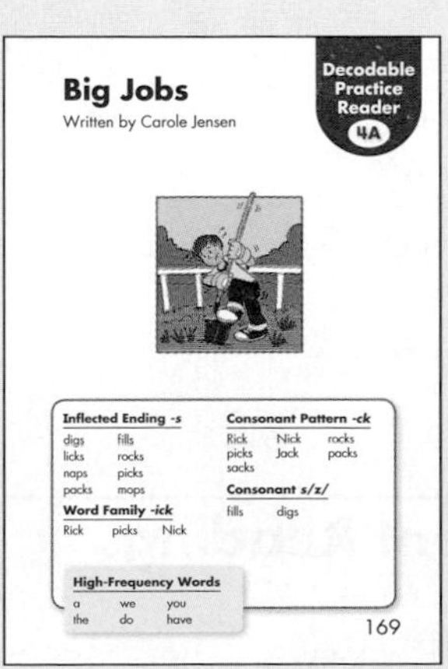

If... children need more scaffolding and practice with phonemic awareness and phonics,
then... use the ELL activities on pp. DI•76–DI•77 in the Teacher Resources section on SuccessNet.

SI
Strategic Intervention

Common Core State Standards

Informational Text 1. Ask and answer questions about key details in a text. **Informational Text 7.** Use the illustrations and details in a text to describe its key ideas. **Foundational Skills 2.b.** Orally produce single-syllable words by blending sounds (phonemes), including consonant blends. **Foundational Skills 3.** Know and apply grade-level phonics and word analysis skills in decoding words. **Foundational Skills 3.f.** Read words with inflectional endings. **Also Foundational Skills 2.**

1 Build Word Knowledge

Reteach Phonemic Awareness

Reteach the lesson on p. 100c to segment and blend phonemes. Use these additional practice items: *hint–hinting, box–boxing, rock–rocking.*

Reteach Phonics

INFLECTED ENDING *-ing* Reteach the lesson on p. 100d to model inflected ending *-ing.* Use these additional words to blend: *willing, mixing, waxing, ticking.*

Make a two-column chart. Label the columns *Ending -ing* and *Ending -s.* Have children read the following words, identify the ending, frame the base word, and write the word in the appropriate column: *telling, rips, tips, ducking, licking, pats, mops, fixing.*

2 Read

A Fox and a Kit

A Fox and a Kit
by Leya Roberts
illustrated by Charles Santore
Genre
Literary nonfiction tells facts about the real world. It is sometimes told like a story. You will read about a fox and her kit at the zoo.
Question of the Week
How do wild animals take care of their babies?
102
103

If you read *A Fox and a Kit* during whole group time, then use the instruction below.

ACCESS TEXT Have children look at the picture on p. 104. Point to the fox in the picture. What else do you see in the picture? (a kit, a clock, a rock, plants, sand/dirt, glass and frame) Reread the sentences on p. 104.

- What time is it? (four) What do the fox and kit do at four? (nap)
- Where are the fox and kit napping? (on a rock)
- How do you know? (The picture shows the fox and kit napping on a rock, and the text says they nap on the rocks.)

If you are reading *A Fox and a Kit* during small group time, then return to pp. 102b–111a to guide the reading.

Corrective feedback	**If...** children have difficulty understanding the section, **then...** read the section aloud using the Access Text Notes.

Independent Reading Options

Trade Book Library

eStreet Interactive
www.ReadingStreet.com

Teacher's Guides available on the Leveled Reader Database.

Strategic Intervention

1 Build Word Knowledge

Reteach Phonemic Awareness

Reteach the activity on p. 112c to count syllables. Use these additional practice items: *eating, sending, jumping, fixing.*

Reteach Phonics

Write these words with inflected endings *-s* or *-ing* and have children blend them with you: *pops, rips, locks, sags, fixing, missing, passing, mixing.*

2 Read

A Fox and a Kit

If you read *A Fox and a Kit* during whole group time, then use the instruction below.

CLOSE READING Reread page 106. Let's read this page to find out what the man is doing.
To help children understand what the man is doing, ask questions related to the text and the picture.

- Look at page 106. What time is it? (five)
- What is the man holding? (a dish of food)
- Is the food for the man or the fox and kit? (for the fox and kit)
- Which sentence tells you that? *(The kit and his mom will eat.)*

Corrective feedback

If... children have trouble answering questions about the text and picture on p. 106,
then... reread the page and have them tell about the picture in their own words. Then compare their summary with the words on the page.

If you are reading *A Fox and a Kit* during small group time, then return to pp. 102–111 to guide the reading.

SMALL GROUP TIME

If... children need scaffolding and practice with the main selection,
then... use the activities on p. DI•81 in the Teacher Resources section on SuccessNet.

Common Core State Standards

Foundational Skills 3.g. Recognize and read grade-appropriate irregularly spelled words. **Speaking/Listening 1.** Participate in collaborative conversations about grade 1 topics and texts with peers and adults in small and larger groups. **Language 4.** Determine or clarify the meaning of unknown and multiple-meaning words and phrases based on *grade 1 reading and content,* choosing flexibly from an array of strategies. **Also Informational Text 1., 7., Speaking/Listening 1.c., 4.**

More Reading for Group Time

CONCEPT LITERACY

Practice
- Concept Words
- High-Frequency Words

BELOW LEVEL

Review
- Main Idea and Details
- High-Frequency Words

Use these suggested Leveled Readers or other text at children's instructional level.

eStreet Interactive
www.ReadingStreet.com

Use the Leveled Reader Database for lesson plans and student pages for *We See Animals* and *Time for Dinner.*

1 Build Word Knowledge

Review Selection Vocabulary

animals	dinner
watch	

SEE IT/SAY IT/HEAR IT Write *dinner.* Scan across the word with your finger as you say it: dinner. Use the word in a sentence. My **dinner** was carrots and chicken.

DEFINE IT How would you tell a friend what *dinner* means? Give a definition when necessary. Yes, *dinner* is the meal you eat in the evening. Restate the explanation. *Dinner* is the meal you eat at night. It is the last meal of the day.

Team Talk What are some good things to eat for dinner? What are some bad things to eat for dinner? Turn to your partner and talk about this. Allow time for children to discuss. Ask for examples. Rephrase their examples for usage when necessary or to correct misunderstandings. Continue with *animals* and *watch.*

2 Text-Based Comprehension

READ ALOUD "A Caring Father" Read "A Caring Father" aloud from *Reading Street Sleuth,* pp. 14–15 as children follow along.

ACCESS TEXT Guide children as they work on the Be a Sleuth section.

Look for Clues Have children look through the text and list information they find about father penguins or penguin eggs.

Ask Questions Have children think about the icy cold Antarctic where penguins live and tell about penguins from what they learned in the selection. Then ask them to create questions about things they would like to find out about penguins. Provide pictures and books to show information to find answers to the questions.

Make Your Case Have children listen as you reread the selection. Then ask what father penguins do and what mother penguins do. Write the key ideas on chart paper. Then ask children to decide which penguin is more important to the penguin egg. Have volunteers tell which penguin they chose and give a reason for their choice.

Strategic Intervention

1 Build Word Knowledge

Review High-Frequency Words

Use the routine on p. 99 to review *eat, four, five, her, this,* and *too.*

Corrective feedback	**If...** children have difficulty with any of these words, **then...** tell them the word and have them repeat it. Have children spell the word and tell what word they spelled. Have them practice in pairs with word cards.

2 Text-Based Comprehension

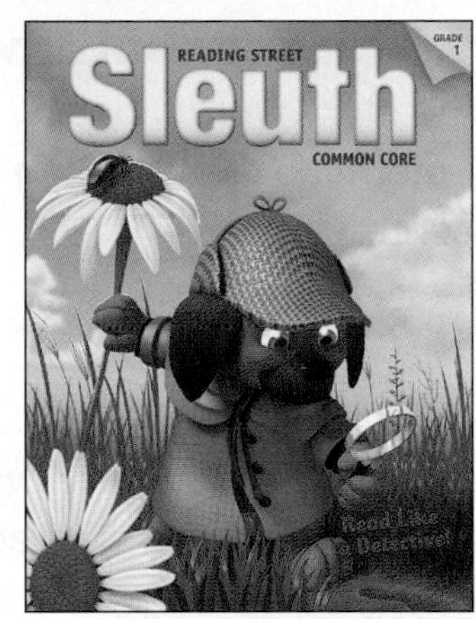

REREAD "A Caring Father" Reread "A Caring Father" aloud as children follow along.

EXTEND UNDERSTANDING Discuss the selection with children. Ask them to think of all the things the father penguin does for the egg. Ask them to think of the things the mother penguin does for the egg. Ask them to think of how difficult life must be for penguins. Remind them that penguins live in Antarctica and it is very cold there.

PERFORMANCE TASK • Prove It! What do you think the mother does while she is looking for food? Where does she go? What kind of food does she bring back? Have small groups write two short sentences that tell where the mother goes and what kind of food she brings back with her. Provide additional books for children to use for research.

COMMUNICATE Have groups present their sentences to the class.

SMALL GROUP TIME

More Reading for Group Time

CONCEPT LITERACY

Practice
- Concept Words
- High-Frequency Words

BELOW LEVEL

Review
- Main Idea and Details
- High-Frequency Words

Use these suggested Leveled Readers or other text at children's instructional level.

eStreet Interactive
www.ReadingStreet.com

Use the Leveled Reader Database for lesson plans and student pages for *We See Animals* and *Time for Dinner.*

Advanced

Common Core State Standards

Informational Text 2. Identify the main topic and retell key details of a text. **Informational Text 10.** With prompting and support, read informational texts appropriately complex for grade 1. **Foundational Skills 3.f.** Read words with inflectional endings. **Also Foundational Skills 3., Speaking/Listening 1.**

1 Build Word Knowledge

Extend Phonics

INFLECTED ENDING *-s* Have children practice with more complex words. Have children write words on cards and sort into groups of one- and two-syllable words. Then have children use several of the words in sentences.

quits	**brings**	**needs**	**throws**	**helps**
happens	**inspects**	**scribbles**	**giggles**	**begins**

2 Read

"Panda Peeks at the World"

TEACH VOCABULARY Before reading, introduce the story words: *peeks, reserve.* Help children determine the meaning of each word using these sentences:

1. She opened the box just a little and **peeked** inside.
2. This park is a **reserve** where the trees and animals are protected.

Panda Peeks at the World

The baby panda peeks out at the world. It is three months old. Its mother holds it. When it was born, it was the size of a stick of butter. A panda grows each day. It is soft now. Its mother licks it and fluffs its black-and-white fur.

Pandas live in just a few places in China. About 1,600 pandas live in the wild. Some pandas live in zoos. Others live in a safe forest called a panda reserve. It is a good place for pandas to have their babies. A baby panda runs and plays with other baby pandas there. There is a giant panda home on the reserve. The home takes pandas that are not able to live in the wild. Maybe one is hurt. Some might be sick. Maybe one was born in a zoo and needs a new home. A panda lives in special rooms while it gets strong. Then it moves from the rooms to the forest.

The panda home uses a camera. Videos of the pandas are fun to watch. A child in another land wants to see pandas. She looks at them on a computer. You can too!

SMALL GROUP TIME

Advanced Selection 4 **Vocabulary:** peeks, reserve

READ Have children read "Panda Peeks at the World" silently. Then have children take turns reading aloud. After reading, have children recall the two most important ideas of the selection using details from the text.

3 Inquiry: Extend Concepts

IDENTIFY QUESTIONS Have children survey the many forms an animal part, such as a beak, a tail, or a wing, may take among different animals. During the week, they will learn more about the animal part they pick. On Day 5, children will present what they have learned. Guide children in brainstorming possible choices.

- How does an animal part such as a tail look alike on different animals? How does it look different?

If... children need practice with phonics,
then... use the ELL activities on pp. DI•76–DI•77 in the Teacher Resources section on SuccessNet.

Panda Peeks at the World

The baby panda peeks out at the world. It is three months old. Its mother holds it. When it was born, it was the size of a stick of butter. A panda grows each day. It is soft now. Its mother licks it and fluffs its black-and-white fur.

Pandas live in just a few places in China. About 1,600 pandas live in the wild. Some pandas live in zoos. Others live in a safe forest called a panda reserve. It is a good place for pandas to have their babies. A baby panda runs and plays with other baby pandas there. There is a giant panda home on the reserve. The home takes pandas that are not able to live in the wild. Maybe one is hurt. Some might be sick. Maybe one was born in a zoo and needs a new home. A panda lives in special rooms while it gets strong. Then it moves from the rooms to the forest.

The panda home uses a camera. Videos of the pandas are fun to watch. A child in another land wants to see pandas. She looks at them on a computer. You can too!

Advanced Selection 4 **Vocabulary:** peeks, reserve

A

Advanced

Common Core State Standards

Informational Text 2. Identify the main topic and retell key details of a text. **Informational Text 7.** Use the illustrations and details in a text to describe its key ideas. **Foundational Skills 3.f.** Read words with inflectional endings. **Language 5.a.** Sort words into categories (e.g., colors, clothing) to gain a sense of the concepts the categories represent. **Also Informational Text 1., Foundational Skills 3., Writing 7., Speaking/ Listening 1.**

1 Build Word Knowledge

Extend Phonics

INFLECTED ENDING *-ing* Have children practice with additional words with ending *-ing.* Have them write each word, cover its ending, and read the base word. Then have children blend the entire word. Point out words that double the final consonant or drop *e* before adding *-ing.*

cracking	**chirping**	**singing**	**running**	**petting**
chasing	**riding**	**making**	**flying**	**breaking**

2 Read

A Fox and a Kit

A Fox and a Kit
by Leya Roberts
illustrated by Charles Santore
Genre
Literary nonfiction tells facts about the real world. It is sometimes told like a story. You will read about a fox and her kit at the zoo.
Question of the Week
How do wild animals take care of their babies?
102
103

If you read *A Fox and a Kit* during whole group time, then use the instruction below.

ACCESS TEXT Have children silently reread *A Fox and a Kit,* summarize the selection, and identify the main idea and details. (Main Idea: A wild fox and kit live together at a zoo. Supporting Details: They sleep, eat, and play together. The fox makes sure her kit is happy by playing with him and safe by removing him from danger.)

DISCUSS GENRE Discuss what makes *A Fox and a Kit* literary nonfiction. Point out that this selection tells facts about the real world.

If you are reading *A Fox and a Kit* during small group time, then return to pp. 102b–111a to guide the reading.

3 Inquiry: Extend Concepts

INVESTIGATE Guide children in choosing materials at their independent reading levels.

LOOK AHEAD Help children decide how they will present their surveys, such as a pictograph or other graphic organizer, collage, illustrated poster, or written format.

Independent Reading Options

Trade Book Library

eStreet Interactive
www.ReadingStreet.com
Teacher's Guides available on the Leveled Reader Database.

A

Advanced

eStreet Interactive
www.ReadingStreet.com
Pearson eText
• Student Edition

1 Build Word Knowledge

Develop Vocabulary

REREAD FOR VOCABULARY Have children reread *A Fox and a Kit* and make a three-column chart listing the words that name living things, words that name nonliving things, and words that name actions.

Living	Nonliving	Actions
fox kit man	rocks dinner	naps, sits, fixing, eat, licking, playing, spots, watch

2 Read

A Fox and a Kit

A Fox and a Kit
by Leya Roberts
illustrated by Charles Santore
Genre
Literary nonfiction tells facts about the real world. It is sometimes told like a story. You will read about a fox and her kit at the zoo.
Question of the Week
How do wild animals take care of their babies?
102
103

If you read *A Fox and a Kit* during whole group time, then use the instruction below.

CLOSE READING Reread pp. 108–109. Have children look at the pictures on the pages. What are the fox and kit doing on page 108? (playing) Why do you think the fox is playing with her kit? (She wants her kit to be happy.) Look at page 109. What is the fox doing with her kit? (She is picks him up with her mouth to get him off the rocks.) Why do you think the fox moves her kit off the rocks? (She wants him to be safe.) Have children look through the rest of the selection and tell why the fox and kit do certain things. Ask children if they have seen other animals, like pets, do similar things.

If you are reading *A Fox and a Kit* during small group time, then return to pp. 102–111 to guide the reading.

3 Inquiry: Extend Concepts

INVESTIGATE Give children time to investigate their topics by reading and studying pictures. Tell children they should begin preparing their information.

ELL

If... children need more scaffolding and practice with the main selection, **then...** use the activities on p. DI•81 in the Teacher Resources section on SuccessNet.

Advanced

Common Core State Standards

Speaking/Listening 1. Participate in collaborative conversations about grade 1 topics and texts with peers and adults in small and larger groups. **Speaking/Listening 4.** Describe people, places, things, and events with relevant details, expressing ideas and feelings clearly. **Language 1.** Demonstrate command of the conventions of standard English grammar and usage when writing or speaking. **Language 5.c.** Identify real-life connections between words and their use (e.g., note places at home that are *cozy*). **Also Writing 7., Speaking/Listening 5.**

More Reading for Group Time

Life Science
Baby Animals in the Rain Forest
by Melissa Burke
illustrated by Burgandy Beam

ADVANCED

- Extend Concept Vocabulary
- Review Target Skill

Use this suggested Leveled Reader or other text at children's instructional level.

eSTREET INTERACTIVE
www.ReadingStreet.com

Use the Leveled Reader Database for lesson plans and student pages for *Baby Animals in the Rain Forest.*

1 Build Word Knowledge

Extend Amazing Words and Selection Vocabulary

observe	wild	parent
canopy	screech	million
native	reserve	

animals	dinner	watch

Team Talk Have children ask each other questions using the Amazing Words and the Selection Vocabulary, such as: Where is a good place to observe animals?

2 Text-Based Comprehension

READ "A Caring Father" Have children track the print as you read "A Caring Father" from *Reading Street Sleuth,* pp. 14–15. Then have children read the selection independently.

ACCESS TEXT Guide children as they work on the Be a Sleuth section.

Look for Clues Have children find details that show what the father penguin does for the egg. Have them list other ways the father penguin may help.

Ask Questions Have children create a list of questions they have about penguins and tell where they could find answers to their questions. Then ask them to work in groups to answer some of their questions.

Make Your Case Have children create a Venn diagram to show what a father penguin does, a mother penguin does, and what both do. Ask them to use their diagrams to decide which penguin is more important to the egg. Have them present their choice.

3 Inquiry: Extend Concepts

ORGANIZE INFORMATION Give children time to continue reading and preparing information. Provide art supplies for children, such as poster board, nature magazines with photographs, scissors, and markers.

Advanced

1 Build Word Knowledge

Declarative Sentences

IDENTIFY DECLARATIVE SENTENCES Have children return to the text "A Caring Father" to find declarative sentences. Have children work independently to identify as many declarative sentences as they can from the selection. Ask children to explain what makes each a declarative sentence.

2 Text-Based Comprehension

REREAD "A Caring Father" Have partners reread "A Caring Father."

EXTEND UNDERSTANDING Discuss the selection together. Ask children to think of all the ways the father penguin cares for the egg. Ask children to think of ways the mother penguin cares for the egg. Ask them if other animal parents care for their young in similar ways. Have children list these ways.

PERFORMANCE TASK • Prove It! What do you think the mother does while she is looking for food? Where does she go? What kind of food does she bring back? Have each child write a short paragraph that tells where the mother goes, how she hunts, and what kind of food she brings with her. Allow time for research. Encourage children to include relevant details in their paragraphs.

COMMUNICATE Have children present their paragraphs to the class. Encourage children to ask questions and discuss each paragraph.

3 Inquiry: Extend Concepts

COMMUNICATE Have children present their survey projects to share what they have learned about how a body part can vary among different animals.

SMALL GROUP TIME

More Reading for Group Time

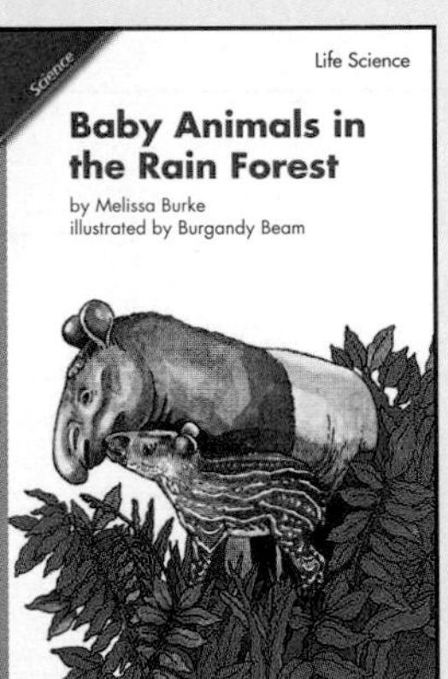

ADVANCED

- Extend Concept Vocabulary
- Review Target Skill

Use this suggested Leveled Reader or other text at children's instructional level.

eStreet Interactive
www.ReadingStreet.com

Use the Leveled Reader Database for lesson plans and student pages for *Baby Animals in the Rain Forest.*

TEACHER NOTES

Indiana Common Core Edition ©

This Week's Target Skills and Strategies

Target Skills and Strategies	© Common Core State Standards for English Language Arts
Phonemic Awareness **Skills:** Distinguish /e/ Segment and Blend Phonemes Segment and Blend Onset and Rime	**CCSS Foundational Skills 2.b.**Orally produce single-syllable words by blending sounds (phonemes), including consonant blends. **(Also CCSS Foundational Skills 2.c., CCSS Foundational Skills 2.d.)**
Phonics **Skill:** Short *e: e* **Skill:** Initial Consonant Blends	**CCSS Foundational Skills 3.** Know and apply grade-level phonics and word analysis skills in decoding words. **(Also CCSS Foundational Skills 2.b., CCSS Foundational Skills 3.b., CCSS Language 2.d.)**
Text-Based Comprehension **Skill:** Main Idea and Details	**CCSS Literature 2.** Retell stories, including key details, and demonstrate understanding of their central message or lesson. **(Also CCSS Literature 1.)**
Strategy: Story Structure	**CCSS Literature 1.** Ask and answer questions about key details in a text. **(Also CCSS Literature 2.)**
Fluency **Skill:** Appropriate Phrasing	**CCSS Foundational Skills 4.b.** Read on-level text orally with accuracy, appropriate rate, and expression on successive readings.
Listening and Speaking Give Descriptions	**CCSS Speaking/Listening 4.** Describe people, places, things, and events with relevant details, expressing ideas and feelings clearly.
Six-Trait Writing **Trait of the Week:** Organization	**CCSS Writing 3.** Write narratives in which they recount two or more appropriately sequenced events, include some details regarding what happened, use temporal words to signal event order, and provide some sense of closure.
Writing Realistic Story	**CCSS Writing 5.** With guidance and support from adults, focus on a topic, respond to questions and suggestions from peers, and add details to strengthen writing as needed. **(Also CCSS Writing 3.)**
Conventions **Skill:** Interrogative Sentences	**CCSS Language 1.j.** Produce and expand complete simple and compound declarative, interrogative, imperative, and exclamatory sentences in response to prompts.

This Week's Cross-Curricular Standards and Resources

Cross-Curricular Indiana Academic Standards for Science and Social Studies

Science
IN 1.3.4 Describe how animals' habitats, including plants, meet their needs for food, water, shelter and an environment in which they can live.

Social Studies
IN 1.3.4 Identify and describe physical features and human features of the local community including home, school and neighborhood.

Reading Street Sleuth

Look Out for Coyotes!
pp. 16–17

Follow the path to close reading using the Super Sleuth tips:

- Look for Clues
- Ask Questions
- Make Your Case
- Prove it!

More Reading in Science and Social Studies

Concept Literacy

Below Level

On Level

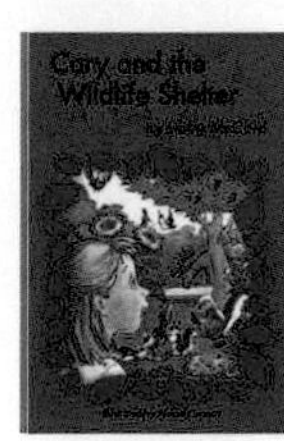

Advanced

ELL

ELD

ISBN-13: 978-0-328-73376-7 ISBN-10: 0-328-73376-8

Your 90-Minute Reading Block

	Whole Group	Formative Assessment How do I make my small groups flexible?	Small Group OL On Level SI Strategic Intervention A Advanced What are my other students reading and learning every day in Small Groups?
DAY 1	**Content Knowledge** Build Oral Language/Vocabulary **Phonemic Awareness/Phonics** **Read Decodable Reader** **Phonics/Spelling Pretest** **High-Frequency Words** **Text-Based Comprehension** Teacher Read Aloud **Research and Inquiry** Step 1–Identify and Focus Topic	**Monitor Progress** Formative Assessment: Check Word Reading	Differentiate Phonics OL **Practice Phonics** More Short *e* Words SI **Reteach Phonics** Blend Short *e* Words A **Extend Phonics** More Challenging Short *e* Words OL SI **Decodable Reader Read** *Jeff the Cat* A **Advanced Selection** "Why Woodpeckers Peck" A Inquiry Project ELL Access Phonemic Awareness and Phonics
DAY 2	**Content Knowledge** Build Oral Language/Vocabulary **Phonemic Awareness/Phonics** **Read Decodable Reader** **Phonics/Spelling** **High-Frequency Words/Selection Words** **Text-Based Comprehension** **Read** Main Selection, using Access Text Notes **Research and Inquiry** Step 2–Research Skill	**Monitor Progress** Formative Assessment: Check Word Reading	Differentiate Comprehension OL **Practice Phonics** Additional Words with Initial Consonant Blends SI **Reteach Phonics** Additional Words with Initial Consonant Blends A **Extend Phonics** Additional Words with Initial Consonant Blends OL SI A **Access Text Read** *Get the Egg!* A Inquiry Project ELL Access the Comprehension Skill
DAY 3	**Content Knowledge** Build Oral Language/Vocabulary **Phonemic Awareness/Phonics** **Phonics/Spelling** **High-Frequency Words/Selection Words** **Text-Based Comprehension** **Reread** Main Selection, using Close Reading Notes **Fluency** **Research and Inquiry** Step 3–Gather and Record Information	**Monitor Progress** Formative Assessment: Check High-Frequency Words **Monitor Progress** Check Retelling	Differentiate Close Reading OL **Reread to Develop Vocabulary** SI **Build Word Knowledge** Blend Words with Short *e* and Initial Consonant Blends A **Reread to Extend Vocabulary** OL SI **Close Reading Reread** *Get the Egg!* A **Extend Concepts Reread** *Get the Egg!* A Inquiry Project ELL Access the Main Selection
DAY 4	**Content Knowledge** Build Oral Language/Vocabulary **Phonemic Awareness/Phonics** **Read Decodable Reader** **Phonics/Spelling** **Read Content Area Paired Selection with Genre Focus** **Fluency** **Research and Inquiry** Step 4–Synthesize	**Monitor Progress** Fluency Check	Differentiate Vocabulary **Build Word Knowledge** OL Develop Language A Extend Amazing Words and Selection Vocabulary SI **Review Vocabulary** Review/Discuss Selection Vocabulary OL SI A **Text-Based Comprehension Read** *Reading Street Sleuth,* pp. 16–17 or Leveled Readers A Inquiry Project ELL Access Vocabulary
DAY 5	**Content Knowledge** Build Oral Language/Vocabulary **Phonemic Awareness/Phonics** **Phonics/Spelling Test** **Let's Learn It!** Vocabulary/Fluency/Listening and Speaking **Text-Based Comprehension** **High-Frequency and Selection Words** **Genre** **Assessment** Phonics, High-Frequency Words, Fluency **Research and Inquiry** Step 5–Communicate	**Monitor Progress** Formative Assessment: Check Oral Vocabulary **Monitor Progress** Word and Sentence Reading	Differentiate Reteaching OL **Practice Interrogative Sentences** SI **Review Vocabulary** High-Frequency Words A **Extend Interrogative Sentences** OL SI A **Text-Based Comprehension** **Reread** *Reading Street Sleuth,* pp. 16–17 or Leveled Readers A Inquiry Project ELL Access Conventions and Writing

Daily Independent Options

What do my other students do when I lead Small Groups?

★ **Independent Reading**
Suggestions for this week's independent reading:

- Informational texts on last week's science topic: How do wild animals take care of their babies?
- Nonfiction selections about how wild animals take care of their babies
- Nonfiction book by a favorite author

Book Talk
Foster critical reading and discussion skills through independent and close reading.

Students should focus on discussing one or more of the following:

- Key Ideas and Details
- Craft and Structure
- Integration of Ideas

Pearson eText
- Student Edition
- Decodable Readers
- Leveled Readers

Trade Book Library

Materials from School or Classroom Library

Independent Stations
Practice Last Week's Skills

★ Focus on these activities when time is limited.

Listen Up!
★ **Word Work**
Read for Meaning
Let's Write!
Words to Know
★ **Get Fluent**

Assessment Resources

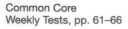

Common Core Weekly Tests, pp. 61–66

Common Core Fresh Reads for Fluency and Comprehension, pp. 61–66

Common Core Unit 1 Benchmark Test

Common Core Success Tracker, ExamView, and Online Lesson Planner

Focus on Common Core State Standards

Main Selection, pp. 128–137

Science in Reading
Genre
How-to Article
A how-to article is procedural text that tells you how to make or do something.
A how-to article is usually a set of directions.
The directions in a how-to article are often numbered. They are listed in the order you should do each step, from first to last.
If you follow the directions as they are written, you will be successful.
Read "Help the Birds." As you read, think about what you've learned about how-to articles.
Help the Birds
Birds like to eat.
You can help.
1 Get a small twig.
2 Dip it here.
3 Dip it in this.
4 Clip it to your tree.
Watch the birds come.
Birds I saw
142
143

Paired Selection, pp. 142–143

Text-Based Comprehension

Main Idea and Details
CCSS Literature 2.

Story Structure
CCSS Literature 1., CCSS Literature 2.

Fluency

Appropriate Phrasing
CCSS Foundational Skills 4.b.

Writing and Conventions

Trait: Organization
CCSS Writing 3.

Writing Mini-Lesson: Realistic Story
CCSS Writing 3., CCSS Writing 5.

Conventions: Interrogative Sentences
CCSS Language 1.j.

Oral Vocabulary

habitat	**hatch**
survive	**chirp**
croak	**moist**

CCSS Language 5.c.

High-Frequency Words

saw	**small**
tree	**your**

CCSS Foundational Skills 3.g.

Phonemic Awareness

Distinguish /e/
Segment and Blend Phonemes
Segment and Blend Onset and Rime
CCSS Foundational Skills 2.b., CCSS Foundational Skills 2.c., CCSS Foundational Skills 2.d.

Phonics and Spelling

Short *e*: *e*
Initial Consonant Blends
CCSS Foundational Skills 3., CCSS Foundational Skills 3.b., CCSS Language 2.d.

men	**red**	**step**
ten	**net**	**leg**
jet	**sled**	**wet**
bed		

Listening and Speaking

Give Descriptions
CCSS Speaking/Listening 4.

Preview Your Week

Which wild animals live in our neighborhood?

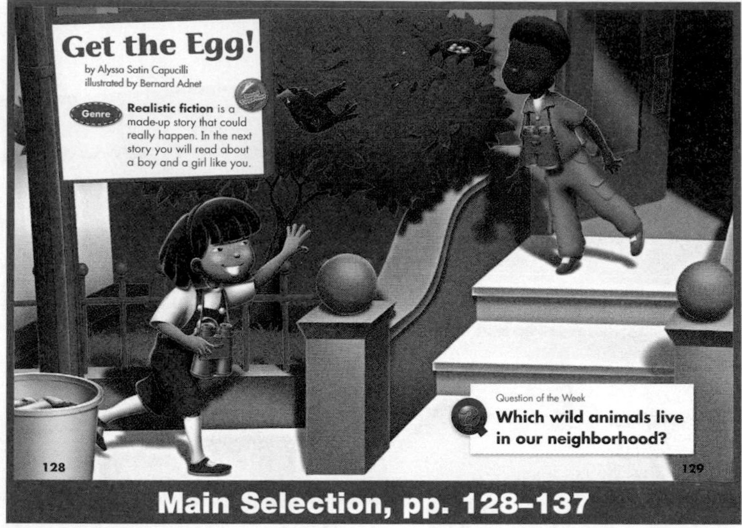
Get the Egg!
by Alyssa Satin Capucilli
illustrated by Bernard Adnet
Genre
Realistic fiction is a made-up story that could really happen. In the next story you will read about a boy and a girl like you.
Question of the Week
Which wild animals live in our neighborhood?
128
129
Main Selection, pp. 128–137

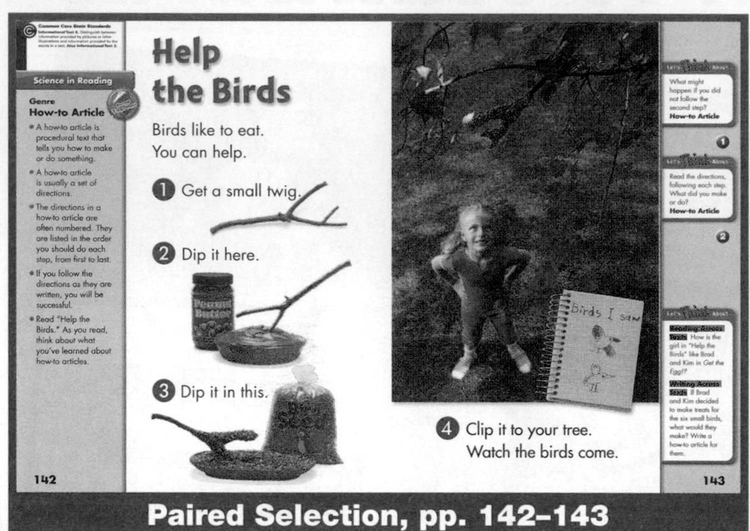
Science in Reading
Genre
How-to Article
Help the Birds
Birds like to eat.
You can help.
1 Get a small twig.
2 Dip it here.
3 Dip it in this.
4 Clip it to your tree.
Watch the birds come.
142
143
Paired Selection, pp. 142–143

Genre: Realistic Fiction

Phonics: Short *e: e,* Initial Consonant Blends

Text-Based Comprehension: Main Idea and Details

Science in Reading

Genre: How-to Article

Build Content Knowledge

Zoom in on

TIME FOR Science

KNOWLEDGE GOALS
Children will understand that:

- all kinds of animals live in our neighborhood
- neighborhood animals need different kinds of food and shelter

THIS WEEK'S CONCEPT MAP
Develop a concept-related graphic organizer like the one below over the course of this week.

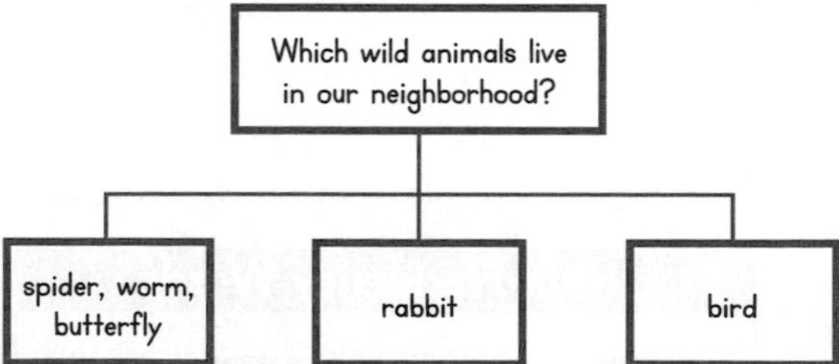
Which wild animals live in our neighborhood?
spider, worm, butterfly
rabbit
bird

BUILD ORAL VOCABULARY
This week, children will acquire the following academic vocabulary/domain-specific words.

Amazing Words

habitat	chirp
hatch	croak
survive	moist

OPTIONAL CONCEPT-BASED READING Use the Digital Path to access readers offering different levels of text complexity.

Neighborhood Animals
Concept Literacy

At Your Vet
by Zachary Cohn
Below Level

What Animals Can You See?
On Level

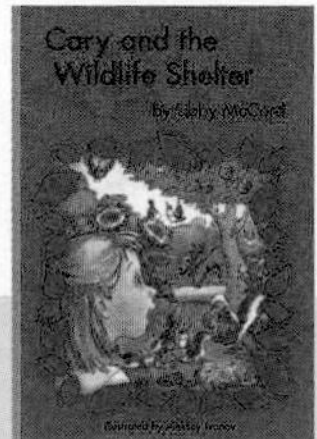
Cary and the Wildlife Shelter
Advanced

ELL

ELD

This Week's Digital Resources

eStreet Interactive
www.ReadingStreet.com

Get Ready to Read

Background Building Audio CD This audio CD provides valuable background information about why robins build nests to help children read and comprehend the weekly texts.

Concept Talk Video Use this video on the Digital Path to build momentum and introduce the weekly concept of neighborhood animals.

Interactive Sing with Me Big Book "Time to Hatch," sung to the tune of "I've Been Workin' on the Railroad," introduces the Amazing Words with a catchy, concept-related song.

Interactive Sound-Spelling Cards With these interactive cards on the Digital Path, children see an image, hear the image name, and see the spelling for short *e* spelled *e* and initial consonant blends.

Pearson eText Use the eText for the Decodable Readers on the Leveled Reader Database for phonics and fluency support.

Letter Tile Drag and Drop Using this interactive tool on Pearson SuccessNet, children click and spell words to enhance their phonics skills.

Read and Comprehend

Envision It! Animations Use this colorful animation on the Digital Path to explain the target comprehension skill, Main Idea and Details.

Pearson eText Read the eText of the main selection, *Get the Egg!*, and the paired selection, "Help the Birds," with audio support on Pearson SuccessNet.

Story Sort Use the Story Sort Activity on the Digital Path after reading *Get the Egg!* to involve children in summarizing.

Journal: Word Bank Use the Word Bank on the Digital Path to have children write sentences using this week's high-frequency words.

Vocabulary Activities A variety of interactive vocabulary activities on the Digital Path help children practice high-frequency and concept-related words.

Language Arts

Grammar Jammer Choose a whimsical animation on the Digital Path to provide an engaging grammar lesson that will capture children's attention.

Pearson eText Find the Student Edition eText of the Let's Write It! and Let's Learn It! pages with audio support on Pearson SuccessNet.

Additional Resources

Teacher Resources DVD-ROM Use the following resources on the TR DVD or on Pearson SuccessNet throughout the week:

- Amazing Word Cards
- Reader's and Writer's Notebook
- Writing Transparencies
- Daily Fix-It Transparencies
- Scoring Rubrics
- Grammar Transparencies
- Research Transparencies
- Let's Practice It!
- Graphic Organizers
- High-Frequency Word Cards
- Vocabulary Transparencies

This Week's Skills

Phonics
- Short *e* Spelled *e*
- Initial Consonant Blends

Comprehension
- **Skill:** Main Idea and Details
- **Strategy:** Story Structure

Language
Vocabulary: Sort Words
Conventions: Interrogative Sentences

Fluency
Appropriate Phrasing

Writing
Realistic Story

5-Day Planner

DAY 1

Get Ready to Read

Content Knowledge 120j
Oral Vocabulary: *habitat, hatch, survive*

Phonemic Awareness 122–123
Distinguish /e/

Phonics/Spelling 123a
Short *e: e*
READ Decodable Reader 5A
Reread for Fluency
Spelling Pretest

Monitor Progress
Check Word Reading

Read and Comprehend

High-Frequency Words 125
saw, small, tree, your

Text-Based Comprehension 125a
Main Idea and Details

Language Arts

Conventions 125c
Interrogative Sentences

Writing 125d
Realistic Story

Research and Inquiry 125f
Identify and Focus Topic

DAY 2

Get Ready to Read

Content Knowledge 126a
Oral Vocabulary: *chirp*

Phonemic Awareness 126c
Segment and Blend Phonemes

Phonics/Spelling 126d
Initial Consonant Blends
Review Short Vowels
READ Decodable Reader 5B
Reread for Fluency
Spelling: Short *e* Words

Monitor Progress
Check Word Reading

Read and Comprehend

High-Frequency Words 127
saw, small, tree, your

Selection Vocabulary 128a
bird
Strategy: Sort Words

Text-Based Comprehension 128b
READ *Get the Egg!*—1st Read

Literary Text 137b
Sensory Details

Language Arts

Conventions 137c
Interrogative Sentences

Writing 137d
Realistic Story

Handwriting 137f
Letter *Ee*/Letter Size

Research and Inquiry 137g
List

DAY 3

Get Ready to Read

Content Knowledge 138a
Oral Vocabulary: *croak*

Phonemic Awareness 138c
Rhyming Words

Phonics/Spelling 138d
Build Words
Blend and Read
Spelling: Dictation

Read and Comprehend

High-Frequency Words and Selection Words 138g
High-Frequency Words: *saw, small, tree, your*
Selection Word: *bird*
Monitor Progress Check High-Frequency Words

Text-Based Comprehension 138h
READ *Get the Egg!*—2nd Read
Monitor Progress Check Retelling

Fluency 139b
Appropriate Phrasing

Language Arts

Conventions 140a
Interrogative Sentences

Writing 140–141
Realistic Story

Listening and Speaking 141b
Give Descriptions

Research and Inquiry 141c
Gather and Record Information

DAY 4

Get Ready to Read

Content Knowledge 142a
Oral Vocabulary: *moist*

Phonemic Awareness 142c
Distinguish /e/

Phonics/Spelling 142d
Review Inflected Endings *-s* and *-ing*
READ Decodable Reader 5C
Spiral Review Fluent Word Reading
Spelling: Short *e* Words

Read and Comprehend

Science in Reading 142i
READ "Help the Birds" —Paired Selection

Fluency 143b
Appropriate Phrasing
Monitor Progress Fluency Check

Language Arts

Conventions 143c
Interrogative Sentences

Writing 143d
Realistic Story

Research and Inquiry 143f
Synthesize

DAY 5

Get Ready to Read

Content Knowledge 144a
Review Oral Vocabulary
Monitor Progress Check Oral Vocabulary

Phonemic Awareness 144c
Review Segment and Blend Onset and Rime

Phonics/Spelling 144c
Review Short *e: e,* Initial Consonant Blends
Spelling Test

Read and Comprehend

Listening and Speaking 144–145
Vocabulary 145a
Fluency 145a

Text-Based Comprehension 145b
Review Main Idea and Details

Vocabulary 145b
Review High-Frequency and Selection Words

Genre 145c
Review How-to Article

Assessment 145d
Monitor Progress Word and Sentence Reading

Language Arts

Conventions 145g
Review Interrogative Sentences

Writing 145h
Realistic Story

Research and Inquiry 145j
Communicate

Wrap Up Your Week! 145k

Access for All

What do I do in group time?
It's as easy as 1-2-3!

1 TEACHER-LED SMALL GROUPS → 2 INDEPENDENT PRACTICE STATIONS → 3 INDEPENDENT READING

Small Group Time

Bridge to Common Core

SKILL DEVELOPMENT
- Initial Consonant Blends
- Short *e: e*
- Main Idea and Details
- Story Structure

DEEP UNDERSTANDING

This Week's Knowledge Goals

Children will understand that:
- all kinds of animals live in our neighborhood
- neighborhood animals need different kinds of food and shelter

1 Small Group Lesson Plan

	DAY 1 Differentiate Phonics	DAY 2 Differentiate Comprehension
On-Level pp. SG•70–SG•74	**Practice Phonics** More Short *e* Words **Decodable Reader** Read *Jeff the Cat*	**Practice Phonics** Additional Words with Initial Consonant Blends **Access Text** Read *Get the Egg!*
Strategic Intervention pp. SG•75–SG•79	**Reteach Phonics** Blend Short *e* Words **Decodable Reader** Read *Jeff the Cat*	**Reteach Phonics** Blend Words with Initial Consonant Blends **Access Text** Read *Get the Egg!*
Advanced pp. SG•80–SG•85	**Extend Phonics** More Challenging Short *e* Words **Advanced Selection** "Why Woodpeckers Peck"	**Extend Phonics** Additional Words with Initial Consonant Blends **Access Text** Read *Get the Egg!*
Independent Inquiry Project	**Identify Questions**	**Investigate**
ELL **If...** children need more scaffolding and practice with...	**Phonemic Awareness and Phonics, then...** use the Phonics Transition Lessons on pp. 249–345 in the *ELL Handbook.*	**the Comprehension Skill, then...** use the ELL activities on p. DI•101 in the Teacher Resources section on SuccessNet.

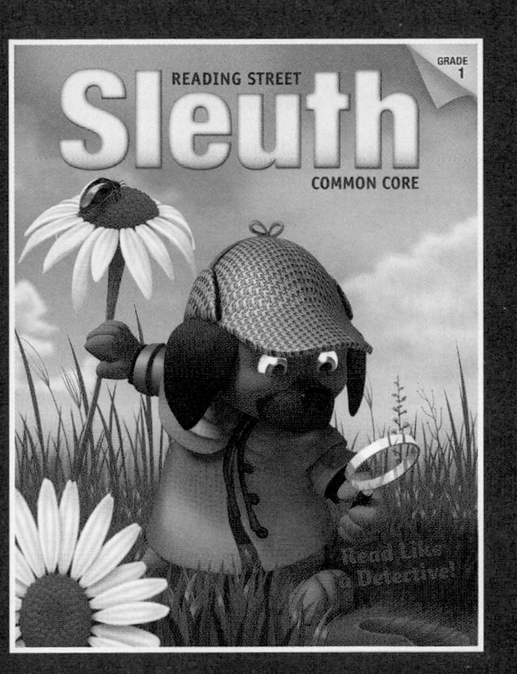

Reading Street Sleuth

- Provides access to grade-level text for all children
- Focuses on finding clues in text through close reading
- Builds capacity for complex text

Build Text-Based Comprehension

Get the Egg!

Optional Leveled Readers

Concept Literacy

Below Level

On Level

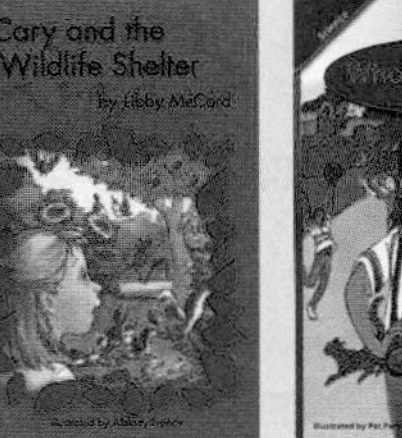

Advanced

ELL

ELD

DAY 3	DAY 4	DAY 5
Differentiate Close Reading	**Differentiate Vocabulary**	**Differentiate Reteaching**
Reread to Develop Vocabulary **Close Reading** Reread *Get the Egg!*	**Build Word Knowledge** Develop Language **Text-Based Comprehension** Read *Reading Street Sleuth,* pp. 16–17 or Leveled Readers	**Practice Interrogative Sentences** **Text-Based Comprehension** Reread *Reading Street Sleuth,* pp. 16–17 or Leveled Readers
Build Word Knowledge Blend Words with Short *e* and Initial Consonant Blends **Close Reading** Reread *Get the Egg!*	**Review Vocabulary** Review/Discuss Selection Vocabulary **Text-Based Comprehension** Read *Reading Street Sleuth,* pp. 16–17 or Leveled Readers	**Review Vocabulary** High-Frequency Words **Text-Based Comprehension** Reread *Reading Street Sleuth,* pp. 16–17 or Leveled Readers
Reread to Extend Vocabulary **Extend Concepts** Reread *Get the Egg!* **Investigate**	**Build Word Knowledge** Extend Amazing Words and Selection Vocabulary **Text-Based Comprehension** Read *Reading Street Sleuth,* pp. 16–17 or Leveled Readers **Organize**	**Extend Interrogative Sentences** **Text-Based Comprehension** Reread *Reading Street Sleuth,* pp. 16–17 or Leveled Readers **Communicate**
the Main Selection, **then...** use the activities on p. DI•102 in the Teacher Resources section on SuccessNet.	**Vocabulary,** **then...** use the routine on pp. xxxvi–xxxvii in the *ELL Handbook.*	**Conventions and Writing,** **then...** use the activities on pp. DI•104–DI•105 in the Teacher Resources section on SuccessNet.

2 Independent Stations

Practice Last Week's Skills

Focus on these activities when time is limited.

ACCESS FOR ALL
- ● Below-Level Activities
- ▲ On-Level Activities
- ■ Advanced Activities

LISTEN UP!

Add phonemes to spoken words.

OBJECTIVES
- Add final /s/, final /z/, and /ing/ to spoken words.

MATERIALS
- *Listen Up!* Flip Chart Activity 5

Modeled Pronunciation Audio CD

● With a partner, children say two verbs. Then repeat a verb with the addition of the final sounds from *walks, runs,* or *sing.*

▲ With a partner, children say five verbs. Children have their partner repeat a verb with the addition of the final sounds from *walks, runs,* or *sing.*

■ With a partner, children say "I *walk.* He *walks.*" Identify the sound at the end of *walks.* They can repeat this exercise with *run, runs,* and with *run, running.*

WORD WORK

Build and read words.

OBJECTIVES
- Add endings *-s* and *-ing* to verbs.
- Read words with inflected endings.

MATERIALS
- *Word Work* Flip Chart Activity 5, Letter Tiles

Interactive Sound-Spelling Cards

Letter Tile Drag and Drop

● Children build the words *picks, fills,* and *bending* with Letter Tiles and read each word.

▲ Children build the words *pick, fill,* and *bend* with Letter Tiles. They first add the consonant *-s* to each word, and then the inflected ending *-ing.* Children read the new words.

■ Children build six new verbs with Letter Tiles. Then they add the endings *-s* and *-ing* to each verb and read the new words.

LET'S WRITE!

Write sentences.

OBJECTIVES
- Write declarative sentences.

MATERIALS
- *Let's Write!* Flip Chart Activity 5, paper, pencils

Grammar Jammer

● Children write a declarative sentence about a wild animal.

▲ Children write two declarative sentences about a wild animal.

■ Children write a short story about a wild animal. Then underline the declarative sentences in the story.

WORDS TO KNOW

Alphabetize words.

OBJECTIVES
- Identify high-frequency words *eat, her, this, too, four, five.*
- Alphabetize words to the first or second letters.

MATERIALS
- *Words to Know* Flip Chart Activity 5, paper, blank cards, pencils

Vocabulary Activities

Teacher Resources
- High-Frequency Word Cards for Unit 1, Week 4

● Children place the words from the Word Cards in alphabetical order to the first or second letter.

▲ Children write the words from the Word Cards in a list in alphabetical order.

■ Children write the words from the Word Cards in a list in alphabetical order. Then they write new words on the blank cards, put them in alphabetical order and include them in the list.

READ FOR MEANING

Use text-based comprehension tools.

OBJECTIVES

- Identify the main idea of a selection.
- Identify the details that support the main idea.

MATERIALS

- *Read for Meaning* Flip Chart Activity 5, Leveled Readers, paper, pencils, crayons

 **Pearson eText**
- Leveled eReaders

 **Envision It! Animations**

● Children read *Time for Dinner.* First, they write a sentence that tells the main idea. Then they write the details.

▲ Children read *Which Fox?* First, they write a sentence that tells the main idea. Then they write the details.

■ Children read *Baby Animals in the Rain Forest.* First, they write a sentence that tells the main idea. Then they write the details.

GET FLUENT

Practice fluent reading.

OBJECTIVES

- Read aloud with accuracy at an appropriate rate.

MATERIALS

- *Get Fluent Flip* Chart Activity 5, Leveled Readers

 **Pearson eText**
- Leveled eReaders

● Children work with a partner to take turns reading from *Time for Dinner.*

▲ Children work with a partner to take turns reading from *Which Fox?*

■ Children work with a partner to take turns reading from *Baby Animals in the Rain Forest.*

Manage the Stations

Use these management tools to set up and organize your Practice Stations:

Practice Station Flip Charts

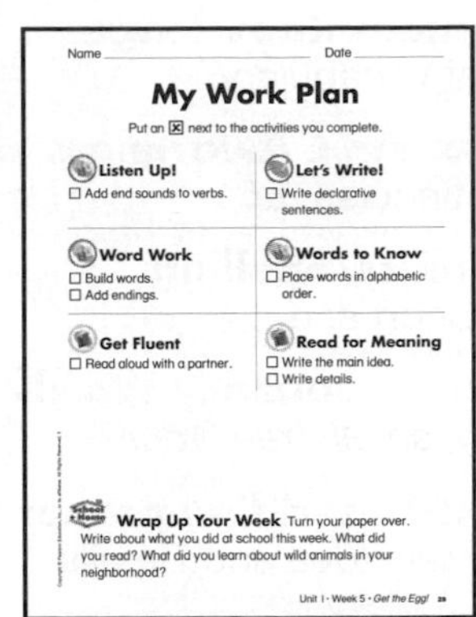
Name ______ Date ______

My Work Plan

Put an ☒ next to the activities you complete.

Listen Up! ☐ Add end sounds to verbs.	**Let's Write!** ☐ Write declarative sentences.
Word Work ☐ Build words. ☐ Add endings.	**Words to Know** ☐ Place words in alphabetic order.
Get Fluent ☐ Read aloud with a partner.	**Read for Meaning** ☐ Write the main idea. ☐ Write details.

Wrap Up Your Week Turn your paper over. Write about what you did at school this week. What did you read? What did you learn about wild animals in your neighborhood?

Unit 1 • Week 5 • Get the Egg!

Classroom Management Handbook for Differentiated Instruction Practice Stations, p. 29

3 Independent Reading

Children should select appropriately complex texts to read and write about independently every day before, during, and after school.

Suggestions for this week's independent reading:

- Informational texts on last week's science topic: How do wild animals take care of their babies?
- Nonfiction selections about how wild animals take care of their babies
- Nonfiction book by a favorite author

BOOK TALK Have partners discuss their independent reading for the week. Tell them to refer to their Reading Log and paraphrase what the selection was about. To focus the discussion, prompt them to talk about one or more of the following:

Key Ideas and Details
- Who is the author? Why did he or she write the work?
- What did I learn from this text?

Craft and Structure
- Did I understand the information?
- Did the author use words that were interesting and clear?

Integration of Ideas
- Did the information seem believable? Why or why not?
- Was this book like others I have read?

 **Pearson eText**
- Student Edition
- Decodable Readers
- Leveled Readers

 **Trade Book Library**

 **Materials from School or Classroom Library**

Content Knowledge
Oral Vocabulary

Phonemic Awareness
Distinguish /e/

Phonics/Spelling
Short *e: e*

High-Frequency Words
saw, small, tree, your

Text-Based Comprehension
Main Idea and Details

Conventions
Interrogative Sentences

Writing
Realistic Story

Research and Inquiry
Identify and Focus Topic

Materials

- Student Edition
- Sing with Me Big Book
- Sound-Spelling Cards
- Decodable Reader 5A
- Reader's and Writer's Notebook

Bridge to Common Core

INTEGRATION OF KNOWLEDGE/IDEAS

This week children read, write, and talk about neighborhood animals.

Texts This Week

- "Time to Hatch"
- "The Pecking Hen"
- *Jungle Drum*
- *Get the Egg!*
- "Help the Birds"
- "Maisie Caught a Toad Today"

Science Knowledge Goals

Children will understand that

- all kinds of animals live in our neighborhood
- neighborhood animals need different kinds of food and shelter

Street Rhymes!

I saw a tiger on our street,
And an elephant with big round feet,
A gorilla that was huge and hairy—
Well, I guess those were imaginary.
There are lots of squirrels and rabbits though,
And birds and deer and a big black crow.

- To introduce this week's concept, read aloud the poem several times and ask children to join you.

Content Knowledge

Neighborhood Animals

CONCEPT TALK To help children gain knowledge and understanding, tell them that this week they will talk, sing, read, and write about wild animals that live in their neighborhoods. Write the Question of the Week, *Which wild animals live in our neighborhood?,* and track the print as you read it.

Build Oral Language

TALK ABOUT NEIGHBORHOOD ANIMALS Have children turn to pages 120–121 in their Student Edition. Read the title and look at the photos. Use these questions to guide discussion and create the "Which wild animals live in our neighborhood?" concept map.

- These photographs show wild animals that may be found in our backyards. Which animal is building a web? (spider) Which animal makes tunnels in the dirt? (worm) What emerges from a cocoon? (butterfly) Let's add these animals to our map.
- What other animals do you see in these photographs? (rabbits) The rabbits survive by digging shallow burrows in the ground to sleep. Let's add *rabbit* to the map too.

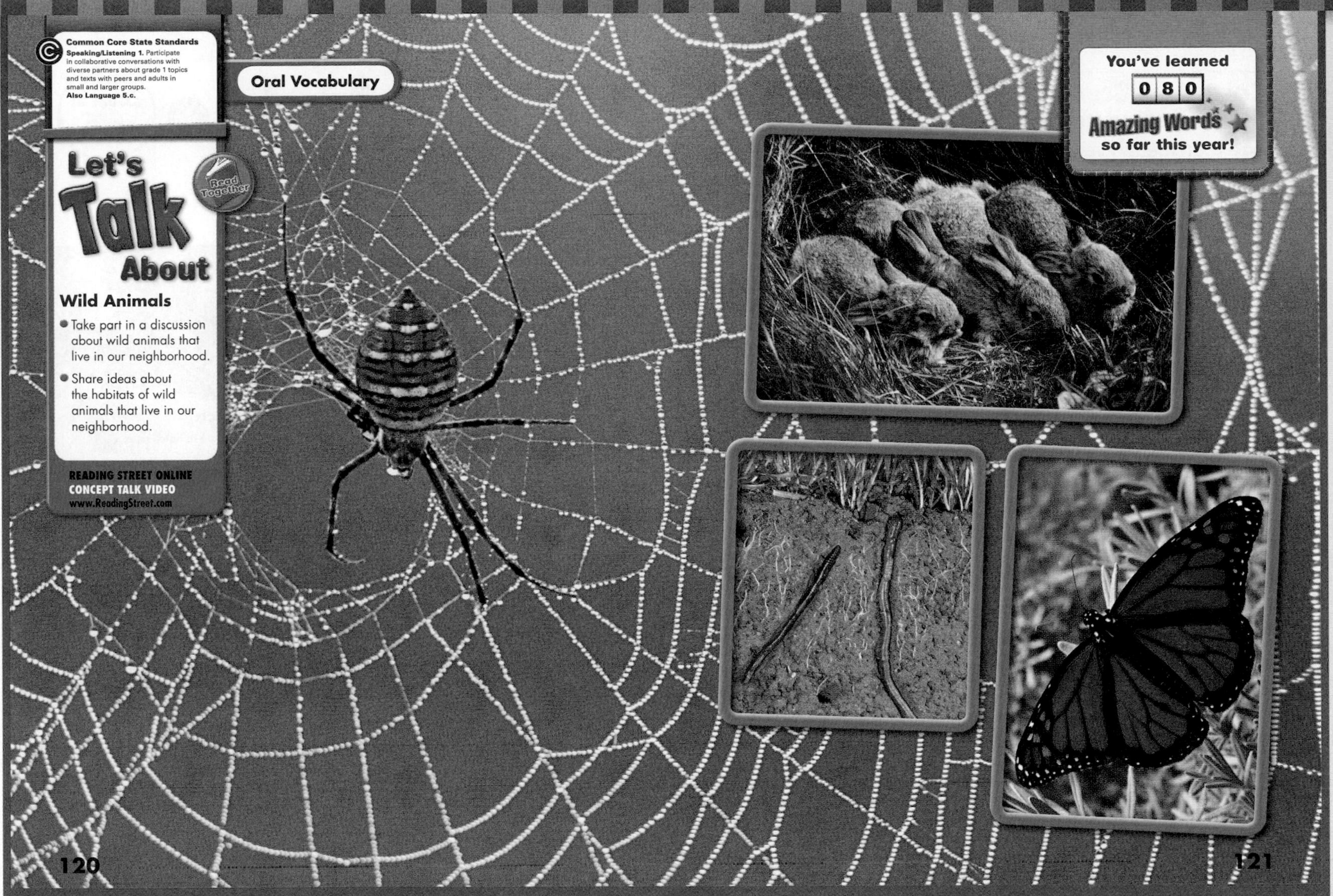

Common Core State Standards
Speaking/Listening 1. Participate in collaborative conversations with diverse partners about grade 1 topics and texts with peers and adults in small and larger groups.
Also Language 5.c.
Oral Vocabulary
Let's Talk About
Read Together
Wild Animals
• Take part in a discussion about wild animals that live in our neighborhood.
• Share ideas about the habitats of wild animals that live in our neighborhood.
READING STREET ONLINE
CONCEPT TALK VIDEO
www.ReadingStreet.com
You've learned
0 8 0
Amazing Words
so far this year!
120
121
Student Edition, pp. 120–121

CONNECT TO READING Explain that this week children will read about two friends that help a bird. Let's add *bird* to our map.

Which wild animals live in our neighborhood?

- spider, worm, butterfly
- rabbit
- bird

eStreet Interactive
www.ReadingStreet.com

Pearson eText
- Student Edition

Concept Talk Video

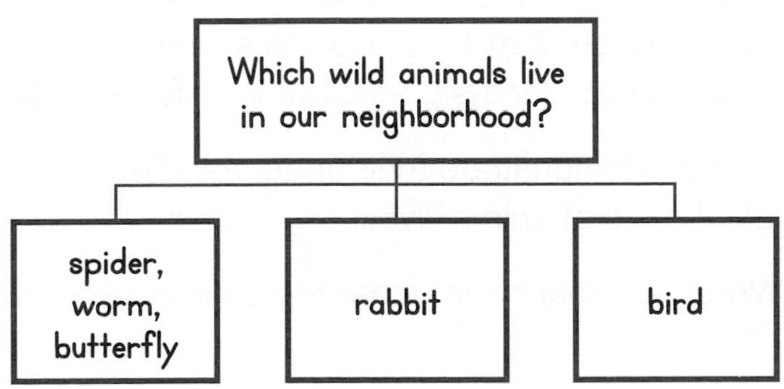

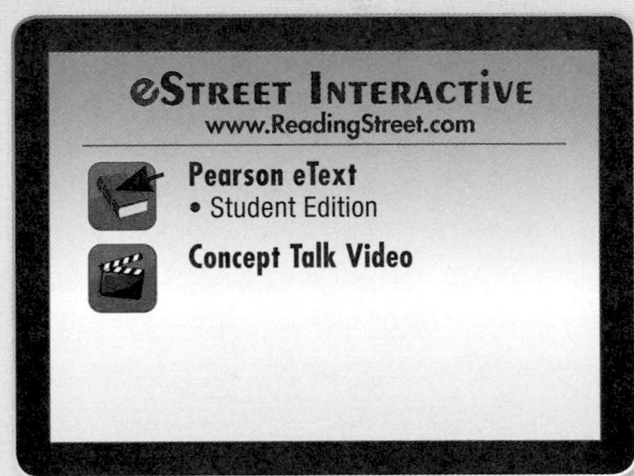

ELL

Preteach Concepts Use the Day 1 instruction on ELL Poster 5 to build knowledge and oral vocabulary.

ELL Support Additional ELL support is provided in the *ELL Handbook* and in the *ELL Support Lessons* on the *Teacher Resources DVD-ROM.*

Common Core State Standards

Language 5.c. Identify real-life connections between words and their use (e.g., note places at home that are *cozy*).

Amazing Words

You've learned 080 words so far.

You'll learn 006 words this week!

habitat	chirp
hatch	croak
survive	moist

Content Knowledge

Build Oral Vocabulary

INTRODUCE AMAZING WORDS Display page 5 of the *Sing with Me* Big Book. Tell children they are going to sing "Time to Hatch," a song about how baby birds learn what they need in order to live. Ask children to listen for the Amazing Words *habitat*, *hatch*, and *survive* as you sing. Sing the song again and have children join you.

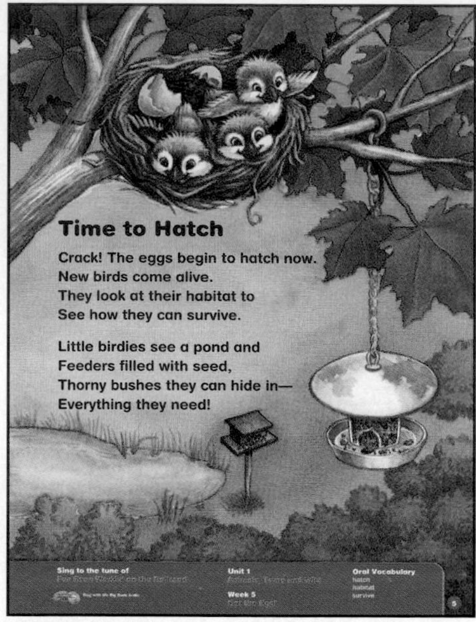

Time to Hatch
Crack! The eggs begin to hatch now.
New birds come alive.
They look at their habitat to
See how they can survive.
Little birdies see a pond and
Feeders filled with seed,
Thorny bushes they can hide in—
Everything they need!

Sing with Me Big Book, p. 5

Amazing Words — Robust Vocabulary Routine

1. **Introduce the Word** Relate the word *habitat* to the song. The song says that baby birds look at their *habitat.* Supply a child-friendly definition. A *habitat* is the place where an animal or plant lives. Have children say the word.
2. **Demonstrate** Provide examples to show meaning. Different kinds of animals live in different *habitats.* The *habitat* for a fish may be a lake, or a pond, or the ocean. A forest may be a rabbit's *habitat.* The dirt in a garden may be a worm's *habitat.* Cactus plants live in a desert *habitat.*
3. **Apply** Have children demonstrate their understanding. Name an animal and the *habitat* where that animal lives.
4. **Display the Word** Run your hand under the chunks *hab-i-tat* as you read the word.

See p. OV•5 to teach *hatch* and *survive.*

Routines Flip Chart

AMAZING WORDS AT WORK Have children look at the picture on pages 120–121.

- What do you think rabbits eat? What else do they need to live? Use the word *survive* in your answer. (Possible response: Rabbits eat grass and other plants. They need food, water, and shelter to survive.)
- The butterfly hatches from a cocoon. What animal in the picture hatches from an egg? Use the word *hatch* in your response. (Spiders hatch from eggs.)
- What other animals can you think of that might live in a backyard habitat? Use the word *habitat* in your answer. (Possible response: Squirrels and mice might live in a backyard habitat.)

APPLY AMAZING WORDS Have children demonstrate their understanding of the Amazing Words by completing these sentences orally.

I watched a ______ **hatch** from an egg.

______ can't **survive** without food or water.

The ocean is a good **habitat** for ______.

Corrective feedback | **If...** children have difficulty using the Amazing Words, **then...** remind them of the definitions and provide opportunities for children to use the words in sentences.

Access for All

SI Strategic Intervention

Sentence Production If children's oral sentences lack subject-verb agreement, then say each sentence several times and have children repeat it.

Pronunciation Children may have difficulty hearing and reproducing stressed and unstressed syllables correctly. If children have difficulty with multisyllable words, use soft and loud hand-claps to help children hear the pacing of stressed and unstressed syllables in words such as *habitat* and *survive.*

Common Core State Standards
Foundational Skills 2.c. Isolate and pronounce initial, medial vowel, and final sounds (phonemes) in spoken single-syllable words. **Also Foundational Skills 2.b., 2.d.**

Phonemic Awareness

Let's Listen for

Sounds

- Find three things that rhyme with *tack*.
- Find five things that contain the short *e* sound. Say each word.
- Find something that rhymes with *best*. Say each sound in that word.
- Find something that starts with the sounds /spr/.

Read Together

READING STREET ONLINE
SOUND-SPELLING CARDS
www.ReadingStreet.com

122 123

Student Edition, pp. 122–123

Common Core State Standards

Foundational Skills 2.c. Isolate and pronounce initial, medial vowel, and final sounds (phonemes) in spoken single-syllable words. **Foundational Skills 3.** Know and apply grade-level phonics and word analysis skills in decoding words. **Also Foundational Skills 2.b., 2.d.**

Skills Trace

Short *e*: *e*

Introduce U1W5D1

Practice U1W5D3; U1W5D4

Reteach/Review U1W5D5; U1W6D4

Assess/Test Weekly Test U1W5
Benchmark Test U1

KEY: U=Unit W=Week D=Day

Phonemic Awareness

Distinguish /e/

INTRODUCE Read the second bulleted point on page 122 of the Student Edition. What is in the nest? (eggs) The first sound in *eggs* is /e/. I also see a bird. What color is the bird? (red) The middle sound in *red* is /e/. Have children identify other items that contain the /e/ sound. (elf, steps, dress, sled, bell)

MODEL Listen to the sounds in the word *red:* /r/ /e/ /d/. There are three sounds in *red.* Let's blend those sounds to make a word: /r/ /e/ /d/, *red.* Continue modeling with *eggs.* Guide children as they look for more words that contain the initial or medial /e/ sound. *(envelope, jet, pet)*

Corrective feedback	**If...** children make an error, **then...** model by repeating the short *e* sound in other words, and have them repeat the sound and the word after you.

Phonics

Short *e: e*

CONNECT Write the words *sit* and *hot.* Ask children what they know about the vowel sounds in these words. (The vowel sounds are short. *Sit* has the short vowel sound /i/ and *hot* has the short vowel sound /o/.) Explain that today they will learn how to spell and read words with the short vowel sound /e/.

Sound-Spelling Card 6

USE SOUND-SPELLING CARD Display Card 6. Point to *e.* The short *e* sound, /e/, can be spelled *e.* Have children say /e/ several times as you point to *e.*

MODEL Write *ten.* In this word, the letter *e* stands for the sound /e/. Segment and blend *ten;* then have children blend with you: /t/ /e/ /n/.

GROUP PRACTICE Continue the process. This time have children blend with you. Remind children that *e* often spells the short *e* sound, /e/.

beg	vet	deck	sell	mess	red
peg	pen	tell	web	less	get

REVIEW What do you know about reading these words? (The letter *e* at the beginning or in the middle of a word can spell the sound /e/.)

Access for All

SI Strategic Intervention

Short Vowel Words If children have difficulty distinguishing the short vowel sounds for *i, o,* and *e,* pronounce and then have children repeat words such as *pit, pot,* and *pet.*

A Advanced

Extend Blending Involve children in a rhyming game by saying a short vowel word such as *bell* and inviting children to name words that rhyme with it.

Vocabulary Support

You may wish to explain the meanings of these words.

beg ask somebody for something

vet an animal doctor

peg a nail or hook in a wall used to hang things on

Sound-Symbol Correspondence Double final consonants such as *ss* or *ll* do not exist in Spanish. Speakers of Spanish may need extra spelling practice with words such as *yell, bell, fell, mess,* and *less.*

Pronounce /e/ In Spanish, the letter *e* is pronounced /ā/. If children tend to pronounce short *e* as long *a,* say such words slowly and distinctly, emphasizing the sound /e/ to help children develop the generalization.

Common Core State Standards

Foundational Skills 3. Know and apply grade-level phonics and word analysis skills in decoding words. **Foundational Skills 3.b.** Decode regularly spelled one-syllable words.

Spelling Pattern

/e/ Spelled *e* The sound /e/ is usually spelled *e* at the beginning or in the middle of a word.

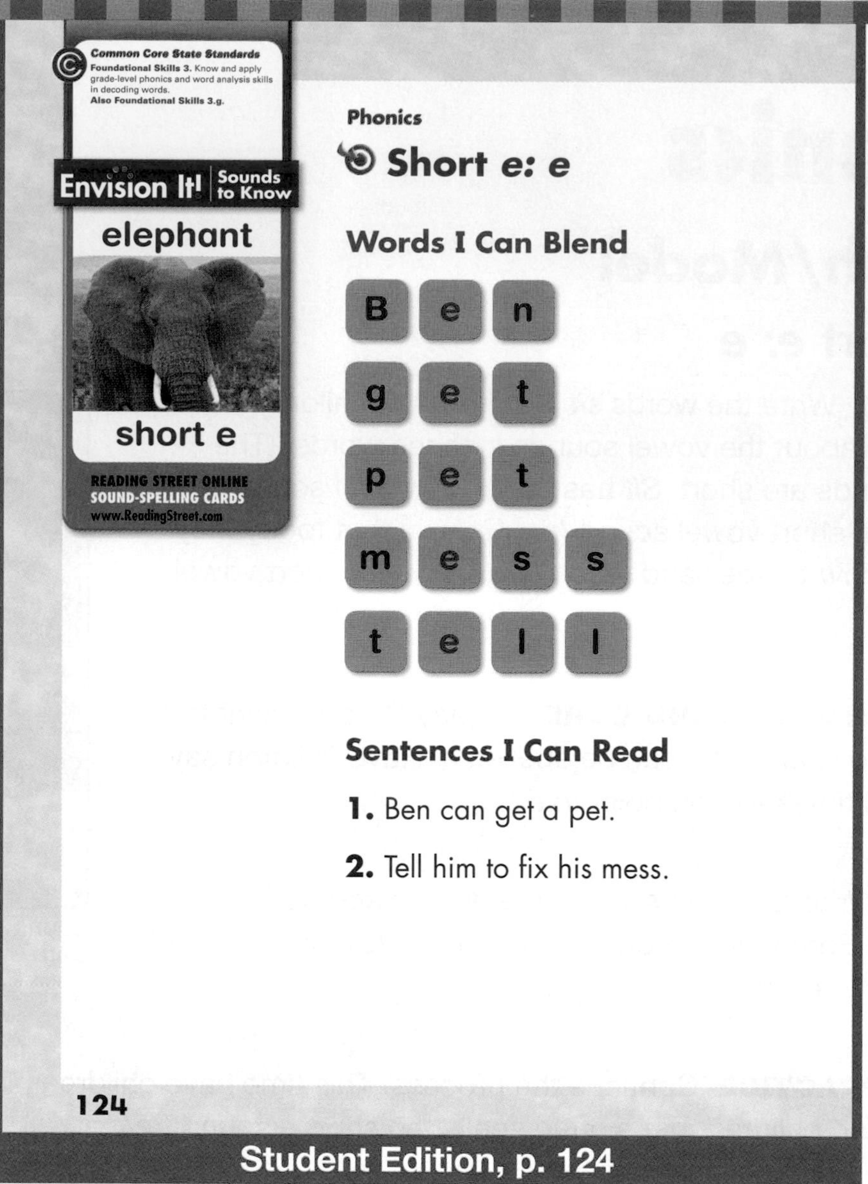

Student Edition, p. 124

Phonics

Guide Practice

BLEND WORDS Have children turn to page 124 in their Student Edition. Look at the picture on this page. I see a picture of an *elephant.* When I say *elephant,* I hear /e/ at the beginning. In *elephant,* short *e* is spelled *e.*

GROUP PRACTICE For each word in "Words I Can Blend," ask for the sound of each letter or group of letters. Make sure that children identify the correct sound for short *e.* Then have children blend the whole word.

Corrective feedback	**If...** children have difficulty blending a word, **then...** model blending the word, and ask children to blend it with you.

DECODE WORDS IN ISOLATION After children can successfully segment and blend the words, point to words in random order and ask children to read them naturally.

DECODE WORDS IN CONTEXT Have children read each of the sentences. Have them identify words in the sentences that have the short *e* sound.

Team Talk Pair children and have them take turns reading each of the sentences aloud.

ON THEIR OWN Use *Reader's and Writer's Notebook,* p. 185.

MONITOR PROGRESS Short *e: e*

FORMATIVE ASSESSMENT Write the following words and have the class read them. Notice which words children miss during the group reading. Call on individuals to read some of the words.

					Spiral Review
pet	hen	egg	bed	pen	
pick	bell	six	get	miss ←	Row 2 contrasts short *e* and short *i*.
deck	rag	fell	win	lock ←	Row 3 reviews short *a, e, i,* and *o*.

If... children cannot blend words with the short *e* sound at this point,

then... use the Small Group Time Strategic Intervention lesson, p. SG•75, to reteach short *e* spelled *e*. Continue to monitor children's progress using other instructional opportunities during the week. See the Skills Trace on p. 122–123.

Access for All

SI Strategic Intervention

Pronounce /e/ If children tend to pronounce short *e* as short *i*, especially before the letter *n*, as in *pen, den,* and *Ben,* say such words slowly and distinctly, emphasizing the sound /e/ to help with formal pronunciation.

A Advanced

Extend Blending Provide children who can segment and blend all the words correctly with more challenging words such as *pencil* and *center.*

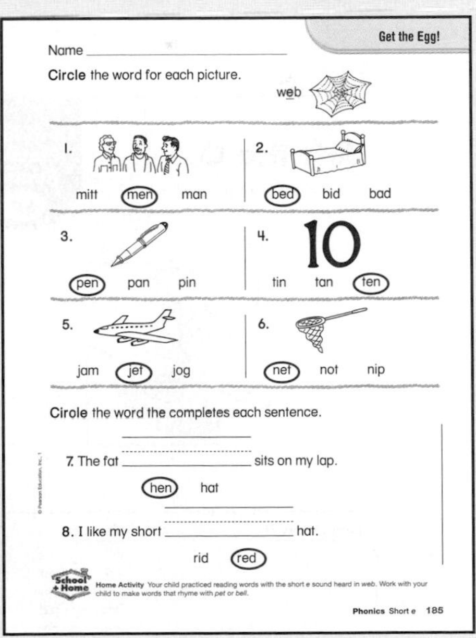
Get the Egg!

Name

Circle the word for each picture.

web

1. mitt (men) man
2. (bed) bid bad
3. (pen) pan pin
4. 10 — tin tan (ten)
5. jam (jet) jog
6. (net) not nip

Circle the word the completes each sentence.

7. The fat ______ sits on my lap.
(hen) hat

8. I like my short ______ hat.
rid (red)

Phonics Short e 185

Reader's and Writer's Notebook, p. 185

Pronunciation Children whose first language is Spanish may need support with initial short *e* sounds in words such as *egg* and *enter.*

Common Core State Standards

Foundational Skills 3. Know and apply grade-level phonics and word analysis skills in decoding words. **Foundational Skills 3.b.** Decode regularly spelled one-syllable words. **Foundational Skills 3.g.** Recognize and read grade-appropriate irregularly spelled words. **Foundational Skills 4.** Read with sufficient accuracy and fluency to support comprehension.

Decodable Reader 5A

If children need help, then...

Read *Jeff the Cat*

DECODE WORDS IN ISOLATION Have children turn to page 193. Have children decode each word.

REVIEW HIGH-FREQUENCY WORDS Review the previously taught words *a, here, the, he, like(s),* and *to.* Have children read each word as you point to it on the Word Wall.

PREVIEW DECODABLE READER Have children read the title and preview the story. Tell them they will decode words with the short vowel sound *e.*

DECODE WORDS IN CONTEXT Pair children for reading and listen as they decode. One child begins. Children read the entire story, switching readers after each page. Partners reread the story. This time the other child begins.

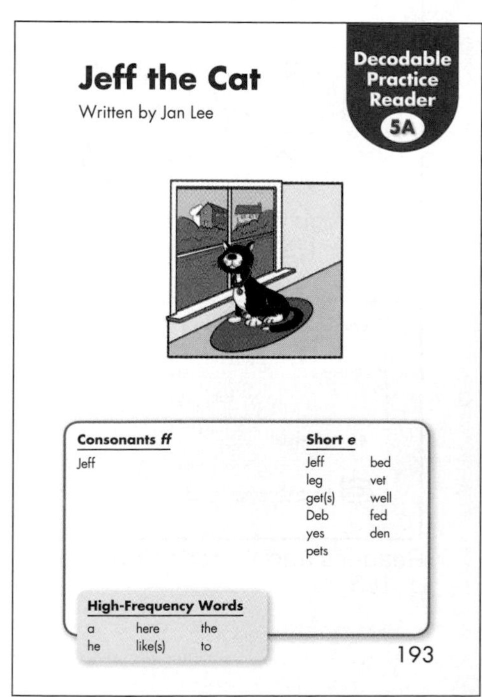
Jeff the Cat

Written by Jan Lee

Decodable Practice Reader 5A

Consonants ff	Short e	
Jeff	Jeff	bed
	leg	vet
	get(s)	well
	Deb	fed
	yes	den
	pets	

High-Frequency Words

a	here	the
he	like(s)	to

193

Decodable Practice Reader 5A

Jeff is a cat.
Jeff sits here.

194

Jeff naps on the bed.
He likes the bed.

195

Jeff licks a lot.
He is licking his leg.

196

Jeff is at the vet.
Jeff gets his tags.
He is well.

197

Deb fed Jeff.
Jeff ran to his mat.

198

Can Jeff get here?
Yes, he is in his den.

199

Deb pets Jeff.
He likes it.

200

Corrective feedback	**If...** children have difficulty decoding a word, **then...** refer them to the Sound-Spelling Cards to identify the sounds in the word. Then prompt them to blend the word. • What is the new word? • Is the new word a word you know? • Does it make sense in the story?

CHECK DECODING AND COMPREHENSION Have children retell the story to include characters, setting, and events. Then have children find words with the short *e* sound in the story. Explain that story words with this letter will have the short *e* sound at the beginning or middle of the word. Children should supply *Jeff, bed, leg, vet, gets, well, den, fed, pets, Deb, get,* and *yes.*

Reread for Fluency

REREAD DECODABLE READER Have children reread Decodable Practice Reader 5A to develop automaticity decoding words with the short *e* sound.

Routine Oral Rereading

1. **Read** Have children read the entire book orally.
2. **Reread** To achieve optimal fluency, children should reread the text three or four times.
3. **Corrective Feedback** Listen as children read. Provide corrective feedback regarding their fluency and decoding.

Routines Flip Chart

Access for All

Main Idea and Details After reading, have children tell about the main idea of the story, *Jeff the Cat.* Ask them to give a detail from the story that supports the main idea.

Short *e*: *e*

Beginning Before children read, lead them on a picture walk through the story. Point out and pronounce the words that have the short *e* sound. Then write a pictured word and have children pronounce it and find its picture.

Intermediate After reading, have children read the words with the short *e* sound. Monitor children's pronunciation.

Advanced After reading, have children find the words with the short *e* sound and use them to make up their own sentences about what they think will happen with Jeff after he comes home from the vet's office.

Common Core State Standards

Foundational Skills 3.g. Recognize and read grade-appropriate irregularly spelled words. **Language 2.d.** Use conventional spelling for words with common spelling patterns and for frequently occurring irregular words. **Language 2.e.** Spell untaught words phonetically, drawing on phonemic awareness and spelling conventions.

Access for All

A Advanced

Extend Spelling Challenge children who spell words correctly to spell more difficult words such as *denim, dress, exit, speck, tennis,* and *welcome.*

Phonics/Spelling Generalization

Short *e* Each spelling word is a short *e* word, which has the short *e* sound.

Name ______________ Get the Egg!

Short e Words

Look at the word. **Say** it. **Listen** for the short *e* sound.

	Write each word.	Check it.
1. bed	bed	bed
2. men	men	men
3. red	red	red
4. step	step	step
5. ten	ten	ten
6. net	net	net
7. leg	leg	leg
8. jet	jet	jet
9. sled	sled	sled
10. wet	wet	wet

Words to Read

11. saw saw 12. your your

DVD•62 Spelling Short e Words

Let's Practice It! TR DVD•62

Spelling Pretest

Short *e* Words

DICTATE SPELLING WORDS Dictate the spelling words and read the sentences. Have children write the words. If needed, segment the words for children, clarify the pronunciations, and give meanings of words. Have children check their pretests and correct misspelled words.

1. men	The **men** helped us move into the new house.
2. red*	Leah wore a **red** dress.
3. step	My little sister took her first **step** today.
4. ten	We leave in **ten** minutes.
5. net*	I used a **net** to catch a goldfish.
6. leg	An ant crawled up my **leg.**
7. jet	We took a **jet** to visit grandma and grandpa.
8. sled	I love to **sled** down the hill in winter.
9. wet	I fell in the pool and got **wet.**
10. bed	I cleaned my room and made my **bed.**

* Words marked with asterisks come from the selection *Get the Egg!*

ON THEIR OWN Use Let's Practice It! p. 62 on the *Teacher Resources DVD-ROM.*

ELL

If... children need more scaffolding and practice with **Phonemic Awareness and Phonics, then...** use the Phonics Transition Lessons on pp. 249–345 in the *ELL Handbook.*

Day 1 SMALL GROUP TIME • Differentiate Phonics, p. SG•69

OL On-Level

- **Practice Phonics** Additional Short *e* Words
- **Read** Decodable Reader *Jeff the Cat*

SI Strategic Intervention

- **Reteach Phonics** Blend Short *e* Words
- **Read** Decodable Reader *Jeff the Cat*

A Advanced

- **Extend Phonics** More Short *e* Words
- **Read** Advanced Selection for Short *e* Words
- **Introduce** Inquiry Project

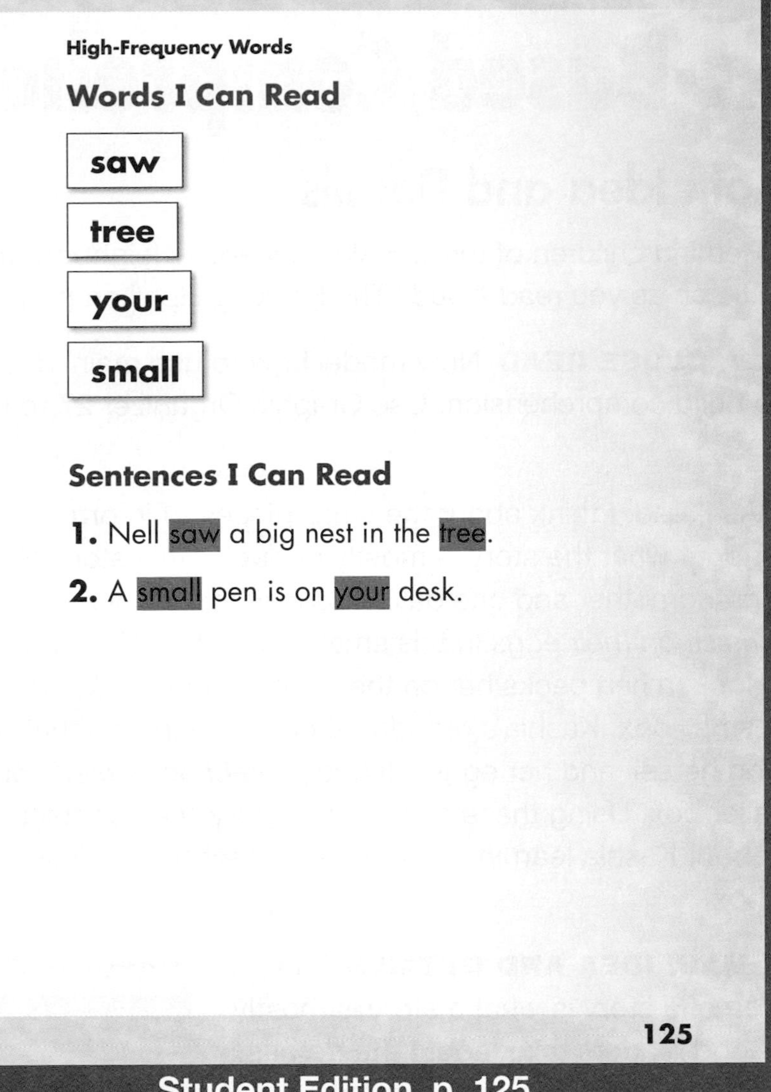
High-Frequency Words

Words I Can Read

saw

tree

your

small

Sentences I Can Read

1. Nell saw a big nest in the tree.

2. A small pen is on your desk.

125

Student Edition, p. 125

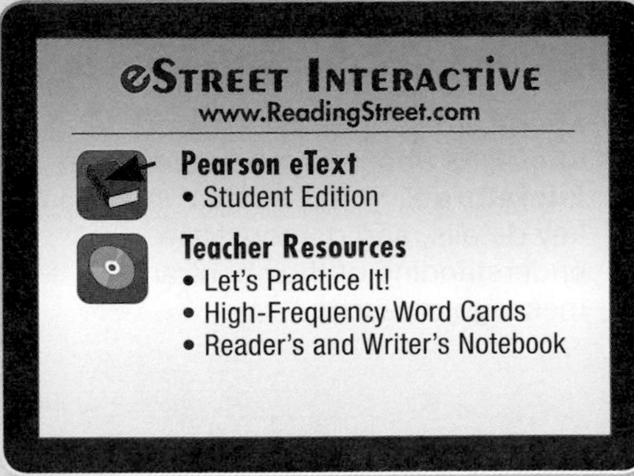

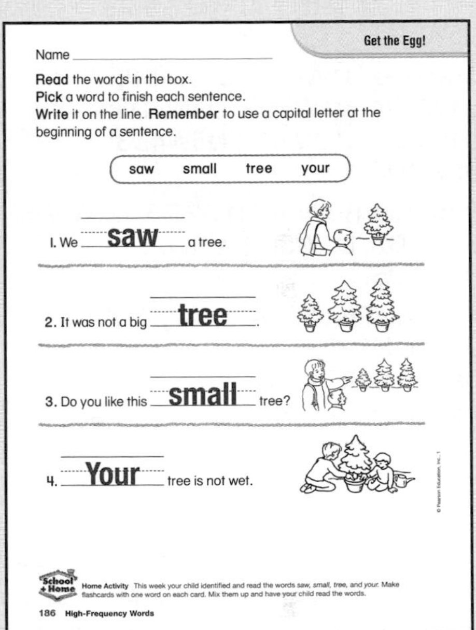
Name

Get the Egg!

Read the words in the box.
Pick a word to finish each sentence.
Write it on the line. Remember to use a capital letter at the beginning of a sentence.

saw small tree your

1. We saw a tree.

2. It was not a big tree.

3. Do you like this small tree?

4. Your tree is not wet.

186 High-Frequency Words

Reader's and Writer's Notebook, p. 186

High-Frequency Words

Routine Nondecodable Words

1. **Say and Spell** Some words we learn by remembering the letters. Point to *saw.* The letters in *saw* are *s-a-w, saw.* Have children say and spell each word.

2. **Identify Familiar Letter-Sounds** Point to the first letter in *saw.* What is this letter and what is its sound? (*s*, /s/)

3. **Show Meaning** Tell me a sentence using the word *saw.* Repeat.

Routines Flip Chart

READ Have children read the page aloud. Add the words to the Word Wall.

ON THEIR OWN Use *Reader's and Writer's Notebook,* p. 186.

Survival Vocabulary Have children use the word *saw* to talk about people at school. Children might say, *I* ***saw*** *Mr. Mead on the playground.*

DAY 1

Common Core State Standards

Literature 1. Ask and answer questions about key details in a text. **Literature 2.** Retell stories, including key details, and demonstrate understanding of their central message or lesson.

Skills Trace

Main Idea and Details

Introduce U1W4D1; U1W5D1; U5W4D1

Practice U1W4D2; U1W4D3; U1W4D4; U1W5D2; U1W5D3; U1W5D4; U5W4D2; U5W4D3; U5W4D4

Reteach/Review U1W4D5; U1W5D5; U1W6D2; U2W3D2; U5W2D2; U5W4D5

Assess/Test Weekly Tests U1W4; U1W5; U5W4
Benchmark Test U1; U5

KEY: U=Unit W=Week D=Day

Academic Vocabulary

main idea what the story is mostly about

details small pieces of information

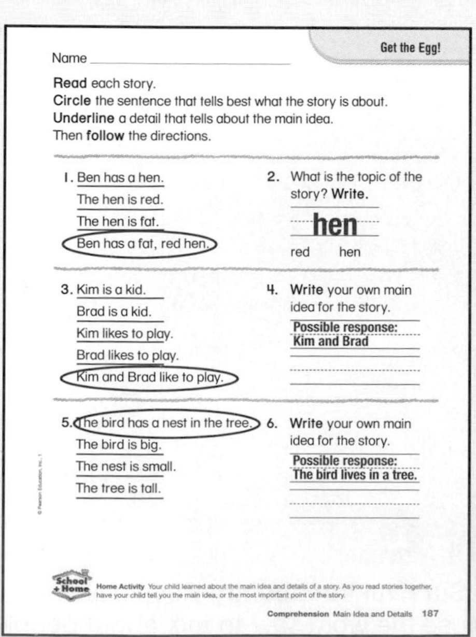

Name ________ Get the Egg!

Read each story.
Circle the sentence that tells best what the story is about.
Underline a detail that tells about the main idea.
Then **follow** the directions.

1. Ben has a hen. The hen is red. The hen is fat. Ben has a fat, red hen.
2. What is the topic of the story? **Write.** hen (red hen)
3. Kim is a kid. Brad is a kid. Kim likes to play. Brad likes to play. Kim and Brad like to play.
4. **Write** your own main idea for the story. Possible response: Kim and Brad
5. The bird has a nest in the tree. The bird is big. The nest is small. The tree is tall.
6. **Write** your own main idea for the story. Possible response: The bird lives in a tree.

School + Home **Home Activity** Your child learned about the main idea and details of a story. As you read stories together, have your child tell you the main idea, or the most important point of the story.

Comprehension Main Idea and Details 187

Reader's and Writer's Notebook, p. 187

Zoom in on

Text-Based Comprehension

Main Idea and Details

READ Remind children of the weekly concept—Neighborhood Animals. Have children listen as you read aloud "The Pecking Hen" on page 125b.

MODEL A CLOSE READ Now model how to use main idea and details as a tool to build comprehension. Use Graphic Organizer 27 to organize your thoughts.

As I read, I think about the small pieces of information that tell more about what the story is mostly about. In this story, Kashia visits her grandmother and one day, a huge white hen was sitting on a nest. I'll write *hens sit on their eggs* in this small box. When Kashia bends down to get a better look, a hen pecks her on the nose. I'll put *pecks Kashia's nose* in another small box. Kashia's grandmother then explains that the hen was protecting herself and her eggs. I'll add *protecting herself and her eggs* in the last smaller box. Using these parts of the story, we can tell that the story is mostly about Kashia learning how hens protect themselves. I'll write that in the big box.

TEACH MAIN IDEA AND DETAILS The **main idea** of a story is what a story is mostly about. Good readers think about the **details,** or small pieces of information, in a story to find the main idea.

Have children turn to p. EI•3 in their Student Edition. These pictures show an example of the main idea and details. Discuss these questions using the pictures:

- What does the "Details" picture show? (the inside of a house, a mother and children, a cat on the couch)
- What does the "Main Idea" picture show? (the outside of a house)
- How do the details connect to the main idea? (They show a family doing things at home.) The main idea is a family doing things at home.

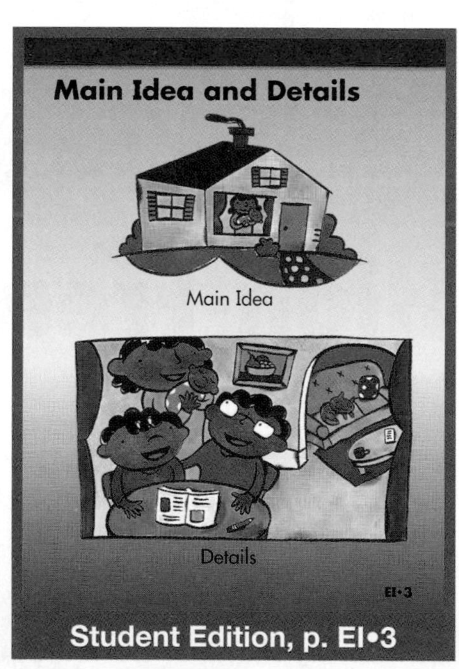

Student Edition, p. EI•3

GUIDE PRACTICE Now reread "The Pecking Hen." After rereading the story, have children choose one of the details from the Main Idea chart and draw it. Then have children share their drawings with the class, using the words *details* and *main idea* as they describe their pictures.

APPLY Use *Reader's and Writer's Notebook,* p. 187.

Teacher Read Aloud

The Pecking Hen

Grandma Bess lived in a big, old, white house in the country. Kashia, who lived in the city, always learned something new when she visited her grandmother.

Grandma Bess had a wonderful garden. She planted tomatoes, carrots, okra, corn, and green beans. Kashia loved to help her grandmother pick the fresh vegetables. It was like shopping at the grocery store for free!

Grandma Bess also had a pen where she kept hens. Each morning, she went inside the pen and gathered eggs. One morning, Kashia went with her. Kashia saw a huge white hen sitting on a nest, waiting for her eggs to hatch. Kashia bent her head near the hen to get a getter look.

Peck! Peck! Squawk! Squawk!

"Ouch!" cried Kashia.

Grandma Bess turned to Kashia quickly and said, "What's wrong?"

"The hen pecked me on the nose! It hurts!"

Grandma Bess chuckled. "That's what a hen does to survive. She protects herself and her habitat from danger."

"It's not funny!" Kashia said. "And I'm not dangerous!"

"No, you're not, Kashia, but the hen doesn't know that. The same thing happened to me when I was your age. I got too close to a hen too. It pecked me right on the nose," said Grandma Bess. "Hens use their beaks to protect themselves and their eggs."

"I guess I learned my lesson," Kashia said. "From now on, I'll keep my nose out of the hen's business!"

Grandma Bess and Kashia laughed.

Bridge to Common Core

KEY IDEAS AND DETAILS

As children explore the content of the selection, they identify the main idea and the details that support the main idea. Retelling the selection helps children focus on the content and the main idea. Asking questions about the selection helps children better understand the key ideas of the selection and the related details.

Support Listening Comprehension
To increase understanding of the academic vocabulary heard in the Read Aloud, use visuals to preview words children may not know such as *okra, green beans,* and *pecked.*

Common Core State Standards

Foundational Skills 1.a. Recognize the distinguishing features of a sentence (e.g., first word, capitalization, ending punctuation). **Writing 3.** Write narratives in which they recount two or more appropriately sequenced events, include some details regarding what happened, use temporal words to signal event order, and provide some sense of closure. **Language 1.j.** Produce and expand complete simple and compound declarative, interrogative, imperative, and exclamatory sentences in response to prompts. **Also Language 1., 2.b.**

Academic Vocabulary

interrogative sentence a group of words that ask a question

characters the people or animals in a story

realistic story a made-up story that could happen in real life

setting where and when a story takes place

Daily Fix-It

1. ten men sat on a jett.
   Ten men sat on a jet.
2. your redd sled is wet.
   Your red sled is wet.

Discuss the Daily Fix-It corrections with children. Review sentence capitalization and the spelling of words with short *e*, such as *jet* and *red.*

Conventions

Interrogative Sentences

MAKE CONNECTIONS This week you listened to a story called "The Pecking Hen." Kashia learns something about hens from Grandma Bess. What would you ask Grandma Bess about hens? Write children's questions on the board. All of these are interrogative sentences because they ask something.

TEACH Explain that an **interrogative sentence** is a sentence that asks something. Interrogative sentences are also called questions. An interrogative sentence begins with a capital letter and ends with a question mark.

Help children recognize that questions use words in a different order than most declarative sentences. Rather than *Pam can run fast,* a question puts a verb before the subject: *Can Pam run fast?* When they practice, help children ask questions with appropriate subject-verb inversion.

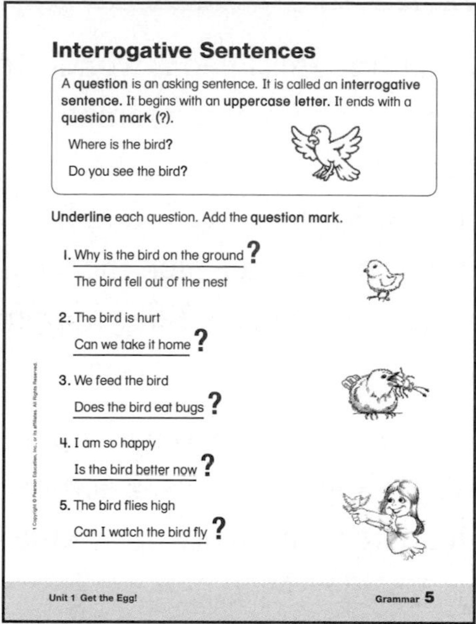

Interrogative Sentences

A **question** is an asking sentence. It is called an **interrogative sentence.** It begins with an **uppercase letter.** It ends with a **question mark** (?).

Where is the bird?

Do you see the bird?

Underline each question. Add the **question mark.**

1. Why is the bird on the ground?
   The bird fell out of the nest
2. The bird is hurt
   Can we take it home?
3. We feed the bird
   Does the bird eat bugs?
4. I am so happy
   Is the bird better now?
5. The bird flies high
   Can I watch the bird fly?

Unit 1 Get the Egg! Grammar 5

Grammar Transparency 5 TR DVD

MODEL Display Grammar Transparency 5. Read the definition aloud. Model why each example is an interrogative sentence. Then read the directions and model number 1.

GUIDE PRACTICE Continue with items 2–5, having children identify which group of words is a question and adding a question mark.

APPLY Have the class complete these sentence frames orally with the words *what, why,* and *where.*

> _______ **do you see wild animals?**
> _______ **do you like to watch animals?**
> _______ **wild animals can you see?**
> _______ **are some wild animals?**

Team Talk Pair children and have them ask each other questions about animals. Have them say "Question" before they ask a question and "Answer" before they respond to a question.

Realistic Story

Mini-Lesson Read Like a Writer

■ **Introduce** This week you will write a **realistic story.** A realistic story is made up, but it is like real life. **Characters** in a realistic story do things that real people and animals do.

Prompt Think about animals in neighborhoods. Write a realistic story about two friends seeing an animal.

Trait Organization

Mode Narrative

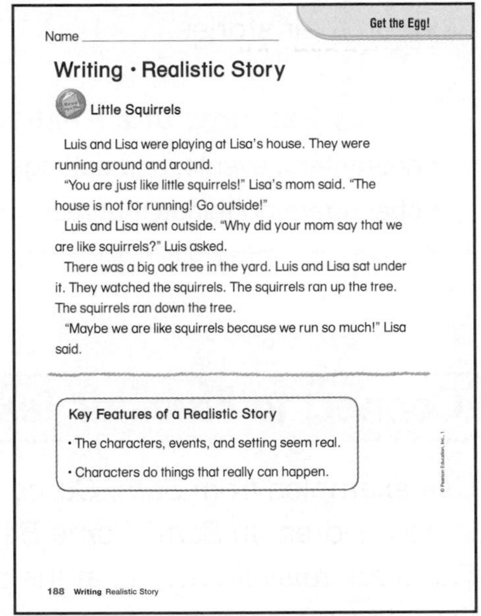

Name ____________ Get the Egg!

Writing • Realistic Story

Little Squirrels

Luis and Lisa were playing at Lisa's house. They were running around and around.

"You are just like little squirrels!" Lisa's mom said. "The house is not for running! Go outside!"

Luis and Lisa went outside. "Why did your mom say that we are like squirrels?" Luis asked.

There was a big oak tree in the yard. Luis and Lisa sat under it. They watched the squirrels. The squirrels ran up the tree. The squirrels ran down the tree.

"Maybe we are like squirrels because we run so much!" Lisa said.

Key Features of a Realistic Story

- The characters, events, and setting seem real.
- Characters do things that really can happen.

188 Writing Realistic Story

Reader's and Writer's Notebook, p. 188

■ **Examine Model Text** Let's listen to a realistic story. Track the print as you read aloud "Little Squirrels" on *Reader's and Writer's Notebook,* p. 188. Have children follow along.

■ **Key Features** Who are the three characters in this story? (Luis, Lisa, and Lisa's mom) Help children find and circle the names. Ask if Luis and Lisa act like real children. (yes) Help children underline short phrases in the story that tell about the characters acting like real children, such as *They were running* and *Luis and Lisa sat.* Then ask what the **setting** is—where and when the story takes place. (Lisa's house and yard during the day) Point out the word *yard.* Ask if yards in real life have big trees and squirrels. (yes)

This story has characters who are like real people. The writer told events that are like things that can really happen. The place is like someone's real home.

The story has a beginning, middle, and end. At the beginning, Luis and Lisa play. In the middle, they go outside and watch the squirrels. At the end, Lisa answers Luis's question.

Writing to Sources Use More Connect the Texts on pp. 221–259 to guide children in writing text-based responses within various forms and modes.

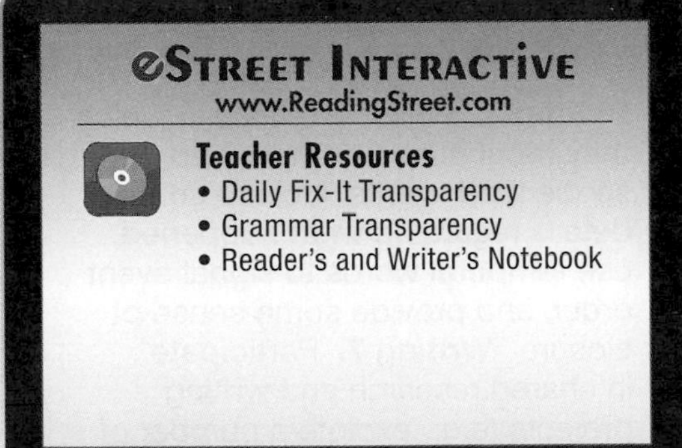

Write Guy *by Jeff Anderson*

What Do You Notice?

When children are examining the model text, ask, *What do you notice?* By giving children the responsibility of commenting on what they find effective in the text, they build self-confidence and often begin to notice features of the writing they might not have otherwise.

Bridge to Common Core

TEXT TYPES AND PURPOSES

This week children write a realistic story about two friends watching an animal.

Narrative Writing

As children develop writing skills for creating a realistic story, they write about real experiences and events. The activities help children develop well-chosen details and well-structured event sequences as they write about friends seeing an animal in their neighborhood.

Throughout the week, children will improve the range and content of their writing through daily mini-lessons.

5-Day Plan

DAY 1	Read Like a Writer
DAY 2	Organization
DAY 3	Writer's Craft: Time and Order Words
DAY 4	Revise: Adding a Sentence
DAY 5	Proofread

Common Core State Standards

Writing 3. Write narratives in which they recount two or more appropriately sequenced events, include some details regarding what happened, use temporal words to signal event order, and provide some sense of closure. **Writing 7.** Participate in shared research and writing projects (e.g., explore a number of "how-to" books on a given topic and use them to write a sequence of instructions). **Writing 8.** With guidance and support from adults, recall information from experiences or gather information from provided sources to answer a question.

Writing

Review Key Features

Review key features of a realistic story with children. You may want to post these key features in the classroom to allow children to refer to them as they work on their stories.

Key Features of a Realistic Story

- characters, events, and settings seem real
- characters do things that really can happen

Connect to Familiar Texts

Use examples from *Sam, Come Back!* (Unit 1) or another realistic story familiar to children. In *Sam, Come Back!,* the characters are people and their pets. There are realistic events at the beginning (Sam the cat sits on a woman's lap), the middle (Sam runs around the yard and house), and the end (Sam comes back to sit on the woman's lap). The setting, a house and yard during the day, is a realistic place for people and their pets.

Routine Quick Write for Fluency

Team Talk

1. **Talk** Read these questions aloud, and give children two minutes to name as many animals as they can think of.
   What animals live around our school?
   What animals live around your home?
2. **Write** Have children write one short sentence about an animal that lives around the school and one about an animal that lives around their home.
3. **Share** Partners can read their sentences to one another.

Routines Flip Chart

Research and Inquiry

Step 1 Identify and Focus Topic

TEACH Display and review the concept map about this week's question: *Which wild animals live in our neighborhood?* How might you find out which wild animals live in our neighborhood? Ask children to share their ideas. Point out that they can learn by observing.

Think Aloud **MODEL** When I observe, I watch carefully with a purpose in mind. If I want to find out about the wild animals in our neighborhood, I might look out the window and observe the animals that pass by. As I observe the animals, questions come to mind. For example, if I see a bird, I might ask myself, *What kind of nest does this bird have?* If I see a squirrel, I might ask, *What does the squirrel eat?*

GUIDE PRACTICE Guide children to think of other questions. Record children's questions in a chart.

Name ______ Get the Egg!

Look at the lists.
Follow the directions and **answer** the questions.

Wild Animals	Pets
bear	cat
fox	dog
frog	fish
lion	frog
tiger	hamster

1. Think of two more wild animals. Write the animal names. **Accept any wild animals**
2. Think of two more pets. Write the animal names. **Accept any pets**
3. Circle the animal that you would like to know more about. Share your choice with the class. **Responses will vary.**
4. Think about what else you want to know about your animal. Write two questions. **Questions will vary. Possible responses: Where do tigers live? What do tigers eat?**

Home Activity Your child learned how to identify topics and ask questions about a topic. Ask your child to make up another question about one of the topics above.

194 Research Identify Topics

Reader's and Writer's Notebook, p. 194

ON THEIR OWN Use *Reader's and Writer's Notebook,* p. 194.

eStreet Interactive
www.ReadingStreet.com
Teacher Resources
• Let's Practice It!
• Reader's and Writer's Notebook

21st Century Skills

Internet Guy *Don Leu*

Weekly Inquiry Project

STEP 1	Identify and Focus Topic
STEP 2	Research Skill
STEP 3	Gather and Record Information
STEP 4	Synthesize
STEP 5	Communicate

Wrap Up Your Day!

- ✔ **Phonics: Short *e*: *e*** Write *met* and *egg*. Ask children what sound the *e* in *met* and the *e* in *egg* has. (short *e*)
- ✔ **Spelling: Short *e* Words** Have children name the letter that spells each sound in *red* and write the word. Continue with *net, leg,* and *bed.*
- ✔ **Content Knowledge** Ask children to recall the Read Aloud "The Pecking Hen." How does the hen protect itself? (It pecks.)
- ✔ **Homework** Send home this week's Family Times Newsletter from Let's Practice It! pp. 57–58 on the *Teacher Resources DVD-ROM.*

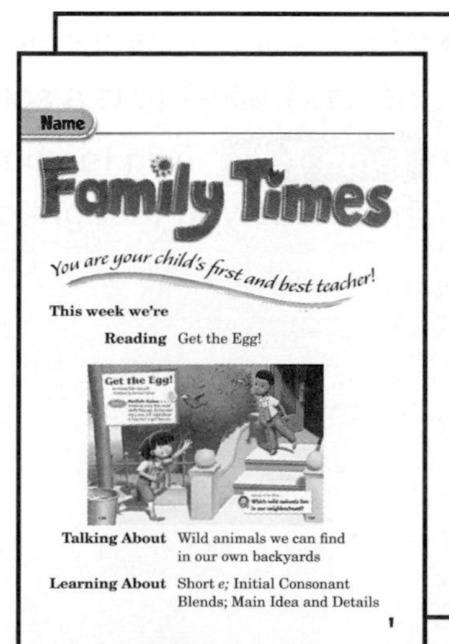
Name
Family Times
You are your child's first and best teacher!
This week we're
Reading Get the Egg!
Talking About Wild animals we can find in our own backyards
Learning About Short *e*; Initial Consonant Blends; Main Idea and Details
1

Let's Practice It!
TR DVD•57–58

Tell children that tomorrow they will read about two children who help a family of birds that live in their neighborhood.

DAY 2 at a Glance

Content Knowledge
Oral Vocabulary

Phonemic Awareness
Segment and Blend Phonemes

Phonics/Spelling
Short *e: e*
Initial Consonant Blends

High-Frequency Words
saw, small, tree, your

Selection Vocabulary
bird
Sort Words

Text-Based Comprehension
Main Idea and Details
Story Structure

Conventions
Interrogative Sentences

Writing
Realistic Story
Writing Trait: Organization

Handwriting
Letter *Ee*/Letter Size

Research and Inquiry
Research Skill: List

Materials

- Student Edition
- Sing with Me Big Book
- Big Book
- Sound-Spelling Cards
- Decodable Reader 5B
- Reader's and Writer's Notebook

Common Core State Standards

Speaking/Listening 2. Ask and answer questions about key details in a text read aloud or information presented orally or through other media. **Language 5.c.** Identify real-life connections between words and their use (e.g., note places at home that are *cozy*). **Also Language 6.**

Content Knowledge

Neighborhood Animals

EXPAND THE CONCEPT To reinforce concepts and to focus children's attention, have them sing "Time to Hatch" from the *Sing with Me* Big Book. What do the baby birds see? (a pond, feeders filled with seed, bushes where they can hide)

Build Oral Language

INTRODUCE AMAZING WORDS Display the Big Book *Jungle Drum.* Read the title and identify the author and illustrator. Explain that the author uses some Amazing Words in this story. Read the story and have children listen for the word *chirp.*

Big Book

TALK ABOUT SENTENCES AND WORDS Reread this sentence from the Big Book.

The insects stop singing, chirping, buzzing, whining, screaming.

- Have children repeat the sentence with you. What does this sentence mean? (The insects stop making noise.)
- What other words could be used instead of *chirping?* Have children share their suggestions.
- Why do you think the author chose the word *chirping* to describe a sound that insects make? (It is a sound the author must have heard an insect make.)
- 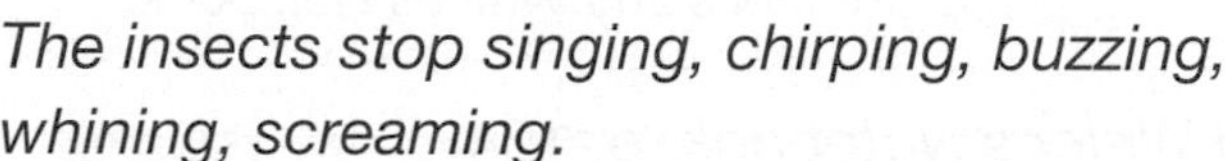 **Team Talk** Turn to your partner and say the sentence again using one of the words you thought of.

Build Oral Vocabulary

Amazing Words — Robust Vocabulary Routine

1. **Introduce the Word** Relate the word *chirp* to the story. The insects sing, *chirp,* and buzz in the jungle. Supply a child-friendly definition. A *chirp* is a short, sharp sound made by a small bird or insect. Have children say the word.
2. **Demonstrate** Provide examples to show meaning. I can hear birds *chirp* in the early morning. Crickets *chirp* in the evening in late summer.
3. **Apply** Have children demonstrate their understanding. What other animals *chirp?* Can you make a *chirping* sound? Let's try it.
4. **Display the Word** Point out the final *p*/p/ in the word.

Routines Flip Chart

ADD TO THE CONCEPT MAP Discuss what children have learned about the animals that live in their neighborhoods.

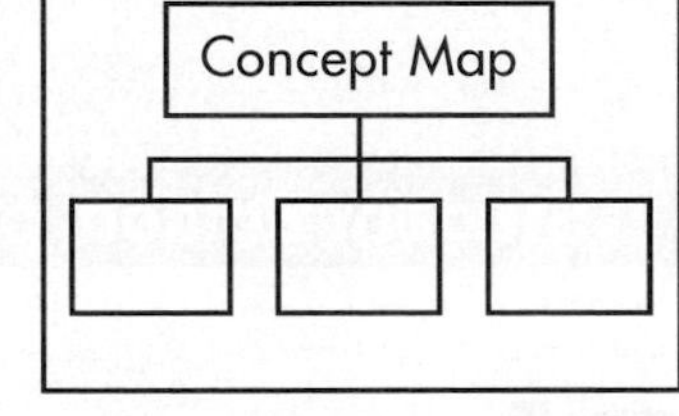

- Recall the song "Time to Hatch." What kind of habitat do the newly hatched birds live in? (a backyard, a park)
- What do the new birds need to survive? (water, food, shelter) What are some things in their habitat that they need? (pond, bird feeders, bushes to hide in) Let's add *pond for water, bird feeders,* and *bushes to hide in* to our map.
- In yesterday's Read Aloud, "The Pecking Hen," what kind of animal did we read about? (a hen) Let's add *hen* to our map. What kind of habitat do the hens live in? (chicken pen) We can add *chicken pen* to the map. How do you think the hen hatches her eggs? (She sits on them.) Let's add *hatches eggs* to the concept map.

Amazing Words

habitat	chirp
hatch	croak
survive	moist

Access for All

SI Strategic Intervention

Sentence Production If children do not pronounce the /ėr/ sound in the middle of the word *chirp,* say the sentence containing the word, stressing the sound /ėr/. Have children repeat it.

ELL

Reinforce Vocabulary Use the Day 2 instruction on ELL Poster 5 to reinforce the meanings of high-frequency words.

Physical Response Teach the word *chirp* by making a chirping sound and having children join you. To reinforce understanding, look for opportunities to recycle language in the day's lessons. For example, invite children to make chirping sounds when they see animals that make chirping sounds outside during recess.

Common Core State Standards
Foundational Skills 2.c. Isolate and pronounce initial, medial vowel, and final sounds (phonemes) in spoken single-syllable words. **Also Foundational Skills 2.b., 2.d.**

Phonemic Awareness

Let's Listen for

Sounds

- Find three things that rhyme with *tack*.
- Find five things that contain the short *e* sound. Say each word.
- Find something that rhymes with *best*. Say each sound in that word.
- Find something that starts with the sounds /spr/.

Read Together

READING STREET ONLINE
SOUND-SPELLING CARDS
www.ReadingStreet.com

122

123

Student Edition, pp. 122–123

Common Core State Standards

Foundational Skills 2.b. Orally produce single-syllable words by blending sounds (phonemes), including consonant blends. **Foundational Skills 2.d.** Segment spoken single-syllable words into their complete sequence of individual sounds (phonemes). **Also Foundational Skills 2.c., 3.**

Skills Trace

Initial Consonant Blends

Introduce U1W5D2

Practice U1W5D3; U1W5D4

Reteach/Review U1W5D5; U1W6D4

Assess/Test Weekly Test U1W5
Benchmark Test U1

KEY: U=Unit W=Week D=Day

Phonemic Awareness

Segment and Blend Phonemes

MODEL Read the last bulleted point on page 122. The boy is spraying the dog. The first sounds in *spray* are /s/ /p/ /r/. Have children find another item whose name begins with /s/ /p/ /r/. (sprinkler)

Listen to the sounds in *spray:* /s/ /p/ /r/ /ā/. There are four sounds in *spray.* Let's blend those sounds: /s/ /p/ /r/ /ā/, *spray.* Continue with *tree* and *steps.*

GROUP PRACTICE Guide children as they segment and blend these words from the picture: *black, blue, sled, spray, steps, frog, tracks.*

Corrective feedback	**If...** children make an error, **then...** model by segmenting the word, and have them repeat.

ON THEIR OWN Have children segment and blend the following words.

bread /b/ /r/ /e/ /d/ **flat** /f/ /l/ /a/ /t/ **speck** /s/ /p/ /e/ /k/

Phonics

Teach/Model

Initial Consonant Blends

CONNECT Write *sip* and *lip.* You studied words like this already. What do you know about the beginning sounds of these words? (They are consonant sounds. The sound /s/ is spelled *s.* The sound /l/ is spelled *l.*) Today you will learn to spell and read words that begin with two consonant sounds.

Sound-Spelling Card 41

USE SOUND-SPELLING CARD Display Card 41. The sounds you hear at the beginning of *train* are /t/ /r/. The sounds /t/ /r/ are spelled *tr.* Have children say /t/ /r/ several times as you point to *tr.*

MODEL Write *slip.* I see that this word has two consonants at the beginning. Point to the letters *s* and *l.* The two sounds /s/ and /l/ are blended together. This is how I blend this word. Segment and blend *slip.* Follow this procedure to model blending *black* and *stop.*

GROUP PRACTICE Continue the process with the words below. This time have children blend with you.

crop	flick	smell	stick	brag	drill
glad	fret	grin	spell	block	prod

REVIEW What do you know about reading these words? (The two consonant sounds at the beginning of each word are blended together.)

eStreet Interactive
www.ReadingStreet.com

Pearson eText
- Student Edition

Interactive Sound-Spelling Cards

Access for All

SI Strategic Intervention

Initial Consonant Blends If children have difficulty blending initial consonant sounds, have them repeat as you pronounce words with initial *bl* and *st* blends, such as *blue* and *stay,* elongating the initial consonant sounds.

A Advanced

Extend Word Blending If children are able to blend words easily and independently, challenge them with more difficult words, such as *snowy, slipper, frighten,* and *broken.*

Vocabulary Support

You may wish to explain the meanings of these words.

fret to worry about something

prod to get someone to do something either by talking to the person or poking the person with your finger

Visual Support Model isolating sounds while using the pictures on pp. 122–123 of the Student Edition as visual support. For example: /p/ /r/ /i/ /n/ /t/ /s/, *prints.* Who can point to the foot*prints*? Now let's say the sounds of *prints* together: /p/ /r/ /i/ /n/ /t/ /s/.

Common Core State Standards

Foundational Skills 2.b. Orally produce single-syllable words by blending sounds (phonemes), including consonant blends. **Foundational Skills 3.** Know and apply grade-level phonics and word analysis skills in decoding words. **Also Foundational Skills 3.a., 3.b.**

Spelling Pattern

Consonant Blends When a blended sound is heard at the beginning or end of a word, two or three consonants spell that sound.

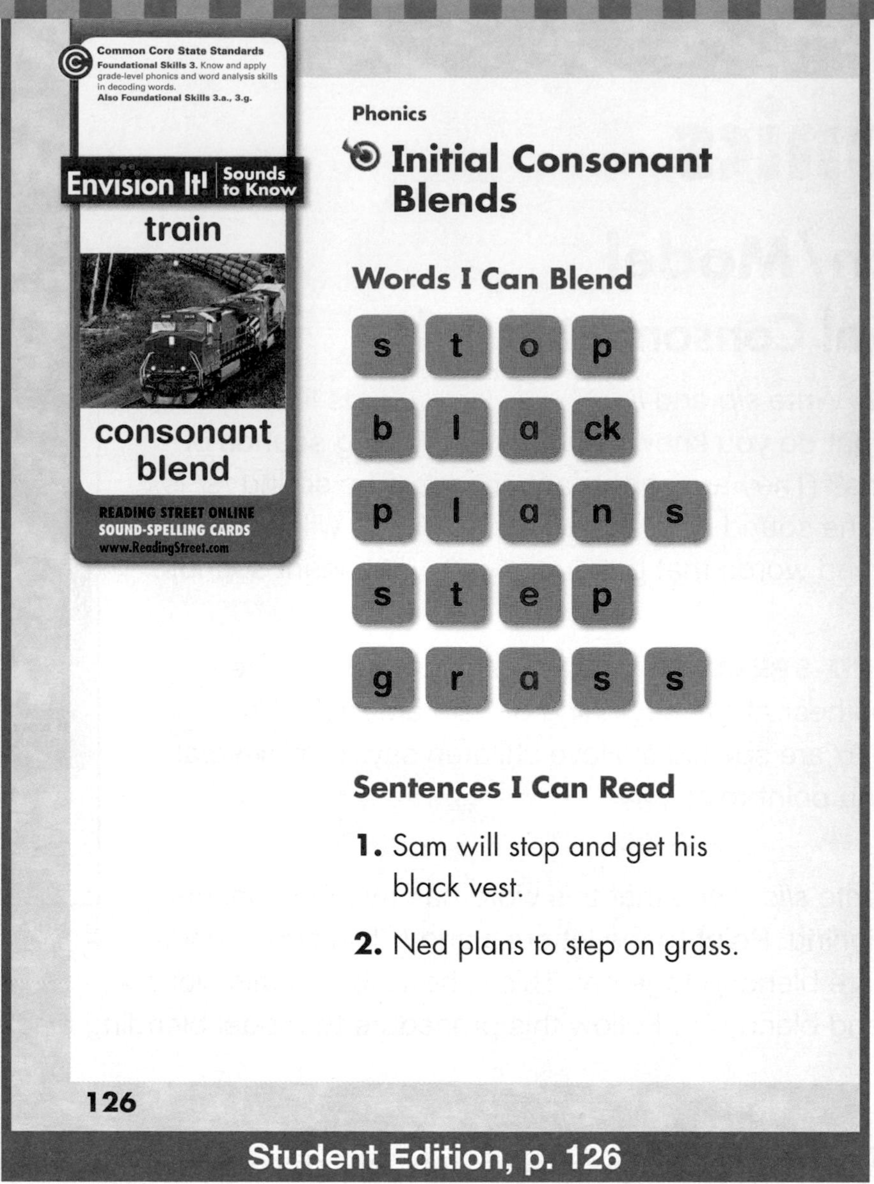

Common Core State Standards
Foundational Skills 3. Know and apply grade-level phonics and word analysis skills in decoding words.
Also Foundational Skills 3.a., 3.g.
Envision It! Sounds to Know
train
consonant blend
READING STREET ONLINE
SOUND-SPELLING CARDS
www.ReadingStreet.com
Phonics
Initial Consonant Blends
Words I Can Blend
s t o p
b l a ck
p l a n s
s t e p
g r a s s
Sentences I Can Read
1. Sam will stop and get his black vest.
2. Ned plans to step on grass.
126

Student Edition, p. 126

Phonics

Guide Practice

BLEND WORDS Have children turn to page 126 in their Student Edition. Look at the picture on this page. The picture shows a *train.* When I say *train,* I hear /t/ /r/ at the beginning. The sounds /t/ /r/ are spelled *tr.*

GROUP PRACTICE For each word in "Words I Can Blend," ask for the sound of each letter or group of letters. Make sure that children identify the correct sounds for the consonant blends. Then have children blend the whole word.

Corrective feedback | **If...** children have difficulty blending a word, **then...** model blending the word, and ask children to blend it with you.

DECODE WORDS IN ISOLATION After children can successfully segment and blend the words, ask them to read the words naturally.

DECODE WORDS IN CONTEXT Have children read each of the sentences. Have them identify words in the sentences that begin with consonant blends.

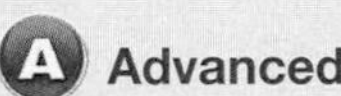

Pair children and have them take turns reading each of the sentences aloud.

ON THEIR OWN Use *Reader's and Writer's Notebook,* p. 189.

Initial Consonant Blends

FORMATIVE ASSESSMENT Write the following words and have the class read them. Notice which children miss words during the group reading. Call on those individuals to read some of the words.

					Spiral Review
flip	**glass**	**clock**	**block**	**slip** ←	Row 1 reviews initial *l* blends.
grin	**frog**	**track**	**crab**	**dress** ←	Row 2 reviews initial *r* blends.
skip	**snap**	**stack**	**spot**	**swim** ←	Row 3 reviews initial *s* blends.

If... children cannot blend words with initial consonant blends,

then... use the Small Group Time Strategic Intervention lesson, p. SG•76, to reteach words with initial consonant blends. Continue to monitor children's progress using other instructional opportunities during the week. See the Skills Trace on p. 126c.

Access for All

A Advanced

Extend Blending If children are able to blend initial consonants easily and independently, then have them work with a partner to create short tongue twisters with words that have initial consonant blends. Children can present their tongue twisters to the class.

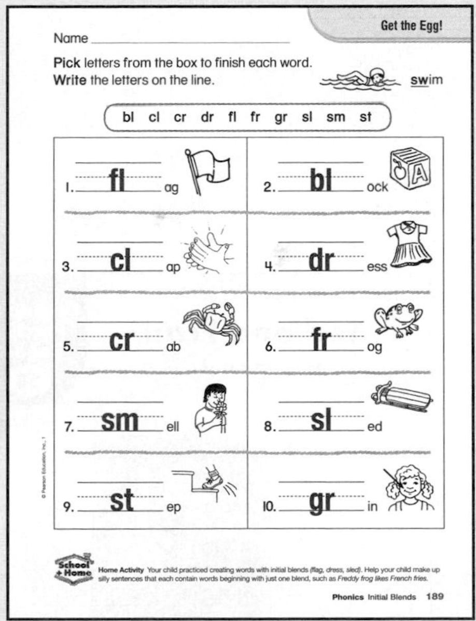

Get the Egg!

Name ______

Pick letters from the box to finish each word.
Write the letters on the line.

swim

bl cl cr dr fl fr gr sl sm st

1. fl ag	2. bl ock
3. cl ap	4. dr ess
5. cr ab	6. fr og
7. sm ell	8. sl ed
9. st ep	10. gr in

School + Home. Home Activity Your child practiced creating words with initial blends (flag, dress, sled). Help your child make up silly sentences that each contain words beginning with just one blend, such as Freddy frog likes French fries.

Phonics Initial Blends 189

Reader's and Writer's Notebook, p. 189

Initial Consonant Blends Initial *s* blends do not appear in Cantonese, Hmong, Khmer, Korean, Spanish, or Vietnamese. Spanish speakers especially may add a short *e* sound at the beginning of words such as *step* and *spin.* Help children practice blending the sounds in words with initial *s* blends, such as *skid, slim, smack, snip, spot, stick,* and *swim.*

Common Core State Standards

Foundational Skills 3. Know and apply grade-level phonics and word analysis skills in decoding words. **Foundational Skills 3.b.** Decode regularly spelled one-syllable words. **Foundational Skills 4.** Read with sufficient accuracy and fluency to support comprehension.

Decodable Reader 5B

If children need help, then...

Read *Ted and Fran*

DECODE WORDS IN ISOLATION Have children turn to page 201. Have children decode each word.

REVIEW HIGH-FREQUENCY WORDS Review the previously taught words *the, you, green,* and *a.* Have children read each word as you point to it on the Word Wall.

PREVIEW Have children read the title and preview the story. Tell them they will read words with initial consonant blends in this story.

DECODE WORDS IN CONTEXT Pair children for reading and listen as they decode. One child begins. Children read the entire story, switching readers after each page. Partners reread the story. This time the other child begins.

Ted and Fran

Written by Peter Ross

Decodable Practice Reader 5B

Initial Consonant Blends

frog grass Fran
black spot(s) flip(s)
flop(s)

Consonants *ss*

grass

High-Frequency Words

a the green you

201

Decodable Practice Reader 5B

Ted is a frog in the grass.
Fran is a hen in the grass.

202

Ted is green with black spots.
Fran is red.

203

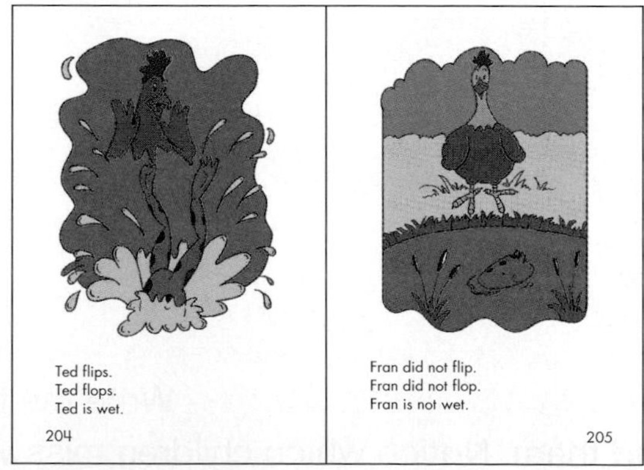

Ted flips.
Ted flops.
Ted is wet.

204

Fran did not flip.
Fran did not flop.
Fran is not wet.

205

Fran gets up.
Can you spot Fran?

206

Ted gets up.
Ted and Fran sat.

207

Ted did not get wet.
Fran did not get wet.

208

Corrective feedback	**If...** children have difficulty decoding a word, **then...** refer them to the Sound-Spelling Cards to identify the sounds in the word. Then prompt them to blend the word. • What is the new word? • Is the new word a word you know? • Does it make sense in the story?

CHECK DECODING AND COMPREHENSION Have children retell the story to include characters, setting, and events. Then have children locate words that have initial consonant blends in the story. List words that children name. Children should supply *frog, Fran, black, spot(s), grass, flip(s),* and *flop(s).* Explain that these words begin with two consonant sounds that are blended together, such as /fr/, /bl/, /fl/, /gr/, and /sp/, followed by a vowel and another consonant.

Reread for Fluency

REREAD DECODABLE READER Have children reread Decodable Practice Reader 5B to develop automaticity decoding words with initial consonant blends.

Routine Paired Reading

1. **Reread** To achieve optimal fluency, have partners reread the text three or four times.
2. **Corrective Feedback** Listen as children read. Provide corrective feedback regarding their fluency and decoding.

Routines Flip Chart

Access for All

SI Strategic Intervention

Retelling If children have difficulty retelling the story, ask them questions regarding events in the story.

Initial Consonant Blends

Beginning Before children read, lead them on a picture walk through *Ted and Fran.* Point out and pronounce the words that have initial consonant blends such as *frog, flips,* and *flops.* Have children say the words aloud.

Intermediate Before reading, help children pronounce the words with initial consonant blends such as *frog, Fran, grass,* and *flip(s).* Then have them use the words to make a prediction about what the story will be about.

Advanced After reading, have children use the words with initial consonant blends to create new sentences such as *Fran's pal is a frog named Ted.*

Common Core State Standards

Foundational Skills 2.d. Segment spoken single-syllable words into their complete sequence of individual sounds (phonemes). **Foundational Skills 3.** Know and apply grade-level phonics and word analysis skills in decoding words. **Foundational Skills 3.b.** Decode regularly spelled one-syllable words. **Language 2.d.** Use conventional spelling for words with common spelling patterns and for frequently occurring irregular words.

Phonics

Review Short Vowels

REVIEW SOUND-SPELLINGS Review the short vowel spelling patterns *a, e, i,* and *o,* using Sound-Spelling Cards 1, 6, 11, and 17.

DECODE WORDS IN ISOLATION Display these words. Have the class blend the words. Then point to the words in random order and ask children to decode them quickly.

set	**pill**	**red**
cat	**hot**	**kiss**
ran	**mad**	**pod**
bin	**peck**	**mess**

Corrective feedback Model blending decodable words and then ask children to blend them with you.

DECODE WORDS IN CONTEXT Display these sentences. Have the class read the sentences.

Team Talk Have pairs take turns reading the sentences naturally.

Ted sat on the **mat.**
Ben will not sit here.
Jan can get a **big pet.**

Spelling

Short *e* Words

GUIDE PRACTICE Tell children that you will segment the sounds in each spelling word. They should repeat the sounds in each word as they write the word. Check the spelling of each word before saying the next word.

1.	/m/ /e/ /n/	**men**	**6.**	/l/ /e/ /g/	**leg**
2.	/r/ /e/ /d/	**red**	**7.**	/j/ /e/ /t/	**jet**
3.	/s/ /t/ /e/ /p/	**step**	**8.**	/s/ /l/ /e/ /d/	**sled**
4.	/t/ /e/ /n/	**ten**	**9.**	/w/ /e/ /t/	**wet**
5.	/n/ /e/ /t/	**net**	**10.**	/b/ /e/ /d/	**bed**

ON THEIR OWN Use *Reader's and Writer's Notebook,* p. 190.

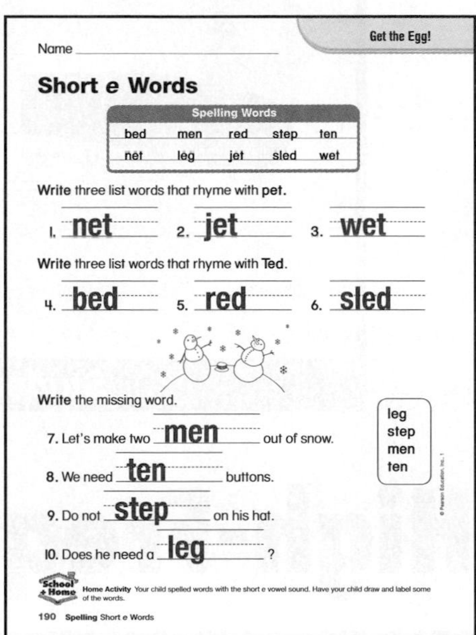
Name ____________ Get the Egg!

Short *e* Words

Spelling Words

bed	men	red	step	ten
net	leg	jet	sled	wet

Write three list words that rhyme with **pet**.

1. net 2. jet 3. wet

Write three list words that rhyme with **Ted**.

4. bed 5. red 6. sled

Write the missing word.

leg step men ten

7. Let's make two men out of snow.
8. We need ten buttons.
9. Do not step on his hat.
10. Does he need a leg ?

School + Home **Home Activity** Your child spelled words with the short e vowel sound. Have your child draw and label some of the words.

190 Spelling Short e Words

Reader's and Writer's Notebook, p. 190

Word Recognition Write the following words on the board: *peg, got, went, well.* Point to and read each word aloud and have children repeat. Tell children to point to the words that contain /e/.

Common Core State Standards

Foundational Skills 3. Know and apply grade-level phonics and word analysis skills in decoding words. **Foundational Skills 3.g.** Recognize and read grade-appropriate irregularly spelled words. **Language 5.a.** Sort words into categories (e.g., colors, clothing) to gain a sense of the concepts the categories represent. **Language 5.b.** Define words by category and by one or more key attributes (e.g., a *duck* is a bird that swims; a *tiger* is a large cat with stripes).

Access for All

Strategic Intervention

Pronunciation If children pronounce the /s/ sound in *saw* and *small* as /TH/, then say each word, clearly pronouncing the /s/, and have children repeat it. If children continue to have trouble, help them practice pronouncing /s/ alone, being certain their tongue is behind their front teeth, not between.

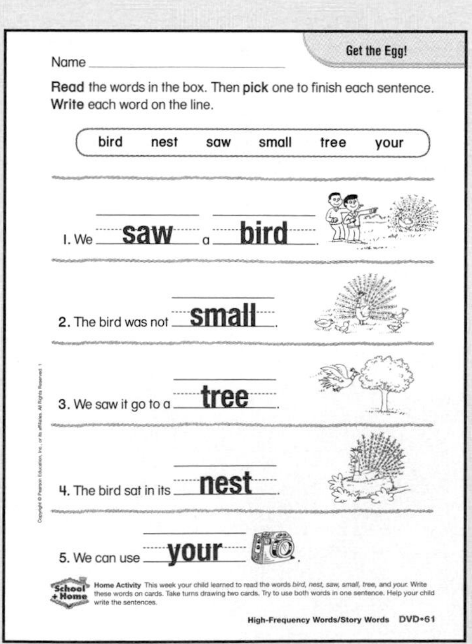
Get the Egg!

Name ________

Read the words in the box. Then **pick** one to finish each sentence. **Write** each word on the line.

bird nest saw small tree your

1. We **saw** a **bird**.
2. The bird was not **small**.
3. We saw it go to a **tree**.
4. The bird sat in its **nest**.
5. We can use **your** .

Home Activity This week your child learned to read the words *bird, nest, saw, small, tree,* and *your.* Write these words on cards. Take turns drawing two cards. Try to use both words in one sentence. Help your child write the sentences.

High-Frequency Words/Story Words DVD•61

Let's Practice It! TR DVD•61

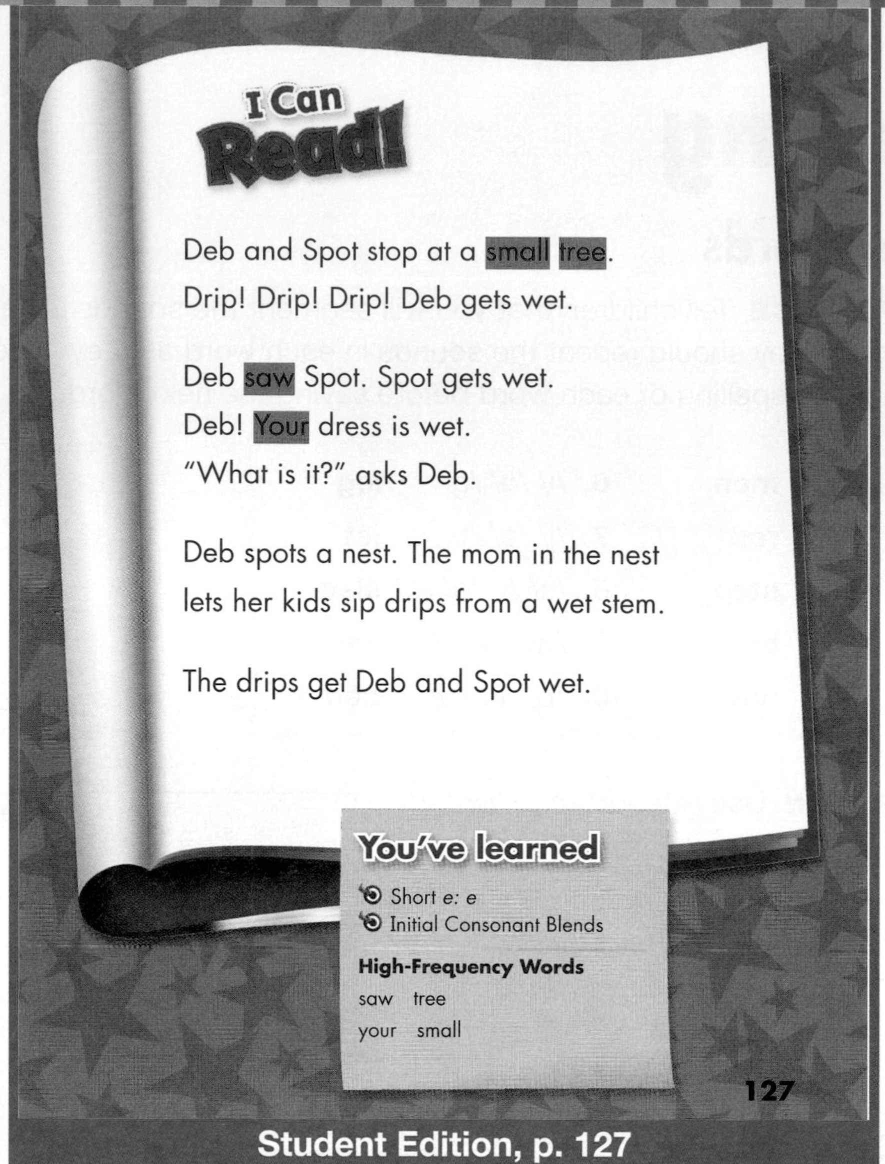
I Can Read!

Deb and Spot stop at a small tree.
Drip! Drip! Drip! Deb gets wet.

Deb saw Spot. Spot gets wet.
Deb! Your dress is wet.
"What is it?" asks Deb.

Deb spots a nest. The mom in the nest lets her kids sip drips from a wet stem.

The drips get Deb and Spot wet.

You've learned

Short *e: e*
Initial Consonant Blends

High-Frequency Words
saw tree
your small

127

Student Edition, p. 127

High-Frequency Words

READ WORDS IN ISOLATION Remind children that there are some words we learn by remembering the letters, rather than by saying the sounds. Then have them read each of the highlighted high-frequency words aloud.

READ WORDS IN CONTEXT Chorally read the "I Can Read!" passage along with children. Then have them read the passage aloud to themselves. When they are finished, ask children to reread the high-frequency words.

Team Talk Have children choose two high-frequency words and give them time to create a sentence in which both words are used properly. Then have them share their sentence with a partner.

ON THEIR OWN Use Let's Practice It! p. 61 on the *Teacher Resources DVD-ROM.*

Selection Vocabulary

INTRODUCE SELECTION WORD Use Vocabulary Transparency 5 to introduce this week's selection word. Read each sentence as you track the print. Frame the underlined word and explain its meaning. Have children read each sentence with you.

bird animal covered in feathers that has wings and two legs

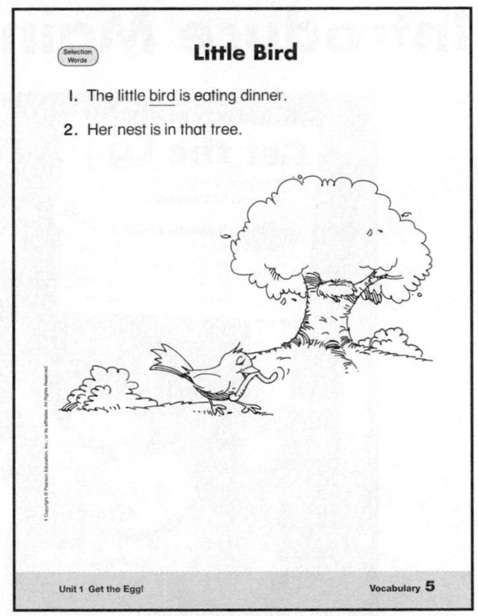
Selection Words

Little Bird

1. The little bird is eating dinner.
2. Her nest is in that tree.

Unit 1 Get the Egg! Vocabulary 5

Vocabulary Transparency 5 TR DVD

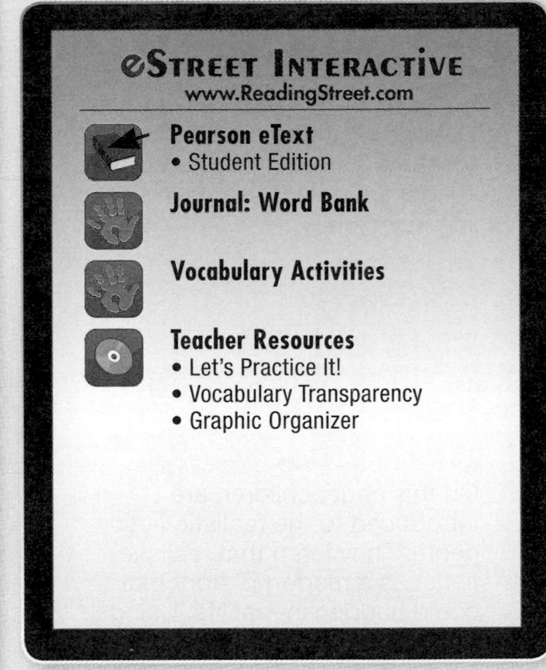

Vocabulary Strategy: Sort Words

TEACH Explain that **sort** means to put things into groups. Draw a three-column chart or display Graphic Organizer 5. Put these headings at the top of each column: *Animals with Fur, Animals with Feathers, Animals with Hard Outer Coverings.* Model how to begin adding animals to the chart.

Animals with Fur	Animals with Feathers	Animals with Hard Outer Coverings

Graphic Organizer 5

Think Aloud We are going to sort wild animals by whether they have fur, feathers, or hard outer coverings. I will name an animal and you will tell me what it looks like. Then we will decide what group it belongs in. I'll begin. Have children turn to page 121 in their Student Edition. These rabbits have fur. I'll write *rabbit* under *Animals with Fur.*

GUIDE PRACTICE Continue naming animals, and have children tell you which column to put them in. If necessary, display the last two pages of *Jungle Drum* to help children think of more animals to sort.

ON THEIR OWN Work with children to name and sort as many animals as possible.

Bridge to Common Core

VOCABULARY ACQUISITION AND USE
As children work with the selection vocabulary for this week, they acquire and use domain-specific words for reading, writing, speaking, and listening. Teaching the strategy of sorting helps children make real-life connections between words and their meanings. As children sort words, they gain a sense of the concepts the categories represent and an understanding of how words can relate.

Academic Vocabulary

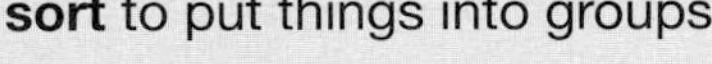

sort to put things into groups

Understand General Meaning
Have children listen as you read aloud p. 127 in the Student Edition. After reading, have them restate the general ideas in the passage using the familiar language of the high-frequency words. Have them ask questions about any unfamiliar situations in the passage.

Zoom in on

Text-Based Comprehension

Introduce Main Selection

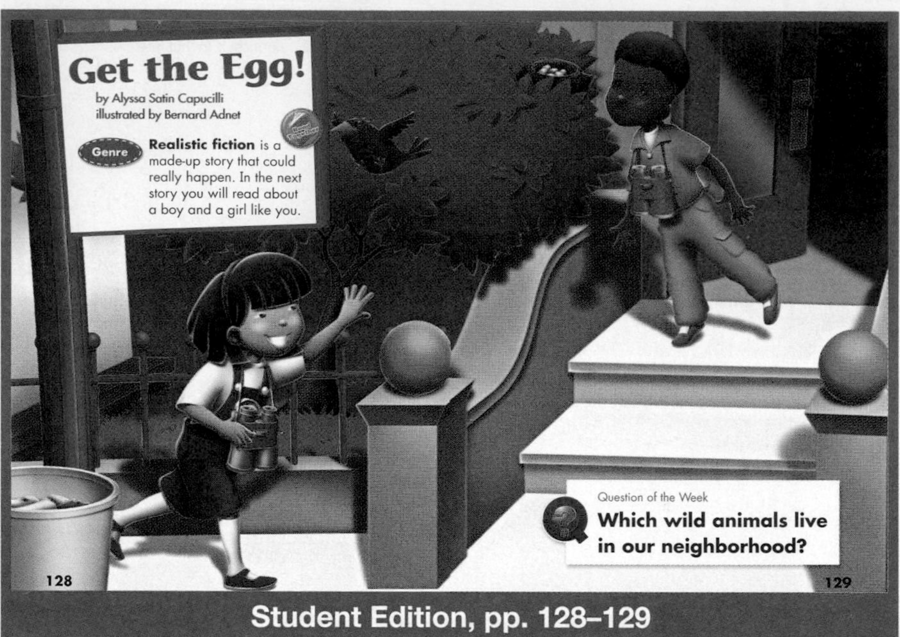
Get the Egg!
by Alyssa Satin Capucilli
illustrated by Bernard Adnet
Genre
Realistic fiction is a made-up story that could really happen. In the next story you will read about a boy and a girl like you.
Question of the Week
Which wild animals live in our neighborhood?
128
129
Student Edition, pp. 128–129

GENRE Realistic fiction is a made-up story that could happen in real life. As they read *Get the Egg!,* children should look for parts of the story that seem realistic to them.

PREVIEW AND PREDICT Have children identify the title of the story, the author, and the illustrator. Have children predict what the story will be about.

PURPOSE Setting a purpose helps us to think and understand more as we read. We will read this story to find out what happens to the egg.

STORY STRUCTURE Explain that good readers use strategies to help them make sense of a story. One strategy is to look for the most important parts of a story, such as the characters, the setting, and what happens. These parts are called the **story structure.** Have children turn to page EI•14 in their Student Edition.

Envision It! Visual Strategies Handbook
Story Structure
Beginning
Middle
End
Let's Think About Reading!
• What happens in the beginning?
• What happens in the middle?
• What happens in the end?
EI•14
Student Edition, p. EI•14

Think Aloud I can see that the characters include a wolf and three pigs. Three main events happen in the story: the wolf blows down the First Piggy's house; then he blows down the Second Piggy's house; but he can't blow down the Third Piggy's house.

Common Core State Standards

Literature 1. Ask and answer questions about key details in a text. **Literature 3.** Describe characters, settings, and major events in a story, using key details.

Bridge to Common Core

CRAFT AND STRUCTURE

On this page, children are introduced to the realistic fiction genre. They learn that realistic fiction is a made-up story that could happen in real life. Using the illustrations, children preview and predict what the selection will be about and set a purpose for reading. As they set a purpose, they analyze the structure of the text and the way the illustrations and text relate to each other to help them understand the content and style of the selection.

Academic Vocabulary

story structure the important parts of a story, including the characters, the setting, and the plot

Strategy Response Log

Genre Have children use page RR17 in their *Reader's and Writer's Notebook* to draw a picture of what they think will be the setting in the story. Have them discuss why they chose to draw their picture.

Access Main Selection

READER AND TASK SUGGESTIONS	
Preparing to Read the Text	**Leveled Tasks**
• Review initial consonant blends. Refer to the phonics lesson on p. 126. • Discuss dialogue in realistic fiction. • Model for children that reading rate may increase slightly during an exciting portion of the text.	• **Structure** If children have difficulty explaining how the text is organized, have them use the words *first, next, then,* and *finally* to retell the story. • **Language Conventionality and Clarity** Challenge children who have a clear understanding of the words used in the selection to identify a word that appeals to the senses.

See Text Complexity Measures for *Get the Egg!* on the tab at the beginning of this week.

READ Tell children that today they will read *Get the Egg!* for the first time. Use the Read for Understanding routine.

Routine Read for Understanding

Deepen understanding by reading the selection multiple times.

1. **First Read**—If children need support, then use the **Access Text** notes to help them clarify understanding.
2. **Second Read**—Use the **Close Reading** notes to help children draw knowledge from the text.

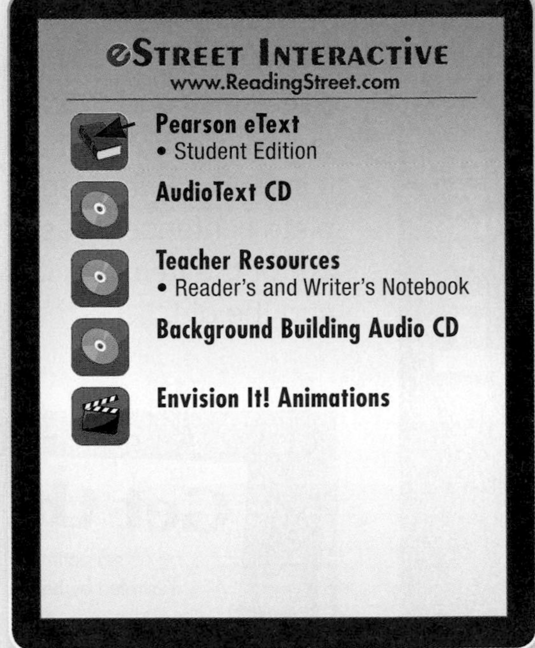

Preview Main Selection Ask children what they already know about birds and nests using the picture on pages 128–129. Then do a picture walk of the selection so children can talk about and see what happens in the nest.

1ST READ

Access Text © If children need help, then…

CONNECT TO CONCEPT Look at the picture on pages 128 and 129. What wild animal do you see? (a bird) Describe what the bird looks like and what it is doing. Encourage children to answer in complete sentences. Yes, the bird is red and flying out of the tree. Ask children to describe the boy and the girl.

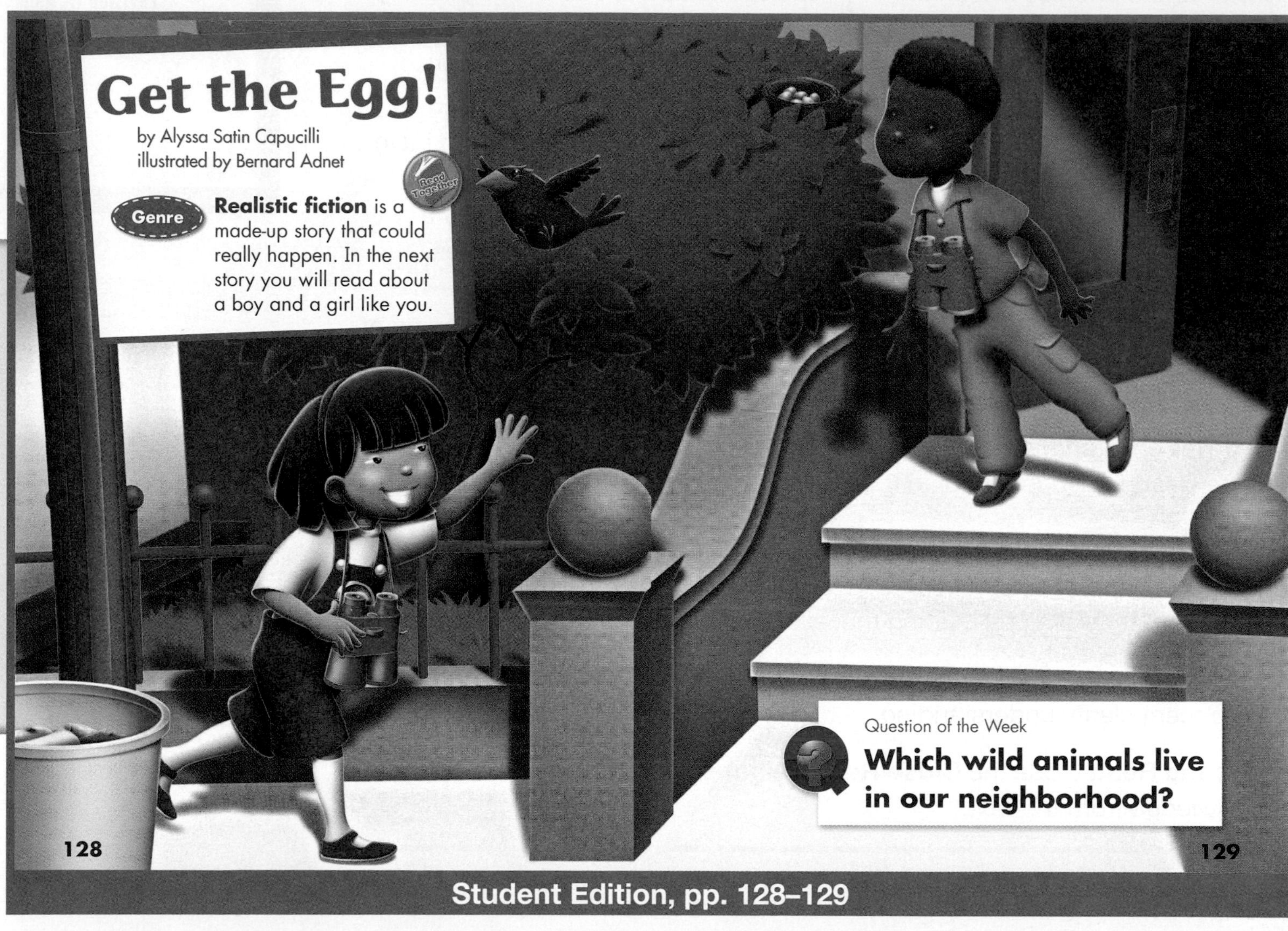

Get the Egg!
by Alyssa Satin Capucilli
illustrated by Bernard Adnet
Read Together
Genre
Realistic fiction is a made-up story that could really happen. In the next story you will read about a boy and a girl like you.
Question of the Week
Which wild animals live in our neighborhood?
128
129

Student Edition, pp. 128–129

2ND READ

Close Reading ©

ANALYSIS I see in the picture on pages 128 and 129 that the bird is leaving its nest. I wonder what will happen to the eggs while the bird is away. Using what you see in the picture, explain what you think may happen to the eggs. (Children should use the picture to explain their prediction, such as the boy and girl will observe the eggs.)

STORY STRUCTURE Remind children that good readers look for the important parts of a story—the characters, the setting, and the plot. Have children name the characters and the setting of the story.

CHECK HIGH-FREQUENCY WORDS How does the picture help you know what *tree* means? (The sentence says Brad is at the tree, and the picture shows Brad standing by leaves.)

Common Core State Standards
Literature 3. Describe characters, settings, and major events in a story, using key details. **Literature 7.** Use illustrations and details in a story to describe its characters, setting, or events.

Kim saw Brad at the tree.
A big red bird is in its nest, Kim.

130

Yes, Brad.
Six eggs sit in the nest.

131

Student Edition, pp. 130–131

ANALYSIS • TEXT EVIDENCE I see that Brad is holding his finger to his lips. What does that mean? (He wants Kim to be quiet and not talk.) Point to the picture and read the words that tell you that.

CONNECT TO SCIENCE Explain that a habitat is where an animal lives. It provides the animal with what it needs.

Team Talk Have partners discuss how the red bird gets what she needs from her habitat.

1ST READ

Access Text ©

If children need help, then...

MAIN IDEA AND DETAILS What are these pages of the story mostly about? What details tell you this? (Brad tries to save an egg that has fallen out of the nest. We know this because a twig hits the egg. Then Brad tries to grab the egg from where it has fallen.)

SORT VOCABULARY Have children recall the animals in *Get the Egg!* and *Jungle Drum.* Discuss how children might sort these animals. Explain that **sort** means to put things into groups.

Snap! A big twig hit the nest!
Snap, snap!
The big twig hit an egg!

132

Stop the egg, Brad. Stop it!
Can you get it?

133

Student Edition, pp. 132–133

2ND READ

Close Reading ©

ANALYSIS • TEXT EVIDENCE I see Brad in the picture on page 133. Where do you think he is? (leaning over the edge of the staircase into the bushes, looking for the egg that fell onto the branches) What clues in the picture tell you that? (He is surrounded by green leaves.)

MAIN IDEA AND DETAILS What is the main idea of this story? What details tell you this? (The story is about how Kim and Brad save a bird's egg. We know that the egg falls from the nest, that Brad uses his net to get it, and that Kim puts it back in the nest.)

STORY STRUCTURE • REREAD CHALLENGING TEXT What happens in this part of the story? What do Brad and Kim do? (Brad gets the egg in his net. Kim sets the egg in the nest.) Have children reread the pages to find the answer.

Common Core State Standards

Literature 1. Ask and answer questions about key details in a text. **Literature 3.** Describe characters, settings, and major events in a story, using key details. **Language 5.a.** Sort words into categories (e.g., colors, clothing) to gain a sense of the concepts the categories represent. **Also Language 5.b.**

The net! Get your net, Brad.
You can help.
Get the egg in your net.
134
Yes! You did it, Brad.
You can help, Kim.
Set the egg back in its nest.
135

Student Edition, pp. 134–135

ANALYSIS What words would you use to describe Brad and Kim? (kind, careful, interested in nature, helpful) Have children give examples of the characters' actions and words to support their ideas. Encourage them to use the pictures too.

1ST READ

Access Text Ⓒ If children need help, then...

SELECTION VOCABULARY Have children locate the selection word *bird* on page 136. Where is the bird in this part of the story? (back in the nest)

CROSS-TEXT EVALUATION

Use a Strategy to Self-Check How did the song "Time to Hatch" from the *Sing with Me* Big Book help you understand this selection?

Continue to DAY 2
Text-Based Comprehension
p. 137a

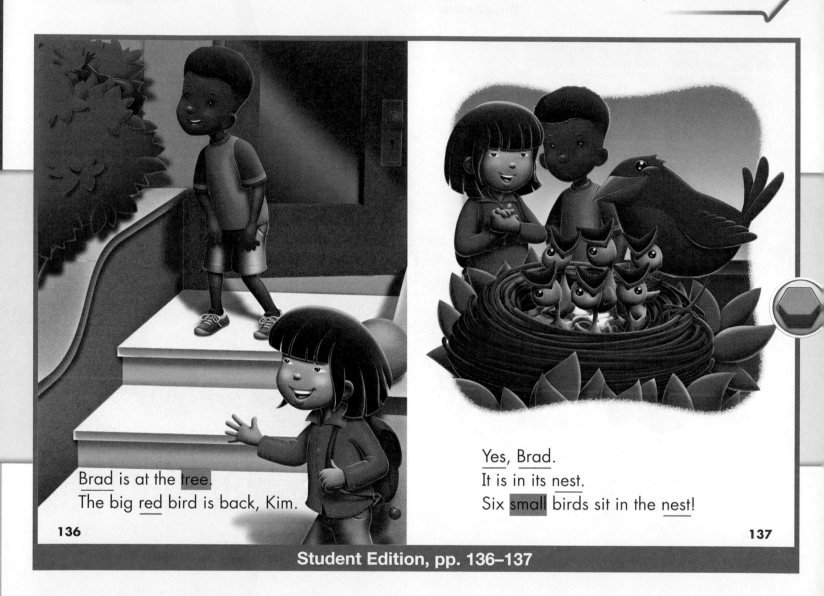

Brad is at the tree.
The big red bird is back, Kim.

136

Yes, Brad.
It is in its nest.
Six small birds sit in the nest!

137

Student Edition, pp. 136–137

2ND READ

Close Reading Ⓒ

SYNTHESIS • TEXT EVIDENCE Using what you learned in this selection, tell about wild animals that live in your neighborhood. Have children cite examples from the text.

Continue to DAY 3
Think Critically
pp. 138–139

Text-Based Comprehension

Check Understanding

Have children discuss each question with a partner. Ask several pairs to share their responses.

- ☑ **Realistic fiction** Do you think this story could happen in real life? (Yes, eggs can fall out of nests, and people can return the eggs safely to their nests if they're careful.)
- ☑ **Character** How do you think Brad and Kim feel at the end of the story? Why? (They're happy because all the eggs hatched safely, even the one that fell.)
- ☑ **Plot** What was the main problem in this story? How was it solved? (The main problem was that an egg fell out of the red bird's nest. It was solved when Brad got the egg into his net and Kim set the egg back in the nest.)
- ☑ **Confirm predictions** How did you use pictures or story clues to predict what would happen next in the story? (The pictures showed what was happening in the story, especially the picture that showed Brad reaching for the egg.)
- ☑ **Connect text to text** Kim and Brad help the bird by putting the egg back in the nest. Tell about other characters we have read about that help. (Ox helps Mom and Pop. The woman with the hat helps Pig.)

Common Core State Standards

Literature 1. Ask and answer questions about key details in a text. **Literature 3.** Describe characters, settings, and major events in a story, using key details. **Literature 7.** Use illustrations and details in a story to describe its characters, setting, or events. **Foundational Skills 4.a.** Read on-level text with purpose and understanding.

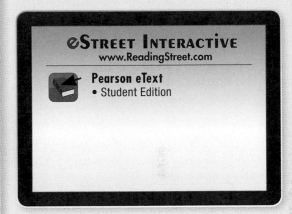

Access for All

SI Strategic Intervention

Story Structure If children have trouble discussing story structure, write *Characters, Setting,* and *Plot* as headings and read them aloud. As each is discussed, write notes under the appropriate heading.

ELL

Support Discussion Ask yes-or-no questions to start children's responses. For example: Are Brad and Kim happy at the end of the story? (yes) Extend language opportunities for children by asking follow-up questions, such as: Why? What has made them happy?

Day 2 SMALL GROUP TIME • Differentiate Comprehension, p. SG•69

OL On-Level	SI Strategic Intervention	A Advanced
• **Practice Phonics** Additional Words with Initial Consonant Blends • **Read** *Get the Egg!*	• **Reteach Phonics** Blend Words with Initial Consonant Blends • **Read** *Get the Egg!*	• **Extend Phonics** More Words with Initial Consonant Blends • **Read** *Get the Egg!* • **Investigate** Inquiry Project

ELL

If... children need more scaffolding and practice with the **Comprehension Skill,**
then... use the ELL activities on p. DI•101 in the Teacher Resources section on SuccessNet.

DAY 2

Common Core State Standards

Literature 4. Identify words and phrases in stories or poems that suggest feelings or appeal to the senses. **Foundational Skills 1.a.** Recognize the distinguishing features of a sentence (e.g., first word, capitalization, ending punctuation). **Language 1.** Demonstrate command of the conventions of standard English grammar and usage when writing or speaking. **Language 1.j.** Produce and expand complete simple and compound declarative, interrogative, imperative, and exclamatory sentences in response to prompts. **Language 2.b.** Use end punctuation for sentences.

Literary Text

Sensory Details

IDENTIFY SENSORY DETAILS IN A STORY Use the story *Get the Egg!* to have children identify sensory details in a story.

- In *Get the Egg!* we read about a bird. What color is the bird? (red)
- Is the bird big or small? (big)
- These details paint a picture of what the bird looks like. They help us see the bird in our mind's eye. Good readers use details from a story to help them visualize, or see, the characters, objects, and setting in their minds.

GUIDE PRACTICE Explain that the class will now think of other examples of details that paint a picture. Use Graphic Organizer 4, and write the heading *Eggs* in the top left column. Let's begin by thinking about the eggs in the nest. How many eggs were there? That's right, there were six. I'll write *six* under the heading *Eggs.* Were the eggs large or small? Yes, the eggs were small, so I'll write *small* in the same column. Repeat this process by directing children's attention to page 132. Write the heading *Twig* in the top right column. Have children identify the words that help them "hear" what happened to the twig. Authors sometimes use words that help us hear what happens. What words would we put in this column? *(Snap, snap!)*

Eggs	Twig

Graphic Organizer 4

ON THEIR OWN Arrange children into small groups and assign each group a previously read story from the Student Edition. Have them identify the details in the story that paint a picture in their minds. Have them share their information with the class.

Conventions

Interrogative Sentences

TEACH Write *Where were you born? I was born in New York.* on the board. Point to each word as you read it. Have children identify which sentence is a question. *(Where were you born?)* Continue with *I am six years old. How old are you? (How old are you?)* A question is an asking sentence. It begins with a capital letter. It ends with a question mark. Write a question mark.

GUIDE PRACTICE Write the following sentences on the board. Have children tell you which words should begin with a capital letter and where to put the question mark in each case.

1. **do you have a pet**
2. **have you seen a bird's nest**
3. **what animals do you like**
4. **have you been to a zoo**

Point out the word order in the questions, such as *Do you have,* rather than *You do have.* As children ask questions, guide them by encouraging appropriate word order in each question.

APPLY Have the class ask questions for which these statements could be answers.

I like a tiger the best.
Many wild animals have fur.
Some wild animals sleep in trees.

ON THEIR OWN Use *Reader's and Writer's Notebook,* p. 191.

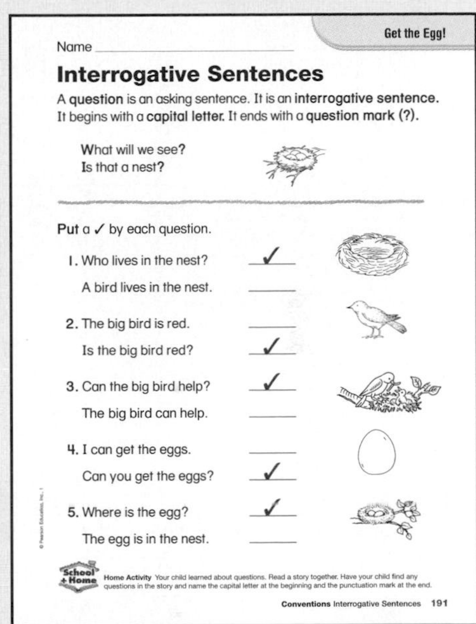
Name ______________ Get the Egg!

Interrogative Sentences

A **question** is an asking sentence. It is an **interrogative sentence.** It begins with a **capital letter.** It ends with a **question mark (?).**

What will we see?
Is that a nest?

Put a ✓ by each question.

1. Who lives in the nest? ✓
   A bird lives in the nest.
2. The big bird is red.
   Is the big bird red? ✓
3. Can the big bird help? ✓
   The big bird can help.
4. I can get the eggs.
   Can you get the eggs? ✓
5. Where is the egg? ✓
   The egg is in the nest.

Home Activity Your child learned about questions. Read a story together. Have your child find any questions in the story and name the capital letter at the beginning and the punctuation mark at the end.

Conventions Interrogative Sentences 191

Reader's and Writer's Notebook, p. 191

Daily Fix-It

3. i saw two men packing a sled
   I saw two men packing a sled.
4. I saw Pop stepp on a weet rock.
   I saw Pop step on a wet rock.

Discuss the Daily Fix-It corrections with children. Review sentence capitalization and punctuation and the spellings of *step* and *wet.*

Questions Unlike English, in Spanish questions begin and end with a question mark. Read the interrogative sentences on the board. Point out that in English, questions end with a question mark but do not begin with a question mark. Have children identify where the question mark belongs in each question.

Writing 3. Write narratives in which they recount two or more appropriately sequenced events, include some details regarding what happened, use temporal words to signal event order, and provide some sense of closure.

Realistic Story

Writing Trait: Organization

INTRODUCE THE PROMPT Review with children the key features of a realistic story. Point out that *Get the Egg!* is a realistic story. Assure them that they can make up a brief story with characters that seem real and a setting like a real place. Explain that today children will plan their own story with events that really could happen. It will be a story with a beginning, middle, and end. Read aloud the writing prompt.

Writing Prompt

Think about animals in neighborhoods. Write a realistic story about two friends seeing an animal.

GENERATE STORY IDEAS

To plan a new story, think of animals in our neighborhoods. Let's make a chart of animals and where they live in our neighborhoods. Display a T-chart or use Graphic Organizer 4. I'll start with the word *squirrel.*

Guide children in identifying animals and where they live in their neighborhoods. Possible ideas are shown. Record the responses, and keep the chart so that children can refer to it as they plan and draft their stories.

Animals in Our Neighborhoods	Where They Live
squirrel	nest, hollow
butterfly	garden
bird	nest
toad	pond
rabbit	warren

Graphic Organizer 4

Have each child choose an animal for a new story. Circulate to guide them. Have them make up names for children who will be their characters.

Mini-Lesson Organization

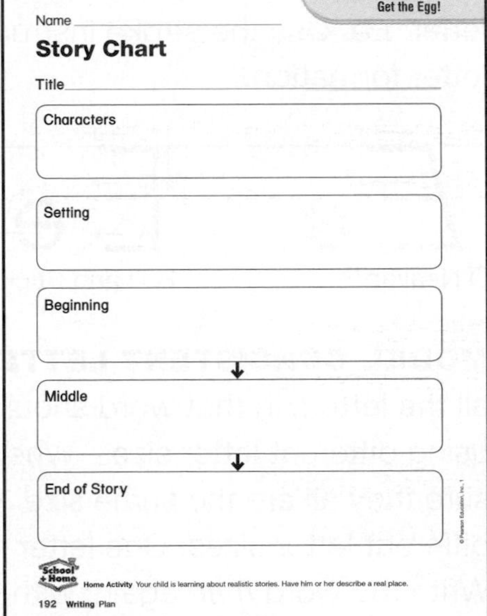
Get the Egg!
Name
Story Chart
Title
Characters
Setting
Beginning
Middle
End of Story
Home Activity Your child is learning about realistic stories. Have him or her describe a real place.
192 Writing Plan

Reader's and Writer's Notebook, p. 192

- **Introduce** Use *Reader's and Writer's Notebook,* p. 192 to model story planning. To plan a story, I can use a chart. I want to write about a butterfly, so I'm going to call my story *The Butterfly.* My characters will be a girl and boy who find a butterfly cocoon in a garden. I'll call my characters Ava and Tyler. I'll write the names in the *Characters* box. In the *Setting* box, I'll write *garden.* Now I will plan what happens in the beginning, middle, and end of my story. I will use the chart to help me put my story ideas in order.
- **Model** At the beginning, Ava and Tyler will find a cocoon in the garden. I'll write that in the *Beginning* box. In the middle of the story, they will put the cocoon in a big jar. They will watch the cocoon break open. I'll write that in the *Middle* box. At the end, they will let the butterfly go. Now I'll write that idea in the *End of Story* box. The chart has helped me put my ideas for the beginning, middle, and end of my story in order. Now plan for your story. Circulate to guide and assist children.

Routine Quick Write for Fluency

Team Talk

1. **Talk** Have children take two minutes to tell their story events to a partner.
2. **Write** Each child writes one short sentence for the beginning, one for the middle, and one for the end of the planned story.
3. **Share** Each child reads the story ideas to the partner.

Routines Flip Chart

eSTREET INTERACTIVE
www.ReadingStreet.com
Teacher Resources
- Graphic Organizer
- Reader's and Writer's Notebook

Write Guy *by Jeff Anderson*

Writers Write!

Young writers succeed in classrooms where they write. Children need to read every day and to write every day. Teachers do not need to read and assess everything that children write.

Access for All

SI Strategic Intervention

Planning Story Ideas If children find it difficult to think of a story idea, have them think about times they have seen an animal in their neighborhood. They can base their story idea on something that really happened.

Support Prewriting

Beginning Have children draw and label three story events (beginning, middle, end) and share with a partner, possibly one who speaks the same home language.

Intermediate Have children write phrases to express three story event ideas (beginning, middle, end). Have them describe the story plan to other children.

Advanced Have children write short sentences in their story charts. As they share the plan with partners, children can clarify and add ideas.

Common Core State Standards

Writing 7. Participate in shared research and writing projects (e.g., explore a number of "how-to" books on a given topic and use them to write a sequence of instructions). **Writing 8.** With guidance and support from adults, recall information from experiences or gather information from provided sources to answer a question. **Language 1.a.** Print all uppercase and lowercase letters.

Name ________ Get the Egg!

E e

Copy the words. Write the letters the correct size.

Emma	Emma	red	red
set	set	ten	ten
leg	leg	vest	vest
bed	bed	hen	hen
fell	fell	jet	jet
net	net	den	den
hem	hem	get	get

Did you write all of your letters the correct size? Yes No

Handwriting 193

Reader's and Writer's Notebook, p. 193

Handwriting

Letter *Ee*/Letter Size

MODEL LETTER FORMATION Display uppercase and lowercase letter: *Ee.* Use the stroke instructions pictured below to model proper letter formation.

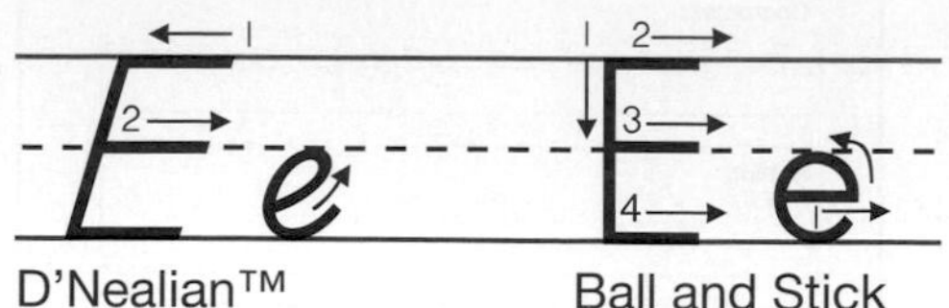

D'Nealian™ Ball and Stick

MODEL CONSISTENT LETTER SIZE Explain that when we write a word, all the letters in that word should be the same size. Write the word *man* using different letter sizes. When I write the letters in a word, I need to make sure they all are the same size. Write another example of the word *man* with different letter sizes. One letter should not be bigger or smaller than another. Write the word *man* again, with letters the same size. When the letters are the same size, the word is easier to read. Ask children which of the three writing samples is easiest to read and why.

GUIDE PRACTICE Write the following words, two with letters of different sizes and two with letters of the same size.

Team Talk Have children work in pairs to discuss which words are written with letters of the same size and which ones are not. Have them discuss how the words need to be fixed. Have them share with the class.

ON THEIR OWN Use *Reader's and Writer's Notebook,* p. 193

Research and Inquiry

Step 2 Research Skill: List

TEACH Tell children that a **list** is a group of words about a topic arranged in order one after the other. Explain that sometimes people make lists to keep track of things to do. Point out that people write lists using words, phrases, or sentences and that lists may be numbered. Write *Books in Our Classroom* and list book titles under the heading. Read the list aloud. Then explain that some lists group things that are alike. Write subheadings such as *Fiction* and *Nonfiction,* and reorganize the titles under the appropriate subheadings.

MODEL First, I read the title of the list. The title tells me what the list is about. I see that the list must be read from top to bottom. So, I start by reading the name at the top. Then I read the rest of the names.

GUIDE PRACTICE Write the heading *Places Where We Might Find Wild Animals.* Read the heading aloud. Have partners work together to make a list of places to look for wild animals.

Academic Vocabulary

list words about a topic arranged in order one after the other

Bridge to Common Core

RESEARCH TO BUILD AND PRESENT KNOWLEDGE

Children will analyze how texts address similar topics in order to build knowledge about a subject through the use of books. They will also:

- learn to choose a title to explore the topic
- how to organize information gathered

Wrap Up Your Day!

✔ **Phonics: Consonant Blends** Write the words *grass* and *spot.* Have children identify the blend at the beginning of each word.

✔ **High-Frequency Words** Write the following sentence: *We saw a small bird in your tree.* Ask children to read the sentence. Ask questions to elicit the high-frequency words, such as *Where was the bird?* (in the tree) *What size was the bird?* (small)

✔ **Content Knowledge** Monitor children's use of oral vocabulary as they respond. What are some habitats in our neighborhood where we might find wild animals? (trees, soil) What do wild animals need in order to survive? (food, water, place to live)

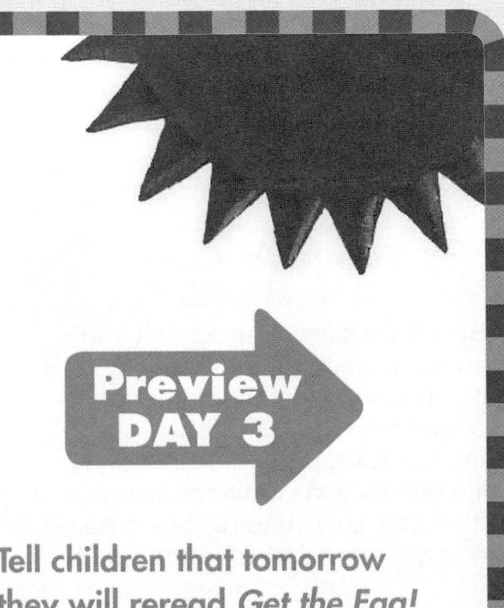

Tell children that tomorrow they will reread *Get the Egg!*

DAY 3
at a Glance

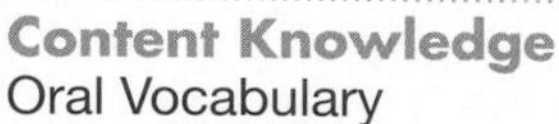

Content Knowledge
Oral Vocabulary

Phonemic Awareness
Rhyming Words

Phonics/Spelling
Short *e: e*
Initial Consonant Blends

High-Frequency Words
saw, small, tree, your

Selection Words
bird

Text-Based Comprehension
Review Character and Setting

Fluency
Appropriate Phrasing

Conventions
Interrogative Sentences

Writing
Realistic Story

Listening and Speaking
Give Descriptions

Research and Inquiry
Gather and Record Information

Materials

- Student Edition
- Sing with Me Big Book
- Big Book
- Letter Tiles
- Reader's and Writer's Notebook
- Retelling Cards

Common Core State Standards

Speaking/Listening 2. Ask and answer questions about key details in a text read aloud or information presented orally or through other media. **Language 5.c.** Identify real-life connections between words and their use (e.g., note places at home that are *cozy*). **Also Language 6.**

Content Knowledge

Neighborhood Animals

EXPAND THE CONCEPT To reinforce concepts and to focus children's attention, have children sing "Time to Hatch" from the *Sing with Me* Big Book. How will the pond help the baby birds survive? (The pond has water, which the baby birds need.)

Build Oral Language

LISTEN FOR AMAZING WORDS Display the Big Book *Jungle Drum.* Read the story and have children listen for the word *croak.* Have them also think about the different sounds the animals make.

- What makes the "Blip!" and "Blop!" sounds? (water drops)
- What animals makes the growling sound? (jaguar)

Big Book

TALK ABOUT SENTENCES AND WORDS Write the following sentence from *Jungle Drum* on sentence strips or on the board.

A tree frog, climbing up a tree, puffs out his throat and croaks, "Creeeeeeee, creeeeeeee!"

- Ask children to read the sentence with you as you track the print.
- Point to and read *puffs out his throat and croaks.* What does this mean? (takes a breath and makes a deep sound) Why did the author use the word *croak?* (It is the best word to use to describe the sound a frog makes.) What word would you use to describe the sound a frog makes?
- What does a frog look like when it puffs out its throat? Ask a volunteer to show or describe it. Why did the author use the word *puffs?*
- **Team Talk** Have pairs fill in the sentence frame below. Encourage them to be creative or silly.

A tree frog ______ his throat and ______.

Build Oral Vocabulary

Amazing Words Robust Vocabulary Routine

1. **Introduce the Word** Relate the word *croak* to the story. The tree frog puffs out its throat and *croaks.* Supply a child-friendly definition. When a frog *croaks,* it makes a rough, deep sound. Have children say the word.
2. **Demonstrate** Provide examples to show meaning. Frogs *croak* as they sit by the pond. I hear frogs *croak* when it's starting to get dark. Toads make a *croaking* sound too.
3. **Apply** Have children demonstrate their understanding. Have you heard a frog *croak?* What does it sound like?
4. **Display the Word** Point out the sound-spelling *cr* /k/ /r/ at the beginning of *croak.* Ask children to say the /k/ sound at the end of the word.

Routines Flip Chart

ADD TO THE CONCEPT MAP Use these questions to discuss wild animals that live in our neighborhood as you add to the concept map.

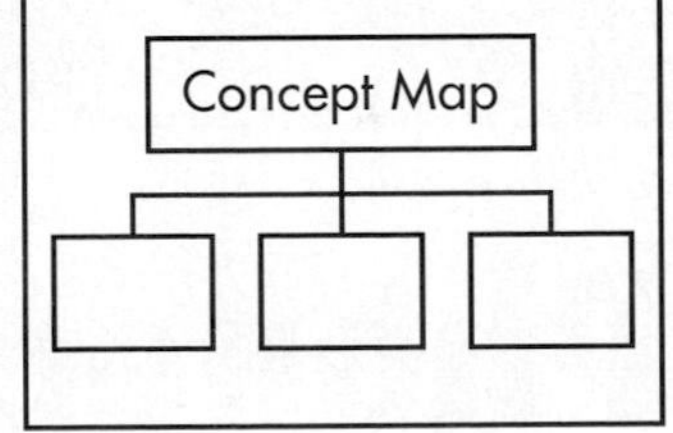

- In *Get the Egg!,* Kim and Brad found an animal that we have listed on our map. What is it? (a bird) What is the red bird's habitat? (It lives in a tree in the yard.) Let's add *lives in tree* to our map.
- The red bird is in a nest. What else is in the nest? (the red bird's eggs) Let's add *nest* and *eggs* to our map.

Amazing Words

habitat	chirp
hatch	croak
survive	moist

Access for All

A Advanced

Amazing Words Allow children to show an understanding of the word *croak* by demonstrating a croaking sound and naming animals that croak.

Expand Vocabulary Use the Day 3 instruction on ELL Poster 5 to expand children's use of vocabulary to communicate about lesson concepts.

Pronunciation Assist children with the articulation of phonemes as they blend sounds, particularly initial consonant blends. Focus on tongue and lip positions when saying words such as *croak.*

Vocabulary Help children understand that the story words *blip* and *blop* are words that sound like what they mean. If possible, demonstrate the sound by dripping water into a bowl. Talk about other words that sound like what they mean, such as *croak.*

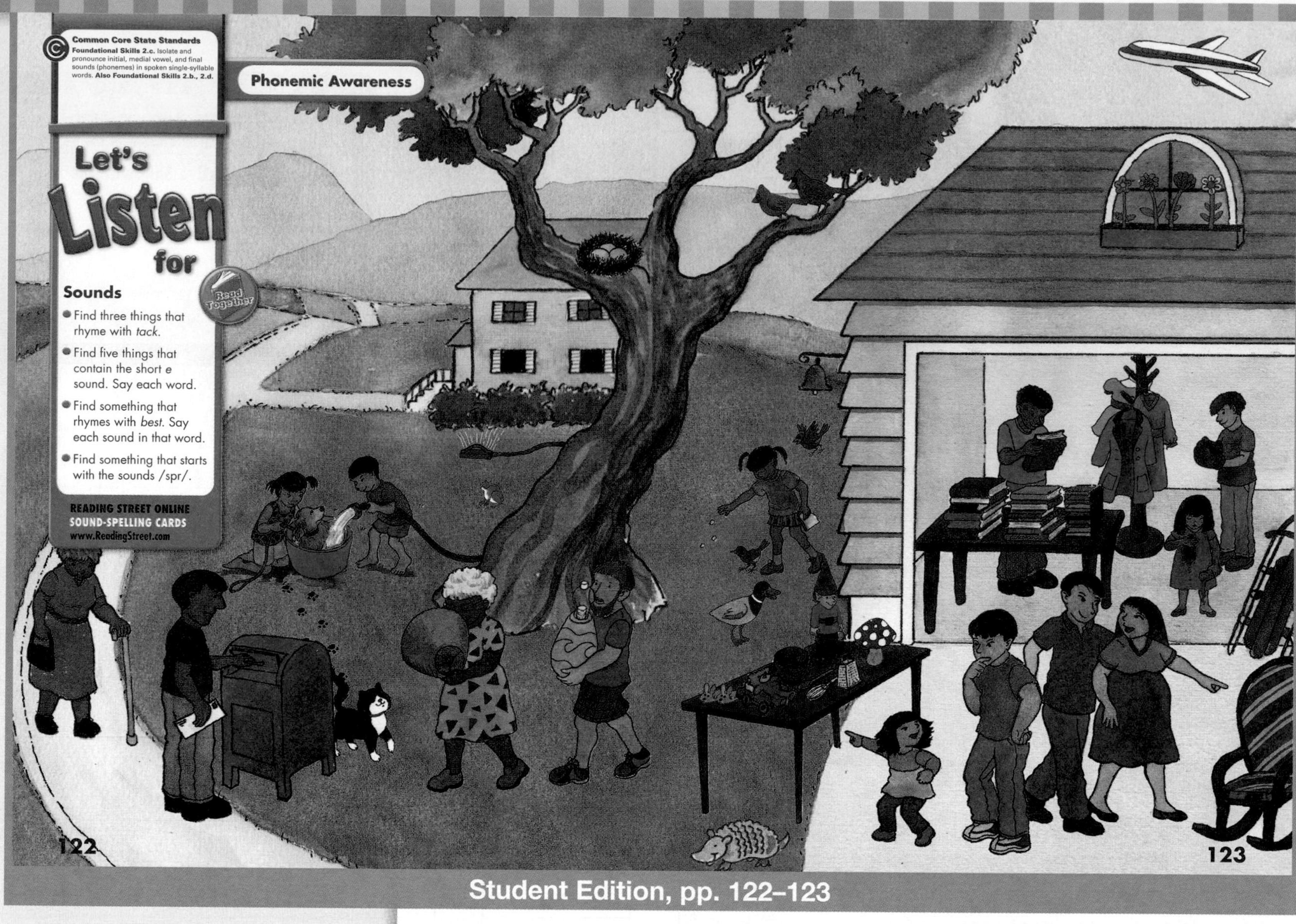
Common Core State Standards
Foundational Skills 2.c. Isolate and pronounce initial, medial vowel, and final sounds (phonemes) in spoken single-syllable words. Also Foundational Skills 2.b., 2.d.
Phonemic Awareness
Let's Listen for
Sounds
Read Together
Find three things that rhyme with *tack*.
Find five things that contain the short *e* sound. Say each word.
Find something that rhymes with *best*. Say each sound in that word.
Find something that starts with the sounds /spr/.
READING STREET ONLINE
SOUND-SPELLING CARDS
www.ReadingStreet.com
122
123

Student Edition, pp. 122–123

Phonemic Awareness

Rhyming Words

MODEL RHYMING WORDS Read the first bullet point on page 122. Remember that **rhyming words** end with the same sounds. Let's find three things that rhyme with *tack*. I see a cat with *black* fur, a *stack* of books, and a *track* left by the cat. *Black, stack,* and *track* rhyme with *tack*. Repeat by reading the third bullet point and finding the rhyming word for *best (nest).*

GUIDE PRACTICE Guide children to use the picture to produce words that rhyme with *red. (sled, bread)*

ON THEIR OWN Have children orally generate words starting with consonant blends that rhyme with the following words. Sample responses are given.

top *(stop, drop, plop, crop)*	**fill** *(still, grill)*	**bee** *(tree, flee)*
sack *(stack, black, track)*	**due** *(blue, true)*	**day** *(play, stay, tray, gray)*

Team Talk Have children create pairs of rhyming words with a partner.

Common Core State Standards

Foundational Skills 2. Demonstrate understanding of spoken words, syllables, and sounds (phonemes). **Foundational Skills 2.b.** Orally produce single-syllable words by blending sounds (phonemes), including consonant blends. **Foundational Skills 2.c.** Isolate and pronounce initial, medial vowel, and final sounds (phonemes) in spoken single-syllable words. **Foundational Skills 3.** Know and apply grade-level phonics and word analysis skills in decoding words.

Academic Vocabulary

rhyming words words that end with the same sounds

Phonics

Build Words

MODEL WORD BUILDING Now we are going to build words with beginning consonant blends. Write *lip* and blend it. Watch me add *f* to the beginning of *lip*. Model blending the new word, *flip*.

GUIDE PRACTICE Have children spell *flip* with letter tiles. Monitor children's work as they build words.

- Change the *f* in *flip* to *c*. Say the new word together.
- Change the *c* in *clip* to *s*. Say the new word together.
- Change the *l* in *slip* to *n*. Say the new word together.
- Change the *n* in *snip* to *k*. Say the new word together.

Corrective feedback	For corrective feedback, model the correct spelling and have children correct their tiles.

Fluent Word Reading

MODEL Write *step*. I know the sounds for *s, t, e,* and *p*. I blend them and read the word *step*.

GUIDE PRACTICE Write the words below. Say the sounds in your head for each spelling you see. When I point to the word, we'll read it together. Allow one second per sound-previewing time for the first reading.

sped	Fred	dress	stress	sled

ON THEIR OWN Have children read the list above three or four times, until they can read one word per second.

Access for All

A Advanced

Blend Words If children are able to blend words with initial consonant blends easily and independently, have them use letter tiles to build these more difficult words with initial blends: *trap, drop, slam, flop, grand.*

ELL

Produce Initial Blends Children whose first language is Spanish may need support with words with initial *s* blends, such as *slip*. Model the formal pronunciation and have children repeat the words.

Common Core State Standards

Foundational Skills 2.b. Orally produce single-syllable words by blending sounds (phonemes), including consonant blends. **Foundational Skills 3.** Know and apply grade-level phonics and word analysis skills in decoding words. **Language 2.d.** Use conventional spelling for words with common spelling patterns and for frequently occurring irregular words.

Phonics

Blend and Read

DECODE WORDS IN ISOLATION Have children turn to page 195 in the *Reader's and Writer's Notebook* and find the first list of words. Each word in this list contains the short *e* sound. Each word in the second list begins with two consonants that are blended together. Let's blend and read these words. Be sure that children distinguish the short *e* sound or pronounce the consonant blend correctly in each word. Next, have children read the high-frequency words.

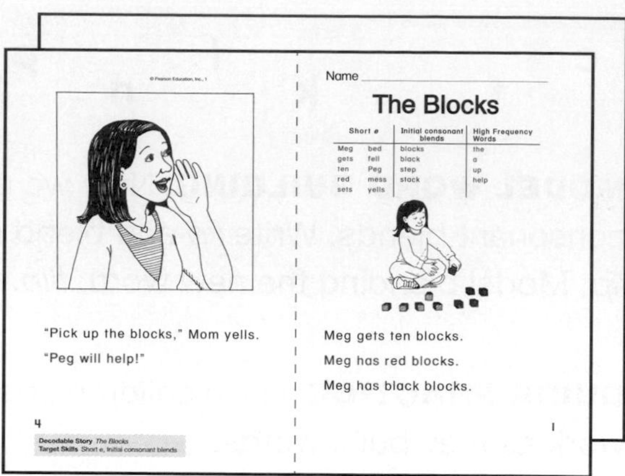

Reader's and Writer's Notebook, pp. 195–196

DECODE WORDS IN CONTEXT Chorally read the story along with children. Have children identify words in the story that contain the short *e* sound or begin with two consonants that are blended together.

Team Talk Pair children and have them take turns reading the story aloud to each other. Monitor children as they read to check for proper pronunciation and appropriate pacing.

ON THEIR OWN To further develop automaticity, have children take the story home to reread.

Spelling

Short *e* Words

SPELL HIGH-FREQUENCY WORDS Write *your* and *saw* and point them out on the Word Wall. Have children say and spell the words with you and then without you.

DICTATION Have children write these sentences. Say each sentence. Then repeat it slowly, one word at a time.

1. **Get your hat.**
2. **I saw Sam and his cat.**
3. **Kim and Kit use the net.**

PROOFREAD AND CORRECT Write each sentence, spelling words one at a time. Have children circle and rewrite any misspelled words.

ON THEIR OWN Use *Reader's and Writer's Notebook,* p. 197.

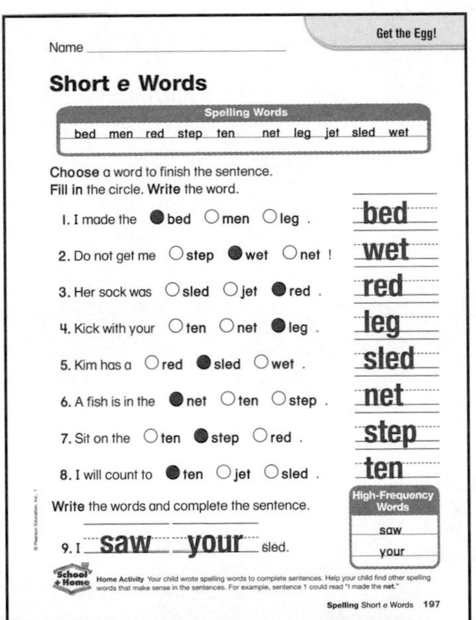
Name ____________ Get the Egg!

Short e Words

Spelling Words: bed men red step ten net leg jet sled wet

Choose a word to finish the sentence. **Fill in** the circle. **Write** the word.

1. I made the ● bed ○ men ○ leg . **bed**
2. Do not get me ○ step ● wet ○ net ! **wet**
3. Her sock was ○ sled ○ jet ● red . **red**
4. Kick with your ○ ten ○ net ● leg . **leg**
5. Kim has a ○ red ● sled ○ wet . **sled**
6. A fish is in the ● net ○ ten ○ step . **net**
7. Sit on the ○ ten ● step ○ red . **step**
8. I will count to ● ten ○ jet ○ sled . **ten**

Write the words and complete the sentence.

High-Frequency Words: saw, your

9. I **saw** **your** sled.

School + Home **Home Activity** Your child wrote spelling words to complete sentences. Help your child find other spelling words that make sense in the sentences. For example, sentence 1 could read "I made the **net.**"

Spelling Short *e* Words 197

Reader's and Writer's Notebook, p. 197

eSTREET INTERACTIVE
www.ReadingStreet.com

Teacher Resources
- Reader's and Writer's Notebook

Spelling Words

Short *e* Words

1. men	**6. leg**
2. red	**7. jet**
3. step	**8. sled**
4. ten	**9. wet**
5. net	**10. bed**

High-Frequency Words

11. your	**12. saw**

ELL

Spelling Dictation Children will benefit from hearing each dictated sentence read three times. First, have children listen to understand the sentence. The second time, they should write what they hear. The third time, they can check their work.

Day 3 SMALL GROUP TIME • Differentiate Close Reading, p. SG•69

OL On-Level
- **Reread** to Develop Vocabulary
- **Reread** *Get the Egg!*

SI Strategic Intervention
- **Blend** Words with Short *e* and Initial Consonant Blends
- **Reread** *Get the Egg!*

A Advanced
- **Reread** to Extend Vocabulary
- **Reread** *Get the Egg!*
- **Investigate** Inquiry Project

ELL

If... children need more scaffolding and practice with reading the **Main Selection,**
then... use the ELL activities on p. DI•102 in the Teacher Resources section on SuccessNet.

Common Core State Standards

Literature 3. Describe characters, settings, and major events in a story, using key details. **Foundational Skills 3.g.** Recognize and read grade-appropriate irregularly spelled words.

High-Frequency Words

saw	tree
small	your

Selection Word

bird animal covered in feathers that has wings and two legs

High-Frequency and Selection Words

READ WORDS IN ISOLATION Display and review this week's high-frequency words and selection words. Have children read the words aloud.

READ WORDS IN CONTEXT Display the following sentence frames. Have children complete the sentences using high-frequency and selection words. Have children read each completed sentence with you.

1. **We _______ the blue eggs in the nest. (saw)**
2. **The nest was up in the _______. (tree)**
3. **A baby _______ hatched from the egg in the nest. (bird)**
4. **The baby was so _______ it fit in my hand. (small)**
5. **Tell Nat about _______ pal Bud. (your)**

Check High-Frequency Words

FORMATIVE ASSESSMENT Point to these words on the Word Wall and have the class read them. Listen for children who miss words during the reading. Call on those children to read some of the words individually.

saw	small	tree	your	**Spiral Review**
are	the	too	you ←	Row 2 reviews previously taught high-frequency words.

If... children cannot read these words,

then... use the Nondecodable Words Routine on p. 125 to reteach the words. Monitor children's fluency with these words during reading and provide additional practice.

Text-Based Comprehension

Read Main Selection

REVIEW CHARACTER AND SETTING Remind children that **characters** are the people and animals in a story. Remind them that the **setting** is where and when the story takes place. Readers better understand a story when they can describe the reasons for a character's actions or feelings, as well as the setting of the story. Have children turn to pages 128–129 in their Student Edition and tell about the characters and setting of *Get the Egg!*

GENRE: REALISTIC FICTION Remind children that realistic fiction is a made-up story about events that could happen in real life. Have children recall facts from *Get the Egg!* that indicate that this story could happen in real life. (An egg can fall out of a bird's nest. People can help return the egg safely to the nest.)

READ Return to pages 128–137 and use the **2nd Read/Close Reading Notes** to reread *Get the Egg!*

Routine Read for Understanding

Deepen understanding by reading the selection multiple times.

1. **First Read**—If children need support, then use the **Access Text** notes to help them clarify understanding.
2. **Second Read**—Use the **Close Reading** notes to help children draw knowledge from the text.

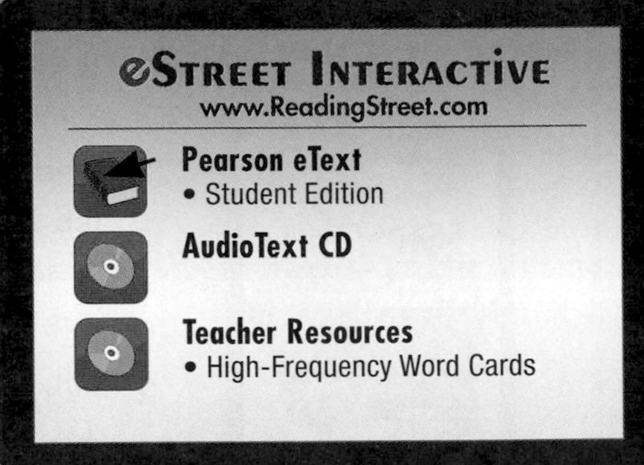

Academic Vocabulary 

character a person or animal in a story

setting where and when a story takes place

Phonics Clues Provide support for children during the sentence frames review activity on page 138g by supplying the initial consonant or consonant blend of the word that completes the sentence.

Common Core State Standards
Literature 2. Retell stories, including key details, and demonstrate understanding of their central message or lesson.
Also Literature 1., Writing 5.
Envision It! Retell
READING STREET ONLINE
STORY SORT
www.ReadingStreet.com

Think Critically

Read Together

1. In *Get the Egg!*, Brad and Kim have an adventure. Find and read one part of the story that reminds you of something exciting that has happened to you. Text to Self
2. Why did the author write this story? Author's Purpose
3. What is this story about? Main Idea and Details
4. Does this story have a happy ending? Explain. Story Structure
5. **Look Back and Write** Look back at pages 134 and 135. Write about how Brad and Kim save the red bird's egg. Provide evidence from the story. Discuss what you wrote with a partner.

Key Ideas and Details • Text Evidence

138

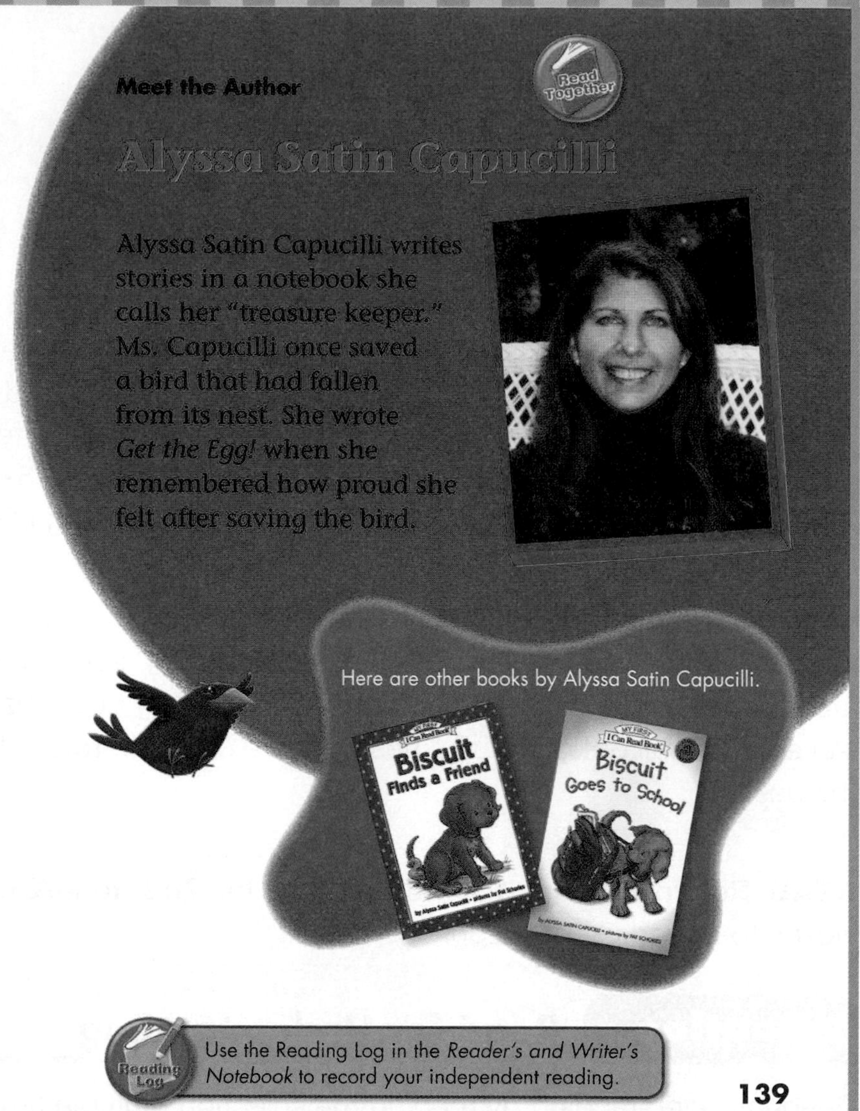

Meet the Author

Read Together

Alyssa Satin Capucilli

Alyssa Satin Capucilli writes stories in a notebook she calls her "treasure keeper." Ms. Capucilli once saved a bird that had fallen from its nest. She wrote *Get the Egg!* when she remembered how proud she felt after saving the bird.

Here are other books by Alyssa Satin Capucilli.

Biscuit Finds a Friend
Biscuit Goes to School

Reading Log

Use the Reading Log in the *Reader's and Writer's Notebook* to record your independent reading.

139

Student Edition, pp. 138–139

Common Core State Standards

Literature 1. Ask and answer questions about key details in a text. **Literature 2.** Retell stories, including key details, and demonstrate understanding of their central message or lesson. **Also Writing 5.**

Bridge to Common Core

KEY IDEAS AND DETAILS

By reading the text multiple times, children will make logical inferences from the text and cite textual evidence when writing or discussing the knowledge they have gained. Use the Think Critically page to ensure a thorough understanding of *Get the Egg!*

Think Critically

1. **TEXT TO SELF** I once found a bird's nest with eggs in it in my neighborhood.
2. **AUTHOR'S PURPOSE** The author wants us to see that we can care for animals.
3. **MAIN IDEA AND DETAILS** The story is about how Kim and Brad save a bird's egg. They discover that a red bird has a nest in a tree. The nest has eggs in it and one falls out.
4. **STORY STRUCTURE** Yes. The story has a happy ending because Brad and Kim are able to save the egg and put it back in the nest.
5. **LOOK BACK AND WRITE • TEXT EVIDENCE** For writing fluency, assign a five-minute time limit. As children finish, encourage them to reread their response and proofread for errors.

Scoring Rubric Look Back and Write

TOP-SCORE RESPONSE A top-score response uses details from the text and the pictures to tell how Brad and Kim saved the egg.

A top-score response might include:
Brad and Kim used the net to get the egg. Then they put the egg back in the nest.

Retell

Have children use the retelling strips in the Student Edition or the Story Sort to retell the selection. Monitor children's retelling.

Scoring Rubric Narrative Retelling

	4	3	2	1
Connections	Makes connections and generalizes beyond the text	Makes connections to other events, stories, or experiences	Makes a limited connection to another event, story, or experience	Makes no connection to another event, story, or experience
Author's Purpose	Elaborates on author's purpose	Tells author's purpose with some clarity	Makes some connection to author's purpose	Makes no connection to author's purpose
Characters	Describes the main character(s) and any character development	Identifies the main character(s) and gives some information about them	Inaccurately identifies some characters or gives little information about them	Inaccurately identifies the characters or gives no information about them
Setting	Describes the time and location	Identifies the time and location	Omits details of time or location	Is unable to identify time or location
Plot	Describes the events in sequence using rich detail	Tells the plot with some errors in sequence that do not affect meaning	Tells parts of plot with gaps that affect meaning	Retelling has no sense of story

Don't Wait Until Friday

MONITOR PROGRESS Check Retelling

If... children have trouble retelling the selection,
then... use Story Sequence Graphic Organizer 23 and the Retelling Cards/Story Sort to scaffold their retelling.

Writing to Sources

Use Write Like a Reporter on pp. 58–59 to guide children in writing text-based responses using one source.

Strategy Response Log

Story Structure Have children use p. RR17 in their *Reader's and Writer's Notebook* to draw a picture of the most important event in the story. Remind children to include the main characters and the setting in their pictures.

Plan to Assess Retelling

- ☐ **Week 1** Strategic Intervention
- ☐ **Week 2** Advanced
- ☐ **Week 3** Strategic Intervention
- ☐ **Week 4** On-Level
- ☑ **This Week** Assess Advanced children.
- ☐ **Week 6** Assess any children you have not yet checked during this unit.

Meet the Author

Read aloud page 139 as children follow along. Ask children what authors do.

Read Independently

Have children enter their independent reading into their Reading Logs.

Common Core State Standards

Foundational Skills 1.a. Recognize the distinguishing features of a sentence (e.g., first word, capitalization, ending punctuation). **Foundational Skills 4.b.** Read on-level text orally with accuracy, appropriate rate, and expression on successive readings. **Language 1.j.** Produce and expand complete simple and compound declarative, interrogative, imperative, and exclamatory sentences in response to prompts. **Language 2.b.** Use end punctuation for sentences. **Also Language 1.**

Options for Oral Rereading

Use *Get the Egg!* or one of this week's Decodable Practice Readers.

Fluency

Appropriate Phrasing

MODEL FLUENT READING Have children turn to Student Edition page 130. Point to the periods at the end of each sentence. A period shows that it is the end of a sentence. I stop when I come to a period. Point to the comma. When I see a comma, I pause.

GUIDE PRACTICE Have children read the page with you. Then have them reread the page as a group until they read with appropriate phrasing, paying attention to punctuation. Encourage them to stop for each period. Continue in the same way with page 131.

Corrective feedback

If... children have difficulty reading with appropriate phrasing, **then...** prompt:

- Do all of the sentences end in a period?
- Try to read the sentences, stopping when you come to each period.

Reread for Fluency

Routine Choral Reading

1. **Select a Passage** For *Get the Egg!,* use pp. 132–133.
2. **Model** First, have children track the print as you read.
3. **Guide Practice** Then have children read along with you.
4. **Corrective Feedback** Have the class read aloud without you. Monitor progress and provide feedback. For optimal fluency, children should reread three to four times.

Routines Flip Chart

CHECK COMPREHENSION What caused the egg to fall out of the nest? (A twig hit the nest and then hit the egg out of the nest.)

Conventions

Interrogative Sentences

REVIEW Remind children that an interrogative sentence, or question, is an asking sentence. It begins with a capital letter and ends with a question mark.

GUIDE PRACTICE Write this sentence on the board and have children read it aloud.

what do birds eat

How should our question begin? (with a capital letter) Write a capital letter. How should our question end? (with a question mark) Write a question mark.

Team Talk Have partners work together to suggest other questions about birds.

APPLY Have children complete these sentence frames orally. Then have them turn each statement into a question.

1. **I want to know why a zebra ______.**
2. **I want to know how a hippo ______.**
3. **I want to know if an elephant can ______.**

ON THEIR OWN Use *Reader's and Writer's Notebook,* p. 198.

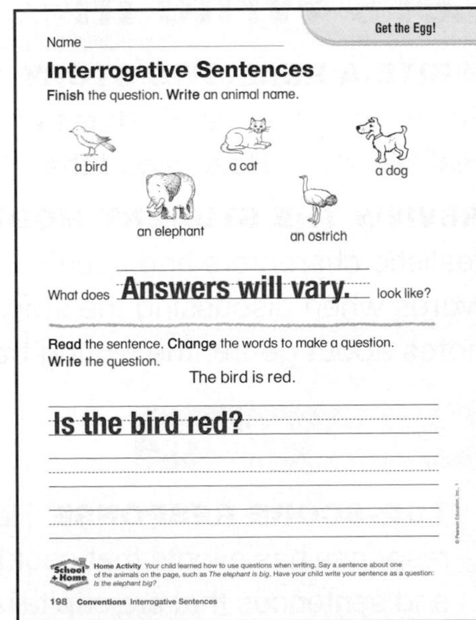

Name ______ Get the Egg!

Interrogative Sentences

Finish the question. **Write** an animal name.

What does **Answers will vary.** look like?

Read the sentence. **Change** the words to make a question. **Write** the question.

The bird is red.

Is the bird red?

Home Activity Your child learned how to use questions when writing. Say a sentence about one of the animals on the page, such as *The elephant is big.* Have your child write your sentence as a question: *Is the elephant big?*

198 **Conventions** Interrogative Sentences

Reader's and Writer's Notebook, p. 198

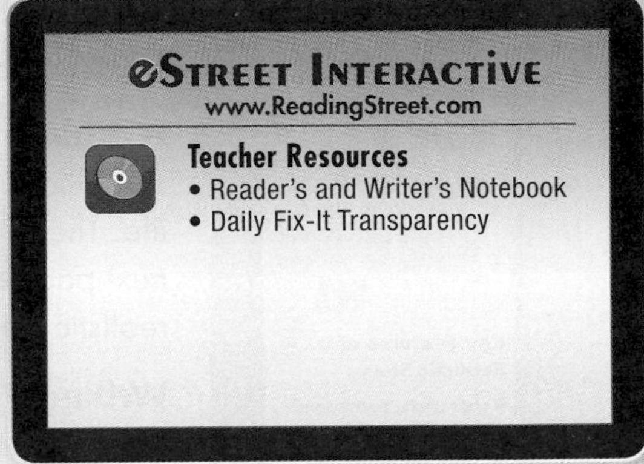

eStreet Interactive
www.ReadingStreet.com

Teacher Resources
- Reader's and Writer's Notebook
- Daily Fix-It Transparency

Daily Fix-It

5. Yor legg got wet in the pond.
Yo<u>u</u>r le<u>g</u> got wet in the pond.

6. We caw Tim get a nett to use.
We <u>s</u>aw Tim get a ne<u>t</u> to use.

Discuss the Daily Fix-It corrections with children. Review the spellings of *your, leg,* and *net* and /s/ spelled *s.*

Professional Development

Questions Using printed materials to identify interrogative sentences helps children recognize them. Provide newspapers or children's magazines for children to use to find questions.

ELL

Interrogative Sentences English language learners may benefit from focusing on question words and their use in interrogative sentences. List question words on the board *(who, what, where, when, why, how)* and read them aloud. Invite children to say or write interrogative sentences that begin with the question words.

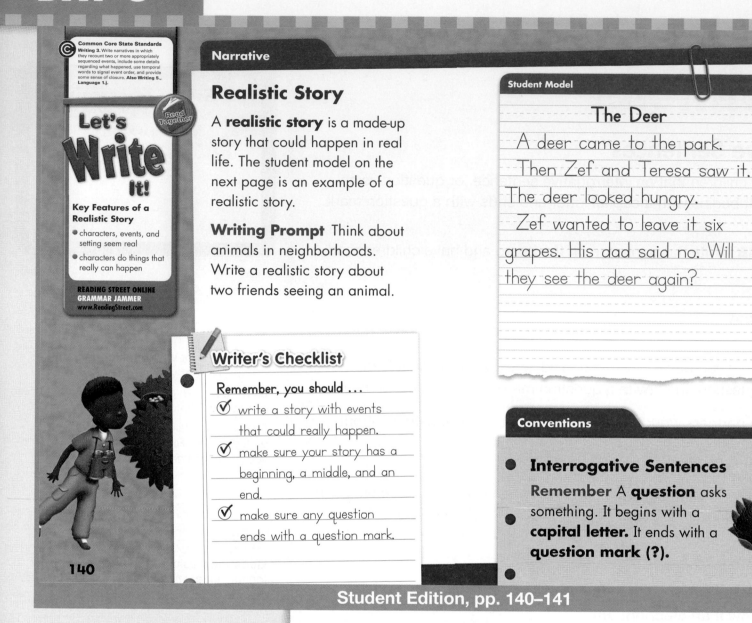

Common Core State Standards **Writing 3.** Write narratives in which they recount two or more appropriately sequenced events, include some details regarding what happened, use temporal words to signal event order, and provide some sense of closure. **Also Writing 5., Language 1.j.**

Let's Write It! Read Together

Key Features of a Realistic Story

- characters, events, and setting seem real
- characters do things that really can happen

READING STREET ONLINE
GRAMMAR JAMMER
www.ReadingStreet.com

Narrative

Realistic Story

A **realistic story** is a made-up story that could happen in real life. The student model on the next page is an example of a realistic story.

Writing Prompt Think about animals in neighborhoods. Write a realistic story about two friends seeing an animal.

Writer's Checklist

Remember, you should ...

- ✓ write a story with events that could really happen.
- ✓ make sure your story has a beginning, a middle, and an end.
- ✓ make sure any question ends with a question mark.

140

Student Model

The Deer

A deer came to the park. Then Zef and Teresa saw it. The deer looked hungry.

Zef wanted to leave it six grapes. His dad said no. Will they see the deer again?

Genre Realistic Story This story tells about an event that could really happen.

Writing Trait Organization The story has a beginning, middle, and end.

This **question** begins with a capital letter and ends with a question mark.

Conventions

Interrogative Sentences

Remember A **question** asks something. It begins with a **capital letter.** It ends with a **question mark (?).**

141

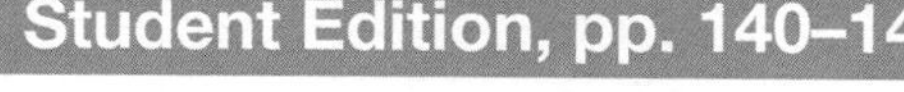

Student Edition, pp. 140–141

Common Core State Standards

Writing 3. Write narratives in which they recount two or more appropriately sequenced events, include some details regarding what happened, use temporal words to signal event order, and provide some sense of closure. **Writing 5.** With guidance and support from adults, focus on a topic, respond to questions and suggestions from peers, and add details to strengthen writing as needed. **Language 1.j.** Produce and expand complete simple and compound declarative, interrogative, imperative, and exclamatory sentences in response to prompts.

Let's Write It!

WRITE A REALISTIC STORY Use pages 140–141 in the Student Edition. Read aloud the Key Features of a Realistic Story and the definition of a realistic story. Read aloud the Writing Prompt and the Writer's Checklist.

REVIEW THE STUDENT MODEL Read aloud "The Deer." Point out the realistic characters and events in the story. Use time and order transition words when discussing the story. Read aloud and briefly discuss the side notes about genre, the writing trait, and questions.

Scoring Rubric

TOP-SCORE RESPONSE Help children understand that a top-score response has events that could really happen; a beginning, middle, and end; and sentences that are capitalized and punctuated correctly. For a complete rubric see Writing Rubric 5 from the *Teacher Resources DVD-ROM.*

CONNECT TO CONVENTIONS Read to children the Conventions note about interrogative sentences. Point out the question in the model story.

Writing

Realistic Story

Mini-Lesson Writer's Craft: Time and Order Words

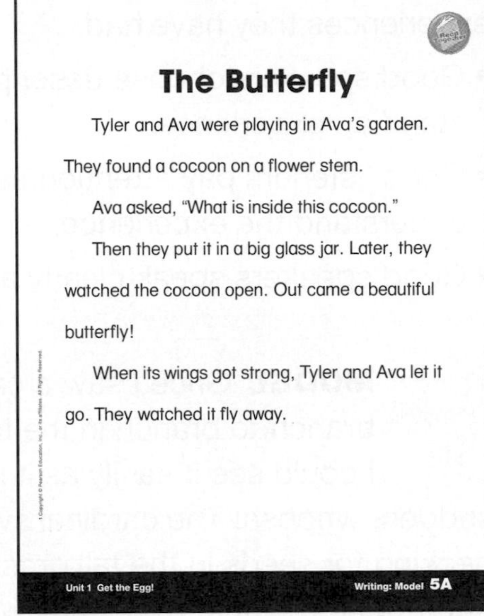

The Butterfly

Tyler and Ava were playing in Ava's garden. They found a cocoon on a flower stem.

Ava asked, "What is inside this cocoon."

Then they put it in a big glass jar. Later, they watched the cocoon open. Out came a beautiful butterfly!

When its wings got strong, Tyler and Ava let it go. They watched it fly away.

Unit 1 Get the Egg! Writing: Model 5A

Writing Transparency 5A TR DVD

- **Introduce** Use your story chart from yesterday and Writing Transparency 5A to model using time and order words when writing story events in sequence. When I write my story, I will use my chart. Yesterday the chart helped me put my ideas for the beginning, middle, and end of my story in order. Today I will write each event in order. I can also use time and order words such as *first, next,* and *last* to make the order of events clear. After Ava wonders what is in the cocoon, *then* they will put it in a big glass jar. *Later,* they will watch the cocoon open. I will use the words *then* and *later* to tell the order of events. Read aloud the draft on the transparency and discuss the order of story events.
- Explain how children can use story events they planned yesterday to draft the story: beginning, middle, and end. Today's goal is to write the story but not to rewrite each word perfectly. They can edit later to correct the words.

GUIDE WRITING Now it is time to write your story. Tell about your characters seeing a neighborhood animal. Have children use their story charts. Help them finish the ideas. Then guide children as they draft the stories.

Routine Quick Write for Fluency

Team Talk

1. **Talk** Have partners take one minute to talk about what children might do with a neighborhood dog.
2. **Write** Each child writes two sentences about children and a dog.
3. **Share** Partners can add time and order words to each other's sentences.

Routines Flip Chart

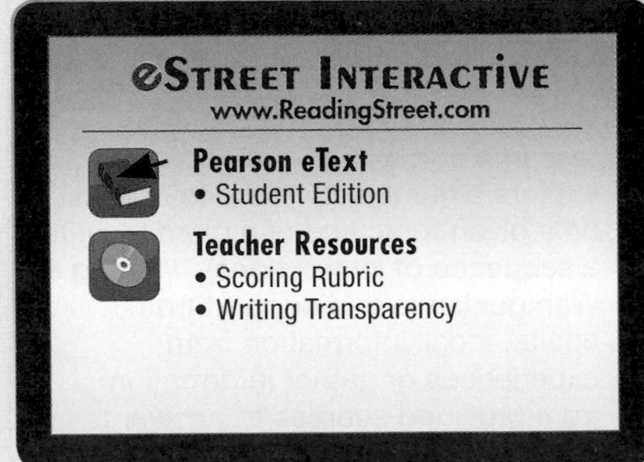

eStreet Interactive
www.ReadingStreet.com

Pearson eText
- Student Edition

Teacher Resources
- Scoring Rubric
- Writing Transparency

Access for All

A Advanced

Developing Sequence Children may include more than one story event in the beginning, middle, or end of the story.

Academic Vocabulary

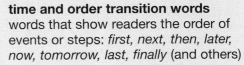

time and order transition words words that show readers the order of events or steps: *first, next, then, later, now, tomorrow, last, finally* (and others)

Listening and Speaking

Give Descriptions

TEACH Ask children what they know about giving descriptions. Remind them that good descriptions tell what something looks like, sounds like, or feels like. Tell children that people often give descriptions of things they have seen or experiences they have had.

- Good speakers choose descriptive words that help listeners better understand an experience.
- Good listeners pay attention as others give descriptions so they can better understand the experience.
- Good speakers speak clearly and at an appropriate pace.

Think Aloud **MODEL** Once I saw a cardinal in my backyard. It was hopping from branch to branch in the tall tree by the fence. It was bright red, so I could see it easily as it moved among the green leaves. All of a sudden, whoosh! The cardinal swooped down to the ground and started pecking for seeds in the tall grass. Then I heard *tap, tap, tap!* It was coming from the tree. There was a tiny woodpecker pecking at the trunk. What a day for birds!

GUIDE PRACTICE Briefly discuss wild animals children have seen in their neighborhoods. Invite children to suggest words that describe the animals. Make a list of animals and related descriptive words on the board. Have children use the words in sentences describing the animals.

ON THEIR OWN Have pairs of children take turns listening to and giving descriptions of wild animals in their neighborhood. Remind children to follow the rules established in Week 1.

Common Core State Standards

Writing 7. Participate in shared research and writing projects (e.g., explore a number of "how-to" books on a given topic and use them to write a sequence of instructions). **Writing 8.** With guidance and support from adults, recall information from experiences or gather information from provided sources to answer a question. **Speaking/Listening 4.** Describe people, places, things, and events with relevant details, expressing ideas and feelings clearly.

Bridge to Common Core

PRESENTATION OF KNOWLEDGE AND IDEAS

As children give descriptions about wild animals in their neighborhoods, they are learning to present detailed information and use supporting evidence to allow listeners to envision the experience. Listeners learn to ask questions about key issues or concepts to clarify and deepen their understanding of the descriptions.

Research and Inquiry

Step 3 Gather and Record Information

TEACH Tell children that today they will write a list of the wild animals they could observe in their neighborhood.

Think Aloud **MODEL** Display the list of places to look for wild animals created on Day 2. Now it's time to make a list of the wild animals we might see in one place in our neighborhood. Think about the list we made yesterday of places where we could see wild animals. Which place do you think would be the best to see animals?

GUIDE PRACTICE Guide children to choose one of the locations they listed to watch for wild animals. Encourage children to write the names of wild animals they would see in that location. Point out that children may think of dogs and other pets, but they should not write the names of these animals because they are not wild animals. Remind children that wild animals live outdoors, not with people. Explain to children that they will use what they write to make their lists.

Access for All

SI Strategic Intervention

Making Lists Some children may have trouble making a list. Tell these children that they do not need to write the names of the animals. They can draw pictures of what they observe and write the names later in the week.

Wrap Up Your Day!

✔ **Main Ideas and Details** Have children think about the main ideas and details of *Get the Egg!* What details did you read about in *Get the Egg!*? What is the story mostly about?

✔ **Story Structure** Have children recall the main characters from *Get the Egg!* What did the characters do? How does remembering the characters and events help you enjoy the story?

Tell children that tomorrow they will read about something that they can do to help wild birds in the neighborhood.

Content Knowledge
Oral Vocabulary

Phonemic Awareness
Distinguish /e/

Phonics
Review Inflected Endings *-s* and *-ing*

High-Frequency Words
Review

Spelling
Short *e* Words

Science in Reading
How-to Article

Fluency
Appropriate Phrasing

Conventions
Interrogative Sentences

Writing
Realistic Story: Revise

Research and Inquiry
Synthesize

Materials

- Student Edition
- Sing with Me Big Book
- Read Aloud Anthology
- Decodable Reader 5C
- Reader's and Writer's Notebook

Common Core State Standards

Speaking/Listening 2. Ask and answer questions about key details in a text read aloud or information presented orally or through other media. **Language 5.c.** Identify real-life connections between words and their use (e.g., note places at home that are *cozy*). **Also Language 6.**

Content Knowledge

Neighborhood Animals

EXPAND THE CONCEPT To reinforce concepts and to focus children's attention, have them sing "Time to Hatch" from the *Sing with Me* Big Book. How will the bird feeders help the baby birds survive? (The feeders have food, which the birds need.)

Build Oral Language

REVIEW GENRE: REALISTIC FICTION Have children tell the key features of realistic fiction: it is a made-up story about people and animals doing things that could really happen. Explain that today you will read about Maisie and her toad in "Maisie Caught a Toad Today" by Tryn Paxton.

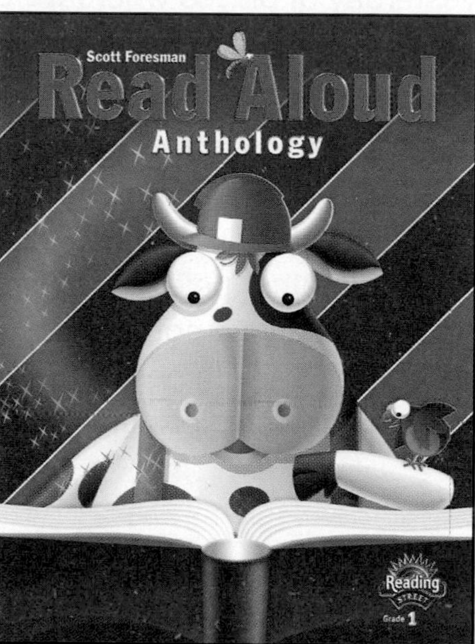

"Maisie Caught a Toad Today"

MONITOR LISTENING COMPREHENSION Recall that Brad and Kim discovered a red bird living in its natural habitat, a tree. Have children listen to "Maisie Caught a Toad Today."

Team Talk **TALK ABOUT NEIGHBORHOOD ANIMALS** Read aloud the second from last paragraph of "Maisie Caught a Toad Today." Display it on the board if possible, and track the print as you read.

- Have pairs generate ideas about why the toad's habitat, or home, needs to have moist soil.
- Add words generated in the discussion to the concept map.

Build Oral Vocabulary

Amazing Words Robust Vocabulary Routine

1. **Introduce the Word** Relate the word *moist* to the story. Maisie used a bucket and *moist* dirt to make a shelter for the toad. Supply a child-friendly definition. When something is *moist,* it is slightly wet or damp. Have children say the word.
2. **Demonstrate** Provide examples to show meaning. The sand was *moist* after it rained. I used a *moist* sponge to clean up the mess. My mom added milk to the oatmeal to make it *moist.*
3. **Apply** Have children demonstrate their understanding. How does something *moist* feel? How do things in nature become *moist?*
4. **Display the Word** Point out the sound-spelling *st*/st/ at the end of *moist.*

Routines Flip Chart

ADD TO THE CONCEPT MAP Discuss wild animals in our neighborhood.

- What kind of animal did Maisie catch? (a toad) What did Maisie do with the toad she caught? (She put it in a bucket with mud and rocks.) What did Maisie's parents tell her a toad needs? (bugs to eat, water to stay moist) Where can we add these ideas to our concept map?

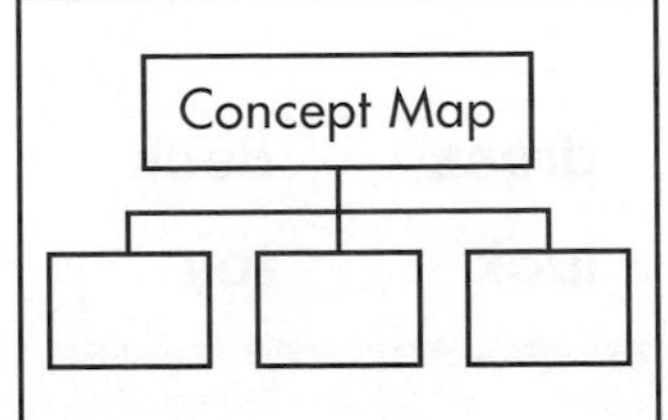

Amazing Words

habitat	chirp
hatch	croak
survive	moist

Access for All

A Advanced

Amazing Words Allow children who demonstrate an understanding of the word *moist* to name things that are moist and explain how they might have become moist.

ELL

Produce Oral Language Use the Day 4 instruction on ELL Poster 5 to extend and enrich language.

Support Listening Use the *Sing with Me* illustration to review the idea of birds being wild animals that live in many neighborhoods. Before reading, ask children: What other wild animals live in the neighborhood? Record their answers on the board.

Common Core State Standards

Foundational Skills 2.c. Isolate and pronounce initial, medial vowel, and final sounds (phonemes) in spoken single-syllable words. **Foundational Skills 3.** Know and apply grade-level phonics and word analysis skills in decoding words. **Foundational Skills 3.f.** Read words with inflectional endings.

Phonemic Awareness

Distinguish /e/

MODEL This week we read about Maisie and a toad. The toad hops out of Maisie's hand and finds a shady spot to *rest.* Listen as I say the sounds in *rest.* Slowly model the sounds in *rest,* /r/ /e/ /s/ /t/. The middle sound in *rest* is /e/.

GUIDE PRACTICE I will say some words, and you can tell me if they have the /e/ sound in the middle or at the beginning. Say each word below, and then guide children to decide whether the /e/ sound is in the middle or at the beginning of each one.

Corrective feedback | If children make an error, model the correct response. Return to the word later in the practice.

nest (middle)	**edge** (beginning)	**step** (middle)
Ben (middle)	**empty** (beginning)	**ten** (middle)

ON THEIR OWN Have children tell you which of the following words contain the /e/ sound.

dress	**deck**	**clam**
luck	**toy**	**egg**

Phonics

Review Inflected Endings -s and *-ing*

REVIEW INFLECTED ENDING -s To review last week's first phonics skill, write *naps* and *tags.* You studied words like these already. What do you know about the ending of these words? (They end in the letter *s.* The letter *s* can stand for the /s/ or the /z/ sound.) When you see a word that ends with *-s,* you know it might be a base word with an *-s* ending.

Corrective feedback	If children are unable to answer the questions about the inflected ending *-s,* refer them to Sound-Spelling Card 129.

REVIEW INFLECTED ENDING *-ing* To review last week's second phonics skill, write *mixing.* You also studied words like this one. When a word ends with *-ing,* you know it might be a base word with an *-ing* ending. In this word, the base word is *mix* and it has an *-ing* ending. What is the word? *(mixing)*

GUIDE PRACTICE Draw a T-chart or use Graphic Organizer 4. When I say a word, hold a hand up high if it has an *-s* ending or down low if it has an *-ing* ending: *yelling, packs, hits, resting, passing, naps, wags, helping, taps, licking.* Write each word in the appropriate column. Read the lists together. Then call on individuals to use words in sentences.

-s	*-ing*
packs	yelling
hits	resting
naps	passing
wags	helping
taps	licking

Graphic Organizer 4

ON THEIR OWN Use Let's Practice It! pp. 59–60 on the *Teacher Resources DVD-ROM.*

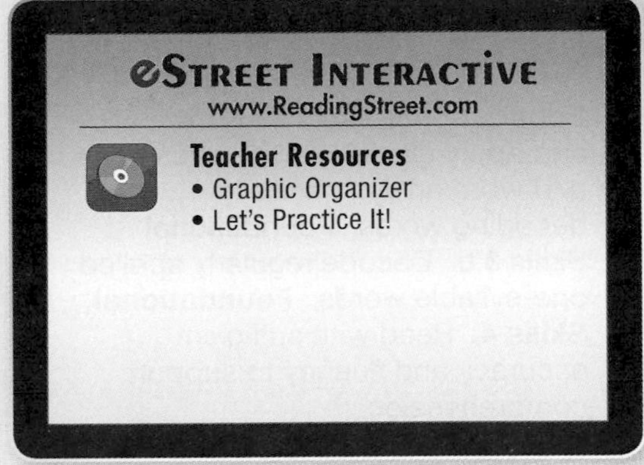

eStreet Interactive
www.ReadingStreet.com
Teacher Resources
• Graphic Organizer
• Let's Practice It!

Access for All

SI Strategic Intervention

Inflected Ending -s If children do not pronounce the inflected ending *-s,* then say each word with and without the inflected ending and have children repeat it.

A Advanced

Using Inflected Endings If children are able to produce words with inflected endings easily and with understanding, give them a base word, such as *pack,* and ask them to create a sentence that has the word with either the inflected ending *-s* or the inflected ending *-ing.*

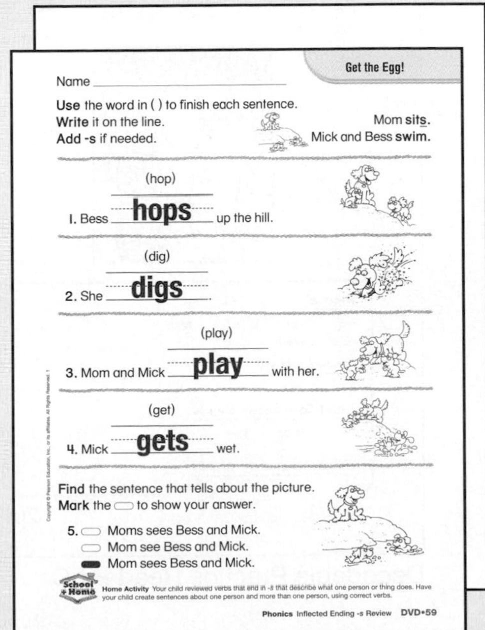
Get the Egg!

Name ______

Use the word in ( ) to finish each sentence.
Write it on the line.
Add -s if needed.

Mom **sits.**
Mick and Bess **swim.**

1. Bess **hops** up the hill. (hop)
2. She **digs** (dig)
3. Mom and Mick **play** with her. (play)
4. Mick **gets** wet. (get)

Find the sentence that tells about the picture.
Mark the ⬭ to show your answer.

5. ⬭ Moms sees Bess and Mick.
⬭ Mom see Bess and Mick.
⬬ Mom sees Bess and Mick.

Home Activity Your child reviewed verbs that end in -s that describe what one person or thing does. Have your child create sentences about one person and more than one person, using correct verbs.

Phonics Inflected Ending -s Review DVD•59

Let's Practice It! TR DVD•59–60

Common Core State Standards

Foundational Skills 3. Know and apply grade-level phonics and word analysis skills in decoding words. **Foundational Skills 3.b.** Decode regularly spelled one-syllable words. **Foundational Skills 4.** Read with sufficient accuracy and fluency to support comprehension.

Decodable Reader 5C

If children need help, then...

Read *The Sleds*

DECODE WORDS IN ISOLATION Have children turn to page 209 and decode each word listed.

REVIEW HIGH-FREQUENCY WORDS Review the previously taught words *little, the,* and *a.* Have children read each word as you point to it on the Word Wall.

PREVIEW Have children read the title and preview the story. Tell them they will read words with short *e* and initial consonant blends in this story.

DECODE WORDS IN CONTEXT Pair children for reading and listen as they decode. One child begins. Children read the entire story, switching readers after each page. Partners reread the story. This time the other child begins.

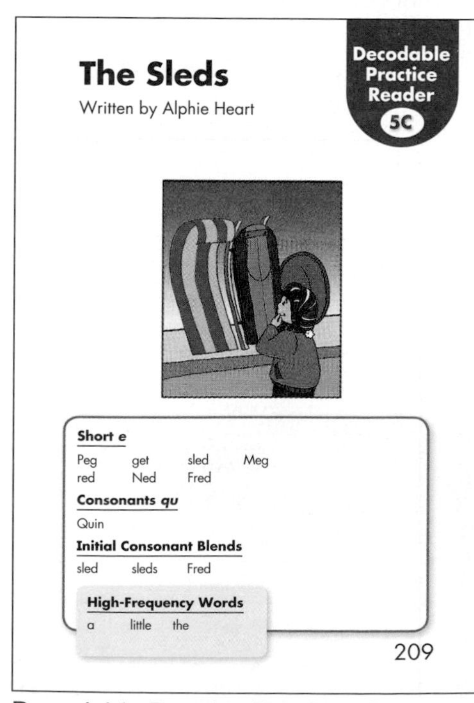

Decodable Practice Reader 5C

The Sleds

Written by Alphie Heart

Short *e*

Peg get sled Meg red Ned Fred

Consonants *qu*

Quin

Initial Consonant Blends

sled sleds Fred

High-Frequency Words

a little the

209

Decodable Practice Reader 5C

Peg can get a sled.

210

Peg can get a little sled.

211

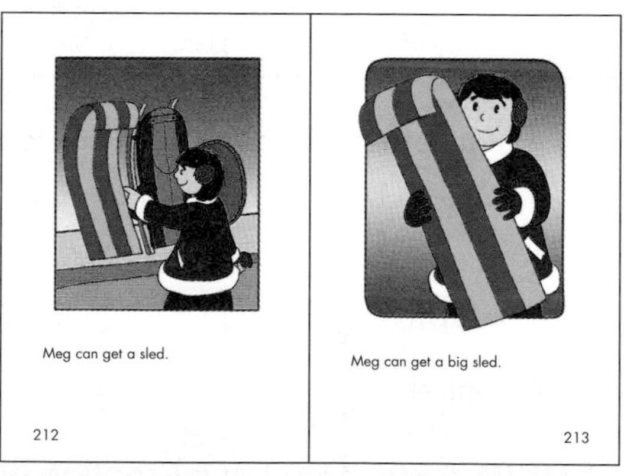

Meg can get a sled.

212

Meg can get a big sled.

213

Quin can get a sled.

214

Quin can get a red sled.

215

Get on the sleds!
Get Ned.
Get Fred.

216

Corrective feedback	**If...** children have difficulty decoding a word, **then...** refer them to the Sound-Spelling Cards to identify the sounds in the word. Then prompt them to blend the word. • What is the new word? • Is the new word a word you know? • Does it make sense in the story?

CHECK DECODING AND COMPREHENSION Have children retell the story to include characters, setting, and events. Then point to a word in the story that has a consonant blend and ask children to say the word. List words that children name. Children should supply *Fred, sled,* and *sleds.* Explain that these words begin with two consonant sounds that are blended together. Point to a word that has a short *e* sound and ask children to say the word. List the words that children name.

Reread for Fluency

REREAD DECODABLE READER Have children reread Decodable Practice Reader 5C to develop automaticity decoding words with the short *e* sound and initial consonant blends.

Routine Oral Rereading

1. **Read** Have children read the entire book orally.
2. **Reread** To achieve optimal fluency, children should reread the text three or four times.
3. **Corrective Feedback** Listen as children read. Provide corrective feedback regarding their fluency and decoding.

Routines Flip Chart

Decodable Practice Reader

Beginning Have children point out the words in the story with initial consonant blends. Have them practice saying the blend sounds together and then say the whole word: *sled* and *sleds*. Have them point out the words with the short *e* sound such as *Peg* and *Ned.* Ask them to say the words aloud.

Intermediate Have children say other words they know with the short *e* sound such as *web* and *bed* and words with initial consonant blends such as *friend, frog, free, fry, slip, slide, slam.*

Advanced After reading, have children think of words with initial consonant blends and words with the short *e* sound and ask them to create sentences with them.

Common Core State Standards

Foundational Skills 3. Know and apply grade-level phonics and word analysis skills in decoding words. **Language 2.d.** Use conventional spelling for words with common spelling patterns and for frequently occurring irregular words.

Spiral Review

These activities review

- previously taught high-frequency words *eat, four, five, her, this, too, where, take, are.*
- inflected endings *-s, -ing;* /a/ spelled *a;* /i/ spelled *i;* /o/ spelled *o.*

Fluent Word Reading

Spiral Review

READ WORDS IN ISOLATION Display these words. Tell children that they can blend some words on this list, and others are Word Wall words.

Have children read the list three or four times until they can read at the rate of two to three seconds per word.

too	**five**	**this**	**are**	**her**
can	**nap**	**four**	**packing**	**eats**
Tom	**Mom**	**black**	**locking**	**hops**
sit	**will**	**pots**	**vans**	**missing**

Corrective feedback — Word Reading

If... children have difficulty reading whole words,
then... have them use sound-by-sound blending for decodable words, or have them say and spell high-frequency words.

If... children cannot read fluently at a rate of two to three seconds per word,
then... have pairs practice the list until they can read it fluently.

READ WORDS IN CONTEXT Display these sentences. Call on individuals to read a sentence. Then randomly point to review words and have children read them. To help you monitor word reading, high-frequency words are underlined and decodable words are italicized.

<u>Where</u> *can Tom sit and nap?*

Mom will* <u>take</u> *six black pots.

Ten men* <u>are</u> *packing and locking vans.

Sal* <u>eats</u> *less and less.

Corrective feedback — Sentence Reading

If... children are unable to read an underlined high-frequency word,
then... read the word for them and spell it, having them echo you.

If... children have difficulty reading an italicized decodable word,
then... guide them in using sound-by-sound blending.

Spelling

Short *e* Words

PARTNER REVIEW Supply pairs of children with index cards on which the spelling words have been written. Have one child read a word while the other writes it. Then have children switch roles. Have them use the cards to check their spelling and correct any misspelled words.

ON THEIR OWN Use *Reader's and Writer's Notebook,* p. 199.

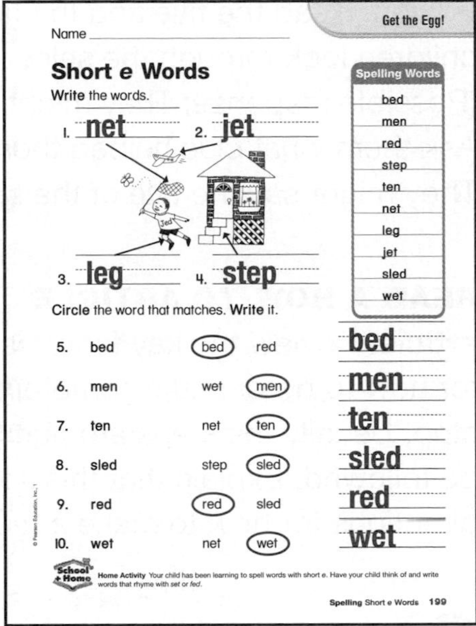

Name

Get the Egg!

Short *e* Words

Write the words.

1. net
2. jet
3. leg
4. step

Spelling Words
bed
men
red
step
ten
net
leg
jet
sled
wet

Circle the word that matches. Write it.

5.	bed	(bed)	red	bed
6.	men	wet	(men)	men
7.	ten	net	(ten)	ten
8.	sled	step	(sled)	sled
9.	red	(red)	sled	red
10.	wet	net	(wet)	wet

© Pearson Education, Inc., 1

School + Home **Home Activity** Your child has been learning to spell words with short *e*. Have your child think of and write words that rhyme with *set* or *fed*.

Spelling Short *e* Words 199

Reader's and Writer's Notebook, p. 199

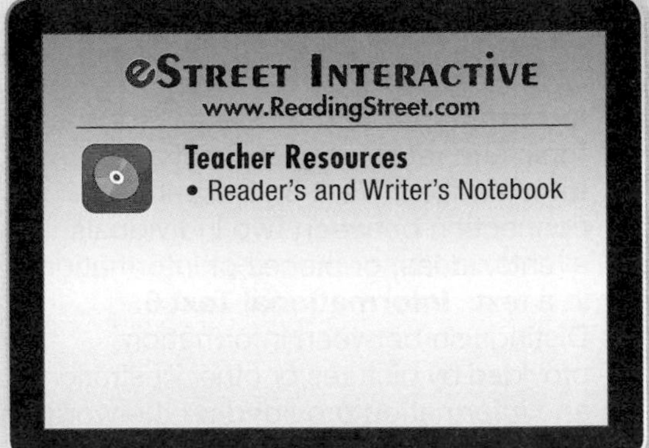

ELL

Fluent Word Reading Have children listen to a more fluent reader say the words. Then have them repeat the words.

Day 4 SMALL GROUP TIME • Differentiate Vocabulary, p. SG•69

OL On-Level

- **Develop** Language Using Selection Vocabulary
- **Read** *Reading Street Sleuth,* pp. 16–17

SI Strategic Intervention

- **Review/Discuss** Selection Vocabulary
- **Read** *Reading Street Sleuth,* pp. 16–17

A Advanced

- **Extend** Amazing Words and Selection Vocabulary
- **Read** *Reading Street Sleuth,* pp. 16–17
- **Organize** Inquiry Project

ELL

If... children need more scaffolding and practice with **Vocabulary,** **then...** use the routine on pp. xxxvi–xxxvii in the *ELL Handbook.*

Common Core State Standards

Informational Text 2. Identify the main topic and retell key details of a text. **Informational Text 3.** Describe the connection between two individuals, events, ideas, or pieces of information in a text. **Informational Text 6.** Distinguish between information provided by pictures or other illustrations and information provided by the words in a text.

Science in Reading

How-to Article

ACTIVATE PRIOR KNOWLEDGE Ask children what they have already learned about birds. (They build their nests in trees. They lay eggs in their nests.)

PREVIEW AND PREDICT Have children turn to page 142 in their Student Edition. Read the title and the first two sentences of the selection. Have children look through the selection and predict what they might learn. (Possible response: They might learn how to help birds get food to eat.) Ask them what clue helped them make that prediction. (Possible response: They might say the title of the selection or the pictures.)

READ A HOW-TO ARTICLE Tell children that they will read a **how-to article.** Review the key features of a how-to article: It is a set of instructions for how to do or make something. The directions often have more than one step. Usually the steps are numbered to show the order in which they should be followed. Explain that this selection is a how-to article because it gives directions for how to make a feeder for birds.

Genre

LET'S THINK ABOUT... As you read "Help the Birds" together, use Let's Think About in the Student Edition to help children focus on the features of a how-to article.

1. The seeds won't stick on the twig.
2. I made a bird feeder.

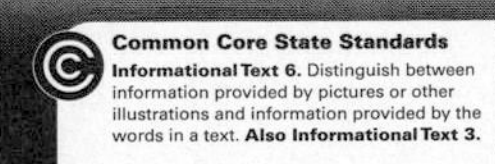

Common Core State Standards
Informational Text 6. Distinguish between information provided by pictures or other illustrations and information provided by the words in a text. **Also Informational Text 3.**

Science in Reading

Genre
How-to Article

- A how-to article is procedural text that tells you how to make or do something.
- A how-to article is usually a set of directions.
- The directions in a how-to article are often numbered. They are listed in the order you should do each step, from first to last.
- If you follow the directions as they are written, you will be successful.
- Read "Help the Birds." As you read, think about what you've learned about how-to articles.

Help the Birds

Birds like to eat.
You can help.

1 Get a small twig.

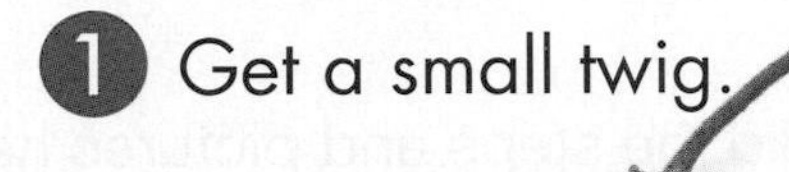

2 Dip it here.

3 Dip it in this.

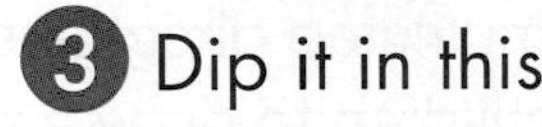

4 Clip it to your tree.
Watch the birds come.

Let's Think About...
What might happen if you did not follow the second step?
How-to Article

1

Let's Think About...
Read the directions, following each step. What did you make or do?
How-to Article

2

Let's Think About...
Reading Across Texts How is the girl in "Help the Birds" like Brad and Kim in *Get the Egg!*?
Writing Across Texts If Brad and Kim decided to make treats for the six small birds, what would they make? Write a how-to article for them.

142 143

Student Edition, pp. 142–143

Access Text

Think Aloud **MAIN IDEA AND DETAILS** The **main idea** is what a selection is mostly about. **Details,** or small pieces of information, tell more about the main idea. In *Get the Egg!* some details were a red bird had a nest in a tree, the nest had eggs in it, and one of the eggs fell out of the nest. The main idea was Kim and Brad saved the egg. As I read "Help the Birds," I will pay attention to the details so I can better understand the main idea.

Think Aloud **MULTISTEP DIRECTIONS** When I read the title of the article and see the numbered steps, I wonder what I will learn to do or make to help birds. Since there are numbers, I know the numbers are in a certain order. I know if I want to learn how to do something, I must follow the steps in the correct order. If I don't, then things will not work out.

eStreet Interactive
www.ReadingStreet.com
Pearson eText
- Student Edition

Academic Vocabulary

how-to article writing made up of numbered instructions for how to do or make something

Science Vocabulary

twig a small branch of a tree

Common Core State Standards

Informational Text 1. Ask and answer questions about key details in a text. **Informational Text 2.** Identify the main topic and retell key details of a text. **Foundational Skills 4.b.** Read on-level text orally with accuracy, appropriate rate, and expression on successive readings.

Writing to Sources

Use Connect the Texts on pp. 60–61 to guide children in writing text-based responses using two sources.

Access Text

MAIN IDEA What is this selection mostly about? (The selection is about how to make a simple feeder for birds.)

STEPS IN A PROCESS What might happen if you didn't do step 2 before step 3? (The birdseed probably wouldn't stick to the twig.)

TEXT STRUCTURE How did the steps and pictures help you to understand how to make the feeder? (The steps told the right order to do things in. The pictures helped show the right materials to use and what the feeder should look like.)

Reading and Writing Across Texts

Children might note that the characters in *Get the Egg!* and the girl in "Help the Birds" both do something to help wild birds in their neighborhood.

Children might write a similar set of multistep directions that they read about in their Student Edition. Suggest to children to draw a picture to go with each step.

Fluency

Appropriate Phrasing

- Have children turn to pp. 134–135 in *Get the Egg!*
- Have children follow along as you read the pages with appropriate phrasing, stopping at each period.
- Have the class read the pages with you and then reread the pages as a group without you until they read with appropriate phrasing, stopping at each period. To provide additional fluency practice, pair nonfluent readers with fluent readers.

Routine Paired Reading

1. **Select a Passage** For *Get the Egg!*, use pp. 136–137.
2. **Model** First, have children track the print as you read.
3. **Guide Practice** Then have children read along with you.
4. **On Their Own** For optimal fluency, have partners reread three or four times.

Routines Flip Chart

MONITOR PROGRESS Fluency Check

As children reread, monitor their progress toward their individual fluency goals. Mid-Year Goal: 20–30 words correct per minute. End-of-Year Goal: 60 words correct per minute. Beginning in Unit 3, children will be assessed to determine WCPM.

If... children are not on track to meet benchmark goals,
then... have children practice with text at their independent level.

Access for All

 Advanced

Rate If children already read at 60 words correct per minute, have them read more challenging text.

Options for Oral Rereading

Use *Get the Egg!* or one of this week's Decodable Practice Readers.

Conventions

Interrogative Sentences

TEST PRACTICE Use *Reader's and Writer's Notebook,* p. 200 to help children understand identifying interrogative sentences in test items. Recall that an interrogative sentence is an asking sentence that begins with a capital letter and ends with a question mark. Model identifying an interrogative sentence by writing this sentence on the board, reading it aloud, and underlining the capital letter and the question mark.

Where do squirrels live?

ON THEIR OWN Then read the directions on *Reader's and Writer's Notebook,* p. 200. Guide children as they mark the answer for number 1.

APPLY After children mark the answers to numbers 1–6, review the correct choices aloud, and have children read each interrogative sentence.

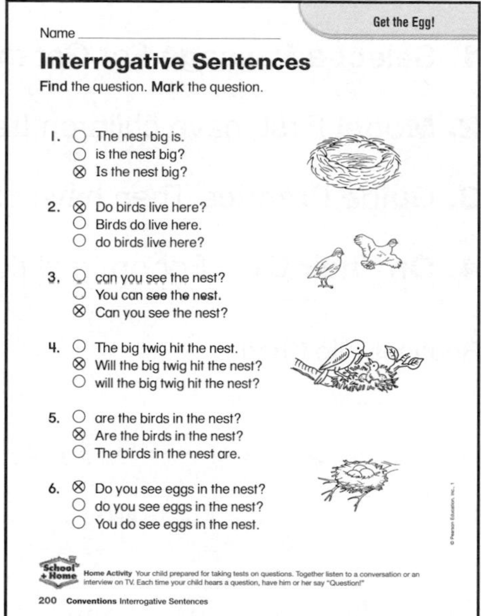

Name ____________ Get the Egg!

Interrogative Sentences

Find the question. **Mark** the question.

1. ○ The nest big is.
   ○ is the nest big?
   ⊗ Is the nest big?
2. ⊗ Do birds live here?
   ○ Birds do live here.
   ○ do birds live here?
3. ○ can you see the nest?
   ○ You can see the nest.
   ⊗ Can you see the nest?
4. ○ The big twig hit the nest.
   ⊗ Will the big twig hit the nest?
   ○ will the big twig hit the nest?
5. ○ are the birds in the nest?
   ⊗ Are the birds in the nest?
   ○ The birds in the nest are.
6. ⊗ Do you see eggs in the nest?
   ○ do you see eggs in the nest?
   ○ You do see eggs in the nest.

School + Home **Home Activity** Your child prepared for taking tests on questions. Together listen to a conversation or an interview on TV. Each time your child hears a question, have him or her say "Question!"

200 **Conventions** Interrogative Sentences

Reader's and Writer's Notebook, p. 200

Common Core State Standards

Foundational Skills 1.a. Recognize the distinguishing features of a sentence (e.g., first word, capitalization, ending punctuation). **Writing 3.** Write narratives in which they recount two or more appropriately sequenced events, include some details regarding what happened, use temporal words to signal event order, and provide some sense of closure. **Writing 5.** With guidance and support from adults, focus on a topic, respond to questions and suggestions from peers, and add details to strengthen writing as needed. **Language 1.j.** Produce and expand complete simple and compound declarative, interrogative, imperative, and exclamatory sentences in response to prompts.

Bridge to Common Core

CONVENTIONS OF STANDARD ENGLISH

In this week's lessons, children learn that an interrogative sentence is a sentence that asks something. They learn that it is often called a question and begins with a capital letter and ends with a question mark. They learn how to change a statement into a question by using appropriate subject-verb inversion. As they do this, they are gaining control of the conventions of standard English grammar, usage, and mechanics.

Daily Fix-It

7. the mix is a hitt.
   The mix is a hit.
8. This mix winz too
   This mix wins too.

Discuss the Daily Fix-It corrections with children. Review sentence capitalization and punctuation, /z/ spelled *s,* the inflected ending *-s,* and the spelling of *hit.*

Realistic Story

Mini-Lesson Revise: Adding a Sentence

- Yesterday we wrote realistic stories about children seeing an animal. Today we will revise to help people who read the stories. One way to make the stories clearer is to add a sentence.

- Display the Revising Tips. Explain that this is a time for making the story clear for anyone who will read it. Tomorrow children will proofread to correct any errors such as misspellings, missing capital letters, or misplaced sentence periods.

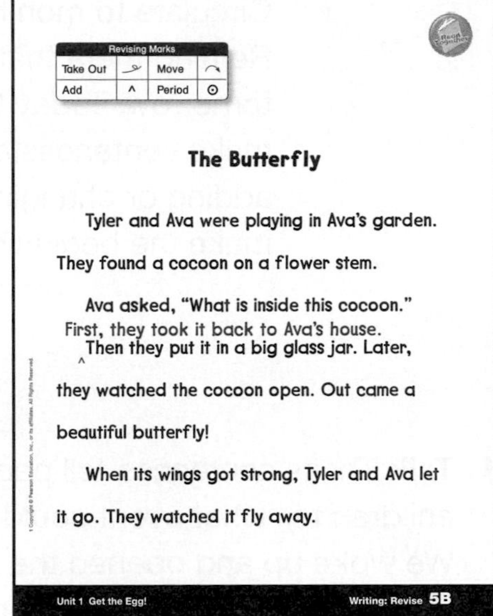
Revising Marks

Take Out		Move	
Add	^	Period	⊙

The Butterfly

Tyler and Ava were playing in Ava's garden. They found a cocoon on a flower stem.

Ava asked, "What is inside this cocoon." First, they took it back to Ava's house. Then they put it in a big glass jar. Later, they watched the cocoon open. Out came a beautiful butterfly!

When its wings got strong, Tyler and Ava let it go. They watched it fly away.

Unit 1 Get the Egg! Writing: Revise 5B

Writing Transparency 5B TR DVD

Revising Tips

✔ Make sure your story events could really happen.

✔ Add sentences to make the story clearer.

- Use Writing Transparency 5B to model adding sentences. In my realistic story "The Butterfly," Tyler and Ava find a cocoon. I'm going to add the sentence *First, they took it back to Ava's house* to the beginning of the third paragraph. Now it is clearer that part of the story happens in Ava's house, not in her garden. Add the sentence to the transparency. Tell children that they can add sentences to their story as they revise.

PEER CONFERENCING • PEER REVISION Pair up children and tell half to read the partner's story. Allow one to two minutes. Then have the readers ask the writers one question about the story. Repeat with second partners reading and asking a question about the other story. Have each writer consider whether a sentence should be added, based on the readers' questions. Circulate to assist children planning to revise their stories. As appropriate, suggest adding sentences to make stories clearer.

Access for All

SI Strategic Intervention

Sentence Production If children have difficulty asking questions during peer conferencing, ask them questions about classroom items. For example: *What is this? How many blocks do we have?* Then encourage pairs to ask each other questions about classroom items.

Subject-Verb Agreement Be sure children understand that plural forms differ from singular forms.

Common Core State Standards

Writing 3. Write narratives in which they recount two or more appropriately sequenced events, include some details regarding what happened, use temporal words to signal event order, and provide some sense of closure. **Writing 5.** With guidance and support from adults, focus on a topic, respond to questions and suggestions from peers, and add details to strengthen writing as needed. **Also Writing 7., 8.**

Writing

GUIDE PRACTICE Have children revise their stories. For those not sure how to revise, have children refer to the Revising Tips or the Key Features of a Realistic Story.

Corrective feedback	Circulate to monitor and confer with children as they write. Remind them that they will have time to proofread and edit tomorrow. Today they can make changes in story events or make sentences clearer. Help them understand the benefits of adding or changing words or sentences. Encourage them to make the beginning, middle, and end interesting.

Routine Quick Write for Fluency

Team Talk

1. **Talk** These sentences tell part of a story. Read them aloud, and have children tell what event could be missing from the story.
   We woke up and opened the shades.
   We were going to need our umbrellas!
2. **Write** Have children write a sentence that could be added to the story to make it clearer.
3. **Share** Partners can read the sentences to one another.

Routines Flip Chart

Research and Inquiry

Step 4 Synthesize

TEACH Tell children that the next step in their project is to review the lists they made to see if they have the information they set out to find. Or, do their lists have information that is not about their topic?

Think Aloud **MODEL** We wanted to make a list of wild animals in our neighborhood. First, we picked a place to watch for animals. Then we wrote the names or drew pictures of the animals we would see there. Now I will look at the list I made. I will see if all the animals on the list are wild animals, not pets. If some of the animals are pets, I can cross them off the list. I will also check the spelling of the animal names on my list. If a word is spelled wrong, I will write the word again with the correct spelling.

GUIDE PRACTICE Have children look at the lists they made during Day 3. Instruct them to work with a partner to go over their lists. If necessary, they can look out the classroom window to look for more wild animals. Finally, tell children that tomorrow they will organize their lists in order to share them with others.

Access for All

A Advanced

Information Sources Give children time to check the spelling of animal names on their lists by providing reference books about animals, such as encyclopedias, nonfiction books, or magazines.

Wrap Up Your Day!

- ✔ **Phonics Review** List several words with the short *e* sound spelled *e*, such as *get, bed,* and *step.* Have children read each word and identify the letter that spells the sound /e/.
- ✔ **Fluency** Write *Mom did hop. Stan can run.* Have the class reread the sentences until they can do so with appropriate phrasing.

Remind children that they heard about Maisie, a girl who caught a toad. Tomorrow they will hear about Maisie and the toad again.

DAY 5 at a Glance

Content Knowledge
Oral Vocabulary

Phonemic Awareness
Segment and Blend Onset and Rime

Phonics/Spelling
Review Short *e: e*
Review Initial Consonant Blends

Text-Based Comprehension
Main Idea and Details

Selection Words
Review

High-Frequency Words
Review

Assessment
Phonics
High-Frequency Words
Fluency

Conventions
Review Interrogative Sentences

Writing
Realistic Story: Proofread

Research and Inquiry
Communicate

Materials

- Student Edition
- Read Aloud Anthology
- Weekly Test

Bridge to Common Core

INTEGRATION OF KNOWLEDGE/IDEAS
This week children have acquired knowledge to further develop the unit concept as they read, wrote, and discussed ideas about wild animals in their neighborhoods. They have developed knowledge from the diverse print and technology resources for the unit topic of Animals, Tame and Wild.

Science Knowledge Goals
Children have learned that

- all kinds of animals live in our neighborhood
- neighborhood animals need different kinds of food and shelter

Content Knowledge

Neighborhood Animals

REVIEW THE CONCEPT This week we have read and listened to stories about animals that live in different habitats. Today you will listen to a story about a toad. Read the story.

- Where did Maisie catch the toad? (in the garden)
- Why does Maisie use moist dirt for the toad's home? (Toads need the moisture to keep from getting dehydrated.)

"Maisie Caught a Toad Today"

Build Oral Language

REVIEW AMAZING WORDS Orally review the meanings of this week's Amazing Words. Then display this week's concept map. Have children use Amazing Words such as *habitat, survive,* and *moist,* as well as the concept map, to answer the question *Which wild animals live in our neighborhood?*

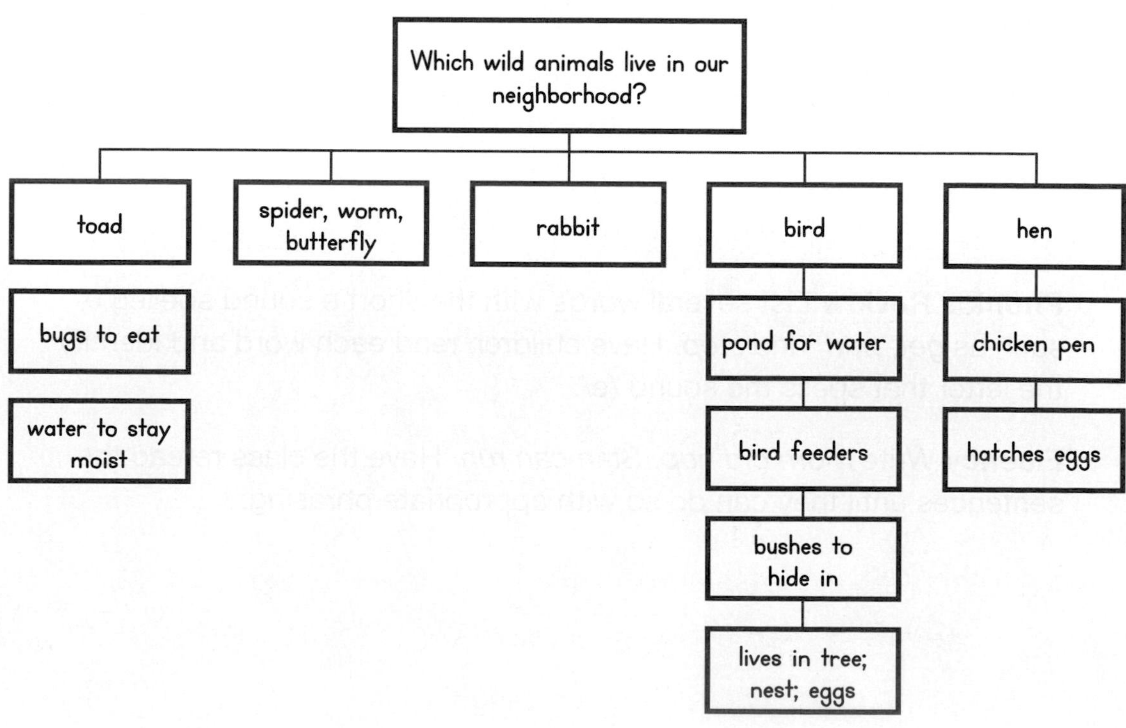

Build Oral Vocabulary

Team Talk **CONNECT TO AMAZING IDEAS** Pair children and have them discuss how the Question of the Week, *Which wild animals live in our neighborhood?,* connects to the question of this unit of study: *How are people and animals important to one another?* Tell children to use the concept map and what they've learned from this week's discussions and reading selections to form an Amazing Idea—a realization or "big idea" about **animals, tame and wild.** Use the following ideas as prompts:

- What neighborhood animals did we read about? (bird, toad)
- Where do these animals lives in our neighborhood?

Then ask each pair to share their Amazing Idea with the class. Encourage children to recall in which selection they learned their ideas.

Amazing Ideas might include:

- Wild animals need food, water, and shelter.
- You can help protect wild animals from danger.

Check Oral Vocabulary

FORMATIVE ASSESSMENT Call on individuals to use this week's Amazing Words to talk about what wild animals need. Prompt discussion with the questions below. Monitor children's ability to use the Amazing Words and note which words children are unable to use.

- **What do birds need in their *habitat* to *survive?***
- **What do you think happens when baby birds *hatch* from their eggs?**
- **Where might you hear birds *chirp?***
- **What does a toad's *croak* sound like?**
- **How can you help keep a toad *moist* so it won't get too dry?**

If… children have difficulty using the Amazing Words,

then… reteach the unknown words using the Robust Vocabulary routines, pp. 121a, 126b, 138b, 142b.

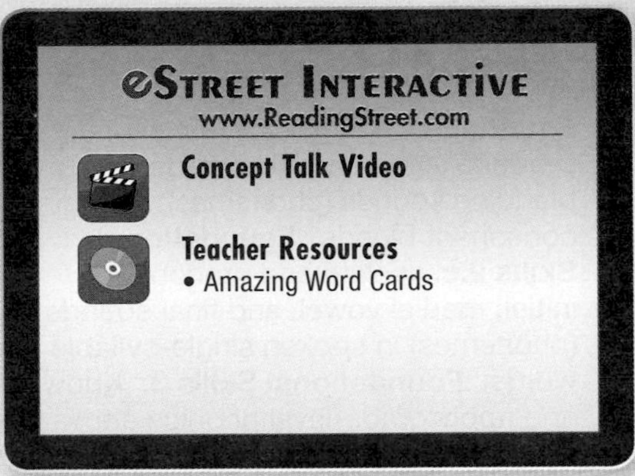

habitat	chirp
hatch	croak
survive	moist

Check Concepts and Language Use the Day 5 instruction on ELL Poster 5 to monitor children's understanding of the lesson concept.

Amazing Words Give children the initial consonant, consonant blend, or digraph *(chirp)* as clues when you review the Amazing Words.

Common Core State Standards

Foundational Skills 2.b. Orally produce single-syllable words by blending sounds (phonemes), including consonant blends. **Foundational Skills 2.c.** Isolate and pronounce initial, medial vowel, and final sounds (phonemes) in spoken single-syllable words. **Foundational Skills 3.** Know and apply grade-level phonics and word analysis skills in decoding words. **Language 2.d.** Use conventional spelling for words with common spelling patterns and for frequently occurring irregular words.

Phonemic Awareness

Review Segment and Blend Onset and Rime

ONSET AND RIME Have children segment and blend the onset and rime in each word below. If children make an error, model the correct response. Return to the word later in the practice.

/b/ -ed **bed**	/m/ -iss **miss**	/p/ -ig **pig**
/s/ -ad **sad**	/f/ -ox **fox**	/r/ -ug **rug**
/d/ -ish **dish**	/j/ -et **jet**	/v/ -an **van**

Phonics

Review Short *e: e;* Initial Consonant Blends

TARGET PHONICS SKILLS Write the following sentences on the board. Have children read each one, first quietly to themselves and then aloud as you track the print.

1. **The crab will get wet.**
2. **Meg has ten blocks and six bricks.**
3. **Get on the black sled.**
4. **Glen can skip, and Ben can swim.**

Team Talk Have children discuss with a partner which words have the short *e* sound and which words have initial consonant blends. Then call on individuals to share with the class.

Spelling Test

Words with Short *e*

DICTATE SPELLING WORDS Say each word, read the sentence, repeat the word, and allow time for children to write the word.

1. men	The **men** will fix the deck.
2. red	Lisa fed the **red** hen.
3. step	**Step** on the dock.
4. ten	**Ten** kids are going.
5. net	Get the bird with a **net.**
6. leg	I hit my **leg** on the rocks.
7. jet	Will you get on the big **jet?**
8. sled	Dad is fixing my **sled.**
9. wet	The dog got **wet.**
10. bed	I nap in my **bed.**

High-Frequency Words

11. saw	I **saw** a big cat.
12. your	Kick the ball with **your** foot.

Assess

- Spell words with short *e.*
- Spell high-frequency words.

Access for All

SI Strategic Intervention

High-Frequency Words To help children recognize the high-frequency words, use them in everyday short sentences that children hear often, such as *Where is your ________?*

Pronunciation If children tend to pronounce short *e* as short *i,* especially before the letter *n,* as in *pen, den,* and *Ben,* say such words slowly and distinctly, emphasizing the sound /e/ to help with correct pronunciation.

Day 5 SMALL GROUP TIME • Differentiate Reteaching, p. SG•69

OL On-Level

- **Practice** Interrogative Sentences
- **Reread** *Reading Street Sleuth,* pp. 16–17

SI Strategic Intervention

- **Review** High-Frequency Words
- **Reread** *Reading Street Sleuth,* pp. 16–17

A Advanced

- **Extend** Interrogative Sentences
- **Reread** *Reading Street Sleuth,* pp. 16–17
- **Communicate** Inquiry Project

If... children need more scaffolding and practice with **Conventions and Writing,**
then... use the activities on pp. DI•104–DI•105 in the Teacher Resources section on SuccessNet.

Common Core State Standards Speaking/Listening 4. Describe people, places, things, and events with relevant details, expressing ideas and feelings clearly. Also Foundational Skills 4.b., Language 5.b.

Let's Learn It!

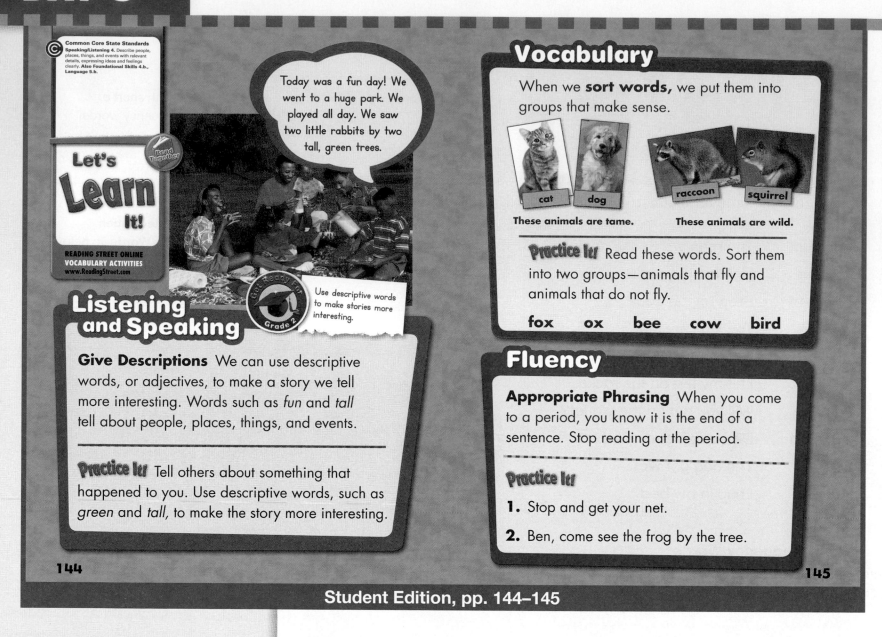

READING STREET ONLINE
VOCABULARY ACTIVITIES
www.ReadingStreet.com

Today was a fun day! We went to a huge park. We played all day. We saw two little rabbits by two tall, green trees.

Get Ready For Grade 2: Use descriptive words to make stories more interesting.

Listening and Speaking

Give Descriptions We can use descriptive words, or adjectives, to make a story we tell more interesting. Words such as *fun* and *tall* tell about people, places, things, and events.

Practice It! Tell others about something that happened to you. Use descriptive words, such as *green* and *tall,* to make the story more interesting.

Vocabulary

When we **sort words,** we put them into groups that make sense.

cat dog

These animals are tame.

raccoon squirrel

These animals are wild.

Practice It! Read these words. Sort them into two groups—animals that fly and animals that do not fly.

fox ox bee cow bird

Fluency

Appropriate Phrasing When you come to a period, you know it is the end of a sentence. Stop reading at the period.

Practice It!

1. Stop and get your net.
2. Ben, come see the frog by the tree.

144 145

Student Edition, pp. 144–145

Common Core State Standards

Foundational Skills 4.b. Read on-level text orally with accuracy, appropriate rate, and expression on successive readings. **Speaking/Listening 4.** Describe people, places, things, and events with relevant details, expressing ideas and feelings clearly. **Also Language 5.a., 5.b.**

Give Descriptions

In addition to using descriptive words to make a story more interesting, children at Grade 2 should also be able to speak clearly at an appropriate rate, sharing ideas that are focused and to the point.

Listening and Speaking

Give Descriptions

TEACH Have children turn to page 144 of the Student Edition. Read and discuss what members of the family said about their picnic. Remind children that good speakers use describing words to make a story more interesting. The first sentence says *Today was a fun day!* What word in this sentence describes the day? The word *fun* describes the day. Have children name the describing words in the remaining sentences.

INTRODUCE PROMPT Read the Practice It! prompt with the class. Remind children that their story should use describing words to make it interesting.

Team Talk Have pairs take turns listening to and speaking about something that happened to them. Tell children that good speakers speak clearly and slowly and in complete sentences.

Vocabulary

Sort Words

TEACH Read and discuss the Vocabulary lesson on page 145 of the Student Edition. Use the model to explain that words can be sorted, or put into groups that make sense. Point to the pictures of the cat and the dog. Why do the cat and the dog go together? The cat and the dog go together because they are both tame. Point to the other pictures. Do the squirrel and the raccoon go together? Yes, because both the squirrel and the raccoon are wild animals, not tame.

GUIDE PRACTICE Read the instructions for the Vocabulary Practice It! activity. Then write the headings *Animals That Fly* and *Animals That Do Not Fly.* Read the first word and have children repeat after you.

Can a fox fly? No, a fox can't fly. So I will say and write *fox* under the heading *Animals That Do Not Fly.*

ON THEIR OWN Have children continue saying and writing the other words under the appropriate heading.

Corrective feedback | Circulate around the room and listen as children say and sort the words. Provide assistance as needed.

Fluency

Appropriate Phrasing

TEACH Read and discuss the Fluency instructions.

READ WORDS IN CONTEXT Give children a moment to look at the sentences. Then have them read each sentence three or four times until they can read each sentence with appropriate phrasing.

Access for All

SI Strategic Intervention

Visualize Skills Some children might find it helpful to see additional visual representations of the vocabulary skill, sort.

Language Production Children may need help identifying the animals in the vocabulary list. Provide photos of a fox, ox, bee, cow, and bird.

Common Core State Standards

Literature 1. Ask and answer questions about key details in a text. **Informational Text 6.** Distinguish between information provided by pictures or other illustrations and information provided by the words in a text.

Text-Based Comprehension

Review Main Idea and Details

Remember that good readers can tell what a story or selection is mostly about. They can tell us its main idea. What do good readers think about to find the main idea in a story? (the details)

CHECK UNDERSTANDING Read aloud the following story and have children answer the questions that follow.

Malia found a beautiful rock to add to her rock collection. But where should she put it? She kept all her round rocks in one bag and all her flat rocks in another bag. Malia also had a bag of rough rocks and a bag of black rocks. Malia's new rock was smooth and black, so she put it in the bag with the other black rocks. What a big rock collection she had!

1. What is this story mostly about? (It is mostly about Malia deciding how to add a new rock to her rock collection.)
2. What tells you this? (Malia has a rock collection. She finds a new rock. She has different types of rocks in different bags. Her new rock is smooth and black.)

Vocabulary

Review High-Frequency and Selection Words

HIGH-FREQUENCY WORDS Review this week's high-frequency words: *saw, small, tree, your.* Provide an example of a rhyming riddle for one of the words for the class to solve, such as: I'm thinking of a word that rhymes with *paw.* (saw)

Team Talk Have children work with a partner to trade rhyming riddles for the remaining three words.

SELECTION WORDS Write the word *bird.* Read it aloud together. Have children tell what the word means.

Corrective feedback	**If...** children cannot tell what the selection word means, **then...** review the definition on page 128a.

Genre

Review How-to Article

HOW-TO ARTICLE Review with children that a how-to article gives step-by-step directions for making or doing something. The steps are numbered to show the order in which they should be followed, and most steps have pictures to help readers understand what to do. The author of a how-to article wants readers to follow the steps carefully and in order. Have children turn to pages 142–143 in their Student Edition.

TEACH In "Help the Birds," the author tells the reader how to make a bird feeder. The steps are numbered, so it's clear what to do first, second, third, and so on. Each step has a picture that shows what to do.

Think Aloud **MODEL** When I look at this article, I see there are four steps altogether. The steps are numbered, so I will read and follow Step 1 first. After I read what to do, I look at the picture. Looking at the picture helps me understand exactly what the author wants me to do. The first picture shows me the kind of stick I should get.

GUIDE PRACTICE Ask the following questions to guide children in understanding a how-to article.

- What do the directions in Step 2 say to do? (Dip the stick.)
- Why is the picture especially important in Step 2? (The picture is important because it shows what to dip the stick in. The words do not give this information.)

ON THEIR OWN Remember, there are four steps in this how-to article. What are the last two steps? (Dip the stick in bird seed. Clip it to a tree.)

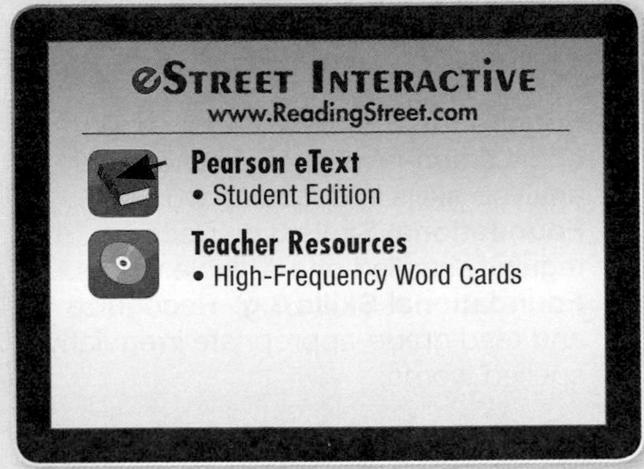

Access for All

SI Strategic Intervention

Connect Text to Pictures If children have difficulty understanding the connection between the text and the picture, ask them questions that help clarify the relationship. For example: What is being dipped in peanut butter? Then where is the twig being dipped? What is being clipped on to the tree? Help children understand that, in each case, the word *it* in the text refers to the twig.

Academic Vocabulary

how-to article writing made up of numbered instructions for how to do or make something

Common Core State Standards

Foundational Skills 3. Know and apply grade-level phonics and word analysis skills in decoding words.
Foundational Skills 3.b. Decode regularly spelled one-syllable words.
Foundational Skills 3.g. Recognize and read grade-appropriate irregularly spelled words.

Assess

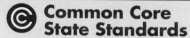

- ◉ Words with Short *e*
- ◉ Initial Consonant Blends
- • High-Frequency Words

Assessment

Monitor Progress

For a written assessment of short *e,* initial consonant blends, high-frequency words, and main ideas and details, use Weekly Test 5, pages 61–66.

WORD READING Use the following reproducible page to assess children's ability to read words in isolation. Call on children to read the words aloud. Start over if necessary.

SENTENCE READING Use the reproducible page on page 145f to assess children's ability to read words in context. Call on children to read two sentences aloud. Start over with sentence one if necessary.

MONITOR ACCURACY Use the Word/Sentence Reading Chart for this unit in *First Stop.*

MONITOR PROGRESS Word and Sentence Reading

If... children have trouble reading words with short *e* and initial consonant blends,
then... use the Reteach lessons in *First Stop.*

If... a child cannot read all the high-frequency words,
then... mark the missed words on a high-frequency word list and have the child practice reading the words with a fluent reader.

Name ______________________________

Read the Words

1. bed
2. Ben
3. small
4. frog
5. traps
6. net
7. saw
8. sled
9. spot
10. tree
11. wet
12. your

MONITOR PROGRESS

- Short *e: e*
- Initial Consonant Blends
- High-Frequency Words

Name ______________________________

Read the Sentences

1. Pop saw ten blocks.

2. Brad, look at your net.

3. The small frog is wet.

4. Meg saw a green spot.

5. We met Fran at the tree.

6. Ted, come and see your frog.

MONITOR PROGRESS

- Fluency
- Short *e: e*
- Initial Consonant Blends
- High-Frequency Words

Conventions

Review Interrogative Sentences

REVIEW Remind children that interrogative sentences ask something. They begin with a capital letter and end with a question mark. Have children give examples of questions.

GUIDE PRACTICE Write the following interrogative sentences. Have children write capital letters and question marks where they belong.

1. **where is the red bird**
2. **what does a toad eat**
3. **when does an owl sleep**

APPLY Display and read the following sentence. Have children work in pairs to ask questions for which the statement could be the answer. Then have them share their responses with the class.

The tiger eats dinner after dark.

ON THEIR OWN Use Let's Practice It! p. 63 from the *Teacher Resources DVD-ROM.*

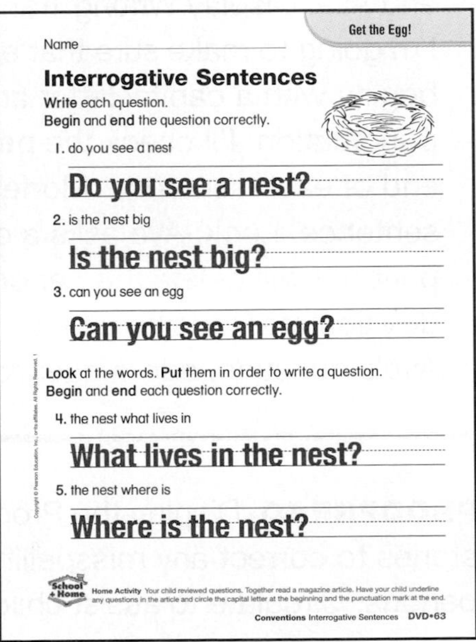
Name ______ Get the Egg!

Interrogative Sentences
Write each question.
Begin and **end** the question correctly.

1. do you see a nest
Do you see a nest?
2. is the nest big
Is the nest big?
3. can you see an egg
Can you see an egg?

Look at the words. **Put** them in order to write a question.
Begin and **end** each question correctly.

4. the nest what lives in
What lives in the nest?
5. the nest where is
Where is the nest?

Home Activity Your child reviewed questions. Together read a magazine article. Have your child underline any questions in the article and circle the capital letter at the beginning and the punctuation mark at the end.

Conventions Interrogative Sentences DVD•63

Let's Practice It! TR DVD•63

Common Core State Standards

Foundational Skills 1.a. Recognize the distinguishing features of a sentence (e.g., first word, capitalization, ending punctuation). **Language 1.j.** Produce and expand complete simple and compound declarative, interrogative, imperative, and exclamatory sentences in response to prompts. **Language 2.b.** Use end punctuation for sentences. **Also Language 1.**

Daily Fix-It

9. You can use my nett
   You can use my ne<u>t.</u>
10. stepp up here to see a bird.
    <u>Step</u> up here to see a bird.

Discuss the Daily Fix-It corrections with children. Review sentence capitalization and punctuation and the spellings of *net* and *step.*

Word Order Point out that in English, questions usually have a different word order than statements. In a question, the auxiliary verb often comes before the subject. Provide additional practice forming statements and questions with the correct word order by having children turn statements such as *The bird flies to the nest* into questions, such as *Where does the bird fly?*

Common Core State Standards

Writing 3. Write narratives in which they recount two or more appropriately sequenced events, include some details regarding what happened, use temporal words to signal event order, and provide some sense of closure. **Writing 5.** With guidance and support from adults, focus on a topic, respond to questions and suggestions from peers, and add details to strengthen writing as needed. **Language 2.** Demonstrate command of the conventions of standard English capitalization, punctuation, and spelling when writing. **Language 2.b.** Use end punctuation for sentences. **Also Writing 6.**

Bridge to Common Core

PRODUCTION AND DISTRIBUTION OF WRITING

As children planned, wrote, and edited their stories throughout the week, they now create a final draft that reflects the changes they made in order to produce clear, coherent, and complete sentences. They focus on correct capitalization, punctuation, and correct use of sequence words for the order of events. Children can make a book or share with a partner.

Writing

Realistic Story

REVIEW REVISING Remind children that yesterday they revised their stories. They may have added sentences to make the events clearer. Today they will proofread their stories.

Mini-Lesson Proofread

Proofread for Questions

- **Teach** In our stories, if we capitalize and punctuate the sentences correctly, readers will know where the sentences begin and end. They will also be able to tell whether a sentence is a telling sentence or a sentence that asks a question. When we proofread, we check to make sure the sentences are correct.

- **Model** Let's look at my story about Tyler and Ava. Display Writing Transparency 5C. I'm going to make sure that each sentence begins with a capital letter and ends with punctuation. I'll check the beginning and end of each sentence. Model checking the beginning and end of each sentence. Look: Ava asks a question, but I ended the sentence with a period. I will delete the period and replace it with a question mark. Use a deletion mark to show that the period should be removed from the end of Ava's question, add a question mark, and then continue to check.

Proofreading Marks

Take Out	⌒	Uppercase letter	≡
Add	^	Lowercase letter	/
Period	⊙	New paragraph	¶
Check spelling	◯	Insert apostrophe	✓

The Butterfly

Tyler and Ava were playing in Ava's garden. They found a cocoon on a flower stem. Ava asked, "What is inside this cocoon?"

First, they took it back to Ava's house. Then they put it in a big glass jar. Later, they watched the cocoon open. Out came a beautiful butterfly!

When its wings got strong, Tyler and Ava let it go. They watched it fly away.

Unit 1 Get the Egg! Writing: Proofread 5C

Writing Transparency 5C TR DVD

PROOFREAD Display the Proofreading Tips. Have children proofread their stories to correct any misspellings, missing capital letters, or errors with periods. Circulate to assist children.

Proofreading Tips

- ✔ Are words such as *first, then,* and *last* spelled correctly?
- ✔ Do sentences that ask end with a question mark?
- ✔ Do sentences that tell end with a period?
- ✔ Do all sentences end with punctuation?

PRESENT Have children use a computer to make a final draft of their stories, with their revisions and proofreading corrections. Help as appropriate. Choose an option for children to present their narratives.

Make a book out of each story by writing the title and drawing an illustration on a separate sheet of paper to create a cover.	Read their stories to a partner.

When children have finished writing their stories, give them a copy of About My Writing, p. RR45 of the *Reader's and Writer's Notebook.* Then have children evaluate their writing by answering the questions on the page.

Routine Quick Write for Fluency

Team Talk

1. **Talk** Have partners take one minute to tell each other about their stories.
2. **Write** Have children write a sentence about what might happen next in their partners' stories.
3. **Share** Partners trade sentences and read them aloud.

Routines Flip Chart

ELL

Support Editing For children to whom the sounds and spelling of English still are not very familiar, look for spelling improvement little by little from week to week rather than rapid development. Help children make progress a word at a time and learn word meanings.

Common Core State Standards

Writing 7. Participate in shared research and writing projects (e.g., explore a number of "how-to" books on a given topic and use them to write a sequence of instructions). **Writing 8.** With guidance and support from adults, recall information from experiences or gather information from provided sources to answer a question. **Speaking/Listening 3.** Ask and answer questions about what a speaker says in order to gather additional information or clarify something that is not understood.

Research and Inquiry

Step 5 Communicate

TEACH Tell children that today they will finish their lists about wild animals that live in the neighborhood and share the list with others.

Think Aloud

MODEL Display the list of wild animals that live in the neighborhood. I will review my list and circle the animals that live in the neighborhood. Those will be the animals I will include in my final list. My list is about wild animals that live in the neighborhood. I will start by writing *Wild Animals That Live in the Neighborhood* as the title of my list. I will write the title at the top of my page. Before I write my list, I will make sure I know that all the animal names on my list are spelled correctly. If I have questions about spelling, I will use a dictionary in the classroom to find the correct spelling.

GUIDE PRACTICE Review children's lists. Work with them to write the title of the list at the top of their page and be sure the names of the animals on the list are spelled correctly.

ON THEIR OWN Have children write a list to share with the class. Suggest they write the title at the top of a sheet of paper and then list the animals. Have children organize themselves into groups. Instruct them to read aloud their lists to one another so they can compare the animals they saw. Remind children how to be good speakers and listeners:

- Good speakers speak clearly so their listeners can understand what they are saying.
- Good listeners pay attention to the speaker and do not talk while someone else is speaking. They ask questions if they don't understand what the speaker says.

Wrap Up Your Week!

Neighborhood Animals

Which wild animals live in our neighborhood?

Think Aloud This week we explored the topic of wild animals in our neighborhoods. In the story *Get the Egg!,* we read about two children who helped save a bird's egg that had fallen out of a nest in a tree. In the how-to article "Help the Birds," we read directions for how to make a bird feeder. Both reading selections told of ways we can help wild animals in our neighborhood.

Team Talk Have children recall their Amazing Ideas about animals. Then have children use these ideas to help them demonstrate their understanding of the Question of the Week, *Which wild animals live in our neighborhood?*

You've learned 006 words this week!

You've learned 086 words this year!

Next Week's Concept

Watching Wild Animals

What can we learn about wild animals by watching them?

Poster Preview Prepare children for next week by using Unit 1, Week 6, ELL Poster 6. Read the Poster Talk-Through to introduce the concept and vocabulary. Ask children to identify and describe objects and actions in the art.

Selection Summary Send home the summary from the *ELL Handbook* of *Animal Park* in English and the child's home language if available. Children can read the summary with family members.

Tell children that next week they will read about what we can learn about animals by watching them.

Preview Next Week

Assessment Checkpoints for the Week

Weekly Assessment

Use pp. 61–66 of *Weekly Tests* to check:

✔ **Phonics** Short *e: e*

✔ **Phonics** Initial Consonant Blends

✔ **Comprehension** Main Idea and Details

✔ **High-Frequency Words**

saw	tree
small	your

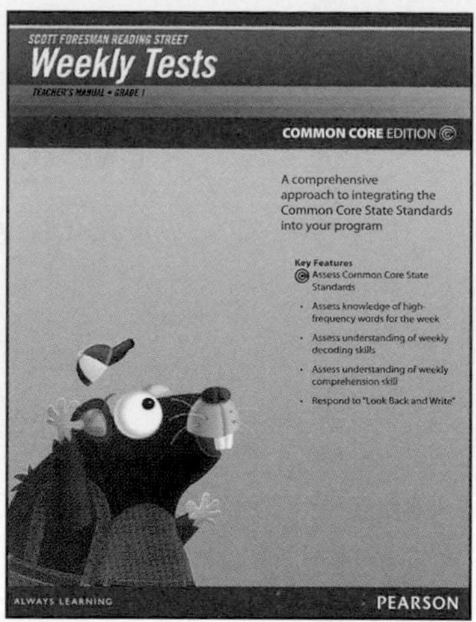

Weekly Tests

Differentiated Assessment

Advanced

On-Level

Strategic Intervention

Use pp. 61–66 of *Fresh Reads for Fluency and Comprehension* to check:

✔ **Comprehension** Main Idea and Details

✔ Review **Comprehension** Character and Setting

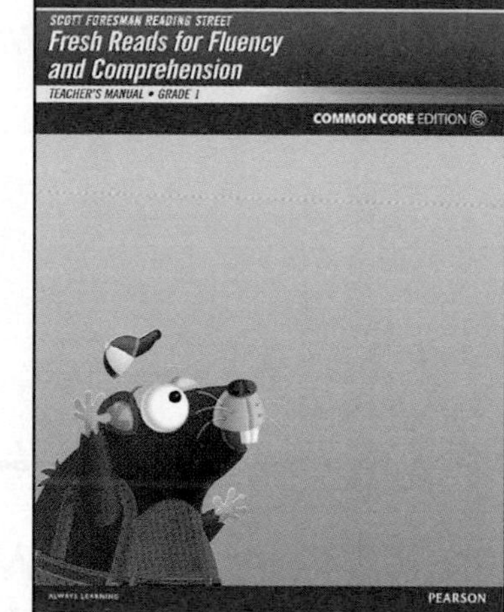

Fresh Reads for Fluency and Comprehension

Managing Assessment

Use *Assessment Handbook* for:

✔ **Weekly Assessment Blackline Masters for Monitoring Progress**

✔ **Observation Checklists**

✔ **Record-Keeping Forms**

✔ **Portfolio Assessment**

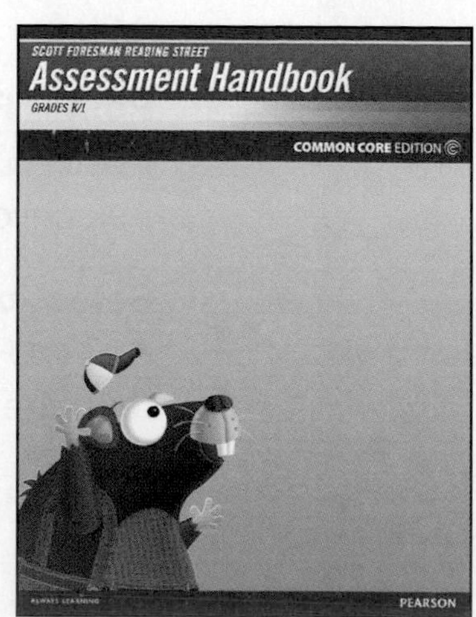

Assessment Handbook

DAY 1 Differentiate Phonics

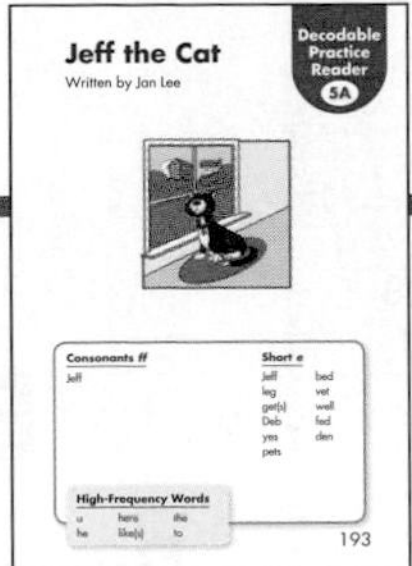

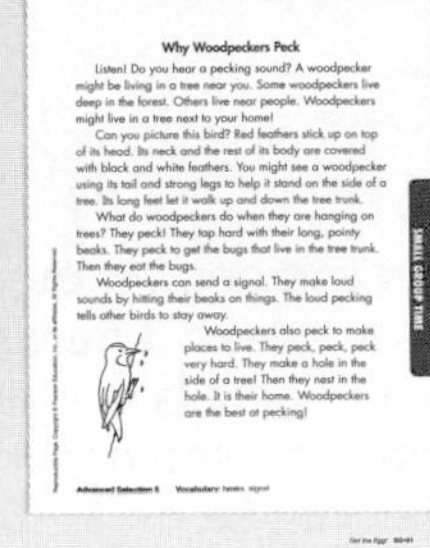

- Short *e: e*
- Decodable Practice Reader
- Advanced Selection "Why Woodpeckers Peck"
- **Inquiry** Identify Questions

DAY 2 Differentiate Comprehension

- Initial Consonant Blends
- **Access Text** Read *Get the Egg!*
- **Inquiry** Investigate

DAY 3 Differentiate Close Reading

- Develop Vocabulary
- **Close Reading** Read *Get the Egg!*
- **Inquiry** Investigate

"Look Out for Coyotes!" pp. 16–17

DAY 4 Differentiate Vocabulary

- Develop Language
- "Look Out for Coyotes!" or Leveled Readers
- **Inquiry** Organize

DAY 5 Differentiate Reteaching

- Phonics and High-Frequency Words
- Conventions
- "Look Out for Coyotes!" or Leveled Readers
- **Inquiry** Communicate

Teacher Guides and Student pages can be found in the Leveled Reader Database.

ELL Place English Language Learners in the groups that correspond to their reading abilities. **If...** children need scaffolding and practice, **then...** use the ELL notes on the page.

Independent Practice

Independent Practice Stations

See pp. 120h and 120i for Independent Stations.

Pearson Trade Book Library

See the Leveled Reader Database for Lesson Plans and student pages.

Reading Street Digital Path

Independent Practice Activities available in the Digital Path.

Independent Reading

See p. 120i for independent reading suggestions.

On-Level

Common Core State Standards

Literature 1. Ask and answer questions about key details in a text. **Literature 7.** Use illustrations and details in a story to describe its characters, setting, or events. **Foundational Skills 3.** Know and apply grade-level phonics and word analysis skills in decoding words. **Foundational Skills 3.b.** Decode regularly spelled one-syllable words. **Foundational Skills 4.a.** Read on-level text with purpose and understanding.

1 Build Word Knowledge

Practice Phonics

SHORT *e: e* Write the following words and have children practice reading words with short *e.*

hen **bell** **fed** **stem**

Spelling

SHORT *e* WORDS Remind children that each spelling word has the letter *e,* which spells the /e/ sound. Clarify the pronunciation and meaning of each word. For example, say: *Men* means "more than one man." Have children identify which of the following words begin with a consonant blend: *red, ten, step, net, sled, wet.*

2 Read

Decodable Reader 5A *Jeff the Cat*

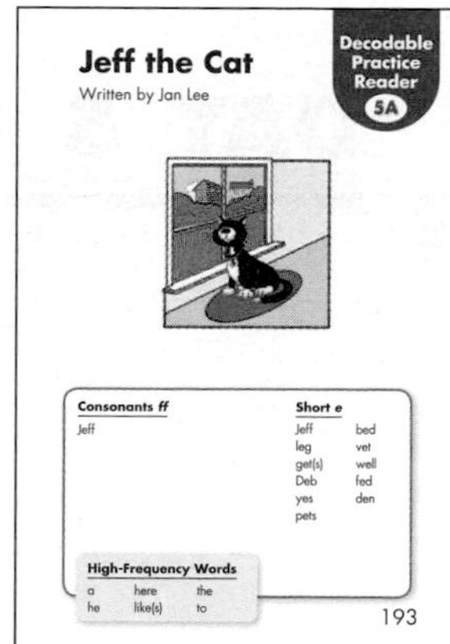

HIGH-FREQUENCY WORDS Have children read the decodable reader. Then have them reread the text to develop automaticity. Have children return to the text and find the previously taught high-frequency words. Help children demonstrate their understanding of the words. Provide sentence frames such as:
My dog _______ to play. (likes)

ELL

If... children need more scaffolding and practice with phonics,
then... use the Phonics Transition Lessons on pp. 249–345 in the *ELL Handbook.*

OL

On-Level

eStreet Interactive
www.ReadingStreet.com
Pearson eText
• Student Edition
• Decodable Reader

1 Build Word Knowledge

Practice Phonics

INITIAL CONSONANT BLENDS Write the following words and have children practice reading words with initial consonant blends.

drip **stack** **trim** **block**

2 Read

Get the Egg!

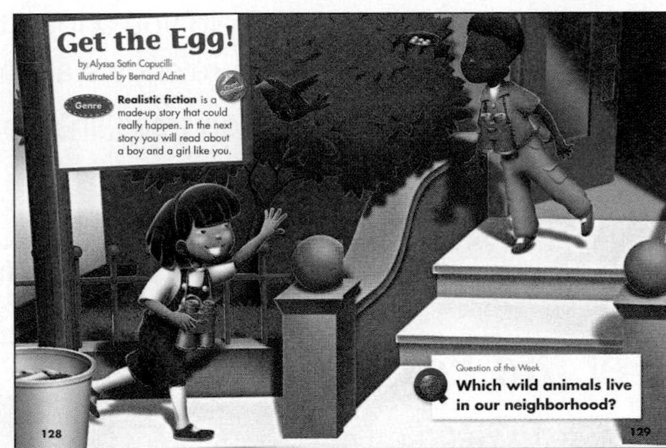
Get the Egg!
by Alyssa Satin Capucilli
illustrated by Bernard Adnet
Genre
Realistic fiction is a made-up story that could really happen. In the next story you will read about a boy and a girl like you.
Question of the Week
Which wild animals live in our neighborhood?
128
129

If you read *Get the Egg!* during whole group time, then use the following instruction.

ACCESS TEXT Have children look at the pictures on pp. 134–136. Reread the sentences on those pages.

- Look at the sentences on page 134. How does Brad help with the egg? (He picks up the egg with his net.)
- Look at the sentences on page 135. How does Kim help with the egg? (She puts the egg in the nest.)
- Look at the picture of Kim and Brad on page 135. Now look at the picture of Kim and Brad on page 136. How are they different? (Kim and Brad are wearing different clothes.) What does that tell us about the story? (This is a different time and day.)

If you are reading *Get the Egg!* during small group time, then return to pp. 128b–137a to guide the reading.

Independent Reading Options

Trade Book Library

eStreet Interactive
www.ReadingStreet.com
Teacher's Guides available on the Leveled Reader Database.

OL

On-Level

Common Core State Standards

Literature 1. Ask and answer questions about key details in a text. **Literature 7.** Use illustrations and details in a story to describe its characters, setting, or events. **Speaking/ Listening 1.** Participate in collaborative conversations about grade 1 topics and texts with peers and adults in small and larger groups. **Language 6.** Use words and phrases acquired through conversations, reading and being read to, and responding to texts, including using frequently occurring conjunctions to signal simple relationships (e.g., *I named my hamster Nibblet because she nibbles too much because she likes that*). **Also Speaking/Listening 4.**

1 Build Word Knowledge

Develop Vocabulary

REREAD FOR VOCABULARY Have children reread *Get the Egg!,* p. 132.

Read the following sentence and discuss words related to nature. (twig, egg)

The big twig hit an egg!

- What does the word *twig* mean? (a small branch)
- What clues in the picture help you understand that the word *twig* is another word for branch? (The picture shows a small branch hitting the nest.)
- Where do you see twigs? (on trees, in a forest, in a yard, in a park)

2 Read

Get the Egg!

Get the Egg!
by Alyssa Satin Capucilli
illustrated by Bernard Adnet
Genre
Realistic fiction is a made-up story that could really happen. In the next story you will read about a boy and a girl like you.
Question of the Week
Which wild animals live in our neighborhood?
128
129

If you read *Get the Egg!* during whole group time, then use the following instruction.

CLOSE READING Reread pp. 130–131. Have children summarize the ideas presented on these pages. Ask questions to guide deeper understanding.

- Why are Brad and Kim at the tree? (They are watching the bird.)
- How can you tell that Brad and Kim are friends? (They watch the bird together. They know each other's names.)

Have children look at the pictures on pp. 130–131 and think of a sentence to describe a detail in one of the pictures. (Brad has a yellow shirt. Kim has black hair. The eggs are blue.)

If you are reading *Get the Egg!* during small group time, then return to pp. 128–137 to guide the reading.

ELL

If... children need more scaffolding and practice with the main selection, **then...** use the activities on p. DI•102 in the Teacher Resources section on SuccessNet.

On-Level

❶ Build Word Knowledge

Practice Selection Vocabulary

Team Talk **LANGUAGE DEVELOPMENT** Have children practice using the selection vocabulary. Ask questions such as: What are some types of birds that you know? What do they look like? Turn and talk to your partner about the types of birds you know.

bird

Allow children time to discuss the word *bird.* Ask for examples or rephrase for usage when necessary or to correct for understanding. Use the Student Edition to provide visual support.

❷ Text-Based Comprehension

READ ALOUD "Look Out for Coyotes!" Lead children in a choral reading of "Look Out for Coyotes!" from *Reading Street Sleuth,* pp. 16–17. Then have partners take turns reading the paragraphs of the selection.

ACCESS TEXT Guide children as they work on the Be a Sleuth section.

Look for Clues Ask children to think about what coyotes look like, what they eat, and where they live. Ask them if they can think of any other details about coyotes that are not mentioned in the text.

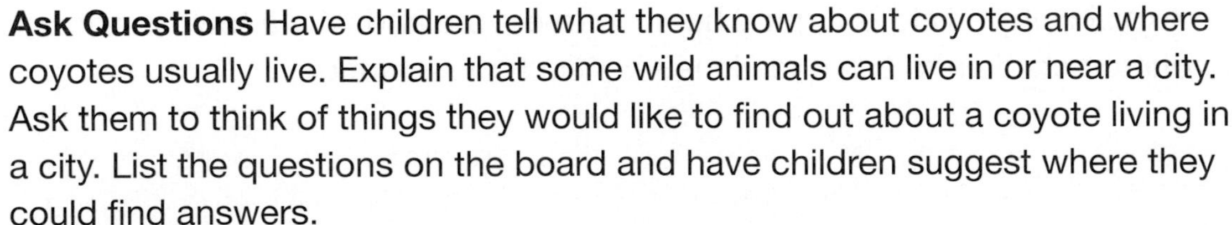

Ask Questions Have children tell what they know about coyotes and where coyotes usually live. Explain that some wild animals can live in or near a city. Ask them to think of things they would like to find out about a coyote living in a city. List the questions on the board and have children suggest where they could find answers.

Make Your Case Have children review a coyote's needs for food, freedom, and open spaces as they reread the selection to gather information about the author's opinion on coyotes. After reviewing the material, have children present their decision about the author's opinion on coyotes and provide supporting evidence for their choice.

SMALL GROUP TIME

More Reading for Group Time

ON-LEVEL

Reviews
- Concept Vocabulary
- Main Idea and Details

Use this suggested Leveled Reader or other text at children's instructional level.

eStreet Interactive
www.ReadingStreet.com

Use the Leveled Reader Database for lesson plans and student pages for *What Animals Can You See?*

On-Level

Common Core State Standards

Informational Text 1. Ask and answer questions about key details in a text. **Foundational Skills 1.a.** Recognize the distinguishing features of a sentence (e.g., first word, capitalization, ending punctuation). **Foundational Skills 2.b.** Orally produce single-syllable words by blending sounds (phonemes), including consonant blends. **Foundational Skills 3.** Know and apply grade-level phonics and word analysis skills in decoding words. **Foundational Skills 4.a.** Read on-level text with purpose and understanding. **Also Speaking/ Listening 4., 5., Language 1.**

More Reading for Group Time

ON-LEVEL

Reviews
- Concept Vocabulary
- Main Idea and Details

Use this suggested Leveled Reader or other text at children's instructional level.

eStreet Interactive
www.ReadingStreet.com

Use the Leveled Reader Database for lesson plans and student pages for *What Animals Can You See?*

1 Build Word Knowledge

Practice Interrogative Sentences

REVIEW If needed, revisit the conventions lesson on p. 137c.

WRITE INTERROGATIVE SENTENCES Have children return to "Look Out for Coyotes!" Ask children to find interrogative sentences in the selection. Point out that the sentences end with question marks. Have children work in pairs to write questions about coyotes. Ask them to identify what makes each an interrogative sentence.

2 Text-Based Comprehension

REREAD "Look Out for Coyotes!" Have partners reread "Look Out for Coyotes!"

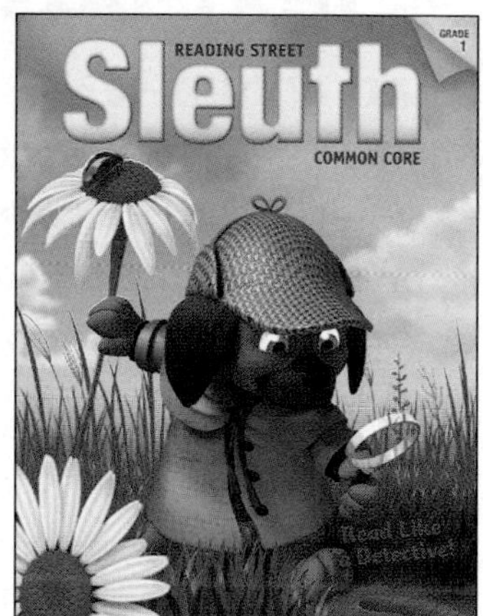

EXTEND UNDERSTANDING Talk about coyotes with children. Discuss details from the selection, such as how coyotes look and sound. Ask children if it is fair for people to not want coyotes nearby.

PERFORMANCE TASK • Prove It! Why would a town be a bad home for a coyote? Why is a field a good home? Have small groups collaborate on illustrated posters that compare the two habitats. Remind them to use details from the text to help them draw details.

COMMUNICATE Have small groups present their posters to the class and explain why a field is a good home for a coyote and why a town is not. Encourage children to ask questions after each presentation.

Strategic Intervention

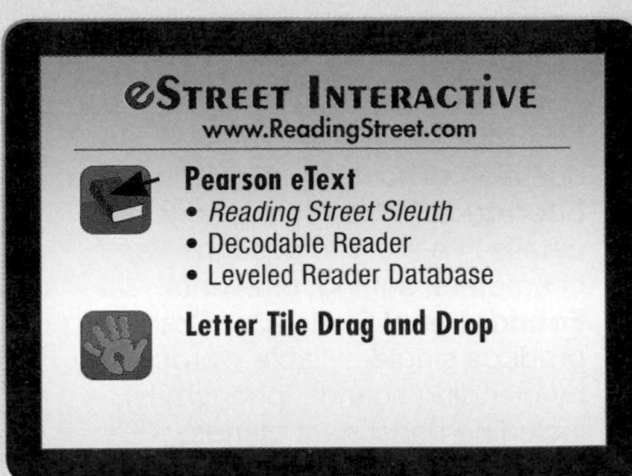

1 Build Word Knowledge

Reteach Phonemic Awareness

Reteach the lesson on p. 122–123 to distinguish /e/. Use these additional practice items.

red **led** **get** **men**

Reteach Phonics

SHORT *e: e* Reteach the lesson on p. 123a, short *e: e.* Use these additional practice words to blend.

bet **met** **tell** **peg** **bed**

Have children spell *peck* using letter tiles. What word did you spell? Let's change letters to make a new word and then read our new word.

- Change the *ck* in *peck* to *st.* What is the new word? p e s t
- Change the *p* in *pest* to *n.* What is the new word? n e s t

2 Read

Decodable Reader 5A *Jeff the Cat*

DECODE WORDS Have children practice reading the words listed on p. 193.

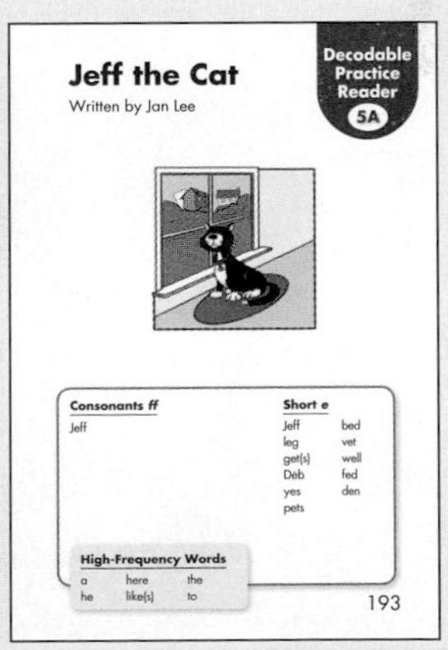

Corrective feedback	**If...** children have difficulty reading the words independently, **then...** reteach the words prior to reading Decodable Reader 5A.

READ IN CONTEXT Have children take turns reading a page in *Jeff the Cat.* Have them reread the text several times to ensure accuracy.

Corrective feedback	**If...** children have difficulty reading the story independently, **then...** model reading a page and have children echo you.

3 Reread for Fluency

Have children reread the text to develop automaticity in their reading.

ELL

If... children need more scaffolding and practice with phonemic awareness and phonics, **then...** use the Phonics Transition Lessons on pp. 249–345 in the *ELL Handbook.*

SI
Strategic Intervention

Common Core State Standards

Literature 1. Ask and answer questions about key details in a text.
Literature 7. Use illustrations and details in a story to describe its characters, setting, or events.
Foundational Skills 2.b. Orally produce single-syllable words by blending sounds (phonemes), including consonant blends.
Foundational Skills 3. Know and apply grade-level phonics and word analysis skills in decoding words.

1 Build Word Knowledge

Reteach Phonemic Awareness

Reteach the lesson on p. 126c to segment and blend phonemes. Use these additional practice items: /s/ /l/ /e/ /d/ ***sled,*** /t/ /r/ /o/ /t/ ***trot,*** /g/ /l/ /a/ /d/, ***glad.***

Reteach Phonics

INITIAL CONSONANT BLENDS Reteach the lesson on p. 126d to model initial consonant blends. Use these additional words to blend: *trip, step, slap, crop, trim.*

Have children spell *tap* using letter tiles. Monitor their work.

- Change the *t* in *tap* to *sl.* What is the new word? **s l a p**
- Change the *s* in *slap* to *c.* What is the new word? **c l a p**

2 Read

Get the Egg!

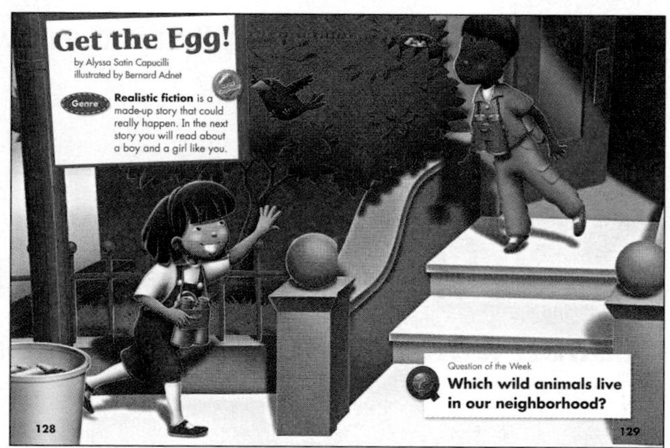
Get the Egg!
by Alyssa Satin Capucilli
illustrated by Bernard Adnet
Genre
Realistic fiction is a made-up story that could really happen. In the next story you will read about a boy and a girl like you.
Question of the Week
Which wild animals live in our neighborhood?
128
129

If you read *Get the Egg!* during whole group time, then use the instruction below.

ACCESS TEXT Have children look at the picture on p. 132. Point to the bird in the picture. What else do you see in the picture? (Brad, Kim, eggs, twig, tree, net, binoculars, wall) Reread the sentences on p. 132.

- What goes *snap?* (a twig)
- What does the twig do? (hits the nest, hits an egg)
- How do you know the twig hits an egg? (The text says a twig hit an egg. The picture shows a twig hitting an egg.)

If you are reading *Get the Egg!* during small group time, then return to pp. 128b–137a to guide the reading.

Corrective feedback	**If...** children have difficulty understanding the section, **then...** read the section aloud using the Access Text Notes.

Independent Reading Options

Trade Book Library

eSTREET INTERACTIVE
www.ReadingStreet.com

Teacher's Guides available on the Leveled Reader Database.

1 Build Word Knowledge

Reteach Phonemic Awareness

Reteach the activity on p. 138c to model words that rhyme. Use these additional practice items: *red/sled; jet/wet; cat/hat; spill/fill.*

Reteach Phonics

Write these short *e* and initial consonant blend words and have children blend them with you: *sped, step, bled, stem, dress, spell, press.*

2 Read

Get the Egg!

If you read *Get the Egg!* during whole group time, then use the instruction below.

CLOSE READING Reread p. 135. Let's read this page to find out what the boy and girl are doing. To help children understand what is happening in the story, ask questions related to the text and picture.

- Who is holding the net? (the boy)
- What is in the net? (an egg)
- Why does the text say, "Yes! You did it, Brad!" (Kim tells Brad he got the egg in the net. She is excited that he did it.)
- Why did he get the egg? (It fell out of the tree.)

Corrective feedback	**If...** children have trouble answering questions about the text and picture on p. 135, **then...** reread the page and have them tell about the picture in their own words. Then compare their summary with the words on the page.

If you are reading *Get the Egg!* during small group time, then return to pp. 128–137 to guide the reading.

SMALL GROUP TIME

If... children need scaffolding and practice with the main selection, **then...** use the activities on p. DI•102 in the Teacher Resources section on SuccessNet.

Strategic Intervention

Common Core State Standards

Informational Text 1. Ask and answer questions about key details in a text. **Foundational Skills 3.g.** Recognize and read grade-appropriate irregularly spelled words. **Speaking/Listening 1.** Participate in collaborative conversations about grade 1 topics and texts with peers and adults in small and larger groups. **Also Speaking/Listening 4., 5., Language 4.**

More Reading for Group Time

CONCEPT LITERACY

Practice
- Concept Words
- High-Frequency Words

BELOW LEVEL

Review
- Main Idea and Details
- High-Frequency Words

Use these suggested Leveled Readers or other text at children's instructional level.

eStreet Interactive
www.ReadingStreet.com

Use the Leveled Reader Database for lesson plans and student pages for *Neighborhood Animals* and *At Your Vet.*

1 Build Word Knowledge

Review Selection Vocabulary

bird

SEE IT/SAY IT/HEAR IT Write *bird.* Scan across the word with your finger as you say it: bird. Use the word in a sentence. I see a **bird** in the tree.

DEFINE IT How would you tell a friend what a *bird* is? Give a definition when necessary. Yes, it is a small animal with feathers and wings. Restate the definition in child-friendly terms. A *bird* is an animal covered in feathers that has wings and two legs.

Team Talk When did you last see a bird? Where was it? What was the bird doing? Turn to your partner and talk about this. Allow time for children to discuss. Ask for examples. Rephrase their examples for usage when necessary or to correct misunderstandings.

2 Text-Based Comprehension

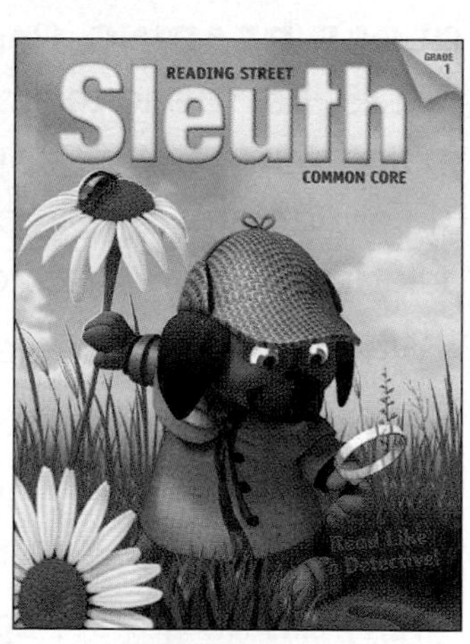

READ ALOUD "Look Out for Coyotes!" Read "Look Out for Coyotes!" aloud from *Reading Street Sleuth,* pp. 16–17 as children follow along.

ACCESS TEXT Guide children as they work on the Be a Sleuth section.

Look for Clues Look through the selection for clues with the class. Read about coyotes together and ask them to think about what coyotes look and sound like.

Ask Questions Have children identify a part of the selection that was confusing or interesting and ask questions about it. Make a list of the questions and have children suggest where they could find answers.

Make Your Case Have children review and restate the information on coyotes given by the author in the selection. Reread the selection if needed. Then ask them to decide if the author thinks coyotes should live in the city or in the wild. Have children tell what they think and give a reason for their choice based on the information in the selection.

1 Build Word Knowledge

Review High-Frequency Words

Use the routine on p. 125 to review *saw, tree, small,* and *your.*

Corrective feedback	**If...** children have difficulty with any of these words, **then...** tell them the word and have them repeat it. Have children spell the word and tell what word they spelled. Have them practice in pairs with word cards.

2 Text-Based Comprehension

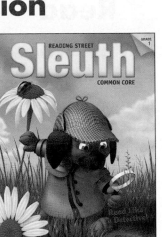

REREAD "Look Out for Coyotes!" Reread "Look Out for Coyotes!" aloud as children follow along.

EXTEND UNDERSTANDING Talk about the selection with the class. Ask children to think of details about coyotes from the selection, such as how they look and how they sound. Ask children if it is safe to have a coyote near a person's home.

PERFORMANCE TASK • Prove It! Why would a town be a bad home for a coyote? Why is a field a good home? Have small groups collaborate on illustrated posters that compare the two habitats. Remind them to use at least one detail from the text in their drawings.

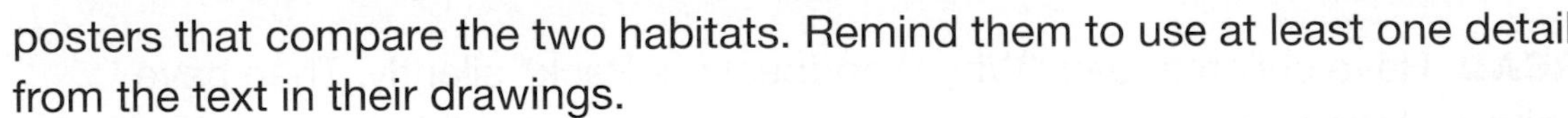

COMMUNICATE Have small groups present their posters to the class and explain why a field is a good home for a coyote and why a town is not. Encourage children to ask questions after each presentation.

SMALL GROUP TIME

More Reading for Group Time

CONCEPT LITERACY

Practice
- Concept Words
- High-Frequency Words

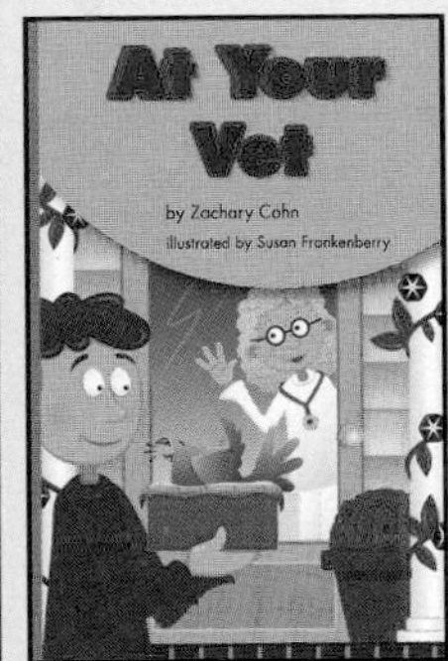

BELOW LEVEL

Review
- Main Idea and Details
- High-Frequency Words

Use these suggested Leveled Readers or other text at children's instructional level.

eStreet Interactive
www.ReadingStreet.com

Use the Leveled Reader Database for lesson plans and student pages for *Neighborhood Animals* and *At Your Vet.*

Advanced

Common Core State Standards

Informational Text 1. Ask and answer questions about key details in a text. **Informational Text 7.** Use the illustrations and details in a text to describe its key ideas. **Foundational Skills 3.** Know and apply grade-level phonics and word analysis skills in decoding words. **Foundational Skills 4.a.** Read on-level text with purpose and understanding. **Speaking/Listening 1.** Participate in collaborative conversations about grade 1 topics and texts with peers and adults in small and larger groups.

1 Build Word Knowledge

Extend Phonics

SHORT *e: e* Have children practice with more complex words. Have children write the words on cards, identify the letters that stand for the short *e* sound, and then sort the words by vowel pattern *e* or *ea.* Then have them use the words in sentences.

them	**edge**	**ever**	**very**	**enter**
meadow	**breakfast**	**weather**	**eggshell**	**bread**

2 Read

"Why Woodpeckers Peck"

TEACH VOCABULARY Before reading, introduce the story words: *beaks, signal.* Help children determine the meaning of each word using these sentences:

1. Birds use their long, sharp **beaks** to eat insects and worms.
2. The bird chirped loudly. It was a **signal** to other birds to stay away.

Why Woodpeckers Peck

Listen! Do you hear a pecking sound? A woodpecker might be living in a tree near you. Some woodpeckers live deep in the forest. Others live near people. Woodpeckers might live in a tree next to your home!

Can you picture this bird? Red feathers stick up on top of its head. Its neck and the rest of its body are covered with black and white feathers. You might see a woodpecker using its tail and strong legs to help it stand on the side of a tree. Its long feet let it walk up and down the tree trunk.

What do woodpeckers do when they are **hanging** on trees? They peck! They tap hard with their long, pointy beaks. They peck to get the bugs that live in the tree trunk. Then they eat the bugs.

Woodpeckers can send a signal. They make loud sounds by hitting their beaks on things. The loud pecking tells other birds to stay away.

Woodpeckers also peck to make places to live. They peck, peck, peck very hard. They make a hole in the side of a tree! Then they nest in the hole. It is their home. Woodpeckers are the best at pecking!

Advanced Selection 5 **Vocabulary:** beaks, signal

SMALL GROUP TIME

Get the Egg! SG•81

READ Have children read "Why Woodpeckers Peck" silently. Then have children take turns reading aloud. After reading, have children recall the two most important ideas of the story using details from the text.

3 Inquiry: Extend Concepts

IDENTIFY QUESTIONS Have children research an author who writes about animals. During the week, they should read two or more selections by this author. On Day 5, children will share what they have learned. Guide children in brainstorming possible choices.

- Look over different books written by the same author. How are they alike? How are they different?
- Which details help you know that the same person wrote these books?

ELL

If... children need practice with phonics,
then... use the Phonics Transition Lessons on pp. 249–345 in the *ELL Handbook*.

Why Woodpeckers Peck

Listen! Do you hear a pecking sound? A woodpecker might be living in a tree near you. Some woodpeckers live deep in the forest. Others live near people. Woodpeckers might live in a tree next to your home!

Can you picture this bird? Red feathers stick up on top of its head. Its neck and the rest of its body are covered with black and white feathers. You might see a woodpecker using its tail and strong legs to help it stand on the side of a tree. Its long feet let it walk up and down the tree trunk.

What do woodpeckers do when they are hanging on trees? They peck! They tap hard with their long, pointy beaks. They peck to get the bugs that live in the tree trunk. Then they eat the bugs.

Woodpeckers can send a signal. They make loud sounds by hitting their beaks on things. The loud pecking tells other birds to stay away.

Woodpeckers also peck to make places to live. They peck, peck, peck very hard. They make a hole in the side of a tree! Then they nest in the hole. It is their home. Woodpeckers are the best at pecking!

Advanced Selection 5 **Vocabulary:** beaks, signal

Advanced

Common Core State Standards

Literature 1. Ask and answer questions about key details in a text. **Literature 3.** Describe characters, settings, and major events in a story, using key details. **Literature 7.** Use illustrations and details in a story to describe its characters, setting, or events. **Foundational Skills 3.** Know and apply grade-level phonics and word analysis skills in decoding words. **Speaking/Listening 1.** Participate in collaborative conversations about grade 1 topics and texts with peers and adults in small and larger groups. **Language 5.a.** Sort words into categories (e.g., colors, clothing) to gain a sense of the concepts the categories represent. **Also Writing 7.**

Independent Reading Options

Trade Book Library

eStreet Interactive
www.ReadingStreet.com

Teacher's Guides available on the Leveled Reader Database.

1 Build Word Knowledge

Extend Phonics

INITIAL CONSONANT BLENDS Have children practice with additional words with initial consonant blends. Discuss the meanings of unfamiliar words with children. Then have them write each word and circle the initial blend. Point out the three-letter blend in *scramble.*

scramble	**broken**	**smudge**	**pleasant**	**skillet**
skeleton	**freedom**	**breakfast**	**grandpa**	**stoplight**

2 Read

Get the Egg!

If you read *Get the Egg!* during whole group time, then use the instruction below.

Get the Egg!
by Alyssa Satin Capucilli
illustrated by Bernard Adnet
Genre
Realistic fiction is a made-up story that could really happen. In the next story you will read about a boy and a girl like you.
Question of the Week
Which wild animals live in our neighborhood?
128
129

ACCESS TEXT Have children silently reread *Get the Egg!,* retell the selection, and identify the plot. (Beginning: The egg falls out of a nest. Middle: The children get the egg and put it back in the nest. End: The kids see all the eggs hatched.)

DISCUSS GENRE Discuss what makes *Get the Egg!* realistic fiction. Point out that this story could really happen.

If you are reading *Get the Egg!* during small group time, then return to pp. 128b–137a to guide the reading.

3 Inquiry: Extend Concepts

INVESTIGATE Guide children in choosing materials at their independent reading levels.

LOOK AHEAD Help children decide how they will present their author studies. They may wish to use story comparisons, Venn diagrams, or other graphic organizers.

Advanced

1 Build Word Knowledge

Develop Vocabulary

REREAD FOR VOCABULARY Have children reread *Get the Egg!* and make a two-column chart listing *Nouns* and *Verbs.*

Nouns	Verbs
tree	saw
eggs	sit
nest	hit
twig	get
net	help
	set

2 Read

Get the Egg!

If you read *Get the Egg!* during whole group time, then use the instruction below.

CLOSE READING Reread pp. 132–133. Have children look at the pictures on the pages. What happens first on page 132? (A twig hits the nest.) How do Brad and Kim look on page 132? (concerned, worried) Why are Brad and Kim worried? (They don't want anything bad to happen to the nest or the egg.) Have children look through the rest of the selection and tell what happens and how Brad and Kim react. Ask children to explain why Brad and Kim are worried or happy.

If you are reading *Get the Egg!* during small group time, then return to pp. 128–137 to guide the reading.

3 Inquiry: Extend Concepts

INVESTIGATE Give children time to investigate their topics by reading and studying pictures. If needed, demonstrate how to locate other books by the same author.

ELL

If... children need more scaffolding and practice with the main selection, **then...** use the activities on p. DI•102 in the Teacher Resources section on SuccessNet.

Advanced

Common Core State Standards

Foundational Skills 1.a. Recognize the distinguishing features of a sentence (e.g., first word, capitalization, ending punctuation). **Speaking/Listening 1.** Participate in collaborative conversations about grade 1 topics and texts with peers and adults in small and larger groups. **Language 1.** Demonstrate command of the conventions of standard English grammar and usage when writing or speaking. **Language 5.c.** Identify real-life connections between words and their use (e.g., note places at home that are *cozy*). **Also Writing 7., Speaking/ Listening 4., 5.**

More Reading for Group Time

ADVANCED

- Extend Concept Vocabulary
- Review Target Skill

Use this suggested Leveled Reader or other text at children's instructional level.

eStreet Interactive
www.ReadingStreet.com

Use the Leveled Reader Database for lesson plans and student pages for *Cary and the Wildlife Shelter.*

1 Build Word Knowledge

Extend Amazing Words and Selection Vocabulary

habitat	chirp	hatch
croak	survive	moist

bird

Team Talk Have children ask each other questions using the Amazing Words and the Selection Vocabulary, such as: What is a good habitat for a bird?

2 Text-Based Comprehension

READ "Look Out for Coyotes!" Have children track the print as you read "Look Out for Coyotes!" from *Reading Street Sleuth,* pp. 16–17. Then have children read the selection independently.

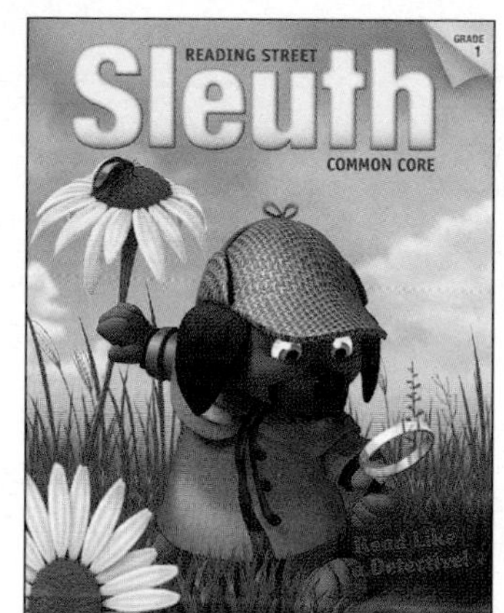

ACCESS TEXT Guide children as they work on the Be a Sleuth section.

Look for Clues Ask children to think about what coyotes look like, what they eat, how they sound, how they behave, and where they live. Ask them if they can think of any other details about coyotes that are not mentioned in the text. Have them make a list of details.

Ask Questions Ask volunteers to think of things they would like to find out about a coyote living in a city. Have children make a list of their questions and suggest books and resources they could use to find answers.

Make Your Case Ask volunteers to tell what they think the author's opinion of coyotes is and present evidence from the selection to support their choice. Have children tell whether they agree or disagree with the author's opinion.

3 Inquiry: Extend Concepts

ORGANIZE INFORMATION Give children time to continue reading and studying books by their chosen authors. Provide any necessary art supplies for children to use in creating their comparisons.

Advanced

1 Build Word Knowledge

Interrogative Sentences

IDENTIFY INTERROGATIVE SENTENCES Have children return to the text "Look Out for Coyotes!" Ask children to find the interrogative sentences in the selection. Point out that the sentences end with question marks. Have children work independently to write questions about coyotes. Tell them to identify the features that make their questions interrogative sentences.

2 Text-Based Comprehension

REREAD "Look Out for Coyotes!" Have partners reread "Look Out for Coyotes!"

EXTEND UNDERSTANDING Talk about coyotes with children. Discuss the details from the selection, such as how coyotes look and sound. Would you be worried if you heard there was a coyote in your neighborhood? Why or why not? Ask children to make a list of reasons explaining their answer.

PERFORMANCE TASK • Prove It! Why would a town be a bad home for a coyote? Why is a field a good home? Have children write a short compare-and-contrast paragraph that discusses both habitats. Remind children to use details from the text and from other sources to make their comparisons clear.

COMMUNICATE Have children present their paragraphs to the class and explain why a field is a good home for a coyote and why a town is not. Encourage the class to ask questions after each presentation.

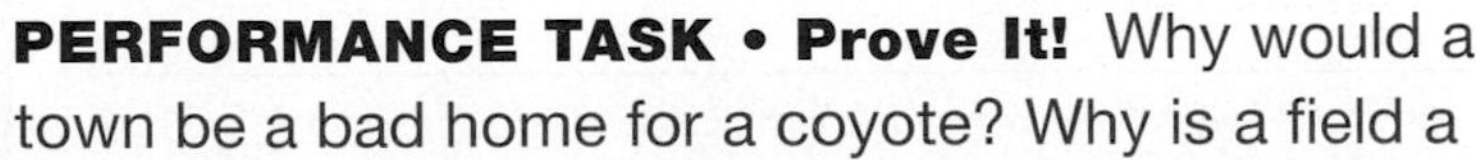

3 Inquiry: Extend Concepts

COMMUNICATE Have children present their author studies and share what they have learned.

SMALL GROUP TIME

More Reading for Group Time

ADVANCED

- Extend Concept Vocabulary
- Review Target Skill

Use this suggested Leveled Reader or other text at children's instructional level.

eStreet Interactive
www.ReadingStreet.com

Use the Leveled Reader Database for lesson plans and student pages for *Cary and the Wildlife Shelter.*

TEACHER NOTES

Indiana Common Core Edition ©

This Week's Target Skills and Strategies

Target Skills and Strategies	© Common Core State Standards for English Language Arts
Phonemic Awareness **Skills:** Distinguish /u/ Segment and Blend Phonemes Segment and Blend Onset and Rime	**CCSS Foundational Skills 2.b.** Orally produce single-syllable words by blending sounds (phonemes), including consonant blends. **(Also CCSS Foundational Skills 2.c., CCSS Foundational Skills 2.d.)**
Phonics **Skill:** Short *u*: *u* **Skill:** Final Consonant Blends	**CCSS Foundational Skills 3.** Know and apply grade-level phonics and word analysis skills in decoding words. **(Also CCSS Foundational Skills 2.b., CCSS Foundational Skills 3.b., CCSS Language 2.d.)**
Text-Based Comprehension **Skill:** Cause and Effect	**CCSS Informational Text 8.** Identify the reasons an author gives to support points in a text. **(Also CCSS Informational Text 3.)**
Strategy: Text Structure	**CCSS Informational Text 8.** Identify the reasons an author gives to support points in a text. **(Also CCSS Informational Text 3.)**
Fluency **Skill:** Appropriate Phrasing	**CCSS Foundational Skills 4.b.** Read on-level text orally with accuracy, appropriate rate, and expression on successive readings.
Listening and Speaking Give Directions	**CCSS Speaking/Listening 1.b.** Build on others' talk in conversations by responding to the comments of others through multiple exchanges. **(Also CCSS Speaking/Listening 4.)**
Six-Trait Writing **Trait of the Week:** Focus/Ideas	**CCSS Writing 2.** Write informative/explanatory texts in which they name a topic, supply some facts about the topic, and provide some sense of closure.
Writing Brief Composition	**CCSS Writing 2.** Write informative/explanatory texts in which they name a topic, supply some facts about the topic, and provide some sense of closure.
Conventions **Skill:** Exclamatory Sentences	**CCSS Language 1.j.** Produce and expand complete simple and compound declarative, interrogative, imperative, and exclamatory sentences in response to prompts.

This Week's Cross-Curricular Standards and Resources

Cross-Curricular Indiana Academic Standards for Science and Social Studies

Science
IN 1.3.1 Classify living organisms according to variations in specific physical features (e.g., body coverings, appendages) and describe how those features may provide an advantage for survival in different environments.
IN 1.3.4 Describe how animals' habitats, including plants, meet their needs for food, water, shelter and an environment in which they can live.

Social Studies
IN 1.3.2 Identify and describe continents, oceans, cities and roads on maps and globes.

Reading Street Sleuth

Look Out for Wildlife
pp. 18–19

Follow the path to close reading using the Super Sleuth tips:

- Look for Clues
- Ask Questions
- Make Your Case
- Prove it!

More Reading in Science and Social Studies

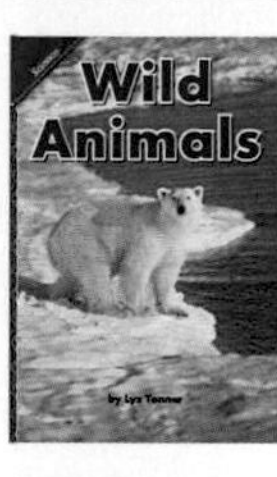

Concept Literacy

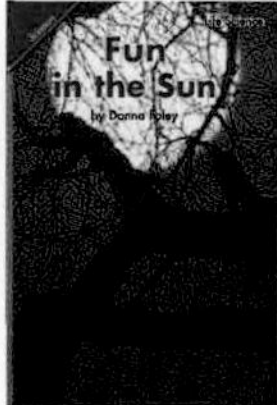

Below Level

On Level

Advanced

ELL

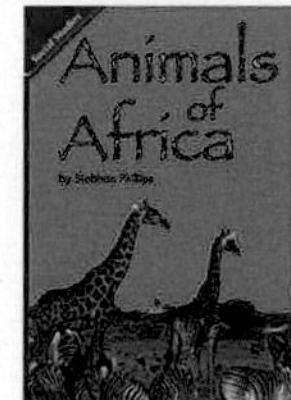

ELD

ISBN-13: 978-0-328-73376-7 ISBN-10: 0-328-73376-8

Your 90-Minute Reading Block

	Whole Group	Formative Assessment How do I make my small groups flexible?	Small Group OL On Level SI Strategic Intervention A Advanced What are my other students reading and learning every day in Small Groups?
DAY 1	**Content Knowledge** Build Oral Language/Vocabulary **Phonemic Awareness/Phonics** **Read Decodable Reader** **Phonics/Spelling Pretest** **High-Frequency Words** **Text-Based Comprehension** Teacher Read Aloud **Research and Inquiry** Step 1–Identify and Focus Topic	**Monitor Progress** Formative Assessment: Check Word Reading	**Differentiate Phonics** OL **Practice Phonics** More Short *u* Words SI **Reteach Phonics** Blend Short *u* Words A **Extend Phonics** More Challenging Short *u* Words OL SI **Decodable Reader Read** *Duck Has Fun* A **Advanced Selection** "Fun With Ducks" A Inquiry Project ELL Access Phonemic Awareness and Phonics
DAY 2	**Content Knowledge** Build Oral Language/Vocabulary **Phonemic Awareness/Phonics** **Read Decodable Reader** **Phonics/Spelling** **High-Frequency Words/Selection Words** **Text-Based Comprehension** **Read** Main Selection, using Access Text Notes **Research and Inquiry** Step 2–Research Skill	**Monitor Progress** Formative Assessment: Check Word Reading	**Differentiate Comprehension** OL **Practice Phonics** Additional Words with Final Consonant Blends SI **Reteach Phonics** Additional Words with Final Consonant Blends A **Extend Phonics** Additional Words with Final Consonant Blends OL SI A **Access Text Read** *Animal Park* A Inquiry Project ELL Access the Comprehension Skill
DAY 3	**Content Knowledge** Build Oral Language/Vocabulary **Phonemic Awareness/Phonics** **Phonics/Spelling** **High-Frequency Words/Selection Words** **Text-Based Comprehension** **Reread** Main Selection, using Close Reading Notes **Fluency** **Research and Inquiry** Step 3–Gather and Record Information	**Monitor Progress** Formative Assessment: Check High-Frequency Words **Monitor Progress** Check Retelling	**Differentiate Close Reading** OL **Reread to Develop Vocabulary** SI **Build Word Knowledge** Blend Words with Short *u* and Final Consonant Blends A **Reread to Extend Vocabulary** OL SI **Close Reading Reread** *Animal Park* A **Extend Concepts Reread** *Animal Park* A Inquiry Project ELL Access the Main Selection
DAY 4	**Content Knowledge** Build Oral Language/Vocabulary **Phonemic Awareness/Phonics** **Read Decodable Reader** **Phonics/Spelling** **Read Content Area Paired Selection with Genre Focus** **Fluency** **Research and Inquiry** Step 4–Synthesize	**Monitor Progress** Fluency Check	**Differentiate Vocabulary** **Build Word Knowledge** OL Develop Language A Extend Amazing Words and Selection Vocabulary SI **Review Vocabulary** Review/Discuss Selection Vocabulary OL SI A **Text-Based Comprehension Read** *Reading Street Sleuth,* pp. 18–19 or Leveled Readers A Inquiry Project ELL Access Vocabulary
DAY 5	**Content Knowledge** Build Oral Language/Vocabulary **Phonemic Awareness/Phonics** **Phonics/Spelling Test** **Let's Learn It!** Vocabulary/Fluency/Listening and Speaking **Text-Based Comprehension** **High-Frequency and Selection Words** **Genre** **Assessment** Phonics, High-Frequency Words, Fluency **Research and Inquiry** Step 5–Communicate	**Monitor Progress** Formative Assessment: Check Oral Vocabulary **Monitor Progress** Word and Sentence Reading	**Differentiate Reteaching** OL **Practice Exclamatory Sentences** SI **Review Vocabulary** High-Frequency Words A **Extend Exclamatory Sentences** OL SI A **Text-Based Comprehension Reread** *Reading Street Sleuth,* pp. 18–19 or Leveled Readers A Inquiry Project ELL Access Conventions and Writing

Daily Independent Options

What do my other students do when I lead Small Groups?

★ **Independent Reading** ©
Suggestions for this week's independent reading:

- Informational texts on last week's science topic: Which wild animals live in our neighborhood?
- Nonfiction selections about which wild animals live in our neighborhood
- Other books by Alyssa Satin Capucilli

Book Talk
Foster critical reading and discussion skills through independent and close reading.

Students should focus on discussing one or more of the following:

- Key Ideas and Details
- Craft and Structure
- Integration of Ideas

Pearson eText
- Student Edition
- Decodable Readers
- Leveled Readers

Trade Book Library

Materials from School or Classroom Library

Independent Stations Practice Last Week's Skills

★ Focus on these activities when time is limited.

Listen Up!
★ **Word Work**
★ **Read for Meaning**
Let's Write!
Words to Know
Get Fluent

Assessment Resources

Common Core Weekly Tests, pp. 66–72

Common Core Fresh Reads for Fluency and Comprehension, pp. 66–72

Common Core Unit 1 Benchmark Test

Common Core Success Tracker, ExamView, and Online Lesson Planner

Focus on Common Core State Standards

Main Selection, pp. 154–163

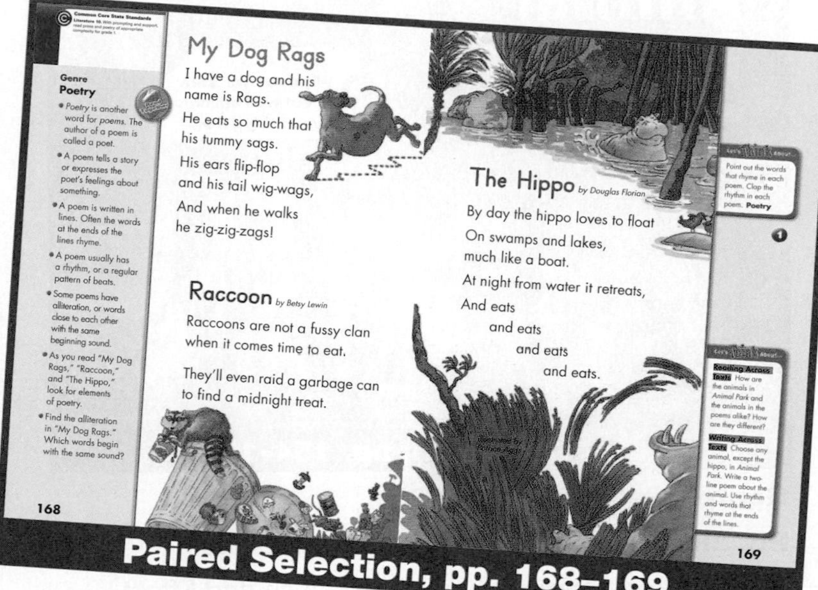

Paired Selection, pp. 168–169

Text-Based Comprehension

Cause and Effect

CCSS Informational Text 3., CCSS Informational Text 8.

Text Structure

CCSS Informational Text 3., CCSS Informational Text 8.

Fluency

Appropriate Phrasing

CCSS Foundational Skills 4.b.

Writing and Conventions

Trait: Focus/Ideas

CCSS Writing 2.

Writing Mini-Lesson: Brief Composition

CCSS Writing 2.

Conventions: Exclamatory Sentences

CCSS Language 1.j.

Oral Vocabulary

Amazing Words

desert	forest
world	chatter
silent	snort
medicine	poisonous

CCSS Language 5.c.

High-Frequency Words

home	into	many
them		

CCSS Foundational Skills 3.g.

Phonemic Awareness

Distinguish /u/

Segment and Blend Phonemes

Segment and Blend Onset and Rime

CCSS Foundational Skills 2.b., CCSS Foundational Skills 2.d.

Phonics and Spelling

Short *u:* *u*

Final Consonant Blends

CCSS Foundational Skills 3., CCSS Foundational Skills 3.b, CCSS Language 2.d.

crust	bump	jump
must	just	dust
trust	dusk	hunt
lump		

Listening and Speaking

Give Directions

CCSS Speaking/Listening 1.b.

Preview Your Week

What can we learn about animals by watching them?

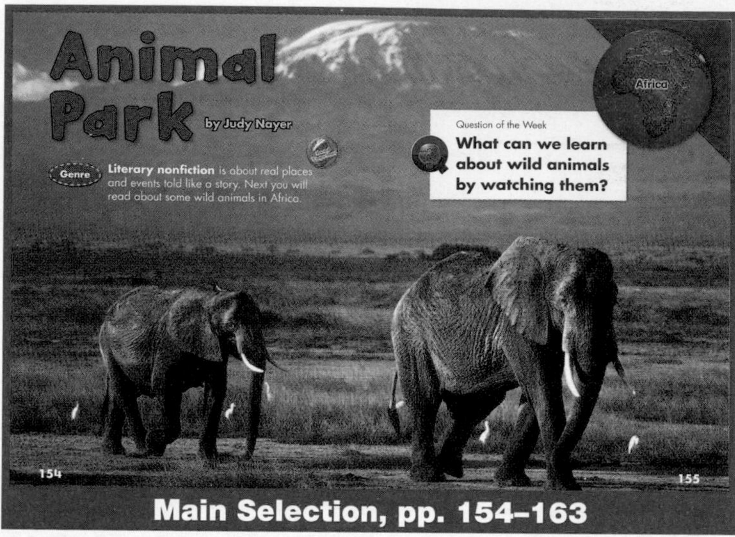
Animal Park by Judy Nayer

Genre Literary nonfiction is about real places and events told like a story. Next you will read about some wild animals in Africa.

Question of the Week
What can we learn about wild animals by watching them?

154 155

Main Selection, pp. 154–163

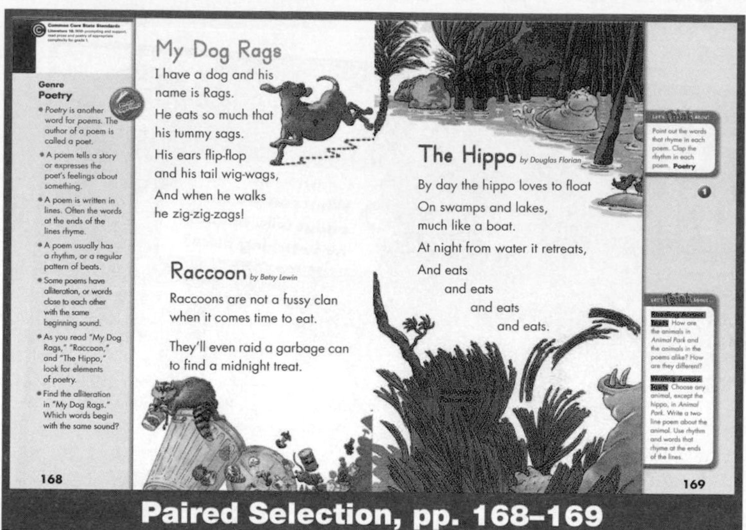
Genre Poetry

168

My Dog Rags
I have a dog and his
name is Rags.
He eats so much that
his tummy sags.
His ears flip-flop
and his tail wig-wags,
And when he walks
he zig-zig-zags!

Raccoon by Betsy Lewin
Raccoons are not a fussy clan
when it comes time to eat.
They'll even raid a garbage can
to find a midnight treat.

The Hippo by Douglas Florian
By day the hippo loves to float
On swamps and lakes,
much like a boat.
At night from water it retreats,
And eats
and eats
and eats
and eats.

169

Paired Selection, pp. 168–169

Genre: Literary Nonfiction

Phonics: Short *u: u,* Final Consonant Blends

Text-Based Comprehension: Cause and Effect

Poetry in Reading

Genre: Poetry

Build Content Knowledge

Zoom in on

TIME FOR Science

KNOWLEDGE GOALS
Children will understand that:

- we can learn about animals by watching them
- wild animals need food, water, and shelter
- we protect animals from danger

THIS WEEK'S CONCEPT MAP
Develop a concept-related graphic organizer like the one below over the course of this week.

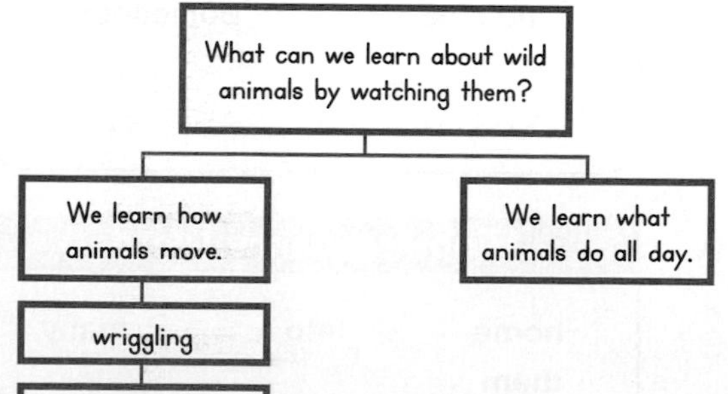
What can we learn about wild animals by watching them?
We learn how animals move.
We learn what animals do all day.
wriggling
climb

BUILD ORAL VOCABULARY
This week, children will acquire the following academic vocabulary/domain-specific words.

Amazing Words

desert	silent	chatter
forest	snort	poisonous
world	medicine	

OPTIONAL CONCEPT-BASED READING Use the Digital Path to access readers offering different levels of text complexity.

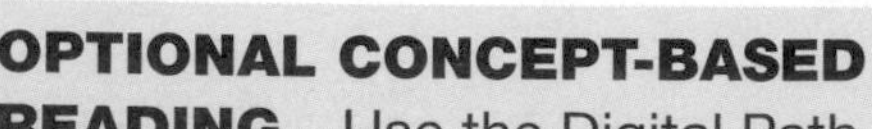

Wild Animals
Concept Literacy

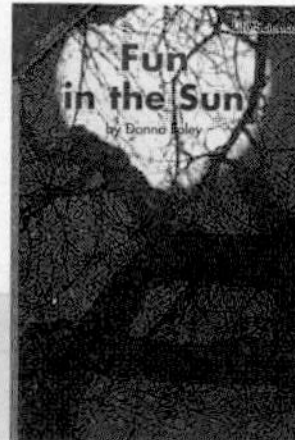
Fun in the Sun
Below Level

Which Animals Will We See?
On Level

Around the World
Advanced

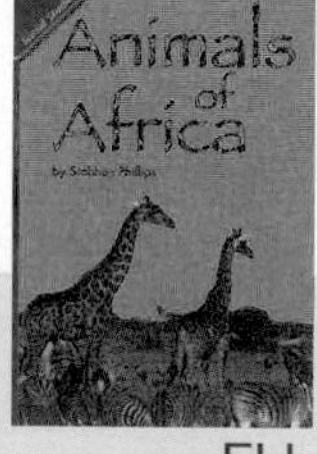
Animals of Africa
ELL

Animals of Africa
ELD

This Week's Digital Resources

eSTREET INTERACTIVE
www.ReadingStreet.com

Get Ready to Read

Background Building Audio CD This audio CD provides valuable background information about what a safari is and the kinds of animals one might see and hear on a safari to help children read and comprehend the weekly texts.

Concept Talk Video Use this video on the Digital Path to build momentum and introduce the weekly concept of watching wild animals.

Interactive Sing with Me Big Book "Big, Round World," sung to the tune of "The Farmer in the Dell," introduces the Amazing Words with a catchy, concept-related song.

Interactive Sound-Spelling Cards With these interactive cards on the Digital Path, children see an image, hear the image name, and see the spelling for short *u* spelled *u* and final consonant blends.

Pearson eText Use the eText for the Decodable Readers on the Leveled Reader Database for phonics and fluency support.

Letter Tile Drag and Drop Using this interactive tool on Pearson SuccessNet, children click and spell words to enhance their phonics skills.

Read and Comprehend

Envision It! Animations Use this colorful animation on the Digital Path to explain the target comprehension skill, Cause and Effect.

Pearson eText Read the eText of the main selection, *Animal Park*, and the paired selection, "Poetry Collection," with audio support on Pearson SuccessNet.

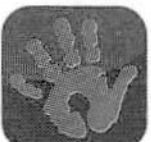
Story Sort Use the Story Sort Activity on the Digital Path after reading *Animal Park* to involve children in summarizing.

Journal: Word Bank Use the Word Bank on the Digital Path to have children write sentences using this week's high-frequency words.

Vocabulary Activities A variety of interactive vocabulary activities on the Digital Path help children practice high-frequency and concept-related words.

Language Arts

Grammar Jammer Choose a whimsical animation on the Digital Path to provide an engaging grammar lesson that will capture children's attention.

Pearson eText Find the Student Edition eText of the Let's Write It! and Let's Learn It! pages with audio support on Pearson SuccessNet.

Additional Resources

Teacher Resources DVD-ROM Use the following resources on the TR DVD or on Pearson SuccessNet throughout the week:

- Amazing Word Cards
- Reader's and Writer's Notebook
- Writing Transparencies
- Daily Fix-It Transparencies
- Scoring Rubrics
- Grammar Transparencies
- Research Transparencies
- Let's Practice It!
- Graphic Organizers
- High-Frequency Word Cards
- Vocabulary Transparencies

This Week's Skills

Phonics
Short *u* Spelled *u*
Final Consonant Blends

Comprehension
Skill: Cause and Effect
Strategy: Text Structure

Language
Vocabulary: Antonyms
Conventions: Exclamatory Sentences

Fluency
Appropriate Phrasing

Writing
Brief Composition

5-Day Planner

DAY 1

Get Ready to Read

Content Knowledge 146j
Oral Vocabulary: *desert, forest, world*

Phonemic Awareness 148–149
Distinguish /u/

Phonics/Spelling 149a
Short *u: u*
READ Decodable Reader 6A
Reread for Fluency
Spelling Pretest

Monitor Progress
Check Word Reading

Read and Comprehend

High-Frequency Words 151
home, into, many, them

Text-Based Comprehension 151a
Cause and Effect

Language Arts

Conventions 151c
Exclamatory Sentences

Writing 151d
Brief Composition

Research and Inquiry 151f
Identify and Focus Topic

DAY 2

Get Ready to Read

Content Knowledge 152a
Oral Vocabulary: *chatter, silent*

Phonemic Awareness 152c
Segment and Blend Phonemes

Phonics/Spelling 152d
Final Consonant Blends
Review Short Vowels
READ Decodable Reader 6B
Reread for Fluency
Spelling: Short *u* Words with Final Consonant Blends

Monitor Progress
Check Word Reading

Read and Comprehend

High-Frequency Words 153
home, into, many, them

Selection Vocabulary 154a
elephants, hippos, park, zebras
Antonyms

Text-Based Comprehension 154b
READ *Animal Park*—1st Read

Genre 163b
Literary Nonfiction

Language Arts

Conventions 163c
Exclamatory Sentences

Writing 163d
Brief Composition

Handwriting 163f
Letters *Uu* and *Qq*/Letter Spacing

Research and Inquiry 163g
Notes

DAY 3

Get Ready to Read

Content Knowledge 164a
Oral Vocabulary: *snort*

Phonemic Awareness 164c
Rhyming Words

Phonics/Spelling 164d
Build Words
Blend and Read
Spelling: Dictation

Read and Comprehend

High-Frequency Words and Selection Words 164g
High-Frequency Words: *home, into, many, them*
Selection Words: *elephants, hippos, park, zebras*
Monitor Progress Check High-Frequency Words

Text-Based Comprehension 164h
READ *Animal Park*—2nd Read
Monitor Progress Check Retelling

Fluency 165b
Appropriate Phrasing

Language Arts

Conventions 166a
Exclamatory Sentences

Writing 166–167
Brief Composition

Listening and Speaking 167b
Give Directions

Research and Inquiry 167c
Gather and Record Information

DAY 4

Get Ready to Read

Content Knowledge 168a
Oral Vocabulary: *medicine, poisonous*

Phonemic Awareness 168c
Distinguish /u/

Phonics/Spelling 168d
Review Short *e* Spelled *e;* Initial Consonant Blends
READ Decodable Reader 6C
Spiral Review Fluent Word Reading
Spelling: Short *u* Words with Final Consonant Blends

Read and Comprehend

Poetry in Reading 168i
READ "Poetry Collection" —Paired Selection

Fluency 169b
Appropriate Phrasing
Monitor Progress Fluency Check

Language Arts

Conventions 169c
Exclamatory Sentences

Writing 169d
Brief Composition

Research and Inquiry 169f
Synthesize

DAY 5

Get Ready to Read

Content Knowledge 170a
Review Oral Vocabulary
Monitor Progress Check Oral Vocabulary

Phonemic Awareness 170c
Review Segment and Blend Onset and Rime

Phonics/Spelling 170c
Review Short *u: u,* Final Consonant Blends
Spelling Test

Read and Comprehend

Listening and Speaking 170–171
Vocabulary 171a
Fluency 171a

Text-Based Comprehension 171b
Review Cause and Effect

Vocabulary 171b
Review High-Frequency and Selection Words

Genre 171c
Review Poetry

Assessment 171d
Monitor Progress Word and Sentence Reading

Language Arts

Conventions 171g
Review Exclamatory Sentences

Writing 171h
Brief Composition

Research and Inquiry 171j
Communicate

Wrap Up Your Week! 171k

Access for All

What do I do in group time?
It's as easy as 1-2-3!

1 TEACHER-LED SMALL GROUPS → 2 INDEPENDENT PRACTICE STATIONS → 3 INDEPENDENT READING

Small Group Time

Bridge to Common Core

SKILL DEVELOPMENT
- Final Consonant Blends
- Short *u: u*
- Cause and Effect
- Text Structure

DEEP UNDERSTANDING

This Week's Knowledge Goals

Children will understand that:
- we can learn about animals by watching them
- wild animals need food, water, and shelter
- we protect animals from danger

1 Small Group Lesson Plan

	DAY 1 Differentiate Phonics	DAY 2 Differentiate Comprehension
OL On-Level pp. SG•87–SG•91	**Practice Phonics** More Short *u* Words **Decodable Reader** Read *Duck Has Fun*	**Practice Phonics** Additional Words with Final Consonant Blends **Access Text** Read *Animal Park*
SI Strategic Intervention pp. SG•92–SG•96	**Reteach Phonics** Blend Short *u* Words **Decodable Reader** Read *Duck Has Fun*	**Reteach Phonics** Blend Words with Final Consonant Blends **Access Text** Read *Animal Park*
A Advanced pp. SG•97–SG•102	**Extend Phonics** More Challenging Short *u* Words **Advanced Selection** "Fun with Ducks"	**Extend Phonics** Additional Words with Final Consonant Blends **Access Text** Read *Animal Park*
Independent Inquiry Project	**Identify Questions**	**Investigate**
ELL **If...** children need more scaffolding and practice with...	**Phonemic Awareness and Phonics,** **then...** use the ELL activities on pp. DI•118–DI•119 in the Teacher Resources section on SuccessNet.	**the Comprehension Skill,** **then...** use the ELL activities on p. DI•122 in the Teacher Resources section on SuccessNet.

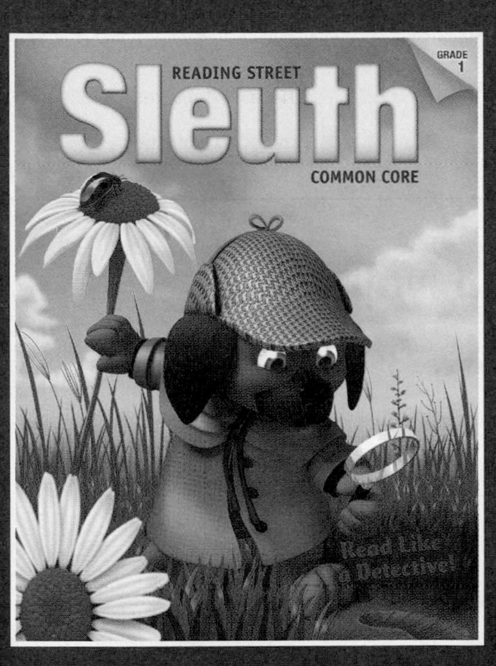

Reading Street Sleuth
- Provides access to grade-level text for all children
- Focuses on finding clues in text through close reading
- Builds capacity for complex text

Build Text-Based Comprehension

Animal Park

Optional Leveled Readers

Concept Literacy

Below Level

On Level

Advanced

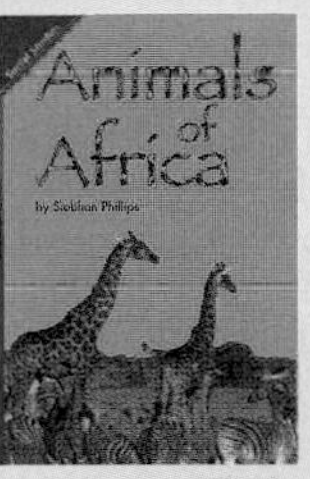

ELL

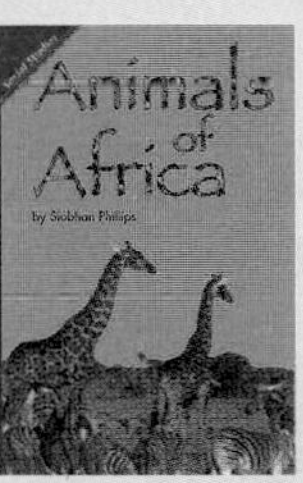

ELD

DAY 3	DAY 4	DAY 5
Differentiate Close Reading	**Differentiate Vocabulary**	**Differentiate Reteaching**
Reread to Develop Vocabulary **Close Reading** Reread *Animal Park*	**Build Word Knowledge** Develop Language **Text-Based Comprehension** Read *Reading Street Sleuth,* pp. 18–19 or Leveled Readers	**Practice Exclamatory Sentences** **Text-Based Comprehension** Reread *Reading Street Sleuth,* pp. 18–19 or Leveled Readers
Build Word Knowledge Blend Words with Short *u* and Final Consonant Blends **Close Reading** Reread *Animal Park*	**Review Vocabulary** Review/Discuss Selection Vocabulary **Text-Based Comprehension** Read *Reading Street Sleuth,* pp. 18–19 or Leveled Readers	**Review Vocabulary** High-Frequency Words **Text-Based Comprehension** Reread *Reading Street Sleuth,* pp. 18–19 or Leveled Readers
Reread to Extend Vocabulary **Extend Concepts** Reread *Animal Park* **Investigate**	**Build Word Knowledge** Extend Amazing Words and Selection Vocabulary **Text-Based Comprehension** Read *Reading Street Sleuth,* pp. 18–19 or Leveled Readers **Organize**	**Extend Exclamatory Sentences** **Text-Based Comprehension** Reread *Reading Street Sleuth,* pp. 18–19 or Leveled Readers **Communicate**
the Main Selection, then... use the activities on p. DI•123 in the Teacher Resources section on SuccessNet.	**Vocabulary, then...** use the routine on pp. xxxvi–xxxvii in the *ELL Handbook.*	**Conventions and Writing, then...** use the activities on pp. DI•125–DI•126 in the Teacher Resources section on SuccessNet.

2 Independent Stations

Practice Last Week's Skills

★ Focus on these activities when time is limited.

ACCESS FOR ALL
- ● Below-Level Activities
- ▲ On-Level Activities
- ■ Advanced Activities

LISTEN UP!

Match sounds and pictures.

OBJECTIVES
- Identify words with initial and medial sound /e/.
- Identify words with initial consonant blends.

MATERIALS
- *Listen Up!* Flip Chart Activity 6, Picture Cards *egg, elbow, elephant, escalator, bed, ten, flag, grape, snail, playground*

 **Modeled Pronunciation Audio CD**

● Children find Picture Cards that have the same beginning sound as *echo* or the same middle sound as *pet.*

▲ Children find Picture Cards that have the same beginning sound as *echo,* the same middle sound as *pet,* or begin with consonant blends.

■ Children find Picture Cards that have the same beginning sound as *echo,* the same middle sound as *pet,* or begin with consonant blends. Then have children write their own words.

★ WORD WORK

Write and read words.

OBJECTIVES
- Write words with short *e* or initial consonant blends

MATERIALS
- *Word Work* Flip Chart Activity 6, pre-cut paper strips, scissors, blue and red markers

 **Interactive Sound-Spelling Cards**

● Children use a red marker for each *e* and *gl* and a blue marker for the other letters as they write *egg, wet,* and *glad* on paper strips.

▲ Children use a red marker for each *e* and *gl* and a blue marker for the other letters as they write *egg, wet,* and *glad* on paper strips. Then they cut apart the letters and a partner builds the words.

■ Children use a red marker for each *e* and *gl* and a blue marker for the other letters as they write *egg, wet,* and *glad* on paper strips. Then they cut apart the letters and a partner builds the words.

LET'S WRITE!

Write sentences.

OBJECTIVES
- Write interrogative sentences.

MATERIALS
- *Let's Write!* Flip Chart Activity 6, paper, pencils

 **Grammar Jammer**

● Children write an interrogative sentence about an animal in their neighborhood.

▲ Children write two interrogative sentences about an animal in their neighborhood.

■ Children write several interrogative sentences about an animal in their neighborhood. Then they will read their questions to a partner to see if they have an answer.

WORDS TO KNOW

Sort words.

OBJECTIVES
- Identify high-frequency words *small, tree, your, saw.*
- Sort words with initial consonant blends.

MATERIALS
- *Words to Know* Flip Chart Activity 6; paper; pencils

 **Vocabulary Activities**

 **Teacher Resources**
- High-Frequency Word Cards for Unit 1, Week 5

● Children sort the Word Cards into two piles: words with initial consonant blends and words without. Then they write the words.

▲ Children sort the Word Cards into two piles: words with initial consonant blends and words without. Then they write the words, underlining the initial blends

■ Children write the Word Cards in two columns: words with initial consonant blends in one column and words without in the other. Then they write sentences using the words.

READ FOR MEANING

Use text-based comprehension tools.

OBJECTIVES

- Identify the main idea of a story.
- Identify the details that support the main idea.

MATERIALS

- *Read for Meaning* Flip Chart Activity 6, Leveled Readers, paper, pencils

 **Pearson eText**
- Leveled eReaders

 **Envision It! Animations**

● Children read *At Your Vet.* First, they write a sentence that tells the main idea. Then they write the details.

▲ Children read *What Animals Can You See?* First, they write a sentence that tells the main idea. Then they write the details.

■ Children read *Cary and the Wildlife Shelter.* First, they write a sentence that tells the main idea inside a circle. Then they write the details on lines that extend from the circle.

GET FLUENT

Practice fluent reading.

OBJECTIVES

- Read aloud with appropriate phrasing.

MATERIALS

- *Get Fluent* Flip Chart Activity 6, Leveled Readers

 **Pearson eText**
- Leveled eReaders

● Children work with a partner to take turns reading from *At Your Vet.*

▲ Children work with a partner to take turns reading from *What Animals Can You See?*

■ Children work with a partner to take turns reading from *Cary and the Wildlife Shelter.*

Manage the Stations

Use these management tools to set up and organize your Practice Stations:

Practice Station Flip Charts

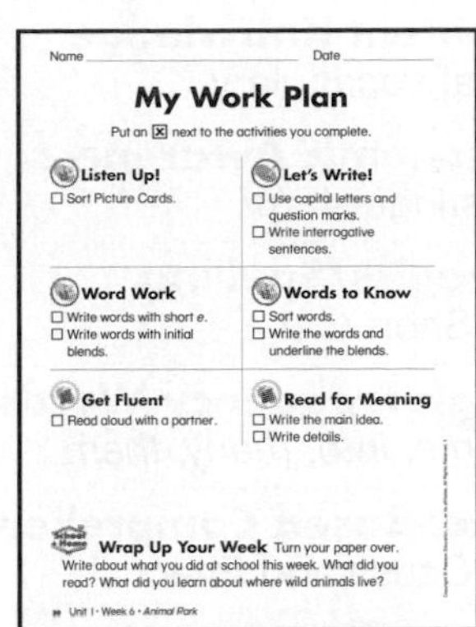

Classroom Management Handbook for Differentiated Instruction Practice Stations, p. 30

3 Independent Reading ©

Children should select appropriately complex texts to read and write about independently every day before, during, and after school.

Suggestions for this week's independent reading:

- Informational texts on last week's science topic: Which wild animals live in our neighborhood?
- Nonfiction selections about which wild animals live in our neighborhood
- Other books by Alyssa Satin Capucilli

BOOK TALK Have partners discuss their independent reading for the week. Tell them to refer to their Reading Log and paraphrase what the selection was about. To focus the discussion, prompt them to talk about one or more of the following:

Key Ideas and Details
- Who is the author? Why did he or she write the work?
- What did I learn from this text?

Craft and Structure
- Did I understand the information?
- Did the author use words that were interesting and clear?

Integration of Ideas
- Did the information seem believable? Why or why not?
- Was this book like others I have read?

 **Pearson eText**
- Student Edition
- Decodable Readers
- Leveled Readers

 **Trade Book Library**

 **Materials from School or Classroom Library**

Content Knowledge
Oral Vocabulary

Phonemic Awareness
Distinguish /u/

Phonics/Spelling
Short *u: u*

High-Frequency Words
home, into, many, them

Text-Based Comprehension
Cause and Effect

Conventions
Exclamatory Sentences

Writing
Brief Composition

Research and Inquiry
Identify and Focus Topic

Materials

- Student Edition
- Sing with Me Big Book
- Sound-Spelling Cards
- Decodable Reader 6A
- Reader's and Writer's Notebook

Bridge to Common Core

INTEGRATION OF KNOWLEDGE/IDEAS

This week children read, write, and talk about watching wild animals.

Texts This Week

- "Big, Round World"
- "The Fox Family"
- *Jungle Drum*
- *Animal Park*
- "My Dog Rags," "Raccoon," "The Hippo"
- "When Animals Are Doctors"

Science Knowledge Goals

Children will understand that

- we can learn about animals by watching them
- wild animals need food, water, and shelter
- we protect animals from danger

Street Rhymes!

Tall giraffes with spotted skin,
Monkeys that can make you grin,
Panda bears with black and white faces,
Elephants from far-off places.
I like seals and tigers too.
My favorite animals are at the zoo.

- To introduce this week's concept, read aloud the poem several times and ask children to join you.

Content Knowledge

Watching Wild Animals

CONCEPT TALK To help children gain knowledge and understanding, tell them that this week they will talk, sing, read, and write about what people learn about wild animals by watching them. Write the Question of the Week, *What can we learn about wild animals by watching them?,* and track the print as you read it.

Build Oral Language

TALK ABOUT WATCHING WILD ANIMALS Have children turn to pages 146–147 in their Student Edition. Read the title and look at the photos. Use these questions to guide discussion and create the "What can we learn about wild animals by watching them?" concept map.

- One thing we can learn by watching animals is how they move. How is the snake in the picture moving? (It is wriggling forward.) Let's add *We learn how animals move* and *wriggling* to our map.
- The animal in the tree is a tarsier. How can it move? (It can climb.) Let's add *climb* to our map.

Common Core State Standards
Speaking/Listening 4. Describe people, places, things, and events with relevant details, expressing ideas and feelings clearly.

Oral Vocabulary

Let's Talk About

Read Together

Wild Animals

- Share information about wild animals from all around the world.
- Discuss what we can learn about animals by watching them.

READING STREET ONLINE
CONCEPT TALK VIDEO
www.ReadingStreet.com

You've learned 0 8 6 Amazing Words so far this year!

146 147

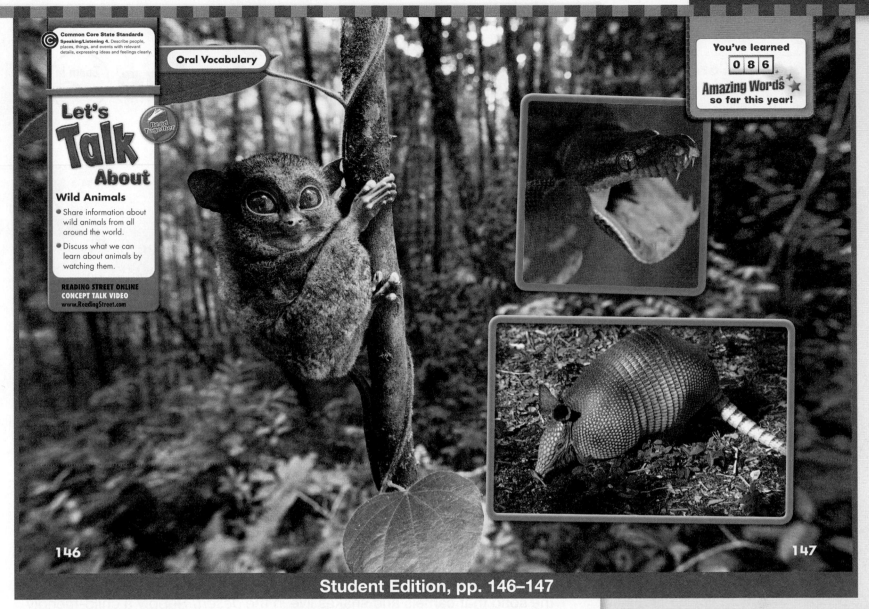

Student Edition, pp. 146–147

CONNECT TO READING Explain that this week children will read about wild animals that live in a special park and what the animals there do all day. Let's add *We learn what animals do all day* to our map.

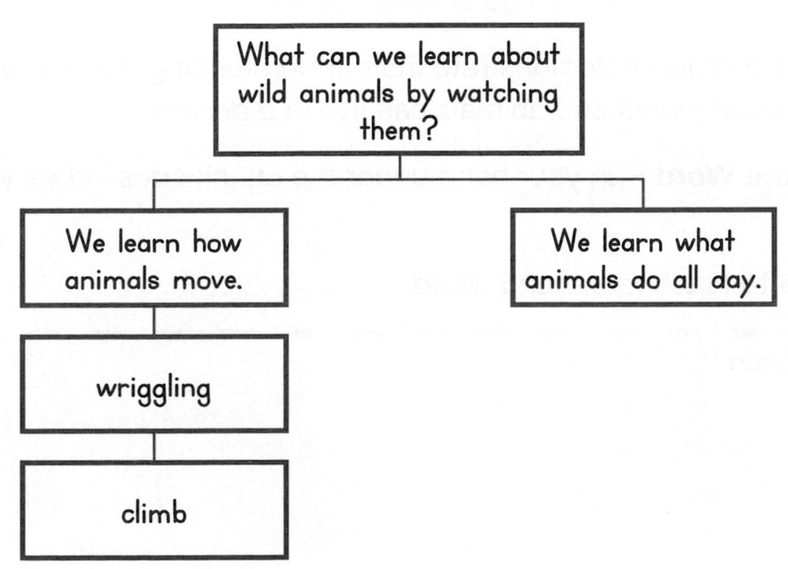

ELL

Preteach Concepts Use the Day 1 instruction on ELL Poster 6 to build knowledge and oral vocabulary.

ELL Support Additional ELL support is provided in the *ELL Handbook* and in the *ELL Support Lessons* on the *Teacher Resources DVD-ROM.*

Common Core State Standards

Language 5.c. Identify real-life connections between words and their use (e.g., note places at home that are *cozy*).

Content Knowledge

Build Oral Vocabulary

INTRODUCE AMAZING WORDS Display p. 6 of the *Sing with Me* Big Book. Tell children they are going to sing about some wild animals and the places where they live. Ask children to listen for the Amazing Words *desert*, *forest*, and *world* as you sing. Sing the song again and have children join you.

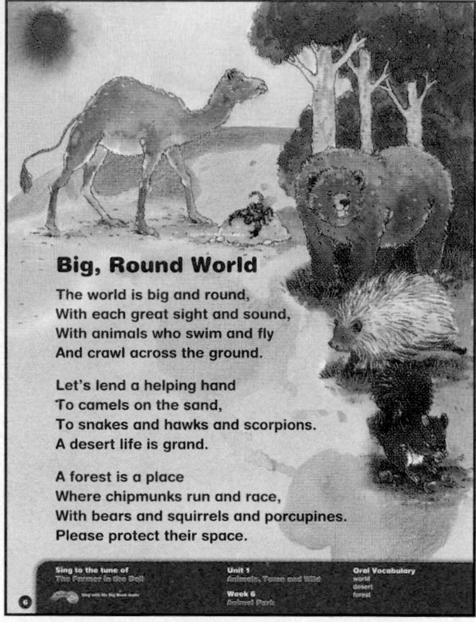

Big, Round World
The world is big and round,
With each great sight and sound,
With animals who swim and fly
And crawl across the ground.
Let's lend a helping hand
To camels on the sand,
To snakes and hawks and scorpions.
A desert life is grand.
A forest is a place
Where chipmunks run and race,
With bears and squirrels and porcupines.
Please protect their space.

Sing with Me Big Book, p. 6

Amazing Words

You've learned 086 words so far.

You'll learn 008 words this week!

desert	silent
forest	snort
world	medicine
chatter	poisonous

Amazing Words — Robust Vocabulary Routine

1. **Introduce the Word** Relate the word *desert* to the song. We know from the song that camels and snakes live in the *desert.* Supply a child-friendly definition. A *desert* is a dry area of land that has very little rain. Have children say the word.
2. **Demonstrate** Provide examples to show meaning. A *desert* is often hot and covered with sand. There are very few plants in a *desert.* People bring water with them when they go across a *desert.*
3. **Apply** Have children demonstrate their understanding. Explain why only some kinds of plants and animals can live in a *desert.*
4. **Display the Word** Run your hand under the chunks *des-ert* as you read the word.

See p. OV•6 to teach *forest* and *world.*

Routines Flip Chart

AMAZING WORDS AT WORK Have children look at the picture on p. 6 of the *Sing with Me* Big Book.

- Which three animals in the picture live in the *forest?* (bear, porcupine, squirrel) What other wild animals might you see in a *forest?* Use the word *forest* in your answer. (Possible response: I might see deer and birds in a forest.)
- Some animals live in many parts of the *world* and some live in only a few places. What is an animal that lives in a different part of the *world* from you? Use the word *world* in your answer. (Possible response: Elephants live in a different part of the world.)
- What might you learn by watching an animal in the *desert?* Use the word *desert* in your answer. (Possible response: I might learn how animals find food in the desert.)

APPLY AMAZING WORDS Have children demonstrate their understanding of the Amazing Words by completing these sentences orally.

Our **world** is home to many _______.

If I go to the **desert,** I will probably see _______.

The **forest** is a great place to _______.

Corrective feedback | **If...** children have difficulty using the Amazing Words, **then...** remind them of the definitions and provide opportunities for children to use the words in sentences.

Visual Support Use the illustrations on p. 6 of the *Sing with Me* Big Book to support children's understanding of animal names and the Amazing Words. Have children name each animal as you point to its picture. Then say and have children repeat these sentences: *The camel and scorpion live in the desert. The bear, porcupine, and squirrel live in the forest.*

DAY 1

Common Core State Standards
Foundational Skills 2.c. Isolate and pronounce initial, medial vowel, and final sounds (phonemes) in spoken single-syllable words. Also Foundational Skills 2.b.
Phonemic Awareness
Let's Listen for
Read Together
Sounds
Find two things that rhyme with trust.
Find five things that contain the short u sound.
Find something that rhymes with dunk. Say each sound in the word.
READING STREET ONLINE
SOUND-SPELLING CARDS
www.ReadingStreet.com
148
149

Student Edition, pp. 148–149

Common Core State Standards

Foundational Skills 2.b. Orally produce single-syllable words by blending sounds (phonemes), including consonant blends. **Foundational Skills 2.c.** Isolate and pronounce initial, medial vowel, and final sounds (phonemes) in spoken single-syllable words. **Foundational Skills 3.** Know and apply grade-level phonics and word analysis skills in decoding words.

Skills Trace

Short *u*: *u*

Introduce U1W6D1

Practice U1W6D3; U1W6D4

Reteach/Review U1W6D5; U2W1D4

Assess/Test Weekly Test U1W6
Benchmark Test U1

KEY: U=Unit W=Week D=Day

Phonemic Awareness

Distinguish /u/

INTRODUCE Read the second bulleted point on p. 148. In the picture, what is shining up in the sky? (sun) The middle sound in *sun* is /u/. Listen as I say the short *u* sound: /u/, /u/, /u/. There are three sounds in *sun:* /s/ /u/ /n/. The middle sound is /u/. There are two sounds in *up:* /u/ /p/. The first sound is /u/.

MODEL Have children identify other items or actions in the picture with the short *u* sound. (mug, skunk, hug, cup, bug) Say *us, egg, ugly, untie,* and *inch.* Have children raise their hands if they hear /u/ at the beginning of the word. Repeat with *cut, bug, bag, rest, rust* for /u/ in the middle.

Corrective feedback	**If...** children make an error, **then...** model by segmenting the word, and then have them repeat the segmenting and blending of the word.

Phonics

Short *u*: *u*

CONNECT Write the words *top* and *jet.* Ask children what they know about the vowel sounds in these words. (The vowel sounds are short. Short *o* is spelled *o.* Short *e* is spelled *e.*) Explain that today they will learn how to spell and read words with short *u,* /u/, spelled *u.*

Sound-Spelling Card 24

USE SOUND-SPELLING CARD Display Card 24. Point to *u.* The short *u* sound, /u/, is usually spelled *u.* Have children say /u/ several times as you point to *u.*

MODEL Write *bug.* In this word, the letter *u* stands for the sound /u/. Segment and blend *bug,* and then have children blend with you: /b/ /u/ /g/. Follow this procedure to model *bud* and *mug.*

GROUP PRACTICE Continue the process. This time have children blend with you. Remind children that *u* usually spells the short *u* sound, /u/.

cut	**rug**	**mud**	**tub**	**run**	**but**
rub	**cup**	**sun**	**nut**	**dud**	**luck**

REVIEW What do you know about reading these words? (The letter *u* can spell the short *u* sound, /u/.)

Access for All

SI Strategic Intervention

Distinguish /u/ If children have difficulty hearing short *u* at the beginning of a word, have them repeat the word *umbrella.* Then ask, Does our new word have the same sound you hear at the beginning of *umbrella?*

Vocabulary Support

You may wish to explain the meaning of this word.

dud something that doesn't work the way it should

ELL

Produce /u/ Because English short vowel sounds do not exist or have only approximations in many languages, English learners may have a hard time hearing the difference between, for example, short *u* and short *o.* Demonstrate the position of the mouth when saying /u/ versus /o/. Provide additional phonemic awareness activities to help children hear and pronounce words with short *u.*

Pronounce /u/ In Spanish, the letter *u* spells the sound /ü/ heard in *ruby.* Spanish-speaking children may therefore read a word such as *mud* as *mood.* Provide extra practice pronouncing /u/ and associating the short *u* sound with the letter *u.*

Common Core State Standards

Foundational Skills 3. Know and apply grade-level phonics and word analysis skills in decoding words. **Foundational Skills 3.b.** Decode regularly spelled one-syllable words.

Access for All

Advanced

Extend Blending Provide children who can segment and blend all the words correctly with more challenging words such as *uncle, summer, funny, study, sunshine,* and *bunch.*

Spelling Pattern

/u/ Spelled u The sound /u/ is usually spelled *u* at the beginning or in the middle of a word.

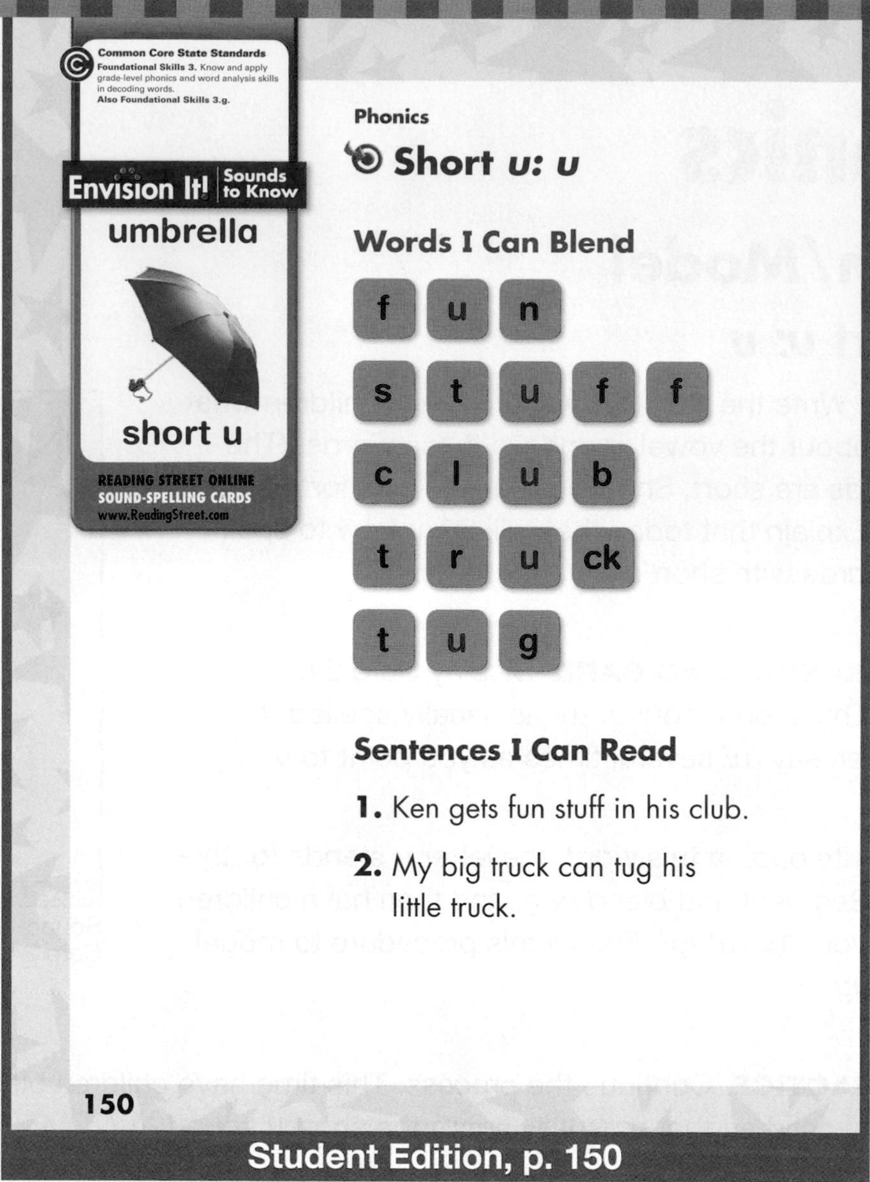

Student Edition, p. 150

Phonics

Guide Practice

BLEND WORDS Have children turn to page 150 in their Student Edition. Look at the picture on this page. I see a picture of an *umbrella.* When I say *umbrella,* I hear the short *u* sound, /u/, at the beginning. The /u/ sound is spelled *u.*

GROUP PRACTICE For each word in "Words I Can Blend," ask for the sound of each letter or group of letters. Make sure that children identify the correct sound for *u.* Then have children blend the whole word.

Corrective feedback	**If...** children have difficulty blending a word, **then...** model blending the word, and ask children to blend it with you.

DECODE WORDS IN ISOLATION After children can successfully segment and blend the words, point to words in random order and ask children to read them naturally.

DECODE WORDS IN CONTEXT Have children read each of the sentences. Have them identify words in the sentences that have the short *u* sound, /u/.

Team Talk Pair children and have them take turns reading each of the sentences aloud.

ON THEIR OWN Use *Reader's and Writer's Notebook,* p. 201.

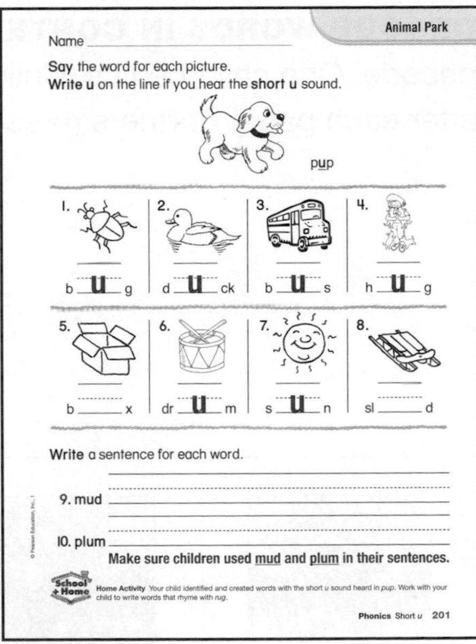

Reader's and Writer's Notebook, p. 201

MONITOR PROGRESS Short *u*: *u*

FORMATIVE ASSESSMENT Write the following words and have the class read them. Notice which words children miss during the group reading. Call on individuals to read some of the words.

					Spiral Review
hum	jug	tub	pup	fun	
box	job	hut	mop	gum ←	Row 2 contrasts short *o* and short *u* words.
hid	ten	pot	cup	bat ←	Row 3 reviews short vowels.

If... children cannot blend short *u* words at this point,

then... use the Small Group Time Strategic Intervention lesson, p. SG•92, to reteach short *u* spelled *u*. Continue to monitor children's progress using other instructional opportunities during the week. See the Skills Trace on p. 148–149.

Common Core State Standards

Foundational Skills 3. Know and apply grade-level phonics and word analysis skills in decoding words. **Foundational Skills 3.b.** Decode regularly spelled one-syllable words. **Foundational Skills 4.** Read with sufficient accuracy and fluency to support comprehension.

Decodable Reader 6A

If children need help, then...

Read *Duck Has Fun*

DECODE WORDS IN ISOLATION Have children turn to page 217. Have children decode each word.

REVIEW HIGH-FREQUENCY WORDS Review the previously taught words *like, they, with, too, to, the,* and *a.* Have children read each word as you point to it on the Word Wall.

PREVIEW DECODABLE READER Have children read the title and preview the story. Tell them they will read words with the short vowel sound *u.*

DECODE WORDS IN CONTEXT Pair children for reading and listen as they decode. One child begins. Children read the entire story, switching readers after each page. Partners reread the story. This time the other child begins.

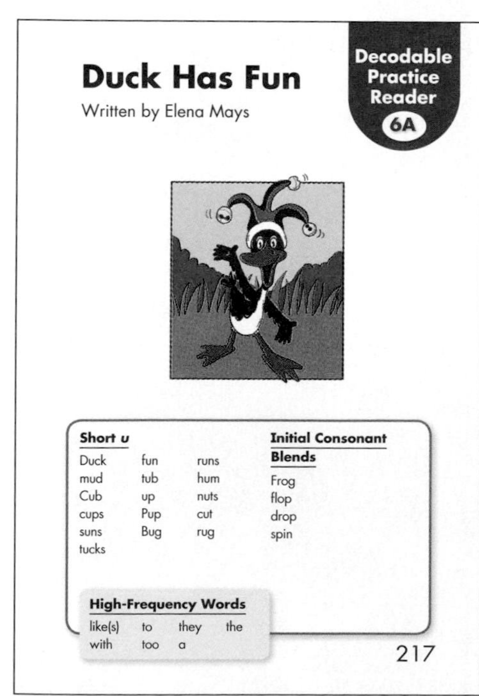

Duck Has Fun

Written by Elena Mays

Decodable Practice Reader 6A

Short *u*			Initial Consonant Blends
Duck	fun	runs	Frog
mud	tub	hum	flop
Cub	up	nuts	drop
cups	Pup	cut	spin
suns	Bug	rug	
tucks			

High-Frequency Words

like(s) to they the
with too a

217

Decodable Practice Reader 6A

Duck likes fun.

218

Duck runs to Frog.
They flop in mud.

219

Duck hops in the tub.
Frog hops in too.
They hum.

220

Duck runs with Cub.
They pick up nuts.
They drop nuts in the cups.

221

Duck sits with Pup.
They cut suns.

222

Duck spots Bug.
They sit on a rug.
They spin tops.

223

Duck gets in bed.
Mom tucks Duck in.
Duck had fun.

224

Corrective feedback	**If...** children have difficulty decoding a word, **then...** refer them to the Sound-Spelling Cards to identify the sounds in the word. Then prompt them to blend the word. • What is the new word? • Is the new word a word you know? • Does it make sense in the story?

CHECK DECODING AND COMPREHENSION Have children retell the story to include characters, setting, and events. Then have children locate short *u* words in the story. List words that children name. Children should supply *Duck, fun, runs, mud, tub, hum, Cub, up, nuts, cups, Pup, cut, suns, Bug, rug,* and *tucks.*

Reread for Fluency

REREAD DECODABLE READER Have children reread Decodable Practice Reader 6A to develop automaticity decoding words with the short *u* sound.

Routine Oral Rereading

1. **Read** Have children read the entire book orally.
2. **Reread** To achieve optimal fluency, children should reread the text three or four times.
3. **Corrective Feedback** Listen as children read. Provide corrective feedback regarding their fluency and decoding.

Routines Flip Chart

Access for All

SI Strategic Intervention

Guide Writing After reading, write the following short *u* words on the board and ask children to pronounce them after you: *mud, tub, gum, hut.* Ask children to write their own sentences using these words. Monitor children's use of each word within their sentences.

Vocabulary Development

Beginning Before children read, lead them through *Duck Has Fun,* identifying Duck, Cub, Pup, and Bug. Point out short *u* words, such as *rug, mud,* and *tub,* and the drawing that illustrates each. Have children say each word aloud.

Intermediate After reading, have children find short *u* words in the story. Ask them to use one or more of the words in a sentence—for example, *It's fun to hum in the tub.* Monitor children's pronunciation.

Advanced After reading, have children act out some of the ways Duck has fun. Have them explain what they are doing. Monitor children's pronunciation.

Common Core State Standards

Foundational Skills 3.g. Recognize and read grade-appropriate irregularly spelled words. **Language 2.d.** Use conventional spelling for words with common spelling patterns and for frequently occurring irregular words. **Language 2.e.** Spell untaught words phonetically, drawing on phonemic awareness and spelling conventions.

Access for All

 Advanced

Extend Spelling Challenge children who spell words correctly to spell more difficult words such as *plump, tusk, pumpkin, stunt, grump,* and *uncle.*

Phonics/Spelling Generalization

Short *u* Each spelling word is a short *u* word, which has the short *u* sound.

Name ______________ Animal Park

Short *u* Words with Final Consonant Blends

Look at the word. Say it. Listen for the short *u* sound.

	Write each word.	Check it.
1. just	just	just
2. dust	dust	dust
3. must	must	must
4. hunt	hunt	hunt
5. crust	crust	crust
6. bump	bump	bump
7. jump	jump	jump
8. trust	trust	trust
9. lump	lump	lump
10. dusk	dusk	dusk

Words to Read

11. many many 12. into into

Home Activity Your child is learning to spell words with the short *u* vowel sound. Practice at home by having your child write each word and circle the *u* in each word.

DVD•70 Spelling Short *u* Words with Final Consonant Blends

Let's Practice It! TR DVD•70

Spelling Pretest

Short *u* Words with Final Consonant Blends

DICTATE SPELLING WORDS Dictate the spelling words. Have children write the words. If needed, segment the words for children, clarify the pronunciations, and give meanings of words. Have children check their pretests and correct misspelled words.

1. crust	Mom can cut the **crust** off my sandwich.
2. bump*	The road has a big **bump** in it.
3. jump	I can **jump** up and down.
4. must	I **must** do my homework.
5. just	I **just** finished reading the book.
6. dust	Look at the **dust** on the table!
7. trust	I **trust** you to tell the truth.
8. dusk	It is **dusk** just before the sun sets.
9. hunt	I have to **hunt** for my mop.
10. lump	The cat made a **lump** under the blanket.

* Word marked with an asterisk comes from the selection *Animal Park.*

ON THEIR OWN Use Let's Practice It! p. 70 on the *Teacher Resources DVD-ROM.*

ELL

If... children need more scaffolding and practice with **Phonemic Awareness and Phonics, then...** use the ELL activities on pp. DI•118–DI•119 in the Teacher Resources section on SuccessNet.

Day 1 SMALL GROUP TIME • Differentiate Phonics, p. SG•86

OL On-Level
- **Practice Phonics** Additional Short *u* Words
- **Read** Decodable Reader *Duck Has Fun*

SI Strategic Intervention
- **Reteach Phonics** Blend Short *u* Words
- **Read** Decodable Reader *Duck Has Fun*

A Advanced
- **Extend Phonics** More Short *u* Words
- **Read** Advanced Selection for Short *u* Words
- **Introduce** Inquiry Project

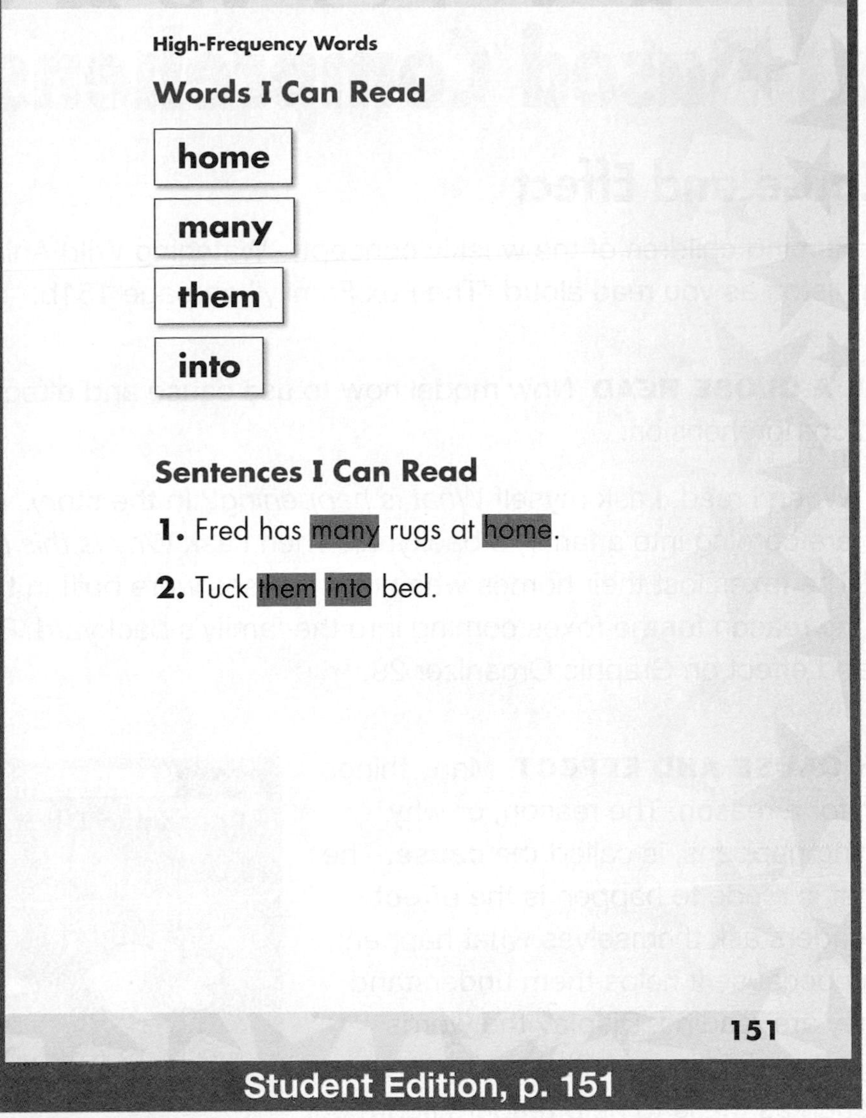

High-Frequency Words
Words I Can Read
home
many
them
into
Sentences I Can Read
1. Fred has many rugs at home.
2. Tuck them into bed.
151

Student Edition, p. 151

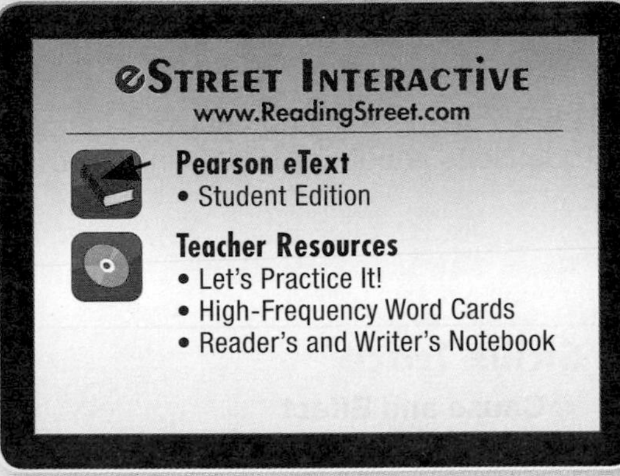

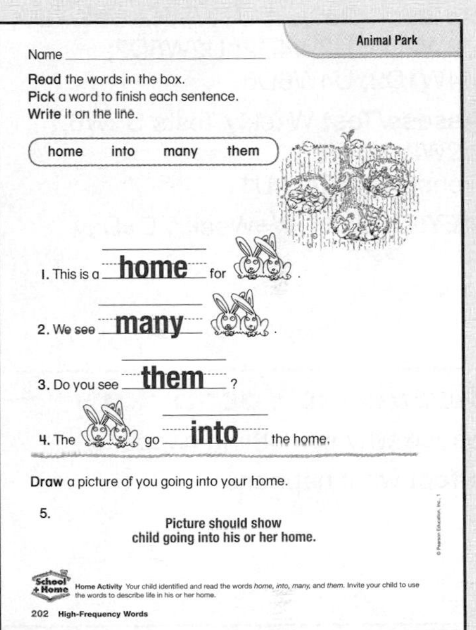

Reader's and Writer's Notebook, p. 202

High-Frequency Words

Routine Nondecodable Words

1. **Say and Spell** Some words we have to learn by remembering the letters. Point to *home.* Have children say and spell each word letter by letter.
2. **Identify Familiar Letter-Sounds** Point to the first letter in *home.* What is this letter and what is its sound? (*h,* /h/)
3. **Show Meaning** Tell me a sentence using the word *home*. Repeat.

Routines Flip Chart

READ Have children read the page aloud. Add the words to the Word Wall.

ON THEIR OWN Use *Reader's and Writer's Notebook,* p. 202.

Survival Vocabulary Have children use the word *home* to talk about where they live. Children might say, *My **home** is nice.*

Text-Based Comprehension

Cause and Effect

READ Remind children of the weekly concept—Watching Wild Animals. Have children listen as you read aloud "The Fox Family" on page 151b.

MODEL A CLOSE READ Now model how to use cause and effect as a tool to build comprehension.

When I read, I ask myself *What is happening?* In the story, wild foxes are coming into a family's backyard. Then I ask *Why is this happening?* The foxes lost their homes when new houses were built in the woods. This is the reason for the foxes coming into the family's backyard. Record the cause and effect on Graphic Organizer 29.

TEACH CAUSE AND EFFECT Many things happen for a reason. The reason, or why something happens, is called the **cause.** The thing that is made to happen is the **effect.** Good readers ask themselves what happens and why because it helps them understand what they are reading. Display the words *because, so,* and *since.* Authors may use clue words such as these to help readers figure out the cause and effect.

Student Edition, p. EI•2

Have children turn to p. EI•2 in their Student Edition. Discuss these questions using the pictures:

- What do you see in the first picture? (a rain cloud)
- What do you see in the second picture? (a wet girl)
- What is the cause and effect? (Rain is the cause; a wet girl is the effect.)

GUIDE PRACTICE Have children choose a previously read story. Ask them to draw one story event on the right side of their paper and its cause on the left. Then have them label their picture with the words *cause* and *effect.* Ask several children to share their pictures with the class.

APPLY Use *Reader's and Writer's Notebook,* p. 203.

Common Core State Standards

Literature 1. Ask and answer questions about key details in a text.

Skills Trace

Cause and Effect

Introduce U1W6D1; U2W2D1; U4W6D1

Practice U1W6D2; U1W6D3; U2W2D2; U2W2D3; U2W2D4; U4W6D2; U4W6D3; U4W6D4

Reteach/Review U1W6D5; U2W1D2; U2W2D5; U2W4D2; U2W5D2; U4W1D2; U4W6D5

Assess/Test Weekly Tests U1W6; U2W2; U4W6
Benchmark Test U1

KEY: U=Unit W=Week D=Day

Academic Vocabulary

cause why something happens
effect what happens

Animal Park

Name

Look at the picture that shows what happened.
Circle the picture that shows why it happened.

1.

2.

3.

Read the two story sentences. **Circle** the one that tells what happens.

4. Val is tan. The pup ran.

5. Sam is sick. Sam naps in bed.

Home Activity Your child learned about cause (why something happens) and effect (what happens). Look for cause and effect with your child. For example, you might point out that when the temperature drops in the fall, frost forms.

Comprehension Cause and Effect 203

Reader's and Writer's Notebook, p. 203

Teacher Read Aloud

The Fox Family

"Mom! Mom!" Jake cried when he saw the red and white furry animal that sat on the grass. "Look at that funny little dog in the backyard!"

Jake's mom moved to the window and looked out.

"Now there are two of them! One is small, and one is big! Maybe one is the mother and one is the baby!"

Jake's mom said, "Those aren't dogs, Jake. Those are foxes. And yes, one is the parent, and the smaller one is the baby. We call a baby fox a kit."

"But why is a wild fox in our backyard?"

Jake's mom looked sad. "We live in a place that was once country and forests. Every year more and more people are building houses here. When people build houses, the foxes lose their homes. We have so many trees in our backyard, I guess they feel safe here."

"Are they dangerous?"

"Not really. They eat beetles, earthworms, mice, and sometimes rabbits."

"What else do they do?"

"Watch and find out," Jake's mom said.

"Can I pet them?"

"No, Jake, foxes are not pets. It's okay to observe them, but we should always remember they are wild animals."

eStreet Interactive
www.ReadingStreet.com
Pearson eText
• Student Edition
Teacher Resources
• Reader's and Writer's Notebook
• Graphic Organizer
Envision It! Animations

Bridge to Common Core

KEY IDEAS AND DETAILS

Children explore the events in the selection to understand what happens and why it happens. Studying these cause-and-effect relationships helps children understand the content of the selection. Retelling the selection helps children focus on the events. Asking questions helps them better understand these elements of the selection.

Support Listening Comprehension
Find places to stop reading in order to discuss the characters, setting, and events that have occurred. Have children retell what has happened in their own words.

Common Core State Standards

Foundational Skills 1.a. Recognize the distinguishing features of a sentence (e.g., first word, capitalization, ending punctuation). **Writing 2.** Write informative/explanatory texts in which they name a topic, supply some facts about the topic, and provide some sense of closure. **Language 1.j.** Produce and expand complete simple and compound declarative, interrogative, imperative, and exclamatory sentences in response to prompts. **Language 2.b.** Use end punctuation for sentences.

Academic Vocabulary

exclamatory sentence a group of words that shows a strong feeling; ends with an exclamation mark

brief composition writing that tells about real things

topic what the composition is all about

Daily Fix-It

1. junp onto a bus to go home.
   Jump onto a bus to go home.
2. many of them sit in sunn.
   Many of them sit in sun.

Discuss the Daily Fix-It corrections with children. Review sentence capitalization, the difference between *m* and *n,* and the spelling of *sun.*

Conventions

Exclamatory Sentences

MAKE CONNECTIONS In the story we listened to today, Jake showed strong feelings about the foxes that were in his yard. What kinds of things did Jake say? What would you say if you were Jake and saw foxes in your yard? Write children's suggestions on the board. These sentences are called *exclamatory sentences.*

TEACH Review that a declarative sentence tells something and ends with a period and that an interrogative sentence asks something and ends with a question mark. Explain that an **exclamatory sentence** shows strong feeling and ends with an exclamation mark. *That is the biggest bird I ever saw!* is an exclamatory sentence.

MODEL Display Grammar Transparency 6. Read the definition and example aloud. Point out the capital letter and exclamation mark. Then read the directions and model number 1.

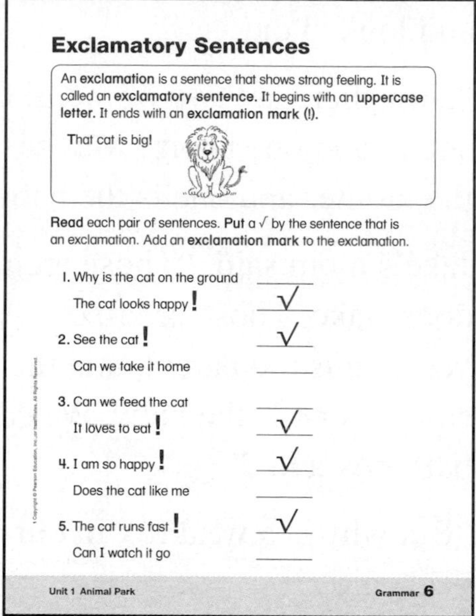

Exclamatory Sentences

An **exclamation** is a sentence that shows strong feeling. It is called an **exclamatory sentence.** It begins with an **uppercase letter.** It ends with an **exclamation mark** (!).

That cat is big!

Read each pair of sentences. **Put** a √ by the sentence that is an exclamation. Add an **exclamation mark** to the exclamation.

1. Why is the cat on the ground
   The cat looks happy! √
2. See the cat! √
   Can we take it home
3. Can we feed the cat
   It loves to eat! √
4. I am so happy! √
   Does the cat like me
5. The cat runs fast! √
   Can I watch it go

Unit 1 Animal Park — Grammar 6

Grammar Transparency 6 TR DVD

GUIDE PRACTICE Continue with items 2–5, having children identify the exclamatory sentence in each pair and write the exclamation mark.

APPLY Read each sentence below. Have children identify the sentence type and name the end punctuation mark. Then have children discuss why these end marks are used.

Did his cat nap in the sun?
Jen has a big dog.
That dog can swim fast!

Team Talk Pair children and have them talk about some amazing things they have seen animals do. Have them make up and write two exclamatory sentences about the animals. Remind them to use an exclamation mark at the end of each sentence.

Brief Composition

Mini-Lesson Writing for Tests: Read Like a Writer

■ **Introduce** This week you will write a **brief composition.** A composition tells about real things.

Genre	Brief Composition
Trait	Focus/Ideas
Mode	Expository/Informative/ Explanatory

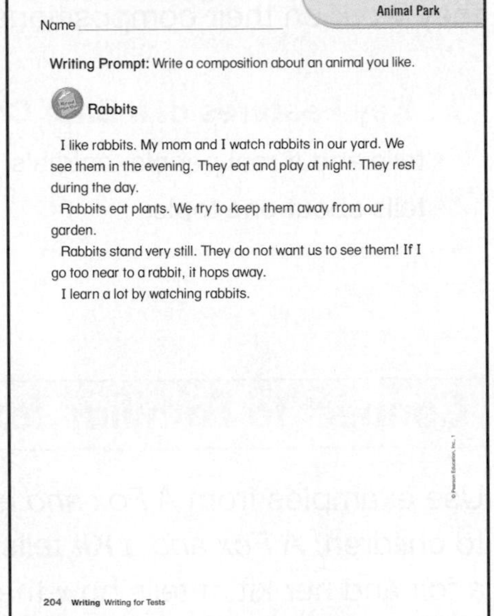

Animal Park

Name ____________

Writing Prompt: Write a composition about an animal you like.

Rabbits

I like rabbits. My mom and I watch rabbits in our yard. We see them in the evening. They eat and play at night. They rest during the day.

Rabbits eat plants. We try to keep them away from our garden.

Rabbits stand very still. They do not want us to see them! If I go too near to a rabbit, it hops away.

I learn a lot by watching rabbits.

204 Writing Writing for Tests

Reader's and Writer's Notebook, p. 204

■ **Examine Model Text** Let's listen to a brief composition. This composition is written to answer a test question. Track the print as you read aloud "Rabbits" on *Reader's and Writer's Notebook,* p. 204. Have children follow along.

■ **Key Features** What is the topic of this composition? (rabbits) Help children find and underline sentences that tell real things about rabbits, such as *They eat and play at night* and *Rabbits eat plants.* Ask children if they can find any made-up things in the composition. (no)

This composition tells real things about rabbits. It tells when rabbits eat and play. It tells what they eat. It tells that they like to be left alone.

The author of this composition tells about only one topic. The composition is only about rabbits. The author also tells only real things, not made-up things.

Writing to Sources Use More Connect the Texts on pp. 221–259 to guide children in writing text-based responses within various forms and modes.

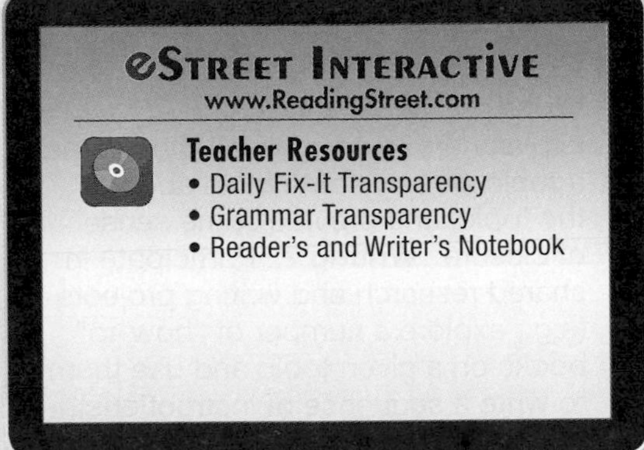

Write Guy *by Jeff Anderson*

The Sunny Side

I like to look for what's *right* in children's writing rather than looking for things I can edit or fix. Most children don't write flawlessly, but they will learn what they are doing well if we point it out.

Bridge to Common Core

TEXT TYPES AND PURPOSES

This week children write a brief composition about things people learn by watching animals.

Informative/Explanatory Writing

As children develop skills for writing a brief composition, they learn to give information about a topic by telling facts and details. When children write about what people learn from watching wild animals, they demonstrate understanding of the subject they are studying.

Throughout the week, children will improve the range and content of their writing through daily mini-lessons.

5-Day Plan

DAY 1	Read Like a Writer
DAY 2	Narrowing Your Topic
DAY 3	Writing Trait: Focus/Ideas
DAY 4	Know Your Purpose
DAY 5	Proofread

Conventions To provide children with practice with exclamatory sentences, use the modified grammar lessons in the *ELL Handbook.*

Common Core State Standards

Writing 2. Write informative/explanatory texts in which they name a topic, supply some facts about the topic, and provide some sense of closure. **Writing 7.** Participate in shared research and writing projects (e.g., explore a number of "how-to" books on a given topic and use them to write a sequence of instructions).

Writing

Zoom in on ©

Introduce Key Features

Review the key features of a brief composition with children. You may want to post these key features in the classroom to allow children to refer to them as they work on their compositions.

Key Features of a Brief Composition

- tells about real people, animals, or things
- tells about one topic

Connect to Familiar Texts

Use examples from *A Fox and a Kit* (Unit 1) or another nonfiction text familiar to children. *A Fox and a Kit* tells about real animals. It tells real things about a fox and her kit. It tells how the fox takes care of her baby. It does not tell made-up things.

Routine Quick Write for Fluency

Team Talk

1. **Talk** Read these titles aloud, and have children discuss which one sounds like the title of a composition and why.
   Penguin Babies
   The Penguin That Flew Around the World
2. **Write** Have children write a sentence explaining what kinds of things a composition might tell about.
3. **Share** Partners can read their sentences to one another.

Routines Flip Chart

Research and Inquiry

Step 1 Identify and Focus Topic

TEACH Display and review the concept map about this week's question: *What can we learn about wild animals by watching them?* What would you like to learn about an animal by watching it? Ask children to share their ideas. Point out that they can learn about an animal in the neighborhood by observing.

Think Aloud **MODEL** One way to learn about an animal is to spend time observing it. When I find an animal I want to watch, I don't look away even for a second. I stay very still and quiet. As I am watching my animal, I ask myself questions about my animal. I keep watching to find the answers to my questions. Later, I will share these answers with other people.

GUIDE PRACTICE Give children time to think about an animal to observe any questions about the animal. Record children's questions in a chart.

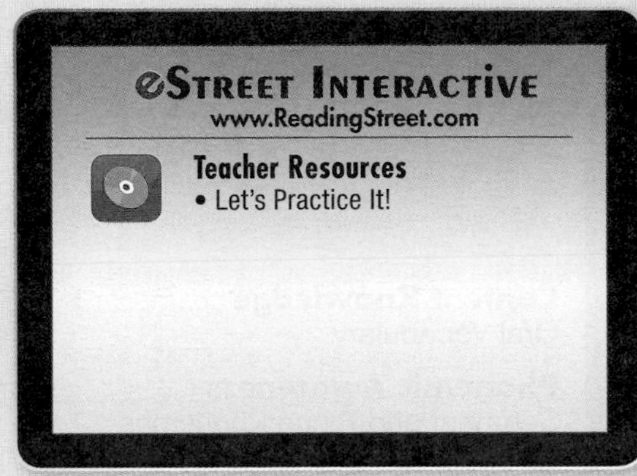

21st Century Skills

Internet Guy *Don Leu*

Weekly Inquiry Project

STEP 1	Identify and Focus Topic
STEP 2	Research Skill
STEP 3	Gather and Record Information
STEP 4	Synthesize
STEP 5	Communicate

Wrap Up Your Day!

✔ **Phonics: Short *u*: *u*** Write *cup* and *ugly.* Ask children what sound the letter *u* spells in each word. (short *u*)

✔ **Spelling: Short *u* Words with Final Consonant Blends** Have children name the letter or letters that spell each sound in *dunk* and write the word. Continue with *rust, sunk,* and *pump.*

✔ **Content Knowledge** Ask children to recall what happened in the Read Aloud "The Fox Family." What do you think Jake will learn if he observes the fox and kit in his yard? (Possible response: what they do during the day, what they eat, where they go)

✔ **Homework** Send home this week's Family Times Newsletter from Let's Practice It! pp. 65–66 on the *Teacher Resources DVD-ROM.*

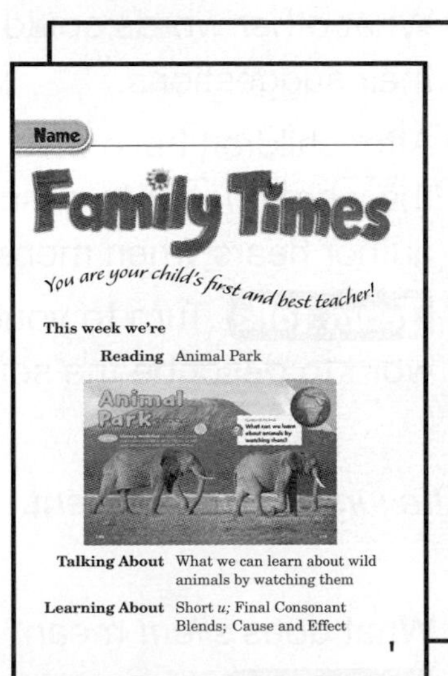

Name
Family Times
You are your child's first and best teacher!
This week we're
Reading Animal Park
Talking About What we can learn about wild animals by watching them
Learning About Short u; Final Consonant Blends; Cause and Effect
1

Let's Practice It!
TR DVD•65–66

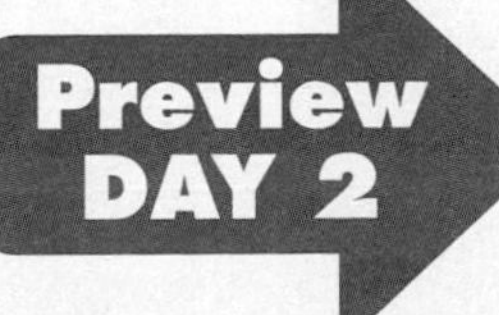

Tell children that tomorrow they will read about wild animals that live in an animal park.

DAY 2 at a Glance

Content Knowledge
Oral Vocabulary

Phonemic Awareness
Segment and Blend Phonemes

Phonics/Spelling
Short *u*: *u*
Final Consonant Blends

High-Frequency Words
home, into, many, them

Selection Vocabulary
elephants, hippos, park, zebras
Antonyms

Text-Based Comprehension
Cause and Effect
Text Structure

Conventions
Exclamatory Sentences

Writing
Brief Composition

Handwriting
Letters *Uu* and *Qq*/Letter Spacing

Research and Inquiry
Research Skill: Notes

Materials

- Student Edition
- Sing with Me Big Book
- Big Book
- Sound-Spelling Cards
- Decodable Reader 6B
- Reader's and Writer's Notebook

Common Core State Standards

Speaking/Listening 2. Ask and answer questions about key details in a text read aloud or information presented orally or through other media. **Language 5.c.** Identify real-life connections between words and their use (e.g., note places at home that are *cozy*). **Also Language 6.**

Content Knowledge

Watching Wild Animals

EXPAND THE CONCEPT To reinforce concepts and to focus children's attention, have them sing "Big, Round World" from the *Sing with Me* Big Book. Where do the chipmunks in the song live? (in the forest) What could you watch them do there? (run and race)

Build Oral Language

INTRODUCE AMAZING WORDS Display the Big Book *Jungle Drum.* Read the title and identify the author. Explain that in the story, the author uses some Amazing Words. Read the story and have children listen for the words *chatter* and *silent.*

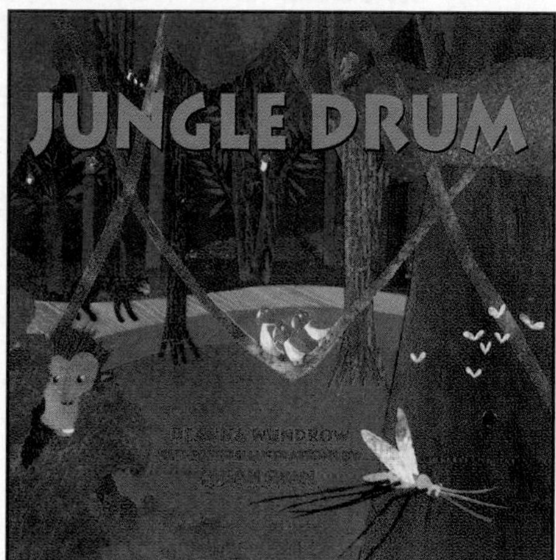

Big Book

TALK ABOUT SENTENCES AND WORDS Reread this sentence from the Big Book.

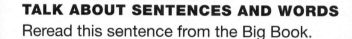

And the trees are full of monkeys chattering.

- Have children repeat the sentence with you. What does this sentence mean? (There are a lot of monkeys making noise in the trees.)
- What other words could we use in place of *chattering?* Have children share their suggestions.
- After children have tried other words, ask: Why do you think the author chose the word *chatter* to describe the sound monkeys make? (That is what the author hears when monkeys make noise.)
- **Team Talk** Turn to your partner and say the sentence again using another word to describe the sound that monkeys make.

The jungle drum is silent.

- What does *silent* mean? (quiet)
- **Team Talk** Have pairs show how monkeys would *chatter* and then how monkeys would be *silent.*

Build Oral Vocabulary

Amazing Words Robust Vocabulary Routine

1. **Introduce the Word** Relate the word *silent* to the book. When the drum plays, the animals are *silent.* Supply a child-friendly definition: *Silent* means "quiet." It means "not making a sound." Have children say the word.

2. **Demonstrate** Provide examples to show meaning. An empty house is *silent.* Your room at night is *silent.* When you turn the TV off, it is *silent.*

3. **Apply** Have children demonstrate their understanding. Name some times when you try to be *silent.*

4. **Display the Word** Run your hand under the chunks *si-lent* as you read the word.

See p. OV•6 to teach *chatter.*

Routines Flip Chart

ADD TO THE CONCEPT MAP Discuss how watching wild animals can help us learn where animals live and what sounds they make.

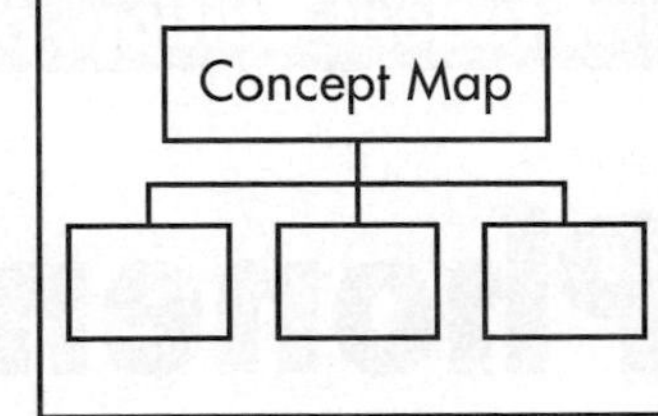

- What does the song "Big, Round World" tell us about the places animals live? (They live in the desert and in the forest.) Let's add *We learn where animals live* to our map. Then I'll write *desert* and *forest* under that.
- The Big Book *Jungle Drum* describes another place that animals live. Where do the animals in that story live? (They live in the jungle.) Let's add *jungle* to our map.
- What sounds do the parrots in the jungle make? (They screech.) What sounds do the monkeys make? (They chatter.) Let's add *We learn what sounds animals make* to our map. Then I'll write *parrots screech* and *monkeys chatter.*

Amazing Words

desert	silent
forest	snort
world	medicine
chatter	poisonous

Access for All

A Advanced

Using Amazing Words Have children fold a sheet of drawing paper in half. Ask them to draw a desert on one side and a forest on the other, including the appropriate plants and animals. Have children add the labels *desert* and *forest.* Then have them add speech balloons to show what sounds the animals make. For example, they might write *chatter* above a squirrel.

Reinforce Vocabulary Use the Day 2 instruction on ELL Poster 6 to reinforce the meaning of high-frequency words.

Physical Response Teach the words *chatter* and *silent* by acting them out and having children join you. To reinforce understanding, look for opportunities to recycle the words during the day. For example, you might note that children are *chattering* during peer writing conferences or that they should be *silent* when you are giving instructions.

Common Core State Standards
Foundational Skills 2.c. Isolate and pronounce initial, medial vowel, and final sounds (phonemes) in spoken single-syllable words. Also Foundational Skills 2.b.
Phonemic Awareness
Let's Listen for
Sounds
Find two things that rhyme with trust.
Find five things that contain the short u sound.
Find something that rhymes with dunk. Say each sound in the word.
Read Together
READING STREET ONLINE
SOUND-SPELLING CARDS
www.ReadingStreet.com
148
149
Student Edition, pp. 148–149

Common Core State Standards

Foundational Skills 2.b. Orally produce single-syllable words by blending sounds (phonemes), including consonant blends. **Foundational Skills 2.c.** Isolate and pronounce initial, medial vowel, and final sounds (phonemes) in spoken single-syllable words. **Foundational Skills 3.** Know and apply grade-level phonics and word analysis skills in decoding words.

Skills Trace

Final Consonant Blends

Introduce U1W6D2

Practice U1W6D3; U1W6D4

Reteach/Review U1W6D5; U2W1D4

Assess/Test Weekly Test U1W6
Benchmark Test U1

KEY: U=Unit W=Week D=Day

Phonemic Awareness

Segment and Blend Phonemes

MODEL Look at the picture. I see a boy who has a bug crawling on his *wrist.* I hear two consonant sounds at the end of *wrist,* /s/ and /t/. I also see a *tent.* I hear the two consonant sounds /n/ and /t/ at the end of *tent.* Listen to the sounds in the word *wrist:* /r/ /i/ /s/ /t/. There are four sounds in *wrist.* Let's blend those sounds to make a word: /r/ /i/ /s/ /t/, *wrist.* Continue with *tent.*

GROUP PRACTICE Guide children as they segment and blend these words from the picture: *crust, bump, camp, last, dump, rust.*

Corrective feedback	**If...** children make an error, **then...** model by segmenting the word, and have them repeat.

ON THEIR OWN Have children segment and blend the following words.

/f/ /a/ /s/ /t/	**fast**	/b/ /e/ /l/ /t/	**belt**	/m/ /i/ /s/ /t/	**mist**

Phonics

Final Consonant Blends

CONNECT Write the word *ten.* You studied words like this already. What is the consonant sound at the end of *ten?* (/n/) Today you will learn about words that have two consonant sounds at the end.

Sound-Spelling Card 38

USE SOUND-SPELLING CARD Display Card 38. Point to the word *lamp.* The letters *mp* at the end of *lamp* stand for the sounds /m/ /p/. Have children say /m/ /p/ several times as you point to *mp.* Explain that the letters *mp* make a consonant blend whose sounds blend together at the end of a word.

MODEL Write *tent.* In this word, the letters *nt* stand for the sounds /n/ /t/. Segment and blend *tent;* then have children blend with you: /t/ /e/ /n/ /t/. Follow this procedure to model *fast.*

GROUP PRACTICE Continue the process. This time have children blend with you. Remind children to blend the sounds of the last two consonants together.

rust	**pant**	**romp**	**gift**	**bend**
milk	**belt**	**camp**	**pond**	**desk**

REVIEW What do you know about reading these words? (The sounds of the two consonant letters at the end of each word are blended together.)

Access for All

A Advanced

Extend Blending Provide children who can segment and blend all the words correctly with more challenging words such as *friend, shrimp, myself, August, frost,* and *spent.*

Vocabulary Support

You may wish to explain the meanings of these words.

rust a reddish-brown coating on metal that is caused by air and water

romp to play in a way that is lively

Visual Support Model isolating sounds while using the pictures on pp. 148–149 of the Student Edition as visual support. For example: /b/ /u/ /m/ /p/, *bump.* Who can point to a bump on the tree trunk? Now let's say the sounds of *bump* together: /b/ /u/ /m/ /p/.

Common Core State Standards

Foundational Skills 3. Know and apply grade-level phonics and word analysis skills in decoding words. **Foundational Skills 3.b.** Decode regularly spelled one-syllable words.

Academic Vocabulary

consonant blend two or more letters whose sounds are blended together when pronouncing a word

Spelling Pattern

Final Consonant Blends Each sound in a consonant blend is represented by a letter.

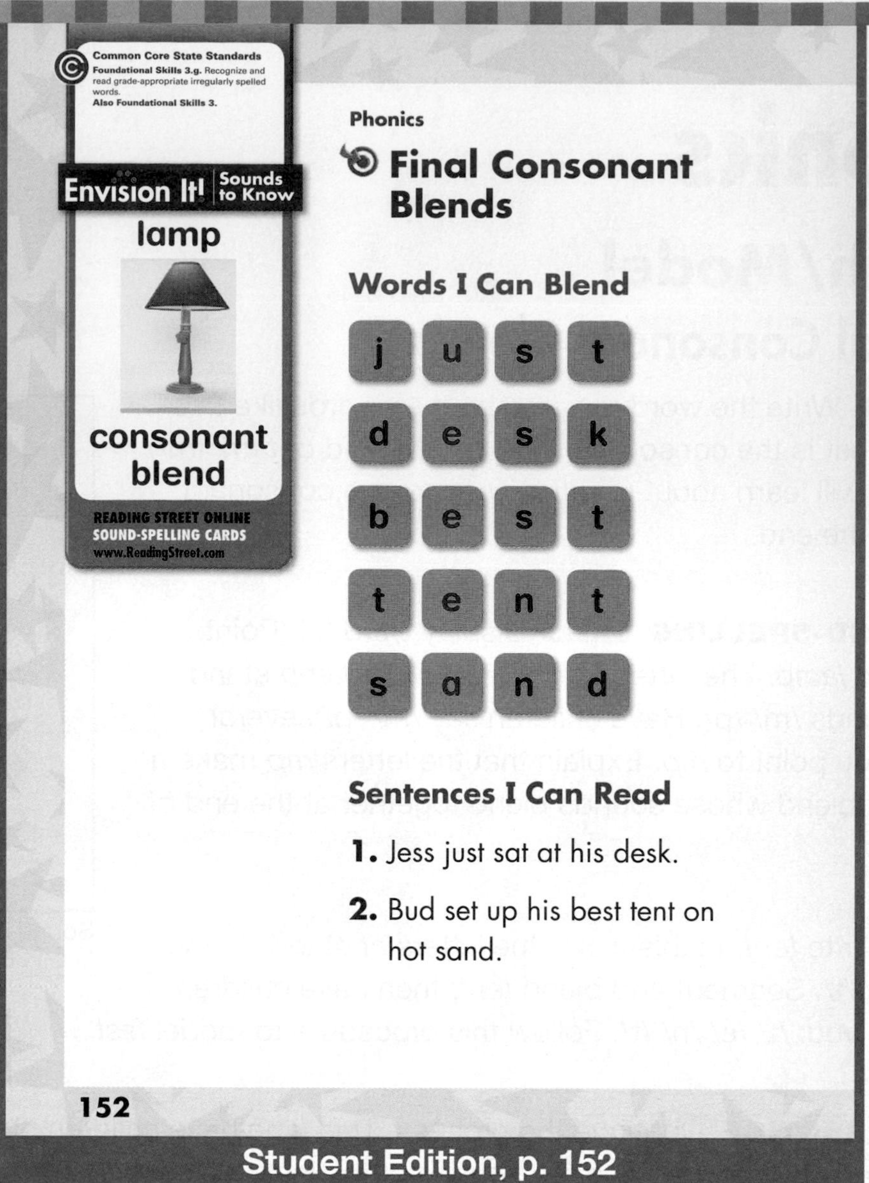

Common Core State Standards
Foundational Skills 3.g. Recognize and read grade-appropriate irregularly spelled words.
Also Foundational Skills 3.
Envision It! Sounds to Know
lamp
consonant blend
READING STREET ONLINE
SOUND-SPELLING CARDS
www.ReadingStreet.com
Phonics
Final Consonant Blends
Words I Can Blend
j u s t
d e s k
b e s t
t e n t
s a n d
Sentences I Can Read
1. Jess just sat at his desk.
2. Bud set up his best tent on hot sand.
152

Student Edition, p. 152

Phonics

Guide Practice

BLEND WORDS Have children turn to page 152 in their Student Edition. Look at the picture on this page. I see a picture of a *lamp.* The word *lamp* ends with two consonants, *m* and *p.* When I say *lamp,* I blend the two consonant sounds together, /m/ /p/.

GROUP PRACTICE For each word in "Words I Can Blend," ask for the sound of each letter or group of letters. Make sure that children identify the correct sounds for each final consonant blend.

Corrective feedback	**If...** children have difficulty blending a word, **then...** model blending the word, and ask children to blend it with you.

DECODE WORDS IN ISOLATION After children can successfully segment and blend the words, ask them to read the words naturally.

DECODE WORDS IN CONTEXT Have children read each of the sentences. Have them identify words with final consonant blends in the sentences.

Team Talk Pair children and have them take turns reading each of the sentences aloud.

ON THEIR OWN Use *Reader's and Writer's Notebook,* p. 205.

MONITOR PROGRESS — Final Consonant Blends

FORMATIVE ASSESSMENT Write the following words and have the class read them. Notice which children miss words during the group reading. Call on those individuals to read some of the words.

					Spiral Review
bend	help	stump	pond	last	
truck	raft	sick	black	held ←	Row 2 contrasts final consonant blends and final *-ck.*
drift	plan	clasp	must	stamp ←	Row 3 reviews initial and final consonant blends.

If... children cannot blend words with final consonant blends,

then... use the Small Group Time Strategic Intervention lesson, p. SG•93, to reteach final consonant blends. Continue to monitor children's progress using other instructional opportunities during the week. See the Skills Trace on p. 152c.

Access for All

A Advanced

Listing Words with Blends Give children one or two common final consonant blends, such as *-st.* Have partners list as many words as they can that end with that blend. For example, children might list *fast, last, nest, chest, first, worst, feast, beast, mist, twist, lost, frost, most, toast, just,* and *trust.*

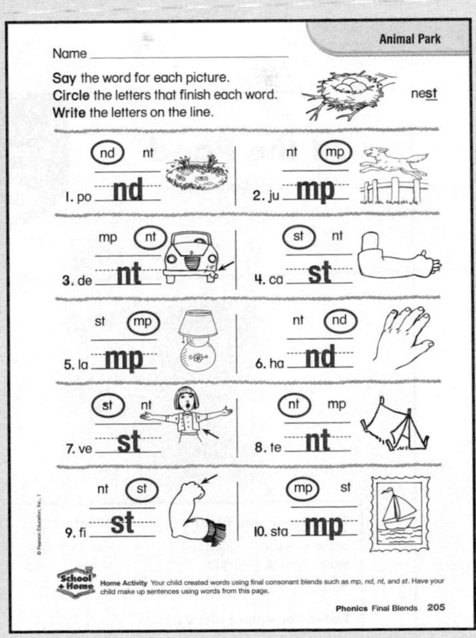
Animal Park

Name ______

Say the word for each picture.
Circle the letters that finish each word.
Write the letters on the line.

nest

nd nt — 1. po nd	nt mp — 2. ju mp
mp nt — 3. de nt	st nt — 4. ca st
st mp — 5. la mp	nt nd — 6. ha nd
st nt — 7. ve st	nt mp — 8. te nt
nt st — 9. fi st	mp st — 10. sta mp

School + Home — **Home Activity** Your child created words using final consonant blends such as *mp, nd, nt,* and *st.* Have your child make up sentences using words from this page.

Phonics Final Blends 205

Reader's and Writer's Notebook, p. 205

Common Core State Standards

Foundational Skills 3. Know and apply grade-level phonics and word analysis skills in decoding words. **Foundational Skills 3.b.** Decode regularly spelled one-syllable words. **Foundational Skills 4.** Read with sufficient accuracy and fluency to support comprehension.

Decodable Reader 6B

If children need help, then...

Read *At the Pond*

DECODE WORDS IN ISOLATION Have children turn to page 225. Have children decode each word.

REVIEW HIGH-FREQUENCY WORDS Review the previously taught words *the, a, see, small,* and *that.* Have children read each word as you point to it on the Word Wall.

PREVIEW Have children read the title and preview the story. Tell them they will read words with final consonant blends.

DECODE WORDS IN CONTEXT Pair children for reading and listen as they decode. One child begins. Children read the entire story, switching readers after each page.

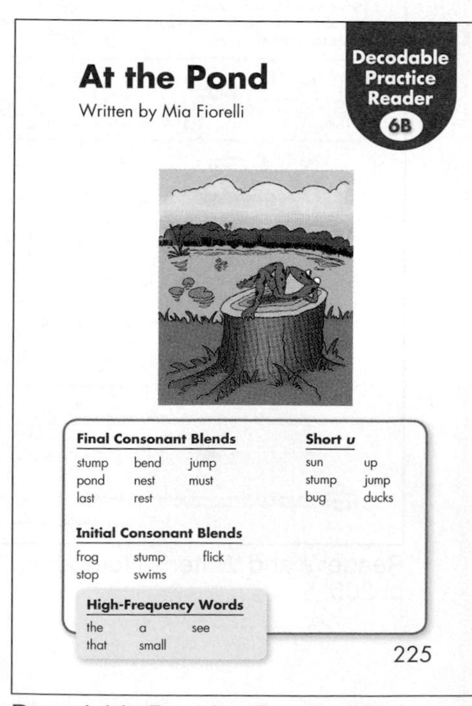
Decodable Practice Reader 6B

At the Pond

Written by Mia Fiorelli

Final Consonant Blends

stump bend jump
pond nest must
last rest

Short *u*

sun up
stump jump
bug ducks

Initial Consonant Blends

frog stump flick
stop swims

High-Frequency Words

the a see
that small

225

Decodable Practice Reader 6B

The sun is up.
Frog sits on a stump.

226

Frog can bend his legs.
Frog can jump in the pond.

227

Frog can see a bug.
Flick!
Stop that bug!

228

Frog can see a nest.
It has small ducks in it.

229

A big duck swims at him.

230

Frog must jump.
Frog gets back on the stump.

231

At last, Frog can rest!
Frog is on his stump.

232

Corrective feedback	**If...** children have difficulty decoding a word, **then...** refer them to the Sound-Spelling Cards to identify the sounds in the word. Then prompt them to blend the word. • What is the new word? • Is the new word a word you know? • Does it make sense in the story?

CHECK DECODING AND COMPREHENSION Have children retell the story to include characters, setting, and events. Then have children locate words that end with consonant blends in the story. List words that children name. Children should supply *stump, bend, jump, pond, nest, must, last,* and *rest.*

Reread for Fluency

REREAD DECODABLE READER Have children reread Decodable Practice Reader 6B to develop automaticity decoding words with final consonant blends.

Routine Paired Reading

1. **Reread** To achieve optimal fluency, have partners reread the text three or four times.
2. **Corrective Feedback** Listen as children read. Provide corrective feedback regarding their fluency and decoding.

Routines Flip Chart

Access for All

SI Strategic Intervention

Retelling If children have difficulty retelling the story, ask them questions regarding events in the story.

ELL

Final Consonant Blends

Beginning Before children read, lead them on a picture walk through the story. Point out and pronounce the words that end with consonant blends. Then write a pictured word and have children pronounce it and find its picture.

Intermediate Write words from the story with final consonant blends on the board, such as *bend, jump, nest,* and *pond.* Say them aloud and then ask children to repeat them after you.

Advanced Have children find words that end with consonant blends in the story and use them in sentences.

Common Core State Standards

Foundational Skills 3. Know and apply grade-level phonics and word analysis skills in decoding words. **Foundational Skills 3.b.** Decode regularly spelled one-syllable words. **Language 2.d.** Use conventional spelling for words with common spelling patterns and for frequently occurring irregular words. **Language 2.e.** Spell untaught words phonetically, drawing on phonemic awareness and spelling conventions.

Phonics

Review Short Vowels

REVIEW SOUND-SPELLINGS Review the short vowel spelling patterns *a, e, i, o,* and *u,* using Sound-Spelling Cards 1, 6, 11, 17, and 24.

DECODE WORDS IN ISOLATION Display these words. Have the class blend the words. Then point to the words in random order and ask children to read them quickly.

wet	**tag**	**dot**	**spin**
twig	**job**	**flap**	**pup**
drum	**truck**	**men**	**quick**

Corrective feedback Model blending decodable words and then ask children to blend them with you.

DECODE WORDS IN CONTEXT Display these sentences. Have the class read the sentences.

Team Talk Have pairs take turns reading the sentences naturally.

I saw a little **red bug** go **in** your **sock.**

My **black and** yellow **hat has** a **rip in it.**

It is too **hot** to **run, but** we **can still** have **fun.**

Spelling

Short *u* Words with Final Consonant Blends

GUIDE PRACTICE Tell children that you will segment the sounds in each spelling word. They should repeat the sounds in each word as they write the word. Check the spelling of each word before saying the next word.

1.	/k/ /r/ /u/ /s/ /t/	**crust**	**6.**	/d/ /u/ /s/ /t/	**dust**
2.	/b/ /u/ /m/ /p/	**bump**	**7.**	/t/ /r/ /u/ /s/ /t/	**trust**
3.	/j/ /u/ /m/ /p/	**jump**	**8.**	/d/ /u/ /s/ /k/	**dusk**
4.	/m/ /u/ /s/ /t/	**must**	**9.**	/h/ /u/ /n/ /t/	**hunt**
5.	/j/ /u/ /s/ /t/	**just**	**10.**	/l/ /u/ /m/ /p/	**lump**

ON THEIR OWN Use *Reader's and Writer's Notebook,* p. 206.

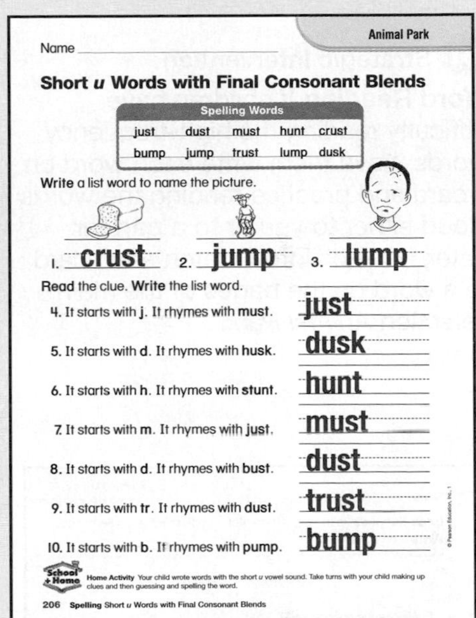

Name ______ Animal Park

Short *u* Words with Final Consonant Blends

Spelling Words				
just	dust	must	hunt	crust
bump	jump	trust	lump	dusk

Write a list word to name the picture.

1. crust 2. jump 3. lump

Read the clue. **Write** the list word.

4. It starts with **j**. It rhymes with **must**. just
5. It starts with **d**. It rhymes with **husk**. dusk
6. It starts with **h**. It rhymes with **stunt**. hunt
7. It starts with **m**. It rhymes with **just**. must
8. It starts with **d**. It rhymes with **bust**. dust
9. It starts with **tr**. It rhymes with **dust**. trust
10. It starts with **b**. It rhymes with **pump**. bump

School + Home **Home Activity** Your child wrote words with the short u vowel sound. Take turns with your child making up clues and then guessing and spelling the word.

206 Spelling Short u Words with Final Consonant Blends

Reader's and Writer's Notebook, p. 206

Pronunciation Remind children that when they pronounce short *u*, their mouths are open, and their tongues are down. Have children practice saying the sound in isolation. Then have them practice with the spelling words, if needed.

Common Core State Standards

Foundational Skills 3.g. Recognize and read grade-appropriate irregularly spelled words. **Foundational Skills 4.** Read with sufficient accuracy and fluency to support comprehension. **Language 5.** With guidance and support from adults, demonstrate understanding of word relationships and nuances in word meanings.

Access for All

SI Strategic Intervention

Word Reading If children have difficulty reading the high-frequency words, have them write each word on a card and practice reading the words aloud either to you or to a partner. Later, have children match each card to a word on the pages of the main selection *Animal Park.*

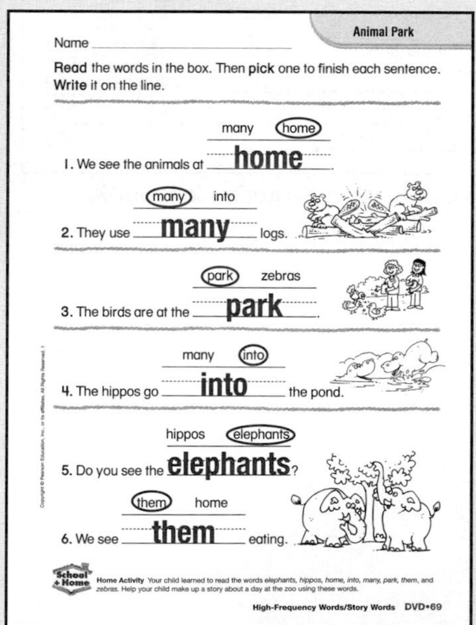

Animal Park

Name

Read the words in the box. Then **pick** one to finish each sentence. **Write** it on the line.

many (home)
1. We see the animals at **home**.

(many) into
2. They use **many** logs.

(park) zebras
3. The birds are at the **park**.

many (into)
4. The hippos go **into** the pond.

hippos (elephants)
5. Do you see the **elephants**?

(them) home
6. We see **them** eating.

School + Home **Home Activity** Your child learned to read the words *elephants, hippos, home, into, many, park, them,* and *zebras.* Help your child make up a story about a day at the zoo using these words.

High-Frequency Words/Story Words DVD•69

Let's Practice It! TR DVD•69

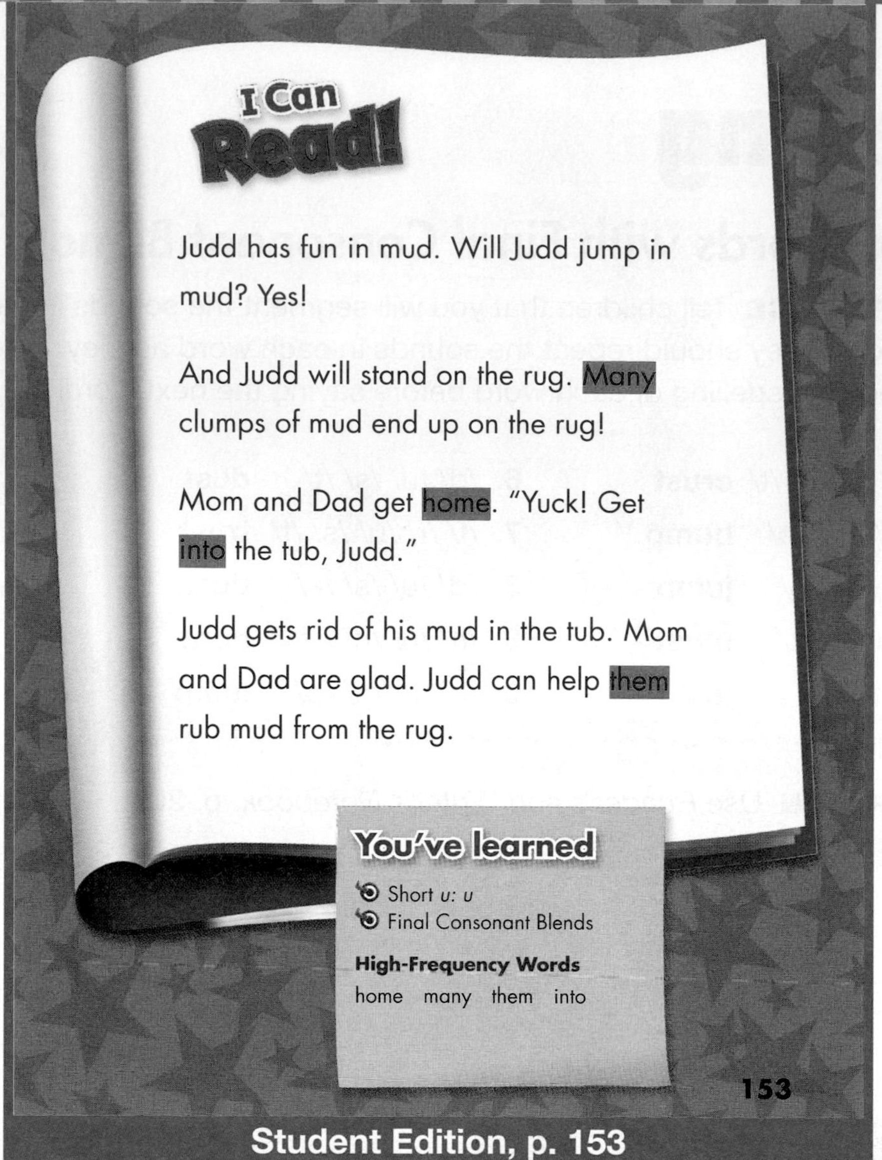

I Can Read!

Judd has fun in mud. Will Judd jump in mud? Yes!

And Judd will stand on the rug. Many clumps of mud end up on the rug!

Mom and Dad get home. "Yuck! Get into the tub, Judd."

Judd gets rid of his mud in the tub. Mom and Dad are glad. Judd can help them rub mud from the rug.

You've learned

Short *u: u*
Final Consonant Blends

High-Frequency Words
home many them into

153

Student Edition, p. 153

High-Frequency Words

READ WORDS IN ISOLATION Remind children that there are some words we learn by remembering the letters rather than by saying the sounds. Have them read each of the highlighted high-frequency words aloud.

READ WORDS IN CONTEXT Chorally read the "I Can Read!" passage along with children. Then have them read the passage aloud to themselves. When they are finished, ask children to reread the high-frequency words.

Team Talk Have children choose two high-frequency words and give them time to create a sentence in which both words are used properly. Then have them share their sentence with a partner.

ON THEIR OWN Use Let's Practice It! p. 69 on the *Teacher Resources DVD-ROM.*

Selection Vocabulary

INTRODUCE SELECTION WORDS Use Vocabulary Transparency 6 to introduce this week's selection words. Read each sentence as you track the print. Frame each underlined word and explain its meaning. Have children read each sentence with you.

Selection Words

At the Park

1. We like to go to the park.
2. The elephants are big.
3. The zebras are fast.
4. Three hippos sit in the mud.

Unit 1 Animal Park Vocabulary 6

Vocabulary Transparency 6 TR DVD

park	land set aside for people to enjoy nature
elephants	huge, strong land animals with gray skin and long trunks
zebras	black-and-white striped animals that look like horses
hippos	a short word for hippopotamuses, which are large animals with short legs, thick skin, and wide mouths

Vocabulary: Antonyms

TEACH Explain that **antonyms** are words that have opposite meanings. Draw a T-chart or display Graphic Organizer 4. List these words in the left column: *stop, win, top, sad, pull.* Explain that each word in the left column has an antonym.

stop	go
win	lose
top	bottom
sad	happy
pull	push

Graphic Organizer 4

I see the word *stop.* The opposite of *stop* is *go.* So *stop* and *go* are antonyms. I'll write *go* in the right column, so I can see the antonyms together.

GUIDE PRACTICE Have a volunteer give the antonym for *win* and write it in the right column. *(lose)* Repeat the procedure for the remaining words.

ON THEIR OWN Have children think of and write pairs of antonyms on cards, writing one word on each card. Then have partners switch card sets and see if they can match the words that are antonyms.

eStreet Interactive
www.ReadingStreet.com

Pearson eText
- Student Edition

Journal: Word Bank

Vocabulary Activities

Teacher Resources
- Let's Practice It!
- Vocabulary Transparency
- Graphic Organizer

Bridge to Common Core

VOCABULARY ACQUISITION AND USE
When children interact with this week's selection vocabulary words, they are learning to recognize the concepts related to the vocabulary words *elephants, hippos, park,* and *zebras.* Teaching about antonyms, or opposites, helps children understand word relationships.

Academic Vocabulary

antonym a word that means the opposite of another word

ELL

Multilingual Vocabulary Lists
Children can apply knowledge of their home language to acquire new English vocabulary by using the *Multilingual Vocabulary List* (*ELL Handbook,* pp. 465–476).

Zoom in on 

Text-Based Comprehension

Introduce Main Selection

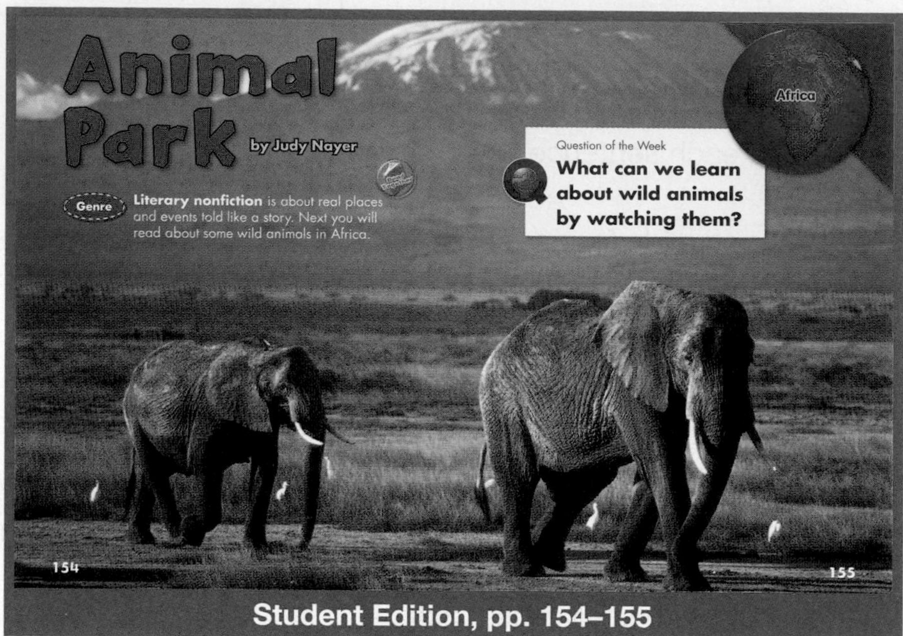

Student Edition, pp. 154–155

GENRE **Literary nonfiction** tells about real-life people, animals, or events. The setting is real. As they read *Animal Park,* children should identify text features that indicate this is a true story about real people, animals, events, and places.

PREVIEW AND PREDICT Have children read the title of the story and the names of the author and illustrator. Have children look through the selection and predict what visitors see in the animal park.

PURPOSE Good readers read for a purpose. Setting a purpose helps us to think and understand more as we read. Guide children to set a purpose for reading the selection.

TEXT STRUCTURE Explain that one way good readers understand what they are reading is to think about how a story is organized. They look at titles, labels, diagrams, maps, pictures, and the order that the author tells readers information. Have children turn to page EI•16 in their Student Edition.

What is happening in the first set of pictures? (A tadpole changes into a frog.) What happens in the second set of pictures? (The seed changes into a plant.) As I read *Animal Park,* I will pay attention to how the selection is organized.

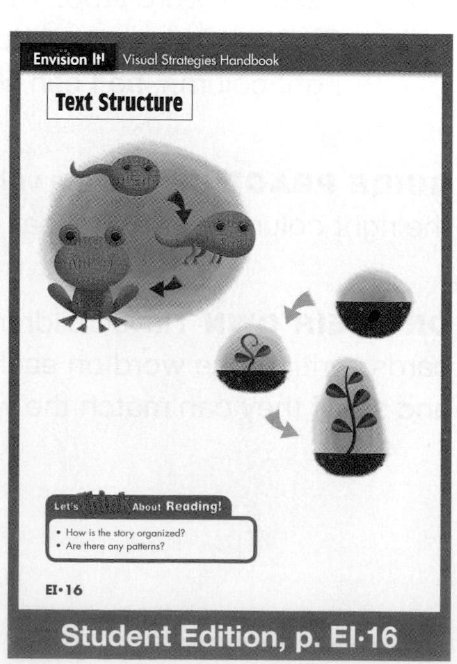

Student Edition, p. EI•16

Common Core State Standards

Informational Text 5. Know and use various text features (e.g., headings, tables of contents, glossaries, electronic menus, icons) to locate key facts or information in a text. **Informational Text 10.** With prompting and support, read informational texts appropriately complex for grade 1.

Bridge to Common Core

CRAFT AND STRUCTURE

On this page, children are introduced to the literary nonfiction genre. They learn that a literary nonfiction selection tells about real-life people, animals, or things. Using a walk-through of the text, children can preview and predict what the selection will be about and set a purpose for reading, which helps them analyze the structure of the text. As they read, children can use these structures to help them understand the content and style of the selection.

Academic Vocabulary

author a person who writes books, stories, poems, or plays

cause why something happens

effect what happens

nonfiction writing that tells facts about something real

Strategy Response Log

Genre Have children use p. RR18 in their *Reader's and Writer's Notebook* to identify the characteristics of literary nonfiction.

Access Main Selection

READER AND TASK SUGGESTIONS	
Preparing to Read the Text	**Leveled Tasks**
• Review antonyms. • Discuss with children how to tell if a selection is fiction or nonfiction. • Remind children that slowing their reading rate can help them read nonfiction text more fluently.	• **Language Conventionality and Clarity** Encourage children who have trouble understanding the verbs in the selection to use the illustrations to tell what the animals do. • **Levels of Meaning • Evaluation** If children have trouble with the story-like features of this nonfiction selection, have them explain what makes the text nonfiction.

See Text Complexity Measures for *Animal Park* on the tab at the beginning of this week.

READ Tell children that today they will read *Animal Park* for the first time. Use the Read for Understanding routine.

Routine Read for Understanding ©

Deepen understanding by reading the selection multiple times.

1. **First Read**—If children need support, then use the **Access Text** notes to help them clarify understanding.
2. **Second Read**—Use the **Close Reading** notes to help children draw knowledge from the text.

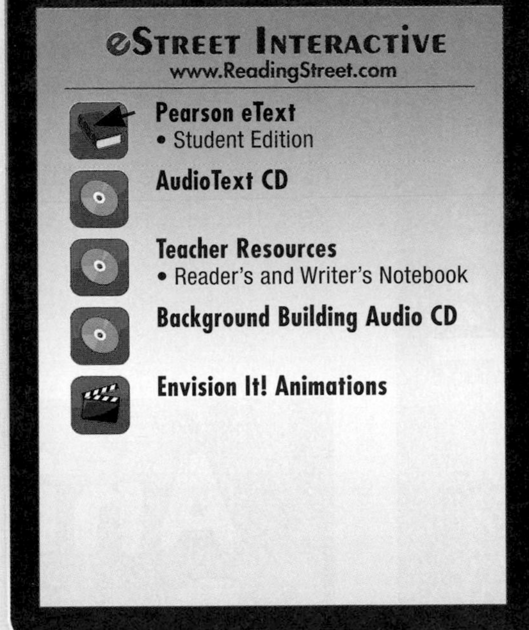

Preview Main Selection Ask children to describe the setting they see on pages 154–155. Then do a picture walk of the selection so children can talk about and see the animals in one African animal preserve.

1ST READ

Access Text © If children need help, then...

CONNECT TO CONCEPT Look at the pictures on pages 154 and 155. Look at the elephants. Describe what they look like. Encourage children to answer the question in complete sentences. Yes, the elephants are big and have trunks.

Ask children to tell how they learned something about the elephants by looking at them.

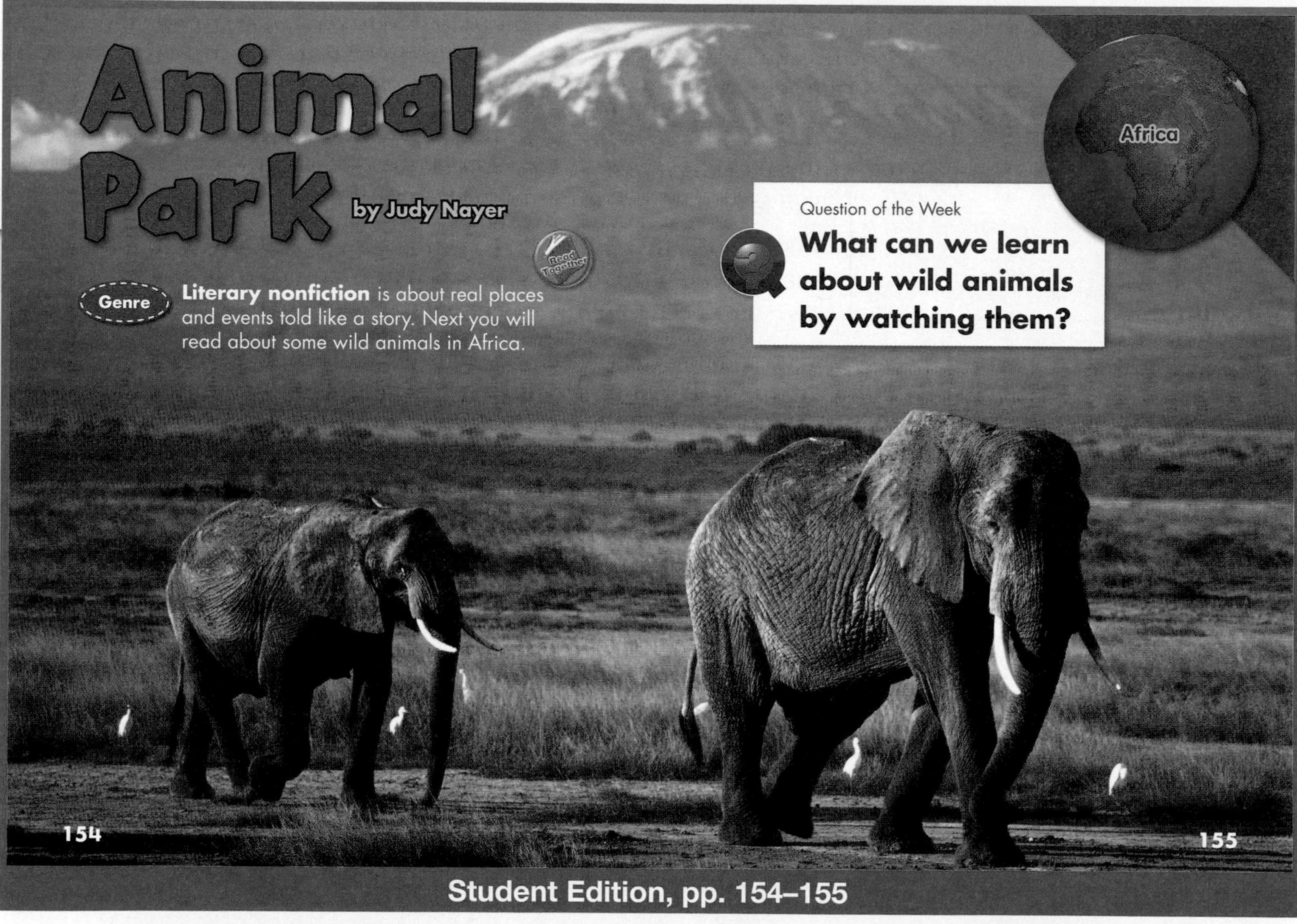

Animal Park
by Judy Nayer
Read Together
Genre
Literary nonfiction is about real places and events told like a story. Next you will read about some wild animals in Africa.
Africa
Question of the Week
What can we learn about wild animals by watching them?
154
155

Student Edition, pp. 154–155

2ND READ

Close Reading ©

SYNTHESIS • TEXT EVIDENCE Look at the elephants and their surroundings. What can you tell about the elephants' habitat? (I see grass and mountains. I think they live in an open area where there are few trees.)

USE TEXT FEATURES Remind children that good readers look at titles, labels, maps, and pictures to help them understand what they are reading. Have children tell what they know so far about the story: What will it be about? Where does it take place? Which animals live in the park? Ask children to explain which text features provide this information.

Common Core State Standards

Informational Text 1. Ask and answer questions about key details in a text. **Informational Text 7.** Use the illustrations and details in a text to describe its key ideas.

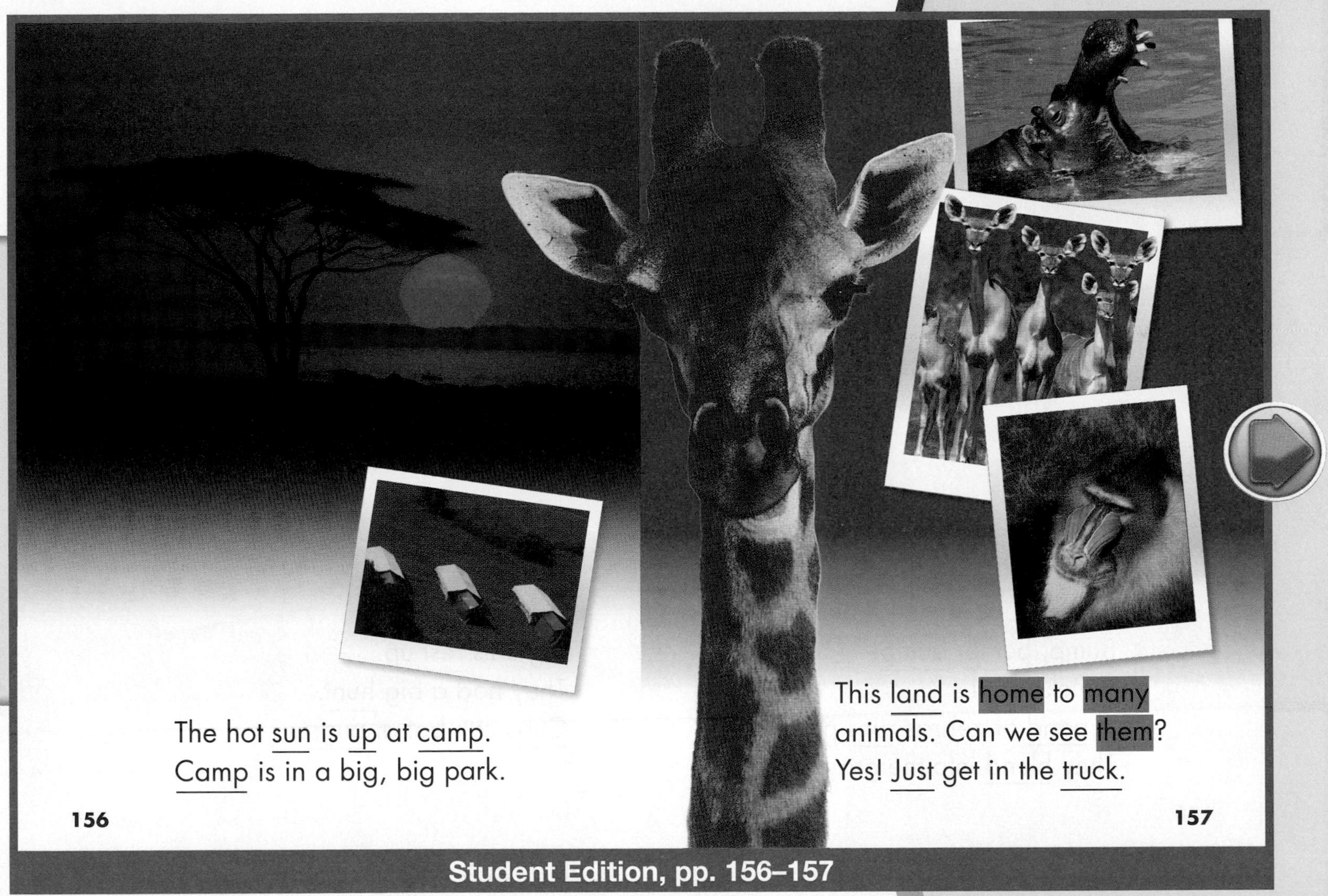

The hot sun is up at camp.
Camp is in a big, big park.
156
This land is home to many animals. Can we see them? Yes! Just get in the truck.
157

Student Edition, pp. 156–157

ANALYSIS What kind of camp is the author writing about on page 156? What clues tell you this? (I can tell from the small photograph that this isn't a summer camp. It's the kind of camp people stay in when they visit the park.)

SYNTHESIS The author says that this is a "big, big park." Why do you think the park is so big? (The park must have room for many animals, some of which are very big and need lots of space.)

1ST READ

Access Text If children need help, then...

TEXT STRUCTURE Remind children to pay attention to the order an author tells events. Describe what has happened so far, in order. (The visitors are staying in a camp. They get into a truck. They see a band of zebras. Then they see big cats and cubs.)

CAUSE AND EFFECT • REREAD CHALLENGING TEXT The big cats are resting on part of a tree. What caused them to be so tired? (They are tired from hunting.) Read the sentence that tells you that. *(They had a big hunt.)*

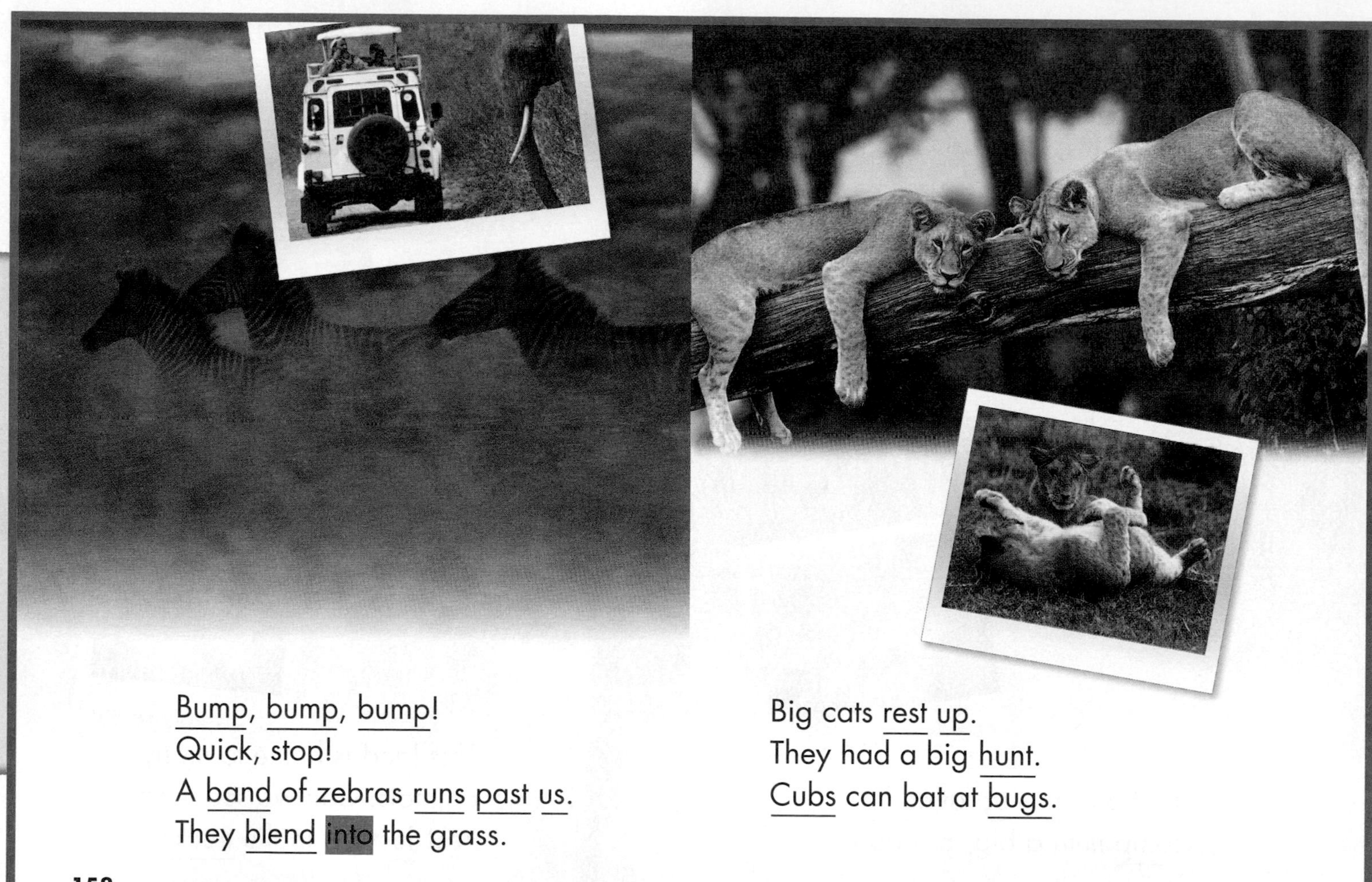

Bump, bump, bump!
Quick, stop!
A band of zebras runs past us.
They blend into the grass.
158
Big cats rest up.
They had a big hunt.
Cubs can bat at bugs.
159

Student Edition, pp. 158–159

2ND READ

Close Reading

ANALYSIS • TEXT EVIDENCE Look at the photograph on page 158. Why do you think the truck goes "bump, bump, bump"? (The road is dirt, so it is probably bumpy, not smooth.)

Time for Science **CONNECT TO SCIENCE** Many animals have developed features that help protect them. The vertical stripes of a zebra, for example, help it hide in the tall grass of the African savanna.

Team Talk Have partners discuss other animals whose coloring helps them hide.

USE ANTONYMS The words *stand* and *sit* are antonyms. What word on page 160 is the antonym of *slow? (fast)* What word on page 161 is the antonym of *dry? (wet)* What word on page 161 is the antonym of *cold? (hot)*

CAUSE AND EFFECT The hot sun has caused the air in the animal park to be very warm. What effect does this have on the hippos? (They sit in mud to try to cool off.)

Common Core State Standards

Informational Text 1. Ask and answer questions about key details in a text. **Informational Text 6.** Distinguish between information provided by pictures or other illustrations and information provided by the words in a text. **Also Informational Text 3., 7.**

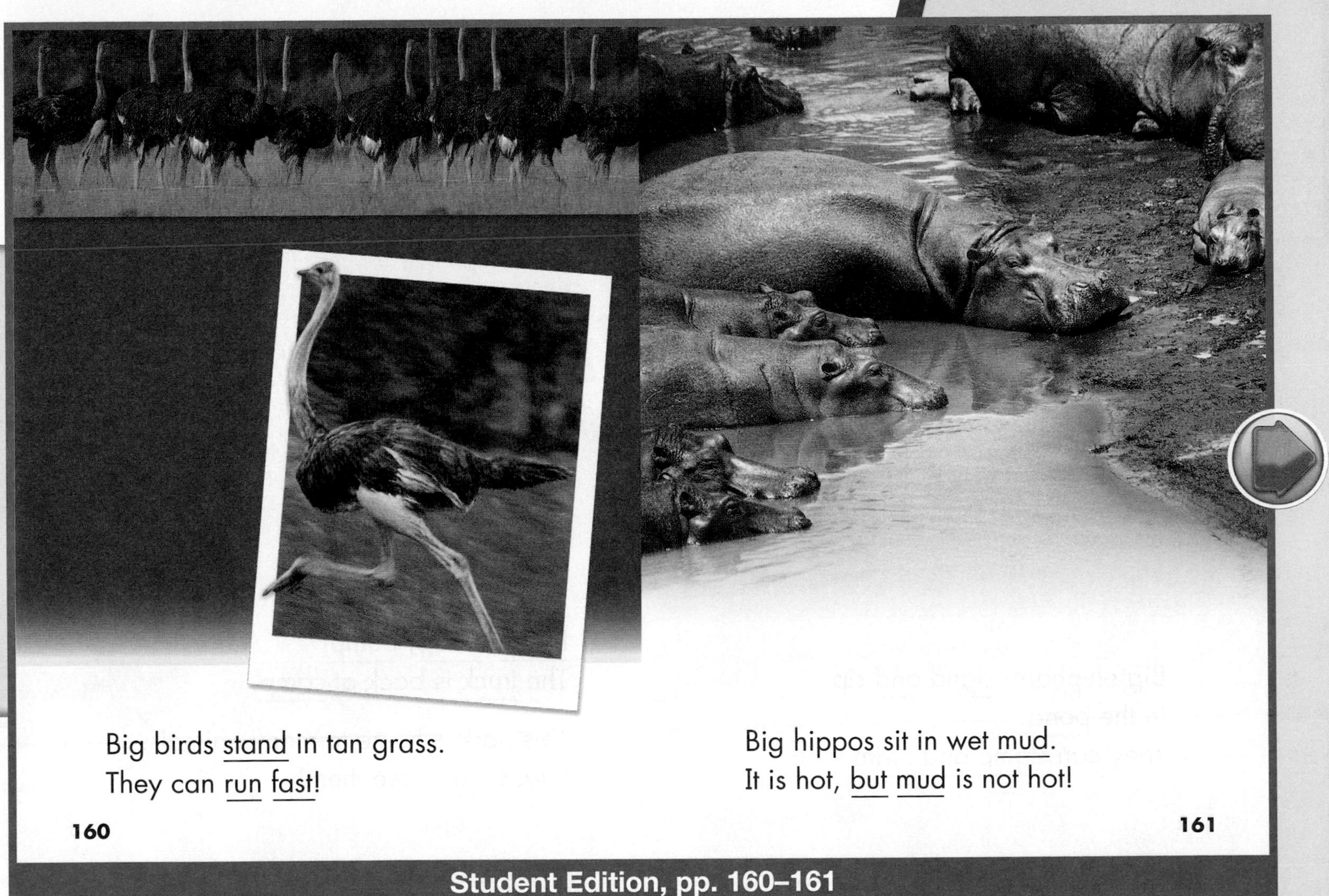

Big birds stand in tan grass.
They can run fast!
160
Big hippos sit in wet mud.
It is hot, but mud is not hot!
161

Student Edition, pp. 160–161

EVALUATION The animals in the park do different things. Compare what the big birds are doing with what the hippos are doing. (The big birds are active. They're running fast. The hippos are not active. They're resting.) Read the words and point to the pictures that show that.

1ST READ

Access Text © If children need help, then...

DEVELOP LANGUAGE Have children find the word *many* on page 163 and reread the sentence. What words could I use in place of *many*? Reread the sentence. Does the sentence still make sense?

CROSS-TEXT EVALUATION
Use a Strategy to Self-Check How did the selection *A Fox and a Kit* help you understand this selection?

Continue to DAY 2
Text-Based Comprehension
p. 163a

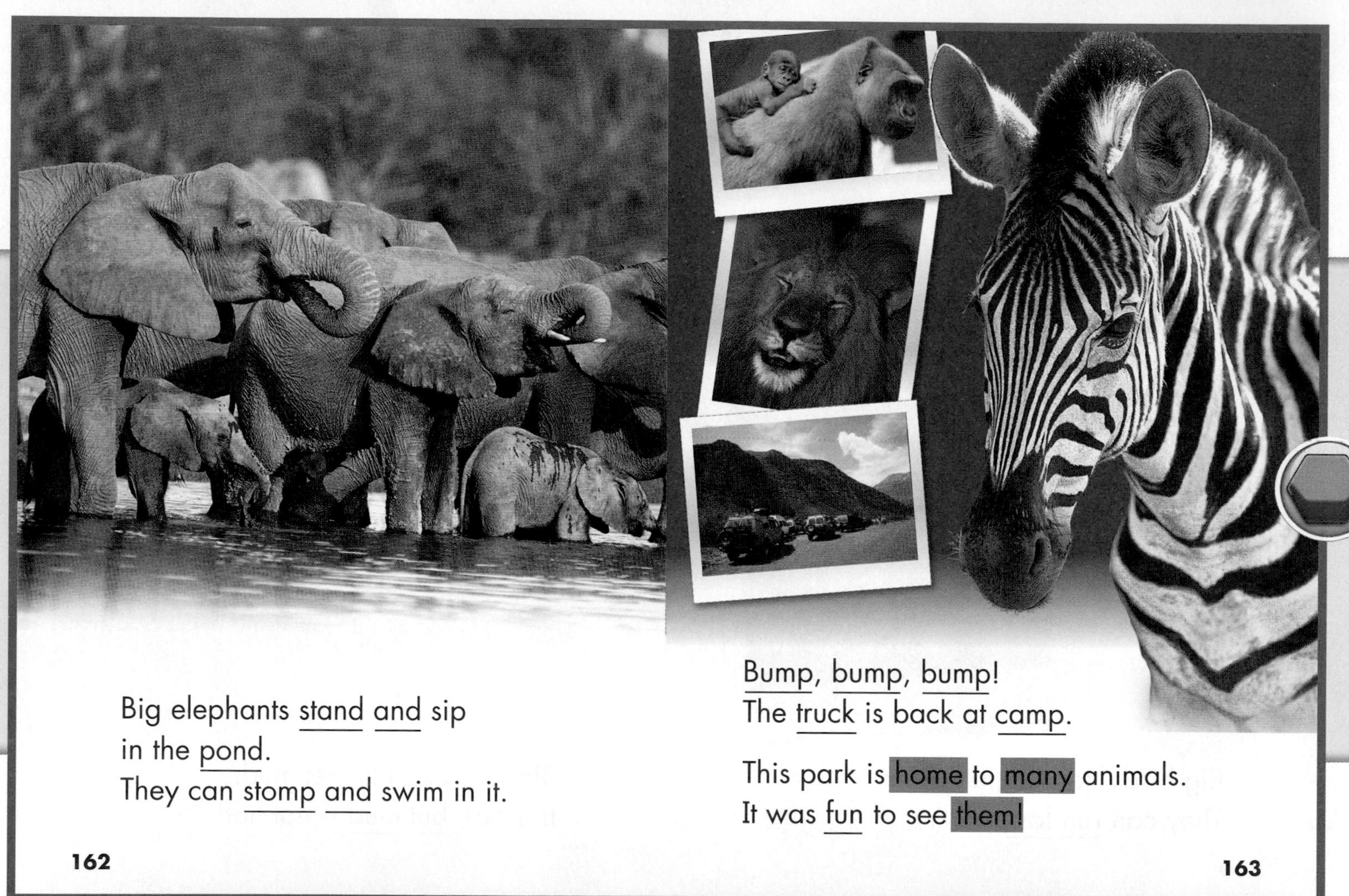

Big elephants stand and sip
in the pond.
They can stomp and swim in it.
162
Bump, bump, bump!
The truck is back at camp.
This park is home to many animals.
It was fun to see them!
163

Student Edition, pp. 162–163

2ND READ

Close Reading ©

ANALYSIS On page 162, the author says that the elephants sip, stand in, stomp in, and swim in the pond. Why do you think they are doing this? (Because it is very hot out, the elephants are thirsty and they want to cool off in the water.) What clues tell you this? (Children should tell how on page 161 it says it is hot.)

SYNTHESIS • TEXT EVIDENCE Using what you learned in this selection, tell what you can learn about wild animals by observing them. Have children cite examples from the text.

Continue to DAY 3
Think Critically
pp. 164–165

Text-Based Comprehension

Check Understanding

Have children discuss each question with a partner. Ask several pairs to share their responses.

☑ **Literary nonfiction** How is *Animal Park* different from a fantasy story about animals? (In *Animal Park,* the animals are real, and the author tells about things that really happened.)

☑ **Confirm predictions** How did you use pictures or other clues to predict what visitors see at the animal park? (I could tell what animals the visitors see by looking at the pictures.)

☑ **Setting** What is the setting for the selection *Animal Park?* (The setting is a hot day in an African animal preserve.)

☑ **Summarize** Summarize what happens in the selection. (People go to an animal park in Africa to see wild animals. They get in a truck and drive through the park. They see giraffes, zebras, lions, and many other animals.)

☑ **Draw conclusions** Why do people come to the animal park? (The people come to watch and observe the wild animals.)

Common Core State Standards

Informational Text 1. Ask and answer questions about key details in a text. **Informational Text 2.** Identify the main topic and retell key details of a text. **Informational Text 7.** Use the illustrations and details in a text to describe its key ideas.

ELL

Support Discussion Help children state their opinions by providing them with this sentence frame: *I think* ______ *because* ______. Explain that first children should tell their opinion and that after the word *because* they should give their reason or reasons.

Day 2 SMALL GROUP TIME • Differentiate Comprehension, p. SG•86

OL On-Level	SI Strategic Intervention	A Advanced
• **Practice Phonics** Additional Words with Final Consonant Blends • **Read** *Animal Park*	• **Reteach Phonics** Blend Words with Final Consonant Blends • **Read** *Animal Park*	• **Extend Phonics** More Words with Final Consonant Blends • **Read** *Animal Park* • **Investigate** Inquiry Project

If... children need more scaffolding and practice with the **Comprehension Skill,**
then... use the ELL activities on p. DI•122 in the Teacher Resources section on SuccessNet.

Common Core State Standards

Literature 5. Explain major differences between books that tell stories and books that give information, drawing on a wide reading of a range of text types. **Informational Text 9.** Identify basic similarities in and differences between two texts on the same topic (e.g., in illustrations, descriptions, or procedures). **Foundational Skills 1.a.** Recognize the distinguishing features of a sentence (e.g., first word, capitalization, ending punctuation). **Language 1.j.** Produce and expand complete simple and compound declarative, interrogative, imperative, and exclamatory sentences in response to prompts. **Also Language 1., 2.b.**

Genre

Literary Nonfiction

IDENTIFY FEATURES OF LITERARY NONFICTION Use *Animal Park* to have children identify the features of literary nonfiction. Remind children that nonfiction selections give information and fiction selections tell stories.

- *Animal Park* tells about real people and animals. Who are the people in the selection? (the author and other park visitors) What kinds of big animals do they see in the park? (elephants, hippos, giraffes)
- The setting of the selection is real too! Where is this animal park? (It is in Africa.)
- The selection tells about real events. How do the visitors travel around in the park? (They ride in a truck on bumpy roads.)

GUIDE PRACTICE Explain that the class will now compare two nonfiction texts that the class has read. Display a T-chart or use Graphic Organizer 4. Write the titles *Animal Park* and *A Fox and a Kit* at the tops of the columns. Record real-life people, animals, places, and events for each selection. Ask children to tell you what to write in each column. Once the chart is complete, have children compare and contrast the selections, discussing how the two selections are alike and different.

Animal Park	A Fox and a Kit

Graphic Organizer 4

ON THEIR OWN Arrange children into small groups and assign each group a previously read nonfiction selection. Have them identify the features that tell the selection really happened. Have them share their information with the class.

Conventions

Exclamatory Sentences

TEACH Write *His frog is the best pet!* on the board. Point to each word as you read it. Ask children to identify the end punctuation mark. (exclamation mark) An exclamatory sentence begins with a capital letter and ends with an exclamation mark. What does the exclamation mark tell us about the writer's feelings? (The writer has strong feelings.)

GUIDE PRACTICE Discuss feelings. Have children suggest the kinds of feelings that might cause someone to exclaim. List the feelings on the board. Then have children brainstorm events that might make them feel that way. Record what children might exclaim next to the appropriate emotion and event, for example:

Feeling	Event	Exclamatory Sentence
happy	winning a game	We won!

APPLY Explain that some declarative sentences can be changed to exclamatory sentences by changing the end punctuation. Have the class say these sentences once as a declarative sentence and once as an exclamatory sentence. Have them listen to the difference in their voices.

A black bug is on his leg.	**A black bug is on his leg!**
It is hot in here.	**It is hot in here!**

ON THEIR OWN Use *Reader's and Writer's Notebook,* p. 207.

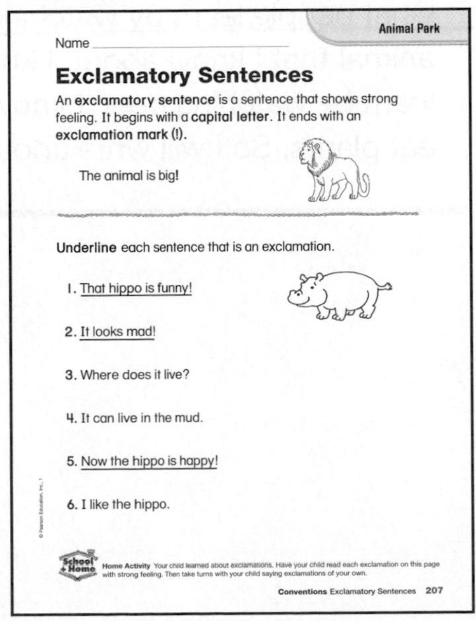

Animal Park

Name ______________________

Exclamatory Sentences

An **exclamatory sentence** is a sentence that shows strong feeling. It begins with a **capital letter**. It ends with an **exclamation mark** (!).

The animal is big!

Underline each sentence that is an exclamation.

1. That hippo is funny!
2. It looks mad!
3. Where does it live?
4. It can live in the mud.
5. Now the hippo is happy!
6. I like the hippo.

© Pearson Education, Inc., 1

School + Home **Home Activity** Your child learned about exclamations. Have your child read each exclamation on this page with strong feeling. Then take turns with your child saying exclamations of your own.

Conventions Exclamatory Sentences 207

Reader's and Writer's Notebook, p. 207

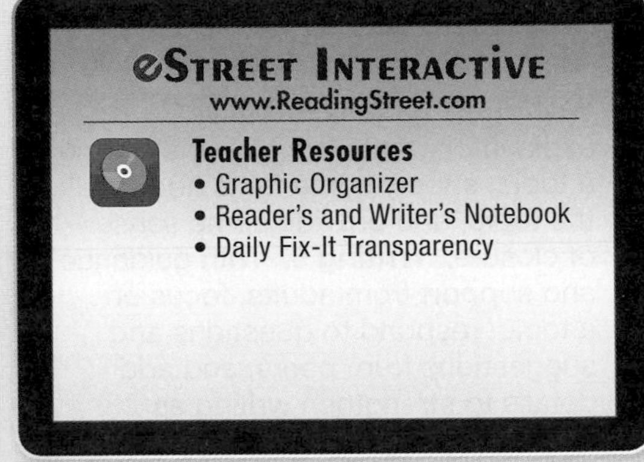

Daily Fix-It

3. my buss ran into a bump.
   My bus ran into a bump.
4. Frogs ren intoo the pond.
   Frogs run into the pond.

Discuss the Daily Fix-It corrections with children. Review sentence capitalization, the spelling of *bus* and *into,* and /u/ spelled *u.*

Access for All

SI Strategic Intervention

Support Conventions Ask children to draw a favorite scene from the Big Book *Jungle Drum.* Below their drawing, have them write two simple exclamatory sentences about their illustration. Ask them to explain what strong feeling each sentence shows and what punctuation mark they used at the end of each sentence.

ELL

Intonation If English learners have difficulty making declarative and exclamatory sentences sound different, model the sentences for them. Then have them sit when they say a statement and stand up when they say an exclamation.

Common Core State Standards

Writing 2. Write informative/explanatory texts in which they name a topic, supply some facts about the topic, and provide some sense of closure. **Writing 5.** With guidance and support from adults, focus on a topic, respond to questions and suggestions from peers, and add details to strengthen writing as needed.

Brief Composition

INTRODUCE THE PROMPT Review with children the key features of a brief composition. Explain that today children will write their own composition. Read aloud the writing prompt.

Writing Prompt

Think about wild animals. Write a composition about what people learn by watching wild animals.

Mini-Lesson: Writing for Tests: Narrowing Your Topic

- **Teach** A good composition tells about just one topic. By writing about just one topic, the author helps readers understand the ideas in the composition. All the ideas are about one thing. To write an answer to the prompt, we should first choose just one topic to write about. One way to do this is to list the topics we could write about and then choose just one from the list.
- **Model** Let's write a list of topics we could write about. Write *Wild Animals We Watch* as a heading for the list. I'll think of wild animals I have seen. I see birds everywhere. I'll write *birds* at the top of my list. Add *squirrels, lizards, raccoons, deer, frogs, spiders,* and other animals children suggest to the list. Next, I'll reread the prompt. The prompt asks me to write about what people learn by watching wild animals. So I should write about an animal that I know about. I know things about deer. I can tell what people learn by watching deer. I know that they live in the woods. I know that they eat plants. So I will write about deer. Circle *deer* on the list.

DISCUSS RUBRIC Explain the rubric on *Reader's and Writer's Notebook,* p. 208. Tell children that their writing this week will be evaluated using the rubric. Track the print as you read aloud the rubric, focusing on the trait of Focus/Ideas. Have children follow along.

SAMPLE TEST Have children get paper and pencil ready to take a writing test. Display the writing prompt and give children time to write to the prompt. Remind children to allow themselves a few minutes after writing to reread what they have written and make changes or additions.

Name ______ Animal Park

Composition
Top-Score Response

Focus/Ideas	A good composition tells about one topic.
Organization	A good composition tells important ideas in an order that makes sense.
Voice	A good composition tells about the topic in a way that is interesting.
Word Choice	A good composition uses clear words.
Sentences	A good composition is written in complete sentences.
Conventions	A good composition has sentences that are punctuated correctly.

School + Home **Home Activity** Your child can begin to learn about writing on writing tests. Ask how writing a composition about a topic such as real animals is different from making up a story.

208 Writing Writing for Tests

Reader's and Writer's Notebook, p. 208

Routine Quick Write for Fluency

Team Talk

1. **Talk** Have children take two minutes to tell what they did to narrow their topic.
2. **Write** Have children write one sentence telling what they did to narrow their topic.
3. **Share** Partners trade sentences and read them aloud.

Routines Flip Chart

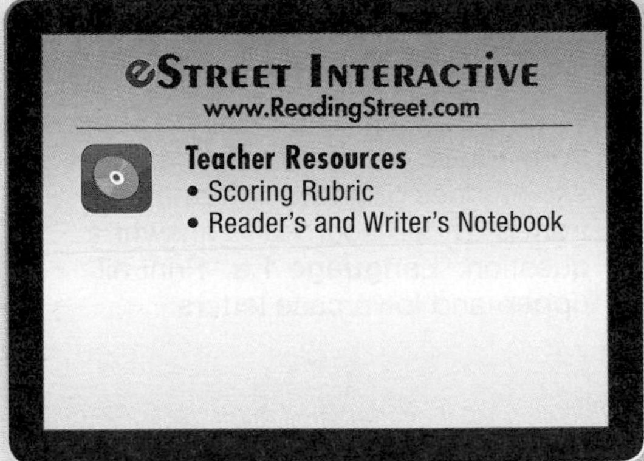

Access for All

SI Strategic Intervention

Writing for Tests If children are overwhelmed by the task, tell them that writing even just one sentence is good. They will be able to practice again later in the week.

Support Prewriting

Beginning Have children write one sentence telling about their topic.

Intermediate Have children write one sentence telling what their topic is and at least one more sentence telling about their topic.

Advanced Have children write one sentence telling what their topic is and at least two more sentences telling about their topic.

Common Core State Standards

Writing 8. With guidance and support from adults, recall information from experiences or gather information from provided sources to answer a question. **Language 1.a.** Print all upper- and lowercase letters.

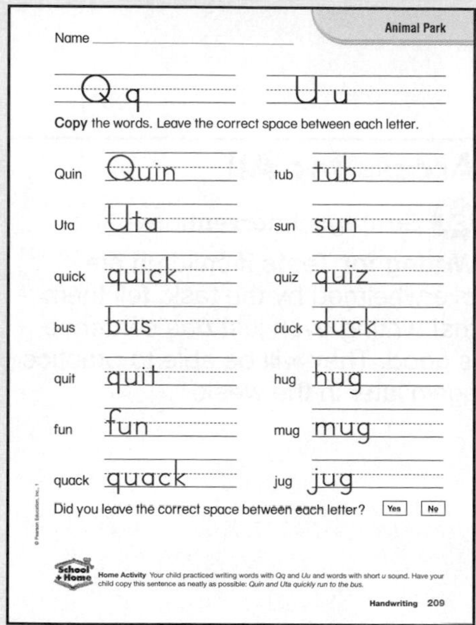

Animal Park

Name ____________

Q q   U u

Copy the words. Leave the correct space between each letter.

Quin	Quin	tub	tub
Uta	Uta	sun	sun
quick	quick	quiz	quiz
bus	bus	duck	duck
quit	quit	hug	hug
fun	fun	mug	mug
quack	quack	jug	jug

Did you leave the correct space between each letter? Yes No

School + Home **Home Activity** Your child practiced writing words with *Qq* and *Uu* and words with short *u* sound. Have your child copy this sentence as neatly as possible: *Quin and Uta quickly run to the bus.*

Handwriting 209

Reader's and Writer's Notebook, p. 209

Handwriting

Letters *Uu* and *Qq*/Letter Spacing

MODEL LETTER FORMATION Display uppercase and lowercase letters: *Uu, Qq*. Use the stroke instructions pictured below to model proper letter formation.

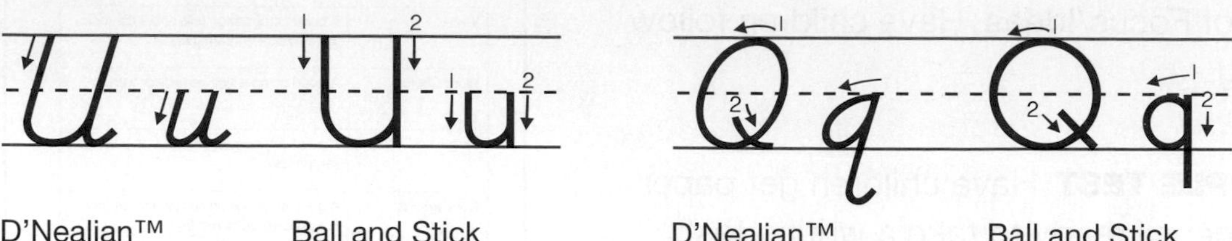

D'Nealian™   Ball and Stick   D'Nealian™   Ball and Stick

MODEL LETTER SPACING Remind children that when they write a word, all the letters should be evenly spaced. Write the word *bump* using correct spacing. When I write a word, I write the letters with just a small space separating them. I make sure I'm leaving the same amount of space between my letters. Write *bump* again, making some letters touch. The letters shouldn't be so close that they touch one another. Write *bump* a third time with the letters too far from one another. When I make my letters too far apart, it's hard to tell that they spell a word. Write *bump* a fourth time, using inconsistent letter spacing. Point out the places where the letter spacing is too large or too small.

GUIDE PRACTICE Write the following sentence, using letter spacing that is inconsistent: *Gus the duck runs and quacks.*

Team Talk Have children work in pairs to discuss what is wrong with the sentence and how it needs to be fixed. Have them share with the class.

ON THEIR OWN Use *Reader's and Writer's Notebook,* p. 209.

Research and Inquiry

Step 2 Research Skill: Notes

TEACH Tell children that **notes** are words and groups of words written about a topic. Explain that people make notes so they can remember information about the topic. Notes may be words, phrases, sentences, or drawings. Write *Our Classroom* on the board. Add two or three notes that describe the room, such as the number of seats, the color of the walls, and so forth. Read the notes aloud as children track the print.

Think Aloud **MODEL** When I write notes, I always start by writing the topic of my notes. The topic tells me what the notes are about. My notes may be words, groups of words, or even drawings. Each note is a bit of information about my topic, so I write each note on a separate line.

GUIDE PRACTICE Have children work with a partner to write two or three more notes about the classroom. As children share their notes, add them to those already on the board.

Academic Vocabulary

notes words and groups of words written about a topic so information about the topic can be remembered

Bridge to Common Core

RESEARCH TO BUILD AND PRESENT KNOWLEDGE

Children will gather information by writing notes to use for their research project. They will also:

- learn how to take notes
- learn how to use the notes when writing

Wrap Up Your Day!

✔ **Phonics: Final Consonant Blends** Write the words *last* and *rest.* Have children identify the blend at the end of each word.

✔ **High-Frequency Words** Point to these words on the Word Wall: *home, many, them, into.* Have children read each word and use it in a sentence.

✔ **Content Knowledge** Monitor children's use of oral vocabulary as they respond. Ask: Is it better to chatter or be silent when you observe animals? (It is better to be silent so you don't scare away the animals.) Why would you observe an animal you are curious about? (to learn about the animal) What could you learn by observing a parent animal? (how it takes care of its babies)

Tell children that tomorrow they will reread *Animal Park.*

DAY 3 at a Glance

Content Knowledge
Oral Vocabulary

Phonemic Awareness
Rhyming Words

Phonics/Spelling
Short *u: u*
Final Consonant Blends

High-Frequency Words
home, into, many, them

Selection Words
elephants, hippos, park, zebras

Text-Based Comprehension
Review Main Idea and Details

Fluency
Appropriate Phrasing

Conventions
Exclamatory Sentences

Writing
Brief Composition
Writing Trait: Focus/Ideas

Listening and Speaking
Give Directions

Research and Inquiry
Gather and Record Information

Materials
- Student Edition
- Sing with Me Big Book
- Big Book
- Letter Tiles
- Reader's and Writer's Notebook
- Retelling Cards

Common Core State Standards

Speaking/Listening 2. Ask and answer questions about key details in a text read aloud or information presented orally or through other media. **Language 5.c.** Identify real-life connections between words and their use (e.g., note places at home that are *cozy*). **Also Language 6.**

Content Knowledge

Watching Wild Animals

EXPAND THE CONCEPT To reinforce concepts and to focus children's attention, have them sing "Big, Round World" from the *Sing with Me* Big Book. How can watching wild animals help us know how to protect the places where they live? (Possible response: We can learn what they need to eat and how they make their homes.)

Build Oral Language

LISTEN FOR AMAZING WORDS Display the Big Book *Jungle Drum.* Read the story and have children listen for the word *snort.* Have them also think about the other wild animals that make noise in the jungle.

- What sound does the mosquito make? (She says, "Hmmmmmmmm.")
- Who puffs out his throat and croaks? (a tree frog)
- Which animal growls? (a jaguar)

Big Book

TALK ABOUT SENTENCES AND WORDS
Write the following sentence from *Jungle Drum* on sentence strips or on the board.

On the ground, wild boars make a snorting sound.

- Ask children to read it with you as you track the print.
- Point to and read *wild boars make a snorting sound.* How can we figure out what a *boar* is? Have children share their suggestions, such as look at the picture or ask an adult.
- What does *snort* mean? (make a noise with your nose) Why do you think the author used the word *snorting?* (It is how the author can describe the sound a boar makes.)
- What word would you use? Ask a volunteer to imitate the sound they think a boar would make.
- **Team Talk** Now have children work with a partner to replace key words to create sentences about other animals and the sounds they make. Use the following sentence frame.

  On the ground, wild ______ make a ______ sound.

Build Oral Vocabulary

Amazing Words Robust Vocabulary Routine

1. **Introduce the Word** Relate the word *snort* to the book. The wild boars in the jungle *snort.* Supply a child-friendly definition. When you *snort,* you make a sound through your nose. Have children say the word.
2. **Demonstrate** Provide examples to show meaning. A pig *snorts.* Sometimes people *snort* when they laugh. The angry horse *snorted* and kicked.
3. **Apply** Have children demonstrate their understanding. Make a *snorting* sound. What other animal might *snort* at you?
4. **Display the Word** Point out the initial consonant blend *sn*/s/ /n/. Read the word and have children repeat after you.

Routines Flip Chart

ADD TO THE CONCEPT MAP Use these questions to discuss what we can learn by observing animals as you add to the concept map.

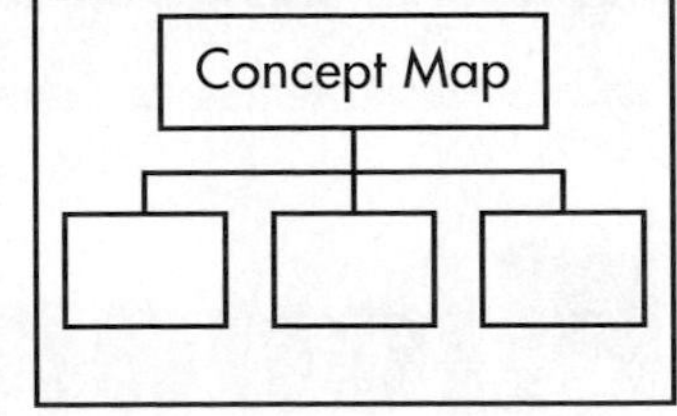

- In *Animal Park,* the visitors see some big cats resting after a long hunt. Let's add *big cats hunt* to our concept map.
- What do the visitors see the hippos doing? (They are sitting in wet mud.) Let's add *hippos sit in mud* to our concept map.
- Next, the visitors watch some elephants in a pond. What do the elephants do there? (The elephants sip, stand in, stomp in, and swim in the pond.) Let's add that to our concept map too.

Amazing Words

desert	silent
forest	snort
world	medicine
chatter	poisonous

Physical Response To support children's understanding of what the animals in the park do, pantomime the animals' actions and have children join you. For example, pantomime *sip, stand, stomp,* and *swim* to demonstrate what the elephants do in the pond.

Common Core State Standards Foundational Skills 2.c. Isolate and pronounce initial, medial vowel, and final sounds (phonemes) in spoken single-syllable words. Also Foundational Skills 2.b.

Phonemic Awareness

Let's Listen for Sounds

- Find two things that rhyme with *trust*.
- Find five things that contain the short *u* sound.
- Find something that rhymes with *dunk*. Say each sound in the word.

Read Together

READING STREET ONLINE
SOUND-SPELLING CARDS
www.ReadingStreet.com

148 149

Student Edition, pp. 148–149

Common Core State Standards

Foundational Skills 2. Demonstrate understanding of spoken words, syllables, and sounds (phonemes). **Foundational Skills 2.b.** Orally produce single-syllable words by blending sounds (phonemes), including consonant blends. **Foundational Skills 3.** Know and apply grade-level phonics and word analysis skills in decoding words.

Academic Vocabulary

rhyming words words that end with the same sounds

Phonemic Awareness

Rhyming Words

MODEL PRODUCING RHYMING WORDS Read the first bullet point on p. 148. Remember that **rhyming words** are words that end with the same sounds. Let's find two things that rhyme with *trust.* When I look at the picture, I see a *crust* of bread, and I see some old trucks with *rust* on them. The words *crust* and *rust* rhyme with *trust.*

GUIDE PRACTICE Guide children to use the picture to produce words that rhyme with *dunk. (skunk, trunk, junk)*

ON THEIR OWN Have children produce words that rhyme with the following words.

bug tub dump cut must fun

Team Talk Have children create pairs of rhyming words with a partner.

Phonics

Build Words

MODEL WORD BUILDING Now we are going to build words that end with a consonant blend. Write *hand* and blend it. Watch me change *h* to *b*. Model blending the new word, *band*.

GUIDE PRACTICE Have children spell *band* with letter tiles. Monitor children's work as they build words.

- Change the *a* in *band* to *e*. Say the new word together.

- Change the *d* in *bend* to *t*. Say the new word together.

- Change the *n* in *bent* to *s*. Say the new word together.

- Change the *b* in *best* to *r*. Say the new word together.

Corrective feedback	For corrective feedback, model the correct spelling and have children correct their tiles.

Fluent Word Reading

MODEL Write *hunt.* I know the sounds for *h, u, n,* and *t.* I blend them and read the word *hunt.*

GUIDE PRACTICE Write the words below. Say the sounds in your head for each spelling you see. When I point to the word, we'll read it together. Allow one second per sound-previewing time for the first reading.

mud dust pup tusk lump bunt

ON THEIR OWN Have children read the list above three or four times, until they can read one word per second.

Access for All

 Advanced

Build Rhyming Words If children are able to rhyme words easily and independently, ask partners to use letter tiles to build a word with short *u*. Then have them see how many rhyming words they can build by changing the first letter tile to another consonant or consonant blend.

ELL

Pronounce Final Blends Final consonant blends may be challenging for speakers of Greek, Italian, Spanish, and some other languages. Provide additional practice in segmenting and blending words with final consonant blends.

Common Core State Standards

Foundational Skills 3. Know and apply grade-level phonics and word analysis skills in decoding words. **Foundational Skills 3.b.** Decode regularly spelled one-syllable words. **Language 2.d.** Use conventional spelling for words with common spelling patterns and for frequently occurring irregular words.

Phonics

Blend and Read

DECODE WORDS IN ISOLATION Have children turn to pages 211–212 in the *Reader's and Writer's Notebook* and find the first list of words. Each word in this list has the short *u* sound. Have children point to the second list of words. Each word in this list has a final consonant blend. Let's blend and read these words. Be sure that children identify the correct sounds in short *u* words and words that end with a consonant blend. Next, have children read the high-frequency words.

© Pearson Education, Inc., 1

Bud got the sums.

Bud did his best.

Bud did well!

4

Decodable Story The Test
Target Skills Short u, Final Consonant Blends

Name ______

The Test

Short u		Final Consonant Blends	High-Frequency Words	
Huff	fun	test	the	said
Bud	stuck	must	a	is
sum	sums	best		

"The class will get a test," said Miss Huff.

"The class will add."

1

Reader's and Writer's Notebook, pp. 211–212

DECODE WORDS IN CONTEXT Chorally read the story along with children. Have children identify words in the story that have short *u* and/or a final consonant blend.

ON THEIR OWN To further develop automaticity, have children take the story home to reread.

Spelling

Short *u* Words with Final Consonant Blends

SPELL HIGH-FREQUENCY WORDS Write *many* and *into* and point them out on the Word Wall. Have children say and spell the words with you and then without you.

DICTATION Have children write these sentences. Say each sentence. Then repeat it slowly, one word at a time.

1. **The cat ran into the net.**
2. **I sat in the dust.**
3. **I just got many rocks on the walk.**

PROOFREAD AND CORRECT Write each sentence, spelling words one at a time. Have children circle and rewrite any misspelled words.

ON THEIR OWN Use *Reader's and Writer's Notebook,* p. 213.

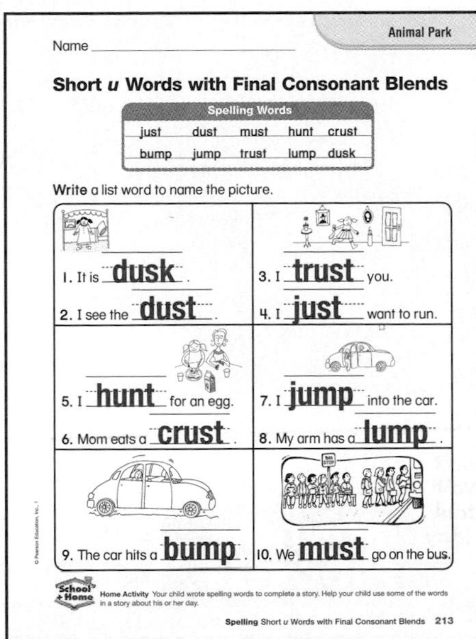
Name ________________ Animal Park

Short *u* Words with Final Consonant Blends

Spelling Words				
just	dust	must	hunt	crust
bump	jump	trust	lump	dusk

Write a list word to name the picture.

1. It is **dusk**.
2. I see the **dust**.
3. I **trust** you.
4. I **just** want to run.
5. I **hunt** for an egg.
6. Mom eats a **crust**.
7. I **jump** into the car.
8. My arm has a **lump**.
9. The car hits a **bump**.
10. We **must** go on the bus.

School + Home **Home Activity** Your child wrote spelling words to complete a story. Help your child use some of the words in a story about his or her day.

Spelling Short *u* Words with Final Consonant Blends 213

Reader's and Writer's Notebook, p. 213

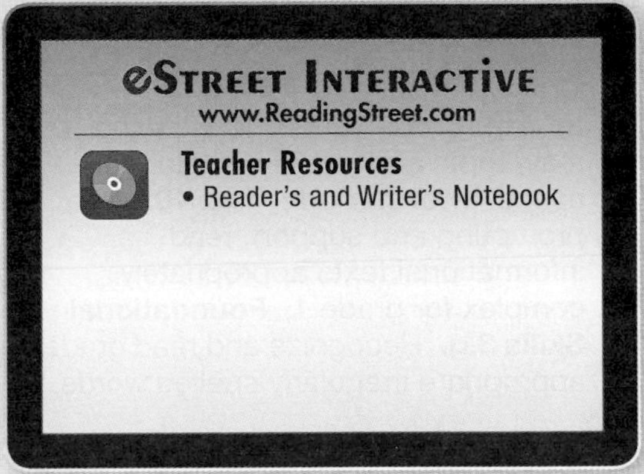

Spelling Words

Short *u* Words with Final Consonant Blends

1. crust	**6. dust**
2. bump	**7. trust**
3. jump	**8. dusk**
4. must	**9. hunt**
5. just	**10. lump**

High-Frequency Words

11. many	**12. into**

Spelling Dictation Children will benefit from hearing each dictated sentence three times. First, have children listen to understand the sentence. The second time, they should write what they hear. The third time, they can check their work.

Day 3 SMALL GROUP TIME • Differentiate Close Reading, p. SG•86

OL On-Level	SI Strategic Intervention	A Advanced
• **Reread** to Develop Vocabulary • **Reread** *Animal Park*	• **Blend** Words with Short *u* and Final Consonant Blends • **Reread** *Animal Park*	• **Reread** to Extend Vocabulary • **Reread** *Animal Park* • **Investigate** Inquiry Project

If... children need more scaffolding and practice with reading the **Main Selection,**
then... use the ELL activities on p. DI•123 in the Teacher Resources section on SuccessNet.

Common Core State Standards

Informational Text 2. Identify the main topic and retell key details of a text. **Informational Text 10.** With prompting and support, read informational texts appropriately complex for grade 1. **Foundational Skills 3.g.** Recognize and read grade-appropriate irregularly spelled words.

High-Frequency Words

home	many
into	them

Selection Words

elephants huge, strong land animals with gray skin and long trunks

hippos a short word for hippopotamuses, which are large animals with short legs, thick skin, and wide mouths

park land set aside for people to enjoy nature

zebras black-and-white striped animals that look like horses

High-Frequency and Selection Words

READ WORDS IN ISOLATION Display and review this week's high-frequency words and selection words. Have children read the words aloud.

READ WORDS IN CONTEXT Display the following sentence frames. Have children complete the sentences using high-frequency and selection words. Have children read each completed sentence with you.

1. **Nan and Ken got ______ his black truck.** **(into)**
2. **Yes, *many* fast ______ ran past Mom and Dad.** **(zebras)**
3. **Big ______ can stomp and swim in the *park*.** **(elephants)**
4. **Will ______ sit in the mud if the sun is hot?** **(hippos)**
5. **Jack went ______ and fed his dog.** **(home)**
6. **Kim gets six blocks and stacks ______.** **(them)**

MONITOR PROGRESS Check High-Frequency Words

FORMATIVE ASSESSMENT Point to these words on the Word Wall and have the class read them. Listen for children who miss words during the reading. Call on those children to read some of the words individually.

many	into	home	them	**Spiral Review** Rows 2 and 3 review previously taught high-frequency words.
they	from	this	saw	←
are	with	what		←

If... children cannot read these words,

then... use the Nondecodable Words Routine on p. 151 to reteach the words. Monitor children's fluency with these words during reading and provide additional practice.

Text-Based Comprehension

Read Main Selection

REVIEW MAIN IDEA AND DETAILS Remind children that the **main idea** of a selection is what the selection is mostly about and **details** are small pieces of information about the main idea. Paying attention to the main idea helps us understand the information we are reading. What is the selection *Animal Park* mostly about? (It is about seeing wild animals that live in an animal park.) What detail, or fact, did we learn about some big birds that live in the park? Find the page the detail is on. (On page 160, it says the big birds can run fast.)

GENRE: LITERARY NONFICTION Remind children that literary nonfiction tells about real-life people, animals, or events and that the setting is real. Have children point out text features that helped them know that *Animal Park* is about real people, animals, events, and places. (The pictures show real animals and the words tell what real animals do.)

READ Return to pages 154–163 and use the **2nd Read/Close Reading Notes** to reread *Animal Park.*

Routine Read for Understanding

Deepen understanding by reading the selection multiple times.

1. **First Read**—If children need support, then use the **Access Text** notes to help them clarify understanding.
2. **Second Read**—Use the **Close Reading** notes to help children draw knowledge from the text.

Academic Vocabulary

main idea tells what the selection is mainly about

details small pieces of information

Sentence Production In preparation for their second reading of *Animal Park,* have children choose two or three animals pictured in the text. Ask them to point to a photo and say a short sentence that explains what the animals are doing. For example, children might point to the elephants on p. 162 and say, "The elephants sip water."

Think Critically

1. Put yourself in the animal park. Read the part of the selection that tells about the animals you would like to see. Text to Self
2. Does the author seem to like animals? Explain why or why not. Author's Purpose
3. Why do hippos sit in the mud? Cause and Effect
4. Which animals does the author see before the hippos? Text Structure
5. **Look Back and Write** Look back at the photographs in the selection. Choose an animal that was in the big park. Use facts from the selection to write about the animal you choose. Key Ideas and Details • Text Evidence

164

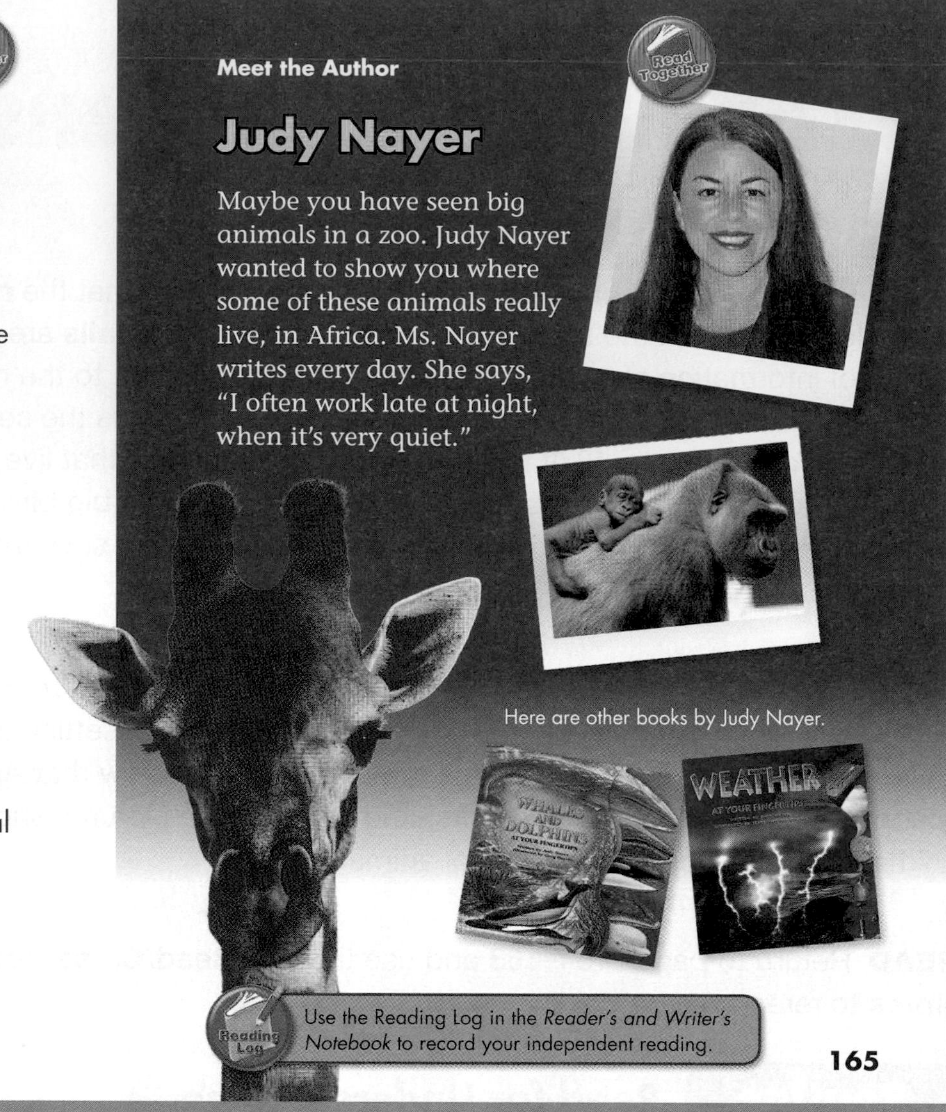

Meet the Author
Judy Nayer
Maybe you have seen big animals in a zoo. Judy Nayer wanted to show you where some of these animals really live, in Africa. Ms. Nayer writes every day. She says, "I often work late at night, when it's very quiet."
Here are other books by Judy Nayer.
WHALES AND DOLPHINS
WEATHER
Use the Reading Log in the *Reader's and Writer's Notebook* to record your independent reading.

165

Student Edition, pp. 164–165

Common Core State Standards

Informational Text 1. Ask and answer questions about key details in a text. **Informational Text 2.** Identify the main topic and retell key details of a text. **Also Writing 5.**

Bridge to Common Core

KEY IDEAS AND DETAILS

By reading the text multiple times, children will make logical inferences from the text and cite textual evidence when writing or discussing the knowledge they have gained. Use the Think Critically page to ensure a thorough understanding of *Animal Park.*

Think Critically

1. **TEXT TO SELF** I would like to see the elephants on p. 162 stomping and swimming in the pond.
2. **AUTHOR'S PURPOSE** The author really likes animals. She goes on a special trip to see them and is happy when she spots different kinds.
3. **CAUSE AND EFFECT** Hippos sit in the mud because it helps them stay cool in the hot sun.
4. **TEXT STRUCTURE** She sees some big birds just before she sees the hippos.
5. **LOOK BACK AND WRITE • TEXT EVIDENCE** For writing fluency, assign a five-minute time limit. As children finish, encourage them to reread their response and proofread for errors.

Scoring Rubric Look Back and Write

TOP-SCORE RESPONSE A top-score response uses details from the text and the pictures to tell about an animal pictured in the selection.

A top-score response might include:
Some big hippos are sitting in the mud. It is hot out. The wet mud keeps the hippos cool.

Retell

Have children use the retelling strip in the Student Edition or the Story Sort to retell the selection. Monitor children's retelling.

Scoring Rubric Expository Retelling

	4	3	2	1
Connections	Makes connections and generalizes beyond the text	Makes connections to other events, texts, or experiences	Makes a limited connection to another event, text, or experience	Makes no connection to another event, text, or experience
Author's Purpose	Elaborates on author's purpose	Tells author's purpose with some clarity	Makes some connection to author's purpose	Makes no connection to author's purpose
Topic	Describes the main topic	Identifies the main topic with some details early in retelling	Identifies the main topic	Retelling has no sense of topic
Important Ideas	Gives accurate information about ideas using key vocabulary	Gives accurate information about ideas with some key vocabulary	Gives limited or inaccurate information about ideas	Gives no information about ideas
Conclusions	Draws conclusions and makes inferences to generalize beyond the text	Draws conclusions about the text	Is able to tell some learnings about the text	Is unable to draw conclusions or make inferences about the text

Don't Wait Until Friday

MONITOR PROGRESS Check Retelling

If... children have trouble retelling the selection,

then... use Main Idea Graphic Organizer 27 and the Retelling Cards/Story Sort to scaffold their retelling.

Writing to Sources

Use Write Like a Reporter on pp. 62–63 to guide children in writing text-based responses using one source.

Strategy Response Log

Text Structure Have children use p. RR18 in their *Reader's and Writer's Notebook* to draw and write what the author saw at the animal park right after she saw the zebras.

Plan to Assess Retelling

- ☐ **Week 1** Strategic Intervention
- ☐ **Week 2** Advanced
- ☐ **Week 3** Strategic Intervention
- ☐ **Week 4** On-Level
- ☐ **Week 5** Strategic Intervention
- ☑ **This Week** Assess any children you have not yet checked during this unit.

Meet the Author

Read aloud page 165 as children follow along. Ask children what authors do.

Read Independently

Have children enter their independent reading into their Reading Logs.

Common Core State Standards

Foundational Skills 1.a. Recognize the distinguishing features of a sentence (e.g., first word, capitalization, ending punctuation). **Foundational Skills 4.b.** Read on-level text orally with accuracy, appropriate rate, and expression on successive readings. **Language 1.j.** Produce and expand complete simple and compound declarative, interrogative, imperative, and exclamatory sentences in response to prompts. **Language 2.b.** Use end punctuation for sentences. **Also Language 1.**

Options for Oral Rereading

Use *Animal Park* or one of this week's Decodable Practice Readers.

Professional Development

Fluency Children who are able to mark sentence endings with pauses and appropriate pitch are better able to comprehend what they are reading.

Fluency

Appropriate Phrasing

MODEL FLUENT READING Have children turn to Student Edition page 158. Point to an exclamation mark. This is an exclamation mark. It tells me that I should read this sentence with excitement.

GUIDE PRACTICE Have children read the page with you. Then have them reread the page as a group until they read with appropriate phrasing, paying attention to the exclamation marks. Point out how your voice changes when you read the exclamation. Continue in the same way with page 160.

Corrective feedback	**If...** children have difficulty reading with appropriate phrasing, **then...** prompt: • Did you look at the end marks? • How should your voice sound when you read a sentence that ends with an exclamation mark? • Read the sentence as if you are very excited.

Reread for Fluency

Routine Choral Reading

1. **Select a Passage** For *Animal Park,* use pp. 159–160.
2. **Model** First, have children track the print as you read.
3. **Guide Practice** Then have children read along with you.
4. **Corrective Feedback** Have the class read aloud without you. Monitor progress and provide feedback. For optimal fluency, children should reread three to four times.

Routines Flip Chart

CHECK COMPREHENSION How are the big birds different from the big cats? (The big cats are resting and the big birds are running.)

Conventions

Exclamatory Sentences

REVIEW Remind children that an exclamatory sentence shows strong feeling and ends with an exclamation mark: *Those giraffes are so tall! I love watching animals!*

GUIDE PRACTICE Write this sentence on the board and have children read it aloud.

Big cats can run fast!

Guide children in describing the sentence. What kind of sentence is this? (an exclamatory sentence) What punctuation mark is at the end? (an exclamation mark) What does that punctuation mark tell you about the writer's feelings? (The writer has a strong feeling about something.)

Team Talk Have pairs look at the photographs in the selection *Animal Park.* Ask them to generate exclamations they might have said if they had been riding on the truck and seeing these animals.

APPLY Have children say these sentences with the appropriate intonation.

That was such a great surprise!
I am so excited!
I'm very worried about the test!

ON THEIR OWN Use *Reader's and Writer's Notebook,* p. 214.

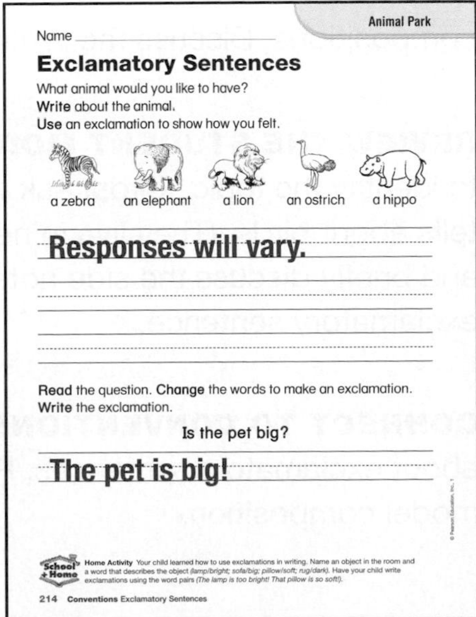
Name ______ Animal Park

Exclamatory Sentences

What animal would you like to have?
Write about the animal.
Use an exclamation to show how you felt.

a zebra an elephant a lion an ostrich a hippo

Responses will vary.

Read the question. **Change** the words to make an exclamation.
Write the exclamation.

Is the pet big?

The pet is big!

Home Activity Your child learned how to use exclamations in writing. Name an object in the room and a word that describes the object (lamp/bright; sofa/big; pillow/soft; rug/dark). Have your child write exclamations using the word pairs (*The lamp is too bright! That pillow is so soft!*).

214 **Conventions** Exclamatory Sentences

Reader's and Writer's Notebook, p. 214

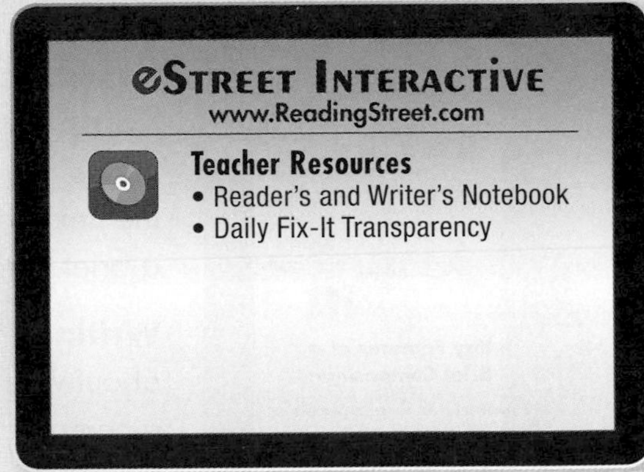
eStreet Interactive
www.ReadingStreet.com

Teacher Resources
- Reader's and Writer's Notebook
- Daily Fix-It Transparency

Daily Fix-It

5. Jummp up for a nutt
Jump up for a nut.

6. she kut a rug up
She cut a rug up.

Discuss the Daily Fix-It corrections with children. Review sentence capitalization and punctuation, /m/ spelled *m,* /t/ spelled *t,* and /k/ spelled *c.*

ELL

Punctuation Children with literacy skills in Spanish may be accustomed to writing an introductory (upside-down) exclamation mark at the beginning of an exclamation. Point out that in English, the exclamation mark appears only at the end.

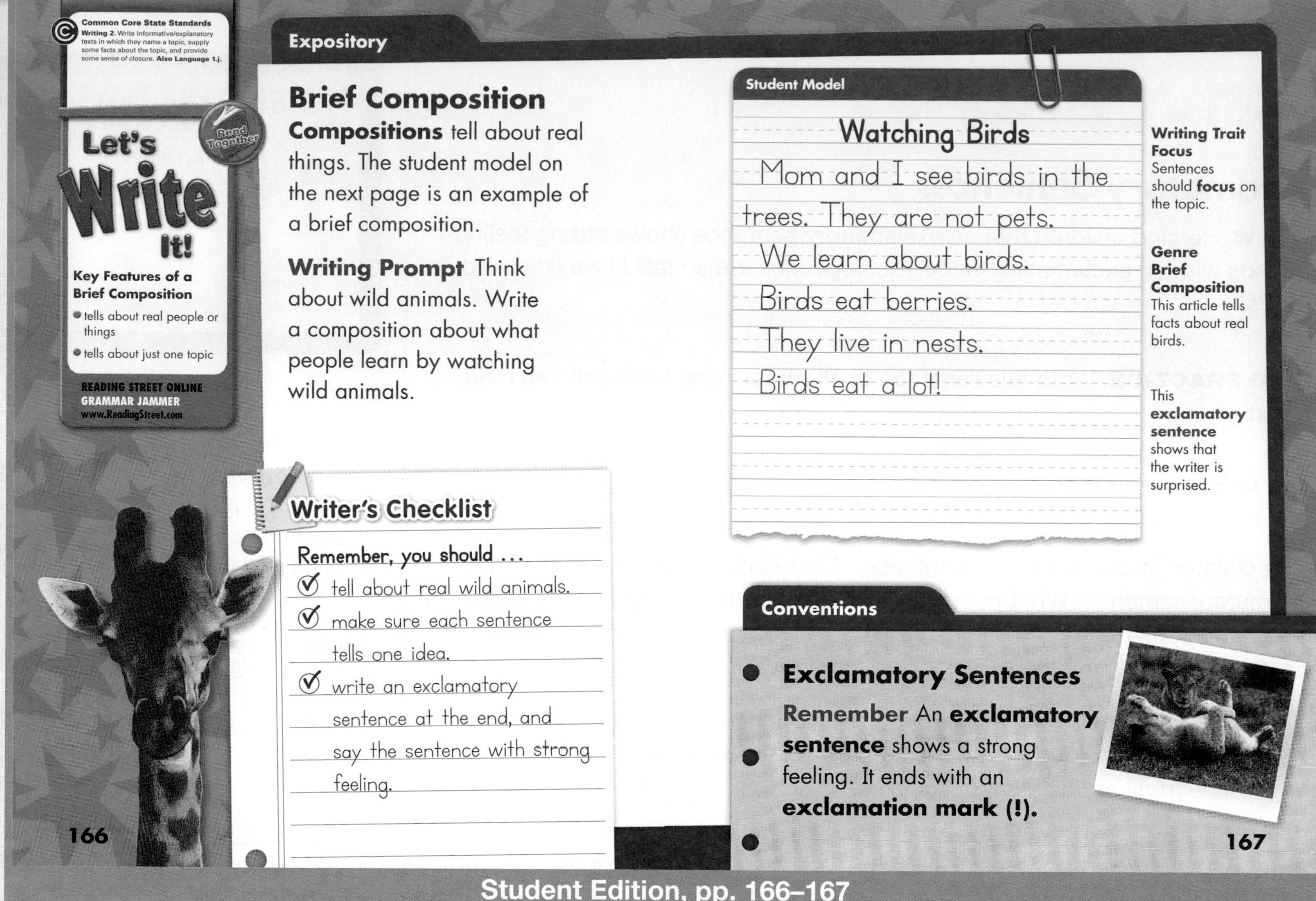

Common Core State Standards Writing 2. Write informative/explanatory texts in which they name a topic, supply some facts about the topic, and provide some sense of closure. Also Language 1.j.
Let's Write It!
Read Together
Key Features of a Brief Composition
• tells about real people or things
• tells about just one topic
READING STREET ONLINE
GRAMMAR JAMMER
www.ReadingStreet.com
Expository
Brief Composition
Compositions tell about real things. The student model on the next page is an example of a brief composition.
Writing Prompt Think about wild animals. Write a composition about what people learn by watching wild animals.
Writer's Checklist
Remember, you should ...
tell about real wild animals.
make sure each sentence tells one idea.
write an exclamatory sentence at the end, and say the sentence with strong feeling.
166
Student Model
Watching Birds
Mom and I see birds in the trees. They are not pets.
We learn about birds.
Birds eat berries.
They live in nests.
Birds eat a lot!
Writing Trait Focus Sentences should focus on the topic.
Genre Brief Composition This article tells facts about real birds.
This exclamatory sentence shows that the writer is surprised.
Conventions
Exclamatory Sentences
Remember An exclamatory sentence shows a strong feeling. It ends with an exclamation mark (!).
167

Student Edition, pp. 166–167

Common Core State Standards

Writing 2. Write informative/explanatory texts in which they name a topic, supply some facts about the topic, and provide some sense of closure. **Writing 5.** With guidance and support from adults, focus on a topic, respond to questions and suggestions from peers, and add details to strengthen writing as needed. **Language 1.j.** Produce and expand complete simple and compound declarative, interrogative, imperative, and exclamatory sentences in response to prompts.

Let's Write It!

WRITE A BRIEF COMPOSITION Use pages 166–167 in the Student Edition. Read aloud the Key Features of a Brief Composition and the definition of compositions. Discuss the Writing Prompt and Writer's Checklist with children.

REVIEW THE STUDENT MODEL Read aloud "Watching Birds." Ask children to identify the topic. (birds) Ask them to identify the real things the composition tells about birds. (They live in nests, eat berries, and eat a lot.) Read aloud and briefly discuss the side notes about genre, the writing trait, and the exclamatory sentence.

CONNECT TO CONVENTIONS Read to children the Conventions note about exclamatory sentences. Point out the exclamatory sentence in the model composition.

Writing

Brief Composition

Mini-Lesson Writing for Tests: Writing Trait: Focus/Ideas

■ **Introduce** Have children turn again to the rubric on *Reader's and Writer's Notebook,* p. 208. Track the print as you read aloud the description of a top-score response for the trait of Focus/Ideas. Have children follow along.

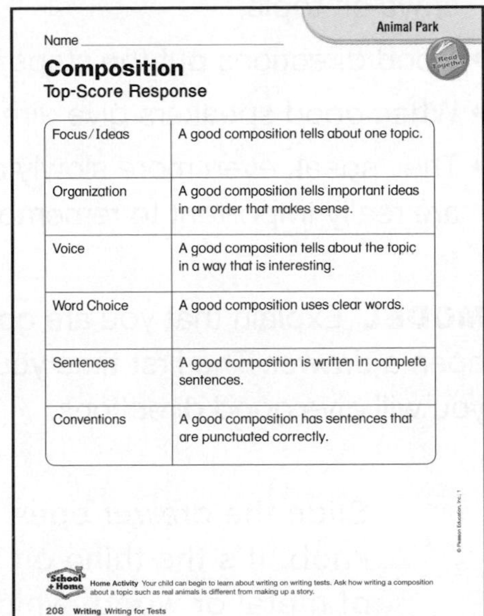

Name ______ Animal Park

Composition
Top-Score Response

Focus/Ideas	A good composition tells about one topic.
Organization	A good composition tells important ideas in an order that makes sense.
Voice	A good composition tells about the topic in a way that is interesting.
Word Choice	A good composition uses clear words.
Sentences	A good composition is written in complete sentences.
Conventions	A good composition has sentences that are punctuated correctly.

School + Home **Home Activity** Your child can begin to learn about writing on writing tests. Ask how writing a composition about a topic such as real animals is different from making up a story.

208 **Writing** Writing for Tests

Reader's and Writers Notebook, p. 208

■ **Teach** When I evaluate a composition, I check that all of the ideas are about the topic of the composition. I reread each sentence and then ask myself if the sentence tells about my topic.

■ Explain that children can follow a similar process to check their compositions for Focus/Ideas or for other traits. They can reread each sentence and then ask themselves if the composition matches the trait.

■ Your composition may receive a high score for each trait. Or you may need to try to improve one or some of the traits. Different scores on the traits will help you see which parts of your writing you should give more attention.

■ Now it is time to evaluate your compositions. Have children use the rubric to evaluate their compositions. Circulate to guide children.

Routine Quick Write for Fluency — Team Talk

1. **Talk** Have partners take two minutes to discuss the best part of the writing they did.
2. **Write** Have each child write a sentence about one strength of his or her composition.
3. **Share** Partners can read their sentences to one another.

Routines Flip Chart

eStreet Interactive
www.ReadingStreet.com

Pearson eText
- Student Edition

Teacher Resources
- Scoring Rubric
- Reader's and Writer's Notebook

Access for All

Developing Evaluation Children may share their compositions with a partner and identify one strength in their partners' compositions. Based on this evaluation, have them tell how they could improve their own compositions.

Write Guy *by Jeff Anderson*

Life in a Fishbowl

When a teacher can't confer with every child, a "fishbowl conference" with one willing child can allow other children to observe, listen, and learn. It's important to reflect what the child is doing well and how a draft might be revised and improved.

Common Core State Standards

Writing 7. Participate in shared research and writing projects (e.g., explore a number of "how-to" books on a given topic and use them to write a sequence of instructions). **Writing 8.** With guidance and support from adults, recall information from experiences or gather information from provided sources to answer a question. **Speaking/Listening 1.a.** Follow agreed-upon rules for discussions (e.g., listening to others with care, speaking one at a time about the topics and texts under discussion).

Bridge to Common Core

COMPREHENSION AND COLLABORATION

In this week's lesson, children develop listening and speaking skills that focus on how to give directions. Children participate in a range of conversations and collaborations to learn to organize their directions to give step-by-step procedures in short and simple sentences. The activities also provide opportunities for children to evaluate good and bad directions.

Listening and Speaking

Give Directions

TEACH Explain that people often give each other directions for how to do something.

- Good directions are given step by step. Each step is short and simple, and it stays on topic.
- Good directions put the steps in the correct order.
- When good speakers give directions, they speak clearly and slowly.
- They speak even more slowly and loudly when they are saying words that are really important to remember.

MODEL Explain that you are going to give two sets of directions for how to open a drawer. The first time you will give bad directions, and the second time you will give good directions.

Slide the drawer open with your hand. Put your fingers on the knob. It's the thing on the front of the drawer, and it's made of metal or wood, which comes from a factory where lots of people work.

Here's the second set of directions. Step 1: With your hand, grab the *knob.* This is the piece of wood or metal sticking out from the front, flat part. Step 2: *Pull* the knob *toward* you gently. Step 3: Stop pulling when the drawer is open far enough that you can see what's inside.

Discuss the differences between the two sets of directions.

GUIDE PRACTICE Arrange the children into pairs. Draw a T-chart on the board, and have each pair draw their own T-chart on a sheet of paper. Label the columns *Good Directions* and *Bad Directions.* Work with children to write words or phrases to fill each column to give directions for writing capital *A.* Then have children work in pairs to add to their own charts. Walk around the room and provide feedback as needed. Then have volunteers share their work with the class.

ON THEIR OWN Have children practice giving directions for how to make their favorite snack or sandwich.

Research and Inquiry

Step 3 Gather and Record Information

TEACH Tell children that today they will think about an animal they have observed in the neighborhood and write notes about what they observed. The notes they make will help them remember what they learned.

Think Aloud **MODEL** Display the list of questions the class created on Day 1. When we write about our animals, we will need the list of questions we made two days ago. We will think about whether we can use what we saw to answer any of our questions. We will write notes that will answer the questions.

GUIDE PRACTICE Tell children that they will now write notes about the animals they observed. Suggest that children write the name of the animal they observed at the top of their paper. Remind children that their notes can be words, groups of words, or drawings. Have them write any bits of information they remember from when they observed their animals. Explain to children that they will use the notes they write about their animal later.

Access for All

SI Strategic Intervention

Writing Notes Some children may have trouble writing notes. Tell these children that they can draw pictures of what they observe instead of writing words. Later in the week they can use the pictures to write their notes.

Wrap Up Your Day!

- ✔ **Cause and Effect** Why might it be harder to observe animals in the winter than in the summer? (The weather is colder in winter so some animals hibernate.)
- ✔ **Text Structure** Have children explain how the picture on each page of *Animal Park* helps them know, in advance, what they will be reading about on that page.

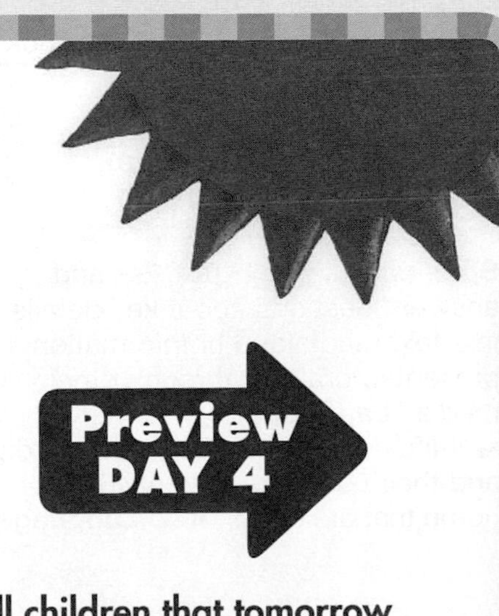

Tell children that tomorrow they will read poems about more animals.

DAY 4 at a Glance

Content Knowledge
Oral Vocabulary

Phonemic Awareness
Distinguish /u/

Phonics
Review Short *e: e*
Review Initial Consonant Blends

High-Frequency Words
Review

Spelling
Short *u* Words with Final Consonant Blends

Poetry in Reading
Poetry

Fluency
Appropriate Phrasing

Conventions
Exclamatory Sentences

Writing
Brief Composition

Research and Inquiry
Synthesize

Materials

- Student Edition
- Sing with Me Big Book
- Read Aloud Anthology
- Decodable Reader 6C
- Reader's and Writer's Notebook

Common Core State Standards

Speaking/Listening 2. Ask and answer questions about key details in a text read aloud or information presented orally or through other media. **Language 5.c.** Identify real-life connections between words and their use (e.g., note places at home that are *cozy*). **Also Language 6.**

Content Knowledge

Zoom in on

Watching Wild Animals

EXPAND THE CONCEPT To reinforce concepts and to focus children's attention, have them sing "Big, Round World" from the *Sing with Me* Big Book. What are some great animal sights and sounds you might notice in a desert? (Possible response: I might see huge camels and hear snakes hiss.)

Build Oral Language

REVIEW GENRE: EXPOSITORY TEXT Have children tell the key features of expository text: It tells facts about something real. Explain that today you will read about how some real animals take care of themselves in "When Animals Are Doctors," by Deborah Churchman.

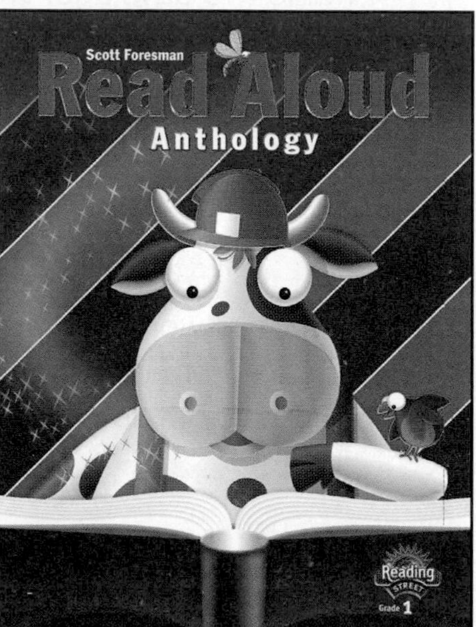

"When Animals Are Doctors"

MONITOR LISTENING COMPREHENSION Recall that in *Animal Park,* the wild animals do things such as run fast, hunt, and swim. Have children listen to "When Animals Are Doctors" to find out what some other wild animals do to stay healthy.

Team Talk **TALK ABOUT WATCHING WILD ANIMALS** Read aloud the first three paragraphs of "When Animals Are Doctors." Display it on the board if possible, and track the print as you read.

- Have partners generate questions about how watching animals helps us learn more about them.
- Add words generated in the discussion to the concept map.

Build Oral Vocabulary

Amazing Words Robust Vocabulary Routine

1. **Introduce the Word** Relate the word *medicine* to the story. A doctor gives you *medicine* if you're sick. Supply a child-friendly definition. *Medicine* is something that helps you feel better or makes you well. Have children say the word.

2. **Demonstrate** Provide examples to show meaning. My doctor gave me *medicine* for my sore throat. Never take *medicine* without an adult present. Scientists work to discover new *medicines.*

3. **Apply** Have children demonstrate their understanding. Describe a time when your parents helped you take *medicine.*

4. **Display the Word** Run your hand under the chunks *med-i-cine* as you read the word.

See p. OV•6 to teach *poisonous.*

Routines Flip Chart

ADD TO THE CONCEPT MAP Discuss how animals take care of themselves.

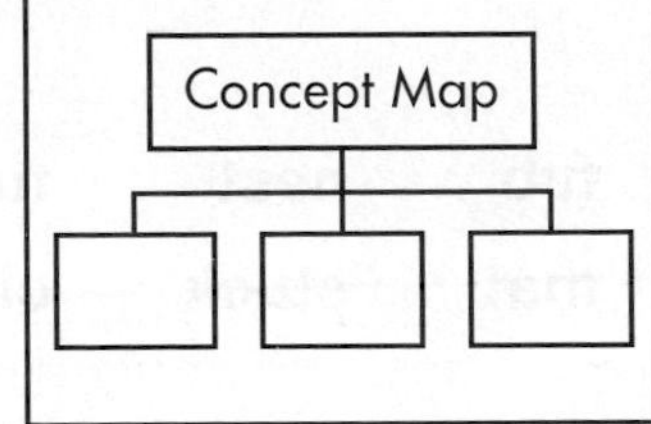

- We just read about something else we can find out about wild animals by watching them. We can learn how they stay healthy. Where can we add that to our concept map?
- What unusual thing do elephants eat? (mud) Why do they eat it? (to get minerals) Let's add to our concept map *elephants eat mud.*
- What unusual thing do macaws eat? (clay) Why do they eat that? (The clay keeps poisonous food from harming them.) Let's add *macaws eat clay* to our concept map.

Amazing Words

desert	silent
forest	snort
world	medicine
chatter	poisonous

Access for All

Advanced

Extend Amazing Words Ask questions such as the following:

- Why do scientists work to discover new *medicines* for animals?
- Why is it important to keep animals away from *poisonous* plants?

Encourage children to use the words in discussion and writing.

Produce Oral Language Use the Day 4 instruction on ELL Poster 6 to extend and enrich language.

Support Listening To prepare children for vocabulary they will encounter in "When Animals Are Doctors," demonstrate the words *swallow, nibble,* and *chew.* Then point out and/or explain *foot, stomach,* and *bone.* Have children repeat the words after you.

Common Core State Standards

Foundational Skills 2.b. Orally produce single-syllable words by blending sounds (phonemes), including consonant blends. **Foundational Skills 2.c.** Isolate and pronounce initial, medial vowel, and final sounds (phonemes) in spoken single-syllable words. **Foundational Skills 3.** Know and apply grade-level phonics and word analysis skills in decoding words.

Phonemic Awareness

Distinguish /u/

MODEL This week we read about how hippos sit in mud. Listen as I say the three sounds in *mud.* Slowly model the sounds in *mud:* /m/ /u/ /d/. The middle sound in *mud* is /u/. Now we're going to say some other words and listen for the sound /u/.

GUIDE PRACTICE I will say a word. Repeat the word after me. Raise your hand if you hear the /u/ sound at the beginning of the word.

Corrective feedback | If children make an error, segment the word and model the correct response. Return to the word later in the practice.

up	**it**	**uneven**	**ever**	**umpire**
apple	**uncle**	**odd**	**unsafe**	**use**

Now I will say some more words. Repeat each word after me. Raise your hand if you hear the /u/ sound in the middle of the word.

Corrective feedback | If children make an error, segment the word and model the correct response. Return to the word later in the practice.

tub	**nest**	**tusk**	**dunk**	**milk**
mat	**stuck**	**club**	**stop**	**bud**

ON THEIR OWN Have children say each word and tell if they hear the /u/ sound at the beginning or in the middle of the word.

hut	**undo**	**trust**	**upon**	**hunt**
us	**brush**	**run**	**usher**	**skunk**

Phonics

Review Short *e* Spelled *e*; Initial Consonant Blends

REVIEW SHORT *e* SPELLED *e* To review last week's first phonics skill, write *pen.* You studied words like this one last week. What do you know about the vowel sound you hear in *pen?* (The vowel sound is /e/ spelled *e.*)

Corrective feedback	If children are unable to answer your question about the short *e* sound in *pen,* refer them to Sound-Spelling Card 6.

REVIEW INITIAL CONSONANT BLENDS To review last week's second phonics skill, write *trip.* You also studied words like this. What do you know about the consonant sounds you hear at the beginning of *trip?* (You blend the sounds /t/ and /r/ together.)

Corrective feedback	If children are unable to answer your question about the initial consonant blend in *trip,* refer them to Sound-Spelling Card 41.

GUIDE PRACTICE Draw a T-chart or use Graphic Organizer 4. Write *Short e* and *Not Short e* as headings. When I say a word, hold a hand up high if it has a short *e* sound, or shake your head no if it does not have a short *e: net, six, sled, dress, bug, grill, step, black, ten, snap.* Write each word in the appropriate column. Then have children identify which words have initial consonant blends and underline them. Finally, have children read the lists aloud.

Short *e*	Not Short *e*
net	six
<u>sled</u>	bug
<u>dress</u>	<u>grill</u>
<u>step</u>	<u>black</u>
ten	<u>snap</u>

Graphic Organizer 4

ON THEIR OWN Use Let's Practice It! pp. 67–68 on the *Teacher Resources DVD-ROM.*

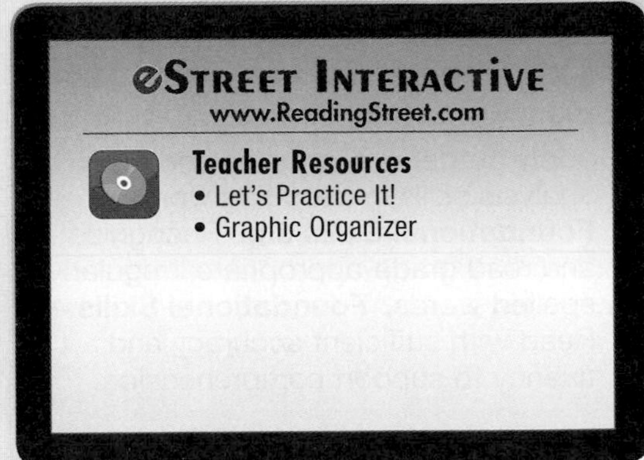

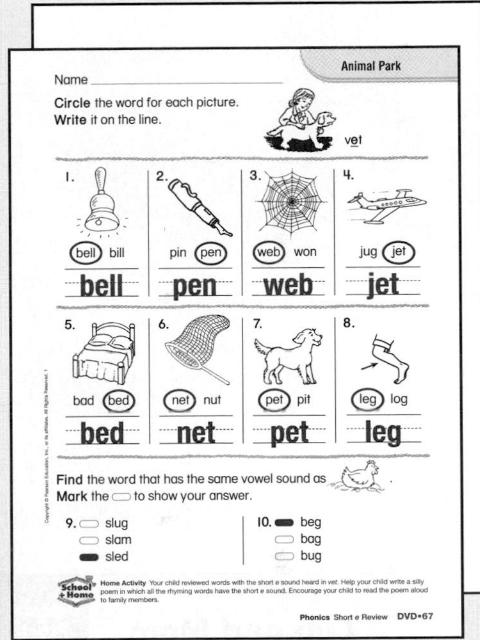
Animal Park

Name

Circle the word for each picture. Write it on the line.

vet

1. bell bill — bell
2. pin pen — pen
3. web won — web
4. jug jet — jet
5. bad bed — bed
6. net nut — net
7. pet pit — pet
8. leg log — leg

Find the word that has the same vowel sound as [picture]. Mark the ⊂⊃ to show your answer.

9. slug / slam / sled
10. beg / bag / bug

Phonics Short e Review DVD•67

Let's Practice It! TR DVD•67–68

Initial Consonant Blends Consonant blends in English words are often challenging for English learners because their home languages may not combine consonant phonemes in similar ways at the beginnings of words. For example, Spanish speakers may add the sound /e/ at the beginning of words with *s*-blends, saying "esled, estep," etc.

Common Core State Standards

Foundational Skills 3. Know and apply grade-level phonics and word analysis skills in decoding words. **Foundational Skills 3.g.** Recognize and read grade-appropriate irregularly spelled words. **Foundational Skills 4.** Read with sufficient accuracy and fluency to support comprehension.

Decodable Reader 6C

If children need help, then...

Read *Cub and Mom at the Pond*

DECODE WORDS IN ISOLATION Have children turn to page 233 and decode each word listed.

REVIEW HIGH-FREQUENCY WORDS Review the previously taught words *a, the, home,* and *many.* Have children read each word as you point to it on the Word Wall.

PREVIEW Have children read the title and preview the story. Tell them they will read words with the short *u* sound and consonant blends in the story.

DECODE WORDS IN CONTEXT Pair children for reading and listen as they decode. One child begins. Children read the entire story, switching readers after each page. Partners reread the story. This time the other child begins.

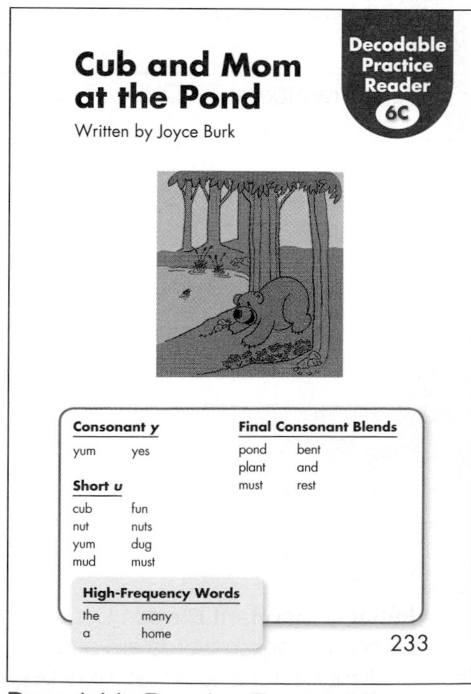

Cub and Mom at the Pond
Written by Joyce Burk
Decodable Practice Reader 6C
Consonant y
yum yes
Short u
cub fun
nut nuts
yum dug
mud must
Final Consonant Blends
pond bent
plant and
must rest
High-Frequency Words
the many
a home
233

Decodable Practice Reader 6C

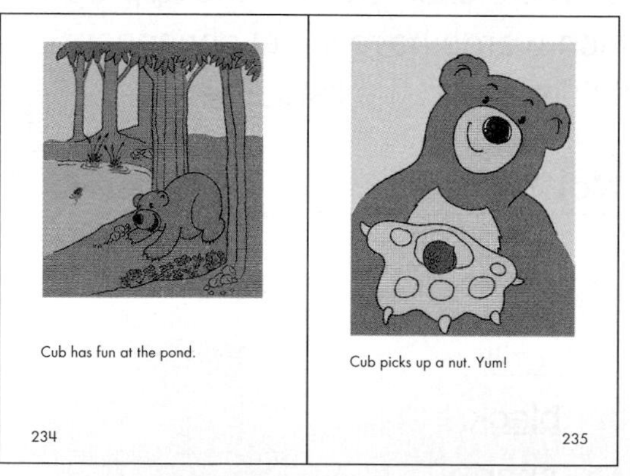

Cub has fun at the pond.
234
Cub picks up a nut. Yum!
235

Mom has many nuts. Yum! Yum!
236
Mom bent.
Mom dug in the mud.
237

Yes, Mom can get the plant.
238
Cub and Mom must rest.
239

Cub and Mom can nap at home.
240

Corrective feedback	**If...** children have difficulty decoding a word, **then...** refer them to the Sound-Spelling Cards to identify the sounds in the word. Then prompt them to blend the word. • What is the new word? • Is the new word a word you know? • Does it make sense in the story?

CHECK DECODING AND COMPREHENSION Have children retell the story to include characters, setting, and events. Then have children locate words that have the short *u* sound and words that end with consonant blends in the story. List words that children name. Children should supply *Cub, fun, pond, up, yum, nut, bent, dug, mud, plant, must,* and *rest.* Ask children how they know that some of these words end with consonant blends and some have the short *u* sound. (There are two consonants together at the end of some of the words and some words have the letter *u* in them.)

Reread for Fluency

REREAD DECODABLE READER Have children reread Decodable Practice Reader 6C to develop automaticity decoding words with the short *u* sound and final consonant blends.

Routine Oral Rereading

1. **Read** Have children read the entire book orally.
2. **Reread** To achieve optimal fluency, children should reread the text three or four times.
3. **Corrective Feedback** Listen as children read. Provide corrective feedback regarding their fluency and decoding.

Routines Flip Chart

ELL

Decodable Practice Reader

Beginning Before children read, lead them through *Cub and Mom at the Pond.* Ask them to identify Cub and Mom. Point out words with the short *u* sound and those with final consonant blends and say them aloud. Have children repeat them after you.

Intermediate Refer children to the list of words with final consonant blends and those with the short *u* sound. Have them choose words and ask them to use them in sentences.

Advanced Have children read a sentence and then use an illustration to elaborate on it. For example, "Cub and his mom have had a busy day. They are both tired because they are yawning. They will take a nap now."

Fluent Word Reading

Spiral Review

READ WORDS IN ISOLATION Display these words. Tell children that they can blend some words on this list, and others are Word Wall words.

Have children read the list three or four times until they can read at the rate of two to three seconds per word.

cluck	**saw**	**red**	**small**	**was**
that	**big**	**tree**	**your**	**sled**
five	**green**	**like**	**pond**	**hens**
stuck	**see**	**frogs**	**Fran**	**where**

Corrective feedback — Word Reading

If... children have difficulty reading whole words,
then... have them use sound-by-sound blending for decodable words, or have them say and spell high-frequency words.

If... children cannot read fluently at a rate of two to three seconds per word,
then... have pairs practice the list until they can read it fluently.

READ WORDS IN CONTEXT Display these sentences. Call on individuals to read a sentence. Then randomly point to review words and have children read them. To help you monitor word reading, high-frequency words are underlined and decodable words are italicized.

I like to see *frogs at* the *pond*.
***Fran* saw your small green tree.**
***"Cluck, cluck," went* the five *red hens*.**
Where was that *big sled stuck*?

Corrective feedback — Sentence Reading

If... children are unable to read an underlined high-frequency word,
then... read the word for them and spell it, having them echo you.

If... children have difficulty reading an italicized decodable word,
then... guide them in using sound-by-sound blending.

Common Core State Standards

Foundational Skills 3. Know and apply grade-level phonics and word analysis skills in decoding words. **Language 2.d.** Use conventional spelling for words with common spelling patterns and for frequently occurring irregular words.

Spiral Review

These activities review

- previously taught high-frequency words *that, see, to, like, saw, your, small, green, tree, five, where, was.*
- short vowels, initial blends, and /k/ spelled *-ck.*

Spelling

Short *u* Words with Final Consonant Blends

PARTNER REVIEW Supply pairs of children with index cards on which the spelling words have been written. Have one child read a word while the other writes it. Then have children switch roles. Have them use the cards to check their spelling and correct any misspelled words.

ON THEIR OWN Use *Reader's and Writer's Notebook,* p. 215.

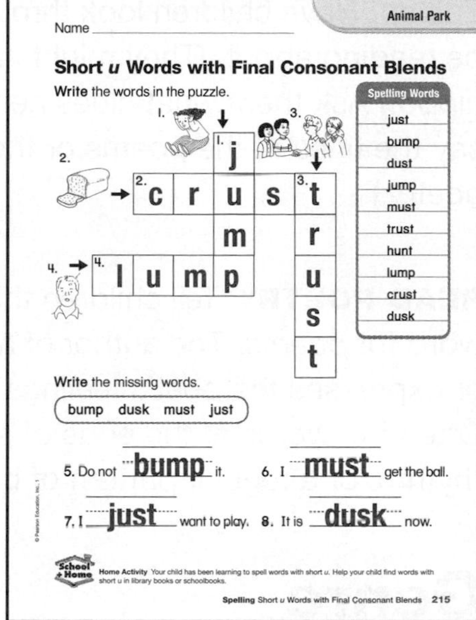
Animal Park

Name

Short *u* Words with Final Consonant Blends

Write the words in the puzzle.

Spelling Words: just, bump, dust, jump, must, trust, hunt, lump, crust, dusk

1. jump
2. crust
3. trust
4. lump

Write the missing words.

bump dusk must just

5. Do not bump it.
6. I must get the ball.
7. I just want to play.
8. It is dusk now.

Home Activity Your child has been learning to spell words with short u. Help your child find words with short u in library books or schoolbooks.

Spelling Short u Words with Final Consonant Blends 215

Reader's and Writer's Notebook, p. 215

eStreet Interactive
www.ReadingStreet.com

Teacher Resources
- Reader's and Writer's Notebook

ELL

Fluent Word Reading Have children listen to a more fluent reader say the words. Then have them repeat the words.

Day 4 SMALL GROUP TIME • Differentiate Vocabulary, p. SG•86

OL On-Level	SI Strategic Intervention	A Advanced
• **Develop** Language Using Selection Vocabulary • **Read** *Reading Street Sleuth,* pp. 18–19	• **Review/Discuss** Selection Vocabulary • **Read** *Reading Street Sleuth,* pp. 18–19	• **Extend** Amazing Words and Selection Vocabulary • **Read** *Reading Street Sleuth,* pp. 18–19 • **Organize** Inquiry Project

ELL

If... children need more scaffolding and practice with **Vocabulary, then...** use the routine on pp. xxxvi–xxxvii in the *ELL Handbook.*

Common Core State Standards

Literature 4. Identify words and phrases in stories or poems that suggest feelings or appeal to the senses. **Literature 10.** With prompting and support, read prose and poetry of appropriate complexity for grade 1.

Poetry in Reading

Poetry

ACTIVATE PRIOR KNOWLEDGE Ask children to name some of the animals they read about this week. (hippos, elephants, zebras) Ask where the animals lived. (in an animal park; in Africa)

PREVIEW AND PREDICT Have children turn to page 168 in their Student Edition. Have children look through the selection and predict what they might be reading about. (They might say: Poems about a dog, a raccoon, and a hippo.) Ask them what clues helped them make their predictions. (They might say the titles of the poems or the pictures and recall some of the elements of poetry.)

READ POETRY Tell children that they will read poetry. *Poetry* is another word for *poems.* The author of a poem is called a poet. A poem tells a story or expresses the poet's feelings about something. A poem is written in lines. Often the words at the ends of some lines rhyme. A poem usually has a rhythm, or a regular pattern of beats.

Genre

LET'S THINK ABOUT... As you read the poetry selections together, use Let's Think About in the Student Edition to help children focus on features of poems.

1. In the poem "My Dog Rags," the words *Rags, sags, wags,* and *zags* rhyme. In the poem "Raccoon," the words *clan* and *can* rhyme; so do *eat* and *treat.* In the poem "The Hippo," the words *float* and *boat* rhyme, and the words *retreats* and *eat* rhyme.

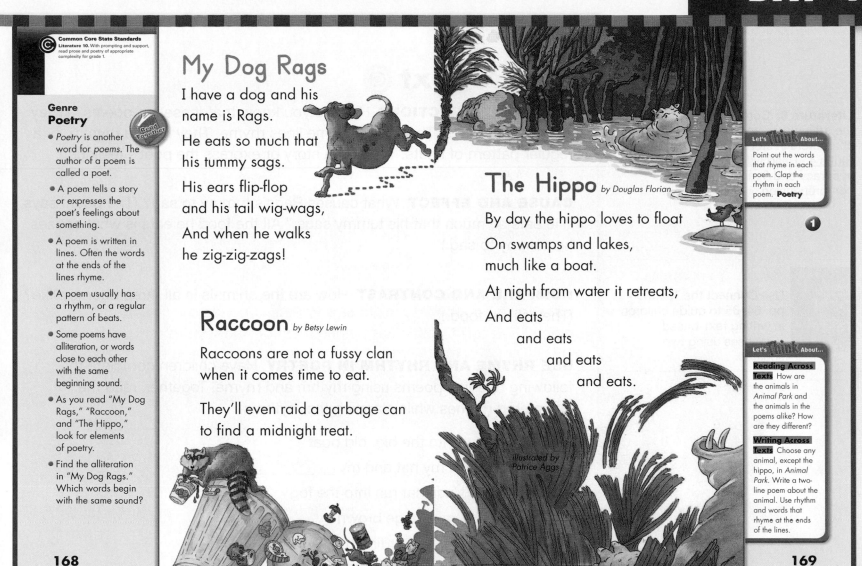

Common Core State Standards
Literature 10. With prompting and support, read prose and poetry of appropriate complexity for grade 1.

Genre
Poetry

Read Together

- *Poetry* is another word for *poems*. The author of a poem is called a poet.
- A poem tells a story or expresses the poet's feelings about something.
- A poem is written in lines. Often the words at the ends of the lines rhyme.
- A poem usually has a rhythm, or a regular pattern of beats.
- Some poems have alliteration, or words close to each other with the same beginning sound.
- As you read "My Dog Rags," "Raccoon," and "The Hippo," look for elements of poetry.
- Find the alliteration in "My Dog Rags." Which words begin with the same sound?

168

My Dog Rags

I have a dog and his
name is Rags.
He eats so much that
his tummy sags.
His ears flip-flop
and his tail wig-wags,
And when he walks
he zig-zig-zags!

Raccoon *by Betsy Lewin*

Raccoons are not a fussy clan
when it comes time to eat.

They'll even raid a garbage can
to find a midnight treat.

The Hippo *by Douglas Florian*

By day the hippo loves to float
On swamps and lakes,
much like a boat.
At night from water it retreats,
And eats
and eats
and eats
and eats.

illustrated by Patrice Aggs

Let's Think About...
Point out the words that rhyme in each poem. Clap the rhythm in each poem. **Poetry**

1

Let's Think About...
Reading Across Texts How are the animals in *Animal Park* and the animals in the poems alike? How are they different?
Writing Across Texts Choose any animal, except the hippo, in *Animal Park*. Write a two-line poem about the animal. Use rhythm and words that rhyme at the ends of the lines.

169

Student Edition, pp. 168–169

Access Text

Think Aloud **MONITOR AND CLARIFY** When I read "My Dog Rags," I wonder what "he zig-zig-zags" means. How can I find out? I look at the picture for a clue. I see that Rags walks first one way, then the other way, then back again, over and over.

VISUALIZE When I read "The Hippo," I imagine what the hippo looks like. I see a picture in my mind of a happy hippo floating on a swamp.

Academic Vocabulary

rhythm a beat that repeats

Science Vocabulary

swamp wetlands with trees and grass growing out of water

Common Core State Standards

Literature 9. Compare and contrast the adventures and experiences of characters in stories. **Foundational Skills 4.** Read with sufficient accuracy and fluency to support comprehension.

Writing to Sources

Use Connect the Texts on pp. 64–65 to guide children in writing text-based responses using two sources.

Access Text

CONFIRM PREDICTIONS How do you know that these are poems? (They are written in lines. The ends of some lines rhyme. They have a rhythm, or a regular pattern of beats. They tell a story or express the poet's feelings.)

CAUSE AND EFFECT What causes Rags's tummy to sag? (The poem says "He eats so much that his tummy sags." All the food he eats is what causes his tummy to sag.)

COMPARE AND CONTRAST How are the animals in all three poems alike? (They all eat food.)

USE RHYME AND RHYTHM IN POETRY Have children complete the following two-line poems using rhythm and rhyme. Together, read the completed rhymes while clapping the rhythms.

I walked onto the big, old boat
Dressed in my hat and my ____________.
The big black cat ran into the fog
Followed by a large brown ____________.
You will never, ever find me
Hiding behind the big oak ____________.

Reading and Writing Across Texts

Have children use pictures, words, and sentences to tell how the animals in the poems and *Animal Park* are alike and different.

Children might write *Big birds run; in the hot sun!*

Fluency

Appropriate Phrasing

- Have children turn to page 161 in *Animal Park.*
- Have children follow along as you read the page with appropriate phrasing.
- Have the class read the page with you and then reread the page as a group without you until they read with appropriate phrasing. To provide additional fluency practice, pair nonfluent readers with fluent readers.

Routine Paired Reading

1. **Select a Passage** For *Animal Park,* use page 162.
2. **Model** First, have children track the print as you read.
3. **Guide Practice** Then have children read along with you.
4. **On Their Own** For optimal fluency, have partners reread three or four times.

Routines Flip Chart

MONITOR PROGRESS Fluency Check

As children reread, monitor their progress toward their individual fluency goals. Mid-Year Goal: 20–30 words correct per minute. End-of-Year Goal: 60 words correct per minute. Beginning in Unit 3, children will be assessed to determine WCPM.

If... children are not on track to meet benchmark goals,
then... have children practice with text at their independent level.

Access for All

Advanced

Rate If children already read at 60 words correct per minute, have them read more challenging text.

Options for Oral Rereading

Use *Animal Park* or one of this week's Decodable Practice Readers.

Conventions

Exclamatory Sentences

TEST PRACTICE Use *Reader's and Writer's Notebook,* p. 216 to help children understand exclamatory sentences in test items. Recall that an exclamatory sentence shows strong feeling. It begins with a capital letter and ends with an exclamation mark: *That baby elephant is so cute!* Model identifying an exclamatory sentence by writing this sentence on the board, reading it aloud, and underlining the capital letter and the exclamation mark.

My truck got stuck in mud!

ON THEIR OWN Read the directions on *Reader's and Writer's Notebook,* p. 216. Guide children as they mark the answer for number 1.

APPLY After children mark the answers to numbers 1–6, review the correct choices aloud. Have children read each exclamatory sentence with the proper intonation.

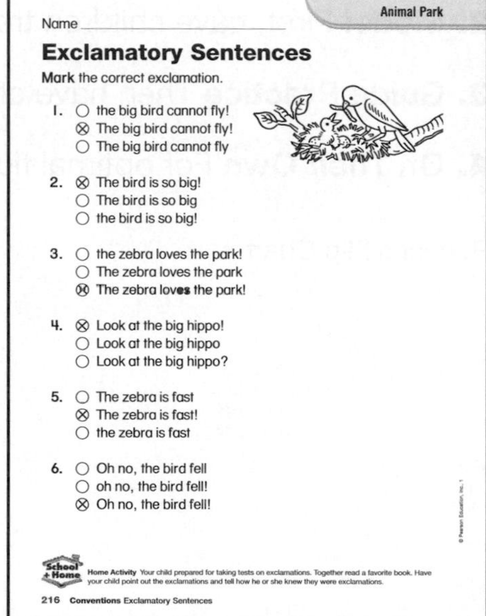
Animal Park

Name

Exclamatory Sentences

Mark the correct exclamation.

1. ○ the big bird cannot fly!
⊗ The big bird cannot fly!
○ The big bird cannot fly

2. ⊗ The bird is so big!
○ The bird is so big
○ the bird is so big!

3. ○ the zebra loves the park!
○ The zebra loves the park
⊗ The zebra loves the park!

4. ⊗ Look at the big hippo!
○ Look at the big hippo
○ Look at the big hippo?

5. ○ The zebra is fast
⊗ The zebra is fast!
○ the zebra is fast

6. ○ Oh no, the bird fell
○ oh no, the bird fell!
⊗ Oh no, the bird fell!

School + Home **Home Activity** Your child prepared for taking tests on exclamations. Together read a favorite book. Have your child point out the exclamations and tell how he or she knew they were exclamations.

216 **Conventions** Exclamatory Sentences

Reader's and Writer's Notebook, p. 216

Common Core State Standards

Foundational Skills 1.a. Recognize the distinguishing features of a sentence (e.g., first word, capitalization, ending punctuation). **Writing 2.** Write informative/explanatory texts in which they name a topic, supply some facts about the topic, and provide some sense of closure. **Language 1.j.** Produce and expand complete simple and compound declarative, interrogative, imperative, and exclamatory sentences in response to prompts. **Language 2.** Demonstrate command of the conventions of standard English capitalization, punctuation, and spelling when writing. **Language 2.b.** Use end punctuation for sentences.

Bridge to Common Core

CONVENTIONS OF STANDARD ENGLISH

In this unit, children have developed understanding of the concept of a sentence and they have studied declarative and interrogative sentences. In this lesson, they learn that an exclamatory sentence is a group of words that shows a strong feeling and ends with an exclamation mark. Children learn to produce exclamatory sentences with the conventions of standard English grammar, usage, and mechanics.

Daily Fix-It

7. did you jump onto the bus
Did you jump onto the bus?

8. Can you take the bus heme.
Can you take the bus home?

Discuss the Daily Fix-It corrections with children. Review the capitalization and punctuation of questions and the spelling of *home*.

Writing

Brief Composition

Mini-Lesson Writing for Tests: Know Your Purpose

- Yesterday we evaluated brief compositions about what people learn by watching wild animals. Today we will use what we learned from our evaluations to write another brief composition.

- When you don't have a lot of time to plan, write, revise, and edit a composition, it helps to know your **purpose,** or reason for writing. For example, my reason for writing a composition is to tell real things about a topic.

- Think Aloud Let's say I am choosing a topic for a composition about what people learn by watching wild animals. I am interested in writing about lions or about turtles. How can I choose which topic to write about? I know that my reason for writing a composition is to tell real things about my topic. I've never seen a lion. I like stories about lions, but I don't know many real things about them. Lions are probably not a good topic. What about turtles? I have seen turtles. I also know a few real things about them. I know that they have shells. I know that they live all over the world. I know that many of them live in water. Turtles would be a good topic for me.

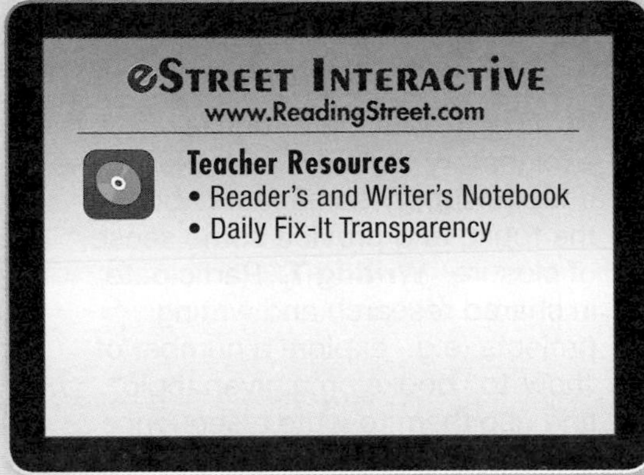

Access for All

SI Strategic Intervention

Test Formats Help children understand and follow the directions on the *Reader's and Writer's Notebook* test-practice page. Children will practice both the conventions skill and test-taking skills.

Capitalization of Titles Tell children that the title of a composition tells its topic. Be sure they understand that important words in a title are capitalized.

Common Core State Standards

Writing 2. Write informative/explanatory texts in which they name a topic, supply some facts about the topic, and provide some sense of closure. **Writing 7.** Participate in shared research and writing projects (e.g., explore a number of "how-to" books on a given topic and use them to write a sequence of instructions). **Writing 8.** With guidance and support from adults, recall information from experiences or gather information from provided sources to answer a question.

Writing

Zoom in on ©

WRITE Review with children the key features of a brief composition. Then have children get paper and pencil ready to take a writing test. Display the writing prompt and give children time to write to it. Remind children to allow themselves a few minutes after writing to reread what they have written and make changes or additions.

Writing Prompt

Write a composition telling what you know about a kind of animal you have seen outside or at a zoo.

Routine Quick Write for Fluency

Team Talk

1. **Talk** Have children discuss which animals they would like to see at an animal park.
2. **Write** Have each child write a sentence about the animal they would most like to see.
3. **Share** Partners trade sentences and read them aloud.

Routines Flip Chart

Research and Inquiry

Step 4 Synthesize

TEACH Tell children that the next step in their project is to review their notes to see if they have the information they set out to find. Or, do their notes contain information that is not about their animal.

Think Aloud **MODEL** We observed an animal and wrote notes about what we observed to help us remember. Now I will look at the notes I made. I will see if all my notes are about my animal. If some of the notes are about other animals or other things I observed, I will cross them out. I will also check my spelling. If a word is not spelled correctly, I will write the word again with the correct spelling.

GUIDE PRACTICE Have children look at the notes they made during Day 3. Instruct them to work with a partner to go over their notes. Remind children to be sure all their notes are about their animal and that the words are spelled correctly. Finally, tell children that tomorrow they will organize their notes in order to share them with others.

ON THEIR OWN Use *Reader's and Writer's Notebook,* p. 210.

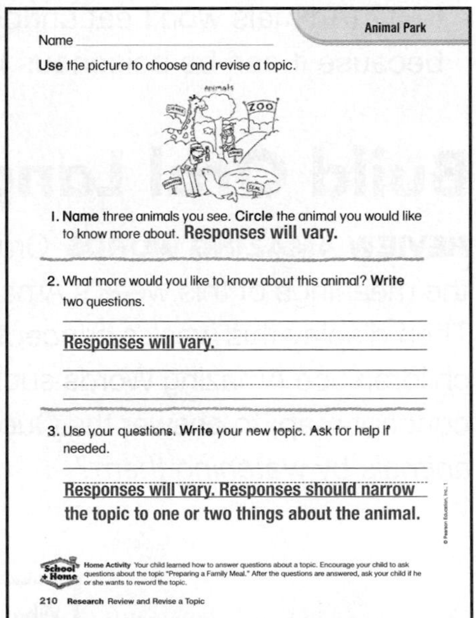
Animal Park

Name ______________

Use the picture to choose and revise a topic.

1. **Name** three animals you see. **Circle** the animal you would like to know more about. **Responses will vary.**

2. What more would you like to know about this animal? **Write** two questions.

Responses will vary.

3. Use your questions. **Write** your new topic. Ask for help if needed.

Responses will vary. Responses should narrow the topic to one or two things about the animal.

© Pearson Education, Inc., 1

School + Home **Home Activity** Your child learned how to answer questions about a topic. Encourage your child to ask questions about the topic "Preparing a Family Meal." After the questions are answered, ask your child if he or she wants to reword the topic.

210 **Research** Review and Revise a Topic

Reader's and Writer's Notebook, p. 210

Access for All

SI Strategic Intervention

Check Spelling If children have difficulty deciding if a word is spelled correctly, give them time to check the spelling by looking up the word in a dictionary.

Wrap Up Your Day!

✔ **Phonics Review** List several words with the short *u* sound spelled *u* and final consonant blends, such as *must* and *dump.* Have children read each word and identify the letter that spells the sound /u/.

✔ **Fluency** Write *Can Bud run back? At last!* Have the class reread the sentences until they can do so with appropriate phrasing.

Remind children that they heard about animals that are like doctors. Tomorrow they will hear about these animals again.

DAY 5 at a Glance

Content Knowledge
Oral Vocabulary

Phonemic Awareness
Review Segment and Blend Onset and Rime

Phonics/Spelling
Review Short *u: u*
Review Final Consonant Blends

Text-Based Comprehension
Review Cause and Effect

Selection Words
Review

High-Frequency Words
Review

Assessment
Phonics
High-Frequency Words
Fluency

Conventions
Review Exclamatory Sentences

Writing
Brief Composition: Proofread

Research and Inquiry
Communicate

Materials
- Student Edition
- Read Aloud Anthology
- Weekly Test

Bridge to Common Core

INTEGRATION OF KNOWLEDGE/IDEAS
Throughout the lessons in the unit, children have acquired knowledge about animals. In this lesson, they explored the topic of watching wild animals. They have developed a wide base of knowledge for the unit topic of Animals, Tame and Wild.

Science Knowledge Goals
Children have learned that
- we can learn about animals by watching them
- wild animals need food, water, and shelter
- we protect animals from danger

Content Knowledge

Watching Wild Animals

REVIEW THE CONCEPT This week we have read and listened to stories about wild animals and the things they do. Today you will listen to find out how watching what wild animals eat helps us understand more about them. Read the article.

- Why won't most wild animals eat unripe fruit? (Animals won't eat unripe fruit because it can be poisonous.)

"When Animals Are Doctors"

Build Oral Language

REVIEW AMAZING WORDS Orally review the meanings of this week's Amazing Words. Then display this week's concept map. Have children use Amazing Words such as *desert, snort,* and *poisonous,* as well as the concept map, to answer the Question of the Week, *What can we learn about wild animals by watching them?*

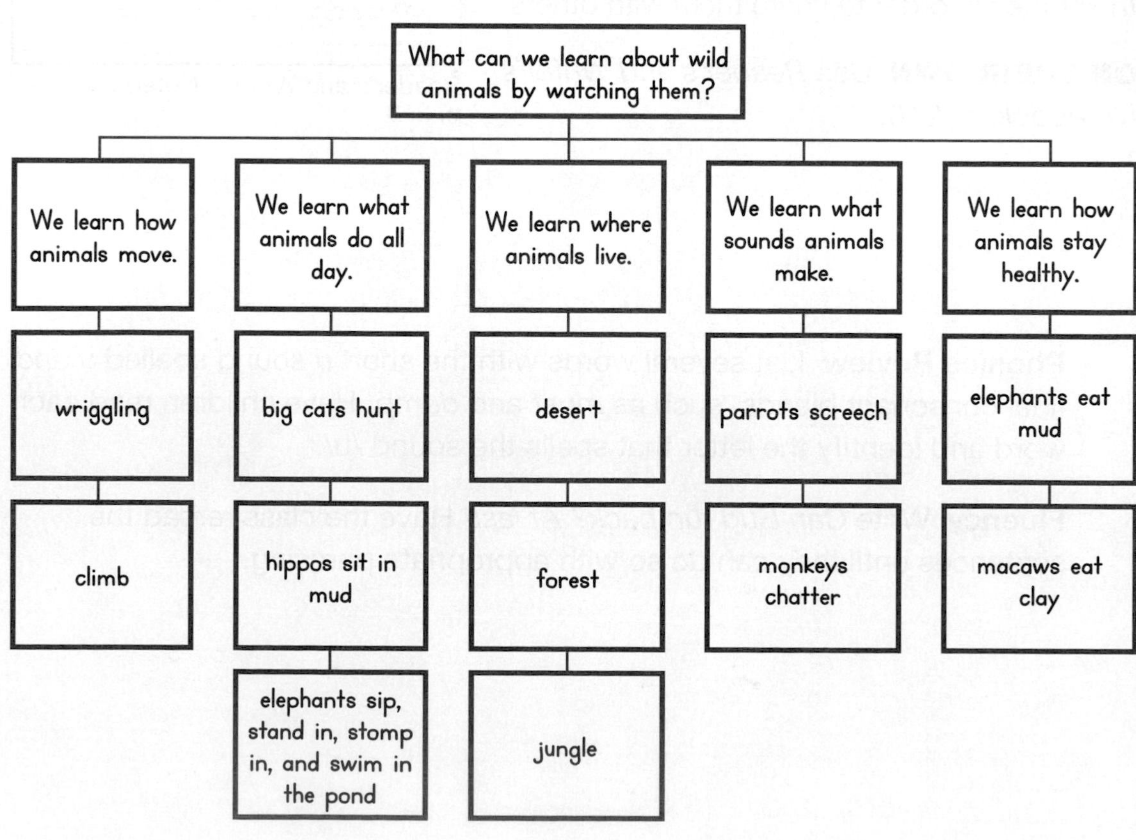

Build Oral Vocabulary

Team Talk **CONNECT TO AMAZING IDEAS** Pair children and have them discuss how the Question of the Week, *What can we learn about wild animals by watching them?,* connects to the question of this unit of study: *How are people and animals important to one another?* Tell children to use the concept map and what they've learned from this week's discussions and reading selections to form an Amazing Idea—a realization or "big idea" about **animals, tame and wild.** Use the following ideas as prompts:

- What are some wild animals we read about? (elephants, zebras, big birds, lions)
- What is something you learn about an elephant by watching it?

Then ask each pair to share their Amazing Idea with the class. Encourage children to recall in which selection they learned their ideas.

Amazing Ideas might include:

- People can protect the places where wild animals live.
- Knowing what plants are poisonous to animals can help people stay safe too.

MONITOR PROGRESS Check Oral Vocabulary

FORMATIVE ASSESSMENT Call on individuals to use this week's Amazing Words to talk about what we learn by watching wild animals. Prompt discussion with the questions below. Monitor children's ability to use the Amazing Words and note which words children are unable to use.

- **What animals could you observe in a *forest*? in a *desert*?**
- **Where in the *world* would you go to see zebras and hippos?**
- **Why do you think some animals *chatter*?**
- **When are animals likely to be *silent*?**
- **What would you do if you heard an animal *snort* nearby?**
- **What kinds of *medicine* do some animals use to protect themselves from *poisonous* foods?**

If... children have difficulty using the Amazing Words,

then... reteach the unknown words using the Robust Vocabulary routines, pp. 147a, 152b, 164b, 168b.

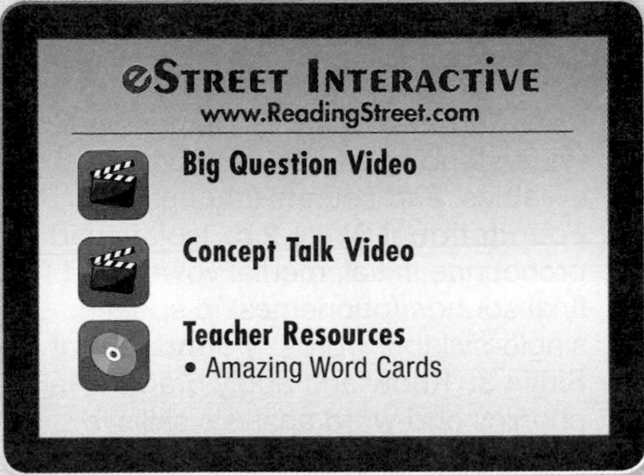

Amazing Words

desert	silent
forest	snort
world	medicine
chatter	poisonous

Check Concepts and Language Use the Day 5 instruction on ELL Poster 6 to monitor children's understanding of the lesson concept.

Amazing Words Provide a sentence frame to help children answer each question, for example: *I could see animals in a ________.*

Common Core State Standards

Foundational Skills 2. Demonstrate understanding of spoken words, syllables, and sounds (phonemes). **Foundational Skills 2.c.** Isolate and pronounce initial, medial vowel, and final sounds (phonemes) in spoken single-syllable words. **Foundational Skills 3.** Know and apply grade-level phonics and word analysis skills in decoding words. **Foundational Skills 3.b.** Decode regularly spelled one-syllable words. **Language 2.d.** Use conventional spelling for words with common spelling patterns and for frequently occurring irregular words.

Access for All

SI Strategic Intervention

Reteach Use sound-to-sound spelling to model blending *bug.* Write *b* and say its sound /b/. Then write *u* and say its sound /u/. Write *g* and say its sound /g/. Then blend the whole word, pointing to each letter as you say its sound.

Phonemic Awareness

Review Segment and Blend Onset and Rime

ONSET AND RIME Have children repeat the onset and rime for each word. Then have them blend the sounds to say the word. If children make an error, model the correct response. Return to the word later in the practice.

/b/ -ug	**bug**	/t/ /r/ -ust	**trust**	/h/ -elp	**help**
/s/ /t/ -ump	**stump**	/b/ -and	**band**	/k/ -ut	**cut**
/d/ -esk	**desk**	/f/ -un	**fun**	/m/ -ilk	**milk**

Phonics

Review Short *u: u;* Final Consonant Blends

TARGET PHONICS SKILLS Write the following sentences on the board. Have children read each one, first quietly to themselves and then aloud as you track the print.

1. **His pup can run fast.**
2. **An ant will step in sand.**
3. **The small bug will drift in the tub.**
4. **Six frogs rest at the pond.**

Team Talk Have children discuss with a partner which words have short *u* spelled *u* and which words have a final consonant blend. Then call on individuals to share with the class.

Spelling Test

Short *u* Words with Final Consonant Blends

DICTATE SPELLING WORDS Say each word, read the sentence, repeat the word, and allow time for children to write the word.

1. crust	The **crust** is the best part of the pie!
2. bump	I fell and got a **bump** on my head.
3. jump	How high can you **jump?**
4. must	I **must** study for the test.
5. just	It is **just** a movie.
6. dust	Can you **dust** the books?
7. trust	I **trust** you to be fair.
8. dusk	It is **dusk** after the sun sets.
9. hunt	Can we **hunt** for my blue socks?
10. lump	I fell on a **lump** of dirt in my yard.

High-Frequency Words

11. many	I saw **many** animals at the zoo.
12. into	I put my toys **into** the box.

Assess

- Spell short *u* words with final consonant blends.
- Spell high-frequency words.

Access for All

Extend Spelling Have children look through the main selection and find as many words as they can with final consonant blends. List the words that children find. Then ask children to write a sentence for each word.

Day 5 SMALL GROUP TIME • Differentiate Reteaching, p. SG•86

OL On-Level

- **Practice** Exclamatory Sentences
- **Reread** *Reading Street Sleuth,* pp. 18–19

SI Strategic Intervention

- **Review** High-Frequency Words
- **Reread** *Reading Street Sleuth,* pp. 18–19

A Advanced

- **Extend** Exclamatory Sentences
- **Reread** *Reading Street Sleuth,* pp. 18–19
- **Communicate** Inquiry Project

If... children need more scaffolding and practice with **Conventions and Writing,**
then... use the activities on pp. DI•125–DI•126 in the Teacher Resources section on SuccessNet.

Common Core State Standards
Speaking/Listening 4. Describe people, places, things, and events with relevant details, expressing ideas and feelings clearly. **Also Foundational Skills 4.b.**

First, I write the letter. Then I put it in the envelope. After I write the address on the envelope, I add a stamp. Then I...

Let's Learn It!

Read Together

READING STREET ONLINE
VOCABULARY ACTIVITIES
www.ReadingStreet.com

Get Ready For Grade 2

Be a good listener when you follow directions.

Listening and Speaking

Follow, Restate, Give Directions When we follow directions, we use good listening skills. We ask the speaker questions. We repeat the directions to show we understand.

Practice It! Listen to your teacher's directions on how to mail a letter. Restate the directions. Then give new directions to a partner. Use sentences.

Vocabulary

An **antonym** is a word that means the opposite of another word.

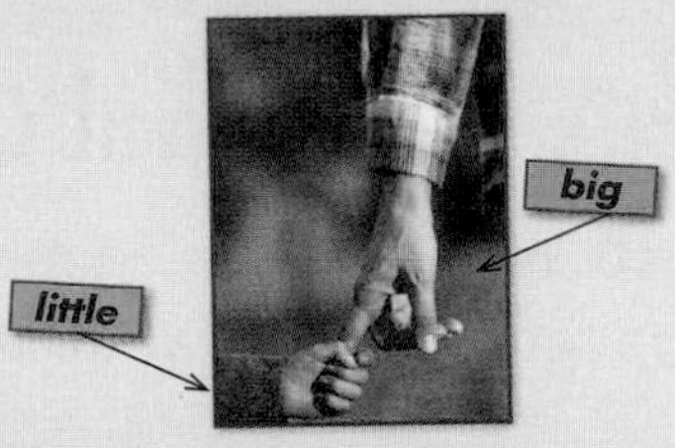

big

little

Practice It! Read these words. Write and say an antonym for each word.

fast in up on back

Fluency

Appropriate Phrasing When you come to a question mark as you read, make your voice go up as if you are asking a question.

Practice It!

1. Can Gus put his frogs into the pond?
2. Where will Bud go to swim?
3. Will the dog run with them at last?

170 171

Student Edition, pp. 170–171

Foundational Skills 4.b. Read on-level text orally with accuracy, appropriate rate, and expression on successive readings. **Speaking/ Listening 4.** Describe people, places, things, and events with relevant details, expressing ideas and feelings clearly. **Also Speaking/Listening 1., 6., Language 5.**

Give and Follow Directions

Children at Grade 2 should be able to give and follow directions of four or more steps.

Listening and Speaking

Give Directions

TEACH Have children turn to page 170 of the Student Edition. Read and discuss the directions the child in the photo is giving. Remind children that good speakers speak in complete sentences. Point out the sequence words *First* and *Then.* Remind children that when we give directions, we tell the steps in order. Ask children what other sequence word they see in the directions. *(After)* Then have them tell, in order, the steps the boy followed to get his letter ready to mail.

INTRODUCE PROMPT Read the Practice It! prompt with the class. Remind children that good listeners listen carefully to directions and ask questions about anything that is unclear.

Team Talk Have children think of something simple that they know how to do well. Ask them to give the directions orally to a partner. Remind them to use sequence words and to tell the steps in order.

Vocabulary

Antonyms

TEACH Read and discuss the Vocabulary lesson on page 171 of the Student Edition. Use the model to explain that antonyms are words that are opposites. Point to the photograph. What word describes the size of the adult's hand? *(big)* What word describes the size of the child's hand? *(little)* Because *big* and *little* have opposite meanings, we call them antonyms.

GUIDE PRACTICE Read the instructions for the Vocabulary Practice It! activity. Read the first word and then have children repeat after you.

I need to think of an antonym for the word *fast.* The opposite of *fast* is *slow.* So, I will write and say the word *slow.*

ON THEIR OWN Have partners continue writing and saying antonyms for the remaining words in the list.

Corrective feedback | Circulate around the room and listen as children say the antonyms. Provide assistance as needed.

Fluency

Appropriate Phrasing

TEACH Read and discuss the Fluency instructions.

READ WORDS IN CONTEXT Give children a moment to look at the sentences. Then have them read each sentence three or four times until they can read each sentence with appropriate phrasing.

Access for All

A Advanced

Visual Support Help children understand antonyms by demonstrating the meanings of opposites, such as *in/out, up/down, stop/go, under/over, left/right, open/close, give/take.*

Physical Response Ask children to demonstrate their understanding of antonyms by physically showing the meanings of the words in each pair. Then have children use this sentence frame to structure their oral response: *The opposite of _______ is _______.*

Common Core State Standards

Informational Text 8. Identify the reasons an author gives to support points in a text. **Foundational Skills 3.g.** Recognize and read grade-appropriate irregularly spelled words. **Literature 10.** With prompting and support, read prose and poetry of appropriate complexity for grade 1.

Text-Based Comprehension

Review Cause and Effect

Remember that good readers ask themselves what happens and why it happens. What do we call the reason, or why, something happens? (the cause) What do we call the result of what happened? (the effect)

CHECK UNDERSTANDING Read aloud the following story and have children answer the questions that follow.

Diego hung two big bird feeders in his backyard and filled them with different seeds. Many wild birds came to the feeders, and Diego would watch the birds for hours. One day Diego noticed that the feeders were suddenly empty. Where had all his seeds gone so quickly? Diego became a detective. What did he discover? Squirrels were leaping off the fence onto his feeders. They gobbled up all the birdseed!

1. What is the cause of the disappearing birdseed? (The squirrels are eating it.)
2. What is the effect on the birds? (The birds don't have anything to eat.)

Vocabulary

Review High-Frequency and Selection Words

HIGH-FREQUENCY WORDS Review this week's high-frequency words: *home, into, many, them.* Write each word on a card. Place the cards in a box or bag. Model pulling out a card, reading the word, and using it in a sentence about wild animals. For example: Camels are at *home* in the desert.

Team Talk Have partners make their own card sets. Ask them to take turns choosing and reading a word and then creating an original sentence.

SELECTION WORDS Write the words *park, zebras, hippos,* and *elephants.* Read them aloud together. Then ask children questions that use the words. For example: What color are *zebras?* Have children respond in complete sentences that include the selection words.

Corrective feedback	**If...** children cannot tell what the selection words mean, **then...** review the definitions on page 154a.

Genre

Review Poetry

POETRY Review with children that a poem is writing that may say things in an unusual way. The words in a poem are usually organized in lines, and some lines may repeat. A poem has a **rhythm,** or beat. And the words often **rhyme**—they end with the same sounds.

TEACH Listen as I read the poem "My Dog Rags." Read the poem on page 168 aloud. As I read, I noticed that the words at the end of each line of the poem rhyme. Write *Rags, sags, wags,* and *zags* on the board. Have children read the rhyming words with you.

MODEL I'm going to read the poem again. This time, I'll clap out the rhythm as I read. Clap out the rhythm as you reread the poem. I can hear that there are four beats in each line of this poem.

GUIDE PRACTICE Use the poem "The Hippo" on page 169 to guide children in understanding rhythm and rhyme in poetry.

- Follow along as I read the poem. Read the poem aloud. Which words rhyme? *(float/boat, retreats/eats)*
- What line in this poem repeats? *(and eats)* How many times is this line in the poem? (four times)
- Listen as I read the first two lines again. I'll clap out the rhythm as I read. How many beats do you hear in each line? (four)

ON THEIR OWN Have children read the poem "Raccoon" on page 168. Ask them to clap out the rhythm as they read. Then have children find and write the words that rhyme *(clan/can, eat/treat).* Finally, ask children to write and illustrate their own rhyming couplet about a favorite animal.

Access for All

SI Strategic Intervention

Words That Rhyme To help children think of rhyming words, have them use letter tiles to spell a familiar phonogram such as *-ag, -ut,* or *-in.* Then ask them to place tiles for different consonants and consonant blends before the phonograms to create rhyming words.

Academic Vocabulary

rhythm a beat that repeats

rhyme ending with the same sounds

Common Core State Standards

Foundational Skills 3. Know and apply grade-level phonics and word analysis skills in decoding words. **Foundational Skills 3.b.** Decode regularly spelled one-syllable words. **Foundational Skills 3.g.** Recognize and read grade-appropriate irregularly spelled words.

Assess

- ◎ Words with Short *u: u*
- ◎ Final Consonant Blends
- • High-Frequency Words

Assessment

Monitor Progress

For a written assessment of short *u: u,* final consonant blends, high-frequency words, and cause and effect, use Weekly Test 6, pages 67–72.

WORD READING Use the following reproducible page to assess children's ability to read words in isolation. Call on children to read the words aloud. Start over if necessary.

SENTENCE READING Use the reproducible page on page 171f to assess children's ability to read words in context. Call on children to read two sentences aloud. Start over with sentence one if necessary.

MONITOR ACCURACY Record scores using the Word/Sentence Reading Chart for this unit in *First Stop.*

MONITOR PROGRESS Word and Sentence Reading

If... children have trouble reading words with short *u: u* and final consonant blends,

then... use the Reteach Lessons in *First Stop.*

If... a child cannot read all the high-frequency words,

then... mark the missed words on a high-frequency word list and have the child practice reading the words with a fluent reader.

Name ______________________________

Read the Words

1. home
2. bus
3. into
4. rest
5. jump
6. many
7. pond
8. hugs
9. stump
10. mud
11. them
12. slug

MONITOR PROGRESS

- **Short *u*: *u***
- **Final Consonant Blends**
- **High-Frequency Words**

Name ___________________________

Read the Sentences

1. Pop runs into the pond.
2. Russ saw them in the sand.
3. Gus is home to rest.
4. The pups hop into the nest.
5. I see many buds on the plant.
6. He went to get many hugs from Mom.

MONITOR PROGRESS

- Fluency
- Short *u: u*
- Final Consonant Blends
- High-Frequency Words

Conventions

Review Exclamatory Sentences

REVIEW Remind children that an exclamatory sentence shows strong feeling and ends with an exclamation mark. Have them give several examples of exclamatory sentences.

GUIDE PRACTICE Write the following sentences without end punctuation. Have children tell you what end punctuation to add and why. If they choose an exclamation mark, have them say what emotion the sentence shows. There will be more than one correct response.

1. Mom is so mad at Ben
2. A big dog bit Brad
3. Fran just got a new red sled

APPLY Display and read the following sentence frame. Have children work in pairs to think of as many ways as they can to complete the exclamatory sentence. Then have children share their responses with the class.

______ is the best ______!

ON THEIR OWN Use Let's Practice It! p. 71 from the *Teacher Resources DVD-ROM*.

Name ______________ Animal Park

Exclamatory Sentences

Read each pair of sentences.
Write the exclamation on the line.

1. The hippo sat in the mud. The hippo is big!
The hippo is so big!
2. Where is the hippo? Look at it run!
Look at it run!
3. The lion is in the park. I like the lion!
I like the lion!

Write each exclamation correctly.

4. the animal is mad
The animal is mad!
5. the lion is the best
The lion is the best!

Home Activity Your child reviewed exclamations. With your child, look through newspaper and magazine ads. Have your child highlight the exclamations he or she finds.

Conventions Exclamatory Sentences DVD•71

Let's Practice It! TR DVD•71

Common Core State Standards

Foundational Skills 1.a. Recognize the distinguishing features of a sentence (e.g., first word, capitalization, ending punctuation). **Language 1.** Demonstrate command of the conventions of standard English grammar and usage when writing or speaking. **Language 1.j.** Produce and expand complete simple and compound declarative, interrogative, imperative, and exclamatory sentences in response to prompts. **Language 2.b.** Use end punctuation for sentences.

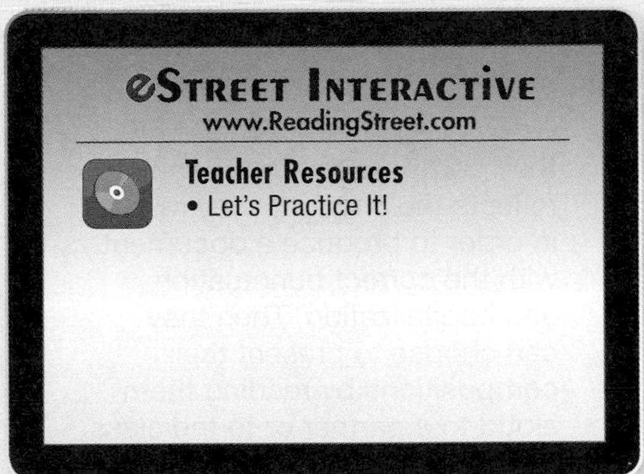

Daily Fix-It

9. Did the bus hit a bummp.
Did the bus hit a bump?
10. Can you see the elephants ruun
Can you see the elephants run?

Discuss the Daily Fix-It corrections with children. Review sentence punctuation, final consonant blend *mp,* and /u/ spelled *u.*

Common Core State Standards

Writing 2. Write informative/explanatory texts in which they name a topic, supply some facts about the topic, and provide some sense of closure. **Language 2.** Demonstrate command of the conventions of standard English capitalization, punctuation, and spelling when writing. **Language 2.b.** Use end punctuation for sentences. **Also Writing 6.**

Bridge to Common Core

PRODUCTION AND DISTRIBUTION OF WRITING

As children create a final draft of their composition, the revision reflects the changes they made in order to produce a document with the correct punctuation and capitalization. Then they can choose to present their compositions by reading them aloud to a partner or to the class.

Writing

Brief Composition

REVIEW EVALUATING Remind children that yesterday they learned more about writing brief compositions and they wrote to a second prompt. Today they will evaluate their writing from yesterday.

Mini-Lesson Writing for Tests: Proofread

Proofread for Sentences

- **Teach** In our compositions, we must capitalize and punctuate each sentence correctly so that readers know where the sentence begins and ends. This will also help readers tell what kind of sentence it is. If it is a telling sentence, it should end with a period. If it is a sentence that asks a question, it should end with a question mark. If it is a sentence that shows a strong feeling, it should end with an exclamation mark.
- **Model** Write the sentence *How funny the giraffes look with their long necks.* I put a period at the end of this sentence. Is it a telling sentence, a question, or a sentence that shows a strong feeling? I think that this sentence shows a strong feeling. It is an exclamation about how funny the giraffes look. I will change the period at the end to an exclamation point. Use a deletion mark and a caret to delete the period and add an exclamation point.
- Explain that when editing compositions, children should check each sentence, think about what kind of sentence it is, and then check the end punctuation.

EVALUATE Now it is time to evaluate your compositions. First, have children evaluate their compositions to make sure their purpose is clear. Then have children use the rubric on *Reader's and Writer's Notebook,* p. 208 to evaluate their compositions. If helpful, they can share their compositions and work with a partner. Circulate to guide children.

When children have finished writing their compositions, give them a copy of About My Writing, p. RR45 of the *Reader's and Writer's Notebook.* Then have children evaluate their writing by answering the questions on the page.

Routine **Quick Write for Fluency** Team Talk

1. **Talk** Have partners take two minutes to discuss what they learned from writing their brief compositions this week.
2. **Write** Have each child write a sentence about what they learned from writing their brief compositions this week.
3. **Share** Partners can read their sentences to one another.

Routines Flip Chart

Support Editing For children to whom the sounds and spelling of English still are not very familiar, look for spelling improvement little by little from week to week rather than rapid development. Help children make progress a word at a time and learn word meanings.

Common Core State Standards

Speaking/Listening 1.a. Follow agreed-upon rules for discussions (e.g., listening to others with care, speaking one at a time about the topics and texts under discussion). **Also Speaking/Listening 1.c., 3.**

Research and Inquiry

Step 5 Communicate

TEACH Tell children that today they will finish the notes about their animal and share the notes with others.

Think Aloud **MODEL** Display the notes about animals in the neighborhood. I will review my notes and circle the words and drawings about my animal. Those will be the notes I will include in my final work. My notes are about the animal I watched. I will start by writing the name of the animal as the title of my notes. Before I write my notes, I will make sure that all the words are spelled correctly. If I have questions about spelling, I will use the dictionaries we have in the classroom to find the correct spelling. I will write each note on its own line. My final work will look a little like a list.

GUIDE PRACTICE Review children's notes. Work with them to write the name of their animal at the top of their page and to be sure the words in the notes are spelled correctly.

ON THEIR OWN Have children write notes to share with the class. Suggest they write the title at the top of a sheet of paper and each note on its own line. Have children break themselves into groups. Instruct them to read aloud their notes to one another so they can learn about other animals. Remind children how to be good speakers and listeners:

- Good speakers speak clearly so their listeners can understand what they are saying.
- Good listeners pay attention to the speaker and do not talk while someone else is speaking. They ask questions if they do not understand something the speaker says.

VISUAL DISPLAY Display children's notes on the classroom bulletin board.

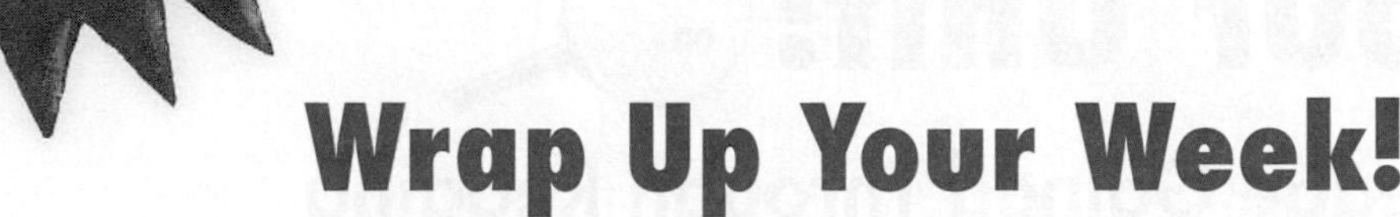

Wrap Up Your Week!

Watching Wild Animals

What can we learn about wild animals by watching them?

Think Aloud This week we explored what we can learn about wild animals by watching them. In the nonfiction story *Animal Park,* we found out what wild animals that live in a special park do. In the poems "Raccoon" and "The Hippo," we learned more about how wild animals behave.

Team Talk Have children recall their Amazing Ideas about watching wild animals. Then have children use these ideas to help them demonstrate their understanding of the Question of the Week, *What can we learn about wild animals by watching them?*

Amazing Words

You've learned 008 words this week!

You've learned 094 words this year!

Next Week's Concept

Family Activities

What does a family do together?

Poster Preview Prepare children for next week by using Unit 2, Week 1, ELL Poster 7. Read the Poster Talk-Through to introduce the concept and vocabulary. Ask children to identify and describe objects and actions in the art.

Selection Summary Send home the summary from the *ELL Handbook* of *A Big Fish for Max* in English and the child's home language if available. Children can read the summary with family members.

Tell children that next week they will read about a family of rabbits.

Preview Next Week

Wrap Up Your Unit! Zoom in on ©

Discuss Content Knowledge Gained Through Reading

How are people and animals important to one another?

SOCIAL STUDIES **WEEK 1**

What do pets need?

Children have learned that pets:

- need food and water
- need shelter
- need exercise
- need love

SOCIAL STUDIES **WEEK 2**

Who helps animals?

Children have learned that:

- pet owners help animals
- vets help animals
- trainers help animals

SOCIAL STUDIES **WEEK 3**

How do animals help people?

Children have learned that animals provide:

- food for people
- transportation for people
- services to people

How are people important to animals?

- keep them busy
- help them get well
- give them something to do
- protection

Discuss with children the selections they have explored surrounding the idea of how people and animals are important to one another. Throughout discussions, children should support their comments and ideas with evidence from the texts.

How are animals important to people?

- *Sam, Come Back!:* Sam the cat keeps the lady company.
- *Pig in a Wig:* Pig dances and is funny.
- *The Big Blue Ox:* Ox helps Mom and Pop.
- *A Fox and a Kit:* People watch the fox and kit.
- *Get the Egg!:* Brad and Kim get to watch the baby birds.
- *Animal Park:* People see the animals in a more natural setting.

WEEK 4

How do wild animals take care of their babies?

Children have learned that wild animals:

- provide food for their babies
- protect their babies from harm

WEEK 5

Which wild animals live in our neighborhood?

Children have learned that:

- all kinds of animals live in our neighborhood
- neighborhood animals need different kinds of food and shelter

WEEK 6

What can we learn about wild animals by watching them?

Children have learned that:

- we can learn about animals by watching them
- wild animals need food, water, and shelter
- we protect animals from danger

Talk about animals.

Tell about an animal that is important to you. What can you do to help that animal? (Responses will vary.)

Team Talk Have children work in pairs to talk about the Amazing Ideas related to animals that they discussed each week. Then have children use these ideas to help demonstrate their understanding of the question, *How are people and animals important to one another?*

You've learned 094 words so far this year!

You've learned 047 words this unit to use as you talk about animals.

Assessment Checkpoints for the Week

Weekly Assessment

Use pp. 67–72 of *Weekly Tests* to check:

- ✔ **Phonics** Short *u: u*
- ✔ **Phonics** Final Consonant Blends
- ✔ **Comprehension** Cause and Effect
- ✔ **High-Frequency Words**

home	many
into	them

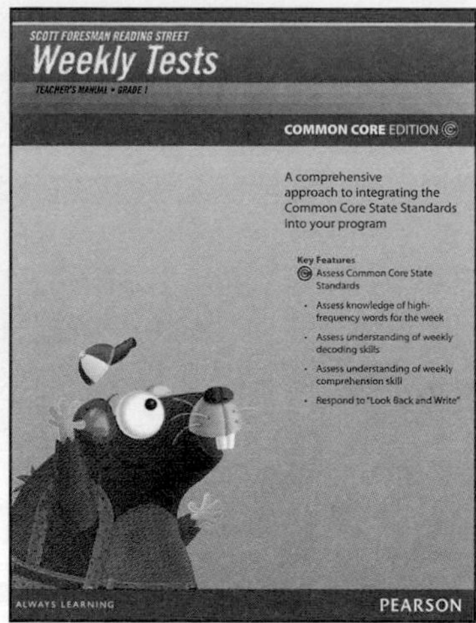

Weekly Tests

Differentiated Assessment

Advanced

On-Level

Strategic Intervention

Use pp. 67–72 of *Fresh Reads for Fluency and Comprehension* to check:

- ✔ **Comprehension** Cause and Effect
- ✔ Review **Comprehension** Main Idea and Details

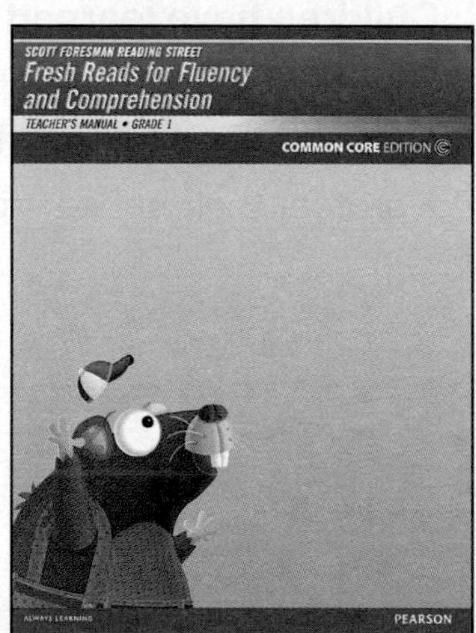

Fresh Reads for Fluency and Comprehension

Unit Assessment

Use the Unit 1 Benchmark Test to check progress in:

- ✔ **Passage Comprehension**
- ✔ **High-Frequency Words**
- ✔ **Phonics**
- ✔ **Writing Conventions**
- ✔ **Writing**
- ✔ **Fluency**

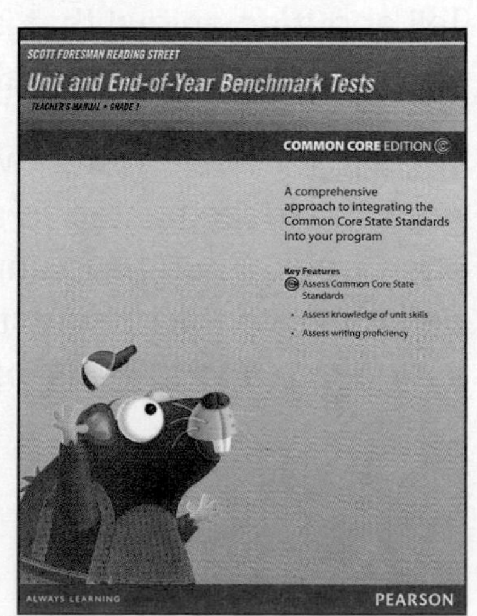

Unit and End-of-Year Benchmark Tests

DAY 1 Differentiate Phonics

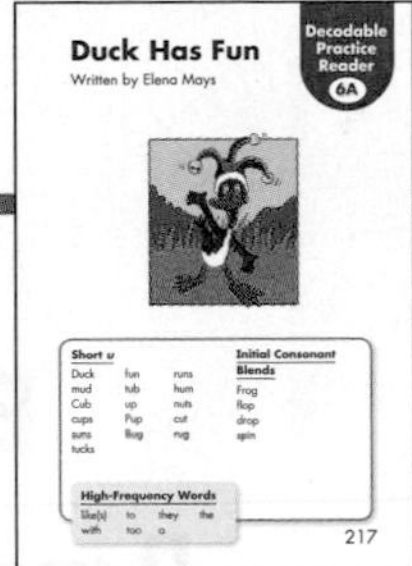

- Short *u: u*
- Decodable Practice Reader
- Advanced Selection "Fun with Ducks"
- **Inquiry** Identify Questions

DAY 2 Differentiate Comprehension

- Final Consonant Blends
- **Access Text** Read *Animal Park*
- **Inquiry** Investigate

DAY 3 Differentiate Close Reading

- Develop Vocabulary
- **Close Reading** Read *Animal Park*
- **Inquiry** Investigate

"Look Out for Wildlife" pp. 18–19

DAY 4 Differentiate Vocabulary

- Develop Language
- "Look Out for Wildlife" or Leveled Readers
- **Inquiry** Organize

DAY 5 Differentiate Reteaching

- Phonics and High-Frequency Words
- Conventions
- "Look Out for Wildlife" or Leveled Readers
- **Inquiry** Communicate

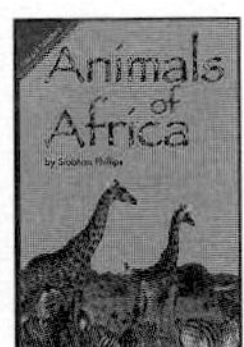
Teacher Guides and Student pages can be found in the Leveled Reader Database.

Place English Language Learners in the groups that correspond to their reading abilities.
If... children need scaffolding and practice,
then... use the ELL notes on the page.

Independent Practice

Independent Practice Stations

See pp. 146h and 146i for Independent Stations.

Pearson Trade Book Library

See the Leveled Reader Database for Lesson Plans and student pages.

Reading Street Digital Path

Independent Practice Activities available in the Digital Path.

Independent Reading

See p. 146i for independent reading suggestions.

On-Level

Common Core State Standards

Informational Text 1. Ask and answer questions about key details in a text. **Informational Text 7.** Use the illustrations and details in a text to describe its key ideas. **Foundational Skills 2.b.** Orally produce single-syllable words by blending sounds (phonemes), including consonant blends. **Foundational Skills 3.** Know and apply grade-level phonics and word analysis skills in decoding words. **Also Foundational Skills 3.b., Foundational Skills 4.a.**

1 Build Word Knowledge

Practice Phonics

SHORT *u*: *u* Write the following words and have children practice reading words with short *u*.

bug **plus** **dust** **fun**

Spelling

SHORT *u* WORDS WITH FINAL CONSONANT BLENDS Remind children that each spelling word has the letter *u,* which spells the /u/ sound, and a final consonant blend. Clarify the pronunciation and meaning of each word. For example, say: *Dusk* is the time of evening just before dark.

2 Read

Decodable Reader 6A *Duck Has Fun*

HIGH-FREQUENCY WORDS Have children read the decodable reader. Then have them reread the text to develop automaticity. Have children return to the text and find the previously taught high-frequency words. Help children demonstrate their understanding of the words. Provide sentence frames such as: My friend wants to go _______ me to the park. (with)

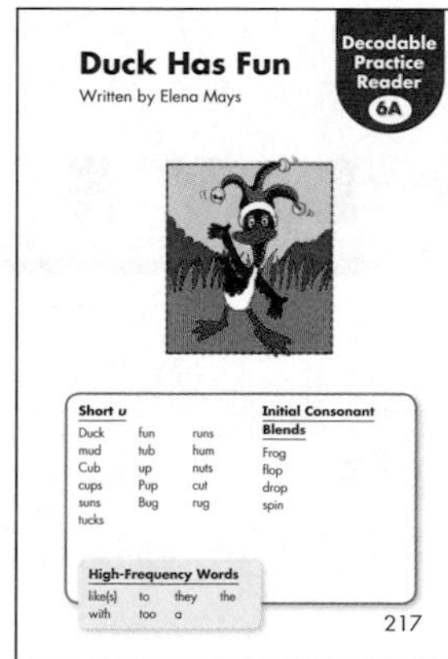

ELL

If... children need more scaffolding and practice with phonics,
then... use the ELL activities on pp. DI•118–DI•119 in the Teacher Resources section on SuccessNet.

OL

On-Level

eSTREET INTERACTIVE
www.ReadingStreet.com
Pearson eText
• Student Edition
• Decodable Reader

1 Build Word Knowledge

Practice Phonics

FINAL CONSONANT BLENDS Write the following words and have children practice reading words with final consonant blends.

hand **best** **sent** **lamp**

2 Read

Animal Park

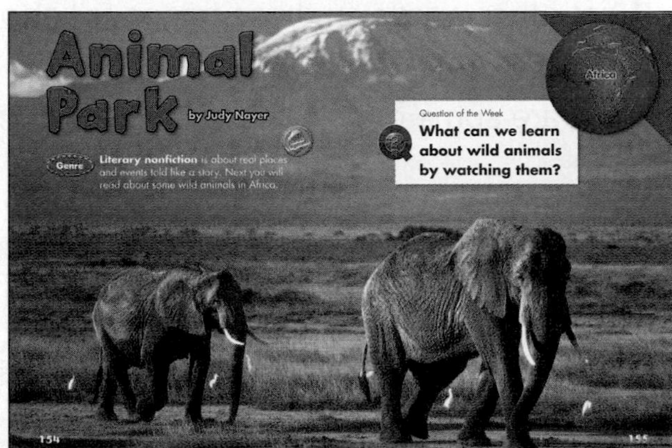
Animal Park
by Judy Nayer
Genre
Literary nonfiction is about real places and events told like a story. Next you will read about some wild animals in Africa.
Question of the Week
What can we learn about wild animals by watching them?
Africa

If you read *Animal Park* during whole group time, then use the following instruction.

ACCESS TEXT Have children look at the pictures on pp. 157–158. Reread the sentences on those pages.

- Look at the pictures on page 157. What animals do you see? (giraffe, baboon, hippo, deer)
- Where do these animals live? (in the park)
- How can people see the animals? (They can get in a truck and drive around the park.)
- Look at page 158. Why does the truck stop quickly? (A band of zebras is running by. They are fast and blend into the grass, so the truck has to stop quickly so the people can see them.)

If you are reading *Animal Park* during small group time, then return to pp. 154b–163a to guide the reading.

SMALL GROUP TIME

Independent Reading Options

Trade Book Library

eSTREET INTERACTIVE
www.ReadingStreet.com

Teacher's Guides available on the Leveled Reader Database.

On-Level

Common Core State Standards
Informational Text 1. Ask and answer questions about key details in a text. **Informational Text 7.** Use the illustrations and details in a text to describe its key ideas. **Speaking/ Listening 1.** Participate in collaborative conversations about grade 1 topics and texts with peers and adults in small and larger groups. **Also Speaking/Listening 4., 6.**

1 Build Word Knowledge

Develop Vocabulary

REREAD FOR VOCABULARY Have children reread *Animal Park,* pp. 158–159.

Read the following sentence and discuss words related to what animals do. (blend)

They blend into the grass.

- What other words on these pages tell about things animals can do? (runs, rest, bat)
- What are some other things animals can do? (hop, sit, swim)

2 Read

Animal Park

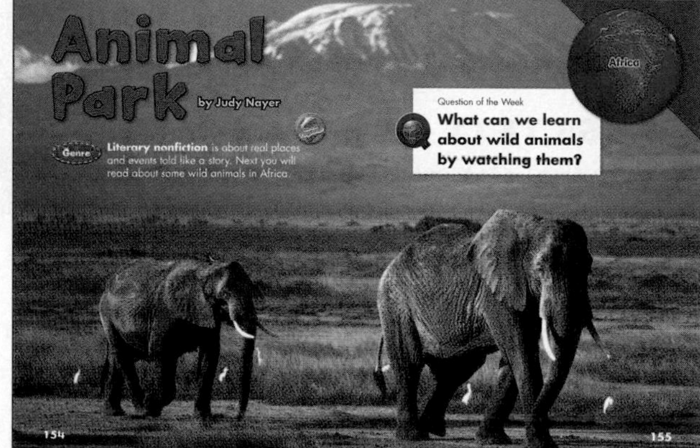

If you read *Animal Park* during whole group time, then use the following instruction.

CLOSE READING Reread pp. 160–161. Have children summarize the ideas presented on these pages. Ask questions to guide deeper understanding.

- What kinds of animals can we find in the park? (birds, hippos)
- Can the birds run slow or fast? (fast)
- Why do the hippos sit in the mud? (It is hot, but the mud is cool.)

Have children look at the picture of the birds on p. 160 and think of a sentence to describe them. (The birds have long necks and long legs. They have black feathers.)

If you are reading *Animal Park* during small group time, then return to pp. 154–163 to guide the reading.

If... children need more scaffolding and practice with the main selection, **then...** use the activities on p. DI•123 in the Teacher Resources section on SuccessNet.

On-Level

1 Build Word Knowledge

Practice Selection Vocabulary

park	elephants
zebras	hippos

Team Talk **LANGUAGE DEVELOPMENT** Have children practice using the selection vocabulary. Ask questions such as: What are some parks that you know? Where are they? Do you see zebras at your park? What kinds of animals do you see at your park? Be prepared to use complete sentences to explain your answers.

Allow children time to discuss each word. Ask for examples or rephrase for usage when necessary or to correct for understanding. Use the Student Edition to provide visual support.

2 Text-Based Comprehension

READ ALOUD "Look Out for Wildlife" Lead children in a choral reading of "Look Out for Wildlife" from *Reading Street Sleuth,* pp. 18–19. Then have partners take turns reading the paragraphs of the selection.

ACCESS TEXT Guide children as they work on the Be a Sleuth section.

Look for Clues Have children look for clues in the text. Ask children to think about where the family was and how the bear responded to the car.

Ask Questions Ask children to tell about a park they know and compare it to a national park like Yellowstone. Have them review the information in the selection and then create a list of questions on things they would like to know about Yellowstone National Park. Have children suggest sources they could use to gather information about a national park.

Make Your Case Ask children to review the selection and identify what the family did and saw at the park. Using this information and other background knowledge, have children decide if the park is a safe place to visit. Have them present their answer to the group and provide information to tell why they made that choice. Have the group ask the presenter questions to be sure the reasons are appropriate.

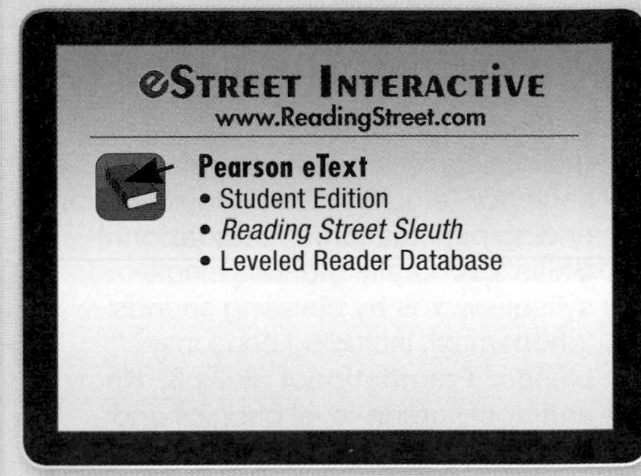

SMALL GROUP TIME

More Reading for Group Time

ON-LEVEL

Reviews
- Concept Vocabulary
- Cause and Effect

Use this suggested Leveled Reader or other text at children's instructional level.

eStreet Interactive
www.ReadingStreet.com

Use the Leveled Reader Database for lesson plans and student pages for *Which Animals Will We See?*

On-Level

Common Core State Standards

Foundational Skills 1.a. Recognize the distinguishing features of a sentence (e.g., first word, capitalization, ending punctuation). **Foundational Skills 2.b.** Orally produce single-syllable words by blending sounds (phonemes), including consonant blends. **Foundational Skills 3.** Know and apply grade-level phonics and word analysis skills in decoding words. **Also Foundational Skills 4.a., Speaking/Listening 4., 5., Language 1.**

1 Build Word Knowledge

Practice Exclamatory Sentences

REVIEW If needed, revisit the conventions lesson on p. 163c.

CREATE EXCLAMATORY SENTENCES Have children return to "Look Out for Wildlife" to create an exclamatory sentence that would fit in the selection. Have children work with a partner to identify the features of their exclamatory sentences.

2 Text-Based Comprehension

REREAD "Look Out for Wildlife" Have partners reread "Look Out for Wildlife."

EXTEND UNDERSTANDING Talk about Yellowstone National Park. Discuss with children all the animals that live there and how large the park is. If necessary, find its location on a map or globe.

PERFORMANCE TASK • Prove It! What is the most interesting animal in Yellowstone National Park? Have partners research other animals in Yellowstone National Park. Then have them choose one animal and collaborate on a short paragraph that tells why it is the most interesting animal in the park.

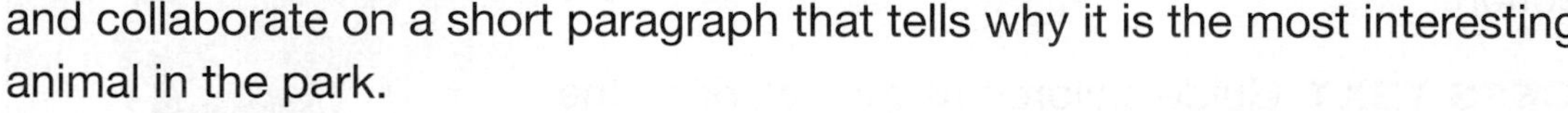

COMMUNICATE Have partners present their paragraphs to the class. Encourage them to include visual aids, such as pictures or drawings, during their presentation. Encourage the class to ask questions about the animal after each presentation.

More Reading for Group Time

ON-LEVEL

Reviews
- Concept Vocabulary
- Cause and Effect

Use this suggested Leveled Reader or other text at children's instructional level.

eStreet Interactive
www.ReadingStreet.com

Use the Leveled Reader Database for lesson plans and student pages for *Which Animals Will We See?*

Strategic Intervention

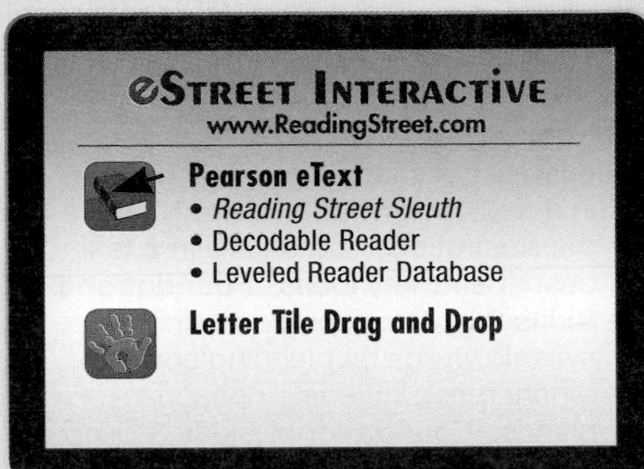

1 Build Word Knowledge

Reteach Phonemic Awareness

Reteach the lesson on p. 148–149 to distinguish /u/. Use these additional practice items.

bug **rub** **hum** **pup**

Reteach Phonics

SHORT *u: u* Reteach the lesson on p. 149a, short *u: u.* Use these additional practice words to blend.

duck **tub** **hut** **slug** **puff**

Have children spell *gum* using letter tiles. What word did you spell? Let's change a letter to make a new word and then read our new word.

- Change the *m* in *gum* to *t.* What is the new word? g u t
- Change the *g* in *gut* to *b.* What is the new word? b u t

2 Read

Decodable Reader 6A *Duck Has Fun*

DECODE WORDS Have children practice reading the words listed on p. 217.

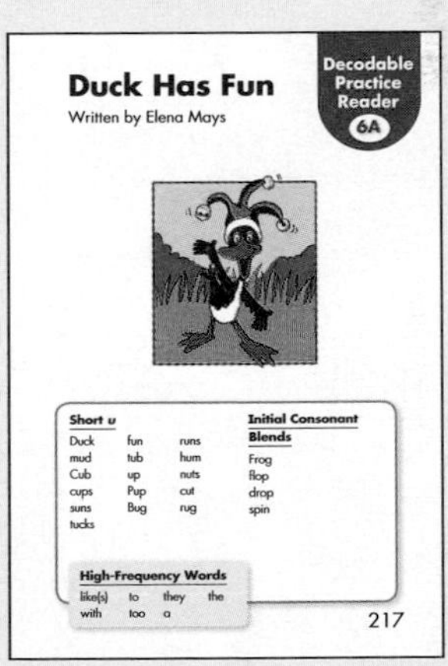

Corrective feedback	**If...** children have difficulty reading the words independently, **then...** reteach the words prior to reading Decodable Reader 6A.

READ IN CONTEXT Have children take turns reading a page in *Duck Has Fun.* Have them reread the text several times to ensure accuracy.

Corrective feedback	**If...** children have difficulty reading the story independently, **then...** model reading a page and have children echo you.

3 Reread for Fluency

Have children reread the text to develop automaticity in their reading.

SMALL GROUP TIME

ELL

If... children need more scaffolding and practice with phonemic awareness and phonics, **then...** use the ELL activities on pp. DI•118–DI•119 in the Teacher Resources section on SuccessNet.

Common Core State Standards

Informational Text 1. Ask and answer questions about key details in a text. **Informational Text 7.** Use the illustrations and details in a text to describe its key ideas. **Foundational Skills 2.b.** Orally produce single-syllable words by blending sounds (phonemes), including consonant blends. **Foundational Skills 3.** Know and apply grade-level phonics and word analysis skills in decoding words.

1 Build Word Knowledge

Reteach Phonemic Awareness

Reteach the lesson on p. 152c to segment and blend phonemes. Use these additional practice items: *band, dent, wind.*

Reteach Phonics

FINAL CONSONANT BLENDS Reteach the lesson on p. 152d to model final consonant blends. Use these additional words to blend: *lamp, hint, lend, fast, jump.*

Have children spell *bent* using letter tiles. Monitor their work.

- Change the *b* in *bent* to *s*. What is the new word? **s e n t**
- Change the *t* in *sent* to *d*. What is the new word? **s e n d**

2 Read

Animal Park

If you read *Animal Park* during whole group time, then use the instruction below.

ACCESS TEXT Have children look at the pictures on pp. 156–157. Point to the sun on page 156. What else do you see on the page? (tree, sky, clouds, tents, grass, rocks) Reread the sentences on p. 157.

- What animals do you see? (giraffe, deer, baboon, hippo)
- What does the author tell about in the text that is not in the pictures? (a truck)
- Do the animals live in a big park or a small park? (big park)

If you are reading *Animal Park* during small group time, then return to pp. 154b–163a to guide the reading.

Corrective feedback	**If...** children have difficulty understanding the section, **then...** read the section aloud using the Access Text Notes.

Independent Reading Options

Trade Book Library

eStreet Interactive
www.ReadingStreet.com

Teacher's Guides available on the Leveled Reader Database.

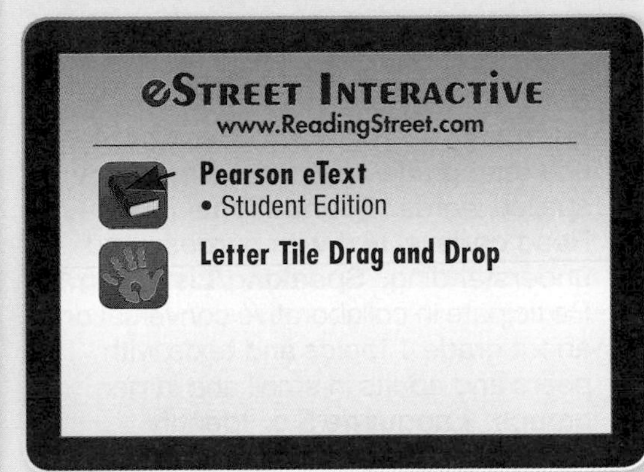

1 Build Word Knowledge

Reteach Phonemic Awareness

Reteach the activity on p. 164c to model words that rhyme. Use these additional practice items: *bug/hug/mug; fun/sun; cut/nut.*

Reteach Phonics

Write these short *u* and final consonant blend words and have children blend them with you: *mud, want, pluck, fast, fuss, twist, nut, gulp.*

2 Read

Animal Park

If you read *Animal Park* during whole group time, then use the instruction below.

CLOSE READING Reread p. 161. Let's read this page to find out what the animals are doing. To help children understand what the animals are doing, ask questions related to the text and picture.

- What do you see in the picture? (hippos, water, mud)
- Is this a hot day or a cold day? (hot day) How do you know? (The text says *It is hot.*)
- Why do the hippos sit in the mud? (The mud is not hot. It cools them off.)
- How does the picture show that the hippos are happy? (They are sleeping and look peaceful.)

Corrective feedback	**If...** children have trouble answering questions about the text and picture on p. 161, **then...** reread the page and have them tell about the picture in their own words. Then compare their summary with the words on the page.

If you are reading *Animal Park* during small group time, then return to pp. 154–163 to guide the reading.

If... children need scaffolding and practice with the main selection, **then...** use the activities on p. DI•123 in the Teacher Resources section on SuccessNet.

Strategic Intervention

Common Core State Standards

Foundational Skills 3.g. Recognize and read grade-appropriate irregularly spelled words. **Foundational Skills 4.a.** Read on-level text with purpose and understanding. **Speaking/Listening 1.** Participate in collaborative conversations about grade 1 topics and texts with peers and adults in small and larger groups. **Language 5.c.** Identify real-life connections between words and their use (e.g., note places at home that are *cozy*) **Also Speaking/Listening 4., 5.**

More Reading for Group Time

CONCEPT LITERACY

Practice
- Concept Words
- High-Frequency Words

BELOW LEVEL

Review
- Cause and Effect
- High-Frequency Words

Use these suggested Leveled Readers or other text at children's instructional level.

eStreet Interactive
www.ReadingStreet.com

Use the Leveled Reader Database for lesson plans and student pages for *Wild Animals* and *Fun in the Sun.*

1 Build Word Knowledge

Review Selection Vocabulary

park	elephants
zebras	hippos

SEE IT/SAY IT/HEAR IT Write *elephant.* Scan across the word with your finger as you say it: elephant. Use the word in a sentence. The big **elephant** has a long trunk.

DEFINE IT How would you tell a friend what an *elephant* is? Give a definition when necessary. Yes, it is a big animal with a long trunk. Restate the definition in child-friendly terms. An *elephant* is a huge, strong land animal with gray skin and a long trunk.

Team Talk When did you last see an elephant? Where was it? What was the elephant doing? Turn to your partner and talk about this. Allow time for children to discuss. Ask for examples. Rephrase their examples for usage when necessary or to correct misunderstandings. Continue with the remaining words.

2 Text-Based Comprehension

READ ALOUD "Look Out for Wildlife" Read "Look Out for Wildlife" from *Reading Street Sleuth,* pp. 18–19 as children follow along.

ACCESS TEXT Guide children as they work on the Be a Sleuth section.

Look for Clues Look through the selection for clues with the class. Read about the incident with the bear and ask what would cause a bear to act like that.

Ask Questions Have children tell things they know about the park from the selection. Then ask them for questions about things they would like to find out about Yellowstone National Park. Help children think of sources to use to gather information about Yellowstone National Park.

Make Your Case Make a list of things that the family did and saw at the park. Have children review the list and decide if the park is a safe place to visit. Have them give their answer and tell why they made that choice.

1 Build Word Knowledge

Review High-Frequency Words

Use the routine on p. 151 to review *home, many, them,* and *into.*

Corrective feedback	**If...** children have difficulty with any of these words, **then...** tell them the word and have them repeat it. Have children spell the word and tell what word they spelled. Have them practice in pairs with word cards.

2 Text-Based Comprehension

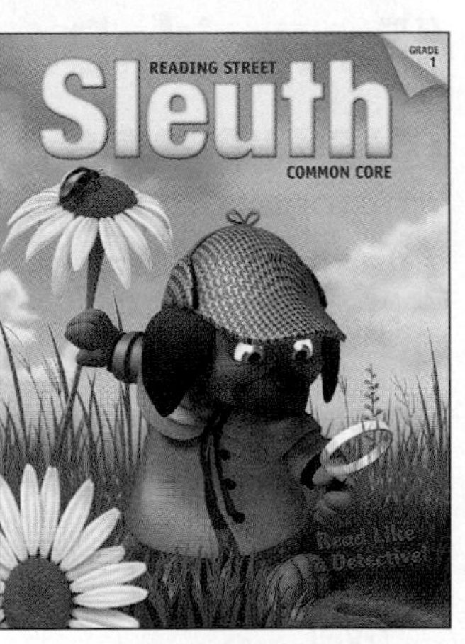

REREAD "Look Out for Wildlife" Reread "Look Out for Wildlife" aloud as children follow along.

EXTEND UNDERSTANDING Talk about Yellowstone National Park with the class. Discuss with children all the animals that live there and how large the park is. Show the class where the park is located if necessary.

PERFORMANCE TASK • Prove It! What is the most interesting animal in Yellowstone National Park? Have partners research other animals in Yellowstone National Park. Then have them choose one animal and collaborate on a picture with a caption that tells why their animal is the most interesting animal in the park.

COMMUNICATE Have partners present their pictures to the class. Encourage the partners to give a short explanation of the animal and why they think it is the most interesting animal in Yellowstone National Park. Encourage the rest of the class to ask questions after each presentation.

SMALL GROUP TIME

More Reading for Group Time

CONCEPT LITERACY

Practice
- Concept Words
- High-Frequency Words

BELOW LEVEL

Review
- Cause and Effect
- High-Frequency Words

Use these suggested Leveled Readers or other text at children's instructional level.

eStreet Interactive
www.ReadingStreet.com

Use the Leveled Reader Database for lesson plans and student pages for *Wild Animals* and *Fun in the Sun.*

Advanced

Common Core State Standards

Literature 1. Ask and answer questions about key details in a text. **Literature 7.** Use illustrations and details in a story to describe its characters, setting, or events. **Foundational Skills 3.** Know and apply grade-level phonics and word analysis skills in decoding words. **Foundational Skills 4.a.** Read on-level text with purpose and understanding. **Speaking/Listening 1.** Participate in collaborative conversations about grade 1 topics and texts with peers and adults in small and larger groups. **Also Language 4.a., Language 5.c.**

1 Build Word Knowledge

Extend Phonics

SHORT *u*: *u* Have children practice with more complex words. Have children use several words in sentences.

uncle	**number**	**funny**	**under**	**summer**
study	**hunter**	**fuzzy**	**sudden**	**unhappy**
disgusted	**hundreds**	**fussing**	**sunshine**	**mushroom**

2 Read

"Fun with Ducks"

TEACH VOCABULARY Before reading, introduce the story words: *munch, paddled.* Help children determine the meaning of each word using these sentences:

1. Hippos like to **munch** on leaves when they are hungry.
2. The ducks **paddled** in the water to cross the river.

Fun with Ducks

Mom led the family up the path. Gus was happy. The forest was beautiful. The sun felt good. Family hikes were fun.

The path ended at a large pond. Near the pond was a picnic table. It was under a tree with a big trunk. "Let's rest here," said Mom. "I have nuts and a bunch of grapes for us to munch. We can drink cups of water."

As the family ate, they saw a mother duck and four little ducks. The ducks marched to the pond in a line. At the muddy edge, the mother duck jumped into the pond. Then she looked back at the little ducks and quacked. The little ducks jumped in too. They each quacked as they jumped.

The mother duck paddled. Then three little ducks paddled in a line. The mother duck looked back. One little duck was not keeping up. The mother duck quacked at it. The little duck quacked and caught up. Gus and his family grinned. The ducks were funny.

Soon the family got up and started to hike again. But Gus was still looking at the ducks. Mom looked back. "Gus!" said Mom. "Quack!"

"Quack!" Gus grinned and ran to catch up.

Advanced Selection 6 Vocabulary: munch, paddled

SMALL GROUP TIME

Animal Park SG•98

READ Have children read "Fun with Ducks" silently. Then have children take turns reading aloud. After reading, have children recall the two most important ideas of the story using details from the text.

3 Inquiry: Extend Concepts

IDENTIFY QUESTIONS Have children learn about one animal that lives in a different part of the world and learn about that animal's habitat. During the week, they should read books and study illustrations to learn about their topic. On Day 5, children will share what they have learned. Guide children in brainstorming possible choices.

- Does your animal live on land or in the ocean? Where could you find this animal? What is its home like?

ELL

If... children need practice with phonics,
then... use the ELL activities on pp. DI•118–DI•119 in the Teacher Resources section on SuccessNet.

Fun with Ducks

Mom led the family up the path. Gus was happy. The forest was beautiful. The sun felt good. Family hikes were fun.

The path ended at a large pond. Near the pond was a picnic table. It was under a tree with a big trunk. "Let's rest here," said Mom. "I have nuts and a bunch of grapes for us to munch. We can drink cups of water."

As the family ate, they saw a mother duck and four little ducks. The ducks marched to the pond in a line. At the muddy edge, the mother duck jumped into the pond. Then she looked back at the little ducks and quacked. The little ducks jumped in too. They each quacked as they jumped.

The mother duck paddled. Then three little ducks paddled in a line. The mother duck looked back. One little duck was not keeping up. The mother duck quacked at it. The little duck quacked and caught up. Gus and his family grinned. The ducks were funny.

Soon the family got up and started to hike again. But Gus was still looking at the ducks. Mom looked back. "Gus!" said Mom. "Quack!"

"Quack!" Gus grinned and ran to catch up.

Advanced Selection 6 **Vocabulary:** munch, paddled

SMALL GROUP TIME

Advanced

Common Core State Standards

Informational Text 1. Ask and answer questions about key details in a text. **Informational Text 2.** Identify the main topic and retell key details of a text. **Foundational Skills 3.** Know and apply grade-level phonics and word analysis skills in decoding words. **Language 5.a.** Sort words into categories (e.g., colors, clothing) to gain a sense of the concepts the categories represent. **Also Writing 7., Speaking/Listening 1.**

1 Build Word Knowledge

Extend Phonics

FINAL CONSONANT BLENDS Have children practice with additional words with final consonant blends. Discuss the meanings of unfamiliar words with children. Then have them write the words on cards and sort by final consonant blends.

find	**child**	**cold**	**count**	**knelt**
myself	**important**	**stunt**	**behind**	**shelf**

2 Read

Animal Park

If you read *Animal Park* during whole group time, then use the instruction below.

ACCESS TEXT Have children silently reread *Animal Park,* summarize the selection, and identify the main idea and details. (Main Idea: Many animals live in the park. Supporting Details: A camp is in the park. Zebras, big cats, big birds, hippos, and elephants live there.)

DISCUSS GENRE Discuss what makes *Animal Park* literary nonfiction. Point out that this selection is about a real place and is told like a story.

If you are reading *Animal Park* during small group time, then return to pp. 154b–163a to guide the reading.

3 Inquiry: Extend Concepts

INVESTIGATE Guide children in choosing materials at their independent reading levels.

LOOK AHEAD Help children decide how they will present what they learn, such as a written report with photographs or an illustrated poster depicting the animal in its habitat.

Independent Reading Options

Trade Book Library

eStreet Interactive
www.ReadingStreet.com

Teacher's Guides available on the Leveled Reader Database.

Advanced

eStreet Interactive
www.ReadingStreet.com

Pearson eText
- Student Edition

1 Build Word Knowledge

Develop Vocabulary

REREAD FOR VOCABULARY Have children reread *Animal Park* and make a two-column chart listing animal words and describing words.

Animal Words	Describing Words
zebras	hot
cats	big
bugs	fast
birds	wet
hippos	fun
elephants	

2 Read

Animal Park

If you read *Animal Park* during whole group time, then use the instruction below.

CLOSE READING Reread pp. 160–161. Have children look at the pictures on the pages. All animals have special ways of staying safe. The big birds can run fast. How does this keep them safe? (They can run from other animals that may hurt them.) The hippos sit in mud. How does this keep them safe? (It keeps them from getting too hot.) Have children look through the rest of the selection and identify ways animals have of staying safe. Ask them to provide details when necessary.

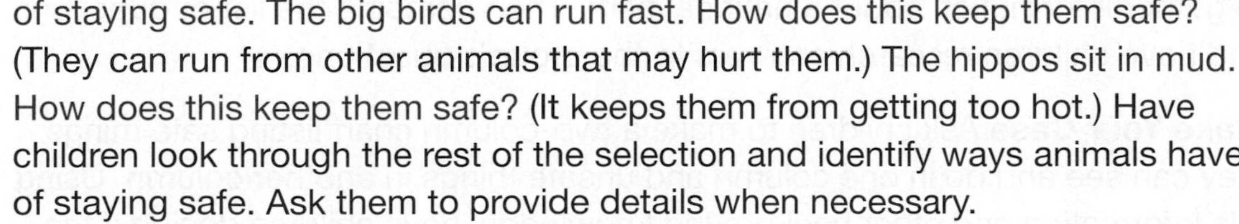

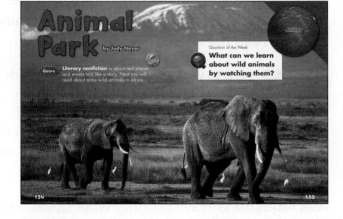

If you are reading *Animal Park* during small group time, then return to pp. 154–163 to guide the reading.

3 Inquiry: Extend Concepts

INVESTIGATE Give children time to investigate their topics by reading and studying pictures. If necessary, provide books such as *One Tiny Turtle* by Nicola Davies or *The Emperor's Egg* by Martin Jenkins.

If... children need more scaffolding and practice with the main selection, **then...** use the activities on p. DI•123 in the Teacher Resources section on SuccessNet.

SMALL GROUP TIME

Advanced

Common Core State Standards

Foundational Skills 1.a. Recognize the distinguishing features of a sentence (e.g., first word, capitalization, ending punctuation). **Speaking/Listening 1.** Participate in collaborative conversations about grade 1 topics and texts with peers and adults in small and larger groups. **Language 1.** Demonstrate command of the conventions of standard English grammar and usage when writing or speaking. **Also Writing 7., Speaking/Listening 4., 5., Language 5.c.**

1 Build Word Knowledge

Extend Amazing Words and Selection Vocabulary

desert	silent	forest
snort	world	medicine
chatter	poisonous	

park	elephants
zebras	hippos

Team Talk Have children ask each other questions using the Amazing Words and the Selection Vocabulary, such as: Is a zebra poisonous?

2 Text-Based Comprehension

READ "Look Out for Wildlife" Have children track print as you read "Look Out for Wildlife" from *Reading Street Sleuth* on pp. 18–19. Then have children read the selection independently.

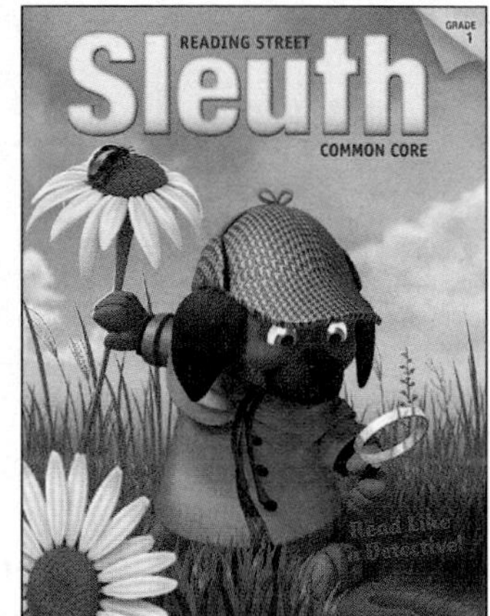

ACCESS TEXT Guide children as they work on the Be a Sleuth section.

Look for Clues Have children list the series of events that took place from the moment the family reached the dead end in the park.

Ask Questions Have children write questions for things they want to know about Yellowstone National Park. Have them suggest sources they could use to gather information about a national park. Then combine the list of questions and have children research answers to the group's questions.

Make Your Case Ask children to make a two-column chart listing safe things they can see and do in one column and unsafe things in another column. Using this information and other background knowledge, have children decide if the park is a safe place to visit. Have them present their answer to the group.

3 Inquiry: Extend Concepts

ORGANIZE INFORMATION Give children time to continue reading and working on their projects. Provide any materials that children need, such as poster board or art supplies.

More Reading for Group Time

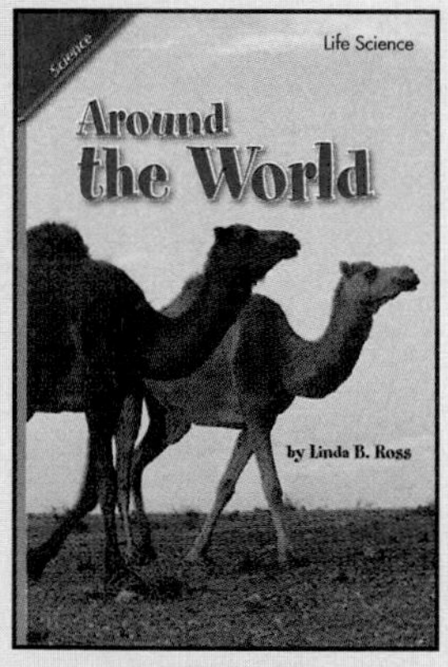

ADVANCED

- Extend Concept Vocabulary
- Review Target Skill

Use this suggested Leveled Reader or other text at children's instructional level.

eSTREET INTERACTIVE
www.ReadingStreet.com

Use the Leveled Reader Database for lesson plans and student pages for *Around the World.*

Advanced

1 Build Word Knowledge

Exclamatory Sentences

CREATE EXCLAMATORY SENTENCES Have children return to the text "Look Out for Wildlife" to create an exclamatory sentences to fit in the selection. Have children work independently to create as many exclamatory sentences as they can. Then have them read their exclamatory sentences aloud using the correct expression.

2 Text-Based Comprehension

REREAD "Look Out for Wildlife" Have partners reread "Look Out for Wildlife."

EXTEND UNDERSTANDING Discuss Yellowstone National Park with children. Talk about the animals, plants, and trees that can be found there. Have children find the park on a map. Have children read about Yellowstone National Park in an encyclopedia and make a list of details they find.

PERFORMANCE TASK • Prove It! What is the most interesting animal in Yellowstone National Park? Have partners read about other animals in Yellowstone National Park. Then have children choose an animal and write a short paragraph that tells why it is the most interesting animal in the park.

COMMUNICATE Have children share their paragraphs with the class. Suggest to children that they include a visual aid, such as a picture with labels, during their presentations. Encourage children to ask questions after each presentation.

3 Inquiry: Extend Concepts

COMMUNICATE Have children present their inquiry projects and share what they have learned about one animal and its habitat.

SMALL GROUP TIME

More Reading for Group Time

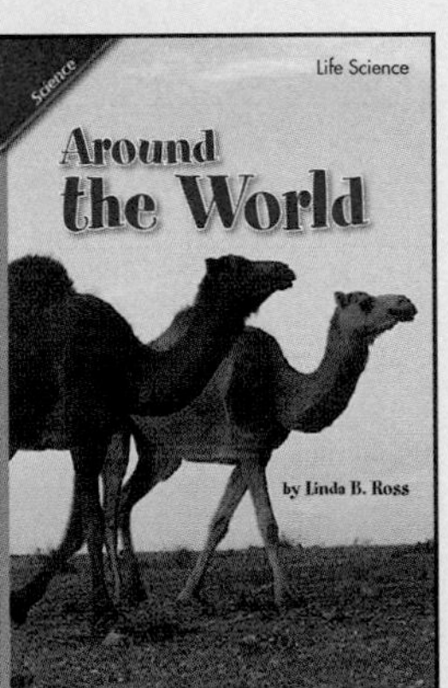

ADVANCED

- Extend Concept Vocabulary
- Review Target Skill

Use this suggested Leveled Reader or other text at children's instructional level.

eStreet Interactive
www.ReadingStreet.com

Use the Leveled Reader Database for lesson plans and student pages for *Around the World.*

TEACHER NOTES

Indiana Writing on Reading Street

Writing Trait Skills Trace

All of the writing traits taught in Scott Foresman Reading Street are dimensions of good writing. The chart below shows you the writing traits taught each week of the unit. In the column on the right, the criteria to achieve the Indiana Writing Applications Rubric top score are identified. For an overview of the Indiana Writing Applications Rubric and the Language Conventions Rubric, see the back of this page.

	Writing Trait of the Week/ Weekly Selection	Indiana Writing Applications/Language Conventions Rubric Top Score Point Criteria **A Score Point 6 paper is rare. It fully accomplishes the task and has a distinctive quality that sets it apart as an outstanding performance.**
Week 1	Voice *Sam Come Back!* **Writing Prompt** Think about a pet you know. Write a story about the pet playing.	**Does the writing sample display a strong sense of audience?** **Does it** • have a unique perspective? It may be original, lively, authoritative, and/or interesting (i.e., have a clear voice).
Week 2	Conventions *Pig in a Wig* **Writing Prompt** Write a fantasy story about a person who helps an animal. Draw a picture for your story.	There are no errors that impair the flow of communication. Errors that appear will generally be of the first-draft variety; they have a minor impact on the overall communication.
Week 3	Sentences *The Big Blue Ox* **Writing Prompt** Think about a kind of animal you know. Write a two-line poem about that animal.	**Is the writing fluent and easy to read?** **Does it** • sound natural? • include varied sentence patterns? (Writing may include complex sentence patterns.)
Week 4	Voice *A Fox and a Kit* **Writing Prompt** Think about a time you watched some animals. Write a narrative about it.	**Does the writing sample display a strong sense of audience?** **Does it** • have a unique perspective? It may be original, lively, authoritative, and/or interesting (i.e., have a clear voice).
Week 5	Organization *Get the Egg!* **Writing Prompt** Think about animals in neighborhoods. Write a realistic story about two friends seeing an animal.	**Does the writing have clear order?** **Does it** • follow a clear sequence with a beginning, a middle, and an end? • have a logical progression of main ideas and support?
Week 6	Focus/Ideas *Animal Park* **Writing Prompt** Think about wild animals. Write a composition about what people learn by watching wild animals.	**Does the writing stay fully focused? Does it** • stay on the topic? • avoid rambling and/or repeating information? **Does the writing sample include thorough and complete ideas?** **Does it** • include in-depth information and supporting details? • fully explore many facets of the topic?

For tips on **Publishing/Presenting** a Personal Narrative, see Step 5 on the Unit 1 Writing Process tab.

Indiana Writing Resources

Use these resources to build writing skills during and after the teaching of Unit 1.

Reader's and Writer's Notebook

Writing Rubrics and Anchor Papers

Digital Resources
- Online Journal
- Online Writing Transparencies
- Grammar Jammer

Teacher Resources DVD-ROM
- Reader's and Writer's Notebook
- Let's Practice It!
- Graphic Organizers
- Writing Transparencies

ISBN-13: 978-0-328-73376-7 ISBN-10: 0-328-73376-8

Indiana Writing Rubrics

Indiana Writing Applications Rubric Overview

The released Indiana Writing Applications Rubric Overview can be used to score the Unit 1 Writing Process Personal Narrative on pp. WP•1–WP•10 and other writing assignments.

Writing Prompt Write about something funny that happened to you and a pet or another animal.

Purpose Entertain

Audience Friend

Score Level	Ideas and Content	Organization	Style
	Does the writing sample	**Does the writing sample**	**Does the writing sample**
6	• stay fully focused? • include thorough and complete ideas?	• have clear order?	• exhibit exceptional word usage? • exhibit writing that is fluent and easy to read? • display a strong sense of audience?
5	• stay focused? • include many relevant ideas?	• have clear order?	• exhibit more than adequate word usage? • exhibit writing that is fluent and easy to read? • display a sense of audience?
4	• stay mostly focused? • include some relevant ideas?	• have order?	• exhibit adequate word usage? • exhibit writing that is readable? • display some sense of audience?
3	• exhibit less than minimal focus? • include few relevant ideas?	• have some order?	• exhibit minimal word usage? • exhibit writing that is mostly readable? • display little sense of audience?
2	• exhibit less than minimal focus? • include few relevant ideas?	• have little order?	• exhibit less than minimal word usage? • exhibit writing that is hard to read? • display little sense of audience?
1	• have little or no focus? • include almost no relevant ideas?	• have little or no order?	• exhibit less than minimal word usage? • exhibit writing that is hard to read? • display little or no sense of audience?

NOTE: This chart is only a brief summary of the score points. It is not appropriate to use this summary as the sole tool in scoring student papers.

Indiana Language Conventions Rubric Overview

Score Level	Command of Language Skills
4	In a Score Point 4 paper, there are no errors that impair the flow of communication. Errors that appear will generally be of the first-draft variety; they have a minor impact on the overall communication.
3	In a Score Point 3 paper, errors are occasional but do not impede the flow of communication; the writer's meaning is not seriously obscured by language errors.
2	In a Score Point 2 paper, errors are generally frequent and may cause the reader to stop and reread part of the writing. While some aspects of the writing may be more consistently correct than others, the existing errors do impair communication. With a little extra effort on the reader's part, it is still possible to discern most, if not all, of what the writer is trying to communicate.
1	In a Score Point 1 paper, errors are serious and numerous; they cause the reader to struggle to discern the writer's meaning. Errors are frequently of a wide variety. There may be sections where it is impossible to ascertain what the writer is attempting to communicate.

PREWRITE DRAFT REVISE EDIT PUBLISH

Personal Narrative

Writing Prompt

Write about something funny that happened to you and a pet or another animal.

Purpose Entertain

Audience A friend

INTRODUCE GENRE AND PROMPT Tell children that in this lesson they will learn about a kind of story called a personal narrative. A personal narrative is a story about you. When you write a personal narrative, you tell a story about something that happened to you.

INTRODUCE KEY FEATURES

Key Features of a Personal Narrative

- tells about an interesting event in your life
- gives details that help readers understand
- uses the words *I, me,* and *my*
- has a beginning, middle, and end

Writing to Sources

Use Prove It! on pp. 66–75 to guide children in completing performance tasks using multiple sources.

Academic Vocabulary

Personal Narrative In a personal narrative, the writer tells about something that happened in his or her own life.

ELL

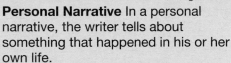

Introduce Genre Point out that a personal narrative is a story that a writer writes about his or her own experience. Explain that the writer uses the words *I, me,* and *my.* Discuss with children the key features of a personal narrative that appear on this page.

Common Core State Standards

Writing 1. Write opinion pieces in which they introduce the topic or name the book they are writing about, state an opinion, supply a reason for the opinion, and provide some sense of closure. **Writing 3.** Write narratives in which they recount two or more appropriately sequenced events, include some details regarding what happened, use temporal words to signal event order, and provide some sense of closure.

1 Plan and Prewrite

Mini-Lesson Reading Like a Writer

- **Examine Model Text** Let's look at an example of a personal narrative. Display and read aloud "My Dog Jet" on Writing Transparency WP1. Point out the words *I* and *My.* Explain that these pronouns show that the writer is writing a personal narrative, or a story about himself. Point out the beginning, middle, and end of the personal narrative. Read aloud the sentences that tell the writer's opinion or how the writer feels: *I was scared! I was happy!* Ask children why the writer first felt scared and then happy.

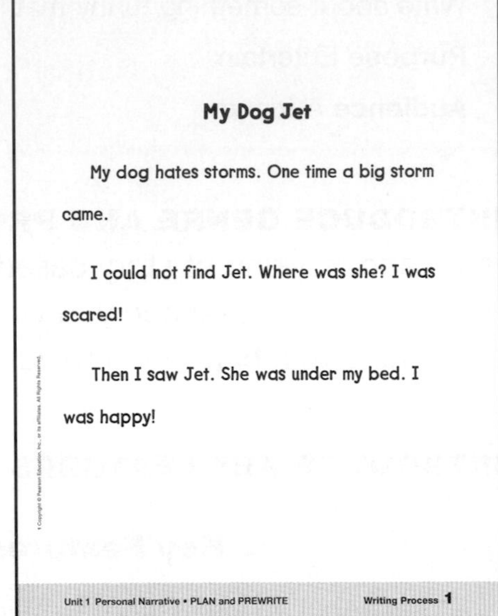

My Dog Jet

My dog hates storms. One time a big storm came.

I could not find Jet. Where was she? I was scared!

Then I saw Jet. She was under my bed. I was happy!

Unit 1 Personal Narrative • PLAN and PREWRITE   Writing Process 1

Writing Transparency WP1, TR DVD

- **Evaluate Model Text** Display "Traits of a Good Personal Narrative" on Writing Transparency WP2. Discuss each trait with children. First, read the name of the trait and remind children what it means. Then read aloud the statement, explaining any unfamiliar words. Finally, help children understand how the statement applies to the model personal narrative.

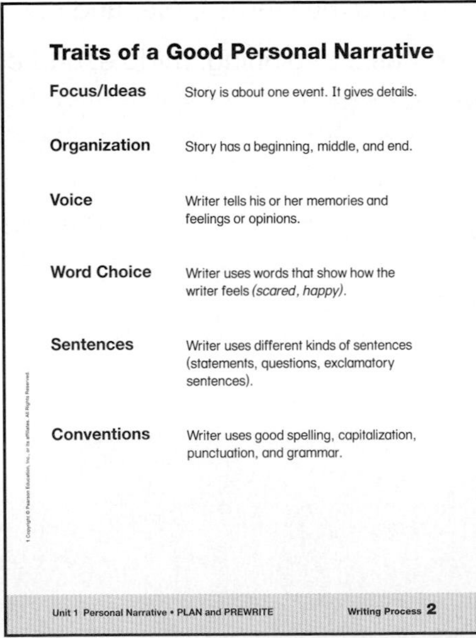

Traits of a Good Personal Narrative

Focus/Ideas	Story is about one event. It gives details.
Organization	Story has a beginning, middle, and end.
Voice	Writer tells his or her memories and feelings or opinions.
Word Choice	Writer uses words that show how the writer feels *(scared, happy)*.
Sentences	Writer uses different kinds of sentences (statements, questions, exclamatory sentences).
Conventions	Writer uses good spelling, capitalization, punctuation, and grammar.

Unit 1 Personal Narrative • PLAN and PREWRITE   Writing Process 2

Writing Transparency WP2, TR DVD

GENERATE IDEAS FOR WRITING Reread the writing prompt to children. The writing prompt asks you to write about something funny that happened to you and an animal.

USE RANGE OF STRATEGIES Encourage children to generate ideas for their personal narratives using these strategies:

✔ Draw pictures of favorite animals. Tell about funny things the animals did.
✔ Share ideas with family members.
✔ Make a list of their best story ideas.

Corrective feedback	**If...** children have difficulty thinking of an animal to write about, **then...** name different animals and ask children about experiences they may have had with these animals.

NARROW TOPIC Have children ask themselves questions about the ideas on their list. They might ask: *Would this idea make an interesting story? Would a friend enjoy reading this story?* Model how to narrow the choices on a list to one topic using the example list shown below.

Think Aloud I thought of three ideas. Now I will choose one. I don't think the raccoon in the yard would make an interesting story because I saw it for only a second. A trip to the zoo is a big topic. I saw many animals there, but it would be best to write about only one animal. I can think of several funny stories about my cat Mack, including the way I got him.

Topic Ideas

raccoon in the yard
trip to the zoo
my cat Mack

Write Guy *by Jeff Anderson*

Use Mentor Texts

Help children remember a narrative they have read that uses the words *I* and *me* or *we,* such as *Animal Park* in this unit (which uses *we*). Children need to hear and remember writing that resembles what they are learning to do. Tell them that they will write a story about something that happened to them, using the words *I* and *me.*

Access for All

SI Strategic Intervention

Alternative Writing Prompt Think about a time when an animal made you smile or laugh. Name the animal. Tell what happened and why you thought it was funny.

A Advanced

Alternative Writing Prompt In your personal narrative, write one thing you said to the animal or another character. Remember to use quotation marks before and after the words you say.

Common Core State Standards

Writing 1. Write opinion pieces in which they introduce the topic or name the book they are writing about, state an opinion, supply a reason for the opinion, and provide some sense of closure. **Writing 3.** Write narratives in which they recount two or more appropriately sequenced events, include some details regarding what happened, use temporal words to signal event order, and provide some sense of closure.

Plan and Prewrite

Mini-Lesson Planning a First Draft

- **Use a Story Chart** Display Writing Transparency WP3 and read it aloud to children.

I write sentences about the events in my story in order on my story chart. I write what happened first in the Beginning box, what happened next in the Middle box, and what happened last in the End box. I think of a good title for my story and write that on the line at the top. Now I can start writing a first draft of my personal narrative.

- Have children use the Story Chart graphic organizer on *Reader's and Writer's Notebook,* page 603 to help them sequence the events in their personal narrative and think of a title. Before you begin writing, decide what events you will tell about and write sentences for the beginning, middle, and end of your story. Also, think of a good title that tells what your story is all about.

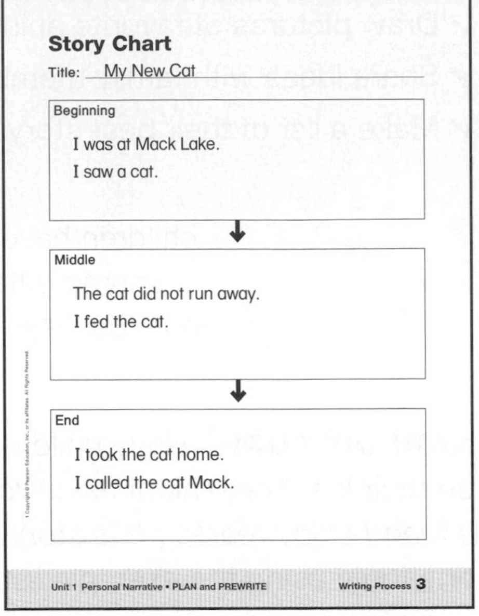

Story Chart

Title: My New Cat

Beginning
I was at Mack Lake.
I saw a cat.

Middle
The cat did not run away.
I fed the cat.

End
I took the cat home.
I called the cat Mack.

Unit 1 Personal Narrative • PLAN and PREWRITE — Writing Process 3

Writing Transparency WP3, TR DVD

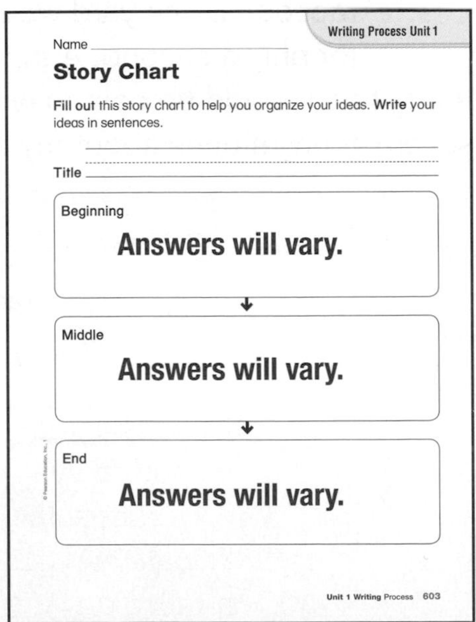

Writing Process Unit 1

Name

Story Chart

Fill out this story chart to help you organize your ideas. **Write** your ideas in sentences.

Title

Beginning
Answers will vary.

Middle
Answers will vary.

End
Answers will vary.

Unit 1 Writing Process 603

Reader's and Writer's Notebook, p. 603

Draft

DISPLAY RUBRIC Display the Scoring Rubric WP1 from the *Teacher Resources DVD-ROM.* Read aloud and discuss with children the traits and criteria that you choose. Encourage children to think about these criteria as they develop drafts of their personal narratives. Tell them that rubrics such as this one are often used to evaluate and score writing.

Scoring Rubric **Personal Narrative**

	4	3	2	1
Focus/Ideas	Reader can understand the story about you	Reader can understand part of the story about you	Reader cannot understand the story very well	Reader cannot understand the story
Organization	Has a good beginning, middle, and end	Has a beginning, middle, and end	Events are out of order	Does not have a beginning, middle, and end
Voice	Clearly shows how you feel or gives your opinion	Shows a little about how you feel or gives your opinion	Does not show very well how you feel or gives your opinion	Does not show how you feel or gives your opinion
Word Choice	Has words that help reader "see" the story	Some words help reader "see" part of the story	Words do not help reader "see" the story	Words are hard to read
Sentences	Sentences not all alike	Sentences are complete	Sentences are not complete	Sentences not complete or clear
Conventions	Uses good spelling and capitalization	Uses fair spelling and capitalization	Uses poor spelling and capitalization	Uses very poor spelling and capitalization

PREPARE TO DRAFT Have children look at the story charts they worked on earlier. Ask them to make sure that their story charts are complete. If they are not, have children finish them now. Use your story chart as you write a draft of your personal narrative. You will have a chance to revise your draft later.

Corrective feedback

If... children do not understand how the Scoring Rubric can be used to evaluate writing,
then... show them how you can use the Scoring Rubric to evaluate and score one or more traits of the model personal narrative on Writing Transparency WP1.

Access for All

SI Strategic Intervention

Plan a First Draft Some children will need additional guidance as they plan and write their stories. You might give them the option of writing a story with a partner under your supervision or pair them with more able writers who can help them with the process.

Prepare to Draft Have children tell you what they want to include in their stories. Help them restate their ideas as complete sentences. Record the sentences on the board and have children copy them.

Common Core State Standards

Writing 1. Write opinion pieces in which they introduce the topic or name the book they are writing about, state an opinion, supply a reason for the opinion, and provide some sense of closure. **Writing 3.** Write narratives in which they recount two or more appropriately sequenced events, include some details regarding what happened, use temporal words to signal event order, and provide some sense of closure. **Writing 5.** With guidance and support from adults, focus on a topic, respond to questions and suggestions from peers, and add details to strengthen writing as needed.

Draft

Mini-Lesson Writing Trait: Voice

- **Use Words That Tell How You Feel** List feeling words on the board. Explain that these words name different emotions or feelings. Act out one of the emotions and have children name the correct feeling word. Remind them to use one or more of these feeling words or other words about feelings in their personal narratives. Explain that a writer should show how he or she feels about the events in a personal narrative.

Feeling Words

Sad
happy
mad
tired
scared

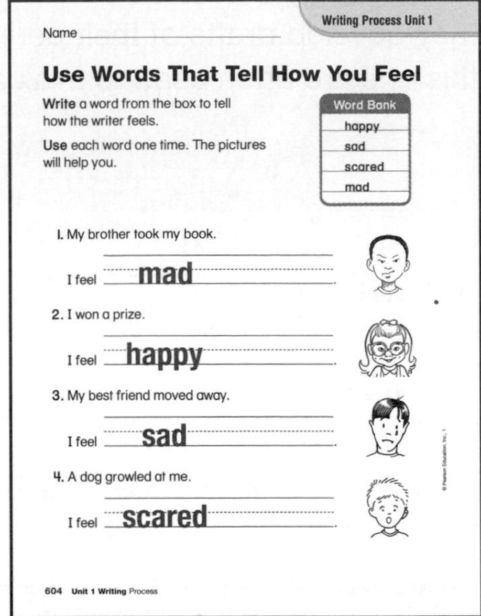

Writing Process Unit 1

Name

Use Words That Tell How You Feel

Write a word from the box to tell how the writer feels.
Use each word one time. The pictures will help you.

Word Bank
happy
sad
scared
mad

1. My brother took my book.
I feel **mad**
2. I won a prize.
I feel **happy**
3. My best friend moved away.
I feel **sad**
4. A dog growled at me.
I feel **scared**

604 Unit 1 Writing Process

Reader's and Writer's Notebook, p. 604

- Have children use *Reader's and Writer's Notebook,* page 604 to practice using words that tell about feelings.

DEVELOP DRAFT Remind children that when they write their first drafts, they just want to get their ideas down on paper. Suggest that they try these drafting strategies:

✔ Close their eyes and visualize the events in the story. Write sentences about what they see.

✔ Start at the beginning. Answer these questions in complete sentences: *Where were you? What were you doing? What happened first?*

Revise

Mini-Lesson Writer's Craft: Adding a Word, Phrase, or Sentence

- Explain to children that when good writers revise, they often add words, phrases, or sentences. They may want to better describe someone or something. They may want to better show their feelings about their topic. Discuss these examples with children.

That is Tabby's food.	The dog lives with me.
That is Tabby's favorite food for dinner.	The greatest dog in the world lives with me.

Writing Process Unit 1

Name ____________

Adding a Word, Phrase, or Sentence

Read each set of sentences. Answer the question.

1. What word did the writer add? Write the word.
   I saw a fish.
   I saw a huge fish.
   huge
2. What phrase did the writer add? Write the phrase.
   The fish swam.
   The fish swam into me.
   into me
3. What sentence did the writer add? Write the sentence.
   Then the fish swam away.
   Then the fish swam away. I laughed.
   I laughed.

Unit 1 Writing Process 605

Reader's and Writer's Notebook, p. 605

- Have children identify the word, phrase, and sentence a writer added on *Reader's and Writer's Notebook,* page 605. Then together discuss how these revisions make the writing more interesting.

REVISE MODEL Use Writing Transparency WP4 to model how to revise a personal narrative.

My first sentence clearly tells where my story takes place, but if I wanted readers to know exactly when my story takes place, I might add a phrase such as *Last month* to my first sentence. I added the adjectives *big* and *yellow* because I wanted readers to "see" the cat. Readers can certainly tell how I feel about him. I told about my feelings or opinion in this sentence: *He is a great cat.*

Revising Marks			
Take Out		Move	
Add	^	Period	⊙

My New Cat

I was hiking by Mack lake. I saw a ^big yellow cat. He did not run away. I gave him my ham sandwich.

I took him home with me. He is a great cat I call him Mack.

Unit 1 Personal Narrative • REVISE Writing Process 4

Writing Transparency WP4, TR DVD

Teacher Tip

Segment the assignment into manageable pieces. To make sure children's writing is on track, check their work at regular intervals, such as after children complete their graphic organizers and after they write their first drafts.

Revise for Voice To help children improve voice in their writing, work with them to develop lists of words and details that show feelings. Encourage them to use beginning dictionaries, if available, to find new words to add to their lists. Children can refer to their lists when they are writing their personal narratives.

Common Core State Standards

Writing 5. With guidance and support from adults, focus on a topic, respond to questions and suggestions from peers, and add details to strengthen writing as needed. **Language 1.** Demonstrate command of the conventions of standard English grammar and usage when writing or speaking. **Language 2.** Demonstrate command of the conventions of standard English capitalization, punctuation, and spelling when writing.

3 Revise

REVISE DRAFT We have written first drafts of our personal narratives. Now we will revise our drafts. When we revise, we try to make our writing clearer and more interesting to read.

PEER CONFERENCING Peer Revision Write the questions you choose from the Revising Checklist on the board. If you elect to use peer revision, help pairs of children exchange and read each other's drafts. Read aloud the checklist, one question at a time. Ask children to answer each question about their own draft or their partner's draft. Remind them to think about where a word, phrase, or sentence could be added to better describe or show feelings.

Help children revise their personal narratives using their own ideas or their partner's comments as well as what they have learned about personal narratives.

Revising Checklist

- ✔ Does the personal narrative tell about an interesting event in the writer's life?
- ✔ Does the story have a beginning, middle, and end?
- ✔ Does the title help tell what the story is all about?
- ✔ Does the writer use the pronouns *I, me,* and *my?*
- ✔ Does the writer use words that show how he or she feels about the event or gives his or her opinion?
- ✔ Will adding a word, phrase, or sentence help make a description better?

Edit

Mini-Lesson Editing Strategy: One Thing at a Time

- Explain this editing strategy to children: Look for one kind of mistake at a time. First look for spelling errors, then look for missing capital letters, and finally look for incorrect or missing punctuation. Model this strategy using Writing Transparency WP5. If you elect to teach proofreading marks, explain what they mean and how they are used as you discuss the errors on the transparency.

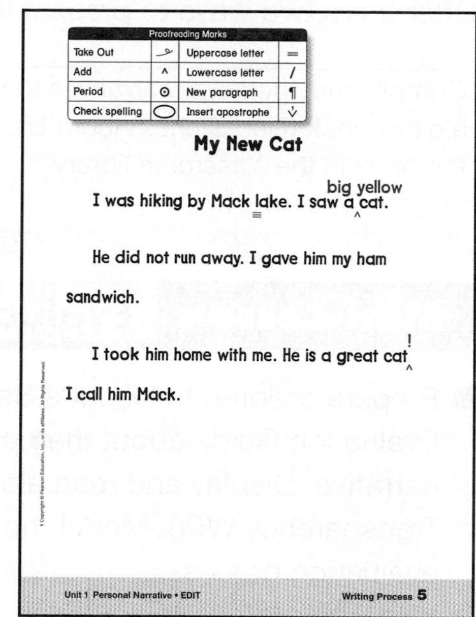

Proofreading Marks

Take Out		Uppercase letter	≡
Add	^	Lowercase letter	/
Period	⊙	New paragraph	¶
Check spelling	◯	Insert apostrophe	∨

My New Cat

I was hiking by Mack lake. I saw a ^big yellow^ cat.

He did not run away. I gave him my ham sandwich.

I took him home with me. He is a great cat^!^

I call him Mack.

Unit 1 Personal Narrative • EDIT — Writing Process 5

Writing Transparency WP5, TR DVD

Think Aloud First, I look for spelling errors. Good, there are no misspelled words. Next, I look for missing capital letters. The word *lake* in the first sentence should begin with a capital letter because it is part of a proper noun, *Mack Lake.* Last, I look for incorrect or missing punctuation. The second-to-last sentence needs a period or an exclamation point at the end after the word *cat.*

- Help children edit their own drafts. Have them check their spelling, grammar, punctuation, and capitalization. Make a simple rubric so children can use it to check the grammar, punctuation, spelling, and capitalization criteria you select for this writing.

Technology Tips

Children who type their personal narratives on computers may find this tip useful as they edit:

✔ Use the print preview or page layout feature when they finish typing. It will show them how their writing will look on a page before they print it.

Access for All

 **Advanced**

Apply Editing Skills As they edit their work, children can consider these ways to improve it.

- Make sure statements end with periods and questions end with question marks.
- Check that every sentence begins with a capital letter.
- Make sure they spelled the pronoun *I* as a capital *I*.

Write Guy *by Jeff Anderson*

Focus Their Editing

In the editing process, children can get bogged down by everything that needs to be fixed. Editing one aspect at a time helps them focus their efforts and concentrate on one task, while making it easier for you as a teacher to fully explain the concept, moving children toward correctness. Sometimes less really is more.

ELL

Support Editing When reviewing a child's draft, focus on ideas more than errors. Keep in mind that a consistent grammatical error may reflect the writing conventions of the home language. Use the appropriate lessons in the *ELL Handbook* to explicitly teach the English conventions.

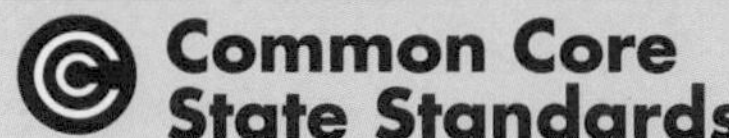

Common Core State Standards

Writing 6. With guidance and support from adults, use a variety of digital tools to produce and publish writing, including in collaboration with peers.

Publish and Present

OPTIONS FOR PRESENTING After children have revised and edited their personal narratives, have them write or use a computer to make a final draft. Offer them two ways to present their work:

Compile their personal narratives to make a class book titled *Stories About Us.* Place the book in the classroom library.	Illustrate their personal narrative with photographs, magazine pictures, or their own drawings. Share the final product with a friend.

Mini-Lesson Evaluating Writing

- Prepare children to fill out a Self-Evaluation Guide about their personal narrative. Display and read aloud Writing Transparency WP6. Model the self-evaluation process.

  Think Aloud In my personal narrative, I used some good words to describe and to show feelings or opinions and actions. I would mark *Yes* for numbers 1, 2, and 3 on my Self-Evaluation Guide. The best part, I think, is about Mack not running away from me. If I wrote this personal narrative again, I would tell about how hungry Mack was. I don't think he had eaten anything for a long time. He really made that sandwich disappear! That would be a good detail to add.

- Have children complete the Self-Evaluation Guide on *Reader's and Writer's Notebook,* page 606 to evaluate their personal narratives. They can save their Self-Evaluation Guides and their work in a portfolio to monitor their development as writers. Encourage them to build on their skills and to note areas to improve.

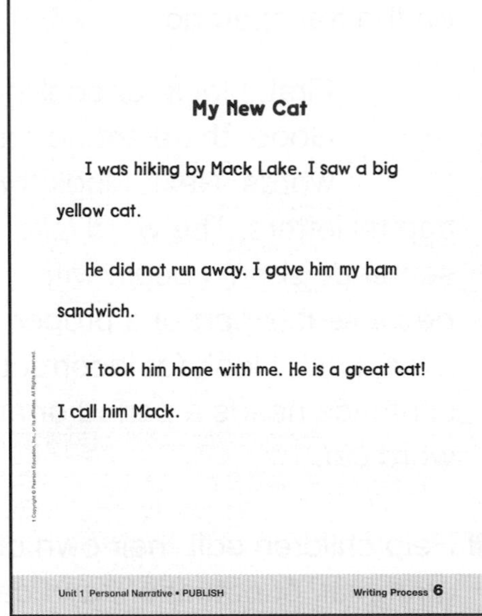

My New Cat

I was hiking by Mack Lake. I saw a big yellow cat.

He did not run away. I gave him my ham sandwich.

I took him home with me. He is a great cat! I call him Mack.

Unit 1 Personal Narrative • PUBLISH Writing Process 6

Writing Transparency WP6, TR DVD

Writing Process Unit 1

Name ____

Self-Evaluation Guide

Check *Yes* or *No* about voice in your story.

	Yes	No
1. I used words that tell feelings or opinions.		
2. I used one or more words that describe.		
3. I used one or more words that show action.		

Answer the questions.

4. What is the best part of your story?

Answers will vary.

5. What is one thing you would change about this story if you could write it again?

Answers will vary.

606 Unit 1 Writing Process

Reader's and Writer's Notebook, p. 606

Looking for Teacher Resources and other important information?

Go online to Pearson SuccessNet

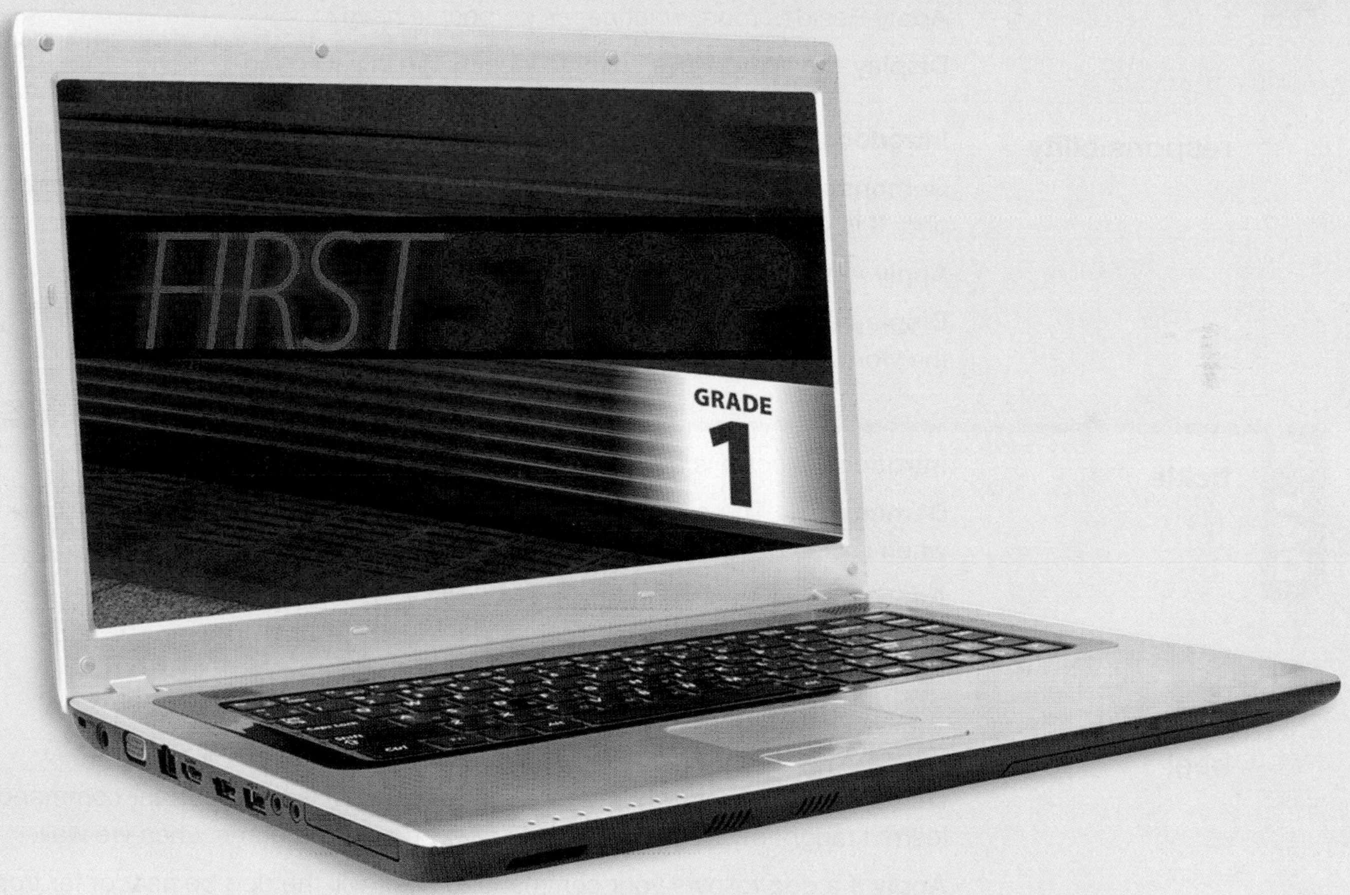

In the ***First Stop*** on Reading Street, you will find the following information.

Oral Vocabulary for Sam, Come Back!

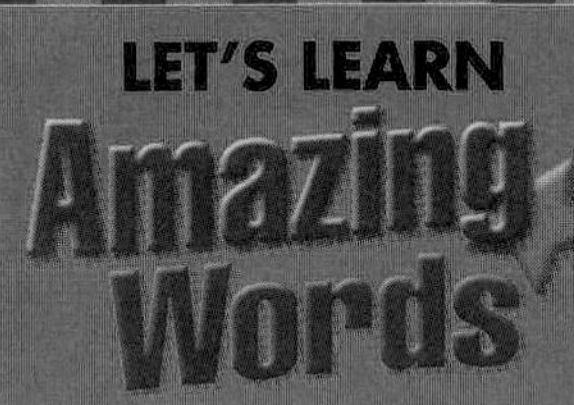

Oral Vocabulary Routine

DAY 1

needs

1. **Introduce** *Needs* are things people, animals, or plants must have to live.
2. **Demonstrate** Food and water are people's *needs.* One of a pet's *needs* is a place to live. Another of a pet's *needs* is water.
3. **Apply** Besides food, what *needs* do people have?
4. **Display the Word** Have children identify the initial sound-spelling *n*/n/.

responsibility

1. **Introduce** *Responsibility* is something you must do.
2. **Demonstrate** It is my *responsibility* to make my bed. It is Mom's *responsibility* to walk the dog. It is your *responsibility* to return books you borrow from the library.
3. **Apply** Act out something that is your *responsibility* each day.
4. **Display the Word** Run your hand under the six word parts *re-spon-si-bil-i-ty* as you read the word.

DAY 2

tickle

1. **Introduce** A *tickle* is a light touch that can make you wiggle or laugh.
2. **Demonstrate** The cat's whiskers *tickle* me when they rub against my cheek. My dog likes it when I *tickle* his tummy. The baby laughs when I *tickle* her feet.
3. **Apply** What is something that might *tickle* you?
4. **Display the Word** Have children identify the medial sound /k/ spelled *ck.*

DAY 4

heel

1. **Introduce** If you teach a dog to *heel,* you teach it to walk beside you.
2. **Demonstrate** I finally taught my dog to *heel. Heel* is an important command for a dog to learn. I taught my dog to *heel* so he won't run ahead of me when we walk.
3. **Apply** If a dog follows your command to *heel,* will the dog be near or far from you?
4. **Display the Word** Have children identify the sound-spellings *h*/h/ and *l*/l/.

Oral Vocabulary for Pig in a Wig

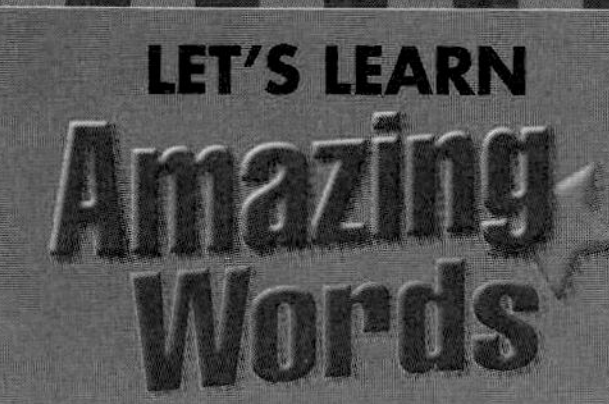

Oral Vocabulary Routine

DAY 1

service

1. **Introduce** *Service* is work done to help others.
2. **Demonstrate** A teacher provides a *service* to help children learn. A mail carrier provides a *service* to deliver the mail. A vet provides a *service* to keep animals healthy.
3. **Apply** Suppose you are a firefighter or a baker. Tell something about the *service* you provide.
4. **Display the Word** Run your hand under the two word parts *serv-ice* as you read the word.

tool

1. **Introduce** A *tool* is something used to help people do work.
2. **Demonstrate** A hammer is a *tool* used to build something. A saw is a *tool* used to cut. A shovel is a *tool* used to dig.
3. **Apply** Listen to the words I say. Pick one that names a *tool* and tell how it is used. Use the word *tool* when you tell about it. These are the words: *rake, pencil, scissors, apple, toothbrush, picture.*
4. **Display the Word** Have children identify the initial sound-spelling *t/t/* and the final sound-spelling *l/l/*.

DAY 2

sloppy

1. **Introduce** If something is *sloppy,* it is wet or messy.
2. **Demonstrate** A *sloppy* eater spills food. If your handwriting is *sloppy,* it will be hard to read. I tucked in my shirt so I wouldn't look *sloppy.*
3. **Apply** Name a word that means the opposite of *sloppy.* Name a word that means about the same as *sloppy.*
4. **Display the Word** Run your hand under the two word parts *slop-py* as you read the word.

DAY 4

comfort

1. **Introduce** *Comfort* means "to make someone feel better."
2. **Demonstrate** My mother sang a song to *comfort* the crying baby. I gave my brother a hug to *comfort* him when he felt sad. When you *comfort* someone, you try to cheer that person up.
3. **Apply** Who is more likely to need *comfort,* someone who won a race or someone who lost? Why?
4. **Display the Word** Have children identify the initial sound-spelling *c/k/*.

Oral Vocabulary for The Big Blue Ox

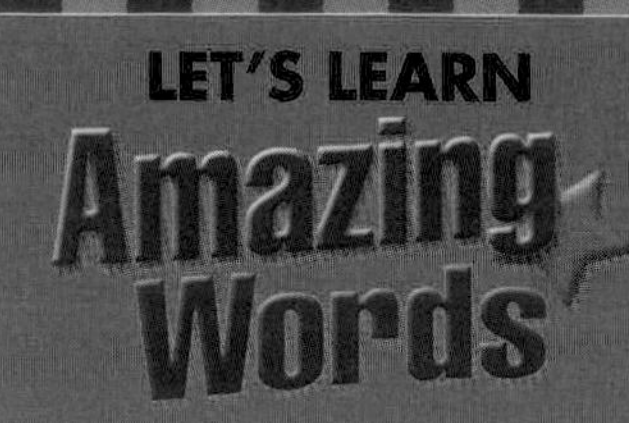

Oral Vocabulary Routine

DAY 1

past

1. **Introduce** The *past* is time that has already happened.
2. **Demonstrate** Anything that happened yesterday happened in the *past.* If something happened in the *past,* it already happened. Things that happened long ago happened in the *past.* In the *past* before there were cars, people rode in wagons pulled by horses.
3. **Apply** Describe a way you can learn about the *past.*
4. **Display the Word** Have children identify the initial sound-spelling *p*/p/.

present

1. **Introduce** The *present* is the time that is happening now.
2. **Demonstrate** Something happening today is happening in the *present.* The *present* time is right now. I am carrying an umbrella now because the *present* weather is rainy.
3. **Apply** Does today's date tell about the past or the *present?* Explain.
4. **Display the Word** Run your hand under the two word parts *pres-ent* as you read the word.

produce

1. **Introduce** *Produce* means "to make or create."
2. **Demonstrate** Factories *produce* cars. Fires *produce* smoke. It takes a lot of work to *produce* a television show.
3. **Apply** Suppose you want to *produce* a picture for the hall outside our classroom. Tell what you would do.
4. **Display the Word** Run your hand under the two word parts *pro-duce* as you read the word.

DAY 2

serve

1. **Introduce** To *serve* means "to work for or to help."
2. **Demonstrate** Some dogs are trained to *serve* people who cannot see or hear. Some dogs *serve* to cheer up people who are in a hospital. A horse *serves* to pull a wagon.
3. **Apply** Have children tell how a seeing-eye dog might *serve* a blind person.
4. **Display the Word** Have children identify the initial sound-spelling *s*/s/.

DAY 4

powerful

1. **Introduce** Something that is *powerful* is very strong.
2. **Demonstrate** Horses are *powerful* animals. A jet engine is *powerful.* A hurricane wind is *powerful.*
3. **Apply** Name a word that means the opposite of *powerful.* Name a word that means almost the same as *powerful.*
4. **Display the Word** Run your hand under the three word parts *pow-er-ful* as you read the word.

Oral Vocabulary for A Fox and a Kit

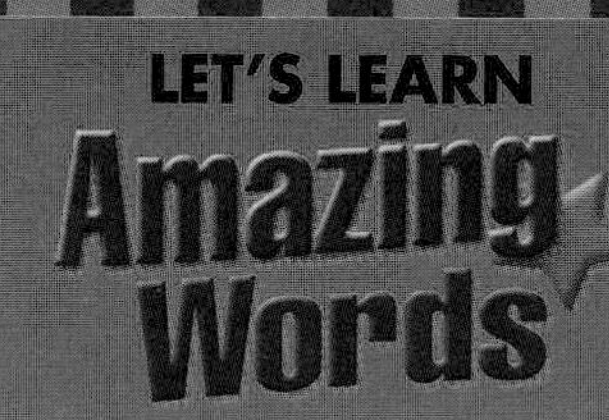

Oral Vocabulary Routine

DAY 1

wild

1. **Introduce** If an animal is *wild,* it lives in nature and is not taken care of by people.
2. **Demonstrate** Foxes are *wild* animals. *Wild* animals often live in the woods. If an animal is *wild,* it takes care of itself.
3. **Apply** Name one kind of *wild* animal. Tell where it lives.
4. **Display the Word** Have children identify the initial sound-spelling *w/w/.*

parent

1. **Introduce** A mother or a father is a *parent.*
2. **Demonstrate** A *parent* takes care of its young. The male sea horse is the *parent* who cares for its young. When they are born, some baby animals do not look like their *parents.*
3. **Apply** What is something a *parent* might do for a child?
4. **Display the Word** Run your hand under the two word parts *par-ent* as you read the word.

DAY 2

canopy

1. **Introduce** A *canopy* is a cover that hangs over something.
2. **Demonstrate** A *canopy* can help shade you from the sun. A *canopy* in the rain forest is like a roof. The tallest trees make a *canopy* in the rain forest. The *canopy* provides shelter for many animals in the rain forest.
3. **Apply** If you were standing, would you look up or down to see a *canopy?*
4. **Display the Word** Run your hand under the three word parts *can-o-py* as you read the word.

DAY 4

reserve

1. **Introduce** A *reserve* is a place set aside for special use.
2. **Demonstrate** An animal *reserve* is a park for animals. A *reserve* provides a safe place for wild animals to live. Endangered animals may be protected in a *reserve.*
3. **Apply** What are some things you might see in a *reserve?*
4. **Display the Word** Run your hand under the two word parts *re-serve* as you read the word.

Oral Vocabulary for Get the Egg!

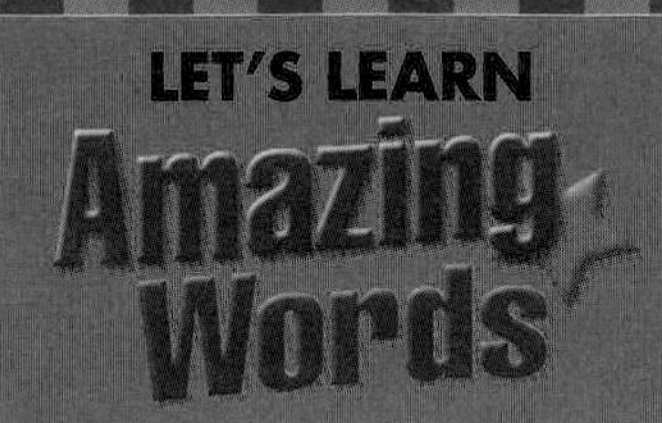

Oral Vocabulary Routine

DAY 1

hatch

1. **Introduce** *Hatch* means "to come out of an egg."
2. **Demonstrate** To *hatch,* a baby chick breaks out of its egg. Snakes and turtles *hatch* from eggs. Some insects *hatch* from eggs.
3. **Apply** If any of the things I name can *hatch,* say "hatch." If not, say nothing: a train, a chicken, a jar of jam, a snake, a turtle.
4. **Display the Word** Have children identify the medial sound-spelling *a/a/*.

survive

1. **Introduce** *Survive* means "to stay alive."
2. **Demonstrate** We hoped the cat would *survive* after it fell from the tree. The man was thankful to *survive* the car accident. Some plants can *survive* with little water.
3. **Apply** Name a word that means the opposite of *survive.* Name a word that means about the same as *survive.*
4. **Display the Word** Run your hand under the two part word parts *sur-vive* as you read the word.

Oral Vocabulary for **Animal Park**

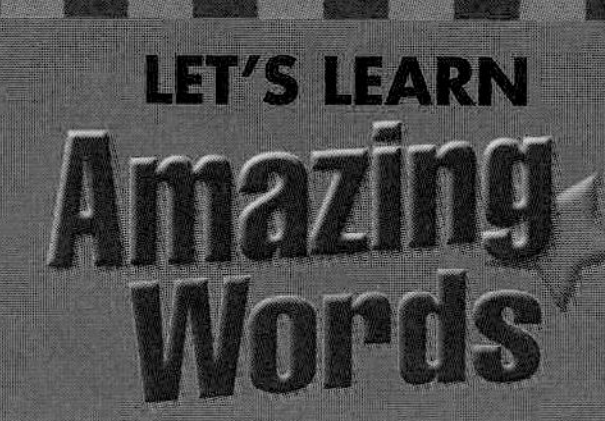

Oral Vocabulary Routine

DAY 1

forest

1. **Introduce** A *forest* is many trees growing together that cover a large area of land.
2. **Demonstrate** A *forest* might have oak trees and maple trees. Wild animals such as squirrels live in the trees in a *forest.* Other wild animals, such as foxes, live in dens in the ground of the *forest.*
3. **Apply** Name a kind of tree or animal that you might find in a *forest.*
4. **Display the Word** Have children identify the initial sound-spelling *f*/f/.

world

1. **Introduce** *World* is the name for the earth.
2. **Demonstrate** People live in different parts of the *world.* A globe is a model of the *world.* Ships can sail around the *world.*
3. **Apply** Tell something about another part of the *world* that you have read in a book or seen on TV. Use the word *world* when you tell about it.
4. **Display the Word** Have children identify the initial sound-spelling *w*/w/.

DAY 2

chatter

1. **Introduce** To *chatter* means "to talk quickly" or "to make quick, sharp sounds."
2. **Demonstrate** Monkeys *chatter.* The *chatter* of the birds made it hard for me to think. The children *chattered* away on the bus ride home.
3. **Apply** Demonstrate how a person or a monkey might *chatter.*
4. **Display the Word** Run your hand under the two word parts *chat-ter* as you read the word.

DAY 4

poisonous

1. **Introduce** Something that is *poisonous* is harmful to your health or life.
2. **Demonstrate** If you eat something *poisonous,* you can get very sick. Some kinds of berries are *poisonous.* Certain animals are *poisonous.*
3. **Apply** Explain why you would not want to eat or touch something *poisonous.*
4. **Display the Word** Run your hand under the three word parts *poi-son-ous* as you read the word.

ACKNOWLEDGMENTS

Student Edition

Student Edition, p. 188

Teacher's Edition

Text

KWL Strategy: The KWL Interactive Reading Strategy was developed and is used by permission of Donna Ogle, National-Louis University, Skokie, Illinois, co-author of *Reading Today and Tomorrow,* Holt, Rinehart & Winston Publishers, 1988. (See also the *Reading Teacher,* February 1986, pp. 564–570.)

Photographs

Cover (B) ©Theo Allots/Getty Images, (T) Getty Images

Every effort has been made to secure permission and provide appropriate credit for photographic material. The publisher deeply regrets any omission and pledges to correct errors called to its attention in subsequent editions.

Unless otherwise acknowledged, all photographs are the property of Pearson Education, Inc.

TEACHER NOTES

TEACHER NOTES

TEACHER NOTES

TEACHER NOTES

Looking for Teacher Resources and other important information?

Go online to Pearson SuccessNet

In the *First Stop* on Reading Street, you will find the following information.

- Research into Practice on Reading Street
- Guide to Reading Street
- Assessment on Reading Street
- Customize Writing on Reading Street
- Small Group Instruction on Reading Street
- ELL on Reading Street
- Customize Literacy on Reading Street
- 21st Century Skills on Reading Street
- Teacher Resources for Grade 1
- Index

Looking for Teacher Resources and other important information?

Go online to Pearson SuccessNet

eSTREET INTERACTIVE
www.ReadingStreet.com

In the *First Stop* on Reading Street, you will find the following information.

- Research into Practice on Reading Street
- Guide to Reading Street
- Assessment on Reading Street
- Customize Writing on Reading Street
- Small Group Instruction on Reading Street
- ELL on Reading Street
- Customize Literacy on Reading Street
- 21st Century Skills on Reading Street
- Teacher Resources for Grade 1
- Index